Practical Share Valuation

'I must enter into a dim world peopled by indeterminate spirits of fictitious or unborn sales'
Danckwerts J (*Holt v IRC* [1953] 1 WLR 1488)

Practical Share Valuation

Seventh edition

Nigel A Eastaway OBE
FCA, FCCA, FCMA, FCIS, CTA (Fellow), MAE, MEWI, CPA, FTIHK, FOI, MRICS, SBV, TEP, AIIT, FRSA, CGMA
MHA MacIntyre Hudson

Diane Elliott
BA (Hons), FCA
BDO LLP

Christopher Blundell CTA
MHA MacIntyre Hudson

Cameron Cook BA ACA CF
MHA MacIntyre Hudson

Contributing author:

Shân Kennedy
MA (Cantab), FCA

Bloomsbury Professional
LONDON • DUBLIN • EDINBURGH • NEW YORK • NEW DELHI • SYDNEY

BLOOMSBURY PROFESSIONAL
Bloomsbury Publishing Plc
41–43 Boltro Road, Haywards Heath, RH16 1BJ, UK

BLOOMSBURY and the Diana logo are trademarks of Bloomsbury Publishing Plc

British Library Cataloguing-in-Publication Data

A catalogue record for this book is available from the British Library.

ISBN: PB 978 1 52650 508 8

Typeset by Evolution Design and Digital Ltd (Kent)

Preface

Our intention in writing this book was to undertake a comprehensive review of the practical aspects of the share valuation problems likely to be faced by the practitioner required to value shares in unquoted companies, whether for commercial or fiscal purposes. Judgment and common sense nevertheless remain the prime qualities of the share valuer, allied to up-to-date knowledge of the latest statutory requirements and developments in case law.

In this seventh edition we include, amongst other things, detailed commentary on the share valuation cases that have been decided by the Courts and Tribunals. We also refer to HMRC's Share and Assets Valuation Manual. The chapters on taxation have been further revised to take account of changes up to and including the Finance Act 2018.

We must thank the partners and staff of MHA MacIntyre Hudson and BDO LLP who have given us much assistance and encouragement.

This book comprises three divisions:

Division A contains the main narrative and is itself divided into three parts:

Part 1 reviews the valuation principles that have emerged from decided cases involving the valuation of shares, partnership goodwill and, in some instances, land and intellectual property, where those valuation principles are pertinent to the value of unquoted shares and intangible assets. Judges' comments on the valuation approach to be adopted are reviewed.

Part 2 concerns statute law, tax law in particular, not only the valuation provisions but also the taxation consequences arising from transfers of unquoted shares on death or during the shareholder's lifetime.

Part 3 looks at valuation in practice in unquoted shares, goodwill and intellectual property for commercial, fiscal, matrimonial and other purposes. The various methods of valuation, negotiating with Shares and Assets Valuation and the influence of Stock Exchanges are all discussed, together with guidance on the preparation of valuation reports and the use of published information.

Division B contains examples of valuation reports and valuations for both fiscal and commercial purposes.

Division C contains a compilation of statistics, public notices and other information of relevance to the valuer of shares, goodwill and intellectual property.

Nigel Eastaway OBE
Diane Elliott
Cameron Cook
Chris Blundell

London
March 2019

Acknowledgements

Extracts from the Final Report from the Expert Group on Intellectual Property Valuation published by the European Commission are reproduced with authorisation from the European Commission © European Union, 2014.

Extracts from IAS 36, IFRS 2 and IFRS 13 are copyright of the IFRS® Foundation in respect of which all rights are reserved. Reproduced by Bloomsbury Professional Ltd with the permission of the IFRS Foundation. No permission granted to third parties to reproduce or distribute. For full access to IFRS Standards and the work of the IFRS Foundation, please visit http://eifrs.org.

Disclaimer: The International Accounting Standards Board®, the IFRS Foundation, the authors and the publishers do not accept responsibility for any loss caused by acting or refraining from acting in reliance on the material in this publication, whether such loss is caused by negligence or otherwise.

Extracts from OECD (2014), *Guidance on Transfer Pricing Aspects of Intangibles, OECD/G20 Base Erosion and Profit Shifting Project*, OECD Publishing (http://dx.doi.org/10.1787/9789264219212-en) are reproduced with kind permission of the OECD.

Extracts from FRS 102 and FRS 105 are adapted and reproduced with the kind permission of the Financial Reporting Council. All rights reserved. For further information, please visit www.frc.org.uk or call +44 (0)20 7492 2300 © Financial Reporting Council Ltd (FRC).

Appendix E: RICS Valuation Global Standards VPGA 3, VPGA 4, VPGA 6, VPGA 7 and VPGA 10 are reproduced by permission of the Royal Institution of Chartered Surveyors who own the copyright.

Appendix F: International Private Equity and Venture Capital (IPEV) Valuation Guidelines, Appendix 1, is reproduced with permission from the IPEV Board (www.privateequityvaluation.com) © IPEV Board.

Appendix F: All rights reserved, subject to permission having been granted to Bloomsbury Professional to include IVS 105, Valuation Approaches and Methods, from the International Valuation Standards 2017 in the publication *Practical Share Valuation* (Seventh Edition). IVS 2017 are the copyright of IVSC.

The International Valuation Standards Council, the authors and the publishers do not accept responsibility for loss caused to any person who acts or refrains from acting in reliance on the material in this publication, whether such loss is caused by negligence or otherwise.

Copyright © 2017 International Valuation Standards Council (IVSC).

No responsibility is accepted by the IVSC for the accuracy of information contained in the text as republished or translated. The approved text of the International Valuation Standards 2017 is that published by the IVSC in the

English language and copies may be obtained from the IVSC, 4 Lombard Street, London EC3V 9AA, United Kingdom (www.ivsc.org).

Appendix H: This appendix reproduces part of the Factsheet Collection available to member expert witnesses of the *UK Register of Expert Witnesses* and is reproduced herein with permission of J S Publications. The *UK Register of Expert Witnesses* Factsheets are regularly updated and you are advised to visit www.jspubs.com/experts/library.htm to ensure you have the latest version.

Appendices I and J: These tables were published in EG Books' publication *Parry's Valuation and Investment Tables* (12th edn) by AW Davidson. The tables reproduced are the Present Value of £1 and The Years' Purchase or Present Value of £1. © EG Books (2003).

All efforts have been made to contact the publishers of other reproduced extracts, and sources are acknowledged here. We welcome approaches from publishers and other copyright holders to discuss further acknowledgements or terms relating to reproduction of this material.

Contents

PART 3 VALUATION IN PRACTICE

DIVISION C APPENDICES

List of Acronyms

AIM	Alternative Investment Market
ASC	Accounting Standards Committee
CISX	Channel Island Stock Exchange
CRR	Cox, Ross and Rubinstein binomial options model
CTA	Corporation Tax Act
EBIT	Earnings Before Interest and Tax
EBITDA	Earnings Before Interest, Tax, Depreciation and Amortisation
EBT	Employee Benefit Trust
EWCA	England & Wales Court of Appeal
FA	Finance Act
FASB	Financial Accounting Standards Board
FCA	Financial Conduct Authority
FMOP	Fair Maintainable Operating Profit
FRC	Financial Reporting Council
FRS	Financial Reporting Standard
FRSSE	Financial Reporting Standard for Smaller Entities
FSMA	Financial Services and Markets Act 2000
FT	Financial Times
FTSE Indices	Financial Times Stock Exchange Indices
FTT	First Tier Tribunal
FV	Fair Value
G20 Guidelines	G20 group of countries' guidelines on transfer pricing
GAAP	Generally Accepted Accounting Practice
HMRC	Her Majesty's Revenue & Customs
IAS	International Accounting Standard
IASB	International Accounting Standards Board
IFRS	International Financial Reporting Standard
IPEV	International Private Equity and Venture Capital Valuation
ISDX	ICAP Securities and Derivatives Exchange
IVSC	International Valuation Standards Council
JV	Joint Venture
LAPM	Liquidity-based Asset Pricing Model
LSE	London Stock Exchange
MTD	Making Tax Digital
OECD	Organisation for European Co-operation and Development
P&L Account	Profit and Loss Account

PAYE	Pay As You Earn tax collection system
PCPI	BDO LLP Private Company Price Index
PEPI	BDO LLP Private Equity Price Index
PSV	Practical Share Valuation Book
RICS	Royal Institution of Chartered Surveyors
RIE	Recognised Investment Exchange
SAV	Shares and Assets Valuation Section of HMRC
SAYE	Save As You Earn
SEDOL	Stock Exchange Daily Official List
SME	Small and medium-sized enterprise
STRGL	Statement of Recognised Gains and Losses
TCC	Take Command Console
TCGA	Taxation of Chargeable Gains Act
TIP	IVSC Technical Information Paper
TV	Terminal Value
UK	United Kingdom
UKFTT	United Kingdom First Tier Tribunal
UKSIC	UK Standard Industrial Classification of Economic Activities
UKUT	United Kingdom Upper Tribunal
VAT	Value Added Tax
WACC	Weighted Average Cost of Capital
WARA	Weighted Average Return on Assets
WWW	World Wide Web

Table of Statutes

All references are to paragraph number, Example number in Division B, and Appendix in Division C.

INDIA

Table of Statutory Instruments

All references are to paragraph number, Example number in Division B, and Appendix in Division C.

Table of European Legislation

All references are to paragraph number, Example number in Division B, and Appendix in Division C.

Table of Cases

All references are to paragraph number, Example number in Division B, and Appendix in Division C.

B

C

D

E

F

J

K

L

M

N

O

P

Q

R

S

T

X

Y

Z

Division A
Main narrative

Part 1: Case law

Part 2: Statute law

Part 3: Valuation in practice

Chapter 1

Introduction

Signposts

1.01 Purpose of valuation

When considering the value of shares in a company the first thing to ascertain is the precise purpose of the valuation. There is no such thing as a value of a share in isolation. There is however a value of a specific number of specific shares in a specific company in a given set of circumstances, real or hypothetical.

1.02 Occasions for valuation

It is clearly necessary to consider the value of shares in a company where there is a proposal actually to buy shares and similarly where there is a real sale. It may also be necessary to value shares on a compulsory acquisition following a take-over under the Companies Act 2006 (CA 2006), s 979 or a court order under CA 2006, ss 994–999,or in connection with divorce, death, or on a gift or sale at an undervalue. It would also be necessary to value shares on a distribution from a trust or on a sale to directors or employees either as part of a share incentive scheme, or otherwise. Commercially there may be occasions for valuation if shares are to be offered as security for a loan or if the shares are to be dealt in on the Stock Exchange, the Alternative Investment Market or elsewhere.

A de-merger or management buy-out involving financial assistance under CA 2006, ss 677–683 could require a valuation, as may the provisions in CA 2006, ss 690–723 to enable companies in the UK to redeem or purchase their own shares. Valuation of shares may also be required in claims for damages arising out of breach of contract, or illegal restrictive practices, or as a result of alleged breach of warranties or indemnities following a sale of shares. Where shares are acquired on a takeover, for shares in the acquiring company a valuation is required under CA 2006, ss 593–609.

Corporate governance may also be enforced through the Insolvency Act 1986 and the Company Directors Disqualification Act 1986, International Financial Reporting Standards (IFRS) and the Financial Conduct Authority (FCA). Unlimited companies are possible but unusual. Limitation of liability may be through a company limited by guarantee but most companies are limited by shares. Charitable organisations may be community interest companies under the Companies Audit, Investigations and Community Enterprise Act 2004. A UK-based business may, at the time of writing, be incorporated under European Company Statutes, or a Societas Europaea, or SE. A few sections of the Companies Acts of 1985 and 1989 remain in force.

Model Articles of Association are deemed to apply, under the Companies (Model Articles) Regulations 2008 (SI 2008/3229), but most companies register their own Articles with bespoke amendments to the model articles. Company formation requirements are set out in CA 2006, ss 7–16.

A transfer or issue of preference shares might be contemplated as might a reconstruction with equity participation by one of the venture capital companies. There may be an issue of share options or fair value assessments for accounting purposes. In each case it will be necessary to value the company's shares.

Variations in class rights among different classes of shares or alleged breaches of such rights may require a valuation.

There will also be occasions where there is a deemed disposal of shares under various taxation statutes calling for a valuation. The particular points arising in each of these cases will be dealt with in more detail in later chapters.

In *Re Press Caps Ltd* [1949] 1 All ER 1013, *Re Hoare & Co Ltd* (1933) LT 374, *Grierson, Oldham and Adams Ltd* [1967] 1 WLR 385 in a take-over bid accepted by 90 per cent of the relevant shareholders, the shares of the dissident minority may be compulsory acquired by the purchaser under CA 2006, ss 979–991, if it is fair to the body of shareholders. Unfairness is not merely that the offer is open to criticism, but it must be 'obviously unfair, patently unfair, unfair to the meanest intelligence': *Re Sussex Brick Co Ltd* [1960] 1 All ER 772. Sufficient information must be given to the shareholders, whose shares are being acquired; the board of that company should take independent advice and so inform its shareholders: *Fiske Nominees Ltd v Dwyke Diamonds Ltd* [2002] EWHC 770 (Ch).

> **Focus**
>
> The reasons for the shares being on the market may affect the value.

1.03 Limited and unlimited companies

A company may be limited by shares if the liability of its members is limited by its constitution to the amount, if any, unpaid on its shares: CA 2006, s 3(2). A company may be limited by guarantee if the liability of its members is limited by its constitution to the, usually nominal, amount which the members undertake to contribute to the assets of the company in the event of it being wound up: CA 2006, s 3(3).

Companies limited by guarantee are usually charities (governed by the Charities Act 2011), or community interest companies under the Companies (Audit, Investigations and Community Enterprise) Act 2004.

A company cannot be formed, or become, a company limited by guarantee with a share capital (since 22 December 1980 in Great Britain and 1 July 1983 in Northern Ireland): CA 2006, s 5.

An unlimited company is one with no limit to the members' liability for its debts: CA 2006, s 3(4). It may be exempt from the obligation to file accounts (CA 2006, s 448), as it is, in effect, an incorporated partnership.

A private company is a company that is not a public company: CA 2006, s 4(1). A public company is one which is incorporated or registered or reregistered as such, CA 2006, s 4(2)–(4). A public company may make an offer of its shares to the public, but is not required to (CA 2006, ss 755–760), and has a trading certificate and a minimum allotted share capital of £50,000: CA 2006, ss 761–767.

Revenue and Customs Brief 87/09 includes a useful summary of the characteristics of ordinary share capital in a UK company under CTA 2010, s 1119 as 'all the company's issued share capital (however described), other than capital the holders of which have a right to a dividend at a fixed rate but have no other right to share in the company's profits'.

The distinction between a company and its shareholders was finally determined by the House of Lords in *Salomon v A Salomon and Co Ltd* [1897] AC 22.

1.04 Different classes of shares

The rights of the holders of shares in a company are set out in the company's articles of association and may not normally be altered without the approval of at least three-quarters of the votes being cast in favour of the alteration. Such an alteration would be by means of a special resolution.

It cannot be too strongly emphasised that it is the rights attaching to the shares which are important, not the name by which they are called. It will be seen below that ordinary shares normally have voting rights but it is perfectly feasible to have non-voting ordinary shares. Indeed, some non-voting ordinary shares are listed securities. It is often assumed that preference shares will have limited voting rights only, but unless this is specifically stated in the articles of association, preference shares will carry one vote per share (see **12.09**). In *Joanne Elizabeth Fletcher v RCC* (2008) SpC 711 the Special Commissioner considered the value of B ordinary shares which had a dividend entitlement to 'such amount as the directors may determine by majority vote up to a maximum of 7%'. The shares held no voting rights and the Commissioner stated:

> 'I must therefore value the B ordinary shares by reference to their liquidation entitlement and to their nebulous dividend right and having regard to the double risk associated with any third party purchase of these shares I cannot put a higher value than 5% on the relevant shares. I was not addressed on whether there would be any company law pressure on the directors to pay reasonable dividends up to the 7% ceiling on the shares were the directors paying large dividends on the other shares. I would however be surprised if the holder of the shares who would have invested in the knowledge that the directors could choose to pay any lower amount of dividend below 7% could complain and seek any remedy if the directors chose to do precisely what it was indicated that they could do.
>
> On a stand alone basis I thus consider that the B ordinary shares were worth only £2,500 when subscribed on 16 May 2003. The 50,000 £1 B ordinary shares had been subscribed for at par by converting a company loan account into shares at a time when the company had significant value.'

1.05 Ordinary shares

Ordinary shares or equity shares are those shares which normally carry votes at company meetings and entitle the holder to a dividend, if declared by the directors. The ordinary shareholders normally will be entitled to any surplus on winding up after all the liabilities and any preference shareholders have been paid. It is sometimes provided by the articles that there are different classes of ordinary shares such as A shares, B shares and C shares. This may be merely for the sake of convenience so that, for example, a dividend could be paid on C shares held by a family trust, but not on A and B shares held by individuals. The rights however may be varied in other ways, and, for example, the A shares might be entitled to dividends but not to vote or to participate in a surplus on liquidation. The B shares might be entitled to vote but not to participate in dividends or a surplus on liquidation, while the C shares might be entitled to the surplus on liquidation but not entitled to vote or participate in dividends. Any combination of name and rights is possible. Such shares are still relatively unusual in practice but are useful as a means of keeping down the value of the shares. It will be appreciated, however, that if more than one class of shares are held by the same shareholder the shares may have to be aggregated if being valued for inheritance tax purposes, see **10.03**.

Other classes of ordinary shares commonly met with are non-voting shares which are often issued to employees.

1.06 Management shares

Management or founder's shares very often carry a majority of the votes even though their nominal value may be but a small proportion of the total ordinary share capital. It is not unusual to find management shares in aggregate carrying one more vote than all the other ordinary shares put together. A certain class of shares could be given the exclusive right to appoint the company's directors, whilst ranking pari passu with other classes in other respects.

Management shares under existing legislation are merely valued at the open market value for fiscal purposes and the basis of valuation might be to calculate what could reasonably be extracted from the company for the benefit of the management shareholders on an earnings per management share basis. This profit per share could take the form of remuneration over and above a reasonable market rate for the work done, but not so high as to enable other shareholders to petition the court under CA 2006, ss 994–996 as unfairly prejudicial conduct or in such a manner as would justify the company being wound up on just and equitable grounds under the Insolvency Act 1986, s 122(1)(g) and the Insolvency (England and Wales) Rules 2016 (SI 2016/1024).

Holt v Holt [1990] 1 WLR 1250 concerned the value of one A share, which alone carried the vast majority of votes but was entitled to one ten-thousandth only of net assets on a winding up. The company owned a farm, and Lord Templeman said, at 1253:

> 'The A shareholder is more nearly in the position of a tenant for life impeachable for waste. He can appoint himself sole director and in that capacity take possession of the farm estate, the farmhouse, the livestock, the machinery and equipment and all the other assets of the company. He can occupy the farmhouse as a family home, he can run the estate as he thinks fit. Unlike a farming manager he cannot be dismissed and is not obliged to consult or take instructions from anyone. He is as much the squire of the Woodah Farm estate as a tenant for life and can even cause the estate to be sold if he pleases. He cannot sell capital assets and put the money in his pocket, he cannot commit waste and he cannot artificially increase the profits of the farm for his own benefit by allowing the condition and state of repair of the estate to deteriorate. But if he would like to farm the estate and enjoy the advantages of being a farmer in the Valley as long as he likes, drawing reasonable remuneration, he cannot be interfered with.'

1.07 Preferred ordinary shares

Preferred ordinary shares are very often similar to participating preference shares which means that as well as being entitled to a fixed dividend they may also participate in a surplus. The rights vary, but it is not unusual to find that the preferred ordinary shares receive a fixed cumulative dividend and if a further dividend is paid on the ordinary shares. Once the ordinary shareholders have received the same rate of dividend as the preferred ordinary shareholders, both classes of shares may then participate in any additional profits distributed by way of dividend either equally or in accordance with some formula set out in the articles.

Preferred ordinary shares could be valued in the same way as ordinary shares on the basis of their entitlement to earnings, dividends and assets, but the dividend entitlement would justify the dividend element in the valuation being weighted more highly than the earnings and assets to take account of the preferred rights. However, in some cases, the rights would be such that it would be appropriate to value them as debt rather than equity.

1.08 Deferred ordinary shares

Deferred ordinary shares are usually those whose rights are deferred for a period of time, often ten to 15 years, during which they are not entitled to votes, dividends, or to participate in any surplus on liquidation, but at the end of the period they acquire the same rights as ordinary shares either immediately or over a period of time. The main purpose of issuing deferred shares would be for inheritance tax purposes where their initial value would be small. If they are issued to existing shareholders and then given away, inheritance tax could be payable on this small value, but in due course they would acquire the same rights as the ordinary shares and acquire a much greater value without there being another transfer of value for inheritance tax purposes. HMRC's Shares and Assets Valuation Section challenged this view in 1991 and for a discussion of the position at the time of writing see **10.06**.

In some cases deferred ordinary shares are merely deferred as regards dividend rights so that they only participate in a dividend after the other shareholders have received their dividend, but these are relatively unusual as they do not have the same tax planning attraction as those whose rights are entirely deferred.

It is suggested that for capital gains tax purposes deferred shares should be valued on the same basis as existing ordinary shares and then discounted for the period of deferral at a suitable rate of discount. If the deferral period is 15 years and a suitable rate of discount is 15% per annum the present value on this basis would be 12.29% on the value of the ordinary shares. At a discount rate of 18% per annum the present value would be 8.35% of the ordinary shares on a 15-year deferral and at a rate of discount of 20% per annum for a similar period the value is 6.49% of the ordinary shares. See Valuation Example 4 in Division B.

Ordinary Shares which may become worthless under a ratchet provision in a management buyout are also referred to as deferred shares.

1.09 Convertible securities

Convertible securities usually consist of loan stock convertible at some future date into equity shares at a predetermined price. For valuation purposes such securities may be valued first of all as a basic fixed interest security and then the conversion rights themselves valued. This would involve making some estimate of the likely share value at the conversion date and discounting this at a suitable rate of interest to its present value. Clearly the further into the future the valuation date the more difficult it becomes to estimate the future value of the shares, but on the other hand, at times of high rates of discounting the accuracy of the future projection becomes less important. If, for example, the conversion right is on the basis of one and half times the current share price and it is anticipated that at the conversion date in, say, 10 years' time, the share price will have trebled, the conversion right at a 20% discount would be some 24% (1.5% + net present value at 20% per annum after 10 years of 0.16) of the estimated ordinary share value; at a 15% discount rate, the conversion right would be some 36% (1.5% + net present value at 15% per annum after 10 years of 0.24) of the estimated ordinary share value, in each case, less the basic fixed interest security value.

1.10 Preference shares

Preference shares normally carry a fixed right to dividend, if declared by the directors, but may be preferred in the case of a liquidation. Preference dividends would normally be cumulative; that is, if they are not paid one year the deficit must be made good in a future year before dividends are paid on ordinary shares, but this presumption may be rebutted if the shares are specifically stated to be non-cumulative or if the articles state that the dividends are to be paid out of the profits of the year. Preference shares do not normally carry votes unless the dividend is in arrears, but will do in all circumstances if the articles of association make no specific provision. Preference shares carrying votes in certain circumstances, such as where the dividends are in arrears, could be of extreme importance for inheritance tax purposes because it could allow the control of the company to change under the provisions of IHTA 1984, s 269(1); see **10.07**.

Preference shareholders will usually be entitled merely to a return of capital in a liquidation, but this would normally be paid in priority to any repayment on the ordinary shares. The articles may however specify that the preference shareholders are entitled to participate in the surplus on a liquidation and in all cases it is important to study the precise provisions of the articles.

Preference shares are normally valued on the basis of the dividend yield by comparison with quoted preference shares, as explained in **12.09**. If there is a cumulative dividend – the cumulative dividends would be valued using discounted cash flow (DCF) calculations – any rights additional to the cumulative dividends would need to be valued separately (eg conversion rights). There may be cases, however, where the voting rights or rights to participate in a liquidation surplus, if any, could be of considerable importance and therefore value, and if there is any doubt as to the continued payment of preference dividends this would also clearly be reflected in the value. Preference shares may also be convertible and the conversion rights would have to be taken into account.

Sometimes, capital described as share capital is actually a liability of the company, so is really part of the debt of a company, notwithstanding that it is called share capital. This issue is addressed thoroughly in IFRS, which provides extensive guidance on how to differentiate debt capital (ie liabilities of a company) from equity capital, although they may be classified as debt, ie liabilities for financial reporting purposes, especially if redeemable, or part debt and part equity under IFRS.

1.11 Participating preference shares

Participating preference shares are really no more than a variation of preferred ordinary shares and would be valued on the same basis.

1.12 No par value shares

In many countries it is possible to issue shares with no par value. Such shares are not permissible in the UK (CA 2006, s 542), but legislation might be introduced to permit the issue of such shares in the future. However, there is no minimum par value so it could be a small fraction of a penny per share. From a valuation point of view the par value of a share is irrelevant except to the extent that it may delineate the right to dividend which is often expressed as a percentage of the par value, or to the return of capital in a liquidation which might again be related to the par value. In the case of no par value shares such particulars are expressed on a per share basis.

Focus

The value of a share depends on its rights and the underlying value of the company concerned.

1.13 Appropriation of profit

Dividends are an appropriation of profits, paid out of income after taxation. The company pays corporation tax on its profits with no allowance for the dividends.

For 2017–18 the tax-free dividend allowance is £5,000, and for 2018–19 it is £2,000 and is applied to the cash dividend received.

The dividend ordinary rate, for dividends otherwise taxable at the basic rate of 20%, is 7.5%.

The dividend upper rate, for dividends otherwise taxable at the higher rate of 40%, is 32.5%.

The dividend additional rate, for dividends otherwise taxable at the additional rate of 45%, is 38.1%.

The starting rate for non dividend savings income is 0% up to £5,000.

Trustees are taxable (at up to 20%, depending on the type of income) on the first £1,000 of income otherwise taxable at the trust rate of 45% or the dividend trust rate of 38.1%.

In the case of a corporate recipient the dividend, having been paid out of profits after corporation tax, is not again subject to corporation tax in the hands of the recipient.

1.14 Loan capital

Other forms of capital issued by a company include debentures which are merely a formal acknowledgment of a loan, debenture stock which is a debenture divided into units to make it marketable by the lenders, and loan stock. Such loan capital may be either secured or unsecured and the interest paid by the borrowing company on the loans would be, in most cases, an allowable deduction for tax purposes under the loan relationship rules. In some cases the borrowing might be directly related to the trade in which case the interest would be allowed as a trading expense rather than as a charge on income. Unless paid to a company subject to corporation tax, yearly interest on UK loans is paid subject to deduction of tax at the basic rate under ITA 2007, s 874. This tax is accounted for under the provisions of ITA 2007, ss 945–962 on form CT61. The recipient receives a net amount and a tax credit for the tax deducted and is liable to higher rate tax on the combined total, which is the gross amount of the interest. The corporate recipient of loan interest is liable to corporation tax on the gross amount received.

Loan capital will normally be repayable at some future date, which may be either fixed or variable according to the terms of issue and this is known as the redemption date. The loan may be repaid either at par or at a small premium and in theory, though not normally in practice, the repayment could be at a small discount.

The security of a debenture or loan stock, if any, may be a fixed charge on the company's freehold or leasehold properties, or more commonly, a floating charge over the company's assets in which case it would rank after a fixed charge but before the unsecured creditors.

Ardmore Construction Limited v HMRC [2018] EWCA Civ 1438 revolves around the source principle that income tax is only payable on income from a source in the UK, now under ITTOIA 2005, s 368 and ITA 2007, s 874 and is longstanding, eg *Colquhoun v Brooks* (1889) 14 App Cas 493. Ardmore submitted that the appropriate test was where the lender was, which was rejected by the First Tier Tribunal, quoting *CIR v Orion Caribbean Limited (in voluntary liquidation)* [1997] STC 923. The Upper Tribunal relied primarily on *Westminster Bank Executors v National Bank of Greece SA* (1970) 46 TC 472, which held that the source was outside the UK, applying the multifunctional test. However, Ardmore still argued that Gibraltar was the source of the interest but the Court of Appeal held otherwise and the source was in the UK.

1.15 Allotment of shares

When shares are issued, the shareholder will normally pay the nominal value of the shares to the company unless the shares are issued at a premium, in which case he pays the amount inclusive of the premium which is shown in the company's share premium account. However, a company may decide to capitalise its reserves by issuing bonus shares. Bonus shares are often issued on renounceable letters of allotment which enable the recipient of the bonus shares to renounce them in favour of some other party, although under FA 1986, s 88 this is subject to stamp duty reserve tax. If a company having shares in issue wishes to raise additional capital it may make what is known as a 'rights issue' to the existing shareholders, which would again normally be on renounceable letters of allotment, under which the existing shareholders are allowed to acquire further shares at less than the value of the existing shares. It will be appreciated that a failure to exercise the rights and take up the shares would allow the shareholding to be diluted by the issue of the additional shares.

Shares may not be allotted at a discount in view of CA 2006, s 580 although may be issued nil or partly paid, the balance being uncalled share capital. Shares may be issued on such terms that they are redeemable and this is particularly common in the case of preference shares. At the date of redemption the company repays the nominal value of the shares, possibly together with a small premium, and capitalises an equivalent amount of reserves under the capital redemption reserve procedure set out in CA 2006, ss 684–689 or out of capital under CA 2006, ss 709–723.

A bonus issue of shares other than for new consideration would not normally be of redeemable shares as the subsequent redemption would be treated as a distribution for corporation tax purposes under the provisions of CTA 2010, ss 1022–1027.

It is not intended in this book to give more than this very brief résumé on the salient features of different types of shares and loan stock. In all cases of valuation of such securities it is absolutely essential to study the debenture trust deed, loan stock agreement or the articles in the case of shares, to find out the precise terms as a first step in arriving at an appropriate value.

1.16 Purchase of own shares

A company may purchase its own shares under the provisions of CA 2006, ss 690–708, provided that its articles of association specifically grant it the power to do so. There are no Companies Act guidelines or specifications for determining the price at which an unquoted company should purchase its own shares, but a price which clearly moves value between shareholders may well fall foul of the capital gains tax value shifting rules (TCGA 1992, s 29 et seq; see **9.21**) or be a transfer of value for inheritance tax purposes (see 10.02). The company's articles of association may prescribe a value without discount for a minority holding on a purchase of own shares, which may or may not be equivalent to open market value for fiscal purposes.

The shares bought back may be cancelled or could be held by the company as treasury shares under CA 2006, ss 724–732.

1.17 Basic valuation principles

The detailed rules and principles involving share valuation laid down by statute, the courts and established valuation practice will be dealt with in some detail in the following chapters. It is however at this stage worth outlining the fundamental aspects which determine the value of a share.

Ultimately the value of anything is what somebody else is prepared to pay for it. In the case of shares in any company the real market is necessarily restricted to those people and institutions prepared to pay for the shares which are basically nothing more than a bundle of rights possessed by the shareholder. For a private company, there is an added restriction in the real market; the restrictions on transfer that are often contained in the articles of association. These rights are delineated by the memorandum and articles of association of the company and by the Companies Acts and court decisions thereon. The shares may entitle the shareholder to participate in dividends that may be declared by the directors, voting in accordance with the rights attached to the shares and to participate in a surplus on liquidation. The shareholder does not possess a proportionate interest in the actual underlying assets of the company. A potential purchaser of such shares is therefore going to consider carefully the rights he would have as the holder of the block of shares being valued. If these were a non-controlling interest the holder would be entitled to such dividends as the directors declare, if any, and he would not be able to exercise sufficient votes to change the board of directors if he thought the dividends paid were ungenerous compared with the available profits. However, merely because dividends may not be declared does not mean that the shares are worthless as profits will be reinvested for the eventual benefit of the shareholders, including the non-controlling shareholders. If, on the other hand, the number of shares on offer are sufficient to give the purchaser voting control he will be able to decide how much of the profit should be paid by way of dividend or reinvested or drawn as remuneration and he is therefore primarily interested in the earnings of the company.

A purchaser of 75% or more of the voting shares could, subject to any specific requirement in the articles or shareholders' agreement, put the company into liquidation and is therefore interested in both the break-up value of the shares and the earnings on the basis of keeping the company as a going concern. He would theoretically be prepared to pay on the basis of whichever of these methods gave the greatest value. A 51% shareholder may be able to do the same in appropriate circumstances.

Valuation calculations are often made on the basis of the historical results of the company, but in reality the purchaser is interested in the future results after he has acquired the shares, not in the past results, and therefore these are only of relevance to the extent that they may be some indication of the likely results that could be expected for the future.

Even a minority shareholder is interested in the asset cover of the company as, if two companies have identical profits and dividends, but one had equity in freehold properties worth £500,000, whereas the other merely had current assets balanced by liabilities, it is likely that a purchaser would pay more for the shares of the company with the freehold property, assuming of course that the anticipated future profits were similar. The reason is simply that such an acquisition would be less speculative, ie have less risk attaching to it, in that, if for any reason the business failed, it would nonetheless still be possible to realise the freehold properties.

It must also be borne in mind that valuations required for specific purposes may be subject to specific rules or considerations and these factors are considered in the following chapters.

1.18 Valuation calculations

The three basic factors which affect the value of a company's shares are its earnings, dividends and asset value and may be evidenced by actual sales at arm's length. The relative importance of these factors will vary in relation to the size of the shareholding being valued. Risk and growth are considered to be key factors.

In many cases in practice it will be found that there are no arm's length transactions, as even in the relatively rare cases where there have been real sales at or about the valuation date it is likely to be shown on investigation that the transfers would be between members of a family or to employees or in other circumstances which could not be classified as an arm's length sale.

When the three basic factors have been ascertained it becomes necessary to consider the influence of each of them on the resulting valuation. There are various ways in which this may be done and one method which is likely to be useful is to convert the earnings and dividends to a capitalised equivalent by applying to them a suitable price/earnings ratio and dividend yield. The three basic valuation approaches are cost, market value and income, as set out in International Valuation Standard (IVS) 300 (see **20.01**).

The problem is always to arrive at a suitable capitalisation ratio or yield and some assistance in determining these figures might be obtained from comparison with quoted public companies and considering the yields available on gilt edged securities and the likely return required by potential purchasers in the real market such as the commercial venture capital companies. This aspect of the correct capitalisation factor is considered later in **Chapter 6** and in **Part 3**.

If it is thought appropriate to adopt the 'hybrid' method of valuation illustrated in Division B, it is then necessary to decide the weighting that should be attached to each factor in the valuation. It might, for example, be appropriate in the case of a substantial minority interest to attach a weighting of say 40% to earnings, 40% to dividends, and 20% to assets. In another case of a controlling interest it might be appropriate to attach a weighting of say 75% to earnings, 5% to dividends, 20% to assets. If more than 75% of the shares are held and the company is asset rich it might be appropriate in the circumstances to attach a weighting of 20% to earnings, nothing to dividends and 80% to assets. Again, in the case of a very small minority interest it might be appropriate to attach say 10% to earnings, 85% to dividends and 5% to assets. The hybrid method is, however, not appropriate in many cases and it may be better to adopt a primary (ie cost, market or income) method and cross-check by a supporting method.

1.19 Discount for lack of marketability

From the raw value per share arrived at as a result of the capitalisation calculations from publicly quoted shares referred to above, it is generally necessary to deduct a discount for lack of marketability in order to value the unquoted shares. It is very difficult to find any justification in the UK for a specific level of discount for lack of marketability. In the case of *Re Holt* (1953) 32 ATC 402 at 405, Mr Benson suggested a 33⅓% discount for non-marketability. In *Re Lynall, Lynall v IRC* (1971) 47 TC 375 at 389, he widened the range and suggested a discount for non-marketability of between 25% and 50%. Shares and Assets Valuation will normally accept a discount for non-marketability of 35% (in *Hawkings-Byass v Sassen* [1996] STC (SCD) 319 the Revenue's expert deducted 35%), although this will vary from time to time. In times of depression, tight money and slow markets there is less competition to buy and the greater difficulty in selling could justify a higher discount and the converse would equally apply.

Research in America on discount for lack of marketability is somewhat easier in view of the existence of letter stock which is not marketable but otherwise ranks pari passu with quoted shares. The Institutional Investor Study Report of the Securities and Exchange Commission on discounts involved in purchases of common stock, published on 10 March 1971, showed that the majority of discounts fell in the 30% to 40% range and an article entitled 'The Impact of Stock Transfer Restrictions on the Private Placement Discount' by Professor John D Finnerty in June 2008, suggests that such discounts reduce with the increase in size of the offering: for a $20million placement, a discount may be between 17.5% and 25%.

In an article in the Journal of Business Valuation and Economic Analysis in 2006, William P Dukes refers to a summary of 11 research efforts which have identified the spread in values between restricted letter stock and actively traded stock which are identical in all other respects, which produced an average discount of about 32.44%. In an article in the *Journal of Finance (USA)* of December 1995, at pp1767–1774, Francis A Longstaff refers to letter stock being typically privately placed at a 30 to 35% discount. It would appear therefore that a discount for lack of marketability of about 35% can reasonably be accepted although it might be worth pushing for a higher discount of up to 50% if for any reason the shares would be particularly difficult to market, although such difficulties would normally be reflected in the capitalisations and yields used and it would not be reasonable to take this into account twice. In the article referred to above Mr Dukes refers to research on the value of marketability as illustrated by Initial Public Offerings and concludes that the average discount for non-marketability shown by such research is 55% in such cases. He points out that smaller companies are more likely to make an IPO than to issue letter stock.

In *Caton's Administration v Couch* [1995] STC (SCD) 34, the Revenue's expert adopted a discount of 60% to 70% to allow for the fact that the shares were unmarketable and that the holding was uninfluential. As he had based the undiscounted value on comparison with shares traded on the Stock Exchange, which are invariably uninfluential holdings, it is not clear why he thought that element of the discount to be necessary. The Special Commissioner nevertheless appeared to consider a 60% discount to be acceptable. It seems likely that factors other than simple lack of marketability influenced the discount.

1.20 Valuation methodology

1. A Company has been valued by reference to the following common valuation approaches:
   1) Market approach, including an analysis of:
      a) comparable transactions (mergers and acquisitions); and
      b) comparable listed companies.
   2) Cost approach, including an analysis of:
      a) replacement cost.
2. The final Valuation has taken account of relevant, commonly applied discounts when valuing shares in privately owned companies.

The Valuation of a company

3. The overall valuation of a business is often termed its Enterprise Value ('EV'); the sum of its total market value of equity (also known as market capitalisation with regard to listed companies) plus preferred shares and net debt (debt, less surplus cash and cash equivalents), as summarised by the diagram below.

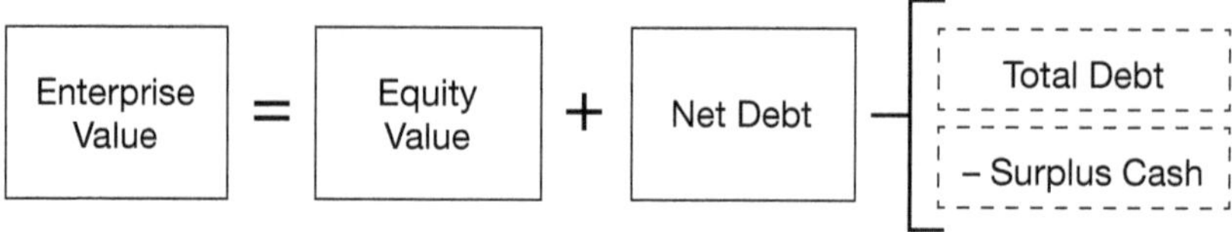

Basis for valuation

4. In order to perform the Valuation in accordance with the instructions, it is usually necessary to assess the Business on the basis of its 'open market value'. In a statutory context, this has been defined as 'the price which those assets might reasonably be expected to fetch on a sale in the open market' s.272(1) TGCA 1992, and similarly defined in s.160 IHTA 1984. Per the 2017 International Valuation Standards ('IVS') report, produced by the International Valuation Standards Council, 'Market Value' is defined (per IVS 104, Paragraph 30.1) as:

> 'the estimated amount for which an asset or liability should exchange on the valuation date between a willing buyer and a willing seller in an arm's length transaction, after proper marketing and where the parties had each acted knowledgeably, prudently and without compulsion'.

5. Each component of this definition is further explained in Paragraph 30.2(a) through (f) IVS 104.
6. The approach adopted in compiling this Report seeks to assess the value that a willing buyer might place on the whole business as a going concern, recognising such willing buyer would assume control over all of the profit and net assets enjoyed by the business, before taking account of specific circumstances related to the valuation of a proportion of the value of a given business.
7. There are a number of accepted methodologies which are routinely used to value a business. These are outlined in this section which sets out the selected bases for valuation applied in compiling this Report, and the assumptions relied upon in so doing.
8. Accepted valuation methodologies fall into the following broadly accepted categories:

- the 'market' approach – provides an indication of value by comparing the asset with identical or comparable (that is similar) assets for which price information is available (Per IVS 105, Paragraph 20.1);
- the 'income' approach – provides an indication of value by converting future cash flow to a single current value (Per IVS 105, Paragraph 50.1); and
- the 'cost' approach – provides an indication of value using the economic principle that a buyer will pay no more for an asset than the cost to obtain an asset of equal utility (incorporating appropriate

deductions for physical deterioration and all other relevant forms of obsolescence) (Per IVS 105, Paragraph 60.1).

9. Some of the more commonly used methodologies which fall under each category are explored hereafter.

<u>The market approach</u>

Market transaction method

10. The market transaction method indicates the fair market value based on sums of consideration paid in actual M&A transactions, applying a capitalisation of future maintainable earnings. In *Parkinson v Eurofinance* [2001] 1 BCLC 720 at paragraph 101 it was observed by Pumfrey J that: 'It will be appreciated that any valuation on a going concern basis depends upon a proper determination of the base earnings figure and the multiplier.'
11. Per IVS 105 (Paragraph 30), when applying this method relevant comparable transactions are identified to permit a consistent comparative analysis of qualitative and quantitative similarities and differences with the subject asset (making adjustments to account for differences identified). Where a sufficient number of comparable transactions can be identified to derive relevant valuation metrics which will identify multiples of earnings before interest and tax ('EBIT') or earnings before interest, tax, depreciation and amortisation ('EBITDA') over net profit (for a subject asset, as well as market comparables) as they are capital structure neutral (ie exclude the impact of leverage) and unique taxation features.
12. Where an insufficient number of directly comparable transactions can be identified, or further validation is required, references to published, aggregated mergers and acquisitions data from third-party sources are utilised to derive relevant valuation metrics or 'multiples'.

Market comparable method

13. The market comparable method seeks to compare the subject business to comparable publicly traded companies. IVS 105 suggests that comparable companies must be sufficiently similar taking account of market segment, geographic area, size in revenue and/or assets, growth rates, profit margins, leverage, liquidity and diversification. The market comparable method seeks to analyse and make adjustments for any material differences between the guideline publicly-traded comparables and the subject asset.
14. Having identified relevant market multiples, they are applied to the subject company's operating results to indicate the value on a marketable, minority basis.

Maintainable earnings

15. The application of the market approaches seeks to identify the level of sustainable earnings of a subject asset, calculated by making adjustments for exceptional and non-recurring income and expenses in order to reflect the true, or 'underlying', earnings of the subject business.
16. 'Maintainable earnings' may be described as 'the level below which in the absence of unforeseen and exceptional circumstances the profits [...] would not be likely to fall in an average year' (such description was accepted by Vinelott J at first instance in *Re a Company (No 002612 of 1984)* (1986) 2 BCC at 99453 (*Re Cumana*))

17. Industry practice seeks to adopt the most reliable indicators of maintainable earnings, usually the most recent available historical information and short-term future projections. Where appropriate, a weighted average of adjusted EBIT or EBITDA is adopted, whereby a higher weighting is placed on years where the information is considered to be more representative of the subject's long-term maintainable earnings. Reasonable judgement is required for determining the weightings which should apply to historical financial information, budgets and forecasts.

The income approach

Dividend yield

18. This method capitalises the level of sustainable dividends at an appropriate dividend yield. For a large number of privately owned companies, dividends paid are either minimal or may form part of a salary sacrifice arrangement (remuneration planning). A dividend yield approach is therefore not one of the most commonly utilised methods for the valuation of privately owned companies, but it can be appropriate in some circumstances.

Discounted cash flow (or 'DCF')

19. Per IVS 105 (Paragraph 50.2), in a DCF the cash flows expected to be generated by a business are discounted to their present value equivalent, using a rate of return that reflects the relative risk of the investment, as well as the time value of money.
20. The reliability of the DCF method is dependent upon the reliability of the forecasts and, as such, is more effective for businesses with strong, predictable income and expense streams and robust forecasting systems.
21. The discount rate, known more formally as the 'weighted average cost of capital' or 'WACC' is an overall rate based upon the individual rates of return for invested capital (equity and interest-bearing debt). The WACC is calculated by weighting the required returns on interest-bearing debt and common equity capital in proportion to their estimated percentages in an expected capital structure.

The discount rate: calculating the WACC

22. The formula for calculating WACC is:
23. WACC = [Kd * (D%)] + [Ke * (E%)]

Symbol	Explanation
WACC	Weighted average cost of capital on invested capital (comprising debt and equity combined)
K_d	After-tax rate of return on debt capital
D%	Debt capital as a percentage of the sum of the debt, preferred and common equity capital ('Total Invested Capital')
K_e	Rate of return on common equity capital
E%	Common equity capital as a percentage of the Total Invested Capital

24. In order to calculate the WACC, the first requirement is to calculate the rate of return on debt and the required return on equity. Explanations for both of these processes are set out below.

Calculating Kd (rate of return on debt) for use in WACC formula

25. The rate of return on debt capital is the rate a likely investor would require on interest-bearing debt of the subject company assuming a typical industry capital structure. Since the interest on debt capital is an allowable deduction for tax purposes, the after-tax interest rate is used in the calculation.
26. The after-tax rate of return on debt capital is calculated using the formula:
27. Kd = K * (1 – t)

Symbol	Explanation
K_d	After-tax rate of return on debt capital
K	Pre-tax rate of return on debt capital
t	Effective tax rate

28. Establishing the cost of debt for private firms is more difficult as they do not generally access public debt markets, and are therefore not rated. Historical debt in the account books is bank debt, and the interest expense on this debt might not reflect the rate at which they can borrow (especially if the bank debt is old). In such circumstances, the cost of debt is estimated by using the cost of debt of similar firms.

Calculating Ke (required return on equity) for use in WACC formula

29. The rate of return on equity capital is estimated using the Modified Capital Asset Pricing Model ('MCAPM'). MCAPM estimates the rate of return on common equity as the current risk-free rate of return on government issued treasury bonds, plus a market risk premium in addition to the risk-free rate of return, multiplied by a 'Beta' for the stock, where Beta ('β') is a risk measure that reflects the sensitivity of a Company's stock price to the movements of the stock market as a whole. Practical application of the MCAPM relies upon the ability to identify publicly traded companies that have similar risk characteristics (ie beta) to the subject company being valued.
30. The MCAPM rate of return on equity capital is calculated using the formula:

$$K_e = R_f + (\beta * (R_m - R_f)) + Ssp + A$$

Symbol	Meaning	Explanation & calculation
K_e	Rate of return on equity capital	n/a
R_f	Risk-free rate of return	The risk-free rate is the theoretical rate of return of an investment with zero risk over a given period of time. It is the starting point for calculating the discount rate as a rational investor will reject any investment yielding amounts below risk-free returns. Practitioners typically use government bonds (also known as Gilts in the UK) as a proxy for the risk-free rate.

$R_m - R_f$	Market risk premium: the expected return on a broad portfolio of stocks in the market (R_m), less the risk-free rate (R_f)	Market risk premiums are based on common stock total returns less risk-free rate of return (as discussed above). Financial theory suggests that investors in common stocks require a premium over the return on Gilts as a reward for incurring additional investment risk. The Market Risk Premium ('MRP') is defined as the excess return that investors expect to receive from investing in shares less bond income returns for Gilts.
Ssp	Small stock premium	The MCAPM rate of return is adjusted by a premium, which reflects the extra risk of an investment in a small company. This premium is derived from historical differences in returns between small companies and large companies.
A	'Alpha': company-specific risk	Alpha is the measure of unsystematic or company-specific risk.

The cost approach

Replacement cost method

31. Per IVS 105 (Paragraphs 70.2 to 70.5), replacement cost is the cost payable to replicate the utility of the subject asset, not the exact physical properties of the asset, taking account of physical deterioration and all relevant forms of obsolescence (the 'depreciated replacement cost'). The replacement cost is generally that of a modern equivalent asset, which provides similar function and equivalent utility to the asset being valued, but which is of a current design and constructed or made using current cost-effective materials and techniques.

Reproduction cost method

32. Per IVS 105 (Paragraphs 70.6 to 70.7), this approach is deemed most appropriate where the cost of a modern equivalent asset is greater than the cost of recreating a replica of the subject asset, or the utility offered by the subject asset could only be provided by a replica rather than a modern equivalent. Where this approach is taken, depreciation related to physical, functional and external obsolescence associated with the subject asset is deducted from the total cost to create a replica of the subject asset.

Summation or 'underlying asset' method

Per IVS 105 (Paragraphs 70.8 to 70.9), this method is typically used for investment companies or other types of assets or entities for which value is primarily a factor of the values of their holdings. The value is equivalent to the sum of the value of each of the component assets comprising the subject asset.

Other considerations when using cost approaches

33. Cost approach methods might normally provide an indication of the minimum value applicable to a business because, where a business is

profitable, the capitalised value of the cash flows, dividends and/or the earnings normally gives a greater value than the value of the assets. They are more reliable if a business is loss-making, in liquidation or in administration, or where a business is generating low or no profits from a substantial asset base.

Goodwill

34. In valuing a profitable business, it is often appropriate to assign additional value to goodwill. Per IVS 210 (Paragraph 20.6), goodwill is described as:

- '[...] any future economic benefit arising from a business, an interest in a business or from the use of a group of assets which has not been separately recognised in another asset.'

35. When adopting a cost approach, it is appropriate to ascribe a value to transferable goodwill based on an assessment of the future 'super-profits' of the business (which represent the profit after making such a charge for the key individuals' or shareholders' salary and other benefits that represent an open market reward for them as employees).

Additional factors for consideration

36. As a matter of standard practice, the following factors should be considered when undertaking valuations:

Cash-free, debt-free, normal working capital

37. Most businesses are acquired on a cash-free, debt-free basis and with a normal amount of working capital. Accordingly, valuations are adjusted downwards to take into account net debt, being the sum of financial debt owed to third parties and related parties, and any surplus assets whose value can be readily realised, and which are not required for the future operations of the business. This then leaves, with the equity value of the business, the sum which shareholders might expect to realise in transferring the asset.

Discounts for lack of marketability ('DLOMs')

38. Per IVS 105 (Paragraph 30.17(a)), a DLOM (often referred to as an 'illiquidity discount') may be applied when the comparables are deemed to have superior marketability to the subject asset. Incorporation of a DLOM reflects the concept that, when comparing otherwise identical assets, a readily marketable asset would have a higher value than an asset with a long marketing period, or restrictions on the ability to sell that asset. Publicly traded securities can be bought and sold nearly instantaneously, but shares in a private company may require a significant amount of time to identify potential buyers and complete a transaction. From this perspective, an investment in smaller and/or unquoted companies is viewed to be a more risky asset, thus attracting a DLOM.

Control premium and discounts for lack of control ('DLOC')

39. Per IVS 105 (Paragraph 30.17(b)), Control Premium and DLOCs are often applied to reflect differences between the comparables and the subject asset with regard to the ability to make decisions and the changes that can be made as a result of exercising control.

40. Shareholders of public companies generally do not have the ability to make decisions related to the operations of the company (they lack control). As such, when applying the public comparable method under IVS guidelines to value a subject asset that reflects a controlling interest, a control premium may be appropriate.
41. Conversely, transactions identified when applying the transaction method under IVS guidelines often reflect transactions of controlling interests. When using that method to value a subject asset that reflects a minority interest, a DLOC may be appropriate.
42. The key control levels in a body corporate are 25%, 51% and 75%, with the latter giving outright control (the ability to pass special resolutions), 51% giving operational control (the ability to pass ordinary resolutions), and 25% giving negative control (the ability to block special resolutions). It is generally recognised that a discount may be applied to reflect the size of a holding in a private company where a minority is being valued, and examples of this concept are to be found in case law (eg *Lloyds Bank plc v Duker* [1987] 1 WLR 1324 per J Mowbray, QC sitting as Deputy High Court Judge; *Irvine v Irvine* [2006] EWHC 583 (Ch); and *Howie v Crawford* [1990] BCC 330).
43. In such instances, the appropriate level of discount takes into consideration other relevant facts to assess the risk associated with a minority shareholding. For example, when valuing a 20% shareholding in a company in which four other shareholders also own 20% each, the best approach is to apply a lower minority discount than when valuing a 20% shareholding in a company in which one other shareholder has an 80% shareholding. In the latter case, the minority shareholder is clearly more at the mercy of the majority shareholder than in the former case where control is effectively shared among all the shareholders.

The strength of minority protections

44. Minority protections may be contained in a shareholders' agreement or in the company's articles and may restrict the actions that the majority shareholder(s) can take without the consent of the minority shareholder(s). If there are strong minority protections in place, the minority discount will be lower (assuming that these protections are transferable to the purchaser). Conversely, the stronger the minority protections, the weaker the control exercised by a majority shareholder and so the higher the discount that would be applied to a majority shareholding.

Dividend rights & restrictions

45. When all shareholders participate in dividends pro-rata to their shareholdings and where a company has a high dividend pay-out ratio, much of the value generated will accrue to the minority shareholder(s) without a discount; thus, the minority discount will be lower than for a company with a low dividend pay-out ratio.
46. Conversely, where differential dividend rights are applied to different classes of shares, for example the right for the Company's board to recommend dividends to be paid on a class of shares (without affecting the rights of another class) or the right to pay differential sums to different classes, such classes may attract a discount taking the facts into consideration as they present themselves.

Selected valuation approach

47. The following valuation methods are commonly used:

- Market Approach – Market Transaction Method; and
- Cost Approach – Replacement Cost Method.

48. A Business which has not produced long-term financial forecasts may not be appropriate for an income approach valuation. If a Business is not paying dividends according to a policy, it is not possible to use the dividend yield method.

Assumptions

49. The following assumptions are normally appropriate:
    i. The Business will continue to operate as a going concern for the foreseeable future and meet its liabilities to third parties and related parties as they fall due;
    ii. There are no planned significant changes in the operations of the Business;
    iii. The Business will continue to achieve financial results in the foreseeable future which are in line with recent historic performance (as adjusted for one-off items);
    iv. Continued investment will be made as required for capital expenditure and working capital requirements to enable the Business to continue to operate at current levels;
    v. There are no significant political or legal issues which could affect the future performance of the Business;
    vi. There are no significant pension issues which could affect the future performance of the Business;
    vii. There are no significant economic conditions which could affect the future performance of the Business;
    viii. There are no significant technological issues which could affect the future performance of the Business;
    ix. There are no new entrants that the Business is aware of, planning to come into the market, which could significantly affect the future performance of the Business;
    x. There are no competitors with plans afoot which could significantly affect the future performance of the Business;
    xi. The relationship with the largest customer is stable and there is no current information which would indicate the largest customer leaving which could significantly affect the performance of the Business;
    xii. In the absence of formal valuations, the book values of assets and liabilities are not materially different from their market values;
    xiii. The Valuation ignores any premium that may be payable by a third party with specific corporate motives for acquisition;
    xiv. The Valuation is based solely on the financial information made available and verbal and written explanations given where requested; and
    xv. Any transactions with related parties are carried out on an arm's length basis.

Conclusion on approach and methodology

50. In assessing the open market value for the whole of a trading company, the most influential methodology is normally the net assets and earnings

basis of valuation. For a minority holding, the dividend yield methodology is considered influential, particularly where there is evidence of a strong dividend policy. In the absence of a strong dividend policy, the value of the whole of the company is the starting point for the minority's proportion, less a discount to recognise the inherent weakness for marketing the shares. Having voting control over all the issued shares in a company entitles the holder to full control over the net assets (and the level of and potential realisation of those net assets) while enjoying the profits of the company into the future.

1.21 Shares Valuation (SV) Fiscal Forum (SVFF) (see Chapter 18)

The Inland Revenue (HMRC) in the late 1990s started holding regular meetings with valuation professionals to discuss issues of interest to both HMRC and professional valuers of shares and other intangibles. Topics discussed included restructuring, changes within HMRC, and SV's aim of getting the technical side right at the outset.

Billows v Hammond [2000] STC (SCD) 430 was referred to (see 3.08), where the SV's expert witness was held to be honest but not independent as he had been involved in the earlier negotiations. Other problems mentioned were where SV had to have a minute that a float was not planned where the shareholding was only 0.15%. SV's performance was discussed.

At the meeting on 24 July 2001, share schemes and options were discussed, particularly EMI (Enterprise Management Incentives) including dilution as a result of higher EMI limits. Pro rata values would be accepted for EMI cases and TA 1988, s 140 was discussed.

HMRC confirmed that their non-HMRC experts were chosen from a competitive tender and appointed for two years with an extra one year option at their discretion. Pre and post valuation checks were discussed.

Non-negligible value meant that, even if an asset had lost a lot of its value, it was unlikely that the reduced value would be negligible. The level of information needed depended on the circumstances of each case.

1.22 SVFF 2002 (1)

The January 2002 meeting discussion referred to proposed legislative changes for substantial shareholdings and intellectual property and an increase in EMI valuations and the Better Quality Secure Review.

The rules for intangible assets were replaced to provide relief for the cost of acquiring the asset, on a consistent basis following the amortisation rate used by companies. On the sale of such assets there is tax on the profit as income, with roll-over for reinvestment in new intangibles, and transitional provisions.

Shares Valuation uses independent neutral expert advice where it considers it appropriate, where the expert may be called as an independent witness.

Employment income valuations usually related to unapproved options and were usually post transaction, although a small number of pre-transaction valuation checks were carried out where shares were being issued to a large number of employees.

1.23 SVFF 2002 (2)

In July 2002 it was confirmed that the SV Manual would not include a section on the valuation of intellectual property. It was pointed out that whether or not a professional valuation was obtained was the prerogative of the tax payer who will be required to submit a reasonable valuation.

HMRC would adopt a more proactive approach in obtaining the information required to conclude a valuation, with more meetings and telephone calls with tax payers and greater use of information powers in IHTA 1984, ss 19A and 20 and greater use of the appeals system.

1.24 SVFF 2003

The next meeting was on 8 April 2003. The Shares Valuation Manual publication was welcomed and would be kept as up to date as was reasonably possible, but it was an internal guidance manual, published as part of government openness, not a definitive manual on all aspects of fiscal valuation, and parts of the published manual had been redacted.

Shares Valuation's view of quasi-partnership did not mean that a minority shareholding is other than at a discount to pro rata of the full going concern or break-up value of the company, as it involves a hypothetical vendor and a hypothetical purchaser. Unfairly prejudicial behaviour is a different matter.

Pre-transaction valuation checks were not available and this applied to Enterprise Management Incentive (EMI) share issues, where the option price may have disregarded the market value. HMRC would only consider a pre-transaction valuation for Schedule E where there was a large number of employees involved.

1.25 SVFF 2004 (1)

In the Fiscal Forum meeting on 8 January 2004, Shares Valuation said that it would consider agreeing the market value of EMI options if an approach was made within six months following the grant.

The taxation of employment-related securities would be resolved with the local inspector who would consult with SV where appropriate. It was accepted that various ambiguities in the legislation were left unresolved. HMRC explained the tendering process of the SV panel of independent expert witnesses.

1.26 SVFF 2004 (2)

In the Fiscal Forum meeting on 12 October 2004 the valuation of jointly owned chattels was discussed following a meeting of interested parties on 17 July 2002, and the rights of a part owner of a chattel differed from those of a part owner of land or property or a shareholder of a company and were written in s 188(1) of the Law of Property Act 1925, on which there was no jurisprudence. The law provided that a part owner of a chattel could apply to the court for an order for division of the chattels, or any of them, according to the valuation or otherwise and as the court may determine.

It was, however, accepted by the parties involved that a negligible discount was untenable and, depending on the circumstances, discounts of up to 75% could be fair and reasonable.

However, a discount of slightly higher than 10% (which has been accepted as appropriate for 50/50 land cases) would be appropriate for joint owners of chattels which have less statutory protection than joint landowners. The Law of Property Act 1925 does not apply in Scotland or Northern Ireland but this does not mean that no discount for joint interests is appropriate. The value of goodwill on incorporation was an increasing workload problem for Shares Valuation, in particular where goodwill of a business was sold to a new company on incorporation, and crediting the vendor's loan account gave rise to a significant tax risk for HMRC. For example, the goodwill may be personal to the individual and not be transferable to a company (eg entertainers and chefs) or if may be overvalued as adherent goodwill which attaches to the premises, such as Public Houses, Nursing Homes etc, not to the transferor personally, which would involve the Valuation Office Agency as well as Shares Valuation.

Ross Marks v Sherred (HMIT) (2004) SpC 418 was considered, in which there was, exceptionally, no premium for control of a 66% shareholding at 31 March 1982, where the profit record was severely hit by the fall in the sterling/dollar exchange rate and the decision was based on the facts of the case and has little general application, except as an example of reference to quoted companies in arriving at an appropriate earnings multiplier.

Also considered was a request for an Employment Income (EI) valuation prior to filing the self-assessment tax returns as a post-transaction valuation check (PTVC), following the decision in *Langham v Veltema* [2004] STC 544.

1.27 SVFF 2005

The SVFF on 10 October 2005 referred to the creation of HMRC on the merger of the Inland Revenue and Customs & Excise.

The chattels valuation issues for jointly owned chattels in Northern Ireland were likely to be the same as those in England and Wales. The discount for joint ownership in Scotland should not exceed 10% as any co-owner can apply to the court for a division on sale of such chattels.

Another point on chattels valuation is where there is an arm's length sale within a year or two of the valuation date. This often applies to the value for inheritance tax where the items are sold at auction shortly after death. The sale price is often declared as the valuation at death and accepted as such by HMRC. The use of subsequent sale price information is not necessarily the same as hindsight and *IRC v Stenhouse Trustees* [1992] STC 103 did not provide support for this point.

Tax privileged pensions would be limited to £1.5 million from 6 April 2006 (£1,030,000 for 2018/19).

HMRC were unhappy with Employment Income post-transaction valuation checks as they took a disproportionate amount of time for HMRC to process. The taxpayers' representatives thought that the system was a good service.

1.28 SVFF 2006

The July 2006 Fiscal Forum stated that SV was now part of Charities Assets and Residence (CAR) directorate, covering inheritance tax, capital gains tax, residency, pensions, savings, employee shares and securities as well as share valuations.

HMRC stated that they did not agree with the Special Commissioners in *Shinebond Limited v Carrol (HMIT)* SpC 522, [2006] STC 147, that there was no contingent tax liability on the leasehold property which was the main asset of the company. HMRC regarded this as inadmissible knowledge of future legislation. The 4th edition of *Practical Share Valuation* was referred to.

Pension Scheme valuations were explained by HMRC and the actual market value applied, not the unrestricted market value.

Where shares were sold at a fair value under the Articles of Association, there would be a tax charge on the excess of the articles valuation over the open market value which would recognise a discount based on the size of the shareholding under TCGA 1992, s 272.

In January 2007 the valuation of adherent goodwill was considered following *Balloon Promotions Limited v Wilson* [2006] STC (SCD) 167, which held that the ownership of goodwill of a franchise business is between the franchisor and the franchisee, and is primarily a question of fact. In this case the goodwill belonged to the franchisee. See also HMRC's Tax Bulletin 83 of June 2006.

There was a discussion on whether a management buy-out created a lower exit value for the vendor than a trade sale, but it all depended on the facts. A shareholders' agreement would be property under IHTA 1984, s 272 and needed to be factored into a valuation in appropriate circumstances.

1.29 SVFF 2008

The Fiscal Forum held on 19 February 2008 covered the points referred to below:

1 and 2. Introduction and Minutes were duly dealt with.

3. The SAV performance and workloads were summarised and a centralised Capital Gains network should result in a better identification of Capital Gains issues and the application of greater expertise. Even excluding adherent goodwill cases, SAV still had 245 cases over two years old. The SAV Edinburgh Office was being closed.
4. Tribunal reform was being introduced from April 2009. The First-Tier Tribunal (FTT) would usually be the court of first instance, with the Upper Tribunal leading on developing the law and administering justice. Permission to appeal from the FTT would usually be on a point of law to the Upper Tribunal, with further appeals only on a point of law to the Court of Appeal or Court of Session.
5. Valuation of adherent goodwill following *Balloon Promotions Limited v Wilson* [2006] STC (SCD) 167 was referred to and HMRC guidelines were being prepared with the assistance of RICS.
6. The valuation of shares quoted on the Alternative Investment Market (AIM) was discussed where there was very low liquidity and a very wide spread and in practice might only be possible on a matched buyer and

seller basis. PAYE valuations at the closing price on the day prior to the transaction would normally be the case and SAV operated the PAYE health check.

7. The structure of the Fiscal Forum was considered.

1.30 SVFF 2009

The Fiscal Forum on 27 January 2009 confirmed that the valuation of trade-related properties had been reconsidered following *Balloon Promotions Limited v Wilson* [2006] STC (SCD) 167, SpC 524, and with the assistance of the Royal Institution of Chartered Surveyors, HMRC recognised that there could be goodwill in these businesses, such as nursing homes. As a result of the credit crunch in 2008 and 2009 the components of discounted cash flow (DCF) valuations, which relied on the calculation of the Capital Asset Pricing Model (CAPM) and the Weighted Average Cost of Capital (WACC), made it very difficult to arrive at a sensible result.

Clarification was sought for the information required for the Enterprise Management Incentive (EMI) Scheme and HMRC agreed to raise the issue with the European Services Strategy Unit (ESSU).

Clarification was sought on the operation of post-transaction valuation checks (PTVCs) which could relate to employment income and chargeable gains and it was confirmed that such requests could be sent to Shares and Assets Valuation at the same time as to the Tax Office responsible for the tax payer.

PTVCs were withdrawn on 3 February 2016 with effect from 31 March 2016.

1.31 SVFF 2010

The 28 June 2010 Fiscal Forum referred to the publication of the SAV Manual/Toolkit in May 2010, in order to help taxpayers submit valuations which would be likely to be accepted without enquiry. At the time of writing, the latest 'Capital Gains Tax for Shares Toolkit', running to 26 pages, was published in April 2018 for 2017–18 Self-Assessment Tax Returns. This can be searched for online and sets out the areas of risk under Capital Gains Tax, such as record keeping, disposals, valuations, expenditure relief, and a 20-point checklist for Capital Gains Tax for shares and an explanation of rights. There is also a 'Capital Gains Tax Land and Buildings Toolkit', of 30 pages, which is outside the scope of this book.

Other points covered in the Forum were the impact on valuation of the dilutive effect of unexercised options under Enterprise Management Incentive (EMI) schemes which, for EMI purposes only, require SAV to consider each valuation on a pragmatic basis and SAV will usually go along with full dilution, ie as if the options had been or were about to be exercised, while reserving the right to argue otherwise when the circumstances justify such a stance. In other cases, normal risk assessment procedures are followed. Referrals to the Valuation Office Agency will only take place if a significant amount of tax is at stake.

The valuation of growth shares may involve the use of modelling using, for example, Black Scholes, Monte Carlo simulation and the Capital Asset Pricing Model (CAPM). SAV do not have a preferred model.

PTVC procedures, both for capital gains and employment income, were discussed. PTVC services under ITEPA 2003 are no longer available at the time of writing, having been withdrawn with effect from 31 March 2016, together with PAYE Health Checks.

Where the value of shares is fixed by the articles or shareholders' agreement or by negotiation and put and call options were discussed, but SAV did not opine on such matters in the absence of a specific case and without consulting the European Services Strategy Unit (ESSU).

SAV provided an update on goodwill in Agent Update 10 in February 2009 as a Proactive Note – Apportioning the Price Paid for a Business Transferred as a Going Concern.

The treatment of personal rights under Part 7 of ITEPA 2003, following *Grays Timber Products v HMRC* [2010] STC 782, was discussed. The format of future Fiscal Forums was also discussed.

1.32 SVFF 7 September 2011

SAV defended its right to request management information in respect of small minority shareholdings and the questions about exit prospects were valid.

S. P Erdal v HMRC [2011] UKFTT 87 (TC) was discussed. HMRC issued CGT assessments on the basis of £1.23 per share but the disposer valued them at £4 each and the First Tier Tribunal applied a 40% discount because of low dividend payments and valued them at £2.42 each.

Marks v HMRC [2011] UKFTT 221 (TC) was also considered, where information reasonably required by a prospective purchaser was not actually available and had to be ignored.

The BDO Private Company Price Index (PCPI), at that date, was considered by SAV to be a useful piece of information but that it was not necessarily decisive and if possible should be used in conjunction with other sources of information. The BDO PCPI compares the private company exit price/earnings ratios and the stock market price earnings/ratios and may not be relevant for minority interests in small companies.

SAV did not feel it appropriate to express a view on a question which was framed with a specific contentious case in mind and the relevant question was withdrawn.

Notices under FA 2008, Sch 36 may require a taxpayer or third party to provide information on documents reasonably required to check a taxpayer's tax position. 'Reasonably required' was considered in *Long v RCC* [2014] UKFTT 199 (TC). Personal bank accounts were 'business accounts' where used for business transactions, in *Beckworth v RCC* [2012] UKFTT 181 (TC).

SAV regarded FA 2008, Sch 36 as effective in reducing response times but would extend the 40-day period if it was justified.

Fiscal valuations within FRS 20/IFRS 2 required valuers to assess the amount for which an asset could be exchanged, a liability settled or an equity interest granted which could be exchanged between knowledgeable, willing parties in an arm's length transaction and is very similar to the fiscal market value standard and any differences would have to be justified.

SAV confirmed that they would not use information from an internal database to argue any case at a tribunal relying on evidence not available outside HMRC, and in fact did not have any such database, only a record of previous agreements reached.

PTVCs for employment income purposes should be sent to the local compliance office in Nottingham, but this may change.

SAV would be prepared to liaise with a local office on behalf of practitioners if it has reason to believe that it would be in everyone's interest to do so.

1.33 SVFF 13 September 2012

Pre-transaction valuations would be considered if the transaction was transparent, the facts were clear and engagement in a valuation was unlikely to lead to prolonged contention and debate and there were over 25 employees and reiterated the policy stated in the Fiscal Forum of July 2001, which was reproduced.

PAYE 'health checks' were, following the share valuation manual SVM 109060, aimed at simple straightforward transactions which could be done quickly in the PAYE timeframe, and are not for complex and high value transactions.

Enterprise Management Incentives (EMI) valuations are given priority by SAV but many VAL 231 forms are not filled out fully and there are many requests for extensions. SAV will provide EMI valuation guidance aimed at smaller companies, subject to being notified of any material change of circumstances.

The basis for calculating the risk-free rate of capital had changed in the USA, but this would not be followed by SAV, which would apply a reasonable rationale checked by benchmarking.

Patent box legislation required determination of a National Marketing Royalty in respect of Marketing Assets which would follow the transfer pricing, governance procedures in HMRC's International Manual and was in accordance with OECD guidelines and methodologies such as the comparable uncontrolled price or profit split. Information sources of comparable company and other data were discussed.

SAV will accept email communications at the taxpayer's risk and, with consent, reply by email and post.

1.34 SVFF 9 September 2013

SAV had suffered a 5% budget cut and new work (Employee Shareholder Employment status and more avoidance work) but a new training course should help to ease the situation in the future.

The general Anti-Avoidance rule would be unlikely to apply and was overseen by a completely independent panel.

HMRC Spotlight 15 is refocused to share loss relief schemes which were at the extreme end of avoidance and should be avoided as they were being looked at by Criminal Investigations.

SAV was working under pressure and there were postal delays which were being investigated.

SAV will respond by email at the taxpayer's risk.

SAV employees at Grades 6 and 7 were accredited associate members of the Royal Institution of Chartered Surveyors (RICS), the Business Valuation Facility, and will become associate members on completion of the RICS ethics test.

SAV were considering secondments to commercial firms of between three and six months. The process for Employee Shareholder Employment status was explained and form VAL 232 was available.

Litigation

HMRC now has RICS-accredited valuers to act as experts before tribunals so SAV can be 'more decisive' in issuing closure notices and using Tribunals for negligible value cases, etc. *Anthony Perry* TC/2012/07357, an unreported criminal investigation, and a minority holding case (*Chartersea Ltd*), were discussed.

SAV's Manual had been amended to include Growth Shares, SVM 114040, SAV's view of 'excepted assets' changed to recognise that it would be sensible to hold more cash during a recession.

HMRC was considering its view on the incorporation of medical practitioners.

SAV's pre-transaction service, to try to agree a value of options before they are granted, is amended to allow 'without prejudice' agreements. If a value is not agreed, the company can issue the options and possibly face a challenge on exercise from HMRC.

The restrictions on transfer in a company's articles have to be taken into account unless there is an Unrestrictive Market Value (UMV) which applies. See 'Disposals for more than Market Value': *Gray's Timber Products Ltd v HMRC* [2010] UKSC 4, see ERSM 80130 for guidance.

Enterprise values should, in general, incorporate hope value, so ordinary shares would still have a hope value even if the debt and preference shares exceed the current enterprise value.

HMRC considered that BDO's Private Company Price Index (PCPI) and the Private Equity Price Index (PEPI) should be used with care and not in isolation. They have been criticised in court cases for lack of detail, which is not in the public domain.

Trade-related property

An updated practice note was issued in October 2013, but there are some fundamental issues of disagreement which are likely to require litigation to resolve, but no cases were on hold.

Crowd funding

The issue price for shares in a crowd funding exercise would normally be acceptable as the taxable market value but SAV would look to see if there was any price distortion.

Any other business: An intellectual property fair value would normally be similar to a share valuation market value, but there could be different values.

1.35 SVFF 29 September 2014

SAV had reduced in size and was aiming to risk-assess better and concentrate on high-risk worthwhile cases and use improved digital services in the future. People were encouraged to fill in the SAV Customer Survey.

Recent litigation

Re Annacott Holdings Limited (AHL); Attwood and others v Maidment [2013] EWCA Civ 119 was an unfair prejudice case under CA 2006, s 994 where one of the 50% shareholders and sole director had transferred the company's entire portfolio of properties to himself at an undervalue. No discount for a 50% interest was appropriate and the claimant was awarded 'quasi interest' on the price of the shares from 1 October 2005 to the date of the Court of Appeal's decision on 26 February 2013 and the contingent liability for corporation tax was valued at the amount actually paid on the disposal at undervalue.

The deduction for selling costs of the actual sales should be allowed.

New ways of working in SAV

SAV agreed to modernise its methods of working to make better use of the telephone and of email and meetings to speed up the valuation process. Part-time valuers at SVD were asked to set out their working days on correspondence. Review of ITEPA PTVCs were considered.

PTVCs

PTVCs and PAYE Health Checks for the Income Tax (Earnings and Pensions) Act 2003 were discussed and many of the submissions were very complex and the checks were subsequently withdrawn on 3 February 2016.

Medical Practitioners

The effect of the incorporation of medical practitioners was under review. Enterprise Management Incentives (EMIs) can be the subject of a request for an agreed value within 92 days of the grant, within the following year.

Employee Shareholder Status (ESS)

SAV had agreed 227 ESS requests up to August 2014, mainly for senior staff.

Time window for post-EMI valuation agreements

SVM110050 allowed a request for an agreed value while the enquiry window remained open. The grant of EMI options must be reported to the Small Companies Enterprise Sector within 92 days and the enquiry window is one year from that date, ie 15 months after the date of grant.

Quoted Share Valuations

The SAV were applying the closing price for quoted share valuations as easier to understand than the 'quarter up price' previously used (and likely to raise more tax revenue).

Information Standards

The confidential information about a business, not in the public domain, could have a material bearing on its value. SAV was regarded as inconsistent in its approach. It was agreed that this was a difficult issue which should be discussed with SAV, who would try and be reasonable in the circumstances, with a referral to the courts if necessary.

If a case is thought to be mishandled, a request can be made for a review by the caseworker's manager.

The treatment of cash as an excepted asset for Business Property Relief in an economic downturn was considered, companies need to demonstrate and justify their business need for cash deposits even in a recession.

1.36 SVFF 8 October 2015

1. Introduction.
2. SAV Workstate
3. New Ways of Working

   The Central Print Service (CPS) means that valuers' letters are printed out centrally and posted from there and are therefore unsigned but do include the valuer's name. The CPS system will show that a particular letter has been posted.

   Digital White Mail (DWM) is the system where incoming post is scanned by HMRC and sent electronically to the appropriate office. SAV is moving towards electronic rather than paper filing.

   Delivery of mail to SAV by courier in office hours should not be a problem. Pro-active caseworking involves SAV making contact with agents by telephone and corresponding by email as part of working cooperatively, identifying points of disagreement and trying to resolve them. Telephone calls will be followed up by letter and will deal only with valuation matters.
4. Litigation update

   A number of recent cases were referred to:

   B G Foods Limited (08560068)
   JD Designs, dissolved 8 December 2015
   Spring Capital Limited v HMRC [2013] UKFTT 41 (TC) (and subsequently [2015] UKFTT 66 (TC) and [2016] UKUT 264 (TC))

   SAV agreed to notify litigation decisions to Fiscal Forum members once the information is in the public domain.

   HMRC referred to Gift Aid cases where shell companies bought new shares in legitimate businesses at a low price (usually 1p per share) with an obligation to buy more shares. The company then placed a small number of shares on AIM or the Channel Island Stock Exchange at a much higher price and some transactions took place. Shares were then gifted to a charity at this higher price and Gift Aid claimed. HMRC challenged this practice and in a criminal case succeeded in alleging this could be fraudulent.
5. Growth/Hurdle shares and clearance work
   HMRC had set out its expectation at the 2014 Fiscal Forum that agents would send forecast information when requesting valuations under the post-transaction valuation check (PTVC) procedure, but in practice these forecasts were often hard to obtain and on 1 February 2016 it was announced that PTVCs would be withdrawn with effect from 31 March 2016. SAV was spending quite a lot of time getting and digesting information and most of the transactions were agreed anyway.

   The ITEPA chapter in the SAV manual was to be rewritten and SAV were reviewing their procedures.
6. Employee Shareholder Put Options
   HMRC was asked for its policy on the valuation of Put Option rights for Employee Share Scheme (ESS) purposes when the actual market value (AMV) was the minimum of £2,000 but SAV considered that it all depended on the facts of each case but generally they took a pragmatic approach, within a two- to three-month exercise period.

7. Goodwill incorporations and Medical Practitioners
   SAV does not accept that there is any transfer of goodwill value arising on the incorporation of a medical practice, and will take a case to Tribunal if necessary.
   Goodwill in trade-related property valuations were covered by Practice Notes in 2009 and 2013 and a nursing home case had been listed for hearing in 2016.
8. AOB
   SAV had appointed three new graduate trainees. The minutes of this meeting should be available within two months.

1.37 SVFF 4 November 2016

1. Welcome by SAV's Deputy Director Sarah Kelsey.
2. SAV Workstate and digitisation
   2015–16 was a good year for SAV with a high level of post response targets being met. Email was being used more often and digital caseworking was introduced across SAV. Staffing retirements were being covered by new recruits.
3. The post-transaction valuation check (PTVC)
   This facility was withdrawn with effect from 1 April 2016.
4. Litigation Update
   HMRC were trying to speed up sending Gift of Shares cases to tribunal where the shares were issued at low prices, then floated on AIM or the Channel Islands Stock Exchange at a much higher price, then gifted to a charity and Gift Aid relief claimed. HMRC considered that the value claimed was too high. Most of these gifts took place more than ten years ago. In *Nicholas Green v HMRC* [2014] UKFTT 396 (TC) the taxpayer claimed £1 per share but the taxpayer's valuer proposed 88p to 93p, HMRC's valuer proposed 25p to 30p per share, and the tribunal judgment figure was 35p per share.
   The *JD Designs* case (*Roger Dyer & Jean Dyer v HMRC* [2013] UKFTT 691 (TC) and [2016] UKUT 0381 (TCC)) confirmed that the shares were worthless as the rights to the trademarks and services belonged to Miss Dyer and the company, where the loans from the company were converted into shares in October 2007.
   Further cases related to a capital loss generation scheme involving the valuation of shares and options and cases on the valuation of goodwill in trade-related properties and medical practitioners were referred to. SAV accepts that a private GP's medical practice could have a goodwill but not sole medical practitioners where the goodwill was personal and could not be transferred.
   HMRC promised to email notification of litigation decisions to Fiscal Forum members once they are final and in the public domain but the authors have not received any to date.
   SAV's panel of independent valuers, currently 13, was explained and it was due to be refreshed in 2017 and delegates were encouraged to consider applying.

5. Penalties
   It was accepted that valuation was an inexact science but there is a range of legitimate issues and, when this can be potentially due to concealment or deliberately including incorrect figures rather than a reasonable negotiated value, penalties are levied. Examples included substantial cash balances (except assets) or carelessly allowing incorrect figures to be used or excluding or mis-describing high-value chattels.
6. Professionalism CPD
   SAV is closely associated with RICS members and the Business Valuation sub-board helping with guidance and training. SAV's new entrants can become associate members of RICS within three years and more senior valuers can become chartered members of RICS. SAV organises Continuing Professional Development (CPD) for staff.
7. AOB
   SAV requested issues for the Fiscal Forum agenda. SAV also had concerns about the historically used rental rate for chattels of 1% which might be underestimated (now 2.5%). A lot of SAV correspondence is now by email and it was likely in future that SAV would accept emails. An invitation was made to join the annual Employment Related Securities Forum.

1.38 SVFF 31 October 2017

1. Welcome by Andrew Knight on behalf of the Royal Institution of Chartered Surveyors (RICS).
2. Overview of SAV by Sarah Kelsey and Barry Roland. SAV is now part of Customer Strategy and Tax Design in the new HMRC structure.
3. Employee Income/Share Schemes
   Tony Spindler explained the SAV involvement in Tax Advantaged Share Scheme (TASS) requests and Employment Income-related valuations. The new rules for Employment Shareholder Status (ESS) had almost eliminated such referrals. The withdrawal of the post-transaction valuation checks in 2016 left the four leading UK employee shares scheme bodies with a vacuum which it was hoped would be partially filled by the new Employee Shares Worked Examples Group (WEG) and inclusion of these examples into SAV guidance. The convoluted mechanics of amending form VAL231 were explained, as were the intentions behind some of the questions involved.

   SAV should only be approached when the company is in a position to grant the options. EMI extension requests were a problem for HMRC.

   The discount for minority shareholding was discussed but discount levels are case specific.

   HMRC's online template replacing form 42 was merely a tool used in conjunction with other data to identify risk.
4. FRS102 implications for calculation of contingent tax
   This was considered to endorse the concept that 'tax follows the accounts'. There was no change in SAV's policy on deductions for contingent Capital Gains Tax or the sale of company property. The Valuation Office Agency will add back any deduction for deferred tax if asked for a view on the Open Market Value of an investment property.

5. Chattels Rental Rates
   The Chattels Fiscal Forum acknowledged the tacit acceptance by HMRC of a chattels rental rate of 1%. SAV now has more information and may start to challenge the 1% figure to see if it is a true commercial rate (F(No 2)A 2017, Sch 9, para 1 introducing TCGA 1992, s 97B which applies the official rate of interest of 2.5% from 6 April 2017, which was increased to 3.25% from 21 August 2018 in cases of default.
6. Litigation Update
   Adrian Kerrison v HMRC [2017] UKFTT 322 (TC). The Excalibur Scheme was a 'bed and breakfast' scheme to generate a capital loss under TCGA 1992, s 106A and to obtain income tax relief for the loss under TA 1988, s 574. HMRC countered by claiming that a loan waiver gave rise to an income tax charge. The First Tier Tribunal held that the value-shifting rules reduced the claimed loss to nil, the special purpose vehicle involved in the scheme was Broadgate Limited which was not a qualifying trading company but the loan waiver did not give rise to an income tax charge under ITTOIA 2005, s 687 as HMRC contended. Therefore the scheme failed but the HMRC closure notice was invalid. However the decision is under appeal.

   In *The estate of M Ross (deceased) v HMRC* [2017] UKFTT 507 (TC) the Tribunal held that the management of holiday cottages where substantial services were provided to holidaymakers was nonetheless an investment activity which did not qualify for business property relief.

   In *The estate of M W Vigne v HMRC* [2017] UKFTT 632 (TC) it was held that a large piece of land on which a horse livery business was carried on was not part of an investment business under IHTA 1984, s 105(3) so business property relief was available under IHTA 1984, s 116. HMRC is appealing this decision.

   In *Jonathan Netley v HMRC* [2017] UKFTT 442 (TC), shares were gifted to a charity at 48p per share based on the price of shares listed on the Alternative Investment Market (AIM) stock exchange. However, the First Tier Tribunal held that the value of the shares was 17.5p per share, the price at which the JBS shares were allotted shortly before the flotation. This was a lead case in a number of AIM and Channel Island Stock Exchange listings where the quoted share value was based on a relatively small number of shares. In this case the taxpayers had paid £10,000 to give rise to a high quoted price where the market value, based on the listed share price, would have given rise to tax relief of £15,866, under ICTA 1988, s 587B.

   SAV has consistently maintained that sales of medical practices do not have a goodwill element as the vendor joins the practice of the purchaser so there is not a sale of the business where the vendor has no further interest in the practice.
7. International Cooperation on Intangibles
   The valuation of intangibles for transfer pricing purposes has proved difficult, particularly where multinational enterprises are involved. OECD is looking at profit splits and hard to value intangibles and there is an EU Joint Transfer Pricing Forum which aims to develop a coordinated approach and block loopholes.

8. AOB
   Feedback on the Fiscal Forum was requested, including completion of the impending SAV Customer Survey.

1.39 SVFF 8 October 2018

At the time of writing, the minutes of this meeting were not available.

1. Welcome by Andrew Knight on behalf of the Royal Institution of Chartered Surveyors (RICS).
2. Overview of SAV and customer survey results was given by Sarah Kelsey and Barry Roland. The Mandatory Performance Framework applied to SAV. The valuation of shares involved proportionality given the value at stake, a degree of professional scepticism, evidence for discount rates etc, consistency and judgement utilising industry knowledge.

   SAV reviewed 12,200 valuations in the previous year of which 6,000 related to Enterprise Management Incentives (EMIs). The tax yield was £230 million and the judicious use of post, telephone and email to enter into an early informed debate resulted in 80% of valuations being completed within 15 days and 98% within 40 days.

   Valuations included those relating to Inheritance Tax, Business Property Relief and other intangible asset issues.

   SAV has 60–65 valuers, half of whom have more than ten years' experience.

   March 1982 valuations represented only a small percentage of cases.

   The pre-transaction disclosure service (PTDS) and other pre-transaction valuations have been discontinued as they were labour intensive and 95% had been accepted without change. EMI extension requests for a further 30 days over the 60-day window were common.

   Multinational thin capitalisation issues revolved around the introduction of a debt cap as a percentage of earnings before interest, tax, depreciation and amortisation (EBITDA).

   The International Compliance Engagement Process applies to multinationals to agree internationally accepted valuations. The European Union is developing a joint transfer pricing forum to agree valuation techniques.

   Transfer pricing in connection with intangibles requires an arm's length price definition and has an administration risk. The US Internal Revenue Service (IRS) is keen on valuing intangibles but HMRC is prepared to challenge foreign tax values.

   In 2019, HMRC is planning to consult on small companies with growth below 5% and freezing the value before outside funding.

   In relation to HMRC's litigation the Expert Witness Panel was mentioned as designed to supplement HMRC's internal expert evidence.

   Negligible value claims were referred to, as were loans converted into shares. A case in the First Tier Tribunal was adjourned in the absence of an expert witness.

   Intellectual Property was apparently being used in avoidance schemes for transferring to a Limited Liability Partnership and whether or not it was trading which involved an expert witness or software.

A low cost valuation of licencing involving discounted cash flow calculations and the internet was not a robust valuation acceptable to HMRC.

HMRC confirmed that a professional valuation was no longer regarded as proof against penalties.

Extracting money from small self-administered pensions in accordance with the valuation of intellectual property may be subject to HMRC challenge, as may the transfer of trade marks and other hard to value assets.

3. Recent Cases

The holiday lettings case of *Anne Christine Curtis Green v HMRC* [2015] UKFTT 334 (TC) referred to *HMRC v Pawson* [2013] UKUT 50 (TCC), *Martin v HMRC* [1995] STC (SCD) 5, *McCall v HMRC* [2009] STC 990, *Best v HMRC* [2014] UKFTT 77 (TC) and *HMRC v Brender* [2010] UKUT 300 (TCC) but it was held that Ms Green's business was mainly one of holding the property as an investment.

Nicholas Green v HMRC [2014] UKFTT 396 (TC) was a tax avoidance scheme which involved subscription in a shell company which acquired a trading company and listed the shares on the Channel Island Stock Exchange (CISX), with the listed price implying a significant uplift in the trading company value based on the placing price and two transactions on CISX. HMRC succeeded in showing that the listed price was not a proper measure of the market value and it was rebased on the value of the underlying trading company. The trades involved did not represent the real market value of the company.

Shares and Asset Valuation had available an expert witness panel whose expertise could be called upon but this has been disbanded and HMRC will call expert witnesses as required.

HMRC confirmed that valuation was not a finite figure but a range of values and there would be no penalty if reputable valuers had advised on a different value to that of HMRC.

HMRC confirmed that business property relief for inheritance tax purposes would include a reasonable amount of cash, up to 20% in most cases.

Employee shares were sometimes valued on a low basis and in due course sold for a much higher price, in which case the taxpayer may have to justify the figures used but there would normally be no penalties unless they were negligently prepared or misleading.

1.40 Chattels Valuation Fiscal Forum, now Chattels Fiscal Forum

The Shares Valuation section of HMRC usually arranges an annual meeting with chattel valuation professionals to discuss issues in connection with 'hard to value' assets such as works of art etc (see **7.14**).

The increase in value of such assets seems to be the primary factor behind the increase but it also reflected an increase in share scheme and heritage work.

HMRC confirmed that they were meeting published customer service targets and post response targets. The average settlement time is 4.5 months per case. However, Colin Gibson added that increasing pressures on staff members and cost might have knock-on effects to service levels.

Jointly Owned Chattels
HMRC delivered a statement that 'The issue here is what level of discount from full pro rata value might be appropriate to reflect the problems of joint ownership'.

At the Fiscal Forum Meeting on 24 July 2001, Colin Gibson announced that he would be setting up a review to try to formulate a line on discounting. This was prompted by an increase in the view that the traditional view, which was to have no discount or very small discount, was unrealistic in some circumstances. The idea was to open channels of communication between interested parties and see if it might be possible to establish a consistent view and publish appropriate guidelines.

A discussion group was formed comprising members from Christies, Sothebys, Bonhams, the legal professional valuation office agencies, Shares Valuation, IR Solicitors Office and the Heritage section of Capital Taxes which was at that time responsible for agreeing these valuations. This group met at Somerset House on 17 July 2002. In legal terms it was noted that a part owner of a chattel does not have the same right as a part owner of land/property or a part owner (shareholder) of a company. In fact the only legislation that gives a part owner any rights is s 188(1) of the Law and Property Act 1925 which states 'where any titles belong to persons in undivided shares the persons interested in moiety or upwards may apply to the Court for an order of a division of the chattels or any of them, according to a valuation or otherwise and the Court may make such an order and give any consequential directions as it thinks fit'.

However, no cases have ever been heard under s 188. It is anyone's guess how the courts might evaluate a particular scenario and no joint ownership valuation cases have been heard before the Commissioners so there is no guidance from that angle either.

Against this background the group discussed a large number of possible scenarios. Should a joint interest in single indivisible chattels be treated differently from easily divisible groups? Should physical possession inform fiscal value? Should the nature of the chattel influence the discount and what about the intentions of other co-owners? There was general agreement that the traditional or very small discount was often untenable and, depending on the circumstances, discounts of up to 75% would be fair and reasonable.

After the July 2002 meeting, further thoughts were invited and scenarios discussed but only one group member made further representations. These were discussed in written exchanges, copied to other group members, but no one else has continued the discussion.

In February 2003, chattels valuation work was transferred to Shares Valuation and a review in May 2004 shows there were 12 live cases on jointly owned chattels at that time, nine of which were 1982 valuations where taxpayers were arguing that no discount was appropriate. Six of the nine cases involved a 50% interest in a family company situation.

We now appear to have reached a point where further exchanges are unlikely to shed any new light. There is general agreement that, when considering an appropriate discount, much will depend on size of interest, likelihood of sale, current agreements and the likelihood of them continuing, age of co-owners and what is likely to happen when they die, which required details of co-owners, exact details of chattels, single chattel/easy divisible group/utilitarian asset etc. Market practice and regulatory agreements affected values.

Many of the valuations that HMRC see relate to 50/50 ownership cases where there are no particularly unusual circumstances and no reason to believe that a newco owner could not reasonably expect to intend to enjoy the fair benefit of joint ownership. In these situations, we would expect to see a discount slightly higher than the 10% which has historically been accepted as appropriate in 50/50 land cases. The higher discount being because s 188(1) of the Law of Property Act 1925 is untested and prima facie does not give 50% plus ownership of chattels as much legal protection as enjoyed by joint owners of land. It should be noted that this view is equally applicable when it is necessary to value a chattel jointly owned by husband and wife for capital gains purposes.

Beyond this type of case, the scenarios that Shares Valuation are faced with vary tremendously and it is common ground that much will depend on the exact circumstances surrounding the chattel or chattels in question. At one end of the spectrum, if there is a ready market for undiscounted part shares, there may be no discount at all. Whilst, at the other end, if there are good reasons to expect difficulties (say, for example, the chattel is in the possession of a mentally unstable third party with a history of refusing access), a discount of 75% or more may be appropriate.

From the Revenue's point of view, the discussions in the last few years have been invaluable in airing views and changing thinking in the most difficult areas. We are very grateful to those practitioners who have given their time to contribute to the debate.

It was pointed out that the Law of Property Act 1925 did not apply in Scotland or Northern Ireland and that it had been argued in consequence that no discount should apply there, but HMRC said that they would need to consider the position in Scotland and Northern Ireland but could not see any logic in the suggestion that the non-application of s 188 led to no discount income. Shares Valuation will consider making an addition to the statement referring to Scotland and Northern Ireland.

Recent meetings:

The April 2015 meeting

This referred to digitalisation of white mail and the availability of requesting bulky reports to be sent direct to SAV via email or a request for a hard copy to be sent on to SAV by post.

The use of other artists as comparables

This was discussed and where direct comparables exist they should be cited. The use of indirect comparables may be appropriate but the reasoning should be explained to SAV.

HMRC enquiries regarding low value items

This can occur where the value retained does not sit within an expected range and an explanation is required.

Sales occurring after the event. What is a reasonable period?

The sale proceeds after the event can provide evidence of value at the date of valuation.

Reservation of benefit – pre-owned assets chattels rentals

These were under review as the rate returned was usually around 1%.

Digitalisation of IHT forms and the paragraph on valuations for probate
Online filing is being introduced for low-risk, low-value excepted estates which will not require an itemised list or professional valuation of chattels. It was supplemented in 2016 for taxpaying and non-taxpaying customers using the IHT400 form which will require more detailed information about chattels.

Any Other Business
The 1982 valuation was becoming increasingly difficult to apply and it was suggested this be changed to the year 2000 and the level for identifying individual chattels from £500 to £1,000. Both these suggestions were subsequently rejected.

Unfortunately the 2008 Chattels Valuation Fiscal Forum minutes in the National Archive cannot be printed but it was noted that SAV Edinburgh had been closed and all chattels valuation work is now being undertaken in Nottingham. SAV rely on other HMRC offices to refer cases to them. Post-transaction valuation checks should be referred to the office dealing with the taxpayer's affairs in the first instance.

The reform of Tribunals into first tier and upper tier was explained.

Chattels values also deal with unquoted share valuations. SAV dealt with 1,483 chattels valuations in 2007–08 involving a total capital value of £81,048,071, with a tax charge of £5,991,654. Taxpayers' valuations were accepted in more than 90% of cases and most were supported by professional valuations. SAV only require supporting evidence if it appears that the valuations submitted appear to be unreasonable.

Art market indices are mainly used as a risk assessment tool or where there is a paucity of sales information. The Retail Prices Index is not considered relevant unlike the Art Market Research (AMR), Invaluable, Art Sales Index (ASI) and artnet.com. Artprice.com was useful for paintings and sculpture. The valuation of chattels sold shortly after death could be of assistance but there could be valid reasons for differences.

Valuations involving SAV are all significant and agents need to provide sufficient information for these to be checked.

23 September 2016 meeting
HMRC's restructuring is likely to have little impact on SAV. SAV assist HMRC's Fraud Investigation Service when so requested.

The benefit charge under ITA 2007, s 731 and TCGA 1992, s 87 on works of art held through offshore trusts was discussed, as were Chattels Rental Rates of 1% where SAV expressed concerns over its continued application, which dated back to the 1970s, and requested input. Discussion included the use of 'attributed to' a particular artist as opposed to 'fully attributed to' at the point of sale, and the withdrawal of the post-transaction valuation check.

The base date for capital gains tax of 31 March 1982 was giving rise to problems of information becoming harder to obtain for that date. HMRC's use of penalties was increasing, as were references to the Tribunal, or Alternative Dispute Resolution which has a 90% success rate.

26 October 2017 meeting
This meeting confirmed that there were no plans to increase the base level of chattels items from £500 to £1,000 or to change the base date from 31 March 1982.

Chattel rentals

The historic acceptance of 1% as a generic rate for chattels rentals gave HMRC concerns and was challenged in F(No 2)A 2017, Sch 9 inserting TCGA 1992, s 97A, which calculated the benefit of a loan or the use of a moveable asset at the official rate of interest in FA 1989, s 178 which is 2.5% from 6 April 2018.

Ivory objects

The question of ivory objects was considered in the light of proposed legislation to prohibit the sale of such objects and HMRC agreed that, as a result, they may become of negligible value when it is illegal to sell them.

Trust reporting rules

Trustees need to register the trustees details with HMRC on an annual basis but a valuation of assets is only provided on its first registration.

Returns and evidence

When original documents are sent to Trusts and Estates they are scanned in black and white and the original copies held for 50 days and SAV requests agents to keep their original copies or a colour scanned or printed copy.

Agent penalties

These will be exceptional but SAV has found some agents to be 'liberal with the truth' and will not apply where an agent has acted ethically and correctly. Penalties may be 30–100% of potential tax revenue.

Obtaining evidence

SAV confirmed that they will look at all relevant and available evidence when considering value.

1.41 Wednesbury unreasonable

A court decision is Wednesbury unreasonable or irrational if no reasonable person acting reasonably could have made it, following *Associated Provincial Picture Houses v Wednesbury Corporation* [1948] 1 KB 223. In this case the plaintiffs, who owned a cinema theatre in Wednesbury, sought a declaration that certain conditions imposed by the corporation on a grant for Sunday performances were unreasonable, ie that 'No children under the age of fifteen years shall be admitted to the entertainment (on a Sunday) whether accompanied by an adult or not'. Lord Greene MR stated that:

> 'The courts must always, I think, remember this: first, we are dealing with not a judicial act, but an executive act; secondly, the conditions which, under the exercise of that executive act, may be imposed are in terms, so far as language goes, put within the discretion of the local authority without limitation. Thirdly, the statute provides no appeal from the decision of the local authority.
>
> ...
>
> When an executive discretion is entrusted by Parliament to a body such as the local authority in this case, what appears to be an exercise of that discretion can only be challenged in the courts in a strictly limited class of case. As I have said, it must always be remembered that the court is not a court of appeal. When discretion of this kind is granted the law recognises that certain principles upon which that discretion must be exercised, but within the four corners of

those principles the discretion, in my opinion, is an absolute one and cannot be questioned in any court of law. What then are those principles? They are well understood. They are principles which the court looks to in considering any question of discretion of this kind. The exercise of such a discretion must be a real exercise of the discretion. If, in the statute conferring the discretion, there is to be found expressly or by implication matters which the authority exercising the discretion ought to have regard to, then in exercising the discretion it must have regard to those matters. Conversely, if the nature of the subject matter and the general interpretation of the Act make it clear that certain matters would not be germane to the matter in question, the authority must disregard those irrelevant collateral matters.

...

It is true the discretion must be exercised reasonably. Now what does that mean? Lawyers familiar with the phraseology commonly used in relation to exercise of statutory discretions often use the word "unreasonable" in a rather comprehensive sense. It has frequently been used and is frequently used as a general description of the things that must not be done. For instance, a person entrusted with a discretion must, so to speak, direct himself properly in law. He must call his own attention to the matters which he is bound to consider. He must exclude from his consideration matter which are irrelevant to what he has to consider. If he does not obey those rules, he may truly be said, and often is said, to be acting "unreasonably". Similarly, there may be something so absurd that no sensible person could ever dream that it lay within the powers of the authority. Warrington L.J. in *Short v Poole Corporation* [1926] Ch 66, 90, 91 gave the example of the red-haired teacher, dismissed because she had red hair. That is unreasonable in one sense. In another sense it is taking into consideration extraneous matters. It is so unreasonable that it might almost be described as being done in bad faith; and, in fact, all these things run into one another.

...

I think Mr Gallop in the end agreed that his proposition that the decision of the local authority can be upset if it is proved to be unreasonable, really meant that it must be proved to be unreasonable in the sense that the court considers it to be a decision that no reasonable body could have come to. It is not what the court considers unreasonable, a different thing altogether. If it is what the court considers unreasonable, the court may very well have different views to that of a local authority on matters of high public policy of this kind. Some courts might think that no children ought to be admitted on Sundays at all, some courts might think the reverse, and all over the country I have no doubt on a think of that sort honest and sincere people hold different views. The effect of the legislation is not to set up the court as an arbiter of the correctness of one view over another. It is the local authority that are set in that position and, provided they act, as they have acted, within the four corners of their jurisdiction, this court, in my opinion, cannot interfere.'

Part 1
Case law

Chapter 2

General principles

Signposts

2.01 Introduction

This chapter is primarily concerned with those principles of valuation which have been considered by the courts and which have application to the valuation of shares. There have been relatively few cases relating to valuation of shares and many of the general principles which apply to share valuation arise from cases dealing with totally different assets.

It should be noted that, as far as the authors are aware, all court cases have been concerned with either 'fair' or 'open market' value. 'Owner' value or 'economic' value has not been considered. Owner value does not attempt to find the price at which the asset in question, whether a building, a project in development or a block of shares, could be sold in an arm's length transaction, but is an assessment of the worth of the asset to its owner or prospective owner. This is usually achieved by a discounted cash flow analysis and for a discussion of valuation; on this basis see **Chapter 13**.

However, when considering what has to be valued it is necessary to consider the reality of the transactions. In *Schofield v RCC* [2012] EWCA Civ 927 a series of put and call options were entered into. The Upper Tribunal stated:

> 'The composite transaction in the present case is not, in our view, a transaction having the nature of a transaction to which s 2 TGCA applies so as to generate a loss. And, whichever analysis one chooses to apply, the options code to which we have referred does not fall to be applied to each Option separately as if each Option existed as a discrete entity on its own apart from the overall scheme to which it owed its existence in the first place.'

In the Court of Appeal Lady Justice Hallett approved the statement in *W T Ramsay v IRC* [1981] STC 074 that:

> 'Where the taxpayer enters into a preconceived series of interdependent transactions deliberately contrived to be self-cancelling, that is to say, to return him substantially to the position he enjoyed at the outset, and incapable of having any appreciable effect on his financial position, no single transaction in the series can be isolated on its own as a disposal for the purposes of the statute.'

She also stated at paragraph 27 that:

> 'Counsel for HMRC took us through the decisions of the House of Lords in *Ramsay* and many of the cases which followed in order to demonstrate the propositions for which he contends. They include, in chronological order, *IRC v Burmah Oil Co Ltd* [1981] STC 30; *Furniss v Dawson* [1984] 1 AC 474; *Craven v White* [1989] 1 AC 398; *MacNiven v Westmoreland Developments Ltd* [2003] AC 311 and *IRC v Scottish Provident Institution* [2004] 1 WLR 3172. In short the submission of counsel for HMRC was that the principle of *Ramsay* clearly applies to the pre-ordained transactions in this case.'

And at paragraph 37 that:

> 'There is nothing in any of the later cases referred to by either party to cast doubt on either the principle enunciated in *Ramsay* or its application in that case. Inevitably the facts with which they were concerned and some of the formulations of principle they contain vary but not in any way supportive of the argument of counsel for Mr Schofield. As Mummery LJ put it in *HMRC v Mayes* [2011] STC 1269, 1287 para 74:
>
> > "*Ramsay* did not lay down a special doctrine of revenue law striking down tax avoidance schemes on the ground that they are artificial composite transactions and that parts of them can be disregarded for fiscal purposes because they are self-cancelling and were inserted solely for tax avoidance purposes and for no commercial purpose. The *Ramsay principle* is the general principle of purposive and contextual construction of all legislation. ICTA is no exception and is not immune from it. That principle has displaced the more literal, blinkered and formalistic approach to revenue statutes often applied before *Ramsay*."'

In *HMRC v Desmond Higgins* [2018] UKUT 280 (TCC), Mr Higgins paid a deposit of £5,000 in 2004 for a new house, off plan. Title problems meant that Mr Higgins could not take up residence until 5 January 2010 and left on 5 January 2012 whereupon he sold the property. HMRC claimed capital gains tax of £61,383 as the property did not exist when he paid the deposit. As his occupation could only begin when the property was habitable, Mr Higgins argued that he could not occupy the property until it was built and his period of occupation should apply, and the First Tier Tribunal agreed with him. However the Upper Tribunal did not, and held that his period of ownership began when he paid the deposit. An off plan purchase must, by definition, contain a pre-occupation building time but that is not what the tax law provides.

In *UBS AG v HMRC; DB Group Services (UK) Limited v HMRC* [2016] UKSC 13, Lord Reed stated:

> '1. In our society, a great deal of intellectual effort is devoted to tax avoidance. The most sophisticated attempts of the Houdini taxpayer to escape from the manacles of tax (to borrow a phrase from the judgment of Templeman LJ in *W T Ramsay Limited v Inland Revenue Comrs* [1979] 1 WLR 974, 979) generally take the form described in *Barclays Mercantile Business Finance Limited v Mawson* [2004] UKHL 51; [2005] 1 AC 684, para 34:
>
> > "structuring transactions in a form which will have the same or nearly the same economic effect as a taxable transaction but which it is hoped will fall outside the terms of the taxing statute. It is characteristic of these composite transactions that they will include elements which have been inserted without any business or commercial purpose but are intended to have the effect of removing the transaction from the scope of the charge."
>
> 2. The present appeals are concerned with composite transactions of this nature, designed to avoid the payment of income tax on bankers' bonuses. They are among a number of cases concerning broadly similar schemes. In each case, the scheme was intended to take advantage of Chapter 2 of Part 7 of the Income Tax (Earnings and Pensions) Act 2003 ("ITEPA"), as amended by Schedule 22 to the Finance Act 2003.
>
> ...
>
> 24. Rather than paying the bonuses directly to the employees, the bank instead used the amount of the bonuses to pay for redeemable shares in a special purpose offshore company set up solely for the purpose of the scheme. The shares were then awarded to the employees in place of the bonuses. Conditions were attached to the shares which were intended to enable them to benefit from the exemptions from income tax conferred by sections 425(2) and 429. Once the exemptions had accrued, the shares were redeemable by the employees for cash. Employees resident and domiciled in the United Kingdom, who were liable to capital gains tax, could however defer the redemption of their shares until they had held them for two years, by which time the rate of tax chargeable, with the benefit of business taper relief, was only 10%.
>
> ...
>
> 98. The error of the Court of Appeal in these cases lies, in my opinion, in adopting a literal construction of Chapter 2, and applying it to a correspondingly formal analysis of the facts. Adopting a purposive construction of Chapter 2, the conditions relied upon in order to bring the shares in question within the scope of the exemption conferred by section 425(2) failed to make provision of the kind required by section 423(1)(a): that is to say, provision having a business or commercial purpose, as distinct from provision whose only purpose was the obtaining of the exemption. That does not however mean that the conditions are to be disregarded for all fiscal purposes. Income tax is payable on the value of the shares as at the date of their acquisition in accordance with *Abbott v Philbin*, account being taken of any effect which the conditions may have had.
>
> 99. I would allow the appeals on that basis, subject to such adjustments to the assessments as may be necessary to reflect any effect which the conditions may have had on the value of the shares as at the date of their acquisition.'

In *Tinta International Limited (in liquidation) v De Villiers Surveyors Limited* [2017] UKSC 77 the Supreme Court overturned the Court of Appeal's judgment where a negligent valuation increased an existing exposure of a lender from £2.56 million to £3 million to the amount of the increase, overturning the Court of Appeal judgment that, because the second loan replaced the then existing loan, the exposure was to the whole of the second loan not just the increased loan, overturning the decision of the High Court.

Jonathan Netley v HMRC [2017] UKFTT 442 (TC) is reviewed at **14.04**. The problem in this case was:

> 'What was the market value of the shares in Frenkel Topping Group plc (FTG) which the Lead Appellant disposed of by way of gift to charity on 28 July 2004 as at that date for the purposes of section 587B ICTA1988 (and on what basis and principles should the market value of such shares be determined)?'

FTG was admitted to the Alternative Investment Market (AIM) on 28 July 2004. The Appellant was one of the shareholders who gifted shares to St Ann's Hospice, a well-known charity at a claimed 48p per share, as quoted on AIM, the Alternative Investment Market. In 2004–05, certain shares were qualifying investments eligible for income tax relief when gifted to charity under ICTA 1988, s 587B on the basis of their market value, if they were listed or dealt in on a recognised stock exchange and had to be valued under TCGA 1992, ss 272, 273. As Forward Link Limited, the share capital was 1,000 £1 shares, each of which, on 27 January 2004, was subdivided into 20,000 shares of 0.005p each.

On 17 February 2004 the authorised share capital was increased to £350,000, being 2,000,000,000 shares of 0.005p and 13,980,000 new ordinary shares of 0.005p per share, at par, raising £699. Some 92% of the shares were held by Richard Hughes, Ian Currie and Keith Salisbury, Stephen Lundy and W H Ireland plc.

On 17 February 2004, 23,000,000 shares were offered for subscription at 5p each which were issued and allotted on 3 June 2004.

Shares were allotted at 17.5p each shortly before the flotation on 28 July at 48p, the price set by the market maker and were quoted at 62p on 20 September 2016 but had gone as low as 14p in the interim. The Tribunal Judge held that the market value of Mr Netley's shares on 28 July were 17.5p per share.

Anne Christine Curtis Green v HMRC [2015] UKFTT 344 (TC) was an Inheritance Tax (IHT) case involving a business called Flagstaff Holidays and 85% of the business was transferred to the Mrs A C Green Settlement (the Trust) in two tranches both of which, it was claimed, qualified for 100% Business Property Relief for IHT, which was challenged by HMRC on the grounds that the business of providing holiday accommodation consisted mainly of making or holding investments and the Tribunal agreed with HMRC. Cases referred to were *HMRC v George* [2003] EWCA Civ 1763, *Weston v HMRC* [2000] STC 1064 and *HMRC v Pawson* [2013] UKUT 50 (TCC).

Nicholas Green v HMRC [2014] UKFTT 396 (TC) is reviewed at 14.04. This case related to two gifts of 118,750 shares of 0.1p each in Chartersea Limited to the National Eczema Society and the Alzheimer's Society on 4 April 2008. Mr Green claimed tax relief under TA 2007, s 434(1) of £237,500 based on a market value of £1 per share. HMRC did not accept that this was the market value of the shares and reduced the claim to 30p per gifted share, ie £71,250 and a reduction of £166,250. Mr Green appealed. HMRC had provided no support for their valuation and the price paid was £1 per share which were quoted on a Recognised Stock Exchange.

Chartersea was the vehicle used to acquire Warwick Development (North West) Limited (WDL) a manufacturer and supplier of PVC windows, doors, sealed glazed units and conservatories. On 1 February 2008, each ordinary share was divided into 1,000 ordinary shares of 0.1p each. 999 shares were issued to Mr Dallimore and 999,500 to Mr Salisbury at par. Chartersea issued a private placing memorandum to issue up to 5,000,000 new shares at 0.1p per 1p share, which were issued on 17 March 2008. 1,000,000 new shares of 0.1p each were issued to Brian Johnson, acting managing director of WDL. He and his brother Gavin with his wife owned 100% of WDL's holding company, Warwick Management Limited (WML). On 10 March 2008, Chartersea issued, in a private placing, 4,998,529 shares in WML. There was a rights issue on 12 March 2008 for 1,649,541 shares at £1 each, and Chartersea's share capital became 9,648,043 ordinary 0.1p shares. On 18 March 2008, Chartersea purchased shares in WML for £4,112,267.90 plus up to £2325,567.32 in respect of book debts. Chartersea had a loan facility from The Cooperative Bank of £2.5 million and an overdraft facility of £461,000. The purchase price for WML was £3,612,267.90 cash plus £500.00 loan rate.

Chartersea's 9,648,043 shares were listed and dealt with on the Official List of the Channel Islands Stock Exchange (CISX). On 4 April 2008, two parcels of 7,000 shares were traded at 101p and 100p. On 4 April 2008, Mr Green gifted all but 134,118 of the Chartersea shares, keeping 134,118 for himself. Not all of his income was taxable at 40% and he claimed to recover £66,500 in tax as a result of his gifts to charity, because not all of the gift was covered at the top rates of tax so he had paid £60,714 for the shares in March 2008 and they were worth £237,500 following the listing on CISX. The net cost, assuming the claimed tax relief was forthcoming, was £28,500. Mr Green had made similar investments in 2004 and 2006 to the same charities who had sold the shares at a profit.

Mr Green claimed that the charities benefited, and he could obtain tax relief and a long-term investment in the remaining shares.

The Tribunal determined the market value of the gifted shares at 35p per share, the relievable amount at £83,125 and the disallowance at £154,375.

Cases referred to included *IRC v Gray* [1994] STC 360, *Marks v Skerred* [2004] STC 362, *Re Lynall deceased, Lynall and another v CIR* (1972) 47 TC 375, *S Patrick Erdol v HMRC* [2011] UKFTT 87 (TC), *Caton v Couch* [1995] STC (SCD) 34, *Solomon Marks v HMRC* [2011] UKFTT 221 (TC), *Bullivant Holdings Limited v IRC* [1998] STC 905, *Salvesen's Trustees v IRC* 1930 SLT 387, *IRC v Clay* [1914] 3 KB 466.

In *The Personal Representatives of the Estate of Maureen W Vigue (deceased) v HMRC* [2017] UKFTT 632 (TC), when Mrs Vigue died on 29 May 2012 she was the sole owner of 30 acres of land, Gavelly Way livery stables. Her personal representatives claimed business property relief under IHTA 1984, s 105 and agricultural property relief under IHTA 1984, s 116. HMRC refused both reliefs and regarded it as holding investments.

IRC v George [2004] STC 147 was considered, which related to a caravan site, and the correct question was not whether a trade was being carried on but whether the deceased's business consisted wholly or mainly of holding investments. A building company case (*Piercy v HMRC* [2008] STC 858) was held not to be a land dealing business. In *McCall v HMRC* [2009] STC 990, letting land for grazing was not a business. *HMRC v Pawson* [2013] UKUT 50 (TCC) was referred to. The Tribunal held that the use of the land was not one of the holding of investments but was a genuine livery business and not agricultural property.

In *Adrian Kerrison v HMRC* [2017] UKFTT 322 (TC), various transactions were carried out in 2006–07 which the appellant claimed gave rise to capital loss of £1,102,655 but claimed income tax relief for £1,083,984 of that loss but HMRC issued a closure notice claiming income tax of £820,222.04, against which the taxpayer appealed. This resulted from a tax avoidance scheme promoted by Premier Strategies Limited, a company in the Tennon group of companies, knows as the Excalibur scheme:

> '4. In outline the steps were as follows:
>
> (1) A new company, Broadgate Trading Limited ("Broadgate"), was incorporated in the Isle of Man and acquired a small UK retail trade.
> (2) The appellant subscribed for 20 shares in Broadgate at their par value.
> (3) The appellant sold his shares to an unconnected company, Braye Finance Limited ("Braye"), for a similar sum and granted Braye a put option to sell the shares back to him within 30 days for their "fair value" plus 9.1%.
> (4) Braye borrowed to subscribe for one share in Broadgate at a very significant premium (the amount reflected the participation of other scheme users as well as the appellant). Broadgate guaranteed the borrowing.
> (5) Braye exercised the option and sold 20 shares back to the appellant for around £1.1m. Braye repaid its borrowing. This step was funded by borrowing by the appellant, which was also guaranteed by Broadgate.
> (6) Broadgate capitalised a British Virgin Islands ("BVI") subsidiary, Broadgate Group Holdings Limited ("Holdings"). Holdings advanced an interest-free loan to the appellant which repaid his bank borrowing. The interest-free loan was subsequently written off.
> (7) The appellant donated his Broadgate shares to a charity.
>
> 5. The intended tax analysis was that the sale and repurchase from Braye would fall within s 106A Taxation of Chargeable Gains Act 1992 ("TCGA"), such that the shares acquired from Braye would be identified with the shares disposed of to Braye for capital gains tax ("CGT") purposes, giving rise to a substantial capital loss on the basis that the appellant had acquired shares for a significant sum and sold them for a nominal amount. The appellant would be entitled to claim relief against income tax in respect of the loss under s 574 Income and Corporation Taxes Act 1988 ("ICTA"). The disposal to charity was a "no gain no loss" disposal (s 257 TCGA).
>
> 6. The relevant legislation, as in force for 2006–07 is [that] s 106A(5) TCGA provides that if within a period of 30 days after a disposal the person making the disposal acquires securities of the same class, then the securities must be identified with securities acquired by him in that period rather than with other securities. Section 574 ICTA permits relief from income tax to be claimed in respect of an allowable loss for CGT purposes which is incurred by an individual on the disposal of shares which he or she subscribed for in a "qualifying trading company".'

HMRC contended that the sale and repurchase of shares was caught by the 'repo' rules in TCGA 1992, s 263A and TA 1970, s 730A, and the value shifting rules in TCGA 1992, s 30 applied to eliminate the loss on the sale and repurchase. The *Ramsay* principle applied to ignore all the transactions and the appellant's subscription for shares and disposal to charity should be respected but the other transactions ignored. The amount paid to reacquire the shares should be ignored. Any capital loss may not be relieved against income tax under TA 1970, s 574 or 575. The waiver of the loan by Holdings is analogous to a dividend paid by Broadgate and is taxable under ITTOIA 2005, s 687.

Cases referred to included *IRC v Scottish Provident Institution* [2004] UKHL 52, [2005] STC 15, *Explainaway v HMRC* [2012] UKUT 362 (TCC), [2012] STC 2525 and *Schofield v HMRC* [2012] EWCA Civ 927, [2012] STC 2019, as well as on *Ramsay* itself (*WT Ramsay Limited v Commissioners of Inland Revenue; Eilbeck (Inspector of Taxes) v Rawling* [1982] AC 300, 54 TC 101) and *Furniss (Inspector of Taxes) v Dawson* [1984] AC 474, 55 TC 324, *UBS AG v HMRC; Deutsche Bank Group Services Limited v HMRC* [2016] UKSC 13 and *Collector of Stamp Revenue v Arrowtown Assets Limited* [2003] UKCFA 46; *Price v HMRC* [2015] UKUT 164 (TCC), *Drummond v HMRC* [2009] EWCA Civ 608, *Samarkand Film Partnership No 3 and others v HMRC* [2017] EWCA Civ 77, *Price v HMRC* [2013] UKFTT 297 (TC), *Ryall v Hoare* (1923) 8 TC 521, *Scatt v Ricketts* [1967] 1 WLR 828, *Property Co v Inspector of Taxes* [2005] STC (SCD) 59, *Leeming v Jones* [1930] 1 STC 333, *Cooper v Stubbs* (1925) 10 TC 29, *Spiritbeam Limited & Others v HMRC* [2015] UKUT 75 (TCC), *Drummond v Collins (Inspector of Taxes)* [1915] AC 1011, 6 TC 528, *Cunards Trustees v IRC* [1946] 1 All ER 159, 27 TC 122, *Stedeford (Inspector of Taxes) v Beloe* [1932] AC 388, 16 TC 505, *Rae v Lagard* 41 TC 1.

The end result was that the court dismissed the appellant's appeal against the refusal of his claim to a capital loss and to relief against income tax in respect of that loss but allowed his appeal against HMRC's assertion that the loan waiver was subject to income tax.

It is also necessary to consider FA 2013, ss 206–215 and Sch 43, which introduced a General Anti-Abuse Rule (GAAR). The GAAR seeks to focus on the most artificial of arrangements rather than 'normal' tax planning and applies to income tax, National Insurance contributions, capital gains tax, corporation tax, inheritance tax, petroleum revenue tax, stamp duty land tax, and the annual tax on enveloped dwellings.

Arrangements may be challenged under the GAAR if they seek to achieve an 'abusive' result. Tax arrangements are 'abusive' if they achieve an outcome of arrangements which cannot 'reasonably be regarded as a reasonable course of action'. This is known as the 'double reasonableness' test, and is intended to be the principal means through which legitimate, non-abusive tax planning arrangements are excluded from the GAAR. In determining whether the arrangements may be regarded as a reasonable course of action, reference is made to all circumstances, including:

(1) whether the arrangements give a result consistent with the principles on which the particular provisions are based (whether express or implied) and the policy objectives of those provisions;
(2) whether the means of achieving those results involves one or more contrived or abnormal steps; and
(3) whether the arrangements are intended to exploit any shortcomings in those provisions.

The legislation specifies that tax arrangements may be abusive where:

(1) the arrangements result in an amount of income, profits or gains for tax purposes that is significantly less than the amount for economic purposes;
(2) the arrangements result in deductions or losses of an amount for tax purposes that is significantly greater than the amount for economic purposes; and
(3) the arrangements result in a claim for the repayment or crediting of tax (including foreign tax) that has not been, and is unlikely to be, paid.

This list is not intended to be exhaustive.

Arrangements are 'tax arrangements' if they have as their main purpose, or one of their main purposes, the achieving of a tax advantage.

A 'tax advantage' includes:

(1) relief or increased relief from tax;
(2) repayment or increased repayment of tax;
(3) avoidance or reduction of a charge to tax or an assessment to tax;
(4) avoidance of a possible assessment of tax;
(5) deferral of a payment of tax or advancement of a repayment of tax; and
(6) avoidance of an obligation to deduct or account for tax.

An independent advisory panel will review and approve HMRC's guidance on the operation of the GAAR, and also provide comment on particular cases where HMRC consider that the GAAR may apply.

HMRC's published guidance, including a number of helpful examples, can be found at: www.hmrc.gov.uk/avoidance/gaar-partd-examples.pdf. The GAAR has effect in relation to arrangements entered into on or after 17 July 2013, the date Finance Act 2013 received Royal Assent.

Even where a company's shares are quoted or a recognised stock exchange the quoted price is not necessarily determinative of the market values: *Nicholas Green v HMRC* [2014] UKFTT 396 (TC), where the quotation on the Channel Islands Stock Exchange was based on artificial transfers.

2.02 Asset being valued – definition of a share and shareholding

A share is defined by CA 2006, s 540 as a 'share in the company's share capital and includes stock (except where a distinction between stock and shares is expressed or implied)'.

The definition of a share has also been considered in the courts and the judgment of Farwell J in *Borland's Trustee v Steel Bros & Co Ltd* [1901] 1 Ch 279 at 288 is probably the most famous:

> 'A share is the interest of a shareholder in the company measured by a sum of money, for the purpose of liability in the first place, and of interest in the second, but also consisting of a series of mutual covenants entered into by all the shareholders inter se in accordance with s 16 of the Companies Act 1862 (CA 2006, s 33). The contract contained in the articles of association is one of the original incidents of the share. The share is not a sum of money settled in the way suggested but is an interest measured by a sum of money and made up of various rights contained in the contract, including the right to a sum of money of a more or less amount.'

Kenny J in the estate duty case of *A-G v Jameson* [1904] 2 IR 644 at 669 stated in considering the judgment in *Borland's Trustee v Steel Bros & Co Ltd* [1901] 1 Ch 279 as follows:

> 'In considering whether that case was rightly decided, it is important to bear in mind the character of the property in question. It is not the property of the company that is subjected to restrictions on alienation. The assets of the company, its premises, stock in trade, etc., are all capable of being disposed of without limitation or fetter of any sort. No shareholder has a right to any specific portion of the company's property, and save by, and to the extent of, his voting power at a general meeting of the company, cannot curtail the free and proper disposition of it. He is entitled to a share of the company's capital and profits, the former, in the words of Farwell J, being measured by a sum of money which is taken as the standard for the ascertainment of his share of the profits. If the company disposes of its assets, or if the latter be realised in a liquidation, he has a right to a proportion of the amount received after the discharge of the company's debts and liabilities. In acquiring these rights – that is, in becoming a member of the company – he is deemed to have simultaneously entered into a contract under seal to conform to the regulations contained in the articles of association (Companies Act 1862, s 16) (CA 2006, s 33). Whatever obligations are contained in these articles, he accepts the ownership of the shares and the position of a member of the company, bound and controlled by them. He cannot divorce his money interest, whatever it may amount to, from these obligations. They are inseparable incidents attached to his rights, and the idea of a share cannot in my judgment be complete without their inclusion. This was the view taken by Farwell J, whose language was adopted by FitzGibbon LJ, in *Casey v Bentley* [1902] 1 IR 376, 383. He could not, nor could his personal representatives, retain the mere money interest and repudiate the contracts entered into in connexion with it. The money interest and the contractual obligations form one whole, and no member could be heard to say that he had a right to retain the former and disclaim the latter.'

Similarly, in the nationalisation case of *Short v Treasury Comrs* [1948] 1 KB 116 at 122 Evershed LJ stated:

> 'Shareholders are not, in the eye of the law, part owners of the undertaking. The undertaking is something different from the totality of the share-holdings.'

Later in the same case at 123:

> 'It is said on the one hand that it is of the essence of the matter that the Crown is, as it is bound to do, acquiring all the shares of the company. That is true; but on the other hand, it is also the fact that the Crown is acquiring shares from a number of individual shareholders. Prima facie, as it seems to us, and apart from any special words in the regulation, each shareholder is entitled to get, and to get only, the value of what he possesses; for that is all that he has to sell or transfer. If an individual shareholder in a company owns such a number of shares in that company as gives him effective control of the company's affairs it may well be that the value to be attributed to that holding on a sale of it as a separate transaction is a figure greater than the sum arrived at by multiplying the number of his shares by the "market" value for the time being of a single share. In such a case the shareholder in question, it may be said, has and is able to sell something more than a mere parcel of shares, each having the rights as to dividend and otherwise conferred upon it by the company's regulations.
>
> In the present case neither of the claimants has such a holding of shares as confers effective control of the company's affairs. No claim on the part of either

> is made on that basis. The claim of each is to have added to the value appropriate to his individual parcel of shares, if being sold separately, a rateable proportion of the added or "control" value belonging to the totality of the shares – an item of value which he, as an individual, does not in fact possess. On 17 March 1943 the first claimant, on the facts as found in the case, could have got 29s 3d for each of his ordinary shares from a willing buyer. He is claiming 41s 9d. The difference represents his share of the extra value which a purchaser, it is said, is prepared to give if he can get hold of all the shares. We can ourselves see no reason in principle why the first claimant should receive more than the value of what he has.'

The valuation difference between a minority and a majority holding was considered in *Lloyds Bank plc v Duker* [1987] 1 WLR 1324, John Mowbray QC commented:

> 'I do not think that a holding of only 574 of the 1,000 issued shares would be as high as 574/1000ths of the value of the hotel, notwithstanding the company's article no 19(A) which gives the holder of a majority of the shares summary power to remove and appoint directors.
>
> In a winding up I think two sets of capital gains tax might be payable and the holder of 574 shares acting alone could not pass a winding-up resolution to unlock the net assets. On the other hand the other shareholders would jump at the chance of joining in such a resolution, for reasons which will shortly appear.
>
> I should expect the asset value of the hotel to find at least a substantial reflection in the value of a holding of 574 shares in the company. The value would also, I think, reflect at least to some extent the after-tax operating profits of recent years, as shown in the audited accounts, even though none have been distributed as dividends. They were about £181,000 in the years to September 1984 and 1985 and have apparently improved since.
>
> The votes of a minor holding of shares, for instance, the 50 shares which would represent Mrs Arnold Smith's 4/80ths, or the 87 which would represent Mr Brian Smith's 7/80ths, could not unlock the assets, so such a holding could not be expected to reflect the asset value to any appreciable extent.
>
> What is more, none of the minority holding can be expected to participate in dividends for the foreseeable future, if Mr Duker takes 574 shares. That appears from a letter which his (and the company's) accountants wrote to Mrs Arnold Smith on 13 February 1986 …
>
> As I understand it, Mr Duker offered £403 a share to all the other beneficiaries, and has subsequently increased this offer to £510 a share (Counsel for the minority beneficiaries confirmed this on instructions.) At that price, the minority's 425 shares would be worth a total of £216,750. The minority could, on any view, insist on their joint holding of 425 shares being sold as a single block, and I think that en bloc they might fetch more than that. None the less, the want of any dividends for the foreseeable future, and the inability of the buyer of any minority block to force a dividend would be bound to have a definite depressing effect on the value of the holding.
>
> Mr Duker could not be expected to join in a winding-up resolution, and he would not need dividends, because he could pay himself a salary as managing director.
>
> So, though the state of the evidence does not enable me to make any precise finding about values, I can find this much, which is all I need for the present purpose: the value per share of a holding of 574 shares in the company is markedly higher than the value per share of a holding even of 425 shares. The

result is that, if Mr Duker takes 574 shares, the value of what he takes will be markedly more than 46/80ths of the aggregate values of his and other holdings.'

In *Irvine v Irvine* [2006] EWHC 583 the defendant had been ordered to buy, or procure the purchase of, the petitioners' shares in the company (CIHL).

> 'The petitioners' shares together represent 49.96% of the issued shares in CIHL. Of that, 49.96% just under half are held by the first petitioner (Patricia) and the balance by the second petitioner (the trust). The shares were acquired from the 50% holding in CIHL formerly owned by Malcolm Irving (Malcolm), Patricia's late husband and Ian's younger brother. Malcolm died on 1 March 1996. In August 1994 Malcolm had given half of his shareholding to the trust. By his will Malcolm had given one share to Ian and the remainder to Patricia. Patricia is one of the two trustees of the trust. The other trustee Michael Thatcher has "delegated" his powers as a trustee to Patricia in relation to the trust. The trust is for the benefit of Patricia's three sons who are now all adults. For all practical purposes Patricia and the trust speak as one voice.
>
> The question which I have to decide is whether in the working out of the buyout order the 49.96% (as effectively it is) is to be valued on a pro rata non-discounted basis to reflect the fact that it is a minority holding. It was agreed by both parties that CIHL had not been a quasi-partnership since Malcolm's death even though it remained a family company. As a result of the gift by Malcolm to Ian of the single share control of CIHL passed to Ian. No conditions were attached to the gift of that share. Ian was not subject to any restriction over and above those contained in CIHL's articles against disposing of his majority holding to an external purchaser. The petitioner's shareholdings constituted a minority holding even though the difference between them and Ian's is so small. There are no circumstances which could be described as exceptional so as to justify a departure from the ordinary assumption that a minority shareholding is valued as such. The fact that the court has found that the manner in which Ian has conducted CIHL's affairs was unfairly prejudicial to the interests of the petitioners so as to establish their entitlement to a buy-out order cannot of itself determine the basis of valuation of the petitioners' shares ... A minority shareholding, even one where the extent of the minority is as slight as in this case, is to be valued for what it is, a minority shareholding unless there is some good reason to attribute to it a pro rata share of the overall value of the company. Short of a quasi-partnership or some other exceptional circumstance there is no reason to accord to it a quality which it lacks. CIHL is not a quasi-partnership. There are no exceptional circumstances. The shareholdings must therefore be valued for what they are: less than 50% of CIHL's issued share capital. The extent of the discount to be applied will be a matter for the valuers.'

In *Howie v Crawford* [1990] BCC 330 the valuation of a 40% interest in a private company had been determined by an arbitrator without any discount for it being a minority interest. Vinelott J stated:

> ' ... the question therefore that I have to decide is whether the arbitrator erred in law in holding that on the true construction of the agreement the expression "the fair market price" means 40% of the fair value as between the parties of the net assets of the company. For my part I do not think the answer to this question admits of any doubt. The market price of an asset is the price which that asset will fetch in the open market between a willing vendor and a willing purchaser. If the asset is a holding of shares in a private company the market price will normally, if not invariably, depend upon the proportion of shares in the company comprised in the holding and on any special rights or restrictions contained in the articles of association of the company as well as on the value of the net assets of the

> company and its profit and dividend record. The addition of the word "fair" adds nothing except to remind the valuer that the market value must be ascertained on the assumption that there is a willing vendor and a willing purchaser that there is a fair market and that no one would be excluded from bidding in it.
>
> ...
>
> The arbitrator as I understand it founded his conclusion on the observation of Nourse J in *Bird Precision Bellows Ltd* which I have cited. However that case concerned a very different situation: the amount to be paid for the shares of a minority shareholder who claimed that the affairs of the company had been conducted by the majority in a way that was unfairly prejudicial to him. He sought an order that the majority should buy his shares at a price ascertained by the court. In such a case the court has a wide discretion and will not, save in very exceptional circumstances, compel a minority shareholder who establishes a claim that the affairs of the company are being conducted in the way which is unfairly prejudicial to him to sell his shares at a price less than an adequate share of the net assets of the company. Such an order would work an obvious injustice, if for instance the minority shareholders' complaint was that the majority shareholder was ensconced as managing director and was using his control of the company by ploughing back all the profits of the company and if the minority shareholder's only remedy under the articles of association was to serve a transfer notice thereby entitling the majority shareholder to purchase his shares at what might be an artificially low value as a result of his use of the control to ensure that no profits were distributed. The judge referred to Oliver LJ's comments in the Court of Appeal in *Bird Precision Bellows Ltd* [1986] Ch 658 and commented: "In that passage Oliver LJ clearly contrasts the basis on which the market price of shares falls to be ascertained when the proportion of the issued shares represented by the size of the holding to be valued must be taken into account, and the ascertainment of the sum to be paid to a successful applicant under (CA 1980) s 75 (CA 2006, s 983) where the court has a wide discretion as to the order to be made and, if the order is that the respondent purchase the appellant's shares, the basis on which the purchase price is to be ascertained..." That principle has no possible application in the present case where what has to be ascertained is the fair market price of Mr Crawford's 40 per cent holding.
>
> In my judgement therefore the arbitrator clearly applied the wrong test.'

Lord MacMillan in the estate duty cases of *Re Crossman, Re Paulin* (1936) 15 ATC 94 at 117 described a share as:

> 'A share in a joint stock company is an entirely conventional creation; the congeries of rights and liabilities of which it consists is the creature of the Companies Acts and the memorandum and articles of the particular company. Within the law the rights and liabilities appurtenant to a share may vary widely. But it cannot exist independently of the inherent attributes with which it has been created.'

In the same case the meaning of a share was also considered by Lord Russell of Killowen at 115:

> 'It is the interest of a person in the company, that interest being composed of rights and obligations which are defined by the Companies Act and by the memorandum and articles of association of the company. A sale of a share is a sale of the interest, so defined and the subject matter of the sale is effectively vested in the purchaser by the entry of his name in the register of members. It may be that owing to provisions in the articles of association the subject matter

> of the sale cannot be effectively vested in the purchaser, because the directors refuse to and cannot be compelled to register the purchaser as shareholder. The purchaser could then secure the benefit of the sale by the registered shareholder becoming a trustee for him of the rights with an indemnity in respect of the obligations.'

Each share is a separate asset capable of being transferred singly. Lord Blanesburgh in *Re Crossman* at 107:

> 'Proceeding now to deal with the case presented by the Crown, my answer to the first question is that the property which so passed here was the deceased's entire legal and equitable interest in his ordinary shares; each share a separate entity – a "property" within the meaning of the Act, charged to duty as it passed "in the ordinary sense of the term from the deceased into the possession and property of another person after his death".'

The rule in *Foss v Harbottle* (1843) 2 Hare 461 encapsulates the point that the court will not interfere in the management of a company which is carrying out the wishes of the majority of the shareholders, through the directors, merely because a minority of shareholders consider that such actions are not in their or in the company's interest. It also extends to any irregularity that arises where that irregularity could be corrected by a resolution of the majority of the shareholders. Only the company can sue to enforce rights of action vested in it and therefore only the directors or the company in general meeting, can sue in the company's name (*Gray v Lewis* (1873) 8 Ch App 1035). This does not of course prevent a member exercising his statutory rights under the Companies Acts to complain of conduct prejudicial to his own interests. He may also seek to restrain the commission of an ultra vires act (*Simpson v Westminster Palace Hotel Company* (1860) 8 HL Cas 712 or where there is a threatened breach of any provisions of the memorandum or articles of the company (*Baschoek Proprietary Co Ltd v Fuke* [1906] 1 Ch 148). A minority shareholder may also take action where inadequate notice had been given for a resolution, where there is fraud or oppression, or breach of directors' or promoter's fiduciary duties.

The rule in *Foss v Harbottle* illustrates the weakness of a minority shareholder's position where the view of the majority prevails and is therefore part of the reason for the discount from a pro rata proportion of the company as a whole which applies in many cases to a minority shareholding. The rule in *Foss v Harbottle* has been partly overridden by the Companies Act 2006 in ss 260–269 which allows any member of a company to bring an action known as a derivative claim in respect of a cause of action vested in the company and seeking relief on behalf of the company. The cause of action may arise from an actual or proposed act or omission involving negligence, default, breach of duty or breach of trust by a director of the company and may be brought against the director or another person or both. In order to continue a derivative claim of this nature it is necessary to have the approval of the court under CA 2006, ss 261–264 in England and Wales and Northern Ireland and under CA 2006, ss 266–269 in corresponding provisions relating to Scotland. These provisions came into force in the autumn of 2007; it is difficult to see what effect this might have in practice on shareholders' rights and whether it has any material affect on the valuation of minority interests. As it is likely to have very limited application it seems probable that it will have no measurable impact on the value of minority shareholdings.

In *Birch v Cropper* (1889) 14 App Cas 525, the House of Lords held that, in the absence of anything in the articles, any liquidation surplus is to be divided among all classes of shareholders, equally according to the number of shares held. Lord Herschell stated:

> 'I am therefore of opinion that the judgment appealed from should be reversed: and that it should be declared that the balance of the proceeds of sale ought to be divided amongst the holders of all the shares in the Bridgewater Navigation Company Limited, in proportion to the shares held by them respectively.'

Lord Fitzgerald agreed:

> 'My lords, I am clearly of opinion that the only equitable principle to be acted on in this case is that of equality. That is an equitable principle and in giving effect to that rule each and every shareholder should receive in respect of his share an equal proportion of this surplus.'

As did Lord McNaughton:

> 'I am therefore of opinion that the judgment of the Court of Appeal must be varied, and that it should be declared that subject to the payment of the costs, charges and expenses on the winding-up, including the costs of all parties in this application here and in the courts below, the assets of the company remaining undistributed other than the reserve fund, which is not the subject of this application, ought to be distributed among all the shareholders in proportion to their shares.'

However, the articles usually provide that on a liquidation, the preference shareholders are to be repaid the amount paid up on their shares and any surplus is then payable to the ordinary shareholders, pro rata: *Seattle Insurance Corporation v Wilson and Clyde Coal Co Ltd* [1949] AC 462; *Re Isle of Thanet Electrical Supply Co Ltd* [1949] 2 All ER 1060.

In *Ward, Cook & Buckingham (Cook's Executors) v IRC* [1999] STC (SCD) 1, it was held that once a building society had issued copies of the transfer document to convert to a limited company, that was a right which was part of the estate, which had enhanced the value of the deceased's interest in the society.

Begum v Hossain and Sunam Tandoori Limited [2015] EWCA Civ 717 involved an Indian restaurant and takeaway in connection with the valuation of the business when one of the shareholders, Ms Hossain, agreed to purchase the shares of the other equal shareholder, Ms Begum, at the valuation of an independent valuer, Neil Oxford of Christie Owen and Davies Limited, being the fair value of the shares at 26 March 2010 between a willing buyer and a willing seller.

The valuation was made on the basis of the Income Approach or Earnings Multiplier applied to maintainable income. However, it appears that the maintainable income in the accounts on which Mr Oxford relied understated the takings, on the basis of the 'handwritten takings'. The account had been relied on for VAT purposes and by the valuer, who drew attention to the possibility of an independent forensic accountant being jointly instructed by both parties to provide alternative figures on which he could base his valuation. However, as he had been instructed to have regard to the books and records of the company, which included the handwritten record of takings, not only the incorrect accounts, he had therefore not followed his instructions and the valuation was set aside.

In *Re Blue Index Limited; Murrell v Swallow and others* [2014] EWHC 2680 (Ch), the Petitioner paid £45,000 for a 3% shareholding, recorded in the books as £2,250, par value.

Mr Murrell petitioned for the purchase of his shares in November 2008, at a fair value, *O'Neill v Phillips* [1999] 1 WLR 1092, ie on a pro rata basis. The maintainable profits were calculated in accordance with the BDO Private Company Price Index as the maintainable Profit Before Tax and Before Directors' Enrolments (PBTBDE). Mr Murrell's 3% of the shares were valued at £300,000 in this case. Director's remuneration to be assumed was based on 10% of turnover.

> **Focus**
>
> Is the value of the shares pro rata to the value of the company as a quasi partnership or subject to a discount for lack of control?

2.03 Memorandum and articles of association

It is obviously important to study the company's memorandum and articles of association in order to ascertain the precise rights attaching to particular shares. There may be various classes of shares each having different rights and the value of any particular shareholding is the value of those rights compared with the totality of the rights of all other shareholders of the various classes of shares.

In *Lyle & Scott v Scott's Trustees, Lyle & Scott v The British Investment Trust* 1959 SC (HL) 64 it was held that where a company's articles provided a mechanism for transferring shares, that mechanism was binding upon the shareholders and that, in view of the wording in the articles, they could not retain the legal title to the shares and dispose of the beneficial interest. Lord Keith of Avonholme stated:

> 'I think that a shareholder who has transferred, or pretended to transfer, the beneficial interest in a share to a purchaser for value is merely endeavouring by a subterfuge to escape from the peremptory provisions of the article. A share is of no value to anyone without the benefits it confers. A sale of a share is a sale of the beneficial rights that it confers and to sell or purport to sell the beneficial rights without the title to the share is in my opinion a plain breach of the provisions of article 9. This, I think, is the view which commended itself to Lord Sourn and I think that he is right. What has happened in the present case is that by virtue of the articles the purchaser is unable to take the seller's name off the register and substitute his own. The defenders have done everything apart from executing a formal instrument of transfer that would be necessary in a normal purchase and sale of shares. They have even done more, for they have executed proxies in favour of the purchaser's solicitors.'

In *Scotto v Petch, re Sedgefield Steeplechase Co (1927) Ltd* [2001] BCC 889, the Court of Appeal upheld the High Court judgement that on a true construction of the articles of association of the company, the transfer by about 76.4% of the shareholders of the beneficial interest in their shares to Northern Racing Ltd did not trigger the pre-emption rights under these particular articles. The beneficial interest was transferred by means of a sale agreement, a vendor's solicitor's letter and a declaration of trust:

> 'The sale agreement was made between the shareholder, ("the vendor") and Northern Racing ("the purchaser"). It recited that the vendor had agreed to sell and the purchaser had agreed to purchase the equitable interest in the vendor's shares on the terms and subject to the conditions of the agreement. By clause 1.1 the word "Rights" was defined to mean the entire equitable interest in the vendor's shares. Clause 2 provided that the vendor shall sell with full title guarantee and the Purchaser shall purchase the Rights. Clause 3 specified the consideration for the sale of the rights. Clause 4.1 provided that the sale and purchase of the rights should be conditional upon the purchaser having entered into agreements with shareholders of the company to acquire equivalent rights in at least 75% of the company. Clause 5.1 provided that the completion should take place on the day on which the condition had been satisfied (in the events which happened, on 30 November 1998). Clause 5.2 provided that, at completion, the vendor should deliver first to the purchaser a duly completed and executed declaration of trust (in a form already agreed); secondly to the vendor's solicitors, the share certificates and other documents of title relating to the shares; and, thirdly to the purchaser's solicitors, the vendor's solicitors' letter.'

The sale agreement also contained various warranties including, in particular, that the vendor's shareholders who retained the legal interest in the shares would vote in accordance with the directions of the purchaser. The vendor's solicitor's letter contained an undertaking to hold the share certificates and not to release them to the purchaser until it was registered as a member of the company. The declaration of trust contained a declaration that the vendor (the trustee) held the shares upon trust for the buyer and contained an undertaking by the trustee:

> 'to transfer, or otherwise deal with the Shares as the Buyer shall from time to time direct and to account to the Buyer for dividends or other monies paid to the Trustee on or in respect of the Shares and to exercise the voting powers and other rights and privileges conferred by the articles of association of the Company in such manner as the Buyer shall from time to time direct save that the Trustee may not be regarded to transfer or otherwise deal with the shares in any way which would contravene any subsisting pre-emption rights contained in the articles of association of the Company in force from time to time.'

The declaration of trust also irrevocably appointed the buyer as the attorney for the trustee for all necessary purposes. The minority shareholder Mrs Scotto, who held 21.3% of the shares, sought a declaration from the court that the disposal of the equitable interest to Northern Racing triggered her pre-emption rights. Her application failed both at first instance and on appeal.

This case was distinguished from cases such as *Lyle & Scott Ltd v Scott's Trustees* [1959] AC 763 and *Owens v GRA Property v Trust Ltd* (unreported) 10 July 1978 where there was an arrangement or option which placed the shareholder under a contractual obligation to execute and deliver a transfer in violation of the rights of pre-emption.

In *Killick & Another v PricewaterhouseCoopers* [2001] Lloyd's Rep PN 17 the claim was made by the executors in respect to the valuation of shares in a company called Benfield Greig Group Plc pursuant to a buy-back provision in the company's articles. The valuers were auditors valuing as experts not an arbitrator. There was a liability cap at £10m. The estate held 16m ordinary shares in the company which the auditors valued at £2.10 per share. The claimants then obtained a report from another firm of accountants, Deloitte & Touche, stating that the right value was in fact £4 a share.

> 'On that basis they contended that the determination of £2.10 per share by the defendant was negligent and they issued the instant proceedings against the defendant for damages of just over £30m based on the difference between £4 and £2.10 per share in relation to the 15,990,990 shares sold pursuant to the valuation.'

As the auditors as valuers had been appointed by the company to perform the valuation they denied any duty of care to the claimants or alternatively that the liability was capped at £10m. One point was whether the Unfair Contracts Terms Act 1977 applied to the liability cap. The problem was the executors were not party to the contract. The judge decided that this was not a question which he could determine at the interlocutory stage and the issue must therefore go to trial. The judge held that the valuers did have a duty of care to the executors. In coming to this conclusion he relied on *Arenson v Casson Beckman Rutley & Co* [1977] AC 405; *Hedley Byrne & Co Ltd v Heller & Partners Ltd* [1964] AC 465; *White Oak v Walker* (1988) 4 BCC 122; the US case of *Glanzer v Shepherd* (1922) 135 NE 275; *Caparo Industries Plc v Dickman & Others* [1990] 2 AC 605; *Cann v Wilson* [1879] Ch 39; and the House of Lords decision in *Smith v Eric S Bush* quoted by Lord Jauncey in *Caparo, and Candler v Crane Christmas & Co* [1951] 2 KB 164.

The other two issues were:

> 'whether the accountant's liability to the selling shareholders can be subject to a limitation clause in the contract between the company and the accountant under which the accountant was appointed to perform the valuation; if so, (b) whether the limitation clause in this case satisfied the requirements of reasonableness in the Unfair Contracts Terms Act 1977.'

These issues were referred to trial. Whether or not the valuation was in fact negligent was not considered at this stage.

> **Focus**
>
> The memorandum and articles of association, with the Companies Acts, constitute the company's rule book.

2.04 Rights under the articles – control

Although it is normally fairly clear from the company's articles of association, the rights of the various shareholders have to be considered in the light of company law generally as amplified by the specific provisions in the articles.

One area which can give a particular problem in practice is where there is an equality of shareholdings and as to whether as a result there is complete deadlock or a particular shareholder has control. Such a case was that of *IRC v B W Noble Ltd* (1926) 12 TC 911. In this case Mr Noble held 500 out of 1,000 ordinary shares. However, he was also chairman of the company and as Rowlatt J stated in judgment at 926:

> 'It seems to be that "controlling interest" is a phrase that has a certain well known meaning. It means the man whose shareholding in the company is such that he is the shareholder who is more powerful than all the other shareholders put together in general meeting. That is really what it comes to. Now this gentleman has just half the number of shares but those shares in the circumstances of this case are reinforced by the position that he occupies of chairman. A position that he occupies not merely by the votes of the other shareholders or of his directors elected by the shareholders, but by contract and so reinforced in as much as he has a casting vote he does control the general meetings, there is no question about that, and in as much as he does possess at least half of the shares he can prevent any modifications taking place in the constitution of the company which would undermine his position as chairman.'

The judge had no hesitation in holding therefore that Mr Noble controlled the company. This could occasionally be important for business property relief for inheritance tax as 50% relief is available for any land or building, machinery or plant, used by a company of which the transferor then had control, under IHTA 1984 s 105(1)(d), and control for this purpose only would include actual control through a chairman's casting vote.

In deciding whether or not somebody has control of the company it is necessary to look closely at the voting entitlement. In the estate duty FA 1940, s 55 case of *Barclays Bank Ltd v IRC* [1960] 3 WLR 280 it was held that where a shareholder held 1,100 ordinary shares in his own right and 3,650 ordinary shares as trustee out of a total of 8,350 ordinary shares, he had control of the company. As Viscount Simonds stated:

> 'As I have said I doubt whether the answer that is given to this primary question is conclusive of the problems raised in this appeal, but it leads me to examine it on the footing that I must ask whether the testator, being under the constitution of the company entitled to vote in respect of both the 1,000 and the 3,650 shares, had control of the company within the natural meaning of those words. My lords in *B W Noble Ltd v IRC* (1926) 12 TC 911 at page 926 (referred to above) the words "controlling interest in the company occurring in the Finance Act 1920" were said by Rowlatt J to mean the interest of:
>
> > "One whose shareholding in the company is such that he is the shareholder who is more powerful than all the other shareholders put together in general meeting."
>
> In other words one who can by his votes control the company in general meeting. His opinion was approved in a later case in this House – see *British American Tobacco Co Ltd v IRC* (1943) 29 TC 49. I see no difference between the natural meaning of two phrases having a controlling interest in the company and having control of the company, though it might be desirable and in the case of the latter phrase was found to be so, to give an extended meaning to the words. If so, I think that your lordships should accept the guidance given by this House in *IRC v J Bibby & Sons Ltd* (1945) 29 TC 167. That case determined that control must be ascertained by reference to the company's constitution and that it is irrelevant that a shareholder who has the apparent control may himself be amenable to some external control. I need not repeat what was said by the noble and learned lords who took part in that appeal. What they said applies with equal force to cases arising under FA 1940 s 55. The Scottish case of *John Shields & Co (Perth) Ltd v IRC* (1950) 29 TC 475 applied the same principle to somewhat different circumstances so did *IRC v Silvers Ltd* (1951) 29 TC 491.'

The fact that a shareholder has control of a company does not mean that the corporate veil can be lifted, for example to assume land is held with vacant possession where both the landlord and the tenant are companies controlled by the same shareholder: *Pyrah (Doddington) Ltd v Northamptonshire County Council* (1982) 263 Estates Gazette 729. Similarly, in *Henderson v Karmel* [1984] STC 572, Nourse J stated:

> 'I will in the first instance assume in favour of the taxpayers that Mrs Karmel's ability to control the company by virtue of her shareholding in it would have enabled her at the material time to procure that vacant possession was given to a purchaser in the open market. It is nevertheless clear that there would still have been two assets to be disposed of; first, the company's tenancy, which would either have had to be assigned to the purchaser or first surrendered to Mrs Karmel and, secondly, the reversion, which would have had to be conveyed by her to the purchaser. The first was an asset of the company and the second an asset of Mrs Karmel. I think it impossible to say that, because Mrs Karmel could in one way or another have extinguished the company's asset, therefore her asset was the unencumbered freehold and not the reversion expectant on the determination of the tenancy.'

A company's share capital may be structured in such a way that voting control is divorced from an entitlement to a majority of the assets on a liquidation. Such structures have often been put in place in order to mitigate vulnerability to taxation, but in the present inheritance tax regime, that allows 100% business property relief for most shareholdings in trading companies, under IHTA 1984, s 105(1)(bb), they may either be unnecessary or possibly even disadvantageous.

An extreme example of a structure of this type featured in *Holt v Holt* [1990] 1 WLR 1250, which concerned the value, in matrimonial proceedings, of shares in a family company in New Zealand. The issued share capital of the company in question consisted of one NZ$1 A share and 999 NZ$1 B shares. The A share carried 10,000 votes, the B shares one vote each, but otherwise the two classes ranked pari passu.

The Privy Council likened the position of the A shareholder to that of a tenant for life, impeachable for waste, with two further advantages not possessed by a tenant for life. First, he could create a further tenant for life by transmitting the A share to, say, his son or to a purchaser who found farming attractive. Secondly, the B shareholders could obtain nothing without the co-operation of the A shareholder. See **12.08** for a discussion of how value might be arrived at in these or similar circumstances.

> **Focus**
>
> Control is a question of fact, ie who can outvote the opposition taking into account more complex situations such as unexercised share options, under IFRS 10.

2.05 Prejudicial conduct

Although the position of a minority shareholder in a limited company tends to be fairly weak there is clearly a limit beyond which the majority may not go without running the risk that the minority shareholder will apply to the court under the provisions of CA 2006, s 994 which provides as follows:

> '994 Petition by company member
>
> (1) A member of a company may apply to the court by petition for an order under this Part on the ground–
>   (a) that the company's affairs are being or have been conducted in a manner that is unfairly prejudicial to the interests of members generally or of some part of its members (including at least himself), or
>   (b) that an actual or proposed act or omission of the company (including an act or omission on its behalf) is or would be so prejudicial.
>
> (2) The provisions of this Part apply to a person who is not a member of a company but to whom shares in the company have been transferred or transmitted by operation of law as they apply to a member of a company.
>
> (3) In this section, and so far as applicable for the purposes of this section in the other provisions of this Part, "company" means–
>   (a) a company within the meaning of this Act, or
>   (b) a company that is not such a company but is a statutory water company within the meaning of the Statutory Water Companies Act 1991 (c58).
>
> 996 Powers of the court under this Part
>
> (1) If the court is satisfied that a petition under this Part is well founded, it may make such order as it thinks fit for giving relief in respect of the matters complained of.
>
> (2) Without prejudice to the generality of subsection (1), the court's order may–
>   (a) regulate the conduct of the company's affairs in the future;
>   (b) require the company–
>   (i) to refrain from doing or continuing an act complained of, or
>   (ii) to do an act that the petitioner has complained it has omitted to do;
>   (c) authorise civil proceedings to be brought in the name and on behalf of the company by such person or persons and on such terms as the court may direct;
>   (d) require the company not to make any, or any specified, alterations in its articles without the leave of the court;
>   (e) provide for the purchase of the shares of any members of the company by other members or by the company itself and, in the case of a purchase by the company itself, the reduction of the company's capital accordingly.
>
> 997 Application of general rule-making powers
>
> The power to make rules under section 411 of the Insolvency Act 1986 (c45) or Article 359 of the Insolvency (Northern Ireland) Order 1989 (SI 1989/2405 (NI 19)), so far as relating to a winding-up petition, applies for the purposes of a petition under this Part.'

In addition the court may put the company into compulsory liquidation under Insolvency Act 1986, s 122(1)(g) if it is of the opinion that it is just and equitable that the company should be wound up.

Earlier legislation in CA 1998, s 210 referred to the powers of an oppressed or potentially oppressed minority to petition the court under these provisions. Although in practice it was usually sufficient to ensure that the majority shareholders did not fraudulently diminish the value of the minority shareholders' shares, it had little to offer the minority shareholder by way of positive action. In *Re Jermyn Street Turkish Baths Ltd* [1971] 1 WLR 1042 additional funds were paid into a company by one shareholder which ended up with the remaining shareholder, who had no available funds, becoming a minority shareholder. Dividends were not paid and substantial remuneration was drawn by the majority shareholder. The minority shareholder petitioned the court. The Court of Appeal's judgment stated:

> 'The fact that the allotment of the shares and the creation of the debentures are dealt with in distinct and separate resolutions seems to us to establish nothing. The company was in dire need of cash. Mr Rowberry and Mrs Peskoff had been told that no money would be available from the Littman estate and that they would have to manage as best they could, or to that effect.' And:

> 'We are concerned only to consider whether the affairs of the company were, when the petition was presented, being conducted in a manner oppressive to some part of the members of the company. What does the word oppressive mean in this context? In our judgment oppression occurs when shareholders, having a dominant power in a company, either (1) exercise that power to procure that something is done or not done in the conduct of the company's affairs or, (2) procure by an express or implicit threat of an exercise of that power that something is not done in the conduct of the company's affairs, and when such conduct is unfair, or to use the expression adopted by Viscount Simonds in *Scottish Co-operative Wholesale Society Ltd v Meyer* [1958] 3 All ER 66 at 71 "burdensome, harsh and wrongful" to the other members of the company, or some of them and lacks that degree of probity which they are entitled to expect in the conduct of the company's affairs. See *Scottish Co-operative Wholesale Society Ltd v Meyer* and *Re H R Harmer Ltd* [1958] 3 All ER 689. We do not say that it is necessarily a comprehensive definition of the meaning of the word oppressive in s 210 [*now CA 2006, s 994*], for the affairs of life are so diverse that it is dangerous to attempt a universal definition. We think however that it may serve us as sufficient definition for the present purpose. Oppressive must, we think, import that the oppressed are being constrained to submit to something which is unfair to them as the result of some overbearing act or attitude on the part of the oppressor. If a director of a company were to draw remuneration to which he was not legally entitled or in excess of the remuneration to which he was legally entitled this might no doubt found misfeasance proceedings or proceedings for some other kind of relief, but it would not, in our judgment, of itself amount to oppression. Nor would the fact that the director was a majority shareholder in the company make any difference unless he had used his majority voting powers to retain the remuneration or to stifle proceedings by the company or other share-holders in relation to it.'

It was explained:

> 'While it is true that no dividend has been paid and that the Littman estate has received no benefit from the company, in the sense of receiving any distribution of capital or profits, it is certainly not true that the Littman estate has not benefited from Mrs Peskoff's efforts. Substantial sums derived from the carrying on of the business have been reinvested in the business. The company's financial position has been enormously improved, the bank overdraft has been eliminated and Mr Littman's guarantee has been discharged without any cost to his estate, and whereas at Mr Littman's death his shares in the company must have been worthless, or very nearly so, they must now have a substantial value notwithstanding that they now constitute a minority shareholding in the company.'

Similarly in *Re Lundie Bros Ltd* [1965] 1 WLR 1051 a director and shareholder who had been forced out of active participation in the company failed in his claim under CA 1948, s 210 (CA 2006, s 994) to prove any case of oppression, although in that case it was agreed that it would be just and equitable to wind up the company as a quasi partnership as in *Re Davis & Collett Ltd* [1935] Ch 693 and *Re Yenidje Tobacco Co Ltd* [1916] 2 Ch 426. The leading case where relief was granted under CA 1948, s 210 is that of *Meyer v Scottish Textile and Manufacturing Co Ltd* 1957 SC 110. In this case two experts in rayon cloth became minority shareholders in a company where the majority shares were held by a wholesale co-operative society. The ability of the individuals was vital to the formation and early success of the business, which prospered. The society subsequently tried to acquire the individuals' shares at less than their true value, and this proving unsuccessful, embarked on a policy of diverting the company's trade to a new department within the society itself. As a result the value of the company's shares was severely diminished. As a result of this application the society was ordered to buy the minority shareholders' shares at the price that they would have had but for the society's oppressive conduct. In the words of Lord Sorn:

> 'It thus appears to me that the society, as majority shareholder participated in its own scheme for the ruin of the business and the devaluation of the shares. Put bluntly what the society did was to put its nominees in control of the company and their job was to see that the company became a passive victim. If that is not oppression by a majority in the conduct of a company's affairs, I do not know what is.'

His Lordship continued:

> 'In the circumstances of this case it is manifest that the only appropriate remedy is to make the majority shareholder, that is to say the society, purchase the petitioners' shares at a fair valuation.'

In *Re Bird Precision Bellows Ltd* [1984] 2 WLR 869, Nourse J stated:

> 'Although both CA 1948, s 210 and CA 1980, s 75 (CA 2006, ss 994–999) are silent on the point, it is axiomatic that a price fixed by the court must be fair. While that which is fair may often be generally predicated in regard to matters of common occurrence, it can never be conclusively judged in regard to a particular case until the facts are known. The general observations which I will presently attempt in relation to a valuation of shares by the court under s 75 are therefore subject to that important reservation.
>
> Broadly speaking, shares in a small private company are acquired either by allotment on its incorporation or by transfer or devolution at some later date. In the first category it is a matter of common occurrence for a company to be incorporated in order to acquire an existing business or to start a new one, and in either event for it to be a vehicle for the conduct of a business carried on by two or more shareholders which they could, had they wished, have carried on in partnership together. Although it has been pointed out on the high authority to which I will soon refer that the description may be confusing, it is often convenient and it is certainly usual to describe that kind of company as a quasi partnership. In the second category, irrespective of the nature of the company, it is a matter of common occurrence for a shareholder to acquire shares from another at a price which is discounted because they represent a minority holding. It seems to me that some general observations can usefully be made in regard to each of these examples.
>
> As to the first, there is a well-known passage in the speech of Lord Wilberforce in *Ebrahimi v Westbourne Galleries Ltd* [1973] AC 360 at 379 where his

Lordship, having observed that it is not enough that the company is a small one, or a private company, identifies three typical elements, one, or probably more, of which will characterise the company as a quasi partnership. They are, firstly, an association formed or continued on the basis of a personal relationship involving mutual confidence, secondly, an agreement or understanding that all or some of the shareholders shall participate in the conduct of the business, and, thirdly, restrictions on share transfers. No doubt these three elements are the most familiar, and perhaps the most important, but they were not intended to be exhaustive. In my view there may be other typical and important elements, in particular the provision of capital by all or some of the participants.

I would expect that in a majority of cases where purchase orders are made under s 75 in relation to quasi partnerships the vendor is unwilling in the sense that the sale has been forced on him. Usually he will be a minority shareholder whose interests have been unfairly prejudiced by the manner in which the affairs of the company have been conducted by the majority. On the assumption that the unfair prejudice has made it no longer tolerable for him to retain his interest in the company; a sale of his shares will invariably be his only practical way out of a winding up. In that kind of case it seems to me that it would not merely be fair, but most unfair, that he should be bought out on the fictional basis applicable to a free election to sell his shares in accordance with the company's articles of association, or indeed on any other basis which involved a discounted price. In my judgment the correct course would be to fix the price pro rata according to the value of the shares as a whole and without any discount, as being the only fair method of compensating an unwilling vendor of the equivalent of a partnership share. Equally, if the order provided, as it did in Re Jermyn Street Turkish Baths Ltd, for the purchase of the shares of the delinquent majority, it would not merely be fair, but most unfair, that they should receive a price which involved an element of premium.

Of the other, I would expect more rare, cases in which the court might make a purchase order in relation to a quasi partnership the arguments of counsel for the respondents require me to mention one. Suppose the case of a minority shareholder whose interests had been unfairly prejudiced by the conduct of the majority, but who had nevertheless so acted as to deserve his exclusion from the company. It is difficult to see how such a case could arise in practice, because one would expect acts and deserts of that kind to be inconsistent with the existence of the supposed conduct of the majority. Be that as it may, the consideration of that possibility has been forced on me by the agreement for the price to be determined by the court without any admission of unfairly prejudicial conduct on the part of the respondents. As will appear, counsel for the respondents submitted that the petitioners did act in such a way as to deserve their exclusion from the company. He further submitted that it would therefore be fair for them to be bought out on the basis which would have been applicable if they had made a free election to sell their shares pursuant to the articles, i.e. at a discount. Assuming at present that the respondents can establish the necessary factual basis, I think that the further submission of counsel for the respondents is correct. A shareholder who deserves his exclusion has, if you like, made a constructive election to sever his connection with the company and thus to sell his shares. That means that evidence of the circumstances in which the petition came to be presented was, perhaps contrary to my expectation on 1 July, properly included, although I propose to deal with that aspect of the case as briefly as I reasonably can.

Next, I must consider the example from the second category of cases in which, broadly speaking, shares in a small private company are acquired. It is not of direct relevance for present purposes, but I mention it briefly in order finally to refute the suggestion that there is any rule of universal application to questions of this kind. In the case of the shareholder who acquires shares from another at a price which is discounted because they represent a minority it is to my mind self-evident that there cannot be any universal or even a general rule that he should be bought out under s 75 on a more favourable basis, even in a case where his predecessor has been a quasi partner in a quasi partnership. He might himself have acquired the shares purely for investment and played no part in the affairs of the company. In that event it might well be fair – I do not know – that he should be bought out on the same basis as he himself had bought, even though his interests had been unfairly prejudiced in the mean time. A fortiori, there could be no universal or even a general rule in a case where the company had never been a quasi partnership in the first place.

In summary, there is in my judgment no rule of universal application. On the other hand, there is a general rule in a case where the company is at the material time a quasi partnership and the purchase order is made in respect of the shares of a quasi partner. Although I have taken the case where there has in fact been unfairly prejudicial conduct on the part of the majority as being the state of affairs most likely to result in a purchase order, I am of the opinion that the same consequences ought usually to follow in a case like the present where there has been an agreement for the price to be determined by the court without any admission as to such conduct. It seems clear to me that, even without such conduct, that is in general the fair basis of valuation in a quasi partnership case, and that it should be applied in this case unless the respondents have established that the petitioners acted in such a way as to deserve their exclusion from the company.'

In *Re Eurofinance Group Ltd (EFG)* [2001] BCC 551, Mr Justice Pumfrey had to deal with a petition under CA 1985, s 459 (CA 2006, s 994) where the founding shareholder held founder's shares, which carried two votes, while the remaining shareholders held ordinary shares with a single vote each, so that the petitioner had voting control of EFG. Nonetheless on 1 May 1998 he was ousted in a boardroom coup, as a result of which the remaining shareholders caused EFG to sell its trading subsidiary, BRC, to a new holding company, (H) on credit, leaving the petitioner's voting control over EFG irrelevant to the future conduct of the business. The petitioner complained that his dismissal as an employee, removal as a director of BRC and the sale of BRC to H were all unfairly prejudicial to his interest as a member of EFG and sought an order that his shares in EFG be acquired by the other shareholders on such terms as the court thought fit.

There were a number of allegations and counter-allegations but Pumfrey J held that the dilution of the petitioner's interest and his exclusion from management of the company were not justified, and that the grounds advanced for his immediate exclusion did not justify summary dismissal, and his dismissal without an offer to purchase his interest was unfairly prejudicial to him. The expert valuers agreed that the petitioner's interest was 51.13% of EFG. Mr Haberman was the expert for the petitioner and Mr Glover for the respondent. The experts' joint report stated:

'(1) we agree that the petitioners shareholding in EFG should be valued on the "fair value" basis, (2) we agree that the working relationship between the petitioner and the individual respondents has carried out through EFG's main operating subsidiary BRC had many of the characteristics of a partnership, (3) we agree that the petitioners' shareholding in EFG…should be valued pro rata to what Mr Glover calls the entirety value of EFG. (4) We agree that the entirety value of EFG should be arrived at by adding the entirety value of BRC to any surplus assets held by BRC. (5) We agree that BRC as a "people business" did not require a substantial assets base. (6) We agree that the combined business of the petitioner and the individual respondent ("the partners") and BRC should generate returns to the partners above the level of earnings which the partners could obtain through employment as individuals elsewhere which Mr Haberman terms "excess profits". (7) We agree that the matters complained of by the petitioner in the petition should be disregarded in the valuation.

Matters where we were unable to agree

There are two areas of disagreement between us: how the entirety value should be arrived at; and the extent to which the dispute between the petitioner and the individual respondent should be taken into account in the valuation.'

Pumfrey J stated that:

'the two valuers proceeded on completely different bases. Mr Haberman valued the company with BRC as a going concern essentially on the basis of a multiple of earnings. Mr Glover considered that in the absence of any restrictive covenants there was no basis for valuing the company on anything other than an assets basis: the "partners" could all walk out tomorrow leaving the company without any value. In summary, Mr Haberman contended that the underlying earnings in the company in 1997/98 were £290,000 and according to a business plan produced by Mr Parkinson prior to his exclusion £462,000 in 1998–99. He took an estimated figure of £400,000 and applied a multiple of 5 to 7 as opposed to a more normal 8 to 10 to reflect the nature of the business so arriving at a valuation of £2m–£2.8m. The valuation advanced by Mr Glover on an assets basis including the non-repayable loan to Mr Parkinson is £387,576 for EFG which assumes an asset value for BRC of £250,000.

Both experts expressed surprise and dismay at the figure arrived at by the other. It seems to me that some of the difficulties can be dispersed by considering the nature of the hypothetical transaction to which the valuation relates. The authorities and in particular *Re Bird Precision Bellows Ltd* (1985) 1 BCC 99467, [1986] Ch 658 make it clear that the court has a wide discretion to order a sale at a price which is fair in all the circumstances of the case. It is a sale by an unwilling seller to an unwilling buyer of a slight majority holding of EFG whose principal assets are about £138,000 net cash and BRC. The seller in this notional sale is the actual seller that is the petitioner, the purchasers are the respondents and the business is that carried on by BRC. I find it difficult to accept the valuation on the basis of a sale to an independent third party can be determinative …

I think that when arriving at a fair value in the absence of a market it is necessary to assume that the notional sale is taking place between the actual participants in the transaction, since the whole purpose of the valuation is to be fair as between the parties. There is no market to provide an objective external criterion. The actual parties must be taken to participate in the sale as willing participants. In my judgement an answer to the problem of lock-in, notice periods and non-competition clauses lies in this proposition. One can expect that there will be a turnover in the directors but it will be relatively slow. Thus far there is a risk of losing one in a year, the risk is not unduly high. It cannot be said that there is a substantial risk of all leaving the day after the sale which would necessarily depress the share price to near nothing. The reason that it cannot be said that they will all leave is that the business belongs to them and they wish to work in it. I consider therefore that the assumption of a third party purchaser is essentially inappropriate in this case …

On the whole I am not confident that the projections prepared by Mr Parkinson for 1998-99 and relied on by Mr Haberman are a sufficiently firm foundation on which to base a valuation for the purpose of these proceedings. I prefer to base myself on the 1997/98 historical figure, while allowing for modest growth, the figure I shall take is £310,000.

The question of the multiplier has next to be considered. Mr Haberman used a substantially reduced multiplier of 5 to 7 with a check to suggest that this does not exceed 7 times historical earnings. He abandoned his earlier suggestion of a multiplier between 8 and 10 after consultation with colleagues at KPMG. I consider that the lower figure is still too high, because of the risk of consultant departure to which I referred and which was accepted by Mr Haberman as relevant. I shall take a figure of 3.5. This gives a valuation of £1.085m which is less than Mr Glover's rule of thumb of one times annual turnover for companies of this description. The valuation of the shareholding is accordingly £550,978.'

Brownlow v G H Marshall Ltd & Others [2001] BCC 152 was another unfair prejudice case under CA 1985, ss 459 to 461 for a family company carried on as a quasi-partnership. The judge held that:

'the findings that I have made justify in my view Mrs Brownlow's claim for an order that her shares be purchased from her by one or more of the respondents. I have not had submissions as to whether that order should be made against the company as claimed primarily by Mrs Brownlow or against the individual respondents. So far as not agreed I will hear argument on this after delivery of this judgment.

There remain however two points upon which I have had argument in writing from Counsel. First at what date should the value of Mrs Brownlow's shares be determined and secondly should there be any discount applied to that value because her holding is a minority one or for any other reason. In giving my reasons for decision on these two aspects of the case I shall not refer in any detail to the helpful written submissions provided since they are fully recorded for all to see if necessary.

(1) Discount

I think that in this respect I am entitled to use as my starting point the views of Lord Hoffmann in *O'Neill & Another v Phillips and Others* [1999] 1 WLR 1092 at page 1107 D-E. There he points out that the offer to purchase that a potential respondent to proceedings such as these should make must be a fair one which will ordinarily be a value representing an equivalent proportion of the total issued capital that is without a discount for it being a minority holding. Lord Hoffmann notes the Law Commissions recommended statutory presumption to this effect and says that this represents the existing practice. With that guidance and with full regard to the submissions advanced on behalf of the respondents I see nothing in these submissions to deflect me from taking what Lord Hoffmann describes as the ordinary course and ordering that the value be determined without discount for the minority nature of the holdings.

(2) Date

On this point Mrs Brownlow submits that the valuation should be at the date that it is made. The respondents admit that the proper date is the date of presentation of the petition. Paragraph 29(iv) of Mrs Brownlow's counsel's outline of argument delivered at the start of the case indicates that she has not had access to financial information that she would otherwise have had as a result of exclusion. However the date suggested by the Respondents indicates as a matter of common sense that the value of the company has probably increased since the commencement of proceedings. In my view two of the arguments of Mr Chivers for Mrs Brownlow on this point are set out in para 8(4) of his submission on valuation weigh with me. I think that it is right that the improvement of fortunes which I think we are entitled to assume are likely to have occurred from the respective stance of the parties (a) would derive in part with the benefit of Mrs Brownlow's share capital (b) would, in large part, be attributable to the senior managers and other staff who are not shareholders (but whose services are paid for equally by all the shareholders).

I am concerned however that the inevitable delays in any contested valuation process should not negate the considerations that have weighted with me in reaching my decision on this point. Equally if I set the date as being the indefinite one of the date on which the value is finally determined that seems to me to be a recipe for constant updating of evidence throughout the process so rendering the task of valuers and of the court a constantly varying one. For my own part I would be inclined (in the interests of certainty) to make an order that the valuation be taken as at the date of delivery of this judgement. However as I am finding in favour Mr Chiver's client in this point I would hear further argument from counsel as to whether the date of judgement or the date of the valuation is the appropriate one.'

Guinness Peat Group Plc v British Land Co Plc & Ors [1998] EWCA Civ 1956, [1999] BCC 536, was an appeal against a strike-out action by a minority shareholder in a public company claiming it had been unfairly prejudiced as a result of the company transferring to its majority shareholder (the respondent) its only asset comprising all the shares held by the company in Broadgate Properties Plc.

The appeal was granted on the basis that:

'at the end of two days of detailed argument focusing on the allegation of undervalue in the petition and on the different approaches to valuation of the shares in the company explained in the expert's reports of Coopers & Lybrand and Ernst & Young no doubt remains about one thing: this is not an appropriate case to strike out the petition. The reasons for this conclusion can be briefly stated.

1 The central issue in the case is whether Guinness Peat as shareholder in the company have been prejudiced by the company's transfer of all its Broadgate shares to British Land.
2 The value of Guinness Peat's minority shareholding in the company is a disputed question of fact. Factual disputes (including those involving big property companies and world experts on share values) are normally resolved in an adversarial system by a trial after pleadings, discovery and oral evidence tested by cross-examination.
3 It is common ground that expert opinion evidence is admissible on the valuation of shares.
4 Coopers & Lybrand and Ernst & Young are both competent experts on the question of valuation of shares. They take different approaches in this case. It is impossible for them both to be right on this question. Until the contrary is demonstrated however it is only fair and reasonable as regards both the parties and the experts to assume that either of them might be right. It is also fair and reasonable to assume at this stage that the conflicting conclusions expressed by the experts are independent opinions honestly formed on the basis of the available material. Both valuers must be well aware of the duty of an expert witness as a witness of the court to give an honest and

independent opinion to the court on matters on which the court requires expert opinion: they are not simply "hired guns" constructing arguments and submissions to bolster the case of a client.

5 In these circumstances it is inappropriate save in the most exceptional circumstances to use the strikeout jurisdiction to reject the relevant opinion evidence of an expert as "incredible". It is not an acceptable way to make a finding on a hotly disputed question of fact. There may be exceptional cases where it can be demonstrated with difficulty that the evidence of the expert is irrelevant to any issue in the action or that the person giving it is not an expert in the relevant fields or that the expert has directed his opinion to the wrong issue or under a misunderstanding as to the issues in the case. That cannot be said here. The most that can be said is that one of them has not adopted the correct method for the valuation of the ordinary shares in the company. An opinion on such a question is difficult involving as it does assumptions readily open to dispute. The dispute at the heart of this case namely the valuation of the large holding of preference shares in the company and its effect on the value of the ordinary shares is so far as this court is concerned without precedent. It is not surprising that in dealing with a novel question there may be scope for differences of approach.'

Earlier in the judgment Lord Justice Mummery stated:

> 'on the central question of valuation of that minority shareholding each side has an expert. British Land's expert is Ernst & Young. Their reasoned opinion of 7 October 1997 is that the shareholding of Guinness Peat was worth nothing at the relevant date of the company's disposition of the shares in Broadgate. They say that "there was no value attaching to the ordinary shares" at any of the relevant dates. It would be an understatement to say that that opinion is not shared by Guinness Peat's expert Coopers & Lybrand. Their reasoned opinion in their reports of 14 July and 16 October 1997 and 13 February 1998 is that the shares had substantial value at the relevant date. The court was informed by Guinness Peat's leading counsel that if this petition is successful then the value of that shareholding will probably run into millions of pounds.
>
> Each side attacks the basis of valuation adopted by the other in almost identical extreme terms. Coopers & Lybrand's "going concern" dividend yield basis of valuation of the preference shares in the company is described by leading counsel for British Land as "contrary to common sense and wholly incredible". Leading counsel for Guinness Peat describes Ernst & Young's "winding up" return of capital basis of valuation of the preference shares as "so contrary to common sense as to be wholly incredible" and castigates British Land's motion to strike out the petition as itself an abuse of process.
>
> At least one thing is clear: Coopers & Lybrand and Ernst & Young cannot both be right although it is not inconceivable that on such a difficult and much debated question as share valuation neither side is wholly right.'

In *Third and Ors v North East Ice and Cold Storage Co Ltd and Anr* [1998] BCC 242 it was held that the company was not a quasi-partnership. The company had originally been formed in 1963 by an uncle of the petitioners and in due course the shares were divided between what may be called, perhaps loosely, the Third family and the West family, who were the majority shareholders. In 1984 the West majority shareholding was sold to Fairlea Investments Ltd, an arm's length purchaser. The Thirds commenced proceedings under CA 1985, s 459, which were discontinued in 1986 in consideration for new service agreements being granted to Andrew and John Third (the first and second petitioners) as managing director and technical director respectively. The subsequent proceedings began in 1996. The judge referred to Lord Wilberforce's definition of a quasi-partnership in *Re Westbourne Galleries Ltd* [1973] AC 360 and continued:

> 'For the purposes of the present case what is important in my opinion is the stress laid by Lord Wilberforce upon the existence of some form of personal relationship of a kind which can be seen to give rise to a right in all shareholders, or at least in the petitioners' shareholders, to participate in the conduct of the business. In my view in the circumstances of this case, the respondent's argument that the acceptance of new service contracts which conferred on the majority shareholders a power to exclude the first and second petitioners from involvement in the management of the company by dismissing them, is wholly inconsistent with the continuance of any such personal relationships. I accept that there might be circumstances in which it could be said that a quasi-partnership or other personal relationship continued notwithstanding a change such as that brought about by the acceptance of the service contracts by the first and second petitioners. For example it might be averred that there was an understanding or an agreement to that effect…I have, therefore, come to the view that the averments as they stand are insufficient to support a case that a quasi-partnership or some other personal arrangement with equivalent effect continued after the acceptance of the service contract. It follows that as the case is pled at present, the averments in support of the claim that the petitioners' shares should be valued on a pro rata business are insufficient and the case cannot proceed upon that footing.
>
> I do not however accept the respondents' contention that the consequence of that finding is that the whole case becomes irrelevant. The exercise of the court's power to make an order for the purchase of shares in a minority in a company is not dependent upon the existence of some quasi-partnership relationship as Lord Wilberforce made clear … In the whole circumstances therefore I have reached the conclusion, that apart from the issue of quasi-partnership, the pleadings do set forth a case of allegedly unfair conduct sufficient to go to enquiry.'

Re London School of Electronics Ltd (1985) 1 BCC 99394, was a case under CA 1980, s 75 on prejudicial conduct (CA 2006, s 994). There was prejudicial conduct notwithstanding that the complainant had himself acted improperly. Nourse J in his judgment stated:

> 'the conduct of the petitioner may be material in a number of ways of which the two most obvious are these. First it might render the conduct of the other side, even if it is prejudicial, not unfair, cf re *RA Noble and Sons (Clothing) Ltd* [1983] BCLC 273. Secondly even if the conduct of the other side is both prejudicial and unfair, the petitioner's conduct may nevertheless affect the relief that the court thinks fit to grant under sub-section 3. In my view there is no independent or overriding requirement that it should be just and equitable to grant relief, or that the petitioner should come to the court with clean hands.'

The majority shareholder in this case was City Tutorial College Ltd and the minority shareholder Mr Lytton.

The judge stated:

> 'in my judgment it was CTC's decision to appropriate the BSc students to itself which was the effective cause of the breakdown in the relationship of mutual confidence between the quasi-partners. Furthermore, that was clearly conduct on the part of CTC which was both unfair and prejudicial to the interests of Mr Lytton as a member of the company.'

In this case it was held, in accordance with normal quasi-partnership rules, that the price must be fixed pro-rata according to the value of the shares as a whole and not discounted.

The case is also of interest in the comments relating to the date of valuation. Nourse J said on this point:

> 'If there were to be such a thing as a general rule I myself would think that the date of the order or the actual valuation would be more appropriate than the date of the presentation of the petition or the unfair prejudice. Prima facie the interest in a going concern ought to be valued at the date on which it is ordered to be purchased. But whatever the general rule might be, it seems very probably that the overriding requirement that the valuation should be fair on the facts of the particular case would, by exceptions, reduce it to no rule at all. That that is so is already suggested by such authorities as there are on this question. In *Scottish Cooperative Wholesale Society Ltd v Meyer & Another* [1959] AC 324 the shares were ordered to be purchased at the value which they would have had at the date of the petition if there had been no oppression. In *Re Jermyn Street Turkish Baths Ltd* [1970] 1 WLR 1194 the order of Pennycuick J discloses that the assets, undertaking and goodwill of the company were to be valued on an enquiry as at the date of the master certificate. In *Re a Company (No 002567 of 1982)* (1983) 1 BCC 98930; [1983] 1 WLR 927, Vinelott J held that the shares of a petitioner who had unreasonably rejected the previous fair offers to purchase them ought to be valued at the date of the valuation, and not the date when he had been excluded from participation in the affairs of the company. However, the learned judge said that he could conceive of many cases where, in an application under s 75 [CA 1980], fairness would require that the valuation should relate back to an earlier date such as, in that case, the exclusion of the petitioner: (1983) 1 BCC 98930 at page 98931. That observation was approved by Mervyn Davies J in *Re OC Transport Services Ltd* (1984) 1 BCC 99068 at p99074 where he held that the facts required the valuation to be made at a date earlier than the date of the petition, in fact at the date when the unfair prejudice had occurred. Finally in *Re Bird Precision Bellows Ltd* (1984) 1 BCC 98992 the valuation was made as at the date of a consent order that the shares should be purchased at such a price as the courts should thereafter determine. That case is not of any real assistance on this point because the date was no doubt implicit in the terms of the consent order.
>
> In the present case I have held that the conduct which was unfairly prejudicial to the interests of Mr Lytton as a member of the company was CTC's decision to appropriate the BSc students to itself. Had that conduct not taken place Mr Lytton would effectively have become entitled to 25% of the profits attributable to the BSc students. Since those profits would not have been earned until the academic year 1983/84, it would not in my view be fair to value Mr Lytton's shares as at 3 June 1983. He is at the least entitled to have them valued at some time during the academic year 1983/84 and, since no other date has been suggested, the date of the presentation of the petition (10 February 1984) is as good as any other. Ought I to go further and order a valuation as at today's date or the actual date of valuation i.e. a date during the academic year 1984/85. It is not clear to me on the evidence whether there has been a significant increase in the number of BSc students this year. I suspect that there may have been. The more important point is that Mr Athanasiou and Mr George have now been able to acquire a greater academic standing for the course in the UK. I find that this has been entirely due to their own efforts and owes nothing to Mr Lytton and, moreover, that it is unlikely that it would have been achieved if Mr Lytton had remained with the company. It would therefore be unfair for Mr Athanasiou and Mr George to order

> a valuation at today's date. I shall direct that Mr Lytton's shares be valued as at 10 February 1984.'

Nourse J further stated:

> 'I am also in no doubt that the valuation ought to be made on the footing that the students which Mr Lytton removed to LCEE remained with the company. Mr Oliver's primary submission here was that Mr Lytton's continued status as a director rendered him accountable to the company in a fiduciary capacity of any profits earned by LCEE in respect of those students. I do not dissent from that submission, but it seems to me that it would in any event be fair to treat those students as having remained with their company, since the whole object of the exercise is that Mr Lytton should be bought out on the footing that the unfair prejudice had never occurred, in which event both he and the students would have remained with the company.'

Re Adlink Ltd [2006] All ER (D) 198 (Oct) is another unfair prejudice case where the petitioner set up a rival business, following which the defendant set up another company to which he transferred the company's trading business without making a goodwill payment to the company, although to his knowledge the goodwill had appreciable value. The judge stated: 'the court's power to grant relief was not limited by the lists or forms of relief set out in s 461(2) and it was entitled to take both the petitioner's and the respondent's conduct into account when deciding on the appropriate relief'.

The judge continued:

> 'prima facie an interest in a going concern ought to be valued at the date on which it was ordered to be purchased, subject to the overriding requirement that the valuation should be fair on the facts of the particular case. In deciding what valuation date was fair on the facts of a particular case there were two main considerations that the court had to bear in mind. One was that the shares should be valued on a date as close as possible to the actual sale so as to reflect the value of what the shareholder was selling. However there were many cases in which fairness (to one side or the other) required the court to take another date.'

In the particular circumstances of this case the court ordered that:

> 'the respondent buy the petitioner's one-half interest in the company at a price equal to one-half of the value of the company at a convenient and suitable date after 1 September 1999 (being the date of the heads of agreement) and assuming the company enjoyed the goodwill of the business transferred to T Ltd. The company would then sell its property interest to the petitioner at a price equal to the value of that property at a convenient and suitable date after 1 September 1999.'

Re Regional Airports Ltd [1999] 2 BCLC 30 was an unfairly prejudicial conduct case under CA 1985, ss 459 and 461 (CA 2006, ss 994–999) in which it was necessary to value the shares in Regional Airports Ltd, which owned 100% of Biggin Hill Airport Ltd, and 80% of London Southend Co Ltd. The company made a profit from letting property owned by the airport companies but losses on actually running the airport: see **2.06**.

Richards v Lundy & Others, Re Apollo Cleaning Services Ltd [1999] BCC 786 is another case where a minority shareholder petitioned under the CA 1985, s 459 as a result of his dismissal from the company. The court ordered the majority shareholders to purchase the petitioner's shares for £162,000, being a pro rata proportion of the value of the company as whole. It is therefore another quasi-partnership case and in fact the business had originally been a partnership prior to incorporation. *Quinlan v Essex Hinge Co Ltd* [1997] BCC 53 and *Re Pectel Ltd* [1998] BCC 739 applied.

After considering the evidence the judge stated:

> 'In the present case in my view the only possible fair basis for the determination of the price of the shares is the pro rata basis. My reasons for this are as follows. First I think that it was always understood between Mr Richards and Mr Lundy that Mr Richards was to have a 10% stake. At the beginning, and at the time of the formation of the company neither was financially sophisticated and I do not think that either would have appreciated that a minority holding could only be sold at a discount. Secondly the conversations to which I have already referred relating to the retention of dividends and the shares being regarded as a pension would make it grossly unfair to make an order on the basis of a minority discount; the result would be that Mr Richards would receive only a small fraction of the value built up in a company by his having foregone dividends. As is submitted by Mr Hollington in his skeleton argument it would reward the unfairly prejudicial conduct with a windfall. Thirdly I have held that Mr Richards was unfairly excluded from his participation in the management of the company and from the income resulting from it. At the time he was 52 years old. Even assuming that he would have retired relatively early, say at 62, his exclusion has resulted in the loss of 10 years salary (representing by a rough and ready calculation assuming no increases in salary but no discount for future payment) a present day value of approximately £175,000. This by itself would greatly exceed the market value of Mr Richards' minority holding even after taking into account the agreed compensation for unfair dismissal …
>
> In view of my findings for fact I do not have to consider what the position would be if Mr Richards had brought his dismissal on himself or contributed to it, as to which there is little authority. In an extreme case no doubt it might be possible that exclusion from the company without an offer to purchase the shares might be fair. In other cases as suggested by Nourse J in *Re Bird Precision Bellows* it may be that an offer to purchase the shares at the market price for a minority holding, i.e. probably at a very substantial discount, may be fair. If however that seems too drastic it seems to me that the wide terms of the section leave it open to the court to order the purchase of the shares at some intermediate figure involving a smaller discount …'

In considering the valuation of the shares the judge stated:

> 'There appears to be no general rule as to the date by reference to which the shares are to be valued but in the present case I propose to take the date of judgment. This seems to me to be fair since Mr Richards has been locked into the company without payment of any dividend until now.
>
> The petitioner's expert witness Mr Rolliston is a partner in Hartley Fowler and has had extensive experience of a large variety of companies of this sort of size and has acted as expert witness on many occasions. In his experience companies of this kind would immediately be valued by adding net assets to goodwill represented in the case of the company by one year's purchase of its gross profit (i.e. sales less cost of sales) and in the case of the subsidiary three times its retained profits after certain adjustments. As at 31 December 1996 the value of the net assets of both companies was £1,198,147. The goodwill in the company was £898,142 and of the subsidiary £198,558. The total was therefore £2,294,847.
>
> However after discussion with the respondent's expert witness, Mr Corner, he agreed – although without resiling from his original method of valuation, that

the value of both companies could be calculated by adding surplus assets not used in the business to goodwill and that the goodwill of both companies could be valued by a multiple of retained profits. They also very helpfully agreed on the adjustments that needed to be made to earnings for the purposes of goodwill. The only dispute was as to the price earnings ratio to be taken for the purposes of the valuation of goodwill.

Mr Rolliston stressed that this was an attractive business in that it had a history of steadily rising profits apart from a recent small dip, large cash reserves and no freehold premises or other major capital assets. It could easily be moved and absorbed into another similar company with considerable economies of scale. He referred to the BDO/Stoy Hayward private company price index prepared by those firms from information available to them suggesting a P/E ratio of 10.5 in 1996 and 12.4 in 1997. The result in round figures was £2.03m for 1995, £2.16m for 1997, not very far from his original valuation. However in his oral evidence he agreed that the size of this transaction made it appropriate to look at a graph referred to by BDO/Stoy Hayward for deals up to £22m suggesting a ratio of 9. His final view was a ratio of between 9 and 10 perhaps nearer 10.

Mr Corner is a partner in the company's auditors. I do not think that his evidence was affected by that. He said that he felt able to give unbiased and independent evidence and I am sure that he did. In his report he said that the majority of transactions attracted ratios in the range 4–8. In his oral evidence although he agreed with Mr Rolliston's view as to the virtues of these companies he said that it was an unexciting sector of business and would not be likely to attract a high ratio. In his report he gave a ratio of 4.5 in his oral evidence he said that a ratio of 5 or at most 5.5 might be achieved.

It is clear that Mr Rolliston has some experience in this kind of business. However so far as the subsidiary with its janitorial supply business is concerned his original evidence (ratio of 3) is not consistent with the final evidence (ratio of 9 to 10). Even after taking into account the difference between net assets and surplus assets. Taking into account the evidence of both experts and the BDO/Stoy Hayward evidence I think it likely that the value of the company's goodwill is somewhere near the BDO/Stoy Hayward graph figure but that of the subsidiary substantially less. I find that the value of the company's goodwill is 8 times, and that of the subsidiary 4.5 times, their respective net earnings. Since the adjustments to profits have for the most part been made to combine profits I have to arrive at one multiplier. Taking into account the rather greater share of profits attributable to the subsidiary I will apply a multiple of 6 to the combined average net profits of both companies for the three years 1995 to 1997. This produces a figure of £672,000. To this must be added surplus assets as at 31 December 1997 of £744,859 plus additional surplus assets resulting from trading between January 1998 and April 1999 which (having regard to the previous years trend) I assess at £180,000 making a total of approximately £1,597,000.'

To this figure the judge added further amounts, in particular the sale of a property at an undervalue to a company owned by Mr Lundy or his family and a loan to his family company without security or interest. He therefore made a further adjustment to take account of the financial loss suffered by the company adding £23,000 to the figure of £1,597,00, making £1,620,000, and ordered the purchase of Mr Richard's shares for £162,000.

Re Ghyll Beck Driving Range Ltd [1993] BCLC 1126 was another case invoking the prejudicial conduct provisions in CA 1985 s 459. The four participators in the joint venture or quasi partnership each owned one share and agreed to lend £25,000 to provide working capital to a company.

The petitioner, Mr Betts, sought an order that the respondents purchase his shares at a price to be ascertained by the court. The judge held that he was so entitled in view of the conduct of the other shareholders and considered the valuation reports prepared by Mr Betts' expert Mr Oakley, a partner in Pricewaterhouse and the respondents relied on a report by Mr Pritchard of KPMG Peat Marwick. The main difference between Mr Oakley and Mr Pritchard lay in their perception of the likely future trend of earnings. The judge stated:

> 'I have reached the conclusion that I should accept Mr Oakley's assessment of future maintainable earnings of £40,000 per annum. I need hardly say that I do not lightly conclude that I should accept the evidence of one of the expert witnesses in its entirety. However Mr Oakley seems to me to approach his task in a balanced and fair minded way. He is familiar with their locality and took the trouble to visit the driving range and use its facilities in his anonymous role as a customer. Mr Pritchard seemed to me to assume too readily the role of advocate and to have accepted uncritically the contentions that the Padleys should be allowed interest on an assumed investment of £55,000 that an investor would require remuneration of £25,000 in addition to a proper return on his investment and that the barn on which considerable sums had been spent would continue as now to be barely utilised.
>
> Mr Oakley took as his starting point four times net profits after tax, a yield of 25% or three times profit before tax, a gross yield of 33⅓%. Mr Pritchard in his written report expressed the opinion that the profits would be nil and would not therefore express any view as to the appropriate yield or multiplier which on his evidence was hypothetical. However in his oral evidence he agreed that the multiplier appropriate to business of this kind would be between four and six times net profits after tax. The difference between the experts lay in their very different assessment of net profit.'

Finally the judge reached the conclusion:

> 'that Mr Betts is entitled to be repaid his loan of £24,990 and to approximately £40,000 for his £1 share. In dividing the £160,000 between the shareholders some adjustment will be needed to reflect the difference in the interest paid on the loan. I trust that that minor adjustment can be agreed and order accordingly'.

In *Elliott v Planet Organic Ltd & Ors* [2000] BCC 611, another case involving prejudicial conduct under CA 1985, s 459 (CA 2006, s 994), it was held that the preference shareholders were mere investors and not quasi-partners so their shares would be subject to a discount from their pro rata value. The preference shares carried a 9% rate of interest plus an entitlement to dividends. They were convertible in the year 2000 to ordinary shares at the rate of 1 ordinary share for two preference shares. If so converted there would be 75,000 further ordinary shares on top of the 200,000 shares held equally by Mrs Elliott and Mr Dwek. However the converted preference shareholders would not hold the balance of power in the company because there is a separate investors' agreement in effect preventing them from doing so. On a winding up the preference shareholders rank above the ordinary shareholders in respect of the return on their money. The preference shareholders were given no voting rights or rights to appoint directors unless dividends were not paid for six months (as in fact they were not). At an earlier hearing Lloyd J gave judgment in cross petitions under CA 1985, s 459 by Mrs Elliott and Jonathan Dwek. They each held 100 shares in the company called Planet Organic Ltd. Lloyd J dismissed

Mr Dwek's petition but held that of Mrs Elliott's succeeded. The circumstances leading to those findings were set out in his judgment. He made the following order, namely, that:

> 'Mr Dwek do sell to Mrs Elliott (or as she may direct) his ordinary shares in the company at a fair price to be agreed between the parties or determined by the court as hereinafter provided'.

He also ordered that identified preference shareholders should sell their preference shares to Mrs Elliott or at her direction at a fair price. The remaining preference shareholders were given liberty to require Mrs Elliott to purchase their shares at the same price. Lloyd J directed that for the purposes of the determination of the value, the valuation date should be the date of his judgment namely 29 January 1999. The case came back to the court because the parties could not agree terms. In the original judgement Lloyd J held that:

> 'as between Mr Dwek and Mrs Elliott it is not in doubt that this is a quasi-partnership company and that the two are and always were equal partners.'

In this case Jacob J confirmed:

> 'there is no dispute that the fair valuation which I must reach in respect of Mr Dwek's shares is to be achieved by valuing the company as a going concern being sold on the open market. There is no discount in respect of Mr Dwek's shares.
>
> The position of the preference shareholders is rather different. They were not undertaking anywhere near as much risk as Mr Dwek and Mrs Elliott. On the contrary, their 9% return irrespective of whether the company was making profits, was good by any standards and of course they had a preference on a winding-up. As a practical matter they were not really expecting to be concerned with the management of the company. Miss Roberts on behalf of Mr Dwek (but I suppose in reality it is urging on behalf of the nine shareholders) urged that the preference shareholders should also be treated as quasi-partners and that there should be no discount in respect of their shares which would be treated as notionally converted.'

The case came before Jacob J who held that:

> 'it by no means follows that a sleeping partner in a private company should be regarded as a quasi-partner and thus given a value on a pro rata basis which would be higher than his shares are worth in the open market. I do not regard the preference shareholders as quasi-partners. Their position is very different from that of Mr Dwek and Mrs Elliott. They were essentially investors in the enterprise of these two individuals not partners in it.'

He also held:

> 'Lloyd J's order merely provides that the sale would be at a fair price. He did not say that the price was to be the same pro rata as that to be paid for Mr Dwek's shares. Nor did he find that the preference shareholders were quasi-partners. On the contrary he merely considered Mrs Elliott and Mr Dwek expressly as quasi-partners leaving the position of the preference shareholders to be dealt with as a matter of fair valuation of their shares. Moreover he concluded his decision by saying "I propose to order that Mr Dwek sell his shares to Mrs Elliott at a fair price to be determined by the court, if not agreed; that the nine preference shareholders who joined in the requisition for the removal of Mrs Elliott as a director do also sell their shares at a corresponding fair price which will, of

> course, take account of their right to any dividend remaining unpaid as well as the other incidents of the preference shares.
>
> I do not read this as precluding me from applying a discount if I think appropriate. S461 (CA 2006, s 996) enables the court to make such order as it thinks fit and that is what I propose to do. The nine preference shareholders whilst they did not appear before me made written representations which I have read and taken into account. They plainly consider that the question of discount or not was open for argument. I am not impressed by Miss Robert's submission that the pleadings in the original petitions refer blindly to quasi-partnership without expressly making it clear that it was between Mr Dwek and Mrs Elliott ... These preference shareholders sought to assist Mr Dwek to oust Mrs Elliott in the manner described in Lloyd J's judgement. I think they should be treated as having brought upon themselves the buy-out of their shares and thus in effect voluntarily selling so there should be a discount.
>
> How much should the discount be? Mr Kabraji (of Grant Thornton, Mrs Elliott's valuer) suggested a discount of 50%. However that was a fairly arbitrary figure. I think it is too much. After all the investment of these preference shareholders helped get the business off the ground and it is a matter to be taken into account in assessing what is fair. I think the appropriate discount should be 30%.'

Jacob J also commented:

> 'The valuation of the company. This is an extraordinarily difficult task. There are no less than four valuations before me. There are the two valuations of Mr Kabraji and Mr Clemence (of BDO Stoy Hayward, Mr Dwek's valuer) respectively valuing the company at £2,270,000 and £6,340,000. There is also a valuation prepared for Mrs Elliott in about July 1998 by an organisation called Corporate Valuations (CV). This valued the company at £4m. Finally the preference shareholders with their written submissions sent a valuation prepared by Pricewaterhouse Coopers suggesting a value of £4,702,500. Mr Kabraji includes in his valuation a figure of £270,000 which he regards as surplus cash already in the business. Mr Clemence's figure for that is £340,000. I think Mr Kabraji is right about this. He took into account all existing liabilities and definite future liabilities in a way in which Mr Clemence did not. I do not think a purchaser buying the company would regard the cash within the company as free unless there were no corresponding liabilities.
>
> I would say one thing more about this cash element. Partly owning to this dispute the remuneration of Mr Dwek and Mrs Elliott was kept artificially low. I think it is only fair to Mr Dwek that account should be taken of this. But how? The artificially low directors' earnings have been removed for the future in reaching the estimated maintainable earnings. They are in fact reflected in this cash element – if proper earnings had been paid the cash element would have been correspondingly less. So by including the cash element in the value one does not take into account the depressed earnings. Of course this may have some unjustified effect on the preference shareholders too – they are getting some benefit from the price including cash which but for the depressed earnings of the directors would be a lesser amount. But it seems to me that the amounts involved are now too small to be worth making a further adjustment. They can be regarded as included in the discount upon which I have already decided.
>
> I should first say something about the PricewaterhouseCoopers valuation. It has come in the most unsatisfactory way just before the hearing. The preference shareholders had copies of the valuations and knew the valuers were to meet. To ignore all of that and to spring a report at the last moment without explanation is

manifestly unsatisfactory. I do not propose to give that valuation any significant weight.

I should also mention one other valuation. Mrs Elliott, as I have said, before the main trial obtained a CV valuation. Also before the main trial, Mr Dwek obtained an informal valuation from Mr Clemence's firm. I was never told what that valuation was, it being covered by privilege. Mr Dwek shortly before the trial, having whatever that valuation was, offered to buy Mrs Elliott out for £1.1m, an offer which was refused.

The main battle therefore is between Mr Kabraji's opinion and that of Mr Clemence. Both witnesses were, I thought, fair and made genuine attempts to be reasonable. The disparity between their valuations reflects not upon their competence but upon the extraordinary difficulty of valuing Planet Organic which really has no comparable, still less a close comparable. The two valuers following their meeting produced a joint letter. They agreed that an approach based on a P/E ratio was appropriate. This approach involved first identifying the "maintainable profits". This is then multiplied by a P/E ratio. That ratio has to be identified by some method or other. Mr Kabraji reached a figure of £252,313 from maintainable profits (E). That of Mr Clemence was £297,000 (CV got to £265,595). The differences were admittedly not great although of course any difference gets multiplied by the overall valuation. I conclude that the appropriate figure is £275,000 which Mr Clemence was prepared to accept as a compromise. Mr Tregear, Counsel for Mrs Elliott, whilst not accepting that figure, did not feel it necessary to argue against it.

That leaves the problem, the near undecidable problem of the P/E ratio. If you have a quoted company you know the share price and you know the earnings per share. The P/E ratio is determined from known figures. (Of course the known P/E ratio may affect market considerations and thus itself affect share price and hence itself, but that is irrelevant here). The problem here is that you have determined (E) maintainable earnings and are trying to find out (P). What the two experts did was to go to quoted companies in the food business. Mr Clemence took the average P/E ratio for the food sector of the Financial Times index and added a factor representing a bid premium: a takeover bid nearly always raises the share value of a quoted company. Mr Kabraji thought that taking the average of all the companies in the food sector which includes giants such as Sainsbury' and Tesco who also sell many things other than food was inappropriate. He selected three companies out of the list Budgen, Iceland and Somerfield on the basis that their shops were much smaller than those of Sainsbury and the like and were food only shops. The truth is however that these companies are nothing like Planet Organic, a little shop with a big name. These companies are what Mr Clemence described as in a depressed state in a depressed sector. On the other hand I do not think taking the average P/E ratio of quoted companies in the FT is any more helpful. None of the companies are like this company. They are metaphorically on a different planet. I cannot imagine any potential investor in Planet Organic considering his investment as in any shape the same sort of investment as in one of the quoted companies.

An investor in Planet Organic would be buying the single shop trading well but at or close to its maximum potential and taking a chance on the possibilities of expansion via other shops. He would plainly be getting the benefit of a very good name on the other hand he would take into account all the problems of competition and possibly limited supply identified by Mr Kabraji but ignored by Mr Clemence. The investment would essentially be a speculative investment. But how does one work out whether there would be many speculators or few and how high would they go? I do not think anyone can come to a certain or even near

> certain answer. One somewhat flimsy guide is the BDO or similar index. These are compiled on a regular basis from information about sales of shares in private companies. Once there has been a sale it may well be possible to find out P and knowing P the actual P/E ratio can be identified. The index is an average of these. It includes obviously good and bad companies. It must be remembered that if the earnings are small but the company has potential people may be prepared to pay a lot of money. Indeed before a company has earnings at all its P/E ratio would be infinite. Mr Clemence suggested that Planet Organic should be taken to have a P/E ratio above that of the average because of the famous name and potential. On the other hand I do not know how the average is made up. It could be a lot of ordinary small companies with no great profitability or expansion potential and a few stars. The safest thing to do I think is to go by the BDO figures. The buyer will be buying one shop, trading very well but with potentially increased competition in the future and an opportunity to exploit the well-known name elsewhere in London and perhaps elsewhere subject to all the competitive influences identified by Mr Kabraji. I propose to take a figure of 11.5 which is slightly above the average p/es reported in Acquisitions Monthly for private companies in the last quarter of 1998 and the BDO index measuring the same thing at 11.9. I think this figure fully reflects what someone would be willing to pay for one shop making profits of £270,000 but with the potential to exploit its name (subject to many market risks) elsewhere. If I have got my figures right this leads to a total of £3,105,000 to which must be added the cash element of £275,000.'

(Actually the judge had not got his figures right as he had originally held that the maintainable profits were £275,000, not £270,000, which would have been £3,162,500 and the cash element was £270,000 not £275,000).

> 'A request for interest to be included in the valuation was denied following *Re Bird Precision Bellows Ltd* (1984) 1 BCC 98992. In this case Lloyd J ordered Mrs Elliott to pay within one month of the determination of the price. Mr Dwek has no entitlement to any money until that date. Indeed he is entitled to, and owner of, the shares until the sale goes through. There is simply nothing upon which interest should run. This forced sale is not like a case where damages has been caused and interest runs on the damages. So I do not include any interest element in my order.'

Irvine v Irvine [2006] EWHC 583 referred to at **2.02** above was another prejudicial conduct non-quasi partnership case where a minority interest discount was applied to the petitioner's shareholding.

It is not prejudicial conduct within CA 2006, s 994 to refuse to enter into a reconstruction under Insolvency Act 1986, s 110 or for the company to refuse to buy out the minority shareholders under CA 2006, ss 690–708: *Re a Company (No 004475 of 1982)* [1983] Ch 178, [1983] 2 WLR 381.

A company can be construed as a quasi partnership even in circumstances where a single individual has control. In *Quinlan v Essex Hinge Co Ltd* [1997] BCC 53 the petitioner was a 'junior partner' holding 500 out of 3,400 shares in issue and the managing director (the second respondent) was the 'dominant senior partner' holding 2,872 shares. The requirements set out by Lord Wilberforce in *Ebrahimi v Westbourne Galleries Ltd* [1972] 2 WLR 1289 (see **2.06**) were met. The court found that the company was a quasi partnership and ordered the petitioner's shares to be purchased by the company on a pro rata basis with no discount for the fact that the holding was a minority. The court ordered the company to be valued by reference to its assets, profitability and future prospects.

Unfairly prejudicial conduct has also been considered in cases such as *Bermuda Cablevision Ltd v Colica Trust Ltd* [1998] AC 198, where criminal conduct was alleged even though the shareholder was aware of the matters complained of when he acquired the shares. The shareholder must have submitted a valid transfer to the company even if it has not been registered: *Re Quickdome Ltd* [1988] BCLC 370. A nominee shareholder may petition under CA 2006, s 994: *Atlasview Ltd v Brightview Ltd* [2004] 2 BCLC 191. A petitioner's own misconduct does not necessarily prevent a petition, but may affect the remedy: *Re London School of Electronics Ltd* [1986] Ch 211. The holder of a single share may bring a petition: *Re Garage Door Associates Ltd* [1984] 1 WLR 35. The cost of prejudicial conduct petitions can be daunting (*Re Unisoft Group Ltd (No 3)* [1994] 1 BCLC 609) and can exceed the value of the assets in dispute: *Re Elgindata Ltd* [1991] BCLC 959. A reasonable offer can cause a petition to be struck out: *Re a company (No 00836 of 1995)* [1996] 2 BCLC 192. The costs of the proceedings may not be paid by the company, except in so far as that they are incurred by the company as a separate person (*Re Kenyon Swansea Ltd* [1987] BCLC 514), although it may voluntarily indemnify a director who successfully refutes the allegations against him: *Branch v Bagley* [2004] EWHC 426 (Ch).

Members of a company may have different interests, as members, such as a lender of funds to a company for working capital (*Gamlestaden Fastigheter AB v Baltic Partners Ltd* [2007] BCC 272), or where the company pays inadequate dividends (*Re Sam Weller & Sons Ltd* [1990] Ch 682) or a rights issue on favourable terms to dilute an impecunious minority shareholder: *Re Cumana Ltd* [1986] BCLC 430. Unfairly prejudicial conduct must be both unfair and prejudicial: *Re Saul D Hawson & Sons plc* [1995] 1 BCLC 14. Unfairness arises where the majority both acted, or is proposing to act, in a manner which equity would regard as contrary to good faith: *Re Guidezone Ltd* [2000] 2 BCLC 321; *O'Neill V Phillips* [1999] 1 WLR 1092. The payment of excessive remuneration to director shareholders, rather than distributing profits as dividends, could be unfairly prejudicial conduct: *Re a Company (No 004415 of 1996)* [1997] 1 BCLC 479. Unfairly prejudicial conduct can arise from misleading information given to shareholders: *Re a Company (No 008699 of 1985)* [1986] BCLC 382. Failure to honour an understanding that major shareholders would not sell their shares without consulting each other was not unfairly prejudicial conduct as it did not relate to the company's affairs: *Re Leeds United Holdings plc* [1996] 2 BCLC 545.

Dismissal of a director of a quasi partnership company may be unfairly prejudicial conduct (*Re Ghyll Beck Driving Range Ltd* [1993] 1 BCLC 1126) unless the director is guilty of misconduct which threatened the company's future: *Woolwich v Milne* [2003] EWHC 414 (Ch).

The quasi-partnership rules do not necessarily apply to valuations required for tax purposes as they are dependent on the members of the company participating in the running of the business and operation, on a practical level as if they were partnerships. If a partner member can show that the affairs of the company were being conducted in an oppressive manner, an application may be made to the court for relief under CA 2006, ss 994–999, which need not result in winding up the company where the majority of members have, or are preparing to act, in a manner which equity would regard as contrary, ie good faith: *O'Neill v Phillips* [1999] 1 WLR 1092.

Where a statutory tax calculation is required under TCGA 1992, ss 272–274; IHTA 1984, ss 160, 168; IHTM18131; and employment-related securities under ITEPA 2003, s 421 it is 'the price which the asset might reasonably be expected to fetch on a sale in the open market': TCGA 1992, s 273(1).

The open market does not assume that a purchasing shareholder has any rights to participate in the management of the company, other than by voting in a general meeting. Therefore a minority shareholder has no right to a value based on a pro rata value of the company as a whole. The open market assumes a hypothetical purchaser and a hypothetical vendor, not necessarily involved in the management of the business, cannot assume that there would be a purchaser, able and willing to pay the pro rata price from his shares and may find himself as a 'detested intruder with a minority interest': *Re Thornley deceased* (1928) 7 ATC 178. HMRC's Shares and Assets Valuations do not regard the quasi partnership analogy as necessarily applicable for tax purpose: Shares Valuation Fiscal Forum Minutes of 8 April 2003. However, the other shareholders could be regarded as special purchasers in some cases and that could be taken into account; see **2.09**.

In *Sally Harding and Rosemary Walton v Elizabeth Edwards and others* [2014] EWHC 247 (Ch) the first three participants were sisters and the other participants were family members and trustees. The parties could not agree on how the company, Brand of Hardings Limited, which owned 242 acres of arable land in Cambridgeshire, should be run and as shareholders and directors the company was run as a quasi-partnership.

Following *Ebrahimi v Westbourne Galleries* [1973] AC 360 and *In re Yenidje Tobacco Co Limited* [1916] 2 Ch 426, in which it was just and equitable to wind up the company, the judge in this case was 'firmly of the opinion that it is just and equitable that the Company should be wound up'.

The Network of Independent Forensic Accountants put out a paper setting tests for a company which was run as a quasi-partnership, ie all directors are shareholders, the directors and owners are close family members, there are no non-shareholders or non-executive directors and there is a close working relationship between the directors and hands-on management style and they agree to declare dividends other than in accordance with their share ownership.

Focus

Prejudicial conduct cases are very dependent on the facts of each case, and often involve quasi partnerships.

2.06 The date of valuation

The date at which shares are to be valued in prejudicial conduct cases is usually, but not invariably, the date of the petition.

In *Re Regional Airports Ltd* [1999] 2 BCLC 30 the judge had to consider whether the valuation of the shares in question should be at the date set out in the petition alleging unfairly prejudicial conduct or the date of trial. In considering this the judge said:

'I was unable to identify anything which had emerged by the time of the trial which would not have been apparent to or at least apprehended by a circumspect purchaser at the date of the petition. Accordingly, so far as it made any difference my preference was for taking the most up to date valuation which was available.

The petitioner's valuers were a chartered surveyor Mr Wolfenden, who valued the properties, and Mr Riddle a partner in KPMG. Mr Wolfenden's conclusion was that the commercial elements at Southend had a value of £5.05m and those at Biggin Hill £4.95m. Different discount rates were used in relation to different rental streams but the average was about 11%.

Mr Riddle (the accountant) then took these figures as data in his principle approach to the valuation of each airport business as a whole. This was that the property based activities at each airport should be valued separately from the airport-related activities. He approached the latter on the basis of a discounted cash flow calculation, explaining that the selection of the appropriate discount rate for this purpose reflected in part the time value of money and in part the degree of risk or uncertainty in predicting the relevant cash flow. His conclusion was that the annual cash flows from the airport related activities at Biggin Hill were minus £290,000 after certain adjustments had been made. The equivalent figure for Southend Airport was minus £340,000. In both cases he concluded that the appropriate discount rate was between 13% and 15%. Capitalised at 13% the airport-related activities in Biggin Hill produced a figure of minus £2.231m and at 15% minus £1.933m. Combining these figures with Mr Wolfenden's (the surveyor) £4.9m produced a range of values from £2.629m to £3.017m. At Southend the range produced by the same exercise was between £2.435m and £2.783m. On this basis the combined values of Biggin Hill and 80% of Southend (which Mr Riddle perceived as being the same as the value of Regional Airports Ltd) ranged from £4.5m to £5.2m.

Mr Riddle eschewed the adoption of any single approach to valuation. In addition to the "activities based cash flow approach" described above, Mr Riddle examined three other approaches. Of these, it is convenient to take first what he describes as the "company based cash flow approach". This differed from the activities based cash flow approach in valuing the cash flows from the property and airport related activities by reference to the same discount rate. In this case he selected 12% as an appropriate discount rate for Biggin Hill and 13% for Southend. The higher rate for Southend being intended to reflect a greater uncertainty over the future of Southend cash flows. The resulting bottom line valuations came out at £1.667m and £1.230m for 80% of Southend giving RAL a value of (£2.897m). Mr Riddle's other two approaches were an adjusted net asset basis (which gave a range of £2.278m to £5.340m depending on the assumptions applied) and a "turnover multiple basis" which gave a range from £5.639m to £8.459m. Stressing that it was unsafe, in the final analysis, to do more than state a range of values Mr Riddle's conclusion was that the value of RAL was in the range of £3m to £5m, the mid-point of which could be expressed as £4m.

The principal expert evidence given on behalf of the respondents consisted of that given by Mr Lomax, the Senior Valuation partner of Drivers Jonas, Property Consultants and Chartered Surveyors. His preferred method was to adopt a discounted cash flow methodology largely because of the difficulty of identifying the reliable comparables in the contemporary market. In approaching his task he applied the same discount rate, 15%, to all revenue and expenditure. He concluded that the value of the leasehold interest in Biggin Hill was £400,000. At Southend, he forecast future cash flows on the basis of three possible scenarios depending on what solution is adopted by management to the perceived problem of the runway. His conclusion was that if the runway has to be shortened the net

> present value of the airport was only some £100,000. in the course of his closing submissions Mr Speller (Counsel) produced a revised sheet of calculations the effect of which was to substitute the figure of £200,000 on this scenario. The second possibility of extending the runway would produce a negative net present value of minus £380,000. The third possibility (in fact comprising the business strategy which Mr Walters currently regards as the most exciting) of the major expansion of the airport to cater for scheduled passenger flights and a rail link he has calculated as producing a negative net present value of minus £2.32m".
>
> In addition to that evidence the respondents adduced expert share valuation evidence from Andrew James Clifford FCA ATII MSPI MEWI Corporate Special Services Partner of Baker Tilly Chartered Accountants. In essence what Mr Clifford did was to take Mr Lomax's figures and put them into an overall asset and liability statement for each company. The result of that process demonstrated that the shares in RAL are, for practical purposes, worth no more than £1 per share.'

Commenting on the various experts' calculations the judge considered that Mr Riddle's approach to his activities based discounted cash flow was not methodologically flawed:

> 'it did however succeed in emphasising the extreme sensitivity of any discounted cash flow calculation to the chosen discount rate and the assumptions made in calculating the relevant cash flow.'

In the end, the judge finally stated:

> 'the conclusion at which I have arrived is that, for the purpose of determining the value at which a court ordered purchase of shares should take place, each RAL share should be valued at £26 (valuing RAL as a whole at £2.6m). There are various routes by which it is possible to reach (or justify) that conclusion and it should be obvious by now that none of them alone can be regarded as wholly satisfactory. The figure is arrived at by taking the value of BHAL to be £1.4m (or £1.75m before making the £350,000 reduction which I have derived from Mr Clifford) and the value of 80% of LSACL (after adjusting for the £230,000) to be £1.2m.'

He then went on to give his reasoning.

In the Court of Appeal in *Re a Company (No 002612 of 1984)* [1986] 2 BCC 99495 Nicholls LJ stated:

> 'Having considered the valuation evidence the judge decided that there were three factors which confirmed or pointed to the date of the petition (18 April 1984) rather than the date of the hearing as the proper date for valuation. The hearing took place in January and February 1985 over 26 working days with judgement being delivered on 3 April 1985. The last practical date for valuation before the commencement of the hearing was 20 December 1984 and in their report the experts valued the shares at that date amongst others. The three factors were: that for reasons set out by the judge the data used in the valuations was more likely to be reliable in respect of a valuation at the earlier date, that valuing the shares at the earlier date made irrelevant the question whether Mr Lewis could compel Mr Bolton to repay part of the pension and bonus payments made to him by Cumana in the summer of 1984 and that Mr Lewis should not suffer from any fall in value of the shares in Cumana after September when he would have been willing to join in selling all the shares in Cumana through a jointly instructed agent, but Mr Bolton had had no genuine intention of doing so (and thus Mr Bolton had only himself to blame if he was unable to sell the shares of

Cumana for the price they would have commanded between April and September 1984).

Finally, when fixing the price of £925,000, the judge observed that it was clear that negotiations for sale or negotiations for raising the necessary sum by other means would take time and he directed that the purchase should be completed on or before 11 October. He gave liberty to apply for an extension before then if there were evidence that negotiations were proceeding for a sale or other transactions which would realise the necessary sum and that they were likely to come to fruition if a further adjournment were given.'

Mr Bolton in this case had sought to argue that a subsequent fall in the share price and inability to sell the share's made the original order inappropriate. Glidewell LJ stated:

'however it is clear that we should only exercise that discretion in favour of admitting the (additional post-trial evidence) if "the basis upon which the case was decided at the trial was suddenly and materially falsified by a dramatic change in circumstances". To quote Lord Hudson in *Mulholland and Anr v Mitchell* [1971] AC 666 at 676G.'

It was argued for Mr Bolton that:

'the effect of the order on Mr Bolton is far more dramatic than the judge anticipated. Effectively it gives him only a choice between going into bankruptcy or remaining at Mr Lewis's mercy for an indefinite period trying to raise the purchase price for the shares while interest on the sum of outstanding amounts.' This received little sympathy. Lawton LJ stated: 'the fact that a wrong-doer is impecunious is no reason why judgment should not be given against him for the amount of compensation due to his victim. What Mr Lewis should do to get money out of Mr Bolton, claiming as he still does that he is impecunious, is a matter for him to decide not the court.'

In *ProFinance Trust SA v Gladstone* [2002] 1 WLR 1024 the Court of Appeal held that:

'the starting point when exercising the discretion as to the date of valuation was that prima facie an interest in a going concern should be valued at the date on which it was ordered to be purchased, subject to the overriding requirement that a valuation should be fair on the facts of the particular case. The Judge had erred in exercising his discretion in the instant case to take the date of the petition as the date of valuation. The fairest case would be to take the agreed value of the share capital of the company as at the time of the hearing before the judge i.e. £215,000 and accordingly to substitute an order that G should purchase P's 40% shareholding for £86,000. Interest should not have been added as no evidence had been put forward that this was the only way, or the best way, to a fair result.'

The date of valuation in prejudicial conduct cases was considered in *Re a Company (No 002612 of 1984)* (1986) 2 BCC 99453 at 99492 in that case, concerning Cumana Ltd, the judge stated:

'I would respectfully agree with Nourse J that there is no rigid rule applicable to all circumstances, though I would at least incline to the view that the date of the petition is the correct starting point, the valuation, of course, being adjusted to take account of unfair conduct which has depreciated the value of the shares (as in *Meyer*) (1959) and that a departure from this date must be justified on the ground of some special circumstance. The date of the petition is the date on which the petitioner elects to treat the unfair conduct of the majority as in effect destroying

> the basis on which he agreed to continue to be a shareholder and to look to his shares for his proper reward from participation in a joint undertaking. If he succeeds in his petition and establishes that the breakdown in the relationship justifies an order for the compulsory purchase of his shares, he has established that the respondents if they had acted fairly would have agreed, following the breakdown in their relationship that his shares should be purchased at fair value. As Mr Evans-Lombe pointed out, if Mr Bolton in this case had agreed, following the presentation of the petition, to purchase Mr Lewis's shares at their fair value it would not have been open to him to have resiled from that bargain if the shares subsequently fell in value and he should be in no better position as a result of having contested the petition. By contrast, if the respondents to a petition contests the petition and continue in effect to employ the value of the petitioner as investment in the company, justice may require that they account to him for an enhanced value of the company's business at the date of valuation unless it can be said that the increase in value is solely attributable to their efforts (as in *Re London School of Electronics Ltd*), that question does not arise for decision and I express no opinion on it.'

Other cases supporting the date of the order as the correct date for the valuation include the Court of Appeal of Queensland, Australia in *Re Golden Bread Pty Ltd* (1977) Qd R44 (1977–1978) CLC 40-437 which concerned a section of the Australian Companies Act similar to s 75 (of Companies Act 1980). In *Re a Company (No 002567 of 1982)* [1983] 1 WLR 927, (1983) 1 BCC 989301, Vinelott J stated:

> 'I expressed the opinion that the shares of a petitioner who had unreasonably rejected previous fair offers to purchase his minority holding ought to be valued at the date of valuation and not at the date when he had been excluded from participation in the affairs of the company.'

However, that was not a case where the court was asked to make an order for the compulsory purchase of shares under s 75. The petitioner had rejected an offer to purchase his shares on the basis of the value at the time of this exclusion. The main question was whether he had acted unreasonably in rejecting the offer and in persisting in seeking an order for the winding-up of the company. It was only later when he had failed to obtain a winding-up order on the grounds that the respondents had at all material times been willing to purchase his shares that he claimed that the valuation should be made at the date of exclusion.

A case where the valuation date was held to be the date of the petitioner's exclusion is in *Re OC (Transport Services) Ltd* (1984) 1 BCC 99068.

Focus

The date of valuation depends on the circumstances.

2.07 Just and equitable winding up

In the case of *Ebrahimi v Westbourne Galleries Ltd* [1972] 2 WLR 1289, in the House of Lords, Lord Wilberforce reviewed in some detail the numerous cases concerning a petition to wind up a company by the court on the grounds that it would be just and equitable to do so under CA 1948, s 222(f) (now Insolvency Act 1986, s 122(1)(g)). Lord Wilberforce admirably summarised the situation:

> 'The just and equitable provision does not as the respondents suggest entitle one party to disregard the obligation he assumes by entering a company nor the court to dispense him from it. It does, as equity always does, enable the court to subject the exercise of legal rights to equitable considerations. Considerations, that is, of a personal character arising between one individual and another which may make it unjust or inequitable to insist on legal rights or to exercise them in a particular way.
>
> It would be impossible and wholly undesirable to define the circumstances in which these considerations may arise. Certainly the fact that a company is a small one or a private company is not enough. There are very many of these where the association is a purely commercial one of which it can safely be said that the basis of association is adequately and exhaustively laid down by the articles. The super-imposition of equitable considerations requires something more which typically may include one or probably more of the following elements.
>
> (1) An association formed or continued on the basis of a personal relationship involving mutual confidence. This element will often be found where a pre existing partnership has been converted into a limited company.
> (2) An agreement or understanding that all or some, or they may be sleeping partners, of the shareholders shall participate in the conduct of the business.
> (3) Restriction on the transfer of the member's interest in the company so that if confidence is lost or one member is removed from management he cannot take out his stake and go elsewhere.
>
> It is these and analogous factors which may bring into play the just and equitable clause, and they do so directly through the force of the words themselves. To refer, as so many of these cases do, to quasi partnership or in substance partnerships, may be convenient but may also be confusing. It may be convenient because it is the law of partnership which has developed the conceptions of probity, good faith and mutual confidence and the remedies where these are absent, which become relevant once such factors as I have mentioned are found to exist, the words just and equitable sum these up in the law of partnership itself. And in many, but not necessarily all cases, there has been a pre existing partnership the obligations of which it is reasonable to suppose continue to underlie the new company structure. But the expressions may be confusing if they obscure or deny the fact that the parties (possibly former partners) are now co-members in a company who have accepted in law new obligations. A company, however small, however domestic, is a company not a partnership, or even a quasi partnership and it is through the just and equitable laws that obligations common to partnership relations may come in.'

Lord Cross summed up the position of the minority shareholders' rights:

> 'What the minority shareholder in cases of this sort really wants is not to have the company wound up, which may prove an unsatisfactory remedy, but to be paid a proper price for his shareholding. With this in mind parliament provided by section 210 of the Companies Act 1948 that if a member of a company could show that the company's affairs were being conducted in a manner oppressive to some of the members, including himself, that the facts proved would justify the making of a winding up order under the just and equitable clause, but that to wind up the company would unfairly prejudice the oppressed members, the court could inter alia make an order for the purchase of the shares by those members or other members or by the company. To give the court jurisdiction under this section

> the petitioner must show both that the conduct of the majority is oppressive and also that it affects him in his capacity as a shareholder. The appellant was unable to establish either of these pre conditions. But the jurisdiction to wind up under section 222(f) continues to exist as an independent remedy and I have no doubt that the Court of Appeal was right in rejecting the submission of the respondent to the effect that a petitioner cannot obtain an order under that section any more than under section 210 unless he can show that his position as a shareholder was being worsened by the action of which he complains.'

However, 'to wind up a successful and prosperous company and one which is properly managed must clearly be an extreme step and must require a strong case to be made': *Cumberland Holdings Ltd v Washington H Soul Pattinson and Co Ltd* (1977) 13 ALR 561.

The case of *Ebrahimi v Westbourne Galleries Ltd* also showed that it is reasonable to assume, in the absence of any evidence to the contrary, that the directors are acting in the best interests of the company. As Lord Wilberforce stated:

> 'It was said that the removal was, according to the evidence of Mr Nazar, bona fide in the interests of the company, that the appellant had not shown to the contrary, that he ought to do so or demonstrate that no reasonable man could think that his removal was in the company's interest. This formula "bona fide in the interests of the company" is one that is relevant in certain contexts of company law, and I do not doubt that in many cases decisions have to be left to majorities of directors to take which the court must assume had this basis.'

In *Re a Company (No 001363 of 1988), ex p S-P* [1989] BCLC 579 the decision in *Ebrahimi v Westbourne Galleries Ltd* was upheld in the Chancery Division of the High Court. A petition was presented to the court to wind up the company on the grounds that it would be just and equitable to do so. The judge dismissed an application to strike out the petition on the grounds that the decision in *Ebrahimi v Westbourne Galleries Ltd* had not been negated by legislation and that the remedy of a 'just and equitable' liquidation is still available to a quasi partner who claims that his equitable rights have been infringed.

Where it might be to the shareholder's advantage to have his shares valued as part of the more controlled winding up process, a winding-up order under Insolvency Act 1986, s 122(1)(g) may be granted. In the Court of Appeal decision in *Virdi v Abbey Leisure Ltd* [1990] BCLC 342 Lord Balcombe said that a valuation under a company's articles of association might be subject to a discount as a minority holding, in a winding up it would not be. The facts of that particular case, where a company had been formed to carry out one venture, lent themselves strongly to a winding-up order. The venture had been completed successfully and the company's assets consisted solely of the profits therefrom. The writers suggest that if the company had been trading as a going concern, Hoffmann J's statements in *Re a Company (No 007623 of 1986)* [1986] BCLC 362 which were dismissed by Lord Balcombe in *Abbey Leisure Ltd* as not relevant to the facts of that case would prevail. He said that 'Certification by the auditors is a swift and inexpensive method to which the parties are contractually bound' and 'Where such machinery is available, it seems to me wrong for a shareholder to insist on the same valuation exercise being undertaken by the court at far greater expense'.

However, a member cannot petition for winding up unless there would be a surplus for members (*Re Rica Gold Washing Co* (1879) 11 Ch D 36; *Re*

Expanded Plugs Ltd [1966] 1 WLR 514); if it is just and equitable to wind up a company, the court must make a winding up order rather than pursuing some alternative remedy such as an application under CA 2006, s 994 (see **2.05**) to buy out the petitioner's interest: *Re a Company No 003843 of 1986* [1987] BCLC 562; *Re a Company No 3096 of 1987* (1987) 4 BCC 80. However, if the valuer is the auditor and not seen to be independent this would not apply (*Re Boswell & Co (Steels) Ltd* (1988) 5 BCC 145) because the auditor's being involved with another associated company enabled the court to overrule a provision in the articles appointing him as valuer.

The Privy Council case of *CVC/Opportunity Equity Partners Ltd and Another v Demarco Almeida* [2002] BCC 684 was under Cayman Islands Law where a shareholder, who had been excluded from the management of the company, petitioned for winding-up on just and equitable grounds. Lord Millett in giving the judgment stated (at para 37):

> 'There are essentially three possible bases on which a minority holding of shares in an unquoted company can be valued. In descending order these are (1) as a rateable proportion of the total value of the company as a going concern without any discount for the fact that the holding in question is a minority holding (2) as before but with such a discount and (3) as a rateable proportion of the net assets of the company at their break-up or liquidation value.
>
> Which of these should be adopted as the appropriate basis of valuation depends on all the circumstances. The choice must be fair to both parties and it is difficult to see any justification for adopting the break-up or liquidation basis of valuation where the purchaser intends to carry on the business of the company as a going concern. This would give the purchaser a windfall at the expense of the seller.
>
> If the going concern value is adopted a further question arises whether a discount should be applied to reflect the fact that the holding is a minority one. An outsider would normally be unwilling to pay a significant price for a minority holding in a private company and a fair price between a willing seller and a willing purchaser might be expected to reflect this fact. It would seem to be unreasonable for the seller to demand a higher price from an unwilling purchaser than he could obtain from a willing one. Small private companies commonly have articles which restrict the transfer of shares by requiring a shareholder who is desirous of disposing of his shares to offer them first to the other shareholders at a price fixed by the company's auditors. It is the common practice of auditors in such circumstances to value the shares between a willing seller and a willing buyer and to apply a substantial discount to reflect the fact that the shares represent a minority holding.
>
> The context in which the shares fall to be valued in a case such as the present is however very different. Mr Demarco is not desirous of disposing of his shares he would rather keep them and continue to participate in the management of the company. It is Opportunity's conduct in excluding him from management that has driven him, however reluctantly, to seek to realise the value of his investment. In this situation the case law in England is that normally the shares should be valued without any discount see for example in *Re Bird Precision Bellows Ltd* (1985) 1 BCC 99467, [1986] Ch 658, *Re Abbey Leisure Ltd* [1990] BCC 60 and *O'Neill v Phillips* [1999] BCC 600, [1999] 1 WLR 1092.'

He further stated:

> 'The rationale for denying a discount to reflect the fact that the holding in question is a minority holding lies in the analogy between a quasi-partnership

> company and a true partnership. On the dissolution of a partnership the ordinary course is for the court to direct a sale of the partnership business as a going concern with liberty for any of the former partners who wish to bid for the business to do so. But the court has power to ascertain the value of a former partner's interest without a sale if it can be done by valuation and frequently does so where his interest is relatively small, see *Syers v Syers* (1876) 1 App Cas 174. But the valuation is not based on a notional sale of the outgoing partner's share to the continuing partners who being the only possible purchasers would offer relatively little. It is based on a notional sale of the business as a whole to an outside purchaser.
>
> In the case of a company possessing the relevant characteristics the majority can exclude the minority only if they offer to pay them a fair price for their shares. In order to be free to manage the company's business without regard to the relationship of trust and confidence which formerly existed between them, they must buy the whole, part from themselves and part from the minority, thereby achieving the same freedom to manage the business as an outside purchaser would enjoy.
>
> …
>
> Their Lordships are satisfied that Opportunity's offer to purchase Mr Demarco's interests at a valuation based on the company's break-up or liquidation value falls far short of a fair offer and fails to remedy his complaint. It is not entitled on this ground to restrain the presentation of a winding-up petition.'

It was stated that by presenting a winding-up petition on the just and equitable ground Mr Demarco was:

> 'invoking the traditional jurisdiction of equity to subject the exercise of legal rights to equitable considerations. If he can make good his contention that the business venture which the parties carried on through the medium of the company possessed the necessary characteristics then equity will not allow Opportunity to exploit its position to make a profit at his expense. If it wants to carry on the company's business as a going concern without him, it must offer to pay him the going concern value of his interest. If it is unwilling to pay him more than the break-up or liquidation value of his interest then the court may order that the company be wound-up. This will not obtain more for Mr Demarco than he already has been offered but it will achieve a fair and just result between the parties by ensuring that they are treated equally.
>
> Their Lordships would wish to emphasise that this does not mean that a minority shareholding can use the threat of winding-up proceedings in order to bring pressure on the majority to yield to his demands however unreasonable. As in *Re a Company* (No 003843 of 1986) demonstrates, the court will be astute to prevent such conduct. In a case such as the present it would be an abuse of the process of the court for a petitioner to commence or continue proceedings after he had plainly received a fair offer for his shares. If he holds out for more the respondent can apply for the proceedings to be restrained or struck-out. The court is fully in control and will not allow its process to be abused. Their Lordships are satisfied that Mr Demarco has not acted unreasonably in rejecting Opportunity's offer to buy his interest and that by continuing to hold out for a fair offer he is not threatening to abuse the process of the court.'

The normal order following a petition is for the majority shareholders to buy the petitioner's shares, and he must offer them to other members at a fair price: *Re Company No 007623 of 1984* [1986] BCLC 362.

In the House of Lords, the decision of *O'Neill v Phillips and Others* [1999] 1 WLR 1092, Lord Hoffmann stated, in relation to an offer to buy the petitioner's shares:

> 'If the respondent to a petition has plainly made a reasonable offer, then the exclusion as such will not be unfairly prejudicial and he will be entitled to have the petition struck out. It is therefore very important that participants in such companies should be able to know what counts as reasonable offer.
>
> In the first place, the offer must be to purchase the shares at a fair value. This will ordinarily be a value representing an equivalent proportion of the total issued share capital, that is, without a discount for its being a minority holding. The Law Commission (paragraphs 3.57-62) has recommended a statutory presumption that in cases to which the presumption of unfairly prejudicial conduct applies, the fair value of the shares should be determined on a pro rata basis. This too reflects the existing practice. This is not to say that there may not be cases in which it will be fair to take a discounted value. But such cases will be based upon special circumstances and it will seldom be possible for the court to say that an offer on a discounted basis is plainly reasonable, so that the petition should be struck out.
>
> Secondly, the value, if not agreed, should be determined by a competent expert. The offer in this case to appoint an accountant agreed by the parties or in default nominated by the President of the Institute of Chartered Accountants satisfied this requirement. One would ordinarily expect the costs of the expert to be shared but he should have the power to decide that they should be borne in some different way.
>
> Thirdly, the offer should be to have the value determined by the expert as an expert, I do not think that the offer should provide for the full machinery of arbitration or the half-way house of an expert who gives reasons. The objective should be economy and expedition, even if this carries the possibility of a rough edge for one side or the other (and both parties in this respect take the same risk) compared with a more elaborate procedure. This is in accordance with the terms of the draft regulation recommended by the Law Commission: see Appendix C to the report (No. 246 (1997)).
>
> Fourthly, the offer should, as in this case, provide for equality of arms between the parties. Both should have the same right of access to information about the company which bears upon the value of the shares and both should have the right to make submissions to the expert, though the form (written or oral) which these submissions may take should be left to the discretion of the expert himself.
>
> Fifthly, there is the question of costs. In the present case, when the offer was made after nearly three years of litigation, it could not serve as an independent ground for dismissing the petition, on the assumption that it was otherwise well founded, without an offer of costs. But this does not mean that payment of costs need always be offered. If there is a breakdown in relations between the parties, the majority shareholder should be given a reasonable opportunity to make an offer (which may include time to explore the question of how to raise finance) before he becomes obliged to pay costs. As I have said, the unfairness does not usually consist merely in the fact of the breakdown but in failure to make a suitable offer. And the majority shareholder should have a reasonable time to make the offer before his conduct is treated as unfair. The mere fact that the petitioner has presented his petition before the offer does not mean that the respondent must offer to pay the costs if he was not given a reasonable time.'

Where the entire scheme of the company is fraudulent, a compulsory liquidation may be justified: *Mahony v East Holyford Mining Co Ltd* (1875) LR 7 HL 869.

Normally, the company would take action against the persons who have defrauded it: *Re Othery Construction Ltd* [1966] 1 WLR 69.

Where a shareholder has been misled into subscribing for shares, the action should be for recession of the allotment of the shares, not winding up: *Re Burlch y Phegm Co Ltd* (1867) 17 LT 235.

Compulsory winding up may be ordered where deadlock exists and there is no other remedy: *Re Expanded Plugs Ltd* [1966] 1 WLR 514. Such cases may involve directors' lack of probity: *Re Concrete Column Clamps Ltd* (1953) 4 DLR 60; *Thomson v Drysdale* 1925 SC 311; *Re Worldhams Park Golf Course Ltd* [1998] 1 BCLC 554. Unfairly prejudicial conduct can lead to relief under CA 2006, ss 994–999, short of winding up. Milking the company by taking excessive remuneration and failing to keep the other shareholders informed can justify compulsory winding up: *Lock v John Blackwood Ltd* [1924] AC 794.

In quasi partnership companies, the exclusion of the petitioner from the management of the company may justify winding it up (*Re Davis and Collett Ltd* [1935] Ch 693), as may the cessation of trust and confidence: *Symington v Symington's Quarries Ltd* (1905) 8 F 121. The completion or abandonment of a single venture for which the company was formed may justify winding it up: *Virdi v Abbey Leisure Ltd* [1990] BCLC 342.

In the case of a partnership, restrictions imposed in the partnership deed must be taken into account in valuing a partner's interest: *Burdett Coutts v IRC* [1960] 1 WLR 1027. A partner's interest is not subject to a discount from the pro rata value of the partnership assets: *Walter v IRC* [1996] STC 68.

Focus

Winding up the company is usually a last resort, but it may be the only fair solution.

2.08 Open market

A valuation may be made on the basis of various assumptions, one of these assumptions being known as the open market value, which is the price the shares would fetch if sold in the open market at the appropriate time. This basis of valuation is the one used for most fiscal purposes, with various statutory modifications. The detailed statutory rules are dealt with in **Chapters 9** and **10**.

There have been a number of cases before the courts on the interpretation of an open market value and a number of rules follow from these decisions.

Cozens-Hardy MR defined open market in the land value duty cases of *IRC v Clay* and *IRC v Buchanan* [1914] 3 KB 466 at 471 in the following terms:

> '"Open market" includes a sale by auction but is not confined to that. It would include property publicly announced in the usual way by insertion in the lists of house agents. But it does not necessarily involve the idea of a sale without reserve. I can see no ground for excluding from consideration the fact that the property is so situated that to one or more persons it presents greater attractions than to anybody else. The house or the land may immediately adjoin one or more landowners likely to offer more than the property would be worth to anybody else. This is a fact that cannot be disregarded.'

In the same case, Swinfen Eady LJ stated at 475:

> 'A value, ascertained by a reference to the amount obtainable in an open market, shows an intention to include every possible purchaser. The market is to be the open market, as distinguished from an offer to a limited class only, such as the members of the family. The market is not necessarily an auction sale. The section means such amount as the land might be expected to realise if offered under conditions enabling every person desirous of purchasing to come in and make an offer, and if the proper steps were taken to advertise the property and let all likely purchasers know that the land is in the market for sale.'

In the estate duty case of *Re Lynall, Lynall v IRC* (1971) 47 TC 375 at 411 Lord Morris of Borth-y-Gest had to consider whether information would be available to hypothetical purchasers and vendors in the open market:

> 'This must mean whether it would be openly available to all potential purchasers and vendors in the market or markets in which the relevant purchases and sales take place. There may be different markets or types of markets for different varieties of property, but in the operation of s. 7(5) of the Finance Act 1894 the market which must be contemplated, whatever its form, must be an "open" market in which the property is offered for sale to the world at large so that all potential purchasers have an equal opportunity to make an offer as a result of its being openly known what it is that is being offered for sale. Mere private deals on a confidential basis are not the equivalent of open market transactions.'

The term open market was also considered in the land value duty case of *Glass v IRC* [1915] SC 449. Lord Johnston stated at 456:

> 'I think the referee is mistaken in assuming that open market necessarily means sale by auction. A sale takes place in open market if the subject is put on the market and the best offer taken, however made.'

The definition of the open market was considered in the excise duty case of *Salomon v Customs and Excise Comrs* [1967] 2 QB 116, [1966] 3 WLR 1223. This was a customs case in which the Commissioners of Customs and Excise sought to define the open market as the open market in the UK; the retail market for one article and the wholesale market for many. Lord Denning MR held that in the context the term 'open market' meant the import market in which a buyer in England buys the goods from a seller overseas.

It is clear that a sale in the open market includes the property with all its advantages and disadvantages. In the stamp duty case of *Stanyforth v IRC* [1930] AC 339, in his judgment at 344, Lord Warrington of Clyffe stated with regard to a sale in the open market:

> 'At such a sale the property would have to be put up with all its incidents, including provisions for defeasance either in whole or in part, powers vested in persons not controlled by the vendor to create charges taking precedence of the property sold and so forth. I really fail to understand, with all respect to those who have taken a different view, how the most drastic power of destroying the property to be sold, vested in persons over whom the purchasers could have no control, could properly be disregarded.'

In the estate duty case of *Duke of Buccleuch v IRC* [1967] 1 AC 506 at 524 Lord Reid stated:

> 'There was some argument about the meaning of "in the open market". Originally no doubt when one wanted to sell a particular item of property one

took it to a market where buyers of that kind of property congregated. Then the owner received offers and accepted what he thought was the best offer he was likely to get. And for some kinds of property this is still done. But this phrase must also be applied to other kinds of property where that is impossible. In my view the phrase requires that the seller must take – or here be supposed to have taken – such steps as are reasonable to attract as much competition as possible for the particular piece of property which is to be sold. Sometimes this will be by sale by auction, sometimes otherwise. I suppose that the biggest open market is the Stock Exchange where there is no auction. And there may be two kinds of market commonly used by owners wishing to sell a particular kind of property. For example, it is common knowledge that many owners of houses first publish the fact that they wish to sell and then await offers: they only put the property up for auction as a last resort. I see no reason for holding that in proper cases the former method could not be regarded as sale in the open market.'

It is apparent from these authorities that all possible purchasers must be considered in the open market, including someone who has some particular interest in acquiring the shares, because, for example, they would give him control of the company – usually known as a special purchaser.

Lord Hoffmann in *Lonsdale v Howard and Hallam Ltd* [2007] UKHL 32, when faced with the problems of how an agent is entitled to be compensated for being deprived of the benefit of the agency relationship held that (at para 11):

'The value of the agency relationship lies in the prospect of earning commission, the agent's expectation that proper performance of the agency contract" will provide him with a future income stream. It is this which must be valued.

12 Like any other exercise in valuation this requires one to say what could reasonably have been obtained at the date of termination of the rights which the agent had been enjoying. For this purpose it is obviously necessary to assume that the agency would have continued and the hypothetical purchaser would have been able properly to perform the agency contract. He must be assumed to have been able to take over the agency and (if I may be allowed the metaphor) stand in the shoes of the agent even if as a matter of contract the agency was not assignable or there were in practice no dealings in such agencies: compare *Inland Revenue Commissioners v Crossman* [1937] AC 26. What has to be valued is the income stream which the agency would have generated.

13 On the other hand as at present advised I see no reason to make any other assumptions contrary to what was the position in the real world at the date of termination. As one is placing a present value upon future income one must discount future earnings by an appropriate rate of interest. If the agency was by its terms or in fact unassignable it must be assumed, as I have said, that the hypothetical purchaser would have been entitled to take it over. But there is no basis for assuming that he would have obtained an assignable asset: compare the *Crossman* case. Likewise if the market for the product in which the agent dealt was rising or falling this would have affected what a hypothetical purchaser would have been willing to give. He would have paid fewer years' purchase for a declining agency than for one in an expanding market. If the agent would have had to incur expense to do work in earning his commission it cannot be assumed that the hypothetical purchaser would have earned it gross or without having to do anything.'

Lord Hoffmann declined to follow the custom of the French courts in awarding compensation at two years' gross commission, because of differences in the commercial markets in England and France. He also looked at the calculation of the compensation in *King v Tunnock Ltd* [2000] SC 424 where the principal ceased the business in which the agent operated. Lord Hoffmann stated:

> 'in view of the closure of the business the agency was worth nothing. No one would have given anything for the right to earn commission on the sales of cakes and biscuits because there would have been none to be sold. Nor had the principal retained any goodwill which the agent had helped to build up. The goodwill disappeared when the business closed. The reason why the business closed is not altogether clear but Mr King's low earnings for the full time work over the previous two years suggests that it was not doing well. Even if one assumes that commission would have continued at the same rate it is hard to see why anyone should have paid for the privilege of a full time job which earned him less than he would have been paid as a bus conductor.'

On the later case of *Barrett McKenzie v Escada (UK) Ltd* [2001] Eu LR 567 in which the judge said, 'it is really a question of compensating for the notional value of that agency in the open market', Lord Hoffmann commented:

> 'I agree that this is what compensation in article 17 (3) means. My only caution is that one must be careful about the word "notional". All that is notional is the assumption that the agency was available to be bought and sold at the relevant date. What it would fetch depends upon circumstances as they existed in the real world at the time: what the earnings prospects at the agency were and what people would have been willing to pay for similar businesses at the time.'

On being urged not to adopt a principle which required valuation evidence, Lord Hoffmann stated:

> 'but I do not see how, if the matter does go to court, the judge can decide the case without some information about the standard methodology for the valuation of such businesses.'

He also made the point:

> 'the hypothetical purchase of the agency does not involve an assumption that the agent gives a covenant against competition. If the situation in real life is that the hypothetical purchaser would be in competition with the former agent and could not have any assurance that the customers would continue to trade with him that would affect the amount he was prepared to pay. If it appeared that all the customers were likely to defect to the former agent (or for that matter to someone else) he would be unlikely to be prepared to pay much for the agency.
>
> What matters of course is what would have appeared likely at the date of termination and not what actually happened afterwards. But I do not see think (sic) that the court is required to shut its eyes to what actually happened. It may provide evidence of what the parties were likely to have expected to happen.'

Focus

The open market is that in which a vendor would seek to sell the asset in question to maximise the sale price, not a private sale to an identified purchaser.

2.09 Special purchasers

Although it is clear that a special purchaser has to be included as a possible purchaser, the point to consider is what effect this would have on the price. In the words of Swinfen Eady LJ in the land value duty case of *IRC v Clay; IRC v Buchanan* [1914] 3 KB 466 at 476, which was a case involving the value of land:

> 'It was then urged by the Solicitor General that if the probability of the special buyer purchasing, above the price, which but for his needs would have been the market price, could be taken into consideration at all, then only one further point or bid could be allowed, and it must be assumed that this special buyer would have become the purchaser upon making this one extra bid. Such an assumption would ordinarily be quite erroneous. The knowledge of the special need would affect the market price and others would join in competing for the property with a view of obtaining it at a price less than that of which the opinion would be formed that it would be worth the while of the special buyer to purchase.'

Glass v IRC 1915 SC 449 on land value duty, although similarly not a case involving shares, is of particular interest in considering the position of a special purchaser. On the 16 October 1911, Robert Glass sold a farm to the Kirkcaldy & Dysart Waterworks Commissioners for the price of £5,000. The farm lay within the drainage area of a reservoir belonging to the commissioners and they did not have but, no doubt, could have obtained, compulsory purchase powers. Mr Glass argued at 450:

> 'That nothing transpired between 30 April 1909 and 16 October 1911 to alter either the total or the site value of this property (Feal) and that the value of the site has not in any way increased since 30 April 1909' and 'further that the total value of the estate at both dates was the price (£5,000) at which it was sold to the Kirkcaldy & Dysart Waterworks Commissioners on the later date and that the site value was also the same at both dates and should be assessed on the original total value as above stated, viz £5,000, as ascertained by sale.'

Mr Glass was merely trying to reduce his liability to duties on land values under F(1909–10)A 1910, s 25. The valuer's total value was £3,379. It was necessary to value the property at 30 April 1909 as if sold at the time in the open market by a willing seller in its then condition. The Water Commissioners did not then have compulsory powers and therefore had to bargain for what lands they required with those who were fairly able to gauge the Commissioners' necessity and were entitled to make use of their knowledge. With regard to the Water Commissioners' position as special purchasers Lord Johnston stated at 456:

> 'But he (the referee) is further mistaken, I think, in that he has forgotten that, where a public body is expected in the near future to require certain property, there are generally found and must be assumed to be, people who are prepared to trade on that fact, and prepared to bid up to a point to which they think they may safely go and leave themselves a chance of profit in turning over the property to the public body. That point would doubtless be below the value to the public body, but where, as here, the public body has no compulsory powers all depends on how near a certainty it is that the Commissioners must acquire. In fact if the acquisition by the public body has become a practical certainty the margin depends on what it would cost the public body to obtain compulsory powers, or to adopt some other course of attaining their end if such is feasible. The phrase

> "willing seller" is not to receive a restricted meaning. He is only hypothetically willing if he gets the advantage of all surrounding circumstances, and this is implied in the further expression "in its then condition".'

Lord Salvesen stated at 458:

> 'It is true that the valuation is to proceed as if it were made at the statutory date, which was more than two years before the actual sale to the commissioners; but the probability of the commissioners requiring the land for the purposes of their undertaking was known long before then. In December 1908 they had actually obtained a provisional order under which they were authorised to acquire any lands within their drainage area for the purpose of securing the purity of the water and of protecting it against pollution. They had already acquired the adjoining estate of Drumain and Holl by purchase for that purpose, and the appellant's being contiguous, formed the next most desirable area to acquire.
>
> It was reasonably certain that within no very long space of time the commissioners would be forced to acquire it in order to preserve the purity of the water in their reservoirs …
>
> These being the facts I am clearly of the opinion that the contingency, and by no means remote contingency, of the Commissioners desiring to purchase the lands, gave them an element of value in excess of what they possessed for merely agricultural purposes … If this farm had been advertised for sale as at 30 April 1909, I cannot doubt that a special point would have been made of the probability of its being required by the Kirkcaldy Water Commissioners at no distant date and of the fact that they possessed only powers of purchase by private agreement. I think it highly probable that in these circumstances more than one speculator would have come forward with offers substantially in excess of the agricultural value in the reasonable expectation that they would sooner or later find a purchaser in the Water Commissioners at a figure that would yield them a profit on the transaction.'

Where property is to be valued, reference must be had not merely to the actual current use to which the property is being put but also to any other use to which it may reasonably be put and which might enhance its value.

This particular point was considered in the Indian compulsory purchase case of *Raja Vyricherla Narayana Gajapatiraju v Revenue Divisional Officer, Vizagapatam* [1939] AC 302, by the Privy Council. In this case the property in question was land which was compulsorily acquired and compensation awarded on a valuation of the land as partly waste and partly cultivated with an allowance for some buildings and trees. This ignored the fact that the land was contiguous to land on which a harbour was being constructed and that it contained a spring which yielded a constant and abundant supply of good drinking water which was required by the harbour. The owner claimed that the land should be valued as building land, but this was rejected as the land was found to be unsuitable for such development. Lord Romer decided that the compensation must be determined by reference to the price which a willing vendor might reasonably expect to obtain from a willing purchaser; at 313:

> 'For it has been established by numerous authorities that the land is not to be valued merely by reference to the use to which it is being put at the time at which its value has to be determined … but also by reference to the uses to which it is reasonably capable of being put in the future. No authority indeed is required for this proposition. It is a self evident one. No one can suppose in the case of land which is certain, or even likely, to be used in the immediate

> or reasonably near future for building purposes, but which at the valuation date is waste land or is being used for agricultural purposes, that the owner, however willing a vendor, will be content to sell the land for its value as waste or agricultural land as the case may be. It is plain that, in ascertaining its value, the possibility of its being used for building purposes would have to be taken into account. It is equally plain however that the land must not be valued as though it has already been built upon … and (it) is sometimes expressed by saying that it is the possibilities of the land and not its realised possibilities that must be taken into consideration.'

The position of the special purchaser was considered as follows at 315:

> 'Proceeding therefore with the imaginary auction at which are present two classes of buyers, namely the "poramboke buyers" (persons who are in no way interested in the land's potentialities) [land set aside for public or communal purpose, a term borrowed from the Indian Raj] and the "potentiality buyers", the former will disappear from the biddings as soon as the "poramboke" value has been reached and the bidding will thereafter be confined to the "potentiality buyers". But at what figure will this bidding stop? As already pointed out it cannot be imagined as going on until the ultimate purchaser has been driven by the competition up to a fantastic price. For he is ex-hypothesis a willing purchaser and not one who is by circumstances forced to buy. Nor can the bidding be imagined to stop at the first advance on the "poramboke value". For the vendor is a willing vendor and not one compelled by circumstances to sell his potentiality for anything that he can get. The arbitrator will, therefore, continue the imaginary bidding until a bid is reached which in the arbitrator's estimate, represents the true value to the vendor of the potentiality. The auction will therefore have been an entire waste of the arbitrator's imagination. If the value of the potentiality be Rs X the imaginary auction will have taken place to ascertain the value of X from the imaginary bidding, and all that can be said is that the bidding will stop at Rs X.
>
> The truth of the matter is that the value of the potentiality must be ascertained by the arbitrator on such materials as are available to him and without indulging in feats of the imagination.
>
> Their Lordships would not have thought it necessary to deal with this question of the imaginary auction at such length were it not for the fact that in the argument before them the respondent's counsel endeavoured to show by reference to such an auction that when there was only one possible purchaser of the potentiality the value of it to the vendor was nil – that is to say that the value of the land with the potentiality was substantially nothing in excess of its value without it …
>
> Upon the question of the value of the potentiality where there is only one possible purchaser there are some authorities to which their Lordships will have to refer. But dealing with the matter apart from authority would seem that the value should be the sum which the arbitrator estimates a willing purchaser would pay and not what a purchaser would pay under compulsion. It was contended on behalf of the respondent that at an auction where there is only one possible purchaser of the potentiality the bidding will only rise above the "poramboke" value sufficiently to enable the land to be knocked down to that purchaser. But if the potentiality is of value to the vendor if there happen to be two or more possible purchasers of it, it is difficult to see why he should be willing to part with it for nothing merely because there is only one purchaser. To compel him to do so is to treat him as a vendor parting with his land under compulsion and not as a willing vendor. The fact is that the only possible purchaser of a potentiality is usually quite willing to pay for it.'

After referring to *IRC v Clay* [1914] 1 KB 339 and *Glass v IRC* 1915 SC 449, which have already been referred to, Lord Romer then went on to consider other authorities at 318:

> 'Of these authorities the first one to which reference should be made is that of *In Re Gough and Aspatria, Silloth and District Joint Water Board* [1904] 1 KB 417. In that case it was not proved that the enquiring authority was the only possible purchaser and it may be that all that the Court of Appeal decided was that it was not incumbent upon the claimant for compensation to specify that any particular body of persons were possible purchasers, though the judgment of Lord Alverstone LCJ seems quite consistent with the view that the potentiality must be valued, even if the acquiring authority be its only possible purchaser. But it is contended that Sir Richard Henn Collins MR expressed the contrary view. After referring to the particular adaptability of the land that was in question and that it ought to find a place in the estimate of the amount of compensation, he said at 423:
>
> > "That view is supported by authority and long practice; but underlying it is the question, which is one of fact which is for the arbitrator, whether there is a possible market for the site, and in determining that the statutory purchase is not to be considered."
>
> But the Master of the Rolls said that the purchase, not the purchaser, was to be left out of consideration. Any enhanced value attaching to the land by reason of the fact that it has been compulsorily acquired for the purpose of the acquiring authority must always be disregarded, and the Master of the Rolls meant no more than that.'

Their Lordships then considered *Re Lucas and Chesterfield Gas and Water Board* [1909] 1 KB 16; *Cedars Rapids Manufacturing and Power Co v Lacoste* [1914] AC 569 at 576; *Fraser v City of Fraserville* [1917] AC 187 at 194 and *Sidney v North Eastern Rly Co* [1914] 3 KB 629, with which they partially disagreed. Lord Romer continued at 323:

> 'For these reasons their Lordships have come to the conclusion that, even where the only possible purchaser of the land's potentiality is the authority that has obtained the compulsory powers, the arbitrator in awarding compensation must ascertain to the best of his ability the price that would be paid by a willing purchaser to a willing vendor of the land with its potentiality in the same way that he would obtain it in a case where there are several possible purchasers and that he is no more confined to awarding the land's "poramboke" value in the former case than he is in the latter.'

The concept that requires the inclusion of all potential purchasers in the hypothetical market is confirmed in the rating case of *Robinson Bros (Brewers) Ltd v Houghton and Chester-Le-Street Assessment Committee* [1938] AC 321 where it was necessary to consider whether the fact that brewers would pay a higher rent for managed houses was a factor that should be taken into account in the valuation for rating purposes. Lord Macmillan stated:

> 'The motives which actuate buyers in a market may be of all kinds, but it is not their motives, but their bids, that matter. In the case of trade premises the competitors for the tenancy are presumably always actuated by a consideration of the profits which they think they can make by utilising the premises and they will have this in view when they make their bids. The brewer who wishes the premises because he thinks he can make money by sub-letting them to a tied tenant is influenced by perfectly legitimate business considerations. He offers the

rent he thinks it worth his while to pay to obtain the tenancy. Why should the rent which he is prepared to pay be excluded from consideration in fixing the market value of the tenancy? He is one of the competitors in the market and the figure which he is prepared to pay is an element which ought clearly to be taken into account in arriving at the market price.'

Although, therefore, it is necessary to include a special purchaser as one of the potential purchasers there is no necessity to assume that he will be blackmailed into paying the maximum which the shares could be worth to him. In the words of the Lord Chancellor in the estate duty cases of *Re Crossman* and *Re Paulin* (1936) 15 ATC 94 at 102:

> 'The evidence which the learned Judge seems to have accepted was that of Lord Plender, who was called on behalf of the petitioners; upon the basis of his figures, the learned Judge fixed the value, on the hypothesis which I have held to be the correct one, at £351 in the Crossman case and £355 in the other. In fixing those figures, it appears from the judgment that Lord Plender "did not exclude anybody or include anybody in particular; he considered the matter generally." In my opinion that is the right way in which to arrive at the value in the open market. But the learned Judge goes on to say that evidence was called for the Crown which indicated that a particular trust company would be willing to give a good deal more than the ordinary market price, because of certain particular attractions which the prospect of getting upon the share register would hold out for such a company. The learned Judge says that he excluded trust companies from the possible buyers because he had evidence to satisfy him that the directors would not have consented to put them upon the register. I cannot think that this is a proper reason in the view which I have taken as to the construction to be put upon the subsection of the Act. On the other hand I think it is a fair construction to put upon the learned Judge's judgment that the extra sum which could be obtained from trust companies was not an element of the value in the open market, but rather a particular price beyond the ordinary market price which a trust company would give for special reasons of its own. I do not think it would be right to appreciate the value of the shares because of this special demand for a special purchase from a particular buyer.'

In this case it had been argued that to a trust company the shares would be particularly attractive and worth £395 a share instead of £355 a share. However, it was not accepted that there was any evidence to show that a trust company would be pushed up to the maximum amount it might in theory be prepared to pay. In the words of Lord Blanesburgh at 113:

> 'I agree with, I believe, all your Lordships in thinking that any possible bid for the shares by a trust company was allowed for by Lord Plender in his estimate of £355 a share accepted by the learned Judge as reliable.'

Harman LJ comments in the Court of Appeal in *Re Lynall, Lynall v IRC* (1971) 47 TC 375 at 396:

> 'It was the taxpayer's argument that directors must be excluded from amongst possible purchasers because they would be "special" purchasers. I do not accept this and am of opinion that this is not an ingredient in the Crossman decision. In Crossman's case it was decided that the fact that a "special" purchaser, namely a trust company, would have offered a special price must be ignored, but this was because that particular purchaser had a reason special to him for so doing. So here a director who would give an enhanced price because he would thus obtain control of the company would be left out of account. But that is not to say that directors as such are to be ignored. All likely purchasers are deemed to be in the market.'

In *Hawkings-Byass v Sassen* [1996] STC (SCD) 319 shareholdings of 9%, 11% and 18% in the sherry producer, Gonzalez Byass were being valued. Shares in the company were spread amongst members of the Gonzalez and Byass families and the Special Commissioners found that two separate groups of shareholders could have been called special purchasers. One of those would 'in all probability' have acquired control of the company on acquisition of the 9% or 11% shareholdings and would have acquired 'clear-cut' control on acquisition of the 18% shareholding. On the basis of those facts and evidence that a multinational drinks company would also have been interested in acquiring any of the shareholdings, the Commissioners adopted discounts from a pro rata proportion of the value of the whole company of 20% for the 18% shareholding and 33% for the two smaller shareholdings. The Commissioners based the discounts on the potential appreciation that would accrue to the special purchasers when entirety value could be achieved. Taking the uncertainties into account, a 50% appreciation was considered appropriate for the two smaller shareholdings and a 25% appreciation for the 18% shareholding.

It was emphasised in *Walton v IRC* [1996] 1 EGLR 159 that someone cannot be identified as a special purchaser if there is evidence that in fact they have no intention of buying the asset in question.

In *Hawkings-Byass v Sassen*, the Special Commissioners appeared to envisage a sale direct to the special purchasers. Previous case law nevertheless suggests that a special purchaser is to be included as a possible purchaser, but it is not to be assumed that the sale would necessarily be to that special purchaser. The existence of a special purchaser could have an appreciatory effect on the price generally, where the existence of the potential special purchaser was known to the general public, but what is the position if the existence of a special purchaser is not so known at the date of valuation?

The approach shown by the cases other than *Hawkings-Byass v Sassen* is that when the existence is known, other persons will estimate the price the special purchaser will pay and bid up to a price which will give them a profit when, in due time, they sell on to the special purchaser. If, however, the existence of a special purchaser is not known – and this is perfectly feasible, eg when a purchaser is buying shares before making a bid for a company – the special purchaser will not affect the price.

Focus

If there is a special purchaser who is known to have a particular interest in acquiring the property, this will be reflected in the value.

2.10 Prior sales

In cases involving the valuation of shares in a private company there may have been previous arm's length sales which may be taken into account in a subsequent valuation. In practice the number of cases where such sales turn out to be truly at arm's length tends to be few and far between.

In the Irish estate duty case of *McNamee v IRC* [1954] IR 214, Thomas McNamee held at the time of his death 175 £1 ordinary shares out of 50,000 ordinary shares in issue in the Convoy Woollen Company Ltd.

Maguire J at 219 stated:

> 'I have imagined a sale in the open market at which this small lot of shares would be offered, the number of prospective purchasers, prudent and cautious, these shares would attract, the exhaustive enquiries into the history of the Company they would make, their examination of the balance sheets, the dividends, the dividend earning capacity of the company, the dividend policy of the directors, the capital resources and liabilities of the company, the company's reserves, the necessity of making provision for worn-out machinery and plant, and the replacement of machinery and plant that was out of date and obsolete, the business difficulties of the Company, its new and vigorous competitors in changing markets, the uncertainties of the woollen trade, the rise and fall of the prices of wool in world markets, the effect of these prices upon the company's stocks of raw material and manufactured goods, the continuance of the company's export business not to speak of other things that might occur to a prudent and cautious investor willing to consider a purchase of these shares with the clog as to alienation attaching to them when the purchase and registration is complete. Strange as it may seem these topics have been the subject of evidence before me. I have in my imagination a large number of interested would-be purchasers, having made these exhaustive enquiries, competing for these shares. But I cannot entirely obliterate another viewpoint in this imaginative effort. Namely that when all these enquiries are made, and the purchase of this lot of 175 shares is considered worth while, there might be few purchasers, some of whom would wish to secure the shares on very favourable terms.'

Some of the evidence quoted by Maguire J (at 221) was that:

> 'The dividend policy is to maintain its dividend at 15% and to maintain its reserves. That policy has been operated for a great many years. Prior to the 15% dividend a 12½% dividend was paid. That was paid for a number of years also. Policy of directors is to maintain and increase reserves. Same policy was in force when the dividend was 12½%. The overdraft is £60,000 at present. There are no circumstances in the trade today to justify departure from the company's policy. Very definitely not at the time of death of McNamee. There is no reason to anticipate a change in that policy or to expect an increase in dividend.'

Later in his judgment Maguire J stated at 228:

> 'The evidence of Mr Francis Cave, Mr Thomas H Scanlan and Mr Abrahamson, who were examined on behalf of the Revenue Commissioners, was given with conspicuous fairness and propriety. It is mostly evidence of opinion and as such I have approached and considered it with the highest respect. It is based on the expectation of a much greater distribution of profits, a much higher dividend, a much smaller appropriation of profits to reserves than has hitherto appeared in any of the annual accounts and balance sheets in the company's history. It has emphasised the profit earning capacity of the Convoy Woollen Company. In that respect it is sound. The profit earning capacity of the company is and must always be of great importance. But its importance must be related to the consistent policy of this company in relation to the limitation of dividends, the conservation of assets, and the appropriation each year of large sums from profits to reserves. It has, I think, overlooked many other but very important matters covered by the evidence of Mr Cromie and Mr Shott. Accepting, as I do, without qualification the evidence of Mr Cromie and Mr Shott, I regret that the evidence of the witnesses for the Revenue Commissioners cannot be reconciled with

that evidence which I have set out at length. It cannot be reconciled with the consistent history, dividend paying policy, conservative policy as to reserves, and cautious provision for the future running through the whole of the company's accounts. Mr Cave, Mr Scanlan and Mr Abrahamson have gone to great trouble to prepare comparative tables of other companies carrying on somewhat similar businesses having stock exchange quotations for their shares. Those have been examined and explained. I am satisfied without going into details, but having considered all the evidence, that the analogies they have drawn from these other companies are far from complete and that they are misleading.

I am satisfied too that the inferences they ask me to draw cannot fairly be drawn in the case of these shares in the Convoy Woollen Company. The affairs of each company must be considered in relation to its own position, its own difficulties, and its own domestic control. The affairs of the Convoy Woollen Company on the evidence before me are unique. I have no evidence of exactly similar companies before me. It would appear that such evidence is not available. I recognise fully that Mr Cave, Mr Scanlan and Mr Abrahamson were doing their best in the difficult circumstances of this case to appraise the value of these shares. If they have failed, as in my opinion they have failed in this case, to convince me of their evidence, they are not at fault. I cannot accept their valuations and I cannot by any effort on my part approximate my valuation of these shares anywhere approaching the figures they have given.

Accepting Mr McNulty's evidence as to the bona fides of the sale of these shares to Mr Kilpatrick and granting that this price of £1.10s.0d. is the highest ever paid for these shares in the history of the company, I still must bear in mind that this was not a sale in any real or an imaginary open market. I must make allowances for the sale in any imaginary open market. It is here I find evidence of Mr Shott and Mr Butler of great value. I have given anxious thought and consideration to this perhaps in some ways the most difficult part of my task. I am satisfied that not more than £1.12s.6d., certainly not more than that, might have been obtained in the open market, an imaginary open market, for this lot of 175 shares. Accordingly I fix and determine the value of these shares at £1.12s.6d. each.'

Mr McNulty's evidence was:

'I purchased 150 of these shares in 1946 at £150. Registration no 248. The parties were at arm's length. The dividend was 10%. Registration no 261. That was a sale at arm's length. Weir to Carless, May 1949; J R Weir to I B Carless, 777 ordinary shares for £971. 5s. 0d. Registration no 266, 19 March 1951, Raphoe Electric Light Co, John Moffat, 100 ordinary shares for £125. They were at arm's length. 19 September 1951, the McNamee sale was registered. In January 1951, the MacNamee sale was negotiated by me. It was not registered until the September following, registration no 269. It was the best price I could get. Mr Kilpatrick had recently been appointed a director. He wanted shares. He knew of the sale of Carless and he offered the same price. I am certain he couldn't have got them at that price. This sale at £1. 10s. 0d. was at arm's length. It was a completely commercial transaction. I am solicitor to the company and I know a fair amount about its affairs. In ordinary cases I would consult the secretary as to the sale. That didn't happen in this case. I knew Mr Kilpatrick wanted the shares. We had a bit of a haggle. I pushed him up to £1. 10s. 0d. I couldn't get any more at all. The most I could get was the £1. 10s. 0d. I did not hawk them around. It was a sale to the most probable purchaser. The directors knew the shares were for sale. I got the highest price in the history of the company.'

This case is often put forward by HMRC as one in which arm's length sales influence the value. It is, however, also a case which clearly demonstrates that it is often difficult to find comparable quoted public companies when trying to value shares in a private company and that an attempt at an unrealistic comparison is merely misleading.

> **Focus**
>
> Prior sale – if at arm's length – may be evidence of the likely value of shares in a hypothetical sale.

2.11 Subsequent sales

Although following *McNamee v IRC* (above) arm's length sales prior to the date of valuation can be of assistance a subsequent sale after the date of valuation does not, of itself, give grounds to reopen the valuation at an earlier time. The most famous estate duty case on this point is that of *IRC v Marr's Trustees* (1906) 44 SLR 647. This case did not concern shares, but a herd of cattle belonging to Mr Marr, who died on 7 June 1904. The cattle were valued on 20 June 1904 at £9,031 by Mr H Ritchie. The herd was subsequently sold at auction on 11 October 1904 for £17,722.17s.

The Commissioners argued – Condescendence 5:

> 'The price fetched in the open market, when the herd was exposed for sale within four months after the deceased's death, affords a reasonable and proper criterion of the value of this portion of the deceased's estate. The amount actually realised formed and falls to be treated as an important asset of the estate, allowance being made for such outlay as was incurred by the defenders, as executors, in the keep and care of the herd. The balance, after making this allowance, represents truly the value of the herd at the deceased's death.'

Lord Johnston distinguished between property which was subject to considerable fluctuation in value and that, such as house property, where a valuation was, at that time, apparently, considerably easier. The judgment is useful in highlighting the factors which may apply to a subsequent sale which may not have been applicable at the date of valuation:

> 'In the case of house property, at any rate, there is a natural time of the year which is regarded as the proper property market, and unless a house has some special attractions it can hardly be said that there is an open market say, in the month of August, should that be the time of the deceased's death. Though the house may not be actually saleable then, yet values change so gradually, that there is no difficulty in a skilled valuator putting a proper value upon the house even in August with his knowledge of past markets and present prospects. There will be no substantial change in the intrinsic value of the house between August, when it may have to be valued and the following February, when it may have to be sold for entry at the ensuing May.
>
> But when one comes to deal with a subject of a fluctuating value, the fluctuation depending upon natural increment or rather on the excess or otherwise of natural increment over natural decrement, a different question arises. Such a subject is a herd of cattle. It is in the definite ascertainable condition at the date of the deceased's death. But in the lapse of months important changes take place. At the date of the death a cow may be two or three weeks from calving. In the course

> of three or four months the risks of calving and the risks to the life of the young calf are over. The cow in calf is one thing, the cow and her calf on its feet and three or four months old is a totally different thing. Again a calf a few weeks old at the date of the death and a calf some months old at a date posterior to the death are also very different things. The calf is over the troubles of its early weeks and every month is developing more of its quality. Similarly a cow may have been put to the bull shortly before the death and in the course of three or four months may prove either to be barren or to be in calf. Again losses by death occur from time to time, and cattle which may be perfectly healthy at the date of the death of the owner may either singly or as a herd be afflicted with disease rendering them valueless at the end of three or four months. It is, I think, therefore obvious that to call for a valuation (and no valuation can be better than actual exposure to sale by auction) at a date three or four months posterior to the date of death would not give the true value of the herd at the date which the statute itself fixes viz, the date of the death.
>
> Now if what I have already said would be true of an ordinary herd of cattle it is true to a greatly enhanced degree in the case of a herd of prize cattle, whose risks and whose variations in individual value are extreme in degree when compared with those of an ordinary herd. Moreover, if what I have said above is true generally there could not be two periods in the year better suited to display the difference in values than the dates with which we are concerned viz 7 June and 11 October. In June the herd is in a transition state. The majority of the calves have been recently dropped, some of the cows are un-calfed and the herd has had none of the benefits of a summer's grass. By October the condition of the herd is set for the season, the cattle have, in agricultural phrase, got the bloom on them, and there can be no question that in the interests of the estate the trustees acted prudently in taking the risk of carrying the herd through the summer and selling it in October, rather than selling it at once, and they also acted prudently in not taking the risk of carrying it through the winter and selling it in February which is the other chief market month for prize cattle, and when if everything had gone well the herd would have been of still greater intrinsic value, though I doubt whether it would have met as good a market.
>
> Even if I had not considered the special circumstances to be immediately adverted to, I should have no hesitation in stating that the herd must be valued at the date of the death, though it might have been imprudent to bring it to the hammer until three or four months later, and that the Commissioners of Inland Revenue were not entitled to have a valuation as in October, when the best market may be anticipated, or a valuation based on the results of actual sale at that period.'

It would appear that the valuer, Mr Ritchie, was a somewhat dour Scot but he nonetheless impressed the Lord Ordinary:

> 'I think it right to state that I was much impressed by Mr Ritchie's appearance in the witness box. He was not a voluble witness and did not always find it easy to put in words a reason for the faith that was in him, but he had lived for years with the herd under his eye, with the markets for Aberdeen prize cattle under his close observation, and with every opportunity of becoming conversant with the ups and downs of the business. I would infinitely rather trust his trained and practical intuition, though it may appear on paper to produce somewhat of a rule of thumb result, than many a more apparently scientific valuation by classification. And I am persuaded that Mr Ritchie's valuation of June is a fair valuation against which the Commissioners of Inland Revenue have no just cause of complaint.'

It would appear that the price realised in the subsequent auction was itself exceptional and this was a further reason for rejecting any attempt to drop back from the subsequent sale price to arrive at the value in June. As Lord Johnston stated:

> 'I think that the sale which actually did take place in October was accompanied by certain adventitious circumstances which, though they rebounded very much to the advantage of the estate, render the sale price obtained a misleading criterion of the true market of the herd at the date of the death, or indeed at any other date. These circumstances were, shortly, that a sudden and unexpected demand had arisen from the great Argentine breeders which sent their agent, Mr Rodger, into the field for the first time with an almost free hand, and that not merely for high grade and mature bulls, to which the Argentine stock growers have chiefly confined themselves, but also for young stock and breeding cows. But even this was not the real cause of the great success of the sale. The real cause of its success was this. Tuberculosis is the great enemy of prize stock. The Argentine Government will not admit it, or indeed any stock, without a careful veterinary examination at their own ports. Consequently their buyers in the UK cannot buy without insuring against the risk of the stock being rejected on its arrival at the Argentine ports. Underwriters are accustomed to insure against this risk provided that they have a reliable veterinary certificate before delivery. This they can rarely get when the sale is in public market, consequently they buy by private bargain and their buyers do not appear as bidders at auction unless in exceptional cases. But Mr Rodger had accidentally found an underwriter who, I assume in ignorance of what he was doing, undertook the risk of rejection on landing in the Argentine without stipulating for the necessary tuberculosis certificate. Hence Mr Rodger was able to intervene in the sale not only with a free hand as to price, but untrammelled by the necessity of obtaining the tuberculosis certificate, and I think that it is not too much to say, as many of the witnesses did, that his advent made the sale. As an illustration of the consequence, the highest priced animal which he bought at a price of 1,200 guineas was rejected on examination and afterwards sold for £100 on account of the underwriters, for show purposes merely. Such adventitious circumstances could not possibly enter into the valuation of the herd as a marketable commodity either at the date of death or at the date of the sale.
>
> I shall therefore assoilzie [absolve] the defenders with [from] expenses.'

Focus

Subsequent sales can, at best, be used only to help substantiate the value at the relevant date.

2.12 Non-arm's length sales – agreements with HMRC

In *IRC v Stenhouse's Trustees* [1992] STC 103, the Scottish Court of Session had to consider transactions in shares in an unquoted company involving members of the same family or trusts or companies in which the family or trusts had an interest, and agreements entered into between the trustees and the Revenue. The court decided that evidence of such sales and agreements was admissible before the Special Commissioners when hearing an appeal involving the value of shares for capital transfer tax purposes. The weight to be given to such evidence was a question of fact. Lord Coulsfield stated:

> 'The general rule of law, which is not in doubt, is that evidence which is relevant to the issue in the case is admissible unless it is excluded by some peremptory rule of law. Evidence is relevant if it is in some way logically connected with the matters in dispute or if it is consistent with, or gives rise to a logical inference regarding, the facts in issue. No peremptory rule of law of evidence was referred to in the present case and the question was argued as one of relevance of evidence. Put shortly, the Crown's contention was that evidence of agreements as to the open market value of shares in the companies and evidence of actual transactions in those shares must be relevant to the issue in the present dispute, even if such evidence might not be determinative or even of very great weight. The trustees argued that the issue between the parties was a hypothetical one, namely the price which would be paid in the open market for the shares under valuation, and that it followed from the nature of that issue that it was correct to take the approach of their witnesses as the primary approach; that regard could only be had to any transactions in the shares to the limited extent allowed by the special commissioner; and that evidence of agreements was not relevant at all.'

He went on to say:

> 'I do not see why, in the present case, the type of evidence admissible should be restricted by the nature of the issue in the way suggested by the trustees. No doubt the best evidence of open market value is evidence of sales of the same or similar property on the open market. It is not, however, necessarily the case that where evidence of open market sales is available, other evidence is excluded. If it is suggested that conditions have changed, in some material respect, the evidence of market sales may have to be qualified by taking account of other evidence. The evidence of market sales is only evidence of value, and is not necessarily conclusive by itself. Similarly, in the case of a hypothetical sale, the calculation made by the trustees' witnesses are, in my view, only evidence of value, and cannot be regarded as, in themselves, conclusive. I therefore do not understand why it is said to follow from the fact that value has to be ascertained on a hypothesis that any evidence of actual transactions should be ruled out as so irrelevant as to be inadmissible. Whether it is correct to start, as the trustees' witnesses did, with the accounts of the companies and information available in the public domain, is, in my opinion a question of fact and opinion, not one of law. Similarly, the question whether any weight, and if so how much, is to be attached to evidence of transactions seems to me to be a question of fact and opinion. Some of the transactions on which the Crown relies may be of no use: but there may be others which took place between parties who were genuinely trying to strike an open market value, and I do not see why such cases should simply be ignored. As I understand the position, the commissioner accepted, as the trustees also did in argument, that it is relevant to lead evidence of some transactions, albeit in a secondary role, as a check or sounding board for a conclusion reached on the basis of their preferred approach. Once that concession is made, it seems to me to be difficult to rule out ab ante the evidence which the Crown seeks to lead as necessarily inadmissible. Whether any particular part of that evidence is of assistance must, in my view, be a question of fact and circumstance.'

He made similar remarks concerning previous agreements with the Revenue but added:

> 'I can see difficulties in dealing with evidence concerning previous agreements if the Revenue are not prepared to reveal the approach which they themselves took in arriving at the value in question, but that is a problem which requires to be dealt with as the evidence is heard.'

See **18.14** for a discussion of the problems arising with previous agreements when considering a value for capital gains tax re-basing purposes.

> **Focus**
>
> Prior valuations agreed with HMRC are not evidence of arm's length transactions.

2.13 Valuation for foreign fiscal purposes

For UK taxation purposes the statutory valuation rules apply to unquoted shares of all companies whether situate here or abroad. HMRC is not bound to adopt a value agreed with an overseas revenue authority. Nevertheless if such an agreed value is based on principles similar to the UK 'open market' concept (especially if agreement was reached after substantive negotiation) then that value may be regarded as some evidence of worth for fiscal purposes in the UK.

The experience of HMRC suggests that there are few cases where taxpayers have fulfilled the conditions mentioned above and have negotiated values abroad which are relevant in the UK. In practice, duplication of effort is less of a problem than it might at first appear for various reasons:

(a) the trend towards investment in companies registered in the 'tax havens';
(b) the taxpayer's total assets in the foreign country may not exceed the taxable threshold there;
(c) the difference in the basis of valuation for UK and foreign taxes, and
(d) the absence of a charge to tax in the foreign country on the event which gives rise to a charge to tax in the UK.

Once the shares in the overseas company have been valued by Shares and Assets Valuation in local currency terms, the London Buying Rate (or the World Value of the Pound Rate) quoted in the *Financial Times*, is used to make the necessary conversion to the sterling equivalent. If the foreign country in question operates exchange controls which adversely affect the repatriation of funds to the UK at the relevant date of valuation, then it may be appropriate to apply a discount to the official rate of exchange in order to allow for the effect of this 'blocking' of assets.

> **Focus**
>
> Valuations for foreign tax purposes are considered in **Chapter 8**.

2.14 Recent valuation cases

A recent and comprehensive case involving a number of valuation issues is *Saltri III Ltd v MD Mezzanine SA Sicar and Others* [2012] EWHC 3025 (Comm), which concerned an enforcement and restructuring of a group of companies known as the Stabilus Group that occurred in early April 2010. At its heart is a battle between a group of senior lenders and a group of Mezzanine lenders and, in the middle, a security trustee. The judge, Mr Justice Eder, ultimately held that at the time of the restructure the Mezzanine debt was 'under water' and had no value. By April 2010 the Stabilus Group owed approximately €409m to its senior lenders and approximately €83m to its Mezzanine lenders. The security trustee was J P Morgan Europe Ltd, which appointed American Appraisal (UK) Ltd (AA) as its valuation experts. The Mezzanine defendants appointed Parmentier Arthur Group as its experts.

At paragraph 153, Eder J stated:

> 'On its face, the AA Report was a substantial and impressive document which had been carefully prepared. As I have stated, its essential conclusion was that the then EV (Enterprise Value) of the Stabilus Group (based on the premise of a going concern and market value) fell within the range of €220m–€230m, including pension liabilities. This conclusion was based upon three separate valuation methodologies as set out in the AA Report viz (i) a DCF (i.e. discounted cash-flow) with an EV in the range €205m–€250m; (ii) market multiples with an EV in the range of €220m–€245m or €215m–€240m (depending on different assumptions); and (iii) a leveraged buy-out with an EV in the range of €210m–€245m.'

The Mezzanine defendants argued that the report was out of date simply because it pre-dated the restructure by two months, which the judged rejected. It was also stated to be based on an outdated business plan. At paragraph 159 the judge commented:

> 'This part of the case advanced by the Mezzanine Defendants was in large part founded upon the evidence of their expert, Mr Lygo. In truth, the main difference between Mr Lygo, on the one hand, and Mr Weaver, Mr Giles and Mr Robinson, on the other hand, was a matter of timing which depended on an assessment as to when and how quickly the world would recover from the downturn after 2008 and what part the Stabilus Group would or might play in such recovery. In that context, it is striking that timing apart, Mr Lygo's approach is not very different from that of the Business Plans in relation to the prospects for recovery. Rather, as appears from a helpful graph produced by Mr Giles, what Mr Lygo has done is essentially to argue (on the basis of 3 months figures, and without taking into account the views of the Management) that the entire projected revenue curve for 5 years should be shifted significantly upwards. In my judgement, the graph serves to demonstrate the speculative nature if not lack of realism of Mr Lygo's evidence. I deal with this further below.'

At paragraph 163, with reference to hindsight the judge stated:

> 'I should mention that in the context of the suggestion that there were very good prospects of recovery for the Stabilus Group in early 2010, Mr Lygo sought to rely at least initially upon events after April 2010 and in particular in the latter part of 2010. In my view, that is a false exercise. It is nothing more than hindsight. Mr Smouha QC bravely sought to support that exercise on the basis that it was, he submitted, a "sense" check. Of course, I accept that it may provide a basis for checking that the assessment made in early 2010 turned out to be correct. But, in my view, it provides no relevant check as to whether the assessment was, or was not, correctly made at the time. That exercise can only be carried out on the basis of information available at the time.'

With regard to the weighted average cost of capital (WACC), Eder J commented at paragraphs 179–180 that Counsel for the Mezzanine lenders, Mr Smouha QC:

> '179 … made a series of attacks with regard to the WACC figure determined by AA which was in the range 11%–12%. I consider the various elements of such attacks below but it is convenient to note at the outset that that range is broadly comparable with other similar figures including that implied by the Paine acquisition (11.3%) as well as that determined by Ernst & Young (11.9%) and by Mr Giles (i.e. 11.9%). The WACC determined by Mr Lygo (8.0% to 8.5%) is an outlier.
>
> 180 The first main element of this series of attacks is that the AA Report overstated the requisite risk free working capital adjustment although again this point was not put to any of JPMEL's witnesses of fact. The risk free rate is the return on an investment that carries no risk. It is common ground that the rate is to be derived from the yield on long-dated German sovereign debt on 8 April 2010. Mr Weaver used a rate of 4% based on the promised yield to maturity of a 20-year German government bond. Mr Lygo used a rate of 3.758%. Mr Giles used a rate of 4.2% derived from the data set out in Exhibit 5.2 to his report and based on the average yield of long dated zero-coupon bonds which is a standard approach. On the other hand, Mr Lygo appears to have used only one bond in order to derive his estimate and he does not provide the source data. Thus, as between Mr Lygo and Mr Giles, it is my view that the evidence of the latter is to be preferred. In any event, there is no proper basis, in my view, for criticising the approach adopted by Mr Weaver. In any event, Mr Lygo accepted that such adjustments are "a matter of valuation judgement". Thus, in my judgement, there is no basis for the suggestion that this was a "flaw"' in the AA Report still less that this was a flaw which was "obvious" or "patent".'

At paragraphs 181–182 the judge commented:

> '181 Fourth, Mr Smouha QC submitted that the AA Report wrongly included a monthly beta rather than a weekly beta. "Beta" is the measure of the systematic risk inherent in a company's investment returns. In other words, it is a measure of the relative volatility or risk of a security as compared with the market as a whole. The beta is derived from identifying comparable companies, calculating leveraged beta from data obtained from sources such as Bloomberg, de-levering the beta and then re-levering the beta to the specific company. For a listed company, its beta is a representation of a relative movement of the price of a share compared with the movement of the price of the underlying share market. A beta of 1 suggests that a company's share price moves at the same rate as the underlying market. Typically, companies which operate in cyclical sectors or sell discretionary products will tend to have betas above 1 and these companies will have higher betas than non-cyclical companies or companies that sell staple goods (which tend to have betas below 1). In addition, companies operating with a high degree of fixed costs also have higher betas. As explained by Mr Robinson, the Stabilus Group, as suppliers of automotive components, would be expected to have a relatively high beta (and certainly a beta higher than 1) as the sector it operates in has a higher systematic risk than the market.
>
> 182 The AA Report used a beta (1.5) derived by utilising returns information from a range of publicity-traded comparable companies relative to a benchmark index i.e. the DJ Stoxx 600 Index; the figure of 1.5 was based on the median of the monthly betas of the publicly traded comparable companies, normalised for different gearing levels and after consideration of correlation statistics.'

The judge went on to explain that the evidence he accepted showed that the use of weekly rather than monthly data frequently leads to a systematic bias and that the use of monthly beta was not flawed.

> '185 Fifth, Mr Smouha QC submitted that the AA Report incorrectly applied what is known as an "alpha factor" which is, in effect, a specific company risk premium and reflects the additional illiquidity and lack of marketability of smaller companies. This was adjudged in the AA Report to be in the range of 2%–3%.
>
> 186 In support of this criticism, Mr Smouha QC again relied upon the evidence of Mr Lygo who did not apply any alpha premium in his calculations. However, as submitted by in particular Mr Knowles QC, it seems to me that the approach of Mr Lygo was flawed and the approach of Mr Giles (and also the AA Report) is to be preferred for the following reasons:
>
> a As appears from the work of Professor Damodaran, an adjustment for illiquidity/lack of marketability is a standard adjustment for smaller companies and unlisted companies: the adjustment reflects the smaller number of potential buyers for such assets and the fact that the assets can be sold less easily than shares in a large listed company. As Mr Giles said, the data is very well established that small companies' trade at lower prices than equivalent large companies and that is because they are less liquid.
>
> b The effect of leaving out an illiquidity premium from the discount rate would be equivalent to assuming that an investment in Stabilus is as liquid as the shares in the largest listed companies. This would seem to be unreasonable.
>
> c Other valuers also added additional premiums for small company risks and company specific risks. For example, ECAS itself included additional premiums of 4% and 5% for small company risks and company specific risks.
>
> d Mr Giles' evidence (which I accept) was that the factor of 2.85% which he used to reflect illiquidity was "very conservative" and would have been greater if market conditions were also being adjusted for. Without an alpha, the assumption would be that Stabilus shares were the most liquid shares on the stock market, "on anyone's judgement, that is unreasonable". Mr Robinson considered that a range of 2% to 3% for a specific company risk premium was appropriate.
>
> e Mr Lygo's contention that this discount is mainly concerned with minority shareholdings is incorrect. The discount is applicable to both minority and controlling interests and reflects characteristics of the Stabilus Group: that it was a smaller company; that its shares were unlisted; that the market for them was more illiquid and they could be bought and sold less easily than shares in a large listed company; and that Stabilus was distressed and it might have been difficult to sell Stabilus in the market at the time. Similarly, Mr Lygo's assertion that insofar as the discount reflects the distressed state of the Stabilus Group as at April 2010 then this is already reflected in the working capital adjustment is not well founded. It is correct that the working capital injection resolves the immediate cash needs of the Group, and therefore removes that element of distress in the sense of the business running short of cash, but it does not resolve the wider issues in terms of the effect of red listing, credit insurer cover, stockpiling and relationships with customers in general.'

Mr Smouha QC also criticised the choice of tax rate used in the AA Report, and the assumption that acquisition finance would be limited, both of which were rejected. He also criticised the failure to take account of tax losses but the judge accepted evidence that such tax losses would not have been usable by a new owner, under German law. The judge also rejected criticism of the failure to apply the last 12 months' EBITDA (earnings before interest, tax, depreciation and amortisation) median multiples, but this was explained as preference for a qualitative not a quantitative analysis as a matter of judgement, which the judge accepted. Eder J summarised the situation in paragraph 207 as follows:

> '207 In essence, the Mezzanine defendants' case was that if a sales and marketing process had been undertaken, this would have opened up the sale to the entire market and created 'competitive tension' resulting in bids in effect worth in excess of the Senior Liabilities. That would have required bidders to come in with bids placing the EV at more than about €400m. Though challenged to do so, the Mezzanine Defendants never produced any evidence of a higher value still less any evidence to suggest that the EV exceeded €400m or that anything like that figure might be achieved in a competitive bidding process. In my judgement, even on the basis that the burden is on JPMEL, any such suggestion is not credible. In my judgement, there was and is no reasonable basis for thinking that anything even approaching that would have been likely or even possible. All the contemporaneous evidence is strongly to the contrary. In particular:
>
> (1) An impairment review undertaken by ECAS itself as at 31 March 2009 which valued the Group at €317m. As a consequence ECAS reduced the value of its investment to nil, at which value it remained.
> (2) A draft valuation prepared by Ernst & Young on behalf of MDM in May 2009 which valued the Group at €186m. Although MDM witnesses sought to criticise Ernst & Young's work as basic, it is clear that ECAS agreed at the time with the methodology used.
> (3) The PwC Interim Report of 10 July 2009 which indicated an EV at 30 September 2009 of between €129.7m and €203.8m.
> (4) The bids made during the Rothschild process in August 2009 which ranged from €130m to €266.3m (ignoring the higher Triton figure for reasons already stated).
> (5) The AXA exit valuation of August 2009 which, on the management case, projected exit valuations of €251.5m in 2011, €289.5m in 2012 and €337.5m in 2013. An equivalent valuation for 2010 (i.e. using the same multiple of 5.0 against EBITDA for 2010 of €44.0m) would be €220m.
> (6) PwC's valuation dated 8 September 2009 of Stabilus GmbH as at 30 June 2009 which indicated a base case EV of €208.1m.
> (7) The impairment review of 30 September 2009 set out in the Stabilus Group's financial statements audited by Deloitte which showed an indicative EV for the Stabilus Group of €226.2m.
> (8) PwC's Restructuring Opinion of 31 March 2010 which showed an indicative exit value in 2010 of between €153.9m and €241.8m.
> (9) The opinion on fair value at acquisition contained in the financial statements of Servus Holdco audited by KPMG which indicated a valuation of €247.2m.
>
> 208 The foregoing is also consistent with the evidence which I have already referred to that throughout this period, the Senior Debt was being traded not only below par but at a very steep discount i.e. between about 40–70 cents which would seem to imply a valuation range of approximately €160m to €280m.
>
> 209 Despite all the above, it was and remained the evidence of Mr Illenberger that if there had been a bidding process, AXA would have been prepared to make an offer of €470m in cash for the Stabilus Group as of March 2010. Mme Levi said that she agreed with that evidence and that such cash bid was "in line" with their

own valuation of the Stabilus Group of €500m. I do not accept that evidence. There is no documentary evidence whatsoever that AXA had considered, let alone decided, paying €470m or anything approaching that figure in cash (or otherwise) for the Stabilus Group in March 2010; and AXA never approached the Senior Lenders or JPMEL with any cash bid for the Stabilus Group, let alone a bid of €470m. On the contrary, the contemporaneous documents show a very different picture which is wholly inconsistent with such evidence.

…

211 In summary:

a By mid-January 2010 the Management would have filed for insolvency unless the Senior Lenders had agreed in principle a restructuring and believed that the restructuring was likely to be delivered;
b Once the Restructure had been agreed in principle it was essential to proceed with the restructuring negotiations and complete them by the deadline of 2 April 2010;
c This was needed not merely to avoid insolvency but also to put the Stabilus Group on a proper commercial footing with its customers and suppliers;
d Running a simultaneous sales and marketing process would have been impracticable, if not impossible;
e Running such a sales and marketing process would also have been potentially damaging;
f There was no reasonable or realistic basis for thinking that a further sales and marketing process would attract any offers better than those being made by Triton in the context of the restructuring negotiations;
g There was no reasonable or realistic basis for supposing that any purchaser would come forward with a cash or equivalent bid within a measurable distance of the Senior Liabilities of about €400m.'

In *Samarkand Film Partnership No 3 and others v HMRC* [2015] UKUT 211 (TCC), the Upper Tribunal, in 68 pages, held that the partners in two partnerships, Samarkand and Partners 'which acquired and leased films under a sale and lease back arrangement were entitled to tax relief in respect of tax losses that, it was claimed, arose from expenditure on the acquisition of films and certain other costs incurred by the partnerships' were not carrying on a trade, which was also the decision of the First Tier Tribunal. The nine badges of trade described in *Marson v Morton* [1986] STC 463 were considered and only one, the nature of the subject matter, pointed towards trading and the FTT found that the partnership was not trading in the period in question and therefore it had no trading losses.

Eclipse Film Partners (No 35) LLP v HMRC [2013] UKUT 639 (TCC), *Edwards v Bairstow* [1956] AC 14, *Ensign Tankers v Stokes* [1989] STC 705, 761, *Icebreaker 1 LLP v HMRC* [2010] UKUT 477 (TCC), *FA & AB Limited v Lupton* [1972] AC 634 were among other cases referred to.

There were also problems with the distribution rights because, although Pathe Slate owned the master negative, it did not own the distribution rights, without which the master negative had no value. However, the FTT had held that the expenditure was incurred for the business of the partnership because it was incurred to set the income stream going, which they were entitled to do.

The tax appeals were dismissed but the doctrine of legitimate expectation was considered and confirmed in *R (GSTS Pathology LLP and Others) v RCC* [2013] EWHC 1801 (Admin), *R v IRC ex parte MFK Underwriting*

Agencies Limited [1989] STC 873 and *R (Davies) v RCC* [2011] UKSC 47, so HMRC's formally published statements, such as IR20, can be relied on by the ordinarily sophisticated taxpayer, unless used for the avoidance of tax.

The Business Income Manual (BIM) is reviewed in considerable detail and it is necessary to have regard to the relevant parts of the BIM as a whole. HMRC reserves the right to scrutinise film schemes etc closely and will not necessarily apply the guidance, which the court regarded as undeniably correct and a reasonable attitude for HMRC to take. The majority of the partnerships were Jersey general partnerships.

The taxpayers' argument of conspicuous unfairness, under *R v IRC ex p Unilever plc* [1996] STC 681 and unreasonableness under *Associated Provincial Picture Houses Limited v Wednesbury Corporation* [1948] 1 KB 223 were referred to and rejected and the application for judicial review was dismissed. However, the appeal was taken to the Court of Appeal – see below.

Samarkand Film Partnership No 3 and others v HMRC [2017] EWCA Civ 77 was a film scheme appeal.

The main issue on these appeals is whether two 'film scheme' partnerships, which were marketed to wealthy individuals resident but not domiciled in the United Kingdom who wished to generate substantial first year losses to set against their taxable income, were carrying on a trade. If the partnerships were not trading, the schemes failed to achieve their fiscal objective in accordance with the relevant legislation governing the grant of tax relief for the financing of films. The First-tier Tribunal (Judge Hellier and John Robinson) ('the FTT'), in a decision released on 20 September 2011 after a ten-day hearing in May 2011, found that the partnerships were not trading, so the schemes failed. The FTT also dealt with a number of subsidiary issues in their long (514 paragraphs) and careful decision: see [2011] UKFTT 610 (TC), reported at [2012] SFTD 1 as *Samarkand Film Partnerships No 3 v HMRC* ('the FTT Decision') [2011] UKFTT 610 (TC).

The Court of Appeal held, having reviewed all the individual grounds of appeal, that none of them should succeed.

It also considered that, if that was wrong and the partnerships were carrying on a trade, it had to be decided whether or not the partnership losses could be set against other income under TA 1988, s 380 or 381. Section 381(4) required that the trade was carried on throughout the relevant period in which the loss was sustained, on a commercial basis in such a way that profits in the trade could reasonably be expected to be realised in that period or within a reasonable time thereafter. The First Tier and Upper Tribunals held that a trade that was found to produce a loss in net present value terms could not be said to be carried on on a commercial basis, ignoring the claimed tax relief. This analysis was rejected by the Court of Appeal which, however, reached the same conclusion, and the availability of loss relief to the individual partners in their personal capacities cannot be a relevant factor in assessing the commerciality of the partnership's business. The ownership of the negative and the residual rights were more or less worthless (no more than 1% of the amount paid) as they had no right to receive any share of the net profits from the film. However, the expenditure was allowed as the purchase of the benefits of the leasing arrangement.

The judicial review was dismissed, as were the taxpayer's appeals and HMRC's cross-appeal.

Patrick Degorce v HMRC [2015] UKUT 447 (TCC) involved the Goldcrest Film Scheme and the question was whether any Schedule D Case 1 loss arose from the sole trader film distribution activity and, if so, the amount allowable for tax purposes. This meant that there were five primary issues: (1) was Mr Degorce, a hedge fund manager, carrying on a trade, (2) on a commercial basis, (3) with a view to or the reasonable expectation of the realisation of profits, (4) in accordance with generally accepted accounting practice (GAAP), and (5) was his expenditure on two films wholly and exclusively expended for the purposes of the trade? Mr Degorce paid a little over £21 million for the rights and claimed a loss for the purchase price and fees of £20,151,186 under TA 1988, s 380(1). The FTT agreed with HMRC that this was not a trading loss.

Reference was made to *Marson v Morton* [1986] STC 463 in which nine badges of trade were identified:

> '(1) That the transaction in question was a one-off transaction. Although a one-off transaction is in law capable of being an adventure in the nature of trade, obviously the lack of repetition is a pointer which indicates there might not here be trade but something else.
>
> (2) Is the transaction in question in some way related to the trade which the taxpayer otherwise carries on? For example, a one-off purchase of silver cutlery by a general dealer is much more likely to be a trade transaction than such a purchase by a retired colonel.
>
> (3) The nature of the subject matter may be a valuable pointer. Was the transaction in a commodity of a kind which is normally the subject matter of trade and which can only be turned to advantage by realisation …? For example, a large bulk of whisky or toilet paper is essentially a subject matter of trade, not of enjoyment.
>
> (4) In some cases attention has been paid to the way in which the transaction was carried through: was it carried through in a way typical of the trade in a commodity of that nature?
>
> (5) What was the source of finance of the transaction? If the money was borrowed that is some pointer towards an intention to buy the item with a view to its resale in the short term; a fair pointer towards trade.
>
> (6) Was the item which was purchased resold as it stood or was work done on it or relating to it for the purposes of resale? For example, the purchase of second-hand machinery which was repaired or improved before resale. If there was such work done, that is again a pointer towards the transaction being in the nature of trade.
>
> (7) Was the item purchased resold in one lot as it was bought, or was it broken down into saleable lots? If it was broken down it is again some indication that it was a trading transaction, the purchase being with a view to resale at profit by doing something in relation to the object bought.
>
> (8) What were the purchaser's intentions as to resale at the time of purchase? If there was an intention to hold the object indefinitely, albeit with an intention to make a capital profit at the end of the day, that is a pointer towards a pure investment as opposed to a trading deal. On the other hand, if before the contract of purchase is made a contract for resale is already in place, that is a very strong pointer towards a trading deal rather than an investment. Similarly, an intention to resell in the short term rather than the long term is some indication against concluding that the transaction was by way of investment rather than by way of a deal. However, as far as I can see, this is in no sense decisive by itself.

(9) Did the item purchased either provide enjoyment for the purchaser (for example, a picture) or pride of possession or produce income pending resale? If it did, then that may indicate an intention to buy either for personal satisfaction or to invest for income yield, rather than do a deal purely for the purpose of making a profit on the turn …'

These are not a comprehensive list but useful guidance.

Eclipse Film Partners (No 35) [2015] EWCA Civ 95 referred to the fact that the conclusion of the tribunal of fact as to whether the activity is or is not a trade can only be successfully challenged as a matter of law if the tribunal made an error of principle or if the only reasonable conclusion on the primary facts found is inconsistent with the tribunal's conclusion. These propositions are well established in case law: *Edwards v Bairstow* [1956] AC 14 at 29–32, 36, 38–39; *Ransom v Higgs* [1974] 3 All ER 949 at 955, 964, 970–971; and *Marson v Morton* [1986] 1 WLR 1343 at 1348.

2.15 International Valuation Standards Council (IVSC)

The IVSC is an independent non-profit-making organisation which aims to improve valuation standards. Its stated objectives are the 'development of high quality international standards and supporting their adoption and use, facilitating collaboration and cooperation among its member organisations, collaborating and cooperating with other international organisations and serving as the international voice for the valuation profession'.

IVSC definitions and guidance are becoming increasingly common as the primary point of reference for valuations both in the UK and overseas. International Valuation Standard 200 (IVS 200) addresses the valuation of businesses and business interests.

Further guidance issued by the IVSC is discussed in paragraphs **18.22**, **18.23**, **20.03** and **21.06**.

2.16 Royal Institution of Chartered Surveyors (RICS)

The valuation of businesses and business interests is covered by the RICS VPGA 3 and adopts the International Glossary of Valuation Terms. It does not deal with the valuation of intangible assets dealt with in VPGA 6. It is necessary as with all valuations, to determine what precisely is to be valued and this should be recorded, as should any assumptions made, and the purpose of the valuation and the basis of value, such as market value or fair value.

Individual assets to be valued which are capable of being independently transferred should, where possible, be valued of their respective market values not as an apportionment of the value of the entire business.

The ownership interest to be valued must be identified, be it the entire business or a part or shares therein and whether it is a legal or beneficial interest and whether a break-up or liquidation basis is appropriate. Ownership interests are equally contained in 'legally binding documents such as articles of association, articles of incorporation, business memoranda, bye-laws, partnership articles or other agreements and shareholders agreements'. These 'may contain transfer restrictions and may state the basis of valuation'.

The purpose of the valuation needs to be identified in order to determine the appropriate basis of valuation; for example TCGA 1992, ss 272–274 set out the basis of valuation for most taxation purposes. 'Ultimately the business that is to be valued is the one that actually exists or the one that could exist on a commercial basis at the valuation date.' As the value is based on 'the profits that the purchaser might expect to accrue from the ownership, these are generally measured after deduction of the commercial costs of managing the business entity'.

VPGA 3 refers to the information available and the reliance put upon it, after an appropriate valuation investigation. Paragraph 6.2 summarises 'the typical information requirements to assist the valuers in understanding the subject company and/or asset(s)', which could include:

- most recent financial statements, and details of current and prior projections or forecasts;
- description and history of the business or asset, including legal protections;
- information about the business or asset and supporting intellectual property and intangibles (eg marketing and technical know-how, research and development, documentation, design graphics and manuals);
- articles of association, company memorandum (for UK pre-Companies Act 2006 entities), shareholders' agreements, subscription agreements, other collateral agreements;
- precise activities of the business, and its associated companies or subsidiaries;
- class rights of all share and debenture classes (security over assets);
- previous valuation reports;
- product(s) dealt in, supported or extended by the business and intangibles;
- company's market(s) and competition, barriers to entry in such markets, business and marketing plans, due diligence;
- strategic alliances and joint venture details;
- whether contractual arrangements can be assigned or transferred in any *intangible asset* or royalty agreement;
- major customers and suppliers;
- objectives, developments or trends expected in the industry and how these are likely to affect the company or asset;
- accounting policies;
- strengths, weaknesses, opportunities and threats (SWOT) analysis;
- key market factors (eg monopoly or dominant market position, market share);
- major capital expenditure in prospect;
- competitor positions;
- seasonal or cyclical trends;
- technological changes affecting business or asset;
- vulnerability of any source of raw materials or supplier arrangement;
- whether there have been any recent acquisitions or mergers in the sector around the *valuation date*, and the criteria that were applied;
- whether there have been any significant developments or changes to the business since the latest accounting date (eg management information, budgets, forecasts);
- offers to acquire the business, or discussions with banks and other sponsors to go public;

- management of research and development (eg non-disclosure agreements, subcontractors, training and incentives).

VPGA 3 then summarises four distinct approaches in the valuation of shares and businesses as 'the market approach (sometimes known as the direct market comparison approach), the income approach, the cost approach and the asset based approach'. It then explains what is involved in each method.

VPGA 3 section 8 sets out the likely contents of a valuation report as:

- introduction;
- purpose and basis of value;
- subject of valuation;
- description and history of the business;
- management and personnel;
- accounting and accounting policies;
- financial statements analysis;
- business and marketing plan analysis, and prospects;
- search results for comparables and comparative transactions;
- industry in which the business operates, economic environment, yields and risk assessment;
- valuation methods and conclusion;
- caveats, disclaimers and limitations.

Focus

See **Appendix E** for RICS Red Book VPGA 3, 4 and 6.

Chapter 3

Open market value

Signposts

3.01 Hypothetical sales

In valuing for statutory purposes on an open market value basis it is important to remember that it is a hypothetical sale that must be assumed. This was simply put by Plowman J in the estate duty case of *Re Lynall, Lynall v IRC* (1971) 47 TC 375 at 377:

> 'It is common ground that the shares must be valued on the basis of a hypothetical sale on 21 May 1962 in a hypothetical open market between a hypothetical willing vendor (who would not necessarily be a director) and a hypothetical willing purchaser on the hypothesis that no one is excluded from buying and that the purchaser would be registered as the holder of his shares but would then hold them subject to the articles of association of the company, including the restrictions on transfer …'

In other words the hypothetical willing purchaser buys in the open market but should he ever need to sell, will sell in the restricted market allowed by the articles. This requirement of selling in the restricted market will usually be a depreciatory factor in a valuation.

Although, in *Re Lynall* [1968] 3 All ER 322, Plowman J referred to 'a hypothetical open market', it is generally accepted that the sale 'should be assumed to take place in the real world' (per Peter Gibson LJ in *Walton v IRC* [1996] 1 EGLR 159). *Walton* concerned the value to a partnership of the agricultural tenancy it held. It was argued for the Revenue that the value should take account of the attitude of a *hypothetical* landlord who might be interested in buying out the tenants. The court disagreed. Evidence of the desires and intentions of the actual landlord had to be taken into account. Lawton LJ's dicta in *Trocette Property Co Ltd v GLC* (1974) 28 P & CR 408 at 420 were quoted with approval:

> 'It is important that this statutory world of make-believe should be kept as near as possible to reality. No assumption of any kind should be made unless provided for by statute or decided cases.'

3.02 Transferee to stand in transferor's shoes – restrictions on transfer

One of the assumptions to be made is that the hypothetical purchaser steps into the shoes of the hypothetical vendor and holds the shares subject to the memorandum and articles of the company and any restrictions contained therein. This principle was first clarified in the judgment of Chief Barron Palles in *A-G v Jameson* [1904] 2 IR 644 at 683. The hypothetical sale and purchase must:

> 'be a sale of the property which the deceased had in the shares at the time of his death, that is of the entire legal and equitable interest therein, of that interest by virtue of which the deceased had been, and had been entitled to be, "a member" of the company in respect of such shares; a sale by virtue of which the purchaser thereat would have been entitled to have had that which he had bought vested in him in the same manner as it had been vested in the deceased, and consequently under which he would be entitled to be registered as a member of the company in respect of those shares.'

Later at 689 he proceeded:

> 'And upon this assumption, which is the supposition the statute directs us to make, we must exclude the consideration of such provisions in the articles of association as would prevent a purchaser at the sale from becoming a member of the company, registered as such in respect of the shares purchased by him at such supposed sale. If we do not, we do not give effect to the assumption that the statute coerces us to make.'

These passages were quoted with approval by Lord Blanesburgh in *Re Crossman* and *Re Paulin* (1936) 15 ATC 94 at 108 and 109. His Lordship also stated at 108:

> 'And, next, if the commissioners' notional sale is to be a sale of the entire share just as it belonged to the deceased immediately before his death, then registration of the share in the name of the notional purchaser must also be offered.'

In the Court of Appeal (1934) 13 ATC 326 at 338 Romer LJ had stated:

> 'It is obvious that for the purpose of ascertaining the principal value of property passing on the death in the manner prescribed by s 7(5) of the Finance Act 1894, the Commissioners must assume that the property can be transferred to the hypothetical purchaser.'

The hypothetical nature of the deemed sale in the open market is emphasised by Danckwerts J in the estate duty case of *Re Holt* (1953) 32 ATC 402 at 403:

> 'The principles on which the value of shares in a private company are to be valued for the purpose of estate duty have been settled by the House of Lords in the case of *IRC v Crossman* [1937] AC 26, 15 ATC 94.
>
> The House of Lords decided in that case (by a majority of three to two) that the fact that a shareholder by the articles of a company may be compelled to sell his shares at the "fair value" ascertained in accordance with the articles, and that by the articles the directors may have power to refuse to register a transfer, must be ignored; but none the less it must be assumed that a purchaser will be bound by the company's articles once he is upon the register of members. The result is that I must enter into a dim world peopled by the indeterminate spirits of fictitious or unborn sales. It is necessary to assume the prophetic vision of a prospective purchaser at the moment of the death of the deceased, and firmly to reject the wisdom which might be provided by the knowledge of subsequent events.'

This judgment was reconsidered and unanimously approved in *Re Lynall, Lynall v IRC* (1971) 47 TC 375 at 405, 408, 412, 413 and 415.

The principle that restrictions on transfer are disregarded for the purposes of assuming a hypothetical sale whilst still taking account in the resultant valuation of the same restrictions continuing in the hands of the purchaser (often referred to as the *Crossman* principle) has been extended to valuations of interests other than shares in unquoted companies. In *Baird's Executors v IRC* 1991 SLT (Lands Tr) 9, concerning an agricultural tenancy that could not be transferred without the landlord's consent, it was assumed for the purposes of the valuation that a sale could take place but the purchaser would hold the tenancy subject to the landlord's veto. *Alexander v IRC* [1991] 2 EGLR 179, CA, concerned the value for capital transfer tax purposes of a leasehold interest in a former council flat that could not be sold within five years of the purchase from the council without a repayment of part of the discount obtained on that occasion. The deceased died within a year of his purchase and his interest was valued on the basis that a sale could take place in the open market but the hypothetical purchaser would be subject to a repayment of part of the discount on any subsequent sale within the five-year period.

Focus

The fundamental point is that in a tax analysis, the transferee is deemed to have exactly what the transferor had.

3.03 Shareholders' agreements

The relationship between the shareholders of a company may also be governed by a shareholders' agreement that stands alongside the company's articles of association. The effect of such an agreement has not been considered in any of the decided cases on valuation for fiscal purposes but the House of Lords in *Russell v Northern Bank Development Corpn Ltd* [1992] 1 WLR 588, when upholding the validity of a shareholders' agreement, decided that the agreement was nevertheless separate and distinct from the company's articles. It did not have the same contractual effect as CA 2006, s 33 (CA 1985, s 14), under which the memorandum and articles bind the company and its members to the same extent as if they were covenants on the part of the company and of each member. The obligations created by the shareholders' agreement were personal to the signatories and would not be binding on the transferee from a party to it, or upon new shareholders. This would suggest that in determining open market value for tax purposes the hypothetical purchaser that has to be imagined could not be said to hold the shares subject to the shareholders' agreement.

The authors take the view, nevertheless, that if the agreement is signed by all shareholders and states that it will bind transferees from the signatories there is a good case for the argument that any new shareholder would be bound by the agreement. The hypothetical purchaser would be no exception. The precise terms of the agreement will of course be crucial.

Harris v Kent & Another [2007] EWHC 463 (Ch) was a case concerning breach of trust arising from an oral agreement under which Mr and Mrs Kent held shares as nominees for Mr Harris.

A breach of trust occurred when the Kent's sold the shares as part of a reconstruction prior to flotation in July 1999. Under the terms of the flotation the founder shareholders were prohibited from disposing of their shares for a period of 12 months. Mr Harris called Mr Keith Eamer, a director in the Share and Business Valuation Department of BDO Stoy Hayward LLP and co-author of Eastaway, Booth & Eamer on *Practical Share Valuation* (4th edition).

> 'In paragraph 9.2.3 of his report Mr Eamer valued the relevant shareholding in Plc as at late August/early September 1999 by beginning with the flotation price of 50p per share, applying a 10% discount for lack of certainty and then a 10% discount for the size of the holding necessitating in his opinion an orderly disposal over a number of months so as to avoid disrupting the market. His value per share was therefore 40.5p which produced a value for the relevant shares of £715,756.50.
>
> In his evidence in chief he said that information obtained only after writing his report demonstrated that because trading in the shares started on 1 September rather than 9 September as he had originally believed there should be no discount for the lack of certainty as to whether the flotation was to go ahead. Since however he had at the same time learnt of the one year restriction on the sale of founders' shares he applied an identical 10% discount for that reason so that his valuation remained unchanged.
>
> The judge held, on the basis of *Target v Redferns* [1995] 3 All ER 785, that "the loss caused by the Kent's breach of trust was therefore that Mr Harris's trustee in bankruptcy (whose claim is being sued upon in this action by way of assignment) was deprived of the opportunity to realise the shares in Plc by then held by the Keats as constructive trustees by way of an orderly sale in the market commencing, but not necessarily concluding, on 19 July 2000. The question what would have been obtained upon such an orderly sale is a matter for expert evidence …"
>
> It remains for me to consider whether the application of the basic equitable principle enshrined in *Target v Redferns* in the manner which I have set out above,

produces any different figure as the true measure of equitable compensation. Mr Eamer valued the same shares in Plc as at 27 November 2000 at £795,285. This was based upon two substantial sales in the market on that date which coincided with a further placing on Ofex of 1,100,000 new shares. Both the sale and the placing were at 50p per share. Mr Eamer applied simply the same large holding discount of 10% since the Kent's were by that stage freed of the one year moratorium on sale. The valuation was not successfully challenged in cross-examination or contradicted by any competing valuation by Mr Platts and I accept it.

My analysis of the correct approach to the application of the basic equitable principle requires the hypothetical assumption that Mr Harris's trustee in bankruptcy would have sought to realise the shares once freed from the one year moratorium i.e. starting in or about July 2000. It seems to me to follow that a prudent realisation starting on that date would have been unlikely to yield less than the value attributed by Mr Eamer to the shares as at 27 November 2000 and I therefore conclude that the sum of £795,285 is the correct measure of compensation derived from the application of the basic equitable principal as the closest reflection of the loss caused by the Kent's breach of trust valued for the purpose of the running of interest as at 19 July 2000.'

3.04 Legal fiction

The open market value for fiscal purposes is a statutory fiction which ignores the impossibility of an actual sale. In the words of Lord Morris of Borth-y-Gest in the estate duty case of *Duke of Buccleuch v IRC* [1967] 1 AC 506 at 535:

'The value of any property must be estimated to be the price which, in the opinion of the Commissioners, the property would fetch if sold in the open market at the time of the death of the deceased. "At the time of the death" must not be paraphrased or altered so as to read "within a reasonably short time of the death". It follows from this that the section is envisaging a hypothetical sale at the time of the death. This is quite inconsistent with the notion that the value of a piece of property is to be estimated by postulating that preparations for an actual sale would be commenced at but after the time of death and that a sale would follow after such preparation. This is not what the section, which is in effect a valuation section, envisages. The section prescribes the criterion for valuation.

The case stated contains a summary of some of the evidence given before the Lands Tribunal. There was evidence to the effect that, with an estate of the size of the Hardwick estate containing as it did some 20,000 acres, it would in practice take several years to effect the sale of it by selling 532 separate units. There was evidence that if it were desired to sell the whole estate within a period of about a year the only way in which in practice this could be achieved would be (after separating a few easily disposable units) to sell the main part of the property as a whole with the result that the only purchaser would be one of a limited class of investors or speculators. Such a person would only pay a sum which would be some 20% less than the aggregate amount which he would consider that he would be able to secure at later dates after arranging for the division of the property into units and after allowing for all the expenses to which he would be put and after allowing for his profit.

In my view the considerations to which this evidence pointed were quite irrelevant. It stands to reason that it would have been impossible in fact to sell the Hardwick estate after the death of the Duke, but on the day of his death, i.e.

> November 26 1950, it would have been impossible there and then to sell it either as a whole or in separate units: equally, it would have been impossible there and then to sell some 46 separate units and to sell the remainder as one entity. Furthermore, it would have been quite impossible there and then to sell either as an entity or as a series of entities all the various estates in England. The total area was just under 119,000 acres or 186 square miles. All this merely serves to emphasise that s 7(5) (of the Finance Act 1894) is a valuation section in that it points to a time by reference to which and a basis upon which values are to be estimated.'

Even the fact that an actual sale would be illegal is ignored in arriving at the open market value. This was confirmed by Eve J in the estate duty case of *Re Aschrott, Clifton v Strauss* [1927] 1 Ch 313 at 322:

> 'At the testator's death part of the property passing under his will consisted of shares saleable in the open market. It is true that, by reason of the subsisting war, he was disqualified, and his executors after his death were disqualified, from transferring the shares, but these shares were only part of the share capital of the several companies in which he was interested, and, in order to ascertain the market price of the shares which were disposed of by his will the broker was bound, I think, to find out at what price some of the shares were being sold and dealt with on the market and to return that as being the correct valuation; it was not open to the valuer to say: "The market price of shares in this particular company is so much, but, in view of the fact that the transferor of these shares is an alien enemy, the market for some of the shares (those which he would be purporting to transfer) would be nil".'

Actual sales around the date of the valuation may be persuasive evidence in arriving at the open market value, see *McNamee v IRC* [1954] IR 214 (at **2.10** above) but are not conclusive as the actual circumstances may differ from those which have to be hypothesised in an open market valuation; see *IRC v Marr's Trustees* (1906) 44 SLR 647 (see **2.11**).

Non-arm's length sales were considered in *IRC v Stenhouse's Trustees* 1993 SLT 243 (see **2.12**).

In *Stephen Marks v HMRC* [2011] UKFTT 221 (TC) the experts disagreed in relation to the provision of information that a prudent prospective purchaser would reasonably require but which was not in fact available:

> 'Miss Hennessey (valuer for HMRC) assumed that it was unlikely that reliable financial information about FCO would have been available to the prospective purchaser on 31 March 1982. Mr Eamer (valuer for Mr Marks) worked on the basis that the purchaser would not be subject to the unsatisfactory state of the accounting information of FCO and assumed that the correct information would be provided. He based this on the statement of the Special Commissioners in *Hawkings-Byass v Sassen* [1996] STC (SCD) 319, 333:
>
> > "Experts and we ourselves alike are at a serious disadvantage through the accounts of GB Cayman being so unreliable. A real potential purchaser in the market on 31 March 1982 would have had the accounts restated."
>
> Mr Gibbon contended that only information actually available was assumed to be provided. We agree with Mr Gibbon. It is inherent in the hypothesis that the information is available to be supplied. The assumption relates to the information that he might reasonably require if he were proposing to purchase the asset from a willing vendor by private treaty and at arm's length. If one assumes a sale by private treaty the purchaser cannot be put in a better position than the seller if

the seller does not have the information that the purchaser reasonably requires. The quotation from *Hawkings-Byass* relates to what a *real* purchaser would have done; the hypothetical purchaser has to take the company in its actual state.'

> **Focus**
>
> It is fundamental that the hypothetical purchaser becomes a member of the company and is thereafter bound by the company's articles.

3.05 Costs

The open market value of shares does not give any allowance for notional expenses on the notional disposal. This was confirmed by Lord Guest in the estate duty case of *Duke of Buccleuch v IRC* [1967] 1 AC 506 at 541, as follows:

> 'The terms of s 7(5) of the Finance Act 1894 have already been quoted. The value of property under this section is to be taken to be at its market value at the date of the death of the deceased. Some things, I think, are reasonably clear. The words "price the property would fetch" in s 7(5) mean that it is not the price which the vendor would have received but what the purchaser would have paid to be put into the shoes of the deceased. This means that the costs of realisation do not form a legitimate deduction in arriving at the valuation. Such a result must follow from the provisions of s 7(3) which allows a deduction of 5% in arriving at the value of foreign property. The doctrine expressio unius exclusio alterius applies and indicates that costs of realisation are not permissible deductions in arriving at the valuation of properties within the United Kingdom.'

On the other hand the purchaser, notional or otherwise, would no doubt take into account his own costs, such as stamp duty and professional valuation fees, in arriving at the price he is prepared to offer.

3.06 Sub-division

It is apparent that the open market value assumes a sale for the best obtainable price, if necessary by sub-dividing the shares. In the estate duty case of the *Earl of Ellesmere v IRC* [1918] 2 KB 735, Sankey J stated at 739:

> 'Now the Act of 1894 says that the value of the property shall be estimated to be the price which it would fetch if sold in the open market. That, in my opinion, does not necessarily mean the price which it would fetch if sold to a single purchaser. There may be many cases where a sale to a single purchaser cannot realise "the price which it would fetch if sold in the open market." Take the case of an owner having property, including a colliery and a draper's shop. It is conceivable that if the colliery and the draper's shop were sold separately the best possible price might be obtained for each. On the other hand a purchaser who was anxious to buy the draper's shop might not wish to be encumbered with the colliery and vice versa, and consequently if the owner insisted upon selling the whole property to one purchaser he would not obtain the market price which the Act contemplates. So, too, with regard to property of the same character situate in different areas. It may well be that if in such a case the vendor insists upon the different parts being all sold to the same person he will not get as good a price as if he allowed

> different persons to buy the portions situate in the different districts. No doubt a sale in one lot of a varied property such as that in the present case may be highly convenient to the vendor. He may want to get the money quickly, he may not care to risk an auction. He may be going abroad, or he may be called up to serve in the Army, and it may be of great importance to him to sell at once. But it does not at all follow that the price which he obtains under such circumstances is 'the price which it would fetch if sold in the open market." What is meant by those words is the best possible price that is obtainable, and what that is, is largely, if not entirely, a question of fact. I can readily conceive cases in which a sale of the whole property in one lot would realise the true market price, but I can equally imagine cases in which it would not.'

This point was again considered in relation to the valuation of land in *Willett v IRC* (1982) 264 Estates Gazette 257. W H Rees, adjudicating in the Lands Tribunal stated:

> 'I should add something with regard to the matter of lotting. Neither valuer had taken it directly into account, but I have done so on the somewhat scanty evidence which was before me. It may be helpful for me to say that in determining the value under s 38 of the Finance Act 1975 ("the price which the property might reasonably be expected to fetch if sold in the open market at that time") it is right to assume that the property is placed on the market in the manner likely to produce the best possible price, so that if an estate might be expected to fetch a better price if sold in a number of lots than if offered as a whole, the valuation must assume that it is suitably lotted. See *Ellesmere v IRC* [1918] 2 KB 735, although that case related to a definition of "principal value" contained in s 7(5) of the Finance Act 1894 – "the price which the property would fetch if sold in the open market at the date of death". I see no substantial difference in the wording of the two relevant sections.'

The requirement to obtain the best possible price must not however be carried to extremes. In the words of Lord Reid in the estate duty case of *Duke of Buccleuch v IRC* [1967] 1 AC 506 at 526:

> 'It is sometimes said that the estate must be supposed to have been realised in such a way that the best possible prices were obtained for its parts. But that cannot be a universal rule. Suppose that the owner of a wholesale business dies possessed of a large quantity of hardware or clothing, or whatever he deals in. It would have been possible by extensive advertising to obtain offers for small lots at something near retail prices. So it would have been possible to realise the stock at much more than wholesale prices. It would not have been reasonable and it would not have been economic, but it would have been possible. Counsel for the respondent did not contend that that would be a proper method of valuation. But that necessarily amounts to an admission that there is no universal rule that the best possible prices at the date of death must be taken.'

Division of a single shareholding into saleable blocks of shares was also considered in *Smyth v IRC* [1941] IR 643, see **3.14** (Adjustments to accounts).

There may be cases where sub-division into easily saleable lots is not practical. In the estate duty case of *Salvesen's Trustees v IRC* (1930) 9 ATC 43 at 45 it was stated by Lord Fleming:

> 'In the course of the proof and also at the hearing attention was directed to Article 12. The terms of that article are very drastic and unusual. It provides for the compulsory retiral from the company of a person holding not more than 10% of the shares of the company and would not therefore apply directly if the whole

> of the testator's shares were transferred to one individual. Nevertheless I am of opinion that this article would have considerable effect in depreciating the value of the shares. Its effect would be to prevent them being sold in lots of less than 10,000 shares. Furthermore a person who was considering what price he ought to offer for the whole of the testator's shareholding would certainly take into account that he could not transfer less than one third of the holding even to one of his own relatives without the transferee being under liability to have his shares transferred compulsorily to the other members of the company at no more than their par value.'

Focus

It is assumed that the deemed transferor takes reasonable and appropriate steps to maximise the value of his assets.

3.07 Consolidation

On the other hand it may be that a better price is obtainable by aggregating shareholdings than by sub-dividing them and the hypothetical sale in the open market can assume a sale of a combined holding of, for example, ordinary and preference shares held by the transferor if this would give rise to a higher price. This is confirmed by Lord Reid's judgment in the estate duty case of *A-G of Ceylon v Mackie* (1952) 31 ATC 435:

> 'In addition to restrictions of a usual character the articles also contained a provision to the effect that holders of not less than nine-tenths of the share capital could at any time call for a transfer of any other shares at a fair value to be fixed by the auditors of the company. It was admitted for the appellant that no purchaser would have paid anything like Rs. 250 per share for the management shares in face of the company's articles unless he could buy at the same time a large block of the preference shares and so have a majority of the votes. But the appellant contends that the respondent must be supposed to have taken the course which would get the largest price for the combined holding of management and preference shares and to have offered for sale together with the management shares the whole or at least the greater part of the preference shares owned by the deceased. In their Lordship's judgment this contention is correct.'

In previous editions of this book the authors have speculated as to whether or not this principle would apply in appropriate circumstances to shares of different companies held by one person, where the combined value of the two shareholdings would be greater than their value in isolation. This speculation was largely answered by the decision of the High Court in *Gray (Executor of Lady Fox dec'd) v IRC* [1994] 38 EG 156. Lady Fox owned the freehold reversion of agricultural land which was let to a partnership in which she had a 92.5% interest. The court held that although the freehold reversion and the partnership interest did not form a 'natural unit' they would nevertheless fetch a greater price if sold together than they would if sold as separate items. That enhanced price constituted the value for capital transfer tax purposes. It is reasonable to suppose that the valuation of the two shareholdings referred to above would be carried out on the same basis for inheritance tax.

HMRC Shares and Assets Valuation, which is a specialist area within HMRC Charities Assets and Residence, has confirmed in an article in Issue 24 of the Tax Bulletin, that the decision in *Gray* relates principally to valuations for inheritance tax purposes and does not necessarily apply to a valuation for capital gains tax purposes, for example. That attitude is to some extent confirmed by the decision in *Henderson (Inspector of Taxes) v Karmel's Executors* [1984] STC 572. The case concerned the valuation of freehold agricultural land tenanted by a company controlled by the taxpayer who owned the freehold. The court decided that the land should be valued without the benefit of vacant possession, as it was thought impossible to assume the procuring of the extinction of the company's tenancy as part of the arrangements preliminary to a sale of the freehold. For the practical implications of their attitude, particularly with regard to valuations for capital gains tax purposes at 31 March 1982, see **18.14**.

In *Stephen Marks v HMRC* [2011] UKFTT 22 (TC) it was held that the consolidation principles, under which the deceased's shareholding of management shares and cumulative preference shares were valued together, which applied for estate duty in *A-G of Ceylon v Mackie* [1952] 31 ATC 435, have no application to capital gains tax. It presumably follows that the similar consolidation for inheritance tax, following *Gray (Executor of Lady Fox dec'd) v IRC* [1994] STC 360 does not apply to capital gains tax either.

The estate concept and the related property rules will often mean that for inheritance tax purposes the combined value of holdings of different classes of share has to be determined (see **10.03**).

> **Focus**
>
> The concept of optimum lotting, which applies for inheritance tax, does not appear to apply for capital gains tax.

3.08 Subsequent events

The valuation must be made at the appropriate date on the basis of the situation at that time and events subsequent to the date of valuation must be ignored.

However, information arising after the date of valuation may help to shed light on the position at that date.

In the estate duty case of *Salvesen's Trustees v IRC* (1930) 9 ATC 43 at 51 Lord Fleming stated:

> 'I quite recognise that the problem I have to deal with must be solved in the light of the information available at or about the time of the testator's death. I think that, however, does not debar me completely from making any reference to the balance sheet at 31 July 1927 which includes a period of nearly three months prior to the testator's death (24 October 1926).'

In *Buckingham v Francis* [1986] 2 BCC 98984 Staughton J remarked:

> 'The Company must be valued in the light of facts that existed at 24 March 1981. (Little or nothing turns on the question whether facts which existed but were not then ascertained or ascertainable should be taken into account.) But regard may

be had to later events for the purpose only of deciding what forecasts for the future could reasonably have been made on 24 March 1981.'

In the estate duty case of *Re Lynall, Lynall v IRC* (1971) 47 TC 375 Plowman J at 383 considered Lord Fleming's judgment in *Salvesen's Trustees v IRC* (1930) 9 ATC 43 and stated:

> 'The facts that he regarded as relevant appear to have been what I have called the published information, particularly the accounts of the company, plus some information as to whether there had been any alteration at the date of death in the position as disclosed by the last published accounts. He permitted himself to look at the accounts for the year in which the death occurred but as this was a document which was not in existence at the date of death he can, I think, have done so only in the context of a check on the profit and dividend forecast which might have been made at the date of death.'

He continued at 385:

> 'I therefore come back to the documents with the admissibility of which I am concerned, and my conclusions are as follows:
>
> (1) The accounts for the year ending 31 July 1962 being post-death documents, are not admissible as evidence of the value of Mrs Lynall's shares at the date of her death, except possibly to the limited extent I have already mentioned.
> (2) The Chairman's speech is a post-death document and is not admissible. In any event in my view it added nothing of any material significance to the 1961 accounts themselves.'

In the cases of *Re Bradberry, National Provincial Bank Ltd v Bradberry*, and *Re Fry, Tasker v Gulliford* [1943] Ch 35 Uthwatt J stated at 44:

> 'It was held by the Court of Appeal that although the moment at which the damages in a case under Lord Campbell's Act are to be fixed is the moment of the death, that did not mean that the court was to shut its eyes to subsequent happenings and that the court could, in assessing damages, inform its mind of circumstances which had arisen since the cause of action accrued and which threw light on the realities of the case.'

Later, at 45, he proceeds:

> 'A principle is to be drawn from these authorities, namely, that where facts are available they are to be preferred to prophecies.'

Events taking place after the date of valuation are however to be ignored in the valuation. In the estate duty case of *Re Holt* (1953) 32 ATC 402 at 410, Danckwerts J stated:

> 'I rule out of consideration the knowledge provided by the passage of time since March 11 1948, that the company's dividend on ordinary shares has not been increased from 5% and that the company has been able to avoid a public issue of ordinary shares by launching an exceedingly successful issue of new preference shares in September 1950.'

In *IRC v Marr's Trustees* (1906) 44 SLR 647 a subsequent sale was ignored (see **2.11**).

In the earlier case of *The Bwllfa and Merthyr Dare Steam Collieries (1891) Ltd v The Pontypridd Waterworks Co* [1903] AC 426, Lord McNaghten was eloquent in his defence of the use of hindsight by an arbitrator determining an amount of compensation payable:

> 'In order to enable him to come to a just and true conclusion it is his duty, I think, to avail himself of all information at hand at the time of making his award which may be laid before him. Why should he listen to conjecture on a matter which has become an accomplished fact? Why should he guess when he can calculate? With the light before him, why should he shut his eyes and grope in the dark?'

In *Garner (Inspector of Taxes) v Pounds Shipowners and Shipbreakers Ltd* [1997] STC 551, Lord McNaghten's words were quoted with approval by Carnwath J when considering for capital gains tax purposes the value, at the date of an option agreement, of the obligation of the grantor of the option to procure the release of some restrictive covenants. The judge adopted the amount actually expended some 20 months after the date of the agreement rather than consider a speculative valuation at the actual date.

Joiner v George and others [2003] BCC 298 was an appeal as to the amount of damages which had been awarded:

> 'equal to the value expressed in money which a 51% shareholding in the English company Unigel Ltd would have had to the claimants on 23 November 1994.'

Expert witnesses in connection with the valuation appealed against were Mr Fisher of Bruce Sutherland & Partners on behalf of Mr and Mrs Joiner and Mr Faull of Hilton Sharpe and Clarke on behalf of Mr George and Mr Robinson.

Sir Christopher Slade, in the Court of Appeal, said (at para 31):

> 'Both experts agreed that in determining a value for the holding it would first be necessary to determine what would have been the value of a 100% holding. The judge rejected the submission by Mr Joiner that the purchasers would have been willing to pay a price above 51% of the value of the entirety. The 51% holding in his view fell to be valued at a straight 51% of the value of 100%.'

Sir Christopher pointed out (at para 38) that:

> 'Though there were differences between their detailed valuations, both the experts, Mr Fisher and Mr Faull had accepted as a norm the basic concept of estimating a figure for maintainable profit and multiplying it by a price-earnings ratio. Mr Faull had described a valuation carried out simply by that process as a capitalised earnings valuation. This was the sole method advocated by Mr Fisher. Mr Faull however referred to an alternative valuation method which he called the adjusted net asset valuation method. This differs from the capitalised earnings valuation method in that the maintainable profit times price earnings formula is used to value not the company as a whole but the goodwill of the business. The net book value, positive or negative of the company's other assets and its liabilities is then added or deducted to arrive at a value of 100% of the shares. Mr Faull favoured the adjusted net asset method for Unigel UK because he took the view that if a balance sheet had been drawn up at the valuation date it would have shown net liabilities rather than net assets.
>
> 39 The judge however did not adopt Mr Faull's view on this point. It took into account a proportion of the license fee of 7 ½% of (turnover) payable by Unigel UK to Unigel HK. At the valuation date, no license agreement existed and, even if one had existed the highest fee which the judge would have considered justifiable would have been 2 ½ per cent. At that level of fee Unigel UK's balance sheet would have shown no or negligible net liabilities. In the circumstances the judge thought it right to adopt the capitalised earnings valuation method.
>
> 40 For this purpose he had to begin by estimating the maintainable profit which fell to be calculated in three stages: (1) Take an item for maintainable revenue,

anticipated as at the valuation date; (2) Deduct the direct cost of sales to arrive at the gross profit; (3) Deduct an appropriate amount for overheads.

41 The experts differed on some of these three components of the calculation. As to the first, Mr Fisher (using the discounted future earnings method) had based his calculation on the level of maintainable revenue on a forecast of future revenues made by Mr Joiner in January 1994 so far as the forecast related to the three years ahead. He had then made deductions from these forecast revenues of three years ahead for direct costs and overheads so as to produce a forecast of future profits. From that last figure he had discounted back at ten per cent per annum to the valuation date, to give his figure of anticipated revenue. Mr Faull on the other hand had derived his figure of anticipated revenue from the actual trading figures for the accounting period which was current at that date, taking the period from the last accounting date, March 31 1994, back to the valuation date and annualising the figure.

The judge preferred Mr Faull's approach to the calculation of revenue, saying this:

> "Mr Faull says that actual figures are better than forecasts, and in any case is something of a sore point with Mr Joiner particularly because the forecasts of future sales which he made in 1994 turned out with hindsight to have been reasonably accurate. However hindsight ought to be excluded ... I accept Mr Faull's view that the actual figures should be preferred to a forecast."

44 As to the deduction for overheads, the third element in the calculation of maintainable profit, the judge recorded that there was a marked difference between Mr Faull and Mr Fisher. Mr Fisher based his provision for the overheads required to run the business on the evidence of Mr Bury, a friend and former colleague of Mr Joiner. Mr Faull had taken the actual overheads in the accounts for the accounting period current at the valuation date with certain adjustments. Mr Fisher and Mr Joiner suggested that a number of expenses envisaged by Mr Faull were too high, in particular the remuneration for directors and employees and for travel and subsistence. The judge, however, ultimately accepted Mr Faull's figure for overheads...'.

46 The judge said that the next major stage in the valuation exercise was to select a price-earnings ratio by which to multiply the post-tax maintainable profit. It was more or less common ground for this purpose that the basic approach was to take an average price-earnings ratio from the price-earnings ratio applicable to comparable quoted companies and then to discount it to reflect the differences between such quoted companies and a company like Unigel UK. However, the two experts differed as to the kinds of quoted companies to take as comparable and also to the extent to which the average quoted price earnings ratios should be discounted.

47 The judge agreed with Mr Fisher's view that having regard to the nature of the business at Unigel UK quoted companies in the general manufacturing and chemical sector should be taken as comparables in preference to Mr Faull's view that the comparables should be taken to be the chemicals and telecommunications sectors. Mr Fisher took the average price earnings ratio of companies in his chosen sectors at the valuation date and then took the average of those two averages a process which gave him a ratio of 25.05. The judge accepted and applied this figure of 25.05. However, he thought that the appropriate discount to apply to it was 75% as suggested by Mr Faull rather than 60% as suggested by Mr Fisher, to reflect the unquoted status of Unigel UK and all the other factors which would tend towards caution for the company as it existed at the valuation date.

48 Accordingly the judge concluded that if the applicable price earning ratio was to be derived from the average of two quoted sectors less the discount he would take 25.05 less the discount of 75%. This rounded up to the nearest half produced a figure of 6.5% which he adopted.

49 The conclusion of the judge's exercise involved a simple calculation which he summarised as follows.

> "The post tax maintainable profit must be multiplied by the selected price-earnings ratio to give a value for 100% of the shares of the company. So £38,887 is multiplied by 6.5 producing £252,766 per 100%. I have already said that, to scale this down to a value for Mr and Mrs Joiner's 51% interest I will simply take 51% of it. Therefore I value their interest at £128,910 which I rounded up to £129,000."'

Mr Joiner appealed against this determination on a number of grounds. Those of general application included the relevance of hindsight. Sir Christopher stated (at para 68):

> 'Mr Joiner while accepting that the basic rule in valuing shares in a company is to reject evidence of events which occurred after the valuation date (see *Holt v IR Commissioners* [1953] 2 All ER 1499) relied on certain cases in which the courts have held that it was legitimate to look at later events for the purpose of the particular valuation exercises they were called on to perform. He placed particular reliance on the decision of the House of Lords in *Bwllfa and Merthyr Dare Steam Collieries (1891) Ltd v Pontypridd Waterworks Co* [1903] AC 426.'

The Court of Appeal held that the *Bwllfa* decision was of no assistance to the appellant as the damages fell to be assessed by reference to a fixed date. They also considered *Phillips v Brewin Dolphin Bell Lawrie Ltd* [2001] BCC 864 was of no assistance. However it was stated (at para 72):

> 'In *Buckingham v Francis* [1986] 2 BCC 98984 Staughton J in valuing the shares in a company at a fixed date reiterated the basic rule in saying "the company must be valued in the light of the facts that existed on 24 March 1981" but added "regard may be had to later events for the purpose only of deciding what forecasts for the future could reasonably have been made on March 24 1981. This addition was perhaps the judicial dictum most helpful to Mr Joiner. He relied on it in support of his submission that regard might be had to the post November 1994 sales figures for the purpose of demonstrating that his forecast of sales made in January 1994 had been fairly accurate".
>
> 73 The latter case however is certainly not authority for the proposition that forecasts a future trading made before the valuation date should be preferred to the actual trading results of the company for its most recent period of trading merely because in the event such forecasts happened to tally reasonably well with the company's subsequent trading results. None of the authorities on which Mr Joiner relies support the proposition that for the purpose of valuing shares in a company at a fixed date its trading results after the valuation date should be preferred to its trading results actually known at the valuation date.'

Mr Joiner later on (at para 89) made the point that:

> 'On the one hand the judge disclaimed the use of hindsight. On the other hand he invoked hindsight at least to the extent that he took into the reckoning the overheads of Unigel UK incurred during the period from the valuation date up to March 31 1995.

90 I do not think there is any substance in this point. Any splitting up of the overheads for the year to March 1995 would inevitably have been a quite arbitrary and artificial operation. Furthermore looking at the matter realistically the appellants and the respondents in negotiating a sale and purchase as at the asset valuation date in November 1994 would not in practice have been likely to conclude their negotiations until the overheads for the whole year had been ascertainable.'

It is interesting to speculate whether it can be inferred from this comment that a limited and judicious use of hindsight may be appropriate in some circumstances.

Perhaps Sir Christopher Slade's final comments should be borne in mind.

'101 In conclusion I would make these general observations. The process of valuation of a shareholding in a case such as this cannot be an exact science. Though it ultimately involves a finding of fact elements leading up to such finding may well invoke points on which different minds approaching the matter judicially could quite properly take different views – in other words points to which there cannot be said to be exclusively one correct answer. It could be that on some of the conclusions of fact reached by the judge in his judgement on valuation other minds would have taken a different view. A figure substantially higher or lower than £129,000 might have been the result.'

In *Marks v Sherred* [2004] WTLR 1251, the Special Commissioner was required to determine the value of the taxpayer's shares in Ross Marks Ltd (RML) at 31 March 1982 for rebasing in connection with subsequent disposals. On 31 March 1982 Ross Marks owned 66% of the shares in RML, his mother and brother owned a further 30% and the general manager of the company the remaining 4%. The Commissioner stated

'I was asked to take no account of any possible premium or discount which might, by reason of the taxpayer's holding of the controlling shareholding on the one hand or his having to take into consideration the interests of minority shareholders on the other hand, but instead to value the entire company and to determine the value of the taxpayer's shares as 66% of the resulting figure.'

Presumably this had already been agreed between the taxpayer and HMRC, although it is not immediately apparent why a discount was not considered appropriate. The company was unquoted and therefore the provisions of TCGA 1992, ss 272 and 273 applied.

'In 1982 RML did not have management accounts or any equivalent nor did it undertake budgeting or forecasting. Properly audited annual accounts were produced in the usual way after the year end but as each year proceeded the taxpayer relied on information provided informally to him by the company's bookkeeper on the company's bank statements and on his own feel for how the business was progressing. I do not find it surprising nor a matter for adverse comment that a comparatively small company controlled on a day to day basis by its majority shareholder was run at that time in such an informal manner.

The experts agreed that the appropriate method of valuing the company was the capitalised earnings approach which requires the maintainable earnings of the business to be identified and then multiplied by an appropriate factor. The disagreement between them about the multiplier was relatively modest, Mr Ruse (for HMRC) maintained that 10 was appropriate while Miss Mullen (for the taxpayer) suggested 11 but there was a much greater difference between them about the level of the company's maintainable earnings.'

Counsel for the taxpayer argued that a prospective purchaser would not have available the audited accounts for the year end to 31 March 1982 and that it was unreasonable to base any calculations on the outcome for the year.

> 'Mr Ruse's point, with which I entirely agree was, that the actual figures for 1982 were the best available guide to what the hypothetical purchaser making proper enquiries would have been able to discover from the available information. I accept the validity of the argument advanced by Michael Geddon, counsel for the respondent that Miss Mullen's approach of largely ignoring what actually happened during the course of the year to 31 March 1982 cannot be right.'

After considering a number of factors the Commissioner concluded that:

> 'a fair figure for the net maintainable pre-tax annual profit of the business at 31 March 1982 is £115,000. That figure takes into account the better results of the history of growth to March 1981, the poor results for the year to March 1982, the cost of taking protective measures, Mr Ruse's proposed adjustment of the overheads and the comparatively high level of stock held by RML at 31 March 1982. A calculation of the effective rate of corporation tax which the company actually suffered is no longer possible, as I have mentioned Mr Ruse suggested 15% but on the assumption that – pre-tax profits were £100,000; Miss Mullen did not make any formal suggestion although her figures assume 22%. The effective rate of tax for the three years to March 1982 was 16.6%. It seems to me that adopting a 15% rate is likely to be excessively generous to the taxpayer and I propose to adopt the average rate of 16.6%. Net after tax earnings are therefore £95,910 per year.'

The Special Commissioner also preferred Mr Ruse's suggested multiplier of ten and therefore concluded that the value of the entire company at 31 March 1982 was £959,100 and that the value of the taxpayer's shareholding on the agreed pro rata basis was £633,006.

Billows v Hammond [2000] STC (SCD) 430 is a case where the taxpayer made gifts of 678 shares out of 1000 in Billows Ltd to his children in December 1986 and alleged that the shares were valueless. HMRC however estimated the company's future maintainable profit before tax as at 15 December 1986 as £78,000 to which was applied a price earnings ratio of 5 to produce a value for the company of £390,000. From this was deducted £25,000 additional unquantified tax liabilities arising from an HMRC investigation into the company, reducing the figure to £365 a share to which was applied a discount of 15% to take account of the fact that the number of shares transferred amounted to slightly less than a 70% holding. HMRC's final valuation therefore became £310.25 per share. The Revenue had previously offered a value of £100,000 for the whole company at April 1986 in respect of transfers of 20 shares each to Mr Billows' two children.

The Special Commissioner stated:

> 'Although it is true that turnover and gross profits were increasing throughout the period from 1984 to 1987 it seems to me incredible that the company's value should almost quadruple in a period of 8 months. I am dealing here with a private company with unquoted shares and factors such as a possible takeover which might produce a very rapid rise in the share value of the public limited company do not arise. The suggested steep rise in the company's value seems particularly unlikely bearing in mind the two substantial problems highlighted by the taxpayer but largely discounted by Mr Vassie (witness for HMRC). First there is the problem of the Revenue investigation of the company which was

nearing its conclusion in December 1986 only three months or so before the first hearing before the Commissioners. Secondly there is the accepted fact that at the relevant time towards the end of 1986 a rapid change was occurring in the company's trade and manufacturing processes. Film Montage at that time was a dying art which was rapidly being replaced by digital electronic equipment and the company's plate punch market was also disappearing. With the benefit of hindsight it has become apparent that the company has successfully adapted to the new electronic age but the hypothetical purchaser would not be able to be certain of such success as at December 1986.'

The Commissioner therefore valued the shares at £195 per share but without expanding further on the methodology used to arrive at this figure.

Re a Company (No 002708 of 1989) ex parte W and another; Re a Company (No 004247 of 1989) ex parte Br and Another (1990) Times, 17 March and *Re ESC Publishing Ltd* [1990] BCC 335 concern two cross petitions under CA 1985, s 459 (CA 2006, s 994), which were substantially compromised whereby the shares of W and B the petitioners in one petition were to be purchased by Br, one the two petitioners in the other cross petition. The price per share was to be agreed and determined by an independent valuer in accordance with article 7(c) of the articles of association of the company. The articles stated that 'the prescribed price' shall be a price agreed between the transferring member and all other members or failing such agreement shall be such price as an independent valuer acting as an expert shall nominate for each share. In arriving at the prescribed price per share, no account shall be taken of the number of shares being sold or the effect that the sale may have on control of the company or the fact that the transferring member (if the sale shares are all his shares) may cease to have an interest in the company or of the existence, actual or potential of an offer of a non-member unless that offer is made to all members simultaneously on the same terms.

The judge stated:

> 'As appears from a reading of that paragraph, this article 7 is concerned with members' rights of pre-emption over shares in a private company in a fairly common manner. Broadly the scheme is that a member who wishes to dispose of his shares has to give a transfer notice to the company. The transfer notice constitutes the Board of the company his agent for the sale of the shares, there then follows the process which I have read in article 7(c) of arriving at the prescribed price and thereafter the Board is required to offer the shares which are being disposed of to other members at the prescribed price.
>
> The issue which has arisen is whether the terms of a letter, which it is agreed was received by the recipients after the acceptance fax was sent on 21 February 1990, is material which is admissible before the independent valuer.'

It was held in these circumstances that the valuation date was the date of acceptance. Knox J held on the basis of *Bwillfa & Merthyr Dare Steam Collieries (1891) Ltd v Pontypridd Waterworks Co* [1903] AC 426 and *Segama NV v Penny Le Roy Ltd* (1983) 269 EG 322 that on a sale at a valuation, changes in market price after the valuation date should not be taken into account:

> 'What is far more difficult is drawing the line between the occurrence of contingencies such as a change in the market which are not admissible if they occur after the valuation date, on the one hand, and evidence of a fact or event later in point of time than the valuation date which enables the valuer to assess a state of affairs which actually existed at the valuation date.

> Mr Brisby (of Counsel) argued that … an offer was a change in the market and not a piece of evidence which was a guide to what the market at the valuation date was. It seems to me that this is so only if one assumes that value resides solely in existing transactions and offers. This is not a necessary or accurate assumption. What is being sought is the value of a parcel of shares. Value is in effect what a purchaser will pay. Evidence of an offer one day after the date for valuation seems to me potentially to be evidence of the existence of a bidder on the date of valuation who was just plucking up his courage to bid what he did in fact bid the next day. I say potentially because an offer is only an offer or the more so an offer subject to contract. I am not concerned with those considerations, for which a valuer can and should make such discount as appeared to him to be appropriate. If it was shown that the offer was not genuine no doubt the offer would fall to be wholly ignored but on the question whether it should be regarded as totally inadmissible because it is a post valuation event I prefer what may perhaps be a realist rather than a purist view and do not consider that the valuer should be required to ignore it all together.'

> **Focus**
>
> The proper date for a valuation depends on the circumstances.

3.09 Value fixed by the articles of association

One of the most important estate duty cases on the principles of valuation for fiscal purposes is that of *A-G v Jameson* [1904] 2 IR 644 in the High Court and [1905] 2 IR 218 in the Court of Appeal. This case held that it was to be assumed that the hypothetical purchaser of the shares was to be registered as shareholder in the place of the deemed vendor and thereafter to hold the shares in accordance with the articles.

Article 6 of the company stated:

> 'A share may be transferred or bequeathed to any person who is already a member, but no share shall, save as hereinafter provided, be transferred to a person who is not a member, so long as any member is willing to purchase the same at the fair value.'

Article 9 stated:

> 'The fair value of a share shall be £100, or such other sum as shall from time to time be fixed as the "fair value" by resolution of the company in general meeting.'

The fundamental point was whether the value of 750 shares held at death was, for the purposes of estate duty, necessarily the same as the fair value fixed by the articles of association.

Lord Ashbourne in judgment in the Court of Appeal at 224 stated:

> 'The Finance Act of 1894 enacts that estate duty be levied and paid upon the principal value of all property which passes on the death of any person dying after 1894, (s 1) of which the deceased was competent to dispose (ss 2 and 6) and that the principal value is to be estimated to be the price which, in the opinion of the Commissioners, such property would fetch if sold in the open market at the time of the death of the deceased (s 7(5)).

What is the meaning of this enactment, as sought to be applied to Henry Jameson's 750 shares? The court has no power to ascertain the principal value. The Commissioners have formed no estimate, and expressed no opinion. The Attorney General has filed the information practically to obtain a declaration that the estimate of the defendants is wrong, that the payment already made is insufficient, and that the "fair value" is to be disregarded, and this for the guidance of the Commissioners who have not as yet performed their statutory duty. The course taken by the Crown compels us to consider with care in reference to the 750 shares what passed on the death of Henry Jameson. The only possible answer that can, in my opinion, be given is – the entire property in the shares, so far as he was competent to dispose of them at the time of his death. He was only competent under and pursuant to the articles of association. These articles defined and circumscribed his powers. At the time of his death he was not competent to dispose of the shares without complying with those articles. The articles also prescribed the position of his executors in reference to his shares. Can it for a moment be suggested that the shares were one thing in the hands of Henry Jameson, and something else in the hands of his executors? Surely there must be the same subject matter before and after death.

This was a private company framed with all the pride of success by the Jameson family. Their absolute bona fides is admitted. The idea of *doing* the Revenue or creditors never crossed the minds of the founders. If there was any idea of fraud the court would be strong enough to refuse to be bound by the articles, as in the cases of *Wilson v Greenwood* (1818) 1 Swan 471 and *Collins v Barker* [1893] 1 Ch 578. The general scope of the articles was that there should be in the company, if it were so desired, none but members of the Jameson family. The articles were frankly directed to this end.

The answer to this claimed obligation made by the Crown is that some of the articles are invalid and void. But which of the articles are invalid, and why? The Crown does not come to close quarters on the question. The case was not made in the information. There is no repugnancy in the articles. The owners are given a regulated and controlled freedom of disposition. The suggestion of perpetuity was only faintly hinted at. The bankruptcy contention was indeed suggested by the Attorney General but was met by a convincing argument on the articles of association, and the facts of the case. The defendants also relied on *Borland's Case* [1901] 1 Ch 279, which, however, was far stronger than the present and I do not deem it necessary to discuss this bankruptcy point. I see nothing to induce me to set aside or disparage any of the articles in the Jameson Company on any of the grounds put forward by the Crown. Therefore, I take the case to be that the executor took on his death the same subject matter which Henry Jameson owned in his lifetime, and was at his death competent to dispose of, ie the 750 shares in the Jameson Company, subject to and controlled by its articles of association. To hold otherwise would be to say that the shares were more valuable in the hands of his executors than in the hands of Henry Jameson that he was fettered while they were free – that the articles bound him and could not control them. He deliberately became a shareholder in this family company with its articles and its contracts, and his shares cannot be considered apart from this contractual position. The share cannot be split up and considered apart from its contractual incidents. The articles are part and parcel of the share, and not collateral and separable. He must be assumed to have absolutely bound himself to obey and conform to the articles.

I am unable to see that the provisions as to pre-emption and "fair value" can be ignored and put aside as separate. They must be faced and dealt with as reasonable methods honestly adopted by this company for the safeguarding of the continuance of the Jameson interest in this Jameson Company.

The 9th article gave power to vary the "fair price" from time to time, and that it has not been varied may have been the considered action of the shareholders having regard to the uncertainties of commerce, and the common interest of the shareholders. The defendants resolutely contend, having regard to the circumstances and the facts, and the articles, that the "fair value" is really the soundest way to gauge the price as if the share were sold in the open market.

But these observations are really preliminary to considering the effect of the Finance Act 1894. How can such share in such a company with such articles have their value estimated at the price which, in the opinion of the Commissioners, such property would fetch if sold in the open market? An actual sale in open market is out of the question. A feat of imagination has to be performed. Two suggestions have been put forward in argument. The Attorney General says that the Commissioners should assume an unfettered sale in the open market to the highest bidder, who would be free from the clogs on alienation contained in the articles. The defendants on the other hand contend that the Finance Act is satisfied by taking the par or "fair value" of £100 per share as the Capital value which the Commissioners would estimate as the price which the shares would fetch if sold in the open market. Each side rushes into an indefensible extreme. The argument of the Attorney General, which seeks to brush aside the articles and to vest in the executors a property which Henry Jameson never possessed, would ascribe to the Finance Act the power of making a new subject-matter. The argument of the defendants clings desperately to the articles, and gives really no adequate significance to the words of the Act requiring the Commissioners to estimate the price which the shares would fetch in the open market. The solution lies between the two. The Attorney General must give more weight to the articles and the defendants to the statute. It requires no tremendous imagination to conceive what a purchaser would give in the open market for Henry Jameson's shares, as Henry Jameson himself held them at his death – for the right to stand in his shoes. That is, he held shares earning 20% interest with power of disposition to sons and brothers subject to, but himself possessed of the power of pre-emption; and if that power of pre-emption was not used against him – a most improbable event indeed – he might sell, as he best could at any price, and to any person he could. This, although not so valuable as owning shares absolutely free and unfettered in power of disposition, was obviously much more valuable than the "fair value" of the articles. I am not a valuer or a Commissioner, but I do not see any overwhelming difficulty in estimating the price which such valuable shares would fetch if sold in the open market.'

FitzGibbon LJ at 231 picked up the point that pre-emption clauses can be both appreciatory and depreciatory:

'The right of pre-emption against Henry Jameson's shares in certain events, if legal, is a depreciating incident, but the right of Henry Jameson, or of any person "standing in his shoes," to exercise the corresponding right of pre-emption against the other shares of the company in the like events, is an appreciating incident, of Henry Jameson's property, which, in my opinion, is to be valued as a whole.'

FitzGibbon LJ further stated:

'The Commissioners, when fixing the value of the property for taxation at the price which, in their opinion, it would fetch in the open market, cannot estimate that price on an assumption that the purchaser was to get, and consequently would be willing to pay for what neither Henry Jameson nor any other shareholder past, present or future, in this company ever had or can have, viz

> shares in John Jameson & Co Ltd, freely transferable to any person whomsoever, as distinguished from shares freely transferable only to existing members of the company or to their sons or brothers, and liable to serious restrictions and conditions upon transfer to others.'

Walker LJ at 235 stated:

> 'I think the test of value, under s 7, is what the shares would fetch if sold in "open market" – an hypothetical "open market", upon the terms that the purchaser would be entitled to be registered in respect of the shares but would himself thereafter hold them subject to the provisions of the articles of association, including those relating to the alienation and transfer of them, and that this price is not limited to the "fair value".'

The Court of Appeal in the *Jameson* case supported the dissenting High Court judgment of Palles CB who stated at 689:

> 'The question is, "What passed, or is deemed to have passed?" And on everything within that description duty is payable. At the moment of his death the testator had in him property producing £15,000 a year. Upon his death that property necessarily ceased to be in him, and passed to some person or persons. By what machinery it passed I care not. What value the parties put upon it in their dealings inter se I care not. I hold that duty must be paid on the entire of it, irrespective of these accidental circumstances, and must be paid upon its value, as ascertained in accordance with the Act.
>
> This brings me again to the valuation provisions. By s 7(5), the "principal value of any property shall be the price at which, in the opinion of the Commissioners, such property would fetch if sold in the open market at the time of death of the deceased." I hold, as I have already said, that "such property" there includes the entire property in the shares which were vested in the deceased at the moment of his death; and that, for the purpose of ascertaining the value the question is not whether it is capable of being sold in the open market. If the articles of association are valid, these shares are not saleable in the open market; but under sub-s (5) we are bound to assume that they are capable of being so sold, because the valuation is to be based not upon an actual, but upon a supposed sale, and that supposed sale one in the open market. The question is, assuming that they were capable of being sold in the open market, what would they fetch on such sale? And upon this supposition, which is the supposition the statute directs us to make, we must exclude the consideration of such provisions in the articles of association as would prevent a purchaser at the sale from becoming a member of the company, registered as such in respect of the shares purchased by him at such supposed sale. If we do not we do not give effect to the assumption the statute coerces us to make.'

See **Chapter 4** for a discussion of the meaning of 'fair value' in any particular context.

Focus

A deemed transfer takes place at market value on the basis that the transferee acquires good title to the shares, but the deemed transferee holds the shares subject to any restrictions in the articles of association.

3.10 Restrictions on transfer

Restrictions on transfer can have a depreciatory effect on the value of shares. In the estate duty case of *Salvesen's Trustees v IRC* (1930) 9 ATC 43, article 12 of the company's articles of association provided:

> 'The company may, at any time, by extraordinary resolution, resolve that any shareholder, other than a director or a person holding more than 10% of the shares of the company, do transfer his shares. Such member shall thereupon be deemed to have served the company with a sale notice in respect of his shares in accordance with Clause 6 hereof, and all the ancillary and consequential provisions of these articles shall apply with respect to the completion of the sale of the said shares. Notice in writing of such resolution shall be given to the member affected thereby. For the purpose of this clause any person entitled to transfer an ordinary share under Article 22 of table A shall be deemed the holder of such share.'

Lord Fleming at 54 stated:

> 'The last matter which I have to consider is the effect which the restrictive conditions in the articles would have on the value of the shares. I may have said once that I regard these restrictions as depreciating their value very considerably. Nobody, except a person who was prepared to have his capital locked up for many years, could afford to buy them at more than par value. I imagine that there are a very limited number of persons who would be prepared to pay £5.10s. For a £1 share which might only be realisable at par or less. The prospective buyer at the price fixed by the commissioners would have to be able to find over £152,000 and, in order to avoid a loss on his capital, he would have to be prepared to hold the shares himself for an indefinite period or transfer them to one or more of the persons mentioned in the articles, subject, however, to the condition that no transferee held less than 10,000. All the witnesses were agreed that the restrictions would depreciate the value of the shares, but the only witness who put any money value on this restriction was Mr Robertson Durham who said that in his opinion it might make a difference of as much as 8s.4d. on his value of £1.6s.8d. and, in my opinion, this figure is not by any means excessive.'

The leading estate duty case on restriction of transfer is *Re Crossman* and *Re Paulin* (1936) 15 ATC 94. The Lord Chancellor in this case at 101 stated:

> 'Since the articles forbid a sale in the open market until the rights of pre-emption have been exhausted, all that the executors could sell in the open market at the time of the death was the right to receive the restricted price fixed by article 34(14a) from any shareholder exercising his right of pre-emption. Obviously the value of this could not exceed the sum which such a shareholder would have to pay, and, accordingly, the Court of Appeal have held that that sum, that is the restricted price, is the value in the open market.
>
> My lords, it seems to me that this construction involves treating the provisions of s 7(5) (of the Finance Act 1894) as if their true effect were to make the existence of an open market a condition of liability instead of merely to prescribe the open market price as the measure of value. The right to receive the price fixed by the articles in the event of a sale to existing shareholders under sub-clause 14a is only one of the elements which went to make up the value of the shares. In addition to that right, the ownership of the share gave a number of other valuable rights to the holder, including the right to receive the dividends which the company was declaring, the right to transmit the shares in accordance with article 34(1), (2) and (3) and the right to have the shares of other holders who wished to realise

> offered on the terms of article 34(14a). All these various rights and privileges go to make up a share and form ingredients in its value. They are just as much part of the share as the restriction upon the sale.'

Lord Blanesburgh in this case at 107 stated:

> 'To all the shares here in question I would apply the words already referred to used by Lord Justice FitzGibbon in *A-G v Jameson* [1905] 2 IR 218.
>
> Each of the 750 shares there in question he says, "with all rights and liabilities and all advantages and disadvantages incident in its ownership passed on Henry Jameson's death to his executors as one indivisible piece of property. In conveyancing phraseology, the executors took each share to hold in as full and ample a manner as the same was held by Henry Jameson at his death".'

Lord Roche in the same case at 119 stated:

> 'Upon an actual sale there must be an actual passing of property. Upon a notional sale there must be a notional or assumed passing of property. In so far as the passing or transfer or property is thus notional or hypothetical, no restriction upon actual passing or transfer comes into question, and the articles as to the prescribed price which is to rule under certain circumstances, though it is no doubt a constituent part of the bundle of rights which constitutes a share, does not, as I think, govern such a notional transfer so as to make the notional purchaser no more than a person who acquires an obligation to offer the shares to others at the prescribed price.'

In the estate duty case of *Re Lynall, Lynall v IRC* (1971) 47 TC 375 at 405, Lord Reid stated with regard to restrictions on transfer:

> 'No fair value had been fixed by the company. So the position at Mrs Lynall's death was that the shares were not transferable until they had been first offered to her husband at £1 per share, and even if he did not want them they were only transferable to a purchaser accepted by the directors.
>
> A similar situation occurred in *IRC v Crossman* [1937] AC 26. The appellants asked us to reconsider that decision. I have done so, and I agree with the decision of the majority in this House.'

Focus

Their Lordships in *Lynall* were unanimous in confirming the *Crossman* decision that the hypothetical purchaser was deemed to be registered as a shareholder and would thereafter hold the shares subject to the company's memorandum and articles of association.

3.11 Willing seller

The assumed sale in the open market is on the basis of a sale between a hypothetical willing seller and a hypothetical willing, prudent and cautious buyer.

Harman LJ in *Re Lynall, Lynall v IRC* (1971) 47 TC 375 at 392 stated:

> 'The sale envisaged by the section is, as is agreed, not a real but a hypothetical sale and must be taken to be a sale between a willing vendor and a willing

> purchaser, see for instance the speech of Lord Guest in *Winter (Sutherland's Trustees) v IRC* (1961) 40 ATC 361 at 369. It is true that the so called willing vendor is a person who must sell: he cannot simply call off the sale if he does not like the price, but there must be on the other side a willing purchaser, so that the conditions of the sale must be such as to induce in him a willing frame of mind.'

In the same case Lord Morris of Borth-y-Gest commented at 409:

> 'It became common ground that the price to be decided upon was that which would have been paid (a) by a hypothetical willing purchaser (b) to a hypothetical willing vendor (c) in the open market (d) on 21 May 1962.'

In the land value duty cases of *IRC v Clay; IRC v Buchanan* [1914] 3 KB 466, 'willing seller' was defined for the purpose of F(1909–10)A 1910, s 25(1) by Swinfen Eady LJ at 476 as follows:

> 'A sale by a willing seller is distinguished from a sale which is made by reason of compulsory powers, where the vendor frequently obtains an addition to the price by reason of being under compulsion to sell. It does not mean a sale by a person willing to sell his property without reserve for any price he can obtain. Mrs Buchanan was a willing seller when she accepted £1,000. The fact that she was persuaded or induced to agree voluntarily to sell at that price did not make her any the less a willing seller. There was no evidence of any compulsion; there was friendly bargaining, some discussion, some haggling about price, and then an agreement come to. This is the normal course of most private contract sales. She was nonetheless a willing seller because she had not previously put the property into the hands of an agent for sale. She was willing to sell at a price, she was offered a price less than the maximum which the intending purchasers were willing to give, and she took it.'

F(1909–10)A 1910, s 25(1) specifically referred to a sale in the open market by a willing seller, whereas most of the legislation merely assumes the sale in the open market at a particular date.

Lord Guest's comment referred to above in the estate duty case of *Winter (Sutherland's Trustees) v IRC* (1961) 40 ATC 361 at 369 was:

> 'the purpose of s 7(5) of the Finance Act, 1894, is to value the property. As Lord Evershed said "It does not require it to be assumed that the sale … has occurred …" It simply prescribes, as the criterion for value, price in the open market as between a willing seller and a willing buyer which is a familiar basis of valuation.'

This comment was also quoted with approval by Lord Reid in the estate duty case of *Duke of Buccleuch v IRC* [1967] 1 AC 506 at 515.

It has been argued that because the vendor is deemed to sell he cannot be assumed to be a willing seller. In *Duke of Buccleuch v IRC* [1967] 1 AC 506 at 525 Lord Reid stated:

> 'But here what must be envisaged is sale in the open market on a particular day. So there is no room for supposing that the owner would do as many prudent owners do – withdraw the property if he does not get a sufficient offer and wait until a time when he can get a better offer. The Commissioners must estimate what the property would probably have fetched on that particular day if it had then been exposed for sale, no doubt after such advance publicity as would have been reasonable.'

But as with Harman LJ's comment in *Lynall* quoted above this merely defines the market and the time of the deemed sale not that the seller must be assumed to be an unwilling or forced seller at any price he can command, he must be assumed to be in a willing frame of mind.

Prior to *Lynall*, there had been no specific reference in any case to a 'hypothetical' willing seller. Some commentators take the view that whilst the supposition of a hypothetical vendor was correct in the context of the dispute in *Lynall*, it is not of general application. Reference to a 'hypothetical' vendor has, however, been made in subsequent cases such as *Holt v Holt* [1990] 1 WLR 1250 and *Re Charrington* (1975) unreported (Hong Kong Supreme Court) and does now appear to be of general application.

> **Focus**
>
> The transaction assumes the seller is willing to sell at the price stated and is not a forced seller.

3.12 Willing buyer

So far as the purchaser is concerned, Lord Fleming stated in the estate duty case of *Salvesen's Trustees v IRC* (1913) 9 ATC 43 at 50:

> 'A person who was being invited to acquire a third of the shares in a private company which imposed stringent conditions on the right of transfer would certainly wish to ascertain the value at which the assets had been entered in the last balance sheet. As a prudent person he would of course keep in view that he was purchasing the shares in October 1926 and that the balance sheet shows the affairs of the company as at June 1926, and he would make inquiry as to the alterations in its financial position which had taken place between these two dates.'

In the estate duty case of *Re Holt, Holt v IRC* (1953) 32 ATC 402 Danckwerts J stated at 410:

> 'I think the kind of investor who would purchase shares in a private company of this kind, in circumstances which must preclude him disposing of his shares freely whenever he would wish, (because he will, when registered as a shareholder, be subject to the provisions of the articles restricting transfer) would be different from any common kind of purchaser for shares on the Stock Exchange, and would be rather the exceptional kind of investor, who had some special reason for putting his money into shares of this kind. He would, in my view, be the kind of investor who would not rush hurriedly into the transaction, but would consider carefully the prudence of the course, and would seek to get the fullest possible information about the past history of the company, the particular trade in which it was engaged and the future prospects of the company.'

Lord Fleming in the estate duty case of *Findlay's Trustees v IRC* (1938) 22 ATC 437 at 440 stated:

> 'In estimating the price which might be fetched in the open market for the goodwill of the business it must be assumed that the transaction takes place between a willing seller and a willing purchaser; and that the purchaser is a person of reasonable prudence, who has informed himself with regard to all the relevant facts such as the history of the business, its present position, its future

> prospects and the general conditions of the industry; and also that he has access to the accounts of the business for a number of years.'

In the estate duty case of *Battle v* IRC [1979] TR 483, Balcombe J stated:

> 'Once it is established that the method of valuation is on the basis of a sale in the open market what is contemplated is a notional sale between a notional vendor and a notional purchaser: one does not postulate a particular vendor or a particular purchaser. See *IRC v Crossman* [1937] AC 26 at 50 per Lord Blanesburgh and *Re Lynall, Lynall v IRC* (1971) 47 TC 375 (see above). One cannot assume that the hypothetical vendor of a minority holding of shares in a company would only sell his holding in conjunction with the other holders so that its value should be assessed on the basis of a sale of all the shares. Cf the nationalisation case of *Short v Treasury Comrs* [1948] 1 KB 116.'

In The French Connection Group case of *Stephen Marks v HMRC* [2011] UKFTT 221 (TC) it was held that where shares were held in two companies at 31 March 1982, one of which (FCO) was sold to the other (SMHL) in exchange for shares in SMHL, the shares in SMHL had two base values at 31 March 1982: those issued in exchange for FCO shares were valued on the basis of FCO shares at 31 March 1982 and the remaining SMHL shares were valued on the basis of the SMHL shares at 31 March 1982. The tribunal judge, John F Avery Jones CBE, quoted Peter Gibson, LJ, in *Walton v IRC* [1996] STC 68:

> 'It is not necessary for the operation of the statutory hypothesis of a sale in the open market of an interest in a tenancy that the landlord should be treated as a hypothetical person, and it is a question of fact to be established by the evidence before the tribunal of fact whether the attributes of the actual landlord would be taken into account in the market. I would add that the same logic requires that in the case of a deceased partner owning an interest in a tenancy which is a partnership asset, regard should be had to the actual intention of the actual surviving partner and not to a hypothetical partner.
>
> 28. Applying the same principle here, the statutory hypothesis does imply the existence of a hypothetical purchaser but does not require one to ignore the characteristics of any actual potential purchasers. It is inherent in the recognition of a special purchaser in *IRC v Clay* [1914] 3 KB 466 that a real prospective purchaser, where the owner of the neighbouring property which wanted to extend it, was known to be in the market. There is also no doubt that the Appellant's separate ownership of the two groups would be known to the other potential purchasers in the market. As Hoffmann LJ said in *IRC v Gray* [1994] STC 360 at 372 also in relation to a valuation of land:
>
> > "The hypothetical vendor is an anonymous but reasonable vendor, who goes about the sale as a prudent man of business, negotiating seriously without giving the impression of being either over-anxious or unduly reluctant. The hypothetical buyer is slightly less anonymous. He too is assumed to have behaved reasonably, making proper inquiries about the property and not appearing too eager to buy. But he also reflects reality in that he embodies whatever was actually the demand for that property at the relevant time. It cannot be too strongly emphasised that although the sale is hypothetical, there is nothing hypothetical about the open market in which it is supposed to have taken place. The concept of the open market involves assuming that the whole world was free to bid, and then forming a view about what in those circumstances would in real life have been the best price reasonably obtainable. The practical nature of this exercise will usually mean that

although in principle no one is excluded from consideration, most of the world will usually play no part in the calculation. The inquiry will often focus on what a relatively small number of people would be likely to have paid. It may have to arrive at a figure within a range of prices which the evidence shows that various people would have been likely to pay, reflecting, for example, the fact that one person had a particular reason for paying a higher price than others, but taking into account, if appropriate, the possibility that through accident or whim he might not actually have bought. The valuation is thus a retrospective exercise in probabilities, wholly derived from the real world but rarely committed to the proposition that a sale to a particular purchaser would definitely have happened."

"On that basis there seems no need to exclude an actual potential purchaser from the market. It is interesting that the RICS Red Book relating to valuations of land does include the actual owner as a potential purchaser and so this is recognised in other valuation contexts. One further problem that arises in relation to share valuation is that the actual owner's information about the asset being valued is bound to be greater than the information that a prudent prospective purchaser might reasonably require. However, there is no theoretical difficulty in assuming that that the actual owner cannot use any information beyond that reasonably required in deciding how much to offer."

29. We do not consider that the presence of the Appellant, with his knowledge treated as limited to what a prudent prospective purchase would reasonably require, would affect the value of each company viewed in isolation because all potential purchasers would use a similar valuation method based on a multiple of earnings. Where we consider that it would make a difference is that if the Appellant, as owner of FCO, is in the market as a potential purchaser of SMHL from a hypothetical vendor (and vice versa). As owner of the company not being valued he has an interest in buying the company being valued from the hypothetical vendor so that he can continue to own both companies and continue the existing relationship between them. For example, on a valuation of FCO and treating it as a vehicle for SMHL selling outside the UK, the Appellant, as owner of SMHL, would want to continue to have such a sales outlet rather than set up a new one; and he would want to continue to have Briardene Enterprises (an FCO group company) continued function as purchasing agent for the SMHL group. And on a valuation of SMHL the Appellant, as owner of FCO, would want to continue to be able to continue to use the trade marks owned within the SMHL group. We consider that this factor removes any issue of each group being worth less because it needs the existence of the other to continue to make profits in the same way as in the past. For example, it could be argued that FCO is worth less to an independent buyer because its established turnover is of French Connection clothes which the buyer would have to replace from another source and then persuade the existing customers to buy under another label. Similar arguments could be made that FCO did not have an assured continuation of its existing funding. But if the Appellant, as owner of SMHL is in the market as a potential purchaser of FCO he will value FCO on the basis that it will continue to be able to sell "French Connection" clothes to existing customers, and that the funding of the FCO group by the SMHL group will continue. In other words, the valuation is on the basis that the business will continue as before.'

30 A similar issue relates to what assumption should be made about the management of the two groups. In the real world we have no doubt that the Appellant, as a typical successful entrepreneur, would not work for either group if he were not substantially the owner. The law is silent on this, perhaps

> because it has developed mainly in relation to death duties, but we consider that we should assume the continuation of the present management. We note that the Special Commissioner in *Marks v Sherred* [2004] STC (SCD) 362 made the same assumption at [20]. Fortunately Miss Hennessey (valuer for HMRC) proceeds on this assumption and so the possibility of the management leaving is not in issue as a reason for reducing the value.'

The FTT valued SMHL at £3,709k and FCO at £443k, a total of £4,152k, and commented that, 'The valuation is a particularly difficult one because first, one has to value something nearly 30 years ago when recollections are poor or non-existent and documents no longer available, to say nothing of the completely different economic scene then applying (for example that clearing banks base rate was 13% at 31 March 1982); secondly, it makes no commercial sense to view the two groups separately when they were run as one, the Appellant being the sole shareholder and director of both; they were put together on the flotation on the Unlisted Securities Market in October 1983, immediately before which SMHL took over FCO on a share for share exchange: the first issue will be whether they can be treated as one or whether a separate valuation of each is required by the tax legislation; thirdly, the Appellant would not have sold the companies at 31 March 1982 when their growth was at an early stage (as we know with hindsight from the fact that they were floated in October 1983 at which time the profits had increased enormously since 31 March 1982); and fourthly, the experts are far apart in their valuations: £8.425m for SMHL and FCO combined by the expert called by the Appellant and £3.1m for SMHL and a nominal £100 for FCO by the expert called by HMRC.

Focus

The transaction assumes that the buyer is ready, willing and able to complete the purchase, but is under no compulsion to do so.

3.13 Time of hypothetical sale

Also in the estate duty case of the Duke *of Buccleuch v IRC* [1967] 1 AC 506 Lord Reid propounded at 524:

> 'The section must mean the price which the property would have fetched if sold at the time of death. I agree with the argument of the respondents that "at the time of death" points to a definite time – the day on which the death occurred: it does not mean within a reasonable time after the death.'

Lord Guest confirmed:

> '"at the time of the death" means at the moment of death, not within a reasonable time after the death.'

And Lord Reid continued:

> 'But here what must be envisaged is a sale in the open market on a particular day. So there is not room for supposing that the owner would do, as many prudent owners do – withdraw the property if he does not get a sufficient offer and wait until a time when he can get a better offer. The Commissioners must estimate

what the property would probably have fetched on that particular day if it had been exposed for sale, no doubt after such advance publicity as would have been reasonable.'

3.14 Adjustments to accounts

In the Irish estate duty case of *Smyth v IRC* [1941] IR 643 it was held that where a testator held 18,501 shares out of 23,007, ie 80.41% of the ordinary shares, it was permissible to recalculate the remuneration of the directors in arriving at the maintainable earnings of the company. Hanna J stated at 653:

> 'Now, as to the remuneration: until 1907 they were getting dividends on whatever shares they held, and Mr Weber Smyth had a comparatively small salary. In that year a difference was made in the income tax on earned and unearned income, and it was arranged that the benefit of the reduction in tax on earned income could be obtained by giving a salary which in the first instance, was varied in proportion to the number of shares held. In 1918 this variation was abandoned and fixed salaries were given at £1,500 to the deceased and £750 to Mr Weber Smyth. In 1920 these were raised to £2,000 and £1,000, and, save for a short period when they were slightly reduced, these salaries continued until the death of Mr Weber Smyth senior. Being a family company in which no one was really interested except the two directors, the profits could be divided up either as salaries or as dividends as they liked and they preferred to give them as salary. The result of this was that for the last six years the actual dividend paid averaged 5.3%, a rate of dividend which the Revenue Commissioners submitted was illusory as a test of the profit earning capacity of the company. In this I think the Commissioners are right.
>
> The first question presented for consideration on the petition is whether the dividend earning capacity of the company is the sole or the proper test of the value of the shares in the hypothetical open market. The Revenue Commissioners submit that not only is it not a test, but, even if it is to be considered at all, the figures presented by the petitioners must be severely criticised. The contention of the Revenue Commissioners is that the earning capacity of the company is not represented by the average of 5.3% for the last six years' trading but by a figure of 12%. On this subject the principal item in dispute is the method and amount of remuneration for two directors. The witnesses for the Revenue submitted that the directors' remuneration at a figure of £3,000 per annum, for such a business was out of all proportion to the value of their services or the nature of the business, and was such as no public company would pay, running the business on a commercial basis. In this I must agree: but, on the other hand, considerable weight must be given to the view put forward by the petitioners that it was a family company, where greater latitude would be given on the remuneration of the directors, who were the principal owners; and that it was a unique business, in which both the directors had special knowledge, and to which they gave constant daily attention and had a special personal relationship with the majority of the customers. A purchaser in a hypothetical market of any of these shares would recognise the value of these factors, and make due allowance for much more than the ordinary remuneration. The evidence of either side went into great detail and after the consideration of it I think that this company can be fairly regarded as one capable of earning on a commercial basis 10% on its capital, and I so find. But, if this is to be taken as the principal test it must be subject to consideration, on the one hand, of the restriction upon the transfer of the shares, and, on the other, of the added value by reason of the splendid security of the company's position.

> There is only one measure of value in this case that is almost agreed upon. It is clear from the evidence of the stockbrokers and accountants who were called as witnesses that in the case of a private trading company with a restriction such as this on the transfer of the shares, a 10% dividend is generally regarded as giving par value to the shares. Being of opinion that the contention of the petitioners, namely, that the dividend earning capacity is the only test, cannot be sustained and that these other matters I have mentioned must be taken into consideration, I am also of opinion on the evidence that the principal matter that influences a purchaser in such case is the return upon the money invested by him in the purchase of the shares.
>
> The Revenue Commissioners have presented a contrary view substantially in the following form: they say that the most likely purchaser of the shares in this case would be someone desiring a block of shares, buying them en bloc for the purpose either of obtaining control of the firm, so as to extinguish it, or to amalgamate it with some other firm, or for the purpose of pure speculation, to wind up and take his profit on the excess of the realisable assets over liability. On this assumption there is undoubtedly much in the view they submitted, as such a purchaser would not pay much attention to the dividend-earning capacity of the company. If such a purchaser were in existence the Revenue contend, on the figures which have been submitted to me, that he could safely give 27s or 30s per share. Their submission (and there is some evidence to support it) is that where 80% of the shares of the company are put up for sale the most likely purchaser would be one of this character … Undoubtedly a share in a limited company gives the holder the right not only to participate in the division of the profits, but also to participate in the division of the capital.
>
> I think that the weakness underlying the submission of the Revenue Commissioners is the assumption that the shares in this case would be necessarily or even likely to be sold en bloc to one purchaser. I do not think that the section of the Act contemplates in the term "open market", not only a market which is hypothetical, but also only hypothetical purchasers wanting a block of shares. In my judgment, you must take into consideration the possibility of the shares being divided up among several purchasers, either members of the family or of the public. In visualising this hypothetical open market I consider that it may contain some persons looking merely for a return of their money in a going concern, or some members of the family anxious to buy, and perhaps willing to give more than the ordinary buyer, in order to keep the business in the family, as well as the block purchaser, who wants to wind up the company for some reason, or to have a profit on his speculation. When you have all these assembled – and you must contemplate such a possibility – it is not easy to determine with arithmetical accuracy what price would be obtained for, under s 7, that "price" is the "value" of the shares, as Lord Justice FitzGibbon points out in his judgment in *A-G v Jameson* [1905] 2 IR 218.'

Hanna J continued at 656:

> 'From the point of view of their pleadings each party has taken up an extreme view, and elects to stand upon one point. The petitioners, on the actual profit-earning capacity based on the past balance sheets; and the Revenue, on the value of the shares in relation to the capital, disregarding the figures in the balance sheets. In this I think both are wrong. In my opinion, in estimating the price, every advantage and disadvantage of the company, and every benefit and clog attaching to the share, as well as the nature of the particular company, must be considered.
>
> Accordingly as the facts differ more weight will be given to one element than to another. You must consider the profit-earning capacity, the return for the

> purchaser's investment, the general solvency of the company, the extent of the security in the shape of assets, the nature of the management, the objects of the company, its methods of business, the capital value of the assets of the company, the restrictions upon the transfer of the shares, and the amount of liabilities. On some of these elements persons accustomed to value can place a relevant figure, but the test for some of the others is merely general business experience. In my judgment the profit-earning capacity of the shares is the most important item, and would be most prominent in the mind of the purchaser in this case. When I say "profit-earning capacity" I mean profit earning on a reasonable commercial basis for a company such as may be under consideration, not necessarily as appearing in the balance sheets which may, for reasons of the proprietors, be prepared on a particular basis. But while this is in the foreground you must consider as a definite and well marked background the capital value of the shares. It may operate either to increase or decrease the price as the case may be.
>
> I find that the shares, taking into consideration the restriction upon the transfer are about par value on a suitable profit-earning basis; but what consideration in addition must be given for the ratio to capital value? I think the returns given in evidence for the Revenue which are on the basis of a sale as a going concern or at break-up values are too high. I am not sure that the purely arithmetical basis is satisfactory as there are some elements of security that do not appear in balance sheets. Mr Brock estimated the value of the strength of the company as worth an additional 25% on the price of the share. Mr Walkey, the petitioners' accountant added 3s to his 12s per share for what he called security and solvency. These percentages give me some guide and would bring my figure over that fixed by the Commissioners (22s 6d), but I do not propose to alter their value, which, from every point of view, seems to me to have been carefully arrived at as a fair value on the terms of s 7.'

The question of adjustment from excessive directors' remuneration was also considered in the Hong Kong case of *Donnett v Cheung Cheung-Shui* (29 February 1988, unreported), Supreme Court of Hong Kong, where MacDougall J stated:

> 'A question that arises is whether the levels of remuneration that the first four defendants voted to themselves for the years ended 31 July 1985 and 1986 truly reflected their emoluments or whether a dividend element was also included in these payments. For the purpose of valuing a class A share in the company this distinction is important for the reason that the higher the net profit of the company in a particular year, the greater is the sum available for distribution of that profit among the shareholders by way of dividend. This would have a direct bearing on the valuation of a share in the company.
>
> Mr Morrison said that the fact that the sums paid as remuneration increased five fold in the years ended 31 July 1985 and 1986 from that of the preceding year coupled with the fact that despite having different job titles, responsibilities, and qualifications, each director received the same remuneration, indicates that those sums contained a dividend element.
>
> The first four defendants claim that the remuneration paid to them in the two years ended July 1985 and 1986 represents a true market value for the services they performed. However, in a report dated 4 September 1987 the auditor stated that he was of the view that the directors had been underpaid during the formative years of the company and that "in 1985 and 1986, because of the extraordinary increase in turnover, generating more profits, [they] were able to receive a more substantial remuneration to compensate themselves for what they should have received in earlier years".

> A Mr Rowell of Boyden Associates Ltd submitted a report on behalf of the defendants in which he expressed the view that there is no generally followed or accepted standard by which remuneration for the directors of a company is determined, but that persons engaged in specialist services work done by a company are normally remunerated on a basis commensurate with the profitability of the work performed by them.
>
> According to him, how much of the annual profits of a company is distributed to its directors depends on the individual circumstances and policy of the company concerned, and this varies considerably. Where uncertain market conditions lead to wide fluctuations in profitability, these wide variations are frequently reflected in the remuneration paid.
>
> Mr Rowell was unaware of the existence of any company similar to the fifth defendant with regard to capital, shareholding, directors, and business or market conditions. He was therefore unable to draw any direct comparison with other companies. Given his premise that there are neither rules nor guidelines for the remuneration of executives in companies such as the fifth defendant, he came to the firm conclusion that the remuneration paid to the first four defendants for the years ended 31 July 1985 and 1986 was not unreasonable or excessive. He expressed the view that since the company was operating a high risk business and the directors had run it like a partnership, had put in effort and had generated the profit, they were entitled to share the entire profit.
>
> This means that, on the basis employed by the auditor in performing his valuation, had the directors' remuneration equalled the company's net income for the three of the five years used by him in which the company made profits, the value of a class A share would have been nil. Indeed, it is difficult to escape the conclusion that the effect of Mr Rowell's testimony, at least in the case of the company, is that the income left for distribution as dividends would almost invariably be nil and thus the value of a class A share calculated on a new profit basis would likewise almost invariably be nil. This approach does not commend itself to me. I consider that for the purpose of a share valuation a serious attempt should be made to determine what constitutes a *fair* remuneration for the work done by the directors.'

HMRC Shares and Assets Valuation Manual (at SVM06050) emphasises that when adding back excessive directors' benefits regard must be had to the circumstances of each individual case. The Manual does suggest that a pension contribution of up to 20% of the total directors' remuneration package is reasonable.

Where accounts have not been prepared on generally accepted practice, for example because of the omission or undervaluation of stock and work in progress, they need to be amended, and disclosure made to HMRC if necessary, as in *Leslie Smith v HMRC* [2010] UKFTT 92 (TC). Otherwise, any comparison on published information of comparable companies would be misleading.

Focus

Where the valuation is based on profits, non-arm's length remuneration levels and other adjustments need to be made to arrive at a market level of profits.

3.15 Sale at undervalue

In the estate duty case of *Re Thornley* (1928) 7 ATC 178 the Inland Revenue argued that a sale of 9,800 shares from father to son for £10,500, following an exceptional dividend, was a partial gift and the shares were worth £4 13s each.

By the articles of association the transfer of shares was drastically restricted. By articles 22 to 28 in effect the shares were subject to pre-emption, the father's by the son, and the son's by the father 'at a fair value', as fixed at the previous ordinary general meeting, or failing that by the auditor. The pre-emption option had to remain for two months, after which the owner could sell them elsewhere within two months, but not at less than the 'full value', without again offering them to the members. By article 30 the registration of any transfer might be refused without reason given by the directors. By article 40 the shares of the first to die of the father and the son were to become converted into 5% preference shares, which by a later article the survivor had an option to purchase at par. By article 96 the father and son were to be permanent directors with power (article 99) to appoint and remove ordinary directors. Article 102 gave the directors power to determine their own remuneration, and no dividend was to exceed the amount recommended by the directors.

Rowlatt J was not convinced that there was any element of bounty attached to the sale, and so held.

Under the sale agreement by which a business was transferred to the company only some 4,000 of the 9,800 shares could have been sold to third parties, which caused the learned judge to comment, at 181:

> 'I had an eminent accountant's evidence that these shares were saleable privately on a 15% basis and were worth perhaps £4 each, notwithstanding that the permanent director might take all the profits by way of remuneration. I dare say from an accountant's point of view that is quite correct. If it were a matter of arranging for a new shareholder coming in under circumstances of cordiality between all concerned and perhaps with an understanding that articles might have to be altered and so on, I can understand it. But the imagined purchaser of the 4,000 shares of the deceased in this case would find himself a detested intruder with a minority interest and under articles already summarised, and I wonder very much whether anyone could be found to take the position on lucrative terms to the seller of the shares. He would have to be found in two months from the expiry of the members' option under the articles, and after all he might very likely not be found at all, or the deceased might die (as in fact he did) before there had been time enough to get all this done. Meanwhile the petitioner would have been antagonised.'

This merely emphasises the importance of considering all the surrounding circumstances, including the uncomfortable position of a minority holder in a family company.

See **10.02** for details of a capital transfer tax case, *IRC v Spencer-Nairn* [1991] STC 60, where the sale of agricultural property at less than open market value was nevertheless not a transfer of value for capital transfer tax purposes.

In *Re Baroness Bateman* [1925] 2 KB 429 a sale of furniture by a mother to her son, at undervalue, was being considered. Rowlatt J stated:

> 'Looking at the figures I cannot think that £5,100 was really the full value of the furniture at the time of the transaction (in 1906) and I shall take it that that sum represented 80% of the full value. That brings me to the last question. The Crown

> have allowed the sum that was paid by the son at the date of the settlement against £45,000 (the sale proceeds in 1918) as being the value of the consideration under s 3, sub-s 2, of the Act, and if that is right the matter is concluded. I do not think that this method is right, because the effect is to compare two entirely different things, which would lead to this absurdity, that if I find that £5,100 was the full value, nothing would be payable, while if I find that it is only 99% of the value, £5,100 will be set off against £45,000. Am I then to say that the amount to be deducted is to be arrived at by a process of interest or discount? I think not. The only alternative is that for which the respondent contends, which I may describe as the proportional method. The object of s 3, sub-s 2, is to see how much of this property is passing by way of bounty and how much by way of purchase. That can only be done by ascertaining what proportion of the property was the subject of purchase and what proportion is represented by gift. Under that interpretation the words "the value of the consideration' mean 'the value which corresponds to the consideration", that is to say, the value in the article partially bought which was bought by the consideration. In other words, this proportion can be allowed as a deduction from the value of the property. It is necessary to find the piece of property which is being taxed, and if it passes partially by reason of purchase for consideration in money or money's worth, then such part of the value as corresponds to the consideration must be deducted from the value of the whole property. I think that the consideration represented four-fifths of the value at the time of purchase, and it follows that estate duty is payable in respect of one-fifth of the value of the property.'

Focus

Whether, and if so, to what extent there is a sale at an undervalue depends on the circumstances of each case.

3.16 Warranties

There are no provisions under which it is to be assumed that the vendor will give any of the warranties or indemnities which would normally apply in the case of an actual sale. Nor is it to be assumed that key employees would enter into service agreements and could therefore be free to set up in competition. The hypothetical sale is therefore considerably removed from any actual sale.

3.17 Sale proceeds

In an actual sale there are often extensive warranties and deferred terms for payment of the sale proceeds and negotiable paper such as loan stock or shares in the acquiring company are offered, usually to postpone the vendor's capital gains tax liability. A hypothetical sale would be on the basis of an immediate cash sale of the shares with no warranties other than as to ownership of the shares sold.

3.18 Reviewing the situation

In *Executors of Ian Campbell McArthur (dec'd) v RCC* [2008] SpC 700 the Special Commissioner had some useful comments on share valuation principles. The issue was the proper valuation of certain majority and minority shareholdings of the deceased in three private family companies. The Special Commissioner stated (at para 61):

> 'I have no wish and would not presume to attempt to add to the anthology of dicta of guiding principles to be applied to share valuation for the purpose of inheritance tax. Suffice it to say that at the end of the day there was no real dispute between the parties that (i) the valuation date is immediately before the deceased's death, (ii) the hypothetical buyer and seller are both wiling participants in the hypothetical sale, (iii) the buyer acts prudently and reasonably and seeks and obtains all relevant information to enable him to make an informed offer; he will be diligent in his enquiries; the seller is assumed to respond to all reasonable enquiries with such reasonable responses as might reasonably have been made (iv) the prudent prospective purchaser acts with reasonable foresight but without the benefit of hindsight (v) the sum deemed to have been offered and accepted is the sum the shares could reasonably be expected to fetch in the open market (vi) the shares and conversion rights are all sold together as a package (vii) the sale is assumed to take place in the real world i.e. the only assumptions to be made are the statutory ones or those derived from case law and (viii) the sale is assumed to be carried into effect i.e. the shareholding bought is assumed to be registered in the name of the notional purchaser not withstanding any obstacles in the Articles of Association.'

Counsel for HMRC submitted (at paras 37 and 38) that:

> 'the existing shares and the options to take further shares fall to be valued as one (*IRC v Gray The Executor of Lady Fox* [1994] 38 EG 156, *AG v Mackie* [1952] 2 All ER 775 at 777, *Duke of Buccleugh v IRC* [1967] 1 AC 506; that is the course a prudent, hypothetical vendor would have adopted in order to obtain the most favourable price without undue expenditure of time and effort. Sale on the open market had to be assumed; no improvements are to be deemed to have been made prior to sale (*AG v Jameson* (1905) 2 IR 218 at 226, 230 and 240, *IRC v Crossman* [1937] AC 26 at 54, Duke of Buccleugh at 525, Gray at 372. *In re Lynall (dec'd)* (1971) 47 TC 375 at 406, 408, 409, 411 and 412, *Caton v Couch* (1995) ATC (SCD) 34 at 49–50; *Salvesen v IRC* 1930 SLT 387 at 391, 392 ... Valuation must be carried out without the benefit of hindsight (in *Re Holt* [1953] 1 WLR 1488 at 1492 and 1493. The hypothetical sale is assumed to take place in the real world (*Walton v IRC* [1996] 1 EGLR 159). Insofar as possible (*Trocett Property Company Ltd v GIC* (1974) 28 P&CR 408 at 420). Mr Eamer's deduction of 12.5% for lack of marketability of the majority shareholdings was justified (*Goldstein v Levy Gee* [2003] EWHC 1574 (Ch)). A discount of 25%–40% for a minority holding is common (in *Re Lynall* [28%], *Dymonds Capital Taxes* para 23.374 [20%], *Caton v Couch* [1995] STC (SCD) 34 [60%–70% – a trading company]). Quoted investment companies typically traded at discounts of around 30%".

The Special Commissioner stated (at paras 76–81)

> 'Mr Eamer's approach in relation to discount for lack of marketability, majority and minority shareholdings in unquoted companies, was to review the evidence in such case law as existed. He noted that shares in quoted investment companies typically traded at discounts of between 10% and 20% from net asset backing. The discount was a little higher for quoted property investment companies and was usually around 30%.
>
> For lack of marketability, he made a deduction of 50% and supported this by reference to the current edition of Dymond's Capital Taxes paragraph 23.374,

(20% or so), *Caton v Couch* 1995 STC (SCD) 34 (60–70% for a holding under 25% in a trading company).

As for majority shareholdings in unquoted property investment companies, he referred to *Goldstein v Levy Gee* [2003] EWHC 1574 (Ch), to illustrate to support the view that 12.5% was a reasonable deduction to make. He noted that both the shareholdings in New Inverness and Chapman (on the assumption that the options are enforceable) would be less than 75%. A special resolution could therefore not be passed without co-operation from other shareholders. In cross-examination he stated that the 12.5% deduction was for both lack of marketability and the inability to secure the passing of a special resolution.

In relation to minority shareholding over 25%, he added back 50% as a nuisance factor and referred to the decision at first in instance in *Re Lynall* (28% shareholding in a trading company). In relation to Cape Wrath he acknowledged that, as a minority holding, tax disadvantages might have to be taken into account. He had not taken such disadvantages into account. An appropriate figure would be up to 5%.

In relation to Cape Wrath's holding in New Inverness (on the assumption that the options were enforceable) he adopted the 25% deduction for lack of marketability but without the addition of the nuisance factor. He adopted a similar approach in relation to Chapman's Shareholding (on the same assumption) in New Inverness but as on this basis the shareholding of Chapman is 51%, the deduction made is 12.5%.

Mr Eamer acknowledged that if there were a doubt about prescription, a further discount would have to be made which might vary between 5% and 45% depending on the strength of the doubt. Likewise if there were a real doubt about the documentation of the loans and options, he thought that an overall deduction of 5–10% might be made.'

The Special Commissioner continued (at para 83):

'Both Mr Sutherland and Mr Eamer included in their Reports a selection of dicta from cases over the years on valuation principles. Mr Sutherland's selection included cases which emphasised that a purchaser would be an unwelcome or detested intruder in a family company (for example *In re Samuel Thornley (dec'd)* 1928 7 ATC 180, *Salvesen v IRC* (1930) 9 ATC 43 at 54 per Lord Fleming. Mr Eamer also mentioned *Thornley*. However, it seems to me these dicta coloured Mr Sutherland's approach to the valuations and led to him make greater discounts than he might otherwise have done. These dicta are however irrelevant for the purposes of those valuations except perhaps in relation to the motivation of the discount where the detested intruder holds a shareholding of between 25% and 49%. Having regard to the terms of the Agreed Statement, it is of no moment that the purchaser is an intruder (detested or otherwise) because (a) he secures a majority shareholding in two of these companies. The fact that other family members become minority shareholders is of no importance because the purchaser controls the company and its board. It might well have been relevant if these companies were family trading companies where family members had key roles in the management of company business including its staff and whose knowledge of its customer base was important or their personal reputation was significant, and formed part of the goodwill of the company. However, none of these factors is present. Mr Sutherland repeatedly emphasised that all three companies were essentially investment companies or family moneyboxes.'

In relation to the valuation of the minority shareholding of 26.8% in a company called Cape Wroth, the Special Commissioner stated (at para 98):

'Mr Eamer's approach was to consider the valuation of minority shareholdings (above and below 25%) in unquoted companies in a variety of reported cases. He starts by deducting 25% for the fact that shares in quoted investment companies and property investment companies trade at discounts of between about 10–30% of their net asset value (property investment companies being at the higher end of discount). From the resulting 75% he deducts 50% thereof for lack of marketability. From the resulting 37.5% he adds back 50% for what he describes as a nuisance factor because the shareholding exceeds (just) the 25% threshold. This produces a figure of 56.25% which he rounds down to 55%. This produces the discount of 45%. Lynall was said to be the basis for the nuisance factor. The result is the same as Mr Sutherland's standard figure.

99 On the valuation basis under discussion, Cape Wrath has an 8.16% shareholding in New Inverness. Mr Sutherland applies a discount of 70%. Mr Eamer applies 65%.

100 Mr Sutherland's view as that for such a powerless small minority holding in the light of the other factors summarised at paragraph 97 the minimum discounts is 70%. Mr Eamer's approach was as set forth in paragraph 98 except that he made no addition for the nuisance factor as the shareholding was less than 25%. This leads to a figure of 37.5% which he rounds down to 35%. This produces a resulting discount of 65%.

101 Although there is little difference between the experts here, I find Mr Eamer's approach to be preferable and accept it. It is based on such case law as exists and seems to me to be a fair and logical assessment. The factors advanced by Mr Sutherland do not seem to be of sufficient weight to reduce further the general levels of discount advanced by Mr Eamer. But for these factors my impression is again that Mr Sutherland would not have quarrelled with Mr Eamer's figures. A small minority shareholder can never control dividend policy. The fact that the companies are moneyboxes does not it seems to me make them less attractive for minority shareholder or a majority shareholder and therefore seems to me to be irrelevant to the question of discount. Likewise, I struggle to see the particular relevance here (as opposed to generally) of the prospect of sale or liquidation to the question of discount for a minority shareholding. Finally, it seems to me that a shareholding which is just over 25% may well have more value than a shareholding which is just under 25%. Although the business of private companies is not run by the passing of special resolutions, the power to block such a resolution may be a valuable weapon in a minority shareholder's armoury, particularly where, as here, assumed hostility between the hypothetical incoming and the existing shareholders has been emphasised. While the add back of 50% advanced by Mr Eamer may be at the high end of the scale, I am unable to conclude that it is outwith the range of figures which might properly be selected. At the end of the day the two valuations are, overall, similar and in relation to Cape Wrath, the minority shareholding, very similar (Eamer £81,955, Sutherland £59,393). If each is adjusted by 15% the difference is less than £1,500.'

In the First Tier Tribunal case of *Stephen Marks v HMRC* [2011] UKFTT 221 (TC), the tribunal judge, John Avery Jones CBE, reviewed the law on share valuation of *Walton v IRC* [1996] STC 68, an agricultural tenancy was owned in different family proportions to the freehold and the deceased's interest in the tenancy was valued separately from his interest as landlord, following *Trocette Property Co Ltd v Greater London Council* (1974) 28 P&CR 408 at 420 (see **3.01**).

Judge Avery Jones explained (at paragraph 27):

'In *Trocette* the landlord was the planning authority which had a planning intention for the land in question and so a purchaser would know that there was no possibility of its acting in such a way so that a share of the "marriage value" could be obtained for the leasehold interest. In *Walton* Peter Gibson LJ said at 88a:

> "It is not necessary for the operation of the statutory hypothesis of a sale in the open market of an interest in a tenancy that the landlord should be treated as a hypothetical person, and it is a question of fact to be established by the evidence before the tribunal of fact whether the attributes of the actual landlord would be taken into account in the market. I would add that the same logic requires that in the case of a deceased partner owning an interest in a tenancy which is a partnership asset, regard should be had to the actual intention of the actual surviving partner and not to a hypothetical partner".

28. Applying the same principle here, the statutory hypothesis does imply the existence of a hypothetical purchaser but does not require one to ignore the characteristics of any actual potential purchasers. It is inherent in the recognition of a special purchaser in *IRC v Clay* [1914] 3 KB 466 that a real prospective purchaser, there the owner of the neighbouring property which wanted to extend it, was known to be in the market. There is also no doubt that the Appellant's separate ownership of the two groups would be known to the other potential purchasers in the market. As Hoffmann LJ said in *IRC V Gray* [1994] STC 360 at 372 also in relation to a valuation of land:

> "The hypothetical vendor is an anonymous but reasonable vendor, who goes about the sale as a prudent man of business, negotiating seriously without giving the impression of being either over-anxious or unduly reluctant. The hypothetical buyer is slightly less anonymous. He too is assumed to have behaved reasonably, making proper inquiries about the property and not appearing too eager to buy. But he also reflects reality in that he embodies whatever was actually the demand for that property at the relevant time. It cannot be too strongly emphasised that although the sale is hypothetical, there is nothing hypothetical about the open market in which it is supposed to have taken place. The concept of the open market involves assuming that the whole world was free to bid, and then forming a view that what in those circumstances would in real life have been the best price reasonably obtainable. The practical nature of this exercise will usually mean that although in principle no one is excluded from consideration, most of the world will usually play no part in the calculation. The inquiry will often focus on what a relatively small number of people would be likely to have paid. It may have to arrive at a figure within a range of prices which the evidence shows that various people would have been likely to pay, reflecting, for example, the fact that one person had a particular reason for paying a higher price than others, but taking into account, if appropriate, the possibility that through accident or whim he might not actually have bought. The valuation is thus a retrospective exercise in probabilities, wholly derived from the real world but rarely committed to the proposition that a sale to a particular purchaser would definitely have happened.
>
> On that basis there seems no need to exclude an actual potential purchaser from the market. It is interesting that the RICS Red Book relating to valuations of land does include the actual owner as a potential purchaser and so this is recognised in other valuation contexts. One further problem that arises in relation to share valuation is that the actual owner's information about the asset being valued is bound to be greater than the information that a prudent prospective purchaser might reasonably require. However, there is no theoretical difficulty in assuming that the actual owner cannot

use any information beyond that reasonably required in deciding how much to offer."

29. We do not consider that the presence of the Appellant, with his knowledge treated as limited to what a prudent prospective purchase would reasonably require, would affect the value of each company viewed in isolation because all potential purchasers would use a similar valuation method based on a multiple of earnings. Where we consider that it would make a difference is that if the Appellant, as owner of FCO, is in the market as a potential purchaser of SMHL from a hypothetical vendor (and vice versa). As owner of the company not being valued he has an interest in buying the company being valued from the hypothetical vendor so that he can continue to own both companies and continue the existing relationship between them. For example, on a valuation of FCO and treating it as a vehicle for SMHL selling outside the UK, the Appellant, as owner of SMHL, would want to continue to have such a sales outlet rather than set up a new one; and he would want to continue to have Briardene Enterprises' (an FCO group company) continued function as purchasing agent for the SMHL group. And on a valuation of SMHL the Appellant, as owner of FCO, would want to continue to be able to continue to use the trade marks owned within the SMHL group. We consider that this factor removes any issue of each group being worth less because it needs the existence of the other to continue to make profits in the same way as in the past. For example, it could be argued that FCO is worth less to an independent buyer because its established turnover is of French Connection clothes which the buyer would have to replace from another source and then persuade the existing customers to buy under another label. Similar arguments could be made that FCO did not have an assured continuation of its existing funding. But if the Appellant, as owner of SMHL is in the market as a potential purchaser of FCO he will value FCO on the basis that it will continue to be able to sell "French Connection" clothes to the existing customers and that the funding of the FCO group by the SMHL group will continue. In other words, the valuation is on the basis that the business will continue as before.

30. A similar issue relates to what assumption should be made about the management of the two groups. In the real world we have no doubt that the Appellant, as a typical successful entrepreneur would not work for either group if he were not substantially the owner. The law is silent on this, perhaps because it has developed mainly in relation to death duties, but we consider that we should assume the continuation of the present management. We note that the Special Commissioner in *Marks and Sherred* [2004] STC (SCD) 362 made the same assumption at [20]. Fortunately Miss Hennessey proceeds on this assumption and so the possibility of the management leaving is not in issue as a reason for reducing the value.

31. A further issue where the experts disagreed was in relation to the provision of information that a prudent prospective purchaser would reasonably require but which was not in fact available. Miss Hennessey assumed that it was unlikely that reliable financial information about FCO would have been available to the prospective purchaser on 31 March 1982. Mr Eamer worked on the basis that the purchaser would not be subject to the unsatisfactory state of the accounting information of FCO and assumed that the correct information would be provided. He based this on the statement of the Special Commissioners in *Hawkings-Byass v Sassen* [1996] STC (SCD) 319, 333:

> "Experts and we ourselves alike are at a serious disadvantage through the accounts of CB Cayman being so unreliable. A real potential purchaser in the market on 31 March 1982 would have had the accounts restated."

> Mr Gibbon contended that only information actually available was assumed to be provided. We agree with Mr Gibbon. It is inherent in the hypothesis that the information is available to be supplied. The assumption relates to the information that he might reasonably require if he were proposing to purchase the asset from a willing vendor by private treaty and at arm's length. If one assumes a sale by private treaty the purchaser cannot be put in a better position than the seller if the seller does not have the information that the purchaser reasonably requires. The quotation from *Hawkings-Byass* relates to what a *real* purchaser would have done; the hypothetical purchaser has to take the company in its actual state.'

Mr Avery Jones went on to explain the reasons for the tribunal's valuation, and at 34(2) continued:

> 'The PE ratios are on the face of it similar: Mr Eamer 15.4 (including the bid premium) (based on a full tax charge), and Miss Hennessey 18.1 (13.9 adjusted for the bid premium) (based on the actual tax charge). This was in the time of 100% first year allowances and stock relief and so the actual tax charge could be very different from the nominal tax rate on the accounting profit and so the difference between the two bases is significant. For SMHL the actual tax charge for the year to 31 January 1982 was 16% (all deferred tax) compared to the 52% nominal tax rate. Miss Hennessey's PE ratio of 18.1 (after the bid premium) based on the profits after actual tax would equate to a PE ratio of 31.7 based on a full tax charge (the limit of the marginal relief of the small companies rate was £200k). On a consistent full tax charge basis therefore Miss Hennessey's PE ratio is twice that of Mr Eamer's basis and so they are not as similar as they appear at first sight. The PE ratio of Miss Hennessey's comparable, Lee Cooper, was almost the same on both bases: 6.2 on the full tax charge, and 6.2 on the actual tax charge, but the average PE ratios for the companies used as comparables by Mr Eamer was 14.5 on a full tax basis and 9.7 on an actual tax charge basis. We believe that Miss Hennessey, having calculated a PE ratio of 13.9 (before bid premium) as a check on her valuation derived from a turnover multiple then compared it to Hepworth's PE of 23.8 and those of other companies all of which are based on a full tax charge and which are not comparable; the PE ratio for Hepworth based on the actual tax charge was 15.2.
>
> Mr Eamer made a number of adjustments to the PE ratio derived from the average of some quoted companies as set out in paragraph 18 above. He did not provide any evidence of support these and we regard the adjustments as his estimate of a suitable PE ratio. Both experts applied a 30% bid premium for valuing the controlling holding (although as shown above Mr Eamer applied his percentage adjustments successively to the total after the previous adjustments with the 30% bid premium at the beginning of his calculation).
>
> The other significant difference in their valuations is caused by applying their PE ratios to different profit figures: Mr Eamer to an estimated consolidated profit for SMHL and FCO for the year to 31 March 1983 of £1.14m before tax and £547K after a full tax charge; Miss Hennessey the actual profit of SMHL for the year to 31March 1982 of £203K before tax and £171K after an actual tax charge.'

The Commissioner explained the problem with possible comparables and the different assumptions of the experts, explaining at 34(8):

> 'We should like to add a plea to experts in cases like this in future that it would be helpful if they could separate the effect of their using different bases to measure the same thing, such as how PE ratios are calculated, from other differences in their views.'

The Commissioner explained why 'the future was likely to be much more successful than the past', and concluded that:

> 'This gives an "as listed" valuation of £2,853K and a PE ratio of 14.9 based on the three-year average of profits we are using and the actual tax charge (compared to Miss Hennessey's 13.9). Increasing this by 30% for control gives our valuation of SMHL at £3,709K, which is a PE ratio (including bid premium) of 19.4 (comparable to Miss Hennessey's 18.1).'

After receiving the possible comparables he continued:

> 'There is no information in the prospectus about the duration of the contract under which the commission was payable, but it states that "The Directors believe that overseas markets, in particular the United States, offer excellent opportunities for growth and that the Group's high reputation places it in a very strong position to exploit these markets". We infer that the licensing arrangements were not short term otherwise reference would have been made to their expiry in the prospectus. These trading arrangements would have been information available to a purchaser at the valuation date. We do not consider that we should give the Appellant an opportunity to provide further evidence on this and there is no point in asking for further expert evidence on valuation if the expert does not know the facts either. Using the tribunal's knowledge we consider that such commission income would be valued on a discounted cash flow basis of the present value of the expected future income stream. If one discounts a level 5 years' future commission at 40% pa to reflect the then high interest rates (bank base rates were then 13%) and the uncertainty factor of the commission continuing at the same rate because of changes in fashion the result is a value of about two years' commission. Accordingly we value the commission value at £293K. We should mention that in the absence of any information we have not placed any value on Briardene Enterprises Limited, which is part of the FCO group and is the buying agent in Hong Kong for all SMHL and FCO companies.
>
> Our valuation is therefore £3,709K for SMHL and £443K (£150K plus £293K) for SCO and we allow the appeal to the extent of the increase over the valuation used in the closure notice. We leave it to the parties to agree the tax payable with liberty to apply for us to determine this.
>
> We would do a credibility check on these values using the prospectus figures, not to use hindsight but to see how it compares to the offer. Our valuation equates to 27.3p per share compared to Miss Hennessey's 20.4p, and Mr Eamer's 55.4p and the offer price of 123p. For the combined group the offer price represented a PE ratio of 31 (or 40 on a post-bid premium basis comparable to the ones we have quoted) on post-tax profits of £601K for the year to 31 January 1983 (with a forecast pre-tax profit of £2.8m for 1984 (compared to £803K for 1983) which was made after 8 months of trading and which the market would expect would be achieved). We do not consider these circumstances are at all comparable as the combined group achieved considerable growth in profits from the pre-tax figure of £28K and post-tax of £7K for 1982. Another factor is that the stock market had risen between the two dates and the PE ratio for stores was then 55% higher than on 31 March 1982, which suggests that an equivalent PE ratio at 31 March 1982 would have been 20 (or 26 on a post-bid premium basis). If the PE ratio we had arrived at were as high as this we would not have regarded it as being credible, but it does not cause us to review our PE ratio of 14.9 (before the bid premium) or of £3.707m in a transaction between two companies which were wholly owned by the Appellant, although we accept that immediately before a flotation the groups had plenty of access to professional advice and would therefore have used a figure that they considered

to be realistic. But the French companies had become profitable for the first time in the year to 31 January 1983 and so were not in a comparable position. We consider that no credibility check is possible.'

Focus

While each case must be considered on its own facts in the light of the circumstances surrounding the valuation, the purpose for which it is being made and the relevant statute and case law, *Executors of Ian Campbell McArthur (dec'd) v RCC* does provide a useful insight into the judicial process in relation to share valuation.

Chapter 4

Fair value

Signposts

4.01 Valuation in accordance with an agreement

Open market value is not the only basis of valuation for company shares. Many private agreements, and indeed many companies' articles of association, provide that a transfer should take place at a 'fair value', which is often a value to be certified by the auditors.

The main reason for preferring a fair value to an open market value is that it is thought that an open market value discounts minority (or non-controlling) interests excessively. There is no statutory definition of fair value and it does not appear to have been considered in any great detail by the courts. The purpose of the fair value is to enable the valuer to exercise his discretion and judgment in the light of all the circumstances, in order to arrive at a value, which is fair to all parties, which can be a very subjective judgment. In the words of Nourse J in *Re Bird Precision Bellows Ltd* [1984] 2 WLR 869:

> 'While that which is fair may often be generally predicated in regard to matters of common occurrence, it can never be conclusively judged in regard to a particular case until the facts are known.'

What is established from court decisions is that if the parties agree to be bound by the valuer his decision is binding in the absence of negligence, fraud, mistake or miscarriage. In *Collier v Mason* (1858) 119 RR 394, a case involving a valuation dispute, the Master of the Rolls stated at 396:

> 'It is not proved that Mr Englehart (the valuer) did not exercise his judgment and discretion in the best way he could. It may have been improvident as between these parties to enter into a contract to buy and sell property at a price to be fixed by another person, but that cannot avoid the contract. Here the referee has fixed the price, which is said to be evidence of miscarriage, but this court, upon the principle laid down by Lord Eldon, must act on that valuation, unless there be proof of some mistake, or some improper motive, I do not say a fraudulent one: as if the valuer had valued something not included, or had valued it on a wholly erroneous principle, or had desired to injure one of the parties to the contract; or even, in the absence of any proof of any one of these things, if the price was so excessive or so small as to be explainable by reference to some such cause; in any one of these cases the court would refuse to act on the valuation. But I am satisfied that it is not so here, the price does not come up to that: one person, it is true, has valued the property at £2,634 and another at £2,834 and it is said that the valuation of Mr Englehart is nearly double; but I have frequently had to refer to the enormous discrepancy in bona fide valuations, when it is known by each valuer for what purpose the property is to be valued; it is impossible in such cases to avoid a species of bias. I find that £3,100 was offered for the property and refused and this is a test that the vendor did not consider that to be the value. The plaintiff said he would not take less than £3,500 and swears that he laid out £5,200 on the property exclusive of the fixtures and the valuation is £4,957. It does appear to me to be a very high and perhaps an exorbitant valuation, but I cannot say it amounts to evidence of fraud, mistake or miscarriage.'

Care has to be taken to comply with the precise terms of a valuation article, although the exact meaning of those terms is often open to different interpretation. For 'a classic example of how not to conduct an articles valuation of shares in a private company' (per Robert Walker J) the case of *Macro and others v Thompson and others (No 3)* [1997] 2 BCLC 36 is essential reading. Various aspects of that case and two associated cases are discussed in **4.02**.

Where a lease gave the lessees an option to purchase at a price to be agreed by two valuers, one to be nominated by the lessors and the other by the lessees and in default of agreement by an umpire to be appointed by the valuers, the House of Lords held in *Sudbrook Trading Estates Ltd v Eggleton & Others* [1982] 3 WLR 315, overruling a long line of cases up to the Court of Appeal, that the refusal of the lessors to appoint a valuer would give rise to injustice and the option was not a mere agreement to make an agreement. As a result the House of Lords ordered the lessors to convey the property to the lessees at a fair and reasonable price to be determined by the court on hearing the expert evidence of valuers, the lessors having clearly waived their contractual right to have the price assessed by the machinery for which the option clause is provided. The lessees were content also to waive their corresponding right to use that machinery.

In the complex and convoluted case of *Pennington v Crampton and Others* [2004] BCC 611 the judge held that the correct interpretation of the company's articles of association required that:

> 'the fair value to be fixed by the auditors is a value per single share from which it follows, as it seems to me and I so hold, that the auditors must take a fair value for the whole company and divide it between the 2,000 issued shares thereby producing a figure which applies consistently whether the block offered is over

> 50%, is between 25% and 50% or is less than 25% of the issued share capital, whatever may be the size of the holding of any likely buyer and whatever may be the number of shares that the buyer chooses to take up.
>
> In reaching this conclusion I am influenced above all by the consistent and apparently careful use of the singular throughout article 8 (B) and in contrast with article 5 with its use of the plural in relation to a subject matter which though different has some analogy to that in article 8 (B).
>
> The fair value under article 8(B) is a value per individual share and is to be derived from the auditors' assessment of the net value of the entire issued share capital, therefore, on a pro rata basis without regard to the size of the block of shares to be offered.
>
> In assessing the fair value of the company on this basis it is for the auditors to consider all relevant circumstances known to them as to which, what I have said in my judgement, probably amounts to no more than platitudes but it may be of some assistance but the only material point on which I have ruled of relevance is that they should not take into account litigation between the shareholders or between a shareholder (as such) and the company …
>
> One other question was raised by Grant Thornton, namely their status in making their determination. It ought not to affect the figure itself, but it would affect the standing of the figure and the ability of any disappointed party to challenge it. This was not in serious dispute between the parties, rightly in my judgment, because it seems to me plain that the auditors in fixing the fair value do so as experts and not as arbitrators. A valuation made in that way is not entirely beyond challenge but the scope of challenge is much more limited than if it had been the result of an arbitration.
>
> I find nothing in the article which suggests that the role of the auditor is as an arbitrator and everything including the choice of the auditor himself as someone already knowledgeable about the company, to suggest that it is to be an expert determination.'

In *Nugent v Benfield Greig Group Plc and Others* [2001] EWCA Civ 397 one of the shareholders, Mr Harding, was killed in a helicopter crash and on his death the notice in respect of his shares was deemed to have been given so that the company Benfield Greig Group Plc became the petitioner's agent for the sale of the shares. The valuation was carried out by PricewaterhouseCoopers who had been appointed auditors to the company in the autumn of 1998; they valued each share at £2.10. The executors had anticipated a price of at least £4.00, being the minimum price paid in two placements of shares which had taken place in 1987. They therefore sought advice from Deloitte and Touche, who provided a preliminary valuation which indicated a minimum value of £4.00 per share, which was based on limited information. The executors alleged that the offer price of £2.10 per share was not the true market value and was not a value that any reasonable valuer properly appointed and instructed could have arrived at. The judge held that such an allegation was unsustainable in law because the effect of the articles was to make the valuer an expert with the result that the valuation was final and binding; it was this allegation which was being argued on appeal.

Pricewaterhouse Coopers had valued the ordinary shares in December 1998 at £1.50 and the incentive shares to be issued to employees at £1.00, then submitted to the Inland Revenue and confirmed to Benfield that they had been unable to make sense of the placement prices at £4.00 and £4.17 per share. It was held that it was a reasonable argument that the petitioners had been unfairly prejudiced. First, by appointing Pricewaterhouse Coopers as valuers when they were not 'independent', ie they could not reasonably approach the task of valuer without restrictions imposed by the advice that they had given in very different circumstances. In particular, advice for the purposes of persuading the Inland Revenue to disregard the placements at £4.00 and to accept a value at which they had been arrived (sic). Second, they had also acted as advisers to Benfield upon another, but similar, matter that was in dispute between Benfield and the petitioners. In so doing it is arguable that they had compromised their ability to be an independent valuer. The appeal was therefore allowed and the case remitted back to the Companies Court. This case is authority for the contention that it may amount to an abuse of process for a person to issue a petition for unfair prejudice in circumstances where the Articles of Association or Shareholders' Agreement contains a mechanism for offering the claimant's shares to other shareholders at a fair price unless the claimant has first utilised the agreed valuation procedure, but it is not an abuse of process if the valuer is not independent.

The court may order the respondent to buy out the petitioner at a fair value with a price fixed by the court in the light of expert valuation evidence: *Re Curmana Ltd* [1986] BCLC 430; *Re D R Chemicals Ltd* [1989] 5 BCC 39; *Sethi v Patel* [2010] EWHC 1830; *Re Nuneaton Borough AFC Limited* [1989] 5 BCC 792; *Re Nuneaton Borough AFC Limited* [1991] 2 BCC 44. The buyout price has to be fair and may take account of a reduction in the share valuation as a consequence of unfairly prejudicial conduct.

Where the parties agree to abide by an expert's valuation, that valuation will not normally be disturbed by the court: *Burke v Bayne Services (Edinburgh) Ltd* [2011] CSIH 14. A petition for prejudicial conduct would be brought under the Companies (Unfair Prejudice Application) Proceedings Rules 2009, SI 2009/2469.

Where share valuation is referred to a single jointly instructed expert, his determination leads to a binding result. If one party is dissatisfied with the expert's determination there may not be very much that can be done about it. If it is a non-speaking determination of which no reasons are given it is difficult to set aside unless the expert has obviously departed from his instructions: *Jones v Sherwood Computer Services Plc* [1992] 1 WLR 277. So long as the expert has answered the right question and not materially departed from his instructions, it is binding even if the expert has made a mistake: *Nikko Hotels (UK) Ltd v MEPC Limited* [1991] 2 EGLR 103; *Veba Oil Supply and Trading GmbH v Petrotrade Inc* [2001] EWCA Civ 1832. However, if the contract appointing the expert is unconditional, apart from manifest error, it may be possible to set the determination aside on the basis of this decision, if the expert has departed from his instructions. These principles were confirmed in *Halifax Life Limited v The Equitable Life Assurance Society* [2007] 1 Lloyds Rep 528. Unlike arbitration, an expert determination does not grant the expert immunity from litigation: *Currys Group Plc v Martin* [1999] 3 EGLR165. Even though the expert's determination may not be set aside if he has acted negligently he can be sued for damages: *Bernhard Schulte GmbH and Co Kg and Others v Niall Holdings Ltd* [2004] EWHC 977. However, in order to sustain an action for negligence it is necessary to show that the valuation arrived at was outside the range of permissible values: *Merivale Moore v Strutt and Parker* [2000] PMLR 498, Levy.

An expert's determination can be set aside on the grounds of bias, either actual bias (*Re Medicaments and Related Classes of Goods (No 2)* [2001] 1 WLR 700), or an apparent bias, 'whether the fair minded and informed observer, having considered the facts, would conclude that there was a real possibility that the tribunal was biased': *Magill v Porter* [2001] UKHL 67, Lord Hope at paragraph 103.

4.02 Valuer's mistake

If, however, the valuer does make a material mistake the valuation can be revised.

In the valuation dispute of *Jones (M) v Jones (R R)* [1971] 1 WLR 840 it was agreed that the defendants should buy from an old company the shares in a new company at a valuation to be made by a Mr Dunn 'on an assets basis as between a willing vendor and a willing purchaser of a business being carried on as a going concern and otherwise in the manner therein mentioned'. It was specifically provided that Mr Dunn should act as an expert and not as arbitrator and the provisions of the Arbitration Act 1950 should not apply. This is commonly so provided in such cases. Ungoed-Thomas J stated:

> 'So Mr Dunn refers expressly to instructions to Mr Denton Clark and to his having received his valuation. Those instructions and valuations were, as I have concluded, for a break-up valuation instead of, as they should have been, for a going concern valuation. It was established, and as I understand it, it is common ground that a going concern valuation would materially exceed a break-up valuation. There is no reference to the valuation of machinery in Mr Dunn's valuation even though it refers expressly to paragraph 12 of the scheduled terms and provides for it. It was conceded that Mr Dunn did not employ an expert valuer to value the machinery.' And:
>
> 'It appears to be expressly stated by Sir Raymond Evershed MR and to be assumed and implicit in the judgments of Denning LJ and Wynn-Parry J that a valuation wrongly made on a break-up basis, instead of on a going concern basis, is a valuation on an "erroneous principle", within the observations quoted from *Collier v Mason* (1858) 119 RR 394 and *Dean v Prince* [1954] Ch 409. And even apart from authority, I would have no difficulty whatsoever in so concluding. And it seems to me that when a valuation of certain specified assets included in a valuation is directed to be by an expert valuer of such assets then the valuation of such assets by a person who is not such an expert valuer is simply not such a valuation as has been directed. If A and B agree to abide by a valuation by C it is a negation of that agreement to require either of them to abide by a valuation by Z. Such a departure, it seems to me, is clearly erroneous in principle; and the valuation of machinery by Mr Dunn instead of by an expert is therefore erroneous in principle in this case.
>
> Roskill J in *Frank H Wright (Constructions) Ltd v Frodoor Ltd* [1967] 1 All ER 433 at 457 in dealing with an error on the face of the certificate agreed with the general principle stated by Sir Raymond Evershed MR that an immaterial error does not vitiate a valuation. Yet he made it perfectly clear that an error, however small, in what had to be certified was a material error. He said:
>
> > "If this error had been material it would have been enough to vitiate the whole of the certificate, small as it might be, and regrettable as the consequences might be."

> And then he added with regard to the error in the case before him: "this error is not material because it does not affect the result", ie that the valuation and the price accordingly to be paid were nil.'

Ungoed-Thomas J concluded:

> 'The authorities thus to my mind establish that if a valuation is erroneous in principle, it is vitiated and cannot be relied on even though it is not established that the valuation figure is wrong.'

In the Hong Kong case of *Donnett v Cheung Cheung-Shui* (29 February 1988, unreported, Supreme Court of Hong Kong), Macdougall J set aside a speaking valuation as erroneous:

> 'Having heard the auditor's testimony I regret that I am led to the conclusion that, in determining the future maintainable income of the company and in deciding that the valuation should be based on three years purchase of the average profits of the company over the five years prior to his valuation, he did not consider all the relevant matters that he now claims he considered. In particular I do not believe that he really turned his mind to a consideration of whether the directors' remuneration for the years 1985 and 1986 was a fair charge for management, or to whether there had been exceptional, extraordinary or non-recurring profits or losses during the five year period he selected.
>
> In arriving at his valuation I am satisfied that, having dismissed the "net asset value" method, he did no more than apply the rule of thumb "that an average profit or loss over the immediate past five years would fairly describe a company's ability to earn profits" which the auditor stated in his letter of 23 October 1986 to be a principle "generally accepted in the commercial world".
>
> Indeed in his letter to the second defendant of 15 September 1986 the auditor dismissed consideration of the "net asset value" method for the simple reasons that the company did not own any real property and its furniture and equipment might realise only a fraction of their book value in a winding-up situation.
>
> During the course of the trial he was asked to produce the working papers on which his valuation was based. These comprised three pages, the first of which contained figures relating to the average profit method of calculation, and the remaining two concerned the net asset value method. There is nothing in these pages that provides any evidence of the thought processes he employed in arriving at his valuation or why he concluded that the average profit for the five years to July 1986 was a fair representation of the profitability of the company and did not include distorting factors. Nor is there any hint of the considerations that he referred to in the report which he prepared on 4 September 1987 more than seven months after the writ was issued and more than nine months after he issued his certificate of valuation.
>
> An examination of the working paper dated 22 October 1986 discloses an average net assets value of $1,649,453 for the five years on which the auditor based his valuation. This is more than twice the sum at which the auditor valued the class A shares.
>
> As Lord Reid observed in *A-G of Ceylon v Mackie* (1952) 31 ATC 435:
>
> > "No doubt, the value of an established business as a going concern generally exceeds and often greatly exceeds the total value of its tangible assets. But that cannot be assumed to be universally true. If it is proved in a particular case that at the relevant date the business could not have been sold for more than the value of its tangible assets, then that must be taken to be its value as a going concern."

Thus the average net assets for the five year period, including as it did the only two years in which losses had been sustained by the company, should have alerted the auditor that the figure he obtained by applying a simplistic rule of thumb method to calculate the value of a class A share was surprisingly low. When one considers that the net asset value of the company at the 31 July 1985, as disclosed by the last balance sheet available to the auditor when he arrived at his valuation, was $2,006,195, the disparity becomes even greater. Although he would not have had available to him the balance sheet which showed that the net current assets of the company as at 31 July 1986 stood at $3,280,099, he must have realised as the company's auditor, that the net assets were likely to be in that region. There is nothing in the working papers that indicates why the auditor concluded that the value of the class A shares was so much less than the net asset value of the company.

Mr Morrison expressed the view that the correct approach to the valuation of a class A share in the company would have been to have considered both the net asset value and the earnings of the company rather than to have made a choice between the two …

On a full consideration of all the evidence before me and bearing in mind the factors that I have already outlined I have come to the conclusion that the auditor fell into error in making his valuation in that he

(1) Failed to make allowance for the fact that sums paid as remuneration to the first, second, third and fourth defendants for the years ended 31 July 1985 and 1986 included an element which represented compensation for underpayment during the formative years of the company, such years not having been included in the calculation on which the valuation was based.
(2) Failed to make allowance for the fact that the sums paid as remuneration to the first, second, third and fourth defendants for the years ended 31 July 1985 and 1986 included an element which represented a distribution of profits.
(3) Failed to give sufficient weight to the net profit after tax for the years ended 31 July 1985 and 1986.
(4) Gave excessive weight to the net loss after tax for the years ended 31 July 1982 and 1983.
(5) Failed properly to consider the significance of the net asset values for the years ended 31 July 1985 and 1986. In all the circumstances the value of the net assets of the company for the year ended 31 July 1986 should have formed the minimum figure from which his valuation would proceed.

Applying the principles laid down in the authorities I have referred to I am satisfied that this is a proper case for the court to interfere. I therefore declare that the certified valuation of 27 November 1986 does not represent the fair value of a class A share in the company and that such valuation is not binding on the parties for the purposes of Article 25 of the Articles of Association. I also grant an injunction to restrain the defendants from acting on the valuation.'

In *Macro v Thompson (No 2)* [1997] 1 BCLC 626, the auditor of two companies had been instructed to certify the value of shares in those companies, as a result of a judgment in a case brought under s 459 of the Companies Act 1985 (*Re Macro (Ipswich) Ltd* [1994] 2 BCLC 354. In the s 459 case expert property valuers for each side had agreed the values of properties owned by the companies. In their joint report the assets of the two companies were mistakenly transposed. The error was perpetuated in the judgment and the auditor based his valuation on the erroneous report. It was held that as the valuer had arrived at his valuation by reference to the assets of a different company, he had not carried out his instructions. As the fault did not derive from a question of judgement, the valuation was open to challenge by the court.

In *Paratus AMC Ltd & Anor v Countrywide Surveyors Ltd* [2011] EWHC 3307 (Ch) it was held that a property valuation was not negligent. In this case the court determined that an acceptable margin of error was 8% either side of £175,000, ie between £160,000 and £190,000, so the valuation of £185,000 fell within the bracket and was not negligent. Interestingly, the claimant's expert's valuation was £154,000 and the defendant's £175,000. The court did not accept a value in between the two expert's figures but preferred that of the defendant's. However in the case of an acceptable margin of error, the claimant's expert valued the property within a bracket of 4% and the defendant's suggested a bracket of 12.5%, so the acceptable margin adopted by the court of 8% was approximately midway between the two experts' opinions on this point. A 90% loan to value was regarded as acceptable at the time.

In *Boyer Allan Investment Services Limited v HMRC* [2012] UKFTT 558 (TC) it was held that, following *Dextra Accessories Limited v MacDonald (HMIT)* [2005] UKHL 47, and FA 1989, s 43, the discovery assessment was valid and was made on the basis of or in accordance with the practice generally prevailing when it was made.

> **Focus**
>
> A fundamental mistake causes the valuation to be set aside.

4.03 Valuer's explanations

In the High Court valuation dispute case of *Dean v Prince* [1953] 3 WLR 271, Harman J had to consider the case where an auditor certified the fair value in accordance with the company's articles and one of the parties was dissatisfied with this valuation. The auditors were asked to explain their valuation and did so (a 'speaking' valuation) and it was argued that it was not legitimate to go beyond the auditors' certificate and look at explanations subsequently offered by the auditors to show that they proceeded on a wrong basis. In the words of Harman J:

> 'In my judgment there is nothing in that point. It is well settled that those who have a discretion, eg trustees, who have powers to apply income for maintenance and directors who have powers to admit members to a company can maintain a silence in regard to the reason of their decision which the court will not oblige them to break, and that if they do maintain silence no action will lie against them, but if they chose, for whatever reason, to disclose the motives which impelled them to their decision the plaintiff may come to the court to impeach these motives. This seems to me to be analogous to what has happened here. It is true that the auditors are dealing as experts and that they have to arrive at what is their opinion about the fair value. It may well be that their opinion, although wrong in the eyes of the others, may prevail, but if they had founded themselves on an entirely wrong basis and have chosen to explain that basis I cannot see that the provisions of Article 9(g) of the company's articles preclude the plaintiff from attacking it.'

The judge continued:

> 'The plaintiff was extremely dissatisfied with their [the auditors'] valuation but she would in my judgment have been powerless in the matter if the auditors had declined to expand their views. Short of fraud or dishonesty, which no one attributes to the auditors in this action, there was no way of questioning the certificate if the auditors declined to give reasons for the result at which they had arrived as the members of the company had committed themselves to be bound by their opinion. Unfortunately for the defendant the auditors did not keep quiet and being pressed to explain how they arrived at what the plaintiff (who knew a good deal about the company having acted as book-keeper and being the owner of the factory where most of the business was carried on) thought was an incorrect valuation they answered her solicitors.'

In this case the auditor had valued on a break-up basis and had not considered the possibility of a sale as a going concern.

The judge in the High Court therefore held that the valuation was not binding on the parties. However, in the Court of Appeal [1954] 2 WLR 538 the valuation was reconsidered. Article 9, para G of the company's articles of association provided:

> 'In the event of the death of any member his shares shall be purchased and taken by the directors at such price as is certified in writing by the auditor to be in his opinion the fair value thereof at the date of death, and in so certifying the auditor shall be considered to act as an expert, not as an arbitrator, and accordingly the Arbitration Act 1889 shall not apply.'

Sir Raymond Evershed MR stated:

> 'Having regard to the form of the articles it is not in doubt that, were it not for one circumstance, Mrs Dean could not have questioned the validity and conclusiveness of Mr Jenkinson's [the auditor's] certificate since no sort of imputation has been made or could be made of Mr Jenkinson's complete integrity. The one circumstance to which I have referred is this. Mr Jenkinson had (in the laudable hope of achieving agreement between Mrs Dean and the first two defendants) indicated in writing the method which he had adopted in arriving at his valuation.'

In the High Court, Harman J had held that by stating the reasons which had led him to arrive at his valuation Mr Jenkinson had exposed his certificate to examination by the courts into the validity of such reasons. At 753, Sir Raymond quoted with approval Sir John Romilly MR in *Collier v Mason* (1858) 119 RR 394 at 396 (see **4.01**).

Denning LJ:

> 'It [the valuation] can be impeached, not only for fraud, but also for mistake or miscarriage … For instance, if the expert added up his figures wrongly, or took something into account which he ought not to have taken into account, or conversely, or interpreted the agreement wrongly, or proceeded on some erroneous principle – in all these cases the court will interfere. Even if the court cannot point to the actual error, nevertheless, if the figure itself is so extravagantly large or so inadequately small that the only conclusion is that he must have gone wrong somewhere, then the court will interfere in much the same way as the Court of Appeal will interfere with an award of damages if it is a wholly erroneous estimate. These cases about valuers bear some analogy with the cases on domestic tribunals, except of course that there need not be a hearing. On matters of opinion, the courts will not interfere, but for mistake of jurisdiction or

> of principle, and for mistake of law, including interpretation of documents, and for miscarriage of justice, the courts will interfere. See *Lee v Showmen's Guild of Great Britain* [1952] 2 QB 829.'

The Court of Appeal came to the conclusion that the plaintiff had failed to prove that, even if there were any errors in principle by the valuer, it is unlikely that any such errors would produce in all the circumstances a figure of value materially different from that at which Mr Jenkinson arrived.

The distinction between speaking and non-speaking valuations and the previous authorities on the subject were considered in *Jones v Sherwood Computer Services plc* [1992] 1 WLR 277. At 284, Dillon J made the following comment:

> 'and it is convenient to say a little at this juncture about the distinction between speaking and non-speaking valuations or certificates, which to my mind is not a relevant distinction. Even speaking valuations may say much or little; they may be voluble or taciturn if not wholly dumb. The real question is whether it is possible to say from all the evidence which is properly before the court, and not only from the valuation or certificate itself, what the valuer or certifier has done and why he has done it. The less evidence there is available, the more difficult it will be for a party to mount a challenge to the certificate. This may lead of course to questions such as whether it is proper to join the certifier as a defendant in proceedings for the purpose of getting discovery from him, a matter considered by Geoffrey Lane LJ in *Campbell v Edwards* [1976] 1 WLR 403, 408–409, and whether it is proper to administer interrogatories to the certifier to discover his reasons, a matter considered in an analogous field in *Berry v Tottenham Hotspur Football and Athletic Co Ltd* [1935] Ch 718 and *Duke of Sutherland v British Dominions Land Settlement Corporation Ltd* [1926] Ch 746; but those questions do not arise on this appeal.'

The judge pointed out that Lord Denning had changed his views on the matter between *Dean v Prince* [1954] Ch 409 and *Campbell v Edwards* [1976] 1 WLR 403, but this change of opinion was justified because by 1976 the principle had been established that an expert or valuer can be sued for negligence. See **4.05** on this point. He said at 287:

> 'We also therefore are free to look at the matter afresh on principle, and are not bound by the law as stated by common consensus in *Dean v Prince* [1954] Ch 409. On principle, the first step must be to see what the parties have agreed to remit to the expert, this being, as Lord Denning M. R. said in *Campbell v Edwards* [1976] 1 WLR 403, 407G, a matter of contract. The next step must be to see what the nature of the mistake was, if there is evidence to show that. If the mistake made was that the expert departed from his instructions in a material respect – eg, if he valued the wrong number of shares, or valued shares in the wrong company, or if, as in *Jones (M) v Jones (R R)* [1971] 1 WLR 840, the expert had valued machinery himself whereas his instructions were to employ an expert valuer of his choice to do that – either party would be able to say that the certificate was not binding because the expert had not done what he was appointed to do.'

He added at 288:

> 'If the parties to an agreement have referred a matter which is within the expertise of the accountancy profession to accountants to determine, and have agreed that the determination of the accountants is to be conclusive, final and binding for all purposes, and the chosen accountants have made their determination, it does

> not seem appropriate that the court should rush in to substitute its own opinion, with the assistance of further accountants' evidence, for the determination of the chosen accountants.'

The decision of Nourse J in *Burgess v Purchase & Sons (Farms) Ltd* [1983] 2 WLR 361 was disapproved. In that case Nourse J said, at 10:

> 'In my judgment the present state of the law can be summarised as follows. The question whether a valuation made by an expert on a fundamentally erroneous basis can be impugned or not depends on the terms expressed or to be implied in the contract pursuant to which it is made.'

Following the decision in *Jones v Sherwood Computer Services plc* [1992] 1 WLR 277, that no longer appears to be the case.

In *Morgan Sindall plc v Sawston Farms (Cambs) Ltd* [1997] EGCS 118, one of the reasons given by the Court for not allowing a non-speaking valuation of land to be set aside was that there was no evidence on the face of the valuation that a mistake had been made. This further confirms Harman J's comment in *Re a company (No 000330 of 1991), ex p Holden* [1991] BCLC 597 that a non-speaking articles valuation is unpredictable in its outcome but is nevertheless normally immune from challenge.

In *Brian and Doreen Foulser v HMRC* [2015] UKFTT 220 (TC) the value of gifts in an unquoted company, BG Foods, on 24 November 1997 was eventually determined in the First Tier Tribunal on 30 April 2015.

Brian Spence for Mr and Mrs Foulser valued Mr Foulser's 51% shareholding at £6,000,000 and Mrs Foulser's 9% shareholding at £243,750. Christopher Glover for HMRC valued Mr Foulser's shareholding at £20,638,000 and Mrs Foulser's at £2,500,000.

Mr Spence annualised the 5 months' pre-tax profits of £1.503 million and added back £250,000 for improved efficiency and deducted £1 million for foreign exchange profits and reduced interest receivable by £117,000 and increased interest payable by £409,000 on anticipated increased borrowings for the new factory and £10,000 added back for intellectual property. 31% was deducted for tax to arrive at post-tax maintainable earnings of £1.615 million to which a capitalisation factor of 8 to 10 gave rise to a company value of between £12.92 million and £16.15 million. Mr Spence's capitalisation factors came from BDO's Stoy Hayward's Private Company Price Index (PCPI). He referred to the third edition of this book to arrive at a discount of 20% for a 51% shareholding and arrived at a value of £6 million. Mrs Foulser's 9% shareholding was calculated as £243,750 on the basis of a 24% required yield on an assumed dividend return of 9%.

Mr Glover, applying his experience and subjective judgment arrived at an 'as quoted' P/E ratio of 15 which he said is approximately equivalent to the Food Producers Sub Sector P/E ratio of 14.67 discounted by 25%. Mr Glover added a bid premium of 40% to arrive at a control P/E ratio of 21, which, applied to the historical earnings of £1,927,000, produces an entirety value for BG Foods of £40,467,000. An historical P/E ratio of 21 translates into a P/E ratio of 15 on projected earnings of £2,698,000 calculated as the percentage increase in turnover between the six-month periods ended 31 October 1996 and 1997 of 140% of £1,927,000. He justified the P/E ratio of 15 by comparison with private bids. The discount applicable to a bare majority of votes is computed as 15%, valuing Mr Foulser's shareholding as £17,542,000 and Mrs Foulser's 9%

shareholding as £2,185,000 applying discount of 40%. There was an indicative offer for the Foulser shares of £26 million in 1997 for 60% of BG Foods.

The Tribunal considered that the PCPI ratio would not have been used for a valuation of this nature due to lack of transparency and comparability and P/E ratios based on historical earnings not future maintainable earnings. Mr Spence's methodology was therefore considered to be flawed by the Tribunal.

Mr Glover's use of the P/E ratio was endorsed by the Tribunal. Mr Spence argued that a discount of 20% was appropriate, quoting *Practical Share Valuation*, with which the Tribunal agreed. Mr Glover's preferred discount of 40% for the minority discount was amended to 50% by the Tribunal. The Tribunal preferred Mr Glover's methodology over that of Mr Spence. Mr Glover's control premium of 40% was reduced to 35% and the discount from the entity value was increased from 15% to 20% resulting in a valuation of Mr Foulser's shares of £15,920,873 and Mrs Foulser's 9% shareholding, subject to a 50% discount, was valued at £1,755,978.

In *Foulser and Foulser v HMRC* [2013]) UKUT 038 (TCC) the matter which was before the First Tier Tribunal (FTT) was an application by HMRC to summarily dismiss on application for an order effectively debarring HMRC from taking any further part in a tax appeal against an assessment to tax made by HMRC, reported at [2005] STC (SCD) 374 (Special Commissioners), [2006] STC 311 (High Court), and [2007] STC 973 (Court of Appeal) as a result of claims for hold-over-relief.

The appeal against a strike-out was allowed and the case referred back to the FTT.

In *Premier Telecom Communications Group Limited (PTCG) and Darren Michael Ridge v Darren John Webb* [2014] EWCA Civ 994, PTCG was a successful private company, 60% of whose shares were owned by Mr Ridge and 40% by Mr Webb. There was a dispute, and the company and Mr Ridge agreed to buy out Mr Webb's shareholdings.

Grant Thornton accepted the appointment as expert valuers on the terms set out in a letter of engagement dated 4 December 2012. It included the following provisions:

> 'You have asked us to undertake a valuation of the shares of PTCG on the following bases:
>
> - Fair value on a pro rata basis, ie no discount to reflect a minority shareholding.
> - As at 30 June 2012, unless it is our opinion that attempts have been made to artificially manipulate the value of PTCG, whereby we would be entitled to make such adjustments as we see fit.
>
> In valuing PTCG we will assume that the fair value is equal to the market value, which is defined by the International Valuation Standards Board as:
>
>> "the estimated amount for which as asset or liability should exchange on the date of valuation between a willing buyer and a willing seller in an arm's length transaction after a proper marketing and where the parties had acted knowledgeably, prudently and without compulsion".
>
> Further, in performing our valuation we will assume that the relationships in place as at 30 June 2012 continue to exist for the purposes of the valuation …'

The valuation was challenged by PTCG and Mr Ridge.

The court summarised the applicable principles:

> '8. Having considered the leading authorities on challenging expert valuations, including *Jones v Sherwood Computer Services Plc* [1992] 1 WLR 403, *Nikko Hotels (UK) Limited v MEPC Plc* [1991] 2 EGLR 103, *Pontsarn Investments Limited v Kansallis-Osake-Pankki* [1992] 1 EGLR 148, the dissenting judgment of Hoffmann LJ in *Mercury Communications Limited v Director General of Telecommunications* [1994] CLC 1125, *Thorne v Courtier* [2011] EWCA Civ 460 and *Barclays Bank Plc v Nylon Capital LLP* [2011] EWCA Civ 826, [2012] Bus LR 542, the judge summarised the relevant principles in paragraph 40 of his judgment as follows:
>
> > "40. Drawing the threads of the cases together, it seems to me that they support the following principles:
> > (1) Where the parties have chosen to resolve an issue by the determination of an expert rather than by litigation or arbitration, the expert's determination is final and binding unless it can be shown that he acted outside his remit.
> > (2) A distinction must be drawn between the expert who has misunderstood or misapplied his mandate with the consequence that this has not embarked on the exercise which the parties agreed he should undertake, and the expert who has embarked on the right exercise but has made errors in conducting that exercise and has come up with what is arguably the wrong answer.
> > (3) A failure of the first kind means that the determination is not binding because it is not a determination of the kind that the parties have contractually agreed should be binding.
> > (4) A failure of the second kind does not invalidate the determination, but may leave the expert exposed to a claim in negligence.
> > (5) In deciding whether an expert determination can be challenged, the first step is to construe his mandate. This is ultimately a matter for the court.
> > (6) The second step is to ascertain whether the expert adhered to his mandate and embarked on the exercise he was engaged to conduct by asking himself the right question(s) and applying the correct principles.
> > (7) Once it is shown that the expert departed from his instructions in a material respect, the court is not concerned with the effect of that departure on the result. The determination is not binding.
> > (8) Where the expert has made an error on a point of law which is not delegated to him, the error means that the determination will be set aside. (It has yet to be decided whether an error by the expert on *any* point of law arising in the course of implementing his instructions will also justify setting aside the determination – see Lord Neuberger MR in *Barclays Bank v Nylon Capital* [2011] EWCA Civ 826.)"
>
> ...
>
> *Conclusion*
>
> 29. For the reasons I have given, I am satisfied that the questions of construction which underpin the grounds of appeal can properly be decided without the need for a trial. Once they have been decided, I think it becomes clear that there is no real prospect that the claim would succeed at trial. For those reasons I think that the judge was right to grant Mr Webb summary judgment and I would dismiss the appeal.'

The Court of Appeal case of *Begum v Hossain and Sunam Tandoori Limited* [2015] EWCA Civ 717 involved an Indian restaurant and the two founders under which Mr Hossain agreed to purchase Ms Begum's shareholding in the company as independently valued. The valuer's decision was contested by Ms Begum.

The valuer used the Income Approach or Earnings Multiplier under which an 'all risks' yield or multiplier is applied to maintainable income. The multiplier is selected to directly reflect market sentiments.

The valuer relied on the accounts and did not give any consideration to the handwritten takings which appeared to show that the figures in the trading accounts were significantly understated but had been used for VAT purposes.

It was held that the handwritten takings should not have been ignored as the instructions were to base the fair valuation on the books and records of the company which included the handwritten takings and the valuation was set aside as the valuer should have enlisted the assistance of an accountant, at the parties' expense. The appeal was allowed.

> **Focus**
>
> If and when a valuation can be challenged depends on several factors, and it is usually preferable to ask for a speaking valuation.

4.04 Fair value

Denning LJ in *Dean v Prince* [1954] 2 WLR 538 had some interesting points to make on a fair valuation of a majority holding compared with the open market value valuation of such a holding, although he subsequently took a different view in *Campbell v Edwards* [1926] 1 WLR 403 (see **4.03** above):

> '(1) The right to control the company
>
> The judge (in the High Court) said that the auditor should have taken into account the fact that 140 shares were a majority holding and would give a purchaser the right to control the company. I do not think that the auditor was bound to take that factor into account. Test it this way. Suppose it had been Mr Prince who had died leaving only 30 shares. Those 30 shares, being a minority holding, would fetch nothing in the open market. But does that mean that the other directors would be entitled to take his shares for nothing? Surely not. No matter which director it was who happened to die his widow should be entitled to the same price per share, irrespective of whether her husband's holding was large or small. It seems to me that the fair thing to do would be to take the whole 200 shares of the company and see what they were worth and then pay the widow a sum appropriate to her husband's holding. At any rate, if the auditor was of the opinion that that was a fair method, no one can say that he was wrong. The right way to see what the whole 200 shares were worth would be to see what the business itself was worth, and that is what the auditor proceeded to do.
>
> (2) Valuation of the business "as a going concern"
>
> The judge seems to have thought that the auditor should have valued the business as a going concern. I do not think the auditor was bound to do any such thing. The business was a losing concern which had no goodwill, and it is fairly obvious that, as soon as Mrs Dean had sold the one hundred and forty shares to the other two directors – as she was bound to do – she would in all probability call in the

moneys owing to herself and to her husband amounting to over £2,000. The judge said that she was not likely to press for the moneys because that would be "killing the goose that laid the eggs", but he was wrong about this, because as soon as she sold the shares, she would have got rid of the goose and there was no reason why she should not press for the moneys. She was an executrix and the company's position was none too good. It had only £1,200 in the bank to meet a demand for £2,200. In these circumstances, the auditor was of opinion that there was a strong probability of the company having to be wound-up, and he rejected the going-concern basis. For myself, I should have thought he was clearly right, but, at any rate, no one can say that his opinion was wrong.

(3) Valuation of the assets of the business

Once the going-concern basis is rejected, the only possible way of valuing the business is to find out the value of the tangible assets. The judge thought that the assets should have been valued as a whole in situ. It was quite likely, he said, that "some one could have been found who would make a bid for the whole thing, lock, stock and barrel". But the judge seems to have forgotten that no one would buy the assets in situ in this way unless he could also buy the premises, and the company had no saleable interest in the premises. In respect of part of the premises the company had only a monthly tenancy. In respect of the rest, the company had only a contract for the purchase of the premises on paying £200 a year for 25 years. It had no right to assign this contract, and its interest was liable to be forfeited if it went into liquidation, either compulsory or voluntary; and the probability was, of course, that, if it sold all the assets, it would go into liquidation, and hence lose the premises. The company could, therefore, only sell the assets without the premises. That is how the auditor valued them and no one can say that he was wrong in so doing.

(4) Valuation on a "break-up" basis

The auditor instructed the valuer, Colonel Riddle, to value the plant and machinery at the break-up value as loose chattels on a sale by auction. The judge thought that was a wrong basis because it was equivalent to a forced sale. I would have agreed with the judge if the business had been a profitable concern. The value of the tangible assets would then have been somewhere in the region of £4,000 or £5,000, being either the balance sheet figure of £4,070 or Mr Pressley's figure of £4,835. But the business was not a profitable concern. It was a losing concern, and it is a well known fact that a losing concern cannot realise the book value of its assets. There is an element to be taken into account which is sometimes spoken of as "negative goodwill". It comes about in this way. If a business is making a loss, that shows that its assets, regarded as an entity, are not a good investment. A purchaser will decline, therefore, to buy on that basis. He will only buy on a piece-meal basis, according to what the various assets, taken individually are worth, and it is obvious that on a sale of assets piece-meal, the vendor will suffer heavy losses as compared with the book figures. The auditor was, therefore, quite justified in asking the valuer to value the assets as loose chattels sold at an auction. At any rate, if he honestly formed that opinion, no one can say he was wrong.

(5) The special purchaser

The judge thought that someone could have been found to buy the one hundred and forty shares, who would use his majority holding to turn out the two directors, and reorganise the factory and put in his own business. In other words, that the shares would have a special attraction for some persons (namely, the next-door neighbour) who wanted to put his own business into these premises. I am prepared to concede that the shares might realise an enhanced value on that

> account, but I do not think it would be a fair price to ask the directors to pay. They were buying these shares – under a compulsory sale and purchase – on the assumption that they would continue in the business as working directors. It would be unfair to make them pay a price based on the assumption that they would be turned out. If the auditor never took that possibility into account, he cannot be blamed, for he was only asked to certify the fair value of the shares. The only fair value would be to take a hypothetical purchaser who was prepared to carry on the business if it was worth while so to do, or otherwise to put it into liquidation. At any rate, if that was the auditor's opinion, no one can say he was wrong.'

The authors do not agree that a non-controlling holding necessarily has the same value per share as a controlling holding or that a fair value under the articles is necessarily the same as the value of the entire company divided pro rata among the shareholders, as that seems to ignore the fact that the holder of a non-controlling interest is in fact in a much weaker position than a controlling shareholder and imparts on the shares a right they do not in fact possess; see *Short v Treasury Comrs* [1948] 1 KB 116 (see **2.02**). It does, however, depend on the facts and in the case of a quasi-partnership a pro-rata value could indeed be a fair one.

In *Re Castleburn Ltd* [1989] 5 BCC 652, a case where the company's articles of association provided for shares to be valued at 'the fair value thereof at the date of such certificate (supplied by the auditors) on a sale by a willing vendor to a willing purchaser', it was held that the articles did not require the auditors to value the whole of the company's shares in order to arrive at the value of a particular holding. Paul Baker J made the following interesting comments at 656:

> 'Thirdly, under art 9.2 the auditors are required to certify the fair value on a sale "by a willing vendor to a willing purchaser". Thus one has to look at what a vendor would accept and a purchaser offer for the shares being valued, and one would expect this to include an uplift if the shares carried control, or a discount if they were a minority holding. Moreover the discount would vary according to the size of the parcel. One share out of 50,000 shares might be almost valueless, but 20,000 out of 50,000 could be expected to have a value higher than 20,000 times the value of one share, though less than 40% of the value of the entirety of the company's assets.'

The judge's reference to the 'company's assets' can be taken as including goodwill, since it is not suggested elsewhere in his judgment that the going concern value of this trading company should have been arrived at by reference to the tangible net assets.

In *Re a Company (No 006834 of 1988), ex p Kremer* [1989] BCLC 365, it was held that if a valuer was asked to determine a fair value it was for him to decide whether to apply a discount or not. It was also held that in most ordinary cases of breakdown the valuer would be entitled to fix a value which rejected the fact that the majority share-holder was an involuntary buyer as much as the minority shareholder was an involuntary seller. Referring to the position of the majority shareholder, Hoffmann J said:

> 'As majority shareholder he already controls the company and will usually derive his income from earnings rather than dividends. The only advantage of the purchase to him is the possibility of a capital gain on a sale or winding up at some future date. Nevertheless on account of the breakdown, he has unexpectedly

> to find the funds in order to pay out the petitioner. It seems to me that in an appropriate case the valuer should be entitled to fix a value which reflects the involuntariness of the purchase as well as the involuntariness of the sale …'

There are, however, cases where the company is run as a quasi-partnership and a valuation based on a pro rata proportion of the value of the company as a whole is appropriate, as in *Buckingham v Francis* (1986) 2 BCC 98984 and in *Re Bird Precision Bellows Ltd* [1984] Ch 419, [1984] 2 WLR 869. However, even in a quasi-partnership it is not necessarily correct to take a pro rata valuation; in *Whiteoak v Walker* (1988) 4 BCC 122, Terence Cullen QC stated at 126:

> 'Mr Sutherland's report made in February 1987 stated that, using the proper approach to the valuation, a fair value was £140,138. The proper approach in his view was to value the company as a whole on a net asset basis, and to attribute to the plaintiff's shares the proportion they represented of the total issued share capital of the company. This was called the pro-rata basis. This basis was to be used because the company was a quasi-partnership. It is also apparent from para 2(5), 6(2) and 7(5) of the report that at the time it was made Mr Sutherland was proceeding on the basis that the plaintiff had been ousted from the company. This was not so. But nevertheless the contention was initially pursued that failure to value on a pro-rata basis was negligent by the specialist standard.
>
> In cross-examination Mr Sutherland accepted that such failure could not be said to be negligent, even by that standard. I should add that, given the terms of art 19 and the provision that a transfer notice is to operate as a separate notice for each share, it is highly arguable, to say the least, that, as a matter of construction, the valuation must be on a pro-rata basis, but quite rightly, in my view, the plaintiff did not rely on this for his claim in negligence.'

Merely because a company is a quasi-partnership company does not mean that on any sale of the shares the vendor should receive the undiscounted value of his proportionate interest. In *Phoenix Office Supplies Ltd & Others v Larvin* [2003] BCC 11 it was held in the Court of Appeal that, where a member of a company resigned his employment but not his directorship in order to move to another part of the country for personal reasons, it was unreasonable for him to regard failure to supply him with information to check the value of his shares as prejudicial conduct, and even if it were, the remedy was to ask the Court to order the production of the information under CA 1985, s 461(2)(b). It was also apparent that he had retained his directorship merely to achieve as high a price as possible for his shares and he clearly had no intention whatever of discharging any of his duties as a director.

Although it was held on appeal that, in this case, there had not been prejudicial conduct, Lord Justice Auld summarised Lord Hoffmann's analysis in *O'Neill v Phillips* [1999] 1 WLR 1092 in connection with quasi-partnerships as follows:

> '• the unfair prejudice for which ss 459 and 461 provide a remedy is that suffered in the capacity of a company member;
> • a partner in a "quasi partnership" company who has not been dismissed or excluded cannot require his partner's to purchase his shares at a fair value simply because he has lost trust and confidence in them;
> • on the other hand it will almost always be unfair to exclude a minority shareholder without an offer to buy his shares or to make some other fair arrangement;

- the unfairness does not lie in the exclusion alone but in exclusion without a reasonable offer;
- it is therefore very important that participants in such companies should be able to know what counts as a reasonable offer, namely to purchase his shares at a fair value;
- ordinarily, fair value should represent an equivalent proportion of the total issued share capital, that is without discount for it being minority holding; and
- the offer should provide for equality of arms between parties, namely both should have the same right of access to information about the company which bears upon the value of the shares.'

Blackburne J, at first instance, looked at the valuation date on the assumption that there had been oppressive conduct within CA 1985, s 459, which was approved in the Court of Appeal. He stated:

> 'the law on the first issue is conveniently summarised in the recent Court of Appeal decision in *Pro Finance Trust SA v Gladstone* [2002] BCC 356 giving the judgment of the court, Robert Walker LJ said this (at para 60–61):
>
> > "60 … The starting point should, in our view, be the general proposition stated by Nourse J in *Re London School of Electronics Ltd* (1985) 1 BCC 99394 at p 99401:
> >
> > > 'Prima facia an interest in a going concern ought to be valued at the date on which it was ordered to be purchased.'
> >
> > That is, as Nourse J said, subject to the overriding requirement that the valuation should be fair on the facts of the particular case.
> >
> > 61 The general trend of authority over the last 15 years appears to us to support that as the starting point while recognising that there are many cases in which the fairness (to one side or the other) requires the Court to take another date, it would be wrong to try to enumerate all those cases but some of them can be illustrated by the authorities already referred to:
> >
> > (i) Where a company has been deprived of its business, an early valuation date (and compensating adjustments) may be required in fairness to the claimant (*Meyer*).
> >
> > (ii) Where a company has been reconstructed or its business has changed significantly, so that it has a new economic identity, an early valuation date may be required in fairness to one or both parties (*OC Transport* and to a lesser degree, *London School of Electronics*). But an improper alteration in the issued share capital unaccompanied by any change in the business will not necessarily have that outcome (*DR Chemicals*).
> >
> > (iii) where a minority shareholder has a petition on foot and there is a general fall in the market, the court may in fairness to the claimant have the shares valued at an early date especially if it strongly disapproves of the majority shareholder's prejudicial conduct (*Cumana*).
> >
> > (iv) But a claimant is not entitled to what the deputy Judge called a one-way bet, and the court will not direct an early valuation date simply to give the claimant the most advantageous exit from the company, especially where severe prejudice has not been made out (*Elgindata*).
> >
> > (v) All these points may be heavily influenced by the parties' conduct in making and accepting or rejecting offers either before or during the course of proceedings (*O'Neill v Phillips*)."
>
> …

In my judgement Mr Barclay Jones is correct and the valuation date should be taken as at today's date as being the date on which the order is made for Mr Parish and Mr Ogden to purchase Mr Larvin's shares. As the citation from *Profinance Trust* makes clear, that is the starting point.'

This case is also of interest in relation to the judge's comments on the valuation. After discussing the two experts' calculations of pre-tax annual maintainable earnings the judge went on to consider the appropriate price/earnings ratio to be applied. At paragraph 113 he stated:

'Mr Taylor's approach was as follows. Taking the view that there is no relevant industry sector for quoted P/E ratios and finding himself unable to identify any suitable comparators he applied a return on investment approach i.e. the return that a purchaser would require from his investment in a reasonably small private company. He contended that an investor would look to pay a sum equal to 5 × pre-tax profits equivalent to a 20% return on investments (to be compared with a 5% return on long-term UK gilts). A tax rate of 23% – the agreed rate – deals a post tax multiple of 6.5 or thereabouts. He then considered that benchmark return against positive factors that might be thought to increase the P/E ratio for the company (ie factors affecting the company which tend to suggest that the net profits will rise with reasonable certainty in the future) and then measured those factors against negative factors which would point in the opposite direction. He then concluded that although there is currently more business uncertainty in the market sector than there was in September 2000 the company was itself experiencing more uncertainty then than now so that overall the price earnings ratio had not changed. He assessed that ratio at 7.

114 Mr Barclay Jones criticised Mr Taylor's approach as somewhat rigid in that it starts with a benchmark return reached without regard to the company's circumstances. He also criticised some of the negative factors listed by Mr Taylor (such as the fact that the company made a loss in the year to August 31 2000) as being matters which had already been taken into account by him on reaching his figure for maintainable earnings. I consider that there is some force in these criticisms.

115 Mr Hine's approach was wholly different. He disagreed with Mr Taylor's approach as being of a "one size fits all" nature and inconsistent with his experience in the valuation of private companies. His method was to take the most comparable sector of quoted companies for which an average P/E ratio can be stated and then to discount that ratio to obtain the appropriate ratio for a private company in the same industry sector. The discount he applied is derived from an index called the private company price index produced on a quarterly basis by his firm in combination with "Acquisitions Monthly". The PCPI (as it is called) is calculated by reference to a vast number (running into several hundreds) of private company sales. By comparing that index (at the relevant valuation date) with the four month average (immediately proceeding the valuation date) of P/E for so-called FT non-financials (involving 600 quoted UK companies) he was able to arrive at a figure representing the difference in P/E between the two groups of companies (ie quoted non-financials and private companies). The differences intended to reflect the lack of marketability of the private company. That differential is then applied to the P/E ratio of a quoted company in the same market sector as the private company which is to be valued (in this case Phoenix Office Supplies Ltd). The resulting figure (or range of figures) represents the P/E ratio of the company being valued.

116 This method was all very well in theory. Where it tended to break down in the case of Phoenix Office Supplies Ltd was the absence at the relevant valuation

> date (ie currently) of any P/E for equivalent quoted companies. Thus although the discount of 40% (as at February 2002) arrived at by comparing the PCPI at December 2001 (12.6) with the four month average of FT non-financials PE (21.1) can be measured Mr Hinde had difficulty in applying that discount to the P/E of any comparable quoted company. The sector indices (IT, hardware and "distributors") quoted in the Financial Times which he had used in his earlier valuations had been discontinued by February 2002. He therefore attempted to "recreate" those indices and carry them through to February 2002.
>
> 117 The result of this exercise which is then checked against a similar exercise in relation to the P/Es of transactions involving quoted companies in supposedly related fields led him to arrive at a P/E range of 10 to 12. After making downward adjustments in the interests of prudence he reached a P/E of 10.1 for the company as at February 19 2002.
>
> 118 Whilst I do not question the extent to which this technique is used as a method of valuation it becomes as Mr Taylor argued and as I think Mr Hine admitted a somewhat imprecise tool where there is a lack of any P/E data for comparable companies. Its fallibility, to my mind, is well illustrated by considering what the effect is when a P/E of 10.1 is applied to Mr Hine's figures for post tax maintainable earnings as at February 2002 (ie £118,500) when compared with the result of applying the same P/E figure for post-tax maintainable earnings as at September 2000 ie £144,000. The calculation values the company at £1.44m in September 2000 and £1.18m currently. At the earlier date its net assets totalled £410,000. Currently its net assets stand at around £508,000. It is a little strange to suppose that despite the upturn in the company's fortunes since September 2000 as reflected in its increasing profitability and increasing net assets its goodwill value (based on maintainable earnings) should have declined by around £¼m.
>
> 119 I consider that the applicable P/E ratio at the current time lies between Mr Taylor's somewhat conservative figure of 7 and Mr Hind's over-generous figure of 10.1. Doing the best that I can I am of the view that it lies two full points below Mr Hine's figure ie 8.1 or thereabouts. Taking current post-tax maintainable earnings at £107,800 and applying a multiple of 8.1 produces a current valuation of the company of £873,180, say £880,000. 33% of that figure is £290,000. I therefore assess the current value of Mr Larvin's shareholding in that amount.'

The judge's reasoning was approved by the Court of Appeal apart from the fact that he had applied a full value basis without any discount for a minority shareholding. The Court of Appeal did not opine on what that discount should be.

In *Re a Company (No 002612 of 1984)* [1986] 2 BCC 99453 (*Re Cumana Ltd*) the majority shareholder held two thirds of the company's shares and a minority shareholder bringing the case for prejudicial conduct under CA 1980 s75, succeeded on the grounds that he was cut out of discussions on the distribution of profits after the company's business had been deliberately diverted into another company operating under the Cumana name and logo. In the words of Vinelott J:

> 'this diversion of profit from a company in which a petitioner is interested into another company in which he is not, is a classic instance of conduct unfairly prejudicial to him as a member.'

The majority shareholder also attempted to procure the company to make a rights issue for the dominant purpose of reducing the minority shareholder Mr Lewis's proportional stake in the company to under 1%. The remuneration paid to the majority shareholder was plainly in excess of anything he had earned and was so large as to be unfairly prejudicial to Mr Lewis. The judge also made the point that under CA 1980, s 75 (unlike CA 1948, s 210) it is sufficient to show that the affairs of the company have been conducted in a manner unfairly prejudicial to a minority shareholder. It is not necessary to show a continuing state of oppression.

It was suggested that the proper remedy would be to put the company into liquidation but the judge held that it would be unfair that the minority shareholder should be deprived of a share in the going concern value of a company in the formation of which he had participated and to the establishment of the business of which he made a significant if not an indispensable contribution. The judge thought that a liquidation would be inappropriate. He stated:

> 'I think the answer to that submission is that the only difference as regards Mr Bolton between a sale of all the shares in the company to an outside purchaser and a winding-up order is that if the company were wound up Mr Bolton would be in a position to appropriate substantially the whole of the company's business to himself. The senior members of the staff would follow him, he and Mr Mewson have always dealt with the company's suppliers and customers there would be no one able to outbid Mr Bolton if he made an offer to the liquidator for the right to use the company's name and logo". It was also suggested on behalf of Mr Bolton "that the courts should follow the form of order made by Pennycuick J in *Re Jermyn Street Turkish Baths Ltd* [1970] 1 WLR 1194 – that is should make an order giving Mr Bolton the option of purchasing Mr Lewis's shares at the fair value and in default of exercise of the option giving Mr Lewis the right to purchase Mr Bolton's shares at the fair value and providing in default of exercise of either option for the compulsory winding-up of the company. Mr Lewis has not the resources to buy Mr Bolton's shares. He could not sell all the shares and account to Mr Bolton for two-thirds of the proceeds without his full cooperation and in the light of Mr Bolton's past conduct I think he would use every means and pretext to frustrate the sale. An order in these terms would be equivalent to an immediate order for the compulsory winding-up of the company.'

The judge also rejected a submission that:

> 'if there is to be an order compelling Mr Bolton to buy Mr Lewis's shares at a value fixed by the court the valuation should be made on the footing that Mr Bolton is buying a minority shareholding.'

The judge relied on *Re Bird Precision Bellows Ltd* [1984] 2 WLR 869, [1984] BCLC 195. He also stated:

> 'I would add that it would, as I see it, also be inequitable that a majority shareholder whose conduct has found to be unfairly prejudicial to the minority, should be allowed to purchase at investment value shares which in his hands will have a higher value (in that he can sell them as part of a controlling interest).'

The judge therefore preferred 'to consider the evidence concerning the value of Mr Lewis's shares taken as a rateable portion of the value of the entire issued share capital of the company'.

The petitioner, Mr Lewis, was represented by R J Munson, a partner in Coopers & Lybrand, and the defendant, Mr Bolton, was represented by M J Lawrence, a partner in Price Waterhouse. The judge commented:

> 'It is common ground between Mr Munson and Mr Lawrence that in the case of a company like Cumana the assets of which are all employed in the

> business (so that none can be severed and sold separately) and are of little value by comparison with the profits generated by the business. The value of the company is simply the capitalised value of its profit earning capacity; in the often cited words of Holmes J "the commercial value of the property consists in the expectation of income from it" (see *Galveston H & SA Railway Company v Texas* (1908) 210 US 217). That value is normally arrived at by ascertaining the level of maintainable profit and then applying a multiplier derived from the price earnings ratio of comparable companies adjusted to meet the particular circumstances. It is important to bear in mind in this context that maintainable profit means (in Mr Munson's words):
>
> "The level below which in the absence of unforeseen and exceptional circumstances the profits after taxation would not be likely to fall in an average year".'

Mr Lawrence makes the same point, I think, in his report when he stresses that:

> 'the essential point is whether the current level of earnings is maintainable. As noted above the price/earnings ratio makes allowance for the expectation of future growth.'

The Court of Appeal in *Strahan v Wilcock* [2006] BCC 320 summarised with approval the factors which supported the judge at first instance's ruling that the company in question was a quasi-partnership:

> 'First, pursuant to the second option Mr Strahan bought 5 per cent of the company's shares, a not insignificant percentage. The only other shareholder was Mr Wilcock. Secondly the evidence showed that Mr Wilcock agreed to the second option as a reward for Mr Strahan's efforts in the company and as an incentive to him and this is confirmed by the fact that under the second option Mr Strahan had to pay for the shares he acquired out of his bonuses. Thirdly, at the relevant time Mr Strahan was participating in management decisions of the company. Indeed as I have said, Mr Wilcock had in effect become a sleeping partner. Mr Strahan became a signatory and possibly the only signatory on the mandate for the company's bank account. Fourthly the terms of the option agreement were informally agreed between them. The terms were never committed to writing and this reinforces the conclusion that there was a personal relationship involving mutual trust and confidence between the parties. Fifthly, while Mr Strahan was rewarded by the payment of remuneration he also received a share of the profits in the form of his bonus. In addition it was in effect agreed that Mr Wilcock should receive his return from the company in the form of dividends. In point of fact those dividends were substantially greater than Mr Strahan's remuneration. Mr Wilcock's case is that his return was in reality no more than a tax efficient way to pay remuneration. The judge made no finding on that but he found that as a fact that Mr Strahan had waived his right to receive any dividend on his shares whilst he was an employee of the company. The fact that Mr Wilcock and Mr Strahan came to an understanding or agreement as to the form of the return they were each to obtain from the company's profits is indicative that their relationship was more a quasi-partnership relationship than a relationship between a majority shareholder and the company executive. All these factors can be found among the findings of fact made by the judge in his judgment.'

In *G v G* [2002] EWHC 1339 (Fam) a company founded by three people was held to be a quasi-partnership and no discount for a minority interest was applicable in valuing the company for divorce proceedings. Most of the cases involving quasi-partnerships and a proportion of the value of the company as a whole have been either on the basis of such provision in the articles or shareholders' agreement or, most commonly, in the case of prejudicial conduct under CA 2006, s 994.

The fact that each of the shareholders had passed a significant proportion of their shares to Jersey trusts for their families did not impinge upon the nature of the company as a quasi-partnership. The judge stated:

> 'I have no difficulty whatever in finding that this is, and always has been, a quasi-partnership and also in finding that it would be unthinkable that any sale of this shareholding would take place other than in concert with the other main shareholders in the company. That was the situation with the M offer and I am sure it would be the situation if any such offer arose in the future. Either this shareholding will be sold at the same time as the other shareholdings or it will not be sold at all. I cannot seriously envisage a situation where the husband in this case would be forced to sell his interest in the company on the open market in circumstances in which a discount would be forced upon him. It is just conceivable that he might sell to a friendly purchaser but in those circumstances I am quite sure he would get full value. Accordingly I think it is artificial to apply any discount to the value of the husband's shares in this company or for that matter the wife's and I shall not do so. Liquidity of course is another matter which I will consider in a different context.'

Re Pectel Ltd [1998] BCC 405 is another case of unfair prejudice under CA 1985, s 459 in a quasi-partnership. The court found that the minority shareholder had been unfairly prejudiced and the Court of Appeal ordered that the majority shareholder Mr Phillips or the company should purchase the 25% minority shareholding at a price equivalent to one quarter of the fair value of the issued share capital of the company, ie without any discount for a minority shareholding, following *Re Bird Precision Bellows Ltd* [1985] 1 BCC 994, 67. The case confirms that there are three typical elements one or probably more of which will characterise the company as a quasi-partnership: 'they are first an association formed or continued on the basis of a personal relationship involving mutual confidence, second an agreement or understanding that all or some of the shareholders shall participate in the conduct of the business, third restrictions on share transfers'.

In *Re Baumler (UK) Ltd, Gerard v Koby* [2005] BCC 181 a buy-out was ordered as a result of a director, in breach of his fiduciary duty, arranging for a third party to buy a freehold property occupied by the company on terms under which he would participate in the anticipated profit from the transaction.

In *Dalby v Bodilly* [2005] BCC 627 an order under CA 1985, s 459 was given where the sole director and 50% shareholder in a company issued a further 900 shares to himself in an attempt to dilute his co-shareholder's interest from 50% to 5%. The court ordered the shares to be 'bought out at a price to be determined by an independent chartered accountant if necessary appointed by the court. That should be a valuation of Mr Dalby's 50% interest in the company that is to say disregarding the allotment by Mr Bodilly to himself of the further 900 shares'.

As pointed out by Robert Walker J in *Macro v Thompson (No 3)* [1997] 2 BCLC 36 at 70, one of the recurring problems with articles valuations is that the auditor (or other valuer) must produce a single valuation. He will not be able to produce a value that is a fair value in respect of shareholders with holdings of different sizes. A 15% shareholding, for example, is a much more attractive proposition to a 45% shareholder than it is to a 5% shareholder. Robert Walker J solved the problem by directing that fair value should be midway between the values per share of minority and majority holdings. He emphasised strongly, however, that he was not laying down a general rule and that his approach was not the only possible fair approach.

Paul John Murrell v James Ernest Swallow, James Paul Sanders and Blue Index Limited [2014] EWHC 2680 (Ch) was a case where the calculation of the value of the shares and the reasoning behind them are set out at considerable length which justifies a detailed review.

In June 2000, Messrs Sanders and Swallow set up a brokering business, Blue Index Limited, to enable clients to deal in contracts for differences (CFDs). Mr Murrell, a former colleague at Everetts, joined the company on 29 April 2002 and paid £45,000 for a 3% shareholding, recorded in the documentation relating to the share sale as £2,250, par value, of the shares acquired.

However the parties fell out and Mr Murrell was summarily dismissed on 24 October 2002, but he retained his shareholding, although the articles of association were changed to convert his shares into non-voting shares devoid of the pre-emption provisions if Mr Sanders or Mr Swallow wished to sell their shares and executed a Shareholders' Agreement between themselves. In November 2008, Mr Murrell presented a petition seeking an order for the purchase of his shares, at the agreed date of valuation, as at 1 November 2006. Both parties adduced evidence from share valuation experts, which were a long way apart.

The Court of Appeal case of *Re Bird Precision Bellows* [1986] Ch 658, approving the judgment of Nourse J in [1984] Ch 419 that, in order to be fair, no discount for a minority interest was appropriate in that case, was followed, as a quasi partnership, referred to in *Re Westbourne Galleries Limited* [1973] AC 360 and in *Re Jermyn Street Turkish Baths Limited* [1970] 1 WLR 1194. In *O'Neill v Phillips* [1999] 1 WLR 1092 (HL) it was stated that, in cases to which the presumption of unfairly prejudiced conduct applies, the fair value of the shares should be determined on a pro rata basis unless the shares had been purchased at a discount, *Re a company (No 005134 of 1986) ex parte Harris* [1989] BCLC 383.

Mr Murrell was held to be a sleeping partner in the quasi partnership. *Irvine v Irvine (No 2)* [2007] 1 BCLC 445 held that there should be a discount unless Mr Murrell was a quasi-partner in a quasi partnership which was extended in this case to a sleeping partner.

The judgment stated:

> '58. Mr Murrell adduced evidence from Mr Faull of Hilton Sharp & Clarke Forensic Accountants. In his first report, he used the common methodology of valuing the Company as a whole (the capitalised earnings methodology), by assessing its maintainable profits before tax and directors' emoluments ("PBTBDE"), deducting from that what he considered to be a commercial level of remuneration for Mr Sanders and Mr Swallow, then deducting tax (i.e. employers' NIC on their remuneration and Corporation Tax), and then applying a price earnings multiplier taken from comparable quoted companies and applying a discount for non-marketability based on the BDO Private Company Price Index ("PCPI"). He calculated PBTBDE at £1,554,913 – this was agreed.
>
> 59. On each of the two controversial elements in his valuation, he used the following figures:
>
> (i) Commercial level of remuneration = £228,000
> (ii) Multiplier = 18

On this basis he valued the Company as a whole at about £16.5million, of which 3% is about £495,000.

60. Mr Sanders and Mr Swallow adduced evidence from Mr Cottle of BDO LLP. He used both Mr Faull's capitalised earnings methodology and also a quite different methodology based on the dividend-earning potential specifically of Mr. Murrell's 3% shareholding, namely the dividend yield methodology. He much preferred the latter methodology in this case, for two principal reasons: first, this was the way in which minority shares, i.e. in quoted companies, are valued in the real world, and secondly, because it was to be expected that the Company would distribute by way of dividend most of its profits, having no need to retain a significant proportion for working capital for investment or other purposes. He stated that businesses such as the Company, due to low barriers to entry, tended "to make hay when the sun shines" and therefore to distribute dividends as and when profits were generated. Mr Faull did not disagree with this, but he adopted the dogmatic attitude that the dividend yield basis was not appropriate in this case, as I have found, Mr Mallin in his closing submissions came close to agreeing with Mr Faull on this point, since Mr Cottle accepted that a discount for a minority shareholding was inherent in his dividend yield methodology. In other words, Mr Cottle in cross-examination, and Mr Mallin in his closing submissions, came close to accepting that there should be no additional discount for a minority shareholding in his dividend yield methodology.

61. So, I approach the matter on the basis that the appropriate methodology is that adopted by Mr Faull. There may be other reasons for not using the dividend yield methodology, an issue I shall return to. But I will also consider Mr Cottle's dividend yield methodology as a useful comparator.

62. On the capitalised earnings methodology, Mr Cottle arrived at the following figures for the two controversial elements in Mr Faull's valuation:

(i) Commercial level of remuneration = £765,000
(ii) Multiplier = 11.3

On this basis he valued the Company as a whole at about £5.94million, of which 3% is about £178,000. In other words, he valued the Company as a whole at about a third of Mr Faull's figure.

63. On his dividend yield methodology, Mr Cottle valued Mr Murrell's 3% shareholding at about £120,000. The critical and controversial elements in this calculation were, apart from a commercial level of remuneration for Mr Sanders and Mr Swallow:

(i) An applied dividend pay-out rate of 70% of profits.
(ii) An applied dividend yield of 10% (i.e. x10), reached from the starting point of 5.1% (i.e. x20) from listed comparables and effectively halved to take into account the additional risk factors which Mr Cottle lists at paragraph 7.5 to 7.10 of his first report assuming minimal dividend headroom on the basis that the directors' remuneration is assumed to be of the order assessed by Mr Cottle (i.e. £765,000): this crucial component of Mr Cottle's calculation is explained at length, and I may say lucidly, at paragraphs 7.4 to 7.21 of Mr Cottle's 1st report.

64. I begin with the commercial level of remuneration for Mr Sanders and Mr Swallow. I was not impressed by Mr Cottle's approach. His starting point was the earnings of Mr Sanders and Mr Swallow at Everetts, adjusted for average pay increases over the period. In my view, their historic earnings when performing functions probably quite different to those they performed 6 years later in the Company are irrelevant. By November 2006, the Company's business had

matured greatly. It had the 5 senior and highly-paid commission-only traders listed in paragraph 95 of Mr Swallow's statement. It was possible for Mr Sanders to step back from full-time work for family reasons. It is likely in my view that Mr Swallow's functions were even more of a managerial nature by this time than they had been at the outset. Mr Cottle justified his figures by reference to comparable figures from recruitment agents, but I was also not impressed with the reliability of these figures or the comparability of the jobs and positions to which they refer. In contrast, I was impressed by Mr Faull's approach, namely the consideration of comparables in quoted companies. In my view, the starting point in a case such as this must be these comparables. There is, I recognise, some force in the criticisms made of Mr Faull's use of the comparables evidence. I think that he should have taken more account of the similar-sized stockbroking comparables, i.e. Fiske and Jarvis Securities, whose top executives I expect would command more than directors of a business such as the Company in November 2006. Instead Mr Faull relied on London Capital Group, which, on the face of its published accounts, even though it conducted a broking business like the Company, was probably mainly involved in CFD trading as one of the leading market-makers. And I also agree with Mr Mallin's submission that it is not right in this context to take into account the earnings of Mr Sanders and Mr Swallow qua owners from dividends. I think some guidance may also be derived from the estimated total sales commission earned by the 5 senior staff members listed in paragraph 95 of Mr Swallow's 1st witness statement, which Mr Faull calculated at about £125,000 pa each in the tax year April 2006 to March 2007. Doing the best I can from the information before me, and this is not a scientific process, I would increase Mr Faull's figure of £228,000 for a commercial level of remuneration for the services of Mr Sanders and Mr Swallow as at 1st November 2006 to a figure representing 10% of the turnover of the Company, making it of the order of £312,000 for the year ending 30th September 2006. I derive some support for this conclusion from the following factors:

(1) In the year ended 30th September 2003, when they proceeded on the basis that they were 100% owners of the Company, they paid themselves about 10% of the turnover for that year.
(2) Even Mr Cottle thought it right to express a commercial level of remuneration as a percentage of turnover. In my view, this reflected the business model of the Company, namely payment solely by reference to profits.

65. I turn now to the appropriate multiplier. In this context I prefer the evidence of Mr Cottle. I was not impressed by Mr Faull's reliance on LCG, which gave him as a starting point a multiple of 21.22, to which he applied a discount of 15%, little more than the 14% discount required by the PCPI. In my view, LCG was a far more secure business than the Company, in terms of all the risk factors identified by Mr Cottle, and had greater growth prospects. I do not see any reason to depart significantly from the analysis of Mr Cottle and I therefore find that the appropriate multiplier is 12, i.e. Mr Cottle's 11.3 rounded up to the nearest whole number.

66. By my calculation, following Mr Faull's at Bundle D page 214, applying the capitalised earnings methodology, the value of Mr Murrell's 3% shareholding is a little over £300,000, which I would round down to that figure. The parties will no doubt check my arithmetic.

67. I note that, on Mr Cottle's dividend yield methodology, if one assumes a commercial level for the directors' remuneration of 10% of turnover, and an assumed dividend pay-out ratio of 90%, but otherwise applies Mr Cottle's dividend yield requirement of 10%, one arrives at a value for Mr Murrell's shares of about £230,000. But I note that the yield requirement of 10% must

be questionable, given that there was far more headroom for dividends than Mr Cottle had allowed for, when I assess a reasonable level of commercial remuneration for the directors at £312,000, not £765,000 as assumed by Mr Cottle. Indeed, an additional reason why I am doubtful about the usefulness of this methodology in cases such as the present is the lack of verifiable objective evidence which underpins this crucial element, or more precisely how Mr Cottle gets from his 5.1% to his 10%. It is common ground that this methodology becomes even less appropriate the more factors there are in a case which justified the retention of profits.

68. Taking all matters in the round, in my view the fair value of Mr Murrell's 3% shareholding as at 1st November 2006 was £300,000 and I so declare.

69. So far as interest on that purchase price is concerned, these proceedings were held up for about 18 months because of the criminal charges against Mr Sanders and Mr Swallow. That feature of this case provides a powerful reason to award interest. I will award Mr Murrell interest at the standard commercial rate on the purchase price for a period of 18 months to the date of this Judgment. Otherwise, I see no sufficiently powerful reason to award Mr Murrell any interest having regard to the principles set out in *Profinance v Gladstone* [2002] 1 WLR 1024, but I am prepared to view this issue when handing down this Judgment. Mr Mallin submitted that I should not award any interest since his clients had accepted the date of valuation before any claim for interest was pleaded. I do not see that as a reason in itself for awarding no interest, since his clients did not stipulate at the time of their agreement to the date of valuation that it was on the basis that no interest would be awarded. Permission has since been granted to amend the Petition so as to claim interest.

The appropriate compensation for remuneration wrongly paid to the directors

70. I have found that for each of the financial years from that commencing 1st October 2003 Mr Sanders and Mr Swallow acted in breach of their fiduciary duties as directors in determining the levels of their remuneration. In my view, it is clearly wrong in principle that Mr Murrell should receive any compensation for this after the valuation date of 1st November 2006. As for the 3 financial years ending 30th September 2004, 2005 and 2006, in my view Mr Murrell is entitled to be compensated in excess of a fair commercial level of remuneration. That requires in my view the following calculation to be made:

(1) Assume that directors' remuneration, including pension contributions, equalled 10% of turnover for the year in question, i.e. what I consider to be a fair commercial level of remuneration.
(2) Calculate what additional dividends would have been declared in these years which would have left the same amounts by way of retained (i.e. undistributed) profits shown for each of these years. In other words, the amount of the excessive remuneration, plus whatever is saved in tax by assuming lower directors' remuneration, is assumed to have been distributed as dividends.
(3) Mr Murrell is assumed to have received 3% of those additional dividends.

71. I would not award Mr Murrell any interest on this compensation. In my view there may well be an element of rough justice in Mr Murrell's favour in treating a commercial level of remuneration as 10% of turnover in the earlier two financial years, so I would allow for this by awarding no interest.

72. I leave it to the parties to agree a figure for compensation under this head.'

Geoffrey Arbuthnott v James Gordon Bonnyman and others including Watling Street Limited [2015] EWCA Civ 536 is an appeal from the order of Asplin

J dated 8 May 2014 dismissing the petition of the appellant, Geoffrey Arbuthnott, pursuant to section 994 of the Companies Act 2006 ("the 2006 Act") claiming that the affairs of the 19th respondent, Charterhouse Capital Limited ("the Company"), have been conducted in a manner unfairly prejudicial to him as a member of the Company.

The principal issue on the appeal concerns the propriety of the compulsory acquisition of Mr Arbuthnott's shares in the Company by the 18th Respondent, Watling Street Limited ("WSL"), in which other members of the company holding a majority of the Company's shares were interested, at a price of £1,500 per share. That valued the Company as a whole at £15.15 million, which Mr Arbuthnott claims is a gross undervalue.

This was an unfair prejudice claim under CA 2006, s 994(1). Mr Arbuthnott's valuer valued 100% of the equity in the company in the range of £275 million to £321 million but the Court dismissed Mr Arbuthnott's appeal.

The central issue in *Gary Haylett v John Cayton and Caytons Law* [2018] EWHC 1951 (Comm) was the value of Mr Haylett's 50% interest in the profits of Cayton & Co, a firm of solicitors. As Mr Haylett was a Chartered Accountant, not a solicitor, he was not actually a partner in Cayton & Co but a participant in a joint venture and as such entitled to a 50% profit share in Cayton & Co as if it had been sold.

The fees in the five years to 28 February 2011 varied from £402,973, in 2007, to £1,845,946 in 2010 but had fallen to £789,835 in 2011, with projected fees for 2012 of £912,000. In arriving at the relevant figures, a number of excerpts were quoted from the 6th edition of *Practical Share Valuation* and an average fees figure of £1,157,324 was calculated. Maintainable fee income was assumed as £1.15 million with annual costs of £1 million giving maintainable earnings of £150,000. An appropriate multiplier of 3.5 was arrived at, giving a total of £525,000 from which net debt of £100,455 was deducted, leaving £424,545. The judge considered that, based on these calculations, a fair value for Mr Haylett's 50% interest in the profits was £200,000. A final adjustment was a credit note in favour of Cayton & Co of £4,345 plus VAT on the PAYE/NI accrual for Mr Haylett which was deducted.

Focus

The fair value of shares in a company may depend on whether a break-up value or a going concern basis is correct, or whether a discount for the size of shareholding is appropriate or whether it should be a pro rata proportion of the company's value.

4.05 Valuer's liability

In *Dean v Prince* [1954] 2 WLR 538, Denning LJ implied that a valuer is not liable to an action for negligence if his value is disputed unless he is dishonest, and quoted with approval earlier valuation disputes such as *Pappa v Rose* (1872) 27 LT 348 and *Finnegan v Allen* [1943] KB 425.

In *Pappa v Rose* (1872) 27 LT 348 the question of the liability of an adjudicator acting honestly but possibly mistakenly was considered and it was held that such a person had no liability merely because he may have arrived at an incorrect decision. In the words of Kelly CB at 350:

> 'If two parties agree to submit a question to a third, the third party is not bound to give an opinion. But if this third party is in any way a party to the transaction and is acting for hire and reward he is just as much bound to give his opinion as the other two are to abide by it. But when you go further and inquire whether the arbitrator contracts to exercise or even to possess skill in the matter then the analogy fails and the illustration does not apply. If the arbitrator agrees to give an opinion I deny that there is any contract to use skill. No better analogy could be suggested in the present case than the position of an arbitrator. How often does it occur that questions are submitted to the arbitration of persons not at the bar. Is it to be said that if in such reference a difficult question of law arises the arbitrator should be taken to have held himself out as possessing skill in the law? It is for the parties themselves to take care that they fix on a skilful arbitrator. So here these two persons made an agreement and fixed on the defendant to judge between them. They themselves ought to have taken care that their arbitrator possessed the skill to do that which was just and right between them. On that plain and simple ground that there was no contract expressed or implied on the part of the defendant that he was possessed of skill in this matter I am of the opinion that this action which assumes that the defendant was bound to exercise and consequently that he had contracted that he possessed skill is not maintainable.'

Blackburn J stated at 351:

> 'But it was said in the contract that the raisins were to be of fair average quality in the opinion of the defendant. The meaning of that was that the defendant was to give his opinion upon the quality so as to bind both sides and that he has done.'

In *Leigh v English Property Corporation Ltd* [1976] 2 Lloyds Rep 298 it was held that, where the relevant agreement provided that 'the fair value of shares shall be agreed between the parties and in default of agreement shall be as certified by the auditors … (whose decision shall be final and binding on the parties)' meant that, since it was clearly envisaged that the fair value was to be certified by the auditors only in the event that the parties failed to agree, the plaintiff had an arguable case in that the auditors, although not formally so appointed by the agreement, are selected as arbitrators.

Another case regarding an action against a bona fide valuer was that of *Finnegan v Allen* [1943] KB 425. Lord Greene MR pointed out:

> 'The fundamental difficulty about the whole of the plaintiff's case lies in this circumstance. He is in effect wishing to recover damages from a valuer employed to fix a price inter partes, using his skill and knowledge to enable him to do so, for not having valued in the way in which his instructions contemplated that he should value. There is no charge of bad faith. We have therefore to deal with this question on the footing that the defendant, perfectly honestly intending to carry out his instructions, has made an honest mistake – a mistake which may have consisted in misunderstanding his instructions or may have consisted in inadvertently failing to comply with some element. Can such an action be maintained? In my opinion, for the reasons which I shall give in a moment, such an action cannot be maintained.'

Lord Greene then went on to review a number of supporting cases, including *Pappa v Rose* (1872) 27 LT 348; *Tharsis Sulphur and Copper Co v Loftus* (1872) 27 LT 549; *Stevenson v Watson* (1879) 40 LT 485; *Boynton v Richardson* (1924) 69 Sol Jo 107 and *Chambers v Goldthorpe; Restell v Nye* (1901) 84 LT 444:

> 'In my opinion unless and until the plaintiff can bring himself to make a charge of bad faith (and it is quite obvious after what counsel for the respondent has said that he cannot do that and has no intention of doing that in this case) there cannot be any case against the valuer in the circumstances and therefore the statement of claim ought to be struck out and it is not a case in which we should give an opportunity for further amendment.'

However, the principle of a valuer's liability for negligence was reconsidered in a case casting doubt on the decision in *Finnegan v Allen*.

This important case, decided in the House of Lords, is that of *Arenson v Casson Beckman Rutley & Co* [1975] 3 WLR 815.

The facts of this case are summarised by Lord Salmon:

> 'Mr Archy Arenson was the chairman, managing director and controlling shareholder of a private company called A Arenson Ltd. In 1964 he took his nephew, the appellant, into his company's employment. He also made a gift to his nephew of a small parcel of shares in the company on the terms of a letter dated 18 March 1964, which reads as follows:
>
> "18 March 1964
>
> Dear Mr and Mrs Arenson,
>
> *A Arenson Limited*
>
> In consideration of your procuring the company to continue to employ me, I hereby agree the following arrangements concerning the shares of which you have made me a gift:
>
> (1) I will not sell the shares other than to Mr Arenson or to Mrs Arenson should he predecease her.
> (2) Should I wish to dispose of my shares, Mr Arenson will purchase them from me at the fair value, but I shall not require him to purchase from me for five years from the date hereof.
> (3) Should I wish to sell the shares after the death of Mr Arenson I will first offer them for sale to Mrs Arenson, who shall have the right to purchase them at the fair value but she shall not be under an obligation so to do.
> (4) Should Mr Arenson decide to dispose of his shares in the company, then I hereby agree to sell my shares in the company to Mr Arenson at the same price per share as Mr Arenson will be receiving in respect of his shares.
> (5) In the event of my employment with the company terminating for whatsoever reason, I will offer to sell my shares to Mr Arenson and it is agreed that he will purchase them from me at the fair value. Should Mr Arenson be dead then Mrs Arenson shall have the option to purchase the shares from me at the fair value.
> (6) "Fair value" shall mean in relation to the shares in A Arenson Limited, the value thereof as determined by the auditors for the time being of the company whose valuation acting as experts and not as arbitrators shall be final and binding on all parties.
>
> Please indicate your acceptance of the above conditions by signing the carbon copy sent herewith, and returning it to me.
>
> Yours sincerely,
>
> I ARENSON
>
> Enc: We agree to the above terms and conditions. (signed over 6d. stamp)"

Another letter in precisely the same terms, dated 1 October 1968, later passed between the appellant and his uncle. The appellant's employment with Arenson Ltd was terminated on 4 April 1970. Some time prior to 13 May 1970 the company's secretary verbally asked the company's auditors, Casson, Beckman, Rutley & Co, the respondents, to place a value on the shares held by the appellant. From the respondents' letter of 13 May 1970 it appears that they had been put in possession of copies of the letters of 18 March 1964 and 1 October 1968 to which I have referred. The respondents wrote to the company's secretary on 13 May 1970 as follows:

"Casson Beckman Rutley & Co
27 Queen Anne Street,
London W1M 0DA
13 May 1970
AB/PDB

The Secretary
A. Arenson Ltd,
Lincoln House,
Colney Street,
St Albans, Herts.

Dear Sir,

Valuation of shares – I Arenson

(1) We refer to your verbal request to place a value on the shares held by Mr I Arenson in your company in accordance with the letters of the 18 March 1964 and the 1 October 1968.
(2) The shares held by Mr I Arenson in the company are as follows: 1,750 ordinary shares of £1 each fully paid, 500 6% non-cumulative preference shares of £1 each fully paid.
(3) In our view the fair value of these shares on the 4 day of April 1970 was as follows:

(a) The 500 6% non-cumulative preference shares of £1 each fully paid at a valuation of £166.15.4.
(b) The 1,750 ordinary shares of £1 each fully paid at a valuation of £4,750.

Yours faithfully,

(Signed)".'

It will be noted that the auditors did not explain their valuation which was therefore what is normally called a 'non-speaking' valuation.

Lord Salmon continued:

'We do not know whether the respondents were asked to make the valuation on behalf of the company (which presumably was interested in the value of its own shares) or on behalf of Mr Archy Arenson and the appellant; nor do we know whether the respondents charged any fee for this valuation and if so, to whom, or whether they made their valuation as part of their ordinary duties as the company's auditors. Nor do I think that this matters because, since the decision of this House in *Hedley Byrne & Co Ltd v Heller & Partners Ltd* [1964] AC 465, [1963] 2 All ER 575, it is clear that quite apart from any contractual obligation, the respondents must have owed a duty both to Mr Archy Arenson and to the appellant to use reasonable care and skill in making their valuation. On 11 June 1970 the appellant, in reliance on the respondents' valuation, transferred his

> shares to his uncle for £4,916.13s.4d. About three months later, on 10 September 1970, a holding company was incorporated to acquire all the issued share capital of A Arenson Ltd. After about a further four months the shares in the holding company were offered for sale to the public by a prospectus dated 14 January 1971. The prospectus included an accountant's joint report prepared and signed by the respondents and another firm of accountants which placed a value on the company's share capital of £1,699,983. This value, if applied pro rata to the shares formerly owned by the appellant would have made them worth not less than £29,500, that is to say six times more than the value put on them by the respondents only seven months previously. There is an apparently striking disparity between the value placed on the shares by the respondents' valuation of 13 May 1970 and the valuation placed on them by the prospectus of 14 January 1971. This disparity might be attributed to the fact that there is normally a substantial difference between the value per share of a small minority holding and the value per share of the entire holding in a private company; whether this factor could account for a difference of 600 per cent is a question which will have to be decided at the trial. There may also have been a remarkable improvement in the company's fortunes between 13 May 1970 and 14 January 1971, entirely unforeseen on the earlier date, which may help to explain the disparity between the two valuations. However this may be, shortly after the publication of the prospectus, the appellant issued a writ against his uncle and the respondents. The only part of the appellant's claim which is relevant to this appeal is that part which claims damages for negligence against the respondents in relation to their valuation of 13 May 1970. For the purposes of this appeal it must be assumed that the allegations of fact in the statement of claim are correct: that the respondents were negligent in preparing their valuation of 13 May 1970 which as a result was a gross undervaluation causing the appellant substantial damage. On this hypothesis, the important question for your Lordships to decide is whether, in the circumstances, the law confers an immunity on the respondents against being sued for the damage which they caused the appellant by their negligence.'

The case does not indicate whether there was any negligence on the part of the auditors or whether the valuation was entirely correct. What it does establish is that an auditor can be sued for negligence when acting as an expert valuer, as opposed to arbitrator.

The position is admirably summarised by Lord Wheatley:

> '(1) It is clear from the speeches of Lord Reid, at 735, Lord Morris of Borth-y-Gest, at 738, and my noble and learned friend, Lord Salmon, at 756, in *Sutcliffe v Thackrah* [1974] AC 727, [1974] 1 All ER 859 that while a valuer may by the terms of his appointment be constituted an arbitrator (or quasi-arbitrator) and be clothed with the immunity, a valuer simply as such does not enjoy that benefit.
>
> (2) It accordingly follows that when a valuer is claiming that immunity he must be able to establish from the circumstances and purpose of his appointment that he has been vested with the clothing which gives him that immunity.
>
> (3) In view of the different circumstances which can surround individual cases, and since each case has to be decided on its own facts, it is not possible to enunciate an all-embracing formula which is liable to decide every case. What can be done is to set out certain indicia which can serve as guidelines in deciding whether a person is so clothed. The indicia which follow are in my view the most important, though not necessarily exhaustive. They are culled from the speeches in *Sutcliffe v Thackrah* cited by my noble and learned friend, Lord Simon of Glaisdale, and from several other passages therein. In particular I would refer to the following passages.

Lord Morris of Borth-y-Gest, at 745, said, after pointing out that the circumstances of his appointment (including the determination of a dispute) might place a person in the position both of a valuer and arbitrator:

> "But it by no means follows that everyone who has a duty of valuing, a duty which obviously must be fairly and honestly discharged, is an arbitrator. A valuer may not be exercising any judicial function."

Then my noble and learned friend, Lord Salmon said at 739:

> "As in the case of the valuer, it is said that the architect is performing much the same functions and must, therefore, be regarded as being in the same position as a judge or arbitrator and must accordingly be accorded the same immunity. I confess that I can see no more reason for regarding the architect as being in the same position as a judge or arbitrator than there is for so regarding the valuer. No reason has ever been suggested. I suspect that this is because none exists. The description 'quasi-judicial functions' have been invoked but never defined. They cannot mean more than in much the same position as an arbitrator or judge. In reality, however, there are the most striking differences between the roles of the valuer and architect in the circumstances to which I have referred and the role of a judge or arbitrator. Judges and arbitrators have disputes submitted to them for decision. The evidence and contentions of the parties are put before them for their examination and consideration. They then give their decision. None of this is true about the valuer or the architect who were merely carrying out their ordinary business activities."

Then later, Lord Salmon, at 763, after quoting a passage from Cockburn CJ in *Re Hopper* (1867) LR 2 QB 367 at 372, 373 said:

> "In *Re Hopper* Cockburn CJ, with whom Blackburn and Lush JJ agreed, was in effect saying that the question whether anyone was to be treated as an arbitrator depended on whether the role which he performed was vested with the characteristic attributes of the judicial role. If an expert were employed to certify, make a valuation or appraisal or settle compensation as between opposing interests, this did not, of itself, put him in the position of an arbitrator. He might, eg, do no more than examine goods or work or accounts and make a decision accordingly. On the other hand, he might, as in *Re Hopper*, hear the evidence and submissions of the parties, in which case he would clearly be regarded as an arbitrator. Everything would depend on the facts of the particular case. I entirely agree with this view of the law."

I likewise agree with my noble and learned friend's summation of the law.

The indicia are as follows: (a) there is a dispute or a difference between the parties which has been formulated in some way or another; (b) the dispute or difference has been remitted by the parties to the person to resolve in such a manner that he is called on to exercise a judicial function; (c) where appropriate, the parties must have been provided with an opportunity to present evidence and/or submissions in support of their respective claims in the dispute; and (d) the parties have agreed to accept his decision.

(4) Applying the foregoing tests to the present case, it is clear to me that the respondents here cannot pray in aid the appellant's pleadings to satisfy the requirement of immunity. On the contrary, they appear to negative the claim. In this regard I agree with and adopt the analysis and rejection by my noble and learned friend, Lord Simon of Glaisdale, of the submission of counsel for the respondents in support of his contention that the requirements for immunity have been satisfied in the present case. I agree with counsel for the appellant's

> submission that the valuation here was not to decide a dispute or difference but to avoid a dispute or difference. There is nothing in the appellant's pleadings and relevant documents to suggest that a dispute or difference between the parties existed and was being remitted to the respondents for a judicial (or quasi-judicial) determination, and nothing to suggest that the remit was so treated.
>
> (5) The validity of the decisions from *Pappa v Rose* (1872) LR 7 CP 32 onwards on which the respondents' counsel relied has to be considered and tested against (a) what was said in *Sutcliffe v Thackrah* [1974] AC 727, [1974] 1 All ER 859, particularly in the rejection of *Chambers v Goldthorpe* [1901] 1 KB 624 and (b) the indicia to which I have referred. So viewed, I find them difficult to justify. I will only deal with *Finnegan v Allen* [1943] KB 425, [1943] 1 All ER 493 because it is said that for over 30 years it has been the guiding basis on which valuations such as the present one have proceeded, and to overturn it could lead to unfortunate and possibly serious repercussions in relation to past transactions where an action based on negligence may still be open. I recognise that this would be unfortunate and that your Lordships' house would be slow to interfere with an understanding of the law which has regulated such transactions over a long number of years, but if the law has to be restated in a manner which seems to run contrary to that decision, then your Lordships' house will not be deterred from restating it because of the consequences. In my opinion the law requires to be restated, and the consequences may not be so grievous as they might appear to be at first blush, since negligence of a certain nature has to be established before a claim for damages can succeed in circumstances where immunity cannot be established. In my opinion *Finnegan v Allen* cannot pass the test unless, as envisaged by Lord Morris of Borth-y-Gest in *Sutcliffe v Thackrah*, there were present there special facts which placed the valuer in the position of an arbitrator. It would appear from what was said by Lord Greene MR, at 432, in *Finnegan v Allen* that there was a dispute between the parties, and as each case has to be decided on its own facts that factor may have justified the decision, although I personally have doubts about that.'

A later case involving an action against an auditor acting as valuer is that of *Whiteoak v Walker* (1988) 4 BCC 122 during which Terence Cullen QC stated at 126:

> 'The difficulty any plaintiff faces when asserting negligence by a valuer who gives a non-speaking certificate is that he does not know how the valuer arrived at his figure. Initially, all the plaintiff and his advisers can do is to say that the figure is so wildly wrong the defendant must have been negligent. In the present case the plaintiff had been advised that £135,000 was a fair value, so it is easy to see that the defendant's valuation would have appeared to be outside normal differences of opinion.'

In order to determine negligence it is necessary to consider the degree of expertise required from the valuer. In *Whiteoak v Walker* at 125 this point was argued:

> 'I have a situation where the parties have chosen the company's auditor to carry out the task. They require him to express his own opinion as to the fair value. The reason for directing him to act as an expert and not an arbitrator is they want him to act quickly and cheaply. The time in which they expect him to form his opinion is, at most, 14 days. Even assuming that, when the articles were agreed, the members knew that there was a specialist body of share valuers, I fail to see that they envisaged that their auditor would bring a specialist valuer's skill to the task. They would have had the choice between opting for the specialist skills of a share valuer and the special knowledge as to the company's affairs of their own

auditor. As they were seeking a fair result, as to which a specialist valuer would have no necessary advantage over their own auditor, and as they were seeking it quickly and cheaply, I have no doubt that they intended their auditor to apply his skills and did not intend that he should bring to bear the skills of a specialist valuer.

Of course, as the art of share valuation develops, which may very well be due to the existence of a specialist body of valuers, so the standard of skill in valuing to be expected of the accountant in general practice and of auditors will rise.

In my judgment I have to apply the auditor standard as it was in 1982. I therefore reject the plaintiff's contention that the specialist standard is to be applied. I might add that in Mr Sutherland's view the gap between the specialist standard and the auditor standard is so wide that most auditors would not be competent to carry out a share valuation. The result, therefore, of applying the specialist standard would be that most auditors would have to refuse the task or seek the opinion of a specialist valuer, either of which courses would in practice frustrate the parties' desire of obtaining their own auditor's opinion of a fair value in a speedy and economical way.'

And at 127:

'Mr Susman submitted that Mr Sutherland was a specialist valuer and Mr Salmon was merely a chartered accountant who carried out six or seven valuations a year, and therefore I ought to accept Mr Sutherland's view. Mr Davidson possibly had this in mind when he directed me to a textbook published in 1986 entitled *The Valuation of Unquoted Securities* by Mr C Glover. However, while any expert can refer to a textbook to confirm his opinion, I do not consider that Mr Glover's untested views can be taken into account in refuting Mr Sutherland's evidence before me.

Nevertheless, the task of the defendant here was the determination of a fair value of the plaintiff's minority interest. I do not consider that even if the right test is a specialist standard and not, as I have held, the auditor standard, Mr Sutherland's opinion has to be accepted by me in the absence of the tested opinion of another specialist. In my judgment, I can test the content of Mr Sutherland's views both in the light of his cross-examination and in the light of the evidence of the practice of what I might call a general practitioner.

Mr Sutherland abandoned his primary view that in 1982 the only way of determining a fair value in this case was a pro-rata method. That itself weakens the weight I attach to his evidence.

Further, I take into account that having valued the shares in Mr Bentley's hands on an asset basis, providing for the element of accretion, he then adopted the defendant's notional dividend method for valuing the shares in the plaintiff's hands before splitting the difference to arrive at a fair value. This seems to me to show an inconsistent approach to the question of whether an asset basis or a profit-related basis should be chosen, and Mr Sutherland accepted, on reflection, that the use of the defendant's method in such a way was inappropriate. Indeed, it was plainly inappropriate as, in view of the dividend cover used by the defendant and the percentage return on investment used by him, both of which were in Mr Sutherland's hands when he made his report, it was evident that the defendant had made a valuation which was weighted in the purchaser's favour, and therefore not looking at it purely as a minority holding.

Having heard Mr Sutherland's evidence and Mr Salmon's evidence, I do not accept Mr Sutherland's opinion that in 1982 if the pro-rata method was not used

> no competent specialist would have used the notional dividend basis or the price/earnings ratio basis as a method of determining what in his opinion was the fair value of the minority holding in this company.'

In *Omega Trust Co Ltd and another v Wright Son & Pepper and another* [1997] PNLR 424, a case concerning the valuation of land, a loan was provided by the first plaintiff in reliance on the valuer's report. The first plaintiff asked the second plaintiff to provide part of the advance. The valuation report nevertheless made clear that it was for the first plaintiff's purpose only and contained a disclaimer that it was for the private and confidential use of the clients for whom the report was undertaken and that it should not be reproduced or relied on by third parties for any use whatsoever without express authority. In the High Court Morland J held that the defendants owed a duty of care to the second plaintiff which would have been negatived by the disclaimer, but the disclaimer did not satisfy the test of reasonableness under the Unfair Contract Terms Act 1977. The Court of Appeal upheld the valuer's appeal against that decision. There was an express and effective disclaimer, which was not unfair or unreasonable. No duty of care could be implied on behalf of the defendant valuers to an unknown lender. It also held that it was not necessary for it to consider the submission

> 'that under the Hedley Byrne test there had to be a probability that the grant of the loans might not be made solely by the first plaintiff (Counsel for the valuers) addressed us with a forcible and sustained submission on that point and it may be useful for any future occasion when the point may be considered simply to refer to the authorities he cited. *Candler v Crane Christmas & Co* [1951] 2 KB 164, *Hedley Byrne & Co Ltd v Heller & Partners Ltd* [1964] AC 465, *Smith v Eric S Bush (A firm)* [1990] 1 AC 831 (also reported at (1989) 1 EGLR 169, (1989) 17 EG 68 and 18 EG 99, *Caparo Industries Plc v Dickman* [1990] 2 AC 605, *Galoo Ltd v Right Grahame Murray (a firm)* [1994] 1 WLR 1360, *Henderson v Merrett Syndicates Ltd* [1995] 2 AC 145, *White v Jones* [1995] 2 AC 207, *Goodwill v British Pregnancy Advisory Service* [1996] 1 WLR 1397.'

The point was not decided as the court found for the defendants on the disclaimer notice in the valuation.

In *Caparo Industries Plc v Dickman* [1990] 2 AC 605 the company's auditors were asked to prepare a special report for the potential purchaser and were liable to the investor for negligent misstatements in the report. The liability is limited to the losses attributable to the inaccuracy: *MAN Nutzfahrzeuge AG v Ernst & Young* [2005] EWHC 2347 (Comm). It is not the mistake on its own that gives rise to an action for damages to a third party, unless that party knew that the accounts would be relied on by the purchaser. In *ADT Ltd v BDO Binder Hamlyn* [1996] BCC 808, the firm was held liable for £65 million in damages for errors in the audited accounts, which they had assured the purchasers were accurate.

In the negligent valuation claim in *K/S Lincoln and Others v C B Richard Ellis Hotels Limited (No 2)* [2010] EWHC 1156 (TCC) it was suggested that a reasonable margin of a valuation of standard residential property might be plus or minus 5%, a one-off property plus or minus 10%, and where there are exceptional features plus or minus 15%, or even higher in appropriate cases.

Zubaida v Hargreaves [1995] 1 EGLR 127 involved valuation for a rent review, but in the Court of Appeal Lord Justice Hoffmann stated:

'In bringing this appeal Mr Zubaida faces a formidable difficulty in the standard which the law requires for a professional man conducting a valuation like this. In an action for negligence against an expert it is not enough to show that another expert would have given a different answer. Valuation is not an exact science; it involves questions of judgment on which experts may differ without forfeiting their claim to professional competence. The fact that a judge may think one approach better than another is therefore irrelevant. Speaking for myself, and therefore irrelevantly, the valuation strikes me as having been somewhat on the high side. But that is by no means enough to show that Mr Hargreaves did not perform his duty with reasonable professional competence. The issue is not whether the expert's valuation was right in the sense of being the figure which a judge after hearing the evidence would determine, it is whether he has acted in accordance with practices which are regarded as acceptable by a respectable body of opinion in his profession: see *Bolam v Friern Hospital Management Committee* [1957] 1 WLR 582 at page 587, a well-known citation.'

In *Sayers v Clarke-Walker* [2002] 2 BCLC 16 the accountants and auditors of a company were trying to act as facilitators to broker a deal between an employee owning 10% of the company and the retiring 90% shareholder. The firm had pointed out that they could not advise on the commerciality of the agreement as they had a potential conflict of interest but the terms of reference were not delineated with great precision and when the purchaser asked the accounting firm's Mr Chilcott for reassurance about the price he had been told that it was about right. The judge stated:

'Mr Sayers was entitled to rely on Mr Chilcott's reassurances as to price but in the circumstances and for reasons given he was only entitled to the most general guidance which he received and the circumstances demanded no more detailed accuracy than Mr Chilcott achieved.'

However the firm was held to be negligent in not giving taxation advice on the purchase in respect of which the judge stated:

'44 That leaves the issue as to whether Mr Chilcott's failure to advise the parties to adopt the "TopCo" structure for the agreement was negligent. This is really a return to the first issue since I there found the defendant's retainer was wide enough to cover advice on "TopCo". All I need add is that in my judgement it was a breach of the retainer and/or negligent to fail to advise Mr Sayers on TopCo. I accept the experts agreed view that such advice was, or should have been, within the competence of the defendant.

…

47 As to the TopCo advice or lack of it Mr Sayers was entitled to assume that he had received the advice a competent accountant would have given. If it was rash of him to reject the advice to seek specialist tax advice i.e. from Tax Counsel, so be it, but that is a client's choice. He is not bound to pay more for more expert advice. The professional may protect himself against failure to give advice only to be expected of the greater expert not against a failure to display the competence to be expected of him.'

In *Craneheath Securities v York Montague Ltd* [1996] 1 EGLR 130 the plaintiff bank lent money to the owner of a restaurant in a manor house at Kingsdown, Kent, secured as a second charge on the property. The business failed and the bank lost its money. In this case the valuers had valued the business as a going concern at £5.25m but when the business failed the property was sold for a mere £475,000. Balcombe LJ in the Court of Appeal stated:

> 'I am satisfied that there was no material before the judge which could have enabled him to make a finding that Craneheath had discharged the initial burden of proving that the valuation of £5.25m was wrong. I reject Mr Lloyds' submission that if we were satisfied that there were a sufficient number of errors in the way in which Mr Crabtree has carried out his valuation we should in the circumstances of this case infer that his final result was wrong. Valuation is not a science it is an art and the instinctive "feel" for the market of an experienced valuer is not something which can be ignored.
>
> Since Craneheath did not establish that the figure of £5.25m was wrong then I agree with Mr Stow that Craneheath's action must necessarily fail. It would not be enough for Craneheath to show that there had been errors at some stages of the valuation unless they could also show that the final valuation was wrong. If authority was needed for so self evident of proposition it can be found in *Mount Banking Corporation Ltd v Brian Cooper & Co* (1992) 2 EGLR 142. Otton LJ emphasised that it was common ground that Mr Crabtree (the valuer) was correct in attempting to assess future profitability. The judge was not persuaded that Mr Crabtree was wrong in arriving at a potential turnover figure of £1.55m based on a seven-day week an increase of prices by 10% and an increase in reputation of 5%. The judge did not reject the net profit ratio of 35% which gave an annual profit of £542,500. He also accepted a factor of eight as the years purchase giving £4,340,000. On the basis that the base figure of £1.1m was not proved to be wrong and that the final figure of £4.34m was an extrapolation based on the £1.1m it is difficult to see how the Judge could have found that the total was erroneous. The valuation of the premises has not been disputed before this court. The overall total of £5.325m was rounded down by Mr Crabtree to £5.25m.
>
> The end result is that the valuation figure of £5.25m, although out of line with subsequent valuations, was never shown to be wrong. It must follow that there was no basis upon which the defendants could have been found to be negligent.'

Mount Banking Corporation Ltd v Brian Cooper & Co [1992] 2 EGLR 142 was one of a number of cases resulting from the collapse of the property market in 1989.

> 'The effect of the increase in bank base rates from 7.5% in May 1988 to 14% in August 1989; Mr Castle told me that with hindsight the storm clouds should have been seen as looming over the property market but that most of the profession did not see them until much later in 1989. I accept that.'

In this particular case, valuations were provided to bankers to support property based loans and the result of the collapse of the property market caused the borrower to go bankrupt and the property was worth a fraction of what had been lent and the bankers sued the valuers for professional negligence. The case makes some useful comments on the responsibility of professional valuers which may have application to the valuers of unquoted shares. In his judgment, R M Stewart QC sitting as a Deputy Judge of the High Court, stated:

> 'if the valuation that has been reached cannot be impeached as a total then however erroneous the method of its application by which the valuation has been reached, no loss has been sustained because within the *Bolam v Friern Hospital Management Committee* principle it was a proper valuation. I do however accept that where errors are demonstrated either in the approach or in the application of the approach then the judge should look carefully at whether that valuation is, despite those errors, nonetheless an acceptable value within the *Bolam* principle. He quoted with approval Watkins J in *Singer & Freedlander v John D Wood &*

Co in which he stated "the valuation of land by trained, competent and careful professional men is a task which rarely if ever admits a precise conclusion". Mr Stewart therefore held "so there is an acceptable margin of error".'

However, in *Lion Nathan Limited v CC Bottlers* [1996] 1 WLR 1438 the court ignored the point that the income was still within what would have been predicted as the limits of foreseeable deviation on the grounds that the only tolerable forecast is the one which on its facts was prepared with reasonable care. Where the valuer has been negligent the liability is the difference between the valuation and the mean of the acceptable valuations: *South Australia Asset Management Corporation v York Montague Limited* [1997] AC 191:

> 'Liability is to be deduced on a combination of principles deduced from *Hedley Byrne & Co Ltd v Heller & Partners Ltd* [1961] 3 WLR 1225, [1964] AC 465 (the passage cited on page 213) and *Bolam's* case (the passage cited at page 217) … A valuer is not to be adjudged negligent merely because others disagree with his figures or I add, merely because with hindsight his valuation is shown to have been too high.
>
> What can properly be expected from a competent valuer using reasonable skill and care is that his valuation falls within the acceptable range (page 213).
>
> I pause to comment on this. In *Singer & Friedlander* the permissible margin of error was found on the evidence to be 10%. It does not in my judgement follow as a matter of law that the same percentage applies in every case. Indeed Mr Bartlett, counsel for the plaintiffs, in opening conceded that it might be appropriate here to look to a higher margin and the pleadings allow 17½%.
>
> The problem which this raises, it seems to me, is 10% (or whatever margin may be thought acceptable) of what. Applying the *Bolam* test, the real question in my judgement is whether the valuation was that which a competent valuer using proper skill and care could properly have reached. This I take from the question raised by Gibson J in *Coris and Investments v Druct & Co*. If the valuation is too high is it too high by such a margin as to be categorised as negligent? The margin of error approach is thus a useful tool for in most straightforward cases it can reasonably be expected, as Mr Castle the expert for the defendants said, that competent surveyors acting with proper skill and care and thus acting on all relevant evidence will come within a moderate bracket of each other. But there is a danger in the margin of error approach to which I have alluded and this was highlighted in the evidence of Mr Castle. I do not think it proper to apply it mechanistically in any case so as to say that any valuation outside the consensus of the experts or if they differ, outside their average valuation by more than 10% is prima facie negligent. Rather, as Mr Castle said, I think the judge must approach the question first by asking where the proper valuation or bracket of valuation lies, then if the defendant is more than the permitted margin outside that proper figure the inference of negligence should be drawn.'

Late in the judgment, Mr Stewart stated:

> 'valuation is, after all, not a precise science. They show how wide a margin there can be between perfectly competent surveyors doing their honest best. Finally they serve to re-emphasise what, in my judgement must be the right approach. A judge must be cautious in his search for a "right figure". He must look at the component figures properly to be taken into account by the competent surveyor using proper skill and care. From there he must reach a conclusion as to whether in total the valuer complained of erred, and he must then stand back and ask whether that is, by the standards of the profession, a margin of error which

> can be tolerated or which can only sensibly be stigmatised as negligence … I conclude therefore on this section that though there was a fault in the process of calculation, nonetheless a proper and acceptable process could probably have resulted in no or no perceptible difference in the end valuation, that is to say that the figure in fact reached by Mr Cohen was acceptable on the Bolam principle. Mr Cohen's working figures on the residual site value can properly be criticised because he took too high a discount for developer's profits but no discount for owner-occupier money tied up. The two areas do not quite cancel each other out but the resultant figure is still within the acceptable range. While that criticism can properly be made it would in my judgment be a nonsense to say that because there is a flaw in the process, and in the figures, damages should be awarded when the resultant figure remains, as it does in my judgment, within the range that a competent surveyor using proper skill and care and informing himself of all relevant evidence could properly reach.'

The leading case of *Bolam v Friern Hospital Management Committee* [1957] 1 WLR 582 defined negligence, in what was a medical negligence claim, as:

> 'The test is the standard of the ordinary skilled man exercising and professing to have that special skill. A man need not possess the highest skill at the risk of being found negligent. It is well established law that it is sufficient if he exercises the ordinary skill of an ordinary competent man exercising that particular art. I do not think that I quarrel much with any of the submissions in law which are being put before you by Counsel. Counsel for the Plaintiff put it in this way, that in the case of a medical man, negligence means failure to act in accordance with the standards of reasonably competent medical men at the time. That is a perfectly accurate statement as long as it is remembered that there may be one or more perfectly proper standards and if a medical man conforms with one of those proper standards then he is not negligent…Counsel for the defendants admitted that if you are satisfied that they were acting in accordance with the practice of a competent body of professional opinion then it would be wrong for you to hold that negligence was established … A doctor is not guilty of negligence if he has acted in accordance with a practice accepted as proper by a responsible body of medical men skilled in that particular art…putting it the other way round a doctor is not negligent if he is acting in accordance with such a practice merely because there is a body of opinion that takes a contrary view.'

The *Bolam* decision was followed in a leading case of negligence concerning property valuation in *Singer & Friedlander Ltd v John D Wood & Co* [1977] 2 EGLR 84.

The share valuation case of *Goldstein v Levy Gee* [2003] EWHC 1574 is of interest in confirming, after a thorough review of the relevant case law, that there was a permissible range within which the valuation would not be negligent and:

> 'the way to do this is to take all the figures at the lowest end of the spectrum followed by all the figures at the highest end of the spectrum. Although one may instinctively feel that this stacks the figures in the way most favourable to the valuer it seems to me that the logic cannot be faulted. That is therefore what I propose to do.'

The judge held that the permissible range was a value for Mr Goldstein's shares of £3,027,628 (£50.46 per share) at the low end and £3,692,892 (£61.55 per share) at the high end: 'Levy Gee's valuation of £3,151,200 (£52.52 per share) is within the bracket … it follows in accordance with the law as laid down by *Merivale Moore* that it was not negligent'.

Merivale Moore Plc v Strutt & Parker [1999] 2 EGLR 171 concerned a property appraisal and the judge in *Goldstein v Levy Gee* quoted Buxton LJ:

> 'It has frequently been observed that the process of valuation does not admit of precise conclusions and thus that the conclusions of competent and careful valuers may differ, perhaps by a substantial margin, without one of them being negligent, see for instance the often quoted judgment of Watkins J in *Singer & Friedlander Ltd v John D Wood & Co* [1977] 2 EGLR 84 and the House of Lords in *Banque Bruxelles Lambert SA v Eagle Star Insurance Co Ltd* [1977] AC 191. That has led the Courts adopting a particular approach to claims of negligence on the part of valuers.'

In the general run of actions for negligence against professional men:

> 'it is not enough to show that another expert would have given a different answer … The issue is … whether (the defendant) has acted in accordance with practices which are regarded as acceptable by a respectable body of opinion in his profession, *Zubaida v Hargreaves* [1995] 1 EGLR 127, per Hoffmann LJ, citing the very well known passage in *Bolam v Friern Hospital Management Committee* [1957] 1 WLR 582.
>
> However where the complaint relates to the figures included in a valuation there is an earlier stage that the court must be taken through before the need arises to address considerations of the Bolam type. Because the valuer cannot be faulted in any event for achieving a result that does not admit to some degree of error the first question is whether the valuation as a figure falls outside the range permitted to a non-negligent valuer. As Watkins J put it in *Singer & Friedlander*:
>
>> "there is as I have said a permissible margin of error the 'bracket' as I have called it. What can properly be expected from a competent valuer using reasonable skill and care is that his valuation falls within the bracket."
>
> A valuation that falls outside the permissible margin of error calls into question the valuer's competence and the care with which he carried out his task … but only if the valuation falls outside the permissible margin does that enquiry arise …
>
> Various further considerations follow. First the "bracket" is not to be determined in a mechanistic way caused from the facts of the instant case … Second if it is shown even at the first stage that the valuer adopted an unprofessional practice or approach then that may be taken into account in considering whether this valuation contained an unacceptable degree of error…third where the valuation is shown to be outside the acceptable limit that may be a strong indication that negligence has in fact occurred … some caution at least has to be exercised in this respect because the question must remain in valuation as in any other professional negligence cases whether the defendant has fallen foul of the *Bolam* principal. To find that his valuation fell outside the "brackets" is, as is held by this court in *Crane Heath* and also I consider by the House of Lords in *Banque Lambert*, a necessary condition of liability but it cannot in itself be sufficient … it is clear that Buxton LJ holds that in cases where the figures are impugned as figures it is a necessary pre-condition of liability that the impugned figures fall outside the "bracket".'

Further confirmation that the court will consider the whole of the valuers reasoning as well as the end result arose in *Dennard and others v PricewaterhouseCoopers LLP* [2010] EWHC 812 (Ch), confirmed by the Court of Appeal in [2010] EWCA Civ 1437.

The case concerned a company, Ryhurst Ltd, which specialised in Private Finance Initiative (PFI) projects.

An extract from the 61-page High Court judgment makes the following points:

> '3. As the trial progressed, the issues narrowed significantly, so that the central points of contention ultimately concerned only four main matters: the applicability of the limitation clause, the correct discount rate to apply to Discounted Cash Flow ("DCF") valuations of the PFI projects, the correct approach to the valuation of the possible future refinancing of the PFI projects, and the alleged conflicts of interest. As will appear, the parties have agreed a more extensive list of issues, but it is in these areas that the bulk of the evidence and argument has been focused.
>
> ...
>
> 7. It is common ground that the valuation of PFI projects should be undertaken on a DCF basis, and that a DCF valuation is essentially a function of 3 variables: (a) the cash flows which are likely to be produced by each project over its remaining life (perhaps 20 or 30 years), (b) the discount rate, which as a matter of judgement, should be applied to reflect the net present value ("NPV") of the cash flows, and the risks inherent in the project and its operation, and (c) the upsides that should be applied to the valuation to reflect present or future added value, like, for example, the present of cash trapped in the project which could be released, or the possibility that the debt might advantageously be refinanced at lower interest rates, creating a profit margin.
>
> ...
>
> 12. In January 2006, the Claimants sold their shares in Ryhurst (amounting, with the interests of others, to a 72% stake), save that the fourth Claimant, Mr Colin Dixon ("Mr Dixon"), retained some of his shares, to Barclays European Infrastructure Fund ("BEIF), another Barclays subsidiary, for £5,500 per share, indicating a value of £5.5 million for the whole of Ryhurst's interest in RBIL. The price the Claimants accepted was, at least, informed by PwC's valuation in May 2005 of £5,100 per share.
>
> 13. The foundation of the Claimant's complaint in these proceedings is that their shares in Ryhurst were re-sold by BEIF only 11 months later, in December 2006, to Secondary Market Infrastructure Fund ("SMIF") for £40,475 per share, an increase of some 736%. They say that this open market sale value represented the true value of their Ryhurst shares 11 months earlier in January 2006, and they claim the difference between £5,500 and £40,475 per share by way of damages from PwC.
>
> 14. Central to PwC's defence is the contention that its valuation was undertaken with all proper skill and care, and that the later sale to SMIF is in no way comparable to the earlier sale to BEIF. PwC says that Barclays had confidentiality rights under a shareholder agreement between ICL and Ryhurst, and pre-emption rights under the Articles of Association of RBIL, both of which it used or threatened to use to ensure that there was in practice only one purchaser in January 2006. Moreover, in December 2006, Barclays was selling both equity and stapled subordinated debt, which, says PwC, is a far more attractive commercial proposition. At the heart of this case lies the question of whether PwC simply used too high a discount rate in valuing the Claimants' shares.
>
> ...
>
> 58. It appears that during April and May 2005, Ms Daniells and Mr Chris Williams continued working with Mr Nigel Dodds and Ms Montague on various

calculations and models. Ultimately on 17th May 2005, Mr Chris Williams produced a schedule to Mr Dodds and Ms Montague updating the Draft Report showing a revised valuation of £5.1 million of £5,100 per share, and saying "the main difference is obviously a result of the base case models being updated to reflect actuals/reality". The valuation was broken down as to £3.4 million for the "base case", £0.3 million for the "upside of 2.7% inflation", £0.5 million for the "upside of trapped cash", and £0.9 million for the "upside of re-financing". This is the valuation on which the Claimants contend they relied, and it is referred to in this judgment as the "May Valuation".

…

63. On 11th August 2005, Barclays wrote to Ryhurst making a revised non-binding offer for BEIF to acquire Ryhurst's 50% interest in RBIL for £5 million.

…

65. There followed a period of negotiation with Barclays in which Mr Wilkinson, but not Mr Williams, was mainly involved. On 3rd October 2005, Barclays increased its offer to £5.25 million, to take account of insurance savings, and on 7th October 2005, Barclays increased its offer again to £5.5 million, expressed to be final, to take account of sinking fund benefits, provided Ryhurst retained those benefits. Meanwhile, deals were done which allowed Ryhurst management to retain their shares, Ms Montague to increase her shareholding, and Mr Dixon to retain 7% of his 16% holding.

…

74. On 21st January 2006:

(i) Each of the Claimants sold their 160 shares in Ryhurst (save for Mr Dixon who sold 90 shares only) at £5,500 per share to BEIF (880,000) for each of Messrs' Dennard, Turner and Gearon, and £495,000 for Mr Dixon). In total, as I have said, 72% of Ryhurst was sold to BEIF.
(ii) The Claimants sold the Rydon Group, in a management buy-out backed by HBOS, for nearly £40 million, from which Mr Dennard was paid some £12.6 million, Mr Turner some £12.7 million, and Mr Gearon some £7.2 million, because his ex-wife had an interest in his stake.

(Rydon Group were under common control with Ryhurst.)

…

80. On 8th December 2006, the interests previously held by Ryhurst were re-sold by BEIF to SMIF for the equivalent of £40,745 per share. The total price paid for the equity and debt was some £121.9 million, with about £39.9 million for the subordinated debt, making some £82 million for the equity alone.

…

106. Mr Jonathan White of KPMG ("Mr White") gave expert valuation evidence for the Claimants. I am afraid I did not find him a very impressive expert. First, he had plainly not properly understood many of the decisions that his team had taken in preparing aspects of his valuation. Secondly, one could not help but think that his original agenda had been to arrive at the highest possible sustainable valuation, rather than the valuation or a range of valuations which a reasonably competent valuer, using the information available to PwC, might have produced in May 2005. Thirdly, he was strikingly unfamiliar with the parts of his report concerned with refinancing. Fourthly, as his evidence progressed, he admitted that segments of his report were simply wrong, and that many of

the most significant assumptions made by both PwC and Mr Gary Neville ("Mr Neville"), PwC's expert (which had been expressly or impliedly rejected in his reports), were ones that a reasonably competent valuer would have made.

...

111. Mr Gary Neville of Birwood Advisors Limited was a contrast to Mr White. He was careful and methodical and seemed to have an insight into the market with which he was concerned. He has not practised as a professional accountant, but is a Fellow of The Chartered Institute of Management Accountants, who worked for Laing, one of the market leaders in PFI, from 2001-2007. In general, I preferred Mr Neville's evidence, whilst not being able to accept all his views, as will become apparent in due course.

...

113. Mr Neville valued Ryhurst's 50% interest in RBIL as at May 2005 at approximately £5.4 million, made up of £4.2 million for the base case, £1.1 million for the refinancing upside, and £0.1 million for the insurance upside. His own preference, however, would have been to use a blended, rather than a single, discount rate, which takes account of the fact that the discount rate will fall after completion and ramp-up. That method allows greater values during construction and ramp-up, and would add £0.9 million to Mr Neville's valuation making it up to approximately £6.3 million. He was at pains, however, to make clear that he regarded the use of a single discount rate method as a reasonable approach for PwC to have adopted.

...

130. PwC's other arguments on reliance are both unmeritorious and wrong on the evidence. The Claimants were fully entitled to rely on the work PwC was doing for their benefit with Ms Montague and Mr Dodds. PwC gave continuing valuation assistance on various upsides, on which the Claimants reasonably relied when Ms Montague negotiated increases in the price with Barclays through the latter part of 2005. As it turns out, this advice is not, in itself, the subject of specific attack, so these reliance issues are not of any great importance. But I find it surprising that PwC should seek to call into question whether the Claimants were truly relying on their advice in these circumstances, merely because they stood behind their agent, Ms Montague.

131. In my judgment, each of the Claimants actually and reasonably relied on the valuation, as they were contractually entitled to do, when they were agreeing to sell their interests in the RBIL portfolio to BEIF.

...

133. Before dealing with the facts on PwC's alleged negligence, I should say what I understand to be the state of the law as it affects allegedly negligent valuations. The parties were agreed that the decision of Lewison J in *Goldstein v Levy Gee* [2003] EWHC 1574 (Ch), [2003] PNLR 35 neatly summarised the latest position, although Mr Downes reserved the right to argue on appeal that the decision was wrong. Lewison J was unable wholly to reconcile some conflicting authority, but in the end he opted (rightly in my opinion) to follow the Court of Appeal's decision in *Merivale Moore plc v Strutt & Parker* [1992] 2 EGLR 171. In reality, it is that decision that Mr Downes reserved his right to criticise hereafter.

...

179. As I have already indicated in dealing with the expert evidence, the differences lie in the assumptions that are made about the manner in which the proposed refinancing will be undertaken, and the likely upside assumptions. PwC assumed that a margin of 50 basis points was achievable, which was significantly more aggressive than either Mr Neville or Mr White. In other respects, however, PwC made no changes to the portfolio in the assumed refinancing, so the aggressive margin rate change was used in effect, in place of making other assumptions. PwC also, of course, adopted the discount rates that have been criticised above. That fact, in itself, means that PwC's valuation of the refinancing upside was not a satisfactory one. Overall, however, the level of the refinancing upside adopted by PwC does not seem to me to be unreasonable – it was very close to the estimation made by quite a different methodology by Mr Neville. I do, however, think that Mr Neville's assumptions were themselves quite conservative.

…

187. For the reasons I have given, I need only deal with the position as at May 2005.

188. The non-negligent valuer as at that date would have valued the portfolio at £7.4 million for base case plus £1.4 million for the refinancing upside, making a total of £8.8 million. The range of non-negligent values would have been between £4.5 and £10.1 for the base case and £5.6 million and £11.8 million for the total.

189. Thus, PwC's valuation of £5.1 million fell outside (although not far outside) the lower limit of the range I have determined. This is the case whether or not Bexley and Black Country are disregarded, which I take the view they should not be, for the reasons I have given.

…

193. As appears from what I have found above, I do not think that a reasonably competent valuer ought to have valued the portfolio at double the sale price, but rather at approximately £8.8 million. Since I accept the preponderance of the Claimants' evidence that they would have gone ahead with the Barclays sale unless they had received a valuation of something like double the price Barclays were paying, it is clear that the sale to Barclays would indeed have gone ahead.

…

205. The next question is what is the percentage chance that Barclays would indeed have improved its offer to the level I have determined as the most likely, namely £6.5 million. I have thought of this in the light of the evidence I heard about the extensive dealings between Ms Montague, Mr Dodds, Mr Williams, Ms Daniells and Mr Jennings and Mr McClatchey. I think there is a good chance that the offer would have gone up to the level I have determined. I evaluate that chance at 75%.

206. On the basis, therefore, that the Claimants sold 57% of Ryhurst, they have lost 75% of 57% of £1 million, namely £427,500.

207. I should add by way of postscript that it seems to me that the exercise I have adopted takes proper account of the possibilities that Barclays would have increased its offer by both less than and more than £1 million. Plainly, on the findings I have made, there would be a less than 75% chance of the offer being increased by more than £1 million, and a more than 75% chance of the offer being increased to lower levels. It is impossible to say whether the scale is precisely linear or not, but this level of detail cannot matter. This consideration acts as a cross-check on the method I have adopted, and seems to me to make

> it clear that the evaluation I have made fairly compensates the Claimants who would have obtained a higher price from Barclays.
>
> Although not, in the event, relevant, it likely confirmed that the £1 million liability cap would have applied.'

In *Price Waterhouse v The University of Keele* [2004] EWCA Civ 583 the firm accepted that their advice had been negligent and the principal issues at trial were causation and the measure of damages.

Iain Paul Barker v Baxendale Walker Solicitors (BWS) and Paul Baxendale-Walker (PBW) [2016] EWHC 664 (Ch) was a claim for professional negligence in relation to an employment benefit trust (EBT) which, if successful, would have avoided a very significant liability to capital gains tax (CGT) and, eventually, inheritance tax (IHT). This EBT scheme was, many years later, challenged by HMRC which Mr Barker settled with substantial payments of tax and interest. In view of the time gap the claim was only in tort. The claim was resisted on various grounds. BWS had ceased its practice and the claim was against PBW. The court dismissed Mr Barker's claim and held that, although the defendants should have given a "general health warning" about the EBT scheme, Mr Barker would nonetheless have proceeded to enter the scheme and transfer the shares and, in taking the view that the trusts and sub-trust satisfied the conditions of IHTA 1984, s 28, the defendants were not in breach of the duty of care.

Focus

The valuer's liability to damages for an incorrect valuation will depend on the agreement to prepare the valuation and whether it is carried out competently and, if an error or errors are made, the effect, if any, this has on the value arrived at which in turn would influence the damages awarded, if any.

4.06 Par value

In arriving at the value of shares the par or nominal value is totally irrelevant. In the contract case of *McIlquham v Taylor* [1895] 1 Ch 53 property was to be transferred for '£1,000 worth' of shares. The defendant created some worthless shares with a nominal value of £1,000 and these were rejected. In the words of Lindley LJ at 63:

> 'The covenant is by Taylor that he will within twelve calendar months of the date of the document pay £1,000 or hand over to, or otherwise transfer into the names of the plaintiffs £1,000 worth of fully paid up shares in a company to be formed by Taylor, the capital of which is not to exceed £12,000. Now what does that mean? Mr Graham Hastings has invited us to construe it that he will pay £1,000 in cash or in shares meaning that he will transfer shares to the nominal value of £1,000. I do not think that that is the fair meaning of the language used. I put to Mr Graham Hastings another aspect of the case. Supposing these shares had gone up and Taylor had offered and tendered a smaller number than £1,000 in nominal value, but £1,000 worth in the market, what would have been the

> answer. The shares would be taken at their value according to the market. It is the same question from another point of view but it strikes me that the answer to it is clear. No one in the case supposed could have accused Taylor of breaking his contract, he would have done exactly what he said he would do – paid £1,000 worth of shares.'

In the words of Rigby LJ at 64:

> 'What does "worth" mean? It means worth in the sense of the reasonable value to be ascertained in some manner. There can be no difficulty in ascertaining it, it does not mean nominal value. The thing may be of the nominal value of £100,000 or as in this case £1,000 and yet not be worth a farthing.'

4.07 Fraud

In an actual sale of an interest in a company the purchaser will conduct a review of the financial and commercial information available and normally instruct accountants to prepare a due diligence report on the intended acquisition. That report will take account of management accounts and other information made available to the reporting accountants and assurances and disclosures made by directors and staff. These disclosures will normally be backed up by warranties in the sale and purchase agreement and in some cases money will be left in escrow until the warranty period has elapsed or will be released over a period of time. The purchasers may also be indemnified against the happening of specified events such as additional tax liabilities and these will also be incorporated in the sale and purchase agreement. It is very important that management information disclosed to a potential purchaser is accurate and any deficiencies or material uncertainties highlighted. Failure to do so can have disastrous consequences and could lead to allegations of fraud or deceit.

In a very lengthy judgment in *Bottin (International) Investments Ltd v Venson Group Plc* [2006] EWHC 3112, the claimant alleged:

> 'that it was fraudulently induced to invest £10 million in subscribing for one million A Preference Shares in the first defendant, Venson Group plc ("Venson"), equivalent on conversion to 28.57% of Venson's ordinary issued share capital. It seeks to rescind the transaction and recover its investment. In the alternative, it claims damages. In the further alternative it claims damages arising out of what it alleges are breaches of certain warranties contained in the share purchase agreement dated 22 December 1999 ("the SPA") pursuant to which it subscribed its £10 million for the shareholding. It alleges that the second, third and fourth defendants, respectively Grant Scriven ("Mr Scriven"), Clive Lawson Smith ("Mr Lawson Smith") and Simon Frost ("Mr Frost"), were parties to the fraud.'

The problem was (at para 231):

> 'the actual outturn for the year was a loss of £2,226,381, a figure which was reached after allowing for capitalisation and an income accrual of £500,000 resulting from the negotiated settlement with the MPS in 2001 ignoring the £500,000 income accrual the true loss of the year after capitalisation was therefore £2,726,381.
>
> 232 It has not been suggested that the groups audited financial statement for the year to 31 December 1999 ie its statutory accounts for 1999 do not give a

true and fair view of the state of Venson's affairs as at that date. Although by the time the accounts came to be audited a different and more rigorous approach to capitalisation of costs had been adopted. The sum capitalised for the year was £1.850m which was not greatly different from the figure of £2.115m of costs stated in the October management accounts to have been capitalised in reaching the profit before tax figure of £567,000 for the ten months to 31 October.

233 The disparity between the projected profit of £737,000 and the actual outturn was at the very least around £3m. Adjusting for the £500,000 income accrual it was correspondingly greater. On any view the variance was enormous.'

At 236:

'Mr Wardle submitted that the conclusion to which one was driven can only be that the October management accounts massively overstated Vensons' profits before tax for the ten months to 31 October 1999.'

At para 410 the judge stated:

'Mr Wardell submitted that damages should be assessed as at the date when Bottin was induced by fraud to invest in Venson namely 22 December 1999 and that the measure of Bottin's loss is the difference between its investment of £10m and what at that time Venson was truly worth.

411 I agree. I was given no good reason why damages should be assessed at any later date or on any other basis. The only question therefore is to determine what Venson was worth at the time Bottin invested its £10m. On this the two experts disagreed.

412 The opinion of Mr Hobbs the expert on valuation called by Mr Bottin was that at 22 December 1999 Venson was worthless. At paras 441 to 442 of his second supplemental report he stated that "but for Vensons' investment and absent any investment from another investor, Vensons liabilities at 31 December 1999 would have exceeded its (assets) by £2,392,099 and its net current liabilities at that date would have amounted to £4,471,727. In so stating he was drawing information contained in Venson's statutory accounts. He expressed the opinion that if Venson had been forced to cease trading at 31 December 1999 the deficit on a liquidation would have been significantly higher than the £2,392,099 figure. He therefore concluded at para 444 of his report that as 22 December 1999 Venson had no value at all unless it had sufficient resources to fund its activities prior to becoming profitable which in the absence of Bottin it did not.

413 Mr Cowan the defendant's expert on valuation considered that Venson's true value as at 22 December 1999 was £3.4m. He produced elaborate calculations to reach this conclusion. In the course of his examination, however, he agreed that he was unable to attribute any value to Venson based on its actual 1999 result. As regards 2000 and forwards, Mr Cowan's approach was to ignore Vensons actual results for those years, namely an overall operating loss (calculated before tax and interest) of £4.345m in 2000 and operating profits (calculated on the same basis) of only £23,322 in 2001 and no more than £31,289 in 2002. Instead he based his calculation on the profit for £2,000 which Venson itself had projected in the Outline Strategic Plan for 2002/04 namely an operating profit of £2.5m and a profit after tax of £1.75m. He also calculated the operating profit before depreciation for 2000 based on the figures in that Plan. He then proceeded to a valuation by Venson by applying a multiplier to those figures averaging the results and adding in the net value of Bottin's £10m investment i.e. £8.8m reached after deducting £1.2m paid out to redeem CIBC's shareholding. In this way he arrived at a figure of £3.4m.

414 In my view Mr Cowan's is a flawed approach. It is flawed not least because it assumes the correctness of Venson budgeted projections for 2000 when it is obvious that it was hopelessly inflated and also because although accepting that he was unable to assess the impact of the actual result for 1999 on Venson's projections for 2000 he nevertheless felt able to adjust the multiplier applicable to those results in an attempt to reflect that impact while admitting that the was unable to justify how he reached the adjustment.

415 The correct approach in my view is to assess the true value of Venson at the date of Bottin's investment taking into account subsequent events in so far as those subsequent events throw light upon Venson's value at the valuation date. The plain fact of the matter is that apart from suffering a loss of £2.226m in 1999 Venson recorded an even greater operating loss in 2000. This occurred despite having the use of Bottin's £10m. Even allowing for exceptional items the operating loss was £1.3m. There was nothing in the evidence to indicate that the loss was attributable to events whether in the nature of market trades or other factors which only surfaced in 2000 rather than factors already evident in 1999.

…

417 In my judgment, given Venson's actual results for 1999 and 2000 it is quite impossible to attribute any value to Venson as at 22 December 1999. I am reinforced in this view by the minimal operating profits eventually earned in 2001 and 2002 and the fact that Bottin's investment has not so far earned it a penny. It follows that Bottin's loss measured as at 22 December 1999 was the full amount of its £10m investment. To these figures must be added interest. The Defendants will be jointly liable for the sum in question.'

The judge held that the claims in deceit succeeded and 'the loss and damage suffered by Bottin in consequence of the deceit was the same in each case. In the result Bottin is entitled to damages against all four Defendants in the sum of £10m together with interest'.

In *Doughty Hanson & Co Ltd v Roe* [2007] EWHC 2212 (Ch) a fair value argument arose when Mr Roe resigned his directorship in the company and its subsidiaries thereby triggering an obligation to give a transfer notice under the Articles of Association in respect of his shares. He gave a transfer notice and the articles of association provided for accountants, in this case Messrs Price Waterhouse Coopers (PWC), who certified a price per share as being a fair value under the articles of association. PWC issued a final certificate on 2 February 2007 which concluded,

'in accordance with our instructions we set out below our opinion as to the fair value of a single share comprised in the shares for sale as at 22 September 2006;

Value of a single share comprised in the shares for sale: £760.'

That figure would give a value of Mr Roe's entire shareholding of approximately £9.3m. Mr Roe employed Deloitte to submit a long report and they stated their opinion that the value of a participating share was in excess of £8,553, a value of more than 11 times greater than that of PWC. The Articles provided that the valuation was to be on the footing that there was no discount for a minority holding and the valuer acts as expert and not as arbitrator. The procedure was that a proposed transferor gives a transfer notice which specifies a price which is acceptable to the transferor or a willingness to sell at a third party valuation by an investment bank or accountant. That is taken to be an offer which is passed on to the other shareholders. They may accept at either the specified price or elect for a valuation. The valuation if there has to be one is carried out by an investment bank or an accountant who has to certify the fair value. The valuer is to disregard the fact (if it be the case) that the shares are a minority holding and shall positively have regard to the fact (if it be the case) that there is no public market in the shares and shall also have regard to the distributable reserves of the company. Mr Roe attempted to withdraw the transfer notice as he was unhappy with the PWC valuation but was not permitted under the articles to do so. One of the main reasons for the difference between the valuations was PWC's opinion that Messrs Doughty and Hanson had no ongoing obligation to work within the business. PWC therefore valued the single share comprised in the shares for sale as a direct pro rata of the total value which they calculated as the net assets as at 22 September 2006 per the balance sheet, adjusted to reflect the market value of the investments and the timing of transaction fees received plus a degree of option value to reflect the possibility that the business had a greater value than that so calculated.

Mr Roe argued that because Messrs Doughty and Hanson in fact continued to work for the company the valuation should be set aside on the grounds that PWC had not valued the company as it actually was. Mr Roe's attempt to set aside the valuation failed:

> 'because the valuer was doing what he was employed to do, namely to apply such valuation techniques and to make such judgments as are in his view necessary and/or appropriate to value that which he is valuing. If he adopts a hypothesis that would not be adopted by other valuers then he may have made an error in his valuation but it does not mean that he has valued something different. It means he has made a mistake … All that it means is that the right thing has been valued but on an erroneous hypothesis. Such an erroneous hypothesis is a mistake which a valuer acting as an expert is "entitled" to make.'

Mr Roe's counsel relied on *Morgan Sindall Plc v Sawston Farms (Cambs) Ltd* [1999] 1 EGLR 90. However, there was no doubt that the valuer had valued the correct shares in the correct company and the *Morgan Syndal* case demonstrates that only a mistake as to the identity of the subject matter of the valuation would enable either party to be able to say that the certificate was not binding because the expert had not done what he was appointed to do. As under the terms of the articles Mr Roe was not entitled to withdraw his transfer notice he was bound by the PWC valuation.

A case involving alleged fraud is *The Hut Group Limited v Nobahar-Cookson and Barclays Private Bank & Trust Limited* [2014] EWHC 3842 (QB). The Hut Group Limited (THG) claimed damages for breach of warranty regarding a company, Cend Limited, which had been transferred by the defendants to THG, and Barclays Private Bank & Trust Limited ('the Trustees') claimed damages for breach of warranty and deceit.

The earnings of THG before adjustments had been stated at £4.1m but, following adjustment, showed a loss of £1.5m. THG successfully claimed £4,317,089 for breach of warranty and the Trustees successfully claimed £10,800,000 and this was not capped by clause 7.12 of the Sale and Purchase Agreement. However, the Trustees' deceit claim failed.

In *Anthony Bayliss v HMRC* [2016] UKFTT 500 (TC), HMRC alleged fraudulent or negligent behaviour in claiming a capital loss of £539,000 having entered into the "Pendulum Long" capital loss scheme. This involved the purchase of a contract for difference (CFD) from Pendulum Investment Corporation, a company based in the Seychelles.

The total issue value was £850,000 and Mr Bayliss paid 6%, £51,000 for the initial margin and the balance was funded by an interest-free loan from Baybridge Investments Limited of £790,000. Mr Bayliss made a part disposal of the CFD for £550,000 and received £11,000 for this, so he claimed his loss was £539,000. The scheme was disallowed under TCGA 1992, s 16A (Restrictions on allowable losses, where the main purpose is to secure a tax advantage) and TCGA 1992, s 38 (Acquisition and disposal costs etc) and a sham within *Snook v West Riding Investments Limited* [1967] 2 QB 786 and *Hitch v Stone* [2001] STC 214.

The group promoting the scheme were Montpelier Tax Consultants who produced a memorandum which purported to set out "Taxation Considerations in respect of an Investment Opportunity in long term FTSE Contracts" which outlined the structure with illustrative numbers including the loan that an "associated company of Pendulum" was prepared to make.

For the defence, *Gedir v HMRC* [2016] UKFTT 188 (TC) and *Hanson v HMRC* [2012] UKFTT 314 (TC) were referred to as cases where the taxpayer relies on an agent to complete his tax return. HMRC relied on the classic description of fraud in *Derry v Peek* (1889) LR 14 App Cas 337 where a false representation was made "(1) knowingly, or (2) without belief in its truth, or (3) recklessly, careless whether it be true or false'.

The defence focused on dishonesty and referred to *Stuttard and another (trading as de Wynns Coffee House) v Customs and Excise Commissioners* [2000] STC 342, *Royal Brunei Airlines SDN Bhd v Ton* [1995] 2 AC 378, *Barlow Clowes International v Eurotrust International Limited* [2006] 1 WLR 1476 and *Abou-Ramah v Abacha* [2006] EWCA Civ 1492.

Negligence relied on a number of points which, in their view, demonstrated fraud and those which pointed to negligence. However the Tribunal held that HMRC had not discharged its burden of proof to demonstrate negligence and relied fully on a chartered accountant on whom he had relied for a number of years and Mr Bayliss had believed, on his recommendation, in Montpelier's expertise.

Criminal Finances Act 2017, ss 44–58

Part 3 (Criminal Offence of Failure to Prevent Facilitation of Tax Evasion) of this Act makes it a criminal offence to prevent the facilitation of UK or foreign tax evasion offences. It provides guidance about prevention procedures, including its extra-territorial application and jurisdiction. No proceedings for such offences may be instituted in England and Wales without the consent of the Director of Public Prosecutions or the Director of the Serious Fraud Office, with similar provisions for Northern Ireland and by Scottish Ministers for Scotland.

4.08 Fairness opinions

A company may seek a fairness opinion from a valuer in respect of the proposed price at which a potential transaction may proceed. This is particularly relevant for US companies as the US Securities and Exchange Commission requires public companies to obtain a fairness opinion in certain circumstances and also because the directors of a company can held personally liable for a 'wrong' decision or a failure in their duty of care to shareholders.

Typical situations in which a fairness opinion may be sought include:

- the acquisition or disposal of a subsidiary;
- mergers and acquisitions (for both the buyer and the vendor);
- management buyouts;
- buyback of shares;
- restructuring;
- loan covenants; and
- industry regulation.

4.09 Purpose of the opinion

A fairness opinion has three main functions:

1 to assist the Board of Directors in their decision-making process;
2 to mitigate the company's risk in respect of the transaction; and
3 the communicate the findings regarding the proposed transaction.

The opinion does not indicate whether the proposed price is the best available, only that, given the facts and the prevailing economic and business circumstances, that the price is fair. The report cannot advise the directors as to their course of action, but will set out the information considered and the assumptions made in arriving at the opinion. The final decision as to whether to proceed with a particular transaction is the responsibility of the Board.

4.10 Valuation basis

The valuation standard required, as set out in US case law (*Weinberger v UOP Inc* 426 A 2d 1333, Del Ch (1981)) is that of 'entire fairness'. This consists of two components, 'fair dealing' and 'fair price'.

Fair dealing looks at the commercial and practical circumstances of the transaction and the conduct of the parties involved. There is a strict requirement of impartiality on the part of the directors and also the valuer giving the opinion. For example, the SEC has been critical in the past of investment banks providing fairness opinions while being remunerated on a success fee basis. Things to consider include the timing of the transaction and its effect on the business at that time, whether any director or individual benefited personally from the transaction, whether any benefit would be at the expense of the company's performance and profitability and whether the directors (and shareholders, if shareholder approval was required) had been provided with all material information. It is also important that any team negotiating the transaction is impartial.

Fair price considers the financial aspects of the transaction such as the current market value of the shares, the company's earnings and prospects, its asset base and any other pertinent factors which would affect the value of a share at that date. There is no requirement for the company to produce new information for the valuer or for the valuer to undertake a formal audit of the data provided, but the Board is expected to disclose all relevant information as part of this process.

There is no prescribed valuation methodology which must be adopted, provided that that work performed is sufficient and appropriate to meet the fair price requirement. In practice, a number of approaches would usually be considered in order to arrive at a suitable range of values and to cross-check for reasonableness. The fair price requirement is very similar to that of fair value, where a vendor or purchaser is deemed to act on a prudent basis on the assumption that all relevant information has been obtained and considered. The company must consider what it is receiving in relation to what it is giving up.

As the fairness opinion is based on the facts and circumstances in existence at a particular point in time, the opinion is only valid while these facts and circumstances remain unchanged. As more facts emerge or the economic climate changes, then it is highly likely that the conclusions leading to the opinion will change accordingly.

4.11 Fair value for financial reporting purposes

In financial reporting, ie preparation of financial statements (accounts), fair value has a different meaning from that described earlier in this chapter. The meaning of fair value for financial reporting purposes is explained in **Chapter 20** of this book: it is a measure of market, or open market, value.

Chapter 5

Relevant factors

Signposts

5.01 Factors in valuation

When valuing at a particular date, the valuer must consider all the pertinent factors, both those relating to the specific business being valued and also wider factors such as the strength of a particular sector and the state of the local and global economy.

In estimating the value of shares in a company it is important to consider the likely prospects for the company in the future as this will have a material effect on the value of the company's shares. All relevant factors have to be considered.

Readers will note that cases included in earlier editions of this book have been retained, even where they relate to activities, such as whaling or trading in West Africa in the 1940s, that are unlikely to be encountered in current valuations. The current pace of technological change is such that activities that were lucrative in the recent past, such as selling disk drives for BBC computers (see *Re Cumana Ltd, in Re a Company (No 002612 of 1984)*), already appear hopelessly outdated. Basic economic rules do not change, however, and the general conclusions reached could still be relevant and are worth repeating.

5.02 General economic and political situation

The economic climate can have a significant impact on a valuation. This can either be as a general context – are we valuing in a 'boom' or 'bust' – but also can have a specific impact on company results; for example, if a business is exposed to foreign currency fluctuations.

In *A-G of Ceylon v Mackie* (1952) 31 ATC 435 Lord Reid stated:

> 'Evidence was given in the District Court as to the value of the shares. The leading witness for the respondents was Mr Lander, a chartered accountant, who has experience of rubber companies. The gist of his evidence was that a buyer would first ask what was the last dividend and when it was paid, but, as no dividend had been paid for many years, it was impossible to value the shares on a yield basis. He then pointed out that in 1940 the future was unpredictable and it was difficult to find anyone who was willing to invest large sums of money on speculation. He valued the shares on a balance sheet basis because, in his view, no one would have paid more than that at the time. When asked in cross-examination whether a buyer would not have taken into account the probability that the high profits of 1940 would last for some time, he said that the buyer would have needed to know precisely what was going to happen in the world which was devastated by a war the length of which could not be guessed by the man in the street. In other words, if a purchaser could have guessed that there was going to be a long war, no government interference, no form of increased taxation, and that he was not going to have competition from others, he might take that view. He would be a brave man. It would possibly be a gamble. In his view, no goodwill attached to the business. Similar evidence was given by other witnesses for the respondents.'

Similarly, in *Re Holt* (1953) 32 ATC 402 at 405 Danckwerts J quoted a witness who:

> 'said that the West African trade had had a very bad reputation in the last thirty or forty years, and referred to the riots following a boycott of European traders, which occurred in February 1948, shortly before the death of the deceased. He also referred to the devaluation of the French Colonial franc which occurred in January 1948, as another depressing factor.'

Another witness:

> 'had long experience of West African trading, and this led him to describe the trading risks in West Africa as immensely greater than in any other part of the world. These risks, he explained, were due to the prosperity of these territories being based on agriculture, and in some cases on some particular kind only, such as the culture of cocoa or ground nuts, so that they were affected by the wide fluctuations in the prices of the products and by growing conditions. In his view the necessity of traders in West Africa carrying heavy stocks at times of high prices represented a tremendous danger, because it was only a question of time when a break in prices would come. In 1946, 1947 and 1948 Mr Samuel expected

> that a break in prices was imminent, and his opinion was generally shared in the West African trade. Another adverse factor in his view was the growing tendency in West African countries to try to get trade away from European firms.'

Danckwerts J commented at 410 that:

> 'the fluctuating nature of West African trading, would be likely to have a greater effect upon the mind of the hypothetical purchaser than was admitted by the witnesses for the Commissioners of Inland Revenue.'

It will be seen that Mr Lander, as quoted above, referred to government interference and increased taxes, but these are not the only way in which the government's actions are relevant. For example, if the government is concerned at the level of inflation it may be actively engaged in attempts to reduce that level. A key question however, is whether those government activities are likely to increase profitability in the industry or not and this can only be decided when the schemes in operation have been considered in detail.

Generally speaking, such schemes as those designed to encourage the placing of orders in the UK or tax incentives designed to encourage research and development do not have the effect of increasing profitability, so that even a very full order book is no indication that profits are about to accrue. Other relevant factors also need to be taken into account.

Local conditions will be one of the many factors influencing value, but the importance of treating each case on its own merits was emphasised in the Hong Kong estate duty case of *Re Charrington* (Hong Kong Supreme Court 1975). An appeal against a value imposed by the Hong Kong Commissioner of Estate Duty was heard in the first instance in the Supreme Court (Appellate Jurisdiction: Full Court), where Leonard J made the following remarks:

> 'I do not, therefore, consider it possible to place reliance on either the basis of dividend yield or earnings yield. I am convinced that in the highly volatile atmosphere of Hong Kong the ordinary investor is attracted more readily by the possibility of capital gain than by the probability of secure annual returns. This, as much as the fact that there had been no dividends paid over the years but only the interest on shares which the board was obliged by the articles to pay, or the fact that its mounting land values was an important factor in giving its shares a high attraction, leads me to forsake the dividend yield and the earnings yield methods of valuation. I am left with the "asset backing" method and am convinced that any shrewd seller would refuse to calculate a selling price on any other basis in the peculiar circumstances of this company.
>
> I am told by Mr. Ladd that it is common practice for the Estate Duty Office to value even minority interests in private companies by reference to their asset backing and in the peculiar atmosphere of Hong Kong I do not consider this inappropriate. Indeed if one is not to play with figures or to pluck figures arbitrarily out of the air it seems to me to offer the only logically justifiable approach.
>
> This is particularly so in the case of this company for no willing but not anxious seller of its shares could have failed to realize the extent to which its land and builders had appreciated in the period immediately prior to the date of death. Mr. MacWhinnie told me that at that time the price of properties was very inflated and that the "whole picture in land prices was distorted". A purchaser and certainly the type of purchaser envisaged by Danckwerts J. in *Holt's* case would have been aware of, and, perhaps rendered the more cautious by this distortion, but he would nevertheless have appreciated that the most important thing about the company

> was the capital value of its land holdings; its rental incomes and its trading profits while they would have influenced him would have been secondary.'

On appeal against Leonard J's decision, nevertheless, Pickering J in the Supreme Court (Appellate Jurisdiction: Full Court) had this to say:

> 'However, what appears to trouble the appellants just as much as the outcome of this appeal upon its actual facts in relation to this particular company, is a comment made by the learned judge in the course of his judgment which may or may not have been intended as a general observation. The comment was in these terms:
>
> > "I am told by Mr. Ladd that it is common practice for the Estate Duty Office to value even minority interests in private companies by reference to their asset backing and in the peculiar atmosphere of Hong Kong I do not consider this inappropriate. Indeed if one is not to play with figures or to pluck figures arbitrarily out of the air it seems to me to offer the only logically justifiable approach."'

The 'peculiar atmosphere of Hong Kong' to which the learned judge refers is a reference to his earlier statement that in Hong Kong the ordinary investor is attracted more readily by the possibility of capital gain than by the probability of secure annual returns. The whole observation may or may not have been intended to have reference merely to this particular case but the reference to 'common practice' suggests that the observation was intended to be of general application.

> 'Let us say at once that the remark was wholly unnecessary for the purposes of the judgment and that, as such, it can only be considered as an obiter dictum. Its very existence, however, appears to have alarmed the appellants that the observation may be used, by the Commissioner in the future, as legitimising the assets backing approach to the valuation of any shares passing upon death in private limited trading companies. For this reason we think it right to record our view that the observation was mistaken. The assets backing approach is not the only logically justifiable approach in these cases. It was an appropriate approach in the present case but, as we have said, the circumstances of different companies vary appreciably and, in the end, the choice of method adopted must be ascertained by something of an empirical approach dictated by those circumstances.'

5.03 State of the industry

As well as the general economic and political situation the valuer should consider the particular prospects for the industry in which the company is operating and its relative position within that industry. If that industry is composed of a number of sectors for example, as in the engineering and chemical industries, it is that sector in which the company operates that needs to be considered. This was brought out in the case of *Salvesen's Trustees v IRC* (1930) 9 ATC 43 where Lord Fleming included in the relevant facts affecting the valuation of shares of the company, the history of the whaling industry and the prospects of the whaling industry generally at the date of valuation, and of the company in particular. In considering the future prospects of the industry and of the company his Lordship referred to the speculative nature of the industry, the fact that the British government had sent the research ship 'Discovery' to make scientific observations which might serve as the basis for the regulation of the whaling industry, but that no report was yet available. He referred to the government licences of shore based stations and the revocability of licences and prospects of further government control and restrictions. He thought (at 52) that it was important that the directors of the company:

> 'were so confident that there was no immediate prospect either of the disappearance of the whales or of the industry being prejudicially affected by government interference that they had spent large sums of money in recent years on purchasing whaling vessels, though their previous policy had been to hire them, and had also committed themselves to the extent of £300,000 for that season's trading. The evidence of Mr Borley, a naturalist in the employment of the Colonial Office, indicates that, though the matter was engaging attention at this time, there was no evidence to suggest that there was any likelihood of the disappearance or even serious diminution in the number of blue whales and fin whales, which constitute the major portion of the catch. He expressed the view that there was not likely to be any decline or collapse of the industry for a very considerable number of years after 1926, and in point of fact it appears from his evidence, and from the report of the "Discovery" investigations, that the seasons 1926–27 and 1927–28 were very successful.'

Lord Fleming also referred to:

> 'Another disturbing factor in the situation at this time was the commencement of Pelagic fishing. Pelagic fishing is fishing for whales on the high seas and its characteristic feature is that, instead of the whale catchers being based on a shore station, they are based on a factory ship which operates on the high seas and performs all the functions of the shore stations and in particular the boiling of the whale for the purpose of obtaining oil from it. Pelagic Fishing has turned out to be very successful, but it was in its initial stages in 1926 and the only vessel which operated in that year was not very successful. What I am concerned with is not the development of Pelagic fishing since 1926, but the knowledge that an intending investor would probably have of it in that year and whether it would influence his views as to the value of the shares. Mr Borley indicates in his evidence that he thought it was not occasioning much serious concern to those in the industry at that time, and I agree with this view. In 1926 no licences were required for Pelagic fishing and, if it turned out to be successful, it would probably mean more competition in the whaling industry. Companies which had licences from the government, as the South Georgia had, could engage in Pelagic fishing as well as in fishing in territorial waters, but it is in evidence that a very large expenditure would be required to enable them to do so.'

Similarly in *A-G of Ceylon v Mackie* (1952) 31 ATC 435 Lord Reid stated:

> 'The practice of the company was to buy rubber and grade it for re-sale. Its graded rubber, known as Mackie standard, had a high reputation in important foreign markets, and it appears that some 20% or 30% of the whole of the rubber exported from Ceylon was handled by the company. The policy of the company was to hold large stocks, and, as the price of rubber has for long been subject to large and rapid fluctuations, the company's profits varied to an extreme degree.'

Later he continued:

> 'No doubt, the value of an established business as a going concern generally exceeds and often greatly exceeds the total value of its tangible assets. But that cannot be assumed to be universally true. If it is proved in a particular case that at the relevant date the business could not have been sold for more than the value

> of its tangible assets, then that must be taken to be its value as a going concern. In their Lordship's judgment it has been proved in this case that the deceased's holding could not have been sold in September 1940 at a price based on any higher figure than the value of the tangible assets of the company.'

In *Findlay's Trustees v IRC* (1938) 22 ATC 437 Lord Fleming stated:

> 'The decision of this case must accordingly depend upon the figure which is to be adopted for expected profits. I do not doubt that, when one is seeking to ascertain the profits which will probably be earned by a business in the future, it is quite usual to do so by taking an average of the profits actually earned for the three preceding years. This probably operates quite equitably when one is dealing with a well established business, which has normal ups and downs, but has no violent fluctuations in either direction. But if there is a definite trend upwards or downwards, it may be different. If, for example, profits are increasing year by year by large figures an average of three years may be unfair to the seller. If there is a similar movement downwards, it may be unfair to the purchaser …
>
> This prima facie view is, I think, confirmed by consideration of the position of the newspaper industry in the year 1930. That year was a period of general depression which had begun in 1929, and it was certainly not a time at which sellers could expect to get good prices. Trade is said to go in cycles, and "booms" follow "slumps", but there were a number of factors which, apart from the slump, were not favourable to this business in 1930. The competition by what are called the national newspapers with their headquarters in London was in an increasing degree affecting the prospects of the morning newspapers published in the provinces of England and in Scotland. According to the evidence of Sir Bertram Ford and Mr Scott the structure of the "Scotsman" business was not well suited to withstand such competition. In this view the morning newspapers are much more amenable to competition from London than the evening newspapers, and it is accordingly a great advantage to a morning paper to have a strong evening paper associated with it, and this business was criticised on the ground that the "Scotsman" was the predominant partner in the group. Though the "Evening Dispatch" was increasing its circulation at this time, their view was that it was not a sufficiently strong evening paper to counteract any retrograde movement on the part of the "Scotsman", especially as it had to face competition from a well established rival newspaper. Another factor which they regarded as unfavourable was that the "Scotsman" newspaper circulated mainly in a non-industrial area in which the population was not increasing or increasing slowly; and that there was little scope for expansion or development. It was maintained by the appellants that the figure in the other columns in No 14 of Process indicated that the business was declining, and references were made in particular to the figures with regard to newspaper sales, advertising revenue and expenses. The decrease in the volume of newspaper sales, though not great, is certainly not a favourable feature, especially as a reduction in circulation may tend to diminish the advertising revenue … I think however it is impossible to avoid coming to the conclusion that the outlook in 1930 could not be regarded as favourable to the newspaper industry, or for the "Scotsman" business in particular.'

Difficult trading conditions and the world price of a raw material or commodity essential to a company's business would also have to be taken into account, but a reasonable view would have to be taken of how long adverse conditions might be expected to last, as noted by Staughton J in *Buckingham v Francis* [1986] 2 BCC 98, 984:

> 'Proceeding by my preferred method, I must next find what was, on 24 March 1981, the most likely figure or best realistic guess for the future maintainable

profits of the company and make appropriate allowance for risk in doing so. I resolutely exclude after-events, save for the purpose of checking what was a proper estimate at that date. I also give a good deal less weight to high profit figures in the past than they received in Mr Humpage's average. Trading conditions were difficult in March 1981, both nationally and for this particular company; an attempted corner in the world silver markets had quadrupled the price, and silver was one of the company's main raw materials. The company did not have a secure asset base; further capital might be needed. And in 1980 profit was only 1% of turnover, a precarious situation …

Against all that, there were some grounds for optimism. Difficult trading conditions nationally were not expected to last for ever. Both Mr Buckingham and the other directors of the company in fact expected its affairs to become more prosperous, and had some grounds for their expectation.'

In *Hawkings-Byass v Sassen* [1996] STC (SCD) 319, concerning the valuation for capital gains tax purposes at 31 March 1982 of shares in the sherry producing company Gonzalez Byass, the Special Commissioners considered the following aspects of the sherry industry in arriving at their opinion of value:

'As compared with 1988 sales of sherry were greater in 1982. There had been a gentle decline partly owing to a change in United Kingdom taxation in about 1984 which made sherry more expensive. (Geoffrey [one of the taxpayers] attributed the decline to changing habits in the United Kingdom, people eating lighter food and drinking less heavy wine.) Sales had peaked in 1979 but this was an artificial peak created by certain houses in Spain which exported a large amount of sherry of no great quality to qualify for a tax rebate. (Geoffrey gave evidence to the same effect). He did not think that the industry in Spain was, as was stated by Mr Baker [expert witness for the Inland Revenue] in his report 'in the doldrums' in March 1982. Gonzalez Byass certainly was not. It was in a very strong position; it was at its height in 1982 (an opinion held also by Nicholas and by Geoffrey who distinguished between increasing branded sales and bulk unbranded sherry which was in the doldrums). There was over-production in 1980 following the planting up of new vineyards in the 1970s. But, as Mr Hines put it, Gonzalez Byass did not subscribe to the South Sea Bubble; it had not overplanted. It was well run and financially sound; it was not over-extended like Domecq which was ripe for a bid (from a reputable suitor) (see the *Financial Times* 27 March 1982).'

Focus

The popularity or otherwise of a sector can have a significant impact on value. However, even within a 'popular' sector there can be distinct trends. A clear example of this is the social networking site, Bebo, which was sold to AOL in 2008 for $850 million but subsequently went into liquidation. It was then sold on in 2010 for $10 million and finally reacquired by its founders for $1 million in 2013. This significant decline in value occurred even at a time when social network sites such as Facebook and Twitter floated at implied values significantly greater than their revenues would have suggested.

5.04 Profit record

A purchaser of shares in a company is usually concerned with the likely profits which the company will make after his acquisition and the past results of the company are clearly important in estimating the likely future profits. It is, however, necessary to look at each case on its merits.

In *A-G of Ceylon v Mackie* (1952) 31 ATC 435, Lord Reid stated in considering the Revenue case:

> 'Their approach was more theoretical. They assumed that it was possible to estimate the future average maintainable profit by means of an arithmetical calculation from past results and losses, and that a purchaser could have been found who would have paid a price for the shares determined by a further arithmetical calculation from that average maintainable profit. One witness said that "a buyer would concentrate on the last five years' profits because that is most likely to represent what would happen in the future"; and another witness went so far as to say that a prudent buyer would take it for granted that conditions would remain the same. It may be that these assumptions would be justified in many cases. Where the past history of a business shows consistent results or a steady trend and where there has been no disruption of general business conditions it may well be possible to reach a fair valuation by a theoretical calculation. But in this case neither condition was satisfied. The profits and losses of the company had fluctuated so violently in the past that, as the second witness for the appellant admitted, it is impossible to choose any five consecutive years in the company's history, the result of which would be reflected in the next year's profits. It is therefore, in their Lordships' judgment, not possible in this case to derive by an arithmetical calculation from past results anything which could probably have been regarded in 1940 as an average maintainable profit, and in addition there were extremely uncertain conditions in 1940.'

In that case the results were considered for the period from the company's formation in 1922 until the date of the shareholder's death in 1940.

In *Re Holt* (1953) 32 ATC 402 the accounting results for the 36 years from 1912 to the year ending on 30 September 1947 were produced to enable the fluctuations in the company's profits to be appreciated. In this case Mr T A Hamilton Baynes was the only witness to attempt to estimate the future profits. As Danckwerts J said at 408:

> 'He looked at the profits for a period of 10 years up to and including 1947 because that happened to include two pre-war years and two post-war years. He found that the average profits for this period were £524,744. This figure he discounted by 25%, because, as I understood, the very high profits of 1947 were not likely to be maintained, and this gave him a figure of £393,558 which he regarded as approximately twice the pre-war profit. He admitted that the deduction of one-quarter from the average of 10 years was made for no particular reason, but he was trying to get at some kind of guess work figure for the future profits. It seems to me, moreover, that the years to which Mr Baynes confined his average might well produce a misleading result, because the years selected were the war years of exceptionally high profits and the years of post-war inflation; and the two pre-war years, 1937 and 1938, were years of unusually high profits not at all typical of the years between the two wars.
>
> ...
>
> It is clear that if the figure taken by Mr Baynes for the average profit, £393,558, was unreasonable for any reason all his calculations by which he reached his selling price of 30 shillings per share, would be affected. It appears, also, that

> he had not paid any attention to the way in which heavy wartime taxation had affected the ability of the company to place money to reserve to meet future capital expenditure and the possibility of a post-war slump.'

In *Lynall v IRC* (1971) 47 TC 375 the company, Linread Ltd was incorporated in 1925 but the results were considered by the court for the years ending 31 July 1957 to 1961 inclusive with the accounts for the year ended 31 July 1962 being available, although not wholly admissible, as covering a period extending beyond the date of death.

The results were summarised by Plowman J at 379:

> 'This, then, was a substantial high-class private company with a successful profit record, even in a difficult year in industry like 1961, showing growth, a strong liquid position, a high dividend cover and a very satisfactory cash flow (that is to say, aggregate of depreciation and retained profits).'

In *Salvesen's Trustees v IRC* (1930) 9 ATC 43 the profit record of the company was examined from the date of its incorporation on the 24 June 1909 to the date of death on the 24 October 1926. In considering the trend of profits in the *Salvesen* case Lord Fleming succeeded in eliminating an exceptional receipt when he stated at 47:

> 'I should however qualify these figures by stating that, as regards the year 1923–24, the company had a windfall from a PPI insurance of about £50,000 and I understood all the witnesses to be agreed that this windfall should not properly enter the profit and loss accounts at all.'

Where the data is available, a consideration of a minimum of three years' accounts is essential; it may be more but it should not be less, unless in exceptional circumstances such a major restructuring of the business, a change in operational focus or significant acquisitions or disposals which make comparison with historical results meaningless. Further, any exceptional items of receipts or expenditure should be looked at in detail to see whether they should be eliminated (eg the £50,000 referred to in *Salvesen*).

Care should be taken in years where there may be have been changes in reporting requirements for accounting purposes, for example the introduction of FRS 102 or a company's adoption of International Financial Reporting Standards (IFRS). Even a change in a particular accounting policy such as depreciation may have a significant impact on profits. Therefore the need for the valuer to examine accounts to make a judgment as to whether particular abnormal components of the reported profit or loss should or should not be eliminated is even greater.

In *Buckingham v Francis* [1986] 2 BCC 98984 the relevant earnings were set out in the judgment of Staughton J:

> '(5) The figures for sales, gross profit, overheads and profit before taxation from the time when the company started trading to 31 December 1981 were as follows:

Periods ending	**31 December 1977 (19 months)**	**1978**	**1979**	**1980**	**1981**
Sales	£265,495	£371,115	£592,151	£632,144	£645,134
Gross profit	£54,762	£83,274	£132,338	£141,549	£131,759
Overheads	£41,316	£69,063	£109,081	£135,182	£151,594
Profit before taxation	£13,446	£14,211	£23,527	£6,367	£19,835

Some adjustment ought to be made to the figures for 1980 and 1981 if they are to be regarded as comparable to earlier figures, since they conceal a difference in treatment of discounts allowed by suppliers. At one time these were deducted from overheads, at another added to sales; but the difference is relatively small; and it does not affect the bottom line – profit before taxation.

(6) The company must be valued in the light of facts that existed at 24 March 1981. (Little or nothing turns on the question whether facts which existed but were not then ascertained or ascertainable should be taken into account.) But regard may be had to later events for the purpose only of deciding what forecasts for the future could reasonably have been made on 24 March 1981.

(7) It follows that the figures for the year ending 31 December 1981 must be left out of account, save for that limited purpose. The only known or ascertainable figure for 1981 was the profit before tax for the first quarter of £460 (which would be £1,840 per annum). I should, however, mention the figure of £18,735 as the loss before tax for the year to 31 December 1981. That included a sum of £14,636 described as "amounts due from former director" – in fact Mr Buckingham – which was written off. But for that item the loss before tax in 1981 would have been much smaller.

(8) The picture is of a company which grew rapidly until 31 December 1979, and perhaps for six months thereafter. But for 1980 as a whole (and 1981), the revenue from sales did not increase in line with inflation, at any rate as measured by the retail price index. After adjustment for the different treatment of discounts, it in fact fell in 1981. Whether that was because fewer goods were sold, or because the sale price did not increase at the same rate as the retail price index, I do not know. Overheads, on the other hand, did increase at, or more nearly at, the rate of inflation revealed by the retail price index. Whether that was because more items of overhead expense were incurred, or because they cost more, again I do not know.

(9) In the result the profit before tax, having risen sharply to start with, showed an even steeper downward trend. To recapitulate the figures, they are:

1977 (19 months)	£13,446
1978	£14,211
1979	£23,257
1980	£6,367
1981 (first quarter)	£460

Mr Burton in his final speech for the defendants submitted that the figure of £6,367 for profit before tax in 1980 should be adjusted, for this reason: the sum of £14,636 written off in 1981, as already mentioned, was incurred for the most part in 1980; since it was written off, it can no longer be treated as having been incurred for the personal benefit of Mr Buckingham, and must therefore have been money spent on the business of the company; that adjustment would obliterate the profit in 1980, and create a loss for the year of £8,316.

It is possible that Mr Burton's submission is well founded. But there are at least two reasons why I cannot accept it. First, the point was not discussed at all in the oral evidence, although it was touched on in para 3.14(d) of the first report of the defendants' expert. I am by no means confident that, even if the facts are as Mr Burton suggests, it would as a matter of accountancy be right to make the adjustment he contends for. Secondly, I do not know what the true facts are as to the sum of £14,636 – only that it was at one time recorded as due from Mr Buckingham to the company, and later written off. A third reason may be that the shares have to be valued as at 24 March 1981, which was before the debt was written off.'

And he continued:

> 'The task of finding the most likely figure, at 24 March 1981, for future maintainable profits is not for the experts: they merely establish the method, and suggest matters to be taken into account. The finding must be made by me on my evaluation of the evidence as to the company's prospects. I arrive at a figure of £6,000 per annum. I must make it clear that this is not a maximum figure, as was suggested by Mr Burns. He thought the most likely figure to be £3,000 or £4,000. I conclude that £6,000 would have been a purchaser's best guess, or estimate or the most likely figure, after making appropriate allowances for risks.'

In *Re Bird Precision Bellows Ltd* [1984] 2 WLR 869, Nourse J described the valuation process:

> 'As described by Mr Milburn, the first step in an earnings valuation is to establish the maintainable level of profit before tax. The second step is to apply to that figure a multiple which is known as the "profit to earnings ratio" or "P/E ratio" for short, and which represents the yield which a purchaser on a willing buyer willing seller basis would expect on his investment. Mr Foster agreed that these were the two steps in the exercise, but there were fundamental disagreements between him and Mr Milburn as to the correct figures to be assigned to the maintainable level of profit and the multiple respectively.
>
> As to the company's maintainable level of profit before tax, the following basic data was available from the company's audited accounts:

Year ended 31 August	**Profit before tax to nearest £1,000**
	£
1978	80,000
1979	73,000
1980	101,000
1981	125,000

> Both valuers made their valuations as at 25 November 1981 instead of 23 November, but that it is an insignificant point. What is important is to consider what information would have been available as at 25 November 1981 for the purpose of making a reliable estimate of profit before tax in the then current year, ie in that which would end on 31 August 1982. Mr Milburn's estimate was largely based on a cash-flow forecast for the year. He proceeded on the footing that that forecast had been responsibly prepared and from that he produced an estimated profit for 1981–82 of £340,000. In fact it was established in evidence that, although management accounts for the period 1 September to 28 November 1981, which were later produced, were not available on 25 November, nevertheless the basic information and material on which they were prepared was available. Without going into detail it was clear that that information and material would have established that the cash-flow forecast was extremely optimistic. Indeed, it had really been prepared for the purpose of the company's dealings with its bank. I should say in defence of Mr Milburn that he appears to have been handed a copy of the document on his visit to the company in April 1982 without much of an explanation of its function. Further, the much more pessimistic basic information and material was not volunteered to him, although it would certainly have been made available if he had asked for it. He was not helped by the fact that Mr Bird declined to give him any overall view for 1981–82. During the course

of his oral evidence Mr Milburn reduced his estimate for 1981–82 to £233,000, but I am satisfied that that was still too high. In his original report Mr Foster worked on a figure of £175,000, which in January 1981 Mr Bird had told him he considered to be reasonable. Mr Foster was later asked to make further written comments on that figure and he did so at some length, producing one of his own of £165,000. That was an illustration designed to support Mr Bird's £175,000.

In my opinion the views of Mr Bird and Mr Foster are clearly to be preferred to that of Mr Milburn on this point. In my judgment the correct estimate of the profit before tax for 1981–82 was £175,000, and that is the figure which I shall adopt. I should add that the audited accounts for 1981–82 later showed the profit to have been only £120,000, although I think not quite on a comparable basis, but that is something which must be disregarded.

The next difference of opinion between Mr Milburn and Mr Foster was this. Proceeding in his written report on an estimated profit for 1981–82 of £340,000, Mr Milburn recognised that that was greatly in excess of the trend shown by the company's recent trading history. He therefore considered that a purchaser, having regard to the risk factor, would have required a yield of (say) 30%, ie a P/E ratio of 3.3 on his investment. On that basis the capitalised value of £340,000 was £1,132,200 or £37.44 per share. In his oral evidence, while accepting that the figure of £340,000 was too high, Mr Milburn said that that meant that the multiple should be higher and he still maintained that it should be applied only to the estimated profit for 1981–82 and not to an average figure of past and anticipated profits. He said that the latter approach was only correct when profits showed a fluctuation and no discernible trend, such as the upward trend in this case. Next, he said that if the correct figure was £175,000, the purchaser would have been content with a yield of 20% and the multiple should be 5. If the correct figure was £146,000 (I will come to that figure shortly) the multiple should be 5.5. On those bases, the values per share would be £29.16 and £26.76 respectively. Mr Milburn also relied on the appropriate table published in the Financial Times on 25 November 1981, which disclosed the equivalent of a P/E ratio before tax of 6.88 as an average for the 66 quoted companies in the mechanical engineering sector at that date. However, I prefer the view of Mr Foster that that is not a very helpful comparison, principally because quoted companies can be assumed to have had a record of paying significant dividends.

Mr Foster's basic position in regard to the maintainable level of profit was that it was wrong to take only the estimated figure for 1981–82, ie £175,000. He said that you ought to take an average of that figure and the actual figures for the two preceding years. Having done that and added back £12,000 as his estimate of the average excessive director's emoluments, he arrived at a figure of £146,000. He then applied a multiple of 3, and came to an earnings-based valuation of £438,000. Having no doubt then looked at the net tangible asset value of £412,000, Mr Foster expressed the opinion that a valuation of the whole share capital of the company on a willing buyer willing seller basis as at 25 November 1981 was in the range of £400,000 to £450,000. He believed that £435,000 or £14.50 per share on an undiscounted basis would be a fair value. He then went on to say that he considered that there should be a discount. For reasons which will now be apparent, I need not consider that part of his report except to say this. Mr Foster's view was that if there ought to be a discount it should be 45% if the petitioners' holdings were properly to be regarded as one holding of 7,800 shares and 55% if they were properly to be regarded as two holdings of 3,900 shares. The reason for that difference is that a holder of 26% can block a special resolution whereas a holder of 13% cannot. Mr Milburn said that he did not dissent from those percentage discounts. In case this point should ever become a live one, I express my own view that the holdings should properly be regarded as one for the purposes of this case.

Before stating my conclusions on the question of valuation, I must get one further point out of the way. An incidental question which was much explored in the evidence was whether the mind of a willing purchaser, and therefore the value of the shares as a whole, would be affected by Mr Bird's remaining with the company or leaving it as the case might be. Neither valuer mentioned this point in his written report and in the end I do not think that either of them said anything in evidence which requires me to take it into account to any material extent.

In my view the basic approach of Mr Foster to the question of the maintainable level of profit is to be preferred to that of Mr Milburn. In other words, I think that a purchaser would be more likely to take an average of three years actual and anticipated profits rather than to rely only on the most recent figure, particularly since it could only be an estimate and the company was still a young one. I therefore start with Mr Foster's figure of £146,000.'

Vinelott J in *Re a Company (No 002612 of 1984) (re Cumana Ltd)* considered the valuations of both experts at 20 December 1984 as this was the date chosen by both valuers, ie the latest practical date before the hearing, even though the judge held that the appropriate date of the valuation was actually 18 April 1984. Mr Munson (for the petitioner Mr Lewis):

'arrived at his maintainable earnings by reference to (a) the profits for the 14 months to 31 May averaged over one year (£362,000 per annum) (b) the profits shown in the company's unaudited accounts for the period to 30 September 1984 (equivalent to £388,000 per annum). After making adjustments for excess emoluments paid to directors he arrived at a figure of maintainable profits of £385,000 or after tax at an assumed rate of 45 per cent, £212,000.

Mr Lawrence arrived at the maintainable profit by two methods. First he divided the profit for the three months to 30 June 1983 by three; then he deducted the profit for that three month period from the profit for the 14 months period to 31 May 1984 and then he added back one-third of the profit to 30 June 1983. He then adjusted for the excess remuneration paid to Mr Bolton (but not the remuneration paid to Mrs Bolton and Mrs Lewis) and deducted tax at an assumed rate of 40 per cent. The maintainable profit thus arrived at is £176,000. Secondly he averaged the profit for the 14 month period to 31 May 1984 over a 12 month period. After making the same adjustments and deducting tax at the same rate he arrived at a net maintainable profit of £201,000. In his oral evidence Mr Lawrence accepted that the first method has the effect of depreciating the maintainable profits to a figure less than 12/14ths of the profit for the 14 month period and less than four times the profit of the three month period. He was at least inclined to accept that the second method is the more reliable. I think that £201,000 is the minimum net maintainable profit ascertained at 20 December 1984 …

Turning to the price earnings ratio, Mr Munson selected a group of companies quoted on the ordinary Stock Exchange or the USM and in the light of the price earnings ratios of those companies and of other market information which he considered relevant he arrived at a price earnings ratio of 20. For reasons that will appear later I do not need to go further into the way in which the starting price earnings ratio was arrived at. He took the view that the company would not attract a premium price earnings ratio.

Starting with a price earnings ratio of 20 he made the following adjustments:

- he discounted by 20 per cent to allow for the fact that the shares in the company were not quoted. This factor depreciates the value because a purchaser even of all the shares in the company would face delay and difficulty in finding a purchaser whereas the holder of shares in a company quoted on the Stock Exchange or on the USM (from which the price earnings ratio is derived) would normally be able to sell at a price near the quoted price, I will call this the long-term holding factor.

- he discounted by 15 per cent to allow for the fact that the company is a one product company and commented that this factor "which so far has been its strength ... might also become a weakness". I will call this the "one-product factor".
- he added a 20 per cent premium to allow for the fact that the assumed sale is for all the shares of the company whereas the quoted prices from which the price earnings ratio is derived are prices quoted from minority in typically small minority holdings. I will call this the "control factor".
- he discounted by 15 per cent to allow for the fact that the company "appears to be somewhat illiquid and thus may require some form of capital investment in the future". And he commented first that if it had additional free cash resources this discount would not be required and secondly that the discount allowed for the fact that the company had a low asset backing.

These discounts and premiums reduced his multiplier of 20 to 14 which he applied to maintainable earnings of £212,000 giving a value for all the shares of the company of £2,968,000.

Mr Lawrence took as his starting point price earnings ratios of quoted companies in the electronic sector. Like Mr Munson he did not consider that the shares of the company would have commanded a premium rating in December and he disregarded shares in the computer industry which did command a premium rating. His starting point was a price earnings ratio of approximately 17.2, he added three points (15 per cent) to allow for the control factor, he deducted 20 per cent for the long-term holding factor and 10 per cent for the one-product factor. By this means he also arrived at a multiplier of 14 thought at this stage he had not made any deduction for Mr Munson's factor (d) and had allowed a smaller premium for the control factor. He then made a series of further reductions which as explained in his oral evidence are as follows.

Stage 1: he reduced the multiplier of 14 to 10 to allow for the risk to which the company was exposed as a one-product company almost wholly dependent on the BBC micro. He took into account the market limitations inherent in dependence upon a supply to owners of the BBC micro and the possibility that at a time when the computer industry seemed to have reached a plateau the company might face fierce price competition possibly from Acorn (though in the past the company has marketed a more reliable disk drive unit for the BBC micro at a price lower than Acorn). I will call this the "risk factor". Applying his maintainable profit of £176,000 to £201,000 this yielded a value for all the shares of the company between £1.7m and £2m.

Stage 2: he then noted that a price earnings ratio of 10 is mathematically equivalent to a gross earnings yield of 14.3 per annum which is close to the yield on Government stock. He commented in his report that in view of the question mark over the company's future development a prospective purchaser would be particularly concerned with the management's ability to make a success of new ventures and drew attention to the weakness of the existing management team, in particular the fact that Mr Bolton's experience and expertise has in the main been in the development of contact with Far Eastern suppliers and that no one in the company has any experience in the development of computer systems. This led him to revise his valuation down to the range of £1m to £1.5m reflecting a price earnings ratio of 6 to 7.5 (applied to his maintainable earnings of £176,000 to £201,000).

Stage 3: he then expressed the opinion that Mr Bolton's role is crucial to the continued success of the company that if he is unwilling to commit himself by a service agreement to the company the company will lose its major asset and concluded that in the absence of such commitment "the market may be restricted to individuals who are capable and willing to take over Mr Bolton's position in the company". This led him to conclude that "the valuation reflected the likely available assets (and included some residual goodwill) rather than the existing potential of the company would be at best £1m and could be substantially less".

By this process of valuation Mr Lawrence proceeded from an adjusted price earnings ratio of 14 yielding a maximum value of £2.8m to a maximum value of £1m reflecting a price earnings ratio of just over one-third of his starting price earnings ratio of 14.

I have come to the conclusion that the reduction in Stage 1 is justified. I think Mr Munson in his valuation has not taken sufficient account of the company's vulnerability to competition in the short to medium term. The position shortly stated is that while Mr Bolton found and exploited a gap in the market with his disc drive unit which he has built on successfully, acquiring for the company a wide reputation for the quality and reliability of its products and a large market share (approximately 50% of the disc drive units provided to the BBC micro are produced by the company), the company has not been able to develop successfully any new product or even to compete successfully in recent years except in the supply of disc drives to the BBC micro …

On the other hand the reductions made by Mr Lawrence in his second and third stages in my judgment, to some extent duplicate allowances earlier made and to some extent are, I think, unjustified. The likely purchaser of the company would be a company anxious to acquire the company's profits and its name and reputation in the market and which would find some synergy between its own and the company's product. Such a purchaser would be expected to provide its own technical staff and know-how in the creation of other products to sell under the Cumana flag. The fact that the company has no technically qualified staff with a record of successful innovation would not therefore be a deterrent nor I think would the current management weakness which the purchasing company would expect to make good …'

At the actual relevant valuation date of 18 April 1984, the date of the petition, the judge stated:

'Mr Munson in ascertaining the company's maintainable earnings as at 18 April 1984 disregarded the management accounts for the three months to 29 February 1984. He was clearly right to do so (the figures were highly suspect). He also disregarded the audited accounts for the 14 months to 31 May 1984 (which were not available at the time) …

Mr Lawrence in his oral evidence said that the only safe guide is to be found in the audited figures for the 14 months to 31 May 1984. Of course these figures would not have been available on 18 April but it must be assumed that a purchaser would not rely on unaudited figures to 30 June 1983. He would put in his own investigating accountants who it must be assumed would find that profits in April were running at an annual rate equivalent to that actually achieved over the whole 14 month period. So he started with the same range and again accepted that a figure of £200,000 would be the more reliable guide.

I think that Mr Lawrence's approach is in principle the correct one …

Turning to the price earnings ratio Mr Munson started with a ratio of 25 and after making the adjustments I have explained arrived at a multiple of 17.3.

> Mr Lawrence started with a price earnings ratio of 16 (derived from the electronic sector of quoted shares). The December equivalent is 17. He then added a 50 per cent premium because the price at which shares of companies in the computer field were floated or quoted on the USM at that time reflected a very much higher than average price earnings ratio. That "glamour factor" increased his starting price earnings ratio to 24 to which he added 15% for the control factor, bringing his starting price earnings ratio to 26.5 (compared to Mr Munson's 25). Making the same proportionate reductions for the long term holding and one-product factors as before he reduced the 26.5 to 18.5. A further risk factor which led him to reduce his December price earnings ratio of 14 to 10 applied proportionately reduces the 18.5 to 13.2. He made a further reduction to 12 on the grounds that in April there were early symptoms of the need to diversify. This corresponds to what I have described in relation to Mr Lawrence's December valuation as his second stage reduction. I have already given my reasons for rejecting it as a ground for a further reduction in the price earnings ratio and they apply equally to Mr Lawrence's April valuation. A price earnings ratio of 13.2 applied to maintainable profits of £200,000 gives a value of £2,680,000. Mr Lawrence accepted that with maintainable earnings of £200,000 the company was worth £2.4m.
>
> I have so far left (Cumana) Peripherals (Ltd) out of account. In April Peripherals was flourishing. Mr Lawrence accepted that if all its shares had been beneficially owned by the company the consolidation of its profit with the profits of the company would add not less than £9,000 (net of tax) to the company's maintainable earnings giving a total of £210,000. The consolidation of Peripherals would also stiffen the price earnings ratio though not by any measurable amount bearing in mind the specialised nature of the business then carried on by Peripherals. A price earnings ratio of 13.2 applied to a maintainable earnings of £210,000 yields a value of £2,772,000.'

The judge then took one-third of this figure, £924,000, and rounded it up to £925,000.

In *Re Eurofinance Group Ltd (EFG)* [2001] BCC 551 (see also **2.05**), Mr Justice Pumfrey had to consider the expert's view that the earnings element in a valuation as at May 1998 should be £400,000, where earnings in 1997/98 were £290,000 and a business plan showed £462,000 for 1998/99. The judge considered that the projection was not a sufficiently firm foundation on which to base a valuation. He preferred to take the 1997/98 figure plus an allowance for modest growth, which he estimated as £310,000 in total.

> **Focus**
>
> *Re Bird Precision Bellows Ltd* shows the detail in which the judge's thought process and the financial information should be analysed in coming to a conclusion. When making adjustments to profit, the validity of the changes needs to be justified and the overall result assessed for reasonableness.

5.05 Dividend record

If a company has paid dividends on a consistent basis this is an important factor in the valuation of the shares, but not the only factor to be considered even in the case of a minority, or non-controlling, shareholding. In the case of *Salvesen's Trustees v IRC* (1930) 9 ATC 43 Lord Fleming pointed out at 48:

> 'The net profits which were earned during the same period amounted to considerably over £1,000,000, whereas I was informed that there was distributed among the shareholders in dividends about £115,000, the remainder being retained in the business. I feel bound to say that these figures suggest to me very strongly that it would be quite fallacious to value these shares merely on the basis of the dividends paid and without regard to the amount of the profits which were earned but not distributed.'

The case concerned a holding of one-third of the ordinary share capital. Lord Fleming continued at 53:

> 'Mr Robertson Durham and Mr MacFarlan, who gave evidence on behalf of the petitioners, took the view that the prospective purchaser would look for a return of 15% on his investment and on this basis they valued the shares at £1. 6s. 8d. I do not think any exception whatever can be taken to the yield which they thought that the investor was entitled to look for. Sir William M'Lintock and Professor Annan who gave evidence for the Crown were prepared to concede to the prospective investor a return of 40%. The difference between Mr Robertson Durham and Sir William M'Lintock is, however, this. Mr Robertson Durham's figure of 15% is based upon the dividends actually paid to the shareholder and does not take account directly, at all events, of profits actually earned but not distributed as dividends. As I have already pointed out, there was, I think, little risk of the dividend, which the company had been paying, not being maintained in the immediate future. But I cannot think it is right to ignore the very large sums which this company had actually earned but had not distributed as dividends …
>
> Assuming that in the future the company has its ups and downs as it has had in the past, its reserves must ultimately, according to all reasonable probabilities, endure to the benefit of the shareholders.'

Sir William M'Lintock's 40% earnings yield was based on the average amount of profits for the last three years at £220,000. Lord Fleming stated, at 54:

> 'If this profit were maintained in the future it would warrant a price of £5.10s. per share on the basis of a 40% yield. Apparently at the time Sir William fixed this figure as the value of the shares he had only seen the accounts of the company for four years. These four years were the most favourable in the company's existence. Sir William did not see the accounts for the earlier years until the morning of the day he gave his evidence, and I am inclined to think that, if he had seen them earlier, he might have modified his valuation of £5. 10s. per share.
>
> While I think that the intending investor would take a favourable view of the prospects of this company I do not think that there is anything in the evidence which would justify him in forming a confident opinion that the exceptional prosperity which prevailed during the four years prior to the testator's death would be an absolutely safe guide for the future.'

In the event, Lord Fleming fixed the value of the shares on the 24 October 1926 at £3 compared with the £1. 6s. 8d of the taxpayer and the £5. 10s. per share of the Crown.

In *A-G of Ceylon v Mackie* (1952) 31 ATC 435 no dividends had been paid on the management shares for many years and as these shares represented the entire equity share capital an attempt was made to value them on the basis of the capitalised earnings for the last five years, but in view of the highly volatile nature of the profits this was not supported by the court and the shares were valued on the basis of the value of the tangible assets of the company.

In *Re Holt* (1953) 32 ATC 402, 43,698 ordinary shares were held by the deceased out of 697,680 ordinary shares, ie 6.26% of the share capital. The date of death was 11 March 1948. Since 1921 the practice of the company had been to limit distributions on the ordinary shares to 5% less tax and to build up its reserves by accumulating surplus profits in good years.

Danckwerts J at 410 stated:

> 'Now, it is plain that the shares do not give a purchaser the opportunity to control the company, or to influence the policies of the directors to any great extent, as the shares available only represent 43,698 shares out of 697,680 ordinary shares which had been issued. Any purchaser, therefore, would be dependent upon the policy of the directors so long as they should have the support of the general body of the shareholders.'

One of the witnesses for the taxpayer, Mr H A Benson, as he then was, at 405:

> 'thought that having regard to the stated dividend policy of the company a purchaser would count on a dividend at the rate of 5% not being reduced, but on the other hand he would not expect it to be increased. Mr Benson thought that the absence of any quotation of the shares on the Stock Exchange, and the restrictions on transfer to which the purchaser would be subject when he got on the register, were factors which would make a purchaser require a further 1½% of income yield on reaching the appropriate price for the shares …
>
> On this basis Mr Benson reached a figure of 15s. 2d per share and to this he added the sum of 1s. 6d making a figure of 16s. 8d. The addition of 1s. 6d represented Mr Benson's estimate of the allowance which the purchaser might make in his offer for the possibility sooner or later of the company's shares being offered to the public, with the resulting capital accretion in some way to the shares held by a previous purchaser. Mr Benson considered that the time for this event would be later rather than sooner, and this was one of the points on which his evidence differed considerably from that of the witnesses for the Commissioners of Inland Revenue, who considered that the issue of shares to the public would be sooner rather than later, and attributed a much greater value to this factor. Finally Mr Benson added a further 6d to his estimated price as representing the amount of the net dividend likely to be declared in respect of the year 1947. Thus the value which he placed upon the shares was 17s. 2d a share.'

A further witness for the taxpayer was Mr F Samuel, Chairman of the United Africa Company, at 407:

> 'By comparison with the quoted prices of shares in other companies Mr Samuel reached a percentage yield of 4.89, to which he added 1¼% for weakness in the company's position compared with those companies making a total required yield of 6.14%. To this he thought it was necessary to add a further 2.05% to compensate for the lack of quotation and difficulties of transfer, thus producing a yield figure of 8.19%. This was equal to a value of 12s. 2d ex dividend. Mr Samuel could not see any real possibility of capital appreciation sufficient to bring into account and added nothing for this factor.
>
> It was suggested in cross examination to Mr Samuel, and I think it is a fair point, that an ordinary buyer would not have all the information on West African conditions which led him to take such a depressing view. Consequently, in my view Mr Samuel's estimate of the value of the shares, so far as based on the unattractiveness of the company's ordinary shares to him, must be discounted for this consideration.'

A further witness for the taxpayer was Mr M R Norman a partner in Edwards Stein & Co, Merchant Bankers, at 407:

> 'In 1948 he would not have expected the dividend to be increased because he did not think that the profits retained by the company after taxation were adequate by a long way. After looking at the yield on other companies, and the Actuaries Investment Index, Mr Norman thought that, on an expected dividend of 5% the yield of half as much again, 2½% would be looked for. This produced a required yield of 7½% and a price of 13s. 4½d per share. As this is an awkward figure, and as he would have been anxious to help if the company had come to his firm in 1948 for help, he increased the price to 15 shillings which is equivalent to 6⅔% yield on a 5% dividend, and, therefore he considered 15 shillings per share a favourable price. He thought 25 shillings an absurd price and would not have paid anything like it.'

Mr R A Hornby a director of Cazenove, Akroyds & Greenwood, Stockbrokers, anticipated that a 5% dividend was likely to be paid by the company and deducted from a price of 20 shillings, according to the practice of his firm when making valuations, 20% for the absence of quotation on the stock exchange and marketability and for the restrictions on transfer, thus reducing the price to 16 shillings, cum dividend.

A witness for the Crown, Sir Harold Barton, a chartered accountant:

> 'Took the extremely low yield figure of 3% and on this basis reached a price of 33s. 4d to which he added eightpence for the dividend expected for the year 1947, making a price of 34 shillings.
>
> Apparently Sir Harold Barton was impressed by the evidence of the petitioners' witnesses, and in particular Mr Holt's emphasis on the policy of restricting the dividends, to the extent of increasing his yield figure to 4% producing a price of 25 shillings ... A great many of Sir Harold Barton's answers seem to me somewhat vague, and it would appear that he had not examined the position of the company in any great detail. It is not at all clear that Sir Harold Barton considered the effect which the restrictions on transfer of shares contained in the company's articles of association would have on the purchaser.'

A further witness for the Crown was Mr C I R Hutton, at 408:

> 'Mr Hutton's method was to divide his valuation into two parts. (1) a fixed element representing a dividend of 5% and (2) a contingent element, in which he attempted to give effect to his estimates of contingencies affecting the price of the shares. He reached the price of 18 shillings for his fixed element on the basis of a yield figure of just under 4% from the Actuaries Investment Index in respect of 5% preference shares and an addition of 1½% for restrictions on transfer, thus assuming a 5% yield. But having regard to the price of 21 shillings which had been agreed between the parties for the 6½% preference shares of the company he reduced this figure from 18 shillings to 16s. 2d. It appeared that this corresponded in his view with the figure of 15s. 8d reached by Mr Benson (before he added 1s. 6d for the contingencies) and with the 16 shillings reached by Mr Hornby and consequently, so far, there was very little difference between the respective valuations.
>
> But then Mr Hutton proceeded to assume that the dividend must rise to 10% and in his calculations the additional 5% represented a further 16s. 2d. This (contingent) 16s. 2d Mr Hutton discounted by 25% to compensate for delay and uncertainty, and allowing against those contingencies (on the credit side) the prospects of a further issue of shares by the company. It appeared that this

deduction of 25% could not have any mathematical or scientific basis, and was purely guess work. This reduced the second or contingent 16s. 2d to 12s. 1d and made Mr Hutton's valuation 28s. 3d. He said that in March 1948, he would have advised the purchaser to buy at that price, and if offered the shares at 25 shillings he would have marshalled the resources of his family and friends in order to purchase. Mr Hutton discounted the effects of the boycott and riots in West Africa in February 1948 and apprehensions for the future expressed by Mr Holt and Mr Samuel and Mr Hutton actually said that "there are no bad risks in the Commonwealth these days" which I find a somewhat surprising statement.'

Mr T A Hamilton Baynes, also for the Crown, at 408:

> 'thought that the dividend paid by the company was quite unrealistic, having regard to the profits earned, but he thought it very unlikely that the company would remain a private company for long. He reached the conclusion that an investor would require an 8½% yield. He thought that the company would be likely to distribute a third of its profits with a view to a forthcoming issue of shares to the public. This represented a sum of £131,000 which was subject to the preference dividend of £9,004, leaving a figure of £122,000 and a possible dividend on the ordinary shares of 17½%. This gave Mr Baynes, on an 8½% yield, a price of £2. 1s. per share. He thought that the type of investor who would be attracted was the surtax payer, looking for a capital profit. Apparently he thought that such an investor would be prepared to pay 30s. 9d in the expectation of a rise to £2. 1s. and a capital accretion of 10s. 3d or about 33⅓% on his investment. So he took a price of 30 shillings which included the prospective dividend for the year 1947.'

Mr H S Loebl, a stockbroker, was the final witness for the Crown:

> 'He was not troubled with abstruse calculations. The question he asked himself was "is this a firm in which I would like to be a sleeping partner?" Having answered that in the affirmative he reached a price of 28 shillings to 29 shillings per share, as far as I can see, by some process of intuition. Then it occurred to him that the Commissioners of Inland Revenue, by whom he was instructed, would want something more than this and so he looked for some other company to form a guide, and took Brooke Bond & Co Limited. He admitted that many people might think that there was no real basis for comparison in the companies, "but it was the nearest thing in which he held shares." He came to the conclusion that Brooke Bond & Co represented a better investment and so lowered his figure for the shares of John Holt & Co (Liverpool) Limited to 25 shillings per share. He said that he himself would have been prepared to purchase the shares at 25 shillings or a bit more in case of competition; and if Mr Benson had offered him the shares at 17s. 2d he would probably have fainted. Matters like the boycott and riots in West Africa, in Mr Loebl's view, would not affect the price, and non-marketability or restrictions on transfer did not worry him at all. Dividend yield was a matter of indifference to him. He dismissed Mr Samuel's anxieties as to the future with the remark "personally I never think there is a risk of falling prices".'

Despite the cavalier nature of his valuation approach, of all the witnesses for the Crown Mr Loebl arrived at a value that was closest to the 19 shillings per share decided on by the court.

In coming to that figure, Danckwerts J stated at 410:

> 'But I think that the witnesses for the Commissioners of Inland Revenue have over-valued the prospect of an increased dividend and of the issue of ordinary shares in the future on March 11 1948. On the other hand, owing to the fall in the value of money, 5% on the ordinary shares did represent a much smaller return in

fact to the members of the family than that dividend represented in prewar years, and there might have been pressure by the family in 1948 or later to increase the dividend having regard to the ample earnings of the company. Moreover some possible hypothetical purchaser might well have thought that the company would be forced to raise further capital by an issue of further shares to the public instead of adopting the method of an issue of preference shares, or debentures, or unsecured notes. Any such anticipation could have no more certainty than a guess. But I think that the petitioners' witnesses have under valued this element in the price which the hypothetical purchaser might pay in this hypothetical open market.'

The other leading case in which dividend yield has been an important aspect is that of *Re Lynall, Lynall v IRC* (1971) 47 TC 375. At the date of Mrs Lynall's death on the 21 May 1962 she held 67,980 £1 shares out of an issued capital of £241,700, ie 28.125%.

Plowman J at 379 explained:

'The policy of the board was always to pay a small dividend and retain the major part of the profits in the business in order to finance the expansion of the company and the replacement of its assets. For 1957 and 1958 a dividend at the rate of 5% was paid, for 1959 10% and for 1960 and 1961 15%. On average, each of those dividends was covered over six times. Even the 5% dividend for 1957 and 1958 was ten times the equivalent rate for 1952 and 1953. But in the background were the Special Commissioners. Under threat of surtax directions under s 245 of the Income Tax Act 1952 additional net dividends totalling £27,798 were declared and paid in the year ending 31 July 1957 in respect of the years 1949 to 1953 inclusive and from that time on the board's dividend policy was influenced by the desire to avoid the possibility of a surtax direction. In that they were completely successful.'

The 1962 accounts which were completed after Mrs Lynall's death would have confirmed an optimistic profits forecast but frustrated an optimistic dividend forecast as the dividend remained the same at 15% although it was covered over eight times by the available profits.

At 387, Plowman J stated:

'In these circumstances there are, I think, three principal factors which affect valuation: (1) the appropriate dividend yield, (2) the prospective dividend; and (3) the possibility of capital appreciation. The evidence suggests certain general observations which may be made about them.

(1) Dividend yield

Two approaches to the problem of an appropriate yield have emerged during the course of the case. The first is to take a purely arbitrary figure based on experience and expertise and work from that. The other is to ascertain the yield which can be obtained on investments in companies in the same general field of industry in the public sector, and then to apply an arbitrary figure of discount for the fact that one is dealing not with a public company but with a private company. The latter method has the advantage over the former that it at least starts on a factual basis, but it is open to criticism on a number of counts. For example, dividend policy in a private company is likely to be entirely different from dividend policy in a public company; and the regulations affecting the transfer of shares are likely to be entirely different in the two cases. Moreover, it is in the company, Linread Ltd and its management and not in the industry that the hypothetical purchaser is likely to be interested. These are only examples and there are no doubt numerous other factors which influence the stock market but are irrelevant in considering the value of shares in a private company, and in particular this company. It can, however, I think, safely be said that any method of calculation involves the introduction of at least one arbitrary figure somewhere along the line.

(2) Prospective dividend

A number of factors enter into any assessment of the dividend which a company is likely to pay in the future. Past dividends are obviously an important consideration. In the case of the present company the profit and dividend record, the dividend policy of the board and the capital position would have suggested that at the lowest a 15% dividend would be maintained. The likelihood of an increase would have to be judged in the light of the known policy of the directors, but that would not rule out the probability of an increase. A number of factors point in that direction, such as the upward trend of profits, the high dividend cover, the risk of surtax directions, the employment of surplus profits in the expansion of the business which itself might well lead to an increase of profits.

(3) The possibility of capital appreciation

It is common ground that in the present case this need only be considered in the context of a possible flotation. The probability of such a flotation was a matter depending primarily, but not entirely, on the wishes of the board. The board's hypothetical known assessment of the position at Mrs Lynall's death was that the prospect of flotation was "doubtful and remote." But against that attitude must be set the fact that it was at least a tenable view on the published information, including the family nature of the business and the ages of the family shareholders, that the board would be forced willy-nilly to go public sooner or later in order to provide for death duties, or for some other financial reason urged upon them by their advisers, such as the fear (justified by the event) of the imposition of a general capital gains tax. Mr Lynall's subjective view of the situation must be discounted accordingly.'

One of the points at issue in the *Lynall* case was the admissibility of certain documents which recorded the investigations which the board was making into possible ways and means of raising money to pay prospective death duties. They included a memorandum on the subject suggesting various alternatives, including a flotation, and a firm of accountants was commissioned to carry out a survey of the company's undertakings with a view to a public issue. These were referred to in the case as category B documents.

Plowman J summarised the evidence of the various experts at 387 et seq which is included in full in in the transcript of the case.

Pitfall

The basis and nature of dividends paid should be considered carefully before placing reliance on the implied yield. Many owner-managed businesses use dividends as a form of remuneration and therefore the yield may be very different from that for a company where this approach is not adopted. (The profitability of each business may also be very different if a full salary cost is reflected in one and not the other.)

Many companies also suspend dividend payments during periods of economic uncertainty, only to make an exceptional payment once circumstances have improved. Again, this will give a distorted yield figure which may not be sustainable over the longer term.

When considering the appropriate yield, thought also needs to be given to the level of distributable reserves in order to confirm that dividends at this level are capable of being paid over the longer term.

5.06 Directors

The ability of the directors in running the company is clearly a material matter on an acquisition of a non-controlling interest. In *Re Holt* it was pointed out that a 6.26% minority shareholder would not have the opportunity to influence the policy of the directors (1953) 32 ATC 402 at 410. In *Salvesen's Trustees v IRC* (1930) 9 ATC 43 Lord Fleming at 54 stated:

> 'The hypothetical person, who I am to assume is the purchaser of these shares, might be apprehensive that he would find himself in an uncomfortable position as an intruder into a family concern, but I feel confident that in their own interest, if for no other reason, the directors of the company would continue to manage it as successfully in the future as they had done in the past.'

But it is not only those who at present manage the company whose ability must be judged. If the present directors are at or approaching retirement age, then the quality of the apparent succession is very material.

Any special provisions in a company's articles of association regarding the appointment of directors have to be taken into account. In *Hawkings-Byass v Sassen* [1996] STC (SCD) 319 the articles of association gave the ordinary shareholders power to appoint one director for every 1,000 ordinary shares held. The number of directors could not exceed 10 and only males with the surname Gonzalez or Byass could be appointed to the board. The alliances that could be formed between shareholders in order to appoint directors influenced the Special Commissioners in their determination of the values of small minority holdings.

The ease of Internet searches and sites such as LinkedIn now make research into directors' track records much easier.

5.07 Liquidity resources

The company's liquid position and financial commitments must be a relevant factor in any valuation. In *Re Holt* (1953) 32 ATC 402 at 404 Danckwerts J stated:

> 'At this date two of the five ships owned by the company were of an age which demanded their replacement. The company had a large overdraft at its bank which approached £1 million in 1947. It was really common ground that the company was over trading, and that the large figures for profits in the years 1946 and 1947 reflected the contemporary inflation.'

In *Re Lynall, Lynall v IRC* (1971) 47 TC 375 at 379 Plowman J stated:

> 'On the other hand, the company's cash resources (including tax reserve certificates) had risen from £218,783 to £263,200. Its only liability for borrowed money was a small mortgage reducing by £2,000 per annum, which in 1957 stood at £20,000 and in 1961 at £12,000. The ratio of its current assets to its

> current liabilities had gone up from 1.7:1 in 1957 to 2.4: 1 to one in 1961. The company's balance sheet as at 31st July 1961 showed that it was then committed to capital expenditure estimated at £105,000. Up to that time the increase in profits had been roughly proportional to capital expenditure.'

In the case of *Salvesen's Trustees v IRC* (1930) 9 ATC 43 Lord Fleming stated, at 49:

> 'I think it may be taken that the liquid assets of the company, that is to say assets that could be turned into cash at short notice, amounted to over £500,000 …
>
> Prior to the testator's death, the company had made arrangements for trading in the ensuing season and had either expended or committed itself to an amount of about £300,000.'

5.08 Gearing

The effect of gearing has to be considered and whether the existence of loan stock is a burden to the company, or a relatively cheap source of finance to the benefit of the ordinary shareholders. Lord Fleming in *Findlay's Trustees v IRC* (1938) 22 ATC 437 at 439 stated:

> 'It seems to me clear that the circumstance that a considerable part of the capital required to run the business can be raised at a comparatively low rate of interest on the security of the assets cannot have any effect in depreciating the value of the goodwill. On the contrary it would rather appear to me that it might have some effect in increasing its value. There is, however, no evidence to this effect and I take it that the existence of the debentures is an immaterial circumstance in so far as the ascertainment of the value of the goodwill is concerned. But this does not mean that their existence is to be disregarded in fixing the value of the interests of the partners. The debentures are a debt of the business and must be deducted from its value before the interest of the partners can be determined.'

Focus

The complexity of many debt instruments means that the valuer must give particular consideration to the business's ability to repay its debt in accordance with the terms of the loan. Payment in kind (PIK) loans or other instruments where interest is rolled-up to the end of the term can represent significant future liabilities and can bankrupt a business if it does not have the means to repay the compound liability at the end of the term.

The level of gearing, be it actual or target, must also be considered when determining an appropriate capital structure for a discounted cash flow calculation.

5.09 Contingent liabilities and taxation provisions

It is necessary to consider whether the company has any contingent liabilities and in this connection unpaid taxation can be a problem (see **7.11**).

In *Re Duffy, Lakeman v A-G* [1949] Ch 28 it was held that a provision for income tax based on the company's profits in a pre-corporation tax year was not a liability of the company in valuing the shares on an assets basis for estate duty purposes under FA 1940, s 55. However under the Schedule D preceding year basis then in force the income tax claimed as a liability, although based on the profits for the period up to the date of death of the shareholder, would in fact have been assessed in a later period and if there had been a cessation may never have been assessed at all and was therefore not regarded as a liability of the company. Lord Green stated, at 37:

> 'Taking the construction of these words, (an allowance "for all the liabilities of the company") I find it impossible to give them a meaning extended beyond what is always perfectly ascertainable without any doubt whatsoever, namely, an existing legal liability actually existing in law at the relevant date. The words cannot be stretched so as to cover something which in a business sense is morally certain and to which every businessman ought to make provision, but which in law does not become a liability until a subsequent date.'

In the case of *Winter (Sutherland's Trustees) v IRC* (1961) 40 ATC 361 it was held that the potential balancing charge on the disposal of assets constituted a contingent liability at the date of the deceased's death and an estimation of that contingent liability as required by FA 1940 s 50 could be deducted in ascertaining the value of the asset for the purposes of estate duty under FA 1940 s 55. Lord Reid at 362 stated:

> 'So the position of the company at the date of the deceased's death was that, by applying for and accepting allowances in respect of these ships, it had become bound by the statute to pay tax under a balancing charge when it ceased to use the ships in its trade, if the money which it received for them exceeded any expenditure on them which was still unallowed. And I should add, because importance was attached to this in argument, the company would only have to pay tax if the law had not been altered, and if when the question arose, there was in existence a Finance Act determining the rate of income tax. So there were two contingencies that had to be fulfilled, or conditions which had to be purified, before tax could be demanded from the company: the sums received from the ships must exceed the unallowed expenditure, and there must be no relevant change in the law and no failure to enact a Finance Act. The question is whether in these circumstances there was a contingent liability of the company to pay tax.
>
> No doubt the words "liability" and "contingent liability" are more often used in connection with obligations arising from the contracts than with statutory obligations. But I cannot doubt that if a statute says that a person who has done something must pay tax, the tax is a "liability" of that person. If the amount of the tax has been ascertained and it is immediately payable, it is clearly a liability; if it is only payable on a certain future date it must be a liability which has 'not matured at the date of death' within the meaning of (FA 1940, s 50(1)). If it is not yet certain whether or when tax will be payable, or how much will be payable why should it not be a contingent liability under the same section?
>
> It is said that where there is a contract there is an existing obligation, even if you must wait events to see if anything ever becomes payable, but that there is no comparable obligation in a case like the present. But there appears to me to be a close similarity. Take the first stage, if I see a watch in a shop window and think of buying it, I am not under a contingent liability to pay the price; similarly if an Act says that I must pay tax if I trade and make a profit, I am not, before I begin trading, under a contingent liability to pay tax in the event of my starting trading. In neither case have I committed myself to anything. But if I agree by contract to accept allowances on the footing that I will pay a sum if I later sell something

> above a certain price, I have committed myself and I come under a contingent liability to pay in that event. This company did precisely that, but its obligation to pay arose not from contract but from statute. I find it difficult to see why that should make all the difference.'

Commenting on *Re Duffy, Lakeman v A-G* [1949] Ch 28, Lord Reid continued at 364:

> 'The taxpayer sought to bring in as a contingent liability of the company a proportion of its income tax for the year 1943–44 because the earning of profits during the year 1942–43 had engendered a contingent liability for tax for 1943–44. As pointed out by Mr Justice Roxburgh, in a judgment which I find convincing, it had done nothing of the kind. Whether the company would have to pay tax for the year 1943–44 depended entirely on whether it chose to carry on trade during that year, and the profits for 1942–43 were merely the measure of the company's tax liability if it chose to do so. I doubt if the taxpayer could even have stated a plausible case if the old three years average rule had still applied. It seems to me to be verging on the absurd to say that a trader had in June 1942 incurred a contingent liability to pay tax for a year which only began nine months later.'

Lord Reid quoted part of the *Duffy* judgment including:

> 'The words cannot be stretched so as to cover something which in a business sense is morally certain and for which every business man ought to make provision, but which in law does not become a liability until a subsequent date.
>
> I agree with the last sentence of this quotation, and it applied to the facts of *Duffy's* case. The taxpayer had already been allowed to deduct tax for 1942–43, and he sought in addition a deduction of something which was only "morally certain" to become the measure of taxation in the next year – if indeed it would be said to be morally certain that the company would continue trading. But as a general statement of the law I think that the passage is inadequate, because it appears to me to deprive the category of contingent liabilities of all content. That this category is in a special position is made clear by the act, which, in contrast to the provision for computing other kinds of liability, only requires for a contingent liability "such estimation as appears to the commissioners to be reasonable." I cannot reconcile this with a requirement that such a liability must always be perfectly ascertainable as a legal liability actually existing in law at the relevant date. The essence of a contingent liability must surely be that it may never become an existing legal liability because the event on which it depends may never happen.'

Lord Reid implied that it is necessary to discount a potential liability and not deduct the actual amount of tax payable if the assets had been sold at the appropriate price at the date of death, at 364:

> 'But the deduction will not be the sum of £270,079 which would have been payable in tax if the ships had been sold at the date of the death of the deceased. I agree with your Lordships and the Court of Appeal in rejecting the appellants' arguments for this. In my view the case must go to the Commissioners of Inland Revenue in order that they may make the estimation required by [FA 1940] s 50 on the footing that at the date of death the liability to pay under a balancing charge was a contingent liability which would become an immediate liability of the company if it sold or otherwise ceased to trade with the ships and received sums exceeding the expenditure still unallowed. It would not be right for me to suggest to the commissioners how they should carry out their task: they will no doubt have regard to all relevant facts.'

Lord Birkett commented at 365:

> 'It was no less a contingent liability because the sale of the ships might not take place. The true legal position was that from the moment the appellants accepted capital allowances they were at once under a liability to pay tax in the circumstances provided for in the Income Tax Act 1952. That liability was a contingent liability.'

Lord Guest, commenting on Lord Greene's comments in *Re Duffy* quoted above, stated at 370:

> 'With great respect to Lord Greene, if a liability must be an existing legal liability to comply with [FA 1940] s 50(1) that would appear to give no content to the adjective "contingent". The liability is not a legal liability until the contingency has arrived and the section cannot therefore be restricted to "existing legal liabilities".'

In *Cash and Carry v Inspector of Taxes* [1998] STC (SCD) 46, a case concerning valuation at 31 March 1982 for capital gains tax re-basing purposes, a question arose over the inclusion in the company's balance sheet of an amount of deferred taxation. The Special Commissioner said:

> 'The taxpayer accepted Mr Carne's evidence in total as supplemented by Mr Carne's oral evidence. That was to the effect that in his opinion on the balance of probability and in the absence of access to the company's accountants' working papers, the item "deferred taxation" should not have been included in the 1982 accounts of the company and such inclusion represented an error on the part of the company's accountants. His opinion was based on the presumption that the company's accounts showed its state as a going concern. The position would be different in the event of a liquidation.'

In *Goldstein v Levy Gee* [2003] EWHC 1574 (Ch) one of the areas of contention was the deduction that should have been made for the contingent tax (at para 97):

> 'Mr Synett deducted from the value of Marchday's assets the whole of the tax that would have been payable if those assets had been immediately sold. It is agreed that as regards those properties that were held as trading stock he was correct to do so. But as regards those properties that were held as investments Mr Goldstein's case is that it was wrong to deduct the whole of the tax that would have become due on an immediate sale of the entirety of the investment portfolio.
>
> ...
>
> 100 In a valuation that he prepared in September 1997 Mr Epstein made a deduction for the whole of the tax contingently payable but qualified this deduction in a note saying:
>
>> "In order to be prudent for the purposes of this valuation any potential tax that would be payable on the disposal of any of the company's assets shown in the balance sheet should be deducted from the values of those assets. This procedure has been assumed notwithstanding the fact that in an open market negotiation some discount might be given for the deferred element of this taxation liability."
>
> ...
>
> 103 The natural aspiration of the seller would be to achieve no deduction for contingent tax liability. The natural aspiration of the buyer would be to achieve 100% deduction. Both the hypothetical buyer and the hypothetical seller are

> willing. I do not think that anyone suggested any particular reason why one would have a stronger bargaining position than the other. If the parties are of equal bargaining power it seems to me that they would meet in the middle and agree a deduction of 50 per cent of the contingent tax liabilities.'

The judge continued (at para 112):

> 'Where does that leave me? Mr Hindley concedes that 35 per cent is not unreasonable. That I think is the lower end of the bracket. Mr Wolf's bracket is between 50 per cent and 75 per cent. Having regard to the practice of the Inland Revenue (which appears to be a recognised yardstick in share valuation) to Mr Wolf's instinct about the result of a discounted cash flow exercise and also to the fact that the parties are hypothetical I think that 75 per cent is too high. In my judgment the highest figure (and hence the upper end of the bracket) is 65 per cent.
>
> I think that the most likely figure that a valuer would have deducted in the case of a hypothetical buyer and a hypothetical seller is (for the reasons I have given) 50 per cent.'

In the Scottish divorce case of *Dow v Sweeney* 2003 SCLR 85 it was held that capital gains tax which would be payable were shares or business assets to be sold at market value should be deducted from that value:

> 'The defender's shares – and the incidence of capital gains tax
>
> The one matter listed in the schedule on which the parties remained at issue was whether the value of the defender's share portfolio should be assessed net of capital gains tax exigible on a realisation of those shares at the relevant date. For the avoidance of doubt, I record that counsel were agreed that this issue required to be resolved by the court , notwithstanding the terms of apparent agreement as to the value of that share portfolio in joint minute No 31 of Process. There was, further, no evidence led, nor any argument addressed, in relation to potential capital gains tax on realisation of the pursuer's shares.
>
> Section 10(2) of the 1985 Act provides that:
>
> > "The net value of the matrimonial property shall be the value of the property at the relevant date after deduction of any debts incurred by the parties or either of them
> > (a) before the marriage so far as they relate to the matrimonial property, and
> > (b) during the marriage,
> > which are outstanding at that date."
>
> The short but important question which requires to be resolved is whether the value of realisable property such as shares (which, it was agreed, would fall to be valued on the basis of a notional sale at the relevant date) should be taken to be the value after deduction of capital gains tax exigible on any such sale. Different views have been expressed on this matter in the Outer House and it has not – so I was informed – been the subject of decision in the Inner House. In *Latter v Latter* Lord Marnoch was concerned to assess the value of the defender's shareholding in a private family company. Although he assessed the value net of the costs of realisation, he declined to deduct capital gains tax. At p809 he said:
>
> > "However in my opinion there is no reason why such a notional tax should be deducted. In this connection I do not doubt that the reference to 'net value' in the 1985 Act presupposes a hypothetical realisation of the parties' wealth but it is just that, namely a hypothetical realisation, and accordingly

> I cannot see why one should have regard to an optional tax liability which is without foundation in reality".

Lord Osborne agreed with that view in *McConnell v McConnell* at p105. Counsel for the pursuer argued that I should follow the approach adopted in these two cases. By contrast, Lord Abernethy, in the unreported decision of *Bolton v Bolton*, assessed the value of the defender's interest in two companies at the relevant date on the basis that both the costs of realisation and the incidence of capital gains tax required to be taken into account. Although counsel for the pursuer sought to persuade me that the case was special in that the defender's interest in the companies had in fact been realised some years after the relevant date, I was not persuaded by that submission. Further, it seems clear that Lord Sutherland in *Savage v Savage* accepted that the valuation of the pursuer's interest in this business at the relevant date fell to be made under deduction of any capital gains tax exigible on its realisation.

Although there may be arguments either way, I have come to the view that capital gains tax should be taken account of. It seems clear that the purpose of the 1985 Act is to secure a fair division of the wealth acquired in the course of a marriage as a result of the efforts of the parties during it. In assessing the value of the matrimonial property at the relevant date for the purposes of such division, it seems reasonable to assess, so far as possible, the value to the parties, or either of them, of such property. In real terms, the value to any person of marketable assets such as shares, is their value after deduction of capital gains tax, if any, exigible on realisation. I agree with Lord Sutherland in *Savage v Savage* when he said (at p135) that:

> "In the context of endeavouring to value matrimonial property for the purpose of division some degree of realism must be allowed to play its part".

In these circumstances, unless the language of the 1985 Act clearly points in the opposite direction, I would be inclined to include the incidence of capital gains tax in the valuation of realisable assets such as shares. Considering the terms of the Act, there is nothing, in my view, which clearly points against that conclusion. Further, it is not too difficult to envisage circumstances n which injustice could be done if capital gains tax exigible at the relevant date was not taken into account. To take a simple example, if all of the matrimonial property at the relevant date consisted of shares owned by one of the parties to the marriage (that party being a higher rate taxpayer), then all things being equal, the Act could lead to a justifiable award of 50 per cent of the shares' sale value, leaving the owner of the shares, after sale to meet the award and after deduction of capital gains tax, with only 10 per cent. Although in making an order for capital payment, that order requires to be justified not only according to the principles set out in section 9 of the Act but also reasonable having regard to the resources of the parties (section 8(2) of the 1985 Act), and although counsel or the pursuer accepted that the incidence of capital gains tax could properly be taken into account in assessing "the resources" of the parties, the likelihood is that that provision – as it has been interpreted – would not greatly assist the payer of the capital sum in the example given. In particular, even after capital gains tax, he would have resources available to meet the previously assessed fair share of the net value of the matrimonial property at the relevant date. As Lord Keith of Kinkel said in relation to a not dissimilar example in *Wallis v Wallis* at p55C-D "It does not appear that section 8(2)(b) could be applied in such a way as to redress the balance in a situation of that kind". No doubt it is possible to envisage examples where capital gains tax exigible on a sale of property at the relevant date was no longer exigible to the same extent when the time came for a capital sum to be paid, in which case it might be said that the equities pointed in the opposite direction (that is against having regard to capital gains tax at the relevant date). Such a case, however, would not be much different from any case in which matrimonial property increased in value, for whatever reason, after the relevant date, and, as was held in *Wallis v Wallis*, it is in general irrelevant to the assessment of a fair share of the value of matrimonial property that the value of that property or of any of the items comprised within it may have altered between the relevant date and the date of dividends. No doubt it could be argued that the proper place to take account of the incidence of capital gains tax at the relevant date would be as a potential "special circumstance" in accordance with section 10(6)(d) or (e) of the 1985 Act. As to section 10(6)(d), however, while no doubt the incidence of tax could be taken into account along with other factors if it was such as to make it unreasonable to expect part of the matrimonial property to be realised at all (see for example the Lord Justice Clerk (Ross) in *McConnell v McConnell (No 2)* at p 112, paragraph 20), that would be likely to have an impact, it seems, in relatively limited circumstances. Equally, section 10(6)(e) appears to relate to expenses, etc in connection with the divorce and, in any event, its language appears in part to cover liability to tax.

I also agree with counsel for the defender that to take account of the incidence of capital gains tax on the notional realisation of property at the relevant date would not be very different from taking into account the penalties payable to a local authority on the notional sale of certain heritable property at the relevant date, as was done in *Mackin v Mackin* and *Lawson v Lawson*. In addition, it seems to me to be difficult in principle to justify taking into account the expenses of any notional sale and not the incidence of capital gains tax. Finally, although the statutory provisions in England are different, I take some comfort from the fact that it appears to be the case that in assessing, under section 25(2)(a) of the Matrimonial Causes Act 1973, "the property and other financial resources which each of the parties to the marriage has or is likely to have in the foreseeable future", it is, in general, the value of capital assets net of capital gains tax, and the expenses of sale, which is taken to be relevant (see e.g. *Rayden and Jackson, Law and Practice of Divorce and Family Matters* (17th edn) at paragraph 21.35; *O'D v O'D*) although there is, it seems, no hard and fast rule (see *White v White* at p612).

'As to the amount of capital gains tax exigible on a notional sale of the defender's portfolio at the relevant date, Mr Alan Barr, a partner in Brodies WS specialising in tax law, gave unchallenged evidence that the taxable gain would be £184,650. Equally, there seemed little dispute but that, subject to any question of potential mitigation, the tax exigible on the defender, a higher rate taxpayer would have been £73,860. As to potential mitigation there was no convincing evidence (and Mr Barr did not accept) that any significant relief would be available. I therefore assess the relevant capital gains tax at £73,860.'

Focus

The likelihood and quantum of a business realising a contingent liability may be a main point of negotiation in any valuation. The valuer needs to take a pragmatic view of both factors based on the history of the business and the circumstances prevailing at the valuation date.

5.10 Asset base

Other particulars that are clearly relevant in many cases are details of the fixed assets held by the company and in the case of *Salvesen's Trustees v IRC* (1930) 9 ATC 43 Lord Fleming when considering the holding of one-third of the ordinary shares was interested in the fixed assets of the company and the depreciation and replacement policies. At 50 he stated:

> 'Some challenge was, however, made of the value of the assets shown in this balance sheet, and particularly of the value of the steamers. I quite understand the view that on a break-up basis the value of the ships which were entered in the balance sheet at £452,122 might amount to a very small sum. A large number of the vessels were especially fitted out for whaling and it might well happen at any particular time that there was no demand for such vessels and that therefore they would have merely scrap value. But when one comes to regard the matter of the value of the vessels as a going concern, the position seems to me different. A number of the vessels were built and acquired in the years 1925 and 1926, and I do not quite follow why, assuming 10% is a fair rate of depreciation on them – as I think it is – the vessels should be less valuable than the amount to which they have been written down. Having been built quite recently they were presumably up to date vessels and there is nothing in the evidence to suggest that, if the company wished to replace them at the end of ten years, the cost would be any greater than it was at the time they were built (this was in 1930). It must be admitted however that a number of the other vessels are in a different position, they were much older – I may observe parenthetically that the ages of some of them indicate that 10% is a generous rate of depreciation and, as they were quite recently acquired, I find it difficult to understand why their depreciated value should not fairly represent their value to a going concern. But, on the other hand, as they were old vessels it may be presumed they would not last at the longest more than 10 years. If and when they came to be replaced by new vessels, the cost of such new vessels would presumably be much greater than the original cost of the old vessel. A prudent investor who investigated this matter, might come to the conclusion that the allowance for depreciation did not represent replacement costs and that a larger allowance ought to be made for this circumstance. I do not think it is possible upon the material available to estimate this at any specific figure. But even if a larger allowance were made on this head, it seems clear that the balance sheet shows the capital value of each share at a sum in excess of the £5.10s. claimed by the Crown. While I think the circumstance would weigh with the intending investor, I do not mean to say that he would assume that there was any likelihood of the assets of the company being realised say by sale to another company – and of his being paid out the capital value of his share. On the contrary he would, I assume, be informed that if he became a shareholder the only means open to him of realising his capital would be to avail himself of the very restricted rights of transfer given by the articles.'

It is apparent that the intending purchaser would consider the likely value of the company's fixed assets, including premises, whether leasehold or freehold, and if leasehold the terms of the lease and any potential liability for dilapidations at the end of the lease.

> **Focus**
>
> When valuing on a net asset basis, it is imperative to ensure that the balance sheet reflects the position at the valuation date accurately. For example, the value of a property company portfolio is likely to have been very different in 2009 compared with 2007, and likely to have changed materially again by 2018.

5.11 Customers and suppliers

An aspect that does not appear to have been considered in the courts, but is nonetheless of relevance in practice, is the dependence on a single or limited number of suppliers or customers as this is clearly significant in assessing the vulnerability of the company to external pressure and the problems that might arise as a result of, for example, strikes at or takeovers of key suppliers or customers or even a change in policy by these parties.

For the purpose of the measurement of fair values of intangible assets arising following an acquisition under IFRS 3 (Business Combinations) customer contracts and related relationships are treated as separately identifiable intangible assets and therefore their fair values at the acquisition date have to be measured (see **Chapter 21**).

5.12 Sales negotiations

In *Percival v Wright* [1902] 2 Ch 421 it was held that the directors were under no duty to disclose to shareholders a possible sale of the company's undertaking. As Swinfen Eady J said at 426:

> 'It is contended that a shareholder knows that the directors are managing the business of the company in the ordinary course of management and impliedly releases them from any obligation to disclose any information so acquired. That is to say, a director purchasing shares need not disclose a large casual profit, the discovery of a new vein, or the prospect of a good dividend in the immediate future, and similarly a director selling shares need not disclose losses, these being merely incidents in the ordinary course of management … I am therefore of opinion that the purchasing directors were under no obligation to disclose to their vendor shareholders the negotiations which ultimately proved abortive.'

See, however, **8.32**, where it is suggested that this case has no general application.

The treatment of information regarding a possible sale of the company was one of the issues in *Caton v Couch* [1995] STC (SCD) 34 and *Clark v Green* [1995] STC (SCD) 99, both of which concerned the value of shares in the same company at about the same date for capital gains tax purposes. For a discussion of those decisions in the context of the special rules regarding availability of information for capital gains tax and inheritance tax purposes see **9.03**.

5.13 Turnover

Where profit and loss accounts are unreliable or subject to understatement or fiscal distortion, it might be appropriate to have regard to turnover. In *Hawkings-Byass v Sassen* [1996] STC (SCD) 319 shares in a Cayman Islands holding company which had unaudited Spanish activities and a principal UK subsidiary with heavily qualified accounts were valued by reference to turnover, which was accepted by the Special Commissioners. The multiple applied to turnover was arrived at by comparing market capitalisations of similar quoted companies with their turnover.

For start-up companies, or businesses trading in a recession, turnover may be the only positive element in the profit and loss account. A turnover-based valuation gives an enterprise value and will need to be adjusted to arrive at a value for the company's equity.

5.14 Contingent liabilities and taxation provisions

In *Shinebond Ltd v Carrol* [2006] WTLR 697 the Special Commissioner referred to the fourth edition of this book in connection with the deduction for contingent liabilities but concluded that there was no contingent tax liability to take into account in determining the value of the company. He stated:

> 'However the property would have been rebased to its market value in the hands of the company as at 31 March 1982 by virtue of the provisions of s 96 Finance Act 1988 – which has been determined by the Lands Tribunal to be £168,000. In other words if the company sold the property for £168,000 at any time after 31 March 1982 the company would not realise any chargeable gain. Indeed after taking account of indexation allowances it might be treated as realising an allowable loss.'

As Bruce Sutherland has pointed out in an article in *Taxation*, 17 August 2006 at page 559 the Special Commissioner was actually wrong in assuming that there would be no chargeable gain if the company sold the property for £168,000 at 31 March 1982 because the March 1982 valuation was originally used only for the calculation of indexation relief, and rebasing did not come into effect until FA 1988, s 96 came into effect and therefore the deduction for the contingent liability was actually appropriate. However the sums involved were not sufficiently material to take this point to appeal. The fact that HMRC were suggesting the deduction was appropriate, and referred to this book to do so, suggests that it is generally accepted that the commercial reality, which is that purchasers would normally require a deduction for a proportion of the contingent liability, is not contentious and is appropriate for a 31 March 1982 valuation on the assets basis.

5.15 Unintended consequences of tax avoidance schemes

In *R (on the application of De Silva and another) v HMRC* the taxpayers were limited partners in film schemes under which alleged trading losses through investment in films were disallowed. The partners invested in films through marketed schemes under which they took out limited recourse loans under

F(No 2)A 1992, s 42 and claimed under TA 1988, ss 380 and 381 for their share of the partnership trading losses which could be carried back against general income for the previous three years. HMRC enquired into these alleged losses and disallowed most of them. The taxpayers claimed for judicial review which rejected their claim to the Upper Tribunal [2014] STC 2088 which was upheld by the Court of Appeal [2016] STC 1333. The appeal to the Supreme Court [2017] UKSC 74 was based on the claims being chargeable only under TMA 1970, s 8 and were out of time but the taxpayer lost, and *RCC v Cotter* [2013] STC 2480 did not assist them.

5.16 *RFC 2012 plc (RFC) (in liquidation) (formerly the Rangers Football Club plc) v Advocate General for Scotland*

Employees were paid through a remuneration trust to try to avoid being assessed to income tax and NICs. The taxpayers succeeded before the First Tier Tribunal and the Upper Tribunal. HMRC appealed to the Inner House of the Court of Session and argued that the payment to the remuneration trust was a redirection of the employees' earnings and therefore chargeable to income tax.

The employing companies and RFC operated the tax avoidance scheme from 2001/02 to 2008/09. It is stated at paragraph 19 that:

> 'A company within the Murray group of companies which wished to benefit one of its employees made a cash payment to the Principal Trust in respect of that employee. When it did so, the employing company recommended the trustee of the Principal Trust to resettle the sum which it paid on to a sub-trust and asked that the income and capital of the sub-trust should be applied in accordance with the wishes of the employee. The trustee of the Principal Trust had a discretion whether to comply with those requests, but, when an employing company provided the funds, the trustee without exception created a sub-trust for the favoured employee. 108 sub-trusts were established in the name of individual employees, of which 81 were for RFC employees (footballers and executives) and 27 for other Murray group employees. The group companies also used the combination of the Principal Trust and a sub-trust to pay discretionary annual bonuses to employees, other than the footballers whom RFC employed. Since 2005 only RFC used the Principal Trust to remunerate its employees.'

At paragraph 59, Lord Hodge stated:

> 'Parliament in enacting legislation for the taxation of emoluments or earnings from employment has sought to tax remuneration paid in money or money's worth. No persuasive rationale has been advanced for excluding from the scope of this tax charge remuneration in the form of money which the employee agrees should be paid to a third party, or where he arranges or acquiesces in a transaction to that effect.'

5.17 Film schemes

Follower notices and partner payment notices (PPNs) were introduced by FA 2014, ss 204–218 and Schedules 3 and 32, and accelerated payment notices in ss 219–229. These were challenged in *Nigel Row, Alec David Worrall & Others v HMRC* [2015] EWHC 2293 (Admin) by 154 claimants who were members of Ingenious Media plc schemes relating to Ingenious Film Partners

(IFP), Ingenious Film Partners 2 LLP (IFP2) and Ingenious Games LLP (IGames). These LLPs were set up to carry on trades of producing films and by the nature of the film industry, losses arise in the first periods while the film is made and profits hopefully arise from its exploitation. The losses in the partnerships were claimed against other income but HMRC responded by issuing PPNs to the participants requiring upfront payment of tax. The PPNs were upheld by the judge.

The First Tier Tribunal (FTT) judgments in *Ingenious Games LLP (IG), Ingenious Track Productions LLP (ITP) and Ingenious Film Partners 2 LLP (the partnerships) v HMRC* [2016] UKFTT 521 (TC) and [2017] UKFTT 429 (TC) run to 1,824 paragraphs in 342 pages and 90 paragraphs in 19 pages. The tax loss claimed in these cases amounted to some £1,620,000,000 and the tax reclaimed by investors £620,000,000 and with interest and penalties, if applicable. The total amount at stake is £1 billion. The LLPs were involved in 65 films, of which 64 were distributed in cinemas and many of which had a high profile and received critical acclaim.

The partnerships were stated to be carrying on a trade with a view to profit and the expenditure incurred on the films was 100%, of which 30–35% came from the individual members and 65–70% from loans and, under UK GAAP, 100% was expended on trading stock valued in the accounts in accordance with UK GAAP (Generally Accepted Accounting Practice) written down to net realisable value, giving rise to a tax deductible loss. HMRC refuted these contentions. The FTT held in the 2016 judgment that ITP and IFP2 were carrying on a trade but IG was not, and none of the LLPs were carrying on a trade with a view to profit on the Ingenious basis, but on another basis there was a view to profit. However, only 30% or 35% of the budgeted cost was incurred by the partners exclusively for the purpose of their trade. The losses were not computed in accordance with GAAP.

In the 2017 judgment the FTT held 'with misgivings and reluctance that the rights were capital in nature'. In view of the sums involved, it appears likely that these appeals will be taken further (see **7.07**).

5.18 Tax avoidance partnerships

In *Icebreaker 1 LLP v HMRC* [2010] UKUT 477 (TCC), the Upper Tribunal pointed out that the six individual partners in the Icebreaker partnership made capital contributions totalling £1.52 million, 70% of which were funded by the Bank of Scotland and the remaining 30% from the members' own resources. The Upper Tribunal amended the decision of the First Tier Tribunal by:

i) Disallowing the deduction of the sum of £1,064,000 as not being a disbursement or expense wholly and exclusively expended for the purposes of Icebreaker's trade within the meaning of ICTA 1988, s 74(1)(a).
ii) Allowing the entirety of the deduction of £209,866 under s 74(1)(a) as a disbursement or expense wholly and exclusively expended for the purposes of Icebreaker's trade.
iii) Allowing the deduction of £120,000 paid under the Administration Agreement also under s 74(1)(a) as a disbursement or expense wholly and exclusively expended for the purposes of Icebreaker's trade.

iv) Disallowing the deduction of £50,000 paid under the Advisory Agreement as a pre-payment of allowable expenses to be incurred in future tax years.

Acornwood LLP and four other Icebreaker partnerships were selected as lead cases to represent each of the five tax years from 2005/06 to 2009/10. There are a further 46 Icebreaker partnerships and the total amount of losses claimed by all 51 partnerships amounted to £336 million. The tax question was whether these losses were allowable under ITTOIA 2005, s 34 as trading losses. The taxpayers usually provided 20% of the funding from their own resources and borrowed 80% from Barclays Bank on full recourse terms, but it was deposited with the bank as security for a letter of credit which the Tribunal held was a capital payment and not for a trading purpose.

The joint cases of *Samarkand Film Partnership No 3 and Proteus Film Partnership No 1* [2015] UKUT 211 (TCC) before the Upper Tribunal related to whether the partners were entitled to relief in respect of tax losses on the sale and lease back of films under ITTOIA 2005, ss 130–144 and other costs. It was held that the expenditure was of a capital nature.

Chapter 6

The required yield

Signposts

6.01 Comparison with quoted shares

One of the most challenging aspects of any valuation is identifying any comparable companies or transactions against which the subject entity may be benchmarked. The case law guidance in this area, although in some cases decades old, still provides a helpful insight into the key issues which may present the valuer with difficulty.

One of the most difficult problems facing the share valuer is ascertaining the prospective yield, and in this connection it is often helpful to consider some comparison with returns available from quoted securities. This will, at least, give an indication of the general economic and political position and the level of interest rates and yields on equity shares generally. It is unlikely that a quoted company would serve as a direct comparison with the shares being valued but allowance for differences in size and diversity of business can always be made in arriving at the price. Some of the problems of such a comparison have been referred to by Plowman J in his comments quoted above in *Re Lynall, Lynall v IRC* (1971) 47 TC 375 at 387, see 5.05. In the Court of Appeal at 402 in *Re Lynall*, Cross LJ stated:

> 'Another point which was argued in favour of the public information test was that the price of shares quoted on the Stock Exchange depends on the market's assessment of published as opposed to confidential information, and that it was desirable that the same standards should be applied to the valuation of every sort of share. I cannot follow this argument at all for the market of the sale of quoted shares is completely different from the market for the sale of holdings in private companies. No one will be a "willing" purchaser of shares quoted on the Stock Exchange at a price higher than the quoted price, and if he happens to have confidential information showing that the shares are worth less than the quoted price he will not be willing to buy at all.'

It will be noted that Cross LJ states that no one will be a willing purchaser of shares quoted on the Stock Exchange at a price higher than the quoted price – but it is common knowledge that bargains do take place on the Stock Exchange at special prices. Provision is made for a symbol to be placed beside such bargains when they are recorded to denote the fact. Such bargains at special prices may be above or below the quoted price depending on the circumstances. This emphasises that in the application of such statements to a particular valuation the valuer must ascertain all the facts, critically examine the statement in the light of those facts and apply his common sense when deciding whether such statements are relevant to his valuation

In *A-G of Ceylon v Mackie* (1952) 31 ATC 435 Lord Reid stated:

> 'The learned judge of the District Court founded on two lists of rubber companies' shares quoted in 1939 and 1940 showing that in 1940 the investing public were not pessimistic. Their Lordships are unable to draw any conclusion from these lists. No evidence was given about them by the appellant's witnesses. A few questions about them were put to one of the respondent's witnesses, Mr Cuming, in cross-examination. He said "There was business in buying rubber shares in 1940 but not considerable business. There was a feeling that government was going to take-over the buying of rubber and as a result there was a certain amount of business." As the company's business depended on its ability to buy rubber any such feeling could not have helped the sale of its shares. It may be that these share lists show there were more buyers in the market in 1940 than in 1939, but they do not show whether those buyers were prepared to buy large blocks of shares, or whether the prices offered exceeded the break-up value of the shares. Their Lordships cannot agree with the District Judge that these lists diminished the value of the evidence of the respondent's witnesses.'

In *Re Holt* (1953) 32 ATC 402 Danckwerts J stated at 405:

> 'Mr Benson supported his evidence with various tables containing the figures relating to various companies whose shares had a quotation on the Stock Exchange, and other figures obtained from the Actuaries Investment Index. Such tables are not without a value, as they provide some possible basis of comparison for the purpose of checking the calculations of a witness, but it is easy to attack them on the grounds that the varying circumstances of the companies, and the difficulty of applying the prices of quoted shares to the shares of a private company not quoted on the Stock Exchange, may render the comparison of little value …
>
> Mr Benson expressed the view that the prices of ordinary shares tended to follow the price of consols and produced a graph which recorded the rise of consols to a peak in 1946 when ordinary shares in the company were valued for estate duty at 20s. a share and a subsequent fall in the price of consols which, if followed by the company's shares, would bring the price of these to less than 16s. 8d by March 1948. Mr Benson's view was not accepted by the witnesses for the Commissioners of Inland Revenue in this respect.'

At 410:

> 'I think the kind of investor who would purchase shares in a private company of this kind in circumstances which must preclude him disposing of his shares freely whenever he would wish, (because he will, when registered as a shareholder, be subject to the provisions of the articles restricting transfer) would be different from any kind of purchaser of shares on the Stock Exchange, and would be rather the exceptional kind of investor, who had some special reason

for putting his money into shares of this kind. He would, in my view, be the kind of investor who would not rush hurriedly into the transaction, but would consider carefully the prudence of the course and would seek to get the fullest possible information about the past history of the company, the particular trade in which it was engaged and the future profits of the company.'

In *Salvesen's Trustees v IRC* (1930) 9 ATC 43, Lord Fleming stated at 48:

> 'Sir William M'Lintock, in giving evidence for the Crown, contrasted the proportion of earnings distributed as dividend in this company and in certain Norwegian companies, and I think he was successful in showing that this proportion was much higher in the Norwegian companies. The figures shown for the years 1923–24, 1924–25 and 1925–26 in No 27 of Process are very remarkable. The company distributed 17% of its earnings as dividends in the year 1923–24, 4.78% in the year 1924–25 and 5.67% in the year 1925–26, whereas the smallest proportion of similar distributions in the Norwegian companies during these years were 57%, 32% and 35%. I should add that the shares of the Tonsberg Company and Vestfold Company, both Norwegian companies, were quoted in the open market about the date of the testator's death at prices of 272% and 167% respectively. I do not think, however, I have sufficient information with regard to these companies, their histories and balance sheets, to make the figures with regard to the prices of their shares of much value.'

Nourse J commented in *Re Bird Precision Bellows Ltd* [1984] 2 WLR 869:

> 'Mr Milburn also relied on the appropriate table published in the Financial Times on 25 November 1981, which disclosed the equivalent of a P/E ratio before tax of 6.88 as an average for the 66 quoted companies in the mechanical engineering sector at that date. However, I prefer the view of Mr Foster that that is not a very helpful comparison, principally because quoted companies can be assumed to have had a record of paying significant dividends.'

In *Findlay's Trustees v IRC* (1938) 22 ATC 437, Lord Fleming stated at 440:

> 'It is to be presumed that the hypothetical purchaser having obtained all the relevant information would consider in the first place the risks which were involved in carrying on the business, and would fix the return which he considered he ought to receive on the purchase price at a rate per cent. The only other factor which he would then require to determine would be the annual profits which he would derive from carrying on the business. The determination of these two factors would enable him to fix the capital value of the business. A seller looking at the matter from the opposite point of view would deal with it on similar lines. Here we are fortunate in this respect that Mr Geoghegan and Mr Robson are in substantial agreement with regard to the first factor, ie the rate per cent of profits. Mr Geoghegan says it must not be less than 12½% and Mr Robson is prepared to concede that figure. This figure takes account of all the advantages and disadvantages of the interest which passed on the deceased's death.'

The *Findlay's Trustees* case involved the valuation of a partnership rather than a company, but the open market value applies in both cases.

In *McNamee v IRC* [1954] IR 214, Maguire J stated at 228:

> 'Mr Cave, Mr Scanlon and Mr Abrahamson have gone to great trouble to prepare comparative tables of other companies carrying on similar business having stock exchange quotations for their shares. Those have been examined and explained. I am satisfied without going into details, but having considered all the evidence, that the analogies which they have drawn from other companies are far from complete, and that they are misleading. I am satisfied too that the inferences they

> ask me to draw cannot fairly be drawn in the case of these shares in the Convoy Woollen Company. The affairs of each company must be considered in relation to its own position, its own difficulties, and its own domestic control.'

In the Australian case of *Federal Comrs of Taxation v Sagar* (1946) 71 CLR 421 it seems that all the expert witnesses agreed that if the shares had been listed on the Stock Exchange at the date of death, and had they been as well and favourably known as the shares in certain comparable companies, it would have been proper to capitalise the sum which they anticipated would be available for dividend in the future at 5%. In the event the valuation board valued the shares on the basis of a capitalised yield at 5% less a discount for non-marketability of 10% and the court refused to disturb this basis of valuation. It appears from the case report that £16,893 capitalised at 5%, ie £337,860, represented 36 shillings a share, giving 187,770 shares of which the deceased's 7,190 shares represented 3.8% of the share capital of Cohn's Bros Victorian Brewery Co Ltd.

In *Jackson v Armitage Ware Ltd* (unreported), it was agreed by the expert witnesses that a comparison could reasonably be made with three quoted companies in the sanitaryware industry, but not with the yield for the building materials section of the Financial Times Actuaries Share Index as this section included many non-comparable companies.

This case was heard by Buckley J in the Chancery Division on 4 to 12 October 1966. The question at issue related to the position of auditors in fixing a fair value for shares in a company as experts and not as arbitrators.

Armitage Ware Ltd had a provision in its articles empowering the directors to require the personal representatives of a deceased shareholder to sell the shares at a value fixed by the auditors, the company acting as agent for the personal representatives in the sale to the other shareholders.

In this case the plaintiffs were the personal representatives of a shareholder who died in 1964. The auditors, on the basis of a yield of 6¼% on a dividend covered 11 times, valued the shares at two shillings each. The plaintiffs argued for eight shillings.

The grounds of law involved in the action were (a) the auditors acted in a fiduciary capacity for all the shareholders and were disqualified from functioning as experts on behalf of the company (b) the valuation was in any case so low that it must have been made on wrong principles.

The company had gone public in March 1965 at 12s 6d per share on the basis of a 6% yield on a dividend covered twice, so the plaintiffs obviously had a prima facie case. The matter was eventually settled out of court so that Buckley J was not required to deliver judgment.

In considering any comparison with quoted public companies it is worth bearing in mind the comments in *Hinchcliffe v Crabtree* (1971) 47 TC 419, of Russell LJ, stated at 434, in connection with FA 1965, s 44:

> 'But subsection 3 in providing a measuring rod is an extremely useful subsection. It is, I think, designed to reflect the accepted practice in estate duty cases: and, of course, cases may occur of a control holding where mere multiplication of a quoted price for a single stock unit will not represent the price obtainable on a sale of the holding; or there may be cases where the Stock Exchange quotations, due to lack of bargains, are out of date or stale. But there are many factors – ignorance, optimism, pessimism, false rumour, inside information – that contribute to a Stock Exchange quotation and it would obviously be wholly

disruptive of the value of subsection 3 if those matters were to be the subject of analysis on valuation, whether for capital gains tax or for estate duty.'

In the same case at 437 Sachs LJ stated:

'The fact remains that day in and day out there occur on the London Stock Exchange situations in which it may well be said that an announcement should have been made by some company which if made would affect the prices of the quoted shares. This can and does happen in relation to many and various events. For instance, it happens in relation to news of the success or failure of boreholes affecting the prospects of mining companies; to the publication of a company's accounts being deferred beyond the proper time; to the effects of important matters which may only later become public when published accounts appear; or to the imminence of the successful completion of some negotiations resulting in a highly valuable contract. Sometimes the absence of that information may result in the quoted prices on the Stock Exchange being higher than had it been available, and sometimes lower. That all forms part of the pattern of the general circumstances in which the market operates and under which prices are fixed having regard to supply and demand. The Stock Exchange, like other bodies concerned with the good name and best interests in the City, may be taken to do its best to see that as much information as practicable is available to those who deal in the market. It does not, and cannot, guarantee the availability of that information, and having regard to the general circumstances in which it operates, it cannot be said to be a special circumstance merely that in some particular instance information has not become available.'

In the same case in the House of Lords at 445, Lord Morris of Borth-y-Gest stated:

'It is to be remembered that what is denoted by the provisions of [FA 1965] s 44 is not the intrinsic value of shares, but the price that they will fetch in the open market, and that as a matter of practical and administrative convenience the London Stock Exchange quotations (ie quotations in the Stock Exchange Official Daily List) are accepted as the basis to be used in following the directions given by [FA 1965] s 44(3). But in the very nature of things stock exchange prices have to be arrived at without full and complete and up to the minute knowledge of all the circumstances which, if they were known, might affect prices.'

Although the effect of a possible sale of the whole company was an influence on the value determined by the Special Commissioner in *Caton v Couch* [1995] STC (SCD) 34, valuations ignoring the possible sale were also considered. The expert witness for the taxpayer proposed a value based on dividend yield and the Revenue's expert proposed a value based on capitalised earnings, which he cross-checked by reference to dividend yield. The following extracts show the attitude of each expert and the conclusion reached by the Special Commissioner. At 45 (expert evidence for the administrators):

'Mr Sutherland's first valuation of the shares assumed that no information about a proposed sale of the company was available and was based on expected dividends. The board meeting of 27 July 1987 had considered a dividend of 35% of post-tax profits. On a basis of pre-tax profits of £2.25m and corporation tax of 35% this would give a post-tax profit of £1,462,500. Thirty-five per cent of that figure was £511,875 which gave a dividend of 3p net, 4.11p gross. A profit of £3m in the year ending on 31 August 1988 would give post-tax profits of £1.95m and a dividend of one-third of post-tax profits would be £650,000 or 3.65p net per share or 5p gross per share. Because a purchaser of these shares could not readily realise them he would require a yield of at least three times that obtainable on quoted shares. At the relevant date the yield on quoted shares was about 3% so a purchaser of these shares would require a yield of between 9% and 10%. If expected gross future dividends were to be 5p per share, and dividend yield was 10%, then the value of each share would be 50p.'

At 46 (expert evidence for the Revenue):

'Mr Richardson valued the shares on an earnings multiple basis. He took an amount for earnings per share and applied the appropriate price/earnings ratio to produce the price of the share. In calculating earnings he took the estimated pre-tax profit of £2,030,000 and deducted corporation tax to produce post-tax profits of £1,319,500. This represented earnings of 7.4p per share. In oral evidence he said that, if the purchaser knew of profits of £2.25m and a budget estimate of £3m, then earnings would be 8.2p per share. For the price/earnings ratio Mr Richardson looked at the *Financial Times Actuaries Share Index* on 7 September 1987 which gave the following price/earnings ratios:

Capital goods	17.66
Mechanical Engineering	16.33
500 Share Index	18.28

[He thought the ratio rather high at between 16.33 and 18.28. He therefore used a ratio of 12.14. With earnings of 7.4p per share this yielded a price in the range of 85p to £1. He then discounted that price by 60 to 70% to allow for the fact that the holding was uninfluential and unmarketable and reached a value of 35p per share. He agreed that if earnings were 8.2p, if a ratio of 14 were used, and if the discount were 60%, then the value would be 46p per share.

Mr Richardson also considered an alternative approach and looked at the dividend yield. He assumed a net dividend of 2.5 to 3p net and 3.42 to 4.11p gross and earnings of 7.4p per share. A price of 35p per share gave a dividend yield of 9.8 to 11.7% which was not unreasonable.

The views of the administrators

Mr Sutherland disagreed with Mr Richardson's calculations in a number of respects.

He did not agree that the price/earnings ratios for the quoted market were high at 16.33 and 18.28. He referred to the *Investors Chronicle* for 4 September 1987 and 11 September 1987 and to an extract from Eastaway and Booth's *Practical Share Valuation* (2nd edn, 1991) which gave a price/earnings ratio for capital goods as 18.41 on 31 July 1987, although this fell to 12.27 by 31 October 1987 after "Black Monday". He also did not agree that the price should be discounted by 60 to 70% for unmarketability and other factors. That discount might be appropriate for a company which did not pay dividends but the present company paid dividends of 35% of post-tax profits. In his view the discount should be 20 to 25%. He referred to *Dymond's Capital Taxes*, para 23.374 which stated:

> "It is therefore not unreasonable ... to begin with the P/E ratio of comparable quoted companies and deduct the usual 20 per cent or so for unmarketability. If the price so obtained is significantly more or less than the price calculated by reference to dividend yield, the market value is likely to be a compromise between the two. Even with quoted companies, the dividend policy usually has an important effect on the P/E ratio."'

At 51 (part of the Special Commissioner's conclusions as to value):

> 'I first consider the validity of the assumptions made by Mr Sutherland. The first was the assumption that a dividend yield of three times that obtained on quoted shares would be required to compensate for unmarketability etc. This strikes me as being on the high side. *Dymond* at para 23.348 talks about an uplift of between 20 and 30% depending on the provisions in the articles of association relating to unmarketability and restrictions on transfer. In *Lynall* where the restrictions were stringent an uplift of 31% was used. However, as Mr Richardson agreed that a yield of three times that of quoted shares would be required I accept that figure.'

And at 53:

> 'It seems to me that Mr Richardson's valuation has two main defects, namely, that it starts by assuming a level of earnings which is too low and it assumes a price/earnings ratio which is too low. Higher earnings of 8.2p per share, and a higher price/earnings ratio of, say 15, would yield a price of £1.23 which, if discounted by 60% for unmarketability etc, would give a price of 49.2p which is close to Mr Sutherland's valuation.
>
> Having considered the figures as carefully as I can I conclude that a value of 45p would be appropriate if up-to-date information about the management accounts and budget forecasts were made available but if there were no information about a sale.'

Marks v Sherred (HMIT) [2004] STC (SCD) 362 relates to the 31 March 1982 value of Ross Marks Limited (RML).

RML was incorporated in 1972 and within TCGA 1992, s 273, and Mr Marks was deemed to have sold and reacquired at market value his shares in RML at 31 March 1982. He held 66% of the shares. His mother and brother held 30% and the general manager held 4%. Mr Marks had assumed a steady exchange rate, which overstated the actual profit and suggested an earnings multiple of 11 whereas HMRC argued for 10. The net sustainable pre-tax profits at 31 March 1982 were £115,000. The effective rate of tax for the three years to 31 March 1982 was 16.6% and the nearest comparable quoted company, Amstrad Consumer Electronics plc, was based on 11.6 times earnings and a price earnings ratio for this unquoted company was 10. So the company's value was £959,100 and Mr Marks' shareholding was £633,006.

In *Eclipse Film Partners No 35 LLP v HMRC* [2015] EWCA Civ 95, the partners in Eclipse 35 borrowed money to contribute to its capital on which interest was paid. Tax relief was claimed on the interest paid which would only be allowed if Eclipse 35 were carrying on a trade and the borrowed money was used wholly for that trade, under ITTOIA 2005, s 863 and TA 1988, ss 353 and 362. The Eclipse members paid £840 million capital and £293 million in interest. The claimed trade was that of exploiting film rights. HMRC claimed that Eclipse 35 never carried on a trade but merely organised a sophisticated financial model involving licensing and distribution rights in respect of two Disney films designed to give pre-determined cash flows giving rise to interest pre-payment on borrowings to set against otherwise taxable income. Eclipse 35 paid an aggregate licence fee for 20 years in advance of £503 million and a variable royalty and entered into a distribution agreement with Disney. The members paid £840 million, £50 million of their own money and £790 million of loans as capital to the partnership which was used to pay the licence fee etc. The members of the LLP borrowed the £790 million from Eagle, a subsidiary of Barclays Bank.

Although these transactions were not shams, Eclipse 35 never received physical delivery of the films. The transactions entered into were determined at the outset and without reference to the performance of the films and the transactions; there was no realistic or commercially meaningful business.

The Upper Tribunal pointed out that the prior agreements had granted enterprise distribution and other rights to Buena Vista companies and Eclipse 35 did not acquire from Disney any substantive distribution rights.

The Court of Appeal were referred to *The Collector of Stamp Revenue v Arrowtown Assets Limited* [2003] HKCFA 52 at para 35:

> 'the driving principle in the *Ramsay* line of cases continues to involve a general rule of statutory construction and an unblinkered approach to the analysis of the facts. The ultimate question is whether the relevant statutory provisions, construed purposively, were intended to apply to the transaction, viewed realistically.'

The Court held that the payment of £503 million with repayment with interest over 20 years was an investment not a trading transaction, and the possible share of contingent receipts was insufficiently significant to be classed as a trade, and the appeal was dismissed.

Pitfall

Since *Re Lynall* was decided there is now the AIM market and other indices which can provide a market for shares. Some stocks may be thinly or rarely traded and therefore the 'quoted' price for some shares may not be the true market value at a given date.

Focus

- There is a risk that over reliance on data without understanding or interpreting it appropriately will give a misleading result. Any analysis of data accumulated to support a particular argument should be reviewed with a critical eye to mitigate the risk of bias or error.
- The information to which a shareholder may be entitled for valuation purposes is discussed in more detail in **Chapter 16**. The valuer needs to consider both the case law position and also a common sense approach as to what might reasonably be expected in a particular circumstance.

6.02 Comparison with other investments

The prospective investor in shares in an unquoted company, being a careful and prudent investor, would also be influenced by the potential yields and likelihood, or otherwise, of capital appreciations in other forms of investment than equity shares whether quoted or unquoted. These could include gilt edged government securities, local authority loans, single premium bonds, savings certificates, building society and bank deposits, quoted debentures, loan stocks and preference shares. He is likely to be interested in the net of tax return on such investments in comparison with that available on the unquoted shares and such return is therefore going to have some effect on the price which he would be prepared to pay for unquoted shares.

In *Buckingham v Francis* [1986] 2 BCC 98984, Staughton J stated:

> 'Then I turn to the multiplier, or figure which a purchaser would require as a profit/earnings [sic] ratio. Mr Burns proposed a figure of 2. All multipliers which I mention are on a pre-tax basis and not post-tax. In other words Mr Burns considered that a purchaser would only pay a price which could be expected to be recouped in two years, subject to tax, with a return of 50% per annum on his investment. In support of that figure he quoted from an article in issue no 132 of Accountants Digest by Mr Christopher Glover of Messrs Ernst and Whinney, at page 20:
>
>> "The client wants to know what his company is worth and the valuer has to value in a vacuum. He then has to select the capitalisation rate purely from his own experience and judgment. Clearly, however, it cannot be less than the risk free rate of return available on gilts. In the author's experience profitable established, well managed, medium sized companies are generally capitalised on pre-tax profit yields of 20 to 25%. Small, well managed companies would sell on higher yields, generally 30 to 35%. These are only general indications. They would be lower for companies with superior management, high profits, growth and strong asset backing: they could well be much higher if management is bad, the industry background depressed and the asset backing poor. These yields will not be valid for all time. The investment scene is constantly changing."'

(Mr Glover's view of the required yield has relaxed since then. In the 2004 edition of *The Valuation of Unquoted Companies* he wrote:

> 'In a previous work, published in 1992, the author suggested a range of pre-tax profit yields of between 20% and 25% for the small to medium-sized private company. The implied rate of return, which was a function of the expected growth rate, would have been higher than these initial yields. In recent years, however, the investment climate has altered. Gilt yields have fallen appreciably and stock market P/E ratios have risen. The capitalisation rates for small to medium-sized private companies are not immune to these developments. They have accordingly risen, although perhaps not by as much as one might have thought. A pre-tax profits yield of 20% would almost certainly be too high for a profitable well-managed medium-sized company. A yield of 15% would perhaps be more appropriate. On the other hand, the smaller private company may well attract a yield of 20%. The required yield for a "people" business could well be higher. These yields will not be valid for all times. The investment scene is constantly changing'.)
>
> 'I did not, of course, have the advantage of evidence from Mr Glover. So I do not know why he says with such confidence ("clearly") that a purchaser would not accept a lesser yield when buying a private company than he could obtain in the gilt edged market – currently about 1%. Presumably it is assumed that the contemplated yield is a fixed figure, and that there are no prospects of growth. If it is said by Mr Burns that his price/earnings ratio of 2, revealing a prospective yield of 50% on the purchase price, is valid even where the figure for future maintainable profits is the best estimate that can be made, giving appropriate weight to all uncertainties of the future, then I cannot accept his evidence. In my judgment a purchaser of this Company would, on that basis, be content with a yield of 25%, or in other words a price/earnings ratio of 4. Having fully evaluated the risks and prospects in selecting a figure of £6,000 for future maintainable profits, I consider that a price/earnings ratio of 2 would contain a second, unnecessary allowance for risk, and that 4 is the more appropriate figure.

> Frankly I doubt whether businessmen are ruled by accountants when deciding how much to pay for a private company. They no doubt seek the advice of accountants beforehand, and are told what likely price/earnings ratio would emerge from various different figures as the purchase price. And afterwards they are told, no doubt, what is the likely price/earnings ratio on the purchase price which they have decided to pay. But I wonder whether, in the crucial stage between, when they are deciding on a price, business acumen or hunch does not play a far larger part than the calculations of accountants.'

In *Re Bird Precision Bellows Ltd* [1984] 2 WLR 869, Nourse J commented:

> 'What then is the correct multiple to apply to that figure? The rival contentions are 5.5 on the part of Mr Milburn and 3 on the part of Mr Foster. It might be thought to be strange that there could be such a wide difference of opinion between two experienced valuers on a question of this kind. I should say here that other experience and information of one kind or another was available to them within each of their well-known firms. Nevertheless, it is not unusual for the court to be faced with a difference of this order. In the end I have to make my own assessment of the evidence which is before me. In doing that I must start by saying that I think that Mr Milburn's figure of 5.5 is far too high. There was what was to my mind a very convincing passage in the evidence of Mr Foster, when he said that he would seek to do all he could to arrive at a realistic maintainable level of profit so as to eliminate any element of risk. But if he then felt that there was still a significant risk left, he would downgrade the multiple. He accepted that any multiple is a matter of individual judgment. Then he turned to the present case and pictured this small private engineering company at the end of 1981 when the recession had not bottomed out and share prices in the industry were depressed. Mr Milburn agreed that those were the conditions of the period. Mr Foster said that he would have been very surprised to have seen a multiple above 2 or 3 at that time. He thought that he would have been very lucky to find a purchaser who would pay £700,000 to £800,000 for a company of this sort at that time.
>
> While, as I say, I found that evidence very convincing, it does nevertheless seem to me that Mr Foster's views were somewhat on the cautious side. Although I have assumed that a willing purchaser would take an average of the actual or anticipated profits for the three most recent years, he would undoubtedly have looked further back in order to see the earlier record of the company. If he had done that, he would have seen that from 1977–78 onwards, ie from only two years after its birth, the company had been making a profit which, with one slight setback in the following year, had steadily increased from £80,000 to £175,000. I think he would have thought that those figures showed that this was a well run and soundly based company. Even in times of great recession in the industry, he would in my view not have expected a yield of as much as 33% on this investment and would therefore have been prepared to apply a multiple of more than 3. I think that he would have been well satisfied with a yield of something over 25%. In my judgment the correct multiple in this case is 3.75, which reflects a yield of 26.66%. If that is applied to a net maintainable profit of £146,000 it produces a valuation on an earnings basis of £547,500.'

Focus

It should be noted that, in court proceedings, the judge is unlikely to accept the evidence of one expert in its entirety. The value determined will be based on the most persuasive elements of both experts.

6.03 Real sales

In the case of an actual sale of shares between arm's length parties it is normal for the sale to be by way of private treaty rather than auction, and it is normal for the prospective purchaser to be given all the information he may require in order to finalise his offer, including access to the company's records in order to perform due diligence. When a substantial proportion of the issued capital is being sold, it is indeed common for the purchaser to appoint investigating accountants to examine the books and records of the company being purchased in order to assist in quantifying the offer to be made.

In a hypothetical sale on the open market it was held in *Re Lynall, Lynall v IRC* (1971) 47 TC 375 at 407, by Lord Reid:

> 'The case for the Crown is based on evidence as to how large blocks of shares in private companies are in fact sold. There is no announcement that the shares are for sale and no invitation for competitive bids. The seller engages an expert who selects the person or group who he thinks most likely to be prepared to pay a good price and to be acceptable to the directors. If that prospective purchaser is interested he engages accountants of high repute, and the directors agree to co-operate by making available to the accountants on a basis of strict confidentiality all relevant information about the company's affairs. Then the accountants acting in an arbitral capacity fix what they think is a fair price. Then the sale is made at that price. Obviously the working of this scheme depends on all concerned having complete confidence in each other, and I do not doubt that in this way the seller gets a better price than he could otherwise obtain. In my view this evidence is irrelevant because this kind of sale is not a sale in the open market. It is a sale by private treaty made without competition to a selected purchaser at a price fixed by an expert valuer. The 1894 Act could have provided – but it did not – that the value should be the highest price which could reasonably have been expected to be realised on a sale of the property at the time of the death. If that had been the case then the Crown would succeed, subject to one matter which I need not stop to consider. But the framers of the Act limited the enquiry to one type of sale–sale in the open market – and we are not entitled to rewrite the Act. It is quite easily workable as it stands.
>
> No doubt sale in the open market may take many forms. But it appears to me that the idea behind this provision is the classical theory that the best way to determine the value in exchange of any property is to let the price be determined by economic forces – by throwing the sale open to competition when the price would be the highest price that anyone offers. That implies there has been adequate publicity or advertisement before the sale and the nature of the property must determine what is adequate publicity. Goods may be exposed for sale in a market place or places to which buyers resort. Property may be up to auction. Competitive tenders may be invited. On the Stock Exchange a sale to a jobber may seem to be a private sale, but the price has been determined, at least within narrow limits, by the actions of the investing public. In a particular case it may not always be easy to say whether there has been a sale in the open market. But in my judgment the method on which the Crown rely cannot by any criterion be held to be selling in the open market. If the hypothetical sale on the open market requires us to suppose competition has been invited then we would have to suppose that steps had been taken before the sale to enable a variety of persons, institutions or financial groups to consider what offers they would be prepared to make. It would not be a true sale in the open market if the seller were to discriminate between genuine potential buyers and give to some of them information which

> he withheld from others, because one from whom he withheld information might be the one who, if he had had the information, would have made the highest offer.
>
> The Crown's figure of £4 10s. per share can only be justified if it must be supposed that these reports would have been made known to all genuine potential buyers, or at least to accountants nominated by them. That could only have been done with consent of Linread's board of directors. They were under no legal obligation to make any confidential information available. Circumstances vary so much that I have some difficulty in seeing how we could lay down any general rule that directors must be supposed to have done something which they were not obliged to do. The farthest we could possibly go would be to hold that the directors must be deemed to have done what all reasonable directors would do. Then it might be reasonable to say that they would disclose information provided that its disclosure could not possibly prejudice the interests of the company. But that would not be sufficient to enable the Crown to succeed. Not all financiers who might wish to bid in such a sale, and not even all the accountants whom they might nominate, are equally trustworthy. A premature leakage of such information as these reports disclose might be very damaging to the interests of the company, and the evidence in this case shows that in practice great care is taken to see that disclosure is only made to those of the highest repute. I could not hold it right to suppose that all reasonable directors would agree to disclose information such as these reports so widely as would be necessary if it had to be made available to all who must be regarded as genuine potential bidders or to their nominees. So in my opinion the Crown failed to justify their valuation of £4 10s.'

For the purposes of market valuation for capital gains tax the *Lynall* decision is effectively overridden by TCGA 1992, s 273(3) where it is provided that there is assumed to be available to any prospective purchaser all the information which a prudent prospective purchaser might reasonably require if he were proposing to purchase from a willing vendor by private treaty and at arm's length (see **9.03**). It should be noted however that there is still to be assumed an open market valuation, merely that such information as would be made available in a sale by private treaty is to be made available. A similar provision applies for inheritance tax under IHTA 1984, s 168. There is, however, no such assumption for stamp duty purposes.

The problem is to determine what information would be made available and in the case of a sale of a controlling interest it is difficult to see why any relevant information would not be made available to the prospective purchasers.

In the case of a sale of a small minority interest for a modest amount of money, however, it is unlikely that much information beyond the published accounts would be made available, although if the company prepared management accounts and budgets these would often be made available to a prospective purchaser of the shares. In some cases, however, the board might consider that such information could prejudice the company's trade and the information would remain confidential. It would clearly be a breach of confidence if a shareholder divulged such information to a prospective purchaser if he were aware of it in his capacity as director, unless he had the agreement of the board to do so.

If, however, a substantial minority interest were being considered, or if the consideration was substantial, it would be most unusual, in a sale by private treaty, not to make available all the books and records and management accounts and budgets, although even then it is not necessarily a foregone conclusion that all the directors' plans for the future would be divulged in full as each case has to be considered on its own particular facts.

In the case of *Re a Company (No 002708 of 1989)* and *Re a Company (No 004247 of 1989)*, judgment given on 6 March 1990 and reported at (1990) *Times*, 17 March, Knox J, 'taking perhaps a realist rather than a purist view', did not consider that the valuer should be required to ignore altogether an offer to purchase shares in a company made the day after the date upon which the value of the shares was to be assessed by him.

6.04 Possible flotation

In both *Re Lynall, Lynall v IRC* (1971) 47 TC 375 and *Re Holt* (1953) 32 ATC 402 the possibility of the company going public was considered by the court. In the first case Mrs Lynall died on 21 May 1962 and the company did go public on 11 July 1963 with a public issue of 27½% of the shares, which was heavily over-subscribed. In the *Holt* case Mr R L Holt died on 11 March 1948 and the company became a public company on 21 September 1950 in connection with the issue to the public of 650,000 5% first cumulative redeemable preference shares of £1 each.

It is important to note that both companies were in a position to go public at the time of valuation, had it been necessary or desirable to do so, which is clearly a matter of some importance when considering the relevance of, for example, comparisons with public quoted companies.

6.05 Takeover bids

Industry is constantly rationalising itself into more efficient units and this process often results in the takeover of smaller companies. If the company, the shares of which have to be valued, is in an industry in the process of rationalisation and is a likely candidate for a bid, this is clearly a factor which any willing vendor would bring to the notice of the purchaser and he would expect the price to reflect that situation even if only to a limited extent. This is particularly so if it is known that bids have been made although for one reason or another the directors have rejected them.

In the cases of *Caton v Couch* [1995] STC (SCD) 34 and *Clark v Green* [1995] STC (SCD) 99 the Special Commissioners considered the effect on value for capital gains tax purposes of a decision by a board of directors to explore the possibility of permitting the company to be acquired. For a discussion of those cases and the influence of confidential information when considering values for tax purposes see **9.03**.

> **Focus**
>
> A key aspect of any valuation of a private company is to establish its intentions in respect of an exit. For a business with private equity backing it may be assumed that there is likely to be an exit event within three to five years of the original acquisition although the actual timescale may be different. The prospect of an exit on a going concern basis is likely to have an impact on value.

Chapter 7

Asset-related valuations

Signposts

7.01 Break-up value

If the shares of a company or at least 75% of them are held by a single person, valuation will normally be on a going concern basis but there is no requirement that this must always be the basis of valuation in such cases as the shareholder would usually be able to put the company into liquidation. The basis of valuation must depend on the circumstances. This point was considered where valuable farmland had been transferred to a farming company in *M'Connel's Trustees v IRC* 1927 SLT 14. It was stated by Lord Fleming at 15:

> 'The petitioners found upon the facts that for each of the three years after its formation the company made a loss and they say there was never any prospect of the company earning profits or being in a position to pay a dividend. They maintained that the shares must be valued on the footing that the company is a

> going concern, and with references to the provisions of the memorandum and articles of association and also to the past history and future prospects of the company, from a dividend earning point of view. These are all circumstances which fall to be taken into account, but in my opinion they are by no means the only factors in the calculation. A share in a limited company gives the holder a right, not only to participate in the division of the profits, but also to participate in the division of the capital … A purchaser of the shares buying them as an ordinary investment and considering what they were worth, would certainly have been influenced by the fact that the holder of these shares would be in a position to put the company into voluntary liquidation, and to realise the whole assets and divide the value thereof amongst the shareholders. Even if the shares are being sold in a number of different lots, I feel satisfied that the purchasers would all have given a price which was related to the capital value of the undertaking on realisation. A purchaser of a small lot of the shares would naturally have assumed that purchasers of the remaining shares would wish to make the most they could out of their shares and would concur with him in taking the necessary steps to have the assets of the company realised to the best advantage.'

In that case the commissioners estimated the value of the net assets of the company, took 998 thousandths of that estimated value, as the deceased held 998 shares out of a thousand, and deducted therefrom a reasonable sum to cover the estimated expenses of liquidating the company. Lord Fleming approved this method of valuation.

This case dealt with 99.8% of the shares but it will be noted that the judge referred to 'a purchaser of a small lot of shares' and his natural expectations. The authors consider that in any case in which there are valuable assets but no profit or any prospect of a profit, the break-up value of the shares must be a factor in the valuation. The extent of the influence of that factor on the price must depend on the circumstances and in particular on the nature of the assets, the identity of other shareholders and the size of their holdings.

In *A-G of Ceylon v Mackie* [1952] 2 All ER 775 it was the Revenue that were arguing that the company had to be valued on a going concern basis, but the Privy Council held that it had been proved that the deceased's holding of the entire equity share capital could not have been sold at a price based on any higher figure than the value of the tangible assets of the company.

Cash & Carry v Inspector of Taxes [1998] STC (SCD) 46 concerned the valuation for capital gains tax purposes at 31 March 1982 of a 24% shareholding in a wholesale cash and carry business. The company's net profits had deteriorated from £65,462 in 1978 to £23,385 in 1981. A loss of £27,850 was made in the year to 31 March 1982 and thereafter losses became larger. It was agreed between the parties that the value should be based on the company's net asset position. The Special Commissioner considered three likely scenarios:

(1) The company might continue to trade for some time.
(2) The Board might decide to liquidate.
(3) There would be a sale of the company at some time in the future.

The Special Commissioner agreed with the Revenue's expert witness that in the circumstances of the case the third scenario was most likely, but he reduced the Revenue's proposed minority discount of 66.67% to 55%.

> **Focus**
>
> Valuation depends on the facts in every case and there is no one size to fit all circumstances.

7.02 Asset-stripper's profit

In *Re Courthope* (1928) 7 ATC 538 the deceased held 1,900 preference shares out of 4,000 and 2,000 ordinary shares out of 4,000. However, the company, which had been carrying on a brewery business, had sold its business and it was argued that as the company's substratum had gone, a shareholder could have wound it up. Rowlatt J stated at 540:

> 'If you try to find a purchaser for these shares in my view he would probably say to himself, "well this is a thing to buy to wind-up," as Mr Stamp suggested, but I cannot help thinking that he would discount the value rather heavily because he would say, "Well, I may be met with difficulties; I shall not buy a controlling interest. Lawyers tell me that I possibly might be able to compel a winding up. There are cases upon it and all the rest of it, but I do not know how that may be," and so on and so on, and I think myself that he would only from that point of view go in for this purchase on the footing that if he succeeded in getting the company wound up he would make a profit in a few years of something like 50%. On that sort of footing, allowing for everything, I will not go through it all, I think the value of these shares may fairly be put at £13. Treating it as something about £19 or £20 and allowing for a possible profit of 50% if the winding up were carried through without a hitch. I think that is a fair price. Therefore I shall say that they are worth £13.'

In other words, in this case the court was giving allowance for an asset-stripper's profits. In some cases the profit of the asset-stripper would be liable to income tax or corporation tax as a trading profit and he would no doubt take this into account when fixing his required profit and the price he would be prepared to offer. However, in every case the purchaser buys for what he can reasonably expect to accrue to him either by way of dividends and earnings or by way of profit on re-sale or liquidation. If the principal motive for buying is to make a profit by the liquidation of the company, then the profit the purchaser expects or requires must be taken into account in arriving at the price.

> **Focus**
>
> Asset-strippers have to make a living too.

7.03 Goodwill

It should be noted that in the stamp duty case of *IRC v Muller & Co's Margarine Ltd* [1901] AC 217 it was held that an agreement which was executed by the vendor in Amsterdam, but by the purchaser subsequently in England, was regarded as having being executed in England and therefore prima facie liable to stamp duty, although in that particular case, as the agreement related solely to property outside the UK, it escaped charge.

Lord MacNaghten considered the definition of goodwill (at 223):

> 'What is goodwill? It is a thing very easy to describe, very difficult to define. It is the benefit and advantage of the good name, reputation, and connection of a business. It is the attractive force which brings in custom. It is the one thing which distinguishes an old established from a new business at its first start. The goodwill of a business must emanate from a particular centre or source. However widely extended or diffused its influence may be, goodwill is worth nothing unless it has power of attraction sufficient to bring customers home to the source from which it emanates. Goodwill is composed of a variety of elements. It differs in its composition in different trades and in different businesses in the same trade. One element may preponderate here and another element there. To analyse goodwill and split it up into its component parts; to pare it down as the Commissioners desire to do until nothing is left but a dry residuum ingrained in the actual place where the business is carried on while everything else is in the air, seems to me to be as useful for practical purposes as it would be to resolve the human body into the various substances of which it is said to be composed. The goodwill of a business is one whole and in a case like this must be dealt with as such.
>
> For my part, I think that if there is one attribute common to all cases of goodwill it is the attribute of locality. For goodwill has no independent existence. It cannot subsist by itself. It must be attached to a business. Destroy the business and the goodwill perishes with it, though the elements remain which may perhaps be gathered up and revived again. No doubt where the reputation of a business is very widely spread, or where it is the article produced rather than the producer of the article, that has won popular favour, it may be difficult to localise goodwill. But here I think there is no difficulty. We have it in evidence that the firm of Muller & Co had no customers out of Germany, and it is a significant fact that the protected area – the limit within which the vendor is prohibited from setting up in business – is the limit of 50 miles from Gildehaus.'

In the same case Lord Brampton has some useful comments to make on goodwill. At 230:

> 'Granting that a goodwill is property, the question still remains, was the goodwill in this case, when it was purchased by the company, "property locally situate out of the United Kingdom"? The answer to this depends, in my judgment upon whether at the time of the making of the written contract the goodwill was attached to and incorporated with the business premises and formed in the hands of the then vendor an inseparable property, very valuable in its combination as giving to the premises a character and an increase in value which, stripped of the goodwill, they would not have possessed, and which represents the value of the profit-earning quality of those premises, when and so long as they are used by the then occupier, for carrying on in them the business he had created within them, by reason of the attraction of customers which tend to make a prosperous business; for that is what the vendor had to sell, and sold; and the question must be determined having regard to the time when the contract of sale was made, and not regarding anything the vendee might think fit to do with the premises in the future.
>
> This word "goodwill" when used in the connection with the sale and purchase of a trade must, I think, be interpreted, according to its popular acceptation. Taken in its strictest sense, "goodwill" would hardly be a saleable commodity at all.

> I do not say there may not be such a thing as goodwill of a business utterly unconnected with the premises in which the business has been carried on, for it is quite possible that a man retiring from business might wish to retain the premises for his own private use, and merely sell the goodwill, but as was pointed out by Pollock CB in *Potter's* case (*Potter v IRC* (1854) 10 Exch 147) there is a wide difference between the sale of a goodwill, together with the premises in which the trade is then carried on, whereby the value of the premises is enhanced, and the sale of a goodwill without any interest in land or buildings connected with it, and which it is merely the advantage of the recommendation of the vendor to his connections and customers and his covenant to allow the vendee to use his trade name and to abstain from competition with him.
>
> In the first of these cases the trade and the premises are inseparable so long as the trade is therein carried on. The advantages and facilities constituting the goodwill are all more or less derived from them or the profitable results of such goodwill are therein realised. The goodwill of a trade carried on in a shop is as essential to the tradesman as the shop itself which is benefited by it. What is the trade of a shop but the business done in it, and how is that custom brought to the shop but by the goodwill attached to it? The combination of a suitable shop with the trade done in it, and the goodwill inducing that trade, seems to me to be inseverable. In my judgment, it matters not whether the business be a manufacturing one, or that of a shopkeeper, or a publican, or a brewer; in each case the seller of his business premises with his goodwill sells, and the purchaser buys, the outgoing man's premises with, so far as in him lies, the whole business carried on therein as a going concern with the same prospects the vendor himself would have had had he continued it; and I think it immaterial whether the business has been built up by the reason of the personal good qualities of the outgoer, the goodness of his wares or merchandise, the good situation of the premises, or the absence of competition; in each case the business and custom in fact have been attracted to the house or premises, and when the incomer takes possession he takes all the chances offered and conveyed to him by the purchase, of standing, so far as the business is concerned, in the shoes of the outgoer, and he must rely upon his own good qualities and aptitude of his undertaking to continue the prosperity of the business and profit by his bargain.'

In the landlord and tenant case of *Whiteman Smith Motor Co v Chaplin* [1934] 2 KB 35, Scrutton LJ quoting *Simpson v Charrington & Co Ltd* [1934] 1 KB 64 and *Cruttwell v Lye (2)* 1810 7VES 335 said that goodwill was nothing more than the probability that the old customers will resort to the old place even though the old trade of a shopkeeper has gone. He also quoted *Llewellyn v Rutherford* (LR 10 CP 456) stating that:

> 'the premises themselves owing to the old established and successful business carried on by the tenant may acquire a special value which stays with them when the tenant leaves.
>
> A division of the elements of goodwill was referred to during the argument and appears in Mr Merlin's book as the "cat, rat and dog basis". The cat prefers the old home to the person who keeps it and stays in the old home though the person who has kept the house leaves. The cat represents that part of the customers who continue to go to the old shop although the old shopkeeper has gone. The probability of their custom may be regarded as an additional value given to the premises by the tenant's trading. The dog represents that part of the customers who follow the person rather than the place. These the tenant may take with him if he does not go too far. There remains a class of customer who may neither follow the place nor the person but drift away elsewhere. They are neither a

> benefit to the landlord nor the tenant and have been called the rat for no particular reason except to keep the epigram in the animal kingdom. I believe my brother Maughan has introduced the rabbit but I will leave him to explain the position of the rabbit.'

Maughan LJ duly obliged:

> 'If the cat metaphor is to be used I would say that the cat may be attracted away by a gentle stroke on the back and the promise of a bowl of milk. But really there should be a fourth animal, the rabbit to indicate the customers who come simply from propinquity to the premises and if this is borne in mind it will be apparent that the rabbit may be much bigger than the cat who (if indeed it does not wholly vanish) may well shrink to the dimensions of a mouse.
>
> For these reasons I regard the arbitrary division into thirds of the goodwill into cat, rat and dog goodwill as valueless unless all sorts of qualifications are made.'

He also points out:

> 'the tenant naturally starts by giving evidence as to the profits which he has earned from the business during the term. It is obvious that these profits form a very slight guide to the value of the adherent goodwill since they may depend largely or entirely on the skill, the reputation or the personal qualifications of the person or persons who have carried on the business or they may be attributable solely to the advantages of the site or to improved trade conditions.'

Another leading case on the valuation of goodwill where it is regarded as the difference between the capitalised value of the earnings and the net tangible assets, is that of *Findlay's Trustees v IRC* (1938) 22 ATC 437 when Lord Fleming stated, at 441:

> 'The only factor still in dispute is the figure of net profit which the purchaser may reasonably expect to earn from the business. Mr Geoghegan and Mr Robson are agreed with regard to the methods by which the net profits should be ascertained. They both take the view that for this purpose the net profits must include income tax and also the interest payable on debentures. They are also agreed that, when the figure of profits which the purchaser may expect to earn from the business is fixed, it should be multiplied by eight in order to ascertain the *cumulo* value of the whole business. The difference between them is that Mr Robson takes as his figure of expected profits the average of the three years prior to the deceased's death, whereas Mr Geoghegan takes the actual profits for the last of these years. Mr Robson takes the average for three years at £147,510, and multiplies it by eight, which gives him £1,180,080. From that he deducts the value of the tangible assets, £707,680, leaving a balance of £472,400, which he takes to be the goodwill of the whole business. Mr Geoghegan takes the profits for the year ended 1930 as £124,721, and multiplies it by eight, which brings out a figure of £997,768. From this he deducts the value of the tangible assets as before, £707,680, leaving £290,088 as the value of the goodwill. The only point of difference between them is whether Mr Robson's figures of £147,510 or Mr Geoghegan's figures of £124,721 should be multiplied by eight in order to ascertain the value of the business. It is to be observed that Mr Robson's valuation of £472,400 contrasts with the value estimated by the Commissioners, and on which the assessment is based, namely, £426,780. On the other hand, Mr Geoghegan's figure of £290,088 contrasts with the sum of £334,185 (now adjusted to £327,525), which the appellants entered in the accounts given up by them. The Commissioners justify their assessment by Mr Robson's figure, and the appellants their value by Mr Geoghegan's figure. Neither can criticise the

other, as each is seeking to justify the figure on which they rely by a valuation which brings out a more favourable figure.

The decision of this case must accordingly depend upon the figure which is to be adopted for expected profits. I do not doubt that, when one is seeking to ascertain the profits which will probably be earned by a business in the future, it is quite usual to do so by taking an average of the profits actually earned for the three preceding years. This probably operates quite equitably when one is dealing with a well established business, which has normal ups and down, but has no violent fluctuations in either direction. But if there is a definite trend upwards or downwards, it may be different. If, for example, profits are increasing year by year by large figures, an average of three years may be unfair to the seller. If there is a similar movement downwards, it may be unfair to the purchaser. The relevant figures as regards this business are to be found in No 14 of Process, and the figures of adjusted net profit are in column 7. In order to find the figures actually used by Mr Geoghegan and Mr Robson, it is necessary to add to each of the figures in that column a sum of £16,500 representing debenture interest. But the actual figures in the column sufficiently indicate the movements of the business upwards and downwards, so far as profits are concerned, and the remarkable fact is that you have in 1930 a drop in profits of not less than £36,000, which is greater than any other increase or decrease in the column. There are large increases in the years 1922 and 1923, but it is apparent that these increases are explained by the reduction on the amount of one item of expense, namely, the cost of the newsprint. Prima facie the drop in profits in 1930 is of such a large amount as to suggest that it cannot properly be dealt with by the application of what is at best merely a rule of thumb.'

Lord Fleming finally decided, at 442:

'The question, however, remains: what effect as regard the quantum of the price is to be given to the considerations to which I have been referring? I reject as being altogether exaggerated the idea that this business falls to be regarded as moribund in 1930. The Solicitor General criticised with much force the evidence adduced by the appellants, because no witness had been brought from the Scotsman office to speak directly to the effect which the alleged adverse circumstances had upon the business. I am certainly not surprised to find that no one has come from the Scotsman office to say that this was a moribund business. I think, however, it is impossible to avoid coming to the conclusion that the outlook in 1930 could not be regarded as favourable for the newspaper industry, or for the Scotsman business in particular, and I think it is unreasonable to suppose that a buyer would expect to earn profits from this business amounting to the figure of £147,000, or anything approximating to that figure in the immediate future. A prudent buyer would, I think, proceed upon the view that the business would not recover from the serious setback which it had sustained in 1930 for some years.

The respondents, however, argued that ample allowance had been made for this, as they were willing to accept a valuation over £45,000 less than Mr Robson had brought out; and they pointed out, quite correctly, that this was equivalent to diminishing the average annual profit which they had taken, by a sum of over £5,000. I am not satisfied, however, that this is a sufficient allowance. There is still left a wide gap amounting to about £15,000 between their reduced figures and the actual profits earned in 1930, and I suggest to your lordships that we should take as the figure of expected profits a sum of £135,000, which exceeds by more than £10,000 the actual profits in 1930. If the figure of £135,000 be multiplied by eight, and the value of the tangible assets, namely, £707,680 be deducted, there is left to represent the value of the goodwill £372,320.'

> **Focus**
>
> A straightforward example of goodwill, as the capitalised earnings less the identified assets.

In *Buckingham v Francis* [1986] 2 BCC 98984 Staughton J considered the question of goodwill:

> 'There is respectable authority for the method adopted by Mr Humpage for some companies in some circumstances. See the Accountants Digest No 132, para 11.2:
>
>> "Super profits approach. The super profits approach has a long and ancient pedigree and appears in one form or another in most texts. The idea behind it is that there is a normal rate of return that can be earned on assets of a certain type but over a number of years it may be possible to earn profits in excess of this normal level. This method assumes that the purchaser will buy, in addition to the normalised value of the assets, a number of years super profits. The procedure is to estimate the value of the net assets on a going concern basis and to add to this the value of the super profits. The annual super profits are calculated by deducting from maintainable profits a sum which is equivalent to the normal rate of return on net assets. These super profits are then multiplied by a factor representing the number of years purchase. The value of the super profits is entered in the accounts as goodwill.
>>
>> The super profits method has the theoretical attraction that it recognises the transitory nature of above average performance. In practice it has serious shortcomings. The pre-occupation with net asset value, which in practice is based on balance sheet amounts, is unhealthy. Few businessmen would admit that their companies' growth rates were a temporary phenomenon, nor would most of them recognise the concept of super profits. The going rate of return on net assets must be a highly subjective assessment, as must also be the amount and duration of super profits. How is one to know that going rate for the purchase of super profits? This valuation basis leads to highly esoteric arguments divorced from reality."
>
> The objection to this method, apart from its complication, is that in the present case I can see no basis for adopting a figure of 10% as the normal level of profits for this company, or even for this industry. And, if one does adopt that normal level of profits, it is speculative as to how long and by how much it would be exceeded. The prognosis that the annual average for the past 3¼ years would be repeated in the future, and that a buyer of the company would be prepared to pay five years' purchase for that prospect, is unsupported by evidence. Nor can I see much sense in basing even part of the valuation on the book value of net assets. They would have realised far less in a liquidation: and when a company such as this one is valued as a going concern it is earnings and not assets that are significant. I reject this method of calculation. The fact that it leads to a value of £87,650 which I am sure was far more than the company was worth, may be due to a fault in the method or to a fault in the forecast which was used to apply it. But either way the result is wrong. It must be added that Mr Humpage had little or no experience of the valuation of companies, and I did not find his evidence at all convincing.'

In some cases, goodwill is very personal to the proprietors or employees, particularly in service industries such as hairdressing and advertising, and as such is very difficult to sell unless those individuals are likely to remain with the purchasers.

> **Focus**
>
> A valuation of goodwill may be based on a number of years' purchase of the super profits in excess of a normal profit level.

In the Special Commissioner's decision in *Balloon Promotions Ltd and Others v Wilson* [2006] STC (SCD) 169, the taxpayers were Pizza Express franchise holders who claimed rollover relief under TCGA 1992, s 152 on the sale of their businesses to Pizza Express, who acquired them to operate them in-house, as a result of which the franchise was terminated. The taxpayer claimed that the resulting capital gain arose from the sale of goodwill for which rollover relief was available under Class 4 of TCGA 1992, s 155. HMRC contended that the taxpayers' received compensation for the early termination of the franchise agreements which did not attract rollover relief rather than consideration for goodwill. They also alleged that the taxpayers had no goodwill to sell to Pizza Express, as the goodwill in a franchise business belonged in law to the franchisor.

The Commissioner held that the excess of the amount Pizza Express paid for the businesses over the tangible assets properly represented goodwill, which was theirs to sell as they had transferred the businesses as a going concern, complete with the leasehold interests in the restaurants. The restaurant businesses were transferred as going concerns to Pizza Express so no value added tax was chargeable on the assets transferred. The Commissioner quoted with approval the definition of the nature of goodwill in *IRC v Muller & Co Margarine Ltd* [1901] AC 217, and the definition of net adherent goodwill in *Whiteman Smith Motor Co Ltd v Chaplain* [1934] 2 KB 35. In the latter Maugham LJ stated:

> 'I shall use the phrase "net adherent goodwill" as meaning the goodwill, if any, which will remain attached to the premises not including the "site goodwill", that is irrespective of customers who would come to a new tenant starting a new business simply because of their convenient situation. In a sentence it is important not to confuse site goodwill, which is inherent with net adherent goodwill.'

The Commissioner in *Balloon Promotions*, Michael Tildesley, while accepting that 'net adherent goodwill will only pass to the purchaser of the business if the premises are sold together with the business', continued, 'however, *Whiteman Smith Motor Co* was not authority for the proposition that the value of net adherent goodwill will as a matter of course, be incorporated in the valuation of the premises sold'.

He also quoted with approval the statement in *Halsbury's Laws of England* 4th edition, Volume 35, para 1210, regarding the existence or non-existence of a non-compete covenant. *Halsbury's* suggests that if the vendor enters into such a covenant then the goodwill is sold to the purchaser.

Mr Tildesley also quoted with approval Nicolls LJ in *Kirby (Inspector of Taxes) v Thorn EMI Plc* [1988] 1 WLR 445:

> 'the covenant is the means by which, amongst other matters, the vendor, for the benefit of the purchaser, precludes himself from exploiting the reputation he has regarding the trade in question. That reputation, as already mentioned, is a form of goodwill. It is not something possessed by everyone. It has a value, even though of its nature it is not assignable. It can be protected by an action for passing off.'

The Commissioner pointed out that *Kirby* was establishing the general principle that the covenant given by the vendor amounted to a disposal of goodwill. Mr Tildesley, at para 152 stated:

> 'I am satisfied after examining the various submissions and authorities that the accountancy definition is deficient for the purpose of construing the meaning of goodwill for rollover relief under s 152 of the TCGA 1992. The definition under SSAP 22 permits the possibility that intangible assets other than goodwill which cannot be separately identified and assessed to be categorised as goodwill. The central dispute in this appeal is about whether the consideration apportioned to goodwill should instead be apportioned to another intangible asset, namely compensation for early termination of a franchise agreement. Thus goodwill should be construed in accordance with legal not accountancy principles. However, I consider the question whether the sale of the appellants' restaurants was done in accordance with sound accountancy principles will be relevant to my finding of fact about the appellants' purported sale of goodwill.'

The definition of goodwill in the Royal Institution of Chartered Surveyors' Guidance on Goodwill, as laid out in the Red Book (the *RICS Appraisal and Valuation Manual*) did not align with the legal concept of goodwill and in particular with the definitions in HMRC's capital gains tax manual. He also referred to the Land Tribunal decision of *Arbib v Earl Cadogan* [2005] RVR 401 which pointed out:

> 'Firstly however we should draw attention to the specific disclaimer of the Red Book itself which makes it inappropriate to apply it to "valuations in anticipation of evidence and pre-hearing statements in connection with legal and quasi-legal proceedings and those of tribunals, courts and committees for the settlement of property-related disputes".'

(Now restated in the 2017 edition of the *Red Book*, now entitled *RICS Global Valuation Standards*, incorporating the International Valuation Standards. It is important to make a clear distinction between a critical review of a valuation and an audit of a valuation or an independent valuation of a property, asset or liability included in another valuer's report (para 6.2).)

The Commissioner concluded:

> 'TCGA 1992 does not define the term goodwill. Goodwill in the context of TCGA 1992 must be construed in accordance with the principles established by the legal authorities on goodwill. Whether goodwill exists is a question of fact. Goodwill is a type of property. Goodwill should be looked at as a whole and includes whatever adds value to a business by reason of situation, name and reputation, connection, introduction to old customers and absence from competition. The precise composition of goodwill will vary in different trades and in different businesses in the same trade. Goodwill realises profits of the business. Goodwill cannot subsist by itself but must be attached to a business. Goodwill distinguishes an established business from a new business and is built up by years of honest work and investment in the business. Goodwill is created by trading activities. The value of goodwill will be enhanced if the business and

> the premises in which the business is carried on are sold together as a going concern. Goodwill can be sold separately from the premises in which the business is carried on.
>
> The authorities caution against an over-analytical approach to goodwill (see *IRC v Muller & Co.'s Margarine Ltd* and *Whiteman Smith Motor Co*). In view of these authorities I question the applicability of the approach adopted by the respondents in their Capital Gains Tax manual and by their counsel which categorises goodwill into three types with the third type broken into two sub-categories. The thrust of the categorisation is to restrict rollover relief to specific categories of goodwill. The categorisation is partly derived from the zoological definition of goodwill which was considered to be of limited value in *Whiteman*. I prefer the approach advocated by appellant's counsel that goodwill in TCGA 1992 shall be looked at as a whole which I consider to be consistent with the authorities and conforms with the principles of statutory construction.
>
> A covenant restricting the trade of the trader selling the goodwill is a means by which all the advantages that the purchaser was intended to have by taking over the goodwill of the business are secured to him. The existence of such a covenant is indicative that goodwill was sold by the vendor.'

The Commissioner did not accept that the parties themselves are the final arbiters of the legal construction and interpretation of their agreement. HMRC had the legal authority to reapportion the consideration on a just and reasonable basis pursuant to TCGA 1992, s 52(4). Mr Tildesley, in coming to the conclusion that what the vendor sold was goodwill, explained in para 248:

> 'My starting point is that the consideration paid for the appellants' business incorporated an amount representing the excess over and above the true and fair value of the tangible assets. The existence of that excess combined with the profitability of the businesses was indicative that businesses had added value which is an essential characteristic of the legal concept of goodwill. The added value was inseparable from the businesses which were sold as going concerns. They were established businesses not new ones. The facts found demonstrated that the appellants had made a significant contribution to the success of their businesses. They provided the start-up and working capital. They developed a reputation for the businesses at a time when the brand name of Pizza Express was not well known. They developed a customer base through the customer service they offered, the maintenance of standards by their daily presence at the restaurants and the individual designs of their restaurants. They enjoyed considerable freedom in the way they run their businesses. The appellants owned the businesses. The businesses were sold with the benefit of the leasehold interests and suitably designed and equipped properties which enhanced the added value belonging to the businesses.
>
> I conclude from the above analysis that the added value as represented by the excess consideration conforms with the salient features for the concept of goodwill as construed in TCGA 1992. The facts that the added value was attracted to the businesses and the appellants owned the businesses are persuasive that the appellants had goodwill to sell to Pizza Express. This goodwill was separate and distinct from the goodwill owned by Pizza Express in its name and associated intellectual property rights. My conclusion is given added force when the facts found in relation to the accounting treatment of the transactions are taken into account together with the requirement for the appellants to enter into restrictive covenants to protect the Pizza Express's acquisition of the added value attached to the businesses.'

The Commissioner's comments on adherent goodwill at 258 were:

> 'I accept that adherent goodwill is associated with the property and will not be passed to the purchaser if the property is not sold with the business. However where the sale of the business incorporates the interest in the property it does not automatically follow that the value of the adherent goodwill will be subsumed within the value of the property. I say this because:
>
> (1) I consider that counsel has extended too far the ratio of *Whiteman Smith Motor Co* upon which his proposition was based. *Whiteman Smith Motor Co* stated that net adherent goodwill will only arise if the property is sold with the business. *Whiteman Smith Motor Co* was not authority, however, for the proposition that the value of the net adherent goodwill in all circumstances will be subsumed within the property valuation. The value of the adherent goodwill was included in the property valuation in *Whiteman Smith Motor Co* because that was the requirement of the Landlord and Tenant Act, which is not the statute under consideration in this appeal.
> (2) The present edition of the respondent's Capital Gains Tax manual classifies adherent goodwill with separable free goodwill not with inherent goodwill which suggests that adherent goodwill will be valued separately from the property. *Butler v Evans* (1980) 53 TC 558 recognises this fact.
> (3) Counsel produced no evidence to support his proposition that Pizza Express and the appellants included adherent goodwill in their valuations of the leasehold interest transferred. The available evidence from the sales agreement suggests that the only type of goodwill not included in the vendor's goodwill was that inherent in the property.'

HMRC expert's opinion was 'that there was additional value to the business trading as Pizza Express over and above the inherent goodwill'. The Commissioner however rejected this argument:

> 'there was a more fundamental flaw in Mr Watson's argument. His reasoning would make sense if the purchaser of the appellant's restaurant business was another prospective franchisee but in this appeal the purchaser was the franchisor Pizza Express. Mr Watson has failed to explain why Pizza Express would pay more for a brand name that it already owned. Respondent's counsel pointed out in this submission that the franchise agreements did not prevent Pizza Express from opening Pizza Express restaurants next door to the appellant's premises and taking away the appellant's customers. Counsel's submission in my view undermined Mr Watson's opinion rather than supporting it. I fail to understand why Pizza Express would pay significant sums of money for a name and intellectual property rights that it already owned particularly as it could open with impunity other Pizza Express restaurants in the immediate locality of the appellant's restaurants.'

The Commissioner therefore found that the amounts in dispute received by Balloon Promotions Ltd and the other appellants was for the disposal of goodwill which qualified for rollover relief under TCGA 1992, ss 152 to 154 as a disposal of goodwill within the meaning of Class 4: TCGA 1992, s 155.

> **Focus**
>
> A leading case on the valuation of goodwill, which HMRC regards as based on unusual facts.

HMRC regards this case as being decided on the particular facts and sticks to its view that in most circumstances franchisees do not have any interest in goodwill.

Tax Bulletin no. 83, pages 1291–1293, set out HMRC's views. This stated:

> 'We accept the findings of the Special Commissioner that the question of whether a franchisee owns goodwill is principally a question of fact. Where a franchise business is disposed of as a going concern the question of whether there has been a disposal of goodwill will be determined in the light of the relevant facts. These will include a detailed consideration of the terms of the franchise agreement, the extent of control exercised by the franchisor and the terms and conditions relating to the sale. Therefore we do not consider that the decision in these appeals is of general application to other cases involving the sale of franchised businesses.
>
> Our opinion that a franchisee's rights under a franchise agreement are an asset within the meaning of TCGA 1992, s 21(1) and that they are not part of goodwill is unchanged. However we do accept that a franchisee may be able to generate some goodwill in a franchise business. The values of franchised rights and goodwill will depend on the precise facts of each individual case and in particular the level of control exercised by the franchisor.
>
> HMRC agrees with the Special Commissioner's conclusion that, for the purposes of TCGA 1992, the term "goodwill" must be construed in accordance with the principles established by the legal authorities on goodwill and that the accountancy definition is deficient for the purposes of construing its meaning in that context.
>
> In reaching his conclusions the Special Commissioner questioned the approach adopted by HMRC of restricting roll-over relief to specific categories of goodwill. He indicated that he considered that goodwill should be looked at as a whole to include whatever adds value to a business by reason of situation, name and reputation, connection, introduction to old customers and absence from competition. We do not accept that the term "goodwill" in TCGA 1992 embraces all of the various types of goodwill described in the CT manual. We will continue to treat inherent and adherent goodwill as part of an asset in the form of a freehold or leasehold interest in land or buildings.
>
> We are hoping to be in a position shortly to publish an updated version of the goodwill guidance in the CG manual.'

CG68270 'Intellectual Property Rights: franchise rights, dealerships and licences', states:

> 'The concept of a franchise or dealership is fairly simple. It enables the franchisee or dealer to start up in business with the backing of an existing organisation.
>
> **Franchises**
>
> In *Wadlow, the Law of Passing Off*, 3rd edition, 2004 at 475 franchising was described as:
>
>> "a relationship in which numerous legally independent businesses trade under a common style and to common standards as if they were branches of one large enterprise. The franchisor invariably specifies the manner in which each franchised business is to trade, often in great detail, although the day-to-day running is left to the franchisee. The element of operational control typically distinguishes franchising from simple licensing arrangements. The success of any franchise to provide goods or services of a uniform degree of quality. The public may frequently be unable to distinguish franchised

> businesses from those run as branches of a single business, and in some cases there may be a mixture of franchised outlets and branches owned and operated by the franchisor."

A franchise is essentially a contractual arrangement between two independent entities with a view to each making a profit from the synthesis of the franchisor's business format and the franchisee's business.

The franchisor will be the owner of the registered trade marks, intellectual property rights; goodwill and whatever else may be distinctive of the business and will derive income from granting rights to franchisees for the use of those assets for a period of time specified in the franchise agreement. That income may take the form of a lump sum payment on the grant of a franchise and/or a percentage of the franchisee's turnover or profits. In addition, the franchisor may provide premises, equipment, stock or raw materials in return for payments from the franchisee.

The franchisee will normally be the proprietor of the franchised business and will be responsible for the employment of staff, purchase of goods or materials, and the provision of sales and services to customers.

By virtue of the terms of the franchise agreement a franchisee will be in a position to exploit the franchisor's goodwill in the business format although he will not own an interest in it. However, it is possible that some goodwill may be generated in the franchisee's business. This follows from the decision in *Balloon Promotions Limited v Wilson*, SpC 524/06 [2006] STC (SCD) 167 in which the Special Commissioner found that the question of whether a franchisee owns goodwill is determined principally by an examination of the facts concerning the terms of the franchise arrangement and the transactions dealing with its sale. Accordingly, whether a franchisee owns goodwill is a question of fact which will need to be established in each individual case. HMRC's view is that the extent to which a franchisee is able to generate goodwill in a franchised business depends on the specific terms of the franchise agreement and the degree of control exercised by the franchisor.

The rights of a franchisee under a franchise agreement are an asset within the meaning of TCGA92/S21 (1). That asset is separate from any goodwill that may exist in the franchisee's business.

An initial payment on the grant of a franchise will usually be treated as capital expenditure on the acquisition of franchise rights in relation to the franchisee even though it may be treated as an income receipt in the hands of the franchisor, see BIM57600 onwards.

If a franchise agreement indicates that the life of the franchise will not exceed 50 years the wasting asset provisions in TCGA92/S45 – TCGA92/S46 may apply, see CG76700+.

Franchise rights are not within any of the classes of assets within TCGA 92/S155 for roll-over relief purposes.

Where a franchised business is disposed of as a going concern together with the benefit of the rights under a franchise agreement care must be taken to distinguish between the consideration attributable to the disposal of franchise rights and the consideration attributable to the disposal of goodwill. Guidance on the circumstances in which an apportionment or a re-apportionment of consideration can be made is given at CG14771.

Dealerships

A business operated under a dealership agreement may be similar in some respects to a franchised business except that the dealer is likely to have a greater degree of freedom in the operation of his business than is normally the case in a franchised business.

The rights of the dealer under a dealership agreement are an asset within the meaning of TCGA92/S21 (1). That asset is separate from any goodwill that may exist in the dealer's business.

If a dealership agreement indicates that its term will not exceed 50 years the wasting asset provisions in TCGA92/S45 – TCGA92/S46 may apply, see CG76700+.

Licences

In relation to intangible assets, a licence is normally a contract under which in return for recompense or royalty a third party is granted permission to exploit the licensor's intellectual property.

The rights of a licensee under a licensing agreement are an asset within the meaning of TCGA92/S21 (1). That asset is separate from any goodwill that may exist in the licensee's business.

An initial payment on the grant of a licence will usually be treated as capital expenditure on the acquisition of the licence.

If a licence agreement indicates that its term will not exceed 50 years the wasting asset provisions in TCGA92/S45 – TCGA92/S46 may apply, see CG76700+.

Guidance on obtaining valuations of intangible assets including the rights under a franchise, dealership, or a licence is given at CG68300+.

When sending your papers to Shares and Assets Valuation you should make it clear whether you require a valuation of goodwill in addition to a valuation of the rights under a franchise, dealership or licence or whether you require an apportionment of consideration between goodwill and the rights under a franchise, dealership or licence.'

Focus

This is the HMRC official line, which may be open to challenge.

As HMRC did not lodge an appeal in the High Court in relation to this case it should be noted that their alleged intention to continue to treat adherent goodwill as part of the freehold or leasehold interest in land appears to be in direct conflict with the Commissioner's decision that *Whiteman Smith Motor Co Ltd v Chaplin* [1934] 2 KB 35 was not authority for the proposition that the value of net adherent goodwill will as a matter of course be incorporated in the valuation of the premises sold.

Denekamp v Pearce (1998) 71 TC 213 was an appeal to the High Court from the Special Commissioner's decision relating to a valuation of unquoted shares at 31 March 1982 for capital gains tax purposes. The taxpayer was arguing that the Special Commissioner should have taken account of the company's goodwill at 31 March 1982 even though he had not put any evidence before the Commissioner relating to the existence or value of any such goodwill.

Park J refused to query the Commissioner's decision, relying on *Edwards v Bairstow* (1955) 36 TC 207.

As the company actually made a loss of £27,850 in the year to 31 March 1982 it was not necessarily of much value although the judge conceded that it could have been argued that had the company as a whole been sold as a going concern a purchaser would have been prepared to add a goodwill element to the price.

It was, however, clear on a reading of HMRC's valuation that upon the general approach on which Mr Everett substantially based his starting figure of £598,064 the valuer had not included goodwill. If the taxpayer had wished to say that the valuer should have included goodwill he could and should have put material before the Special Commissioner to that effect at that time. This case is a useful reminder that the facts of a case need to be put before the Special Commissioners in full. As the judge phrased it, 'this is not a case where new facts have emerged since the hearing before the Special Commissioner; rather it is a case where on further reflection, after that hearing, the unsuccessful party, in the present case the taxpayer, now wishes to present this case differently. He wants to seek to obtain additional evidence which if obtainable now was equally obtainable when the original hearing took place. In my judgement it would be an improper exercise of the discretion of the court to make an order to that effect.'

In *Condliffe & Hilton v Sheingold* [2007] EWCA Civ 1043 it was held that Ms Sheingold, in her capacity as a former director of Baja Ltd, was liable to account to the assignees from the purchaser from the liquidators of Baja Ltd which ran a restaurant in Truro. Ms Sheingold sold the goodwill of the restaurant which she claimed to own personally, to an arm's length purchaser for £71,837 and was ordered by the Court of Appeal to pay this sum, plus interest, to the appellants, as it belonged to Baja Ltd which ran the restaurant. Her contention that Baja Ltd merely supplied the customers with food and drink but the goodwill belonged to her personally was untenable.

In *Wildin v RCC* 20 February 2014 TC/2010/06391, the First-tier Tribunal had to value the goodwill of the senior partner of an accountancy practice, on its transfer to a limited company, for capital gains tax purposes at 31 March 1982 and 1 April 2003. Mr Wildin's valuations of these dates were £438,624 and £1,585,000 on the basis of multiples of gross recurring fees (GRF), and HMRC's were £63,638 and £740,000, on the basis of multiples of GRF less net assets, of 1 and 0.88 respectively.

At paragraph 71, the tribunal judge stated:

> 'We took from the oral evidence provided to us from Mr Wildin, Mr Smith and Mrs Hennessey and the secondary sources to which they referred that while there is a general commercial approach to valuing goodwill for standard businesses, there is a different approach which is usually applied to professional services firms. Our conclusions from this evidence, including in particular the approach of Jeremy Kitchin in the APMA website referred to, is that in practice goodwill is ascertained in a particular way for businesses. For these businesses goodwill is not "everything else which is not net assets", it is the business. To quote from the Kitchin website "In the case of professional partnerships in general, and accounting practices in particular, a different valuation convention can generally be adopted. A methodology involving a multiple of turnover is normally adopted which, in so far as it is not expressed as a multiple of profit, appears initially to be quite distinct from that used in commercial businesses…"
>
> …

74 The Tribunal has concluded that it cannot be correct that the value of a professional firm's net assets should affect its overall goodwill value. The Tribunal disagrees with HMRC's assertion that there is any necessary link between the net assets of a professional firm and the value of its goodwill. Indeed it is clear that deducting net assets to find the goodwill value can result in anomalies, particularly where freehold properties are involved or where practices have different approaches to profit retention. Taking "client book" as proxy for value of goodwill is a reasonable method of arriving at a goodwill valuation for capital gains tax purposes for professional firms. This is in our view supported by the Jeremy Kitchin APMA information and by Mr Roland's evidence about what was commonly done in practice.

75 For these reasons we have concluded that valuing goodwill on the basis of a multiple of gross recurring fees is a more accurate method of valuing professional firms including small accountancy practices like Wildin & Co and that this is the method which should be adopted for tax purposes for Wildin & Co's goodwill valuation in 1982 and 2003.

…

78 The Tribunal has taken the relatively limited evidence available from 1982 and placed reliance in particular on the information from the SAV database, as the best available independent evidence, to determine a reasonable range for the multiple to be applied to Wildin & Co's goodwill in 1982. We have assumed that while Mr Wildin's practice was successful, and so might have commanded a multiple at the top of the SAV database range; there were nevertheless some risks in his business, including the retention of some newly acquired clients. For these reasons the Tribunal has concluded that a reasonable multiple for Mr Wildin's practice in 1982 is in the range of 1.5–1.75.

…

80 Therefore we agree with Mr Wildin that the 1983 year end numbers give the best available estimate of 1982 turnover and we do not take notice that HMRC did also at one point accept this as a reasonable starting point. However on this basis we do not think that it is correct to include, as Mr Wildin attempted to persuade us, any additional work in progress for 1982. (Represented by Mr Wildin's 0.5 additional multiple). Our conclusion at this point on the calculation of the base cost of Wildin & Co's goodwill in March 1982 is that it is in the range of £147,697 × 1.5 and £147,697 × 1.75.

81 HMRC suggested that if the Tribunal concluded that the correct multiple was in a range which resulted in a range of valuations which did not include either the Taxpayer's or HMRC's suggested valuations, the Tribunal should take the mid-point of their suggested range as the most reasonable valuation to apply. On that basis we are applying a multiple of 1.625 for the purposes of the 1983 goodwill valuation.

…

85 We have concluded from the evidence provided to us in respect of 2003 that it is not clear that Mrs Hennessey's comparison with the consolidator market price and the H&L Bloom sale is necessarily an accurate way of pricing Wildin & Co and that Mr Smith's evidence concerning the wider accounting market in 2003 is to be preferred. Taking Mr Smith's suggestion of a range of 1–2 as a multiple for this period, we have concluded that 1.5 is a reasonable multiple to apply to the Wildin & Co practice. This is also in line with the information from the SAV database and the figure previously accepted by HMRC for the 2003 valuation.

86 There is one further point to clarify in coming to the 2003 valuation which is the correct turn-over for applying the multiple in 2003. Mrs Hennessey's starting point was Wildin & Co's turn over for the previous year (£1,003,828). Mr Smith took a three-year average of Wildin & Co's turn-over, giving him £1,056,540.

87 As between Mr Smith and Mrs Hennessey we have concluded that Mr Smith's approach of taking a three year average turn over provides the best approximation for the 2003 fee valuation and we have therefore concluded that a multiple of 1.5 should be applied to this £1,056,540 valuation to give a valuation of Wildin & Co's goodwill at the time of disposal in April 2003.

Conclusion:

88 For the reasons set out above the Tribunal has concluded that the base cost for capital gains tax purposes of Mr Wildin's share in the goodwill of Wildin & Co at March 1982 should be calculated by applying a multiple of 1.625 to Wildin & C's gross recurring fees as at June 1983 of £147,697, giving a base cost of £240,008.

89 The disposal value of Mr Wildin's share of the goodwill of Wildin & Co in 2003 should be valued on the same basis, applying a multiple of 1.5 to the gross recurring fees of £1,056,540 in 2003 giving a disposal value of £1,584,810 and a resulting gain of £1,344,802 chargeable to capital gains tax, of which £1,141,064 represents Mr Wildin's 84.85% share in the business, subject to any available reliefs.'

> **Focus**
>
> A useful case on the valuation of goodwill in a professional practice.

7.04 Valuation on termination of an agency

In the case of *Lonsdale (t/a Lonsdale Agencies) v Howard and Hallam Limited* [2007] UKHL 32, the House of Lords had to consider the compensation due for damage suffered on a unilateral termination of an agency agreement. Mr Lonsdale had an agency agreement with Howard and Hallam to sell their Elmdale brand of footwear in South-East England. On termination of the agreement by Howard & Hallam giving reasonable notice, Mr Lonsdale had a statutory entitlement to compensation under the Commercial Agents (Council Directive) Regulations 1993, which gave effect to a European Council Directive.

Their Lordships were asked by counsel to Mr Lonsdale to award compensation of thrice the average annual gross commission, a practice adopted by the French courts. That approach was rejected. The European Court of Justice had made it clear that the method of calculation of damages was for each member state to decide.

Lord Hoffmann (at para 11) outlined the approach to be adopted in the UK:

'11. Having thus determined that the agent is entitled to be compensated for being deprived of the benefit of the agency relationship, the next question is how that loss should be calculated. The value of the agency relationship lies in the prospect of earning commission, the agent's expectation that "proper

> performance of the agency contract" will provide him with a future income stream. It is this which must be valued.
>
> 12. Like any other exercise in valuation, this requires one to say what could reasonably have been obtained, at the date of termination, for the rights which the agency had been enjoying. For this purpose it is obviously necessary to assume that the agency would have continued and the hypothetical purchaser would have been able properly to perform the agency contract. He must be assumed to have been able to takeover the agency and (if I may be allowed the metaphor) stand in the shores of the agent, even if, as a matter of contract, the agency was not assignable or there were in practice no dealings in such agencies: compare *Inland Revenue Commissioners v Crossman* [1937] AC 26. What has to be valued is the income stream which the agency would have generated.'

The agency was in fact in terminal decline and their Lordships endorsed the compensation of £5,000 awarded by the judge at first instance on a fairly arbitrary basis.

> **Focus**
>
> Valuation in the UK depends on all the circumstances, not on arbitrary figure based on turnover.

7.05 Accounting for goodwill and intangible assets

Accounting for goodwill and intangible assets arising on an acquisition is covered in **Chapter 21**.

7.06 Asset values

Where it is appropriate to take account of the value of underlying assets in a valuation of shares, for example for a controlling interest on a break-up basis, it will normally be necessary to ascertain the open market value of each individual asset. Although an asset will normally have a positive value it must be borne in mind that where, for example, the rent due under a lease is greater than the market rent or where there are onerous covenants there could be a negative value for the asset.

The Royal Institution of Chartered Surveyors' Valuation Global Standards 2017 (known as the Red Book), in the Glossary and IVS 2017 paragraph 30.1, define 'market value' as:

> 'The estimated amount for which an asset or liability should exchange on the valuation date between a willing buyer and a willing seller in an arm's length transaction, after proper marketing and where the parties had each acted knowledgeably, prudently and without compulsion.'

Normally the valuation would be on the basis of open market value. Where the valuation is on a break-up basis, it would be necessary to consider whether an open market value would encompass the existing, extended or an alternative use of the building.

Land and buildings, in particular, may possess a value differing from their existing use value when the prospective use of the property for some other purpose is reflected, ie alternative use value. Such an alternative use value may have relevance to an overall appraisal of the assets of a company on a break-up basis.

For a business being valued on a going concern basis, where land and buildings are declared by the directors to be surplus to trading requirements they will be assessed on open market value, taking into account any possible alternative use. Similarly land and buildings held as investment or for development will also be valued on an open market basis subject to existing tenancies and this will take into account any alternative use, if appropriate.

It may also be necessary to value properties which come within the category of those rarely, if ever, sold in the open market. Their existing use value can only be arrived at using the depreciated replacement cost method. Examples of the type of properties to which this basis apply are oil refineries and chemical works where, usually, the buildings are no more than structure or cladding for highly specialised plant, power stations and dock installations where the building and site engineering works are related directly to the business of the owner and it is highly unlikely that they would have a value to anyone other than a company acquiring the undertaking, and properties located in particular geographical areas for special reasons, or of such a size, design or arrangement as would make it impossible for the valuer to arrive at a conclusion as to value from the evidence of open market transactions.

The depreciated replacement cost method of valuation requires an estimate of the open market value of the land in its existing use and an estimate of the new replacement cost of the buildings and other site works from which deductions are then made to allow for the age, condition, functional obsolescence and other factors which result in the existing property being worth less than a new replacement. It is a method of using current replacement cost to arrive at the value of the property as existing at the valuation date.

If a formal valuation is obtained, for example, of properties, the RICS Practice Statements recommend that the valuation certificate should be addressed to the directors of the company and the valuation will be dated and the purpose for which it is made identified. For example, a sale of shares or a deemed transfer on death.

The basis of valuation should be stated and defined. This will normally be an open market value. If for some special reason another basis, such as existing use, is adopted, this should be adequately explained.

The valuation certificate will then state the information with regard to the property that has been relied upon by the valuer and the assumptions he has made. It will then detail the general state of repair of the properties and make clear whether or not a structural survey or testing of service installations has been carried out. Any latent defects apparent will be noted and items of plant and machinery included in the valuation will be referred to.

The valuation will normally be before any deduction for taxes that might arise on an actual disposal such as capital gains tax and before any deduction for costs of sale. Government grants and mortgages will not normally be deducted but these would clearly have to be taken into account in finalising the business value.

If the company owns properties overseas local valuations may have to be obtained and the particulars of the conversion into sterling, including the conversion rate and date of conversion, will be stated. The valuer will normally include a non-publication clause and exclusion clause to limit his liability to third parties (see *Omega Trust Co Ltd and another v Wright Son & Pepper and another* (1997) 18 EG 120, referred to at **4.05**) and in most cases the particulars of the individual properties would be scheduled. Such a schedule will normally show the property with a description of its age and tenure, the terms of existing tenancies and the estimated current and net annual rents receivable and the capital value of the property in its existing state.

In property valuations it is normal to capitalise the current rental value of the property on a number of years' purchase of that rent in perpetuity. In the case of a let property it may be necessary to capitalise the rent under the existing lease in accordance with the terms of the lease and to capitalise the anticipated future rent under current conditions discounted to a present value.

In the case of properties in the course of development it is normal to calculate the capital value when completed and let on the basis of the estimated net annual rents when completed and let. From this would be deducted the estimated cost of completing the development in order to arrive at the capital value of the property in its existing state. In certain cases where the development has just started it may be appropriate to value on the basis of the site value plus the value of the work done to the date of valuation.

The whole subject of property valuation is highly complex and would usually require the services of a specialist. HMRC would refer cases involving property values to the District Valuer. The Valuation Office also has specialists in the valuation of mineral rights, plant and machinery etc. to whom HMRC can refer.

Although the value of underlying assets cannot normally be ignored in valuing shares in an unquoted company the cost of a specific professional valuation will, in many cases involving minority interests, not be justified and an estimate will have to be made, possibly by the directors, of the open market value of the assets so far as these can reasonably be ascertained.

Focus

The RICS Red Book 2017 guidance, VPGA 3, 'Valuation of Businesses and business interest', VPGA 4, 'Valuation of individual trade related properties', and VPGA 6, 'Valuation of intangible assets', are reproduced at **Appendix E**.

7.07 Liability for ineffective schemes

In *Brown and Others v InnovatorOne Plc and Others* [2012] EWHC 1321 (Comm) a circular funding scheme was challenged by HMRC which only allowed tax relief on the amount paid by the participant taxpayers, not on the funding, as in *Tower MCashback LLP 1 v RCC* [2011] STC 1143. The investors sued the promoters. The Innovator Schemes, as promoted, included four main features, namely: a tax incentive, gearing, a profit incentive and borrowing ability.

The schemes were structured in such a way that although the vendor of the technology would be paid a 100% price for the technology, to enable the partners to claim tax relief by way of first-year capital allowances for both income and capital gains tax purposes, 80% of the price paid would immediately be placed on deposit to secure the loan, and the vendor would be likely to receive the benefit of that element of the price if the technology was successfully exploited, relying on *MacNiven v Westmoreland Investments Ltd* [2003] 1 AC 311. The stated intention was to qualify for information and communication technology (ICT) capital allowances under CAA 2001, s 5.

Most of the schemes included a valuation of the technology rights.

The allegation that there were no real technology rights acquired by the partnerships was not upheld. The value of the technologies was challenged, the cost approach was dismissed and the discounted cash flow of the anticipated income accepted as was the premise that there was no such thing as proper due diligence in relation to start up technologies. It was a pre-revenue investment, ie a 'high risk punt on a very risky investment'. However, the judge found that 'the technology rights were of real value, that that value was more than minimal and that it did bear relation to the acquisition costs under the Acquisition Agreements … The fact that none of the technologies ultimately succeeded did not mean that genuine efforts were not made to exploit them.'

In his 183-page judgment, Mr Justice Hamblen largely rejected on the evidence the 'core' allegations of conspiracy fraud and associated dishonesty. He also pointed out that:

> 'Further, the Schemes were put together in accordance with a structure which was extensively and expensively advised upon by leading counsel, Mr Bretten QC. That structure was not substantially criticised. Indeed it was similar to that in the Tower MCashback schemes about which no allegations of fraud, conspiracy or dishonesty were apparently made. The essential criticism made by the IR (Inland Revenue) of the Schemes related to their implementation rather than their structure, and in particular the failure to establish sufficient trade within the relevant tax year.
>
> Even if, however, there had been no implementation issues the likelihood is that the Schemes would have faced the same challenge from Mr Frost of the IR as the Tower MCashback schemes, and with the same result – ie tax relief on the partners' cash contributions only.
>
> Although the Claimants were understandably aggrieved to lose their cash contributions and receive back only limited tax relief, there are obvious risks in going into aggressive tax schemes which offer the prospect of almost immediately doubling your money.
>
> In fact, the greatest risk to the Claimants was not losing their cash contribution, but being exposed to repayment of the 80% loan. This had to be a real liability for the tax relief to be claimable, as was reasonably apparent from the IMs (Information Memoranda) and is the logic of a geared investment. However, few Claimants appreciated the reality of the liability and the consequent risk. In the event that risk did not materialise in respect of virtually all Schemes since a hive down to a limited company was achieved, as was anticipated but never assumed. In relation to those Schemes, such as Charit, where no hive down was achieved, the consequence of the contraventions of FSMA may well be that there is no liability. If so, then, ironically, the relevant Claimants will in one sense have benefitted from the FSMA contraventions about which so much complaint was made.

> Whilst the Claimants will no doubt be generally disappointed at the outcome of the litigation, they can be solaced in the fact that a very possible outcome of entering into these highly geared tax Schemes would have been a liability for four times their capital contribution, and that has been avoided. Further, the tax relief obtained (or, in the case of Arte, offered) was probably no more than would have ultimately been achieved, however well these Schemes had been implemented.'

Anthony Bayliss v HMRC [2016] UKFTT 500 (TC) (see **4.07**) was an appeal against penalties under TMA 1970, s 95(1)(a) in respect of incorrect self-assessment returns made in respect of an alleged capital loss which related to a 'pendulum long' scheme.

The scheme involved the purchase of a contract for difference (CFD) from a Seychelles company, Pendulum Investment Corporation, which was linked to the FTSE 100 index after 3, 5, 7 or 10 years at predetermined levels. The initial cost was £51,000 plus the margin balance of £799,000 which was an 80-year interest free loan. Fees were payable at 30% increasing to 75% after 7 years. Pendulum made a written offer to repurchase 65% of the CFD for £11,000. This allegedly gave rise to the claimed loss of £539,000. HMRC disputed this and claimed that the taxpayer had acted fraudulently or negligently, which the tribunal rejected. HMRC had accepted that the scheme failed as the loss was disallowed under TCGA 1992, s 16A, as a capital loss connected with arrangements with a main purpose of securing a tax advantage. It was also caught by TCGA 1992, s 38 as the taxpayer did not in fact incur expenditure of £850,000 as claimed and the arrangements were a sham within the decisions in *Snook v West Riding Investments Limited* [1967] 2 QB 786, *Hitch v Stone* [2001] STC 214 and *Hamilton v Hamilton* [2016] EWHC 1132.

HMRC had to show that Mr Bayliss had acted fraudulently or negligently as in *Derry v Peak* (1889) LR 14 App Cas 337, *King v Walden* 74 TC 45 and *HMRC v Khawaja* [2008] EWHC 1687 (Ch).

The appellant's counsel suggested that the focus should be on dishonesty following *Stuttard and another (trading as de Wynns Coffee House) v Customs and Excise Commissioners* [2000] STC 342, *Royal Brunei Airlines Sdn Bhd v Ton* [1995] 2 AC 378, *Barlow Clowes International Limited v Eurotrust International Limited* [2006] 1 WLR 1476, *Abou-Romah v Abacha* [2006] EWCA Civ 1492 and *Bintu Binette Krubally N'diaye v HMRC* [2015] UKFTT 380 (TC).

HMRC, alleging negligence, relied on *Blythe v Birmingham Waterworks Co* (1856) 20 JP 247, *Anderson v HMRC* [2009] UKFTT 258 (TC), *Colin Moore v HMRC* [2011] UKUT 239 (TCC), *Litman & Newall v HMRC* [2014] UKFTT 089 (TC). Mr Bayliss's counsel referred to *Barker v Baxendale Walker* [2016] EWHC 664 (Ch), *Gedir v HMRC* [2016] UKFTT 188 (TC) and *Hanson v HMRC* [2012] UKFTT 314 (TC).

In *Ingenious Games LLP (IG), Inside Track Productions LLP (ITP), Ingenious Film Partners LLP (IFP2)* [2016] UKFTT 521 (TC) (see **5.17**), the LLPs were engaging in the making of films and video games and the question was whether this was trading with a view to profits; what amount was incurred on the acquisition of rights in respect of films and gains, and what amount was incurred wholly and exclusively for the purpose of any trade and whether profits had been computed in accordance with Generally Accepted Accounting Practice (GAAP) under ITTOIA 2005, s 33 etc.

These companies were appealing against a closure notice issued by HMRC denying claims for trading losses. £100 million or so had been spent on these activities which resulted in trading losses in the early years which could, in appropriate cases, be set against taxable income. The losses claimed were £1,620 million and the tax reclaimed by the investors amounted to £620 million. The amount of tax, interest and penalties at stake was some £1 billion.

The questions were whether the LLPs were carrying on a trade with a view to profit and did they earn expenditure equal to 100% of the budget of the film or gain, and was it wholly and exclusively for the purpose of their trade and were the losses correctly computed in accordance with GAAP. The LLPs were involved in 65 films, 64 of which were distributed in cinemas and had a high profile and received critical acclaim, for example 'Avatar'.

The FTT held that ITP and IFP2 were carrying on a trade but IG was not. They were carrying on a trade on the 30:30 basis, with a view to profit. However, they incurred expenditure with a view to profit as to 35% of the budgeted profit for ITP and IFP2, but 30% for IG. On this basis the expenditure was incurred for the purposes of the trade except for 5% of the budget which was incurred to provide the executive producer's fee.

The profits were not computed in accordance with GAAP, only the 30/35% was. The appeal of IG was dismissed and the appeals of the other two parties were adjourned for the parties to agree the computations.

Ingenious Games LLP, Inside Track Productions and Ingenious Film Partners 2 LLP (Capital or Revenue) v HMRC [2017] UKFTT 429 (TC) is a supplementary decision following [2016] UKFTT 521 (TC) arising from a dispute as to whether or not provisions for the impairment of rights under the relevant agreements were regarded as property deductible for GAAP purposes as impairment for the rights under the relevant agreements under ITTOIA 2005, s 33 or ICTA 1988, s 74(1).

The findings of fact concluded that the LLPs acquired an asset which was the right to payment of a portion of the proceeds of distribution of a film and for use on a continuing basis in the business and so were not current assets for those purposes. In substance the rights were not stock and should be treated as fixed intangible assets and should be accounted for at cost less any impairment (or onerous contract provisions).

HMRC argued, on the basis of *British Insulated and Helsby Cables Limited v Atherton* [1926] AC 205, that expenditure made 'not only once and for all but with a view of bringing into existence an asset or advantage for the enduring benefit of a trade is likely to be capital'.

R (on the application of Vital Nut Co Limited and another) v HMRC [2016] EWHC 1797 (Admin), [2017] EWCA Civ 2105, *Rowe and others v HMRC* [2015] EWHC 2293 (Admin), [2017] EWCA Civ 2105 and *Walapu v HMRC* [2016] EWHC 658 (Admin), [2017] EWCA Civ 2105 are three judicial review cases claiming that Advance Payment Notices (APNs) requiring money to be paid to HMRC are ultra vires, as Employer Financed Retirement Benefit Schemes (EFURBS) rules apply. The claims have been dismissed by the High Court and the Court of Appeal.

Broomfield and others v HMRC [2018] EWHC 1966 (Admin), as a lead case for 342 claimants, was won by HMRC, as was *Huitson v HMRC* [2015] UKFTT 448 (TC), and *R (Locke) v HMRC* [2018] EWHC 1967

(Admin) which was deemed similar to *Eclipse Film Partners No 35 LLP v HMRC* [2015] EWCA Civ 95.

In *John Hardy and Richard Moxon v HMRC* [2017] UKFTT 754 (TC), the appellants were shareholders in companies investing in a general partnership, Vanguard, with the assistance of limited recourse loans which were used to acquire films from producers under distribution sale and purchase arrangements which included put options, held by Vanguard, and call options held by the producers.

A film valuer predicted the income likely to be generated, shortly after release of the films, which served as a basis for the exercise of options, linked to the film budget and actual performance over time. Vanguard was held not to be carrying on a trade under TA 2007, s 137 and there was not a loss for capital gains tax purposes.

Focus

From a valuation point of view the case confirms that the only way to value untried innovation is the present value of the likely future earnings if it is moderately successful, but that it is a 'high risk punt on a very risky investment.'

7.08 Trade-related properties

The Royal Institution of Chartered Surveyors (RICS) Valuation Global Standards 'Red Book' of July 2017, which incorporates the International Valuation Standards, states that 'trade related' is 'any type of real property designed for a specific type of business where the property value reflects the trading potential for that business'.

The relevant RICS Valuation Practice Guidance Application is VPGA 4 (see **Appendix E**). Such properties have been designed and adapted for a specific purpose and because of this the value of the real properties is 'intrinsically linked to the returns that an owner can generate from that use. The value therefore reflects the trading potential of the properties'. This is contrasted with other business properties, which can be used for various businesses such as shops, industrial premises or offices.

The starting point is therefore the actual profits which have been achieved by the vendor, assuming they can be relied on, adjusted for the fact that they reflect the vendor's past results and need to be adjusted for the efficiency, or lack of it, of the vendor and the future potential for improving the business, if any.

There may be occasions where the personality or exceptional skills of the vendor may result in a level of profits, which a purchaser would have difficulty in matching or a potential for increased business which the vendor has not aspired to. Even trade-related properties may have alternative uses, which, if more profitable, should be taken into account.

The RICS recommend the use of the adjusted net profit shown in the accounts, adjusted for abnormal and non-recurring expenditure, finance costs and depreciation related to the property itself and rent where appropriate, in order to arrive at a fair maintainable operating profit (FMOP) relating to the building, which may be different from the earnings before interest, taxes, depreciation and amortisation (EBITDA). What is sought is the FMOP relating to the property that a reasonably efficient operator (REO) would expect to derive from the fair maintainable turnover (FMT). The FMOP should include a proportionate proportion of periodic expenditure such as decoration, refurbishment and replenishments of fixtures, fittings and equipment (VPGA 4, paragraphs 2.2 to 2.5). Paragraphs 2.6 to 2.8 define market rents, market value and operational entity.

The personal goodwill of the current operator is 'the value of the profit generated over and above market expectations that would be extinguished upon the sale of the trade related property, together with financial factors related specifically to the current operation of the business, such as taxation, depreciation policy, borrowing costs and the capital invested in the business … based on the trading potential rather than adopting the actual level of trade under the existing ownership, and it excludes personal goodwill'.

Reasonably efficient operator (REO), tenants' capital, trade-related property and trading potential are defined by VPGA 4, paragraphs 2.10 to 2.13.

The profits method of valuation under VPGA 4, section 3 requires an estimate of the FMT which could be generated by an REO from which an assessment is made of the potential gross profit from which, would be deducted, the costs and allowances which would be expected of the REO to arrive at the FMOP which is capitalised at an appropriate rate of return reflecting the risk and rewards of the property and its trading potential, in the light of relevant comparable market transactions.

> 'It is essential that the valuer review the cumulative results of the different steps in the valuation process. The valuation should be considered having regard to the valuer's general experience and knowledge of the market.'

(VPGA 4, paragraph 3.4.)

VPGA 4 paragraph 5.1 confirms that 'the valuation of a trade-related property as a fully equipped operational entity necessarily assumes that the transaction will be either the letting or the sale of the property, together with the trade inventory, licences etc, and required to continue trading'. VPGA 4, sections 6 to 9 deal with assessing the trading potential, the valuation approach for a non-trading property apportionment and valuation for investment purposes. Paragraph 8.4 recognises that 'apportionments for tax purposes have to be in accordance with specific legislation and are outside the scope' of VPGA 4.

7.09 Goodwill in trade-related properties

In September 2013, HMRC published a note entitled 'Goodwill in trade-related properties', as follows:

> **'Introduction**
>
> Further to the decision in the *Balloon Promotions* case SpC524 ((2006) SSCD 167) (see Tax Bulletin 83) we have met with disagreements in relation to how sums paid in transactions involving businesses carried out from "trade related properties" (e.g. public houses, hotels, petrol filling stations, cinemas, restaurants, care homes etc.) should be allocated between what have

previously been labelled as different categories of "goodwill" (e.g. free, adherent and inherent). The main areas of disagreement relate to Capital Gains Tax and Stamp Duty Land Tax (SDLT) where we accept that the term "goodwill" must be construed in accordance with the principles established by legal authorities. The current situation is that there is a backlog of unresolved interventions.

Revised approach by HM Revenue & Customs (HMRC) for Capital Gains Tax and SDLT

The differing views held in this area prompted a review of our approach to the identification and valuation of goodwill in "trade related properties". In the past we have taken the view that it was unlikely that there would be 'free goodwill' of any significant value in businesses carried out from such properties.

We have now concluded that:

The subdivision of goodwill into different categories such as "inherent goodwill", "adherent goodwill" and "free goodwill" is not helpful as this tends to cause confusion. What used to be called "inherent" and "adherent" goodwill are, in reality, attributes that add value to the property in which a business is carried out and they do not represent goodwill at all. To make this distinction clear in our communications we will now only use the term 'goodwill' and when referring to attributes of the value of a property we will describe these as such.

If a business carried out from a trade related property is sold as a going concern then the sale price is likely to include some goodwill but the sum attributable to goodwill will depend on the facts of each case.

For Capital Gains Tax and SDLT purposes the value of goodwill and any other separately identifiable intangible assets will usually be represented by the difference between the value of the business as a going concern and the value of the tangible assets (the property, fixtures, fittings, chattels etc.).

We have prepared a background note that explains the issues in more detail and a practice note that sets out how we and the Valuation Office Agency (VOA) consider one should go about allocating the price paid for a business as a going concern between goodwill and other assets included in the sale.

HMRC approach for Schedule 29 Finance Act 2002

For Schedule 29 FA 2002 (CTA 2009 part 8 ss711–906) the accountancy definition of goodwill rather than that drawn from interpreting legal authorities is applicable. Our approach in this area is outlined in the Corporate Intangibles Research and Development Manual (CIRD25030). We are seeing some transactions where the appropriate accounting based approach has not been adopted and are making the necessary interventions.

Roll-out to address the backlog of Capital Gains Tax and SDLT interventions

We appreciate that there has been a delay in making progress in these interventions whilst we carried out the review mentioned above. However, we believe that this update provides the necessary clarity on the HMRC position and we now intend to start addressing the backlog by contacting the agents involved. We will be referring to the views outlined in the update to inform our view on how best to make progress on a case by case basis.'

HMRC also published at the same time a background note, as follows:

'Goodwill in Trade Related Properties Background Note

In the past HM Revenue & Customs (HMRC) have taken the view that it was unlikely that there would be 'free goodwill' of any significant value in businesses carried out from trade related properties (for example public houses, hotels, petrol filling stations, cinemas, restaurants, care homes etc.) because the occupation and use of the particular, specially adapted, premises was usually essential and integral to the generation of the business income.

However, it is now acknowledged that when a business is sold as a going concern the sale price will reflect the combined value of the tangible assets together with the benefit of other business assets such as any contracts with customers, staff and suppliers, records of previous customers etc. Substantial value can be realised by combining the tangible and other business assets together for sale as a going concern but this enhanced value may be reduced if the assets are split and sold separately.

In the unusual event of this type of business being transferred without some form of property interest, it would be highly likely that the value otherwise achieved, would be substantially diminished or removed. This is why such businesses are rarely, if ever, transferred without any form of property rights.

It remains important to recognise this distinction from most other businesses where there is no such reliance on a specific property interest and business goodwill can be readily sold and will be of value irrespective of the actual premises. Recently published articles in the professional press do not fully address this important distinction and appear to misinterpret some fundamental valuation issues.

There are a host of real and practical reasons why the assets in such premises cannot be actually separated without depreciating their combined value but HMRC now accept that for taxation purposes HMRC need to recognise the contribution that each asset makes to the combined value.

The attached Practice Note explains the issues in more detail and sets out how HMRC and the Valuation Office Agency (VOA) consider one should go about apportioning the price paid for a business as a going concern between goodwill and other assets included in the sale. The Practice Note reflects the VOA view that the appropriate method of valuing this type of property is by reference to the profit making potential of the premises. The VOA have discussed this valuation approach with the Royal Institution of Chartered Surveyors.'

Statement of Practice 5 of 1992 (SP 5/92) provides as follows:

'**(a) TCGA1992 Sch 5 para 9(3): transactions entered into at arm's length**

12. The condition in Sch 5 para 9(3) is not met where the property or income is provided to the trust under a transaction entered into at arm's length – see para 9(3)(a). This applies irrespective of whether the parties to the transaction are connected persons under TCGA 1992 s 286. Each case depends on its own facts and circumstances but a transaction is, in general, regarded as being at arm's length where all the facts and circumstances of the transaction are such as might have been expected if the parties to the transaction had been independent persons dealing at arm's length i.e. dealing with each other in a normal commercial manner unaffected by any special relationship between them.

13. Solely for the purposes of TCGA 1992 Sch 5 para 9(3)(a), a provision in the document governing the transaction for an appropriate adjustment to the consideration where the value agreed by HMRC differs from the original consideration arrived at by an independent valuer and specified in the sale document is, in general, regarded as falling within the terms of the above definition of an arm's length transaction. The arm's length value of the transaction is to be determined in accordance with the principles set out in para 12 above.

This will usually correspond to the value for capital gains tax purposes except, for example, where TCGA 1992 s 19 would apply.

14. It would also be necessary for the terms of the contract to provide for compensating interest at a commercial rate to be paid in either direction once the arm's length value is determined. For this purpose, the official rate of interest for Taxes Act 1988 s 160 purposes will usually be regarded as equivalent if the circumstances of a particular case warrant this treatment.

15. This practice is, however, subject to the consideration passing on sale being realistically based, ie on a third party valuation by a qualified valuer, all the other terms of the transaction being at arm's length and the compensating interest being timeously paid. The position in a particular case depends on all the facts and circumstances.'

7.10 HMRC guidance

HMRC published a 23-page revised Practice Note on 30 September 2013 from the Valuation Office Agency website, entitled 'Apportioning the Price Paid for a Business Transferred as a Going Concern', and HMRC's summary of the Basis of Valuation for Tax Purposes, in relation to various assets. It is available at www.hmrc.gov.uk/svd/goodwill-overview.htm.

The Background states:

'1.1 An apportionment of the price paid for a business as a going concern between the underlying assets may be required for tax purposes in a number of instances, for example:

- a. For the purpose of calculating the capital gains arising on the disposal of the separate assets in accordance with the TCGA 1992.
- b. On an acquisition for the purpose of calculating the SDLT (Stamp Duty Land Tax) due on the interest in the land and buildings only.
- c. On an acquisition for the purpose of calculating the allowances available against Corporation Tax for Capital Allowances, such as Machinery and Plant Allowances (see Section 3), or for purchased goodwill (Schedule 29, FA 2002).

1.2 The price paid for a business sold as a going concern may include any or all of the following assets:

- a. The land and buildings including landlord's fixtures ('the property').
- b. The trade fixtures, fittings, furniture, furnishings and equipment ('the chattels').
- c. Any transferable licences.
- d. Goodwill.
- e. Other separately identifiable intangible assets (eg registered trade marks).

The purchaser may also separately acquire consumables and stock but these are usually valued separately and will not normally be included in the sale price to be apportioned.

1.3 Some of the principles set out in this Practice Note are applicable to apportionments for all types of businesses but the note deals mainly with the particular issues that have arisen where the property is a 'trade related property' valued using a profits approach (eg public houses, hotels, petrol filling stations, cinemas, restaurants, care homes etc). In these cases there can be particular difficulties in identifying the sum attributable to 'goodwill' and this is fundamental to the apportionment.'

7.11 Property companies

Property companies can be conveniently divided into three main types: the property holding or investment company, a property development company and a property dealing company.

There are of course a number of different types of property involved in property companies. Obviously sub-divisions are offices, warehouses and factories, shops, residential property and specialised properties such as hotels, ice rinks, cinemas etc. Agricultural property is considered separately below at **7.12**.

Commercial property tends to be valued by reference to its income earning capacity and not merely the current rental but the anticipated future rental following the next rent review under the lease where the property is let. The value of the underlying property is also affected by matters such as hope value for alternative and more profitable use and the stability and creditworthiness of the tenant or other potential market tenants. The anticipated future rental can also be affected by likely developments in the area, particularly in the case of shops where the position is of paramount importance and road changes or the development of a new shopping precinct or out of town hypermarket could have an effect on the value of the property.

In the case of residential property, likely legislative changes can also have a marked effect on the value of property as rents tend to be closely controlled, as are the standards of repair and maintenance required which can lead to a highly artificial market.

Earlier versions of HM Revenue & Customs' Shares Valuation Manual at SVM18030 suggested that the appropriate approach to be taken in any particular valuation of shares in a property company will depend upon a variety of factors. Their preferred approach is nevertheless to base the value of such shares on net asset backing, less a discount to reflect the size of the holding. The Manual suggests that the following discounts could be appropriate, after deducting an allowance for contingent tax:

Size of holding	**Discount**
75% or more	0% to 5%
50%+ to 74.9%	10% to 15%
50%	20%
25%+ to 49.9%	25% to 40%

No particular level of discount is suggested for holdings of 25% or less, which are described as the most difficult to value. Experience suggests nevertheless that HM Revenue and Customs' Shares and Assets Valuation section would be likely to suggest discounts in the range of 50% to 70%.

In the case of *MacArthur (executors of) v HM Revenue & Customs* (2008) SpC 700, the Commissioner accepted the following discounts in respect of various holdings in companies that invested in a mixture of property and quoted stocks and shares.

Size of holding	Discount
8.16%	65%
26.8%	45%
51.1% and 69.9%	12.5%

In general, Shares and Assets Valuation try to discourage any deduction for contingent liability to tax on increases in value of investment properties, unless it can be shown that there is a history of regular property disposals. The Manual gives no guidelines but HMRC will nevertheless usually agree to a deduction of between 10% and 30% of the inherent tax liability.

Most public property companies revalue their properties on a regular basis, often yearly, and pay out a large percentage of the earnings by way of a dividend. It is, therefore, relatively easy to compare the results of one company with another by expressing a value based on the quotation as a percentage discount from the net assets value.

In fact the purchaser of shares in a private property company is no different from the purchaser of shares in any other unquoted company. He or she has to consider the likelihood of a capital profit and the ease or otherwise of disposing of his shareholding in due course and the income he is likely to obtain on his investment in the meantime. The valuation of a shareholding in a property company therefore depends, in the same way as for any other company, on the likely future earnings of the company and the amount of those earnings which are likely to come the way of the potential shareholder. The valuation should therefore take account of the earnings potential, the asset cover and the likely dividend stream in the same way as for any other company. There is, of course, in a property company a very close relationship between the future earnings and the asset value, since, as has already been explained, properties are themselves valued by reference to the anticipated future earnings.

Most quoted property companies distribute a very high proportion of their earnings each year and it is by no means uncommon for unquoted property companies to do likewise. Other things being equal, the value of a minority interest in a company paying dividends is likely to be greater than one that is accumulating its earnings, as the investor is getting an immediate return on his shareholding.

As with any other unquoted company, it is necessary for valuation purposes to consider the level of likely future earnings. In the case of a property investment company, it may be a reasonably straightforward exercise to compute the likely level of earnings for the next few years with rather more certainty than in the case of most trading companies.

In the case of a property development company, the situation for each individual company can vary considerably between a company with a single development that may even have been acquired on a speculative basis without planning permission but merely hope value, to the well-established building and contracting group which maintains a bank of land with planning permission and develops this on a regular and orderly basis. The value of the land bank could be an important element in the value of the company's assets which in turn could be an important element in the valuation. A dealing company will normally buy and sell land or buildings in the same state or possibly merely upgrade the planning permission and on-sell the property without becoming involved in the physical development. The value of the land held in stock is obviously a very important element in anticipating the future earnings of the company and is therefore an important element in the valuation.

An aspect which has considerable significance in the valuation of any property company is the element of gearing which the company has, that is the proportion of borrowings to market value, with the interest charged on borrowings also being a relevant factor. If the company has long-term finance and the interest is covered by the rental income received, it is obviously in a much stronger financial position than a company that is much more heavily extended and perhaps is in a marginal or even negative cash position in the short term. If such a company is also financed on short-term borrowings it could be very vulnerable to an adverse change in the level of interest, which in turn could force the sale of part of the company's property assets, perhaps at the very time when the market is itself unduly depressed. This form of liquidity squeeze has happened on various occasions to several property companies and will no doubt happen to many more. Yet another element of considerable vulnerability with property is the level of political interference. This may have a direct bearing on the value of the company's property with major developments in the area such as the high speed rail link to the HS2, new airport development or a new roadway. Where land has been acquired speculatively, such a change may increase considerably or reduce or eliminate the hope of planning permission just as changes to legislation could have a major impact on the value of a company's residential property. Indirect effects would be felt through changes in the taxation system and in recent years there have been special provisions relating to property in the form of betterment levy, the taxation of development gains and development land tax, all of which have been introduced and subsequently abolished, but the possibility of their reintroduction or replacement by something similar or worse has to be borne in mind as it would have a major impact on the value of the shares in a property company.

Focus

The policy for the distribution of profits, the gearing and costs of borrowing can have a material effect on the value of property companies, particularly for minority shareholders.

7.12 Farming companies

A farming company is very often closely controlled within a particular family and the company is very often the beneficiary of a favourable lease from members of the family who own the freehold of the farmland which is let to the farming company on an agricultural tenancy. It is of course possible for a farming company to own the freehold of the land it farms although this is relatively unusual. The market value of farmland tends to increase markedly in times of high inflation and can level off or fall in times of relative stability, but in recent years has always remained at a figure well above that at which it is possible to earn a reasonable return on capital by farming the land. Even an efficient farmer is likely to have difficulty in obtaining a return of more than 1% or 2% on the capital value of his farm.

High capital values apply to farmland itself and the value does depend on the quality of the land, although it would also be affected by any hope value for possible development or if it had any mineral bearing capacity. The high relative value of agricultural land is also reflected in the high value of an agricultural tenancy on that land compared with its earning capacity. This in turn can give rise to problems in valuing shares in a farming company. It would be most unusual in a family farming company to sell shares other than within the family or to employees and therefore an arm's length open market sale of a minority interest is very rarely met with. HM Revenue and Customs' Shares and Assets Valuation section may well approach the valuation on the basis of a discount from the asset basis of the value of the company as a whole, valuing the land whether tenanted or freehold on the basis of the District Valuer's open market value. It is suggested that this basis is likely to prove unrealistic in many cases because the actual rights of a minority shareholder are insufficient to ensure that he could expect a reasonable return on an investment based on a discounted asset value over a reasonable period unless there was a likelihood of the farm being sold and not replaced. It is again important to consider all the factors of valuation including income and dividends and not just the asset value.

In *IRC v Gray (Executor of Lady Fox)* [1994] STC 360, the court had to consider for inheritance tax purposes the freehold value of agricultural land in the estate of the deceased, where the land was subject to a tenancy in favour of a partnership in which the deceased had a 92.5% interest. It was decided that the deceased's interests in the partnership and the land should be treated as a composite asset and the land in effect valued with the benefit of vacant possession. This decision raises the question of the proper treatment of agricultural land owned by a deceased's estate, which also owns shares in a company which is the tenant of the land. In the authors' view the value of shares in the farming company should be based on the level of earnings, dividends and assets applicable to the shareholding under consideration and the ownership of the freehold reversion is irrelevant unless there is power to liquidate the company and realise a marriage value.

The case of *Walton v IRC* [1996] 1 EGLR 159 emphasised that when considering the value of an interest in a farming partnership which holds an agricultural tenancy the attitude of the actual landlord to a purchase of the tenancy should be taken into account. It cannot be assumed that the landlord is a hypothetical person who would be a special purchaser of the tenancy. The same would apply to a tenancy held by a company.

Focus

Farming companies often seem to be assets-rich and profit-poor.

7.13 Works of art, etc

It is not unusual for books, fine art and other chattels to be held in a company, often an overseas company, held by an offshore trust where the asset is enjoyed by a beneficiary in the UK. HMRC has a Chattels Valuation Fiscal Forum, which meets annually, and the recent minutes are published on the Revenue website (see **1.40**). Where it is necessary to consider the capital value of an asset, the minutes of 1 December 2010 confirm that HMRC, Christie's and Sotheby's subscribe to Art Market Research and other dealers have occasional access; 'views were expressed that AMR trends are sometimes questionable', but 'no-one present knew of any other databases that recorded trends in such specific categories and over such a long period as AMR'. HMRC confirmed that the valuation should take all possible factors and possible sale avenues into account. The weight given to any particular avenue would depend on the exact circumstances of each case. Where pictures or other works of art or chattels are enjoyed by a person other than the owner, HMRC confirmed, in the minutes of 7 December 2009, that 'a case very nearly came to the Commissioner's in 2009. A taxpayer was arguing that purely nominal rate represented market rent for very valuable paintings and HMRC had been challenging that … much information was uncovered in preparing for the hearing but, until further notice, HMRC's policy remains essentially the same as that set out at the Chattels Valuation Fiscal Forum of 22 November 2006'. Every case will be treated on its own merits, 'but if there is no meaningful rental market and the other advice set out in the minutes to the 2006 Forum is adhered to, then a rate of 1% is likely to be acceptable'. (This has been increased to the official rate of interest in FA 1989, s 178 under TCGA 1992, s 97A, introduced by F(No 2)A 2017, Sch 9, para 1, currently 2.5% for 2017–18.) The minutes referred to were those of 22 November 2006, where Mike Fowler of HMRC said:

> 'if a meaningful rental market exists there is not usually a problem as all concerned will be guided by the prices achieved in that market. The issue becomes problematical when the assets in question are items, such as, country house chattels or valuable works of art, where there may be no meaningful rental markets. In these cases, HMRC advice has been that the rental rate is unlikely to be challenged, if the taxpayer can demonstrate that it resulted from:
>
> > "A bargain negotiated at arms-length;
> > By parties who were independently advised;
> > Which follows the normal commercial criteria in force at the time it was negotiated."
>
> The facts of individual cases will vary, but against this background, HMRC experience is that an accepted norm of 1% of capital value had arisen but is now displaced by TCGA 1992, s 97A, as explained above. The 1% rate had no robust basis, but was regularly accepted by HMRC, on a without prejudice basis, as an informal way of resolving a difficult issue.'

Mike Fowler advised that some practitioners had argued 'that purely nominal rates are appropriate in respect of particularly important chattels'. He made it clear that, much as every case will be treated on its own merits, HMRC have no sympathy with this line of argument and taxpayers who apply purely nominal rental rates could have expected them to be vigorously challenged.

Edward Manisty, of Christie's, asked if the figure of 1% included costs such as insurance. Mike Fowler said that it didn't. Manisty said that this conflicted with his experience of the 1% dispensation, whereby if the user agreement provided that the donor/lessee was responsible for the insurance, security etc, then those costs were deducted from the 1%.

Dave Goulsbra, of HMRC, said that he had dealt with these issues for HMRC for many years. Arrangements varied, but in his experience, the norm was for 1% per annum of the capital value to be paid to the owner and the costs of ownership to be dealt with separately.

Edward Manisty took issue with the statement that HMRC can be expected to vigorously challenge nominal rent and rates for extremely valuable pieces. He felt that it was obvious that no one would ever pay a rate as high as 1% to rent a piece worth many millions of pounds. Mike Fowler acknowledged the difficulties facing valuers when there is no market, but said that he could do no more than state that HMRC did not accept purely nominal rates were appropriate and warn practitioners that taxpayers who apply them can expect a vigorous challenge. Edward Manisty asked that it be minuted that he strongly disagreed with this approach.

The RICS advice on the valuation of personal property including art and antiques are in VPGA 7, which points out at 3.2 that 'an asset may have a different value at the wholesale level of trade, the retail level of trade or where the trading is by auction'. It recognises at 3.3 that 'online auctions and other forms of e-transactions can open up the market for some types of property to potential buyers', otherwise they may well deter purchasers bids based on constraints of location or time, and that 'collections, if divided, may be worth significantly more or less per item than when held collectively'. However, 'the degree of reliability of previous sales data may be limited'.

The sales comparison approach involves 'comparing sales information of the subject with identical or similar assets for which sales data if available'. The case approval 'provides an indication of value based on the estimated current costs to reproduce or create a property of equal quality utilities and marketability'. The income approval 'provides an indication of value by calculating the monetary benefits (such as a stream of income) for the subject asset'.

In *HMRC v Executors of Lord Howard of Henderskelfe (deceased)* [2014] All ER (D) 166, [2014] EWCA Civ 278, [2014] SWTI 1560, it was held that a painting by Sir Joshua Reynolds sold for £9.4m was plant, and a wasting asset under TCGA 1992, s 44(1)(c) and therefore free of capital gains tax under s 45 which was upheld by the Supreme Court. However, the law was changed by the insertion of TCGA 1992, s 45(3B) by FA 2015, s 40.

Focus

The ownership or sale of works of art can have some unexpected tax consequences.

7.14 Investments

It will be appreciated that if a company includes among its assets shares in another company it may be necessary to value the interest of the company in that other company. If it is a wholly owned subsidiary the full assets and profits can be taken into account. If there is a non-controlling interest owned by a third party the full value, less that applicable to the non-controlling interest, may be included without discount. If, however, it is a minority interest in an unquoted company it will be necessary in the first instance to value the shares in that company reflecting a discount for lack of control in order to arrive at the asset value of the company holding the shares. It would not be appropriate to take into account a pro rata proportion of the investee company's assets (see *Short v Treasury Comrs* [1948] 1 KB 116), but to value the shares in the investee company on the basis of the earnings, dividends, assets and previous sales in the same way as for the investor company.

> **Focus**
>
> The normal arm's length approach to valuations, reflecting a controlling or non-controlling stake, as appropriate, should apply.

7.15 Asset-rich trading companies

Circumstances sometimes arise where the property assets of a company carrying on a trade as a going concern have achieved a separate value in excess of the value of the trade. This often occurs where a company rents out premises or a part of premises formerly used for its trade, whilst continuing its trade elsewhere.

In the case of *Re Charrington* (1975, unreported), Pickering J, in the Hong Kong Supreme Court (Appellate Jurisdiction: Full Court) made the following comment:

> 'Few companies are precisely alike and in the present case, whilst the company was unquestionably a trading company, its assets in the form of real estate were disproportionate to the relatively meagre results of its trading and it would have been unrealistic, despite the wish of the shareholders at the time of Harry Charrington's death to continue as a trading company with tight control of the shares, to ignore the substantial assets of the company.'

The case concerned a 10% holding in a manufacturing company in Hong Kong that let out seven floors of a factory, the remaining two floors of which it occupied for the purpose of its trade. The Hong Kong Appeal Court upheld the value imposed by the judge in the court of first instance, which reflected a 40% discount from the value of net assets adjusted to allow for the open market value of the property. Pickering J added at the end of his judgment:

> 'The assets backing approach is not the only logically justifiable approach in these cases. It was an appropriate approach in the present case but, as we have said, the circumstances of different companies vary appreciably and, in the end, the choice of method adopted must be ascertained by something of an empirical approach dictated by those circumstances.'

As the case was heard in Hong Kong, it does not create a precedent in the UK. Section 13(5)(a) of the Hong Kong Estate Duty Ordinance is nevertheless very similar to the UK valuation provisions:

> 'The principal value of any property shall be estimated to be the price which … such property would fetch if sold in the open market at the time of the death of the deceased.'

Focus

The asset backing may be important even for a trading company.

7.16 Provision for taxation

When the company's assets have been calculated by direct valuation it may be necessary to make an adjustment for taxation in respect of the chargeable gains or the chargeable realised development value which would be taxable if the assets were to be disposed of at the realised value. This adjustment is normally only made in respect of interests in property and, unless the company is being valued on a break-up basis, it will be necessary to take account of the fact that such taxation would not be immediately payable as there would be no actual disposal. It would normally be appropriate to discount the potential tax charge to take account both of the fact that it would be over stating the net asset value of the company to ignore the tax charge, but also to recognise the fact that there is no immediate intention to dispose of the properties concerned and therefore no actual crystallisation of the tax charge.

The extent of the discount on the tax charge depends on the circumstances. If there is very little possibility of the tax charge crystallising, then only a small percentage of the potential tax charge should be deducted but if, for example, a controlling interest is for sale in a company which has no possibility of profits so that it is to the purchaser's advantage to liquidate, then virtually the whole of the potential tax charge could be a valid deduction.

On the same reasoning a proportion of any deferred taxation liability, whether provided for in the accounts or not, would be deducted from the net asset value.

There is also the possibility that a purchaser of shares with the intention of putting the company into liquidation could be liable to tax under ITA 2007, ss 689–691 and CTA 2010, ss 734–746, even though there was an ITA 2007, ss 701–702 and CTA 2010, ss 748–749 clearance on the acquisition, unless this also covered the subsequent liquidation. In the income tax case of *IRC v Joiner* [1975] 1 WLR 1701 Lord Wilberforce stated:

> 'A decision that the sub-code (TA 1970, s 461D now ITA 2007 ss 689-691, CTA 2010 ss 737–739) applies to some types of liquidation might not necessarily involve the more radical decision that this applies to all liquidations including "pure" liquidations, and I do not think that we should decide this question here.'

If there is considered to be a danger and a clearance is not obtained, the purchaser may want a discount on the purchase price for the risk of such a tax liability, although whether a vendor would accede to such a discount is open to doubt.

A tax charge could also possibly arise under the provisions of ITA 2007, ss 752–770 and CTA 2010 ss 815–831, where the clearance provisions of ITA 2007 s 770 and CTA 2010, s 831 are unlikely to be of assistance, and the prospective asset-stripper is likely to discount his offer to take account of any such liability.

The question of contingent tax on capital gains is considered in HM Revenue and Customs' Share Valuation Manual at SVM18100.

> **Focus**
>
> Taxation is a cost which should be taken into account.

7.17 Break-up costs

If a valuation is based on the value of the individual assets or an assumed liquidation it is important not only to deduct the probable costs of the liquidation and the asset-stripper's profit, (see *Re Courthope* (1928) ATC 538 at **7.02**) but also to consider the value of the assets in such circumstances.

Stock, in particular, is likely to realise considerably less than the book value in any forced sale other than in the normal course of business, such losses are commonly 50% or more of the book value.

Debtors are more likely to prove bad in the case of a cessation of trade and work in progress may prove very difficult to dispose of at a worthwhile price.

There will be redundancy costs in many cases which could be substantial.

Continuing contracts, such as equipment on lease, could have heavy early termination penalties, and there could be large dilapidation liabilities on termination of leases of properties.

There could be taxation balancing charges on the disposal of plant and industrial buildings.

All these potential costs and losses must be taken into account when the shares are to be valued substantially on the basis of the value of the underlying assets in the liquidation.

> **Focus**
>
> The market value of assets or a forced sale can be substantially different from the book value.

7.18 Investment-holding companies

In *Battle v IRC* [1979] TR 483, the only asset of the company, Potterhanworth Investments Ltd was a holding in British Gas stock.

Balcombe J in judgment stated:

> 'The evidence for the Crown was that the value of a minority holding of shares in a private company, even a company such as Potterhanworth, with no liabilities and its assets in a readily realisable form, would represent a substantial discount on the asset value of those shares. Convincing reasons are given for that conclusion. Mr Marriott, a partner in Mullen's & Co stockbrokers, sets out his reasons as follows and I quote from his affidavit:

> "I do not consider, however, that a hypothetical purchaser of 49 (out of 100) shares of Potterhanworth would have been prepared to pay as much as the asset value for such a holding. There was no doubt whatsoever of the quality of the assets but a potential purchaser of 49 shares would argue that unless he was offered some inducement in the form of a discount on the asset value he would be better off investing directly in a British Government Stock for the following reasons:
>
> (a) He could buy British Government Stock without incurring the transfer stamp payable on a purchase of Potterhanworth shares.
>
> (b) He could subsequently sell his British Government Stock without any difficulty, whereas a sale of Potterhanworth shares would be subject to the onerous restrictions on transfer in the articles of association of Potterhanworth.
>
> (c) Should he invest in a short dated British Government Stock such as 4% British Gas 1969–72 he would be assured of receiving the redemption proceeds on a fixed date (not later than 8 August 1972 in the case of the British Gas Stock), whereas a liquidation of Potterhanworth would take time and incur some expense which would deplete the ultimate proceeds.
>
> (d) He would have complete control over his holdings of British Government Stock, whereas he would be a minority holder in Potterhanworth and could find himself locked in should the other shareholders decide not to liquidate the company on the repayment of 4% British Gas Stock 1969–72.
>
> Having regard to all these factors I consider that a potential purchaser of 49 shares in Potterhanworth would require a substantial discount on asset value before he would be prepared to complete his purchase. It is impossible to arrive at such a discount by a precise mathematical calculation but my experience in the market and in the valuation of unquoted shares suggests that the discount should be in the region of 10% to 15%. Taking a mid point of 12½% I would value the holding of 49 shares at £42,886.53."
>
> Mr Booth, an assistant controller of death duties at the Capital Taxes Office, with considerable experience in valuing unquoted shares gave evidence to the like effect. He considered that an approximate discount would be in the region of 15% and valued a holding of 49 shares in Potterhanworth on 10 August 1971 at £41,661.20. On this point neither witness was shaken in cross-examination. Indeed Mr Pinsent the principal valuation witness for Antony and Robin, an investment manager with some 15 years experience, in general accepted the principles indicated by Mr Marriott and Mr Booth as to the way in which shares in a private investment company ought to be valued for purposes of estate duty, i.e. on the basis of a sale in the open market.'

It was argued that two 49% holdings of two brothers should be aggregated in view of some understanding between them, but this argument was rejected by Balcombe J who continued (at para 93):

> 'Even if I were wrong on this last point, and the value of each brother's holding of 49 shares in Potterhanworth falls to be valued on the basis of a single block of 98 shares, I am still not satisfied that a holding of 49 shares was on 10 August 1971 worth not less than £49,095.89. The evidence was that even on such a sale a purchaser would require a discount of some 2½% from the net assets value of Potterhanworth, because of the disadvantages of holding shares in a private company as compared with a direct holding of Gas Stock.'

It should perhaps be pointed out that in this case the taxpayer was trying to argue for the highest possible value of his shares as part of an artificial estate duty avoidance scheme and in other circumstances the taxpayer may not have accepted so readily a valuation of a minority interest on the basis of a discounted assets value.

There will certainly be cases where such a company is effectively a private investment trust company and a valuation solely on the basis of discounted assets is the correct procedure. On the other hand if it is a case of a small minority interest in a private investment company, or property investment company the valuation would also have to take account of the earnings and effect of any dividends.

It has already been pointed out that the purchaser of a minority interest does not ignore the asset backing when considering the value of the shares. See for example *Salvesen's Trustees v IRC* (1930) 9 ATC 43 (see **5.10**).

Shares Valuation considers that assets are the single largest factor in the valuation process. It suggests that rough guides to levels of discount are those shown at SVM18060 in respect of property investment companies.

In *Shinebond Ltd v Carrol* [2006] WTLR 697 the Special Commissioner had to determine the market value of Shinebond Ltd's shareholding in Chas Polsky Estates Ltd (CP) at 31 March 1982 in respect of a disposal of the entire share capital in December 1988. At 31 March 1982 Shinebond Ltd owned all the share capital in CP which in turn held a leasehold interest in 165–167 Commercial Road, London E1. The Lands Tribunal, following the reference by the Special Commissioners under TMA 1970, s 46D(1), ordered that the value of the property as at 31 March 1982 was £168,000. Shinebond Ltd argued that the shares in CP at 31 March 1982 should be valued by applying an appropriate yield percentage to its gross income. However HMRC argued that the company should be valued on the basis of its net assets. Shinebond submitted:

> 'that the correct valuation of the company's shares is £252,257. This is based on annual net rental income for the year ended 5 April 1982 of £22,218 (after adjustment to take account of voids and management expenses) and annual interest income of £4,005. Capitalising these using a yield of 10% gives a valuation of £262,224. In addition, the appellant submits that account should be taken of dividends of £3,000 which were paid for each of the financial years ended 5 April 1980 and 1981. This gives £40,000 in value (adopting a yield of 7.5%) in addition to the value of the retained assets (which would, of course, have been depleted by the payment of the dividend). Mr Amin also drew my attention to the letter from Mr Dee of London Ltd, referred to above, in which Mr Dee of London Ltd confirmed that they would have purchased the property in 1982 for £220,000. Accordingly, Mr Amin submits that the valuation of £252,257 adopted in the company's tax computations is correct.'

The Commissioner states (at para 19):

> 'it is interesting to note that the appellant responded on 26 September 1991 to the standard questionnaire issued by the Shares Valuation Division that gave as the explanation for the value of £252,225 placed on the shares: Value of leasehold interest £220,000 plus net current assets £32,225 total £252,225. Thus the appellant originally valued the company on an assets basis but has given no reason for the subsequent change of its methodology.'

The Special Commissioner stated (at para 15):

> 'I am not persuaded that the use of the gross yield basis of valuation is appropriate in the circumstances of this case. No justification was given by the appellant for this approach, which results in a valuation for the shares in the company which exceeds the aggregate value of the property and other net assets by some £52,000.'

The appellant ascribed this difference to goodwill inherent in the site and to the impact of a special purchaser but the Commissioner pointed out that both of these would have been taken into account in the Lands Tribunal determination and to take into account again when valuing the shares would give rise to double counting. Similarly the yield would have been taken into account in the Lands Tribunal valuation. In the Special Commissioner's view:

> 'capitalising dividends is not relevant in valuing a controlling interest in an unlisted property investment company. As the appellant owns all of the shares in the company it controls whether any dividends are paid and if so how much they are. To a great extent the amount paid by way of dividends in any year by a company which is profitable and has significant distributable reserves (such as the company) is at the whim of the controlling shareholder.'

HMRC's approach:

> 'is to aggregate the net assets of the company as at 31 March 1982 namely £168,000 for the property and £32,257 for its other net assets. This results in a valuation of £200,257. The respondent submits that this valuation should be adjusted to take account of the tax liability which would arise in the hands of the company should it dispose of the property. If the company disposed of the property for £168,000 it would realise a gain of £145,000. As at 31 March 1982 the effective rate of corporation tax that would have been charged on the gain would be 30% and the tax liability would therefore have been £43,500. Of course this tax liability is contingent. It would only arise if the company sold the property which might never happen. Accordingly on the basis that the prospective purchaser acquired the company with a view to retaining the property as an investment a discount would be applied to this contingent liability when valuing the company's shares. The respondent suggests that a 30% discount is appropriate (namely 30% of £43,500 which equals £13,050). Taking these factors into account the respondent values the company at £187,207.'

The Special Commissioner found that HMRC's approach to the valuation of the company was more appropriate in the circumstances:

> 'the company is an investment company whose sole business activity is the ownership of the property. Its only other assets are modest amounts of cash (or assets similar to cash such as short term deposits and intra-group loans) and it had no material borrowings. The company exists solely for the purpose of owning the property. The property has a value which is realisable independently of its use in the company's business (in contrast for example with the fixed assets of a trading business). The shares in question represent the entire issued share capital of the company. The owner of 100% of the shares has unfettered control over the company and has the ability to force the company to realise and distribute the value of its assets. In these circumstances a hypothetical prospective purchase would have valued the company by adding the value of the property to its other assets and deducting its liabilities.'

The Special Commissioner was supported in this view by Christopher Glover's book Valuation of Unquoted Companies.

In *Dyer and Dyer v HMRC* [2016] UKUT 381 (TCC), a negligible value claim was excluded on the basis that the family support for their daughter's dress designing activities, which resulted in a loss to her parents and family trusts of some £800,000, was not tax deductible in the absence of any contractual arrangements as there is no such thing as a de facto contract.

The shares in J D Designs Limited (JDDL) had no value when they were acquired on 31 October 2007 as well as on the date of claim on 26 January 2009 and therefore had not 'become' of negligible value, as there had never been a legally binding contract in the lack of a mutuality of obligation and certainty of the intention of entering into a legally binding relationship.

In *Armajaro Holdings Limited (AHL) v HMRC* [2013] UKFTT 571 (TC) it was held that the company was incorporated to provide management services to its subsidiaries and associated undertakings. In July 2002, Armajaro Asset Management LLP (AAM) was incorporated and the partners were AHL and RIA Gower, ARB Ward and N Brennan, contributing £100,000, £5,000, £5,000 and £5,000 respectively, and JM Tilner (JMT) joined on 2 November 2005. On 5 March 2008, N Brennan ceased to be a member of AAM, giving up his right in AAM and selling his interest in AAM to AHL for US$17,593,011. On 6 March 2008, AHL purchased ARB Ward's and RIA Gower's members' interests in AAM for US$6,169,988.55 on their cessation of membership.

A new limited liability partnership agreement of AAM was entered into by AHL, Armajaro Limited and JMT, giving rise to goodwill of $22,553,000 (or $23,335,873, the total consideration paid) amortised over several years, claimed for tax purposes under FA 2002, Sch 29, para 2. The Tribunal held that the intangibles relief did not apply.

Chapter 8

The foreign influence

Signposts

8.01 Introduction

In considering the cases quoted on share valuation it must be remembered that in relatively few cases has the actual valuation itself been considered in any detail by the court. It therefore seems appropriate to consider other jurisdictions where the basic law is not fundamentally different from the United Kingdom and where consideration as to the mechanics of valuation has been given in some detail by the courts. As Lord Wilberforce stated in *W T Ramsay Ltd v IRC* [1981] 2 WLR 449 on being referred to a number of cases in the United States of America:

> 'I venture to quote two key passages, not as authority, but as examples, expressed in vigorous and apt language, of a process of thought which seemed to me not inappropriate for the courts in this country to follow.'

Focus

Valuation approaches in different jurisdictions vary, but it is interesting to see the interpretations of some of the key underlying principles in different countries.

8.02 American case law

The Internal Revenue Service ('IRS') in the USA issues guidelines for the valuation of shares in unquoted companies. A revenue ruling is published by the IRS that offers an official interpretation of the Internal Revenue Code. Revenue Ruling 59-60 provides significant insight into methodology, assumptions, and considerations associated with the valuation of a privately held business interest in connection with estate and gift tax.

A recent case which went to the UK Supreme Court was *Anson v HMRC* [2015] UKSC 44:

> '2 Mr Anson was at all material times a member of the Delaware limited liability company, which was classified as a partnership for US tax purposes. As a member of an entity classified as a partnership, Mr Anson was liable to US federal and state taxes on his share of the profits. Mr Anson remitted the balance to the UK, and was therefore liable to UK income tax on the amounts remitted, subject to any double taxation relief which might be available. The respondent Commissioners decided that Mr Anson was not entitled to any double taxation relief, on the basis, put shortly, that the income which had been taxed in the US was not his income but that of the limited liability company. The question is whether they were correct to do so.
>
> …
>
> 51 … Secondly, domestic tax law – in this case, the relevant double taxation agreements as given effect in UK law – then fell to be applied to the facts as so found. This approach was explained by Robert Walker J in *Memec* at [1996] STC 1336, 1348–1349. It is well illustrated by the contrasting decisions in *Baker v Archer-Shee* [1927] AC 844 and *Archer-Shee v Garland* [1931] AC 212, where the taxpayer lost in the House of Lords in the first case, and then succeeded in the House of Lords in the second case, because of the introduction in the second case of evidence establishing that the trust law of the state of New York differed from English trust law.
>
> …
>
> 119 … It was against that background that the FTT made findings which contradict the premise that the profits belong to the LLC in the first instance and are then transferred by it to the members. Their conclusion, on the contrary, was that, under the law of Delaware, the members automatically became entitled to their share of the profits generated by the business carried on by the LLC as they arose prior to, and independently of, any subsequent distribution. As the FTT stated:
>
> "the profits do not belong to the LLC in the first instance and then become the property of the members … Accordingly, our finding of fact in the light of the terms of the LLC operating agreement and the views of the experts is that the members of [the LLC] have an interest in the profits of [the LLC] as they arise."
>
> 120 As I have explained, the evidence as to Delaware law entitled the FTT to make that finding. The Commissioners challenged it in this court, as they did below, on two bases. The first was that the FTT was describing a proprietary right, as the Upper Tribunal had held. Since there was no basis in the evidence for such a finding, the FTT had erred in law. I reject that criticism for the reasons explained at paras 38–40. Secondly, it was argued that the FTT's finding constituted a holding on domestic law, not a finding of fact on foreign law. I reject that criticism for the reasons explained in paragraph 51.'

Numerous US cases involving valuation concepts can be helpful and insightful for valuation professionals. Although these cases can provide an interesting perspective, valuation professionals are cautioned to not rely on cases in performing a valuation as the courts' decisions were based on the unique facts and circumstances of that particular matter.

Additional sources to cite:

- *Business Valuation and Taxes Procedure, Law, and Perspective* by David Laro and Shannon P. Pratt, 2005.
- *Valuing a Business The Analysis and Appraisal of Closely Held Companies* by Shannon P. Pratt, 5th Edition.

8.03 Capitalised future earnings

In *Cottrell v Pawcatuck Co* 128 A 2d 225 (1957) it was held in the Supreme Court by Southerland CJ that a sale of the undertaking of a company, challenged by a minority shareholder, was not at a grossly inadequate price.

Although the debtors were sold at their face value, patents which had a book value of \$52,828 were sold for \$1 and stock, plant and equipment with a book value of \$5,395,000 was sold for approximately \$2,223,000.

The two important points arising from this case are confirmation that the value of a business sold as a going concern is to a large extent dependent on the capitalised value of its earnings and secondly that future earnings must be estimated in accordance with all available factors and in the absence of evidence to the contrary the best guide to future earnings may be the record of earnings actually achieved in the past. A mere statistical projection extrapolated from past earnings is suspect, but the trend of profit, if it can be discerned, is important.

In *Delaware Open MRI Radiology Associates; PA v Kessler, 898 A 2d 290 (Del Ch 2006)*, the court held that the business's strategy of opening further centres was part of the 'operative reality' at the merger date and therefore should be taken into account for valuation purposes.

8.04 Loss-making business

In *Levin v Midland-Ross Corpn* 194 A 2d 50 (1963) stockholders in Industrial Rayon Corporation were objecting to the take-over of their company by Midland Ross Corporation and were seeking the full value of their shares.

The case was heard in the Court of Chancery of Delaware in 1963 and the final value was arrived at as follows:

Value element	Value per share \$	Weight	Value \$
Earnings value (7 × \$1.26)	8.82 ×	25%	2.20
Asset value	35.67 ×	50%	17.84
Market value	18.69 ×	25%	4.67
			\$24.71

The case is of interest even though Industrial Rayon was a quoted company, as it was a take-over of the entire company and Industrial Rayon had previously been making losses.

There was some argument over the appraiser's asset value of $35.67 per share mainly because the appraiser took the book value of certain assets necessary for the operation of the business, but no evidence was presented as to the actual current value of the items in dispute, although an estimate of their liquidation value was submitted.

8.05 Going concern basis

There was also in this case an argument as to the earnings from investments, the prospective earnings of the manufacturing operation being agreed at $1 per share. The investment income amounted to 26c per share which the appraiser added to the operating earnings and capitalised at seven times total corporate earnings. The petitioners argued that the full dollar value of investments should be substituted for their capitalised earnings value. This argument was rejected by the court.

8.06 Capitalisation factor

There was also an argument as to the capitalisation factor. The court considered Standard and Poor's national stock price earnings ratio (20.2) and compared it with a similar ratio in the rayon textile and cord industry (between 12 and 14) before deciding on a price/earnings ratio of 7.

This is a useful case where the factors making up the valuation are each carefully considered and the weighting to be given to each component part of the valuation is determined in the light of the particular circumstances of the case. It should, however, be noted that this case involved the valuation of a dissenter's stock in proceedings based on title 8 Del C s 262 under which each shareholder is deemed to be entitled to a proportionate interest in the company as a going concern. In UK terms this would correspond to a fair value under the articles rather than a market value for taxation purposes. However, it is suggested that an open market value would merely affect the proportionate weighting depending upon the size of shareholding, rather than the principles involved and the factors considered are all relevant for UK fiscal purposes, except in the exceptional case where the valuation is based entirely on the break-up value.

8.07 Minority interest

Central Trust Co v United States 10 AFTR 2d 6203 (305 F 2d 393) (1962) was a case concerning American gift tax at a time when the company had 245,125 shares of common stock outstanding.

On 3 August 1954 Albert E Heekin made gifts totalling 30,000 shares of stock of the Heekin Can Company. The gifts were composed of 5,000 shares to each of six trusts created for the benefit of his three sons, each son being the beneficiary under two trusts. On 25 October 1954 James E Heekin made gifts totalling 40,002 of Heekin Can Company stock. The gifts were composed of 13,334 shares to each of three trusts created for the benefit of his three children and their families.

Of the total shares in issue 180,510 shares were owned by 79 persons who were related to James Heekin, the founder. Thus the Heekin family owned approximately 71% of all the outstanding stock. The remaining 73,615 shares were owned by 54 unrelated persons, most of whom were employees of the company and friends of the family.

The cases were referred to Saul Richard Gamer, a Trial Commissioner of the court, and eventually his findings were accepted by the parties. The Commissioner's opinion, reported in *Share Valuation Cases*, is worth detailed consideration.

The Commissioner's valuation calculations can be summarised as follows:

Central Trust Co v US

Value element	Value per share $	Weight	Value $
3 August 1954			
Earnings	1.93 × 9.45 =	18.24 × 50% =	9.12
Dividends	.50 × 3.50% =	14.29 × 30% =	4.29
Asset value	33.15 × 83.96% =	27.83 × 20% =	5.57
		100%	18.98
Less deduction for non-marketability		12.17%	2.31
			16.67
Less deduction for special circumstances of comparable companies and prior sales		1.17	
			15.50

Value element	Value per share $	Weight	Value $
25 October 1954			
Earnings	1.79 × 9.84 =	17.61 × 50% =	8.81
Dividends	.50 × 3.56% =	14.05 ×30% =	4.22
Asset value	33.54 × 86.39% =	28.98 × 20% =	5.80
			18.83
Less deduction for non-marketability	12.17%	2.29	
			16.54
Less deduction for special circumstances of comparable companies and prior sales		1.04	
			15.50

This case brings out not only the wide disparity between the professional valuations of the experts involved in the case but also the approach by the Commissioner in including all relevant factors and giving to them what he considered to be the appropriate weight in each case.

8.08 Valuation in practice

One of the more interesting cases in the US is that of the *Kirkpatrick's Estate v CIR* 34 TCM 1490 (1975), and as the valuation process can be followed through, the case report is worth reading almost in its entirety.

The mathematics used by the judge are not divulged in the case report but would appear to be along the following lines:

French Tool

Value element	Value per share $	Weight	Value $
Earnings	54 × 8 = 432 ×	70%	302.40
Asset value	$\frac{2,849,958}{2,512}$ = 736 ×	30%	220.80
			530.20
Discount for lack of marketability	43.63%	232.20	300.00

French Oil

Value element	Value per share $	Weight	Value $
Earnings	55 × 6 = 330 ×	80%	264.00
Asset value	$\frac{1,630,165}{2,000}$ = 815 ×	20%	163.00
			427.00
Discount for lack of marketability		41.45%	300.00
			250.00

8.09 Investment companies

In *Piper Senior's Estate v CIR* 72 US TCR 1062 (1979) the entire share capital of two private investment companies was disposed of. The case is a useful illustration of the adjustments necessary in an asset-based valuation approach. In this case the adjusted net assets value was reduced by 17% on the basis of the discount on net assets in quoted investment trust companies and a further 35% for non-marketability. In the UK the shares would probably have been valued on the basis of a liquidation less costs of winding up – see *Battle v IRC* [1979] TR 483 and **7.18**.

8.10 Investment company – minority interest

An American case where a company which was primarily an investment company was valued on the basis of discounted net assets for a disposal of minority shares was that of *Gallun v CIR* 33 TOM 1316 (1974).

Although the number of shares involved represented only 400 out of 15,722 the valuation was based largely on the considerable investment portfolio held by the company, albeit heavily discounted rather than on the capitalised value of earnings or dividends; the latter would have been more appropriate had the company been mainly a trading company.

The judgment of Wiles J at 1320 attempts to quantify an appropriate discount at 55% from the adjusted market value of the investments as appropriate.

8.11 Subsequent flotations

The American case of *Messing's Estate v CIR* 48 TC WSR 502 (1967) was one involving a gift of shares in an unquoted company where there was a subsequent flotation within a short period. The comments of Tannenwald J at 508 et seq make interesting reading.

He highlighted the difference between private sales and sales through public trading, stating that where there was no public market at the critical tax date, there was a further difference, going to the underlying character of the property. He went on:

> 'In short, a publicly traded stock and a privately traded stock are not, as respondent would have us assume, the same animal distinguished only by the size, frequency or colour of its spots. The essential nature of the beast is different.'

He conceded that the sale price to the public was a factor to be taken into account, but with due regard to all factors that could have affected the proposed flotation. For UK tax purposes, it should be said that the proposed flotation price will influence the value only if it can be shown that it would be made known to the hypothetical willing buyer and hypothetical willing seller at the valuation date.

8.12 Shares of different classes

In *Newhouse's Estate v Comr* 94 TC 14 (1990), the deceased held all ten voting shares of common stock and all 990 shares of non-voting common stock in Advance Publishing. Other family members owned 3,500 shares of non-cumulative preferred stock. The right to voting in connection with the appointment of the Board of Directors rested with the voting common stock. The cumulative preferred stock carried votes only in connection with a liquidation. The shares ranked pari passu for dividends. The preferred shareholders were entitled on a liquidation to the first $187.25 per share with the balance being shared by all the shares equally. There was in existence a number of put options held by the shareholders requiring the company to redeem stock to cover each shareholder's federal estate taxes with restrictions on any purchaser of the preferred stock. There was also a pre-emption arrangement giving the company the right to acquire stock from preferred stock holders in certain circumstances at a fair value determined by Chemical Bank that would be binding on all parties.

Chemical Bank valued the shares for the estate on the basis that the voting A common stock was worth five times as much as the non-voting B common stock which was equal in value to the preferred stock. The ten voting shares of A common stock were worth $8m and the 990 shares of B common stock

$170m. The IRS however, valued the shares at $420m and $811m respectively; a difference of more than a billion dollars. Their valuation approach was to deduct the value of the preferred stock from the value of the company as a whole and split the balance between the A and B common stock.

There were considerable uncertainties and there was conflicting expert evidence in connection with the precise rights of the various classes of shares, in particular the entitlement to participation in dividends declared from a capital surplus and the right of the common stock shareholders to effect a merger and effectively buy out the preference shareholders.

In view of the considerable sums involved, it was concluded that the litigation necessary to clarify such matters could take five to ten years and would obviously affect the rights of the common stock holders vis-à-vis the preferred stock holders.

Goldman Sachs were asked to prepare a further valuation which looked at the general economic conditions, the industry economic factors, Advance's competitive position within the industry, Advance's size (it was the fourth largest publisher in the US), potential anti-trust problems to any possible mergers, and potential accounting problems in view of the differences of opinion over the precise nature of the shareholders' rights. The value of the company as a whole was concluded as being the amount that it could be floated for and not the higher theoretical break-up value which in practice would have resulted in flooding the market and could not have realised the theoretical figures.

Goldman Sachs looked at four potential types of investors:

(1) the passive investor who would have required a 30% discount for illiquidity, lack of control and other certainties;
(2) the active investor looking for a quick return on his investment;
(3) the control investor seeking to acquire 100% of the company who, in view of the shareholders' rights, would assume he could acquire only 22% of the effective equity by purchase of the common stock; and
(4) the public following a flotation.

A flotation could only take place on the basis of a merger of the various classes of stock and the capitalised value would be in the order of $906m. The common stock at 22% of the total would be worth $201m, which, adjusting for a control premium of 7% and a discount for lack of marketability of 15%, would value the two classes of common stock together at $171m, ie very close to the Chemical Bank valuation on behalf of the executors. The IRS valuation was based on the value of the aggregate of the constituent parts amounting to nearly $1.6bn, less the value of the preferred stock on the basis of the IRS view of the shareholders' rights (effectively including $370m per preferred share), with the difference being the value of the common stock.

The court held that the hypothetical willing buyer would be presumed to be aware of all pertinent facts, including the different legal opinions on the rights of the preferred stock holders, and would therefore have considerable uncertainty at best about the common stock holders' ability to reduce the preferred stock holders' share of the total below the pro rata proportion of 78% of the value of the company as a whole.

The court was also unconvinced by the IRS subtraction method and preferred the commercial approach of Chemical Bank and Goldman Sachs as being consistent with the willing buyer/willing seller concept. There was no evidence that a willing buyer would use the subtraction method brought forward by the IRS and the court was unconvinced that the preferred stock could be eliminated in the way suggested by the IRS, finding it an astonishing proposition. The court also referred to the underlying fallacy in the theory of valuation; of the assumption that the sum of the fair market value of the preferred stock and the common stock sold independently to separate buyers must equal the net value of the entire company as a going concern. This assumption was simply not supportable.

The case is of considerable significance because the court supported the executors' valuation and did not attempt to find a midway point between the figures put forward by the executors and the figures suggested by the IRS, which is a useful precedent for producing a properly reasoned valuation in the first instance and sticking to it rather than the haggling approach commonly adopted in dealing with HMRC Shares and Assets Valuation in the UK.

It is noteworthy to point out that significant guidance, including a practice aid, has been published regarding valuations of entities with complex capital structures or multiple classes of equity interests. Much of this guidance relates to valuations for US financial reporting purposes, and no landmark court cases have addressed the methodology used to allocate the value amongst various classes of equity.

8.13 Personal goodwill

In the US case of *Morrison v Rathmell* 650 SW 2d 145 (1983), the Appeals Court was considering the valuation of insurance agencies for matrimonial purposes and, in the absence of employment or non-competition agreements, excluded any value attributable to the personal goodwill of the owner, his time, toil and talent expended after the valuation date and any assumptions with respect to any continued employment or non-competition agreement.

In *McReath v McReath*, 2011 WI 66, 800 N W 2d 399, the Appeals Court held that no reasonable buyer would purchase a professional practice without a non-compete agreement covering the local area. The non-compete agreement would allow for the transfer of some of the personal goodwill in the business to the buyer.

8.14 Price adjustment clauses – US and UK

In *King v United States* 545 F 2d 700 (10th Cir 1976) it was held that a price adjustment clause which stated:

> 'If the fair market value of The Colorado Corporation stock as of the date of this letter is ever determined by the Internal Revenue Service to be greater or less than the fair market value determined in the same manner described above, the purchase price shall be adjusted to the fair market value determined by the Internal Revenue Service'

was not contrary to public policy where the intention was to pay full and adequate consideration without any donative intent.

UK Statement of Practice 5 of 1992 (SP 5/92) provides as follows:

'**(a) TCGA1992 Sch 5 para 9(3): transactions entered into at arm's length**

12. The condition in Sch 5 para 9(3) is not met where the property or income is provided to the trust under a transaction entered into at arm's length – see para 9(3)(a). This applies irrespective of whether the parties to the transaction are connected persons under TCGA 1992 s 286. Each case depends on its own facts and circumstances but a transaction is, in general, regarded as being at arm's length where all the facts and circumstances of the transaction are such as might have been expected if the parties to the transaction had been independent persons dealing at arm's length i.e. dealing with each other in a normal commercial manner unaffected by any special relationship between them.

13. Solely for the purposes of TCGA 1992 Sch 5 para 9(3)(a), a provision in the document governing the transaction for an appropriate adjustment to the consideration where the value agreed by HMRC differs from the original consideration arrived at by an independent valuer and specified in the sale document is, in general, regarded as falling within the terms of the above definition of an arm's length transaction. The arm's length value of the transaction is to be determined in accordance with the principles set out in para 12 above. This will usually correspond to the value for capital gains tax purposes except, for example, where TCGA 1992 s 19 would apply.

14. It would also be necessary for the terms of the contract to provide for compensating interest at a commercial rate to be paid in either direction once the arm's length value is determined. For this purpose, the official rate of interest for Taxes Act 1988 s 160 purposes will usually be regarded as equivalent if the circumstances of a particular case warrant this treatment.

15. This practice is, however, subject to the consideration passing on sale being realistically based, ie on a third party valuation by a qualified valuer, all the other terms of the transaction being at arm's length and the compensating interest being timeously paid. The position in a particular case depends on all the facts and circumstances.'

8.15 Discount for lack of marketability (DLOM)

In 2009, the IRS published a Job Aid for valuers (www.irs.gov/pub/irs-utl/dlom.pdf), which sets out issues to be considered in relation to non-marketability discounts. This source provides an overview of approaches used to quantify discounts for lack of marketability, as well as a listing of strengths and weaknesses of each approach. It also cites relevant court cases.

The valuation of a substantial private company by reference to quoted companies and sectors was considered in *Re Gallo's Estate*, 1985–363 P-H Memo TC, which approved a valuation based on earnings trends after detailed consideration of the company's trading record and prospects. An allegation of excessive remuneration was rejected as were untenable assumptions based on balance sheet ratios. A discount for non-marketability of 36% was approved.

The following was written in the court's decision as specific factors, referred to as 'Mandelbaum Factors', to consider when selecting an appropriate discount for lack of marketability:

'A nonexclusive list of these factors includes: (1) The value of the subject corporation's privately traded securities vis-a-vis its publicly traded securities (or, if the subject corporation does not have stock that is traded both publicly

> and privately, the cost of a similar corporation's public and private stock); (2) an analysis of the subject corporation's financial statements; (3) the corporation's dividend-paying capacity, its history of paying dividends, and the amount of its prior dividends; (4) the nature of the corporation, its history, its position in the industry, and its economic outlook; (5) the corporation's management; (6) the degree of control transferred with the block of stock to be valued; (7) any restriction on the transferability of the corporation's stock; (8) the period of time for which an investor must hold the subject stock to realize a sufficient profit; (9) the corporation's redemption policy; and (10) the cost of effectuating a public offering of the stock to be valued, e.g., legal, accounting, and underwriting fees.'

Mandelbaum v Commissioner of Internal Revenue, TC Memo 1995-255, aff'd 91 F 3d 124 (3rd Cir, 1996) established a benchmark discount for lack or marketability of between 35% and 45%, but emphasised that the appropriate figure depends on the facts of each case.

The IRS and courts have continued to place additional scrutiny on the methodologies utilised, factors considered, and discounts for lack of marketability selected. Simply citing historical ranges of indicated discounts for lack of marketability from restricted stock and pre-IPO studies is not acceptable. Specific facts and circumstances should be elaborated on, and the rationale for the selected discount should be clearly stated.

8.16 Discount for lack of control (DLOC)

An additional discount that may be applicable when valuing a non-controlling interest is referred to as a discount for lack of control or a minority discount. Several sources of data are frequently cited as a starting point for selecting an appropriate lack of control discount based on the specific facts and circumstances of the particular interest being valued. These sources include closed-end funds data and analysis of control premium data. Implied discounts from net asset value are computed for the closed-end funds, and the inverse of the control premium data is computed to indicate an implied discount for lack of control.

Depending on the valuation methodology and inputs that are utilised, the value indication may be on a controlling or non-controlling basis. Valuators should ensure each valuation methodology is yielding a value indication on the same level of value before attempting to weight different value indications. The percentage interest does not always determine if an interest is deemed controlling. For example, not all 51% and above interests would be deemed controlling, even though they do represent a majority interest.

Often the organisational documents or agreements contain the specific rights and privileges that should be considered to determine the degree of control associated with a particular subject interest. Key features would include the ability to vote, what percentage vote is required to approve a decision, ability to call a meeting of the board or managers, approval of the sale of an asset or of the entity, determining distributions or dividend policy, approval of amendments to the organisational documents or agreements, removal of a board member, officer or manager, decisions related to management of the business, approving admission of additional owners, etc.

In *Estate of Dunn v Commissioner*, the court cited a 7.5% lack of control discount for a 62.96% block, which was upheld at a later decision when the case was appealed. In *Adams v United States*, the court used a 20% lack of control discount for a 25% block being valued.

8.17 Canadian case law – fair market value

Fiscal valuations in Canada are necessary for capital gains tax.

The Canadian definition of fair market value, which corresponds with the definition of UK market value, is:

> 'the highest price available in an open and unrestricted market between informed and prudent parties acting at arm's length and under no compulsion to act, expressed in terms of cash (*Re Mann Estate* [1972] 5 WWR 23; on appeal [1973] CTC 561; aff'd [1974] CTC 222).'

8.18 Fair value

There is some useful Canadian jurisprudence in connection with fair value as opposed to market value in which it is held that a pro rata proportion of the value of the company as a whole, and viewed as a going concern, can be a fair value for a minority shareholder (*VCS Holdings v Helliwell* [1978] 5 BLR 265, *Diligenti v R W M D Operations Kelowna Ltd (No 2)* (1977) 4 BC LR 134 (BC SC) and *Brant Investments Ltd v KeepRite Inc* (1967) 60 OR (2d) 737). In certain cases minority shareholders have been given a premium to compensate them for being forced out (for example, in *Domglas Inc v Jarislowsky, Fraser & Co* (1980) 13 BLR 135; confirmed on appeal (1982) 138 DLR (3d) 521). The *Diligenti* case also provided for adjustment for excessive management remuneration taken by the majority shareholders, but not for mere poor business decisions.

8.19 Insider knowledge

In *National System of Baking of Alberta Ltd v R* [1978] CTC 38; on appeal [1980] CTC 237, it was held that a taxpayer's inside knowledge about a likely take-over bid was inadmissible in valuing the shares, and that the quoted price was appropriate following *Crabtree v Hinchcliffe* [1971] 3 All ER 967, HL.

8.20 Personal goodwill

In the Canadian matrimonial dispute of *Crutchfield v Crutchfield* (1987) 10 RFL (3d) 247 in valuing a dental practice, together with shares in a management company which held the lease of the dental premises, held the dental equipment and hired the practice employees, it was proper to value the practice as a whole, including the company as an integral part of the practice. The value effectively ignored the separate existence of the company, for matrimonial purposes. In other cases, and generally the approach accepted by the Canada Revenue Agency, the courts have refused to attach a value to personal goodwill on the grounds that it is not transferable (*Adair v Minister of National Revenue* (1962) 62 DTC 356; *Losey v Minister of National Revenue* [1957] CTC 146; *Young v Minister of National Revenue* (1965) 65 DTC 242).

8.21 Special purchaser

The application of a premium for special purchasers is very rare in Canadian valuation work.

The Canadian view of the special purchaser appears to be that where there is only a single special purchaser he is likely to pay only a nominal amount more than a purchaser without such special interest, and the special value to him should not be taken into account (*Levitt v Minister of National Revenue* [1976] CTC 2307, which also confirmed the irrelevance of a share's par value). In *Cyprus Anville Mining Corpn v Dickson* (1982) 20 BLR 21; revsd (1986) 8 BCLR (2d) 145, the court held that the fact that the purchaser had a special interest in buying as owner of other property in the immediate vicinity should be taken into account. Similarly, a number of special purchasers were assumed to compete with each other as in *R v Hugh Waddell Ltd* [1982] CTC 24; affd [1983] CTC 270.

8.22 Chairman's casting vote

A chairman's casting vote is not the property of the shareholder per se and is therefore ignored in determining whether he controls the company (*Minister of National Revenue v M F Esson & Sons Ltd* [1967] CTC 50), which contrasts with the English decision of *B W Noble Ltd v IRC* (1926) 12 TC 911, where control through the chairman's casting vote was held to be relevant for the purposes of that case.

8.23 Shareholders' agreement

Shareholders' agreements have been instrumental in affecting the degree of control held by shareholders in *Aaron's Ladies Apparel Ltd v Minister of National Revenue* [1966] CTC 330; affd [1967] CTC 50 and *Lou's Service (Sault) Ltd v Minister of National Revenue* [1967] CTC 315, although the court came to an opposite conclusion in *Credit la Verendrye Ltee v Minister of National Revenue* [1972] CTC 2404, where an agreement among the shareholders was held not to be part of the company's byelaws. Shares held through a voting trust were considered in *R v Hugh Waddell Ltd* [1982] CTC 24; affd [1983] CTC 270, in which it was held that the shares had to be valued on the assumption that the market value was not limited to the formula value in the trust deed as the deemed purchaser was standing in the shoes of the vendor following *IRC v Crossman* [1937] AC 26.

8.24 Price adjustment clauses – Canada

Price adjustment clauses in agreements under which the contract price is adjusted to the market value determined by the Shares and Assets Valuation are not unusual and are commonly used in tax reorganisations. In Canada the equivalent agreement has received Revenue approval in *Interpretation Bulletin* IT – 169 of 6 August 1974, provided that a bona fide attempt has been made to arrive at a fair market value. In the absence of such an attempt the price adjustment clause was ignored in *Guilder News Co (1963) Ltd v Minister of National Revenue* [1973] CTC 1.

8.25 Australian case law – general principles

Australia has a common law system and has had at various times estate duty, gifts tax, death duties and stamp duty. Judicial comments quoted by Wayne Lonergan in *The Valuation of Businesses Shares and other Equity* include the following:

> 'The main items to be taken into account in valuing shares are the earning powers of the company and the safety of the capital assets in which the share-holders' money is invested.' (*Perpetual Trustee Co v Federal Comr of Taxation, Re Murdoch* (1941) 65 CLR 573)

> 'The final assessment of the value of the shares must be made principally on the basis of the income yield … but where owing to exceptional circumstances the valuation on this basis presents enormous difficulties it is legitimate … to rely more than usual on the assets value.' (*Abrahams v Federal Comr of Taxation* (1944) 70 CLR 23)

> 'The main items to be taken into account in estimating the value of shares are the earning power of the company and the value of the capital assets in which the shareholders' money is invested. But a prudent purchaser does not buy shares in a company which is a going concern with a view of winding it up, so that the more important item is the determination of the probable profit which the company may be reasonably expected to make in the future, because dividends can only be paid out of profits and a prudent purchaser would be interested mainly in the future dividends which he would reasonably expect to receive on this investment.' (*Gregory v Federal Comr of Taxation* (1971) 2 ATR 33)

Reference is also made to the comment of Kitto J in *Elder's Trustee and Executor Co Ltd v Federal Comr of Taxation* 96 CLR 563:

> 'In a company such as the Beltana Company I think that an investor would expect a very high degree of security for his money as well as expecting a high dividend yield, and would be inclined to make little, if any, allowance in his price for the fact that on book figures the shareholders' funds are much more than adequately represented by assets.'

8.26 Hindsight

A useful comment on hindsight was contained in *Trustees Executors and Agency Co Ltd v Federal Comr of Taxation (Victoria)* (1941) 65 CLR 33:

> 'It may be conceded that the calculation of duty on the deceased's estate is not controlled by events subsequent to the death of the deceased, but subsequent events may be taken into account as evidence of what were the facts at the date of the testator's death.'

In *McCathie v Federal Comr of Taxation* (1944) 69 CLR 1 the question of hindsight was referred to in the context of the valuation of shares in a retail store at 7 August 1940 during the 1939–45 war and after structural alterations to the premises had been carried out.

> 'The accounts for the year ended 15 July 1941 would be admissible in my opinion on the question whether the structural alterations would in the future lead to improved business and whether the grave international situation was going to interfere with the trade of a retail store. These were matters existing and to be taken into account at the date of death and the Court should not be forced to speculate as to their future when the facts are known and can speak for themselves.'

8.27 Willing buyer and willing seller

The question of willing buyer and willing seller was considered in *Spencer v Commonwealth of Australia* (1907) 5 CLR 418, where Griffith CJ stated:

> 'In my judgment the test of value of land is to be determined not by enquiring what price a man desiring to sell could actually have obtained for it on a given day, i.e. whether there was in fact on that day a willing buyer, but by enquiring what would a man desiring to buy the land have had to pay for it on that day to a vendor willing to sell it for a fair price but not anxious to sell.'

This was followed in *Abrahams v Federal Comr of Taxation* (1945) 70 CLR 23:

> 'The Court should endeavour to ascertain the price which a willing but not anxious vendor could reasonably expect to obtain, and a hypothetical willing but not anxious purchaser could reasonably expect to have to pay for the shares if the vendor and purchaser had got together and agreed on a price in friendly negotiation. The basis of the bargaining being that the purchaser would be entitled to be registered as the owner of the shares, but when registered, would hold the shares subject to the provisions of the Memorandum and Articles of Association of the company including any restrictions on transfer which they might contain.'

Williams J in *Kent and Martin v Federal Comr of Taxation* (not reported) stated:

> 'The essence of the matter is to ascertain the real value of the shares at the date of death, having regard to the existing condition and probable future course of the company's business. The success or failure of that business does not depend in any way upon whether the shares are listed, unlisted, or unlistable on the stock exchange. The market for unlistable shares is no doubt strictly limited in comparison with shares that are listed but a purchaser in a limited market cannot expect to acquire the shares at less than their real value to the owner. The fact that such shares are difficult to mortgage or sell makes them unattractive to buyers, who, like the ordinary investor on the stock exchange, attach great importance to negotiability, and they must be regarded as a long term investment. Some discount must, as Lord Hanworth pointed out, be allowed on this account, particularly where the business on which a private company is engaged is hazardous, and the amount paid for the shares is not fully covered by tangible assets. But I am unable to accept the evidence that, taking purchasers as a whole, as opposed to investors on the stock exchange, shares in a private company, as compared with shares in a company listed on the stock exchange, should be depreciated to the extent suggested by some of the appellants' witnesses when both companies are engaged in carrying on similar businesses and own substantially identical assets.'

In this case the judge increased the yield from the 8% available for comparable quoted companies to 9.5% representing a discount for non-marketability of 18.75%.

In *Elder's Trustee and Executor Co v Comr of Succession Duties* (1932) SASR 10 Pipper J stated:

> 'I think buyers and sellers in an open market would be more directly influenced by the apparent earning power than by complex calculations on net assets, but those assets would be regarded generally for assurance that returns would be maintained.'

In *McCathie v Federal Comr of Taxation* (1944) 69 CLR 1 Williams J stated:

> 'A purchaser of shares in a company which is a going concern does not usually purchase them with a view to attempting to wind up the company. A prudent purchaser therefore, while taking care to see that his purchase money is well secured by tangible assets, would look mainly to the dividends which he could reasonably expect to receive on his shares and such a purchaser would no doubt expect to receive such dividends as were appropriate to the nature of the business in which the company was engaged. It follows therefore that the real value of shares which a deceased person holds in a company at the date of his death will depend more on the profits which the company has been making, and should be capable of making, having regard to the nature of its business than upon the amounts which the shares would be likely to realise upon a liquidation.'

8.28 Personal goodwill

In *Comr of Succession Duties (SA) v Executor Trustee and Agency Co of South Australia Ltd* (1947) 74 CLR 358 it was stated:

> 'No doubt outstanding business capacity may be shown in the motion picture business as in most other businesses, but we find it difficult to believe that it is a business in which any particular individual is irreplaceable.'

8.29 New Zealand case law – market value

The concept of market value is in essence the same as that in the UK and UK valuation cases are freely quoted. In the leading case of *Hatrick v Comr of Inland Revenue* [1963] NZLR 641, the fair market value test was considered:

> 'the test has been variously phrased but in essence it calls for an enquiry as to the value at which a willing but not anxious vendor would sell, and a willing but not anxious purchaser would buy.'

8.30 Discounted cash flow

The discounted cash flow approach to earnings was first applied in *Keesing v Comr of Stamp Duties* [1935] GLR 58. The capitalisation rate for valuation purposes is equal to the risk-free rate of return from government securities plus the risk premium, less the growth factor. The discounted cash flow of future projected earnings would include the growth factor.

8.31 Asset basis

With regard to break-up valuation for businesses, the inherent costs of the liquidation should be included (*New Zealand Insurance Co Ltd v Comr of Inland Revenue* [1956] NZLR 501). See also *Keesing v Comr of Stamp Duties* [1935] GLR 58. A liquidation approach is not appropriate to a holding of just over 50% (*Hatrick v Comr of Inland Revenue* [1963] NZLR 641).

In the case of *Holt v Holt* (1985) 4 NZFLR 339, Heron J stated:

> 'In this case the Court is not so concerned with concepts at arriving at a valuation except to say that it was generally agreed that the assets value method was appropriate and shareholders' funds were in the order of $800,000. From that an allowance for profit of 25 per cent was considered appropriate by Mr Hadlee, but so far as I could see, no separate allowance for legal and liquidation costs was included, but I regard the discount of 25 per cent as on the high side. I allow for all the above deductions a figure of 20 per cent which gives the 1,000 shares a value, ignoring differences in voting rights of $640,000 or $640 each.'

8.32 Control holdings

Mahon J in *Coleman v Myers* [1977] 2 NZLR 225 stated:

> 'A share does not constitute an interest in the assets of a company. It only vests in the holders that collection of rights provided by the Memorandum and Articles of the company. Its value will depend not only upon the financial status of the company at a given date, but also upon the extent of the individual holding of which that share forms part. Thus a share will have a value in a minority holding different from that which it will possess as part of a majority holding. In a private company such as this a shareholder owning not less than half the shares has the sole right to appoint directors, and if he owns not less than three quarters of the shares he has the additional right to alter the Articles in such manner as he may think fit, subject only to controlling provisions of the Memorandum and the terms of the Companies Act. Consequently, the acquisition of a controlling interest will generally attract to those shares an additional value by way of premium on their ordinary market value and as a corollary the shares held by minority shareholders will sustain a discount in value.'

8.33 Directors' fiduciary duties

In *Coleman v Myers*, the decision in *Percival v Wright* was discussed at some considerable length with the judge at first instance, Mahon J, concluding that it was wrongly decided. He commented:

> 'applying such considerations to the problem in hand, I reached the unhesitating conclusion that the decision in *Percival v Wright*, directly opposed as it is to prevailing notions of correct commercial practice and being in my view wrongly decided, ought no longer to be followed in an impeached transaction where a director dealt with identified shareholders. I accordingly accede to the submission of Mr Wallace that on the facts of this case where the director of a private company made an offer to shareholders to purchase their shares, he had a duty to disclose to such shareholders any material fact of which, to his knowledge, they were unaware and which reasonably might, from an objective

> viewpoint, materially affect the decision of those shareholders as to whether they would sell or as to the terms of sale.'

These comments were considered by Cooke J in the Court of Appeal.

> 'In *Percival v Wright*, the plaintiffs themselves opened negotiations for the sale of their shares which were ultimately purchased by the chairman and other directors at the revised price sought by the plaintiffs. Later the plaintiffs discovered that at the time of the negotiations, the Board were also being approached by another person who had in mind purchasing the entire undertaking at a price per share considerably above that for which the plaintiffs were willing to sell, but this proposal came to nothing and the Judge was not satisfied on the evidence that the Board ever intended to sell. Nevertheless, the plaintiffs sought to have their sale to the directors set aside for non-disclosure of the would-be purchaser's approach. As reported, Counsel for the plaintiffs conceded that there was no unfair dealing or purchase at an undervalue and also, somewhat surprisingly I think, that the defendants would not have been bound to disclose such things as a large casual profit, or the discovery of a new vein. The argument was that the position was altered as soon as negotiations for the sale of the undertaking were on foot. Swinfen Eady J accepted the concessions but declined to draw the distinction. He held that the purchasing directors were under no obligation to disclose to their vendor shareholders the negotiations which ultimately proved abortive.
>
> 'Swinfen Eady J did not say that directors can never be in a fiduciary position vis a vis shareholders with whom they are dealing. The actual outcome of the case certainly does not shock the conscience. As has been seen, major concessions were made in argument. It was a decision of a single Judge at first instance … It was distinguished in non-committal language by the Privy Council in *Allen v Hyatt* (1914) 30 TLR 444. In so far as it might be thought to lay down a general proposition that no fiduciary duty is owed by a director dealing with individual shareholders to disclose particular inside information acquired by him, that proposition was criticised in England by the Kern Committee in 1945 (CMND 6659, para 86) and by the Jenkins Committee in 1962 (CMND 1749, para 89) … While the result of *Percival v Wright* may have been correct on its facts, the judgment can carry little authority for any general proposition in this country and with respect I do not find it of much help in the present case.'

Casey J at 371 stated: 'like Cooke J, I find *Percival v Wright* of no great relevance here and for the reasons he and Woodhouse J have set out I have no doubt that in this tightly held family company both directors owed a fiduciary duty to the appellants and to the other shareholders'.

8.34 Earnings basis

In *Trathem v Comr of Inland Revenue* (1979) 4 NZ TC 61637, the deceased held 10,001 out of 20,000 shares in the family retailing company. The Revenue valuations in this case were severely criticised on the grounds that they either included a capital profit that had not been made, and was unlikely to be realised, or were based on a notional liquidation of assets which was regarded as 'unreal in so far as a purchaser of the shares could not have been influenced to pay a price on the basis that he could compel a liquidation and there was no evidence that one was contemplated at the date of the deceased's death', or thirdly that the valuation was made:

> 'not on the basis of earnings at the company as it was being, and is now being, operated but he assumed that the purchaser of the shares would sell all trading stock at close to book value and be relying on rental income as a source of return on investment … This basis of valuation is unreal. The trading stock of a closing down sale is unlikely to produce anything like its book value, apart from which no consideration has been given to payments for staff redundancies.'

The judgment continued:

> 'Mr Crimp (Valuer) for the objector based his valuation on earnings yield. He adjusted the average profit for the previous five years to £6,027. After studying market yields of shares at date of death of deceased, Mr Crimp concluded that an earnings yield of at least 20 per cent would be required by the market to produce a dividend of 10 per cent and place 10 per cent in reserve. Based on the 1974 company accounts, the yield on earnings of $5,657 at a price of $1.60 is 17.6 per cent. If the yearly average of $6,247 profit is used, the yield on earnings at a market price of $1.60 is 20 per cent.'

8.35 Damages and hindsight

In *Mair Astley v Giles* (1987) 3 NZ CLC 100120, it was held that where a purchaser of shares refused to complete the purchase, the damage arises at the date of breach and is not affected by the fact that if the vendor retains the shares they may increase or decrease in value between the date of breach and the date of action. The measure of loss was the difference between the contract price and the value of the shares, which was the open market value of what the seller could have sold them for, as a willing but not anxious seller to a willing but not anxious buyer.

On this basis in computing the value of the shares to the plaintiff as at 30 September 1983, the assessment should take into account, in the view of Tipping J, the following matters:

(1) all facts known as at 30 September 1983 and having a bearing on the value of the shares at that date;
(2) all matters which ought reasonably to have been known at that time;
(3) all future events or factors which ought reasonably to have been anticipated or foreseen at that time.

It was argued that:

> 'in establishing future maintainable earnings it is normal to take into account future projections of earnings. The projections which were available at 30 September 1983 have subsequently proven to be unreliable and in these circumstances, we consider it would be commercially unrealistic not to take into consideration the actual earnings subsequent to 30 September 1983.'

To this the judge responded:

> 'while it would certainly have been reasonable and proper to take into account the actual projections available at 30 September 1983, it is not permissible in my judgment to look backwards from the present time and take into account the actual performance of the companies. Assessment must be done as at the date of breach so as to reflect the value of the shares at that date based on the proposition of what the shares were worth to Mair at that date.'

8.36 Management shares

In the case of *Re Burgess Homes Ltd (in liquidation)* (1988) 3 BCR 130, Burgess Homes Ltd changed the voting rights of shares in its subsidiary, Colyer & Green Ltd, to disenfranchise its shares which resulted in the remaining share, which was held by the founder director of the parent company personally, to be reclassified as the 'A' share with all the voting rights. When the parent company went into liquidation it was argued that the company had disposed of an asset, viz, the voting rights, for inadequate consideration and it became necessary to value the voting rights.

It was accepted that the total value of the shareholders' funds in Colyer & Green Ltd at the relevant time was some $400,000. In his judgment Tipping J stated:

> 'as Cooke P said in *Holt v Holt* (1985) 4 NZFLR 339, while not an invariable rule 20–25 per cent of net asset backing at the material date could well represent the fair value of control. Here the control is less than absolute in the temporal sense because of Article 30 [under Article 30 Burgess Homes Ltd could acquire for a nominal $1,000 the golden "A" share on the holder's death or as a pre-emption right on sale]. It is, however, full control during its enjoyment.
>
> 'If there had been an arm's length negotiation between Burgess Homes and Burgess Senior (the holder of the "A" share) for the disposition and acquisition of the voting rights, I do not think that the transaction would have proceeded at a higher sum than $70,000. I think that the hypothetical purchaser at arm's length would probably have been prepared to go that high. That figure represents 17.5 per cent of the shareholders' funds taken at $400,000 and a corresponding percentage discount from asset backing in respect of the "B" shares. The circumstances of this case, particularly Article 30 and Burgess Senior's health problems, justify a lesser figure than the 20–25 per cent range. The liquidator's claim that the value of the voting rights was the difference between the value of all the shares in Colyer & Green Ltd with votes, and the value of the non-voting shares held after the change in the articles, was rejected.'

8.37 Divorce valuation

In *Flett v Flett* (1985) 3 NZFLR 487, shares in a family company had to be valued in the divorce proceedings. The company owned the family farm but did not produce any material profits and the shares had to be valued on the basis of a notional break up. Hardie Boys J stated in his judgment:

> 'if shares are being purchased because of the income return they produce, then their value will normally be determined by reference to their earning capacity. The adoption of an assets basis is appropriate where the earning capacity is low and the assumption must be that the purchaser is acquiring the shares in order to liquidate the company and realise the assets. Thus the costs and expenses of a notional liquidation must always be a proper deduction in an asset backed valuation [*NZ Insurance Co Ltd v Commissioner of Inland Revenue* [1956] NZLR 501, 503] and further there must be some allowance for profit to the purchaser … I see no justification for departing from these principles in a matrimonial property case, certainly one such as the present where the parties are not the only shareholders in the company and so the matrimonial property would comprise only a share of the assets even if it were proper for the existence of

> the company to be disregarded. Methods of valuation are but a means to an end, with the ascertainment of the fair value for the purpose in hand. The particular circumstances of each case must be taken into account … The Court's task … is not merely to value assets, but in the words of the preamble "to provide for a just division" of those assets … the fixing of values is a means to this end not an end in itself … it would be wrong for the wife to be penalised for having participated in the formation of the company … in my judgment, effect will best be given to these considerations by allowing the usual deductions made on asset backing valuation but disallowing that made on account of the minority nature of the wife's holdings. For to allow such deduction would indeed be to penalise the wife on account of what is in reality a rather artificial concept. She must accept some degree of penalisation for the conversion of her property rights from realty to personality because that was done for the benefit of her own family, but she should not be penalised again because of the proportions in which the shares happen to be held.'

The wife's shares were valued at a pro rata proportion of the shareholders' funds less notional liquidation costs and less a further 15% allowance for loss on break up and profit to purchaser.

8.38 Personal goodwill

In the case of *Tremaine v Comr of Stamp Duties* [1942] NZLR 157, Smith J, referred to the importance of the general manager of the company who was largely responsible for the favourable profit record of the company: 'The death or removal from the scene of this single person would very likely have a detrimental effect upon the progress of the company'.

8.39 Valuation of unquoted shares in India

The valuation of unquoted shares is required in relation to the additional issue of shares or transfer of shares. There are various provisions under the Indian regulations with respect to the valuation of unquoted shares which define the method of valuation or, in certain cases, determine the maximum or minimum pricing of such shares. The key provisions set out in corporate law, tax laws and foreign exchange regulations are stated below.

8.40 Valuation under the Companies Act and Rules

The Companies Act 1956 has been replaced by the Companies Act 2013 (the Companies Act). This has introduced the concept of a 'Registered Valuer'. Accordingly, where a valuation is required in respect of any property, stocks, shares, debentures, securities or goodwill or any other assets or net worth of a company or its liabilities under the provisions of the Companies Act, the asset must be valued by a person having such qualifications and experience and registered as a valuer in such manner, on such terms and conditions as may be prescribed and appointed by the audit committee or, in its absence, by the Board of Directors of that company.

Some of the key instances where the valuation of shares by a Registered Valuer is required under the Companies Act include:

- Issue of new/additional shares and conversion of loans into shares (Section 62(3)).
- Arrangement of non-cash transactions involving Directors (Section 192(2)).
- Scheme of Compromise/Arrangement with Creditors/Members and Merger/n of Companies (Sections 230(2)(c)(v), 230(3), 232(2)(d), 232(3)(h)).
- Purchase of Minority Shareholding (Section 236(2)).
- Submission of report by Company Liquidator (Section 281(1)).

Under the Rules the registered valuer must comply with the valuation standards as notified or modified under rule 18 while conducting a valuation. The Central Government will notify and may modify from time to time the valuation standards on the recommendations of the Committee to advise on valuation matters. Currently the Central Government has appointed a committee to draft a set of valuation standards. Until these have been introduced, the valuer must prepare valuations in accordance with either:

(a) internationally accepted valuation standards; or

(b) valuation standards adopted by any Registered Valuer Organisation ('RVO').

Valuations are also required by any entity which has adopted Indian Accounting Standards (IndAS) which require a business to report fair value for financial reporting purposes under Indian AS 113 and other applicable IndAS standards.

8.41 Valuation under the Income Tax Regulations

Under the provisions of the Income Tax Act 1961, if the shares of a closely held company are transferred to an individual, Hindu Undivided Family (HUF), partnership firm or company (being a closely held company) for either nil or inadequate consideration, the difference between the 'fair market value' (FMV) of such shares and the amount of sale consideration is taxed as 'income from other sources' in the hands of the recipient of shares. FMV for the purpose of these sections has been defined to mean value as determined in accordance with prescribed rules.

The Income Tax Rules 1962 ('the IT Rules') provide the methodology of calculating the FMV of shares of an unlisted company and certain definitions in relation thereto. The methodology prescribed for the valuation of unquoted equity shares in such cases is the net asset value method in accordance with the formula provided for in the rules. The IT Rules also provide detailed explanations as to the factors which are to be considered when calculating the book value of assets and liabilities. In the case of unquoted shares other than equity shares, the IT Rules provide that FMV is the price which the shares would fetch in the open market as at the valuation date. Where a closely held company issues shares to a resident at a premium (ie the issue price exceeds the FMV), the difference between the issue price and FMV of such shares is taxed as income from other sources in the hands of the company issuing the shares. In this case, FMV has been defined as the higher of:

- the value as determined in accordance with the prescribed rules; or
- the value substantiated by the company to the assessing officer based on certain prescribed parameters at the time when the shares were issued.

In this case, the IT Rules specify that either of the following methodologies can be adopted at the option of the entity being assessed:

- net asset value method (as discussed above);
- the amount which would be fetched if sold in the open market on the specified date.

8.42 Valuation under the Foreign Exchange Regulations

The Foreign Exchange Regulations are applicable in cases of the transfer of shares of an Indian company by a resident to a non-resident or vice versa. The Foreign Exchange Regulations provide that, where there is an allotment of unquoted securities, the transaction price must not be lower than the fair value of shares determined by a Securities and Exchange Board of India ('SEBI') registered merchant banker or a chartered Accountant using any internationally accepted pricing methodology for valuation on an arm's length basis.

These regulations also state that, in the case of a transfer of shares in an Indian company from a resident to non-resident, the transaction price cannot be lower than the price determined by an internationally accepted pricing methodology. In case of a transfer of shares in an Indian company from a non-resident to an Indian resident, the transaction price cannot be higher than the price determined by any internationally accepted pricing methodology for valuation on an arm's length basis.

Where non-residents make investments in an Indian company in compliance with the provisions of the Companies Act by way of subscription to its Memorandum of Association, such investments may be made at par value.

In the event of a rights issue of unquoted shares, the price offered to non-residents cannot be lower than the price offered to Indian resident shareholders.

In case of share warrants, their pricing and the price/ conversion formula shall be determined upfront and the price at the time of conversion should not be lower than the fair value calculated at the time of issuance of such warrants.

Investment in an LLP, either by way of capital contribution or by way of acquisition/ transfer of profit shares, should not be lower than the fair price calculated in accordance with internationally accepted/ adopted market practice and a valuation certificate to that effect should be obtained from a Chartered Accountant or by a practising Cost Accountant or by an approved valuer from the panel maintained by the Central Government.

The pricing guidelines will not apply for investment in capital instruments by a person resident outside India on a non-repatriation basis. The pricing guidelines will not be applicable for any transfer by way of sale done in accordance with SEBI regulations where the pricing is prescribed by SEBI. A Chartered Accountant's Certificate to the effect that relevant SEBI regulations/ guidelines have been complied with has to be attached to the form FC-TRS filed with the central bank.

The pricing guidelines in the case of investment in a wholly owned subsidiary or a company outside India do not recommend any specific valuation methodology. However, the issue or transfer of shares in accordance with the guidelines should not be more than the fair value as determined by a Category I Merchant Banker registered with SEBI where there is a transfer of funds in excess of US$5 million, or by a Category I Merchant Banker or a Chartered Accountant where the transfer of funds does not exceed US$5 million.

8.43 Valuation under the SEBI Regulations

Under a SEBI Notification, valuation by an independent chartered accountant is mandatory in the case of merger and acquisitions, restructuring, preferential share issues or a substantial acquisition/takeover involving listed companies other than those specifically exempted. A 'Valuation Report from an Independent Chartered Accountant' is not required in cases where there is no change in the shareholding structure of the listed company or new entity.

Although the guidelines do not specifically dictate a specific valuation approach, in the case of a merger valuation the emphasis is on arriving at the 'relative' values of the shares of the merging companies to facilitate determination of the 'swap ratio' and not to arrive at absolute values. Generally, weighted averages of a number of approaches are used to arrive at a fair swap ratio. The key factor is that the swap ratio must be fair to all the shareholders.

The SEBI Substantial Acquisition of Shares & Takeovers Regulations set out the valuation methodology for the direct or indirect acquisition of an Indian listed company.

The SEBI Issue of Capital and Disclosure Requirements Regulations set out the valuation methodology for preferential issue of shares in respect of listed companies.

8.44 Valuation under the Insolvency and Bankruptcy Code

For a company referred under the Insolvency and Bankruptcy Code to the National Company Law Tribunal, the Insolvency and Bankruptcy Code ('IBC') requires that two registered valuers appointed by the insolvency professional under the IBC shall provide the value of the assets computed in accordance with internationally accepted valuation standards. The valuers now need to provide both the 'fair value' as well as 'liquidation value' of the assets.

8.45 Republic of Ireland

The valuation principles used in the Republic of Ireland are very similar to those used in the UK and valuations are required for capital gains tax, capital acquisitions tax and stamp duty.

Interestingly, the Revenue Commissioners in Ireland on Private Company Share Valuation form Q7 used to refer to the hybrid basis based on the US IRS notice 59–60, at Part 8 paragraph 10 as an approved basis but the current form suggests that this is an exceptional basis, although permitted, as in the UK. The Irish Revenue's manual on share valuations suggests the following discounts for minority shareholdings for capital gains tax (*Valuation of*

Shares in Private Companies by B H Giblin – Institute of Taxation in Ireland p 267). In the case of a shareholding of less than 75%, it is necessary to discount for lack of control and marketability. Below is a list of the discounts to be applied:

Size of holding (Percentage)	Reduction (Percentage)
%	%
75 to 100	NIL
51–74	10
50	30
25 to 49	40
15 to 24	60
10 to 14	70
1 to 9	80

However, their Capital Acquisitions Tax Guidance, Part 7, suggests the following approach for determining discounts for CAT purposes:

Size of shareholding

The size of the shareholding passing reflects the amount of control which a shareholder can exercise on the running of a company and the value of a particular shareholding is normally discounted to reflect the advantages/disadvantages attaching to it.

A 75% – 100% shareholder has full control over all matters affecting the company, including the power to wind it up.

A 51% – 74% shareholder has the power (control) to do all things except wind the company up.

A 50% shareholder needs the support of another shareholder to pass an ordinary resolution.

Majority shareholding/influential minority shareholding

Holdings of 50% and above

Value by reference to the value of the whole company less a suitable discount, eg

75%+	Nil discount or perhaps 5% at most
50%+1	10–15%
50%	20–30%
25%+1	35–40%

Minority shareholding

Up to 25% – value by reference to dividends if a realistic level of dividend is being paid. If no dividend has been paid, look at discounted earnings with a discount range of 50%-70%, as these are (not) influential minority holdings.

Reported cases on share valuation issues in Ireland since the creation of the Republic appear to be *McNamee v Revenue Commissioners* [1954] IR 214 (see **2.09**) and *Revenue Commissioners v Henry Young* 51 TR 294 on legislation since repealed.

8.46 The European approach

The civil law countries of Europe adopt either a market value approach to share valuation for tax purposes, as in the Netherlands, or a formula approach, as in Germany. The rules for the main countries for which information is available are shown below.

8.47 Belgium

The value of shares in unquoted companies is not only important for the transfer of a company, but also for a number of other contexts, including group restructuring, fund raising, IPO, value enhancement, impairment testing, shareholder disputes, contribution in kind, succession planning and gift tax filing.

The value of an asset can be determined on the basis of three generally accepted approaches: the cost approach, the income approach and the market approach. These approaches encompass several valuation methods.

The cost approach is based on the principle that an asset is not worth more than the amount originally paid for it. In the field of company valuation, the most commonly used method, fitting with this approach, is the adjusted equity method. This method states that the value of a company corresponds to its net assets, ie the total assets less the liabilities and provisions as shown by the company accounts, adjusted by unrecognised gains or losses on these balance sheet items (and taking account of tax consequences).

The income approach assumes that an asset is worth the income it can generate in the future. On this basis, the value of the company is equal to the discounted value of the future cash flows that are available, either for the shareholders (DCFE method – Discounted Cash Flow to Equity) or for the capital providers, ie both shareholders and banks (DCFF method – Discounted Cash Flow to the Firm).

Under the market approach, an asset can be valued by comparison to the prices at which similar assets were recently bought and sold. With respect to a company valuation, this approach includes two common methods. The first uses a comparison with recent deals in the sector, and the second takes as a basis for comparison the trading prices of listed companies operating in the same sector. Ratios or 'multiples' (P/E, EV/EBITDA, etc.) are then derived from these observable market prices and applied to the financial parameters of the company to be valued.

The choice of approach(es) and method(s) depends on the nature of the business to be valued, as well as the valuation context. Industrial and commercial/services companies are usually valued with income or market-based approaches, whereas the cost approach is more relevant for holding or real estate companies. For businesses which are no longer going concerns, the adjusted equity method is the most relevant, which aggregates the individual market value of all assets and liabilities of the company.

8.48 Denmark

In recent years the Danish tax authorities have had a stronger focus on implementing the existing tax laws, which state that in transactions between related parties or parties with joint interest the value of the transferred shares or transferred enterprise should reflect market value.

The Danish tax authorities published valuation guidelines in 2009, which consist of a description of the most common valuation techniques that are used in practice. The focus is on DCF-valuation and multiple-analysis based on comparable transactions or listed peer group. The methods described in the guidelines are the methods preferred by the Danish tax authorities.

Older guidelines (TSS-circular 2000-9 and TSS-circular 2000-10) are still valid but it is unclear in which circumstances these may still be used. The Danish tax authorities have interpreted the relevant tax law as being the market value of an asset that should be used in transactions between related parties or parties with joint interest. As the TSS-circular calculation is based on historical information (a weighted average of the results in the three latest years before the valuation date), this approach would only calculate a market value for companies that are expected to have same growth and return as they have achieved historically. This approach does not capture, in the valuation, intangible assets such as trademarks, patents or knowhow. Therefore, these limitations restrict the use of the TSS-circulars, resulting in the Danish tax authorities' greater focus on the most common valuation techniques used in practice, which are DCF analysis and a multiples approach.

The use of industry-specific or custom and practice approach is acceptable as long the value is considered to reflect market value.

Further guidance is available from the Danish Tax authority website (in Danish only): www.skat.dk/SKAT.aspx?oId=1813084.

8.49 Germany

Germany currently applies the Standard S1 (Version 2008), Principles for the Performance of Business Valuations. The Standard was originally developed in the 1990s by the *Institut der Wirtschaftsprüfer* (Institute of Public Auditors) with the primary purpose to standardise the determination of shareholders' compensation in squeeze out situations. Even though the Standard is only mandatory for public auditors, nowadays it is widely used, especially if a valuation is to be used in any official context (ie for tax purposes or in court).

The Standard describes different versions of the DCF approach as its primary means of valuation. Of the four variants of the calculation most widely known (flow to equity; WACC approach; APV; and direct cash flow approach), only two are used for the purposes of the Standard and described therein in more detail. The leading approach in Germany is the so-called *Ertragswert*, a dividend discount model. It bases the cash flow streams to be discounted on a standard profit and loss account, deducting taxes (following the tax planning of the company, not just statutory rates) and taking into account the distribution policy of the company as well as any restrictions which might apply from a balance sheet point of view (ie covenants from debt financing, regulatory aspects).

Nevertheless, even if the concept seems to be straightforward, there are some aspects which deviate from UK and/or US approaches. The most significant point is that, for all valuations which do not aim to evaluate a so-called 'entrepreneurial initiative', the Standard requires a post-tax basis to be used. 'Post-tax' means that the personal income tax of the shareholder has to be incorporated into the valuation for the income stream as well as for the discount rate. For the income stream this might be a simple deduction, but for the derivation of the appropriate discount rate the Tax-CAPM has to be applied. The reason for this rather complicated approach is that under German jurisdiction different types of income are taxed at different rates.

The Standard explicitly states that the (objective) value of a share in a company is determined by the value of the company as a whole and the size of shareholding that the share is representing. This means that the use of control premiums in a business valuation is limited to valuations aiming at deriving a subjective value for decision making purposes. They cannot be used for tax purposes or in court.

Another point to note is the hierarchy of valuation methodologies given by the Standard. In Germany, the DCF model will always be the leading approach. Other means like quoted stock prices or multiples can only be used for the cross-check purposes. In some circumstances, this approach is at odds with the approach expected under IFRS.

8.50 Italy

There are a number of methods which may be used for the valuation of listed shares.

Adjusted net asset method

The adjusted net asset method as proposed by doctrine and best practice is based on the assumption that the company's equity value at a certain date (the 'reference date') is equal to the adjusted shareholders' equity. The value of this asset is obtained as a result of assessing the current market value of all assets minus all the liabilities, net of any notional tax arising on the difference.

Using the adjusted net asset method, the company equity value is determined using the following formula:

$$W = PNR$$

where:

W = equity value
PNR = adjusted shareholders' equity

The above calculation is the simple adjusted net asset method. This method is different from the above approach because it evaluates the intangible assets (eg know-how) not already listed in the company financial statements.

Income method (capitalisation of earnings)

The evaluation of a company according to the income method uses the company's expected cash flows to derive the value.

Specifically, the income method is based on the determination of the company's equity value using the income flow that the enterprise could generate in 'normal' conditions, discounting the value by the degree of risk associated with obtaining the income flow.

The income method can be calculated using the following formula:

$$W = R/Ke$$

where:

W = equity value
R = normalised average expected levered net income
Ke = cost of equity

Discounted cash flow method (DCF)

The company value is calculated based on forecast cash flows over the period.

The mixed method

The mixed method is based on the assumption that the current company value, at a certain date, is equal to the sum of the following elements:

- adjusted net worth, which is the result of an evaluation, at current market value, of all activities minus liabilities (surplus assets included), net of the value of marginal tax rate; and
- the difference between the purchase price and the sum of the fair value of the net assets which may lead to goodwill if positive, or negative goodwill.

The first step consists in calculating the current market value of every item listed in the balance sheet in order to arrive at adjusted net worth (surplus assets included).

The asset value found is then adjusted to reflect the company's level of profitability compared with market profitability. This assessment generates a positive or negative difference to be capitalised which represents the adjustment to be made to the standard adjusted net asset approach.

The increase in the value of surplus assets allows the valuer to assess the proper price of those assets which do not affect the profitability of the business.

Using the mixed method, the economic capital value of the company is determined using the following formula:

$$W = K' + a_{n\neg i'} (R - Ke \times K')$$

where:

W = equity value
K' = adjusted net worth (excluding non-operating or surplus assets (SA))
R = normalised net profit
an¬i = the annuity function. (R – Ke × K'), for n years at the rate i per cent
Ke = cost of equity
i' = discount rate

Therefore, an¬i' (R – Ke × K') is the goodwill calculation.

Multiples approach

The standard approach uses maintainable income multiplied by an appropriate multiple.

8.51 The Netherlands

Dutch law requires the valuation of unquoted shares for the purposes of wealth tax, inheritance tax and for certain income tax purposes. The value is the economic value which is basically an arm's length value between willing buyer and willing seller. The normal method is to calculate the value of the company as a whole by reference to its intrinsic value, its potential value and its dividend yield. A discounted cash flow basis is the most common valuation approach. Other methods may be used in specific circumstances.

As in the UK, in the Netherlands it would be necessary to consider special situations such as where the company was likely to be taken over in the short term or, if there are particular restrictions on the company's articles of association, how the remaining shares are held and variations in voting rights.

The Netherlands tax authority resists the application of minority discounts as a general rule and any discount agreed is on a case-by-case basis.

8.52 Portugal

Portugal requires a valuation of unquoted shares for fiscal purposes, particularly in connection with estate and gifts taxes. The valuation is based entirely on historical data, although fixed assets (in particular, real estate) have to be adjusted to the current market value.

In the case of shares in a private limited company, the valuation is calculated from the last balance sheet, duly corrected for market value, apportioned equally to the shares. There is therefore no goodwill element included and no discount for a minority shareholding or premium for control.

In the case of unquoted public limited companies, the nominal value of the shares is taken where the issued share capital does not exceed €500,000, and in other cases a value of the company as a whole is calculated by applying a formula. The value of the individual shareholding is a pro rata proportion of the value of the company as a whole. The formula is:

$$Va = 1/2n\ [S + ((R1 + R2) / 2)\ f]$$

(ie the average of an asset value and an income yield value, all divided by the number of shares in issue)

where:

Va represents the value of each share at the date of transmission.
n is the number of shares representing the capital of the subsidiary.
S is the substantial value of the subsidiary, which is calculated from the accounting value corresponding to the last year prior to the transmission with the adjustments which are justified, considering, where appropriate, the provision for income taxes.

R1 and R2 are the net results obtained by the investee in the last two years prior to the transmission, considering R1 + R2 = 0 where the sum of these results is negative. In this case the 'f' is the factor of capitalisation of the net income calculated on the basis of the interest rate applied by the European Central Bank to its main refinancing operations, as published in the *Official Journal of the European Union* and in force on the date on which the transfer occurs, plus a spread of 4%.

For companies incorporated for less than two years, simplified rules apply.

8.53 Norway

For Norwegian wealth tax purposes, company shares are valued on the basis of the net assets, as adjusted, showing, for example, debtors with a formula deduction for bad debts, stocks and shares held as investments at the quoted value, or market value if unquoted, plant and machinery at cost less depreciation according to the approved declining balance depreciation method, and real estate revalued to the valuation used for rating purposes. Liabilities may be deducted except for accrued interest not yet due, accrued tax not yet due and unpaid dividends. For wealth tax purposes, 65% of the total adjusted net asset value is used and this is divided among the shares with no deduction for minority interest nor premium for control. For estate and gift taxes, the percentage of net asset value is reduced to 30%.

8.54 Switzerland

For tax purposes, Switzerland uses the guidelines of the Swiss tax conference (circular letter 28) for the valuation of unquoted shares: the value of the company normally being computed on the basis of one-third of the net assets plus two-thirds of the capitalised earnings based on the last two or three years. The net assets are based on the last financial statements and are calculated on the basis of the nominal issued share capital plus undistributed profits, plus reserves and the guidelines define the minimum and maximum values of the individual items in the balance sheet. Earnings are calculated on the basis of the profits after tax for the last two or three years and the guidelines define what income statement items must be aggregated or can be eliminated. Depending on the canton, the average profit is either calculated from the last three years or the last two years (in this case, the last year is counted twice). If the average profit is negative, earnings are considered as nil. This (weighted) average profit is then capitalised at an appropriate percentage of, eg, 8%, to give a price/earnings ratio of, eg, 12.5 times, which would be high by UK standards. The Swiss Federal Tax Authorities define the official capitalisation rate each year. For 2017 the rate is 7% for investments in companies in Switzerland. However, the Tax Authorities allow different capitalisation rates within a certain range in specific cases, especially for investments in companies located outside of Switzerland. An official circular letter with interest rates for investments in other currencies is published by the Federal Swiss Tax Authorities on an annual basis.

The use of twice the capitalised earnings in the formula, compared with one times the adjusted net assets, weights the valuation result to a profits basis. If earnings are nil, the value of the company will be deemed to equal one-third of the net asset value.

A property holding company, an asset manager, a holding company or a start-up company is valued based on the net asset value only.

In specific cases, a discount of 30% for a minority shareholding or a lack of marketability is permitted.

It should be noted that these guidelines are not mandatory. Tax authorities may also accept valuations based on a discounted cash flow method and multiples, but this practice differs from canton to canton, as the fiscal sovereignty is with the cantons and their local tax authorities can decide individually whether a different valuation is accepted or not. In certain circumstances, the tax authorities will specifically ask for valuations on a discounted cash flow basis.

8.55 France

According to the *Cour de Cassation*, the real value of shares must be assessed by taking into consideration all available factors in order to obtain a figure which is as close as possible to that which would be obtained in the market under the normal rules of supply and demand. Recent rulings have put emphasis on comparison with real-life transactions.

The French Tax Authorities issued a Valuation Handbook in 2006 setting out the following valuation methods:

(1) *Arithmetic method* (also called patrimonial method) is used to value the shares of holding companies. It involves taking the values as stated in the balance sheet of the company and adjusting them where appropriate to market value. It is commonly accepted that the value of the holding companies is their patrimonial value reduced by a reduction 'for holding companies' in order to take into consideration the following elements:
   - the liquidity of fixed assets;
   - the deferred taxation on these assets;
   - the cost of disposal (legal and transaction fees etc);
   - the potential sub-optimal value related to a lower than average business portfolio mix;
   - the lack of control of the holding company on shareholdings.

(2) *Productivity method* capitalises the average post-tax profits by a factor of between 12% and 15%. This method is favoured when a company practises a policy of self-financing by forgoing the distribution of profits. It is sometimes combined with method (3) below.

$$\frac{\text{after-tax profit} \times 100}{\text{capitalisation rate}}$$

(3) *Return method* is used when a company practises a regular policy of profit distribution in order to value more specifically the value of minority shareholdings. It involves capitalising the average net dividend distributed by the company during the past two to three years. A capitalisation rate of 5% is generally used. This method, which may be combined with (2) above, may only be used when a company practises a regular policy of profit distribution.

$$\frac{\text{distributed profit} \times 100}{\text{capitalisation rate}}$$

The distributed profit figure may be increased by 'excessive' salaries paid to shareholder directors.

(4) *Combined method* is a combination of the previous methods. If, for example, majority shareholdings giving control of the company are being valued then the following formula may be used:

$$\frac{3 \times \text{arithmetic value} + \text{productivity return value}}{4}$$

Conversely, if a minority shareholding is being valued then the following formula may be used:

$$\frac{3 \times \text{productivity return} + \text{arithmetic value}}{4}$$

(5) *Cash flow method* is suitable for significant size companies that show growth prospects because it presents an additional challenge compared to other methods, namely, the reliability of these forecasts, and the ability of the company to achieve them. It involves taking the net profit after tax of the company and adjusting this figure by non-cash items charged in the profit and loss account. The resulting cash flow is divided by a capitalisation factor of between 4% and 10%, depending on the size of the shareholding being valued.

(6) *Comparative value method* involves comparison with previous sales of shares in the same company.

(7) *Goodwill method* is used to value intangible assets. It involves capitalising the super-profits. The super-profits represent that part of the profits which exceed a normal rate of return for capital invested.

Since the handbook's publication there have been many discussions between the French tax authorities and valuation practitioners. Valuation practitioners prefer comparison methods or a DCF basis of valuation. The asset-based approach is reserved for holding companies or real restate valuations. The tax authorities' methods are often applied with a number of arbitrary adjustments, including the weighting applied in the combination method or the discount rate used. Practitioners regard some methods such as the goodwill approach as outdated and the authorities are criticised for seeking to use irrelevant methods (eg a dividend capitalisation approach applied to a small company) or apply an approach that is incorrect (eg the capitalisation of recurring income without an adjustment for debt or cash). Practitioners are unwilling to accept the use of an average value based on a collection of heterogeneous methods, not all of which may be relevant. There is wide agreement within the profession that the valuation method selected should be appropriate (adopting the multi-criteria approach requested by the AMF, the French SEC) and a move away from using average values. There is an expectation that the authorities' approach will gradually evolve and become more aligned to the commercial approach adopted by practitioners.

Part 2

Statute law

Chapter 9

Capital gains tax and corporation tax on chargeable gains, stamp duty and income tax

Signposts

9.01 Introduction

The statutory rules governing valuation for the various taxes differ in detail but are generally derived from FA 1894, s 7(5), which contained the estate duty valuation provisions. In addition, the majority of cases on share valuation for fiscal purposes used to be concerned with estate duty. The text of relevant estate duty legislation is therefore included in **Appendix D** for ease of reference when referring to the appropriate case. The Appendix also contains the text of F(1909–10)A 1910, s 25, concerning now obsolete duties on land values, which can be used for comparison with current fiscal legislation set out in this chapter and **Chapter 10**. Stamp Duty Land Tax is a tax on transactions in land, the valuation of which is outside the scope of this book.

9.02 Valuation provisions

The capital gains tax provisions relating to valuation are to be found in TCGA 1992, ss 272–274 inclusive.

It is to be noted that in TCGA 1992, s 272(1) and (2) 'market value' is the price which would have applied on a sale in the open market with no reduction for unloading all the shares on to the market at the same time.

The provisions of TCGA 1992, s 272 are as follows:

> 'Valuation: general
>
> (1) In this Act "market value" in relation to any assets means the price which those assets might reasonably be expected to fetch on a sale in the open market.
>
> (2) In estimating the market value of any assets no reduction shall be made in the estimate on account of the estimate being made on the assumption that the whole of the assets is to be placed on the market at one and the same time.
>
> (3) Subject to subsection (4) below, the market value of shares or securities quoted in The Stock Exchange Daily Official List shall, except where in consequence of special circumstances prices quoted in that List are by themselves not a proper measure of market value, be as follows:
>
> (a) the lower of the 2 prices shown in the quotations for the shares or securities in The Stock Exchange Daily Official List on the relevant date plus one-quarter of the difference between those 2 figures, or
>
> (b) halfway between the highest and lowest prices at which bargains, other than bargains done at special prices, were recorded in the shares or securities for the relevant date,
>
> choosing the amount under paragraph (a) if less than that under paragraph (b), or if no such bargains were recorded for the relevant date, and choosing the amount under paragraph (b) if less than that under paragraph (a).
>
> (4) Subsection (3) shall not apply to shares or securities for which The Stock Exchange provides a more active market elsewhere than on the London trading floor; and, if the London trading floor is closed on the relevant date, the market value shall be ascertained by reference to the latest previous date or earliest subsequent date on which it is open, whichever affords the lower market value.
>
> (5) In this Act "market value" in relation to any rights of unit holders in any unit trust scheme the buying and selling prices of which are published regularly by the managers of the scheme shall mean an amount equal to the buying price (that is the lower price) so published on the relevant date, or if none were published on that date, on the latest date before.
>
> (6) The provisions of this section, with sections 273 to 274, have effect subject to sections 25A and 41A. These provisions deal with, respectively, deemed disposals of long funding leases of plant or machinery and restrictions of losses on such leases which are fixture for capital allowances. Schedule II Part 1 deals with gifts and transactions between connected persons before 20 March 1985, valuation of assets before 6 July 1973, depreciated valuations referable to deaths before 31 March 1973 and Estate Duty in respect of any property passing on a death after 30 March 1971.'

The treatment for unit trusts in TCGA 1992, s 272(5) also applies to open-ended investment companies: under the Authorised Investment Funds (Tax) Regulations 2006, SI 2006/964, reg 97, introduction and 108. Regulation 108 provides as follows:

> '(1) Section 272 of TCGA 1992 (valuation: general) is modified as follows.
>
> (2) In subsection (3)(a) the words "where a single price is shown in the quotations for the shares or securities in The Stock Exchange Daily Official

List on the relevant date, that price, or" are treated as inserted after "2 figures, or",

(3) After subsection (5) the following subsection is treated as inserted –

> "(5AA) In this Act 'market value' in relation to shares of a given class in an open-ended investment company the prices of which are published regularly by the authorised corporate director of that company (whether or not those shares are also quoted in The Stock Exchange Daily Official List) shall mean an amount equal to the price so published on the relevant date, or if no price was published on that date, on the latest date before that date.'"

On 26 June 2014 HMRC published, in draft for comment, The Market Value of Shares, Securities and Strips Regulations 2014. The Regulations will apply for capital gains tax, corporation tax and income tax to listed securities for the purposes of the TCGA 1992, profits from deeply discounted securities and strips under ITTOIA 2005, Chapter 8, Part 4 and s 445.

They do not apply where the quoted price is not a proper measure of the listed shares or securities.

For CGT purposes, it is the mid point between the two closing prices shown in the Stock Exchange Daily Official List on any day the Exchange is open or if it is closed the latest previous day on which it was open.

> **Focus**
>
> These are the key valuation provisions for most taxation purposes, apart from employees' shares for the taxation of earnings; see **9.31–9.48**.

9.03 Information available

When the Revenue lost the case of *Lynall v IRC* [1971] 3 WLR 759, (1971) 47 TC 375 it was confirmed that the only information to be taken into account was that which would have been made available on a sale in the open market and that an arm's length sale by private treaty was not in the open market. The law was therefore changed and TCGA 1992, s 273 now provides that for capital gains tax purposes, in valuing shares in unquoted companies it is to be assumed that such information is available as the purchaser would reasonably require to be made available on an arm's length sale by private treaty (see **6.03** and below).

What information would be made available in any given case will depend on the facts of the case. A minority shareholder would usually have available the accounts and dividend record and little else unless he were a director, in which case information which he held in that capacity would normally be confidential and not disclosable without the permission of the board of directors.

In most cases, if the shareholding is substantial or the amount involved is material, a reasonable board would allow accountants appointed by the intending purchasers to look through the books and records and to examine the taxation computations. Other historical information would usually be made, as set out in **Chapter 16**.

The directors may be less willing however to divulge any future plans they have for the company (see *Percival v Wright* [1902] 2 Ch 421; **5.12** and **8.32**), which might only become available to a purchaser of a controlling interest, and it is interesting to speculate whether in *Lynall v IRC* [1971] 3 WLR 759, (1971), 47 TC 375, the directors would actually have produced details of a possible flotation to a purchaser of a 28% interest, in a sale by private treaty – the evidence suggests that they would not. The verbatim evidence of Mr Alan Lynall, whose evidence was tendered and accepted as being the evidence of the board of directors, is quoted by Plowman J:

> 'What was your attitude towards the possibility of the company having a public issue? (A) Could you tell me at what time? (Q) During the whole of the period from 1959 to the day before your mother died in 1962. (A) I started with an open mind on the matter, knowing practically nothing about it. As we got information from Thomson McLintock, which gave us a basis for seeing what the effects of a public issue would be on the company, I myself became very much more dubious about the correctness of such an action, and I would say that my attitude really eventually became adverse. (Q) What was it about the project that made you dubious and then subsequently adverse? (A) I felt that the way in which we would have had to have conducted the company as a public company, which would have involved distributing very much more of the company's funds in profits, would have been likely to prevent us continuing to promote the growth of the company from our own resources; so that we would either have had to stagnate or raise money by borrowing – an idea which was most unwelcome, to say the least. (Q) Again wait and see if there is any objection to this question: Do you know what your father's view was on the project? (A) I believe that he started, as I did, with an open mind about it, but I think that his views changed very much in the same way as mine did. Indeed, I think they would probably have been stronger, because, in all honesty, he could see the implications I think very much more clearly than I could. (Q) Supposing that on 21 May 1962, again my gentleman came in and said he was proposing to buy a block of shares in your company – first of all supposing he said he was a banker and that he was proposing to buy a block of shares in your company for his bank and he asked you whether the directors would give him an undertaking to have a public issue within say four or possibly five years, what would have been your attitude to that request? (A) We would not have given such an undertaking. (Q) Supposing that the person we have been talking about, the potential or hypothetical purchaser, asked you what was the likelihood of the company having a public issue in the foreseeable future, what answer would you have given to that question? (A) That I find a very difficult one. I would certainly prefer to say nothing at all; but to say nothing at all I am afraid would have created an impression, so I would have tried then to give as accurate a view as I could of the state of affairs as I saw them, and I would have said then that I regarded the prospect as doubtful and remote. (Q) If the gentleman had said: "Well, look, let me see any minutes of the board of directors or other documents in the possession of the company which might throw any light on the question of whether there would or would not be a public issue", what would you have done in answer to that request? (A) I would have said that all board minutes and other documents were completely confidential and I would certainly not disclose anything. (Q) Supposing that it was not the gentleman who said he was negotiating a purchase of the shares who asked you the question but that it was a partner in a firm of chartered accountants who said: "We are advising a client who is negotiating a purchase of shares in your company", and he had asked the same question about minutes and other documents of the company, what would have been your answer to the partner

> in the chartered accountants? (A) It would have been the same so far as I am concerned, it would have been a breach of confidence.'

The mere fact that a sale is assumed to be by private treaty does not of itself imply that all information possible would be made available. As Danckwerts J stated in *Re Holt* (transcript of proceedings day 3, 22 October 1953, page 56 quoted in *Re Lynall* (1971) 47 TC 375 at 384):

> 'I do not think it matters what they (the board of directors) did so much as what information the outsider would be likely to get.'

TCGA 1992 s 273(3), however, is not concerned with the information which the board would make available but that which a prudent prospective purchaser might reasonably require if he were proposing to purchase.

The purchaser's view of what is reasonable may differ from that of the board of directors of the company whose shares are being sold but the statute assumes their complete co-operation and in Lord Reid's view in *Re Lynall* at 407 this extends to all relevant information and would be assumed to extend to all future plans unless it could be shown that this was completely unreasonable:

> 'The case for the Crown is based on evidence as to how large blocks of shares in private companies are in fact sold. There is no announcement that the shares are for sale and no invitation for competitive bids. The seller engages an expert who selects the person or group whom he thinks most likely to be prepared to pay a good price and to be acceptable to the directors. If that prospective purchaser is interested he engages accountants of high repute, and the directors agree to co-operate by making available to the accountants on a basis of strict confidentiality all relevant information about the company's affairs. Then the accountants acting in an arbitral capacity fix what they think is a fair price. Then the sale is made at that price. Obviously the working of this scheme depends on all concerned having complete confidence in each other, and I do not doubt that in this way the seller gets a better price than he could otherwise obtain. In my view this evidence is irrelevant because this kind of sale is not a sale in the open market. It is a sale by private treaty made without competition to a selected purchaser at a price fixed by an expert valuer.'

(It is interesting in contrast to Lord Reid's use of the influence of accountants on the price to be paid with Staughton J's remarks in *Buckingham v Francis* (1986) 2 BCC 98984 (see **6.02**)).

Lord Harman stated:

> 'This leaves the Crown's contention. Very strong evidence was produced from two leading experts that, where substantial blocks of shares in private companies are in the market, as from time to time they are, it is the invariable practice among boards of directors to answer reasonable questions in confidence to the advisers of the purchaser. In fact, it was said that if such questions are not answered no sale would ever go through, because a purchaser would fight shy if he felt he were being left in ignorance of material facts. This, then, would not produce the willing purchaser which the formula postulates. It was said, further, that where a substantial shareholder was minded to dispose of his shares in such a company the directors would feel a moral duty to assist him by answering reasonable questions. It was argued by the taxpayer that this solution was impracticable because it would depend on the availability of members of the board who could in the last resort, if unwilling to make proper disclosure, be called into the witness box on *subpoena duces tecum* to produce some reasonable information. I suppose such circumstances might conceivably arise, but I am content to leave

> the matter where it is, relying on the almost unchallenged evidence that boards of directors do not behave in that way and that reasonable answers would be forthcoming.'

Lord Cross stated:

> 'On the other hand, the un-contradicted evidence of the experts called by the Crown, Sir Henry Benson and Mr Andrews, shows that substantial minority holdings of shares in private companies are often bought and sold, and that before a price is agreed the purchaser invariably asks the vendor or the board to supply him, or alternatively to supply his advisers, in confidence with information possibly affecting the value of the shares which is not to be found in the accounts – as, for example, the trading results from the date to which the last accounts were made up and information, such as is contained in the category B documents in this case, bearing on the likelihood of a capital appreciation and the time at which one might hope to realise it. Further, the evidence showed that such information is in practice always given to enable the sale to go through. It is, of course, true – as Mr Bagnall pointed out – that the sales of which Sir Henry Benson and Mr Andrews were speaking were sales sponsored, or at least approved, by the board of the company in question. This is necessarily so, for if the board did not wish the shareholder in question to dispose of his holding they would make it clear that they would refuse to register the purchaser. It is in fact a condition of the market for the sale of minority holdings in private companies that the directors co-operate with the vendor.'

The provisions of TCGA 199, s 273 are as follows:

> 'Unquoted shares and securities
>
> (1) The provisions of subsection (3) below shall have effect in any case where, in relation to an asset to which this section applies, there falls to be determined by virtue of section 272(1) above the price which the asset might reasonably be expected to fetch on a sale in the open market.
>
> (2) The assets to which this section applies are shares and securities which are not listed on a recognised stock exchange at the time as at which their market value for the purposes of tax on chargeable gains falls to be determined.
>
> (3) For the purposes of a determination falling within subsection (1) above, it shall be assumed that, in the open market which is postulated for the purposes of that determination, there is available to any prospective purchaser of the asset in question all the information which a prudent prospective purchaser of the asset might reasonably require if he were proposing to purchase it from a willing vendor by private treaty and at arm's length.'

In practice, it is often necessary to determine which of a company's accounts would have been 'reasonably required' by the prudent prospective purchaser at a particular date. The usual approach taken is that for a holding of 25% or less, only audited accounts published by the date of valuation would be available. For a holding of more than 50%, audited accounts for any period ended before the date of valuation would be considered available, whether or not they had actually been published by that date. When considering the value of a holding of that size, it would also be usual to expect management accounts for the period from the end of the last accounting year to the date of valuation to be 'reasonably required'. Any budgets or forecasts actually made prior to the date of valuation would also be available. If no management accounts, budgets etc were produced, it would be usual to look at the audited accounts for the period during which the date of valuation fell and deduce therefrom, bearing in mind the general circumstances of the company, the level of information that a hypothetical vendor would have been in a position to impart to a hypothetical purchaser.

For holdings of more than 25% but less than 50% of a company's share capital, often called influential minority shareholdings, the amount of information that would be reasonably required could depend on a variety of factors. If, for example, the holding being valued represents 49% of the issued share capital and the remaining shares are well spread amongst other shareholders, the 49% shareholder may well have de facto control, in which case the information reasonably required would be much the same as for a holding with de jure control. If, on the other hand, the holding in question represents 26% of the issued share capital and the remaining 74% is all in the hands of one shareholder, the 26% shareholder could exert little influence and would in most circumstances reasonably require no more than published information.

The guidelines are not hard and fast. In two separate cases heard before the Special Commissioners, *Caton v Couch* [1995] STC (SCD) 34 and *Clark v Green* [1995] STC (SCD) 99, both of which concerned shares in the same company at about the same date, the Commissioner found a difference in the level of information that would be reasonably required by a purchaser of a 14.02% shareholding compared with that which would be reasonably required by a purchaser of a 3% shareholding. There were two particular items of unpublished information which would have been of interest to the purchaser: (a) the company's results for the year which had ended less than a month before both dates of valuation and (b) the intention of the company's board of directors to seek a buyer for the whole company. The Commissioner decided that, because of the amount likely to be expended, the purchaser of the larger holding would reasonably require both items of unpublished information. The value of that holding was determined by the Commissioner at about £1.4m.

In the case of the smaller holding, the Commissioner decided that the purchaser would reasonably require up-to-date information about profits and information as to whether that level of profits was maintainable, but not information about a possible sale of the company. In coming to her decision the Commissioner was influenced by the fact that the latest published results were more than a year out of date and approximate results for the latest year were available to the board. The value of the holding was determined by the Commissioner at about £168,000.

No hint was given as to the level at which the information regarding the sale would have become available. The Shares and Assets Valuation Manual (at SVM 113130) notes that in *Canton v* Couch, 'based on prospective outlay of £1 million a prudent purchaser would consult advisers who would advise him that information about a possible exit was important; such a purchaser could, therefore, reasonably require information about approaches for sale, about future prospects of sale, and about up-to-date information from the management accounts and budget forecasts.' The Special Commissioner, at P54 stated that:

> 'If I then discount the price of £1.12 by 50% I reach a figure of 56p per share. That figure is in line with the value of 45p reached on the basis that no information about a sale was in prospect and, in my view, the difference between the two correctly reflects the added value which that information would give, bearing in

> mind the fact that, at 7 September 1987, there was no certainty that a sale would take place at all.
>
> Accordingly I determine the value of the shares at 56p each.'

It would probably be reasonable to conclude that if a holding can be valued at more than £100,000, information about unpublished but available results would be reasonably required and if the value is more than £1,000,000, virtually all available information would be reasonably required. There is nevertheless a large grey area which could lead to prolonged argument with Shares and Assets Valuation.

The following question is also left unanswered. If it is unpublished information that will cause the shares to be worth a substantial amount, should the information be taken into account in considering whether or not a substantial amount is at stake? A common sense approach will, in most circumstances, provide a reasonable answer.

A problem of consistency can arise where the unpublished information is depreciatory, as was the case in *Re Holt*. If both a control and a minority shareholding have to be valued at the same date, it could be that using published information only gives a higher value per share than a value that also takes account of unpublished information.

A further difficulty encountered in practice concerns late publication of accounts CA 2006, s 442 provides that, for a private company, the period allowed for delivering accounts and reports is nine months (after the end of the relevant accounting reference period and, for a public company, six months after the end of that period. Late delivery is punishable by a fine determined by the length of the delay. Accounts are, nevertheless, sometimes delivered late, and when considering the value of a minority holding for fiscal purposes at a date when accounts should have been delivered but have not, would the information contained in those accounts be 'reasonably required' by the prospective purchaser? *Clark v Green* suggests that they would be if the value is more than £100,000. Where the value is less, the answer may well depend on the particular circumstances of the company, but in most circumstances it is suggested that such accounts would reasonably be required.

In *Baker, Harper & Wickes v HMRC* [2011] UKFTT 645, TC 01487 the tribunal judges stated, at paragraph 52:

> 'we have regard to valuable summary of the characteristics of the market to be hypothesised given by Hoffmann LJ in the inheritance tax case of *IRC v Gray* [1994] STC 360 at 372:
>
> > "The hypothetical vendor is an anonymous but reasonable vendor, who goes about the sale as a prudent man of business, negotiating seriously without giving the impression of being either over-anxious or unduly reluctant. The hypothetical buyer is slightly less anonymous. He too is assumed to have behaved reasonably, making proper inquiries about the property and not appearing too eager to buy. But he also reflects reality in that he embodies whatever was actually the demand for that property at the relevant time.
> >
> > It cannot be too strongly emphasised that although the sale is hypothetical, there is nothing hypothetical about the open market in which it is supposed to have taken place. The concept of the open market involves assuming that the whole world was free to bid, and then forming a view about what in those circumstances would in real life have been the best price reasonably

> obtainable. The practical nature of this exercise will usually mean that although in principle no one is excluded from consideration, most of the world will usually play no part in the calculation.
>
> The inquiry will often focus on what a relatively small number of people would be likely to have paid. It may have to arrive at a figure within a range of prices which the evidence shows that various people would have been likely to pay, reflecting, for example, the fact that one person had a particular reason for paying a higher price than others, but taking into account, if appropriate, the possibility that through accident or whim he might not actually have bought. The valuation is thus a retrospective exercise in probabilities, wholly derived from the real world but rarely committed to the proposition that a sale to a particular purchaser would definitely have happened".'

In *Stanton v Drayton Commercial Investment Co Ltd (DCI)* [1982] STC 585, the taxpayer agreed to purchase a portfolio of investments from the Eagle Star Insurance Co Ltd for £3,937,962 in exchange for 2,461,226 ordinary shares of 25p each in DCI at 160p per share. However, the shares in DCI when quoted were priced at 125p per share, which the Revenue argued was the base price for calculating the capital gains tax when DCI sold some of the investments, as this was the value on being granted permission to deal in the shares. The House of Lords held that the cost price was that agreed, ie £3,937,962 at 160p per share on 2,461,226 shares in Eagle Star, not the quoted price for small numbers of DCI shares.

For capital gains tax purposes, shares or debentures of a company incorporated in any part of the UK are situated in the UK, TCGA 1992, s 275(1)(da) otherwise registered shares or debentures are situated where the principal register is situated, TCGA 1992, s 275(1)(e). Renounceable letters of allotment of shares in UK private companies were situated in the UK in *Young and another v Phillips* [1984] STC 520.

In the *Executors of Lord Howard of Henderskelfe (dec'd) v RCC* [2014] All ER (D) 176, (2014) SWTI 1560 it was held by the Court of Appeal, that a valuable painting owned by the Executors, which was exhibited at Castle Howard until its sale, was a wasting asset as plant and machinery within TCGA 1992, s 44(1)(c) with a deemed predictable life of less than 50 years and its disposal was free of capital gains tax under TCGA 1992, s 45(1). It was exhibited in the public part of the stately home which was run as a business by Castle Howard Estate Ltd. This case has been referred to the Supreme Court.

In *Neely v Rourke* [1988] STC 216 a former partner received shares in a company on the sale of his partnership interest and received £30,000, when the shares were acquired by one of his former partners. He was assessed to capital gains tax on £23,470 but successfully argued before the General Commissioner, who accepted that of the £30,000, £5,750 represented notional remuneration £7,000 represented a loan repayment and £6,000 represented a notional salary due to Mr Neely's wife. The disposal proceed for the shares were therefore, £11,250 less legal fees at £2,300 and acquisition costs of the shares of £1,029 so the Commissioners determined the gain to be £7,921. The taxpayer appealed to the High Court, who dismissed the appeal, so he appealed to the Court of Appeal. The taxpayer described the company's accounts as 'rubbish' and the court commented that 'at least to some extent, the Commissioners themselves regarded the accounts as defective'.

The taxpayer 'seemed to believe that it was incumbent upon the Crown to establish by precise evidence the correctness of each of the figures, which had been under challenge ... this belief is ... ill-founded in law':

> 'The evidentiary burden fell, fairly and squarely on him to establish any deductions from that £30,000 figure which he sought to claim.
>
> If there was a cross-appeal by the Crown, we might find ourselves obliged to consider whether, on the basis of their findings of primary fact, the Commissioners were justified in law in finding that any of the deductions of £5,750, £6,000 and £2,300 were permissible. However, in the absence of a cross-appeal, it seems to me that all we have to consider is whether the Commissioners erred in law in not allowing larger deductions than the deductions of £5,750 and £6,000 which are under attack. As I see the position, on the taxpayer's appeal we are concerned only with such errors of law, if any, as the commissioners may have made to his disadvantage. In the absence of a cross-appeal, we are not concerned with any errors of law that the Commissioners may have made which operate in his favour.
>
> The case stated gives me no ground at all for thinking that the taxpayer or the accountant appearing on his behalf was precluded from proving, if he could, that part of the consideration represented a share of the profits due to him for 1975. His difficulty was that he did not have the material to prove it.'

The appeal was dismissed.

In *Fielder v Vedlynn Ltd* [1992] STC 553, the company sold on 22 December 1977 all the share capital in eight subsidiary companies to Minden Securities Ltd, a subsidiary of Lazard Brothers & Co Ltd for £19,529 plus deferred consideration equal to 7.5% of the agreed allowable capital losses of these companies, which were subsequently agreed at £19,465,528, 7.5% of which was £1,429,915.

Vedlynn Ltd sold, on 20 December 1977, its shareholding in Grendon Trust Ltd to the eight subsidiaries, which on sold to Minden. The judge agreed with the Special Commissioner that the definition of consideration was 'as set out in the speech of Lord Lindley giving the advice of the Privy Council in *Fleming v Bank of New Zealand* [1900] AC 577 at 586, quoting from Lush J in 1875 (see *Currie v Misa* (1875) LR 10 Ex 153 at 162)) (who himself was citing *Comyns' Digest* (at B.1-15) going back to the 17th century):

> 'A valuable consideration in the sense of the law, may consist either in some right, interest, profit, or benefit accruing to the one party, or some forbearance, detriment, loss, or responsibility, given, suffered, or undertaken by the other ...'

Counsel for the Crown argued that the guarantees were part of the consideration and asserted that there must be a value to the guarantees. He submitted that the value of the guarantees to the vendor was the difference between the benefit of a fully secured obligation to pay a supplemental sum and a wholly unsecured obligation to pay that sum on the part of a company without realisable assets. Although he accepted that the valuation of the difference would involve some uncertainties he submitted that that was no answer. Valuation often involved uncertainties, and he cited *O'Brien (Inspector of Taxes) v Benson's Hosiery (Holdings) Ltd* [1979] STC 735, [1980] AC 562.

The judge, however, agreed with the Special Commissioner's comment that:

> 'It seems to me to be quite impossible to place a rational value on the guarantees. In effect the rather speculative submissions of the Crown's representative on this

> topic bear this out. How do you value the guarantees in monetary terms? I do not think you can. No evidence was led to suggest that you can. So if the guarantees are part of the consideration given by Minden for the owning companies, that part of the consideration in my opinion "cannot be valued" and one is left with the shares in the owning companies having a market value of £19,529, a figure which in itself has not be challenged.'

The reference to 'cannot be valued' relates to FA 1965, s 22(4), now TCGA 1992, s 17(1)(b).

This case had been delayed on account of *Shepherd v Lyntress Ltd* [1989] STC 617, which held that the *Ramsay* principle (*WT Ramsay Ltd v IRC* [1981] STC 174) did not apply to the acquisition of Lyntress shares by News International plc.

In *E V Booth (Holdings) Ltd v Buckwell* [1980] STC 578 it was held that when there was an arm's length agreement to sell the shares in a company for £35,000 plus the net current assets of £20,969 (total £55,969) in full and final settlement of the balance on the vendor's loan account of £55,839. It was not possible to reallocate the consideration for the sale of the shares for tax purposes to £130 for the shares and £55,839 for the loan account (total £55,969).

The net capital gain of £34,788, £35,000 less the nominal value of the shares of £2 and costs of £210, was therefore chargeable to capital gains tax and the loss on the loan was a non-allowable loss. *Aberdeen Construction Group Ltd v IRC* [1978] STC 127 was distinguished as the sale price in that case reflected both the sale of the shares and the loan amount waiver, and had to be apportioned.

In *McBrearty v IRC* [1975] STC 614 a company, The Howard Cold Storage Co Ltd, held 2,418 shares in Pye of Cambridge Ltd, which cost £1,347.6s, and had a market value at 31.3.66 of £1,964.12s.6d at 16s.3d per share. They were transferred to Mr McCarthy by the liquidators of the company on 6 September 1966 at the market value of £876.10s.6d, which was 7s.3d per share.

Pye was taken over by Philips Electrical Ltd on 5 May 1967 at 12s a share, which produced a short-term gain of £287.2s.9d. Mr McCarthy argued that the 1966 budget day price of 16s a share should have been used to produce a loss as the liquidation had been incorrectly carried out. He lost, as that was irrelevant, and outwith the jurisdiction of the Commissioners. On appeal to the Court of Exchequer in Scotland, he lost again and the gain of £287 was confirmed.

It would appear that if Mr McCarthy's allegations were correct, his actions should have been against the liquidator, not the Revenue.

In *Spectrum International v Madden* [1987] STC 114, Lightman J stated:

> 'The assessment was made in respect of the gain made by the taxpayer company on the sale of Applied Biosystems Inc., a corporation incorporated in California (the purchaser), of 1,000 shares of common stock (the shares), which for practical purposes were the entire issued share capital of its former subsidiary Spectros International Holdings Ltd, a company incorporated in Delaware (the subsidiary). The issue was whether the purchase price for the shares was US$20,001,000 or $1,000. This turns upon the true construction of the sale documents. The subsidiary shortly before the sale borrowed $20m from the Midland Bank (the bank) and used this money to pay a dividend of the same amount to the taxpayer company. The issue turns on whether the sale was of the subsidiary encumbered with this debt to the bank or with the debt discharged. It is common ground that, if the sale was of the subsidiary so encumbered, the

> price and value of the shares was \$1,000. If the sale was of the subsidiary free of the debt, it is clear that the price and value was \$20,001,000. The difficulty in this case arises from the fact that the sale documents were drafted by lawyers in California and are (in the eyes of an English lawyer) in unfamiliar form, and there is no expert evidence of Californian law or other evidence to explain their form or the reasons for such form.'

The result was that:

> 'I conclude, therefore, like the Special Commissioners, that upon the true construction of the three agreements the consideration for the disposal of the shares was \$20,001,000. I see nothing unreal or un-business-like in this view: there may well have been good reason for structuring the transaction this way. I fully accept that it results in a hefty bill for corporation tax which any of a number of alternative structures suggested by Mr Goldberg would have avoided. But that is a matter which should have been (if it was not) taken into account when the form of the agreements was negotiated and agreed.
>
> I wish to make it quite clear that the decision in this case is a decision on its own facts based on the terms of the documentation used. In the ordinary case, where a holding company sells a subsidiary, and the subsidiary is indebted to the holding company or some other person, and the purchaser under the sale agreement agrees to discharge the subsidiary's debt, the payment of the debt will not necessarily or indeed (perhaps) ordinarily constitute additional consideration of monetary value for the shares. The obligation on the purchaser may constitute added value, e.g. if the subsidiary is insolvent and the debt is due to or guaranteed or secured by the vendor. When however the subsidiary is solvent and the shares are sold for full value, no question of added value, let alone added value in monetary terms, will arise. What distinguishes this case is the unusual fact that the parties have here agreed to allocate to the purchase price the sum required to be expended by the vendor in the discharge of the debt and provided for application of that part of the purchase money in its discharge. The parties have chosen this result, and the court must respect their choice.'

Focus

- *Re Lynall* is one of the key valuation cases in respect of the information assumed to be available.
- Directors are assumed to act reasonably, as are potential purchasers.
- TCGA 1992, s 273 is a key valuation section for unquoted shares.
- It is the purchaser and vendor that are hypothetical, not the shareholdings or the market.
- *Stanton v Drayton Commercial Investment Co Ltd* is a useful decision which emphasises that the quoted price is for an uninfluential minority interest.
- The situs of an asset is of particular importance to non-UK domiciled residents.
- Litigation without evidence is unlikely to succeed.
- Consider the taxation consequences of any apportionment of the sale proceeds.
- If you must litigate, litigate against the correct party in the correct forum.
- Where more than one jurisdiction is concerned tax advice needs to be taken in each jurisdiction.

9.04 Series of transactions

TCGA 1992, s 19 deals with the case where assets are disposed of to one or more connected persons, as defined by TCGA 1992, s 286 in a series of transactions, and the total value transferred exceeds the sum of the individual transfers. TCGA 1992, s 20 provides the method of determining the original market value of the assets and the aggregate market value of the assets disposed of. The original market value is the market value which would be the consideration for a capital gains disposal in the absence of the provisions of TCGA 1992, s 19. The aggregate market value is the market value of all the transactions in the series if they had been disposed of by one disposal occurring at the time of the transaction concerned. If the original market value is less than the appropriate share of the aggregate market value, the proportionate part of the aggregate market value is applied to each disposal and the capital gains tax re-computed for all the linked transactions in the series. Transfers may be linked with any earlier transaction within a six-year period.

The most likely application of TCGA 1992, s 19 to shares in unquoted companies is where a few shares are transferred, say, by way of gift to a child, followed by a further transfer within six years of shares in the same company to the same child. If, for example, 10% of the shares were transferred in the first instance and 20% in the second, the valuations would be on the basis of a transfer of 30% of the shares, so that on the occasion of the first transfer the market value would be adjusted to one-third of a 30% interest rather than a 10% interest, and on the second transfer the value would be two-thirds of a 30% interest rather than the value of a 20% interest.

Example: series of gifts of shares

Year	*Company Value* £	*Cumulative Shareholding* £	*Value 10/11* £	*Value 11/12* £	*Value 12/13* £	*Value 13/14* £	*Value 14/15* £
2010/2011	1,000,000	10%	30,000	40,000	50,000	70,000	80,000
2011/2012	1,250,000	20%		50,000	62,500	87,500	100,000
2012/2013	1,500,00	30%			75,000	105,000	120,000
2013/2014	1,750,000	40%				122,500	140,000
2014/2015	2,000,000	50%					160,000
Total			30,000	90,000	187,500	385,000	600,000

Discounts to apply relative to the size of the shareholding, eg

Stake	Discount
10%	70%
20%	60%
30%	50%
40%	30%
50%	20%

Focus

The cumulative effect of a series of transfers can have a significant cost.

9.05 Statement of Practice 5/89 31 March 1982, rebasing

In certain limited circumstances the shares actually held by a taxpayer at 31 March 1982 (see **9.18** and **18.14**) may be aggregated with other shares in order to determine the value per share for rebasing and indexation purposes at that date. This treatment occurs most commonly when shares have been transferred from husband to wife, or vice versa, between 31 March 1982 and a subsequent disposal, but it can also apply to transfers within a group of companies.

Statement of Practice 5/89, published on 25 May 1989 and reproduced below, confirmed the Revenue's interpretation of the legislation:

> 'Capital gains rebasing and indexation: shares held at 31 March 1982
>
> Under TCGA 1992 s 35 and Sch 3 a person is treated as having held an asset at 31 March 1982 if he acquired it after that date by a transfer, or series of transfers, treated as giving rise to neither a gain nor a loss for capital gains purposes, from someone who did hold it at that date. Shares or securities of the same class in any company which are acquired in this way will be added to any shares or securities of the same class in the same company held by the transferee at 31 March 1982. Where, for rebasing and indexation purposes, it is necessary to determine the market value of the shares or securities at 31 March 1982 they will be valued as a single holding.
>
> If the shares or securities in the relevant disposal represent some but not all of those valued at 31 March 1982 then the allowable cost or indexation allowance as appropriate will be based on the proportion that the shares or securities disposed of bears to the total holding.
>
> The no gain/no loss transfers relevant in this context are those listed in TCGA 1992 s 35(3)(d).'

It will be noted that the statement also confirms that on a part disposal of shares held or deemed to be held at 31 March 1982, for rebasing purposes the shares disposed of will not be valued in isolation but as part of the larger holding. This applies to all disposals and not just those where there has been an intervening no gain/no loss transfer (Extra Statutory Concession D34 of 20 May 1989 – see **9.06**). If open market value has to be ascertained on the disposal, however, the shares will be valued in isolation, unless the provisions of TCGA 1992, ss 19 and 20 apply.

The publication of the statement of practice led to the unusual case of *R v IRC, ex p Kaye* [1992] STC 581, where the taxpayer sought judicial review of the Financial Secretary to the Treasury's refusal to allow the statement to be applied retrospectively. Lord and Lady Kaye each held minority interests in their mail order company, but together held control. Prior to selling the company, legal advice had been sought on the question of whether or not the 31 March 1982 value would be based on their combined holding if Lady Kaye were to have transferred her shares to her husband in advance of the sale. The advice received was that at best they would be taxed as if they held their shares separately. They did not therefore proceed. The application for judicial review was in fact dismissed, as it was held that the Revenue had not breached their duty of fairness to the Kayes.

On 31 March 1982, the appellant in *Marks v RCC* (2011) SWTI 1842 (TC 01086), [2011] UKFTT 221 (TC), owned all the share capital in S Ltd and F Ltd. In October 1983 the shares in F Ltd were exchanged for shares in S Ltd, so that F Ltd became a wholly owned subsidiary. The taxpayer contended that at 31 March 1982, the combined value of the two companies was £8,425,000, whereas HMRC valued them separately at £3,100,000 for S Ltd and a nominal £100 for F Ltd.

It was held that the shares in the two companies were separate assets for capital gains tax rebasing of 31 March 1982. Under TCGA 1992, s 126(1)(a), the base value of the new S Ltd shares was the value of the F Ltd shares at that date, and the estate duty and inheritance tax cases, such as *Earl of Ellesmere v IRC* [1918] 2 KB 735, *Duke of Buccleuch v IRC* [1967] 1 All ER 129 and *Gray (Executor of Lady Fox) v IRC* [1994] STC 360, which were optimum lotting cases, did not apply for capital gains tax. The value at 31 March 1982 was held to be £3,709,000 for the S Ltd shares, and £443,000 for the S Ltd shares acquired in exchange for the F Ltd shares, taking into account the fact that S Ltd was a special purchaser of the F Ltd shares at 31 March 1982, in order to continue the commercial relationship between the two companies. This was computed on the basis of a 10% return on wholesale turnover (£150,000) and five years' future utilisation under a licence agreements discounted at 40% per annum, (£273,000).

In *Erdal v HMRC* [2011] UKFTT 87 (TC) the 31 March 1982 value of shares was required, which HMRC valued at £1.23 each and the taxpayers at £4 each. The tribunal judge valued the whole share capital at £4.04 each and applied a 40% discount for the taxpayers' less than 3% shareholding to take account of the lack of marketability and low dividend payments to arrive at a capital gains tax value of £2.42 a share. The judge emphasised that each case should be considered on its own facts and it was neither 'worthwhile nor appropriate to trawl the cases comparing discounts in share valuation cases'. The price earnings ratio used, of 14, was higher than the nearest quoted comparable in the light of the excellent prospects for the company.

Focus

- The 31 March 1982 values in *R v IRC, ex p Kaye* are still important but the relevant information becomes harder to obtain. See **Appendix C**.
- Each case has to be considered on its own particular facts and circumstances.

9.06 Extra Statutory Concession D34 (issued on 20 May 1989)

This concession, reproduced below, confirms that where there is a part disposal from a holding of shares owned at 31 March 1982, the value for rebasing and indexation will not be the value in isolation of the shares disposed of, but their value as a proportion of the total value of the shares held at 31 March 1982:

> 'D34. Rebasing and indexation: shares held at 31 March 1982
>
> Where for the purposes of the rebasing provisions in TCGA 1992 s 35, and the indexation provisions in TCGA 1992 s 55, it is necessary to determine the market value of shares or securities of the same class in any company on 31 March 1982, all the shares or securities held at that date will be valued as a single holding whether they were acquired on or before 6 April 1965 or after that date.
>
> If the shares or securities in the relevant disposal represent some but not all of those valued at 31 March 1982 then the allowable cost of indexation allowance as appropriate will be based on the proportion that the shares or securities disposed of bears to the total holding at 31 March 1982.'

Focus

The 6 April 1965 holding has now ceased to have any relevance for capital gains tax purposes.

9.07 Extra Statutory Concession D44 (issued on 16 March 1993) – 31 March 1982, rebasing

This concession extended the beneficial treatment recognised by Statement of Practice 5/89 to allow a transferee in a no gain/no loss disposal to choose to have their shares valued as the appropriate proportion of the *transferor's* holding at 31 March 1982. It was classified as obsolete by the Enactment of Extra Statutory Concession Order 2010 No 157, but is still in HMRC's Shares and Assets Valuation Manual at SVM 107130 at March 2014.

The text of the concession is as follows:

> 'Capital gains tax rebasing and indexation: shares derived from larger holdings held at 31 March 1982.
>
> For rebasing and indexation purposes, taxpayers are treated as having held an asset at 31 March 1982 if it was acquired after that date by a transfer, or series of transfers, treated as giving rise to neither a gain nor a loss for capital gains purposes, from someone who did hold it at that date. Such "no gain/no loss" transfers include transfers between spouses and between companies in the same group where transfers fell within TCGA 1992 ss 58 or 171(1) or the predecessors of those Sections.
>
> Where, for rebasing and indexation purposes, it is necessary to establish the 31 March 1982 market value of shares or securities of the same class, shares or securities acquired in this way by no gain/no loss transfer are added to any such shares or securities of the same class actually held by the transferee at 31 March 1982 and valued as a single holding.
>
> For the purposes of this valuation, where a claim is made by the taxpayer, the value of the single holding may be regarded as:
>
> – in the case of a disposal by an individual, the appropriate proportion of the value of any larger holding of shares or securities of the same class which

were held by the individual's spouse at 31 March 1982 and from which part or all of the single holding was derived by one or more no gain/no loss transfers within TCGA 1992 s 58;

- in the case of a disposal by a company, the appropriate proportion of the value of any larger holding of shares or securities of the same class which were held by another company at 31 March 1982 and from which part or all of the single holding was derived by one or more no gain/no loss transfers within TCGA s 171(1). This extra-statutory concession applies in relation to:
- all relevant disposals made before 16 March 1993 in relation to which a claim is made before liabilities are finally determined; and
- all disposals made on or after 16 March 1993 provided a claim is made within 2 years of the end of the year of assessment or accounting period in which the disposal is made; or at such later time as the Board of Inland Revenue may allow.'

A simple example would be as follows:

Example

	Husband's shareholding	*Wife's shareholding*
At 31 March 1982	70%	30%
Value per share	£10	£3
Husband transfers 5% to wife on 31/3/86 (no gain, no loss)	65%	35%

The whole company is then sold on 1 April 1993. As a result of the extra-statutory concession, the wife may elect to have all her shares valued at 31 March 1982 as the appropriate proportion of her husband's 70% shareholding, ie, in this example at £10 per share rather than £3 per share which would have applied if there had been no intervening transfer.

It should be noted that for individuals, trustees and personal representatives, indexation allowance has been frozen for periods after April 1998 and abolished from 6 April 2008. For corporation tax purposes, however, the previous indexation allowance rules continue in force.

Focus

There may still be cases where reference to this concession will be appropriate.

9.08 Non-arm's length transfers

The capital gains tax legislation requires market value to be calculated on various occasions other than on death. These include TCGA 1992, s 17, which provides that market value is used for non-arm's length transactions and where the consideration cannot be valued. The legislation ensures that market value shall not be taken as the acquisition cost where there is no corresponding disposal or the corresponding disposal is made by an excluded person, and any consideration in money or money's worth is less than the market value of the asset. This prevents the use as a tax avoidance mechanism of the decision in *Harrison v Nairn Williamson Ltd* [1978] 1 WLR 145, that the issue of shares by a company is not a disposal.

HMRC's Capital Gains manual at CG14542 states:

> 'a transaction is "otherwise than by way of a bargain made at arm's length" when one of the persons involved in the transaction does not intend to get the best deal for themselves from THAT PARTICULAR TRANSACTION. That person enters into the transaction with the subjective intention of giving some gratuitous benefit to the other person.
>
> WHERE ONE OF THE PARTIES TO A TRANSACTION HAS THE INTENTION OF CONFERRING A GRATUITOUS BENEFIT ON ANOTHER PARTY TO THE TRANSACTION THEN THE TRANSACTION IS OTHERWISE THAN BY WAY OF A BARGAIN MADE AT ARM'S LENGTH AND THE MARKET VALUE RULE APPLIES.'

And includes the following:

> 'EXAMPLE
>
> Mr K Brown sells 100 shares in the family trading company to his nephew, Alec Brown, at par, for £1 each. The shares are worth £100 each. Mr K Brown has knowingly sold the shares at undervalue and intended to confer a gratuitous benefit on his nephew. An uncle and nephew are not connected persons so the subjective intention test has to be applied in order to use the market value rule.
>
> The market value of the shares, supplied by Shares and Assets Valuation, should be used as Mr K Brown's disposal proceeds and as Alec Brown's acquisition cost.'

A transfer into settlement is a disposal of the entire property settled. See *Berry v Warnett* [1982] STC 396.

See also *IRC v Spencer-Nairn* [1961] STC 60 and *Postlethwaite's Executors v HMRC* [2007] WTLR 353 on the meaning of gratuitous intent. See also on TCGA 1992, s 17, *Bullivant Holdings v IRC* (198) STC 905, *Mansworth v Jelly* [2002] EWCA Civ 1829, *Whitehouse v Ellam* [1995] STC 503 and *Director v Inspector of Taxes* [1998] STC (SCD) 172.

Focus

The market value rule applies to non-arm's length transactions.

9.09 Trust distributions

TCGA 1992, s 71 provides that there is a deemed disposal for capital gains tax where a person becomes absolutely entitled to trust assets. The appropriate trust assets are deemed to have been disposed of at market value by the trustees and re-acquired by them as nominees of the beneficiary: *Crowe v Appleby*

[1975] STC 502; *Pexton v Bell & another* [1976] STC 301; *Stephenson v Barclays Bank Trust Co Ltd* [1975] STC 151; *Hoare Trustees v Gardner* [1978] STC 89; *Chinn v Collins* [1981] STC 1; *Roome and another v Edwards* [1981] STC 96; as to resettlements, see *Hart v Briscoe and others* [1978] STC 89. An allocation of part of a discretionary trust does not crystallise a capital gains tax charge: *Bond v Pickford* [1983] STC 517. An appointment did not create a new settlement in *Swires v Renton* [1991] STC 490.

On a beneficiary becoming absolutely entitled as against the trustees any unused losses of the trustees may be carried forward and are available to the beneficiary. However, the loss can be set off only against any gain on disposal of the asset concerned by the beneficiary. Where that asset is an estate, interest or right in or over land, the loss can be set against a gain on the disposal of any asset deriving from that asset, eg a gain on the grant of a lease or sublease out of a freehold or superior lease. In any case, the loss must first be set against pre-entitlement gains of the trustee, and only the excess of the loss over such gains is available to the beneficiary.

A pre-entitlement gain is a gain arising on other assets passing to the same beneficiary on his becoming absolutely entitled, and any other gains arising in the same year but before he becomes absolutely entitled. Where gains arise on some assets and losses on other assets, those gains and losses must be netted off.

No claim is necessary. Such losses are not restricted by TCGA 1992, s 18(3) as connected persons. A remainderman becoming absolutely entitled on the death of a life tenant during the period of administration takes the assets at the date of death as if he were a legatee (CCAB Press Release, June 1967).

Statement of Practice SP7/84 deals with Power of Appointment or Advancement.

The Commissioners for HMRC statement of practice SP 9/81, which was issued on 23 September 1981 following discussions with the Law Society, set out the Revenue's views on the capital gains tax implications of the exercise of a power of appointment or advancement when continuing trusts are declared, in the light of the decision of the House of Lords in *Roome & Denne v Edwards* [1981] STC 96. Those views have been modified to some extent by the decision of the Court of Appeal in *Bond v Pickford* [1983] STC 517.

In *Roome & Denne v Edwards* the House of Lords held that where a separate settlement is created there is a deemed disposal of the relevant assets by the old trustees for the purposes of TCGA 1992, s 71(1)). But the judgements emphasised that, in deciding whether or not a new settlement has been created by the exercise of a power of appointment or advancement, each case must be considered on its own facts, and by applying established legal doctrine to the facts in a practical and common-sense manner. In *Bond v Pickford* the judgments in the Court of Appeal explained that the consideration of the facts must include examination of the powers which the trustees purported to exercise, and determination of the intention of the parties, viewed objectively.

It is now clear that a deemed disposal under TCGA 1992, s 71(1) cannot arise unless the power exercised by the trustees, or the instrument conferring the power, expressly or by necessary implication, confers on the trustees authority to remove assets from the original settlement by subjecting them to the trust of a different settlement. Such powers (which may be powers of advancement or appointment) are referred to by the Court of Appeal as 'powers in the wider form'. However, the Commissioners for HMRC consider that a deemed disposal will not arise when such a power is exercised and trusts are declared in circumstances such that:

(a) the appointment is revocable; or
(b) the trusts declared of the advanced or appointed funds are not exhaustive so that there exists a possibility at the time when the advancement or appointment is made that the funds covered by it will on the occasion of some event cease to be held upon such trusts and once again come to be held upon the original trusts of the settlement.

Further, when such a power is exercised the Commissioners for HMRC consider it unlikely that a deemed disposal will arise when trusts are declared if duties in regard to the appointed assets still fall to the trustees of the original settlement in their capacity as trustees of that settlement, bearing in mind the provision in TCGA 1992, s 69(1) that the trustees of a settlement form a single and continuing body (distinct from the persons who may from time to time be the trustees).

Finally, the Commissioners for HMRC accept that a power of appointment or advancement can be exercised over only part of the settled property and that the above consequences would apply to that part. With regard to bare trustees, TCGA 1992, s 60 provides that a trustee is deemed to hold as nominee for a beneficiary who has become absolutely entitled.

Focus

The capital gains tax rules on a distribution by trustees can be complex.

9.10 Termination of life interest

After 5 April 1982 no chargeable gain is to accrue on the termination of a life interest (where the settled property remains intact in the trust) whether the termination is on the death of a life tenant or not. Previously, a termination of a life interest otherwise than on death would have given rise to a chargeable gain (or allowable loss) on the trustees: TCGA 1992, s 72.

On a death, the settled property is treated as having been disposed of and immediately re-acquired by the trustees at market value but no chargeable gain is deemed to accrue.

There is a deemed disposal of the settled property on the death of the life tenant even if his interest is pur autre vie and does not therefore terminate. From 22 March 2006, the exemption for property remaining in trust on the termination of an interest in possession only applies to immediate post-death interests, transitional serial interests, disabled persons' interests, trusts for a bereaved child or age 18-to-25 trusts as defined by IHTA 1984, s 49A, 49B, 89B, 71A or 71D.

Under TCGA 1992, s 73(1) where a beneficiary becomes absolutely entitled to trust assets on the death of a life tenant no chargeable gain accrues on the deemed disposal. After 5 April 1982, if the deceased only had an interest in part of the trust assets in question the exemption only applies to that proportion.

For this purpose a life interest in part of the income of settled property is a life interest in a corresponding part of that property: if no right of recourse to other property in the settlement exists the life interest is deemed to be in a settlement separate from the other property.

In a case where the trust asset was rolled into a settlement under the former holdover rules in FA 1980, s 79, or under the restricted rules now contained in TCGA 1992, s 165 (see **9.17**), the held over chargeable gain crystallises (to the appropriate extent) on the life tenant's death: TCGA 1992, s 74.

The tax free write-up on death to the probate value is also available in respect of the death of a life tenant under the provisions of TCGA 1992, s 73.

Focus

The termination of a life interest can give rise to valuations, depending on the circumstances.

9.11 Bare sales

TCGA 1992, s 105 provides that where there has been a bare sale, in other words the quantity of the securities so disposed of exceeds the quantity of the securities held, then it is to be related to shares acquired subsequently and matched with the next shares of the appropriate type acquired.

Focus

Bare sales usually arise with quoted not unquoted shares.

9.12 Reorganisations

One of the capital gains tax provisions involving the valuation of unquoted shares relates to the provisions where there has been a reorganisation of share capital under TCGA 1992, Sch 2, para 19.

If there has been a reorganisation prior to 6 April 1965 other than a mere bonus issue there is a deemed disposal and acquisition at 6 April 1965. The gain or loss from that date is therefore subject to capital gains tax whether it is more or less than the actual gain on the shares throughout the entire period of ownership. A take-over of a company on a share for share exchange is not a bonus issue but a full reorganisation for this purpose, see *IRC v Beveridge* (1979) 53 TC 178.

If the reorganisation takes place after 6 April 1965 time apportionment will cease to run and a notional gain or loss is computed which is frozen until the shares are in fact sold.

The interpretation of these provisions is clarified by the Inland Revenue Statement of Practice published on 21 December 1979 as SP14/79:

'Unquoted shares or securities held on 6 April 1965

1. This statement concerns the application of TCGA 1992 Sch 2 para 19 to unquoted shares and securities held on 6 April 1965. Where there has been a reorganisation of a company's share capital before 6 April 1965, para 19(1) deems the shares to have been sold and re-acquired at market value on 6 April 1965. Where a reorganisation takes place on or after 6 April 1965, and all or part of the new holding of shares is disposed of without an election for valuation at 6 April 1965 being made, para 19(2) requires the new shares to be valued as at the date of the reorganisation: time apportionment is applied to the gain or loss up to that date and on a disposal this is brought into account as well as the subsequent gain or loss.
2. For the purpose of para 19(1) and 19(2), "reorganisation of share capital" includes not only reorganisation of one company's share capital within TCGA 1992 s 126 or 132, but also certain takeovers, reconstructions and amalgamations involving more than one company within TCGA 1992 s 135 or 136.
3. Para 19(3), however, prevents the application of paras 19(1) or 19(2) where the new holding differs only from the original shares in being a different number, whether greater or less, of shares of the same class as the original shares. The Inland Revenue's practice has been to treat para 19(3) as capable of covering reorganisations involving more than one company; for example, the exchange of shares of a certain class in one company for shares of the same class in another company.
4. The Board of Inland Revenue, have considered this practice in the light of the recent case of *IRC v Beveridge* (1979) 53 TC 178. In accordance with opinions expressed in the Court of Session paragraph 14(3) is no longer considered to apply where the shares comprised in the new holding are shares in a different company from the old shares.
5. This interpretation will be applied to all cases in which the liability had not been finally determined by the date of the Court of Session's judgment (19 July 1979).'

From 6 April 2008 rebasing at 31 March 1982 is mandatory. It should however be noted that ESC D10 provides:

> 'Where in consequence of a reorganisation of share capital before 6 April 1965, computation of a gain by reference to value at that date is required by TCGA 1992 Sch 2 para 19(1) or where under para 19(2) in consequence of such reorganisation after 6 April 1965 time apportionment applies only to the gain or loss up to the date of reorganisation. Capital gains tax is not charged on a disposal of the entire new shareholding on more than the actual gain realised.'

For the purposes of this concession the disposal of the entire new holding by way of a number of separate transactions all within the same income tax year (or in the case of a company the same accounting period) will be treated as a single disposal.

Focus

These rules are likely to have limited application nowadays.

9.13 Negligible value

If an asset, such as shares in an unquoted company, has been claimed to be of negligible value, that valuation will be considered by Shares and Assets Valuation.

The claim would be under TCGA 1992 s 24 which provides:

> '(1) Subject to the provisions of this Act and, in particular to [sections 140A(1D), 140E(7), and 144], the occasion of the entire loss, destruction, dissipation or extinction of an asset shall, for the purposes of this Act, constitute a disposal of the asset whether or not any capital sum by way of compensation or otherwise is received in respect of the destruction, dissipation or extinction of the asset
>
> [(1A) A negligible value claim may be made by the owner of an asset ("P") if condition A or B is met.
>
> (1B) Condition A is that the asset has become of negligible value while owned by P.
>
> (1C) Condition B is that:
>
> (a) the disposal by which P acquired the asset was a no gain/no loss disposal,
> (b) at the time of that disposal the asset was of negligible value, and
> (c) between the time when the asset became of negligible value and the disposal by which P acquired it, each other disposal (if any) of the asset was a no gain/no loss disposal.]
>
> [(2) [Where a negligible value claim is made:]
>
> (a) this Act shall apply as if the claimant had sold, and immediately reacquired, the asset at the time of the claim or (subject to paragraphs (b) and (c) below) at any earlier time specified in the claim, for a consideration of an amount equal to the value specified in the claim.
> (b) An earlier time may be specified in the claim if:
>   (i) the claimant owned the asset at the earlier time; and
>   (ii) the asset had become of negligible value at the earlier time; and either
>   (iii) for capital gains tax purposes the earlier time is not more than two years before the beginning of the year of assessment in which the claim is made; or
>   (iv) for corporation tax purposes the earlier time is on or after the first day of the earliest accounting period ending not more than two years before the time of the claim.
> (c) FA 1994 s 93 and Sch 1 (indexation losses and transitional relief) shall have effect in relation to an asset to which this section applies as if the sale and reacquisition occurred at the time of the claim and not at any earlier time.
>
> (3) For the purposes of [this section], a building and any permanent or semi-permanent structure in the nature of a building may be regarded as an asset separate from the land on which it is situated, but [where a building or structure is so regarded], the person deemed to make the disposal of the building or structure shall be treated as if he had also sold, and immediately reacquired, the site of the building or structure shall be treated as if he had also sold, and immediately reacquired, the site of the building or structure (including in the site any land occupied for purposes ancillary to the use of the building or structure), for a consideration equal to its market value at that time.
>
> (4) For the purposes of subsection (1C), a no gain/no loss disposal is one which, by virtue of any of the no gain/no loss provisions, neither a gain nor a loss accrues to the person making the disposal.'

Although in the past Shares and Assets Valuation has been willing to consider negligible value in terms relating to the value of the original investment, it now treats it as an absolute term, meaning 'next to nothing'. It has not put a figure on 'next to nothing' but in practice it is likely to be about £1,000 or less.

> **Focus**
>
> The negligible value rules, giving rise to a deemed disposal, are strictly interpreted by HMRC.

9.14 Negligible value cases

In *Joanne Elizabeth Fletcher v RCC* (2008) SpC 711 the Special Commissioner had to consider whether TCGA 1992, s 24(2) applied to 50,000 B ordinary shares acquired by capitalising a loan account in circumstances where the B shares were issued to the holder of 400 ordinary shares and he concluded:

> 'that those shares had a very significant value on 16 May 2003. This case is in other words not remotely akin to the line of cases commencing with *IRC v Burmah Oil Co Ltd* (1982) 54 TC 200 where worthless debt was swapped for shares in the tax hope of turning an admitted and non-allowable loss on the debt into an allowable tax loss on shares. The capitalisation here was done without any thought to taxation consequences; at the insistence of SEGF which was injecting £250,000 to fund marketing and did not want half of the amount applied in repaying directors loans and indeed the capitalisation was affected at a time of great excitement and optimism about the company's future. And I repeat that the terms of the third party subscription must render it inconceivable that the ordinary shares and the directors' loan were valueless on 16 May 2003.'

In fact the Commissioner also held in this case that the B shares had been acquired on a company reorganisation within TCGA 1992, s 126 on, the authority of *Dunstan v Young Austen Young Ltd* (1989) 62 TC 448. The loss claimed when the company went into liquidation, and the shares proved worthless, was therefore allowed. This case was followed in *Fletcher v HMRC* (2008) SpC 711.

Barker, Harper & Wickes v HMRC [2011] UKFTT 645 (TC) was a negligible value claim under TCGA 1992, s 24(1B), as a deemed disposal where the owner of an asset which has become of negligible value makes a claim to that effect. TCGA 1992, ss 272(1) and 223 were referred to, defining market value as the price which the assets might reasonably be expected to fetch on a sale in the open market.

Submissions on the law for the taxpayers (at para 7):

> 'It was common ground between the parties that "negligible value" means "worth next to nothing", but not "nil", and that the concept has no room for any notion of materiality in which the previous value of the asset would be taken into account by way of comparison with the value which is said to be negligible. The test in that regard is therefore an absolute one, the same for an asset previously worth a million pounds and an asset previously worth much less. No authority was cited to us for this view, and no attempt was made to translate the concept

into figures so that it could be said with confidence that any particular value would undoubtedly be "negligible" within the meaning of the section – though Mr Gibbon QC for the Crown expressed the view that a value of even £1,000 would not be negligible. It was also common ground that the shares in question did have value on their acquisition.'

Submissions on behalf of HMRC (at para 31(viii)):

'Mr Gibbon (counsel for the Crown) then recalled the various principles which had been established by the courts regarding valuation: that the hypothetical vendor is anonymous (*IRC v Clay* [1914] 3 KB 466, at 473); that the sale also is hypothetical (*Duke of Buccleuch v IRC* [1976] 1 AC 506, at 543 per Lord Guest); that there is a willing vendor and a willing purchaser (*Clay* at 478); that proper marketing and exposure of the asset is to be assumed (*Buccleuch* at 525A–B, per Lord Reid); that the potential purchaser is prudent (*Findlay's Trustees v CIR* (1938) ATC 437, at 440); that the potential purchaser's enquiries would depend on the circumstances (*Lynall* [1972] AC 680 at 698E per Lord Morris); that the common law open market approach did not require confidential information to be made available, whereas s 273 does: *Caton's Administrators v Couch* [1995] STC (SCD) 34 at 49h–50c, per Special Commissioner Brice.'

Conclusions on the law:

'47. … to speak of an asset which has become of negligible value as having a market value makes no sense. The very fact that it has no market value is why it is said to be of negligible value; if the asset has a market value, then its value cannot be negligible. That it may nonetheless have a subjective value to its owner is beside the point: an item of sentimental value to a person may well be nearly priceless as far as that person is concerned, but it would be quite unworkable for the tax base to depend on the accident of personal attachment to an asset rather than upon a value evidenced by an actual or hypothesised arm's length transaction.

48. The test of eligibility for a claim under section 24(2) is therefore: does this asset have a market value? If the answer is "no", a claim may in principle be made; if the answer is "yes", no claim under this provision is appropriate. The draftsman had accordingly no need to specify whether the word "value" in the phrase "negligible value" meant "market value" – or some other type of value – because the reference is to a situation in which there is no objective value. It was rightly accepted by both parties that 'negligible value' meant 'worth next to nothing'; and although it is at first sight odd for a claim for 'negligible' value to be set at nil, it is quite consistent with an approach to the issue which accepts that nil and negligible are so close as to make no difference.

49. It follows that the criteria in sections 272 and 273 must be applicable for the purpose of ascertaining whether a claim falls within section 24(2) or whether it fails *in limine*. We accept the argument that parliament cannot have intended the tribunals and courts to embark upon a fresh course of investigation into a novel and nebulous concept of value when there are clear and well understood rules within the tax code in question, or that it has been left unclear since 1965 when this section was first enacted whether section 272 alone should be in play or whether both these sections are relevant. Section 273 is in terms appended to section 272, and we see no ground for excluding its possible application.

50. Various other conclusions follow. Thus, bearing in mind the possibility admitted by subsection (2)(b) of making negligible value claims two years in arrear, it is apparent that information relevant to the earlier time thus permitted to be used, which is discovered after that date may be taken into account, but

only if it was in fact available at the relevant time and the prospective purchaser would reasonably have requested it. Following *Marks*, we accept therefore that accounts not in existence at the relevant time are not to be treated has having been created at that time, even if they came into existence subsequently and contained information available at the time.

51. Further, since the issue is whether the asset in question had a market value or not, the likely costs of disposal must be taken into account in the usual way it is found that there is a gross market value. The fact that [TCGA 1992] section 38(4) requires no account to be taken of expenditure incidental to the deemed sale and re-acquisition is irrelevant, since that notional transaction takes place after the prior question of whether the asset is of negligible value or not has been dealt with. There cannot be a conflation of the condition precedent to a claim being made and the consequence of its having been made.'

The expert evidence included:

'151. Mr Eamer's evidence considered the basis on which Diligenti had been established, compared the forecasts with the position at 5 April 2001 and the value of Diligenti's investments then, reviewed market conditions at that date and the cash position at that point, and examined in detail the position with regard to each of Diligenti's businesses. It was noted that the investment made by the appellants effectively resulted from the absence of any alternative source of funding, and the crisis at InterX in early 2001 and the falls in its share price were then examined and the conclusion reached that the market capitalisation of InterX at 5 April put the value of its equity in Diligenti at nil.

154. Mr Eamer's evidence continued that by 5 April 2001 Diligenti had been unable to secure any further funding; that any that was secured would have to be used to repay the first instalment of £10m due to InterX on 30 June (and although InterX might have given up hope of getting their money then, that fact would either not get through to a purchaser or he would be inclined to discount it); that the value of all the companies owned by Diligenti with the exception of HESc was nil, and that HESc's goodwill would be no more than £1m. The net asset deficit in Diligenti's balance sheet at that date would therefore be £9.452m. At 5 April, it was clear – both generally, and from InterX's own strategy announcement on 27 March – that the BladeRunner technology could not now be expected to bring value to any of Diligenti's operations and that Diligenti had not adopted any other form of IT integration.

155. Concluding that the value of each of the appellants' shareholdings at 5 April was worth no more than £1, Mr Eamer summarised his opinion as follows: (i) any additional intangible value that had been due to prospects for the BladeRunner technology had disappeared since the side-lining of that by InterX in March 2001, (ii) market values for the types of investment made by Diligenti had had fallen dramatically since they were made, (iii) the forecasts for the first quarter of 2001 had fallen well short, (iv) the 'enterprise value' of InterX at 5 April showed that the market put no value on InterX's investment in Diligenti, and (v) Diligenti was running out of cash and had little prospect of finding new sources.

168. Mr Glover's evidence was that the open market value of a holding of each appellant's shares at 5 April 2001 was not less than £154,000 (£14.66 per share) "and may well have been considerably more". His report reviewed the origins of Diligenti, its financing, the activity of its subsidiaries, the forecasts for turnover and profit/loss, and the position at 5 April 2001 in so far as it could be ascertained by reference to information which would have been available at that time. Valuations on the basis of section 272 and 273, or 272 alone, or on the basis

> that the shares would be sold in an arm's length commercial transaction but with no presumption that the transaction would be in the open market, all reached the same conclusion.
>
> 172. Mr Glover concluded that informed professional opinion at the time was that Diligenti's value was considerably in excess of its costs – over four times as much – and the company's shares must have been worth at least their balance sheet value: thus, the net assets and equity funds shown in the unaudited balance sheet as at 31 March 2001 were £6,189,000 which, given the 441,000 shares than in issue, produced a value per share of £14.03, or £154,330 for 11,000 shares; he rounded these figures down to £154,000 and £14 per share.
>
> 174. Although the notion of "enterprise value" used by Mr Eamer had become a mainstream tool of investment appraisal, it had "no external stock market reality", and the average stock market participant could not have formed a view on the worth of Diligenti since there was no adequate information in the public domain for that purpose.'

There was a 'fundamental flaw' in Mr Eamer's approach stemming from his failure to recognise that because so much information on Diligenti and its subsidiaries was not now available it was impossible to be precise about the value of its shares, and there was very little likelihood that by 5 April 2001 they had become worthless.

The Tribunal's conclusions were:

> '180. The claim by Mr Eamer to use the concept of "enterprise value" to show that Diligenti was valued at nil by the market as of the valuation date is not convincing. As has been pointed out, such a "top down" process is not adequate to value specific assets held by a quoted company, and much commercial activity takes place upon investors perceiving that an underlying asset or assets are indeed worth more than is suggested by the share price of a holding company.
>
> 185 (viii) The unresolved difference between Messrs Eamer and Glover over the value of HESc, the only Diligenti asset for which there is external evidence of value, shows how difficult it would be to get to the bottom of matters. Mr Glover put the value of the HESc shares at between $10.9m and $12.2m, referring to actual trades on NASDAQ on 4 and 6 April 2001, whereas Mr Eamer put the value at $1.5m.
>
> 182. The range of potential purchasers appears to us to have consisted of two groups of persons.
>
> 183. Group one would be composed of an indeterminate number of high net worth individuals interested in a relatively speculative investment in the technology sector. That there were such persons can be inferred from the fact of the American and British indices of shares in the sector still showing a significant degree of investor activity; despite the heavy fall in the value of the stocks over the previous year, the sector was not by any means dead.
>
> 184. Group two would consist of the three appellants, Mr Stafford and Mr Spanoudakis, and InterX. They were the only persons likely to be willing to consider purchasing with a low level of due diligence.
>
> *Decision*
>
> 198. Our decision in the appeals is therefore that each of the appellants' shareholdings would in all probability have been unsaleable at 5 April 2001 in the open market in a sale by private treaty at arm's length. Their value therefore

> was, within the sense of that term as used in the statute, negligible. 'The appeals must therefore be allowed. The parties are at liberty to make an application with regard to costs within 30 days of the release of this Decision.'

In *Williams v Bullivant* [1983] STC 107, a claim to carry back a negligible value claim was refused although amended TCGA 1992, s 24(2), now allows a two-year carry-back before the beginning of the year of assessment in which the claim is made (enacting extra statutory concession D28).

In *Director v HMIT* [1998] STC (SCD) 172 relief under TCGA 1992, s 24(2) was refused on the basis that the taxpayer had agreed that the shares he had been allotted had a nil market value at allotment, as the company liabilities exceeded its assets and it subsequently became insolvent. The s 24(2) claim was rejected as the shares had been allotted at their market value, which was nil and they had therefore not become of negligible value as they had never had a value. A similar decision was reached in *Re Mrs J Dyer v HMRC* [2013] UKFTT 691 (TC), where the taxpayer had acquired, in 2007, some shares in a company which their daughter controlled and in respect of which they claimed negligible value relief under TCGA 1992, s 24(2), which was denied as the shares were worthless of acquisition.

In *Cleveleys Investment Trust Co v IRC (No 2)* [1975] STC 456, a payment under a bank guarantee of £27,351 did not give rise to a negligible value claim as the acquisition of the bank's worthless claim was an incidental consequence of honouring its guarantee.

In *Larner v Warrington* [1985] STC 442, it was held that a negligible value claim in 1978/79 under s 24(2) could not be given against a 1973/74 assessable gain. For there to be relief under s 24, there must be either a disposal or deemed disposal of the relevant shares, which was not the case in *Marks v McNally* [2004] STC (SCD) 503. Income tax sideways loss relief for the disposal of worthless shares under the conversion of securities provisions in ITA 2007, ss131–133 was refused in *Hobart v Willows* [1997] STC (SCD) 330 on an attempt to carry the loss forward, instead of backwards. In *S Joyce v HMRC* [2010] UKFTT 566 (TC), the problem was that the shares had to be subscribed for, not purchased from existing shareholders. A similar decision was reached in *F Fard v HMRC* [2011] UKFTT 63 (TC).

A claim under ITA 2007, s 131 failed on the taxpayer's failure to provide evidence of his subscription for shares, in *J Hadnan v HMRC* [2011] UKFTT 580 (TC), and similarly, in *P Saund v HMRC* [2012] UKFTT 740 (TC).

ITA 2007, s 131 relief was denied under s 134(5) for losses of a Canadian company, which had not carried on its business wholly or mainly in the UK: *Professor Sir P Lachmann v HMRC* [2010] UKFTT 560 (TC).

In *D Harper v HMRC* [2009] UKFTT 382 (TC) the negligible value claim failed because the shares were of negligible value when they were acquired.

Robert Brown v HMRC [2013] UKFTT 740 (TC) was another negligible value claim, under TCGA 1992, s 24(1B), that an asset, in this case shares in Microsharp Holdings Ltd, had become of negligible value at 5 April 2006, giving rise to a capital loss for which income tax relief was claimed under TA 1988, s 574 (now ITA 2007, s 131(3)(c)).

Reference was made to *Barker, Harper & Wickes v HMRC* [2011] UKFTT 645 (TC), [2012] SFTD 244. The company was developing intellectual property and had made substantial losses in each year of trading, and the 2004 accounts showed a deficit of assets of over £2 million. The majority shareholder, Mr Derek Coates, subscribed for a further 2,100,000 10p shares at £1 each on 17 November 2005. HMRC argued that as Mr Coats had injected more funds into the company at £1 per share, they could not have a negligible value.

> 'One of HMRC's contentions is that the company had always been loss making; it was loss making in 2002 and loss making in 2006. Nothing had changed and therefore the fact it was loss making did not mean its shares were of negligible value.
>
> We agree with Mr Povey that this reasoning is not sound. A company cannot continue to be loss making without the value of its shares being affected. The more losses accumulate, the lower the value of the shares.
>
> However, the question is not whether Mr Brown's shares reduced in value: everyone is agreed that they did. The question is whether they were of negligible value as at 5 April 2006 and the fact that the company was always loss making does not prove that either way.
>
> *Earnings valuation*
>
> Mr Povey's case was that there were only two ways of valuing a company: one was to look at the net present value of its assets and the other was to look at its earnings potential.
>
> An investor looking at the shares' earning potential would look at what dividends had been paid in last three years. None had been paid. What is more no dividends could be paid until a sum greater than its accumulated losses of over £15 million had been realised in profits. In his view the company's shares had a nil valuation on the basis of their earnings potential.
>
> *Value of assets*
>
> An investor looking at the net present value of the company's assets would see from the accounts, whether the 2004 or 2005 accounts, that it liabilities exceeded its assets by about £2million. Again, on this basis the shares had a nil value.
>
> *Hope value?*
>
> We did not really understand Ms O'Reilly to dissent from Mr Povey's view of the assets or earnings potential of the company: HMRC's case was that notwithstanding the company's enormous losses and lack of assets, the shares still had "hope" value as at 5 April 2006: there was hope that some of the IPR that it still had would one day realise significant value. HMRC took this view even though in its accounts (audited by a very reputable firm) any value in its IPR had been written off two years before.
>
> *Decision*
>
> HMRC's case seems to be that as at 5 April 2006, Mr Brown's 1000 shares were worth around £1000 (i.e. about £1 each), and Mr Povey's case was that a prudent purchaser would not be prepared to pay anything for the shares. HMRC indicated that they were likely to accept that as of 2013, with an application to strike the company off the register, the shares are now of no value but they do not think this was true in 2006.
>
> In conclusion, on the particular facts of this case, the appellant has discharged the burden of showing that the shares had a negligible value as at 5 April 2006. The appeal is allowed.'

Focus

The case law illustrates that although some cases succeed, there are several that fail for one reason or another.

9.15 Liquidation part disposals – Statement of Practice D3

On the 20 January 1972 the Inland Revenue published a Press Release now renumbered as Statement of Practice D3:

> 'D3. Company liquidations: Shareholders' CGT
>
> 1. During the liquidation of a company the shareholders often receive more than one distribution. For capital gains tax each distribution, other than the final one, is a part disposal of his shares by the shareholder, and the residual value of the shares has to be ascertained in order to attribute a proportion of the cost of the shares to the distribution (unless the Inspector of Taxes accepts that the distribution is 'small' and can therefore be deducted from cost). It has been represented to The Commissioners for Her Majesty's Revenue and Customs that the making and formal agreement of these valuations is holding up the agreement of liabilities and that little if any change in the total tax is involved in the majority of cases.
>
> 2. Where the shares of a company are unquoted at the date of the first or later interim distribution, therefore, the Commissioners for Her Majesty's Revenue and Customs are prepared to authorise Inspectors of Taxes to accept any valuation by the taxpayer or his agent of the residual value of the shares at the date of the distribution, if the valuation appears reasonable and if the liquidation is expected to be completed within two years of the first distribution (and does not in fact extend much beyond that period). The valuation need not include a discount for deferment; and if the distributions are complete before the capital gains tax assessment is made, the Revenue will accept that the residual value of shares in relation to a particular distribution is equal to the actual amount of the subsequent distributions. In the normal way the Revenue will not raise the question of capital gains tax on an interim distribution until after 2 years from the commencement of the liquidation unless the distribution, together with any previous distributions, exceeds the total cost of the shares.
>
> 3. Where time apportionment (shares acquired before 6 April 1965) applies to a case within the scope of this practice, the Commissioners for Her Majesty's Revenue and Customs are prepared to calculate the gain on each distribution by applying the time apportionment fraction as at the date of the first distribution without further adjustment under TCGA 1992 Sch 2, para 16(8).'

Focus

This statement provides a pragmatic solution to a practical problem with little tax effect.

9.16 Connected persons

Transactions between connected persons are dealt with under TCGA 1992, s 18, which in general treats the connected persons as parties to a transaction otherwise than by way of bargain made at arm's length.

TCGA 1992, s 18(6) and (7) provide that:

> '(6) Subject to subsection (7) below in a case where the asset mentioned in subsection (1) above (acquired from a connected person) is subject to any right or restriction enforceable by the person making the disposal, or by a person connected with him, then (where the amount of the consideration for the acquisition is, in accordance with subsection (2) above, deemed to be equal to the market value of the asset) that market value shall be:
>
> (a) what its market value would be if not subject to the right or restriction, minus –
>
> (b) the market value of the right or restriction or the amount by which its extinction would enhance the value of the asset to its owner, whichever is the less.
>
> (7) If the right or restriction is of such a nature that its enforcement would or might effectively destroy or substantially impair the value of the asset without bringing any countervailing advantage either to the person making the disposal or a person connected with him or is an option or other right to acquire the asset or, in the case of incorporeal property, is a right to extinguish the asset in the hands of the person giving the consideration by forfeiture or merger or otherwise, that market value of the asset shall be determined, and the amount of the gain accruing on the disposal shall be computed, as if the right or restriction did not exist.'

These subsections are particularly interesting as they denote cases where it is possible to have a marked difference between the true market value of an asset and its value for capital gains tax purposes which can be useful in capital gains tax planning.

Connected persons are defined by TCGA 1992, s 286.

CG14580 illustrates persons who are so connected:

> 'The following diagram illustrates the provision of TCGA92/S286 (2). All of the people in the diagram are connected with the individual. They are not all connected with each other.

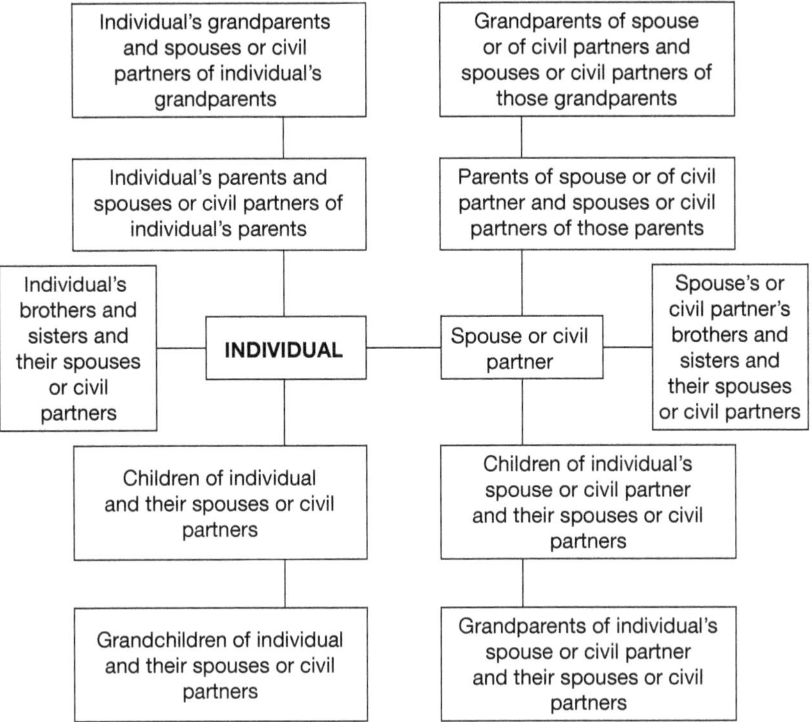

An individual is connected with:

- Husband, wife or civil partner,
- Relatives (= brother, sister, ancestor in lineal descendant) and spouses or civil partners of relatives;
- Relatives of spouse or of civil partner and spouses or civil partners of those relatives.

All the persons in the diagram are connected with the individual.

Excluded are the widows or widowers, or surviving civil partners, of deceased persons, or relatives of a deceased spouse or of a deceased civil partner unless connection can be established by a route not involving the deceased. A dissolution of a civil partnership or a divorce can similarly lead to persons in addition to the former civil partner or spouse ceasing to be connected with the individual.'

Focus

These connected person rules can have a material effect on the chargeable gains which would otherwise arise.

9.17 Holdover relief

The disposal of an asset by way of gift is normally deemed to be for a consideration equal to the market value of the asset disposed of, which may lead to a capital gains tax liability. FA 1980, s 79 (as amended) provided widespread holdover relief which allowed the tax liability to be deferred until a disposal for a valuable consideration. FA 1980, s 79 was repealed by FA 1989 in respect of disposals made on or after 14 March 1989 but holdover relief was retained in a restricted form (TCGA 1992, s 165). The relief is now applicable, inter alia, to gifts of business assets, which include shares or securities of a trading company or of the holding company of a trading group where the shares or securities are not quoted on a recognised stock exchange but are dealt in on the Alternative Investment Market (AIM), or the trading company or holding company is the transferor's family company. Under TCGA 1992, s 260, holdover relief is also available where the disposal is an immediately chargeable transfer for inheritance tax purposes, even if the transfer falls within the inheritance tax nil rate band or is reduced in value to nil as a result of 100% business property relief.

In Statement of Practice 8/92, issued on 26 October, the Revenue announced that it was to allow inspectors of taxes to accept holdover relief claims in most circumstances without the need to value the asset transferred. This is a voluntary measure and the taxpayer may still require HMRC to agree valuations and calculate the held over gain.

One point to consider is the base cost which would be applicable to the recipient of the shares following the transfer. The number of shares transferred might only represent a fraction of the transferor's original holding and therefore the base cost transferred is the relevant proportion of that original shareholding. Thus, if the transferor originally held a 60% stake, but only transfers 10%, then the base cost would be 10/60 of the original acquisition (or March 1982, as appropriate) value.

SP8/92 provides as follows:

> 'Valuation of assets in respect of which capital gain tax gifts holdover relief is claimed.
>
> Introduction:
>
> 1. This statement sets out HMRC's practice for dealing with the valuation of assets in respect of which a claim to capital gains tax gifts holdover relief has been made. It applies to both new claims to holdover relief and existing claims in relation to which valuation negotiations with HMRC may already have started.
>
> Circumstances in which capital gains tax gifts holdover relief is available:
>
> 2. Subject to an appropriate claim, gifts holdover relief is available where:
>
> - an individual makes a disposal not at arm's length of-
> - an asset used for the purposes of a trade, profession or vocation carried on by the transferor, his personal company or a member of a trading group of which the holding company is the transferor's "personal" company – TCGA 1992, s 165(2)(a); or
> - shares in a trading company or holding company of a trading group which are either unlisted or are in the transferor's "personal" company – TCGA 1992, s 165(2)(b); or
> - agricultural property as defined by IHTA 1984 – TCGA 1992, Sch 7, para 1;
> - the trustees of a settlement make a disposal of certain settled property – TCGA 1992, Sch 7, paras 2, 3;
> - an individual or the trustees of a settlement make a disposal of an asset not at arm's length which is either a chargeable transfer under IHTA 1984; or is one of a specified range of exempt transfers – TCGA 1992, s 260(2).

What is the held over gain?

3. In the absence of a claim to holdover relief, TCGA 1992, s 17 would treat both the acquisition and disposal of the assets transferred to be for a consideration equal to their market value. Where a valid claim is made the effect is that the transferor's chargeable gain is reduced to nil and the transferee's acquisition cost is reduced by the amount of the held over gain.

4. The held over gain is the amount of the chargeable gain which would have accrued to the transferor, but for the claim to holdover relief. To compute the chargeable gain, and hence the held over gain, it is necessary to establish the market value of the asset at the date of the transfer.

5. Where no other reliefs are involved, holdover relief will be available where the market value of the asset transferred exceeds the transferor's allowable expenditure and the amount of indexation allowance due up to the date of disposal. If holdover relief is claimed and no consideration is paid then the transferee's acquisition cost will be equal to the sum of the transferor's allowable expenditure plus indexation to the date of transfer. In holdover relief cases, assuming none of the restrictions described in paras 6 and 13 below apply, agreement of the market value of the asset at the date of transfer has no bearing on the immediate capital gains tax liability of the transferor.

Position where consideration is paid by the transferee:

6. Additional rules apply which affect the amount of the held over gain where actual consideration is given to the transferor. Full holdover relief is only available if the actual consideration received does not exceed the transferor's allowable expenditure (TCGA 1992, s 38). If the actual consideration received exceeds the transferor's allowable expenditure on the asset, the holdover relief is restricted by that excess (TCGA 1992, ss 165(7), 260(5)).

7. Where consideration is given, the transferee's acquisition cost will be equivalent to the sum of the transferor's allowable expenditure, the indexation allowance due to the date of disposal by the transferor and the gain immediately chargeable on the transferor.

Circumstances where in future market value at disposal need not be agreed with HMRC:

8. Subject to the following conditions, HMRC will admit a claim for holdover relief without requiring a computation of the held over gain in any case where the transferor and transferee complete the second page of the claim form attached to the Help Sheet IR 295. In particular this requires:

- a joint application by the transferor and the transferee;
- provision of details concerning the asset and its history or alternatively a calculation incorporating informally estimated valuations if necessary; and
- a statement both parties have satisfied themselves that the value of the asset at the date of transfer was in excess of the allowable expenditure plus indexation to that date.

The further conditions are that-

- once a claim made on this basis has been accepted by HMRC it may not be subsequently withdrawn;
- if after acceptance by HMRC it emerges that any information provided or statement made by either the transferor or transferee was incorrect or incomplete, in each case their capital gains tax position in relation to the asset will be computed in accordance with the relevant statutory provisions and assessments made as appropriate.

It should be noted that for years 1996-97 onwards all claims to holdover relief are to be made on the claim form attached to Help Sheer IR 295 or a copy of it.

9. Where, under the terms of this statement of practice, a claim is admitted without the held over gain being computed,, this does not mean that HMRC accept as factually correct or will subsequently be bound by any information or statements given by any person, whether expressly or by implication, in connection with the claim. Neither HMRC nor the claimants are bound in any way by any estimated values shown on the claim form or in any calculations.

Assets held on 31 March 1982:

10. Unless actual consideration is given by the transferee, this practice will also apply to assets held by the transferor on 31 March 1982. It will only be necessary to agree a value at 31 March 1982 when the transferee disposes of the asset.

11. If the transferor has made an election under TCGA 1992, s 35(5), the transferee's acquisition cost of the asset will be equal to the 31 March 1982 value plus indexation up to the date of the transfer. If there is no election under TCGA 1992, s 35(5), the transferee's acquisition cost of the asset will be equal to the transferor's original cost plus indexation up to the date of the transfer or the 31 March 1982 value plus indexation up to the date of transfer – whichever is greater.

12. If the transferee has given some consideration for the asset it will be necessary to agree the 31 March 1982 value immediately. This is so that the excess over the allowable expenditure – which is chargeable to capital gains tax immediately – can be determined. However, HMRC will still be prepared to accept a holdover relief claim without undertaking a valuation as at the date of transfer.

'Circumstances in which a valuation may be required:

13. There are certain cases where TCGA 1992, Sch 7, paras 5, 6 and 7 restrict the amount of the held over gain. These are cases where an asset has at some time during the transferor's ownership been used for non-business purposes, or has only been used in part for business purposes, and cases involving shares etc. in a company which has non-business assets. This statement of practice cannot apply in any of these cases, because it is necessary to compute the chargeable gain before holdover relief. Otherwise, HMRC's expectation is, subject to the circumstances described in paras 8 and 10 to 12, that it will rarely be necessary to determine the market value at the date of the gift. However, a valuation may become necessary as a result of the interaction of the held over gain with other capital gains tax reliefs. It is not expected that even in these cases will it be necessary to establish the market value immediately. Instead, it is more likely that a valuation will not be required before, for instance, a later disposal of the asset by the transferee. The following paragraphs cover these common circumstances.

Retirement relief:

14. Holdover relief is not available in the case of a disposal of an asset to the extent that any gain benefits from retirement relief (TCGA 1992, s 165(3)(a), (b); TCGA 1992, s 260(5), Sch 6). This means that holdover relief may be claimed if the market value at the date of transfer is at least equal to the sum of the transferor's allowable expenditure, indexation allowance to the date of disposal and the retirement relief due.

15. Unless requested by the claimants, the agreement of the market value of the asset will be deferred until either–

- it is necessary to determine the quantum of the retirement relief due. (Normally this will be when the transferor makes another disposal which attracts retirement relief), or
- it is necessary to determine the transferee's cost of the asset

Relief in respect of deferred charges on gains before 31 March 1982 (TCGA 1992, Sch 4):

16. In the case of an asset acquired before 31 March 1982 and transferred before 6 April 1988 it is necessary to compute any held over gain in order to give the benefit of the 50 per cent reduction available under TCGA 1992, Sch 4. To the extent that the market value of the asset at the date of transfer has not already been determined HMRC are prepared to defer the need for a valuation until disposal by the transferee.

Time apportionment in the case of assets held on 6 April 1965:

17. In the case of an asset held at 6 April 1965 chargeable gains and allowable losses arising on disposal are "time apportioned" so that only those accruing since 6 April 1965 are recognised for capital gains tax purposes. If holdover relief is claimed in relation to the gift of such an asset it is always necessary to agree a valuation at the date of transfer in order to apply time apportionment to the deferred gain. HMRC are content to defer this valuation until the asset is disposed of by the transferee.

Application of statement of practice to existing holdover relief claims:

18. In relation to existing holdover relief claims, valuation negotiations with HMRC may have commenced, but not yet been completed. Taxpayers who want to take advantage of the practice in relation to such claims should write to the inspection of taxes to whom they were submitted.'

> **Focus**
>
> This is one of the areas where the capital gains tax legislation is modified in practice to make it work as intended.

9.18 31 March 1982 – rebasing

Except in certain circumstances, detailed below, gains on the disposal of assets which were held on 31 March 1982 are measured by reference to their increase in value since that date less an indexation allowance for inflation under TCGA 1992, s 35 and Sch 3. For non-corporate taxpayers the indexation allowance runs to April 1998 but not beyond. For corporate taxpayers the allowance runs for the whole period from 31 March 1982 to the date of disposal (see **9.19**).

A difficulty arises with regard to valuation where on a sale the shareholder has received a pro-rata proportion of the value of the company as a whole but his shareholding has to be valued at 31 March 1982 in accordance with its size.

The value of a minority holding will almost invariably be less than a pro rata proportion of the value of the whole company so the shareholder will in effect be taxed not only on the growth in value of the company but also on the change in the nature of his interest.

The gain prior to 6 April 2008 may still be measured by reference to the cost of an asset acquired before 31 March 1982, or its value at 6 April 1965 where rebasing at 31 March 1982 would give rise to an increase in the gain or loss as compared with the gain or loss which would have arisen under the rules in force before FA 1988. An election can nevertheless be made to have all pre-existing assets rebased to 31 March 1982 under TCGA 1992, s 35(5).

Where a shareholder disposes of part only of his holding, the Revenue have acknowledged that the base value at 31 March 1982 of the holding disposed of will be calculated as a pro rata proportion of his holding at that time (see **9.06**).

Focus

Rebasing is a useful mechanism although even the value at 31 March 1982 – far less at 5 April 1965 – may be difficult to calculate in practice due to the possible absence of the necessary records.

9.19 Indexation

The gain arrived at after deducting allowable expenditure following a disposal is termed the 'unindexed gain'. For assets acquired before April 1998, there is then deducted an indexation allowance which is the market value multiplied by (RD – RI) ÷ RI where –

RD is the retail prices index for the month in which the disposal occurs; and

RI is the retail prices index for March 1982 or the month in which the acquisition was made, whichever is the later.

If the asset was acquired before 31 March 1982, it is normally assumed that on that date the asset was sold by the person making the disposal and immediately reacquired by him at its market value on that date.

For disposals on or after 30 November 1993, indexation cannot increase or create a loss on a disposal, but can do no more than reduce the unindexed gain to nil. Indexation was abolished by FA 2008, s 8, Sch 2 from 6 April 2008 except for companies where indiscretion still applies.

Focus

The indexation allowance from March 1982 to March 1998 was 1.047, but is now merely of historical interest except for companies, where the RPI has increased from 79.4 in March 1982 to 254.8 at March 2014, an increase of 2.207 times the March 1982 value.

9.20 Rebasing at 6 April 1965

One of the fundamental reforms to capital gains tax introduced by the Finance Act 1988 was the bringing forward of the base date from 6 April 1965 to

31 March 1982. Unless, however, the taxpayer elects under TCGA 1992, s 35(5) for the computation of all relevant disposals to be based on 31 March 1982 values, it still may be necessary to have regard to values at 6 April 1965 where rebasing at 31 March 1982 would give rise to an increase in the gain or loss as compared with the gain or loss which would have arisen under the rules in force before the Finance Act 1988. TCGA 1992, Sch 2, para 17 provides for an election for the gain to be based on the market value of the shares at 6 April 1965 instead of normal time apportionment.

In the context of the valuation of shares in unquoted companies, 6 April 1965 value can give rise to the same difficulties as described at **9.18** in respect of valuation at 31 March 1982. If all the shareholders sell their shares in the company and as a result achieve a sale price related to a pro rata proportion of the value of the company as a whole and then elect for the value at 6 April 1965 they may be under a fundamental misconception as to the method of valuation at that date when each individual shareholder's holding will be valued in accordance with the normal rules for the size of the holding. HMRC do not want to treat an irrevocable 6 April 1965 election as being irrevocable if the taxpayer makes this election under such a fundamental misconception. Form CG 21 was devised which explains the method of valuation and if the election is made on this form the taxpayer would be stopped from claiming fundamental misconception as to the basis of valuation. If, however, the election is made before form CG 21 is issued, the fundamental misconception problem could still arise in which case HMRC may be prepared to accept the withdrawal of the election.

Focus

In most cases the relevant rebasing date is to 31 March 1982.

9.21 Anti-avoidance

It may also be necessary to calculate the market value for capital gains tax purposes under the value shifting provisions of TCGA 1992, ss 29–34.

If a shareholder exercises his control over a company to allow value to pass out of his (or a connected person's) shares into other shares in or rights over the company, he is treated as making a disposal of those shares at the market value before the rights passed out. Losses are disallowed to the extent that they are attributable to the value passing out of assets.

The exercise of control for these paragraphs does not necessarily require a conscious action; inaction, for example, in failing to subscribe for a favourable rights issue would appear to come within the provisions, in spite of *Nicols v IR Comrs* [1973] STC 497; *Floor v Davis* [1979] STC 379. Under IHTA 1984, s 3(3) an inheritance tax charge can also arise on failing to act.

A tax avoidance scheme involving the exporting of shares outside the UK by a reorganisation and renounceable letters of allotment to avoid capital transfer tax was held to be caught by both s 29(2) and the effect of TCGA 1992, s 137(1): *Young v Phillips* [1984] STC 520.

HMRC accepts that gift of business assets hold-over relief may apply to a gain under these sections if the relevant conditions of TCGA 1992, s 165 are satisfied.

HMRC v Paul Newey (T/A Ocean Finance) [2018] EWCA Civ 791 was an EU abuse of law case where Ocean Finance, a loan-brokering partnership, incorporated and restructured the business in Jersey. Ocean Finance was an 'exempt trader' and could not offset input tax mainly in respect of advertising which became an irrecoverable cost. The loan-brokering services were supplied to lenders in the UK by the Jersey company through Mr Newey's office in the UK.

HMRC argued that Mr Newey, and not the Jersey company (Alabaster CI Limited), actually supplied the loan-brokering services in the UK under VATA 1994, s 8(1) or alternatively the supplies of advertising services were made to Mr Newey and not to Alabaster and the arrangements were an abuse of law under EU law. The FTT held that this was not the case following *Halifax plc and others v Customs & Excise Commissioners* [2006] STC 919 and the Court of Appeal in *WHA Limited v RCC* [2007] STC 1695.

HMRC appealed to the Upper Chamber and referred to the CJEU which held that contractual terms are not decisive if they do not reflect economic and commercial reality. The Upper Tribunal held for the taxpayer but referred the case to the Court of Appeal on the basis that the Supreme Court decision in *Pendragon plc v RCC* [2015] STC 1225 might have supported an abuse of law although the FTT was the primary tribunal of fact under the House of Lords decision in *Edwards v Bairstow* [1956] AC 14.

The case was remitted to the First Tier Tribunal to reconsider the factual analysis and it would be open to them, if they considered it necessary or helpful to do so having received submissions for the parties, to admit written or oral evidence at a resumed hearing.

In *Davis and Others v RCC* [2018] UKFTT 559 (TC), ABP Properties Limited, a company registered in Mauritius wholly owned by CSLP, acquired investment properties in the UK which were developed or sold and it was held that the profits were subject to UK tax under TA 1988, ss 739 and 741 or ITA 2007, ss 720 and 721 or ITTOIA 2005, ss 461–463. CSLP was Credit Suisse Life & Pensions (Bermuda) Limited which issued life policies for premiums at £3,000 each to the appellants and it was held that they were taxable on the profits arising as a result of paying the premiums to CSLP, procuring the finance for ABP and providing their own personal goodwill and services.

See also *Adrian Kerrison v HMRC* [2017] UKFTT 322 (TC) at **2.01**.

These two cases concerned transfers of assets abroad under TA 1988, s 739 and ITA 2007, s 720 and the UK/Mauritius double tax agreement.

HMRC argued that the appellants were liable to income tax on the profits of ABP Properties Limited (ABP), a company registered in Mauritius. The appellants argued that they were subject to UK tax on their life policies, the policies were linked to ABP and that tax had been paid in Mauritius and the double taxation treaty with the UK meant that they were not subject to UK income tax as assessed. *Britcom Holdings Limited v IRC* 70 TC 272 and *Strathalmond v IRC* [1972] 1 WLR 1511, 48 TC 537 were quoted in support. It was held that it was impossible to conclude that the arrangements were not designed to avoid tax and were caught by the transfer of assets abroad rules.

Focus

These sections are complex and need to be referred to in cases where value shifting may have taken place.

9.22 Taper relief

As part of the 'simplification' of capital gains tax contained in the Finance Act 1998, the indexation allowance for individuals, trustees and personal representatives was frozen at April 1998 and retirement relief was phased out. In their place a taper relief was introduced at two rates, the higher of which applies to 'business assets' under TCGA 1992, s 2A and Sch A1. Business assets for this purpose include shares in an individual's 'qualifying company', which has to be a trading company or the holding company of a trading group in which originally either: (i) at least 25% of the voting rights were exercisable by the individual; or (ii) at least 5% of the voting rights were exercisable by an individual who is a full-time working officer or employee of the company. This was amended from 6 April 2000 to include such companies where the company was unlisted or the individual was an employee of the company or a connected company or at least 5% of the voting rights were held by the individual. The relief was abolished by FA 2008 on the reintroduction of a flat rate capital gains tax of 18% for 2008/09 for gains above the capital gains tax annual exempt amount. From June 2010, this changed such that gains above the capital gains tax annual exempt amount are charged at 18% for basic rate tax-payers and at 28% for higher rate tax payers. There are separate rates for trustees and estates and for gains qualifying for Entrepreneurs' Relief.

Focus

The effective tax rate on many capital gains is 28%.

9.23 Appeals

TMA 1970, s 57 gives HMRC power to make regulations for the conduct of capital gains tax appeals and these are the Capital Gains Tax Regulations 1967, SI 1967/149, as amended by the General and Special Commissioners (Amendment of Enactments) Regulations 1994, SI 1994/1813, and the Transfer of Tribunal Functions and Revenue and Customs Appeals Order 2009, SI 2009/56.

In *Mr Alan Anderson v HMRC* [2016] UKFTT 335 (TC) the Revenue raised a discovery assessment for £830,387 under TMA 1970, s 29(4) on the basis that capital gains tax on the sale of his 50% shareholding in Anson Limited on 4 April 2008 was at an undervalue and was brought about by careless behaviour. However, he had been advised by PwC that an offer of £36 million for his shareholding on the basis of an offer from the Weir Group and the fact that shares had been sold in 2009 at a higher figure was irrelevant, as the value of his shareholding at 4 April 2008, when it was sold, was based on a third party offer of £72 million for the company and the fact that, on 2 April 2009, Mr Anderson and his brothers sold their entire shareholdings for £88,607,734 was irrelevant.

> **Focus**
>
> The detailed procedural rules for tax appeals are outside the scope of this book.

9.24 Alternative Investment Market

The Inland Revenue confirmed in a Press Release dated 20 February 1995 ((1995) SWTI 343) that companies listed on the Alternative Investment Market are considered to be unquoted companies for United Kingdom tax purposes.

> 'The Stock Exchange alternative investment market (AIM) – tax reliefs for investment in companies joining AIM:
>
> In a speech to representatives of the venture capital industry the Financial Secretary to the Treasury, Sir George Young Bt MP, said:
>
> > "Last week the Stock Exchange announced details of the new securities market which it is launching in June, the Alternative Investment Market (AIM). AIM hopes to attract a wide range of new, small and growing companies.
> >
> > The Exchange and market professionals have been concerned about the availability of the various tax reliefs for unquoted securities and for investment in unquoted companies – these reliefs include inheritance tax relief, capital gains tax reinvestment relief, and reliefs under the enterprise investment scheme and the new venture capital trust scheme.
> >
> > I am now pleased to be able to confirm that these unquoted reliefs will be available for AIM securities; the Revenue will be issuing a Press Release to publicise this point. We will monitor the progress of the new market carefully."
>
> DETAILS
>
> 1 There are a large number of references in tax legislation to securities which are listed or quoted on the Stock Exchange or other recognised stock exchanges. As the Financial Secretary's speech makes clear, securities on AIM will not fall to be treated as quoted or listed for tax purposes. They will therefore qualify for the various tax reliefs available for unquoted securities.
>
> 2 It follows that AIM securities will not be eligible to be held directly by individual investors in PEPs. They will, however, count towards unit trusts' and investment trusts' own qualifying investments for PEP purposes.
>
> 3 The reliefs for unquoted securities include–
>
> - inheritance tax business property relief (IHTA 1984, Part V, Ch 1)
> - income relief for losses on shares subscribed for (CTA 2010, ss 68–73)
> - capital gains tax reinvestment rollover relief (TCGA 1992, ss 164A–164N)

- capital gains tax holdover relief for gifts of business assets (TCGA 1992, ss 165–169)
- the enterprise investment scheme (ITA 2007 s 1031, Sch 3, para 2)
- venture capital trusts (TCGA 1992, Sch 5B, ITA 2007, ss 261–232).'

> **Focus**
>
> This is the authority for AIM shares not being regarded as quoted for tax purposes.

9.25 *Lynall*, transitional rules

There are transitional provisions where there was an acquisition prior to 6 July 1973 enabling the taxpayer to recalculate his acquisition value on the basis of open market value with information available as on a sale by private treaty, where his disposal takes place after that date, as under the new rules applicable from that date under TCGA 1992, s 273. This also applies where there has been a part disposal for example, in liquidation, where each distribution is treated as a part disposal, or part of a series of transactions under TCGA 1992 s 19.

These provisions are set out in TCGA 1992, Sch 11.

> **Focus**
>
> Schedule 11 deals with a number of transactional provisions and savings.

9.26 Deaths between 6 April 1965 and 30 March 1975

A death between 6 April 1965 and 30 March 1971 gave rise to both an estate duty charge and also a potential capital gains tax charge which was normally based on the value for estate duty purposes under FA 1965, s 26(3). However, if the shares were valued for estate duty purposes on the assets basis under FA 1940, s 55, under the provisions of FA 1965, s 26(4), the estate duty value was not to apply for capital gains tax purposes, and the open market value would then apply under FA 1965, s 44(1). If, therefore, someone has inherited shares on a death between these dates the acquisition value will be the open market value either as determined under the estate duty rules, or in the case of an assets valuation as separately determined for capital gains tax on the open market value basis. The asset basis valuation under FA 1940, s 55 would not be the base value for a subsequent capital gains tax acquisition.

In respect of deaths after 30 March 1971 and before 30 March 1975, FA 1971, s 59 and Sch 12, para 15 introduced a new FA 1965, s 26(1) which provided that the estate duty value was in all cases to be the acquisition value for capital gains tax purposes for the legatee. If the estate duty value is calculated on the assets basis under FA 1940, s 55 that is the acquisition value for subsequent capital gains. In other cases the estate duty value is the capital gains tax acquisition value subject to an increase to the market value which would have been determined had the provisions of TCGA 1992, s 273 been in force prior to 6 July 1973. From this date the decision of *Lynall v IRC* [1971] 3 All ER 914, 47 TC 375 was overruled to provide that for valuation purposes all information which a prudent prospective purchaser of the shares might reasonably require if he were proposing to purchase from a willing vendor by private treaty at arm's length was available. It is therefore possible in arriving at the acquisition value for capital gains tax purposes in respect of a death between 30 March 1971 and 6 July 1973 to re-compute the acquisition value as if this information were available.

Similarly if there was a part disposal of shares treated as a part disposal prior to 6 July 1973 the market value of the amount remaining may be re-computed on the basis that the current rules, assuming information available as on a sale by private treaty at arm's length, had applied to the original acquisition and previous part disposal.

Focus

These provisions now have limited application following the adoption in most circumstances of 31 March 1982 as the base valuation date for capital gains tax purposes.

9.27 Death after 30 March 1975

In respect of death after 30 March 1975 these transitional problems no longer apply and the acquisition value for subsequent gains is the probate value for inheritance tax purposes before any reduction for business relief that may apply under IHTA 1984, s 103 et seq.

TCGA 1992, s 62(1)(b) provides that assets passing on death, including those under TCGA 1992, s 62(5) by way of donatio mortis causa, shall not be subject to capital gains tax. However TCGA 1992, s 62(1)(a) provides that the assets of which a deceased person was competent to dispose shall be deemed to be acquired on his death by the personal representatives or other person on whom they devolve for a consideration equal to their market value at the date of the death. This is amplified by TCGA 1992, s 274 which makes it clear that the market value at death is the probate value for inheritance tax purposes.

TCGA 1992, s 274 provides as follows:

> 'Value determined for inheritance tax
>
> Where on the death of any person inheritance tax is chargeable on the value of his estate immediately before his death and the value of an asset forming part of that estate has been ascertained (whether in any proceedings or otherwise) for the purposes of that tax, the value so ascertained shall be taken for the purposes of this Act to be the market value of that asset at the date of the death.'

HMRC take the view (RI 110) that a value has not been 'ascertained' unless it has been referred to and accepted by Shares and Assets Valuation. Thus the values of unquoted shares that have been included in an HMRC Account on the death of a shareholder, but not negotiated because inheritance tax 100% business property relief or spouse relief applies, are not considered to have been ascertained. It can, therefore, be necessary to negotiate date of death values for capital gains tax purposes as the base cost on a subsequent disposal by the beneficiary of the deceased's estate. In those circumstances the inheritance tax related property provisions do not apply.

Focus

This view of the meaning of 'ascertained' can be contrasted with the court's view for the purposes of TCGA 1992, s 38(2), discussed at **9.28**.

9.28 Acquisition and disposal costs

TCGA 1992, s 38(1) provides that:

> '(1) Except as otherwise expressly provided, the sums allowable as a deduction from the consideration in the computation of the gain accruing to a person on the disposal of an asset shall be restricted to–
>
> (a) the amount or value of the consideration, in money or money's worth, given by him or on his behalf wholly and exclusively for the acquisition of the asset, together with the incidental costs to him of the acquisition or, if the asset was not acquired by him, any expenditure wholly and exclusively incurred by him in providing the asset,
>
> (b) the amount of any expenditure wholly and exclusively incurred on the asset by him or on his behalf for the purpose of enhancing the value of the asset, being expenditure reflected in the state or nature of the asset at the time of the disposal, and any expenditure wholly and exclusively incurred by him in establishing, preserving or defending his title to, or to a right over the asset.
>
> (c) the incidental costs to him of making the disposal.'

It was held in *Blackwell v HMRC* [2014] UKFTT 103 (TC) that expenditure for the purpose of enhancing the value of an asset and reflected in its state included payment of £17.5 million by a share-holder to release him from an earlier agreement under which he had agreed to do or not do certain things connected with his A shares in return for a payment of £1 million.

TCGA 1992, s 38(2) provides that, in the case of a disposal, costs reasonably incurred in making any valuation required for the purposes of the computation may be deducted, including in particular expenses reasonably incurred in ascertaining market value where required by the Act. HMRC's view of this section, expounded in the February 1994 issue of *Tax Bulletin*, is that it allows deduction of costs incurred in *making* the valuation but not those incurred in *agreeing* the valuation with, for example, Shares and Assets Valuation or the District Valuer, or, indeed, those incurred in litigation. This view was upheld by the Court of Appeal in *Caton v Couch* [1997] STC 970. The court decided that to allow all reasonable costs would be a positive deterrent to reaching a sensible agreement with HMRC as to the quantum of the liability, despite powerful arguments that a correct reading of the section would allow the deduction.

> **Focus**
>
> The court's reasoning appears to ignore the fact that only costs 'reasonably incurred' can be deducted, but the decision is now definitive.

STAMP DUTY

9.29 General and special provisions

In the Chancellor's 1990 Budget statement it was announced that all stamp duties on transactions in shares were to be abolished from a date late in 1991–92. Following the collapse of the Taurus project, however, abolition was initially postponed but now appears to have been put on permanent hold. The position thus remains that for stamp duty purposes duty on a conveyance or transfer on sale is calculated on the consideration, and in the case of a gift F(1909–10)A 1910, s 74(1) provided that:

> '(1) Any conveyance or transfer operating as a voluntary disposition inter vivos shall be chargeable with the like stamp duty as if it were a conveyance of transfer on sale with the substitution in each case of the value of the property conveyed or transferred for the amount or value of the consideration for the sale.'

This was interpreted as meaning the same as the value on a sale on the open market for estate duty purposes under FA 1894, s 7(5), in *Stanyforth v IRC* [1930] AC 339, see 2.07. Stamp duty chargeable on a gift inter vivos by virtue of F(1909–10)A 1910, s 74 was, however, abolished by FA 1985, s 82.

It is worth nothing that a sale at an under value was stamped as a voluntary disposition at the ad valorem rates on the market value of the property and not on the actual consideration although on an arm's length sale. This applied whenever the amount paid was substantially less than the market value even where there was no gratuitous intent on the part of the vendor; *Lap Shun Textiles Industrial Co Ltd v Collector of Stamp Revenue* [1976] 2 WLR 817. This particular case involved a sale of land in Hong Kong and was a Privy Council decision on the Hong Kong legislation corresponding to F(1909–10)A 1910, s 74(5).

In this case, Lord Wilberforce stated:

> 'First it does not in the least follow that if the collector succeeds in the present case every conveyance or transfer on sale will require an official valuation of the property or an adjudication of the stamp duty. Any stamp authority has to start from the point that valuation of much, if not most, property, is a matter of judgment and is only possible within fairly broad limits and that sound, if not the best, evidence of value is to be found in bona fide arm's length dealings. It is for this reason that when s 27(4) authorises the substitution of the agreed consideration of the real value it requires that a substantial benefit for the transferee should be found to exist. In the great majority of cases the normal procedure of presentation for stamping and routine stamping according to the stated consideration will continue to be followed. Such cases as the present will continue to be exceptional.'

> **Focus**
>
> Stamp duty on a sale of shares is levied at 0.5% of the consideration.

It is to be noted that the stamp duty legislation does not contain any special prohibition against a deduction for flooding the market, as for capital gains tax, TCGA 1992, s 272(2) and inheritance tax, IHTA 1984, s 160. Nor is there any provision assuming information would be available as for a sale by private treaty, as for capital gains tax, TCGA 1992, s 273(3) and for inheritance tax, IHTA 1984, s 168. If these factors increase the value for capital gains tax or inheritance tax they should be ignored for stamp duty purposes and a separate lower value arrived at, if the difference in duty is material.

In the *Pollen Estate Trust Company Limited and Kings College London (KCL) v HMRC* [2013] EWCA Civ 753, it was held that, when KCL bought a flat jointly with a professor in the proportions 46.3% for KCL and 53.7% by the professor, the KCL share was exempt from stamp duty and the professor's share was chargeable.

> **Focus**
>
> Stamp duty valuations do not follow the statutory assumptions which apply for capital gains tax and inheritance tax.

9.30 Stamp Duty Land Tax

Stamp Duty Land Tax (SDLT) applies in England and Northern Ireland. Land and Building Transaction Tax applies in Scotland and Land Transaction Tax applies in Wales. The current threshold for SDLT on the purchase of real property is £125,000 for residential property and £150,000 for non-residential land and properties. There are various reliefs such as for first-time buyers.

There are various reliefs but the rate in England is 12% above £1.5 million purchase price plus a 3% surcharge if buying an additional new residential property.

SDLT valuations will usually be carried out by land valuers such as Chartered Surveyors and are outside the scope of this book.

However, in *Project Blue Limited v HMRC* [2018] UKSC 30, SDLT of £50 million was payable on the purchase of the former Chelsea Barracks from the Ministry of Defence. The tax issues concerned sub-sale relief under FA 2003, s 45 and the anti-avoidance provisions in FA 2011, s 82 and Sch 21 in the case of ijara finance by way of sub-sale in accordance with Sharia law.

INCOME TAX

9.31 Introduction

The valuation rules that apply for other fiscal purposes such as income tax are now considered.

9.32 Employee shares

If shares are issued by an employer to employees, those employees will usually be taxable on the market value of those shares or the amount by which those shares' market value exceeds what the employee pays for them if they purchase them. There have been a number of cases which established this principle: *Weight v Salmon* (1935) 19 TC 174; *Ede v Wilson and Cornwall* [1945] 1 All ER 367, 26 TC 381 and *Patrick v Burrows* (1954) 35 TC 138.

What the value is on which the employee pays tax and how it is determined depends on whether the shares are shares which are restricted (within the meaning of ITEPA 2003, s 423) or unrestricted. If they are not restricted shares, the shares will be taxed on the employee under ITEPA 2003, s 62 by reference to their money's worth. There is no statutory definition of market value in such cases but money's worth is the shares' value when taking into account the personal circumstances and rights over those shares of the holder. It is usually postulated for section 62 purposes that it would contemplate an arm's length sale of the shares in the open market in the same way as for capital gains tax, except that there would be no assumption of information being made available as would be available in respect of a sale by private treaty under TCGA 1992, s 273(3) and there would be no statutory prohibition reducing the value as a result of flooding the market as in TCGA 1992, s 272(2). In many cases in practice there would be no material difference between the capital gains tax value for the transferor and the value charged as employment income on the transferee. However, in cases of a transfer of shares to an employee followed soon afterwards by a public flotation or takeover the difference in value could be material as it was in *Lynall v IRC* (1971) 47 TC 375.

It should be noted that if shares are issued on preferential terms to an employee in the course of a flotation, the value of that preference, in other words the difference between the price at which the employee can buy and the issue price, is taxable as employment income following *Tyrer v Smart* [1979] 1 WLR 113.

Exceptionally in the case of *Bridges v Hewitt; Bridges v Bearsley* (1957) 37 TC 289 it was held that gifts of shares to a director by the other shareholders were unrelated to the employment and therefore were not chargeable as emoluments. In such a case the market value as computed for capital gains tax would be the applicable value both for the transferor and for the transferee, under TCGA 1992, s 17, in the absence of an election for the donee to take over the donor's base value under TCGA 1992, s 165, if appropriate.

In *Ede v Wilson and Cornwall*, referred to above, the court accepted that the market value should be reduced because of additional restrictions attaching to the employee's shares.

Under the restricted securities rules in ITEPA 2003, ss 422–432, UBS AG entered into a carefully planned tax avoidance scheme which was designed to enable it to provide substantial bonuses to employees in the tax year 2003/04 in a way that would escape liability to both income tax and national insurance contributions (NIC).

In *UBS AG and another v HMRC* [2016] UKSC 13, the scheme that was set up was described. It involved setting up an offshore company held by an unconnected charity which issued shares which were purchased by UBS, and beneficial interests in these shares were transferred to the employees UBS intended to benefit. As restricted shares within ITEPA 2003, s 423, the argument of the taxpayer was that they were exempt from tax and NIC under s 425 and when the restrictions were removed the exemption in s 429 applied. HMRC argued that the amounts paid into the scheme were earnings and taxable on the employees at that stage. The Supreme Court disagreed with HMRC that the scheme was simply a vehicle for paying cash to employees free of income tax and NIC as the employees did receive shares. Nonetheless, the Supreme Court found in favour of HMRC on the basis that, when purposively viewed, the shares were not restricted shares and so the exemptions in ITEPA 2003, ss 425 and 429 that had been relied on in the planning did not apply. As such, the employees were taxable on the value of their shares when they received them.

A very similar scheme, heard by the Supreme Court at the same time, *HMRC v Deutsche Bank Group Services (UK) Ltd*, was also found in favour of HMRC.

In the absence of specific rules to the contrary, the right to use an asset or otherwise benefit from it, is only taxable as a benefit in kind, if it is a money payment or convertible into money: *Tennant v Smith* (1892) 3 TC 158.

In *Bentley v Evans* (1959) 39 TC 132, the taxpayer agreed in October 1953 to purchase shares in his employer company at 15% below the market value, in instalments. The Revenue argued that there was a taxable benefit of the difference between the market-value and the amount paid at the date of each instalment, but the court held that the benefit arose when the contract was entered into in October 1953, ie on the then 15% discount.

In *Parker v Chapman* (1927) 13 TC 677 the taxpayer was issued shares in lieu of cash as commission earned. The amount credited to him and used to purchase the shares was taxable income.

In *Paul Richards (PR) and Keith Purves (KP) v I P Solutions Group Limited (The Company)* [2016] EWHC 2599 (QB), PR (CEO of I P Solutions) and KP (Sales Director), both 30% shareholders, were dismissed on 29 July 2015 and on 18 January 2016. The Company required them to sell their shares for £1 under the bad leaver provisions in The Company's Articles. PR and KP claimed for wrongful dismissal, damages, and a declaration that they continued to hold their shares in The Company, which is a unified communications provider which has won a number of awards. It entered into negotiations with Living Bridge (LB), a private equity house, to provide investment and become an equal shareholder in a holding company which would acquire the shares in The Company. PR and KP sold their shares to The Company for £2 million each and a 30% shareholding.

The Company's Articles of Association included bad leaver and good leaver provisions which were enforceable but the claimants had been wrongfully dismissed and were entitled to damages and/or further declarations.

In *Christa Ackroyd Media Limited v HMRC* [2018] UKFTT 69 (TC) it was held that Ms Ackroyd was an employee of her personal service company, CAM Limited, and caught by 'IR35', ITEPA 2003, ss 48–61, and payments to CAM Limited should have been treated as payments to Ms Ackroyd and subject to PAYE and NIC.

Mr Alan Anderson v HMRC [2016] UKFTT 335 (TC) was an appeal against a discovery assessment under TMA 1970, s 29(1) for £830,387 in respect of capital gains tax for 2007/08 on the sale of the appellant's shares in Anson Limited. This was a 50% shareholding in a company which manufactured and marketed specialist oil and gas field products. The shares were sold to ANS (1002) Limited in exchange for shares therein. The shares in Anson were considered to be worth £72 million in total, based on an offer made by the Weir Group on 25 March 2008. HMRC claimed that the market value was higher. On 2 April 2009 the shares were sold for £88,607,734, of which the appellant's share was £44,303,867. The failure of the taxpayer to obtain a further independent valuation in April 2008 did not cause an insufficiency of capital gains tax and HMRC were not entitled to issue a discovery assessment out of time.

In *J P Whitter (Wales Well Engineers) Limited v HMRC* [2018] UKSC 31 the Supreme Court upheld the decisions of the Upper Tribunal and Court of Appeal against the cancellation of the company's registration for gross payments under the VAT Construction Industry Scheme in FA 2004. It noted that the legislation does not require the consideration of the impact of loss of gross payments on the individual taxpayer and therefore the loss of around 60% of the company's turnover and the dismissal of about 80% of its employees was irrelevant and proportionate.

Focus

Well before the advent of ITEPA 2003 in April 2003, if an employee acquired shares for less than their worth, an income taxable amount would arise. There was no statutory valuation basis, however.

9.33 Employee shares under ITEPA 2003

As already said above, with the introduction of the Income Tax (Earnings and Pensions) Act 2003 ('ITEPA 2003') in April 2003, how the market value of a share is determined for tax purposes differs depending on whether it is a restricted share (within the meaning of ITEPA 2003, s 243) or an unrestricted share. If it is a restricted share, whether or not an election is made under ITEPA 2003, s 431(1), its 'market value' for tax purposes is now defined by TCGA 1992, s 272 and the same information standards applicable to capital gains tax valuation apply: ITEPA 2003, s 421.

As well as defining that a restricted share's market value is determined using the methodology set out in TCGA 1992, s 272, ITEPA 2003 brought in the concept of 'restricted' and 'unrestricted' securities and their respective values. The value of a share taking into account all its restrictions is known as the actual market value (AMV) of a share. The value of a share ignoring any restrictions imposed by the Articles or other document, like a Shareholders' Agreement, is the unrestricted market value (UMV). Typical restrictions include:

- directors' veto on share transfer;
- pre-emption rights;
- bad leaver provisions;
- valuation formulae;
- fair value requirement.

Almost all shares in privately owned companies will be restricted securities.

There is no formal guidance from HMRC as to the effect of these 'standard' restrictions on the UMV on a share. However, in practice, HMRC's Shares and Assets Valuation ('SAV') team will normally accept an AMV which is approximately 10% lower than the UMV of a share.

If tax is due on an employee's acquisition of shares, for example, because they were acquired at less than their market value, then the liability will be calculated on the basis of the AMV, unless an election is made under ITEPA2003, s 431, in which case the tax liability will be calculated on their UMV.

Gains made by exercising a right or option to acquire securities by reason of a right or opportunity available to an employee are charged to income tax. Securities options are widely defined and could include earn-out rights in certain circumstances. Payments to associated persons are charged on the employee.

Managed Service Companies

In the First Tier Tribunal case of *Christianuyi Limited and others v HMRC* [2016] UKFTT 272 (TC) the tribunal held that the determinations under regulation 80 of the Income Tax (Pay As You Earn) Regulations 2003, SI 2003/2682, and liability for National Insurance Contributions under section 8 of the Social Security Contributions (Transfer of Functions) Act 1999 were correctly made. The services provided by the owners and sole directors of personal service companies were held to be Managed Service Companies (MSCs) within ITEPA 2003, Chapter 9, Part 2, s 61B(2), inserted by FA 2017 with effect from 6 April 2007, and Costelloe Business Services Limited (CBS) was an MSC provider, as was its associated company, i4 Group Limited, based in the Isle of Man ('i4 IOM'). i4 IOM offered an offshore product aimed at UK contractors to minimise UK PAYE and NICs. i4 Group (UK) Limited was incorporated in 2006. There were a number of associated companies. The taxpayer's appeal against regulation 80 determinations were not allowed.

> **Focus**
>
> Part 7 of ITEPA2003 introduces the concept of a share having two values, an unrestricted market value (UMV) and a restricted or actual market value (AMV).

9.34 Restricted securities

Where employees acquire securities or interests therein, such as options, by reason of their employment, any restrictions or conditions such as the risk of forfeiture would depress the value of the asset acquired. The rules in ITEPA 2003, Part 7, Chapter 2, ss 422–432 charge the employee to income tax (and possibly NIC if the share is a Readily Convertible Asset or 'RCA') on any benefit on the original acquisition and on the enhanced value on any subsequent lifting of a restriction. This applies to assets acquired on or after 16 April 2003. The lifting of each restriction constitutes a 'chargeable event' for tax purposes. The formula aims to tax the increase in value of the proportion of the security which has not yet been subject to tax at the date of each chargeable event and is set out as follows:

Taxable amount = UMV × (IUP – PCP – OP) – CE, where

UMV is the unrestricted market value immediately after the chargeable event arises

IUP (Initial Uncharged Proportion) is the Initial UMV multiplied by any Deductible Amounts (DA) (any consideration paid or charged to income tax) divided by the Initial UMV, ie

IUP = IUMV – DA/IUMV

IUMV is the initial unrestricted market value of the employment-related securities at the time of acquisition.

PCP (Previously Charged Proportion) is the Initial UMV less any Previously Charged Proportion and any Outstanding Proportion (OP), ie

PCP = IUMV – PCP – OP

OP (Outstanding Proportion) is the current UMV less the AMV immediately after the chargeable event divided by the UMV.

CE (Consideration and Expenses) is any amount paid in respect of, or expenses incurred in the lifting of the restriction.

DA (Deductible Amounts) are:

- the amount of any consideration given for the employment related security;
- any amount that constituted earnings or employment income in respect of the acquisition of the employment related security;
- if the employment related security was acquired on the conversion of another employment related security then the amount that counted as employment income on the conversion;
- if the employment related securities were acquired pursuant to a securities option, any amount that counted as employment income under ITEPA 2003, s 476.

Where the value of an employment-related security is depressed by means of non-commercial transactions, the reduction in value is taxed on the employee, either at the time of acquisition or at the following 5 April, as if there had been the lifting of restrictions. The artificial depression is ignored in calculating the market value for restricted or convertible securities. If the value of an employment-related security is taxed on the following 5 April or disposal if earlier, ITEPA 2003, Part 7, Chapters 3A to 3D, ss 446A–446Z apply.

Focus

Shares in most unquoted companies are restricted shares for the purposes of ITEPA 2003 because of standard restrictions on transfer contained in the articles.

9.35 Acquisitions and disposals not at market value

Employee-related securities acquired at less than market value give rise to a notional loan on which the notional interest is taxable as a benefit. The amount of tax payable will be calculated by reference to the AMV of the shares unless a 'Section 431' Election has been made.

Where a disposal is made at more than market value, the excess proceeds over market value are subject to income tax and National Insurance contributions (both employer's and employee's). This situation can commonly arise in circumstances where the Articles contain a formula which determines the price payable to employees leaving the company, particularly if there is no discount factor to reflect the size of the shareholding to be valued, or in cases where special arrangements are in place, such as in the case of *Gray's Timber Products Ltd v HMRC* [2010] UKSC 4, [2010] STC 782.

Employee-related securities disposed of for more than market value by an associated person are taxable on the employee.

Gray's Timber Products Ltd v HMRC is an important case in that it established for certain that rights attaching to the shares, which would not flow through to a hypothetical purchaser, were to be ignored in establishing the value of those shares. In brief, the managing director of Gray's Timber Products, Mr Gibson, was able to subscribe for shares in the parent company representing 6% of the issued share capital, but a shareholders' agreement provided that he would be entitled to 25% of the sale proceeds. The parent company was bought by Jewsons for £6 million. Mr Gibson received just over £1.4 million for his shares when his pro-rata value based on shareholding percentages would have been just under £400,000. The question for the courts was whether the £1 million difference in value should be taxed at the lower rate of capital gains tax or be subject to income tax and National Insurance contributions. This in turn depended on the shares' market value.

The Supreme Court determined that the extra rights attaching to Mr Gibson's shares in the shareholders' agreement did not have to be taken into account in establishing the value of his shares for tax purposes because the rights were not in the Articles. Even had the rights been included in the shares, because they were in the Articles, the hypothetical purchaser would only be concerned about the total price payable for the shares not how the consideration was split amongst the shareholders.

A hypothetical purchaser would not pay anything extra for the rights attaching to Mr Gibson's shares, as they were personal to him. This would be the case regardless of whether the rights were attached to the shares or not. The extra value paid to Mr Gibson did not derive from the shares, and so was liable to income tax under ITEPA 2003, ss 446X–446Z and National Insurance contributions.

Focus

The existence of an agreement stating that an employee will get a certain amount for their shares does not make that their market value for tax purposes.

9.36 'Section 431' elections

If shares or options are to be acquired at less than their unrestricted market value, an employee may enter into a 'Section 431' election (under ITEPA 2003, s 431) within 14 days of acquiring the shares (or at any time before acquisition). The effect of this election is that the employee pays any tax liability arising based on the higher UMV, thus increasing the initial tax charge. However, by paying a higher amount of income tax at the outset, full capital treatment is assured (provided that the shares are not sold for more than market value). The additional tax charges arising as restrictions lift, set out above, would not apply.

There is no formal wording required in respect of the election and suggested examples are provided by HMRC on their website. Completed elections are now reviewed as part of the PAYE health check procedure and those which have not been entered into within the required 14-day post-transaction period are confirmed as invalid. Tax repayments of the initial income tax are made where appropriate and the shares will then be subject to a mixture of capital and income treatment going forward.

It should be noted that, should the value of the shares fall following acquisition, the employee will have paid more tax and national insurance than may actually be due ultimately. This excess is not recoverable and no relief is available. For this reason, advice as to whether an election should be completed is regarded as constituting investment advice.

Focus

This election needs to be made within 14 days of acquiring the shares. Careful consideration is needed as to whether an election needs to be made. Such an election must, though, always be thought about when an employee acquires shares in their employer.

9.37 Post-acquisition benefits

ITEPA 2003, when it came in in April 2003, replaced the post-acquisition benefits relating to restricted securities, dependent subsidiaries and 'special benefits'. Post-acquisition benefits from employment-related securities not otherwise taxed are now charged under ITEPA 2003, Part 7, Chapter 4, ss 447–450. These changes are no longer confined to higher rate taxpayers. 'Benefit' is not defined in the legislation and therefore these sections may be widely applied. Some exceptions exist for employee controlled and other companies.

In respect of ratchet arrangements, which are particularly common in venture capital backed entities, HMRC issued a joint Memorandum of Understanding in conjunction with the British Venture Capital Association on 25 July 2003 (SVM109080, ERSM30520, 30530), which states that no further liability would arise from the operation of the ratchet, provided that:

- there are no performance conditions attaching to the ratchet;
- the ratchet arrangements were in place at the date when the venture capitalist acquired shares;
- the employees paid a price for the shares that reflect their maximum potential entitlement.

HMRC subsequently confirmed that, provided that conditions set out in the Memorandum of Understanding are met, no income tax charge would arise on a ratchet which is effective on an exit. Any gain would instead be subject to capital gains tax. However, if the conditions set out in the Memorandum of Understanding are not met, then income tax charges may arise.

> **Focus**
>
> The tax treatment of employment related securities can become complex and are outside the scope of this book; see ITEPA 2003, Parts 7 and 7A, ss 417–554Z21.

9.38 Convertible securities

Where convertible securities are acquired by reason of the employment the rules will treat these as two assets, the security itself, ignoring the right to convert, and the right to acquire another security as if it were similar to a securities option. Tax is charged on the basis that, at acquisition, the security is regarded as not convertible: ITEPA 2003, ss 435–44.

On conversion, tax is charged on the profit on exercising the notional option as if the market value of the securities being converted was the cost of the option.

> **Focus**
>
> If value is delivered to an employee via shares, if it is not caught by the general provisions or the restricted securities provisions, it is usually caught by one of the provisions at **9.35**, **9.37** or **9.38**.

9.39 'Spin-out' companies

The restricted securities and special benefits legislation was considered counter-productive in relation to research institution spin-out companies and relieving measures were introduced in FA 2005, ss 20–22, ITEPA 2003, Part 7, Chapter 4A, ss 451–460.

9.40 Annual share scheme returns

A company must complete an annual share scheme return in respect of the tax year ended 5 April if a 'reportable event' occurs in that tax year. Since the

2014/15 tax year, these returns have had to be filed online via an employer's HMRC Online Services account. Prior to 2014/15, the return was a paper return known as a Form 42.

Reportable events include:

- an acquisition by an individual of shares, options, an interest in securities or an exercise of options acquired by reason of employment;
- the occurrence of a chargeable event relating to restricted or convertible securities or interests therein;
- anything which artificially enhances the value of the securities;
- the discharge of a notional loan relating to securities acquired at less than market value;
- disposals of shares at more than market value;
- the receipt of any benefit arising from securities giving rise to a taxable amount counting as taxable income.

A formally agreed valuation is not required for the completion of the form. HMRC guidance is that the market value used should be the best available at the time of the relevant transaction.

From 2014/15 there are automatic penalties for failing to file by the 6 July deadline and penalties if the submitted share scheme return has material inaccuracies.

Focus

The online share scheme return gives HMRC the information to calculate or check any tax charge arising.

9.41 Share option and acquisition schemes

There are many different kinds of share schemes for employees, which essentially may be divided into HMRC approved schemes, and other share option or share acquisition schemes. FA 2000 introduced two new schemes, Share Incentive Plans (SIPs) and Enterprise Management Incentive Schemes (EMIs) described below. HMRC guidance can be found on their website in the Employee Share Schemes user guide as follows:

(a) ESSUM 20000: Share Incentive Plans (SIP);
(b) ESSUM 30000: Approved Save as You Earn Share Option Schemes (SAYE);
(c) ESSUM 40000: Approved Company Share Option Plans (CSOP);
(d) ESSUM 50000: Enterprise Management Incentive Scheme (EMI).

The tax consequences of each vary and are examined briefly below.

9.42 Approved company share option schemes (CSOP)

These schemes under ITEPA 2003, Part 7, Chapter 8, ss 521–526 and Sch 4 involve options over either quoted or unquoted shares. There is a limit (which has not changed since November 1995) on the value of shares over which an individual may hold an option. In testing whether this limit is reached, for options granted before 17 July 2013, the basis of valuation is to take into account any restrictions and risks of forfeiture to which the shares are subject ie the shares are valued on an AMV basis. For CSOP options granted on or after 17 July 2013, the basis of valuation for the £30,000 limit is to ignore any restrictions to which the shares are subject and value the shares on a UMV basis.

For options to qualify as CSOP options, the exercise price under the option must not be manifestly less than the market value of the shares at the date of grant. This value takes into account restrictions so is on an AMV basis.

Income tax is generally not due on either the grant or the exercise of a CSOP option. That being said, a charge can arise in certain circumstances, for example, on the exercise of an option where the conditions for a 'tax free' exercise are not met. Likewise a charge can arise on some early exercise options (ITEPA 2003, s 524 as amended by FA 2003, Sch 21). ITEPA 2003, s 701(2)(c) provides that PAYE and NIC are to be charged in such cases. The gain subject to income tax is the value of the shares at the date of exercise, less the price paid. Where quoted shares are involved, the employee should have no problem in completing his return since the valuation will be a matter of public record. Where unquoted shares are concerned, and the shares are sold, the taxpayer will likewise have a value for the computation, being the sales figure (albeit one which HMRC may be entitled to challenge).

Focus

If a company can award CSOP options, income tax and NIC can be avoided on its exercise of such options, provided that they are within the approved limits.

9.43 Share Incentive Plans (SIP)

ITEPA 2003, Part 7, Chapter 6, ss 488–515 and Sch 2 as amended by FA 2003, Sch 21 contain the law relating to Share Incentive Plans (SIPs), a share plan intended to be open to all employees and to be taken up by unquoted as well as quoted companies. Essentially, the scheme allows shares to be given or sold to employees without a tax charge. The key points of the scheme are:

(a) The scheme applies to shares given to employees ('free shares'), shares bought by employees ('partnership shares'), additional shares given to employees buying partnership shares ('matching shares'), and shares acquired from dividends from free, partnership and matching shares ('dividend shares') so long as the main purpose is not tax avoidance.

(b) A plan may cover free shares, partnership shares or both. If it offers partnership shares, it may also offer matching shares, but need not do so.

(c) A plan may be set up by a single company, or by a parent company to cover all or some of its subsidiaries.

(d) The plan must be open to all employees, on the same terms, who meet the criteria and must not have features that would discourage employees from participating. There is no minimum length of employment required and if one is set by the plan it cannot exceed 18 months for free shares (the period is extended for other shares if there is an 'accumulation period'). From 17 July 2013, an employee with a material interest (25 per cent before that date) can participate in a SIP. Where a minimum period of employment is set, it may be satisfied by employment with a group company.

(e) An employee may be awarded up to £3,600 of free shares a year (in valuing shares to test whether they are within this £3,600 limit, restrictions are disregarded and the shares are valued on a UMV basis). The number of shares awarded may be linked to performance in certain specified ways. After being awarded, the shares must be held in trust for three to five years (with a lifting of the restriction where there is a general offer for the company).

(f) Partnership shares are to be purchased under 'partnership share agreements' which provide for the deduction of part of the employee's salary to be used to buy the shares. The amount deducted must not exceed £1,800 pa or 10% of the employee's annual salary, whichever is lower. The deduction must be paid to a trustee as soon as practicable; the trustee may then either buy shares immediately or accumulate for a period of up to 12 months, depending on the terms of the trust. The maximum number of shares that can be bought for each employee may be capped.

When partnership shares are purchased or dividends are reinvested, it is necessary to establish the market value of the shares if they are unquoted. The basis of valuing the shares in this respect is the capital gains tax basis outlined in TCGA1992, s272: the shares are valued taking into account all restrictions, ie on an AMV basis.

(g) Matching shares must be of the same class as the partnership shares to which they relate, and be awarded on the same day. The rules of the scheme may specify any ratio up to two matching shares for each partner's share.

(h) In general, only ordinary share capital may be used. The shares must be fully paid up and not redeemable. Certain restrictions are allowed, however, including limits on voting rights, forfeiture in certain circumstances (except of partnership shares) and pre-emption conditions.

(i) There is no income tax charge on free shares provided that they remain in trust for at least five years. Sums deducted from the employee's salary to buy partnership shares are not charged to income tax. There is an employment income tax charge if the shares are withdrawn from the plan, or a capital sum received in respect of them, within five years of the award. This also covers the disposal of the beneficial interests in the shares by the employee. The employee is treated as being absolutely entitled to the shares as against the trustees from the outset and there is no CGT charge on a transfer of shares from the trustees to the employee.

(j) Dividends from free shares, partnership shares and matching shares may be reinvested each year. There is no limit on the dividends that can be reinvested (since 6 April 2013). No tax will arise on these dividends, if the dividend shares are kept for at least three years.

(k) The employer company is given a deduction for the market value of shares acquired by the trustees pursuant to the scheme.

The Employee Share Schemes Act 2002 allows companies to enable their employees to become more involved in a SIP by setting up a Board of Trustees, which can include company representatives.

> **Focus**
>
> A SIP, in appropriate cases, can be a worthwhile incentive for employees.

9.44 Enterprise Management Incentive Scheme

The Enterprise Management Incentive (EMI) Scheme (ITEPA 2003, Part 7, Chapter 9, ss 527–541 and Sch 5), as it is now drafted, allows a company to grant tax-favoured EMI options provided that the maximum value of unexercised options within the scheme amounts to no more than £3 million (valued ignoring restrictions and any risk of forfeiture). Essentially, the scheme allows employees to hold options over shares worth up to £250,000 at the date of grant (this limit was previously £100,000, increased to £120,000 with effect from 6 April 2008 and to £250,000 from 16 June 2012). There are restrictions on the size of company involved, and the activities it undertakes. In testing whether the individual limit is reached, shares are again valued ignoring restrictions on them and any risk of forfeiture. The other main points are:

(a) The options must be granted for commercial reasons in order to recruit or retain an employee in the company and not as part of a scheme or arrangement the main purpose of which (or one of the main purposes of which) is the avoidance of tax. (Before amendment by FA 2001, the options had to be granted to recruit or retain a 'key' employee.)

(b) If an employee holds unexercised options worth £250,000, further options do not qualify for relief and where qualifying options with a total value of £250,000 have been issued, no options granted within three years of the last qualifying options will themselves qualify (even if sufficient options have been exercised in the interim to bring the employee back below the £250,000 threshold).

(c) The issuing company must be independent (i.e. neither a 51% subsidiary of, nor controlled by, another company). It cannot itself have any subsidiaries except those in which it: (i) owns 51% of the shares (i) controls 51% of the voting power; (iii) is entitled to 51% of the assets; and (iv) is entitled to 51% of the profits. Nor must there be arrangements in place under which any of the 51% tests would be failed. The required percentage for options granted before 17 March 2004 was 75%, reduced to 51% by FA 2004, s 96. Property management subsidiaries have to be 90% owned (ITEPA 2003, s 5, Schs 11A and 11B).

(d) The gross assets of the issuing company cannot exceed £30 million (SI 2001/3799).

(e) The issuing company must be carrying on (or preparing to carry on) a 'qualifying trade' (ie one that does not include 'non-qualifying activities').

Non-qualifying activities include dealing in land or financial instruments, banking, leasing, receiving royalties or licence fees (unless from intellectual property developed in house), legal or accountancy services, property development, farming, operating hotels or nursing homes, and providing facilities for another business.

(f) The employee must be a full-time employee (as defined, in detail) and must not have a 'material interest' in the issuing company. A 'material interest' for these purposes is a 30% beneficial shareholding.

(g) The options must be capable of being exercised within ten years and must be over ordinary, non-redeemable fully paid-up share capital. The terms must be agreed in writing and the rights cannot be assignable.

(h) There is no income tax charge on the grant of an EMI option. There is a charge on exercise to the extent that the exercise price is below the market value of the shares at the time the option was granted (the valuation basis for market value in this context is AMV). However, if there has been a 'disqualifying event' (if, broadly, the company or the options cease to meet the criteria outlined above) the relief is lost unless the option is exercised within 90 days of the event (40 days prior to 17 July 2013).

(i) The CGT base cost is the amount paid for the shares. Prior to April 2012 there was no particular CGT relief for EMI options. For EMI options exercised after 6 April 2012, the shares deriving from these options automatically qualify for Entrepreneurs Relief notwithstanding that they may not represent 5 per cent of the ordinary share capital. Furthermore, the 12-month qualifying period for such shares starts not when the option is exercised but when it is granted.

(j) Since 21 July 2008, a company must have fewer than 250 full time equivalent employees.

9.45 Anti-avoidance

In *Macdonald v Dextra Accessories Limited* [2004] STC 339 (CA); [2005] STC 111 (HL) it was held that payments by the employing company to the trustees of an Employee Benefit Trust were taxable as potential enrolments under FA 1989, s 43(11). This decision was followed in *Boyer Allan Investment Services Limited v HMRC* [2012] UKFTT 558 (TC).

UBS AG v HMRC; DB Group Services (UK) Limited v HMRC [2016] UKSC 13 involved a tax avoidance scheme to take advantage of ITEPA 2003, Part 7, Chapter 2 as amended under which employees would receive redeemable shares in a company, Z, in an offshore jurisdiction, which were subject to a short-term restriction involving an unlikely contingency. The banks paid the amount of the employees' bonuses to company Z as the price of the shares which were allocated to the employees which were said to be restricted securities. The restriction was, a short time later, removed and the employees could redeem their shares or, if UK resident and domiciled, redeem them after two years to qualify for taper relief. Company Z was then wound up. UBS subscribed £91,880,000 for the shares in company Z which were awarded to the employees. There were other conditions to make the shares restricted securities. The error of the Court of Appeal decision in favour of the taxpayers was to adopt a literal construction, whereas the Supreme Court held that

ITEPA 2003, s 423(1)(a) required there to be a genuine business or commercial purpose as distinct from a provision whose only purpose was the obtaining of the exemption. Income tax was payable on the value of the shares at the date of their acquisition in accordance with *Abbott v Philbin* [1961] AC 352, account being taken of any effect which the conditions may have had.

Focus

The basis of valuation for the overall limits for HMRC approved share plans is UMV – and £3m, the £30,000 limit for CSOP, the £250,000 and £3m limit for EMI, the £3,600 limit for SIP. The basis of valuation for ensuring an exercise price is not less than market value in a SAYE, CSOP or EMI option or a shares market value in a SIP is AMV.

9.46 Unapproved schemes: options and shares acquired at less than their value

For share options, there is now no income tax charge on the grant of an option even if it is capable of being exercised for many years. By contrast if shares are actually purchased (without any option) at an undervalue, an income tax charge will arise on this undervalue. When an unapproved option is exercised, there will be a charge to income tax. In the case of shares acquired at an undervalue, the measure of the charge will be the value of the shares on the date the shares are acquired, less anything paid for them. In the case of an option exercise, the charge will be on the value of the shares at the date of exercising the option, less the exercise price paid under the option for the shares: ITEPA 2003, Part 7, Chapter 5, ss 471–484. Similar considerations as to the determination of the taxable amount apply as with CSOPs (see **9.42** above).

Prior to the introduction of what is now ITEPA 2003, s 472 and since May 1966, a share option was assessed to tax on the value of the option when granted and any subsequent profit would have been a tax-free capital gain. This was confirmed in the case of *Abbott v Philbin* (1960) 39 TC 82. These rules were to an extent perpetuated by TA 1988, s 135(2) which applied where an option was granted that was capable of being exercised later than ten years after it was obtained. Section 135(2) was effectively repealed when FA 2003 introduced ITEPA 2003, s 475, which stipulates that no income tax arises on the grant of an option no matter how long after grant it can be exercised.

HMRC's updated guidance on the capital gains tax treatment of options following *Mansworth v Jelley* [2002] EWHC 442 (Ch) can be found in IRPR, 17 March 2003. The case confirmed that HMRC's interpretation of TCGA 1992, s 17 was flawed, which gave some taxpayers an unexpected capital loss and others an unexpected charge on the application of the market value rule. As a result HMRC's interpretation was confirmed by TCGA 1992, s 144ZA, inserted by FA 2003, s 158, which generally results in capital gains tax or income tax on the actual profit realised. This legislation appeared to open the door to new avoidance opportunities and further amending legislation was introduced by F(No2)A 2005, s 35 and Sch 5.

> **Focus**
>
> Since April 2003, there is no income tax charge on the grant of an employment-related option.

9.47 Employee shareholder status shares

In September 2013 a new employment status of 'employee shareholder' (ES) was introduced. Because shares worth £2,000 could be awarded free of income tax and NIC to those who took up ES status and because those shares could then be sold completely free of capital gains tax (CGT), this led to a raft of Employee Shareholder Share (ESS) plans being introduced to award tax-efficient equity to employees willing to take on ES status.

This planning was effectively stopped when legislation was introduced preventing shares awarded to employees on or after 1 December 2016 in consideration of them taking on ES status from benefiting from the ESS income tax and CGT reliefs. Holders of ESS shares which had been awarded before 1 December 2016 continued to benefit from the ESS CGT reliefs on their shares.

The ESS CGT exemption was unlimited for shares awarded between 1 September 2013 and 16 March 2016 and then restricted to a lifetime limit of £100,000 for shares awarded after 16 March 2016 until the relief was completely abolished on 1 December 2016.

> **Focus**
>
> The income tax and capital gains tax reliefs for Employee Shareholder Shares ceased to be available for all ESS shares issued on or after 1 December 2016.

9.48 Save as you earn share option schemes

Approved Save As You Earn (SAYE) share option schemes are dealt with under ITEPA 2003, Part 7, Chapter 7, ss 516–520 and Sch 3. The Schemes apply to options granted to employees, and exempts them from income tax if held for at least three years, provided that avoidance of tax or NIC is not a main purpose of the scheme.

> **Focus**
>
> SAYE and CSOP option plans as well as SIPs can now be implemented without HMRC having to approve these plans first.

9.49 Trading receipts

Occasionally a trader will receive payment in specie, in the form of shares, for the sale of some business interest or property. If this is a capital receipt, where an asset is transferred in exchange for shares, as in *Wolf Electric Tools Ltd v Wilson* [1969] 2 All ER 724, 45 TC 326, the shares received in exchange would have to be valued in accordance with the open market value rules for capital gains purposes. If, however, the shares are received in exchange for trading assets the value of the shares would be a trading receipt and in that case it is again necessary to arrive at the market value of the shares but the capital gains rules would have no application. Viscount Simon stated in *Gold Coast Selection Trust Ltd v Humphrey* [1948] 2 All ER 379 at 384, 30 TC 209:

> 'In my view the principle to be applied is the following. In cases such as this when a trader in the course of his trade receives a new and valuable asset, not being money, as a result of sale or exchange, that asset, for the purpose of computing the annual profits or gains arising or accruing to him from his trade, should be valued as at the end of the accounting period in which it was received, even though it is neither realised nor realisable till later. The fact that it cannot be realised at once may reduce its present value but there is no reason for treating it for the purposes of income tax as though it had no value until it could be realised. If the asset takes the form of fully paid shares the valuation will take into account not only the terms of the agreement but a number of other factors such as prospective yields, marketability, the general outlook for the type of business of the company which has allotted the shares, the result of a contemporary prospectus offering similar shares for subscription, the capital position of the company and so forth. There may also be an element of value in the fact that the holding of the shares give control of the company. If the asset is difficult to value but is nonetheless of a money value the best valuation possible must be made. Valuation is an art, not an exact science. Mathematical certainty is not demanded nor indeed is it possible. It is for the Commissioners to express in the money value attributed by them to the asset their estimate and this is a conclusion of fact to be drawn from the evidence before them.'

The case concerned whether the shares received in exchange for assets held as trading stock should be valued at the cost of the trading stock disposed of, the par value of the shares, or the market value of the shares. Evidence had been led that it would have been impossible to dispose of 3,200,000 shares in Marlu Goldmining Areas Ltd which had been issued to the company in exchange for the transfer of trading stock. This evidence was summarised by Somervell LJ:

> 'The shares were dealt with on the Stock Exchange at prices which varied between 17s.3d and 7s.3d between 1934 and 1938. The percentages of shares dealt in were small, never exceeding 4% of those issued, after the shares had been allotted to the trust on 30 November 1934.'

The trust called a number of witnesses of experience in Stock Exchange transactions and financial dealings. They gave evidence that an attempt to sell these large blocks of shares on the Stock Exchange 'would probably kill the market altogether'. It might have been possible to get a syndicate or financial house to take 250,000 at par, but if a bid were asked for a million it would probably be at a very low figure. If the trust had offered 3,200,000 Marlu shares people 'would have been very wary of dealing with them at all'. Mr Allen, a director of the trust, said that there has not been much opportunity to sell but shares of this kind held by the trust 'were given as security for loans and had a marketable value'. He also said that 'a concession, after it was proved, was worth a great deal more than the out of pocket expenses'. Some of these sentences quoted above emphasised to our minds that it is in no sense conclusive of the arguments. The difficulty is applying the kind of test for which Sir Cyril contends in cases of this kind. The whole transaction as known to financial and mining circles was on the basis that the Trust had confidence in the value of the property and were taking the shares not for immediate realisation, though they contemplated realising parcels over the years as and when they wanted the money for their business. If one assumes a financial company with the necessary liquid resources equally interested in this form of undertaking there seems no reason why they should not purchase the shares as worth £800,000 which was admittedly an honest estimate by highly skilled people of the value of the rights and property transferred. In transactions such as these there will not usually be a possible purchaser of this kind. If the trust suddenly tried to place the whole block of shares on the market everyone would want to know why. We are prepared to accept the view that there might in practice have been great difficulty in disposing of the whole block shortly after the purchase at a price which reflected the intrinsic value of the shares.'

In the case of an open market value for capital gains tax or inheritance tax purposes it is not permissible to deduct anything for a delay in disposing of the assets. See *Duke of Buccleuch v IRC* [1967] 1 AC 506, [1967] 1 All ER 129 referred to previously at **3.05**. It is also statutorily provided for capital gains tax under TCGA 1992, s 272(2) that there can be no reduction for flooding the market and a similar rule applies for inheritance tax under IHTA 1984, s 160 (see **10.05**). These provisions do not apply to a disposal for trading purposes and the depreciatory effect of a disposal of a large quantity of shares would be a relevant factor in discounting the value to the market value on a real disposal. It is therefore necessary to estimate what could have been disposed of over a period and to discount this back to the present value. This is dealt with by Viscount Simon:

> 'It seems to me that it is not correct to say that an asset such as this block of shares cannot be valued in money for income tax purposes in the year of its receipt because it cannot in a commercial sense be immediately realised. That is no reason for saying that it is incapable of being valued, though if its realisation cannot take place promptly that may be a reason why the money figure set against it at the earlier date should be reduced in order to allow for an appropriate interval. Supposing for example the contract conferring the asset on the taxpayer included the stipulation that the asset should not be realised by the transferee for five years and that if an attempt was made to realise it before that time the property in it should revert to the transferor. This might seriously reduce the value of the asset when received, but it is no reason for saying that when received it must be regarded as having no value at all. The commissioners, as it seems to me, in fixing what money equivalent should be taken as representing the asset, must fix an appropriate money value as at the end of the period to which the appellant's accounts are made up, by taking all the circumstances into consideration. It is a relevant circumstance that £800,000 was the figure fixed upon the appropriate consideration to be satisfied by fully paid shares. But it is also a relevant consideration that the asset could not be realised at once.'

In *Rajesh Gill v HMRC* [2018] UKFTT 245 (TC), regarding losses arising from the appellant dealing in financial instruments and securities, it was held by the Tribunal that he had been trading, on a commercial basis, with a view to profits and his loss claim was allowed. In the course of the appeal, HMRC had produced a 600-page tax book, 300 pages of various academic articles, various graphs, disclosed electronically and a series of spreadsheets, printed double-sided and incomplete. A lot of the recalculated data included errors and was flawed. The extra material was therefore excluded, at HMRC's cost.

Mr Gill was a trader buying and selling stocks and shares as a full-time job. He made a profit of over £1 million in the year ended 31 March 2001. He incorporated offshore trading companies in the Bahamas.

However it transpired that Matthew Bamford, a senior broker of Union Cal Limited, on whom Mr Gill relied heavily, had fraudulently lied about the results of his trades, placing unauthorised trades and failing to execute trades. Mr Gill's multi-million pound trading fund had fallen to £817,000 whereas he had been told by Mr Bamford a few months earlier that it was £9.27 million. He sued and was ultimately awarded approximately £9.3 million plus costs and entered into a contract settlement with HMRC.

Not surprisingly, Mr Gill was held to be trading, although this is unusual for an individual investor. *Salt v Chamberlain* [1979] STC 750 (non-trading) and *Cooper v C&J Clark Limited* [1982] STC 335 and *Lewis Emanuel & Sons Limited v White* (1965) 42 TC 369 were considered and trading losses were allowed.

> **Focus**
>
> The capital gains tax and inheritance tax rules do not apply to trading receipts.

9.50 Pre-owned assets

The charge to income tax on benefits received by former owners of property under FA 2004, Sch 15, usually referred to as the Pre-Owned Assets Tax (POAT) was aimed largely at land and chattels. However a charge can arise where intangible property, which would include shares in a company, is held in a settlement in which the chargeable individual has retained a benefit within ITTOIA 2005, s 624, apart from benefits arising purely through a spouse's interest in the settlement. The charging section is FA 2004, Sch 15, para 8. The amount chargeable is determined under para 9 and is N – T where N is the amount of the interest which would be payable for the period if interest were payable at the prescribed rate on an amount equal to the value of the relevant property at the valuation date, and T is the amount already subject to income tax or capital gains tax under ITTOIA 2005, ss 461 or 624, ITA 2007, ss 720 to 730 or TCGA 1992, ss 77 or 86, in respect of the property enjoyed by the settlor. Regulations may provide for a valuation of the relevant property by reference to an adjusted earlier valuation date. These are the Charge to Income Tax by Reference to Enjoyment of Property Previously Owned Regulations 2005, SI 2005/724, which provide for the valuation date to be 6 April in the relevant fiscal year, and the prescribed rate is the official rate of interest at the valuation date, 6.25 per cent from 6 April 2007. The taxable period is the whole or part of the fiscal year in which the benefit arises. A transfer into a settlement in which a spouse or former spouse or civil partner retained an interest in possession under a court order is ignored for these purposes under FA 2004, Sch 15, para 10 (1)(c). Where the property remains part of the settlor's estate for example as an interest in possession, it is exempt from the POAT charge under FA 2004, Sch 15, para 11.

HMRC's Pre-Owned Assets Guidance gives the following example.

Mr A is the UK resident and domiciled settlor of a non-resident settlor interested settlement. (You should assume that Mr A has not reserved a benefit in the settled property nor has an interest in possession in the trust and is therefore subject to the POAT charge).

The settlement comprises 'intangible' property of cash and shares with a value of £1,500,000 at the valuation date. In the tax year 2005/06 the trustees receive income of £60,000 which is chargeable to income tax on Mr A under s 624. A further £150,000 Capital Gains are realised which are deemed to be Mr A's gains by virtue of TCGA 1992, s 86. In these circumstances £24,000 Income Tax is payable on the £60,000 and £60,000 in CGT on the £150,000. The tax allowance (T) against the potential Schedule 15 charge is therefore £84,000. The chargeable amount (N) is 5% (the prescribed rate in SI 2005/06) × £1,500,000 = £75,000. Since the tax allowance is greater than the chargeable amount, a charge under Sch 15 will not arise.

Focus

The POAT rules are complex and easily overlooked.

Chapter 10

Inheritance tax

Signposts

10.01 The scope of the tax

The tax on assets transferred on death and on chargeable lifetime transfers has been known since 25 July 1986 as inheritance tax, although the major changes to the capital transfer tax regime on which it was built were contained in the March 1986 Budget statement, and are effective from 18 March 1986. Capital transfer tax itself replaced estate duty in respect of deaths after 20 March 1974. The capital transfer tax legislation was consolidated in 1984 into an Act which is now known as the Inheritance Tax Act 1984. FA 1986, s 101 introduced the concept of potentially exempt transfers for transfers made on or after 18 March 1986, which means in effect that most lifetime gifts will not be subject to inheritance tax unless made within seven years of the transferor's death. There are exceptions to the rule, which are dealt with briefly later in this chapter. A non UK domiciliary is not taxable on excluded property located outside the UK (IHTA 1984, s 6), including settled property (s 48). FA 2012, s 210 introduced anti-avoidance provisions to prevent the purchase of an interest in settled property with a non UK domiciled settlor being used to avoid inheritance tax, by inserting IHTA 1984, ss 74A–C. FA 2012, Sch 38 was introduced to penalise the dishonest conduct of tax agents. FA 2013, s 177 introduced an irrevocable election for a non UK domiciliary to be treated for IHT as UK domiciled under IHTA 1984, ss 267ZA and 267ZB.

FA 2013, s 178 increases the exemption for gifts to a non-UK domiciled spouse to the nil rate band limits, and ss 206–215 introduced the General Anti-Avoidance Rule (GAAR). FA 2013, ss 218 and Schs 4, 5 and 6 bring in the Statutory Residence Test and the abolition of 'ordinary residence'.

The impact of inheritance tax, particularly as far as unquoted shares in trading companies are concerned, was considerably reduced by the introduction in 1992 of 100% business property relief for most shareholdings carrying more than 25% of votes, which was extended to any size of shareholding for transfers after 5 April 1996 (see **10.09**).

Focus

The tax applies on death or on making a chargeable lifetime transfer or deemed transfer.

10.02 The basic rules

IHTA 1984 s 1 provides for inheritance tax to be 'charged on the value transferred by a chargeable transfer'. A chargeable transfer is a transfer of value made by an individual which is not an exempt transfer (IHTA 1984, s 2). IHTA 1984, s 3 defines a transfer of value as:

> 'a disposition made by a person (the transferor) as a result of which the value of his estate immediately after the disposition is less than it would be but for the disposition; and the amount by which it is less is the value transferred by the transfer.'

It will be seen therefore that inheritance tax is payable on the reduction in value in the estate which means that if, for example, the transferor held 8,000 out of 10,000 ordinary shares in a company and gave away 2,000 he would end up with 6,000 shares. The transfer that has to be valued for inheritance tax purposes is not 2,000 shares in isolation, as it would be for capital gains tax, but is the difference between 8,000 shares originally held and 6,000 remaining after the transfer.

It will be appreciated that if a further 2,000 shares were to be transferred the holding would come down from 6,000 to 4,000 shares and again the value for capital gains tax purposes would be the value of 2,000 in isolation (unless they were to connected transferees in which case TCGA 1992, ss 19 and 20 may be in point) but for inheritance tax the value is the difference between 6,000 shares before the transfer and 4,000 after the transfer. It will also be appreciated that in these two disposals the shareholding has come down from 80% which may be on a largely assets based valuation to 60% which may be on an earnings based valuation as a controlling interest down to 40% which may be largely based on a dividend yield as a minority interest. The value for capital gains tax would be for 2,000 shares on a largely yield basis as a smallish minority interest.

It should be noted that for inheritance tax purposes there can be a reduction in the estate on failing to exercise a right under IHTA 1984, s 3(3) above, which could apply for example on a rights issue for shares not taken up. Such an omission could allow the existing shareholding to be devalued and inheritance tax would be payable on the value passing out of the estate. A similar provision would apply for capital gains tax under the provisions of TCGA 1992, s 29 (value shifting) referred to in **9.21**.

A disposition is not a transfer of value if it is shown that it was not intended to confer any gratuitous benefit on any person and was either made in a transaction at arm's length between persons not connected with each other, or was such as might be expected to be made in a transaction at arm's length between persons not connected with each other (IHTA 1984, s 10(1)). Section 10(2) provides that s 10(1) does not apply to a sale of unquoted shares or unquoted debentures unless it is shown that the sale was at a price freely negotiated at the time of the sale or at a price such as might be expected to have been freely negotiated at the time of the sale. In *IRC v Spencer-Nairn* [1991] STC 60, the court held that in a disposition to a connected person, disparity between the price received and the open market value was no more than a single factor to be taken into consideration. On the particular facts of that case it was decided there was no transfer of value despite such disparity.

The rate of inheritance tax may be reduced by making a qualifying gift to a charity under FA 2012, s 209, inserting IHTA 1984, Sch 1A.

Shares are situated for tax purposes where they could be effectively transferred: *R v Williams and Another* [1942] 2 All ER 95. Where the shares are registered in two countries, they are situated where, in the ordinary course of affairs, they would be dealt with by the registered owner: *Treasurer for Ontario v Aberdeen* [1947] AC 24; *Standard Chartered Bank Ltd v IRC* [1978] STC 272. Bearer securities are situated where the certificate of title is held (*Winans and another v A-G (No 2)* [1910] AC 27), unlike for capital gains tax under TCGA 1992, s 275(1)(da).

Speciality debts are normally situated where the document of title or deed is kept: *Royal Trust Co v A-G of Alberta* [1930] AC 144. However, on 23 January 2013 HMRC amended IHTM 27079 ('Foreign property specialty debts, bonds and debentures under seal') to read as follows:

> 'A speciality debt is:
>
> - a debt made by deed, or
> - a deed which records or creates obligations, or
> - a debt incurred by way of statute, or
> - a certain type of debt that is given the nature of a speciality debt by statute.'

In the past, HMRC's approach to the situs of specialty debts has been that this depends on where the relevant document is found. We now believe this may not be the correct approach in all cases involving specialty debts; specifically that many such debts are likely to be located where the debtor resides, or where property taken as security for the debts is situated. Any cases involving situs and a specialty debt must be referred to Technical. For example, any claim that a debt secured on UK assets is not UK situs property must be sent to Technical.

It appears that HMRC Technical may take the following approach:

Where the debt is secured on land or other tangible property in the UK, HMRC will treat the specialty debt as situated where the property providing the security is located, which is generally agreed to be the correct treatment.

Where the speciality debt is unsecured, HMRC appears likely to treat the debt as situated where the document evidencing the debt is found, but where the creditor and debtor are both in the UK but the deed has been taken offshore, HMRC may consider that the debt was situated in the UK.

Similar treatment may apply to insurance policies issued under seal to policyholders domiciled outside the UK and there is no evidence to suggest artificiality in the location of the deed, and to Treasury Bills and British Savings Bonds. This is also likely to apply for the remittance basis, but otherwise has no impact on capital gains tax or income tax.

Focus

The tax is usually charged on the reduction in value of the estate as a result of the transfer, or, on death, on the value of the property passing as a result of the death.

10.03 Related property

For inheritance tax purposes it is necessary to include related property when evaluating the reduction in the transferor's estate. IHTA 1984, s 161 defines related property as:

(a) property in the estate of a person's spouse or civil partner, or
(b) property which is, or has during the preceding five years, been (IHTA 1984, s 23) owned by a charity or held on trust for charitable purposes only or (s 24) a qualifying political party or (s 25) certain national bodies, or, (s 24A) in the case of land transferred after 13 March 1989, to a registered housing association, following an exempt transfer made by the person or his spouse or civil partner.

IHTA 1984, s 176 provides that related property does not have to be included for valuation purposes where there is an arm's length disposal within three years of a death on which the property has to be valued for inheritance tax purposes, provided that the related property is not also disposed of.

Focus

Related property is included to compute the reduction in value of the estate as a result of the transfer.

10.04 Associated operations

Another section that has to be taken into account in deciding what is to be valued for inheritance tax purposes is IHTA 1984, s 268 dealing with associated operations. This provision was enacted to prevent a transfer being effected by a series of transfers which would have a combined value less than the total value transferred.

The effect of the related property and associated operations provisions may be illustrated by some examples.

Example

If the transferor held 45% of the shares in an unquoted company, his wife held 10% of the shares and his charitable trust, set up after the 15 April 1976, held 15% of the shares he would be deemed to have held 45/70ths of a 70% interest in the company. If therefore within seven years of his death he transferred say, 10%, of his shares to his son, reducing his own shareholding from 45% to 35%, this would be valued for inheritance tax purposes on the difference between 45/70ths of a 70% interest, before the transfer, including related property, and 35/60ths of a 60% interest after the transfer.

If, however, his spouse had made the transfer within seven years of her death, of 10% of the shares to their son, she would have been deemed to have had 10/70ths of a 70% holding before the transfer and nothing at all after the transfer so the value of the transfer would be 10/70ths of a 70% interest.

This might, subject to the possible application of the associated operation provisions in IHTA 1984 s 268, be useful in certain cases. For example, if the husband held 49% of the shares and the wife 2% of the shares, if he were to give away 2% of his shares to their son there would be a reduction in his estate from 49/51sts of a 51% interest before the transfer to 47/49ths of a 49% holding after the transfer. The 51% holding would be valued as a controlling interest, but the 49% could be valued largely on a yield basis owing to the absence of control. If on the other hand the wife gave her 2% shareholding to the son there would be a reduction in her estate from 2/51sts of a 51% shareholding before the transfer to nothing after the transfer and therefore the value of the transfer would be limited to 2/51sts of a 51% holding. For example:

	£
Value of 51% interest	85,000
Value of 49% interest	45,000
Chargeable transfer, 2%	
Father to son	
49/51 × £ £85,000 before transfer	81,667
47/49 × £45,000 after transfer	43,163
Chargeable	38,504

	£
Mother to son	
2/51 × £85,000 before transfer	3,333
Nil after transfer	–
Chargeable	3,333

If, however, the father started off with 51% and gave 2% to his wife as an exempt inter spouse transfer, and the wife then gave them to their son, the associated operations provisions would probably be applied and the mother's transfer would be subject to inheritance tax as if it were her husband's transfer.

These transfers are all potentially exempted and there would be no charge to inheritance tax provided that the transferor survives the transfer by seven years.

If the company's business did not consist wholly or mainly of dealing in securities, stocks or shares, land or buildings, or making or holding investments, 100% business property relief could in any event reduce the chargeable amount to nil (see **10.09**).

Focus

The value transferred is the reduction in the value of the estate as a result of the transfer.

10.05 Valuation rules

The statutory valuation provisions for inheritance tax are contained in IHTA 1984, s 160 which provides as follows:

> 'Except as otherwise provided by this Act the value at any time of any property shall for the purposes of this Act be the price which the property might reasonably be expected to fetch if sold in the open market at that time; but that price shall not be assumed to be reduced on the grounds that the whole property is to be placed on the market at one and the same time.'

With regard to unquoted shares and securities IHTA 1984, s 168 provides that:

> 'In determining the price which unquoted shares or unquoted securities might reasonably be expected to fetch if sold in the open market it shall be assumed that in that market there is available to any prospective purchaser of the shares or securities all the information which a prudent prospective purchaser might reasonably require if he were proposing to purchase them from a willing vendor by private treaty and at arm's length.'

This is the equivalent of the capital gains tax provisions in TCGA 1992, s 273(3) dealt with at **9.03**, and similar comments apply.

It will be noted that in the inheritance tax legislation there is no equivalent to TCGA 1992, s 272(3) which deals with the value of listed securities for capital gains tax purposes. Nevertheless the same value as that arrived at under s 272(3) will usually be accepted for inheritance tax.

In *A-G v Ralli and Others* (1936) 15 ATC 523 it was held that partnership reserves which, under the partnership deed, accrued to the remaining partners on a partner's death or retirement, was not part of the deceased's estate for estate duties, and presumably for Inheritance Tax purposes. It was not a gift, merely an ordinary commercial transaction.

The value of a joint interest in property may be subject to a discount of 15%: *Wight & Moss v IRC* (1982) 264 EG 935 (Lands Tribunal); *JDP Barrett (Barrett's Personal Representative v HMRC Lands Tribunal* (23 November 2005, unreported). However, a 10% discount may apply: *Cust v IRC* (1917) 91 EG 11; *St Claire-Ford (Youlden's Executor) v Ryder*, Lands Tribunal (22 June 2006, unreported); see *Tolley's Tax Cases 2014*, 72.102–72.104.

Focus

The valuation rules are the same as for capital gains tax, but it is the reduction in the estate as a result of the transfer rather than the value of the shares transferred that is taxed.

10.06 Close companies

Other inheritance tax provisions which have to be considered on the valuation of shares in unquoted companies are those relating to transfers by close companies and alterations in their share structure under IHTA 1984, s 94 et seq.

In September 1991, the following announcement by the Inland Revenue appeared in various professional journals:

> 'Following recent legal advice, the Inland Revenue's interpretation of section 98, Inheritance Tax Act 1984 has changed.
>
> Until now the capital taxes offices have taken the view that when deferred shares came to rank equally with another class of shares there would be no alteration in the rights of the shares within the meaning of section 98(1)(b). But there would be an alteration in the company's share capital within the meaning of section 98(1)(a).
>
> The Board of Inland Revenue has now been advised that an alteration of rights, within the meaning of section 98(1)(b), occurs when deferred shares come to rank equally with another class of shares. Accordingly, claims for inheritance tax will be raised where deferred shares, issued after 5 August 1991, subsequently come to rank equally, or become merged, with shares of another class.'

The Revenue originally stated that this change in interpretation would make no practical difference to tax liabilities. They subsequently amended that statement to the effect that the change of approach would make no practical difference in cases of deferred shares issued prior to, or on, 5 August 1991, but could affect schemes entered into after 5 August 1991. This statement was subsequently amplified when the Revenue confirmed that in relation to deferred shares *issued before 6 August 1991* no claims to inheritance tax would be raised under either s 98(1)(a) or s 98(1)(b).

The full text of s 98 is as follows:

> **'98. Effect of alterations of capital, etc.**
>
> (1) Where there is at any time–
>
> (a) an alteration in so much of a close company's share or loan capital as does not consist of [quoted shares or quoted securities]
>
> (b) an alteration in any rights attaching to [unquoted shares in or unquoted debentures of a close company],
>
> the alteration shall be treated as having been made by a disposition made at that time by the participators, whether or not it would fall to be so treated apart from this section, and shall not be taken to have affected the value immediately before that time of the [unquoted shares or unquoted debentures].
>
> (2) In this section "alteration" includes extinguishment.
>
> [(3) The disposition referred to in subsection (1) above shall be taken to be one which is not a potentially exempt transfer.]'

The description 'deferred share' is applied to various types of share, but in this instance the Revenue were referring to shares which have minimal rights for a number of years, say ten, 15 or 20, after which period they rank pari passu with ordinary shares. They are usually issued as bonus shares to existing shareholders, who then typically transfer their entitlement to family trusts. Prior to the Revenue's announcement of September 1991, it was thought that for inheritance tax purposes there would be a charge on the transfer of the bonus issue, but no charge at the time the shares achieve parity with the other shares in the company.

The Revenue's announcement raises more questions than it answers; for example, who will be assessed to inheritance tax at the maturity date? Who is responsible for reporting the disposition? Is the Revenue compiling a list of companies with deferred shares and maintaining a diary of dates when claims will be issued? Is there still considered to be a charge to inheritance tax on the original disposal of the bonus shares? It may be that it will be necessary to wait until maturity dates are reached before answers to these questions will be forthcoming. There appears to be no jurisprudence at the time of writing.

It is generally agreed that value accrues gradually to deferred shares between the date that they are issued and the date they achieve parity. If that is so, the change in value of a deferred share on the precise day that parity is achieved would be minimal and a charge under s 98(1)(b) would be similarly insignificant.

HMRC Shares and Assets Valuation had, prior to the issue of the September 1991 statement, adopted different views of the value transferred for inheritance tax purposes on the disposal of a bonus issue of deferred shares, depending on the size of the transferor's holding prior to the disposal. If the transferor had control of the company and would retain it until the deferred shares matured, the Revenue were apt to suggest a relatively small loss to the transferor's estate, since the transferor would remain at liberty to appoint directors, fix directors' remuneration and carry out day-to-day management of the company, provided that he did not defraud the other shareholders.

If a minority holding was being considered, Shares and Assets Valuation were likely to argue for a relatively large initial drop in the value of the transferor's estate, particularly if the company had no history of paying dividends, since the minority shareholder was likely to have been in a position where he may well have been unable to sell his shares or receive any income therefrom in the period before the deferred shares were to mature. The downside of that argument from the HMRC's point of view was that in those circumstances a minority holding of ordinary shares is itself worth very little.

Correspondence took place between the Chartered Institute of Taxation (CIOT) and HMRC on Inheritance Tax Act 1984, s 98 and HMRC Press Release dated 11 September 1991 in relation to deferred shares.

In September 2012 HMRC confirmed its agreement to the terms of the final paragraphs of a letter from CIOT, the full text of which is reproduced below:

> 'CIOT requests confirmation from HMRC on the proper interpretation of the 11 September 1991 Press Release that deals with s.98 IHTA. The 1991 Press Release deals with HMRC's view of when there can be an alteration of rights within the meaning of IHTA 1984 s 98(1)(b) in the context of deferred shares coming to rank pari passu with another class of shares. We do not discuss here the technical validity of this view but rather how the Press Release should be interpreted.
>
> The 1991 Press Release indicates that where shares were issued before 5 August 1991, there will not be a claim to IHT when deferred shares subsequently come to rank pari passu with another class of shares.
>
> However, the 1991 Press Release does not expressly deal with the not infrequent situation where the company in question has issued the shares carrying the deferred rights, before 5 August 1991, and afterwards, for commercial reasons, but before the deferred shares can rank pari passu with another class of shares, there is a reconstruction of the company. In the course of the company's reconstruction, the company is liquidated in accordance with s 110 of the Insolvency Act 1986 and its businesses and trades are transferred to new companies, pursuant to TCGA 1992 s 139. Naturally and in accordance with statutory clearances, pursuant to TCGA 1992 s 136, shares are issued by the new companies which are identical in their rights and in all relevant respects to the original deferred shares issued by the company. These shares effectively stand in place of the original deferred shares issued by the company and have exactly the same rights as the original deferred shares. Similar results can occur where a company's shares are sold in exchange for the issue of shares by the purchaser bearing the same rights.
>
> This appears to be the situation arising in an increasing number of commercial situations particularly where the deferral period is very long and subsequent reconstructions have occurred as a result of commercial considerations. It seems to us, that for the purposes of the 1991 Press Release, the shares issued by the new companies should be treated as shares issued before 5 August 1991 given that to all intents and purposes the rights attaching to the new shares are unaltered from those attaching to the old shares but should be grateful for your confirmation on this point.
>
> In these cases the new share capital is issued after 5 August 1991, simply because the reconstruction happens after that time. But there has been no creation of deferred rights after 5 August 1991, as these rights existed previously by the creation of deferred shares prior to 1991 and there is no new transfer of value.
>
> We should be grateful for your confirmation that HMRC interpret the Press Release such that provided the new deferred shares, issued as part of the sale or reconstruction post 1991 mirror the rights of the pre-1991 deferred shares and there is no transfer of value or change in the deferral period, there should be no inheritance tax due as a result of s 98 when the shares come to rank equally with another class of shares and the taxpayer can rely on the Press Release to ensure that no IHT arises.'

However, as explained above, Counsel has confirmed that there are arguments against HMRC's view that there is an alteration of rights on deferred shares coming to rank pari passu with another class of shares.

A suggested method for valuing deferred shares is included at Example 4 in Division B and is useful for valuing deferred shares for capital gains tax purposes. For inheritance tax, however, there are the factors referred to above to be taken into account and, as ever, the precise circumstances of each valuation occasion will have to be examined.

HMRC's Shares and Assets Valuation's attitude to deferred shares is set out in their Manual at SVM 108280:

> 'IHTA 1984 Section 98 serves to stop avoidance by the alteration of a company's capital or the rights attaching to it. It achieves this by treating the alterations as if they had been effected by dispositions made by the participators (normally the shareholders). To give rise to a liability one is looking for a situation where, after the company has altered its capital or varied share rights, the value of an individual's holding after the event is less than it was before. A common case involves the creation of new classes of shares which are not issued pro rata to existing shareholders.'

Example

A company has issued share capital of 100 ordinary shares owned 60% by A, 20% by B and 20% by C.

The company issues two further classes of shares:

- 20 deferred shares (acquiring rights to votes and to 50% of the income and capital after five years) to C;
- 80 20% preference shares (absorbing much of the current income) to C.

Although control remains with A the value of his holding is substantially diminished and s 98 is in point. A further claim under s 98 will arise when the deferred shares actually acquire voting, and other, rights in five years' time or new shares are issued which vary the proportions in which the capital is held.

However, the Employee Share Scheme User Manual (ESSUM 43240) states:

> 'Deferred shares may be ordinary share capital. An example might be a company with two classes of share, ordinary shares and deferred shares. The two classes may have identical rights except that for a period of ten years the deferred shares bear no dividends. After the ten year point the two classes merge and have the same rights to dividends as the original ordinary shares. The fact that the deferred shares have no rights to dividends during a particular period does not mean they are not ordinary share capital. Deferred shares are often created for commercial reasons, to enable private investors to take capital growth instead of dividend income.
>
> New schemes proposing to grant options over deferred shares should be referred to the ESSU (Employee Shares Scheme User) operations manager.
>
> Deferred shares given scope for abusing the approved scheme legislation but their use as scheme shares in approved schemes is not common. The scope for

abuse stems from the fact that at the outset (when the options might be granted and the option prices fixed) the value of deferred shares will be much less than the value of comparable ordinary shares (which have dividend rights) and with which they will, in due course, merge. Because of their inherent rights to receive dividends after the merger of the two classes of shares, the value of the deferred shares is therefore capable of increasing irrespective of any improvement in the company's performance.'

In *Bruce-Mitford v HM Revenue & Customs* [2014] UKFTT 954 (TC) the First Tier Tribunal held that deferred shares were convertible securities within ITEPA 2003, s 436, as amended and chargeable to income tax as employment-related convertible securities within ITEPA 2003, ss 438, 439 and 440.

10.07 Control

It can be important for inheritance tax purposes to determine whether a shareholder has control of a company the valuation of shares for control is defined by IHTA 1984, s 269, which reads as follows:

> '1. For the purposes of this Act a person has control of a company at any time if he then has the control of powers of voting on all questions affecting the company as a whole which if exercised would yield a majority of the votes capable of being exercised on them.
>
> 2. For the purposes of this Act shares or securities shall be deemed to give a person control of a company if, together with any shares or securities which are related property within the meaning of Section 161 above, they would be sufficient to give him control of the company (as defined in subsection (1) above).
>
> 3. Where shares or securities are comprised in a settlement, any powers of voting which they give to the trustees of the settlement shall for the purposes of subsection (1) above be deemed to be given to the person beneficially entitled in possession to the shares or securities (except in a case where no individual is so entitled).
>
> 4. Where a company has shares or securities of any class giving powers of voting limited to either or both of–
>
> a the question of winding up the company, and
>
> b any question primarily affecting shares or securities of that class,
>
> the reference in subsection (1) above to all questions affecting the company as a whole shall have effect as a reference to all such questions except any in relation to which those powers are capable of being exercised.'

See *Walding (Executors of Walding, deceased) v IRC* [1996] STC 13, and *Walker's Executors v IRC* [2001], STC (SCD) 86, where the 50% shareholder's casting vote as chairman was sufficient to give her control of the company and her shares therefore qualified for business property relief on her death under the law at the time.

Focus

Control affects the value of the shares, although this is no longer a requirement for 100% business property relief. See **10.09**.

10.08 Payment by instalments

It is necessary to determine whether a person has control of a company in order to ascertain whether it is possible to pay inheritance tax by ten equal yearly instalments beginning six months after death under the provisions of IHTA 1984, s 228(1)(a).

It is possible to pay inheritance tax by instalments on other unquoted shares and securities in the circumstances provided for by IHTA 1984, ss 227 and 228. Interest is charged from the date each instalment is due: FA 2009, Sch 53, para 7.

> **Focus**
>
> Payment by instalments not only reduces the cash flow problem but may avoid having to dispose of the shares.

10.09 Business property relief

One of the most important reliefs for inheritance tax so far as it applies to unquoted shares is that relating to relief for business property in accordance with IHTA 1984, ss 103 to 114.

Relevant business property is defined by IHTA 1984, s 105(1)(a) as including property consisting of a business or interest in a business and, under s 103(3), business includes a business carried on in the exercise of a profession or vocation but does not include a business carried or otherwise than for gain. Business is defined under the Fair Trading Act 1973, s 137(2) as including a professional practice and any other undertaking carried out for gain or reward or which is an undertaking in which goods on services are supplied, otherwise than free of charge: *Re Ogilby* [1942] Ch 28; *Stevenson v Rogers* [1999] QB 1028; *In Town Investments Ltd v Department of the Environment* [1984] AC 359, quoted with approval in *C & E Commissioners v Apple & Pear Development Council* [1984] STC 296, where it was stated that 'the word "business" is an etymological chameleon: it suits its meaning in the context in which it is found'. See also *National Water Council v C & E Commissioners* [1979] STC 157. In *C & E Commissioners v Morrison's Academy Boarding Houses Association* [1978] STC 1, it was held that the word 'business is wide enough to include the deliberate carrying on, continuously, of an activity or activities or an occupation or profession' and 'wide enough to embrace any occupation or function actively pursued with a reasonable and recognisable purpose' and 'where the tax in question relates to profits or gains, I can well appreciate that that is such a context of the word "Business" should relate to those activities which normally have the purpose or objective of the promotion of profits or gains'.

The aspects of that activity which are to be considered, as being indicia or criteria for determining whether the activity is a business are six in number and were listed by counsel for the Crown in *C & E Commissioners v Lord Fisher* [1981] STC 238 as follows:

'(a) whether the activity is a 'serious undertaking earnestly pursued', a phrase derived from the judgement of Widgery J in [1967] 2 QB 65 at 76, or 'a serious occupation, not necessarily confined to commercial or profit-making undertakings', a phrase derived from the speech of Lord Kilbrandon in *Town Investments Ltd v Department of the Environment* [1977] 1 All ER 813 at 835, [1978] AC 359 at 402, both of them cited to and referred to by the tribunal in their decision; (b) whether the activity is an occupation or function actively pursued with reasonable or recognisable continuity: per Lord Cameron in *Morrison's Academy* [1978] STC 1; (c) whether the activity has a certain measure of substance as measured by the quarterly or annual value of taxable supplies made: again, per Lord Cameron; (d) whether the activity is conducted in a regular manner and on sound and recognised business principles: again, per Lord Cameron; (e) whether the activity is predominantly concerned with the making of taxable supplies to consumers for a consideration: per the Lord President; (f) lastly, whether the taxable supplies are of a kind which, subject to differences of details, are commonly made by those who seek to profit by them: per the Lord President and per Lord Cameron.'

The relief is a percentage reduction in the value transferred by the transfer of value. It applies to transfers both in lifetime and on death and to those occasions where tax is chargeable under the provisions relating to settlements see **10.18**. The main provisions relating to unquoted shares are as follows:

(a) Qualifying business. Shares in a company do not qualify if the business of the company consists wholly or mainly of dealing in securities, stocks or shares, land or buildings or making or holding investments, unless the business is wholly that of a UK market maker or discount house, or that of a holding company of one or more companies whose business does qualify.
(b) Nature of the relief. The relief takes the form of a percentage reduction of the value transferred. For transfers of value and other events occurring after 5 April 1996 the following rates of relief under IHTA 1984, s 104 apply:
    (i) securities of a company which are unquoted and which either by themselves, or together with other such securities owned by the transferor and any unquoted shares so owned, gave the transferor control of the company immediately before the transfer: 100%;
    (ii) any unquoted shares in a company: 100%;
    (iii) shares in or securities of a company which are quoted and which (either by themselves or together with other such securities owned by the transferor) gave the transferor control of the company immediately before the transfer: 50%.
(c) Unlisted Securities Market. Between 17 March 1987 and 10 March 1992 shares in companies dealt in on the Unlisted Securities Market were not treated as unquoted shares for the purposes of business property relief, before 17 March 1987 and after 9 March 1992 until the demise of the USM in December 2006 such shares were treated as unquoted (SVM09060). Shares dealt with on the Alternative Investment Market (AIM), opened on 19 June 1995 are regarded as unquoted, SVM 09070, as are those dealt with on Ofex or, while it lasted, the Over-the-Counter market.
(d) Binding contracts for sale. Unless the sale of shares or securities is for the purpose of reconstruction or amalgamation, such shares or securities

will not qualify as relevant business property if at the time of the transfer a binding contract for sale has been entered into: IHTA 1984, s 113.

(e) Minimum period of ownership. Shares in unquoted companies will not qualify for relief unless they were owned by the transferor for a minimum period of two years immediately preceding the transfer or they replaced other property which qualified immediately before the replacement and was owned by the transferor for at least two years out of the five years immediately preceding the transfer, IHTA 1984, ss 106–109.

Assets which are neither used wholly or mainly for the purpose of the company's business nor required at the time of the transfer for future use for those purposes are 'excepted assets'. The part of the value of shares that is attributable to the excepted asset or assets does not attract business property relief. In *Barclays Bank Trust Co Ltd v IRC* [1998] STC (SCD) 125, a trading company with annual turnover of around £600,000 had cash in hand of £450,000. The Commissioner accepted the Inland Revenue's argument that no more than £150,000 was being used for the purpose of the company's business or was required for future use. The Commissioner was not asked, however, to determine either the value of the 50% shareholding or the proportion of that value that was to be attributed to the excepted asset.

In circumstances where a company's business does not consist wholly or mainly of the excluded activities referred to at (a) above, but does have, for example, investment properties, the Inland Revenue accept that the holding of such investments is a business in itself. Those assets are therefore required for the purpose of the company's business and cannot be 'excepted assets'. Full business property relief would apply in those circumstances.

In the *Barclays Bank* case the taxpayer did not argue that the holding of cash in the bank also constituted a business, but unless the cash was in a non-interest-bearing current account it was certainly being used to generate income.

In *Brown's Executors v IRC* [1996] STC (SCD) 277 the Commissioner accepted that the proceeds of sale of a company's previous business were required for the future use of the business, as it was intended to buy a further business with those proceeds.

It should be noted that if an investment asset is held in a separate subsidiary company, IHTA 1984, s 111 could apply to restrict business property relief in shares in the holding company to the extent of the value of the subsidiary.

The pro rata valuation of a company, under the quasi-partnership provisions does not apply to a shareholder acquiring the shares under an inheritance at a minority valuation: *Re Saul D Harrison & Sons plc* [1995] 1 BCLC 14.

In *Grimwood Taylor v IRC* [2000] STC (SCD) 39, it was held that the shares in the deceased's estate did not qualify for business property relief. Nafisa Investments was an unlimited Irish company controlled by the deceased, as was Barton Blount Estates, an unlimited English company resident in Jersey, and Nether Hesleden Farms Ltd and Clayview Ltd, English incorporated and resident companies. They were respectively a non-trading former farming loss making company, a property-owning company, a farming company with a deficiency of assets and an insolvent property-owning company. The companies did not constitute a group under IHTA 1984, ss 111 and 112, and merely carried on otherwise than for gain, and were excluded from business property relief by IHTA 1984, s 103(3).

A landlord holding properties as a business of letting them out to tenants is carrying on an investment business, whatever the degree of his personal involvement: *Martin & Horsfall (Moore's Executors) v IRC* [1995] STC (SCD) 579 and *Burkinyoung (Executors of Burkinyoung deceased) v IRC* [1995] STC (SCD) 29. Business property relief is therefore denied under IHTA 1984, s 105(3). A similar result was applied to a caravan park in *Hall & Hall (Hall's Executor's) v IRC* [1997] STC 126 and *Powell & Halfhide (Pearce's PRs) v IRC* [1997] STC (SCD) 181, but was allowed in *Furness v IRC* [1999] STC (SCD) 232 where less than half the caravan park's profits came from letting sites.

IHTA 1984, s 105(3) denies business property relief if the business consists wholly or mainly of dealing in securities, stocks or shares, land or buildings or making, or holding investments, whether active or passive: *Martin & Horsfall (Moore's Executors) v IRC* [1995] STC (SCD) 5; *Burkinyoung (Burkinyoung's Executors) v IRC* [1995] STC (SCD) 579; *Hall & Hall (Hall's Executors) v IRC* [1997] STC 126; *Powell & Halfhide (Pearce's Personal Representative) v IRC* [1997] SSCD 181; *Weston (Weston's Executor) v IRC* [2000] STC 1064; *Clark & Southern (Clark's Executor v HMRC* [2005] STC (SCD) 823; *PN McCall & BJA Keenan (Personal Representatives of Mrs E McClean v HMRC* (2009) 79 TC 990; *HMRC v Lockyer & Robertson (Mrs N V Pawson's Personal Representative* [2013] STC 976; *Trustees of David Zetland Settlement v HMRC* [2013] UKFTT 284 (TC).

However, it is possible, in some cases, to obtain business property relief on, for example, caravan parks where the trading activities exceed those relating to rental income: *Furness v IRC* [1999] STC (SCD) 232; *George & Loochin (Stedman's Executors) v IRC* [2004] STC 163; *Farmer & Giles (Farmer's Executors) v IRC* [1999] STC (SCD) 232; *DWC Pierce's Executors v HMRC* [2008] STC (SCD) 858.

The definition of holding investments did not apply to a money-lending business: *Phillips v HMRC* [2006] STC (SCD) 639. Where a business was sold and cash was held pending reinvestment the Special Commissioners accepted that it was not an investment holding company in *Brown's Executors v IRC* [1996] STC (SCD) 277.

Whether or not a company's business consisted wholly or mainly of making as holding investments under IHTA 1984, s 105(3) was considered in *Phillips v HMRC*. The company was incorporated as a property investment company, but it sold its properties and made informal loans to family companies and two individuals, at 2.5% above base rate. It was held that the company was not a property investment company and was eligible for inheritance tax business property relief.

Reference was made to the Court of Appeal decision in *IRC v George* [2004] STC 147, which related to a business which operated a caravan site, which held that the business should be considered in the round and that there was no decisive factor which would indicate whether a business consisted wholly or mainly of the making or holding of investments, and that interest on cash balance was regarded as non-investment income as obtaining interest was not a business in itself. Money-lending is not normally regarded as an investment.

In *The Personal Representatives of the Estate of Maureen W Vigue (deceased) and HMRC* [2017] UKFTT 632 (TC), when Mrs Vigue died on 29 May 2012 she was the sole owner of 30 acres of land, Gravelly Way livery stables. Her personal representatives claimed business property relief under IHTA 1984, s 105 and agricultural property relief under IHTA 1984, s 116. HMRC refused both reliefs and regarded it as holding investments.

IRC v George [2004] STC 147 was considered, which related to a caravan site, and the correct question was not whether a trade was being carried on but whether the deceased's business consisted wholly or mainly of holding investments. A building company case, *Piercy v HMRC* [2008] STC 858, was held not to be a land dealing business. In *McCall v HMRC* [2009] STC 990, letting land for grazing was not a business. *HMRC v Pawson* [2013] UKUT 50 (TCC) was referred to.

The Tribunal held that use of the land was not one of the holding investments but was a genuine livery business and not agricultural property.

Anne Christine Curtis Green v HMRC [2015] UKFTT 334 (TC) was an Inheritance Tax (IHT) case involving a business called Flagstaff Holidays and 85% of the business was transferred to the Mrs A C Green Settlement (the Trust) in two tranches, both of which it was claimed qualified for 100% Business Property Relief for IHT, which was challenged by HMRC on the grounds that the business of providing holiday accommodation consisted mainly of making or holding investments and the Tribunal agreed with HMRC. Cases referred to were *HMRC v George* [2003] EWCA Civ 1763, *Weston v HMRC* [2000] STC 1064, and *HMRC v Pawson* [2013] UKUT 50 (TCC).

In *Executors of the Estate of Marjorie Ross (deceased) v HMRC* [2017] UKFTT 507 (TC) the question to be answered was whether let holiday cottages, despite the high level of services provided, were an investment in land and therefore not eligible for business property relief under IHTA 1984, s 104 or relevant business property within s 105. The court held that what the guests really wanted was access to a property to call their own in a beautiful part of Cornwall to enjoy for a specific period, and business property relief was refused.

Cases referred to were *A C Curtis Green v HMRC* [2015] UKFTT 334 (TC), *IRC v George and Another* [2004] STC 147, above, and *HMRC v Lockyer and another (as personal representatives of Pawson, deceased)* [2013] UKUT 50 (TCC).

Focus

As business property relief may be 100% for unquoted shares in a non-excluded company, it is a very valuable relief.

10.10 Agricultural property relief

In the case of a farming company, agricultural relief may be available, which takes precedence over business relief. The relevant provisions are contained in IHTA 1984, s 115 et seq. The relief is a percentage reduction of the value transferred by a transfer of value and is limited to agricultural property within the UK, Channel Islands and Isle of Man and any European Economic Area state (FA 2007, s 122). There are two rates of relief, which were increased to

100% and 50% in FA 1992. If shares in a company are transferred, agricultural relief is available to the extent that the value is attributable to the agricultural value of agricultural property which forms part of the company's assets and can be attributed to the value of the shares provided that the transferor had control of the company. Shares in a company can qualify for business property relief for the non agricultural value.

> **Focus**
>
> The combination of agricultural and business property relief will often take the whole value of a farming company out of inheritance tax.

10.11 Transfers on death

The main occasions for a charge for inheritance tax purposes are the lifetime charge on a non-exempt transfer of value, already considered, and on death under IHTA 1984, s 4(1). This section provides:

> 'On the death of any person tax shall be charged as if, immediately before his death, he had made a transfer of value and the value transferred by it had been equal to the value of his estate immediately before his death.'

This means that any shares held by the deceased would be valued for inheritance tax purposes as part of his estate, taking into account any related property, unless eligible for agricultural or business property relief.

> **Focus**
>
> The value of the estate is its entire value except to the extent covered by reliefs.

10.12 Lotting

For inheritance tax purposes, it may be necessary to add together assets of a deceased's estate if the combined value of those assets is greater than their value in isolation. *Gray (Executor of Lady Fox) v IRC* (1994) 38 EG 156, concerned the correct method of valuing for capital transfer tax purposes the deceased's 3,000 acre estate and her 92.5% interest in a farming partnership which was the tenant of the estate. The Lands Tribunal had held that the interest in the estate should be valued without the benefit of vacant possession, but the Court of Appeal decided that, for the purposes of FA 1975 s 38, the freehold reversion and the partnership share could be treated as a single unit of property and valued accordingly. It was not important that the two items together did not form a 'natural unit'. Allowances were made in the overall value for the interests of the other partners and the delay and uncertainty the hypothetical purchaser might face in obtaining vacant possession.

The case raises questions concerning the correct method of valuing a shareholding in a company that rents land owned by the shareholder. At present, business and agricultural property relief at 100% render the problem less pressing, but the point would still be important where no such relief is available. It appears that unless the shareholder has winding-up control, the overall value would not reflect the value of the property with the benefit of vacant possession.

It should be remembered that if, in these circumstances, 100% agricultural or business property relief is due on the death and the value is not 'ascertained' for inheritance tax purposes, the base value for capital gains tax purposes on any subsequent sale would be arrived at on capital gains tax principles. In that case, the two assets would be valued in isolation.

Focus

Different taxes may produce different values for the same assets.

10.13 Surviving spouse exemption

An exemption is available where a beneficial interest in property was left by a deceased person in trust for a surviving spouse. If the settlor died prior to 13 November 1974, estate duty would have been payable on the first death and the equivalent of the surviving spouse exemption will apply on the subsequent death of the transferee under IHTA 1984, Sch 6, para 2.

Focus

It is unlikely that this relief will still be relevant.

10.14 Effect of death

IHTA 1984, s 171 provides:

> '(1) In determining the value of a person's estate immediately before his death changes in the value of his estate which have occurred by reason of the death and fall within subsection (2) below shall be taken into account as if they had occurred before the death.
>
> (2) A change falls within this subsection if it is an addition to the property comprised in the estate or an increase or decrease of the value of any property so comprised, other than a decrease resulting from such an alteration as is mentioned in section 98(1) above; but the termination on the death of any interest or the passing of any interest by survivorship does not fall within this subsection.'

The effect of this provision is that if there is a fall in the value of shares in a company as a result, for example, of the death of a managing director who was the driving force of the company, the effect of this death would be taken into account in arriving at the value of his shares for the purposes of inheritance tax on his death.

The valuer will, of course, be fully aware that if it is asserted to HMRC that the deceased's death will cause a marked fall in the value of the shares, he will need to prove that assertion. One way of so doing is to produce the profit figures after the death; if they have markedly fallen, it is evidence of the effect of the death. It is appreciated that in *Holt* (see 3.08) it was stated that knowledge of subsequent events must be firmly rejected but the subsequent profit figures are being used as evidence of a fact before the death i.e. that the deceased was the driving force.

It will be noted that in (2) above it is stated 'other than a decrease resulting from such an alteration as is mentioned in section 98(1) above'; in other words a change of rights attaching to the shares or an alteration in the company's share or loan capital. Had this provision not been included, if the deceased had a holding of ordinary shares, it would have been possible to provide in the articles that immediately before his death his shares would become (say) 1% preference shares without votes with the consequent effect on a valuation.

Where land is sold within three years of death at less than the probate value, a claim may be made by the personal representatives to substitute the net proceeds for the probate value under IHTA 1984, s 191; see also ss 190–198 and *Stoner & Mills (Dickinson's Executor) v IRC* [2001] STC (SCD) 199 and *Jones & Another (Balls' Administrators) v IRC* [1997] STC 358.

Where other assets, such as shares, are sold within 12 months of death at less than the probate value, the sale proceeds may be substituted under IHTA 1984, s 178–189; see *Lee & Lee (Lee's Executors) v IRC* [2003] STC (SCD) 4.

Focus

These statutory provisions provide some relief if assets are sold at less than the probate value.

10.15 Interests in possession and reversions

It should be noted that so far as settled property is concerned IHTA 1984, s 49(1) provides that a person beneficially entitled to an interest in possession in settled property shall be treated as beneficially entitled to the property in which the interest subsists. The converse of this is that under IHTA 1984, s 48(1) a reversionary interest is excluded property, unless:

(a) it has at any time been acquired (whether by the person entitled to it or by a person previously entitled to it) for a consideration in money or money's worth; or
(b) it is one to which either the settlor or his spouse is or has been beneficially entitled; or
(c) it is the interest expectant on the determination of a lease treated as a settlement by virtue of IHTA 1984, s 43(3).

Where a person becomes beneficially entitled to an interest in possession on or after 22 March 2006 these rules only apply to an immediate post-death interest

(IPDI) (IHTA 1984, s 49A), a disabled person's interest (DPI) (IHTA 1984, s 49A) or a transitional serial interest (TSI) (IHTA 1984, ss 49B–49E). Where shares are held in such trusts they are treated as part of the estate of the beneficiary provided that he has a qualifying interest in possession. The meaning of interest in possession was considered at length in the case of *Pearson v IRC* [1980] 2 WLR 872 where it was held to mean an entitlement to the income or part of the income of the trust and excluded cases where there was a discretionary interest or where the income was accumulated.

The termination of an interest in possession which is treated as a transfer of the interest under IHTA 1984 ss 51–53 makes it necessary to value any shares held by the trust on the termination of such an interest. The Capital Taxes Office used to take the view that any shares held by the settlement would be aggregated with shares held in the free estate of the beneficiary and with any related property in determining the value for inheritance tax purposes. For example, A holds 40% of the shares in a private company, his wife 20% and A also has an interest in possession in a settlement holding 15% of the share capital. If someone other than A or his wife becomes absolutely entitled to the shares on the termination of the trust, the valuation would be on the basis of 15/75ths of a 75% controlling interest. It has been argued that IHTA 1984, ss 51–55 specifically state that the termination of such an interest in possession is not a transfer of value and therefore the quantum of the deemed transfer would be the settlement's own 15% shareholding without aggregation with the shares held by A and his wife. The Revenue subsequently advised the Institute of Chartered Accountants (as reported in the May 1990 edition of *Accountancy* magazine) that they take the view that when the interest in possession comes to an end during the lifetime of the person entitled to it the settled property in which the interest subsisted should be valued in isolation without reference to any similar property.

Where a person entitled to an interest in possession in settled property is entitled to part only of the income (if any) of the property, and, under IHTA 1984, s 50(1)–(3) his interest is taken to subsist in a proportionate part of that property, what falls to be valued as forming a part of his 'estate' for inheritance tax purposes (by virtue of the combined effect of IHTA 1984, ss 5(1) and 49(1) is that part of the property in which his interest subsists.

If therefore the trust held say 60% of the shares in Corsair Ltd and Christopher Angus had a life interest in 25% of the trust fund, on termination of the interest in possession it would be necessary to value a 15% interest in Corsair Ltd, (25% of 60%) and not value a 60% interest and charge 25% of the result, provided that Mr Angus held no other interest in Corsair Ltd as part of his free estate.

Where a reversioner acquires a beneficial interest in the relevant property for money or money's worth, he is treated as having made a disposal of the reversionary interest which is not a potentially exempt transfer under FA 2010, s 52 introducing IHTA 1984, s 81A.

Focus

A change of view by HMRC results in a more sensible interpretation of the law.

10.16 Lifetime transfers

IHTA 1984, s 7(2) provides that tax charged on the value transferred by a chargeable transfer made before the death of the transferor shall be charged at one-half of the rate on death. This, however, merely affects the amount of inheritance tax payable, not the valuation of the assets transferred and therefore is outside the scope of this book.

> **Focus**
>
> Whether or not the transfer is a lifetime transfer affects the rate of tax chargeable.

10.17 Grossing up

Whether an asset is given subject to inheritance tax or free of inheritance tax, in which case the tax itself is an additional gift and the net gift has to be grossed up, is a question of calculation affecting the tax payable, not one of valuation.

10.18 Relevant property settlements

IHTA 1984, ss 58 to 69 contain the inheritance tax legislation concerning relevant property settlements ie post-22 March 2006 life interests which are not IPDIs, DPIs or TSIs (see **10.15**), or settlements with no interest in possession, that it is to say those settlements where no beneficiary is entitled to receive the income, or a share of income, such as accumulation and maintenance trusts settled before 22 March 2006 and remaining so settled; beneficiaries under 25, are excluded by s 71 as are trusts for bereaved minors (ss 71A–71C) age 18–25 trusts (ss 71D–71H) and charitable trusts under s 70 and certain employee trusts are excluded by ss 72–76. If a company is entitled to the income from a settled property, under s 59(2), the settlement will fall within the inheritance tax relevant property regime, unless the company's business consists wholly or mainly of buying interests in trusts and the interest in point was purchased from a beneficiary for full consideration.

Transfers into relevant property trusts are not potentially exempt but are chargeable transfers, suffering tax at one-half the rate applicable on death on the amount exceeding the taxable threshold, which is £325,000, until April 2018 under FA 2014, Sch 21, para 2. Tax on death is currently 40%, and 20% on lifetime transfers.

Attempts to avoid this charge by purchasing at full value an interest in an existing trust are caught by FA 2010, s 53.

Under s 64 there is a charge to tax on the value of property in discretionary trusts every ten years, at 30% of the lifetime rate. This is known as the principal or periodic charge and is intended to levy, over the period of a generation the total amount of inheritance tax that would be payable at the rate applying on death. The first principal charge is made on the tenth anniversary of property first becoming comprised in the settlement, which will usually be ten years from the date on which the settlement was created. The rate of the ten-yearly charge is at the time of writing 6% (30% × 40% × 50%). It remains to be seen whether or not the legislation will remain in force long enough to achieve the aim of charging the equivalent of tax at death rates on property in relevant property trusts.

Where property is added to a settlement during a ten-year period, tax payable thereon is reduced, under s 67, by a fraction representing the part of the ten-year period the property was not in the settlement, expressed to the nearest fortieth. FA 2014, Sch 25, para 4 provides that income arising in the five years prior to the ten-year charge which remains undistributed is to be added to the capital value at that date and is liable to the full charge, unless it is an exempt gilt or the settlor was not UK domiciled when the settlement was made and it is situated outside the UK or a holding in an authorised unit trust or OIC.

Focus

The ten-year charge on a settlement can be overlooked if it is not diarised and kept under review.

10.19 Distributions

To prevent avoidance of the ten-year charge by taking property out of trust, s 65 provides that a proportion of the ten-year charge becomes payable when trustees make capital distributions of trust property. Settlements made before the introduction of capital transfer tax on 27 March 1974 have special treatment, discussed at **10.24**. Settlements made on or after 27 March 1974 are subject to tax on the loss in value to the trust as a result of the distribution, similar to the 'loss to the estate' principle which applies to transfers by individuals. The loss to a settlement on a transfer of company shares will therefore require a valuation of the settlement's shareholding both before and after the distribution. Business property relief under ss 103–114 is due where appropriate but it has to be remembered that the two-year qualifying period of ownership starts from the date the *settlement* acquired the shares.

Focus

A capital distribution from a relevant property trust is subject to IHT on the reduction in value as a result of the distribution.

10.20 Rate of tax on distributions

Under IHTA 1984, s 68 the trustees of a relevant property settlement acquire the same cumulative total of transfers as that of the settlor on the day before the settlement was made. The rate of tax suffered by the trustees is the rate that would be incurred by a person with that cumulative total making a lifetime chargeable transfer equal to the initial value of all sums previously transferred to the settlement. If the settlor has used up his nil rate band with other chargeable transfers before making the settlement, the rate will be a simple 20%. If none or part of the nil rate band has been used, to calculate the rate of tax on a distribution it is necessary to find:

(a) the value of the settled property immediately after the settlement was first made (making no deduction for business or agricultural property relief);
(b) the value of additions (before the date of the relevant calculation) to the settlement immediately after they were put in;
(c) the initial value of any related settlement, which is defined by s 62 as any settlement, other than a purely charitable trust, made by the settlor on the same day as the relevant property in question. The total of these three values forms the basis from which the trustees calculate the tax they would have to pay thereon at lifetime rates, assuming that their previous cumulative total is equal to the settlor's chargeable transfers made in the seven years up to the date the settlement was made, excluding other transfers made on that date or before 27 March 1974. To the rate of tax so calculated, it is then necessary to apply the appropriate fraction, which is 30% multiplied by the number of complete quarters which have passed since the settlement was made.

Under s 65(4), distributions in the first quarter of a ten-year period attract no liability.

If the settlor dies having made a potentially exempt transfer within seven years of his death but before the date of the settlement, it will be necessary to revise the calculation to take account of that transfer which has become chargeable, as a gift inter vivos.

Focus

Where unquoted shares are transferred into or out of a relevant property trust, there will be a requirement to value the shares as the reduction in value as a result of the transfer.

10.21 Ten-yearly charge ('the principal charge')

For relevant property settlements created after 27 March 1974 it is also necessary to work out the notional rate of tax which the trustees would pay if they made a lifetime transfer. In this instance, in addition to taking into account the settlor's cumulative total prior to the making of the settlement, any additions to the settlement during the ten-year period have to be included. If the trustees paid the tax on those transfers, it is the grossed up figure which is added to the trustees' deemed cumulative total.

The trustees' deemed chargeable transfer on the ten-year anniversary is the total of:

(1) the value of the property in the settlement on the anniversary date; less agricultural and business property relief;
(2) the initial value of any property remaining in the settlement but which has never been 'relevant property', as provided by s 66(4)(b), such as property

in which there has been an interest in possession since the beginning of the settlement;

(3) the initial value of any related settlement.

The tax which would be payable by a person making that chargeable transfer with a previous cumulative total as described above is used to find the effective rate of tax. The effective rate of tax multiplied by 30% multiplied by the value, after any business or agricultural property relief, of the relevant property in the settlement, results in the tax payable by the trustees.

> **Focus**
>
> Trustees needs to be prepared for the ten-year charges and ensure that they have the necessary liquid funds or facilities to pay the tax due.

10.22 Added property

If the settlor has added property to the settlement after it was first created but before the ten-year anniversary, it is the settlor's cumulative total at that date, less any part attributable to property which was initially put into the settlement which is used to calculate the trustees' addition to the trust, which would have to be grossed up if the settlor did not pay the inheritance tax on the gift.

Section 66(2) allows the rate of tax payable on an anniversary to be reduced if any part of the settled property on that date can be attributed to property added by the settlor in the ten-year period. The reduction is made by reference to the number of quarters which passed before the addition was made.

> **Focus**
>
> Added property in a settlement is only chargeable, pro rata, on the next ten-year charge.

10.23 Charges between ten-year anniversaries

The rate of tax on distributions from the trust after the ten-year anniversary is calculated under s 69 as the effective rate of tax charged on the settled property on the ten-year anniversary multiplied by the number of quarters that have passed since the anniversary date and divided by forty.

If there have been additions to the settlement in the ten years up to the last anniversary date or since the last anniversary, adjustments have to be made. If the addition was before the last anniversary date, no allowance is made for the part of that ten-year period that the property was not in the settlement. If the addition was after the anniversary, it is necessary to work out what the effective rate of tax would have been on that anniversary if the additions had been in the settlement on the anniversary date.

If the rates of inheritance tax have been reduced since the anniversary it is necessary to calculate what the effective rate of tax would have been on the anniversary date, using the reduced scale.

> **Focus**
>
> As a result of the complexities of additions to an existing settlement it may be simpler to create a new settlement for the additional property.

10.24 Relevant property settlements made before 27 March 1974

Relevant property settlements made before the introduction of capital transfer tax on 27 March 1974 were given special treatment. As the settlor could not have made chargeable transfers prior to the creation of such a settlement, there could be no counting of the settlor's cumulative total at the time the settlement was created.

If the settlor adds property to a settlement made before 27 March 1974, the settlor's cumulative total at that date gives the trustees a deemed cumulative total which is taken into account thereafter.

Distributions by the trustees prior to the first ten-yearly charge suffered tax at 30% of the rate of tax which would have been payable on the distribution if it had been a chargeable transfer by a person with a cumulative total equal to the amounts on which previous distribution charges have arisen to the trustees under FA 1975 or FA 1982 rules.

On the first ten-year anniversary date of a relevant property settlement made before 27 March 1974, the tax payable was 30% of the effective rate of tax which would be payable on the value of the settled property under FA 1975 or FA 1982 rules. The trustees were assumed to have a cumulative total equal to their distributions in the previous ten years. Related settlements and non-relevant property were disregarded.

For subsequent ten-year anniversaries the same rules apply as for settlements made on or after 27 March 1974.

> **Focus**
>
> These provisions are largely of historic interest only.

10.25 Pre-owned assets tax

FA 2004, s 84 and Sch 15 introduced an income tax charge where people continued to enjoy the use of an asset, having disposed of their interest in it, if it was not caught by the gift with reservation rules in FA 1986, ss 102–102C. Under Sch 15, paras 21–23 it may be possible to elect for the asset in question to remain in the inheritance tax net on making the appropriate election; see **9.50.**

Part 3
Valuation in practice

Chapter 11

Valuation approaches

Signposts

11.01 Introduction

There are several possible methods available to value a business. However, as explained in IVS 200, Businesses and Business Interests, all will fall into one of three main approaches: the market approach; the income approach; or the cost approach. IVS 200 also notes that the cost approach is rarely appropriate in the case of businesses, except for early-stage or start-up businesses, for which there is little other information available.

This chapter sets out the two methods used most commonly: the capitalisation of earnings method and the discounted cash flow method. The valuer must consider which method is the most appropriate and which secondary method(s) should be used as a cross-check.

11.02 Market approach

The market approach seeks to value a business by reference to real transactions in similar businesses for which price information is available. The acknowledged difficulty of this approach is that directly comparable transactions have seldom occurred within reasonable proximity to the valuation date required. It is possible to consider the prices at which similar businesses are being offered at that date, even if no transaction has taken place. However, it is likely that adjustments to any publicly available data will be needed to reflect the relative strengths and weaknesses of the business to be valued compared with the entity for which the market data is available.

Many valuations of private companies will also use market data for quoted companies in order to arrive at an appropriate multiple for the business. This approach, sometimes called the Public Company Market Multiple Method (PCMMM), takes quoted multiples data from comparable listed entities and, after suitable adjustments to reflect the differences between the subject and the quoted comparators, applies this multiple to the earnings of the business to be valued.

11.03 Income approach

The focus of this approach is on the income-producing capability of a business and generally estimates a capital value on the basis of the cash flows expected to be generated in the future. In the majority of income-based valuation methods, a discount rate is applied to the cash flows in order to reflect the present value of the future income stream, after adjusting for factors such as risk and inflation. Valuation techniques which use the income approach include discounted cash flow analysis (DCF), option-pricing and dividend yield.

11.04 Cost approach

The application of the cost approach to the valuation of businesses involves adding up the values of the underlying assets less liabilities – it is, in effect, a net assets valuation. The individual assets and liabilities may themselves have been valued using a cost, market or income approach. This approach is sometimes used to value investment businesses (incorporating the sum of the values of their investees) and property businesses.

11.05 Market multiples method – a market approach

Under the market multiples method, an estimate of the 'maintainable' earnings of the business being valued is made. A multiple is then applied to this figure in order to arrive at the value of the entire business. At its simplest, this approach demonstrates the number of years of profits which a purchaser would be willing to pay to acquire the business. As the choice of multiple relies on comparison with information from the market, this is a method within the market approach.

The market multiples valuation method is usually best suited for companies that have relatively stable or mature earnings and in sectors in which there are a number of comparable quoted companies. It is difficult to apply the earnings multiples method to start-up, high-growth, or turnaround businesses as relatively bold assumptions often have to be made with regards to a 'maintainable' level of earnings given the initial high earnings growth profile for these businesses.

11.06 Calculating earnings

Maintainable earnings represent an estimate of the annual earnings of the business which are likely to be achievable on an ongoing basis. The estimate can be based on historical or forecast earnings, although any unusual or non-recurring income and expenditure should be eliminated from the estimate. When historical earnings are considered, if the business has experienced rapid growth or its earnings stream is maturing, the historical earnings can be weighted by placing greater emphasis on more recent results.

Unlike the DCF approach described in **11.11**, a multiples-based methodology is a relative valuation methodology in that the multiple selected may be based upon the observed trading multiples of quoted comparable companies. As such, the value of the business is assessed in relation to quoted comparable companies.

Determining the appropriate measure of 'earnings' for this purpose is key as explained below. For tax valuation purposes, for example, 'earnings' were traditionally profits after tax. However, given the variability of companies' marginal tax rates and the fact that, during periods of prolonged recession, many companies were loss-making at a pre-and post- tax level, valuations on the basis of EBITDA (earnings before interest, tax, depreciation and amortisation), EBIT (earnings before interest and tax) or, in some circumstances, revenue, are all acceptable bases of valuation, provided they are meaningful in the context of the business to be valued.

The key driver in determining the appropriate measure of earnings for the purposes of valuation is to identify both the figure which is most likely to be stable in the business's profit or loss account, and also to adopt the measure which is most commonly used by the quoted comparable companies, as the overall valuation will rely on the data relating to these entities. For many commercial transactions, EBITDA is considered the most suitable measure of performance as it calculates value before any account is taken of an individual company's capital structure and, hence, is likely to be comparable from one business to another. EBITDA is also considered to be a rough approximation for free cash flow and therefore this approach can avoid some of the complexities of DCF but still arrive at a comparable value.

Certain business sectors will use different profitability measures; for example, for companies which have a significant rental cost, EBITDAR (earnings before interest, tax, depreciation amortisation and rent) is often a key earnings performance indicator.

It should be noted that EBITDA is not always an appropriate basis and EBITA may be more relevant in certain cases, as shown in *S v S* [2006] EWHC 2339, discussed at **23.12**.

Other points to note in the identification of an appropriate maintainable earnings figure are specific matters pertaining to the subject business. For example, if directors' remuneration is paid by way of dividend, then the profits of the company will be proportionately higher than those of the comparator companies.

11.07 Weighted average

When calculating maintainable earnings, it is desirable to base the calculation on the anticipated future earnings of the company, as a purchaser of the company's shares is interested in what he might be received in the future rather than what has happened in the past. Where forecasting is unreliable or problematic, for example, for cyclical businesses, a common method, which has little to recommend it except convenience, is to take the average earnings for the past three to five years (depending on the extent to which profits fluctuate) and to take the arithmetic mean of these figures. However, if there is a marked trend in the earnings, be it upwards or downwards, taking a simple average is not only incorrect as a basis of calculating potential earnings, but positively misleading. Unless there is evidence to suggest that the historical trend will not continue, it is necessary to extrapolate this pattern into the future, that is, if the trend is upwards, future earnings are likely to be higher than those of the current year. If the profits fluctuate wildly or go in cycles it may be sensible to average over a longer period. The trouble with any substantial period of averaging is that inflation can mean that results of several years ago are unlikely to be a valid indication of current figures. One practice which tries to cater for this is by applying a 'sum of the years' digits' average to the earnings of the past three or five years.

Example

An estimate of the average profits of Dewoitine Productions Ltd is required for the years 2014–2018.

Year	*Profits*	*Weighting*	*Weighted profit*
	£		£
2018	1,022,873	× 5	5,114,365
2017	862,504	× 4	3,450,016
2016	1,347,206	× 3	4,041,618
2015	763,540	× 2	1,527,080
2014	502,175	× 1	502,175
	4,498,298		14,635,254
Mean	4,498,298/5	= £899,660	
Weighted average	14,635,254/15	= £975,684	

The above calculation results in an earnings figure lower than the results actually achieved in 2018. The valuer must consider whether this is a reasonable result, eg if the business is truly cyclical or if the results achieved in 2018 were exceptional. Averaging the results over a three-year period would give a mean of £1,077,528 and a weighted average of £1,023,472. Therefore the valuer needs to be able to justify the rationale for selecting a particular averaging period and method of calculation as the differences which result can be material.

A more precise calculation might possibly be to adjust the profits for earlier years for inflation in accordance with, for example, the general index of retail prices, and to take the average of these profits. This could be a reasonable means of arriving at the anticipated future profits of a static business but is unlikely to take account of one where a considerable degree of growth is apparent. The combination of the sum of the years' digits with inflation adjusted profits would give more weight to the most recent profits and therefore take account of the profit trend to some extent.

It is essential that the earnings and the multiples are derived on a consistent basis, ie both on a historical basis or both on a prospective basis.

11.08 Determining an appropriate multiple

The choice of an appropriate earnings multiple reflects, inter alia, expectations about the prospects for growth of the business; a higher multiple generally reflects higher growth and/or lower risk expectations (and vice versa).

The selection of the earnings multiple depends on what is being valued. For commercial transactions, where the valuation is of the whole business or a controlling interest in its issued capital, the appropriate earnings multiple will generally be the EV/EBITDA multiple, which uses EBITDA as the basis of maintainable earnings. In this, EV represents enterprise value, which is the sum of the values of debt and equity in the company. EBITDA is generally viewed by valuers as the best proxy for enterprise free cash flow because it incorporates both the revenue and operating costs of a business, but not the non-cash depreciation and amortisation. EBITDA multiples are calculated as enterprise value divided by EBITDA. As might be expected, a valuation performed using this multiple results in an enterprise value and therefore, in order to arrive at an equity value, the value must be adjusted for net debt as described in **11.10** below.

If a valuer were seeking a multiple for a listed company to use as a comparator, enterprise value would need to be calculated at the valuation date. This is the sum of the market value of the equity and the value of debt. Whilst the share price will be published and often so will market capitalisation, the value of the debt is harder to obtain. Frequently, the valuer will need to resort to the most recent published annual or interim accounts and assume that the level of debt has not changed since that date, being careful to reflect any repayments obviously due as disclosed in the accounts. If interest is paid at above or below a market rate, the market value of the debt will differ from its nominal amount.

Despite the popularity of an EBITDA basis of valuation, EBITDA multiples for quoted companies are not readily available without a subscription to financial data websites such as Capital IQ or Bloomberg. However, a company's last reported EBITDA is usually detailed in the investor information section of its website and enterprise value can be calculated as described above.

Some commercial transaction reports will also provide an implied EBITDA multiple applicable to the transaction. Again, this may provide a reasonable starting point to any calculation, although the valuer should be mindful that the figures will be based on reported information, not necessarily the actual transaction price, and any adjustments for deferred consideration or warranties may have a significant impact on the final figure.

Price/earnings (P/E) ratios for listed companies are published in the *Financial Times*, and the Actuaries Share Index also gives sector averages, which can be useful if no individual comparator companies can be identified. The *Investors Chronicle* uses a method of a calculating a price/earnings ratio in which pre-tax profit is reduced by corporation tax at the standard rate (19% at the time of writing). The difference between the P/E ratio published in the *Investors Chronicle* and that published in the *Financial Times* can be quite marked at times when the corporation tax regime permits significant allowances against tax (see **18.14** on valuation at 31 March 1982).

Focus

Unless given in relation to a transaction, quoted multiples relate to small minority shareholdings. Historically, it was always considered necessary to adjust these multiples for a control premium for valuations of a controlling stake. However, recent theory is that this is not always the case and that many quoted company multiples already include an implicit control premium, so no adjustment is required. Page 34 of the International Private Equity and Venture Capital Valuation (IPEV) Guidelines (68 pages, December 2018) makes clear that they presume that market-based multiples are indicative of the value of the company as a whole and do not require a control adjustment.

11.09 Adjustments to the quoted multiple

It is rare to find a directly comparable listed company or transaction to the business or asset being valued and therefore it is likely that adjustments to the market data will be required. The need for a control premium will need to be considered on a case-by-case basis. Substantial, easily accessible research has been undertaken into this topic recently. The valuer should familiarise himself with up-to-date research before deciding on the appropriateness and size of any control premium. A discount for lack of liquidity is likely to be appropriate.

The necessity for other adjustments will depend on the subject entity and the purpose of the valuation. For example, a valuation calculated for the purpose of a commercial transaction between known parties may adjust for specific synergies identified between the parties or tax benefits or liabilities which are expected to arise. These special circumstances would not be reflected in a market-based valuation, where both the vendor and the acquirer are hypothetical individuals or entities. Other adjustments are likely to be required to reflect differences in size and operations of the subject entity compared to the quoted comparators, which may be much larger, more diverse and operate in a different range of geographical locations.

Pitfall

If a control premium or discount is to be applied to quoted company data, care must be taken to ensure that the premium is applied to the equity value or market capitalisation of the company and not to the enterprise value. A purchaser would not pay a premium for any debt or cash in the business, nor would these be discounted.

11.10 Enterprise versus equity value

As noted in **11.08** above, valuations based on multiples of enterprise value to revenue and EBITDA (and its variants) derive an enterprise value. If the valuation required is that of the company's equity then an adjustment to enterprise value must be made in order to arrive at an equity value. Any surplus or non-operating items are added, surplus cash (if any) is added back and interest bearing debt deducted in order to arrive at the value attributable to equity. Depending on their rights, preference shares may well need to be treated as debt in this calculation.

These adjustments should be made based on appropriate figures as close as possible to the valuation date and taken from the subject company's records.

11.11 Discounted cash flow method – an income approach

The fundamental tenet of the income approach is that the value of a business reflects the present value of the future income flows attributable to the business in the form of cash flows. While an acquirer of a business will review the business's historical financial performance, the price that they are willing to pay will be dictated by the *future* cash flows that they can reasonably expect the business to generate.

DCF is the most widely used of the income-based valuation approaches. It determines the present value of the business by reference to the future cash flows expected to be generated by it. Forecasts are prepared for each of the years for which results may reasonably be foreseen and an appropriate discount rate is applied to arrive at the net present value of the future cash flows. A residual or 'terminal' value may be added to represent value after the end of the chosen period or the cash flows can be modelled on an annual basis until the end of the life of the business.

Historically, DCF was most often used in the acquisition of capital assets or in respect of capital projects where returns could be predicted with reasonable certainty. However, this is now a standard valuation method for many commercial transactions, particularly private equity investment, notwithstanding the difficulties of preparing forecasts sufficiently far in advance to make the calculations meaningful.

DCF is also becoming a more common valuation method in the cases heard before the Courts. A DCF calculation was used, with the court's approval, by one of the expert witnesses in the US case of *Newhouse's Estate v Comr* (1990) TC No 14 at 2711. In the UK, *Saltri III Ltd v MD Mezzanine SA Sicar & Ors* [2012] EWHC 3025 (Comm) concentrated on the DCF cash flows prepared by the experts and this approach was also the accepted approach in *Re Charterhouse Capital Limited; Arbuthnott v Bonnyman* [2014] EWHC 1410 (Ch). In this case a shareholder failed in an attempt to remedy alleged prejudice and obtain a pro rata value for his shareholding in Charterhouse Development Capital Limited. The shareholders' agreement allowed for the minority to be bound by the price agreed by a disinterested majority. 'Valued on a minority basis, Mr Arbuthnott's shareholding was valued in the region of £0.4789m to £1.3m and the offer to buy the shares was worth £1.35m and Mr Arbuthnott could not complain as to the process or the value placed upon the shares'.

The decision in this case was confirmed in *Arbuthnott v Bonnyman and others* [2015] EWCA Civ 536.

The DCF method is often used to value start-ups or businesses in a turnaround situation where historical information (if any) is unlikely to have any bearing on the future performance of the business. As explained in **21.05**, DCF is the method stipulated when measuring value in use for impairment testing for financial reporting in both IFRS and UK GAAP. The methods set out in **Chapter 21** for the valuation of intangible assets – principally relief from royalty and excess earnings – are both variants of the DCF method.

While a DCF exercise comprises two elements – a forecast of cash flows and a discount rate – there are a number of component parts to each element for which assumptions need to be made.

11.12 Forecast information and assumptions

The quality of the forecast information will have a significant impact on the credibility of the resulting valuation. As growth assumptions tend to be calculated on a cumulative basis, the effect of any delay or shortfall in the cash flows generated will have an impact on the expected results in later years, the aggregate effect of which may be substantial.

If growth is expected over a number of years, the forecasts should reflect any additional capital expenditure and changes in working capital which may be required to sustain the business in its expansion.

For start-up enterprises, in particular, it can be extremely difficult to predict the quantum and timing of cash flows arising as there is limited historical data and a generally unproven business model. Therefore, in this situation, forecasts should be treated with caution and sensitivity analysis performed to assess the effect of a delay in the timing of receipt and/or a shortfall in the amount of revenue generated.

11.13 Enterprise versus equity cash flows

The DCF calculation can be prepared using enterprise cash flows or equity cash flows, although it is generally prepared on an enterprise value basis. Enterprise cash flows are on a pre-debt basis, so represent those amounts available for distribution to the debt and equity investors. Enterprise cash flows are discounted using a weighted average cost of capital (WACC) that incorporates both the cost of debt and cost of equity (ie the estimated returns demanded by debt and equity investors to account for the risk of investing in the business). If using enterprise cash flows, the resulting net present value reflects the enterprise value of the business. In order to determine the equity value, the third-party debt (net of any surplus cash) required to fund the enterprise cash flows is subtracted from the enterprise value and any surplus or non-operating assets should be added.

Equity cash flows are on a post-debt basis, so represent those amounts available after the repayment of principal and interest to the debt investors. As such, they are the free cash flows available *solely to equity investors*. Equity cash flows are discounted using a cost of equity and the resulting net present value is the equity value of the business.

The resulting equity value should not differ whether enterprise free cash flows (discounted using a WACC) or equity-free cash flows (discounted using a cost of equity) are used.

11.14 Forecast period and terminal value

Under DCF the forecast free cash flows are discounted back to the valuation date using an appropriate discount rate, thus generating a net present value of those future cash flows. This initial forecast period, known as the explicit forecast period, should be long enough to enable the business to achieve a stabilised level of earnings, although, as noted above, if appropriate, a terminal value at the end of the explicit forecast period (estimating the value of the business into perpetuity) is then determined and the resulting terminal value is discounted back to the valuation date and added to the net present value of the cash flows forecast for the explicit period to arrive at an overall value for the business. Many businesses will not continue into perpetuity, due to termination of a lease, takeover or the normal course of business and so consideration needs to be given as to the extent to which cash flows should extend beyond the explicit forecast period.

A terminal value may include inflationary and/or other growth assumptions, or cash flows may be assumed to remain flat throughout the terminal period (which is an effective decline if no inflation adjustment is made).

Pitfall

Valuing cash flows into perpetuity can result in a very large part of the business's value accruing in the terminal value element. This can dominate the overall valuation. Before attributing a perpetual life to a business or income stream the valuer should give careful consideration as to whether this assumption is reasonable in the circumstances.

11.15 Discount rate

The rate at which future cash flows are discounted (the discount rate) should reflect not only the time value of money, but also the risk associated with the business future operations and the achievability of those cash flows.

The discount rate should correspond to the assessed riskiness in the cash flows, in particular the risk inherent in: (a) achieving the quantum of cash flows; and (b) doing so in the time frame anticipated (reflecting the time value of money). Risk factors impacting the successful execution of future cash flow plans include (but are not limited to) the competitive and economic landscape, the reasonableness of revenue and profit growth assumptions, management's historical track record, and the implementation and successful execution of strategic initiatives driving the future growth expectations.

If discounting enterprise cash flows, the appropriate discount rate is a WACC. This captures the estimated rate of return for both debt and equity investors in a business, weighted on a reasonable estimate of its optimal capital structure (ie the proportion of debt and equity that maximises the value of a business). If discounting equity cash flows, then the appropriate discount rate is the cost of equity.

11.16 Calculating the WACC

Algebraically, the WACC is represented as:

WACC = ke (E / (D + E)) + kd (D / (D + E)), where:

- ke represents the cost of equity, ie the return required by a shareholder to compensate them for the assessed risks, including the company's ability to repay the anticipated debt financing (ie credit risk);
- kd represents the after tax cost of long-term debt, ie the return required by debt holders to compensate them for the company's assessed credit risk;
- E / (D + E) represents the estimated optimal level of equity in the capital structure; and
- D / (D + E) represents the estimated optimal level of long-term debt in the capital structure.

A range of parameters can materially influence the outcome of the assessment of a WACC. Selecting those parameters necessarily involves the application of judgement. Therefore, where possible, it is important to cross-check the calculated WACC with broker notes provided for comparable quoted entities. It is also important to consider a range of sources for each parameter which forms an input to the WACC.

11.17 Calculating cost of equity

The cost of equity is commonly estimated using the Capital Asset Pricing Model (CAPM). This model hypothesises that the required rate of return on equity is equal to the risk-free return plus a market risk premium adjusted to reflect the volatility of the relevant company, as compared with the market as a whole. The CAPM is a globally recognised and applied model for estimating the cost of equity.

For the purposes of valuation, the CAPM is represented as Ke = Rf + (Beta × M) + S + C where:

- Rf represents the risk-free rate (usually taken as the market yield on a government bond of the same maturity as the investment being considered);
- Beta represents the relative risk (measured by volatility) of the company being valued compared to the risk of the market as a whole – for instance a beta of 1 indicates an expected change in value in line with the market, whereas a company with a beta of less than 1 would be less volatile (in terms of volatility of returns) than the market as a whole and vice versa;
- M represents the equity (or market) risk premium, ie the return a market equity portfolio is expected to generate in excess of Rf;
- S represents the small company premium; and
- C represents the country risk premium.

The small company premium and country-specific risk premium are additional adjustments that are made to the base CAPM estimate for companies to reflect the additional risk inherent in small companies or in specific locations. In addition, there may be a company-specific risk which should also be reflected in the calculation. These adjustments – S, C and any further specific risk adjustment – are often known generically as 'alpha' adjustments.

Pablo Fernandez, a professor at the University of Navarra in Spain, publishes regular surveys on the equity risk premium in different countries and other parameters required when using CAPM. These are available at www.papers.ssrn.com.

For companies operating overseas in developing markets an international CAPM needs to be considered. This adjusts the mature market cost of equity to reflect the specific risks associated with investing in assets in a developing market.

11.18 International CAPM

There are three generally recognised CAPM methods of calculating an international cost of equity. These are:

- Global CAPM – this utilises a global risk-free rate, a global Equity Market Risk Premium (EMRP) and a beta measuring covariance with respect to the global equity market. This assumes that investors hold fully diversified international portfolios made up of stocks from around the world.
- Home CAPM – this utilises a home risk-free rate, a home EMRP and a beta measuring covariance with respect to the home equity market. The betas should relate to foreign companies operating in the national market of the target investment. Home is defined as the country where the investor is located.
- Foreign CAPM – this utilises a foreign risk-free rate, a foreign EMRP and a beta measuring covariance with respect to the foreign equity market. 'Foreign' means the country where the investment is located.

Performing DCF exercises in foreign currencies can be complex and is outside the scope of this book. As a general rule, cash flows should be forecast in the same currency as that used for measurement of the discount rate.

11.19 Risk-free rate

A generally accepted approach for assessing a risk-free rate is to adopt the rate of return (based on the yield) on a government bond as a proxy. The government bond should have a similar time to maturity as the period of the cash flow forecasts. Where a perpetuity value has been included in the cash flow forecast, the bond life should be the longest available (ie 20 or 30 years depending on the currency). As noted at **11.18**, it is usual to match the currency of the risk-free rate with the currency of forecast cash flows. By doing this, inflation is modelled consistently between the forecast cash flows and the risk-free rate. Therefore, if a forecast is prepared in US dollars, this would suggest that a US treasury bond with a similar life to the forecast cash-flow period is an appropriate guide to the risk free rate.

11.20 Beta

Beta is a measure of systematic risk in the CAPM. It reflects the relationship between the rate of return on equity in a company and the rate of return on the overall market as a whole, measured on the basis of the volatility of the respective prices. Companies with a beta greater than 1 generally have more volatility in their returns than the market, which by definition has a beta of 1.

Betas are available for listed companies. Betas for unlisted entities can be estimated based on betas available for comparable listed entities, and adjusted to reflect the level of target debt assumed in the optimal capital structure for the company being valued.

Betas can be raw or adjusted. An adjusted beta includes an adjustment to reflect empirical studies which demonstrate that betas have a tendency to move towards a value of 1 over time.

The most common method for assessing a beta is to regress the excess stock return (over the risk-free rate) against the excess market return. As with the risk-free rate and the CAPM basis adopted, it is important to consider which market index is appropriate for the regression analysis. If a Home CAPM is used for a US company then the index used should be the US index.

When considering a beta, it is also important to consider the period over which the beta is assessed and the frequency of assessment, ie weekly or monthly.

Assuming a long-term investment horizon, the beta should be measured using a sufficient period of time and data points thereby reducing the impact of short-term fluctuations. Empirical research supports five years as the appropriate measurement period and both Morningstar Ibbotson and the London Business School, main data providers, assess beta on a monthly basis over five years. This approach was also confirmed in *Saltri III Ltd v MD Mezzanine SA Sicar & Ors* [2012] EWHC 3025 (Comm).

Listed companies similar to the subject entity must be identified and betas obtained. 'Geared' betas reflect the capital structure (debt v equity) of the listed entity. These are then 'ungeared' to eliminate the effect of the different debt and equity structures in the various comparable companies selected. In order to calculate the cost of equity, the ungeared betas must then be re-geared based on the estimated target capital structure applicable to the subject company using the following formula, known as the Hamada formula:

Re-geared beta = Ungeared beta × [1 + {debt/equity × (1 – tax rate)}]

The debt/equity ratio reflects the proportion of net debt in relation to the market value of the company's equity, the following formula is used:

D/IC = 1/(1+{1/[D/E]}) where:

- D = the debt;
- IC = invested capital (total debt plus equity);
- E = equity.

Example

Alexander Limited wishes to estimate the value of a product which is expected to have a remaining life of six years before being superseded. The company has calculated its post-tax cash flows after adjusting for all necessary costs of cessation as follows:

Year to 31 December	*2019*	*2020*	*2021*	*2022*	*2023*	*2024*
Post-tax cash flows (£000)	550	485	350	240	210	185

As the product division is small, the company has decided to value it using Alexander's own cost of capital.

Alexander Limited has identified a number of global comparator companies which produce similar products. The company has an optimal gearing structure of 20% debt to 80% equity and effective tax rate of 24.5%. It is ranked in the lowest percentile of companies by size, has significant operations in a developing country but otherwise no firm specific risks.

It has calculated an appropriate beta as follows:

Company	*Currency*	*Geared beta*	*Gearing (D/E)*	*Ungeared beta*	*Net debt (D)*	*Market capitalisation (E)*	*Tax rate*
A	EUR	1.4	21.0%	1.23	2,385	11,359	33.3%
B	EUR	0.8	0.0%	0.80	(1,157)	10,592	33.3%
C	WON	1.5	27.8%	1.28	1,069,347	7,430,694	27.5%
D	USD	1.6	60.4%	1.20	343	567	40.0%
E	USD	1.2	0.0%	1.23	(2,984)	29,081	21.2%
F	YEN	1.2	88.1%	0.78	1,031,686	1,170,656	40.7%
G	EUR	1.0	47.3%	0.77	5,203	11,002	33.3%
H	EUR	1.1	22.0%	0.99	9,034	41,093	29.5%
Average			**33.3%**	**1.03**			
Selected data for subject			**25.0%**	**1.10**			**24.5%**

The selected beta of 1.1 has then been re-geared as shown below:

Re-geared beta = Ungeared beta × [1 + {debt/equity × (1 – tax rate)}]

Re-geared beta = 1.10 × [1+ (0.25 × (1 –.24.5%)]
= 1.10 × [1+0.18875]
= 1.307625

11.21 Equity risk premium

The equity risk premium represents the average incremental return required by investors for investing in the stock market as opposed to risk free investments such as government bonds. This figure is measured in empirical studies by reference to the actual excess returns generated by the market over a selected period of time and can also be implied from forecast information.

Many data providers produce equity risk premium data and information may also be found on the Internet.

11.22 Country risk premium

The country risk premium reflects the additional risks presented by particular equity markets in certain countries and also captures the additional currency and inflationary risks in these countries. When there are international factors affecting the cash flows, it may be appropriate to apply a country risk premium. Details of the premium which might be applicable to a particular country are published on an annual basis by Professor Aswath Damodaran (www.damodaran.com) and are also available from other sources.

11.23 Small company premium

The need for a small company premium reflects the fact that investors generally regard small companies as a riskier investment than larger enterprises. Therefore, investors require a higher rate of return to invest in such companies. The perception of higher risk stems from the fact that smaller companies tend to be less diversified and have higher operational risk and hence are more vulnerable to a whole host of factors including undue dependence on specific suppliers, customers or products.

Small company premium information is available from a number of data providers, although there is generally a charge for this information.

11.24 Company-specific risk

There may specific uncertainties relating to the subject company which require a further adjustment to the cost of equity. These may include dependence on a single customer or supplier, legal risk or potential market obsolescence of a main product.

Example

Having calculated beta, Alexander Limited's cost of equity has been calculated as follows:

Cost of equity capital:	
Beta (re-geared)	1.31
Equity risk premium	6.00%
Risk-free rate	3.00%
CAPM cost of equity	10.85%

Add/(deduct): unsystematic risk factors:	
Small company premium	7.50%
Country risk premium	1.75%
Firm-specific risk	0.00%
Cost of equity capital to the company	**20.10%**

11.25 Cost of debt

The cost of debt should reflect the actual cost of debt that is applicable to the business as at the valuation date. If the company has no debt at the valuation date, a proxy for the cost of debt may be obtained by using published commercial loan rates.

Example

Alexander Limited has debt with an interest rate of 5.5%. Therefore, the cost of debt has been calculated as follows:

Cost of debt capital:	
Interest rate	5.50%
Tax rate of the company	24.5%
Cost of debt capital to the business	**4.15%**

Alexander Limited's WACC is as follows:

Weighted average cost of capital

	Debt	*Equity*
Cost of capital (after tax) to the company	4.15%	20.10%
Selected capital structure	20.00%	80.00%
Weighted-average cost of capital	0.83%	16.08%
Weighted average cost of capital (0.83% + 16.08%)	**16.91%**	

Accordingly, the company has calculated the net present value of its product at 31 December 2019 as follows:

Year to 31 December	*2019*	*2020*	*2021*	*2022*	*2023*	*2024*
Post-tax cash flows (£000)	550	485	350	240	210	185
Months in period	12	12	12	12	12	12
Mid-year discount period	0.50	1.50	2.50	3.50	4.50	5.50
Mid-year discount factor	0.925	0.791	0.677	0.579	0.495	0.423
Present value of single cash flows	509	383	237	139	104	78
Net present value of cash flows	1,450					

11.26 Performing a cross-check

As with any valuation calculation, a cross-check of the final WACC calculated should be undertaken in order to assess the reasonableness of the discount rate calculated. Cost of capital information is sometimes included in analyst reports, although this may often be a cost of equity figure, rather than a WACC. Therefore, where possible, information for the companies used as comparators should be obtained in order to compare the results with the calculation prepared for the subject company.

If there is debt capital in a company, it should be noted that the WACC applicable to that entity will generally be lower than the cost of equity because the return demanded by debt holders is lower than that demanded by equity-holders. There are two main reasons for this:

- debt holders usually have priority over shareholders if the company becomes bankrupt. Therefore, debt is regarded as being safer than equity and warrants a lower return; for the company, this translates into an interest rate that is lower than the expected total shareholder return on equity; and
- interest paid on debt is tax deductible, and a lower tax bill effectively creates cash for the company and reduces the effective borrowing cost.

For highly geared companies, however, the WACC will increase as debt in a company increases beyond its optimal level. This is because increasing debt correlates with an increasing risk that shareholders will receive no value. Therefore the cost of equity increases accordingly, particularly if the company's leverage reaches a level which is considered unsustainable given its cash flows; if the company is unable to service its debt obligations then there is significant uncertainty as to whether the business will be able to continue.

Focus

In the example above, had Alexander Limited been unable to find suitable comparable companies or beta information, the company may have chosen to use a simple 'build-up' model to estimate its cost of equity as shown below; ie effectively assuming a beta of 1.

Equity risk premium	6.00%
Risk-free rate	3.00%
Small company premium	7.50%
Company risk premium	1.75%
Firm specific risk	0.00%
Cost of equity	18.25%

Weighted average cost of capital:

	Debt	*Equity*
Cost of capital (after tax) to the company	4.15%	18.25%
Selected capital structure	20.00%	80.00%
Weighted average cost of capital	0.83%	14.60%
Weighted average cost of capital (0.83% + 14.60%):		**15.43%**

In this case, the WACC calculated is lower than using the full calculation and the impact on the valuation is as follows:

Year to 31 December	*2019*	*2020*	*2021*	*2022*	*2023*	*2024*
Post-tax cash flows (£000)	550	485	350	240	210	185
Months in period	12	12	12	12	12	12
Mid-year discount period	0.50	1.50	2.50	3.50	4.50	5.50
Mid-year discount factor	0.931	0.806	0.699	0.605	0.524	0.454
Present value of single cash flows	512	391	245	145	110	84
Net present value of cash flows	1,487					

While this shortened calculation approach is not appropriate for commercial transactions or situations where the values need to be precise, it may be suitable in situations where a broader approximation of value is sufficient.

Chapter 12

Other methods of valuation

Signposts

12.01 Introduction

In addition to the two most widely used methods of valuing a business described in **Chapter 11**, there are further techniques which may be used to establish value, particularly for minority shareholdings or specific instruments.

There are several other methods available to value unquoted shares. While the two methods set out in **Chapter 11** focus on the value of the entity as a whole (ie incorporating 100% of the equity), the methods discussed in this chapter mainly identify the value of a single share and therefore may be suitable for the valuation of minority shareholdings or as a cross-check to one of the two methods discussed in **Chapter 11**.

12.02 Earnings yield – income approach

The earnings yield can be significant in the valuation of unquoted company shares where, in the majority of cases, dividends are either not declared at all or are a purely nominal amount.

The earnings yield is calculated by taking the profit after corporation tax and dividing this by the total capitalisation (the nominal share capital multiplied by the price per share) and multiplying by 100 to give the earnings yield percentage.

Example

Tornado Ltd, motor vehicle component factors, had the following results for the year ended 31 December 2019.

	£
Turnover	1,800,000
Operating profit before taxation	64,000
Profit after taxation	48,000
Share capital	50,000
Value per £1 share	3
No of shares in issue: 50,000	
Earnings yield	$\frac{48{,}000 \times 100}{3 \times 50{,}000}$
=	32%
Earnings yield on par value of the share	$\frac{48{,}000 \times 100}{1 \times 50{,}000}$
=	96%

The valuer must then determine an appropriate earnings yield for the subject company. If, starting with an earnings yield but not knowing the share price and bearing in mind the earnings yield of other companies in similar businesses and any factors peculiar to the subject company – for example, the quality of the management – the valuer considers an earnings yield of 32% reasonable, the price per share will be £3, eg:

$$\frac{48{,}000}{0.32 \times 50{,}000} = £3$$

12.03 Earnings per share

Earnings are also expressed in pence per share, which is simply the profit after tax divided by the number of shares in issue. It is important in computing the earnings per share to ensure that the post-tax profits are divided by the correct number of ordinary shares in issue, particularly where the nominal value of each share is other than £1.

Example

If Tornado Ltd's share capital was divided into 200,000 shares of 25p each, the earnings per share would be:

Profit after taxation:	£48,000
Number of shares:	200,000
Earnings per share:	= 24p

Where the number of shares in issue has varied during the year, it may be appropriate to use the weighted average number of shares in issue during the year.

Tornado Ltd had 120,000 shares in issue on 1 January 2019 and made a bonus issue of 2 for 3 on 1 April 2019. The weighted average number of shares in issue was:

120,000 for 12 months	120,000
80,000 for 9 months	60,000
	180,000

so earnings per share becomes:

$$\frac{48,000}{180,000} \; 26.7p$$

The weighted average number of shares in issue is often used in practice to calculate earnings per share, but a valuer must be extremely careful in using it. They are valuing the shares after the bonus issue and looking to the past as a guide to the future. So far as the shares being valued are concerned, the past results indicate future earnings per share of 24p, not 26.7p.

If instead of the bonus issue there had been an allotment of 80,000 shares, either at par or at a premium, the valuer needs to consider what effect the additional cash injected will have on the profit figure. For example, if the cash received were used to pay off an overdraft thereby saving (say) £9,000 of interest charges, the anticipated future profit, based on past figures, would be £48,000 plus £9,000 less any additional taxation. If all other things are equal, the anticipated earnings per share would change.

12.04 Dividend yield – income approach

As a dividend is normally declared as a percentage of the nominal value of the share this has to be related to the market value to give the actual true yield. This is arrived at by dividing the nominal value of the shares in pence by the price of the share in pence and multiplying by the dividend as a percentage to give the yield as a percentage.

Example

Tornado Ltd for the year ended 31 December 2019 paid a dividend of 36% on the 25p shares. The shares were valued at 75p per share. Dividend yield =

$$\frac{25 \times 36}{75 \times 100} = 12\%$$

The required yield can also be used to arrive at a value per share. If the required yield were 12% and the actual dividend 36%, the value per 25p share would be:

$$\frac{25 \times 36}{12} = 75\text{p per share}$$

In many cases, the dividend is declared at a rate per share and the dividend yield obtained by dividing the actual dividend in pence by the price of the share in pence and multiplying by 100 to give the net dividend yield per cent.

Example

For the year ended 31 December 2019, Tornado Ltd paid a dividend of 9p per share on the 25p shares. The shares were valued at 75p per share.

$9/75 \times 100 = 12\%$

The required yield and the dividend per share can be used to arrive at a value per share.

$9 \times 100/12 = 75$p per share

In considering the value of a share it is important to look not only at the actual dividends paid and the appropriate dividend yields but also to consider the likelihood of future dividend changes, and it may be possible to calculate the prospective or likely future dividend which in turn would enable the prospective yield to be calculated.

Example

Tornado Ltd was expected to pay a dividend of 10p per share for the year ended 31 December 2019. If the price is 75p per share the prospective yield becomes

$10/75 \times 100 = 13.33\%$

If the required yield were 12% the share would be valued at:

$10 \times 100/12 = 83.33$p per share

In order to value a share from a dividend yield it is merely necessary, as illustrated above, to reciprocate the fraction which then becomes the dividend amount in pence divided by the required dividend yield per cent, to give the price per share in pence. The valuer must compare like with like. It is pointless to arrive at a dividend yield for A Ltd based on last year's total dividend and attempt to compare it with B Ltd's dividend calculated on last year's final dividend and this year's interim.

It will be observed that in the above examples a required dividend yield of 12% is assumed, but one of the difficulties facing the valuer is to arrive at that required yield on a reasoned and logical basis. It is of course perfectly possible simply to adopt a dividend yield on the basis of experience, but such a yield would be very difficult to justify before, for example, the courts, where objective observable data tends to be more persuasive.

For fiscal purposes, valuation in the open market is necessary and there is, in fact, no better open market for shares than a stock market, such as the London Stock Exchange (LSE). If, on the LSE, an exactly comparable company to Tornado Ltd were listed and the price quoted for it showed a net equivalent dividend yield of 8.8%, what would be the required dividend yield for Tornado Ltd? In this example, since the companies are exactly comparable, the only difference is that the comparable company is listed so that there is a ready market for its shares while Tornado does not enjoy that benefit. The extent of the allowance for that difference must depend on the time, circumstances and the conditions in the market. There is a wealth of research into appropriate levels for the lack of liquidity discount – this is often taken as being above 50%.

It is, however, extremely unlikely that there will be an exactly comparable company. It is much more likely that there will be a number of listed companies showing similarities to the business under consideration, but also showing variations in size, geographical focus, dividend policy, earnings, range of product, etc. A valuer can make suitable allowance for differences in the companies to arrive at a dividend yield for the particular company on an 'if quoted' basis. Allowance for lack of marketability can then be made and the value reduced accordingly.

Some professionals consider that there is absolutely no comparison between a listed and an unlisted company. When they reject comparability, they must prefer the arbitrary selection of a required dividend yield (unless they consider dividend yield is of no consequence in valuation) but the difficulty of defending an arbitrary selection of the required dividend yield is obvious.

It will be appreciated that so far as valuation is concerned a prospective purchaser of shares is interested in the future dividends he is likely to receive after his purchase and the dividends previously paid are merely evidence of the previous dividend policy of the company and as such an indication to its likely future dividend policy. However, there may be many reasons why the past dividend policy is unlikely to be a reliable guide to the future policy. For example, the company might be trying to resist a takeover bid and therefore increasing its dividends to its existing shareholders. On the other hand, the new management and shareholders might be more or less interested in providing an immediate return in the form of dividends than the previous management and shareholders. Therefore, it is important to remember that past dividends are, at best, a mere indication of likely future dividends and it is important to take account of all available evidence in estimating the size of future dividends.

Pitfall

Many owner-managed businesses use dividends as remuneration for the owner and therefore the amounts paid are not representative of sums which would be payable to passive shareholders. In addition, many companies do not pay dividends during an economic downturn as they prefer to pay down debt or retain funds for security. Therefore, when a dividend is paid, this can be a 'catch-up' payment and not necessarily reflective of the company's dividend policy going forward.

12.05 Notional dividends

So far as dividend yield calculations are concerned, where no dividend is actually paid it is suggested that the best approach is to assume that the board of the company had to consider the payment of a dividend, in view of the existence of hypothetical outside shareholders, and to decide what dividend would be declared by a reasonable board in such circumstances.

In his book entitled *Share Valuations* (2nd edn), the late T A Hamilton Baynes at p 125 referred to this treatment:

> 'The problem was raised by Halmer Hudson FCA, in a public discussion with H Booth, a chief examiner (who was not necessarily expressing the view of the Shares Valuation Division). Halmer Hudson proposed a company which refused to pay a dividend and instead paid income tax on shortfall. The examiner accepted that there would be little that the holder of say 10% of the equity could do. The shares would have a value because the controlling share-holders would themselves have in mind a minimal value which they would be prepared to pay. He accepted the uncertainty of threatening action under section 210 (of the Companies Act 1948). Halmer Hudson suggested a method of valuing the shares by assuming that the company had paid a normal dividend. The valuation arising from such an assumed dividend would be discounted by 70%. The examiner preferred a discount of about 50%.'

In commenting in an actual case on this concept, HMRC's Shares and Assets Valuation division stated:

> 'I think you will agree that the view expressed by Mr Booth during the course of the dialogue between himself and Halmer Hudson is his own personal view-point and is not binding upon the Revenue. However, the division does accept that a valuation has to be made of shares in a company trading very successfully but not paying dividends. To solve this problem, and as you wish to adopt the line advanced by Booth and Halmer Hudson also, I propose to fall in with your wishes in this particular valuation to produce an early settlement.'

And again later:

> 'I said that I would like the opportunity to consider the result of the dialogue which took place between Mr Booth (formerly of this office) and Mr Halmer Hudson. Having considered the results of such dialogue it is apparent to me that the process leading to a valuation in companies where no dividend is being paid is to assume the amount the company could afford to pay arrive at a value and then discount for non-payment. I note this is the approach you have adopted and I have accepted the same.'

The problem with the notional dividend approach is to decide what would be the appropriate dividend in the circumstances and it might normally be appropriate for a trading company to distribute, say, one-third of its post-tax profits by way of dividend. This is very much a generalisation and what would be reasonable in the circumstances must be considered having regard to the company's cash flow and the requirement to use reinvested profits within the company as well as wider economic circumstances. It may be that a reasonable board of directors in the circumstances of a particular case would recommend a distribution of the vast majority of the available profits, for example, if it were a property investment company, or declare a purely nominal dividend if the company is over-trading or likely to require retained profits for the maintenance and development of its business.

The notional dividend method received a measure of judicial approval in *Whiteoak v Walker* [1988] 4 BCC 122 at 129:

> 'Finally, on notional dividend assessment, Mr Sutherland's report criticised the defendant for deducting from the 1981 profit the difference between the valuation of certain factory property and its balance sheet value. The criticism was twofold. First, it assumed that the property was a fixed asset and it was therefore said that no deduction should have been made. Secondly, it presumed that the valuation was made by Mr Bentley and was therefore not to be relied upon. In fact, the property was trading stock and in 1981, when it could not be sold, it was let and turned into investment property, so that the loss on the notional realisation was a proper deduction, and the valuation was made by a firm of chartered surveyors. This valuation was disclosed on discovery months before Mr Sutherland's report and the nature of the asset was known to the plaintiff himself. Both criticisms were completely unjustified. Mr Sutherland had a valid criticism that the factory property was not shown at the reduced value in the 1982 accounts and the defendant as auditor did not qualify the accounts. However, the valuation was, as I have said, a professional valuation, and the criticism is one that lies against the defendant in his conduct of the audit, not in respect of his deduction when making his valuation.
>
> It follows that in my judgment the defendant did not fall below the required standard, whether the specialist standard or the auditor standard, in applying the notional dividend method so as to arrive at a fair value of the relevant shares.'

It is important, however, not to disregard the general circumstances of the company and any other influences on value. In *Re Charrington* (Hong Kong Supreme Court 1975), the valuer for the estate proposed a notional dividend based value for a 10% shareholding which resulted in a figure of $250 per share, whereas net asset backing was $19,105 per share. The court imposed a value of $11,463 per share, taking account of the particular factors that affected the case.

12.06 Dividend cover

If the earnings yield is divided by the dividend yield this gives the cover for the dividend- that is, the number of times the net dividend could be paid out of the current net profit. The identical figure is of course given by dividing the earnings per share by the dividend per share.

Example

Tornado Ltd has an earnings yield of 32% for the year ended 31 December 2019 and a dividend yield of 12%.

The dividend cover is:

32/12 = 2⅔ times

Alternatively, on the basis of earnings per share of 24p and a dividend per share of 9p:

The dividend cover is:

24/9 = 2⅔ times

It will be noted that if the weighted average number of shares in issue is used to calculate the earnings per share, 26.7p as previously calculated, it would be necessary to recalculate the dividend per share on the basis of the average capital:

200,000 × 9p	= £18,000 (net dividend payment)
Average number of shares in issue	180,000
Dividend per share	10p
Cover	26.7/10 = 2.67 times

It will be appreciated that the greater the dividend cover the more secure the dividend is and therefore if all other factors are equal a company with a greater dividend security is likely to be more valuable as being less speculative than one with a lower dividend cover. However, it is extremely rare that all other things are equal.

Pitfall

When considering dividend yields and cover it should be noted that at various times in the past the Government has restricted the amount that can be paid by way of dividend, which means that the past dividend record may be a poor guide to the prospective future dividends once those restrictions have been removed.

12.07 Trend line analysis

It may be worth looking at the earnings of a company to see whether there is a predictable trend in the results, although any such statistical exercise must be viewed with a good deal of caution. It would be unusual to find a company where mere extrapolation of a trend line based on past results gave an accurate estimate of the future profit level.

Computer models are often used to examine trends these days. See Division B, Example 2.

Most spreadsheets have statistical and financial functions which can automatically produce a trend line and calculate the correlation coefficient.

12.08 Special rights

If shares are entitled to dividends but not to votes and the company has a history of paying regular dividends it may be reasonable to value the shares on the basis of an appropriate dividend yield, with a discount of, say, 15% for lack of voting rights. Experience of non-voting shares on the Stock Exchange where shares which are otherwise identical but carry votes are also quoted would suggest that a discount of this order is reasonable.

If, however, shares are entitled to dividends, but the company does not pay dividends, the shares might be valued on the basis of a hypothetical reasonable dividend discounted by say 50% for non-payment with a further discount of 15% for lack of voting power.

If shares are entitled to votes, but not to participate in dividends, it is suggested that a valuation on the normal basis of ordinary shares should be made subject to a further discount for lack of dividend rights. In the case of a controlling interest the lack of dividend rights would not be so important, as the profits could within reason be extracted by way of remuneration and a discount of say 15% might be reasonable. In the case of a minority interest however the shareholder who was not on the board of directors and who had no rights to obtain a seat on the board, and had no rights to a dividend could well expect a discount of a further 40% or more compared with similar shares with dividend rights.

If the shares only have rights to participate in a liquidation surplus with no voting or dividend rights it would be necessary to consider whether there was any likelihood of a liquidation taking place. In most such cases there would be little or no likelihood and it is suggested that a method of valuation would be to calculate the asset value per share, assuming an immediate liquidation, and to discount that figure for say 20 years at a market rate of interest of, say, 5% per annum in order to arrive at a realistic value. Such a discount would very heavily reduce the value of such shares but then the real value in such circumstances would be very low. £100 discounted for 20 years at 5% per annum amounts to approximately £38 and, discounted at 15% per annum, amounts to just over £6.

The lack of a right to participate in a surplus, however, as far as the other shares are concerned, would justify a further discount of say 15%. It will be appreciated that by structuring a company in this way it may possible to depreciate substantially the overall value of the shares. However, in respect of employee shares, the Income Tax (Earnings and Pensions) 2003 introduced the concept of 'actual market value' ie considering the value of the shares including any restrictions placed upon them, as well as 'unrestricted market value', which ignores restrictions. When considering a valuation for taxation purposes, the valuer now has to consider which value he or she is attempting to calculate. Shares and Assets Valuation have not attributed a specific discount to any of the main restrictions eg bad leaver provisions, lack of voting rights etc. which may be seen in relation to employee shares, but the current trend is for a differential of between 10% and 12% between unrestricted and actual market value to be agreed in respect of 'standard' restrictions. Both the unrestricted and actual market values were required to be shown on Form 42, the HMRC form requiring details of employee share transactions from employers, which applied up to and including 2013–14 which had to be submitted to HMRC by 6 July 2014.

12.09 Employment-related securities

From 2014–15 all employment-related securities (ERS) schemes must be registered with HMRC, including one-off awards or gifts of shares.

A new tax-advantaged scheme should be registered by 6 July following the tax year it was established. The following schemes cannot be registered after 6 July:

- Share Incentive Plans (SIPs);
- Save As Your Earn (SAYE); and
- Company Share Option Plans (CSOPs).

It is only necessary to register non-tax-advantaged schemes when there is a reportable event, for example acquiring or disposing of securities, or assigning or releasing securities options.

To tell HMRC about an ERS scheme (www.gov.uk/employment-related-securities-files), a Government Gateway user ID and password are needed (a user ID can be created when the service is used).

After HMRC has been informed, a scheme reference number will be sent by HMRC within 7 days.

An ERS return must be submitted electronically (www.gov.uk/guidance/submit-your-employment-related-securities-ers-return) for each registered ERS scheme every year, even if there is no reportable event.

For Enterprise Management Incentive (EMI) schemes, HMRC must be told about a grant of an EMI option (www.gov.uk/guidance/submit-an-enterprise-management-incentives-emi-notification) within 92 days of the grant.

HMRC need to be told that an ERS scheme has ceased (www.gov.uk/employment-related-securities-files), using the Government Gateway user ID and password used when informing HMRC about the scheme, and a final event date must be provided.

Any outstanding returns must be submitted (www.gov.uk/guidance/submit-your-employment-related-securities-ers-return) until the date of cessation.

12.10 Preference shares

Average yields for quoted preference shares were also included in the fixed interest section of the Financial Times Actuaries Share Index until the end of 1990 and therefore this information might be useful if a March 1982 valuation is required. An uplift of, perhaps, 20% would be given to allow for non-marketability, although it may be possible to agree a higher non-marketability discount of up to one-third with Shares and Assets Valuation division. A greater uplift might also be necessary if there was some doubt as to the financial viability of the company and its ability to continue preference dividend payments.

Preference shares are generally categorised as debt and therefore their value derives from the company's ability to pay the preference dividend and, if the shares are redeemable, its ability to redeem the shares are the relevant date. This would therefore be valued on a discounted cash flow (DCF) basis applied to the DCF with forecast interest and principal payments discounted at the required rate of return.

Not all shares described as 'preference' shares will have the characteristics normally associated with such shares, ie a right to a fixed dividend, no voting rights in normal circumstances and no right to participate in any surplus on a winding up. The company's articles of association should be read carefully to ascertain the precise class rights. If the articles do not say that 'preference' shares carry no votes, the shares will carry one vote each. Preference shares may be shown as equity on the balance sheet or included in the account notes for creditors, depending on the facts in each case.

12.11 Valuation of fixed-interest securities

For fixed interest securities with a fixed redemption date, such as debentures, it will first be necessary to calculate the yield to redemption. However, if the debentures are redeemable at a variable date (such as on the death of the debenture holder) it would be necessary to estimate this actuarially in order to ascertain the probable redemption date. Similarly, if the redemption period is within a period of time at the borrower's option it would be necessary, having regard to current interest rates, to estimate whether the company would be likely to redeem the debentures at the earliest or latest available date under the debenture deed.

The flat or running yield of a debenture is merely the nominal price divided by the market price multiplied by the percentage rate of interest to give the interest yield per cent. It is clearly necessary to know the coupon rate of the debenture or loan stock and whether interest is paid yearly, half-yearly or at other intervals. The redemption terms will also be required as it is possible that the debenture may be repaid at a discount or premium rather than at par. Yields of debentures and loan stock are always quoted as gross yields.

Leading firms of stockbrokers publish lists of corporation stocks showing the values of quoted debentures. HMRC would normally accept a relatively small discount of, say, £5 per £100 stock of the nearest comparable quoted stock as appropriate for valuation purposes. In most cases, the list of redemption yields is compiled on the basis of the annual coupon rate of interest which, because the interest is in fact paid half-yearly, is rather less than the true annual equivalent. For example, a redemption yield of 16% is in reality 8% per half year which on a true annual basis is equivalent to a rate of interest in excess of 16.6%.

The yield to redemption can also be found from compound interest tables such as Parry's valuation tables applying the formula:

$$V = A = An\ \grave{u}\ i$$

$$A = M\ (I + i)^{n}$$

$$An\ \grave{u}\ I = IM \times \frac{I - (I + i)^{-n}}{i}$$

Where

A = present right to value of repayment

M = future maturity value

i = effective rate of interest (required yield)

I = nominal rate of interest
N = number of periods
An ù I = present value of interest payments
V = value of debenture

The majority of computer spreadsheet programmes have financial functions which readily compute the present value of a bond. For example, if the applicable rate is 18% payable half-yearly and the debenture stock matures in 25 years' time, it is necessary to enter the number of half-yearly periods ie 50, and the half-yearly required yield, ie 8.63% and the redemption value, say £10,300, and then calculate the present value of the capital repayment at the chosen rate of interest ie £138.52. To this figure must be added the present value of the half-yearly payments at the chosen rate of interest.

12.12 Apportionment of income (pre-March 1989)

Prior to accounting periods beginning after 31 March 1989, close companies had to distribute their investment income unless they could show that profits could be retained for the maintenance and development of the business within the provisions of TA 1988, Sch 19, paras 8 and 9. Similarly, closely held property companies had to distribute 50% of their estate income under TA 1988, Sch 19, para 2(1), again subject to the requirements of the company's business which did not include the acquisition of further investments. Consequently, when considering the significance of dividends in relation to a valuation as at 31 March 1982, these factors meant that unquoted investment companies and property companies were likely to distribute a substantial proportion of their profits. Trading companies, on the other hand, might normally wish to retain their profits in the company, so far as possible, and therefore the dividends might be small or non-existent, with the proprietors being rewarded by remuneration which would be taxed in their hands as earned income.

12.13 Brand valuation

Chapter 21 considers intangible asset valuations including brand valuations for accounting purposes.

Part of the continuing controversy surrounding brand valuation centres on the precise definition of the term and whether or not it can be or should be distinguished from goodwill in general.

Put simply, a brand may be regarded as a product or service with a recognised name, which may or may not be protected by a trademark, which has an established earnings stream created by consumer loyalty over the long term.

It is the commercial value attributable to the intangible asset that is considered here, but it is important to remember that in any actual sales of brands some or all of the means of production may well be included as part of the deal. For example, Jaguar and Land Rover car 'brands' were sold in 2008 for $2.3 billion. However, this price would have undoubtedly included other intangible assets such as technical know-how, customer and supplier contracts and a global distributor network. If a comparison with market values is to be adopted, an allocation of the sale price between tangible and the various types of intangible assets will have to be attempted. Lack of information will make this difficult. It could also be the case that no such allocation had been made by vendor or purchaser, although many transactions now require a Purchase Price Allocation to be disclosed in the acquiring company's financial statements.

12.14 Excess earnings valuation approach

The income approach is based upon the estimated future income streams associated with the brand, consideration of the remaining life of the asset, the average expected annual return (if available) and the actual market rate of return. The future income stream is then discounted at an appropriate rate to arrive at a present value.

These calculations can be performed in a variety of ways. The 'excess earnings' method, states that the value of an intangible asset is determined by the present value of the earnings it generates, net of a reasonable return on the assets contributing to that stream of earnings. This method is considered in more detail in **Chapter 21**.

12.15 Relief from royalty valuation approach

Relief from royalty is also an income approach and is used more frequently than excess earnings. This method is now considered to be one of the primary valuation methods for brands and is a method within the income approach. The royalty represents the amount that the manufacturer of a product similar to the branded product would pay to use the brand name. The value of the brand is arrived at by discounting the future royalty stream to its net present value.

In addition to the discount rate and the cash flows deriving from the asset, in this method of valuation there is a third subjective element, namely the royalty rate itself. In the US the royalty will usually be paid by reference to net sales, depending on the asset under consideration and the geographic and sector markets in which it operates. Various organisations collect details of royalty rates from arm's length transactions which can be used for comparison, and this data is relatively straightforward to obtain. This method is considered in more detail in **Chapter 21**.

12.16 Market transactions

The market approach is based on the price of comparable assets recently sold. Using comparables, adjustments are made, based on the transactions being considered, to the sales price of the brand being valued. Market prices are an indicator of the likely market value of a comparable asset, as there is an underlying assumption that market transactions are conducted between willing buyers and willing sellers in arm's length transactions. When a number of sales of similar assets occur, a pattern of definable prices is established and this increases reliability.

As market-based methods rely on evidence from actual reported transactions, they can often provide the best evidence of the value of an asset. However, it is often difficult to determine exactly what was acquired as part of a reported transaction as full details are rarely provided. Also, there may be synergies or cost-savings arising from a particular acquisition of, or disposal of, a brand within a large global portfolio and these benefits might be reflected in the price paid, giving the transaction the character of a 'special purchaser'. In addition, it is rare to find a directly comparable brand to that which is under consideration and therefore further adjustments are likely to be required. Thus, these methods can be difficult to apply in practice. However, where comparable transactions exist, the data available can be used as a starting point or cross-check with other valuation methods, as explained in **Chapter 21**.

12.17 Interbrand method

Interbrand positions its approach as a strategic tool for ongoing brand management. The focus is as much on the insight and analysis of the subject brand as the value itself. An Interbrand valuation aims to demonstrate how the brand is contributing to business results today, as well as delivering a roadmap of activities to increase the strength and value of the brand going forwards.

It focuses on the three stakeholder groups that Interbrand believe have the most influence on business performance, namely (current and prospective) customers, employees and investors. Their logic is that strong brands: influence customer choice and create loyalty; attract, retain and motivate talent; and lower the cost of financing; and their approach takes these factors into account. They also use valuation techniques to conduct business case modelling, evaluating strategic branding options (such as brand positioning or brand architecture) and making the business case for a change of brand strategy or greater levels of brand investment.

For more financially driven valuations (for investor relations, pension fund planning, tax etc) their objective is to add value by providing strategic branding recommendations as well as a defendable valuation.

Interbrand was the first company globally to have its methodology certified as compliant with the requirements of ISO 10668 – requirements for monetary brand valuation.

There are three key components to their approach:

- FINANCIAL ANALYSIS
  This quantifies the forecast financial return to an organisation's investors, or its 'economic profit'. Economic profit is the after-tax operating profit of the brand minus a charge for the capital used to generate the brand's revenues and margins.

- ROLE OF BRAND
  Role of Brand measures the portion of the purchase decision attributable to the brand, as opposed to other factors (for example, purchase drivers like price, convenience or product features). The Role of Brand Index ('RBI') quantifies this as a percentage. Typically this is derived using quantitative research.

- BRAND STRENGTH
  Brand Strength measures the ability of the brand to create loyalty and, therefore, sustainable demand and profit into the future. Brand Strength analysis is based on an evaluation across ten factors that Interbrand believes make a strong brand. Performance on these factors is assessed relative to competitors. The Brand Strength analysis delivers a snapshot of the strengths and weaknesses of the brand and is used to generate a roadmap of activity to enhance the strength and value of the brand in the future.

Interbrand brand valuation methodology

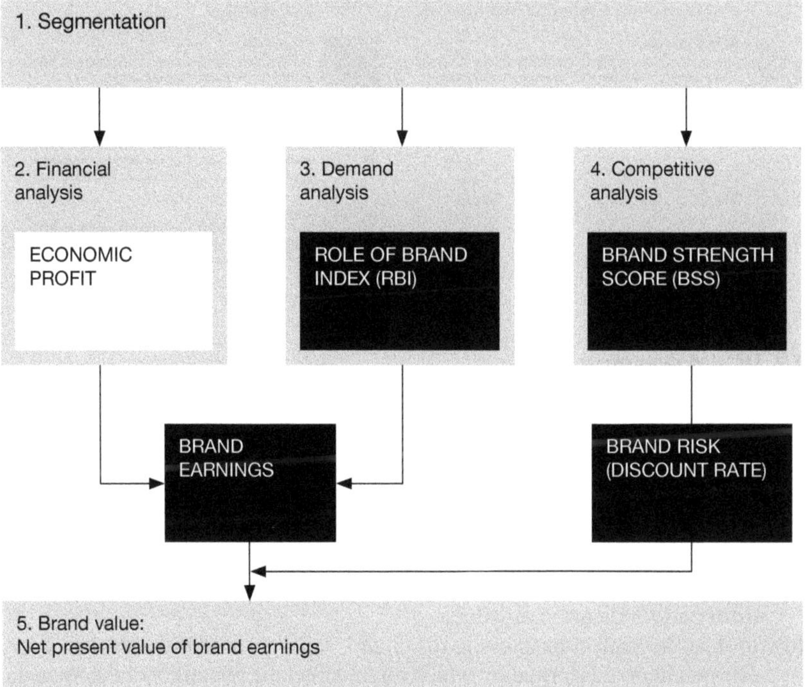

Brand Strength factors

Interbrand's Brand Strength framework

Internal factors

Clarity
Clarity internally about what the brand stands for in terms of its values, positioning and proposition. Clarity too about target audiences, customer insights and drivers.

Commitment
Internal commitment to the brand, and a belief internally in its importance. The extent to which the brand receives support in terms of time and influence.

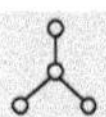

Governance
The degree to which the organization has the required skills and an operating model for the brand that enables effective and efficient deployment of the brand strategy.

Responsiveness
The organization's ability to constantly evolve the brand and business in response to, or anticipation of, market changes, challenges and opportunities.

External factors

Authenticity
The brand is soundly based on an internal truth and capability. It has a defined story and a well grounded value set. It can deliver against the (high) expectations that customers have of it.

Relevance
The fit with customer/consumer needs, desires, and decision criteria across all relevant demographics and geographies.

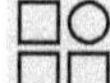

Differentiation
The degree to which customers/consumers perceive the brand to have a differentiated proposition and brand experience.

Consistency
The degree to which a brand is experienced without fail across all touchpoints or formats.

Presence
The degree to which a brand feels omnipresent and is talked about positively by consumers, customers and opinion formers in both traditional and social media.

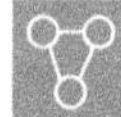

Engagement
The degree to which customers/consumers show a deep understanding of, active participation in, and a strong sense of identification with, the brand.

12.18 Assessing value

In assessing value, the valuer should:

(a) identify the asset to be valued, the purpose of the valuation and the valuation;
(b) consider the most appropriate primary basis of valuation and an appropriate cross-check;
(c) identify comparable companies and/or transactions which may provide third party indicators of value;
(d) look at the subject business in detail and, as far as possible, ascertain every relevant item of information which might affect the reliability of the financial data provided or the overall quality of the business or asset to be valued;
(e) consider whether any special method of valuation is appropriate, eg for property companies, investment companies, start-ups, distressed businesses (companies making no profit and/or without any prospect of doing so in the future), control holdings.

Having arrived at the valuation, the valuer should then consider the following:

(1) Would they recommend that a client sell a holding of shares in this company or the asset being valued at the price indicated by the valuation? If not, at what price would the recommendation be made?
(2) Would they advise a client to buy a holding of shares in this company or the asset being valued at the price indicated by the valuation? If not, at what price would the recommendation be made?

The answers to each question are unlikely to be the same, but form the range within which the valuation will lie. Where within the range the precise value falls is a matter of choice and experience.

In defending the valuation either in correspondence or in negotiation the valuer will need to justify any negative response to the above questions which would be generated by the value selected. Therefore it is helpful to document the rationale for the valuation judgement at the time of preparing the calculations in order to confirm that the crucial factors in the valuation have been identified, the weight attached to them crystallised and to ensure that the valuer has prepared cogent evidence in support of the valuation.

It must be emphasised that valuation is not a precise science; notwithstanding the valuation approach adopted, it is impossible to calculate the price with certainty. Valuation is always a matter of opinion, based on the context of the valuation, backed by experience and research. However, provided appropriate information has been received and reviewed with a professional eye, it should be possible to arrive at a value within an appropriate range.

Chapter 13

The influence of the London Stock Exchange

Signposts

13.01 Introduction

As many valuations rely on the use of comparable data from listed entities, this chapter outlines some of the key features of the London Stock Exchange and the data produced. Many of the atypical events which can impact a listed share price need to be considered if we are using an entity as a comparator for an unquoted business. For example, if the share price has fallen, is this because profits are declining or has there been a dilution of the share capital? Similarly, if a stock is highly volatile, we must consider whether this is typical for the sector or is company-specific (perhaps due to illiquidity or limited trading in the shares).

It is widely accepted that value is best determined by the marketplace through the creation of a price. The price is an agreed level between a willing buyer and a willing seller. A valuation can only be an estimate of what that price might have been, without testing it. Accordingly, the accepted way of establishing a 'valuation' is to find a comparable circumstance where the 'price' has been established. This is not to say that a price always reflects true value.

Where a particular company or security is sufficiently individual, or where the purchase demand is unknown, an auction ensures the best price. Valuing such an entity is very difficult. In the case of company shares, a valuer would look at the price at which the shares of a quoted company are changing hands and make allowances for any particular characteristics of the unquoted company. Accordingly, the valuer would look to the Stock Exchange in order to seek a company or companies most closely matching the private share.

13.02 Regulation

The Financial Services Act 2012 (FSA 2012) introduced a new financial regulation framework and made significant changes to the Financial Services and Markets Act 2000 (FSMA 2000), with effect from 1 April 2012.

It replaced the Financial Services Authority by the Financial Conduct Authority (FCA) and the Prudential Regulation Authority (PRA). The FCA (www.fca.org.uk) supervises the conduct of over 50,000 financial service firms and regulates their prudential standards by assessing their conduct, monitoring their products, dealing with threats to the integrity of the industry and ensuring that firms compensate consumers where necessary.

The FCA is operationally independent of the Government, but is accountable to the Treasury and through them, to Parliament. The FCA is funded entirely by the financial services firms it regulates. It is the UK Listing Authority.

All businesses which, in any way at all, carry out any form of financial transaction or provide investment advice must be authorised to do so by the FCA. The FCA Register is a public record of financial services firms, individuals and other bodies which fall or have come under the FCA's regulatory jurisdiction as defined in FSA 2000. Anyone is able to search for firms, individuals and other bodies using the search facility on the FCA website: https://register.fca.org.uk/ The PRA website (www.bankofengland.co.uk/prudential-regulation) states:

> 'The Prudential Regulation Authority (PRA) regulates and supervises around 1,500 banks, building societies, credit unions, insurers and major investment firms.
>
> The PRA has three objectives:
> 1. We promote the safety and soundness of the firms we regulate.
> 2. We contribute to securing an appropriate degree of protection for insurance policyholders.
> 3. We have a secondary objective to facilitate effective competition between firms.'

The Financial Policy Committee of the Bank of England aims to identify, monitor and take action to address systemic risk in the financial sector.

13.03 Recognised investment exchanges ('RIEs')

The following organisations are currently recognised as investment exchanges on the Financial Services Register:

- The London Stock Exchange plc;
- The London Metal Exchange Limited;
- ICE Futures Europe;
- NEX Exchange;
- Euronext London Limited; and
- Cboe Europe Limited.

The rules applying to recognised Investment Exchanges are also determined by the EU Market in Financial Instruments Directive (MiFID) which came into force as European legislation in 2004. It was included within UK law in 2007 and revised by MiFID II which took effect in January 2018.

The revision was designed to improve the functioning of financial markets in the light of the 2008 financial crisis and to strengthen investor protection.

Recognised overseas investment exchanges

The FCA has recognised and supervises a number of recognised overseas investment exchanges ('ROIEs') under FSMA 2000. In order to be recognised, ROIEs must satisfy the requirements of FSMA 2000, s 292(3). These include:

- Australian Securities Exchange Limited;
- Chicago Mercantile Exchange Inc.;

- Chicago Board of Trade (CBOT);
- EUREX;
- ICE Futures US, Inc.;
- NASDAQ;
- New York Mercantile Exchange Inc. (NYMEX);
- SIX Swiss Exchange AG.

Designated investment exchanges

An investment exchange which does not carry on a regulated activity in the United Kingdom and is not a regulated market may apply to the FCA to be included on the FCA's list of designated investment exchanges. Before adding an investment exchange to the list of designated investment exchanges, the FCA will consider the rules of the exchange and undertake a public consultation.

Designation allow firms to treat certain types of transactions effected on a designated investment exchange in the same way as they would treat transactions effected on a RIE.

These include, amongst many others:

- Australian Stock Exchange;
- Bermuda Stock Exchange;
- Johannesburg Stock Exchange;
- New York Futures Exchange;
- Tokyo Stock Exchange.

A recognised or designated stock exchange, other than the London Stock Exchange is not within TCGA 1992, s 272(3) for valuation purposes: *Nicholas Green v HRMC* [2014] UKFTT 396 (TC), para 88.

Regulated markets

Under Article 47 of the Markets in Financial Instruments Directive (2004/39/EC) the FCA is responsible for maintaining the list of regulated markets for which the UK is the home member state. A market may ask to be added to the list of regulated markets it if satisfies the requirements set out in Title III of MiFID. MiFID II has developed these regulations further.

13.04 The history of the London Stock Exchange

The Stock Exchange evolved in London in the seventeenth century from informal gatherings of stocks and share dealers in the coffee houses around the Royal Exchange. Records of daily price lists go back as far as 1698. In the nineteenth century other stock exchanges opened up outside London and in 1965 these joined with London to form the Federation of Stock Exchanges in Great Britain and Ireland. In 1973 all were amalgamated to form the Stock Exchange.

A major change took place in 1986 with the deregulation of the market, known as 'Big Bang'. From this date, the Exchange itself became a limited company, minimum scales of commission were abolished, all firms could become brokers/ dealers and able to operate in a dual capacity and trading could now be conducted by telephone and computer via dealing rooms.

The Alternative Investment Market (AIM) was launched in 1995 as an international market for smaller companies. A wider range of businesses are listed on AIM ranging from young, venture capital-backed start-ups to well-established, mature organisations looking to expand. Since its launch in 1995 to 2018, almost 4,000 companies have joined AIM – raising more than £111billion in the process, both through initial public offerings (IPOs) and further capital raisings.

The Exchange became a publicly quoted company in 2000 and merged with the Borsa Italiana in 2007 to become the London Stock Exchange Group.

The main market has approximately 1, 200 listed companies with a combined market capitalisation of over £4 trillion. AIM has more than 900 listed companies with a combined market capitalisation of £115 billion.

13.05 Trading mechanisms

The London Stock Exchange has a global hosted platform for matching, validation and reconciliation services, UnaVIsta. The company also provides real time market data.

13.06 Leading stock markets by capitalisation

It was in 1927 that for the first time the value of the shares quoted on the American market exceeded those quoted in London. Since that time the gap has grown by a very wide margin. The development of the 'emerging markets' of India and China mean that these exchanges are as large as some of the more established markets in terms of their capitalisation.

At the end of 2017, the ten largest stock markets in the world were:

Exchange	*Market capitalisation ($US trillion)*
	2017
New York	30
NASDAQ	12
LSE	5.8
Tokyo Stock Exchange Shanghai	5.5
	5.05
Euronext	4.18
Hong Kong Exchange	4.14
Shenzhen	3.65
Bombay Stock Exchange	2.2
TMX Toronto	1.8

The total market capitalisation of the world's exchanges (equities only) is forecast to reach r $100 trillion by 2020.

13.07 Official List of the London Stock Exchange

In the UK, the market is provided by the London Stock Exchange and comprises those companies which have been granted admission to the Official List of the Stock Exchange (full listing). The Daily Official List (DOL) is a daily publication of official quotations for all securities traded on the London Stock Exchange. The DOL price is presented in a bid-and-ask format and is widely used in a variety of calculations including pension portfolio valuations and for probate, as recommended by HMRC. The DOL Valuation Report provides a daily file of securities traded on these markets, and includes the 'quarter-up' price calculated from the DOL price. The FCA, in its capacity as the UK Listing Authority, maintains the Official List. The London Stock Exchange is also responsible for a second market, the Alternative Investment Market (AIM). The requirement for admission is set out in the UK Listing Authority's Listing Rules, available from the FCA's website: https://www.londonstockexchange.com/companies-and-advisors/main-market/rules/regulations.htm The FCA website also lists the rule for prospectuses and the disclosure and transparency rules.

Focus

The London Stock Exchange website retains historical share prices for pension and probate purposes, which is very helpful when completing the necessary returns.

13.08 Application for listing

A company applying for listing must appoint a sponsor. Sponsors will normally be corporate brokers or investment banks but may also be other professional advisers. A list of sponsors is available on the FCA website: https://www.fca.org.uk/markets/ukla/sponsor-regime/list

Special modified listing rules apply to mineral and research-based companies, which might not be profit-making for a number of years.

A company may have a primary or secondary listing allocated by the FCA. Only equities can have a primary listing, but both equity and depositary receipts (for overseas-incorporated companies only) may have a secondary listing.

13.09 Methods open to applicants without equity shares already listed

Applicants without equity shares already listed may bring equity shares to listing by means of an introduction or by methods which are dependent on the value at the offer price of the portion of the equity shares being offered or placed in the UK.

13.10 Offer for sale or subscription

An offer for sale is an invitation to the public by, or on behalf of, a third party to purchase securities of the issuer already in issue or allotted (and may be in the form of an invitation to tender at or above a stated minimum price).

An offer for subscription is an invitation to the public by, or on behalf of, an issuer to subscribe for securities of the issuer not yet in issue or allotted (and may be in the form of an invitation to tender at or above a stated minimum price).

In an offer for sale or subscription:

(1) not more than 50% of the securities being offered may be 'placed firm' with clients of the sponsor and any security house assisting with the offer, (but the Exchange may allow a greater proportion of the issue to be so placed in the case of a substantial issue and in exceptional circumstances);
(2) no securities may be 'placed firm' with connected clients either of the sponsor or any securities house assisting with the offer, unless placed with a market-maker or fund manager for the purpose of its business as such;
(3) the issuer must ensure that letters of allotment or acceptance are all issued simultaneously and numbered serially.

Preferential allocations may be made to existing shareholders, directors, employees and past employees of the issuer up to a maximum of 10% in aggregate of the value of the offer price of the securities not placed firm.

13.11 Placing

A placing is a marketing of securities already in issue but not listed or not yet in issue, to specified persons or clients of the sponsor or any securities house assisting in the placing, which does not involve an offer to the public or to existing holders of the issuer's securities generally.

13.12 Intermediaries' offer

An intermediaries' offer is a marketing of securities already or not yet in issue by means of an offer by, or on behalf of, the issuer to intermediaries for them to allocate to their own clients.

13.13 Introduction

An introduction is a method of bringing securities to listing not involving an issue of new securities or any marketing of existing securities because the securities are already widely held by the public.

13.14 Exchange Market Size

The hallmark of the market is the visibility of the transactions that are taking place. Originally all securities quoted on the market were categorised into four basic systems of dealing, known as alpha, beta, gamma and delta. These categories were determined by the number of market-makers operating in each stock. This approach was replaced with the concept of Normal Market Size, now amended to Exchange Market Size. It is defined as 'the minimum quantity, as specified by the Exchange, of securities for which a market-maker is obliged to quote a firm two-way price on the trading system'. For each listed company, the Exchange Market Size is defined by the London Stock Exchange based on a percentage of the share's average daily turnover in the previous year. Quoted prices on SEAQ (the Stock Exchange Automated Quotation system) only have to be honoured for an order up to the Exchange Market Size. It is this feature which is pertinent to this book since a low level of marketability can lead to sharp price movement on any announcement or other circumstance which changes the previously known situation. A transaction of, say, 10,000 shares may not be significant for a company which has millions of shares in issue, but may have a significant impact for a company in which the shares are thinly traded.

A large order waiver is permitted under the London Stock Exchange regulations to permit transactions above the Exchange Market Size to take place.

13.15 Indices

The market is broken into the various indices. The FTSE 100 share index is the index most often quoted when referring to movement in the London Stock Exchange. The FTSE 100 share index comprises the companies whose market capitalisation is the largest of those companies quoted on the London Stock Exchange. This index is regularly reviewed, smaller companies drop out and new companies with increased market value are included. The significance of these changes will become apparent later in this chapter. The next 250 companies, largest in size after the first 100, is known as the mid cap index, and the 350 cap index is the sum of these two. The All Share Index comprises over 640 companies, including investment trusts and accounts for over 98% of the UK's market capitalisation. A separate All Share Index excluding investment trusts is also produced, as well as Small Cap, Fledgling and AIM Indices for smaller companies.

13.16 Equity derivatives

Trading in equity derivatives has grown dramatically during the last few years. Derivatives, as the name implies, derive from the ordinary shares of a listed company or a combination of shares, and cover such securities as unsecured loan stocks convertible into ordinary shares, preference stocks convertible into ordinary shares, warrants which carry the right to buy an underlying share at a fixed price at a future date, conventional options, traded options and financial futures. It is the growth in the latter categories that has given rise to a degree of volatility in the marketplace.

Derivative trading hit the spotlight in 2008 in relation to shares in Volkswagen (VW) and the 'short-selling' widely undertaken by many investment funds. Short-selling is the practice of selling securities or other financial assets which are not currently owned, in the hope of buying the assets in the market at a lower price in order to cover the obligation. If the share price falls, then the trader makes a profit since the purchase price of the asset is lower than the amount received for the short sale. However, if the share price rises, the trader will make a (potentially unlimited) loss. In the case of VW, there had been extensive short-selling activity; however, when Porsche revealed it had built up a 74% stake in the company, the share price increased dramatically and the short-selling funds lost an estimated €40 billion. Porsche, which sold some shares to alleviate the sudden share shortage, made an exceptional profit of €6 billion, which had the effect of increasing its profit to twice its revenue. The funds took Porsche to court, but the company was cleared of any wrongdoing.

13.17 Traded options

Some of the companies comprising the FTSE 100 index would also be traded on the options market. Traded options are broken down into two categories:

(a) A call option provides the holder with the right to purchase the underlying stock until a fixed date in the future at a pre-determined price (the exercise price). The option exercise prices are spread around the current market price. This gives the purchaser of a call option a variety of prices and exercise dates from which to choose. The price in terms of the premium which will be paid for each option will vary in accordance with the margin between the exercise price and the market price, the length of time to the expiry of the option, and the assessed volatility of the share price. Other factors are the dividend flow and the current rate of interest.

(b) A put option provides a similar right for the holder of that option to sell at a known price in a stated time cycle.

On the opposite side of this transaction is the writer of the option who receives the premium, and enters into an obligation to satisfy the demand of the purchaser. Thus, if a share price increases, and the purchaser of a call option exercises the right to purchase the stock, the writer of the option is obliged to deliver the holding. Similarly, if the purchaser of a put option exercises that right as the share price falls away, the writer of that option is obliged to purchase the underlying security from the purchaser of the put option.

An option class simply means that all the calls and puts are on the same underlying instrument, and the option series are all the puts and calls in the same option class having the same expiry date and exercise price. During the period prior to the expiry date the value of the option will vary in accordance with the share price, and may be traded on the traded option market.

A traded option also exists based on the value of the FTSE 100 share index. Accordingly the purchaser of a call option, or the writer of a call option, is trading in a fixed number of shares in each security, which collectively makes up the FTSE 100 Index.

13.18 Futures

Futures were originally created around commodities, thus enabling, for example, a farmer to trade wheat still growing in the fields, in the futures market, for delivery at a future date. Consequently, the farmer may have secured an advantageous price prior to a surplus of wheat on the market, but runs the risk that the combine breaks down and he is unable to deliver. A futures contract is a contractual agreement to buy or sell commodities or financial instruments at a predetermined price in the future. Futures contracts exist in many areas of the financial markets, as they are effectively derivatives, but for the purposes of this book the important futures contract is that which reflects the FTSE 100 share index.

13.19 Share analysis

There are basically three forms of share analysis. By far the most extensive form is fundamental analysis, involving the assessment of the prospects of an individual company against its marketplace by analysts who are expert in that particular sector. The output of research from the major security houses in London, particularly as regards the shares comprising the FTSE 100 share index is quite phenomenal. The degree of research carried out for smaller companies essentially diminishes in accordance with the interest displayed by investors in any particular stock. However, it should be possible to obtain research on every company quoted on the London Stock Exchange and there are many websites, including companies' own investor relations pages, which provide historical information and analysts' forecasts.

Technical analysis is the use of charts to anticipate the next movement in the share price. Clearly, since charts reflect past activity there is a certain lag between the appearance of a trend and the ability to recognise it as such, but it is regarded by many as a means of reflecting market sentiment. In an efficient market, a 'trend is your friend'.

Quantitative analysis is a systematic approach using a high level of numerical and statistical analysis. In its simplest form it is the identification of under-valued or over-valued shares through the use of computer systems to analyse data fed into the system. For example, an analyst might believe that a cheap share is one which has an asset value higher than the current share price, stands on a price/earnings ratio 25% less than the market average, has an earnings yield greater than the market average or has gearing of less than 25% etc. Use is made of a computer to analyse and identify the shares which fit the relevant criteria. In a more sophisticated form it is the identification of the cheapest method of purchasing a share, particularly when used to replicate an index.

13.20 Acquiring an interest

The example below shows the various methods of acquiring an interest in BP, where there are traded options as well as the shares listed on three exchanges. All are available to provide the intended interest in the underlying company, in this case BP. If, in replicating an index, it is possible to acquire the appropriate representation from a derivative on cheaper terms than by buying the shares, then an out-performance of the index will be achieved.

Example

BP

The alternatives:

- buy ordinary $0.25 shares;
- buy 8% £1 preference shares;
- buy 9% £1 preference shares;
- buy American depositary shares (ADS);
- buy traded options (NASDAQ).

Shares are listed in London, Frankfurt and New York.

13.21 Disclosure of information

Ever since the Financial Services Act was originally introduced in 1986 (followed by FSMA 2000 as amended by the FSA 2012), the objective of the authorities has been to increase the disclosure of information which would enable a shareholder or a potential shareholder to assess the value of a company. Earlier in this chapter, reference was made to the stringent requirements applied by the London Stock Exchange when bringing a company to listing and the FCA states that, 'providing clear information is essential to delivering fair outcomes for consumers'.

13.22 Asset values

Private companies tend to pay a great deal of attention to the net asset value. This is not unnatural since it is an obvious benchmark indicating the health of the company. As private companies tend to retain a greater proportion of profits within the business the asset value might be considered to be a reflection of this. The asset value of a quoted company is less relevant, probably because an individual shareholder rarely has sufficient power to crystallise that asset value. That is not to say that it is immaterial, and of course an asset backing provides some credibility to a market price. If a company has made low profits or losses for some time and the market price has fallen as a consequence, an asset value higher than the market price might well attract a purchaser for the company, since a bidder may well believe that better management of those assets might reap a higher reward. However, a quoted company is driven by the earnings prospects rather than by the asset backing.

This leads to the crucial difference between the valuation of a public company and that of a private company. As mentioned earlier, a vast amount of research is carried out on quoted securities. Clearly the degree of research is a function of the size and marketability of the business, but all companies would have some degree of analytical research carried out on them. Accordingly, a company's prospects are the overriding criteria leading to the rating of a company's share price. Comparing historical figures from a private company with the historical figures of a quoted company, and looking at the share price to gauge the rating, may well be an inappropriate exercise. It is important to ascertain the prospects for the private company, preferably on a two-year view, and to make a comparison of those figures with the appropriate comparison or comparisons in the quoted company.

13.23 Market movements generally

The flows of capital around the world can substantially increase the valuation offered by some smaller markets. High levels of liquidity can lead to abnormal valuations. Markets are moved by supply and demand, and when the demand for assets by the investing institutions cannot be met from supply, prices may be pushed to unrealistic and unsustainable levels. This may be seen most clearly in some AIM shares, where liquidity is relatively low and therefore the scarcity of shares on the market can create considerable share price volatility. Conversely, in times of economic turbulence, share prices can fluctuate significantly from day to day as investors seek to minimise losses or find safe havens for their investments.

13.24 UK market

In 2008, the main financial markets saw some of the highest levels of volatility in their history, with falls of up to 10% in a single day. There has been unprecedented government involvement in this sector, from the effective nationalisation of Northern Rock to the injection of billions of pounds into the financial markets to stabilise the banking industry. Interest rates were cut as the threats of recession and a lack of market confidence are seen to outweigh that of inflation. Yields in respect of safe investments such as gilts fell as investors sought low-risk investments in the light of potential bank failures. However, in early 2014 the FTSE 100 exceeded the peak achieved in October 2007, leading many economists to speculate whether this was a recovery or a 'bubble'. After some fluctuations, the index has continued to rise and reached a new record high in 2018.

Many aspects of the economy are inter-related, and it is difficult to know which influences which, but it might be argued that politics determines the ongoing level of inflation, the level of inflation determines the real yield at the long end of the gilt market, short-term interest rates through their influence on borrowing ultimately determine the level of inflation, all of which gives rise to a level of confidence in the marketplace, and that indefinable but major factor, market sentiment. Collectively these aspects of the economy impinge on the level of the currency in relation to other world currencies. Of course there are other factors which might be brought to bear on any one of these items, and since they are inter-related one will not move without influencing others. Thus, if there is a balance-of-trade problem, this will impinge on the currency, which may force interest rates higher, which will impinge on GDP growth, which may alter inflation prospects, bringing down the level of confidence which may ultimately change the colour of politics. The UK's housing market can also have an effect on the economy (particularly inflation) to an extent which may not be seen in other countries.

Confidence in the government of the day is of paramount importance to the overall level of the market, and uncertainty brought about by an election can lead to volatility. In a capitalist society the market used to view a socialist administration as one likely to operate against the shareholder in the long term, and traditionally regarded the Conservative Party as the one most likely to favour shareholders. While the high levels of economic growth experienced under the Labour regime in the first decade of the twenty-first century would suggest an unwillingness to return to the brand of socialism rolled back during the 1980s when privatisation issues particularly in the UK were much in favour, at the time of each election, whole sectors of the stock market might be nervous of the outcome. What the market turmoil of 2008 and subsequent factors such as Brexit risk show are the truly global interrelationship between the world's primary markets and how the impact of events in one country can trigger a worldwide financial response. Market confidence – or, rather, the lack of it – resulted in the collapse of several major global financial institutions and perhaps a permanent change in the regulatory banking landscape.

The second obvious influence of politics is at the time of the Budget. The -Budget and subsequent Spring Statement set out the spending plans for the coming year and the methods by which the expenditure will be financed. Increases in direct and indirect taxation are undesirable to the profitability of companies such as tobacco companies, wine and spirits companies, brewing companies, gambling companies and oil stocks. All will be influenced by changes in taxation, and share prices can become volatile over the period around the budget announcement. Such announcements are not confined to the UK, since many of our domestic companies trade in international markets, and are thus influenced by local taxation.

Finally, politicians have influence over certain segments of the economy where they seek to maintain control, and the obvious example of this is in the media sector. Control of television licences is of paramount importance to a TV company.

The allocation of rail franchises is another example of government influence.

13.25 Futures market

The futures market represents an easy means by which institutions can acquire a stake in the entire list of shares comprising the FTSE 100 share index in one go. Thus, with the desire to invest in the UK equity market, an institution can, by buying a future contract, inject a substantial amount of cash into the market very quickly. There is no need to purchase, individually, the shares comprising the 100 share index. As a consequence of this, the future may trade at a premium to the value of the underlying market, known as the cash market. In these circumstances the value of the ordinary shares comprising the index rise in order not to move too far out of line with the value of the futures contract. Conversely, the market can be driven down by selling the future contract when institutions anticipate a falling market. As a consequence of this a 2% or 3% movement in the market on a daily basis is by no means unheard of.

Whilst discussing the influence on the market generally of the instruments traded on the Intercontinental Exchange Group (ICE), which acquired the NYSE Euronext exchange (formerly LIFFE) market the potential for volatility in individual shares should be addressed. The composition of the various indices is important. A large section of the pension fund market is managed in such a way as to precisely replicate the various indices. Thus, if a fund wishes to hold 62% in the FTSE 100 stocks, the manager is obligated to invest exactly that proportion of the fund in the shares comprised in the FTSE index in accordance with their representation of that index. Thus if a company falls in value, and its inclusion in the top 100 ceases, there are automatically a vast number of funds wishing to sell that stock since there is now no need to hold it. Conversely, a stock that has risen in value, and thus will start to be included in the 100 share index, has an automatic flow of funds directed towards it, thus ensuring accurate representation. Such circumstances occur with the 100 share index, the 250 share index, and the All Share Index. Additions to the All Share Index can present a problem, since the marketability of these smaller companies can be limited, and the demand for stock by the index funds can be greater than the market can bear. Representation in these companies is essential for an index fund in order to ensure that the tracking error to the index is minimal. Volatility can occur with stocks moving in, or out, of the FTSE 100 index, where the increase in liquidity is more than matched by the increase in size of transaction from the index funds. It is estimated that UK pension funds held assets in excess of almost £3 trillion at the end of 2017, of which 47% were equities.

13.26 Branded products

Companies spend a great deal of money establishing a brand name in the marketplace. Following a number of takeover bids in the 1980s it became important for companies to reflect the value of their brand names in the valuation placed on the business. Share price volatility can occur when the value of branded products is brought into question. The most dramatic example of this was displayed by Philip Morris, when the announcement of a 40% reduction in the price of Marlboro cigarettes in the face of competition from generic bands, led to a 25% reduction in the share price of Philip Morris in the space of a few hours. Similarly, any quality issues or product recalls by a major manufacturer can have a significant effect on the share price. When Cadbury was bought by Kraft in 2010 many commentators observed that the value of the various Cadbury brands had not been recognised fully in the transaction price and speculation has continued as to whether the brand value of Cadbury's 'Britishness' has been eroded since the sale to a multinational business. Conversely, while Volkswagen's share price plummeted in October 2015, following the diesel emissions scandal, the company has since recovered over $40 billion of value since that date.

13.27 Patented products

The value of a patent is particularly important to pharmaceutical stocks. The cost and time involved in bringing a successful drug to the market is considerable, and as a consequence the price of the drug reflects not only the cost of manufacture, but also the cost of development. Protection of the patent is therefore of paramount importance, as is the length of that patent protection. When the patent for a major branded drug expires, revenues are likely to be affected adversely and a corresponding impact on the company's share price is anticipated.

13.28 Contract awards or cancellations

Companies can become vulnerable to the value of exceptionally large orders. Defence contracts are invariably of such potential to a company that the winning, or losing, of a contract could seriously affect long-term earnings. In the construction industry the winning of a substantial contract may well mean long-term employment for key personnel on a project making very little profit, but still perhaps avoiding redundancy and other costs of downsizing, which may have been the result of losing the contract.

13.29 Company announcements

Clearly, the announcement of company results is a time when disclosures of profitability may be reflected in the share price. As mentioned earlier in this chapter, a great deal of research effort is now carried out on companies quoted on the London Stock Exchange. As a consequence there is an expectation of the results about to be disclosed. It is often the case that very poor results do not lead to a down-turn in the share price, since these will generally have been preceded by a profits warning or other market announcement and therefore anticipated by the market. However, surprises can still occur. A company is not entitled to reveal forecasts or trends within two months of the announcement of results, and, during this period, new situations might arise which the company is unable to signal to the market. Furthermore, the actual dividend pay-out should be decided by the board of directors on the day of the board meeting, and as a consequence the actual announcement may come as a surprise.

Many companies now offer an online subscription service so that investors or any interested parties may receive email copies of any news items or market announcements made.

13.30 Research, downgrades or upgrades

Research analysts wish to be as well informed of a company's prospects as possible. Knowledge of the sector, of market trends, and the abilities of the managers of businesses, is extremely important. The practice of interviews with chief executives has generally ceased, given the potential for parties to be in possession of inside information, but on a collective basis it is in the interest of corporate management to ensure that the City is appraised of the prospects of the business, thus keeping surprises to a minimum. However, as a result of corporate contact, or other research information, a company could have its prospects downgraded, or upgraded, by an analyst in the City. The share price may react to this new information, which may be outside the company's control, depending on the quality of the research.

13.31 Takeover bids

Clearly a takeover bid for a company will lead to a sharp movement in the share price. Directors should ensure that the market is made aware of any approach, at the earliest opportunity. As a consequence, a company may announce that an approach has been made which may or may not lead to an offer for the company. Clearly no one will know the outcome of any subsequent discussion, but it would be unusual if the share price were not to rise in anticipation of a bid being made to all shareholders at a price higher than that ruling prior to the announcement.

13.32 Stake building

A bidding company may well seek to acquire a foothold in the target company prior to making any approach. The degrees by which a bidding company may acquire ordinary shares in a target company are clearly defined. However, in the UK, prior to any announcement a bidder may acquire up to 3% of the target company.

13.33 Large or significant shareholdings

The changes in circumstances of any large shareholders may lead to price volatility. The prospect of a substantial stake being placed on the market could have a depressing effect on the price, whilst the forced disposal of a blocking shareholding may well make a company vulnerable to a full bid. The disposal of large tranches of shares by any of the company's management team might also be seen as significant and may depress the share price accordingly, and for this reason many share incentive arrangements restrict the amount of shares which can be sold at any one time.

13.34 Rights issues

The announcement by a company of a rights issue would normally lead to a reduction in the share price. Very often a rights issue is announced at the same time as company results, and it may be that the results are sufficiently in excess of expectations to offset the naturally depressing effect of the requirement of existing shareholders to subscribe for additional shares in the company. A rights issue is normally underwritten, and those underwriters carry the risk for movements in the market generally, which may mean that a rights issue is not fully subscribed. If, for one reason or another, underwriters are called upon to subscribe for the bulk of the issue then it might be expected that a share price may be depressed for a long period whilst the unwanted position is unwound. However, in the normal course of events, a successful rights issue, whilst depressing the price pending the call, should see a recovery once the rights issue is subscribed for.

13.35 Press comment

Given the pervasive nature of data available online, press comment is much less of an influence in the marketplace than was the case perhaps ten years ago. Communication is now so rapid that screen-based share price data is available throughout the City, and accordingly, recommendations from newspapers are less influential than has been the case in the past. However, original information will be reflected in the share price. Online data sources are now much more influential due to the speed with which information can be updated and disseminated to a global audience. In particular, social media campaigns and comments on sites such as Twitter can have a significant and rapid influence on a company's behaviour and reputation with a corresponding impact on share prices.

13.36 The effects of the economic cycle

A potential purchaser of shares is far more concerned with the future prospects of a company than with details of its past. Research results in forecasts of a two year horizon and as a consequence historical ratings can look extremely cheap or expensive. The quality of earnings is reflected in a company's rating, and volatility of earnings equally so. Consequently, the shares of the house building sector are sharply influenced by the economic cycle, whilst it would be anticipated that food retailing and manufacturing are less so.

13.37 Overseas earnings

Many companies operate internationally. Overseas earnings have two major influences. First, they exist outside the economic cycle of the UK (but are clearly subject to the economic cycle of the country of activity), and should not therefore be compared to a company within the UK wholly dependent on the UK economic cycle. And secondly, overseas earnings are subject to a currency translation on remittance to the UK. Clearly, at a time of strength in sterling, a lower valuation is placed on companies deriving profit outside the UK.

13.38 Quality of earnings

A higher rating is placed on a company listed on the London Stock Exchange where the quality of earnings is high. Again, a comparison with an unquoted company may well be that an individual within a private business places great store on a large one-off profit, whereas a stock market may pay less heed to such an event.

13.39 Summary

As can be seen, there are a wide variety of reasons why short-term movements in share prices occur. In choosing a company with which to make a comparison to an unquoted company it is essential that a degree of investigation is carried out. A valuer needs to be content with the accurate comparison with the quality of earnings, the source of earnings, the comparison of the cash position or the gearing position. In short, the valuer has to treat like with like. It is worth investigating the position of the comparison company in terms of market capitalisation in order to check that the selected company is not about to leave, or has recently left, one of the major indices, and finally that the chosen comparative company is not the subject of either take-over speculation, or actual stake building. In these circumstances it may be worthwhile waiting for a few weeks. When valuing a company at an historical date, it is beneficial to obtain general market information about the wider economic position prevailing at that time, so that any specific company information is put into a wider context.

In conclusion, it will be appreciated that in an efficient market, and the UK is generally regarded as such a market, the value placed on a company reflects all the circumstances known about that company at that time, and represents an equilibrium between buyers and sellers. Prices change when the known circumstances change, for whatever reason, and if the price movement is disproportionate when compared with the movement of the market as a whole, then it is advisable to establish the reason.

Chapter 14

The real market for shares and valuation for specific purposes

Signposts

14.01 Finding a buyer

One of the problems of valuing shares in unquoted companies is that these are so often done on a hypothetical basis for purely fiscal purposes or financial reporting that it is sometimes difficult to remember that it is possible to sell shares in private companies in suitable cases.

It is not possible to generalise on the best method of finding a potential purchaser for shares. In some cases there will be employees or members of the family able and willing to buy shares and it must not be overlooked that a company, subject to conditions, is able to buy its own shares. This, while the company is a going concern, will tend to put a floor on the price of the shares i.e. the price below which the company as a whole is not prepared to see its shares change hands. In other cases private investors may be known to the company's auditors or to outside accountants, stockbrokers or merchant bankers. The directors of a company may know, through their knowledge of the trade, a company which could be interested in acquiring shares and a direct approach to such company may be made either by the directors or by an intermediary on their behalf.

> **Focus**
>
> Finding a buyer is fundamental to a sale of any securities.

14.02 Private Equity and Venture Capital

There are a number of institutions that seek to invest in suitable private companies. In the UK, The British Private Equity and Venture Capital Association (BVCA) represents more than 500 such entities.

The managers of a fund that invests in unquoted companies will normally receive part of their return from a percentage of the profit made on disposal of their investments, the so-called 'Carry' or 'Carried Interest'. In simple terms the usual practice is that once the third-party investors have been paid their original investment the fund managers receive a percentage, eg 20% of the excess. Favourable taxation treatment of the carried interest in the UK has become a political issue.

Valuation guidelines

These provide that an unlisted portfolio should be valued at fair value in accordance with the guidelines set out by the International Private Equity and Venture Capital Valuation Guidelines (December 2012) (the IPEV Guidelines), which extend to 62 pages and are available at www.privateequityvaluation.com. Section three summarises the Valuation Methods.

The IPEV Guidelines define fair value as:

> 'The price that would be received to sell an asset in an Orderly Transaction between Market Participants at the Measurement Date.'

This is identical to the definition of the fair value of an asset in International Financial Reporting Standards (IFRS); see **20.1**. Thus, similarly to IFRS, the IPEV Guidelines use the term 'fair value' to refer to what is generally known in tax valuations as 'open market value' and referred to by the International Valuation Standards Council as 'market value'.

Section three of the IPEV Guidelines summarises the Valuation Methods as follows:

> **'3.1 General**
>
> 3.1 (i) In determining the Fair Value of an Investment, the Valuer should use judgement. This includes consideration of those specific terms of the Investment which may impact its Fair Value. In this regard, the Valuer should consider the economic substance of the Investment, which may take precedence over the strict legal form.

3.1 (ii) Where the reporting currency of the Fund is different from the currency in which the Investment is denominated, translation into the reporting currency for reporting purposes should be done using the bid spot exchange rate prevailing at the Measurement Date.

3.2 Selecting the Appropriate Valuation Technique

Valuers should exercise their judgement to select the valuation technique or techniques most appropriate for a particular Investment.

3.3 Price of Recent Investment

In applying the Price of Recent Investment valuation technique, the Valuer uses the initial cost of the Investment itself, excluding transaction costs, or, where there has been subsequent investment, the price at which a significant amount of new Investments into the company was made, to estimate the Enterprise Value, but only if deemed to represent Fair Value and only for a limited period following the date of the relevant transaction. During the limited period following the date of the relevant transaction, the Valuer should in any case assess at each Measurement Date whether changes or events subsequent to the relevant transaction would imply a change in the Investment's Fair Value.

3.4 Multiples

In using the Earnings Multiple valuation technique to estimate the Fair Value of an Enterprise, the Valuer should:

(i) Apply a multiple that is an *appropriate* and *reasonable* indicator of value (given the size, risk profile and earnings growth prospects of the underlying company) to the *maintainable* earnings of the company;

(ii) Adjust the Enterprise Value for surplus or non-operating assets or excess liabilities and other contingencies and relevant factors to derive an Adjusted Enterprise Value for the Investee Company;

(iii) Deduct from this amount any financial instruments ranking ahead of the highest ranking instrument of the Fund in a liquidation scenario (e.g. the amount that would be paid) and taking into account the effect of any instrument that may dilute the Fund's Investment to derive the Attributable Enterprise Value;

(iv) Apportion the Attribution Enterprise Value appropriately between the relevant financial instruments using the perspective of potential Market Participants. Judgement is required in assessing a Market Participant perspective.

3.5 Net Assets

In using the Net Assets valuation technique to estimate the Fair Value of an Investment, the Valuer should:

(i) Derive an Enterprise Value for the company using the perspective of a Market Participant to value its assets and liabilities (adjusting, if appropriate, for non-operating assets, excess liabilities and contingent assets and liabilities);

(ii) Deduct from this amount any financial instruments ranking ahead of the highest ranking instrument of the Fund in a liquidation scenario (e.g. the amount that would be paid) and taking into account the effect of any instrument that may dilute the Fund's Investment to derive the Attributable Enterprise Value; and

(iii) Apportion the Attributable Enterprise Value appropriately between the relevant financial instruments using the perspective of potential Market Participants. Judgement is required in assessing a Market Participant perspective.

3.6 Discounted Cash Flows or Earnings (of Underlying Business)

In using the Discounted Cash Flows or Earnings (of Underlying Business) valuation technique to estimate the Fair Value of an Investment, the Valuer should:

(i) Derive the Enterprise Value of the company, using reasonable assumptions and estimations of expected future cash flows (or expected future earnings) and the terminal value, and discounting to the present by applying the appropriate risk-adjusted rate that captures the risk inherent in the projections;
(ii) Adjust the Enterprise Value for surplus or non-operating assets or excess liabilities and other contingencies and relevant factors to derive an Adjusted Enterprise Value for the Investee Company;
(iii) Deduct from this amount any financial instruments ranking ahead of the highest ranking instrument of the Fund in a liquidation scenario (e.g. the amount that would be paid) and taking into account the effect of any instrument that may dilute the Fund's Investment to derive the attributable Enterprise Value;
(iv) Apportion the Attributable Enterprise Value appropriately between the relevant financial instruments using the perspective of Market Participants. Judgement is required in assessing a Market Participant perspective.

3.7 Discounted Cash Flows (from the Investment)

In using the Discounted Cash Flows (from an Investment) valuation technique to estimate the Fair Value of an Investment, the Valuer should derive the present value of the cash flows from the Investment using reasonable assumptions and estimations of expected future cash flows, the terminal value or maturity amount, date, and the appropriate risk-adjusted rate that captures the risk inherent to the Investment. This valuation technique would generally be applied to Investments with characteristics similar to debt.

3.8 Industry Valuation Benchmarks

The use of industry benchmarks is only likely to be reliable and therefore appropriate as the main basis of estimating Fair Value in limited situations, and is more likely to be useful as a sanity check of values produced using other techniques.

3.9 Available Market Prices

(i) Instruments quoted on an Active Market should be valued at the price within the bid / ask spread that is most representative of Fair Value on the Measurement Date. The Valuer should consistently use the most representative point estimate in the bid / ask spread.
(ii) Blockage Factors that reflect size as a characteristic of the reporting entity's holding (specifically, a factor that adjusts the quoted price of an asset because the market's normal daily trading volume is not sufficient to absorb the quantity held by the entity) should not be applied.
(iii) Discounts may be applied to prices quoted in an Active Market if there is some contractual, Governmental or other legally enforceable restriction attributable to the security, not the holder, resulting in diminished Liquidity of the instrument that would impact the price a Market Participant would pay at the Measurement Date.'

Venture Capital Trusts

Venture Capital Trusts (VCTs) introduced in 1995, provide a tax-efficient method for private individuals to invest in unquoted companies. VCTs have to invest 70% of their money in 'qualifying holdings' within three years of their launch: ITA 2007, ss 258–332.

Qualifying companies are essentially trading companies not involved in asset backed or financial activities, including those quoted on the Alternative Investment Market or ISDX.

> **Focus**
>
> Private Equity and Venture Capital Trusts are major markets for unquoted shares.

14.03 European regulated markets

In November 2012 the interdealer broker ICAP bought PLUS-SX and its derivative operations and later sold the technology division, PLUS-TS, to Forum Trading Solutions. ICAP Securities and Derivatives Exchange (ISDX) is an equity market for small and medium sized companies to finance and grow their businesses. It allows companies to come to the public markets for the first time to enable them to raise equity finance or existing listed companies to raise further finance. It is a recognised investment exchange under the Financial Services and Markets Act 2000 and recognised stock exchange under ITA 2007, s 105(1)(b).

PLUS, formerly OFEX, was an independent quote-driven trading platform that supported trading in over 800 small and midcap companies. Most had market caps of less than £10m but also included were larger, well-known companies such as the brewers Shepherd Neame and Newbury Racecourses, as well as Arsenal FC.

ISDX operates the following market segments:

ISDX Main Board is a EU-regulated market with officially listed securities which are regulated by the UK Listing Authority or another EU competent authority and are subject to the ISDX Main Board Admission and Disclosure Standards (primary market).

The ISDX growth market is a market for unlisted securities with a regulatory framework dedicated to the needs of smaller companies – an SME market (primary market). The growth market offers cost-effective access to capital for businesses seeking the first step on to a public market. The market is supported by a growth-driven trading platform, with competing two-way prices at all times.

The ISDX secondary market is a trading venue for both listed and unlisted (ie non-regulated market) securities admitted to trading on other EU markets.

GXG Markets is a European Regulated Market focussing on small and medium enterprises, which provides an over-the-counter trading platform, a multilateral trading facility or a regulated market.

The Channel Island Securities Exchange (CISX) is, since 20 December 2013, a recognised stock exchange under CTA 2010, s 1137 and licenced to operate as an investment exchange under the Protection of Investors (Bailiwick of Guernsey) Law 1987. Shares quoted on CISX are quoted shares and are valued for tax purposes on the basis of the open market value under TCGA 1992, s 272(1) not as unquoted shares under s 273 nor as shares or securities quoted in the Stock Exchange Daily Official List under s 272(3). Under s 272(1) the value is 'the price which those securities might reasonably [have been] expected to fetch on a sale in the open market', which is not necessarily the same as the listed price on CISX. (*Nicholas Green v HMRC* [2014] UKFTT 306 (TC), paragraphs 88 and 125 – see **14.04**).

> **Focus**
>
> These may provide a step towards flotation on the Stock Exchange.

14.04 Alternative Investment Market

The Alternative Investment Market (AIM) of the Stock Exchange was introduced in 1995 to encourage a wider range of companies to go public by reducing the associated costs and obligations. There are no minimum conditions relating to the size of the company, market capitalisation, the percentage of shares in public hands or the length of trading record. AIM applicants do not have to comply with pre-set criteria but are required to disclose an accurate and comprehensive description of their businesses in order to allow investors to make an informed assessment of the risks and rewards of the proposed investment.

Although there are no specific entry criteria, companies with existing pre-tax profit in excess of £500,000 are likely to generate greater interest. An initial market capitalisation of at least £5m would also be required to ensure reasonable liquidity in the shares.

Securities listed on AIM are treated as unquoted for tax purposes.

Nicholas Green v HMRC [2014] UKFTT 396 (TC) related to two gifts of 118,750 shares of 0.1p each in Chartersea Limited to the National Eczema Society and the Alzheimer's Society on 4 April 2008. Mr Green claimed tax relief under TA 2007, s 431 of £237,500 based on a market value of £1 per share. HMRC did not accept that this was the market value of the shares and reduced the claim to 30p per gifted share, ie £71,250 and a reduction of £166,250. Mr Green appealed. HMRC had provided no support for their valuation and the price paid was £1 a share which were quoted on a Recognised Stock Exchange.

Chartersea was the vehicle used to acquire Warwick Developments (North West) Limited (WDL), a manufacturer and supplier of PVC windows, doors, sealed glazed units and conservatories. On 1 February 2008, each ordinary share was divided into 1,000 ordinary shares of 0.1p each. 999 shares were issued to Mr Dallimore and 999,500 to Mr Salisbury at par. Chartersea issued a private placing memorandum to issue up to 5,000,000 new shares at 0.1p per 1p share, which were issued on 17 March 2008. 1,000,000 new shares of 0.1p each were issued to Brian Johnson, acting managing director of WDL. He and his brother Gavin, with his wife, owned 100% of WDL's holding company, Warwick Management Limited (WML). On 10 March 2008, Chartersea issued, in a private placing, 4,998,529 shares in WML. There was a rights issue on 12 March 2008 for 1,649,541 shares of £1 each and Chartersea's share capital became 9,648,043 ordinary 0.1p shares. On 18 March 2008, Chartersea purchased shares in WML for £4,112,267.90 plus up to £235,567.32 in respect of book debts. Chartersea had a loan facility from The Cooperative Bank of £2.5 million and an overdraft facility of £461,000. The purchase price for WML was £3,612,267.90 cash plus £500,000 loan note.

Chartersea's 9,648,043 shares were listed and dealt with on the Official List of the Channel Islands Stock Exchange (CISX). On 4 April 2008, two parcels of 7,000 were traded at 101p and 100p. On 4 April 2008, Mr Green gifted all but 134,118 of the Chartersea shares, keeping 134,118 for himself. Not all of his income was taxable at 40% and he claimed to recover £66,500 in tax as a result of his gifts to charity, because not all of the gift was covered at the top rates of tax as he had paid £60,714 for the shares in March 2008 and they were worth £237,500 following the listing on CISX. The net cost, assuming the claimed tax relief was forthcoming, was £28,500. Mr Green had made similar investments in 2004 and 2006 to the same charities who had sold the shares at a profit.

Mr Green claimed that the charities benefited, he could obtain tax relief and a long-term investment in the remaining shares.

The Tribunal determined the market value of the gifted shares at 35p per share, the relievable amount at £83,125 and the disallowance at £154,375.

Cases referred to included *IRC v Gray* [1994] STC 360, *Marks v Sherred* [2004] STC 362, *Re Lynall deceased, Lynall and another v CIR* (1972) 47 TC 375, *Erdal v HMRC* [2011] UKFTT 87 (TC), *Caton v Couch* [1995] STC (SCD) 34, *Stephen Marks v HMRC* [2011] UKFTT 221 (TC), *Bullivant Holdings Limited v IRC* [1998] STC 905, *Salvesen's Trustees v IRC* 1930 SLT 387 and *IRC v Clay* [1914] 3 KB 466.

The problem in *Jonathan Netley v HMRC* [2017] UKFTT 442 (TC) was:

> 'What was the market value of the shares in Frenkel Topping Group plc ("FTG") which the Lead Appellant disposed of by way of gift to charity on 28th July 2004 as at that date for the purposes of section 587B ICTA1988 (and on what basis and principles should the market value of such shares be determined)?'

FTG was admitted to the Alternative Investment Market (AIM) on 28 July 2004. The Appellant was one of the shareholders who gifted shares to St Ann's Hospice, a well-known charity, at a claimed 48p per share, as quoted on the Alternative Investment Market (AIM). In 2004–05, certain shares were qualifying investments eligible for income tax relief when gifted to charity under ICTA 1988, s 587B on the basis of their market value, if they were listed or dealt in on a recognised stock exchange and had to be valued under TCGA 1992, ss 272, 273. Forward Link Limited's share capital was 1,000 £1 shares, each of which, on 27 January 2004, was subdivided into 20,000 shares of 0.005p each.

On 17 February 2004 the authorised share capital was increased to £350,000 being 2,000,000,000 shares at 0.005p and 13,980,000 new ordinary shares at 0.005p per share, at par, saving £699. Some 92% of the shares were held by Richard Hughes, Ian Currie and Keith Salisbury, Stephen Lundy and W H Ireland plc.

On 17 February 2004, 23,000,000 shares were offered for subscription at 5p each which were issued and allotted on 3 June 2004.

Share were allotted at 17.5p each shortly before the flotation on 28 July 2004 at 48p, the price set by the market maker, and were at 62p on 20 September 2016 but had gone as low as 14p in the interim. The Tribunal Judge held that the market value of Mr Netley's shares on 28 July 2004 were 17.5p per share.

Focus

An alternative step towards flotation.

14.05 Full listing

In order to obtain a full listing as a public company quoted on the Stock Exchange the company must be of sufficient size to enable a reasonable market to be made in the shares. The costs of a flotation are such that it would be unusual for a company to attempt to dispose of less than say £2m worth of shares on a full listing.

A full listing can be obtained on an introduction to the market if the shares are already widely held, and although a full prospectus and accountants' report has to be prepared it does not have to be published in the press.

A placing is done through an issuing house.

Larger companies will go for an offer for sale where the full prospectus and accountants' report are published in the financial press and the sponsoring house will undertake that all the shares to be issued at the offering price will be taken up and this risk will be underwritten.

In order for a company to be suitable for flotation it is desirable to have a consistent record of increasing profits. The company must be in a business where demands for its services or products are likely to continue and there should be a likelihood that the company's business will continue to grow. This is clearly in the proprietors' interest as although they will be disposing of at least 25% of their shares in order to obtain a full listing, they will normally retain a substantial holding which means that they have a vested interest in the company's share price continuing to increase after the flotation.

A company in a particularly high risk area of activity is difficult to float successfully as investors like to see a reasonable diversification of risk.

It is also essential that the company is financially sound and has sufficient working capital for its activities for the immediate future, taking account of any sums being raised by the flotation itself.

In many cases it will be necessary to reorganise the structure of the company prior to flotation in order to present to the share buying public a simple and readily comprehensible structure. In many family businesses it will have been desirable to have a number of trading companies, and possibly partnerships, held by various members of the family and it might be necessary to incorporate the business into a simple group structure prior to flotation.

The management of the company should have both experience and depth. It is never desirable to float a company where key management decisions are made by one person, particularly if he or she is on the point of retirement. The sponsors will wish to ensure that the management are aware of their responsibilities for running a quoted public company and this will influence their decision as to whether or not to back the issue.

In the case of a company coming to the market the principal factors affecting the issue price will be the price/earnings ratio, the dividend yield and the asset cover, which are the main factors affecting the valuation of shares in a private company in any circumstances. In addition the prices and multiples at which other companies are quoted around the date of issue is relevant. This is a case therefore where the influence of the prices quoted on the London Stock Exchange and the multiples implicit in those prices for comparable companies has a distinct bearing on the value of the shares.

In some cases the issuing house merely fixes a minimum price and invites potential investors to tender an offer for the shares at or above this minimum price. When all applications have been received the issue price is fixed at the price at which the offers at and above that price equate with the shares to be issued. This automatically avoids over subscription and ensures that anyone making a ridiculously high bid is going to acquire shares, although at the issue price, which is the same for all tenderers at and above that price. An offer for sale by tender usually only takes place in a bull market.

Focus

Only substantial groups will be able to go directly for a full flotation.

14.06 Enterprise Investment Scheme

The Enterprise Investment Scheme in ITA 2007, ss 156–257 replaced the Business Expansion Scheme, which came to an end at the end of 1993. The EIS applies from 1 January 1994 and from 6 April 2012 allows relief at 30% on investments of up to £1,000,000 a year, as well as capital gains tax exemption on the first disposal of shares. Capital gains tax incurred on disposal of a different asset can also be deferred indefinitely, where disposal of the asset was less than 36 months before the EIS investment or less than 12 months after it. Companies are limited to raising £5m per year on which relief will be given.

In relation to shares issued after 19 July 2012, the value of the company's gross assets must not exceed £15m immediately before the issue of EIS shares and must not exceed £16m immediately afterwards. Eligible shares have to be held for at least five years and qualifying companies are unquoted trading companies which carry on a qualifying activity for a minimum of three years. The current scheme extends to companies trading in the UK, whether or not they are incorporated and resident there, and to investors liable to UK tax whether or not resident there.

The Seed Enterprise Investment Scheme in ITA 2007, ss 257A–257HJ gives tax relief at 50% of qualifying investments up to £100,000. FA 2014 introduced tax relief for social investments under ITA 2007, ss 257J–257TE and TCGA 1992, ss 255A–255E and Sch 8B.

Focus

These are the main tax reliefs for investment in unquoted companies.

14.07 Valuation for specific purposes

Previous chapters have dealt with valuations for various fiscal purposes and the fair value under the Articles of Association. There are many other occasions for valuation, the most common of which are considered below.

14.08 Management buy-outs / buy-ins

In the third quarter of 2013, the Centre for Management Buy Out Research (CMBOR) reported 276 European exits for the year to date with a value of €51 billion. At the peak of the market in 2007, there were 1,244 deals with a combined valued of €177.6 billion. By 2010, this figure had fallen to 871 deals with a value of €53.8 billion.

Buy-outs take several different forms and attract various acronyms, such as MBI (management buy-in) and BIMBO (buy-in management buy-out). The feature common to most is the creation of a new company, funded largely by equity and debt put in by a private equity provider that acquires an existing entity. Managers from that entity and/or new management brought in from outside will also acquire equity, sometimes on favourable terms, which can cause tax valuation problems (see **Chapter 9**). The previous owner might also retain a small holding in the new entity or have entitlement to further consideration based on the ongoing performance of the company.

The buy-out could be of a company that was itself the vehicle for an earlier buy-out (secondary buy-out, tertiary buy-out, and so on) or of a company quoted on the stock market (public to private).

The value of a public-to-private buy-out will take the market capitalisation as a starting point, but the price to be paid for a private company will be largely a question of negotiation, driven by returns required by the private equity provider in the light of a business plan drawn up by or on behalf of the management team.

The business plan is normally prepared by the compilation of detailed budgets and cash flow forecasts for period of five years or more on the basis of the information available. Private equity providers usually expect an exit within five years and will have to be convinced that they will achieve their required return within that period. The exit could be a secondary buy-out, a trade sale to another company or, more rarely, a flotation.

Focus

Private equity involvement in management buy-outs and buy-ins has been considerably reduced in the last few years, but is still an important element of unquoted company funding.

14.09 De-mergers

A company can normally only de-merge by going into liquidation and distributing assets in specie to shareholders under the provisions of the Insolvency Act 1986, s 84 et seq or by entering into a reconstruction with the approval of the court under the provisions of CA 2006, s 900, or by a capital distribution in specie of shares in a subsidiary company. There are relieving provisions for income tax, capital gains tax and stamp duty under the provisions of TCGA 1992, s 192. The distribution must, under CTA 2010, s 1051(4)–(7), be wholly or mainly for the purpose of benefiting some or all of the trading activities and it may be necessary to prepare valuations of the companies or businesses involved in order to show that there is a bona fide commercial arrangement. There are, however, no specific statutory provisions relating to valuation in the circumstances of a de-merger.

Focus

This is sometimes a useful means of dividing the assets of a company among different shareholder interests.

14.10 Receiverships and liquidations

If a receiver is appointed or a company is put into liquidation it may be possible to sell off the whole or part of the business as a going concern which would often involve the creation of a new company and the transfer of the saleable assets to that new company.

The receiver or liquidator would then have to value the saleable business and find a buyer at the appropriate price or persuade the debenture holders, creditors or shareholders to continue the business in its restructured form or accept a distribution in specie at the appropriate valuation. Depending upon the circumstances of each case the valuation would be on the basis of the capitalised value of the projected future earnings, or the realisable value of the underlying assets.

Focus

A common way of securing something from a financial wreckage, or a shareholder dispute, is to wind up the existing structure.

14.11 Estate planning

If it is desired to reorganise a shareholder's estate, possibly by the transfer of shares to members of his family or by the creation of appropriate family settlements, it would be necessary to arrive at the value of the shares in order to decide on the estate planning tactics. The valuation would be done on the basis of a disposal at market value for capital gains tax estimates. For inheritance tax, if the gift is to be a chargeable transfer to a discretionary trust, or a potentially exempt transfer which will not become chargeable unless the transferor dies within seven years of the gift, the basis for valuation is the reduction in the value of the transferor's estate, as on an actual transfer. It might also be necessary to consider the question of valuation of other interests in the company if for example deferred shares were to be issued or preference or management shares created. These valuations would take place along normal capital gains tax, stamp duty and inheritance tax lines, as appropriate.

Focus

A single transaction may involve different valuations for different taxes.

14.12 Company buying its own shares

CA 2006, ss 690–737 enable a company to issue redeemable shares and to purchase its own shares. Such a redemption, repayment or purchase of shares is not a distribution for tax purposes which it otherwise would be under CTA 2010, ss 1030–1032, in view of CTA 2010, s 1033 the company is an unquoted company. An unquoted company includes one dealt in on the Alternative Investment Market, provided that it is a trading company or a holding company of a trading group. The redemption, repayment or purchase must be made wholly or mainly for the purposes of benefiting a trade carried on by the company or by any of its 75% subsidiaries. It must not be part of a scheme or arrangement to enable shareholders to participate in the profits of a company without receiving a dividend or for the avoidance of tax. It is also necessary to comply with the provisions of CTA 2010, ss 1034–1043.

If, however, the whole or substantially the whole of the payment is applied in discharge of an inheritance tax liability on death and is applied within two years of the death and it can be shown that the inheritance tax liability could not be met otherwise without undue hardship, the payment does not have to be for the purpose of benefiting the trade.

The following conditions, set out in CTA 2010, ss 1034–1043 et seq must otherwise be complied with:

(1) The vendor must be resident and ordinarily resident in the UK as must any nominee.

(2) The shares must have been owned by the vendor throughout the five years ending with the disposal. Shares inherited from a previous owner may include his period of ownership and that of the personal representatives. Where shares are acquired at different times a first in, first out basis is applied and any previous disposal shall be assumed to have been on a last in, first out basis. The capital gains tax acquisition rules for reorganisation etc are applied *mutatis mutandis*.

(3) The vendor's interest as a shareholder must be substantially reduced on the company's purchase or redemption and must not exceed 75% of what

it was before the sale. His interest in profits available for distribution must be reduced by a similar amount.

(4) Where an associate owns shares the combined holdings of the vendor and his associates must be substantially reduced as if the vendor was also entitled to his associate's shares.

(5) Where a group is involved it is necessary to look at all companies in the group in which the vendor owns shares immediately before and after the purchase. The group is defined as a company with one or more 51% subsidiaries which is not itself a 51% subsidiary of any other company. Where there has been a transfer of the business within three years the company purchasing its own shares and the successor company are treated as being in the same group. A company which has left a group continues to be a member of the group if arrangements exist under which it could again become a subsidiary.

(6) If an associate owns shares in any company in the group the combined interests of the vendor and his associates must be aggregated to see whether the appropriate substantial reduction in the combined holdings has taken place.

(7) After the purchase the vendor must not be connected with the company making the purchase or with any other member of the same 51% group. Connected for this purpose is more than a 30% interest as defined under CTA 2010, ss 1062–1063.

(8) The purchase must not be part of a scheme or arrangement which would disqualify the vendor if the ultimate result had been achieved immediately on the purchase.

(9) The vendor may qualify even though he does not himself satisfy the tests if he has to sell shares to the company in order to enable an associate to qualify.

In *Russell Baker v HMRC* [2013] UKFTT 394 (TC 02790) the purported purchase of its own shares from one of the shareholders, as a result of a dispute, was void under CA 1985, s 143(2) as being in breach of CA 1985, ss 159–181 and the company was entitled to recover the amount paid following *Kleinwort Benson Ltd v Lincoln City Council and Others* [1999] 2 AC 349 on the ground of mistake of law. *Kinlan v Crimmin* [2006] EWHC 779 (Ch) was distinguished as the only breach was the prohibition of deferred payment for a company buyback and would have been paid in full on completion had the parties realised the necessity to do so. At paragraph 60 it was stated:

> 'We discount entirely any suggestion that the Appellant should be taxed on the basis of the 'economic reality' of what has taken place. Such a submission has a degree of unreality about it, bearing in mind the approach taken by HMRC in the sad appeals from defrauded investors in complicated life insurance bonds who have lost most or all of their investment but are still being taxed by HMRC on entirely fictitious gains arising under the life policy "chargeable events" rules.'

Focus

A company buying its own shares can be complex from both a company law and taxation perspective.

14.13 Administration

Application may be made to HMRC before a redemption, repayment or purchase by a company of its own shares and they have 30 days within which to request further particulars. Full details of the transaction have to be provided for the clearance to be effective. A return must be lodged to the inspector within 60 days after making the payment. Any person connected with the purchase has a similar liability to inform HMRC. HMRC may require the company to furnish particulars of any suspected scheme or arrangement. The standard penalties for failing to submit a return are applied. An associate is defined and includes a husband and wife living together, a minor child, a person connected with the company and vice versa, a company under the control of another company, trustees with the settlor or an associate of his or the beneficiaries, a legatee or nominee but not the trustees of an exempt approved pension scheme. A beneficiary is only associated where he has a significant (greater than 5%) interest in the trust or estate.

A person is connected with a company if he directly or indirectly possesses or is entitled to acquire more than 30% of the issued ordinary share capital of the company or loan capital and issued share capital or voting power of the company, or is entitled to receive more than 30% of the assets available for distribution or otherwise has control of the company.

It may still be essential to obtain clearances under TA 1988, s 703 from being a transaction in securities under ITA 2007, s 682 et seq, and other clearances, for example, under ITA 2007, s 770, CTA 2010, s 831 and TCGA 1992, s 138 may also be required.

There are commonly a number of complex taxation problems to be dealt with on a reconstruction of this nature, which are not dealt with here. From a valuation point of view there are no specific provisions except for the need to capitalise the amount spent by the company on the redemption, repayment or purchase by way of a capital redemption reserve under CA 2006, s 733.

Focus

It is important to follow the correct procedures and obtain any necessary tax clearances.

14.14 Take-overs

If shares in a company are being purchased, the intending purchaser will obviously have to consider a valuation of the company in order to determine the price to be offered. In practice what usually happens is that the board of the acquiring company approaches the board of the target company to be acquired and suggests that it could be in their mutual interest to arrange for the take-over. If the parties are in agreement in principle, information will be provided either to the acquiring company itself or to accountants or valuers appointed on its behalf with a view to supplying the information required to agree a price. The valuation would then proceed along the normal lines, although the emphasis would be primarily on the earning potential of the target company. Obviously the keener the acquiring company is on the acquisition the higher the price/earnings ratio it is prepared to offer. If reference is made to reports in the *Financial Times* and the comments of Lex in that paper, or to the *Investors Chronicle* it will be seen that the P/E ratio in such circumstances (referred to, as often as not, as the exit P/E) expresses the price paid in such deals as a multiple of the current or forecast profit before tax in actual take-overs. (Strictly speaking, however, earnings are defined as profit after tax, so a P/E ratio should be based on profit after tax.) The normal P/E ratio of a quoted public company in, for example, the Financial Times Share Information Service is based on a small minority interest and is not necessarily applicable in the case of a take-over, where the whole company is being acquired. These days, many price multiples are expressed in terms of enterprise value (ie the sum of the equity price and the debt in the target) to EBIT (earnings before interest and tax) or EBITDA (earnings before interest, tax depreciation and amortisation), rather than as P/E ratios.

In view of the importance of earnings it is not unusual for some of the consideration to be contingent on the acquiree company achieving stated profit targets. In such circumstances it is necessary to value the right to the additional consideration, if the profit targets are met, as there will be a part disposal on the initial takeover followed by a further disposal when the deferred consideration is quantified: *Marren v Ingles* [1980] STC 500, [1980] 3 All ER 95 and *Marson v Marriage* [1980] STC 177. This type of earn-out arrangement can prevent a complete capital gains tax roll-over under TCGA 1992, s 135 as the value of the right is not itself shares.

In some cases, the acquiring company considers that the acquiree company has surplus assets and will consider the market value of those assets. It may be, for example, that the acquiree company has a reasonable profit potential in its existing premises, but that the land it is occupying could be more profitably used for a property development of some kind. In such circumstances it would be necessary to value the land and estimate the costs either of winding up the existing business or transferring it to another location.

The ability of the acquiring company to purchase compulsorily shares of dissident shareholders where it acquires at least 90% of the outstanding shares under the provisions of CA 2006, s 979 can be important in the case of a takeover.

> **Focus**
>
> Take-overs may proceed with or without the consent of the existing management if the shareholders approve the deal.

14.15 Nationalisation

Until recently it seemed unlikely in the present political climate that there would be any large scale nationalisation or re-nationalisation. Changes in the political climate can be as sudden and unexpected as changes in the climate in the geographical sense, however, and the effects of nationalisation may once again be on the political agenda.

The terms on which shareholders may be compensated on the nationalisation of their company depends very much on the rapacity of the government for the time being. The terms may be based on an open market value of the shares, but in some cases have been linked to the Stock Exchange prices for minority interests in the company being nationalised, or other companies of a like character. The value therefore might bear no relationship to the underlying value of the entire business. In each case it would be necessary to consider in detail the legislation under which the expropriation takes place.

Focus

Recent partial nationalisations have been rescues for businesses deemed too big to fail, such as high-street banks.

14.16 Non-cash share issues: CA 2006, ss 593–597

Subject to certain exceptions, a public company must not allot shares otherwise than in cash unless the consideration for the allotment has been independently valued.

The valuer has to be someone who is eligible for appointment as a statutory auditor and also meets an independence requirement. The valuer may nevertheless rely on a valuation made by a person other than himself, provided that it appeared reasonable to him. The valuer's report has to state the nominal value of the shares, the amount of any premium, a description of the consideration, the method used to value it, the date of valuation and the extent to which the nominal value and premium are treated as paid up by the non-cash consideration, and any cash consideration. The valuer also has to confirm that the value of the consideration and any cash consideration is not less than the aggregate of the nominal value and any premium treated as paid up by the consideration and any cash.

Focus

Normally, non-cash issues are related to an acquisition of another company.

Chapter 15

Published data

Signposts

SHARE INDICES

15.01 The importance of published information

It is almost impossible to undertake any type of valuation without needing to access information held in the public domain. For taxation purposes, consideration must be given to the information to which a hypothetical purchaser would be expected to have access. Commercial valuations will usually be more meaningful if market multiples, including, where possible, transaction data, can be incorporated.

The development of the internet means that more information is available than ever before. No case has yet been heard to test the effect of online data on the information deemed to be required, but it would now be taken as a given that the hypothetical purchaser would undertake an Internet search as part of any prudent enquiries into the suitability or otherwise of a potential purchase. As more companies post material online, it has become much easier for the valuer to obtain reference materials. However, the same health warnings apply to documents sourced from the internet as those obtained by more traditional methods, ie it should be ensured that the information was available at the valuation date and that the source of the information is credible.

Reference is often made to a company's beta or beta coefficient which indicates whether an investment is more or less volatile than the market as a whole. A beta of less than one is less volatile than the market as a whole and a beta of more than one is more volatile.

Focus

When considering the value of a business, a valuer will look to market information to provide a cross-check to the assumptions made in the calculations. The significance and relevance of such information depends on the quality of the data and an understanding of the data presented.

15.02 The FT 30 Index

The FT 30 Index, originally known as the Financial Times Industrial Ordinary Share Index, began on 1 July 1935 and is the oldest continuous share price index in the UK. According to the *Financial Times* it was designed to 'test the feel and changing moods of the equity market', based on the share prices of the most prominent and actively traded shares. Although largely superseded by the launch of the FTSE 100 in 1984 (see **15.03** below), the index differs from the FTSE indices in that it is not governed by the Stock Exchange and the fact that the calculation methodology applies an equal weighting to all constituents of the index. In addition, in contrast to the FTSE 100, an FT 30 constituent is only changed when a company no longer exists, eg following a takeover or business cessation or if the company is no longer UK-owned. Only two of the original 1935 companies, GKN (now owned by Melrose Industries) and Tate and Lyle, still remain in the index. While the FT 30 is no longer used as an indicator of short-term market trends, it remains useful as an indicator of longer-term trends. It can also be used as an indication of the general economic and political climate at the date of valuation. These factors must be of importance in arriving at the value of any shareholding. A final factor is that the index was in existence at 31 March 1982, and therefore can be of use when considering valuations as at that date.

15.03 Financial Times Stock Exchange (FTSE) Indices

The FTSE 100 (also known as 'Footsie') index began in January 1984 and comprises the 100 largest UK companies based on their market capitalisation. Market data suggest that companies in the index represent a combined market capitalisation of circa £2 trillion. The list of eligible companies is reviewed on a quarterly basis and up to ten companies may join or leave the index each quarter. The index is weighted on the basis of constituents' market capitalisation. The FTSE 250 is also a weighted index based on the market capitalisation of traded 'mid-market' companies. Launched on 12 October 1992, the index excludes companies included in the FTSE 100.

The FTSE All-Share Index began in 1962 as the FT Actuaries All-Share Index. Considered by many experts as the best UK market performance indicator, the index is calculated on the basis of participants' 'free-floating' market capitalisation i.e. any shares held by restricted shareholders or family shareholders which are unlikely to be traded are ignored. The index includes the constituents of the FTSE 100, FTSE 250 and FTSE Small Cap indices. At 31 October 2018, the all-share index comprised 638 companies and represented a market capitalisation of circa £2.3 trillion.

15.04 Financial Times Stock Exchange (FTSE) Actuaries Share Indices

The Financial Times Actuaries Share Indices are compiled by the joint investment research committee of the Faculty of Actuaries and the Institute of Actuaries for the *Financial Times* – see **Appendix A**. They are published daily from Tuesday to Saturday in the *Financial Times* and have the advantage of breaking down the equity market into various groups and also showing the overall performance in the FTSE Actuaries All Share Index and other sector indices. Dividends and earnings of the constituent companies are aggregated to arrive at the figures for each sector – see **Appendix B**.

15.05 Basis of compilation of the FTSE UK Indices

The earnings yield percentage is calculated on declared dividends of a company to produce an 'actual yield'. Earnings are the sum of the latest two half years' earnings. Tax calculated at the average rate of the declared profits. The price-earnings (P/E) ratio is the market value divided by the net earnings.

It will be appreciated, when using the FTSE to assist in the valuation of shares in private companies, that it is important to remember the underlying bases on which the figures are compiled as otherwise a direct comparison may be misleading.

The indices are based on the historical cost accounts of the constituent companies. The main features of the indices set out in the FTSE Guide to Calculation Methods for the FTSE UK Index Series: www.ftse.com/products/downloads/FTSE_UK_Index_Series_Guide_to_Calc.pdf.

It should be noted that the sectors are redefined from time to time and therefore the constituent companies will probably not be the same at different valuation dates.

Pitfall

When valuing the same business at a number of different dates, the valuer needs to ensure that the comparable data is consistent and appropriate at each date.

SHARE PRICES

15.06 Financial Times London Share Service

The share price details published by the *Financial Times* for individual companies are often referred to in share valuation and it is important to appreciate precisely what figures have been published.

Since1975 the price/earnings ratio has been based on figures updated to take account of interim statements. The figures are therefore based on the latest annual report and accounts, but where the interim statement shows sufficient detail the earnings for the first six months of the current year replace the first six months of the preceding year, so that the earnings are the latest available earnings on a moving annual basis. The number of shares dealt in on any particular day is also shown.

The Financial Times London Share Service includes a separate section for shares listed on the Alternative Investment Market. The information supplied is the same as for those companies with a full listing.

Individual companies are listed by sector. The constituents or each sector and the sector categories themselves change from time to time and consequently, when valuing shares in a company at a number of dates, it is possible that the same comparable companies will be in different sectors at different times.

15.07 Stock Exchange Daily Official List (SEDOL)

This has been briefly referred to in **13.07**. The official list gives the quotation of a pair of prices, known as the going out prices (the closing bid and offer prices), for each quoted security. The spread between the quoted going out prices will normally be considerably wider than that involved in actual prices made by market-makers.

If there has been little activity in a share the quoted going out prices may be stale if there has been a significant movement in the market or if further information has been published but not reflected in the quotation. However, merely because a quoted price is purely nominal does not mean that it is necessarily stale. Occasionally a broker will object to a price shown in the official list and normally the market-maker will make the appropriate alteration, although there is an appeals procedure in cases of dispute.

As well as showing the quoted going out prices the official list also shows a series of bargains done at various prices. These come from the marking of actual bargains, which, although largely optional, is in fact compulsory for certain classes of bargains. As marking is largely optional the list of bargains done is incomplete but there is no indication as to how incomplete it may be. From 2012, there are specific SEDOL codes for warrants and derivatives.

It should be noted that the exchange remains open until 4.30 pm and the prices that appear in the Stock Exchange Daily Official List are the prices at that time.

The prices quoted in the daily newspapers, such as the Financial Times Share Information Service (**Appendix C**), include a single quotation which represents the middle price being made by market-makers at or near the close of business.

After hours dealing, ie after the exchange officially closes at 4.30 pm, is perfectly legitimate and covered by the normal rules of the exchange.

The Stock Exchange Daily Official List is recognised for capital gains tax purposes under TCGA 1992, s 272(3). Up to 5 April 2015, the market value of shares for capital gains tax purposes was calculated as the lower of (a) the quarter up basis, which is the lower of the two quoted going out prices plus one-quarter of the difference between the two figures or (b) half way between the highest and lowest bargains reported, other than bargains done at special prices, but including bargains reported late which appear in the next list. From 6 April 2015, market value is calculated as the lower of the two prices shown in the Stock Exchange Daily Official List for that day as the closing price, plus one half of the difference between those two figures.

A bargain done at a special price is indicated by a distinguishing mark in the Stock Exchange Daily Official List and would normally consist of either a very large or very small parcel of shares outside the normal range of prices.

If the Stock Exchange is closed on the relevant valuation date, then data for the nearest previous day on which the exchange was open should be used.

There is no statutory basis of valuation for quoted securities for inheritance tax purposes but in practice the capital gains tax rules are applied. The London Stock Exchange website, www.londonstockexchange.com, includes a 'probate calculator' in respect of quoted shares to assist with the completion of IHT Form D7 which relates to stocks and shares. It also offers a historic price service for securities which have been traded on the London Stock Exchange for dates going back to 1 January 1982.

Online data is available from www.sedol.co.uk.

15.08 BDO LLP Private Company Price Index/Private Equity Price Index (PCPI/PEPI)

The PCPI/PEPI tracks the relationship between the current four-month rolling average FTSE Non-Financials Enterprise Value/EBITDA multiples currently being paid on the sale of private companies to trade and private equity buyers. The FTSE Non-Financials multiple is calculated from the data published in the *FT*. The private company multiple is calculated from publicly available financial information on deals that complete in the quarter. For the third quarter of 2018, the PCPI indicated that on average, private companies were being sold at an Enterprise Value of 10 times their historical EBITDA. The PEPI indicated that, on average, private companies were being sold to private equity buyers at an Enterprise Value of 12 times their historical EBITDA.

As private companies are generally owner-managed, reported or disclosed earnings tend to be suppressed by various expenses that may be non-recurring under a new owner. This will have been factored into the price the purchaser paid, but may not be reflected in the profits declared to the public. The effect of this is that the multiple paid as calculated from the publicly available information may be over stated. The PCPI/PEPI tracks the discount between how the public and private companies are being valued. This discount enables valuers to use enterprise multiples from the prices at which public companies are trading in the market and apply them to private companies in the same sector. It should be noted that the index excludes companies that are loss-making at an EBITDA level and therefore the average figure published will be higher than the true deal average if all transactions were included.

The PCPI/PEPI is calculated as the arithmetic mean of the Enterprise Value/EBITDA multiples for deals where sufficient information has been disclosed. For the third quarter of 2018, the included deals for the PEPI have a mean deal size of £40m. For the PCPI, the mean deal size over the same period has been £16m. Therefore, if a company is smaller than this, a further discount may be applicable.

The PCPI/PEPI is an average measure and guide, not an absolute measure of value, as there are many other factors that can have an impact on value.

In *Mr & Mrs Foulser v HMRC* [2015] UKFTT 220 (TC), a long-running dispute, since 1997, that reached the First Tier Tribunal in 2015:

> '*Capitalisation factor*
>
> 150. We have set out above the reasons why Mr Spence considered that it was inappropriate to use published quoted company P/E ratio or industry sector averages. However, our view is that the PCPI ratio would not have been used by a willing prudent purchaser.
>
> 151. In our view it is unsafe to rely on the PCPI for a valuation of this nature. Our reasons, which reflect our acceptance of Mr Glover's evidence in this regard, are as follows:
>
> (1) There is no transparency of the PCPI. No information is available as to the number of private company acquisitions on which the average P/E ratio is based. Nor is anything known about the companies concerned, including their activity and size. It is thus impossible to take any view on comparability.
> (2) An approach based on future maintainable earnings requires as its concomitant a market P/E ratio based on such a calculation of earnings. The PCPI is based on reported (historic) earnings. No adjustment has been made to reflect future maintainable earnings.
>
> 152. In support of the capitalisation factor which Mr Spence derived from the PCPI, Mr Spence placed reliance upon the views of the "industry experts" who provided witness statements in these proceedings. We do not consider that any

support should be derived from that source. As Mr Glover explained, the use of comparable transactions as a guide to value is properly confined to actual transactions. It does not include opinions of persons who are not themselves expert valuers. Mr Myerson sought to undermine Mr Glover's evidence in this regard by reference to a passage in Mr Glover's book and certain remarks made by Mr Glover in cross-examination. We are satisfied, however, that these criticisms go nowhere. As Mr Glover says in his book, it is for the expert valuer to take a view as to the industry background, and references to the views of others are to be confined to actual purchasers, or as Mr Glover put it "those assumed to be". We shall examine later the extent to which we consider that latter concept can be applied in this case by reference to the October 1997 offer and the Mermaidlogic deal.

Conclusion of Mr Spence's methodology

153. We find that there are serious flaws in the methodology adopted by Mr Spence in relation to the valuation of Mr Foulser's 51% shareholding, both as regards the concept of future maintainable earnings and his use of a capitalisation factor derived from the PCPI.'

In *Ingram & Hall v Ahmed* [2016] EWHC 1536 (Ch) at paragraphs 103–105 it was noted that:

'Miss Longworth also accepted that the Private Company Price Index ("PCPI"), published by BDO, from which she derived her multiples, was jettisoned by BDO in 2013 in favour of Enterprise Value ("EV") multiples, which was, according to BDO, a "less subjective" measure of profitability, on the basis that they are based on all disposals taking place in the relevant quarter, rather than being sector specific, so that the PCPI multiples would not match the business sector of Hornby, Wembley or Continental. Miss Longworth accepted that she no longer uses PCPI but EV for her other valuations. Her explanation for using PCPI in this case was that at the relevant dates the PCPI was a recognised basis for valuation and an accepted methodology. The EV/EBITDA ratio only became the accepted method in 2013.

However I find that the current valuations should be made according to the most recent methods and that this is no breach of the hindsight principle. The court seeks to determine the true value of the Shares not what a valuer would have said on 5th June 2007 was the value of the Shares.

Miss Longworth valued the earnings attributable to equity holders only by reference to equity multiples derived from PCPI and not earnings attributable to both equity and debt holders. However the effect of a small percentage variation in profit before interest and tax in an indebted company is significant compared with a company that has low indebtedness.'

Pitfall

The PCPI/PEPI index is widely used, but consideration must be given to the size of the business being valued compared to the average deal size reported in any given period. It should also be noted that the index now reports Enterprise Value/EBITDA multiples, but historically (up to 4th Quarter 2012) it reported P/E ratios. Therefore, if using the index to value a business at different dates, the user will need to ensure that the multiple derived from the index is applied to the correct profit measure.

15.09 Private Company Price Earnings Ratio Database (PERDa)

The PERDa (info@perda.net) is based on information for private company deals to provide historical and current price/earnings ratios. As at the first quarter of 2018, the average P/E ratio was 8 times.

TRACING COMPARABLE COMPANIES

15.10 A standard industrial classification

One way of finding a company which may be reasonably comparable, in so far as a quoted company is ever comparable with an unquoted one, is to ask the directors which companies are its competitors. If this fails, it may be necessary to define the standard industrial classification within which the company operates. The standard industrial classification was last revised in 2007 and took effect from 1 January 2008 and is published by the Office of National Statistics as 'UK Standard Industrial Classification (UKSIC) of Economic Activities', which gives fuller particulars of the breakdown of each classification. This is available online at www.statistics.gov.uk; email: classifications.helpdesk@ons.gov.uk.

If, for example, the company to be valued is a company which has as its main activity the production of sand and gravel from gravel pits which it operates it will be possible to look in the index under say, 'gravel pit', which gives the Standard Industrial Classification 08120. Not surprisingly, if 'sand pit' is referred to, the same Standard Industrial Classification is arrived at. If, however, the company also wholesales the sand and gravel it extracts, the index will show that sand and gravel merchants are classified under Standard Industrial Classification 46130 which in fact covers wholesale distribution of timber and building materials. This classification includes dealers in hardwood, softwood, plywood casks, staves etc, dealers in sand and gravel, bricks, slates, tiles, cement, glass, clay, granite, marble and other stone, builders' hardware, plumbers' goods etc. It is always important to remember, when tracing comparable companies in this way, that the more specialised the company's activities, the more difficult it is to find a realistic comparison.

If the company has a land bank of gravel bearing land it may well also farm the land prior to extracting the gravel and in this case the index will show that farming has the Standard Industrial Classification 01500.

Many information services, for example FAME (fame.bvdinfo.com), maintain an index of classified companies, listing companies in accordance with the Standard Industrial Classification appropriate to their various activities. In some cases a company will be listed under several headings.

15.11 Trade directories and magazines

Another way of finding comparable companies would be to consult classified directories. Many of these such as *Key British Enterprises* (https://solutions.dnb.com/kbe) are available online, although a fee may be payable for some Internet searches.

Also published by Dun & Bradstreet Ltd is *Who Owns Whom* (https://solutions.dnb.com/wow).This details the corporate links between over 7.5 million companies. Industry codes are assigned to the parent of each group of companies. There is also a section on consortia.

15.12 Trade journals

Trade journals could be consulted to see who is advertising products or services similar to the company to be valued in order to identify possible comparable companies. Such publications also often report recent transactions within the specialist sector which can provide indicative multiples.

15.13 Trade associations

A further method of identifying possible comparable companies would be to obtain a list of members of trade associations. This can also be a useful resource when establishing any recent trends and 'custom and practice' approaches to valuing a particular type of business.

15.14 Special reports

A very useful source both for identifying comparable quoted companies and obtaining details of the companies themselves and the recent history and likely prospects for the industry itself and the particular companies in it, are the various business surveys produced by leading firms of stock-brokers from time to time. Other sources of useful surveys are Factiva (https://global.factiva.com), IBISworld (www.ibisworld.co.uk) and Mintel (www.mintel.com).

The Financial Times (www.ft.com) and Thomson Reuters (http://thomsonreuters.com) also provide market reports in respect of particular industry sectors and geographic regions. HM Revenue and Customs also published general industry reports (Business Economic Notes). While these have now been archived, access to these documents is still available via their website (www.hmrc.gov.uk/bens) and can provide useful historical background information on a particular sector.

15.15 Company sources

It might be possible to obtain from the directors of the company being valued a list of companies engaged in similar activities, and in some cases the company will maintain files on its major competitors which could produce useful information.

15.16 Other online databases

Companies House information can now readily be obtained from its website www.companieshouse.gov.uk, which also provides to links to the equivalent organisations in other countries. Similar data is also available from Morningstar (www.morningstar.co.uk), among others. Bloomberg (www.bloomberg.com) and S&P Capital IQ (www.capitaliq.com) also provide subscription-based services giving access to large amounts of financial and other company information.

Whilst maintaining their own library of cuttings from national and international publications, Shares and Assets Valuation division now also makes extensive use of press searches. Other databases are more specialised, such as Lexis Nexis, Westlaw and BAILII, which contain legislative and case law information, and Jordans, which provides detailed information on the financial status of more than 1.6 million registered companies. Details of mergers and acquisitions are available from Mergermarket (www.mergermarket.com) and other corporate finance sites.

When researching a business in a particular geographic area, it can often be useful to research the website of any local newspapers for interviews or other relevant information.

Other online databases include:

BVB Insights (Business Valuation Benchmarks Limited) E: cservice@bvbenchmarks.com T: 0203 092 2471

European Industry Market-Multiples Duff & Phelps LLP The Shard 32 London Bridge Street London SE1 9SG T: 0207 089 4700 T (Mathias Schumacher): 0207 089 4720

Parmentier Arthur Group Limited 90 Long Acre Covent Garden London WC2E 9RZ T: 0207 849 3018 E: Steve.leggo@parmentierarthur.com

MarktoMarket Valuations Limited Codebase 38 Castle Terrace Edinburgh Scotland EH3 9SJ T: 0131 510 2880 M (Bertie Wilson): 07849 578 166 E: bertie@marktomarket.io www.marktomarket.io

Interbrand (brand valuation) www.interbrand.com bestglobalbrands.com E: mike.rocha@interbrand.com (methodology) E: charles.trevail@interbrand.com (CEO) E: liz.moe@interbrand.com (global marketing & communications)

15.17 Cuttings services

Many companies now offer a cuttings and updates service. Information is also available from the online archives of most major publications. It is also possible to set up internet alerts for articles and press commentary about a particular company.

15.18 Stock Exchange Daily Official List and Financial Times London Share Service

The Stock Exchange Daily Official List and the Financial Times Share Information Service are each divided into various sectors which might help to identify particular comparable companies to investigate further. Periodic redesignations reduce the number of companies in each sector, but the largest section is still 'Support Services' which includes a highly diverse range of companies from recruitment businesses to waste management companies.

Therefore this sector needs to be analysed with care in order to ensure that non comparable companies are excluded from any analysis.

15.19 Industry ratios

One of the purposes of trying to identify comparable quoted companies is to use the share price, dividend yield, P/E ratio, Enterprise value/EBITDA or other financial multiples of the quoted company as a basis to arriving at a possible price for the unquoted company share. This means it is necessary to compare the company being valued with the quoted company and with performance in the industry generally. Many financial information companies, including Bloomberg and Dun & Bradstreet, provide the profit or loss and balance sheet items of a particular company, and its principal business ratios, for comparison with industry ratios for the relevant sectors. It is therefore possible to obtain such particulars of specific quoted companies which may have been identified as being reasonably comparable with the company to be valued. These reports identify various ratios relating to profitability, financial structure, asset utility and employees and are based on the published accounts.

15.20 London Business School Risk Measurement Service

This quarterly guide lists estimated data for every quoted company by sector and also alphabetically. The Industry Tables summarise the estimated risks and returns for the quarter for each industry group and also provides average marketability and performance measures of individual shares. The average expected betas and P/E ratios are also shown for each share. In the Company Tables, the SEDOL Number for each quoted company is listed, together with expected yields and price/earnings ratio. Market capitalisation is also published.

15.21 Thomson Reuters

Thomson Reuters provides a subscription based financial information service, which enables the user to access real time global information in respect of a particular company, as well as historical information and broker data. The service can also perform analysis in respect of the chosen shares and provide international money market information.

Thomson DataStream International (www.thomsonreuters.com/datastream) has over one billion data files from over 170 countries dating back to 1965, including:

- national and international equities;
- company accounts and corporate fundamentals;
- estimates
- stock market sectors and indices;
- exchange rates.

15.22 Company accounts

If a quoted company appears to be reasonably comparable with a company to be valued it is worthwhile obtaining copies of the financial statements as a study of these will assist highlighting the similarities or differences between the quoted company and the company to be valued. Almost all quoted companies now have an 'Investor relations' section on their websites from which financial information and press releases may be downloaded, or alternatively, the information can be obtained from Companies House, which also provides an online service.

15.23 Accounts of comparable unquoted companies

The accounts of unquoted companies can sometimes be useful in comparing the performance of the company whose shares are being valued with those of competitors. Obviously as the comparison is with an unquoted company it does not lead directly to a valuation, but it would show whether the company's position is more or less favourable than its competitors and this in turn could help to determine whether a relatively low or high P/E or Enterprise Value/ EBITDA ratio is appropriate. Copies of accounts could be obtained from Companies House. However, it should be noted that smaller companies are only required to file abbreviated accounts and therefore the profit or loss account information available may be extremely limited.

15.24 The Society of Share and Business Valuers

The Society of Share and Business Valuers (SSBV) (www.ssbv.org) was formed in 1996 to provide a unique forum for specialist valuers in the United Kingdom. The SSBV provides members with a learning and business network.

The SSBV provides a lecture programme, representation and networking for its members who are professionals specialising in the valuation of shares and derivatives, businesses, intellectual property and other intangibles. Members advise their clients on valuations for commercial, taxation, dispute resolution and financial reporting purposes. Many members also act as expert witnesses.

Full members of the SSBV are amongst the most experienced and senior practitioners in the field of share and business valuation.

Chapter 16

Unpublished information and company records

Signposts

16.01 Company data

In order to proceed with the valuation of shares in an unquoted company it will clearly be necessary to obtain information concerning the history and future prospects of the company. The amount of information to be obtained in each case will be determined by the purpose of the valuation and the size of the shareholding. Depending on the purpose of the valuation, it may be uneconomic to spend a lot of time and money on a small minority interest expected to be of nominal value. This chapter sets out the main areas of information which may be examined in greater or lesser detail depending upon the circumstances of each case.

16.02 Memorandum and articles of association and shareholders' agreements

It is necessary to study the precise wording of the company's memorandum and articles in order to find out the rights of the shareholders and in particular the voting power, rights to dividends, including accumulation of dividends in arrears, redemption rights, if any, voting rights, if any, rights on a liquidation and whether or not the shareholder has any right to participate in a surplus on winding up, and all other rights attaching to the shares such as the ability to appoint directors. In addition the articles will normally set out the restrictions on transfer and although it may often be assumed that a hypothetical purchaser will be entered on the register it is nonetheless clear that he holds the shares subject to the articles in respect of any possible future transfer of shares. Restrictions contained in a shareholders' agreement have to be taken into account when considering actual market value for the purposes of employment-related securities under ITEPA 2003. The articles will also set out the transmission rights on death.

The precise terms of any relevant rights and restrictions contained in articles of association or a shareholders' agreement have to be studied carefully if a valuation has to be carried out by reference to their provisions.

In *Paul Richards and Keith Purves v IP Solutions Group Limited* [2016] EWHC 2599 (QB), the valuation of the claimants' shareholdings was required:

> '7. The parties agreed that as employees who were wrongfully dismissed, the Claimants are entitled to be treated as "Good Leavers" under the Company Articles of Association and were entitled to be paid the "Market Value" of their shares. "Market Value" is defined in the Articles as:
>
> > "such value as the transferor and (with Investor Consent) the Company shall agree within ten days after the date of the relevant Transfer Notice (or such longer period as shall be agreed between the transferor and (with Investor Consent) the Company) or, failing such agreement, such value as the Independent Expert shall determine pursuant to Article 18.4."
>
> 8. The critical provision for these purposes is Article 18.4, under which the Independent Expert is required to determine the Market Value:
>
> > "… on the basis which, in the Independent Expert's opinion, represents the market value of the Leaver's Shares at the Leaving Date as between a willing seller and a willing buyer as if the entire issued share capital of the Company were being sold in accordance with these Articles and, in making such determination, the Independent Expert shall ignore the fact that such Leaver's Shares may represent a minority interest and may be subject to the compulsory transfer requirements of Articles 17 (Transfer of Shares) and 20 (Tag Along and Come Along)".
>
> Further, by Article 18.4.3:
>
> > "the certificate of the Independent Expert shall, in the absence of manifest error, be final and binding".
>
> 9. The parties were unable to agree the Market Value (as defined) of the Claimants' shares, accordingly they jointly instructed Ernst & Young ("E&Y") to act as Independent Expert in accordance with the Articles. Notwithstanding that appointment, there remain, it seems, two issues for me to determine: (i) the date to be taken for the valuation, being either 29 July 2015 when the Claimants' employment was (wrongfully) terminated or 29 January 2016 when their contractual period of notice would have otherwise have expired; and (ii) whether the provisions of Article 13.3 are properly to be taken into account in determining Market Value.
>
> …
>
> 15. Clause 13.3 of the Articles ("the redemption premium provision") provides as follows:
>
> > "13.3 Exit Provisions
> > On a Share Sale the Proceeds of Sale shall be distributed in the order of priority set out in Article 13.2 unless the aggregate Proceeds of Sale distributed to the Living Bridge Investors is less than two times the Living Bridge Investment Amount in which case:
> >
> > 13.3.1 the holders of the A Ordinary Shares shall be paid the Issue Price of each such Share, together with a sum equal to any arrears or accruals of any dividends calculated down to and including the date of actual payment ('the A share proceeds');

> 13.3.2 the holders of the B Ordinary Shares shall be paid the B Share Prices of each such Share, together with a sum equal to any arrears or accruals of any dividends calculated down to and including the date of actual payment (the 'B Share Proceeds') plus an additional amount (the 'Additional B Share Proceeds') such that the A Share Proceeds, the B Share Proceeds and the Additional B Share Proceeds plus the Previous Distribution Amount in aggregate equal two times the Living Bridge Investment Amount; and
>
> 13.3.3 the balance of such assets shall be distributed amongst the holders of all the Equity Shares (other than the A Ordinary Shares) in proportion to their respective nominal values by reference to the total nominal value of those Equity Shares in aggregate, provided that the amount payable to the holders of the A Ordinary Shares and the B Ordinary Shares pursuant to the Article 13.3 shall not be subject to the 49.9% limit set out in Article 13.2.2
>
> For the purposes of Article 13.3.3 the Equity Shares shall be deemed to have the same nominal value being 0.1p per share."

16. Article 13.3 in effect directs that on sale of a controlling interest in the Company, the holders of other than Class A or B shares will not receive any distribution until the value of the equity is at least twice the amount invested by the holders of the A shares and B shares (i.e. the LB investment companies). The intention was clearly to provide a priority return for LB's investment.

…

21. Mr Leiper submitted that the result of such a construction – rendering his clients' shares of negligible value – made no commercial sense given that the Claimants had sold their shares in IPS for just under £2 million each some 6 months previously, being left with a 30% shareholding in the Defendant. In response to this Mr Quinn made the point that the shares which the Claimants sold were shares in IPS, that purchase being part of an investment deal which saw the incorporation of a new Company, namely the Defendant. The Claimants' shareholdings in the (new) Company were thus different shareholdings, held on entirely new terms agreed as part of the investment deal. Mr Quinn pointed out that in these circumstances Mr Leiper was not comparing like with like; in any event, he argued, the Articles in general and Article 13.3 in particular formed part of the overall deal documentation which had been finalised followed extensive negotiations and in relation to which the Claimants had had the benefit of expert legal advice. If the provisions which they had agreed operated disadvantageously, or proved uncommercial, to them then they may have a claim elsewhere, but it did not justify the court in "reading down" the clear wording of that agreement.'

It must be remembered that the articles are a contract which binds the shareholders.

Focus

The value of the shares depends on the rights attached to them.

16.03 Annual accounts

The annual accounts, at least of a larger unquoted company, would normally contain the chairman's statement with his views on the immediate past performance and future prospects of the company. Such a statement is unlikely to be available for smaller companies. The directors' report would normally summarise the results for the year and set out the directors' interests in the company's shares. The directors' report may comment on fixed asset valuations, charitable and political contributions, export sales, number of staff employed, policy with regard to the employment of disabled people, the reappointment of auditors and other matters of interest to shareholders or required by statute.

If the accounts have been audited, the audit report should highlight any particular areas where the auditors have reservations on the accounts of the company. The balance sheet and profit or loss account, which could both be in consolidated form if the company is the holding company of a group, together with the notes thereon will be set out in the accounts and will need to be studied.

For companies reporting under UK GAAP's (Generally Accepted Accounting Principles), FRS 102 (see **Chapter 20**), a statement of cash flows is required. This provides information about the changes in cash and cash equivalents of a company over the course of the financial year, showing separately changes from operating activities, investing activities and financing activities. It is reconciled to the profit or loss account either at a net (ie to net profit) or at a gross (ie reconciling sales, cost of sales, etc figures separately) level.

Small UK companies reporting under the FRSSE 2015 (see **Chapter 20**) are encouraged, but not required, to provide some cash flow information to reconcile reported profit to changes in cash for the year.

Companies reporting under FRS 102 have the choice of presenting gains or losses that are not included in the profit or loss account as either:

- items of Other Comprehensive Income within the single Statement of Comprehensive Income; or
- items making up the Statement of Comprehensive Income together with the result for the year from the profit or loss account.

Small UK companies reporting under the FRSSE 2015 report gains or losses that are not part of the profit and loss account, if any, in a separate Statement of Total Recognised Gains and Losses.

Many small UK companies do not need to be audited. Since October 2012, the audit exemption applies to companies satisfying at least two of the following:

- annual turnover of no more than £6.5 million;
- assets worth no more than £3.26 million;
- 50 or fewer employees on average.

However, if 10% or more of the shareholders request an audit, then an audit must be performed.

Any unaudited company satisfying at least two of the specific criteria can submit annual accounts to Companies House in an abbreviated form – that includes simply an abbreviated balance sheet and reduced notes.

On 22 January 2014, HMRC published two overview papers on the tax implications of the new UK GAAP (see **Chapter 20**).

16.04 Interim accounts for shareholders

Listed companies are required to produce interim accounts, which must:

- be issued within two months of the period end; and
- include condensed financial statements that comply with IAS 34, Interim Financial Reporting.

There must also be an interim management report containing an indication of important events that have occurred during the first six months of the financial year, and their impact on the condensed set of financial statements, and a description of the principal risks and uncertainties for the remaining six months of the financial year. There must be a responsibility statement.

Unquoted companies are not required to prepare interim accounts and rarely do so.

> **Focus**
>
> The most recent management accounts should be reviewed for unquoted companies, alongside interim accounts if there are any.

16.05 Budgets

The valuer will be seeking in many cases to estimate the maintainable future profit of the company for the purposes of his valuation and in this connection he will look at the company's budgetary control records, if any, and cash flow forecasts for the immediate future in order to see whether these can assist him in forming a view as to the likely future profitability of the company. Clearly if the company has been producing budgets for many years and has been meeting these budgets within a reasonable degree of accuracy it will be much more likely that the budgets for the immediate future period will be reasonably meaningful.

> **Focus**
>
> Some companies' budgets are consistently achieved within a realistic margin of error, but others are more aspirational than reliable.

16.06 Corporation tax return

Under the corporation tax self assessment system, companies have to complete return form CT600. The CT600, accounts and computation normally have to be submitted within 12 months of the end of the accounting period.

Most companies are required to pay their self-assessed corporation tax within nine months and one day after the end of their accounting period. Large companies are required to pay in the course of the current year, in up to four quarterly instalments, based on a company's estimated liability.

> **Focus**
>
> A comparison of tax returns with the accounts may highlight deferred taxation liabilities, reliefs or non-tax-deductible expenses.

16.07 Other tax returns

Other tax returns for example, forms P35 and P14 in respect of tax and National Insurance deducted from employees' wages and form CT61 in respect of payments made under deduction of income tax, would also be available. Forms P11D in respect of directors' expenses and benefits should be referred to as they should highlight any case where assets or resources are used for the personal benefit of directors which might require adjustment on any valuation of the company's shares.

Focus

In an owner-managed business, a purchaser of a minority shareholding may find himself regarded as a 'detested intruder' in a family company.

16.08 Management accounts

If the company prepares management accounts these should be analysed to see whether they can easily be reconciled with the audited financial accounts for past periods and if so whether they can be used to give an accurate view of the company's current position. This is important even where the shares are being valued some considerable time after the date to which the valuation relates as the valuation must be made on the basis of such information that was available at the valuation date, or could reasonably have been made available at the date of valuation.

Focus

The reliance to be placed on management accounts depends on their quality and availability.

16.09 Stock lists

Although the valuer is not attempting an audit he is nonetheless interested in the level of stocks carried by the company and the extent to which these may be obsolescent or slow moving and the provisions, if any, which have been made for stock write-down. Unsold fashion goods, for example, may be worth only a small fraction of their cost price because they have become virtually unsaleable.

From the accounts, the number of times the stock is turned over can be calculated (see **16.39**).

Focus

Such secondary information is particularly important where the accounts are not subject to audit.

16.10 Aged list of debtors

A list of debtors as close as practicable to the valuation date should be obtained and this should be analysed showing the period for which debts have been outstanding and any provisions made for doubtful debts. An aged list of debtors is often divided into those debts less than one month old, one month to two months, two months to three months, three months to six months and over six months.

> **Focus**
>
> Are there valid explanations to ensure any old debts are still recoverable?

16.11 Aged list of creditors

This list is merely the equivalent of the aged list of debtors and will show those creditors which have been outstanding for an abnormal length of time. The explanation for abnormally large creditors may be either that the company has specially favourable credit terms agreed with suppliers or that the company is in financial difficulty and having to make payments on account rather than be able to settle its liabilities as they become due.

> **Focus**
>
> Check the reason for the presence of old creditors on the list.

16.12 Property register

A register of properties owned by the company should be obtained, together with a summary of the terms on which such property is held, ie whether leasehold or freehold and, if leasehold, the terms of the lease and any potential liabilities for dilapidations or forthcoming rent reviews. Any provision for depreciation or amortisation should be analysed, property by property.

> **Focus**
>
> Property assets may contain substantial liabilities which need to be identified and allowed for.

16.13 Plant register – including fixed plant in buildings

A register of plant maintained by the company analysed by year of purchase, together with the accumulated depreciation, should be maintained which will help to show the valuer whether the plant is likely to be obsolete and whether the company is likely to have difficulty in replacing plant at the most opportune time.

A problem may arise in connection with the market value of plant and machinery where it is necessary to consider the age and adequacy of depreciation charged to the accounts and to consider the replacement cost of such equipment. Except in the case of a probable liquidation the valuer will be concerned with the value of such equipment to the business on a going concern basis and not with the realisable value on a forced sale.

> **Focus**
>
> Plant in buildings may qualify for capital allowances, provided that the appropriate claims have been made.

16.14 Dividend history

If dividends have been paid by the company a list of the dates on which they have been paid, together with the amount before and after tax, should be compiled.

If a minority (non-controlling) interest is being purchased the valuer will consider the dividends which the company has paid in the past, if any, or, as is likely in the absence of any dividends, the likely reasonable dividend which the company could pay to an unconnected minority shareholder having regard to the company's financial position and future cash requirements.

Consider the position of a third-party investor and the likelihood of his being able to obtain a regular dividend or return on his investments. The oppression of minority interests relief may be difficult or expensive to enforce.

> **Focus**
>
> What realistic return will an investor receive on his investment, if he is acquiring less than a controlling interest? There may be other ways that the non-controlling interest will receive a return, such as if an IPO or trade sale is planned in the future.

16.15 Directors' remuneration

A schedule of remuneration and pension contributions of directors and in some cases also of senior management should be obtained as, in the case of small companies in particular, it used to be common practice to take out a large proportion of the profits in the form of remuneration or pension premiums and this could have a significant effect on the value of the company's shares. However, it is now common practice for shareholder directors to take dividends in order to obtain the imputation credit and avoid the National Insurance on remuneration for both the employee and employer.

If an open market valuation is required for tax purposes, an estimate will be needed of the market rate of remuneration for directors and senior management. An effort should be made to decide the extent to which remuneration would be commercially justifiable for the work done and whether this represents a reward for labour rather than an entrepreneurial profit, taken by way of dividend.

If there are any material loans to directors, or for that matter, by directors to the company, these should be analysed and any taxation consequences considered.

> **Focus**
>
> If looking to acquire a small shareholding, consideration should be given to the position of an investor with a minority interest, particularly if not an employee or director.

16.16 Management personnel

It may be important to obtain a list of managers involved in the company, together with a brief synopsis of their careers to date and particular expertise. The list would obviously show their ages and remuneration and a synopsis of any service contracts they have with the company and whether they are particularly important to the company's business or could be replaced without undue difficulty if necessary. It would also be important to discover whether they are protected in any way by key man accident insurance, which would enable the company to ride a disruption caused by the loss of a key member of the management team.

The quality of management should also be assessed.

> **Focus**
>
> The object of the exercise is to evaluate, in respect of continuity of management, the risks to which the potential purchaser of shares will be exposed.

16.17 Employees

Particulars of the company's work force should be obtained, together with details of any significant agreements with unions and the level of skill and experience of the work force. These should be reviewed in the light of the ability to add to or reduce the workforce should circumstances require. If, for example, the company is engaged in a business where it takes five years to train personnel it may not be possible to make part of the workforce redundant because of a short-term reduction in orders without severely restricting the company's ability to benefit from a subsequent increase in business which would necessitate recruiting and training skilled personnel. Conversely a company which relies mainly on part-time or casual unskilled employees could relatively easily adjust the workforce to the work on hand. It should also be ascertained whether the company's employees are unionised and if so whether any major pay claim has been, or is about to be, submitted.

Focus

Workforce skills and availability are potentially major factors in risk assessment for the would-be purchaser of shares.

16.18 Pension scheme

The company's pension scheme, if any, should be examined both from the point of view of the likely contentment and future loyalty of the employees and the extent to which, in the case of a small self administered scheme for example, there have been interconnected transactions with the company, such as where the pension fund owns premises occupied by the company, or where loans have been made from the pension fund to the company within the authorised limits for small self-administered schemes. There may also be a liability to pay further increasing premiums, and the funding basis of the scheme may have to be examined and discussed with the actuaries involved.

In *Gareth Clark v HMRC* [2016] UKFTT 0630 (TC), pension funds were held in Mr Clark's self-invested pension scheme (SIPP) with Suffolk Life and were transferred to a new scheme, Laversham Marketing Limited Pension Scheme, and from there to Laversham Marketing Limited (LML) and then Cedan Investments Management Limited (CIM), out of which sums were lent to Mr Clark and funds were placed with an investment management firm, Quilter & Co.

Mr Clark came across as a man who had been trying to do his honest best to improve the investment performance of his pension funds, but who had had the misfortune to become involved with an organisation, Aston Court Chambers, whose attitude and operation might fairly be described as unprofessional, a circumstance that Mr Clark now deeply regretted.

Mr Clark's approach was against a notice of assessment dated 25 March 2014 issued by HMRC for the year ended 5 April 2010 in relation to an unauthorised payments charge and an unauthorised payments surcharge pursuant to Part 4 of the Finance Act 2004 ('FA 2004'). The assessment, which was a discovery assessment under s 29 of the Taxes Management Act 1970 ('TMA'), was in respect of an alleged unauthorised member payment by a registered pension scheme within the meaning of FA 2004, s 160(2). The alleged unauthorised payment was in the sum of £2,115,049.68; the sum assessed was the aggregate of £846,019.87, being 40% of the alleged unauthorised payment, and a 15% surcharge of £317,257.45.

The court concluded that:

> '(1) The trust constituting the LML Pension was void for uncertainty.
>
> (2) The LML Pension was not a registered pension scheme within s150 FA2004.
>
> (3) Consequently, the transfer of funds by LML Pension to LML in May 2009 was not a payment by a registered pension scheme and that payment was not an unauthorised member payment within the meaning of s160(2) FA2004.
>
> ...
>
> (a) The Suffolk Life SIPP was a registered pension scheme of which Mr Clark was a member;
>
> (b) In respect of the transfer of funds by the Suffolk Life SIPP to the LML Pension on 21 April 2009, a resulting trust of those funds arose in favour of the Suffolk Life SIPP;
>
> (c) Notwithstanding that, that transfer of funds was a "payment" within the meaning of that term in s160(2); and
>
> (d) That payment was in respect of Mr Clark, a member of the Suffolk Life SIPP.
>
> (6) Consequently, the transfer of funds by the Suffolk Life SIPP to the LML Pension was a payment by a registered pension scheme in respect of a person who was or who had been a member of the pension scheme, and was not authorised by s 164 FA 2004. Accordingly, that payment was an unauthorised member payment within s 160(2) FA 2004.
>
> **Determination**
>
> 142. By finding that there was an unauthorised member payment in respect of Mr Clark in the tax year 2009–10, we have determined the substantive issue in this case in favour of HMRC. Mr Clark is chargeable to both the unauthorised payments charge and the unauthorised payments surcharge. However, the question remains whether we should confirm the assessment.
>
> 143. In the rather exceptional circumstances of this case, that question is not one we consider we should resolve without further submissions. Although, in answer to a question from the Tribunal at the outset of the hearing, the parties confirmed that, notwithstanding that the assessment on Mr Clark had been a discovery assessment, there was no issue on the validity of the assessment itself, or the application of s 29 of the Taxes Management Act 1970, in the events which happened the nature of the substantive issue itself developed well beyond the pleaded cases of the parties. The original case had been concerned exclusively with the question of the application of s 160(2) FA 2004 to the transfer of funds by LML Pension to LML. In that respect we have found for Mr Clark. But in doing so, the issue of the initial transfer of funds from the Suffolk Life SIPP to the LML Pension fell to be considered, and it is in that respect that we have found in favour of HMRC, and in respect of which the chargeability of Mr Clark to tax has arisen.
>
> 144. Although we received some, fairly brief, submissions on the assessment question were we to find that the only unauthorised member payment was the transfer of funds from the Suffolk Life SIPP to the LML Pension, that was only one of the possible outcomes of our consideration of the case. In the circumstances, we should give Mr Clark the opportunity, should he be so advised, of disputing the validity of the assessment so far as it is said to relate to the transfer of funds by the Suffolk Life SIPP to the LML Pension, and in the light of the conclusions we have reached on the substantive issue.'

> **Focus**
>
> The workforce pension arrangements could notably affect the value of the shares, particularly if defined benefit schemes are involved.

16.19 Order backlog

The valuer should obtain a schedule of outstanding orders. If the company has a reasonable backlog of orders, which remains fairly constant over time, this is an indication of a stable trading position. If the backlog of orders is increasing it implies that steps will have to be taken to expand production, which in turn means increased capital investment if such orders are not to be lost to competition. A reducing order backlog might mean that the company's products are losing their attraction to customers and that if no positive steps are being or can be taken there may soon be a problem requiring a corresponding cut back in production. A very long order book however does not necessarily portray a healthy company because it could arise if orders are being placed protectively to reserve a place in the queue. It can then be found that a large proportion of such orders are later cancelled as the customer makes alternative arrangements.

> **Focus**
>
> Risk is reduced where the customer requirements and the company's ability to meet them are in balance.

16.20 List of customers

It may be helpful to obtain a list of active customers, together with a list of the approximate monetary amount of purchases by customer in the last 12 months. This would give an indication of the concentration of sales to particular customers. Ideally it would be desirable to analyse sales on a monthly basis over the previous 12 months; this would also indicate any particular seasonal trends, which might require further investigation. It is normally risky for a company to be supplying goods or services to a single or small number of key customers. However, a retail business may only be able to provide information relating to, say, the average number and size of transactions.

> **Focus**
>
> This is part of the process of evaluating risk.

16.21 List of suppliers

A list of suppliers, together with the purchases therefrom over the previous 12 months, again analysed by month if possible, would be interesting in showing the degree to which purchases had been concentrated with particular suppliers and whether or not there is a seasonal trend. If supplies are obtained from a small number of key suppliers the valuer may need to identify whether alternative suppliers can readily be found and, if so, the penalty in terms of cost or quality which has led to the concentration of orders with existing suppliers.

> **Focus**
>
> In general terms, the wider the spread, the lower the risk, but it does depend on the circumstances applicable to the particular business.

16.22 Insurance records

The valuer is interested in insurance records, not only to see that the company is fully covered for all likely claims, but also to check that values of assets for insurance purposes are not too dissimilar to the values shown by the asset schedules used in his valuation. In many cases the potentially significant claims for which insurance is required are not so much fire and consequential loss, but are those related to product liability and professional negligence.

> **Focus**
>
> Assessing and minimising risk is important for any business, and the difference between current value and replacement cost could be material.

16.23 Professional valuations

In some cases the directors will have commissioned a professional valuation of, for example, real estate property, for the purpose of financial reporting and these would obviously be useful to the valuer of the company's shares. However, it would be worth discussing the values with the valuer if at all possible to see whether the basis of valuation adopted is appropriate for a valuation of the company's shares. If, for example, all the shares were being valued and a break-up basis were being considered the property would need to be valued on a forced disposal basis rather than on the basis of the value to the company if it continues to be used for its existing purposes. There can be considerable differences between values on an alternative use basis following the winding up of a company and on an existing use basis within the company's business. If the company's property interests are leasehold, the cost of dilapidations at the end of a lease could be material, as could be the benefits of the capital allowances on integral fixtures.

> **Focus**
>
> A valuation is relevant for the purpose for which it is commissioned, and may not be applicable in different circumstances.

16.24 Contractual obligations

Contracts take many forms and may or may not be recognised in the financial statements (accounts), depending on factors such as whether they are executory (ie.neither party has yet performed) and also the GAAP (eg UK GAAP, IFRS) adopted.

Companies frequently enter into normal trading arrangements such as leases for property or plant, which could have onerous conditions on early termination. In the case of real property there may be potentially significant dilapidations and, in the case of plant, early termination might require the payment of all outstanding contractual rental premiums due possibly with a nominal discount for early payment. These onerous conditions are of particular significance if the company is being valued on a break-up basis.

The valuer should therefore be aware of such contracts and may need to assess the effects of early termination.

The company may, on the other hand, be the beneficiary of favourable contracts, for example, agency or franchise arrangements with other parties, and such contracts should be listed so that the valuer can consider the likelihood and the effect of termination of one or more of such contracts. This is particularly important where a substantial change in the shareholding is contemplated and it may be appropriate in such cases to obtain confirmation from the supplier or franchisor concerned that the agreement will not be terminated on the change of share ownership.

Claims under contractual arrangements may be significant. For example, in the construction industry there are often material claims as a result of delays in supplying goods or equipment by other parties, or unforeseen problems in the nature or state of land on which development is taking place. The valuer should seek a list of contracts subject to claims, together with an estimate of the amount of each claim and the likely settlement figure. There may also be insurance claims outstanding and again these should be listed and quantified.

Focus

Identify and quantify contractual risk.

16.25 Contingent liabilities

The company may have a liability, legal or moral, to pay pensions or redundancy payments to former employees; such potential liabilities should be listed and analysed so that the likely effect on the business can be taken into account in the valuation.

If the company is engaged in litigation, either in respect of damages that it is seeking, or claims that are being made against it, the particulars of the outstanding law suit should be considered and the likely outcome of the litigation estimated so far as possible.

> **Focus**
>
> Identify and quantify risk arising from litigation.

16.26 Contingent assets

The valuer should seek a list of assets not shown on the balance sheet or shown purely at a nominal figure. Internally generated goodwill is one such asset, but that will normally be dealt with in the valuation itself. Other such assets, however, might consist of various forms of intellectual property that have been developed internally rather than purchased from a third party; the requirements for when these are recognised vary according to the type of intellectual property involved and the GAAP (eg UK GAAP, IFRS) adopted. Again, according to the GAAP adopted, some purchased intangible assets may be recognised separately on the balance sheet and some may be assumed within purchased goodwill.

Significant categories of intellectual property include patents, trademarks and registered designs. The valuer should discuss the importance of these items with management.

Care must be taken in considering the value of patents and similar items in order to avoid double counting. If, for example, a patent is useful for the purpose of the company's trade, that value would be reflected in the company's actual and forecast profits and, hence, is included in any capitalised value of those profits. If, on the other hand, the patent in question has been licensed to some other party, the royalties received and the capitalised value thereof would be reflected in results and forecasts. If an agreement has been entered into but material royalties have yet to be received the past results might require adjustment for the future royalties receivable from the patent.

> **Focus**
>
> Consider whether there are contingent assets that require valuation separately from the business.

16.27 Brochures and catalogues

The valuer should review the company's website and should also ask for copies of the company's current sales literature and those for the recent past as the purpose of the appraisal is to enable the valuer to consider the future profitability of the company. In order to do so he has to be familiar with the products of the company and sales literature, including that available online, is a useful means of obtaining this background information. It would also tend to show whether the company's product line changes markedly year by year which in turn will help when deciding whether stock has been correctly valued as it would be unusual to show finished products in the inventory at full value if they were no longer in the current sales catalogue.

> **Focus**
>
> Understand the business of the company.

16.28 Trade associations

In **Chapter 15**, it is noted that trade associations and trade magazines may be a useful source of information both to identify possible comparable quoted companies and to consider the financial prospects for the industry. This information may well be available within the company itself, or readily obtainable through the company's membership of the appropriate trade association. A valuer would normally be able to obtain such information more easily through the company itself than externally.

> **Focus**
>
> All relevant information helps to identify and quantify risk and growth which together drive value.

16.29 Company history

The valuation report will normally include a brief history of the company in order to put into context its likely future results. This information might well be obtainable directly from the company from, for example, anniversary literature which would only require updating and editing by the valuer. It will obviously be necessary to confirm that the history is factually correct.

> **Focus**
>
> It is important to understand the business being valued.

16.30 Company visit

As well as examining the written information made available to him the valuer will normally find it useful to visit the company's premises and see for himself the activities undertaken. During the course of this visit it will often be helpful to discuss with the various managers their activities within the overall company framework and find out from them the likely constraints on the company's future growth. This will both serve to confirm the projected future results and help in assessing the impact of the individual managers. It will also enable the valuer to see plant in operation and for example see whether recently acquired equipment is running satisfactorily or is giving rise to unexpected teething troubles.

16.31 Auditors

Where the valuer is not already auditor to the company it may be possible to arrange a visit to the auditors to consult their working papers and to discuss with them the recent history and prospects of the company. The degree to which it is reasonable to seek the auditors' co-operation would of course depend very much on the purpose of the valuation and the number of shares being valued. In the case of a commercial take-over, for example, there would normally be a detailed accountants' report on which the valuation would subsequently be based.

Focus

The auditors will only be able to co-operate with the valuer if the other shareholders and management support the proposed transfer of the shares being valued.

16.32 Solicitors

The company's solicitors would often be consulted if litigation were pending in order to confirm the company's views as to the likely outcome of the litigation.

Focus

Check and quantify risk. The vendor's co-operation is essential if confidential information is involved.

16.33 Bankers

In certain cases it would be appropriate for the valuer to discuss with the company's bankers the existing facilities and the extent to which further working capital would be forthcoming should it be required.

Focus

Bankers, like other professionals working for the company, will only be able to assist if so instructed by management of the company being valued.

16.34 Third parties

If it is possible to obtain information about a company from customers, suppliers or competitors it is obviously helpful to do so as they are likely to be able to give a fairly clear cut view of many of the company's strong and weak points. In practice it is not very common to be able to arrange discussions with such parties where the valuation is confidential. However, information may be in the public domain through trade associates, Internet search, etc.

> **Focus**
>
> The fuller the information, the more reliable the valuation.

16.35 Accounting ratios

Accounting ratios can be useful in highlighting trends by comparison with previous years of the same company, to show whether certain areas are improving or getting worse, and by comparison with quoted companies or other unquoted companies to show how the company compares, be it favourably or unfavourably, with other companies engaged in broadly similar activities. For published accounting ratios, see **15.18–15.19** and **Appendix E**.

It may be necessary to adjust for differences in accounting policy, especially where different GAAP is involved, to compare like with like.

> **Focus**
>
> Past results may or may not be an indication of likely future profits. It may be helpful to consider the accounting ratios described in **16.36–16.45** below.

16.36 Percentages

A very simple accounting ratio comparison technique is to convert balance sheet and profit and loss account figures into appropriate percentages in order to make relevant comparisons.

16.37 The credit ratio

The credit ratio is computed as follows:

Trade creditors/cost of sales

The ratio can be multiplied by 365 to show the average length of credit taken in days or by 52 if the information is wanted in weeks or by 12 if in months.

Where the credit ratio is high it usually means either that the company is in a very strong position and can force its suppliers to make interest free money available through trade credit or that it is living from hand to mouth and having considerable difficulty in paying creditors as they fall due. The distinction is of some importance.

16.38 The debtor ratio

This is calculated as follows:

$$\frac{\text{Debtors, including bills receivable}}{\text{Sales}}$$

Again this proportion can be multiplied by 365, 52 or 12 to show the average length of credit granted to customers in days, weeks or months. A high debtor ratio may indicate that the company has difficulty in collecting its debts as they fall due and may mean that some of the debts are doubtful.

16.39 Rate of stock turnover

The rate of stock turnover is computed as follows:

$$\frac{\text{Cost of sales}}{\text{Average stock}}$$

Cost of sales will be computed on the basis of opening stock, plus purchases, less closing stock, in the case of a trading organisation and include manufacturing costs in the case of a manufacturer. This ratio may be converted into the time taken to turnover stock by dividing it into 365, 52 or 12 depending on whether the answer is required in days, weeks or months.

The stock ratio can be broken down into a raw material ratio which is the closing stock of raw material divided by the value of production, and a work in progress ratio which is the closing value of work in progress divided by production, and a finished stock ratio which is the closing stock divided by sales.

16.40 Working capital

Working capital ratio is usually arrived at as follows:

$$\frac{\text{Working capital}}{\text{Sales}}$$

The working capital consists of the current assets less current liabilities.

16.41 The return on capital employed (ROCE)

There are many different ways of calculating this figure. Typical approaches include

- EBIT (earnings before interest and tax)/total capital

where capital comprises the net figure for balance sheet assets less liabilities.

As an alternative, ROCE may be measured as:

- Profit before (or after) tax/equity capital

It is important to be consistent between the numerator and denominator when establishing a preferred measurement of ROCE. Thus, if earnings before interest are measured in the numerator, (ie the return is to the providers of both debt and equity capital) then the denominator must include debt capital as well as equity capital. Conversely, if earnings are measured after interest in the numerator (ie the return is to the providers of equity capital only), then the denominator should be a measure of equity capital only.

There are also different ways of measuring total capital: it may be on balance sheet measures or it may be based on value. Many companies have developed their own specific approach to measurement of ROCE that they consider to be most appropriate to their business.

16.42 Current ratio

This is calculated on the following basis:

$$\frac{\text{Current assets}}{\text{Current liabilities}}$$

It is usually shown as a proportion say, 1.5 to 1.

If the ratio is less than unity, eg 0.75 to 1, the reason for the low ratio must be carefully examined. It could indicate that more working capital should be injected into the company and this, of course, would be a depreciatory factor in the valuation.

16.43 Liquid asset ratio (acid test ratio)

This is calculated on the basis of:

$$\frac{\text{Current assets minus stock}}{\text{Current liabilities}}$$

and is usually shown as a proportion.

Again, a ratio of less than unity could indicate that the company is, in theory, insolvent, ie not able to pay its debts as they fall due. This could be a major factor in the valuation if anyone with the requisite sized claim could be capable of initiating liquidation.

16.44 Cash ratio

The cash ratio, ie cash divided by current liabilities is not commonly used these days.

16.45 Dividend cover and fixed interest charges cover

Dividend cover has already been considered in some detail at **12.06**. Fixed interest charges cover is represented by:

$$\frac{\text{Net income plus net interest after tax}}{\text{Net load interest after tax}}$$

Preference dividend cover is calculated according to whether the preference shares and their dividends fall to be recognised as debt, equity or as a hybrid of the two. When preference shares and their dividends are treated as debt (eg set rate of dividend payable on mandatorily redeemable preference shares), their dividend cover should be measured as for fixed interest shown above.

16.46 Earnings per share

Earnings per share have already been considered, see **12.03.**

Chapter 17

Valuation of intellectual property and other intangibles

Signposts

17.01 Introduction

Intellectual property protection is given by law in respect of patents, trade marks, service marks, copyright, registered design rights, moral rights, plant breeding rights and so on. Guernsey has recently introduced laws allowing the registration of image rights and endorsement fees thus facilitating the registration of image rights by sportsmen and other performers under the Image

Rights (Bailiwick of Guernsey) Ordinance 2012. See also *Agassi v Robinson* [2006] STC 1056. The law allows the owner of intellectual property to proceed against anyone using the protected property without permission, and a normal remedy would be an injunction and damages. Know-how, secret processes and confidential information may be protected under specific or implied confidentiality agreements and in some cases there may be mileage in an action for 'passing off', for example, in relation to brand names. In the *Advocaat* case, *Erven Warwick BV v J Townsend & Sons (Hull) Ltd,* [1980] RPC 31, [1979] 2 All ER 927, Lord Diplock described 'passing off' as including:

(1) a misrepresentation;
(2) made by a trader in the course of his trade;
(3) to prospective customers of his or ultimate consumers of goods and services supplied by him;
(4) which is calculated to injure the business or goodwill of another trader (in the sense that it is a reasonably foreseeable consequence);
(5) which causes actual damage to a business or goodwill of the trader by whom the action is brought or will probably do so.

Although it is sometimes possible to challenge intellectual property agreements on the grounds of unfair competition, for example, under the anti-trust laws in the USA or the provisions of Articles 81 and 82 of the Treaty of the European Community, the protection given to the holder of intellectual property and allied rights is normally effective in the sense that it prevents or inhibits third parties from making use of such property without payment. What intellectual property protection cannot do, however, is, of itself, to give any value to those rights. The protection is purely negative in the sense of preventing competition and cannot give value to a copy of a work or a patented invention, if there are no customers wishing to buy.

With a patented invention, it is quite common for the patent holder to be involved in the manufacture and distribution of the invention. It is also common practice for the original inventor to license the invention to an established manufacturer, or new business set up for the purpose, and the terms of such a licence may vary enormously. It can be limited as to time or by reference to the geographical area within which the goods may be manufactured or sold, and may be an exclusive licence which would prevent anyone else, including the inventor, from exploiting the invention, or the licencee may be one of many people authorised to produce the goods. Finance Act 2012, Sch 2 introduced CTA 2010, Part 8A, ss 357A–357GE, the UK's Patent Box legislation to compete with other EU countries, such as Luxembourg, Ireland, Netherlands, Belgium and others. This is likely to encourage UK businesses to patent the results of their research and development (R&D), where possible. This is dealt with in some detail in *Intellectual Property Law and Taxation* by Eastaway et al, published by Sweet & Maxwell. With copyright material, it is usual for the author to licence a specialised publisher to produce books or recordings rather than to do it himself. In some cases the originator of the intellectual property assigns it outright for a lump sum rather than granting a licence for a royalty. However, an assignment may also be in consideration for an ongoing royalty or a lump sum, so the means of exploitation is not restricted in any particular way.

Intellectual property rights depend for their value on the income that can be generated from exploiting the invention, or publishing the work, or franchising with the benefit of the trade mark, therefore the value of the rights is, normally, the present value of that earning capacity.

There are really two aspects to the valuation of intellectual property. One is the royalty value which is the amount which the licensor could expect to receive on sale of each item of product, and the other is capital value which could be received on outright assignment. Obviously the capital value is directly related to the royalty value in that it is the discounted present value of the likely future royalty stream from licensing the product. There is an infinite number of variables between licensing entirely for royalties and outright assignment for a lump sum. A common solution in practice is for a reduced lump sum and an ongoing royalty of a lesser amount, ie a mixture of lump sum and royalty payments.

Valuations of intellectual property may be required for commercial or accounting purposes or for fiscal purposes. It may be necessary to show that the proposed royalty level is reasonable for transfer pricing purposes and that the lump sum, if any, is at market value, on an assignment or deemed assignment of intellectual property rights giving rise to a tax charge.

As with any valuation of property, the first step is to identify what is being valued: in this case, the precise intellectual property rights and the basis on which they are protected (see *Borland's Trustee v Steel Bros & Co Ltd* [1901] 1 Ch 279; *Short v Treasury Comrs* [1948] 1 KB 116). A valuation for fiscal purposes will assume that the rights are capable of assignment and that the assignee would acquire a valid title to those rights, subject to any rights or restrictions, actually attached to the intellectual property (*Re Crossman* (1936) 15 ATC 94). It is by no means uncommon to find that, in the course of licensing intellectual property to a licensee, it will also be necessary to obtain permission from another owner of intellectual property in order to exploit the product commercially. A film script based on a book is itself copyright but would require the acquisition of the film rights or a licence from the author of the book before a film could be made based on the script.

A patent may be assigned or licensed while the application is still pending. Copyright, under the Copyright, Designs and Patents Act 1988, s 91, may be dealt in before the work has been created, as a future copyright, and licensed or assigned as such.

Some of the financial reporting (ie accounting) requirements of intellectual property are discussed in **Chapter 20**.

Focus

Commercial, financial and fiscal problems with the valuation of intellectual property are introduced.

17.02 Open market value

Whether the transfer or licence is for a lump sum or periodic royalty payment, or a combination of the two, the open market value is the price which the licence or assignment would be expected to fetch if sold in the open market at the appropriate time. This applies for fiscal purposes for inheritance tax (IHTA 1984, s 160), chargeable gains (TCGA 1992, s 272), and where taxable as income (*Gold Coast Selection Trust Ltd v Humphrey* [1948] 2 All ER 379). For fiscal purposes open market value is likely to be similar to a commercial market value, as there are no deeming provisions for the valuation of intellectual property as there are for unquoted shares and securities, for example, in relation to the information assumed to be available, under either TCGA 1992, s 273 or IHTA 1984, s 168.

As with unquoted shares, the problem in the valuation of intellectual property is very often to find a meaningful comparison where the market is limited.

An open market assumes a hypothetical willing buyer and a hypothetical willing seller (*Lynall v IRC* (1971) 47 TC 375). The open market implies that the property is offered for sale to the world at large, so that all potential purchasers have an equal opportunity to make an offer as a result of it being openly known what it is that is being offered for sale (*Lynall v IRC* (1971) 47 TC 375 at 411). The open market means the market in which the property in question would normally be dealt with (*Salomon v Customs and Excise Comrs* [1966] 3 All ER 871; *Glass v IRC* 1915 SC 449; *Duke of Buccleuch v IRC* [1967] 1 AC 506). The contrast is between an open market where all potential purchasers are assumed to be around and a closed market where there is a sale on a confidential basis, for example between associated companies (*IRC v Clay* and *IRC v Buchanan* [1914] 3 KB 466).

The market value assumption that there is a willing seller who is not forced to sell (*Lynall v IRC* (1971) 47 TC 375) is counter-balanced by the assumption that the purchaser is a man of prudence and not someone perhaps carried away in the throes of an auction (*Salvesen's Trustees v IRC* (1930) 9 ATC 43; *Caton's Administrators v Couch* [1995] STC (SCD) 34; *Clark v Green* [1995] STC (SCD) 99; *Holt v IRC* (1953) 32 ATC 402). As a prudent purchaser, he will have made all reasonable enquiries concerning the property being acquired, for example whether the patents are being challenged in any way (*Findlay's Trustees v IRC* (1938) 22 ATC 437).

The open market will take into account the fact that there might be special purchasers. For example, a brilliant invention for the improvement of an existing product might be dependent for its commercial exploitation on a licence from the patent holder of the original product; which may mean that the original patent holder is likely to offer a special price, or conversely that the subsequent inventor needs to offer a high price to the original patent holder in order to exploit his improvements. Where the existence of a special purchaser is common knowledge or can be reasonably inferred it may well have an effect on the market value (*Hawkings-Byass v Sassen* [1996] STC (SCD) 319; *Raja Vyricherla Narayana Gajapatiraju v Revenue Divisional Officer Vizagapatam* [1939] AC 302; *Robinson Bros (Brewers) Ltd v Houghton and Chester-le-Street Assessment Committee* [1938] AC 321; *IRC v Clay, IRC v Buchanan* [1914] 3 KB 466; *Glass v IRC* 1915 SC 449 and *Lynall v IRC* (1971) 47 TC 375).

Although the special purchaser may in this way enter into the valuation consideration, the actual identity of the purchaser or seller is irrelevant in determining the market value (*Battle v IRC* [1979] TR 483).

Focus

Identify the intellectual property, the hypothetical buyer and what he would be prepared to pay; identify the hypothetical seller and what he would be prepared to part with his rights for; where these coincide is the market value. Danckwerts, J described this as 'a dim world peopled by indeterminate spirits of fictitious or unborn sales' (*Re Holt* (1953) 32 ATC 402 and 403).

17.03 Evidence of open market value

In spite of the open market value requirements for tax purposes, the fact is that most intellectual property licensing agreements and assignments are by their nature private transactions between a purchaser and seller on a confidential basis and the terms are seldom made public. Although, therefore, real deals form the best evidence of market value (*McNamee v IRC* [1954] IR 214), it is necessary to consider whether there are any special circumstances affecting the deal (*Stanyforth v IRC* [1930] AC 339; *IRC v Marr's Trustees* (1906) 44 SLR 647; *Holt v IRC* (1953) 32 ATC 402). In practice, information relating to real deals in intellectual property are hard to come by, although they may sometimes be inferred from articles in trade magazines or take-overs and management buyouts, where intellectual property is a major portion of the target company's assets.

Market value in private deals becomes of increasing importance as a result of the revision of the transfer pricing rules in FA 1998, ss 108–111 and Sch 16 (inserted as TA 1988, s 770A and Sch 28AA) which significantly widen the categories of persons regarded as connected for transfer pricing purposes, and passes the responsibility onto the parties to make the appropriate declarations of non-arm's length transactions as a result of self assessment for companies.

When valuing intellectual property rights for fiscal purposes, it is normally necessary to look at the entire bundle of rights being dealt with in an actual transaction (or, where there is no such transaction, a deemed disposal), and it is to be assumed that the real or hypothetical vendor is putting together the most attractive package of rights available. Most inventions are covered not by a single patent but by a master patent, with additional subsidiary patents protecting additional inventive steps that have been introduced in the course of production and development. Clearly, although each patent is an individual intellectual property right it is interdependent in order to exploit the full commercial value. There may also be production drawings which are copyright, designs which are registered and know-how which is necessary for proper commercial exploitation. This bundle of rights is often referred to as 'optimum lotting' and received judicial support in *Earl of Ellesmere v IRC* [1918] 2 KB 735. However, it is not necessary to consider every unlikely combination of rights in order to arrive at a maximum market value, as the exploitation has to be assumed to be reasonable in the circumstances (*Duke of Buccleuch v IRC* [1967] 1 AC 506; *Smyth v IRC* [1941] IR 643; *Salvesen's Trustees v IRC* (1930) 9 ATC 43; *A-G of Ceylon v Mackie* [1952] 2 All ER 775).

As with valuation generally, the benefit of hindsight is not available (*Lynall v IRC* (1971) 47 TC 375; *Holt v IRC* (1953) 32 ATC 402; *Salvesen's Trustees v IRC* (1930) 9 ATC 43; *Buckingham v Francis* [1986] 2 All ER 738; *Re Bradberry, National Provincial Bank Ltd v Bradberry* and *Re Fry, Tasker v Gulliford* [1943] Ch 35).

As with the valuation of shares, the general state of the economy, industry sector etc. will have an effect both on the discount rate to be applied in calculating a present value and on the estimate of the future royalty stream which could be earned by the intellectual property concerned.

The relevant factors in choosing the appropriate discount rate will depend upon the rate of interest available on risk-free investments such as gilts, the anticipated rate of inflation and the appropriate premium for risk, including the risks of obsolescence. In many cases, the weighted average cost of capital of a hypothetical buyer or seller for the asset will be a reasonable starting point – the necessity of adding a premium to this figure should then be considered.

In calculating the likely future royalty stream, it is obviously necessary to consider the estimated commercial life of the intellectual property concerned. This could range from the unexpired term of a patent with a life of 20 years to copyright which may have a life of 70 years plus the remaining life of the author, or trademarks which typically have an indefinite life. However, the copyright work may have a realistic commercial life of very much less than the remaining life of the copyright, eg, a pop record, while a patent may continue to be commercially useful through the development of additional patents covering design improvements, long after the original master patent has expired. Anticipated royalties will also depend on the profitability of the product, the likely competition, the general economic climate and the requirement for capital to develop a product.

> **Focus**
>
> Much of the case law relating to share sales can be applied to intellectual property.

17.04 Case law – tax avoidance schemes

Assets which need to be valued in order to arrive at the value of the shares or business include intellectual property such as patents, which were considered in *RCC v Tower MCashback LLP 1* [2011] STC 1143 in which the Supreme Court found for HMRC. The case concerned a claim for capital allowances for software rights acquired by two limited liability partnerships as part of a marketed tax avoidance scheme. At [25] of the judgement Lord Hope explained that:

> 'the investor members of the LLPs were individuals with large incomes who themselves put up only 25% of the consideration said to have been paid for acquiring rights in software. The remaining 75% was provided by interest-free loans on non-recourse terms, made to the investor members by special purpose vehicles set up for the purpose. HMRC rely strongly on the circularity of these

transactions as more fully described below. The essential issue (simply stated but not simply resolved) is whether the LLPs incurred capital expenditure, to the whole stated consideration, in acquiring software rights for the purpose of their trades.'

And at [32]:

'Apart from the three main groups of participants' two banks, both based in Guernsey, were involved in the arrangements. These were R&D Investments Ltd ('R&D') and Janus Holdings Ltd ('Janus'). As explained in more detail below, R&D held security deposits placed with it by MCashback, which R&D in turn deposited with Janus as security for a loan by Janus to a Tower Finance company (described in the scheme's explanatory material as the 'Lending SPV'). The Tower Finance company made interest-free non-recourse loans to individual investor members of the LLPs.'

And at [74]:

'HMRC has now abandoned the soft finance argument as such. But it has not vanished completely, as appears from para 66 of HMRC's printed case, quoted at para 25 above. Before this Court Mr Prosser argued (though this is probably an oversimplification of his more subtle arguments) that even if an investor member did spend the money which he borrowed (say £225,000) as well as his own money (say £75,000) he did not incur expenditure of £300,000 on acquiring software rights, because only £50,000 of the money reached MCashback, and £225,000 went into a loop from which MCashback received no immediate benefit at all. If in the future money were to flow back to MCashback out of the loop it would be because of its own commercial success in generating clearing fees. Whatever the £225,000 was spent on, it was not spent on acquiring software rights from MCashback, because the £225,000 never reached MCashback. (I leave open for the present the expenditure, in this example, of the £25,000 on fees and expenses).'

And at [75]:

'The judge was right to emphasise that the transaction was the subject of tough negotiation between MCashback and Tower (whose founder members stood to make a large gain, when the investor members' rights had been fully satisfied, if the M Rewards scheme was as successful as both sides hoped it would be). The negotiations were tough because MCashback (unlike BGE in *BMBF*) really did need up-front finance in order to roll out its software and give effect to its business plan. It saw itself as parting with potentially very valuable rights indefinitely (the investor members dropped out after ten years, but the founder members did not) for only a modest part (just over 18% before fees and expenses, or just under 17% after fees and expenses) of the total capital apparently being raised. That was because 75% of the capital raised, although not simply a sham, was really being used in an attempt to quadruple the investor members' capital allowances. That is what the tough bargain which Tower struck with MCashback enabled Tower to offer to its investor members. I have already (para 47 above) quoted Lord Goff in *Ensign* [1992] STC 226 at 245–246. The facts of that case were different, since in that case there was not "in any meaningful sense" a loan at all. In this case there was a loan but there was not, in any meaningful sense, an incurring of expenditure of the borrowed money in the acquisition of software rights. It went into a loop in order to enable the LLPs to indulge in a tax avoidance scheme. Despite the shortcomings in his decision, the Special Commissioner was essentially right in his conclusion in para 138 (quoted in [56], above).'

And finally concluded at [78]:

> 'I would direct the conclusions and amendments in the closure notices to be amended to allow 25% only of the FYAs claimed. That is in one way generous to the LLPs, since in fact about one-third of their contribution (the £25,000 in the example give above) was devoted to fees and expenses. But I think it would, in all the circumstances, be the fair outcome in a confusing case.'

In this case at first instance (*Tower MCashback LLP v RCC* [2008] STC (SCD) 1) the Special Commissioner, Howard Nowlon, stated:

> '99. I have no hesitation whatsoever in concluding that the market value of the software acquired by the appellants was very materially below the price ostensibly paid for it.
>
> '100. The factor that most obviously supports this conclusion is that whether the form of the various transactions stands up to scrutiny (and that yet remains to be seen), the transactions were in economic substance contingent instalment sales where MCashback would only eventually receive the full price over a ten-year period, and indeed would receive it (assuming no sale and there was no arrangement for any sale) only if the figures of clearance fees assumed in the business plan *were materially exceeded.* As a consequence, at the date of sale, MCashback would only have at its disposal an amount equal to 18.2% of the gross capital contributions made to the LLPs. If the software intended to be sold to the four LLPs was in fact worth the £143m, aggregate price, why did MCashback not find the willing purchaser ready to pay this price, and why did it instead choose to proceed via a complex transaction that was only expected to deliver at the outset approximately £26m? In fact of course it produced far less than £26m because the lack of appetite on the part of genuine investors for the transaction resulted in no completion of the sales occurring until January 2005, the LLP3 transaction being completed on an instalment basis at a later date still, and by far the largest transaction, that involving LLP4, never being completed at all. And the 'outside' funds contributed into LLP1 amounted to only £700,000.
>
> '101. Consistently with the fact that whatever the form of the transactions, the deal was economically a contingent instalment sale from both the perspective of the seller and the buyers, no serious attention was ever given to the valuation issue. A business plan was produced containing staggering rising figures of revenues over a ten-year period for a software concept that had at the point of the preparation of the figures been sold to no one. I saw absolutely no evidence that ever addressed whether the figures in the business plan were carefully calculated and cautious estimates, or whether they were 'away with the fairies'. In reality it did not particularly matter whether the figures could be supported because the proposed transaction was only ever going to be put to investors on the basis that their ceiling exposure would be for 25% of the price paid, and the expected tax relief (that could even be carried back to the previous year) was expected and represented to be worth not 25% of gross price paid, but 40%. I am not suggesting that the transaction was a fraudulent one where the aim was to sell capital allowances in relation to a fictitious sale of near worthless software. But I certainly say that the reality of the transactions meant that nobody had to give that figure, or indeed any figure that should not be more than underwritten by the tax relief expected from the exchequer.
>
> '102. It was suggested in argument by Counsel for the Appellants that the software was worth the full price paid on the assumption of an outright purchase by a purchaser providing the entire purchase price of his own resources. And it was then contended that if the transaction had instead been an instalment sale the

> price would have been higher. I am simply unable to understand how this could be advanced as an argument. I note that this argument did at least recognise the inevitable difference in price between the price command in an outright sale, and that in an instalment (or I would say 'a highly contingent instalment') sale. Why it is supposed however that the parties would have failed to note that notwithstanding its form, this transaction was economically identical to a contingent instalment sale I simply cannot understand …
>
> '108. My conclusions on the valuation issue are that:
>
> > I do not purport to have any clear idea what the 13% interest in the software was worth in 2004, and I heard no evidence that could enable an experience valuer, let alone me, to make that judgement.
> >
> > I consider that the actual figures bandied around, and inserted into the business plan, were highly optimistic, untested and unreliable aspirations. Some people might have genuinely believed them, but their approach to valuation would inevitably have been influenced by the fact that the proposed transaction meant that no-one would have to rely on the figures or pay either anything approaching the full price on an outright basis, or indeed even as much as the projected front-end savings, in tax;
> >
> > In my view it is ridiculous to try to support a market valuation of the software by reference to the proposition that independent people gave percentages of £143m for it, when no-one gave anything other than 25% on a very contingent instalment basis; no-one expected to spend more than 62% of their projected tax savings on their total capital contribution to the project; several investors backed off; and the sum raised from outside investors in LLP1 at as late a date as January 2005 was only about £700,000;
> >
> > In short, the appellants' valuation arguments fail to establish their case by a very wide margin indeed.'

In *Acornwood LLP and others v HMRC* [2014] TC 03545, UK FTT 416 (TC), it was held that 51 Icebreaker limited liability partnerships to exploit films and other forms of intellectual property, on which tax relief on losses of £336,187,867 had been claimed, were tax avoidance schemes, which failed to give rise to losses offsettable against other income as the partnerships' trades were uncommercial; the members were non-active. Relief claimed under TA 1988, ss 380 and 381 and ITA 2007, ss 64, 66, 72, 74 and 74ZA–74D was disallowed. The Partnership (Restriction on Contributions to a Trade) Regulations, SI 2005/2017 were not in point. In deciding whether there were tax avoidance arrangements in place, under ITA 2007, s 74ZA, the tribunal judge referred to *Snell v RCC* [2008] STC (SCD) 1094; *Lloyd v RCC* [2008] STC 681; *IRC v Brebner* [1967] 2 AC 18; *A H Field Holdings Ltd v RCC* [2012] UKFTT 104 (TC); *IRC v Trustees of Sema Group Pension Scheme* [2002] STC 276.

In *R (on the application of Silva and another) v HMRC* [2014] All ER (D) 66, which was a judicial review case, HMRC challenged a film partnership scheme by an enquiry into the returns of the partnership which was subsequently settled by agreement under TMA 1970, s 54 by reducing the losses available for relief. HMRC so informed the individual partners who argued that their loss claims were not to be regarded as claims made in a personal tax return under TMA 1970, s 8, but were standalone claims under TMA 1970, Sch 1A and HMRC were out of time to amend such claims. The Upper Tribunal held that the challenge under s 8 was appropriate and dismissed the taxpayers' claims.

Clavis Liberty 1 LP (acting through Mr D J Cowen) v HMRC [2016] UKFTT 253 (TC) was an income tax avoidance scheme promoted by Mercury Tax Strategies Limited under which a partnership purchased the rights to certain dividends which were received but were excluded from the computation of income of the partnership for tax purposes, which, it was claimed, resulted in a loss under TA 1988, s 730. This claim was rejected as the partnership was held to be trading in short dated securities but this did not include the purchase of dividend rights and the scheme fees of £761,363 paid to Mercury were not a deductible trading expense.

In *Premier Telecom Communications Group (PTCG) and D M Ridge v D J Webb* [2014] EWCA Civ 994, the Court was asked to value Mr Webb's 40% shareholding on the basis of fair value on a pro rata basis without a discount to reflect a minority shareholding. The Court held that this was exactly what the valuers, Grant Thornton, had done and dismissed the appeal.

Seven Individuals v HMRC [2017] UKUT 132 (TCC): the *Acornwood LLP v HMRC* case was appealed to the Upper Tribunal at [2016] UKUT 361 (TCC) and *Bastionpark LLP v HMRC* [2016] UKUT 425 (TCC).

The present case relates to individual referrors as a representative of about 900 members in all and about half had joined the Icebreaker Members Action Group (IMAG). The seven members were members of different schemes in 2006–07 to 2009–10. The basis of the relevant schemes had been summarised in [2016] UKUT 361 (TCC).

The FTT found that none of the LLPs had come close to earning a commercial rate of return on its members' personal contributions. Acornwood, for example, had gross receipts of £37,952 in the years to 31 March 2011 and the amount subscribed was £5,355,000, of which 75% was borrowed and the balance of 25%, £1,338,750, contributed by its members. ITTOIA 2005, s 863 applies to a limited liability partnership if it carries on a trade, profession or business with a view to profit under TA 1988, ss 380–384, in which case it is a transparent entity and its activities are treated as carried on in partnership by its members (and not by the limited partnership as a separate entity).

HMRC, however, accepted that the trades were carried on with a view to profit and TA 1988, ss 380–384 or TA 2007, ss 64–74 applied to restrict the loss relief to the income received in the first four years of trade. Non-active partners' relief was restricted further by TA 1988, ss 118ZE and 118ZH unless at least an average of 10 hours a week was personally engaged in activities carried on for the purposes of the trade in order to set the losses against other income.

ITA 2007, s 747ZA applies to post-21 October 2009 cases to deny tax relief for tax-generated losses with a main purpose of obtaining sideways loss relief or capital gains relief.

Wannell v Rothwell [1996] STC 450 referred to 'a serious interest in profit is at the root of commerciality', while 'a view to profit' is referred to in *Ingenious Games LLP v HMRC* [2016] UKFTT 521 (TC).

The Supreme Court, in [2016] UKSC 13, considered the joined cases of *UBS AG v HMRC* and *D B Group Services (UK) Limited v HMRC* involving schemes designed to avoid the payment of income tax and NICs on bankers' bonuses under ITEPA 2003, Chapter 2, Part 7 as amended by FA 2003, Schedule 22.

In *Barclays Mercantile* [2002] EWCA Civ 1853, [2003] STC 66, schemes such as these 'draw their lifeblood from real world transactions with real world economic effects'. In *Collector of Stamp Revenue v Arrowtown Assets Limited* (2003) 6 ITLR 450, paragraph 35, it was stated that, where schemes involve intermediate transactions inserted for the sole purpose of tax avoidance, it is quite likely that a purposive interpretation will result in such steps being disregarded for fiscal purposes, but not always. Examples include *Inland Revenue Comrs v Burmah Oil Co Limited* 1982 SC (HL) 114, *Furniss v Dawson* [1984] AC 474, *Carreras Group Limited v Stamp Comr* [2004] UKPC 16, [2004] STC 1377, *Inland Revenue Comrs v Scottish Provident Institution* [2004] UKHL 52 and *Tower M Cashback LLP 1 v Revenue and Customs Comrs* [2011] UKSC 19, [2011] 2 AC 457. In this case, their Lordships decided that:

> 'Income tax is payable on the value of the shares as at the date of their acquisition in accordance with *Abbott v Philbin*, account being taken of any effect which the conditions may have had.'

In *Nigel Rowe, Alec David Worrall & Others v HMRC* [2015] EWHC 2293 (Admin), the appellant's claim for judicial review to challenge the legality of partner payment notices (PPNs) under FA 2014, s 219 failed.

The schemes referred to were those of Ingenious Media Plc, Ingenious Film Partners, Ingenious Film Partners 2 LLP (IFP2) and Ingenious Games LLP (IGames). The schemes themselves were being litigated in the First Tier Tribunal by the managing partners of IFP2, IGames and Inside Track Productions Limited. HMRC issued closure notices which were under appeal and the LLPs did not have relievable losses.

PPNs were anti-avoidance measures, like the Disclosure of Tax Avoidance Schemes (DOTAS) in FA 2004, ss 306–318 and the General Anti-Abuse Rule (GAAR) in FA 2013, ss 206–215 and Schedule 43 (see **2.01**). The PPNs were challenged on the grounds of natural justice, unlawfulness, legitimate expectation, irrationality, breach of Convention rights, and Article 6 of the Convention for the Protection of Human Rights and Article 1 of the First Protocol (the right to protection of property) (AIPI).

Rangers RFC 2012 plc (in liquidation) (formerly The Rangers Football Club plc) (RFC) v Advocate General for Scotland [2017] UKSC 45 was a major victory for HMRC and heralded the end of many widely sold tax avoidance schemes.

It consisted of an arrangement under which its parent company, Murray International Holdings Limited, through a subsidiary, Murray Group Management Limited, set up a 'remuneration trust (RT)' under which a group company made a payment to RT and asked it to resettle the sum on a sub-trust, the income of which should be applied in accordance with the wishes of the employees, ie the players and senior executives of RFC. In theory, this was merely a request but on every occasion RT created the sub-trust as requested.

The employee was a protector of his sub-trust and had powers to change its beneficiaries and could borrow from the sub-trust and receive more than the net sum he would have received after tax under PAYE and National Insurance Contributions (NICs) had he been paid through RFC. The trust fund was held for the benefit of the player's family, as he specified, and on his death the loans and interest would be repayable out of his estate which would reduce its value for inheritance tax purposes.

However, the Supreme Court held that ITEPA 2003, s 62(2), which includes gratuities and incidental benefits and anything else which constitutes an emolument, applied, and tax and NICs were payable as if the payments to the remuneration trusts had been emoluments subject to tax under PAYE.

The Privy Council decision in *Hadlee v CIR* [1993] STC 294 was quoted in support and a reference in the tax statutes to a payment to an employee included a payment to a third party.

Payments to the Principal Trust should have been subject to income tax under PAYE as earnings, and *Sempra Metals Limited v RCC* [2008] STC (SCD) 1062 and *Dextra Accessories Limited v Macdonald (HMIT)* [2002] STC (SCD) 413 had wrongly excluded payments to a third party from being earnings.

In *David Ingram and Michaela Hall v Ealisham Ahmed and others* [2016] EWHC 1536 (Ch) the judge stated:

> '103. Miss Longworth also accepted that the Private Company Price Index ("PCPI"), published by BDO, from which she derived her multiples, was jettisoned by BDO in 2013 in favour of Enterprise Value ("EV") multiples, which was, according to BDO, a "less subjective" measure of profitability, on the basis that they are based on all disposals taking place in the relevant quarter, rather than being sector specific, so that the PCPI multiples would not match the business sector of Hornby, Wembley or Continental. Miss Longworth accepted that she no longer uses PCPI but EV for her other valuations. Her explanation for using PCPI in this case was that the relevant dates the PCPI was a recognised basis for valuation and an accepted methodology. The EV/EBITDA ratio only became the accepted method in 2013.
>
> 104. However I find that the current valuations should be made according to the most recent methods and that this is no breach of the hindsight principle. The court seeks to determine the true values of the Shares not what the valuer would have said on 5 June 2007 was the value of the Shares.'

In *Andrew Davies, Paul McAleen and Brian Evan-Jones v HMRC* [2018] UKFTT 559 (TC) the appellants each took out life policies with Credit Suisse Life & Pensions (Bermuda) Limited (CSLP) and paid a premium of £3,000 each. The life policies were owned by ABP which was wholly owned by CSLP.

HMRC claimed that the appellants had made a transfer of assets by the payment of premiums to CSLP, processing finance for ABP and/or providing their personal services and had power to enjoy the trading income of ABP under TA 1988, s 739(2), ITA 2007, s 721(2). The appellants claimed the protection of TA 1988, s 741 and ITA 2007, s 739. The appellants claimed that the life policy arrangements were liable to UK tax and ABP had paid tax in Mauritius which was treaty protected under the UK/Mauritius double taxation agreement, and the arrangements were entered into for bona fide commercial purposes. They claimed that *Bricom Holdings Limited v IRC* 70 TC 272 and *Strathalmond v IRC* (1972) 48 TC 537 supported this, under TIOPA 2010, s 6. The taxpayer's appeal was dismissed.

David Mark Kyte v HMRC [2018] EWHC 1146 (Ch) involved a film tax mitigation scheme from Scion Structured Products for certain rights in the well-known film 'Frost/Nixon' (Mr Kyte also invested in two other such schemes, 'Goldcrest' and 'Ingenious Film Partners 2', which were not involved in this case). The claim was that a binding contract had been entered into with HMRC on 12 January 2016 to settle his tax liabilities from the Scion Scheme, which HMRC denies, on the basis that there was no offer, no acceptance of an offer, no legal certainty and were 'subject to contract'.

The Scion Scheme required a total capital contribution of £1,481,122 made up of two elements, one of £311,036 made 'in cash', the other out of a limited recourse interest earning loan of £1,170,086 provided under the scheme. The scheme entitled the investor to certain Minimum Annual Payments ('the MAPs') derived from a leaseback of the rights to 'Frost/Nixon'. The MAPs were mandated to the lender and offset against the loan. The claimant submitted tax returns from 2007/08 to 2012/13, claiming sideways loss relief for 2007/08: HMRC disputed whether participation in the scheme gave rise to allowable losses and whether loan interest was deductible. Mr Kyte sought declarations that there was a binding contract with HMRC on 12 January 2016 and that payment of £316,995.30 satisfied his tax liabilities under the contract. The claim that there was a binding settlement contract on 12 January 2016 was dismissed.

In *Christa Ackroyd Media Limited v HMRC* [2018] UKFTT 69 (TC) it was held that Ms Ackroyd was an employee of her personal service company, CAM Limited, and caught by 'IR35', ITEPA 2003, ss 48–61, and payments to CAM Limited should have been treated as payments to Ms Ackroyd and subject to PAYE and NIC.

In *Dr A Jones v HMRC* [2018] UKFTT 260 (TC), reference was made to *Customs and Excise Commissioners v Steptoe* [1992] STC 757 at 765 and *ETB (1914) Limited v HMRC* [2016] UKUT 424 (TCC) in defining a reasonable excuse for late payment of VAT because of insufficiency of funds which, although it cannot of itself constitute a reasonable excuse, the underlying cause of that insufficiency – the underlying cause of the taxpayer's default – might do so, under VATA 1994, s 71(1)(b). The HMRC's Compliance Handbook recognises that a shortage of funds which 'occurred despite the person exercising reasonable foresight and due diligence, having given proper regard to their tax due date obligations'.

Mr Alan Anderson v HMRC [2016] UKFTT 335 (TC) was an appeal against a discovery assessment under TMA 1970, s 29(1) for £830,387 in respect of capital gains tax for 2007/08 on the sale of the appellant's shares in Anson Limited. This was a 50% shareholding in a company which manufactured and marketed specialist oil and gas field products. The shares were sold to ANS (1002) Limited in exchange for shares therein. The shares in Anson were considered to be worth £72 million in total, based on an offer made by the Weir Group on 25 March 2008. HMRC claimed that the market value was higher. On 2 April 2009 the shares were sold for £88,607,734, of which the appellant's share was £44,303,867. The failure of the taxpayer to obtain a further independent valuation in April 2008 did not cause an insufficiency of capital gains tax and HMRC were not entitled to issue a discovery assessment out of time.

Focus

- These were schemes which mainly failed by being both over-ambitious and uncommercial.
- Most tax avoidance schemes which seem too good to be true are just that.

17.05 Trademarks

In *Iliffe News and Media Ltd & Others v Revenue & Customs Commissioners* [2013] SFTD 309 the valuation was considered of five-year licences of 'various unregistered trademarks (UTMs) being titles of local newspapers and other periodicals, referred to as 'mastheads' (which) were assigned from the respective subsidiaries … to their parent company INML and were then licenced back to the subsidiaries by INML for consideration of various sums payable as being sums totalling £51,400,000' (para 5). Ernst & Young (E&Y) were the companies' valuers. At para 93 it was stated that:

> 'Three methodologies of valuation were considered, all assuming a 5 year licence. These were: the royalty relief methodology ("RRM") – which we understand to be a computation of the present value of royalty payments saved through the ownership of the licence; the elimination methodology "EM") – sometimes called "the residual value approach", which is a method based on allocating the correct proportion of the determined value of the entire intangible assets and goodwill of a business to the assets licenced, and determining the proportion of that value attributable to the licences by application of the RRM; and the market methodology ("MM") – ascertaining the proportion of enterprise value represented by mastheads in transactions in the market place (or the price paid for mastheads sold in isolation), applying such proportion to the value of the relevant Subsidiaries' businesses and determining the proportion of the resultant ascertained value attributable to the licences by application of the RRM.
>
> 94. E&Y regarded the MM as being the 'primary analyses. The MM was the ascertainment of market value for the licences, based on a hypothetical sale of a licence to use the masthead by a willing vendor to a willing purchaser, 'each of whom is acting for self-interest and gain and both of whom are equally well informed about [the masthead] and the market place in which it operates'. It can be seen that the adoption of the MM made the question of what proportion of the enterprise value was represented by the mastheads of prime importance in reaching a valuation.
>
> 95. E&Y's valuation of 5 year licences of the HENL portfolio was between £13m and £18m, their valuation of 5 year licences of the CNL portfolio was between £16m and £21m, and their valuation of 5 year licences of the SNL portfolio was between £5m and £8m. [ie a range of £34-£47m]. As stated above, the figures adopted in the relevant licences were: HENL – £15.5m; CNL – £18.5m; and SNL – £6.5m [total £40.5m]. In other words, valuations mid-point in the ranges suggested by E&Y were adopted as the consideration for the grants of the licences in question.
>
> 96. Mr Burns (the appellants' independent valuation expert) stated that in his opinion the MM represented the most robust and accurate method of valuation. He concluded that substantially all of the value of the intangible assets of HENL, CNL and SNL could be attributed to their mastheads. He accepted in cross-examination that he had based everything on the premise that virtually all the value of the intangible assets of the Subsidiaries was attributable to the values of their respective mastheads. He put values on the licences involved in the 2003 transactions as follows: HENL – between £14m and £21m; CNL – between £11m and £20m; and SNL – between £5m and £8m [total £30–£49m]. He put values on the licences involved in the 2005 transactions in the range of between £5.3m and £11m. It will be recalled that INML charged CNL £299,000 for the grant of the licence of the UTMs sought to be assigned by CNL in 2005, and INML charged LSN £10,641,000 for the grant of the licence of the UTMs sought to be

assigned by LSN in 2005. These figures total just under £11m. Mr Burns said in evidence that he thought the E&Y valuation in 2003 was "a competent piece of professional work". E&Y valuation of 2005 however, focussed on the RRM, and Mr Burns, concluding that although his value range for the 2005 licences came within E&Y's valuation, considered that E&Y's valuation 'pretty near the top of it' and that, in relying on the RRM, he considered that 'intellectually, [E&Y were] flying in fairly thin air

…

98. The evidence was that the EM and the MM were similar methodologies focussing on an attribution of a proportion of enterprise value to the licences, whereas the RRM was different, and focussed on the present value of royalty expenditure saved by ownership of the licences. A difficulty faced by both Mr Burns and Mr Ryan was that there was not much relevant evidence of licences or sales of mastheads having taken place in the open market, as opposed to sales and purchases of newspaper businesses as a whole or, more usually, the companies carrying on the businesses (examples being INML's acquisition of Acorn in 2004 and LSN in 2005), although we note that Mr Burn's opinion was that when a newspaper business was acquired, the acquirer regarded the masthead as the sole asset it was seeking to acquire.

99. Mr Ryan (HMRC's independent valuation expert) stated in his original report that he regarded the RRM as the most suitable method to value the licences in issue, but he cross-checked his valuation of the UTMs by considering what proportion of intangible asset value the licences represented and the replacement cost of a local newspaper masthead. He identified what he regarded as appropriate royalty rates (5% – 6% for the HENL, CNL and SNL licences and 2% for the LSN licence, because LSN publishes free newspapers only). He initially (in his written evidence) valued the licences involved as follows: HENL – £2.1m to £2.5m; CNL – £3m to £3.6m; SNL – £1.4m to £1.7m; and LSN – £1m.

100. Mr Ryan made the point that the value given by the RRM would be appropriate only if one did *not* accept his view that in the market in which the licences were granted the most likely acquirer of the licences from INML would be the existing publisher of the newspaper concerned. (He thought, having considered the position of the newspaper publishers in nearby areas which could be said to be most likely to wish to expand into the Subsidiaries' areas, that "the incumbent would pay the maximum value because if it purchases the masthead or the licence nobody else is going to – you go back to the position that you were in".) Mr Ryan's view was that if one accepted this point then the value of the licences would be unlikely to be significantly higher than the cost of recreating the UTMs concerned (ie rebranding), which would give a lower value than that achieved by application of the RRM). He rejected the MM as the primary valuation methodology because, as with the most intellectual property valuations, there were not enough reference points to apply a "top-down" valuation in a rigorous way.

101. Mr Ryan produced his Second Supplementary Report dated 12 October 2011 in the light of transcripts of evidence given at the hearing on 10 and 11 October 2011. In it he referred to evidence which Mr Richard had given which in his view emphasised the dominant nature of the paid-for newspapers (the most important of the totals concerned) operated by the appellants in their local markets. This evidence suggested to Mr Ryan that the existing publisher would be the only credible acquirer of the licences in the hypothetical market being considered and that therefore a valuation based on the costs of recreating the UTMs concerned might be a more appropriate valuation methodology.

102. In Mr Ryan's Second Supplementary Report he also considered clause 3.8 of the licences (see: paragraph 70 above), which he said he had overlooked when he wrote his two earlier reports. Clause 3.8 concerns the entitlement of the licensor (INML) from time to time at its sole discretion on at least 30 days' notice to remove any UTMs from the licence on payment of a *pro rata* refund of the licence fee attributable to UTMs so removed.

103. Mr Ryan stated that clause 3.8 significantly increased the likelihood that an existing publisher would be the only credible acquirer of the licences, essentially because of the investment needed in the business which the licences would permit, and the uncertainty attendant upon possible exercise by the licensor (INML) of its entitlement under clause 3.8. He stated his opinion that the replacement value of the UTMs which were subject to the licences was £10.8m and, on the basis that the Tribunal found that the existing publishers (notionally deprived of the right to use the relevant mastheads) were the only credible acquirers of the licences, he suggested that the appropriate valuation was based on that figure, but discounted to take account of the uncertainty created by possible exercise of the power of removal under clause 3.8. He suggested a figure of up to 35% of the cost of recreating the UTMs. This methodology gave a total valuation of £3.8m for all the licences in issue, as compared with £7.5m to £8.8m if the RRM was applied. Mr Ryan added that if the Tribunal found that the existing publishers were *not* the only credible acquirers of the licences, then he would confirm his valuation adopting the RRM method.

...

107. Mr Jones, in cross-examining Mr Burns, explored whether the fact that no non-competition covenant had been given by the Subsidiaries in assigning the UTMs to INML and that INML had not given any non-competition covenant on granting the licences to the Subsidiaries had had any effect on the value of the licences. Mr Jones' point was that the Subsidiaries, although without the right to use the various mastheads, remained as incumbents in their respective areas and must be assumed (as was the fact) to have retained their employees, local office facilities, distribution networks and advertiser relationships, and were therefore in a position immediately to recommence publishing, albeit under a different title, the Cambridge Star, say, instead of the Cambridge Evening News.

...

109. Mr Burns regarded the RRM as of no assistance, because the transactions providing the basic data necessary to apply it were drawn from "non-comparable transactions in a non-comparable period a long time ago in different jurisdictions". The cross-checking he employed for the purpose of his valuation on MM was against actual sales of companies running newspaper businesses in possession of mastheads, and for this purpose he attributed the whole of the value of the intangible assets of such companies to their mastheads. Mr Jones put to him that his begged the question of whether it was correct to make that attribution. He then said (without much enthusiasm) that instead of the RRM one could look at the expected split of profits between a licensor and a licencee, and make a cross-check of the valuation on that basis.

110. Mr Burns was disposed to agree that the non-exclusive nature of the licence between INML and LSN concluded as part of the 2005 Transactions would have had an impact on the value of that licence.

111. Mr Ryan thought it was neither possible nor realistic to regard all (or virtually all) the value of the Subsidiaries other than that attributable to tangible assets to be attributable to their respective mastheads. He made the point that a

masthead was essentially a brand (Mr Richard had described it as such) and a specialist brand consultancy called Interbrand had valued the Coca-Cola brand at 50% of the value of the Coca-Cola company's intangible assets – for the McDonalds brand, the figure said to be 40%, for the Apple brand it was 10%. In the light of that he thought it very unlikely that any brand could be worth 100% of the owning company's intangible asset value. Instead he suggested a value of 20% to 30% – which he described as 'a relatively hefty amount, in my experience', regarding at least 50% of the company's intangible asset value as attributable to its incumbency – that is, the relationships it has because it is in place as the local newspaper publishing company – which Mr Ryan regarded as distinct from brand loyalty. A newspaper brand – a masthead – told the purchaser something about what to expect in terms of the editorial comment and the style of the newspaper. It was not the newspaper itself. Thus the value of a masthead had to be supported by, for instance, editorial staff, although Mr Ryan accepted that this was less important with a free newspaper, which did not rely on the reader making a conscious decision to take (and pay for) the newspaper. On the other hand, the value of the masthead of a free newspaper was connected to the value of the newspaper's relationship with its advertisers. He made the point that the relationships supporting the value of a masthead needed to be maintained, and could dissipate rapidly 'if the editorial content is not longer there to support it'. On the other hand, he acknowledged that if one could 'replace everything overnight' then one 'would be able to capture a lot of [the] business', adding that Mr Richard's evidence had been that it would be impossible for a newcomer to a local newspaper market to do that.

112. Mr Ryan considered that it was very advantageous to check a valuation of an intellectual property asset against other valuations of the asset computed on different methodologies. Thus, he considered it appropriate to check a valuation arrived at by the MM (a "top-down" methodology arrived at by taking an overview of the value of the business) against the RRM or a discounted cash-flow methodology which is 'a bottom-up method which really relies on getting to grips with the business and how it works'.

113. Mr Ryan, disagreeing with Mr Burns, thought that a newspaper business which had disposed of its masthead, but otherwise retained its business intact, would "rebrand" – that is, publish under a different name – rather than close down or 'exit' the market. He thought (based on competition surveys which had been carried out) that it was quite possible that there could be a significant take-up of a new brand.

114. Mr Ryan's view was that the royalties implied in the licence fees charged to the Subsidiaries by INML were too high to be commercial – having regard to the alternatives available to the Subsidiaries, namely to enter the market with rebranded titles. The licence fees as a percentage of the licencees' profits were, in Mr Ryan's view, too high to be commercial – and far higher than any intellectual property valuation that he had been involved in. Even on Mr Burn's estimate (of 60% to 70% of the licencees' profits) the licence fees were too high to be commercial, in Mr Ryan's view.

That level of profit split would suggest that the product being licenced was very profitable (like a "blockbuster pharmaceutical product") and that the market risks and the functions to be performed by the licencee were minimal.

115. Mr Ryan, differing from Mr Burns, did not regard the factor of synergies (the ability for an acquirer to make more profit out of existing assets, or to save costs) or a "bid premium" on the licensing of the UTMs as likely to increase the market value of the licences, because he regarded the parties most likely to

> pay the most for the licences to be the existing publishers (the Subsidiaries) and therefore "there are clearly no synergies because all you are doing is making it whole, effectively". And there would be no logical basis to add a "bid premium". If, alternatively, a third party newspaper publisher acquired the licence and could achieve synergies by "sweating [its assets] more", Mr Ryan's view was that those synergies would be counterbalanced by the loss of revenue it would experience by competing in the market with the existing publishers' rebranded newspapers. He acknowledged that synergies might boost the value of the licences if one could assume that the Competition Commission reports had stated that many local newspapers were in effect able to operate a monopoly in a competitor for paid-for titles with a distribution network and other relationships which could give rise to synergies …'

In its judgment the tribunal stated:

> '192. We however have to consider an artificial (from a commercial point of view) state of facts where only the masthead (the UTM) is alienated by a newspaper operating business, and no non-competition covenant is given by the existing publisher.
>
> 193. In that context, Mr Burns sought to support his valuation of a newspaper masthead by making the assumption that the existing publisher (who has notionally alienated only the masthead) would not try to remain in the market, and so would not be a potential purchaser of a licence of the masthead. Mr Burns thought it would be more logical for the existing publishers to distribute the proceeds of sale to their shareholders than to contemplate re-entry into the market by taking licences of the titles which they had recently disposed of (see above, paragraph 104).
>
> 194. Mr Ryan, on the other hand, was of the view that the existing publisher would be the only credible acquirer of the licence in the hypothetical market being considered (see above, paragraph 101). Indeed he thought that the existing publisher, even if unsuccessful in acquiring the licence, would be likely to use its existing business apparatus to publish under a different name ("rebrand") rather than close down (paragraph 113). This course would be particularly attractive in relation to free newspapers (such as those operated by LSN). The fact that the Subsidiaries had not given covenants not to compete when assigning the UTMs to INML, and the fact that the licence taken by LSN was on a non-exclusive basis supported this view.
>
> 195. On this important issue, we favour the approach of Mr Ryan and reject that of Mr Burns. In particular we cannot understand the basis on which Mr Burns makes his assumption that the existing publisher would "exit the business" rather than acquire the licence and in this way continue to derive value, and profit, from its existing (and notionally retained) employees, local office facilities, distribution networks and advertiser relationships. It seems to us that there is no basis to assume that, if they had, they would not have considered re-investing a part of that value in the acquisition of the licences. On the contrary, the assumed business realities seem to us (as they did to Mr Ryan) to point to the existing publishers being the most likely acquirers of the licences, because they retained the necessary business facilities in place to derive immediate and maximum benefit from the licences, once acquired. Any other purchaser, for example a newspaper publisher in a nearby area, or one who could achieve synergies by "sweating [its assets] more" (*cf.* Above, paragraph 115), would inevitably require a period of adjustment before it could enter the market using the licenced masthead, and this would leave a time-gap which could be exploited by the existing publisher – particularly in the area of free newspapers.

> …
>
> 198. We regard Mr Burn's use of the MM to value mastheads sold in isolation to be flawed because we do not accept his underlying assumption that the masthead represents the entirety of the intangible asset value of a newspaper business. We regard the RRM as being, in principle, an appropriate valuation methodology to use, concentrating, as it does, on the present value of royalty payments rendered necessary by the ownership of the licence. However, having reached the view that in the hypothetical market in which the licences were granted the most likely purchasers would be the existing publishers of the newspapers concerned, we are persuaded by Mr Ryan's view that the cost of recreating the UTMs concerned (ie rebranding), which would give a lower value than that achieved by application of the RRM (see above, paragraph 100).
>
> 199. In the light of Mr Ryan's evidence about the values assigned by Interbrand to the Coca-Cola brand, the McDonalds brand and the Apple brand, we would not in any event have accepted a value for the UTMs in this case which exceeded 30% of the relevant Subsidiaries' intangible asset value. We accept Mr Ryan's point that the bulk of that value is attributable to the Subsidiaries' incumbency – the relationships it has, because it is in place as the local newspaper publishing company – and his point that this is distinct from brand loyalty, or masthead value (see above, paragraph 111).
>
> …
>
> 205. In the result, we accept Mr Ryan's evidence (at paragraphs 1.19 to 1.21 of his Second Supplemental Report) that the value of the various licences equated to 35% of the cost of recreating the relevant UTMs which gives a total value of £3.8m, allocated between the licences as follows: HENL – £1.4m; CNL – £1.1m; SNL – £900,000; and LSN £400,000. The fees paid for the relevant licences were: HENL – £15.5m; CNL – £18.759m (£18.5m in 2003 and £259,000 in 2005); SNL – £6.5m; and LSN – £10.641m; [a total of £51.4m]. Comparison of these figures gives amounts paid by the various Subsidiaries to INML in excess of the market values of the licences concerned as follows: HENL – £14.1m; CNL – £17.659m; SNL – £5.6m; and LSN – £10.241m. These are the figures we take into account when considering the amounts which may (or may not) rank as distributions for company law purposes by the Subsidiaries concerned to INML.
>
> 206. If we had not determined that the correct valuations were linked to the cost of recreating the relevant UTMs, we would have preferred valuations calculated by the use of the RRM, as prepared by Mr Ryan. An advantage of Mr Ryan's approach using the RRM, as against Mr Burn's approach using the MM (which we have rejected), is that Mr Ryan has cross-checked his valuations against the proportions of intangible asset value which they represented and the resultant profit split between licensor and licencee. This, in our view, added to the robustness of Mr Ryan's RRM-based valuations.'

Lengthy extracts from the judgement in this case have been included because the valuation of intellectual property is rarely considered in detail in taxation cases. In fact, the exercise was irrelevant because of 'issue a', in paragraphs 14, 15 and 161:

> '14 The appellants submit that by each assignment in issue both UTMs (Unregistered Trade Marks) and the goodwill attaching to them were assigned, so that we do not have any attempted assignment of an UTM in gross (that is, a transfer of an UTM independently of the underlying business and goodwill to which it relates). They further submit that the UTMs were assigned intra-group and that therefore there was no risk of the assignments deceiving the

public. They submit that HMRC's approach is to attempt to extend the law limiting assignments of UTMs well beyond the situations for which the rule was developed to circumstances where there is no rationale in preventing assignment.

15. HMRC submit that the purported assignments of UTMs in this case are purported assignments in gross, and that a UTM (as opposed to a registered trade mark) cannot, as a matter of law, be assigned in gross. The TMAs in this case are, in HMRC's submission, ineffective. Further HMRC originally contended that a UTM is not an intangible asset within the meaning of Schedule 29 FA 2002 (which gives 'intangible asset' the meaning it has for accounting purposes and includes, in particular, any intellectual property, which for these purposes includes "any … trade mark … or any licence or other right in respect of [any trade mark]" paragraph 2, Schedule 29, FA 2002). However, this latter point was withdrawn by Mr Jones in the course of argument – see: paragraphs 163 to 165 below.'

Issue *a*: conclusion:

'161. Our conclusion in relation to issue *a* therefore is that the purported assignments of UTMs in this case by the respective Subsidiaries to INML were assignments in gross and were void for mistake as to the assignability of the subject matter of the purported assignments (see: *Halsbury's Laws, 4th Edition 2007 Reissue, Vol. 13, Deeds and other instruments* paragraph 71 and the cases there cited). It follows that no UTM, has been validly transferred to INML or licenced back by INML and on this basis the Subsidiaries' appeals in relation to their claims to write down for tax purposes the acquired licences of UTMs fall to be dismissed.'

Focus

This case demonstrates that experienced valuers can arrive at substantially different figures: £51.4m and £3.8m (paras 5 and 106). It also demonstrates that a purported assignment of an unassignable asset is void for mistake (para 161).

17.06 Transfer pricing

The transfer pricing provisions in TA 1988, Sch 28AA have been rewritten to the Taxation (International and Other Provisions) Act 2010 (TIOPA 2010), Part 4, ss 146–217 and the Advance Pricing Agreements in FA 1998, ss 85–88 to TIOPA 2010, Part 5, ss 218–230 and Tax Arbitrage in F (No 2) A 2005, ss 24–31 to TIOPA 2010, ss 231–259.

TIOPA 2010, ss 208–211 put the onus on the taxpayer to self-assess in relation to transfer pricing and to notify HMRC of any transfer pricing adjustments required. Central control of transfer pricing is maintained by requiring transfer pricing adjustments to the taxpayer's declared figures in a self assessment return to have the prior approval in writing of an Officer of Revenue and Customs, which in practice means approval by International Division, not at district level.

TIOPA 2010, s 210 requires HMRC to notify the other party to a transfer pricing adjustment where they would have been entitled to make a corresponding relief claim under TIOPA 2010, ss 174–175. TIOPA 2010, ss 218–223 provided for written Advance Pricing Agreements to be made between HMRC and multi-national groups regarding the attribution of profits to a UK permanent establishment, branch or agency, wherever situated, and the extent to which income is treated as arising outside the UK, where the matter is not covered by a double taxation agreement and the operation of the transfer pricing rules for transactions between associated companies. Where such a transfer pricing agreement is reached between the companies concerned and HMRC, and is implemented, it should ensure that the transfer pricing will not apply to the transactions covered by the agreement. HMRC have published a statement of practice SP2/2010 which sets out the procedures to be followed and the information required in order to apply for an Advance Pricing Agreement. Advance Pricing Agreements include compliance and other provisions, which, if not complied with, would make the agreement inoperable or give HMRC the right to revoke it under TIOPA 2010, s 225. Such an agreement is void altogether if it is based on false or misleading information provided fraudulently or negligently and HMRC so notify the company concerned under TIOPA 2010, s 226. Companies entering into Advance Pricing Agreements are required to make reports to HMRC regarding the operation of the agreement. There is a penalty of up to £10,000 under TIOPA 2010, s 227 for fraudulently or negligently making false or misleading statements in connection with the application for an Advance Pricing Agreement or in its preparation. The normal penalty provisions of TMA 1970, s 98 apply to any failure to make a return under an Advance Pricing Agreement and for an incorrect return: TIOPA 2010, s 221.

TIOPA 2010, s 222 enables a person who is not a party to an advance pricing agreement, but is the other party to a transaction covered by such an agreement, to prevent economic double taxation of profits by applying TIOPA 2010, ss 174–190 as though the agreed prices had been imposed under those provisions.

Although the necessity to change the transfer pricing legislation was to make it compatible with corporate self assessment, the opportunity was taken both to widen the provisions and the circumstances in which it might apply, to try and bring the rules closer to the OECD Model Tax Convention, Article 9, and to provide specifically that the legislation is to be interpreted in accordance with these provisions.

The reference to interpretation in accordance with Article 9 of the OECD Model Tax Convention (associated enterprises) is given by TIOPA 2010, ss 164. This effectively gives statutory authority to an appropriate associated enterprises article in an actual double tax treaty and to the *OECD Transfer Pricing Guidelines For Multinational Enterprises and Tax Administrations* (5th edn, 2010). The effect of this section is to enable the double taxation treaty to impose taxation in the sense that expenses could be disallowed on a non arm's length agreement which would not otherwise be disallowed under, for example, the general provisions of CTA 2009, ss 53, 54, 59, 68, 103 and 231.

The basic rule in TIOPA 2010, ss 147–148, refers to 'provisions', which is used not in the accounting sense, but in the sense of conditions made or imposed between the parties. The parties have to be connected in that either one was directly or indirectly participating in the management, control or capital of the other, or was a third party so participating in both parties. In such cases the actual terms and conditions are compared with those which would have been made between independent enterprises referred to as the 'arm's length provision'. This is the equivalent to transactions taking place at market value between a willing buyer and a willing seller and can extend to the totality of the inter-party arrangements. For example, if interest is paid by a thinly capitalised taxpayer, under finance arrangements guaranteed by affiliates, the whole of the interest would be disallowed on the basis of an argument that such a loan would not be made between parties at arm's length and therefore no interest would have been paid. It would not be confined, therefore, to cases where the actual rate of interest was excessive. Given that HMRC seems to assume, as a starting point in negotiations, a debt equity ratio of 1:1 as being the norm, this could provide scope for considerable argument in practice.

The 'provision', to which the new legislation refers has to be made by a transaction or series of transactions, a term very widely defined by TIOPA 2010, ss 150. There does, however, need to be participation in the management, control or capital as the connection between the parties. This is defined by TIOPA 2010, ss 158–163 to include potential participants, who are assumed to have the rights which they are entitled to acquire at a future date. Control is construed in accordance with TIOPA 2010, ss 1124, as voting control or powers given by the articles, or actual ability to direct the affairs of the company, including control through directly owned rights and those owned by relatives and connected settlements. Control in this context has to be at company meeting level, not at board meeting level (*Irving v Tesco Stores (Holdings) Ltd* (1982) 58 TC 1), and in determining control of a trust holding it is necessary to consider the terms of the trust, not merely the first named trustee who actually votes (*IRC v Lithgows* (1960) 39 TC 270). Where there is a joint venture and each of two participants own 40% or more of the entity, there is common control with other parties owned by either participant.

In order to give rise to a transfer pricing adjustment, it is necessary to show that there has been a 'tax advantage' (defined by TIOPA 2010, s 155) which effectively means a loss to the UK Exchequer as a result of the artificial transfer prices used. TIOPA 2010, ss 165–173 give exemptions for dormant companies and small or medium sized entities.

Transfer pricing adjustments will only be required to nullify the effect of such a tax advantage. This excludes most intra-UK transactions, as a loss to one party is a profit to the other, provided that the party making the advantage is resident in the UK and within the UK charge to tax, and not otherwise exempt or entitled to double taxation relief. There are special rules for life assurance companies.

For intra-group transactions which remain within the charge, double counting is eliminated by TIOPA 2010, ss 174–190, as adjusted for what would then become excessive double tax relief. As the legislation relating to foreign exchange and financial instruments contains its own arm's length provisions, the transfer pricing rules are not used to make adjustments in this area, although loan relationships are clearly within the revised legislation.

Appeals in relation to transfer pricing adjustments are made to the Special Commissioners under TIOPA 2010, s 212.

There are special provisions relating to oil companies under TIOPA 2010, ss 147, 205–217. The transfer pricing rules do not extend to capital gains or capital allowances, which have their own rules, in TIOPA 2010, ss 213–214.

In practice, although the cases to which transfer pricing adjustments can apply have been extended, the calculation of any adjustments will not change substantially as the Inland Revenue have been applying the OECD rules under the press release of 26 January 1981 on the Transfer Pricing of Multi-National Enterprises and the confirmation in Tax Bulletin, Issue 25, October 1996, which specifically confirmed that the Revenue will follow the recommendations in the OECD report, *Transfer Pricing Guidelines for Multinational Enterprises and Tax Administrations* (given statutory effect by TIOPA 2010, s 164).

The main concerns with regard to transfer pricing and corporate self assessment are in relation to the record keeping requirement, summarised in the consultative document *A Modern Approach to Transfer Pricing*, published in October 1997. The Government made it clear in the Finance Bill Standing Committee debates on 9 June 1998 (Hansard column 659) that there would be no automatic penalties on transfer pricing adjustments in the absence of fraud or neglect, that transfer pricing is not an exact science and in most circumstances there will be an acceptable range of outcomes.

As most transfer pricing challenges will be directed to cross border transactions, one of the main problems, in practice, will remain the avoidance of economic double taxation which arises where an adjustment is made to recover a perceived tax advantage in one country, without there being a corresponding adjustment, accepted by the tax authorities in the other. In fact, it is by no means unknown for the tax authorities in both jurisdictions to make transfer pricing adjustments in their favour, hitting the taxpayer with irrecoverable additional taxation in both jurisdictions. In such cases, it may be possible to invoke the competent authority provisions of a double taxation treaty to try and persuade the Revenue authorities in both countries to agree a common arm's length price, but this has proved to be an unwieldy procedure in practice. Statutory authority is available for making adjustments to the UK tax liabilities where the mutual agreement procedure has been successfully invoked by TA 1988, s 815AA on making an appropriate claim. As a result, within the European Community, an Arbitration Convention on the Elimination of Double Taxation in connection with the Adjustment of Profits of Associated Enterprises was entered into (90/436/EEC) and came into force on 1 January 1995 for an initial five year period, subsequently extended, and given statutory authority within the UK by TIOPA 2010, ss 126–127.

Under the Convention the authorities have to agree a common transfer price, or to make such other adjustments as result in the same tax liability arising as if a common transfer price had been agreed.

In the field of intellectual property, the market value and arm's length price rules are used to consider whether transactions between connected parties are such as would have taken place between unconnected parties, and if not, to tax them as if they had been. This obviously means looking at the combination of any lump sum and/or royalty payable and the services provided, which normally takes the form of a licence or assignment of the intellectual property concerned, including any related know-how. This is where the OECD *Guidelines for Multinational Enterprises and Tax Administrations* are intended to provide the practical ground rules.

Focus

Transfer pricing is merely substituting an arm's length value for that adopted by the parties – but what is that value?

17.07 OECD Transfer Pricing Guidelines for Multinational Enterprises and Tax Administrations

Publication of these guidelines began in 1995 and is continuing. The latest report at the time of writing is that of 10 July 2017 as amended up to 9 May 2018. The difficulty with transfer pricing in practice is that very often the transactions to be considered would not actually take place between unconnected parties, making the problem of arriving at an arm's length value that is likely to be fair both to the company concerned and to the Revenue authorities in both countries, a complicated matter. Transfer pricing comparisons may be either transaction based or profit based.

Focus

The OECD Guidelines suggest ways to value the property being transferred.

17.08 Transaction-based methods

The three main transaction-based methods referred to in the report are the comparable uncontrolled prices method (CUP), the resale price method and the cost plus method. The object of the exercise is to identify an uncontrolled third party transaction, or transactions, which is or are broadly compatible with the transaction being investigated, and in respect of which it is possible to adjust for those differences which will inevitably apply. This does not, however, get over the problem of identifying a comparable transaction in respect of which information is in the public domain. Tax authorities are prevented by the rules of confidentiality from disclosing one taxpayer's commercial transactions to another, in order to substantiate alleged third party transactions.

Focus

The three transaction-based methods are set out in **17.09** to **17.11** below.

17.09 Comparable uncontrolled price (CUP)

In order to identify a comparable transaction in the fields of intellectual property, it is necessary to consider not only the type of property involved, for example, a patent licence in connection with a drug, but also all the other attributes which affect the commercial prospects of such a licence. For example, in the case of a drug, it would be necessary to look at the potential market, so that, for example, a drug that might cure BSE related CJD, might be extremely desirable for the victims, but the market would appear to be tiny, and the profit potential likewise. Conversely, a cure or treatment for Alzheimer's disease, where the sufferers are measured in hundreds of millions and increasing, the potential market is enormous, and the profit potential likewise. It is also necessary to consider whether preventative treatment is already available, and if so the advantages of the product under consideration compared with existing products. These advantages may relate to the cost of production, efficacy of treatment or reduction of side effects.

It is also necessary to consider the likely future competition. Knowledge as to whether other drugs are being worked upon by rival companies would obviously be relevant, as would the state of clinical trials, and the state of approval from the drug control authorities in the appropriate jurisdictions in which the drug is likely to be marketed.

These and other factors have to be taken into account when considering what is a comparable uncontrolled price, and have to be estimated in advance on the basis of the best information available, and the pricing decisions duly documented. This emphasises the importance of record keeping in transfer pricing provisions. Hindsight may show that, for innumerable reasons, the projections were wide of the mark, but hindsight is not a factor that ought to be taken into account in any valuation, even though it may be available at the time when the transaction has to be considered by the fiscal authorities.

The problem with intellectual property based transfer pricing is that the conclusion arrived at is based almost entirely on the perceived commercial prospects of the product and not on the costs of development, although clearly the CUP would take into account direct costs such as brand name and advertising which, in practice, may justify a substantial premium compared with an unbranded product.

Focus

Intellectual property is by definition unique, so to find a meaningful comparison is difficult.

17.10 Resale price

The resale price method looks at the sale price and costs in each jurisdiction and seeks to ensure a reasonable gross margin in each case. Again, this is difficult to do in practice, for example, a compact disc costs almost nothing to produce compared with its retail sale price, which will vary within relatively small limits depending on the type of product being supplied and the sale price of competing products. The volume produced may vary enormously from sales of an obscure classical piece or recording by an unknown group measured in the low thousands to sales of established popular artistes or groups measured in the tens of millions. Resale prices will also differ in each market, but the royalty payable to the composer, publisher or artiste is likely to increase as a percentage of the retail sales as those sales increase for established performers. In this case, the commercial market allows a higher proportion of the final profit to be taken by the creators of intellectual property, although other areas, say, product royalty, may well decrease as a percentage as production increases.

> **Focus**
>
> Allocation of profit by reference to the salc price compared to cost seems reasonable at first, but can given an unfair advantage to, perhaps, the input of material and labour as apposed to the ingenuity of the idea.

17.11 Cost plus

The cost plus method assumes that at each stage in a transaction it is possible to allocate the overall profit to the various stages of production by reference to the costs incurred in the various jurisdictions. This method is particularly inappropriate for intellectual property, where the commercial value of the product tends to bear little or no correlation to the costs of development. The Internal Revenue Service in the USA tends to argue that the royalty level for intellectual property should be commensurate with the income generated which, applying a cost plus method, would effectively allocate the whole of the super profit beyond a reasonable return on capital to the intellectual property. This method is not normally regarded as an arm's length price by the other members of the OECD.

> **Focus**
>
> Opinions differ as to whether the costs of production bear any relationship to the value of the end product to the user.

17.12 Profit methods

Profit based methods tend to be used where a comparable transaction cannot be identified, and the most popular solution is the profit split method under which the profit of the total transaction is allocated among the connected parties on a rational basis in accordance with the contribution of each to the overall profit. This raises innumerable problems in practice as to what that contribution might be, particularly in relation to the intellectual property involved. The profit per product is often split by reference to a functional analysis of items such as management, administration and finance, manufacturing, assembling and processing, testing, research and development, packaging, labelling, warehousing, preserving, storing, distribution, branding, marketing, wholesaling, retailing, transportation, advertising, after sales servicing, warranties and guarantees; ownership of intellectual property, brand names and capital employed. The analysis of risk should take account of the commercial link between the entities, parent company guarantees and support, liabilities to third parties and employees, product and environmental risk, financing, economic, political and currency risks. Again the problem is that many of these risks are simple to recognise as existing but difficult to quantify.

The profit split analysis also has to take account of unsuccessful research and development. It would clearly be inappropriate to look at the direct costs of developing a marketable patent if only one in ten ideas which are developed actually result in a commercially useful, patentable invention at the end of the day.

A profit split method may also have to take into account launch costs for a new product, which may well give rise to a loss in the initial period whilst the product is being established on the market.

The comparable profit method also uses functional analysis to try and arrive at an arm's length price by looking at the return on capital employed, and other financial ratios such as net profits to sales in order to arrive at a profit norm for such products. This suffers from the same problem as the CUP method of finding suitable comparisons to establish the norm.

The rate of return method, which is not specifically referred to as such in the OECD 1995 Report, is a variant of the comparable profits method which looks at the return on equity or net assets of the connected parties, compared with those of unconnected parties, to try and establish the effect on connected parties of the transfer prices used. The problem here is to take account of assets used for different purpose by the connected parties and also finding the bench mark comparisons. It is also difficult to compare the accounts of different companies which have acquired assets at different times and in different ways. For example, a company which has bought its intellectual property rights may have a very different return on capital from one which has developed those rights in house over a substantial period of time.

Global methods of profit allocations such as by reference to turnover, labour costs etc. have the advantage that they are easy to calculate but are almost entirely arbitrary in their application to an arm's length price for an intellectual property right.

Focus

The successful products have to cover the cost of the unsuccessful, otherwise the producer goes bankrupt.

17.13 Arm's length range

Both the OECD and HMRC recognise that it is impossible to specify in any given set of circumstances a particular price which is the one and only arm's length price and that there is a danger in Revenue officials trying to substitute their own commercial judgement for that of the enterprise which they are examining and using the benefit of hindsight, which was not available when the prices were fixed. In practice, the connected parties should record how they have arrived at the price and their reasons for doing so, and the information available to them, and any attempt to adjust this price should be resisted in the absence of compelling reasons to do so.

The documentation which HMRC will expect taxpayers to prepare and retain includes that which identifies any relevant commercial or financial relations falling within the scope of the transfer pricing legislation, the nature and terms (including prices and quantum), of relevant transactions (including transactions which form a series), and any relevant offsets. It should include the method or methods by which the nature, terms and quantum of relevant transactions were arrived at, including any study of comparables undertaken. It should also show how that method has resulted in arm's length terms etc., or, where it has not, what computational adjustment is required and how it has been calculated. This will usually include an analysis of market data or other information on third party comparables. It should also record the terms of relevant commercial arrangements with both third party and group customers. These will include contemporaneous commercial agreements (e.g. service or distribution contracts, loan agreements) and any budgets, forecasts or other papers containing information relied on in arriving at arm's length terms etc., or in calculating any adjustment made in order to satisfy the requirements of the transfer pricing legislation.

> **Focus**
>
> The problem is that the intellectual property is unique as otherwise it would not be protectable as intellectual property.

17.14 Intangible rights

The OECD Report distinguishes between production intangibles, such as patents, know-how, designs, models etc. and marketing intangibles, such as trade marks, trade names, logos, service marks etc. A further distinction can be drawn between the transfer of intellectual property by way of sale or licence or the sale of goods or products protected by intellectual property where that value is reflected in the sale price. In the transfer pricing context, where the intellectual property is not separately licensed or assigned, the transaction will be regarded as a transfer of goods or services, not a transfer of intellectual property. It is quite common for companies to commission other connected companies to carry out research and development in certain areas on their behalf and on such terms that the intellectual property resulting belongs to the commissioner. In the context of transfer pricing, it is clearly difficult to substantiate a substantial profit accruing to a company in a tax haven which licences intellectual property rights to connected or unconnected companies within the group at a cost which is substantially more than the cost of developing those products, where the development has been sub-contracted to other companies in the group, perhaps on a cost plus a fixed percentage basis. HMRC would be likely to challenge such a position under the series of transactions rules in TIOPA 2010, s 150.

In intellectual property terms, in the OECD Report, the emphasis is very much on the arm's length royalty which would have been paid by an unconnected licensee to an independent licensor and it rejects the American concept of the 'Super Royalty' under which the royalty due to the licensor should be commensurate with the actual income which can be generated from the licensed rights. Transfer pricing cases rarely end up in court on the basis of the valuation, but an exception is *Chen Hsong Machinery Co Ltd v IRC* (D52/96) before the Hong Kong Board of Review, where a trade mark was valued on the basis of a capitalised value, using a multiple of 5, of a notional royalty of 6% less 1% for the maintenance of the trademark, ie 5% net, applied to the projected turnover for the forthcoming year.

17.15 Royalty comparisons in practice

In many cases, industry practice will dictate a reasonable commercial royalty in a given set of circumstances which is relatively easy to justify from trade magazines, sector analysis reports and other information likely to be available to companies within the industry concerned.

Where the market value of the intellectual property is required, a hypothetical royalty rate is the usual starting point, from which can be ascertained a capital value on the basis of the net present value, at a reasonable discount rate, of the anticipated royalty cash flows, on the basis of the arm's length royalty rate applied to the anticipated production.

The IVSC TIP 3 paragraph 16 states that 'The relief-from-royalty, or royalty savings, method estimates the value of an intangible asset by reference to the value of the hypothetical royalty payments that would be saved through owning the asset, as compared with licensing the asset from a third party. It involves estimating the total royalty payments that would need to be made over the asset's useful life, by a hypothetical licensee to a hypothetical licensor. Where appropriate, the royalty payments over the life of the asset are adjusted for tax and discounted to present value.'

Example

Lebedev Ltd, Valuation of Patent Rights

Instructions
We have been asked to consider the market value of Lebedev Ltd.'s rights under the patents listed on the schedule headed 'Status Report on Patent Applications'. The date of valuation has been taken as 1 October 2014.

Purpose of valuation
The valuation is required for the purposes of corporation tax on chargeable gains in order to establish the value of the patent rights to be acquired by a connected company within TCGA 1992, s 18(1), ITA 2007 s 993 and CTA 2010, s1122.

Basis of valuation,
Open market value, which is defined under TCGA 1992, s 272 as the price which those assets might reasonably be expected to fetch on a sale in the open market.

Valuation approach
We consider it reasonable to arrive at the current value of the company's patent rights by estimating the net present value of the future royalties which the company could reasonably expect to achieve if it were to license its patent rights to another manufacturer.

Valuation
We have been provided by the company with a forecast of its turnover in the five-year period from 2014 to 2018. At present the company achieves gross margins (after allowing for costs of sale, which include manufacturing costs) in the region of 60%. We therefore consider that the company could reasonably expect to receive a royalty on turnover of about one-half of that gross margin, say 30%. In view of the uncertainty involved, however, we would reduce that rate to 20% after the first three years.

As the company is forecasting a considerable increase in turnover over the next five years, arising in part from contracts which have yet to be awarded, we consider it prudent to adopt relatively high discount rates in arriving at the net present value of the assumed royalty income. We would therefore apply a discount rate of 25% over the five years covered by the forecast.

The company's patents will run out by the year 2022. We have therefore added a further four years' turnover to the company's forecast, at the same level of turnover as in 2018, the last year of the company's forecast, except for the final year where sales are predicted to fall as a result of the anticipated end of the patent protection. We have, nevertheless, increased the discount rate for those final four years to 35%, to reflect the increased risk of achieving the forecast royalty, as well as other factors.

On that basis, the net present value is as follows:

Year	*Turnover*	*Royalty level*		*Discount factor*		*Net present value of royalty £000s*
		30%	*20%*			
	£m	£m	£m	*@ 25%*	*@ 35%*	
2014	2	0.6		0.8		480
2015	4	1.2		0.64		768
2016	8	2.4		0.512		1,229
2017	10		2.0	0.409		818
2018	12		2.4	0.327		785
2019	12		2.4		0.165	396
2020	12		2.4		0.122	293
2021	12		2.4		0.091	219
2022	8		1.6		0.067	107
						5,095
Corporation tax at 20%						1,019
After corporation tax						4,076

We therefore put the value of the company's patent rights at £4,076,000.

17.16 HMRC International Manual – transfer pricing

The HMRC International Manual covers transfer pricing in INTM480000 et seq (18 July 2018) under the general headings of:

INTM480500	Introduction: contents
INTM481000	Governance: contents
INTM482000	Risk assessment: contents
INTM483000	Working an enquiry: contents
INTM484000	Examining transfer pricing reports: contents
INTM485000	Evidence gathering: contents
INTM486000	Interaction with indirect taxes: contents
INTM489000	Derivation and destination tables: contents
INTM480510	Scope of the original guidance
INTM480520	Alternatives to consider before transfer pricing
INTM480530	Giving transfer pricing advice to customers
INTM480540	Real time working of transfer pricing issues (excluding thin capitalisation)
INTM480550	Real time working of transfer pricing issues: thin capitalisation

'Transfer Pricing: Operational guidance: scope of the operational guidance

This operational guidance consists of the following chapters.

Governance

The chapter beginning at INTM481000 sets out the governance for transfer pricing work and explains how it applies to the stages of an enquiry. It also describes the role of the Transfer Pricing Group and how they can help.

Risk assessment

The chapter beginning at INTM482000 explains the principles of assessing tax risk in applying transfer pricing rules. It considers such issues as building an understanding of the business, the amount of tax at risk, resources, and specific factors that might influence pricing.

Working a transfer pricing case

The chapter beginning at INTM483000 looks at some practical and compliance issues involved in working a transfer pricing case, from opening the case, deciding on the information and documents needed, through to settlement.

Examining transfer pricing reports

The chapter beginning at INTM484000 is concerned with examining transfer pricing reports. In many cases case teams will be presented with a transfer pricing report prepared for the business under review. A good transfer pricing report can be a great help in resolving concerns promptly. But in practice such reports vary greatly in scope and quality. The guidance will help teams to evaluate the information and conclusions in a report and indentify what is missing from it.

Establishing the arm's length price – evidence gathering

The chapter beginning at INTM485000 provides practical guidance on how to establish the transfer price. If flaws are found in the transfer pricing used by a business, case teams will need to propose a better alternative approach to put in its place. This chapter looks at establishing the facts and how to find and use comparables.

Transfer pricing: Operational guidance: alternatives to consider before transfer pricing

How does TIOPA10/Part 4 interact with other legislation?

There are alternative ways of challenging the position if it appears that a group may not have followed the arm's length principle in determining its transfer pricing. Compared to TIOPA10/Part 4 these alternatives can sometimes be more straightforward and less time-consuming. The points below are not listed in any order of prominence.

UK Residence

A company which states it is resident outside the UK and which is transacting business with a UK resident person, may be vulnerable to a fundamental challenge to its residence status. If it can be established that the central management and control of that company is in the United Kingdom, it can be taxed accordingly. This subject is dealt with in detail at INTM120000 onwards.

Non-resident companies

Even if subsidiary companies are not resident in the UK, the Controlled Foreign Companies ('CFC') legislation may apply. Detailed guidance on the UK's CFC regime can be found at INTM190000 onwards.

When faced with a non resident company outside the scope of the CFC legislation, it is usually sensible to concentrate on transactions between the non-resident company and its UK affiliates applying all relevant legislation (whether or not it is transfer pricing specific).

Permanent establishment

A permanent establishment ('PE') is "a fixed place of business through which the business of an enterprise is wholly or partly carried on" (as stated in Article 5 of the OECD Model Tax Convention). Facts and circumstances may indicate that a foreign business operating in the UK through an agency, a branch or an associated or subsidiary company may have a UK PE. There is detailed guidance about PEs at INTM281000 onwards.

Capital Transactions

Characterising transactions as being on capital account is particularly pertinent in the case of companies in start-up mode. 'Once and for all' payments can sometimes be properly disallowed on capital/revenue grounds.

Asset Transfers – Capital Gains

The TCGA 1992 legislation on the transfer of assets applies only to transactions on capital account. But, by applying the arm's length standard to non-arm's length transactions, it effectively deals with profit shifts that occur by virtue of the transfer pricing of asset transfers.

For guidance on TCGA92/S18 (Transfers of assets between connected persons) and TCGA92/S173 (Transfers of assets within groups) see CG14480 onwards.

Asset Transfers – Distributions

CTA10/S1020 (formerly ICTA88/S209(4)) can be useful in certain cases. It deals with the situation where a company transfers an asset (or liability) to one of its members at undervalue (or overvalue). Unless both are companies resident in the UK, CTA10/S1020 treats the difference as a distribution. Notwithstanding that transfer pricing principles may be applied to uplift the UK profits, a deemed distribution under CTA10/S1020 is a 'qualifying distribution'.

Inward Financial Transactions – ITA2007/S874

See the guidance on Thin Capitalisation (INTM510000 onwards) and Intra-group funding (INTM500000 onwards) for advice on the use of ITA07/S874 (formerly ICTA88/S349) in circumstances where the terms of a loan would have been different at arm's length but the requisite control test of TIOPA10/Part 4 is not satisfied. It may be possible to establish an income tax charge on the recipient (and deny any request for the interest to flow gross) if the amount of interest can be shown to be excessive by virtue of a special relationship between the parties. But this will depend on the precise terms of any relevant tax treaty.

Financial Avoidance – CTA09/S441

Where financial avoidance is involved, it may be appropriate to consider use of the anti-avoidance provision at CTA09/S441 (formerly FA96/SCH9/PARA13). It operates by disallowing debits where in an accounting period a loan relationship has an unallowable purpose.

Whilst CSTD Corporation Tax and Business Income Tax has assumed responsibility for overall policy and domestic operation of the legislation, Business, Assets & International should always be consulted before the section is used in relation to cross-border transactions.

CTA09/S54 and other computational rules

Before applying TIOPA10/Part 4 consideration must be given to the normal computation rules, in particular CTA09/S54 (previously ICTA88/S74(1)(a)) which prohibits the deduction of disbursements or expenses not wholly and exclusively laid out or expended for the purposes of the trade. If there are specific rules denying a deduction for particular expenditure, then these rules take precedence; there is no need to consider the arm's length nature of the particular provision in question.

Broadly for any trade, profession or vocation expenditure is subject to CTA09/S54. Expenditure not incurred wholly and exclusively for business purposes is not allowable. So for example, a UK company may be recharged the cost of a particular service by another group member. If the company did not actually receive that service, any payment would be disallowed under CTA09/S54. If the company did receive the service then the question of price would be subject to TIOPA10/Part 4; even if nothing was actually charged or, conversely, if the arm's length price turned out to be nil.

Alternatively if a UK company, trading as a service provider for other group companies, incurs expenditure on behalf of those group companies as part of its trade, the quantum of the recharge will be considered under TIOPA10/Part 4.

The fact that the original recharge was zero is insufficient, of itself, to establish that the transaction is not within the UK company's trade. Thus, in such situations, the matter would be considered under TIOPA10/Part 4, unless other factors suggest that the transaction is not within the UK company's trade.

This flowchart illustrates the process which should be followed in considering whether CTA09/S54 (or CTA09/S1219 in respect of management expenses – see CTM08180) applies in situations to which TIOPA10/Part 4 would otherwise apply:

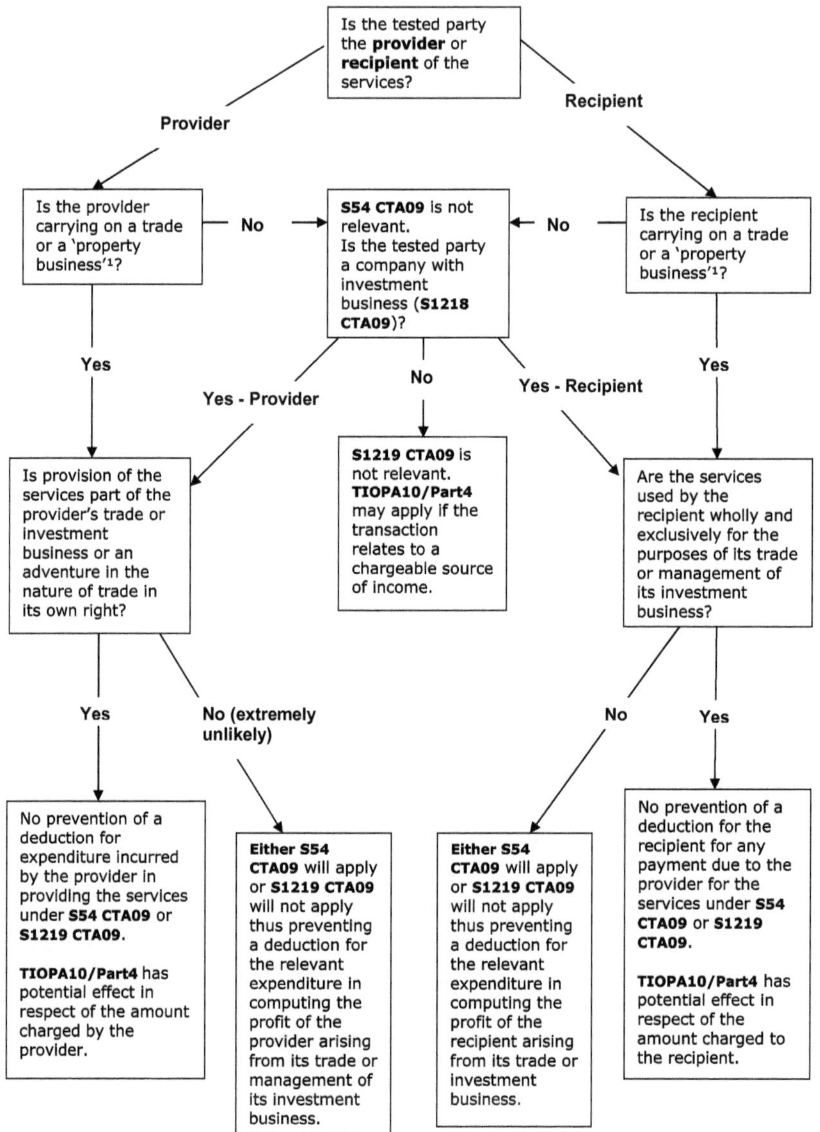
TIOPA/Part 4: S54 or S1219 CTA09 Interaction – Flowchart
This flowchart applies when costs are incurred (or should be incurred) in the provision or receipt of intra-group services.
Is the tested party the provider or recipient of the services?
Provider
Recipient
Is the provider carrying on a trade or a 'property business'[1]?
No
S54 CTA09 is not relevant. Is the tested party a company with investment business (S1218 CTA09)?
No
Is the recipient carrying on a trade or a 'property business'[1]?
Yes
Yes - Provider
No
Yes - Recipient
Yes
Is provision of the services part of the provider's trade or investment business or an adventure in the nature of trade in its own right?
S1219 CTA09 is not relevant. TIOPA10/Part4 may apply if the transaction relates to a chargeable source of income.
Are the services used by the recipient wholly and exclusively for the purposes of its trade or management of its investment business?
Yes
No (extremely unlikely)
No
Yes
No prevention of a deduction for expenditure incurred by the provider in providing the services under S54 CTA09 or S1219 CTA09.
TIOPA10/Part4 has potential effect in respect of the amount charged by the provider.
Either S54 CTA09 will apply or S1219 CTA09 will not apply thus preventing a deduction for the relevant expenditure in computing the profit of the provider arising from its trade or management of its investment business.
Either S54 CTA09 will apply or S1219 CTA09 will not apply thus preventing a deduction for the relevant expenditure in computing the profit of the recipient arising from its trade or investment business.
No prevention of a deduction for the recipient for any payment due to the provider for the services under S54 CTA09 or S1219 CTA09.
TIOPA10/Part4 has potential effect in respect of the amount charged to the recipient.
[1] Within the meaning of S204 CTA09

Other computational rules may also be in point, such as CTA09/S1298 regarding business entertaining expenditure. If an affiliate provides entertaining to a company, no deduction could be claimed for any recharge to the company.'

HMRC International Manual

INTM481010	Introduction
INTM481020	What types of enquiry are within the governance?
INTM481030	The stages of an enquiry
INTM481040	The selection stage
INTM481050	The progress stage
INTM481060	The resolution stage
INTM481070	The Transfer Pricing Group
INTM481080	Case teams and the wider transfer pricing community
INTM482010	Introduction
INTM482020	Issues to consider before starting a transfer pricing enquiry: resources
INTM482030	Issues to consider before starting a transfer pricing enquiry: tax at risk
INTM482040	Transfer pricing risk indicators: general
INTM482050	Transfer pricing risk indicators: effective tax rates
INTM482060	Transfer pricing risk indicators: transfer pricing rules in other countries
INTM482070	Transfer pricing risk indicators: comparing the results of the company and the group
INTM482080	Transfer pricing risk indicators: losses over a number of years
INTM482090	Transfer pricing risk indicators: payment of significant management or service fees
INTM482100	Transfer pricing risk indicators: payment of royalties
INTM482110	Transfer pricing risk indicators: ownership of intellectual property
INTM482120	Transfer pricing risk indicators: business reorganisations
INTM482130	Conducting a transfer pricing risk assessment: detailed process
INTM482140	Conducting a transfer pricing risk assessment: review of information from other sources
INTM482150	Conducting a transfer pricing risk assessment: lack of information
INTM482160	Conducting a transfer pricing risk assessment: range of issues

INTM482170	Summary and conclusions
INTM483010	Opening the case
INTM483020	Working the case
INTM483030	Transfer pricing documentation
INTM483040	Initial information request
INTM483050	Dealing with the initial response
INTM483060	Exchange of information
INTM483070	Reaching a settlement
INTM483080	How many years?
INTM483090	Assessments and enquiry closure notices
INTM483100	Interest
INTM483110	Penalties
INTM483120	Penalties: negligence or carelessness
INTM483130	After the settlement
INTM484010	Overview
INTM484020	Report contents
INTM484030	Legislation
INTM484040	Information in a report – functional analysis
INTM484050	What transactions are covered?
INTM484060	OECD methodologies
INTM484070	OECD methods
INTM484080	Using other methods
INTM484090	Arm's length range
INTM484100	Dealing with global transfer pricing
INTM485010	Overview
INTM485020	Establish the facts
INTM485022	Comparability Analysis
INTM485023	Economically relevant characteristics
INTM485024	Risk allocation
INTM485030	Accurate delineation of the actual transaction: full process
INTM485021	Using the most appropriate method
INTM485040	Using a test year
INTM485050	Bargaining power
INTM485060	Searching for comparables
INTM485070	Searching for comparables: internal comparables
INTM485080	Searching for comparables: public information

INTM485090	Searching for comparables: UK or global companies?
INTM485100	Searching for comparables: using commercial databases
INTM485110	Searching for comparables: making adjustments to potential comparables
INTM485120	Searching for comparables: range of results
INTM485130	Industry standards
INTM485140	General research
INTM486010	Interaction with VAT

Focus

HMRC's views set out in their manuals are a helpful synopsis, but are not binding on taxpayers and are regularly updated.

17.17 EC report on intellectual property valuation

On 29 November 2013, the European Commission published the Final Report from the Expert Group on Intellectual Property Valuation.

After the introduction there is a review of intellectual property valuation approaches, methods and standards followed by reviews of intellectual property valuation and raising finance, intellectual property valuations and accounting and reporting, and intellectual property valuation in litigation. There are also recommendations for possible policy actions, conclusions and appendices. It is recognised that 'there is a clear need to increase market actors' confidence and certainty in intellectual property valuation methods as a way to stimulate' intellectual property transactions, to support, intellectual property based financing and to give companies the tools to provide information about their IP'. It is recognised that 'the uniqueness of IP makes comparisons with other IP difficult, thereby limiting the usefulness of comparison based pricing':

> 'The Expert Group recommends a number of policy actions that could have a significant impact on reducing the identified barriers in order to increase the efficient use of IP valuation and to make such valuation flexible, transparent and reliable to respond to market requirements:
>
> - Establishing a data source containing information for use by valuation professionals, as a way to enhance credibility of valuations by improving data and available information on IP transactions;
> - Creating an organisation to oversee IP valuation practice as a way to increase confidence in the quality of valuations being performed and to ensure that valuations are in line with generally accepted principles and standards;
> - Introducing a risk sharing scheme for banks to facilitate IP secured lending to innovative companies, especially SMEs;
> - Introducing an additional reporting section for intangible assets and IP that would increase the transparency of IP value within company accounts, providing important information to lenders, investors and stakeholders.'

International Accounting Standard IAS 38 defines an intangible asset as 'an identifiable non-monetary asset without physical substance'.

The accounting for intangible assets is discussed further in **Chapters 20** and **21**.

However, where, under EU rules, a company has to produce a management report with the accounts, this should include an indication of the activities in the field of research and development.

Appendix 2 of the EC report includes the following at page 75:

> **'Supplementary information on IP valuation methodology**
>
> **Section 1: Relief from royalty methods**
>
> The primary income-based approach used in the valuation of IP is the relief from royalty approach. The methodology is based on the economic theory of deprival value. Based on this theory, the value of the IP is equal to the capitalised amount of the royalties that would be payable if the IP was not owned but had to be licensed at arm's length from a third party.
>
> In other words, the Relief from Royalty approach posits intangible value based on a royalty savings hypothesis, essentially asking: "over the useful life of the intellectual property, what would a person or business save by owning, rather than licensing, the intellectual property under consideration?"
>
> The primary steps involved in applying this method are:
>
> - Identifying the appropriate royalty rate;
> - Calculating royalty cash flows (by applying the royalty rate to an appropriate "royalty base", often projections of revenues derived from use of the IP); and
> - Capitalizing periodic royalty payments, generally on a post-tax basis, by discounting at a suitable discount rate.
>
> A number of assumptions have to be made, notably as to a reasonable royalty rate, the reasonable remaining useful life of the IP, and an appropriate discount rate (or weighted average cost of capital, taking risk into account) by which to obtain the present value of these future, hypothetical royalty savings.
>
> The relief from royalty method is generally used to measure the overall value of an IP asset, and so the calculation is usually based on royalty cash flows projected into perpetuity. In some cases, IP assets are licensed for a period of time (often several years) in return for an upfront payment. One advantage of the relief from royalty method is that it can also be used to consider the value of such a licence (by capitalising projected cash flows over the licence period only).
>
> There are two commonly used ways of establishing an appropriate royalty rate for use of a particular piece of IP, including:
>
> - Comparable royalties; and
> - Economic benefits analysis.
>
> *Comparables approach to determining an appropriate royalty rate*
>
> The comparable royalties approach is often regarded as the best approach to establishing a suitable royalty rate. Negotiations between willing licensors and willing licensees, in like circumstances, will, at least in theory, provide the best available information about the level of an appropriate royalty for the IP in question.

In practice, however, it may not be possible to identify perfect comparables. In this case, it may be necessary to adjust the comparables available to reflect important differences, taking into consideration factors such as the IP being licensed, specific rights of use granted to the licensee, specific terms of the license, etc.

In practice, with the exception of experienced IP valuation professionals who often have access to their own databases of licence agreements, it can be challenging to identify even imperfect comparables for many IP assets.

Economic benefits approach to determining an appropriate royalty rate

IP generally provides, or is intended to provide, an economic benefit to the user. One view of an appropriate royalty is that it provides a means to share that benefit between the user of the IP and its owner. This approach is most useful where it is possible to identify the specific economic benefits created through use of the IP. A royalty rate can then be derived by considering how these benefits should be shared between licensor and licensee.

The economic benefit created through use of the IP is the incremental benefit a business derives through using the IP, compared with using the next best alternative. In many cases, it is difficult to measure this incremental benefit. In such circumstances, it is possible instead to consider the overall profits a business derives from the operations that utilise the IP (the 'available profits'), and to consider how these are shared between licensor and licensee.

What split of incremental benefits, or overall profits, is appropriate between licensor and licensee will depend on the costs incurred, assets contributed, risks borne, and the functions performed by each party. It is particularly important when dividing overall available profits (as apposed to specific incremental benefits) to take into account the other assets that contribute to earning the profits of the business, and which party is providing these.

Input data required

In addition to the data sets required for income based approaches generally, the following valuation inputs may be required in the relief-from-royalty method.

- An estimate of the hypothetical royalty rate that would be paid if the asset were licenced from a third party,
- Projections for the royalty base, e.g. revenues that the royalty rate would be applied to over the life of the IP together with an estimate of the life of the IP,
- Rate at which tax relief would be obtainable on hypothetical royalty payments,
- The cost of marketing and any other costs that would be borne by a licensee in utilising the asset and,
- An appropriate discount rate or capitalisation rate to convert the asset's hypothetical royalty payments to a present value.

Potential sources of input data

In addition to the sources of data required for income based approaches generally, the following sources of data may be used in the relief-from-royalty method:

- Databases of licence agreements,
- IP valuation professionals,
- IP transfer professionals.

Section 2: Premium profits method

The IVSC defines the premium profits (sometimes referred to as incremental income) method as:

> "The premium profits, or incremental income, method indicates the value of an IP asset by comparing an estimate of the profits or cash flows that would be earned by a business using the asset with those that would be earned by a business that does not use the asset. The forecast incremental profits or cash flows achievable through use of the asset are then calculated. Forecast periodic amounts are brought to a present value through use of either a suitable discount factor or suitable capitalisation multiple."

Input data required

In addition to the data sets required for income based approaches generally, the following valuation inputs may be required in the premium profits method (adapted from IVSC Professional Board Meeting documents, 3 November 2011).

- Forecast periodic profit, cost savings or cash flows expected to be generated by a market participant using the intangible asset,
- Forecast periodic profit, cost savings or cash flows expected to be generated by a market participant not using the IP and
- An appropriate capitalisation multiple or discount rate to capitalise forecast periodic profit or cash flows.

Potential sources of input data

In addition to the sources of data required for income based approaches generally, the following sources of data may be used in the premium profits method:

- Financial reports and data of the organisation utilising the IP,
- Sales data, forecasted sales data of products and services with an IP component,
- Market research data and documents,
- Any entities, using similar or identical intangible assets for which information is available publicly and,
- Proprietary databases of the valuer.

Section 3: Excess earnings method

The excess earnings method determines the value of IP as the present value of the cash flows attributable to the subject IP after excluding the proportion of the cash flows that are attributable to other assets.

It is a method that is often used for valuations used in financial reporting when there is a requirement for the acquirer to allocate the overall price paid for a business between tangible assets, identifiable intangible assets and goodwill.

The excess earnings method can either be applied using several periods of forecast cash flows – the "multi-period excess earnings method" or using a single period of forecast cash flows – the "single-period excess earnings method". In practice, because an intangible asset will normally bring monetary benefits over an extended period, the multi-period excess earnings method is more commonly used.

Input data required

In addition to the data sets required for income based approaches generally, the following valuation inputs may be required in the excess earnings method (adapted from IVSC Professional Board Meeting documents, 3 November 2011):

- Forecast cash flows obtainable from the business to which the subject intangible asset contributes to cash flows – this will involve allocating both income and expenses appropriately to the pertinent business or group of assets of the entity that includes all the income derivable from the subject intangible asset,
- Contributory asset charges in respect of all other assets in such business(es), including other intangible assets,
- An appropriate discount rate to enable expected cash flows attributable to the subject IP alone to be brought to a present value and
- If appropriate and applicable, a calculation of tax amortisation benefits.

Potential sources of input data

In addition to the sources of data required for income based approaches generally, the following sources of data may be used in the excess earnings method:

- Financial reports and data of the organisation utilising the IP.

Section 4: Residual value methods

The residual value method takes as its starting point the value of a business as a whole, and allocates this between the various assets employed in it, commensurate with their contribution to the overall value.

Once part of the value of the business has been allocated to its tangible assets, the residual value is considered to relate to intangibles. This approach is easier to apply where all the intangibles of the business are being valued collectively. Where an individual IP is to be valued, it is necessary to allocate the residual value identified among the various intangible assets employed in the business. Although there are some methods that can be used to make such an allocation, the data and skills required to apply these methods reliably are often unavailable. The residual value method is therefore most suited to a valuation of all the intangible assets of a business.

The key steps in this method are to:

- Value the business in which the IP is being used, arriving at an "enterprise value";
- Ascertain the market or fair value of tangible assets;
- Deduct the value of tangible assets from enterprise value to obtain the value of intangible assets (the "residual value"); and
- Allocate this residual value amongst the various intangibles if required.

To obtain the residual value, it is the market value of tangible assets that should, in theory, be deducted from enterprise value. In practice, the value of intangible assets is usually recorded in accounting statements, which value most assets at historical cost, and are often the only source of data available. In such circumstances, to the extent that book value is lower than market value, the residual value calculated will be overstated.

Once the residual value has been estimated, it can be allocated between intangibles in one of the following ways:

Value chain analysis

This requires an understanding of all the value-adding activities undertaken by the business. From this, the intangible assets that contribute to the business making profits can be identified, and their relative importance understood, using benchmark returns for comparable companies. Where it is possible to perform such an analysis, this method has the advantage of taking into account the specific circumstances in which the IP is being used. The difficulty, however, can be to perform this analysis in a quantitative rather than qualitative way.

Market reference points

Where other, comparable, companies have performed a similar allocation exercise, this can provide a reference point that can be applied to the residual value calculated. One situation in which companies often perform such an analysis is when they require assets in a business combination. However, the allocation of assets in an acquisition can be affected by accounting practice, which can vary over time and from one jurisdiction to another, and so care must be taken when interpreting the results of such an analysis.'

Focus

The valuation of intellectual property is problematic as comparables, and their values are difficult to identify, as pointed out in this 100-page report.

17.18 OECD/G20 guidance on transfer pricing aspects of intangibles

In September 2014, the OECD published this guidance as part of the work on the Base Erosion and Profit Shifting (BEPS) project.

'Section A – Identifying Intangibles

6.6 In these guidelines, therefore, the word "intangible" is intended to address something which is not a physical asset or a financial asset, which is capable of being owned or controlled for use in commercial activities, and whose use or transfer would be compensated had it occurred in a transaction between independent parties in comparable circumstances. Rather than focusing on accounting or legal definitions, the thrust of a transfer pricing analysis in a case involving intangibles should be the determination of the conditions that would be agreed upon between independent parties for a comparable transaction.

6.7 Intangibles that are important to consider for transfer pricing purposes are not always recognised as intangible assets for accounting purposes. For example, costs associated with developing intangibles internally through expenditures such as research and development and advertising are sometimes expensed rather than capitalised for accounting purposes and the intangibles resulting from such expenditures therefore are not always reflected on the balance sheet. Such intangibles may nevertheless be used to generate significant economic value and may need to be considered for transfer pricing purposes. Furthermore, the enhancement to value that may arise from the complementary nature of a collection of intangibles when exploited together is not always reflected on the balance sheet. Accordingly, whether an item should be considered to be an intangible for transfer pricing purposes under Article 9 of the OECD Model Tax Convention can be informed by its characterisation for accounting purposes, but will not be determined by such characterisation only. Furthermore, the determination that an item should be regarded as an intangible for transfer pricing purposes does not determine or follow from its characterisation for general tax purposes, as, for example, an expense or an amortisable asset.

6.16 Certain categories of intangibles are, however, commonly referred to in discussions of transfer pricing matters. To facilitate discussions, definitions of two such commonly used terms, "marketing intangibles" and "trade intangibles" are contained in the Glossary and referred to from time to time in the discussion in these Guidelines. It should be emphasised that generic references to marketing or trade intangibles do not relieve taxpayers or tax administrations from their obligation in a transfer pricing analysis to identify relevant intangibles with specificity, nor does the use of those terms suggest that a different approach should be applied in determining arm's length conditions for transactions that involve either marketing intangibles or trade intangibles.

The Glossary of these Guidelines is amended by deleting the definition of the term "marketing intangible" and replacing that definition with the following language:

> "Marketing intangible
>
> An intangible (within the meaning of paragraph 6.6) that relates to marketing activities, aids in the commercial exploitation of a product or service, and/or has an important promotional value for the product concerned. Depending on the context, marketing intangibles may include, for example, trademarks, trade names, customer lists, customer relationships, and proprietary market and customer data that is used for aids in marketing and selling goods or services to customers."

6.17 In certain instances these Guidelines refer to "unique and valuable" intangibles. "Unique and valuable" intangibles are those intangibles (i) that are not comparable to intangibles used by or available to parties to potentially comparable transactions, and (ii) whose use in business operations (e.g. manufacturing, provision of services, marketing, sales or administration) is expected to yield greater future economic benefits than would be expected in the absence of the intangible.'

Section B deals with the ownership of enhancement, intangibles and transactions involving the development, enhancement, maintenance, protection and exploitation of intangibles.

> '6.41 In identifying the legal owner of intangibles, an intangible and any licence relating to that intangible are considered to be different intangibles for transfer pricing purposes, each having a different owner. See paragraph 6.26. For example, Company A, the legal owner of a trademark, may provide an exclusive licence to Company B to manufacture, market, and sell goods using the trademark. One intangible, the trademark, is legally owned by Company A. Another Intangible, the licence to use the trademark in connection with manufacturing, marketing and distribution of trademarked products, is legally owned by Company A. Another intangible, the licence to use the trademark in connection with manufacturing, marketing and distribution of trademarked products, is legally owned by Company B. Depending on the facts and circumstances, marketing activities undertaken by Company B pursuant to its licence may potentially affect the value of the underlying intangible legally owned by Company A, the value of Company B's licence, or both.
>
> 6.42 While determining legal ownership is an important first step in the analysis, that determination is separate and distinct from the question of remuneration under the arm's length principle. For transfer pricing purposes, legal ownership

> of intangibles, by itself, does not confer any right ultimately to retain returns derived by the MNE group from exploiting the intangible, even though such returns may initially accrue to the legal owner as a result of its legal or contractual right to exploit intangible. The return ultimately retained by or attributed to the legal owner depends upon the functions it performs, the assets it uses, and the risks it assumes, and upon the contributions made by other MNE group members through their functions performed, assets used, and risks assumed. For example, in the case of an internally developed intangible, if the legal owner performs no relevant functions, uses no relevant assets, and assumes no relevant risks, but acts solely as a title holding entity, the legal owner will not ultimately be entitled to any portion of the return derived by the MNE group from the exploitation of the intangible other than arm's length compensation, if any, for holding title.'

The suggestion that the legal owner may have no entitlement to any portion of the return attributable to the intangible seems untenable. If Company A commissions and makes a film or musical recording and licences it to a distributor, it may have no further involvement in the product. However, it will probably be entitled to a royalty from the distributor, whether a group company or not, even though that company makes contributions to further enhance the value of the intangible. This applies whether or not the distributor is part of the group.

The guidance goes on to consider the functions, assets and risks related to intangibles.

Section C deals with transactions involving the use or transfer of intangibles.

Section D provides supplemental guidance for determining arm's length conditions in cases involving intangibles, setting out general principles and dealing with comparability of intangibles or rights therein. Matters to be considered include exclusivity, extent and duration of legal protection geographic scope, useful life, stage of development, rights to enhancements, revision and updates, and expectation of future benefit. It is also necessary to consider the comparison of risk in cases involving transfers of intangibles or rights in intangibles, comparability adjustments with regard to transfer of intangibles or rights in intangibles and the use of comparables drawn from databases, and the importance of conducting a comparability analysis.

Supplemental guidance is given on transfer pricing methods in matters involving the transfer of intangibles or rights therein, which would usually involve the comparable uncontrolled price method, although profit split methods may be appropriate. There is guidance on the use of valuation techniques such as the discounted value of projected cash flows, which emphasises the importance of accurate projections, growth rates, useful life and terminal values.

There is also supplemental guidance for transactions involving the use of intangibles in connection with the sale of goods or provision of services.

The annex includes examples of the application of the transfer pricing guidelines in hypothetical cases.

17.19 Brand valuation

A business brand, such as Apple, Google, Microsoft, Facebook or Amazon, the world's most valuable brands, have been given values in the tens of billions of dollars. However, many businesses have well-recognised brands which have a more modest but recognisable value. The development of a brand costs money and a successful brand can be worth a lot, and can cost a lot to develop and maintain.

This cost can be capitalised if it can be shown to be of value, ie if the branding brings in greater profits than the unbranded production or service it has a measurable value such as the cost of replicating a new brand or the amount for which comparable brands have been sold.

Another method of valuing a brand is the present value of the super-profits, if any, which the brand attracts, on the price at which it could be sold in the market, by comparing similar transactions for which details are available.

Alternatively, a brand can be valued at the present value of the future net earnings attributable to the brand, taking into account the costs of maintaining or developing the brand.

Other valuation methods are the relief from royalty method, ie the royalty which would have to be paid to produce the same results, or the in-house development of the brand, the discounted present value of future cash flows as a result of the brand. If the brand enables the product to be sold for a higher price than would otherwise be the case, the value is the present value of the super-profits, often referred to as the 'excess earnings method'.

The price premium method is based on the capitalised future super-profits attributable to a branded as opposed to an unbranded product.

In some cases, the value is based on the capitalisation of profits attributable to the brand.

Other methods apply a price/earning method based on the multiple derived from reported brand values. The cost of developing the brand could in appropriate cases be capitalised. The replacement cost method is based on the cost of building a similar market share for a similar product from scratch.

One or more of these methods may enable a realistic value to be placed on the brands which have been or are being developed.

Interbrand states that:

> 'Leading brands are driven by their desire to be useful, to create products, tools and services that actually solve customer problems, and to use their marketing to serve and not just sell.'

Focus

The guidance seems to ignore the legal rights in respect of ownership but concentrates on 'important functions', which are poorly defined and likely to lead to considerable uncertainty.

17.20 Image rights

Entertainers, sportspersons and other celebrities often exploit, individually or via a company, which they own or are contracted to the right to use their appearance in a photograph, film or video or in person to endorse a product. These are usually referred to as 'image rights' and their payment as 'endorsement fees'. In the UK, a celebrity's likeness is effectively protected at common law by libel, defamation, passing off or in some cases breach of copyright or trademark. However, in Guernsey, The Image Rights (Bailiwick of Guernsey) Ordinance 2012 provides that a personage, a natural person, a legal person, two or more such persons as a joint personality or group or a fictional character, wherever resident, may be registered as a registered personality, and protected as a form of intellectual property. The extent to which other countries will take account of registration in Guernsey remains a matter of conjecture, but it is an indication of the commercial value of a person's 'name and likeness' in endorsement of goods and services.

Image rights are valued in the same way as many intellectual property rights, ie as the present value of the anticipated fees that advertisers are prepared to pay for the endorsement, which is often linked to the individual performer's success in his chosen field, which, in turn, makes them hard to value.

Under the non-resident entertainers and sportsmen provisions, HMRC currently regard a visiting sportsperson's endorsement income, as well as fees for appearances, as subject to tax in the UK on a proportion of the worldwide income from endorsement, calculated by reference to the person's relevant performance and training days in the UK as a proportion of their relevant performance and training days worldwide. In *Agassi v Robinson* [2006] STC 1056 the House of Lords held that payments for endorsement contracts through non-UK companies not remitted to the UK were nonetheless taxable under these provisions even though they would not have been taxed on Andre Agassi had he been tax resident in the UK, unless remitted to the UK, in view of his non-UK domicile. This peculiar state of affairs means that a non-resident sportsman or entertainer can pay more tax in the UK than his or her earnings from appearing in the UK. It also indicates that the income of a successful celebrity from endorsement, etc can easily exceed their direct earnings as a performer.

In *Hull City AFC (Tigers) Limited v HMRC* [2017] UKFTT 629 (TC), the appeal related to image rights of football player Geovanni Gomez who was taxed under Regulation 80 of the Income Tax (Pay As You Earn) Regulations 2003 and Decisions under section 8 of the Social Security Contributions (Transfer of Functions) Act 1999 for tax years 2008/09 to 2010/11 inclusive. These rights were paid to Joniere Limited, a British Virgin Islands company. The agreements related to two Premier League contracts. The taxpayer claimed that 'the amounts (assessed) relate to image rights payments under a bona fide commercial arrangement' and no NIC or PAYE were payable. HMRC argued that the payments were for salary, wages or other emoluments of the employment.

HMRC argued that the amount of the payments was too excessive to be commercial and were part of remuneration as a football player.

HMRC referred to *Autoclenz Ltd v Belcher* [2011] UKSC 41 and the Upper Tribunal in *Acornwood & Ors v HMRC* [2016] UKUT 361 (TCC), especially paragraph 59, and concluded that Joniere Limited was a nominee of Mr Gomez. The decision, so far, is merely that HMRC must serve its evidence first, not that the burden of proof lies with HMRC or that there is a general obligation on HMRC to serve its evidence first.

Chapter 18

HMRC Shares and Assets Valuation

Signposts

18.01 Background

HM Revenue and Customs Shares and Assets Valuation section (SAV), formerly Shares Valuation and before that Shares Valuation Division, is responsible for HMRC's valuation of shares in companies that do not have a quotation on a reorganised stock exchange anywhere in the world. As the name suggests, SAV also values many other assets, including goodwill and other intangibles, foreign land, livestock, wine and spirits.

Since the introduction of capital gains tax in 1965, SAV has lived through the abolition of estate duty and the introduction of an all-embracing capital transfer tax, followed by its relaxation and transformation into inheritance tax; the introduction and abolition of capital duty; the prospect of wealth tax; the abolition of stamp duty on gifts inter vivos and the current popularity of share option schemes, including Enterprise Management Incentives (EMI), growth share arrangements and Save As You Earn schemes.

This section considers the specific issues relating to valuations to be submitted to HMRC including whether the valuation may be submitted in advance of a transaction or post-transaction. It also reminds us of the main case law principles which apply to fiscal valuations and practical matters including the information which should be submitted with the valuation.

18.02 Submitting a valuation to HMRC

Pre-transaction clearance is available for EMI and Employee Shareholder Status (ESS) schemes and is required for Company Share Ownership (CSOPs) schemes. The reduction in the amount of tax relief available under ESS was reduced with effect from 17 March 2016. From this date, only gains over £100,000 in respect of ESS shares are subject to CGT. However, the ESS arrangements are still in place and values may be agreed pre-transaction, which in certain circumstances may be of use. Valuations submitted for EMI purposes must be accompanied by Form VAL231, which can be downloaded from HMRC's website. The form also lists the additional information which should be submitted with the valuation report. Similarly, applications for agreement to an ESS valuation must be accompanied by Form VAL232.

It should be noted that there is no requirement to advise SAV of the individual awards to be made under EMI when the valuation is submitted. However, for ESS, details of the individual share awards and the recipients must be provided when the valuation is submitted, together with the Employee Statement of Particulars.

No special form is required for CSOP valuations.

The current mailing address for correspondence with SAV is: Shares and Assets Valuation, HMRC, BX19 1BJ.

Correspondence may also be sent by email to savexternal.mailbox@hmrc.gsi.gov.uk. Care should be taken when sending a large number of attachments as there is a data limit and, if correspondence by email or telephone is preferred, the initial email sent should explicitly state that the sender is happy to receive correspondence in these forms.

The mechanism for agreeing PAYE health-checks and the informal arrangement for post-transaction agreements for share awards requiring a value for Income Tax (Earnings and Pensions) Act 2003 (ITEPA 2003) purposes were withdrawn with effect from 31 March 2016.

In *MDCM Limited v HMRC* [2018] UKFTT 147 (TC) it was held that Mr Daniels, the appellant's principal employee, should be treated as an employee of the ultimate contracting company under Parts I to IV of the Social Security (Contributions and Benefits) Act 1992, commonly known as IR35.

HMRC issued determinations under regulation 80 of the Income Tax (Pay As You Earn) Regulations 2003 on the basis that the intermediaries legislation applied to the appellant's contract with an independent introductory company, Solutions Recruitment Limited; and its contract with a construction company, STC, was a contract of employment between Mr Daniels and STC. The Tribunal held that it was not, due to lack of control over Mr Daniels and lack of employee-type benefits. It was held that the hypothetical contract was one of personal services with no right of substitution with mutuality of obligations, not one of employment.

Valuations for capital gains tax (CGT) and corporation tax purposes may still be submitted for post-transaction agreement (the PTVC procedure). Form CG34 sets out details of the office to which the valuation should be sent.

Focus

The bases of value required for EMI schemes are the unrestricted market value and actual market value of the shares; for CSOP the required basis of value is open market value.

18.03 The Shares and Assets Valuation Manual (SVM)

The manual is available online at the HMRC website. It was designed as a general introduction to the work of SAV for new entrants to that office, but is also used by existing members as a source of reference and guidance.

The current version of the manual was published on 13 March 2016 and is continually updated, the latest update (at the time of writing) being on 9 July 2018.

It explains how HMRC works out the value of shares and assets in unquoted companies for inheritance tax and capital gains tax purposes. This manual is now comprehensive and helpful, in our opinion.

SVM101000	Introduction: contents (www.gov.uk/hmrc-internal-manuals/shares-and-assets-valuation-manual/svm10100)
SVM102000	Files and forms: contents
SVM103000	Correspondence and Customer Service: contents
SVM105000	Self Assessment: contents
SVM107000	Capital Gains Tax Procedures: contents
SVM108000	Inheritance Tax: contents
SVM109000	ITEPA: contents
SVM110000	Share Option Schemes: contents
SVM111000	IHT Business Property Relief: contents
SVM112000	IHT Agricultural Property Relief: contents
SVM113000	The Statutory Open Market: contents
SVM114000	Information Standards: contents
SVM115000	Liaison with the Valuation Office Agency and other offices: contents

SVM117000	The Litigation and Technical Advice Team (LTAT): contents
SVM118000	Statutory Notices: contents
SVM119000	Other Compliance Matters: contents
SVM120000	Case Selection, Handling and Settlement: contents
SVM150000	Additional guidance

SVM UPDATES
Update index (www.gov.uk/hmrc-internal-manuals/shares-and-assets-valuation-manual/svmupdate001 etc).

> **Focus**
>
> The SVM gives a number of examples. It should be remembered that these are for illustrative purposes and the approach is not mandatory. Since the withdrawal of PTVCs for ITEPA 2003 purposes, the Worked Examples Group of practitioners has been established to assist valuers by submitting and agreeing proforma valuation calculations with HMRC.

18.04 Case law assumptions

As discussed in the preceding chapters of this book, the basis of valuation for fiscal purposes is derived from a century of case law. In its Introduction, SAV's guidance summarises the main case law assumptions as follows:

- 'the sale is a hypothetical sale
- the vendor is a hypothetical, prudent and willing party to the transaction
- the purchaser is a hypothetical, prudent and willing party to the transaction (unless considered a "special purchaser")
- for the purposes of the hypothetical sale, the vendor would divide the property to be valued into whatever natural lots would achieve the best overall price (this is the principle of "prudent lotting")
- all preliminary arrangements necessary for the sale to take place have been carried out prior to the valuation date
- the property is offered for sale on the open market by whichever method of sale will achieve the best price
- there is adequate publicity or advertisement before the sale takes place so that it is brought to the attention of all likely purchasers
- the valuation should reflect the bid of any "special purchaser" in the market (provided they are willing and able to purchase).'

18.05 Information to be submitted

SAV's website lists the following information which should be considered for the purposes of valuing unquoted shares:

- 'The company's performance and financial status as shown in its accounts for, say, the last three years before the date of valuation, and any other information normally available to its shareholders. In the case of foreign companies you will need to provide copies of the accounts for the three years before the date of valuation.

- The size of the shareholding, and shareholders' rights. If, for example, the holding is one that would give control of a company, it may be necessary to agree the value of all the company's assets and to have much more information about the company's performance and prospects than is in the published accounts.
- The company's dividend policy.
- Appropriate yields and price earnings ratios of comparable companies or sectors.
- The commercial and economic background at the valuation date.
- A full explanation as to how the suggested value has been calculated, including:
  - the valuation approach adopted, for example Earnings, Assets, Dividend Yield or industry specific valuation method
  - any assumptions or adjustments made
  - all the supporting evidence used.
- Any other relevant factors.'

Focus

There may be circumstances where the information listed above would not be available to a small minority shareholder. The valuer must then decide whether they wish to adhere to the 'deemed' information which would be available or provide the additional documentation which might expedite agreement to the valuation.

Valuations should reflect the information available at the relevant valuation date. It is possible that a company's circumstances may change significantly in a relatively short period of time, eg following an offer for the business. If there is a significant mismatch between a value agreed for the shares (eg for EMI purposes) and a subsequent third party transaction, then HMRC are likely to review the valuation originally submitted in order to confirm that all relevant information was reflected in the value at that date. In particular, EMI valuations are agreed on a 'without prejudice' basis and HMRC will set aside a previously agreed valuation in circumstances where they believe that full and accurate disclosure was not originally provided. Agents may also be subject to penalties.

Pitfall

HMRC will review share values in the light of subsequent transactions or financial reporting disclosures and may enquire further if there is significant disparity between the values.

18.06 Small minority holdings

When preparing a valuation, the valuer should always take into account how much a potential buyer can control, influence and get enjoyment from the asset.

Usually, if the buyer does not control 100% of the asset, the value of the percentage share that the buyer would own would be lower than the pro rata proportion of the asset's total value, to reflect the lower degree of control.

For unquoted shares, there are various degrees of control, usually based on the voting power of a particular block of shares, ranging from power to liquidate a company to a small or non-existent influence over the company's affairs of a minority shareholding.

The price per share of shares that are part of a minority holding will be lower than the price of a share that forms part of a majority holding.

The level of detail to use when preparing a valuation for UK fiscal purposes is linked to the size and influence of the shareholding. The greater the influence, the more detailed and sensitive information about the company can be used together with the company's accounts and other published information.

SAV tends to divide holdings into various classifications according to the size of the shareholding. Small minority holdings are those of 25% or less in which it is accepted that a holder can do little to influence the running of the company and would not have a reasonable expectation of a seat on the board. It must be remembered that what is being valued are 'the shares' and not 'the shares plus a seat on the board because of the special expertise of the shareholder'. The shareholder would therefore be primarily concerned with the yield they would receive on their investment and the shares should be valued on the basis of a dividend yield if a dividend is paid, but with some regard paid to earnings or on an earnings yield or price/earnings ratio basis if there is no dividend.

For non-dividend paying companies, a capitalised earnings approach is generally adopted unless the company is financially unable to pay a dividend. The notional dividend approach is not usually considered because of the additional imponderables introduced into the valuation.

18.07 Influential minority holdings

SAV considers holdings of more than 25% but less than 50% to be influential minority holdings, where the shareholder can block a special resolution for which a 75% majority is required under CA 2006, s 283. Although it is accepted that, in practice, this ability to block a special resolution is unlikely to have of itself a significant value, the value per share would generally be higher than for a small minority holding. The premium for voting influence depends largely on the facts of the particular case. The size of the holding compared to other holdings is considered the most important factor and a premium of 10% is apparently considered to be the minimum. In practice, when it is remembered that the dividend yield required when there is a 'consistent reasonable dividend' should also take into account the size and influence of the holding and that dividend yields of comparable companies (based on the sales of small minority holdings) would need to be reduced to allow for the size of the holding involved, there may be little, if any difference between a dividend-based and an earnings-based valuation.

18.08 50% holding

In the case of a 50% holding it would seem that SAV would normally argue that although there would be a potential deadlock if the other shares were held by another 50% shareholder there would nonetheless be an assumption, following *Ebrahimi v Westbourne Galleries Ltd* [1973] AC 360 (see **2.06**) that the shareholders would act for their mutual benefit and the valuation should be by reference to the company as a whole.

If, however, the other 50% of the shares are held in small numbers by many other shareholders, then clearly the 50% shareholder has de facto but not de jure control. Value by reference to the value of the company as a whole is again reasonable. In the view of HMRC this apparently still requires a discount to the proportionate going concern value of the company as a whole provided, of course, that the company is a going concern.

It will be recalled that in *Battle v IRC* (see **7.18**) that the Revenue's witnesses suggested in evidence that a discount of 12½% from the net assets value of the shares was reasonable in arriving at the value of a 49% holding. The company in that case was an investment company holding first class securities and a different and larger discount may need to be considered for a trading company, which, in any event, would be unlikely to be valued on a net assets basis.

A purchaser of a 50% shareholding would expect to play an active part in the running of the company and would be comforted by the fact that no one party could have a larger shareholding. Previous HMRC guidance suggested that the discount from a pro rata value should be between 20% and 30% depending on how the remaining 50% of the equity was held. The discount could be greater than 30% if, for example, the articles of association refer to a chairman's casting vote or the position of a life chairman.

18.09 Majority holdings

A controlling holding of over 50% and under 75% of the voting capital is one which should be valued by reference to the overall value of the company based on either earnings or net assets as appropriate. Consideration may need to be given to applying a discount depending on the specific facts and circumstances.

If a net asset value valuation approach is used, then the intangible assets, goodwill, know-how, etc, have to be valued and included in the net assets. One method of valuing the goodwill and intangible assets is to capitalise the profits of the business, then deduct the net value of the tangible assets. What remains is the value of the goodwill and intangible assets; this method of valuation is perfectly reasonable when it is remembered that the benefit of those assets to the company is reflected in the profit figures.

Sometimes, the profits are insufficient to pay adequate remuneration to the directors together with a fair return on the assets although the company may reasonably anticipate a return to profitability. In other words liquidation or break up is not anticipated. The most reasonable way of arriving at the value of such a company is to capitalise the existing profits.

Generally, a company that is a going concern should be valued by reference to either the market or income approach The International Valuation Standards Council (IVSC) describes these approaches as follows:

> 'The market approach provides an indication of value by comparing the subject asset with identical or similar assets for which price information is available.
>
> The income approach provides an indication of value by converting future cash flow to a single current capital value.'

Under the income approach, the value of an asset is determined by reference to the value of income, cash flow or cost savings generated by the asset. A cost approach may be appropriate for early stage businesses or start-ups where cash flows are unreliable and there are no meaningful comparators. It may also be appropriate for businesses which are no longer a going concern, situations where an entity's net asset value exceeds the business value, or for investment or holding companies.

The BDO Private Company and Private Equity Price Index showed, up to 4th quarter 2012 the average price/earnings ratio apparent from published details of sales of UK unquoted trading companies. From the 1st quarter 2013, it shows Enterprise/EBITDA multiples. Although the sample on which the Index is based is inevitably rather small and is dependent on the number of transactions reported in a quarter, its consistent results demonstrate that it can be a useful reference point. P/E ratios or Enterprise/EBITDA multiples used in arriving at the average could be based on historical results, or an average of historical and forecast or warranted earnings where the purchase consideration is dependent on future performance. Earnings can be adjusted for items such as non-recurring levels of directors' remuneration.

The application of a multiple to pre-tax profit gives the capitalised value of the whole of the company so that when the valuer is considering the value of a bare majority, a discount from the value of the entirety is appropriate. The level of discount to be applied depends on the circumstances of the particular holding and the company. A 50.1% holding would normally command a larger discount than a 74.9% holding if only because the 74.9% holding only requires the support of a very small shareholder to secure the passing of a special or extraordinary resolution. The 12½% for the 49% holding suggested by the Revenue in *Battle v IRC* (see above and **7.18**) for an investment company with good investments is of no relevance to a trading company. Listed investment companies are normally valued by a discount on net assets (see **18.17**). For a trading company a 50.1% holding would command a discount of, at least, 20% to 25% in normal circumstances and a 74.9% holding of, at least, the 15% mentioned below.

When the figure of 75% or more of the voting shares is reached, it is indisputable that the whole value of the company on an earnings or assets basis, as appropriate, and as calculated above, is the correct method of valuation. The SAV's traditionally offered discount of 5% is unlikely to be acceptable to the taxpayer and indeed would only appear appropriate when 90% or more of the shares are to be valued on a sale in the open market so that it is possible to acquire the remaining shares by compulsory purchase at the same price. If the holding to be valued is precisely 75%, admittedly it has the power to force through a special resolution but there is, in fact, little practical difference between this holding and a 74.9% holding. Company business is not conducted by the passing of special resolutions and a discount of 10% for this size of holding cannot be considered unreasonable for the average trading company.

18.10 Break-up value

In certain circumstances, it might be appropriate to look at the break-up value on a supposed liquidation and adjust for the liquidation expenses, but it would not be accepted that a valuation of the company as a whole should be subject only to a 5% discount, in the majority of cases, as it would be argued that any purchaser would wish to see an immediate return on their investment of more than this amount. It should be remembered that in *Re Courthope* (1928) 7 ATC 538 (see **7.02**) the court suggested a discount of approximately 33⅓% on the estimated realisable value for a 50% shareholder when liquidation was probable, although not inevitable.

It is suggested that a reasonable discount on a break-up basis of valuation would be between 10% and 15% for a holding of between 75% and 90% of the ordinary shares, and because of the compulsory purchase powers under CA 2006, s 979 a discount of between 5% and 10% for a holding in excess of 90%.

Where a break-up value is relevant, valuers should adjust assets to their realisable values, to take account of taxation consequences, redundancy and professional costs and the asset-stripper's profit. It also contains guidelines on valuation practice where a company is actually in liquidation.

18.11 Adjustments to accounts

SAV accepts that it may be necessary to adjust the earnings shown in the accounts to take account of for example, notional interest on interest free loans to the company, or excessive directors' remuneration. Unless, however, a controlling interest is being acquired it is unlikely that HMRC will argue that any excess remuneration should be added back in calculating the company's earnings, because in the absence of an oppression on the minority under CA 2006, s 994 there is little that a minority shareholder could do even if the remuneration were not entirely justified. This is accepted by SAV. Similarly it is unlikely that it would be suggested that a minority shareholder would automatically acquire a seat on the board, although it may be shown in practice that this may happen.

18.12 Imminent disposal

Where at the valuation date the company is about to be subject to a flotation, taken over or put into liquidation, the value would normally be based by SAV on the figures which the flotation take-over or liquidation would produce, subject to an appropriate discount for uncertainty as to whether or not such disposal would take place.

18.13 31 March 1982

The valuation of shares in unquoted companies at this date has been one of the most contentious areas for practitioners negotiating with SAV. The same valuation criteria apply as for valuations at any other date but since it is on this occasion in the taxpayers' interests to negotiate as high a value as possible, the professional adviser and SAV find themselves faced with the arguments they would normally expect to be defending. It is easy to sympathise with the taxpayer who cannot understand why their 10% shareholding, for which they received a pro rata 10% of the proceeds on the sale of a company, has to be valued as a small minority holding at 31 March 1982. The capital gain on which they have to pay tax arises to a large extent not because of an increase either in the value of the company or in the value of their minority holding, valued as such, but because of the difference between the value of a small minority holding on the statutory basis and its value as a proportion of the whole company. It was presumably not Parliament's intention to penalise minority shareholders whilst allowing shareholders with controlling interests to have their shares valued at 31 March 1982 in a more even-handed manner. No doubt the possibility of avoidance devices and the consequent necessity of counter legislation would be put forward by HMRC as reasons not to propose legislation which would allow shareholders receiving pro rata sale proceeds to have their shares considered as a proportion of the value of the company as a whole for re-basing purposes.

Included in **Appendix B** are the Financial Times Actuaries Share Indices as at 31 March 1982 and details published in the *Investors Chronicle* of 9 April 1982 of the companies which were, at that date, the constituents of each of the FTASI sectors. It should be remembered that the price/earnings ratios quoted by the *Investors Chronicle* reflect a full notional corporation tax charge whereas price/earnings ratios published in the *Financial Times* are based on the net distribution method of calculating earnings, which gives an accurate calculation of all actual tax liabilities. If comparison with a quoted company or companies is considered pertinent and maintainable earnings for the company being valued have been arrived at on a fully taxed basis, it would be appropriate to have regard to price/earnings ratios published in the *Investors Chronicle* rather than those in the *Financial Times*.

Where valuation of a minority shareholding in a company with a wide spread of shareholders is required at 31 March 1982, it may be that a value has already been agreed between a taxpayer (or in some cases the company itself) and HMRC. It is reasonable to ask the company secretary if he has any record of such an agreement and, if so, for the details including the size of the holding. (HMRC no longer divulge any details of values agreed with other taxpayers and, under data protection laws, records are generally only retained for six years.) The size of the holding is important because the value per share of a 1% holding is hardly relevant to the value per share of a 49% holding and even less relevant to the value per share of a 51% holding.

If there has been an agreed value, there can be little doubt that HMRC would not wish to depart from it for a similar sized holding. There are good reasons for this attitude; it is very unlikely that any fact or factor now known was not known at the earlier date and taken into account while the conditions surrounding the valuation would be easier to ascertain at the earlier date. The *Stenhouse* case (see **2.12**) shows that details of the previously agreed values can be used as evidence but will not necessarily be conclusive. (It is not clear whether or not the SAV would divulge details before the First Tier Tribunal which they had refused to divulge in correspondence with the taxpayer.)

It may also be the case that a value has been agreed at or around 31 March 1982 for capital gains tax, capital transfer tax or stamp duty on a disposal at that date of a holding of a similar size to that for which a value is required for re-basing. Unless the earlier agreement with SAV was reached on a without prejudice basis, it will be difficult to negotiate a value at 31 March 1982 that is not in line with other values already agreed. The practitioner should attempt to discover any other valuations agreed for whatever purpose at or around 31 March 1982 so that he can, if necessary, distinguish them from the value he is proposing. SAV should in strictness ignore any agreements at dates after 31 March 1982, but in practice they will not wish to agree a value at 31 March 1982 that is fundamentally at odds with the previously agreed value of a similar size of shareholding at a date one or two years later, unless there was a substantial change in the company's fortunes between 31 March 1982 and the later valuation date.

18.14 6 April 1965

When a valuation as at 6 April 1965 for capital gains tax purposes is necessary, it may again be that a value has already been agreed between a taxpayer (or in some cases the company itself) and HMRC. It will usually be beneficial to opt to re-base at 31 March 1982, although it may be preferable to opt for a valuation at 6 April 1965 under TCGA 1992, Schedule 2, paragraph 17.

In such cases the principles set out above for valuations at dates other than 6 April 1965 will apply, but the parameters of the valuation have changed simply because the dividend yield, earnings yield etc demanded by the investor are different now from what they were in 1965. If a dividend yield of 12½% to 15% is now reasonable then 10% to 12% was reasonable in 1965 with consequent lower earnings yields and higher price/earnings ratios.

All relevant factors must be taken into account and the value must be arrived at in the conditions prevailing and on the information available at that time. It is still necessary firmly to reject the knowledge of subsequent events.

It can be assumed that a relatively high value at 6 April 1965 is in the taxpayer's interest so that in a small case a dividend yield of say 10% may well be acceptable to the taxpayer. If there are no dividends it could be advisable to take a notional dividend on the basis of a distribution of a reasonable proportion of the profit, say one-third, and argue for a dividend yield of, say, 10% as appropriate at that time. There is no doubt, however, that HMRC would seek to discount the resulting value on the grounds of a notional dividend only.

18.15 Comparison with quoted companies

SAV does attempt to find reasonably comparable companies but would, of course, reject as comparable any companies which are grossly out of line, were the subject of a bid, had a stale quotation or particularly unmarketable shares and if HMRC attempt to use such a company, the facts should be brought to their notice and the calculations adjusted.

18.16 Investment companies

In the case of investment holding companies, the actual market does appear to value the shares on the basis of a discount from net assets as is well illustrated by the analyses of such companies produced regularly by some stockbrokers. It must, however, be remembered that for these listed companies it is usual for the company to distribute a large proportion of its income while the actual discount depends on the quality of the portfolio and its spread by type of industry and location, both nationally and internationally.

For the private investment company these factors are still of importance but it will usually be that the portfolio is not of the same high quality and will not have the same spread. Further the private company may not distribute the same proportion of its income.

If the private company does have a good portfolio and does distribute a realistic proportion of its income, then the same discount from net assets value is a reasonable basis of valuation provided that there is a further discount to allow for the relative unmarketability of the shares.

If, however, the quality of the portfolio leaves much to be desired or the distribution is relatively small, the discount should be much higher and a valuation based solely on net assets should be resisted for a small minority holding and greater weight attributed to the dividends. For a larger holding and certainly for a control holding, a discounted assets basis is probably acceptable.

Based on discounts from assets of listed property investment companies. In the past, SAV suggested a range of 25% to 40% for discounts for influential minority holdings but did not lay down any guidelines for uninfluential minority holdings in property investment companies. In practice, however, a range from 60% to 70% is likely to prove acceptable. Shares in quoted property companies have generally traded at discounts ranging from 20% to 40%, although most have been concentrated within the 25% to 35% range.

If the valuation is a very material one, an analysis of listed companies in the sector as at the relevant date should be undertaken in order to ascertain which of the listed companies most closely resembles the particular company. This could well adjust the suggested discount in the taxpayer's favour. The taxpayer should not overlook the fact that the shares to be valued may not enjoy a ready market and allowance for this should be claimed in the price.

HMRC will recognise that investors usually require dividends and therefore when valuing a small holding in a property company due consideration should be given to the yield which should reflect the likelihood and amount of return that the investor can look forward to.

In the case of a property investment company where the shareholding is in excess of 25% SAV may wish to refer the value of the underlying properties to the District Valuer for confirmation. It may not be appropriate to supply the information to enable this to be done if it is thought that a discounted asset basis is inappropriate in the circumstances.

18.17 Other classes of company

So far as property development companies are concerned, HMRC may view these as property holding companies in embryo and would be interested not only in the assets currently held but the likely rentable value of those assets in the course of construction. Therefore, in order to ascertain the correct basis of valuation it is important to ensure that the precise nature of the business' activities is set out in detail.

Property dealing companies on the other hand are regarded as trading companies, albeit in view of the sometimes wild fluctuations in profits, a profit record of five years rather than three years may be more appropriate.

Family holding companies, sometimes known as 'money box companies', may be investing in assets not required for the purposes of the trade and could be broken down into their trading and investment constituents for valuation purposes.

Investment trusts will often be valued on a discount on the asset basis. Quoted investment trusts often show a discount on underlying assets of between 10% and 30% and the tax rules for such companies are beneficial in that they do not now suffer capital gains tax on reinvestment, whereas an unquoted investment trust would do so. This would justify a higher discount compared with a quoted investment trust to account for this factor. There would also be an increased discount because of unmarketability. The degree of discount however will also be directly related to the size of shareholding in that a controlling or near controlling interest would probably justify a relatively small discount on assets of between say 10% and 20%. It is worth noting that in the case of *Battle v IRC* [1979] TR 483 (see **7.18**) it was accepted that a discount of only 12½% from net asset value would have been appropriate for a 49% shareholding on the particular facts of that case, although it must be borne in mind that in that case the taxpayer was attempting to show that no discount at all was appropriate and HMRC were more than delighted to have judicial approval to a minimal discount in such a case. Previous SAV guidance contained a rough guide to levels of discount for investment companies or trusts which suggested 50% to 60% for holdings of 10% or under and 35% to 45% for holdings of 10% to 25%. It is not clear why such a discrepancy was thought appropriate. A discount of 20% to 30% is suggested for holdings of 25.1% to 49.9%. The Special Commissioners case of *McArthur (Executors of) v Revenue & Customs* [2008] STC (SCD) 1100 adopted discounts of 12½% for holdings of between 50% and 75%, 45% for a holding of 26.1% and 65% for a holding of 8.1%.

The 'normal' company for share valuation purposes which has been the subject of consideration in this chapter is the trading or manufacturing company. The other main class recognised by SAV is the talent exploitation company, such as an employing company for an entertainer, or an advertising agency. Such companies normally have very little by way of asset backing and make high profits over a short period taken out in the form of remuneration rather than dividend. It may be that the company's personnel are such that there is a likelihood of continuing earnings over a reasonable period and a valuation along normal lines can be made to take account of this earning potential. This is of course particularly so in the case of, say, an advertising agency where the client connections are capable of being transferred and therefore a substantial goodwill element may be present.

It should also be borne in mind with certain talent exploitation companies that there may be a continuing source of income, for example, from copyright royalties or artistes' royalties irrespective of the continued employment of the personnel and this stream of future income will have a marketable value.

18.18 Growth shares

A growth, hurdle or flowering share is a class of equity to which value flows only if certain performance criteria are achieved. Typically, these performance targets are profit or enterprise value based, but this does not have to be the case.

Any condition which is capable of definition, measurement and is applicable to the shares as a class could be used as the hurdle or trigger for participation in value.

As previously discussed, the information standard applicable to small minority shareholdings generally means that the acquirer of an uninfluential shareholding would have to base their investment decision on published historical data and market information which is in the public domain. This presents a practical difficulty for the valuation for growth shares which, by their very nature, have value based on the achievement of targets likely to be met (or not) at some date in the future. Therefore, a hypothetical purchaser of these shares would reasonably require some insight as to the likelihood of the targets being achieved. Put simply, in making their investment decision, the shareholder will need to assess the likely level of return, the timescale to realisation, and the risks which might diminish the prospect of any return.

The most appropriate method of estimating the value of a growth share is to calculate the expected return to the shareholder, ie the value likely to accrue to the shares at the point of realisation, discounted for the risk of non-achievement, the time value of money and the size of the shareholding. In the absence of forecasts, a useful guide to assessing the risk attaching to the prospective results is the company's own historical performance against the original budget for a given year. If a company habitually underperforms against budget then it is not unreasonable to assume that may be a continued risk for the future.

It is possible to forecast the likely future return by using option pricing techniques, such as Monte Carlo simulation, but this is not necessarily required, provided suitable estimates can be made and a suitable valuation approach adopted.

Often, the recipient of a growth share expects that the initial market value of the share will be minimal, particularly if the performance targets are challenging. This may well be the case, although not necessarily if the return on the share once the hurdle is achieved is disproportionate. However, while the upfront value may be low, in the hypothetical scenario required for fiscal purposes, it is unlikely that the vendor (in this case, the company) would merely give the shares away as there is likely to be an element of hope that the targets might be achieved and value flow into the shares. Therefore, it is not uncommon that a token additional value is attributed to the shareholding in order to reflect this 'hope value'.

Conversely, some calculations of future value may result in an extremely high value for the shares, particularly in cases where a company is in a turnaround or high growth phase or the overall equity value at the current date is low. The valuer should always assess whether the calculated value for the growth share, which generally has a restricted entitlement to capital, is reasonable in comparison to the current value of the ordinary equity which should include the value of the growth prospects of the company and has more advantageous capital rights. On the date of issue, it would be highly unusual for a growth share to have a higher market value than an ordinary share.

18.19 Shares with special rights

Some companies have share classes where the voting and capital rights are not aligned. As an extreme example, a company may have two classes of share, one which has all the income and capital rights but not voting entitlement, and another which has full voting rights but no entitlement to income or capital. In this situation, the valuer needs to be mindful of the decision in *Holt v Holt* [1990] 3 NZLR 401 which ascribed a value of about 20% to voting control alone. Even where the voting shareholding to be valued does not have absolute control, it is likely to have nuisance value of up to, say, 5% of the whole company value, depending on the size of the holding.

For shares which have income or capital rights but no votes, while the shareholder has an entitlement to value, they may be unlikely to effect the realisation of this value if they are unable to control dividend policy or a sale. Accordingly, a discount will be applicable to the shares depending on the precise rights of the share class.

Pitfall

Care must be taken with share classes where the rights are unusual. HMRC will generally consider the judgment in *Holt v Holt* in relation to any shares with voting rights only. Therefore, the lack of income or capital rights does not necessarily result in a minimal value for shares of this type.

18.20 Negotiations with Shares and Assets Valuation

Where shares are being valued for fiscal purposes the manner in which the valuer acting for the taxpayer will proceed will depend in many ways on the personal preferences of the valuer.

Some valuers consider that the most favourable valuation is achieved by deciding whether a high or low value is required for the taxpayer's best advantage and preparing a valuation setting out all the relevant factors that point to a low or high valuation as appropriate, and then to argue in support of these contentions by correspondence with SAV over a period of years. Other valuers will prefer to prepare a short valuation setting out the factors that have been considered in the valuation and ending up with the final figure without showing the arithmetic calculations which might have been made in arriving at the figure. The valuer will then endeavour to meet with SAV and discuss the valuation in order to achieve a value which he considers will be in the interests of the taxpayer. The method preferred by the authors is to prepare a detailed valuation report listing all the relevant factors and to show the calculations taking into account the dividends, earnings, assets and other transfers as appropriate in order to arrive at an acceptable valuation. If this work is done properly it is contended that the valuation can be agreed reasonably quickly and within an acceptable valuation range as the value has been placed into context. It is not accepted that horse trading from a ridiculously high or low figure will give the most beneficial valuation, although it must be appreciated that the valuation of shares in unquoted companies is not a precise science and there is no such thing as a single correct valuation. There is, however, in the authors' opinion a relatively narrow band within which the correct valuation lies which is arrived at by a valuation on the lines proposed in this book.

If a full valuation is submitted at the start it should merely be necessary to clarify any areas of uncertainty or explain why a particular view has been taken on the likelihood or otherwise of some future happening as a result of which the valuation should be capable of agreement by SAV. In those cases where there is a fundamental difference of opinion between the valuer and SAV, for example, on the degree to which the underlying property values are important in the case of a minority interest in a property investment company, a full valuation report will at least enable the areas of disagreement to be isolated and the argument can then proceed by correspondence or interview, as appropriate. In the final analysis it may be necessary to refer the value to the First Tier Tribunal for their determination. If the valuation has been fully thought out in the first instance the chances of success before the Tribunal are likely to be improved.

There is clearly room for a difference of opinion between the valuer and SAV for example, as to whether a particular quoted public company or sector of the Financial Times Actuaries Share Index is relevant to a particular disposal, and as has been shown there are few cases where there is a truly comparable quoted public company. In most cases such disputes can be disposed of by agreement and only rarely will it be necessary to refer the matter to the commissioners.

Unfortunately in many cases the valuation presented on behalf of the taxpayer does not take into account the factors required by statute and case law, which results in needless delay while the valuer learns the facts of life from SAV. On the other hand an inexperienced or inflexible examiner at SAV may prove immoveable even in the face of well-reasoned argument and in rare cases it becomes necessary to refer to SAV's Appeals Team or the Tribunal for a decision.

18.21 Appeals

An appeal before the Tribunal on cases involving the valuation of unquoted shares has been exactly the same as any other appeal on a taxation matter. Normally the valuer or a barrister acting on their behalf would put forward the taxpayer's evidence on the basis of the statutory provisions and the case law referred to in this book. Witnesses would be called to give evidence and comparisons with other companies or previous values propounded or distinguished as appropriate.

The examiner or a barrister acting on their behalf for HMRC would put forward the reasons why SAV consider the value should be different and refer to any statute or case law which they consider relevant. The valuer on behalf of the taxpayer has a right of reply and would sum up on behalf of the client. Where witnesses are produced the examination in chief is conducted on behalf of the party producing the witness who is then open to cross examination and re-examination. The taxpayer is usually the appellant and is therefore required to open the proceedings by setting out the details of the case to the commissioners. The normal rules of evidence apply (see **3.12** for details of evidence that was considered admissible in the *Stenhouse* case).

The Tribunal's decision on a point of fact is final and conclusive, but on a point of law a case could be referred to the courts.

If a case is to be taken to appeal it would be worthwhile studying in detail all the relevant published decisions of the Special Commissioners and Tribunal in share valuation cases to gain an understanding of the approach they are likely to take.

If a case involves the value of land and that value cannot be agreed with the District Valuer or Mineral Valuer, as appropriate, the land value would be referred to the Lands Tribunal.

Following the merger between Revenue and Customs the Solicitor's Office have split their duties between advisory and litigation. The advisory officer might contact the taxpayer or his agent with a view to reaching a settlement. If no settlement is reached and the case is thought worthwhile, it is referred to the litigation officer who will then begin to prepare the case for a hearing before the tribunal. That will usually require the appointment of counsel from outside the Solicitor's Office. Before referring the case to the Solicitor's Office it is likely that SAV will have commissioned a report from one of their panel of outside experts. That expert will also have to provide an expert witness report for the hearing.

Unsurprisingly, very few appeals are eventually decided by the tribunal. Of those that are so decided, a fair proportion have been brought by taxpayers determined to have their day in court but which shed little light on the grey areas of valuation. Only a handful of cases have been decided since the publication of Special Commissioners' Decisions began in 1992.

Chapter 19

Valuation reports

Signposts

19.01 Introduction

In considering the valuation of shares in an unquoted company it will usually be desirable to prepare a detailed written report relating to the valuation.

This report should be prepared even where only the final conclusion will be communicated to the interested parties (following *Dean v Prince* [1954] 1 All ER 749) (see **4.03**) as it enables the valuer to make sure that he has considered all the necessary aspects of the valuation, although there will be cases where the sums involved do not justify a full valuation and a more rough and ready approach has to be adopted.

A valuation may be scrutinised several years after it was originally prepared. Documenting any assumptions and conclusions made in the report and retaining source documentation is of paramount importance. The valuer must be prepared to defend and explain the work prepared.

The valuer must consider the elements of the report which are appropriate for the asset to be valued. For example, the current value of the business' real estate is unlikely to have an effect on a valuation of intellectual property but may have a significant impact if valuing the company as a whole.

The International Valuation Standards Council (IVSC) have published a number of general standards including IVS 103 Reporting.

This recommends the:

(a) identification of the author;
(b) identification of the client and other intended users;
(c) purpose of the valuation;
(d) identity of asset to be valued;
(e) basis of value;
(f) valuation date;
(g) extent of investigation;
(h) nature and source of the information relied on;
(i) assumptions and special assumptions;
(j) restrictions on use, distribution or publication;
(k) confirmation that the assignment has been undertaken in accordance with the IVS;
(l) valuation approach and reasoning;
(m) amount of the valuation or valuations; and
(n) date of the valuation report.

19.02 Addressee

The report should begin by identifying the persons for whom it is prepared such as the transferor, in the case of a gift of shares, or the personal representatives if it is a transfer on death.

19.03 Identification

The next important thing is to set out precisely what has to be valued. It may be for example that it is a transfer on death and the deceased's shareholding at the date of death has to be valued or it is a capital distribution from a discretionary trust where again it may be the amount of the shares transferred that has to be valued. On the other hand it may be that the deceased's spouse also held shares in the company, or there is a charitable trust or other related property so that the matter to be valued would be a proportion of the larger shareholding. In the case of a lifetime transfer the shares to be valued may be a specific number of shares being the subject of the transfer for stamp duty purposes, with a proportionate valuation for capital gains tax purposes taking into account previous transfers under TCGA 1992, s 19. For inheritance tax purposes the shares to be valued could be the proportionate value of the transferor's own shares and related property before and after the transfer.

A single transfer therefore could give rise to four distinct valuations for tax purposes each in accordance with the appropriate statutory rules.

If the valuation is for the purposes of a commercial transaction such as an intended take-over or flotation it is again necessary to identify the shares which will be disposed of. For example, in the case of a flotation it may be a disposal of say, 30%, of the ordinary share capital on an offer for sale, which then become available for sale in very small stakes rather than as the 30% floated as one parcel, whereas in the case of a sale to one of the venture capital companies it could be a disposal of a specific number of preferred ordinary shares.

19.04 Valuation date

The report should clearly state the date (or dates, as appropriate) at which the asset is being valued.

19.05 Basis of valuation

The basis of valuation must be set out. This may be, say, for stamp duty purposes, on the open market value; or for capital gains tax purposes on the market value with such information available as would normally be made available in a sale by private treaty at arm's length. For inheritance tax purposes again it is the market value with information available as for a sale by private treaty at arm's length, but if it is a valuation by the auditors for the acquisition of shares under pre-emption rights it may be on the basis of a 'fair value' as determined by the articles. In each case it is usually helpful to repeat, or at least to refer to the precise legislation or clause in the articles or sale agreement, which gives rise to the valuation.

Other bases of valuation could be an investment value or a special purchaser value, for example to someone who would have control of the company if he acquired the shares, perhaps in competition, if say, two 49% shareholders were being offered the 2% balance to the highest bidder.

Focus

As there are many different bases of value, not all of which have a formal definition, setting out the basis of valuation required and the definition of this – or the interpretation given to the definition by the valuer – makes it clear to the user of the report the context in which the valuation has been prepared.

19.06 Capital structure

If valuing an interest in shares, the various classes of shares issued by the company should be identified and the proportion of the appropriate shares should be valued, calculated on the basis of the issued share capital of the company as a whole and of shares of that class. Bear in mind that the latest annual return filed with Companies House will not reflect any share transactions which have taken place since the filing date. Many companies will also have issued loan stock or have secured or unsecured short- or long-term loans in place.

19.07 Definition of rights

The provisions in the company's memorandum and articles relating to the share structure and the rights attaching to the various classes of shares should be repeated or referred to. It is important to ensure that the articles used for reference are still in force at the valuation date and whether there are any additional agreements in place between the shareholders.

19.08 Sources of information

It is helpful to define the sources of information used in the valuation both in relation to the company records and those of any comparable companies. It is only necessary in the introduction to summarise these sources and to state, for example, whether in appropriate cases the company's premises have been visited and the management interviewed. It might also be appropriate to mention whether additional information had been obtained from the company's auditors, solicitors or bankers, any websites used for research and whether information on the industry had been obtained from any appropriate trade organisation. For a valuation prepared for litigation purposes that might end up in court, full copies of all documentation relied upon and its source will have to be included as appendices to the valuation report.

19.09 Valuation approach

All valuations will have been prepared using at least one of a cost, market or income approach. The primary and any supporting approach should be set out, together with the selected methods within each approach.

19.10 Valuation conclusion

The final value for the appropriate shareholding or asset previously identified will be stated, and in the case of a lifetime transfer, for example, the value will be stated for each of the various purposes, for example, the open market value for stamp duty, the open market value for capital gains tax, the value included in the transferor's estate before the transfer, the value included in the transferor's estate after the transfer and therefore the value of the reduction in the transferor's estate as a result of the transfer for inheritance tax purposes.

19.11 The reasoning behind the valuation

The valuation report will have to explain why the particular values arrived at are considered appropriate, unless it is a non-speaking valuation. Consequently, calculations should generally be supplied and explained. These would include spreadsheets where they have been used.

19.12 General economic conditions

It will normally be appropriate in a valuation to consider the general economic conditions under which the company is operating. It may be operating in anything from a worldwide market to a single product for a single customer, but normally the company's sales will be concentrated in particular areas and the economic outlooks for those areas should be considered. The company's activities may be confined to the UK or even to a local area within the UK, and in each case the general economic conditions of the area will merit consideration. Such things as the economic growth rates in the particular areas of operation and the rate of inflation will be obvious economic factors bearing upon the performance of the company as will such matters as interest rates and the level of unemployment. The anticipated trend of interest rates and, if the company is exporting or importing or has overseas borrowings or investments, foreign exchange rates and any assumptions about expected future rates will also be of considerable importance. The analysis will normally include not only the immediate levels but those in the recent past and anticipated levels for the immediate future.

Regional development plans for the area in which the company is operating will also be appropriate, particularly if it is in an area which attracts additional grants or incentives.

If the company operates in various locations each of these in turn could be considered, if appropriate.

19.13 Outlook for the industry

The industry or industries within which the company operates should be considered and the immediate future prospects of those industries examined. These may be affected by such things as commodity prices or oil prices or likely over or under capacity and the recent performance of leading companies within the industry. The Financial Times Actuaries Indices could be analysed over the past say, three years, to see whether the sector as a whole is highly regarded by the Stock Market and whether the rate of growth is greater or less than the average for then economy as a whole. This can be a very useful comparison as the performance of the industry relative to the market generally is not going to be distorted by the short-term influences which cause the share prices on the Stock Exchange to fluctuate.

The effect of inflation on the industry should be considered and the indices for raw materials and wholesale prices considered for the company's main products.

Any particularly significant trends or technical developments within the industry should be considered as should marketing trends in appropriate cases, for example, the growth of self service or take away businesses or the influence of the do it yourself market. It will also be important to compare the profitability of the industry with that of the economy generally and again the Financial Times Actuaries Indices could be helpful here.

If the company is engaged in a number of different activities the profit margin expected for the industry as a whole for such activities should be examined and whether or to what extent these margins are likely to be squeezed or expanded in the foreseeable future.

19.14 Company history

A brief history of the company prior to and up to the valuation date should be included, together with any constituent businesses taken over or incorporated into the group. If the company has subsidiaries or associated companies a brief history of each of the main operating companies should also be set out, together with particulars of non-controlling interests where the subsidiaries are not wholly owned.

If the group structure is at all complex it is helpful to include a group structure chart.

The main shareholders in the company should be listed, together with details of the trustees and main beneficiaries of settlements and the beneficial owners of shares held by nominees, if the facts can be ascertained. Family relationships should be indicated.

The operations of the company at the valuation date should be described in some detail and the major competitors and particular advantages or areas of vulnerability which the company has. Dependence on a limited number of suppliers or customers should be noted as should any excessive involvement in particular geographical areas or particular areas of the market. The mix of products or services supplied should be ascertained and any anticipated future technical developments which could help or hinder the company's relative position mentioned.

19.15 Management

Depending on the purpose of the valuation, the company's directors and senior managers may need to be listed, together with their ages and particular areas of expertise. The remuneration drawn and any pension arrangements or additional benefits should be disclosed as this, together with the shareholdings already listed, should show to what extent profits that might otherwise be distributed by way of dividend to an outside shareholder are in fact drawn by the proprietors in the form of remuneration and benefits.

The management of a company sold for its ability to earn profits is clearly of vital importance and areas such as the dependence on one or a small number of key figures and the extent to which they are committed to the company through shareholdings and service agreements should be examined, together with the likely development of future management.

The section of the report dealing with management would obviously be of relatively little importance in the case of a company being taken over entirely where the existing management is likely to be replaced, but in cases where the existing management is likely to remain in place the consideration of a company's management and its potential is an important area of the report.

19.16 Workforce

The extent to which the company relies on skilled personnel, and its labour requirements generally, should be examined in the light of the employment situation in the areas in which the company operates and the shortage or otherwise of people with the appropriate skills required by the company.

Where there are key individuals in a business, the holding of 'key man' insurance policies may be important to note.

FINANCIAL INFORMATION

Focus

Depending on the purpose of the valuation, not all of the financial aspects detailed in this section may require analysis. The valuer needs to apply judgement to determine the relevant elements to include and whether the omission of a particular area of analysis is likely to result in the report being misleading or unclear to the reader.

19.17 Annual accounts

The company's annual accounts for the preceding three or five years will normally be analysed in tabular form. These will usually consist of the profit and loss account and balance sheet on the historical cost basis. A note of dividends paid in each period may also be helpful, depending on the purpose of the valuation, and how it has been performed.

A note will be made of the adjustments to the published accounts in order to make the comparison between the years consistent. For example, if a further company had been brought into the group during the period it might be appropriate to include the results of the new subsidiary for a period before it became a member of the group in order to show the comparable position of the currently subsisting group over the period; alternatively, it may be desirable to eliminate these results from the current figures and to show them separately.

The valuer will not normally make subjective adjustments to the accounts such as for example, eliminating excessive directors' remuneration, unless a controlling interest is to be valued and remuneration at the previous level is unlikely to be drawn in the future. This recognises the comparative vulnerability of a minority shareholder to the power of the directors and controlling shareholders and the fact that it is extremely unlikely that a minority shareholder could in practice do anything about the remuneration drawn by the directors merely because it seemed on the face of it to be excessive. Only if there was an oppression on a minority shareholder sufficient to justify a winding-up order on just and equitable grounds under Insolvency Act 1986, s 122(1)(g) or an order on the grounds of unfairly prejudicial conduct under CA 2006, s 994 (formerly CA 1985, s 459) would it be necessary to make any such adjustment. Only in exceptional cases would the court consider action justifiable under these provisions.

It may also be necessary to value the shares in other companies in which the company has an interest in order to value the shares in the company itself.

19.18 Assets and liabilities

The valuer may comment in his report on the values of assets such as debtors and plant and the evidence he has accepted as to their values. Any significant movement in values within a short space of time, particularly an increase in liabilities, is likely to require further explanation.

19.19 Properties

In the case of freehold or leasehold properties owned by the company the valuer will state whether it has been necessary to obtain a professional valuation, or whether the directors have been able to produce an acceptable estimate of the asset value sufficient for the valuer's purposes. Clearly this depends on the company, the size of the shareholding being valued and the degree to which the company's premises have a significant impact on value. If the company's properties consist of leasehold premises with short leases or onerous terms, it is probably not necessary to have a professional valuation. Similarly if a minority interest in a trading company is being purchased the asset value will be of only limited importance and the directors' estimate may well be sufficient to give comfort to the purchaser. However, in the case of a property investment company where the main asset consists of the properties, it is likely that a professional valuation will be required by the valuer, particularly if a majority interest is being acquired or if the last valuation was several years previously.

19.20 Profit forecasts

The valuer may be able to rely on company budgets to arrive at a reasoned forecast of future profits. Where the company has no formal budgeting system or where previous budgets have proved vague and unreliable, however, an estimate will be needed of the future profitability of the company, on the basis of past financial information available, budgets and market data.

19.21 Capital commitments

Future capital projects for which the company is already committed, or to which it is likely to become committed in the near future, would be referred to, together with the effect, if any, of these projects on the company's cash flow and future profitability.

19.22 Order book

The valuer will also refer to the company's order backlog and the degree to which it is dependent upon a restricted source of supply of goods or materials, or dependent on a restricted number of customers whose allegiance may be transferred elsewhere.

19.23 Insurance

It is important that the company is adequately insured and the valuer may refer to the insurance values in relation to the current value of the company's assets. The valuer will also report the existence or otherwise of any insurance of key members of the company staff and the extent to which any such insurance proceeds would remain with the company in the event of an employee's demise or incapacity.

19.24 Intangible assets

The valuer may wish to refer in his report to those items which, under current accounting practice, are usually excluded from the accounts or shown at a purely nominal figure. For instance, under both UK GAAP and IFRS, the value of internally generated brands and publishing titles are excluded.

19.25 Contingent liabilities

The valuer should perform a search for contingent liabilities, whether or not recognised in the balance sheet, and ensure that they are reflected in his valuation. For instance, some companies may have a potential liability with regard to a defined benefit pension scheme.

19.26 Accounting ratios

As well as setting out the accounts figures in a suitable comparative form the valuer in his report may calculate the profit and loss account and balance sheet figures as percentages and compare them with the average for comparable businesses.

Which accounting ratios will be included for the company being valued and other comparable companies will depend on the circumstances (see **Chapter 16**), but the usual ratios to be considered include:

- current ratio: current assets/ current liabilities;
- quick ratio ('acid test'): (current assets less stock)/current liabilities;
- gross profit margin: gross profit/turnover × 100%;
- net profit margin: net profit/turnover × 100%;

- breakeven point: fixed costs/gross profit margin;
- return on assets: net profit/net assets × 100%;
- dividend cover: earnings per share/dividend per share;
- interest cover: EBIT/net interest payable;
- return on capital employed (ROCE): EBIT/capital employed (often defined as total assets minus current liabilities).

19.27 Comparable companies

Any comparison included in the report would usually, but not necessarily, be with quoted companies. However, it may be appropriate to compare the company being valued with other companies in the sector even if unquoted to show whether it is on the whole more or less attractive than its competitors.

If the comparable companies are quoted companies, the report would certainly show the price at which they were trading on the appropriate stock market.

The comparison should endeavour to show the extent to which the company to be valued represents a more or less attractive long-term investment than the quoted companies.

If may be, however, that the company operates in such a specialised area that there is no company with which the company can be compared directly and in this case it may be marginally helpful to include a comparison with a number of companies in the broader sector in which the business operates.

19.28 Valuation

The valuation conclusion should be clearly set out.

Focus

The report prepared for any valuation needs to be appropriate for the purpose to which it is being put. It is unlikely that a tax valuation for Enterprise Management Incentive purposes would require all of the above elements to be considered. However, for a contentious valuation or one where there are potentially large sums at stake, the valuer should be able to demonstrate that all material aspects of the business or asset to be valued have been considered.

Chapter 20

Fair value for financial reporting purposes

Signposts

20.01 Meaning of fair value

International Financial Reporting Standards (IFRS) is the set of standards adopted by most countries globally for the preparation of the financial statements, ie accounts, of listed companies. The key exception to this is the USA where US Generally Accepted Accounting Principles (US GAAP) are still required for domestic registrants, ie US companies, although IFRS may be adopted by foreign registrants, ie companies registered other than in the USA but with listings on one of the US stock markets.

Many countries still retain their own local Generally Accepted Accounting Principles (GAAP) for private (unlisted) companies, for subsidiaries of listed companies and for submission of accounts to their local tax authorities. In the UK, we are permitted to use UK GAAP in the statutory accounts of private companies and subsidiaries of listed companies.

The International Accounting Standards Board's (IASB's) IFRS 13, 'Fair Value Measurement', has been in force since 2013. This standard defines 'fair value' as:

> 'the price that would be received to sell an asset or paid to transfer a liability in an orderly transaction between market participants at the measurement date.'

IFRS 13 separately defines an 'orderly transaction' as one:

> 'that assumes exposure to the market for a period before the measurement date to allow for marketing activities that are usual and customary for transactions involving such assets or liabilities; it is not a forced transaction (eg a forced liquidation or distress sale).'

IFRS 13 also provides a lengthy definition of market participants: principally they are buyers and sellers in the appropriate market (there is further guidance on identifying the appropriate market – see **20.03** below) for the asset or liability that are independent of each other, knowledgeable, able to enter into a transaction and willing but not forced or compelled to enter into a transaction.

In 2015, UK GAAP underwent something of a metamorphosis: all the existing standards (Financial Reporting Standards (FRSs) and Statements of Standard Accounting Practice (SSAPs)) were replaced by a single composite standard, FRS 102.

FRS 102 defines 'fair value' in the same way as IFRS did before the issue of IFRS 13:

> 'the amount for which an asset could be exchanged, a liability settled, or an equity instrument granted could be exchanged, between knowledgeable, willing parties in an arm's length transaction.'

In practice, there is little difference between the IFRS 13 and the FRS 102 definition of fair value. The only difference that is potentially of substance is that the FRS 102 definition is silent as to whether an entry or exit price is required (the asset could be 'exchanged'), whilst the IFRS 13 definition is clear that an exit price is required ('received to sell an asset').

An identical standard to IFRS 13 was introduced into US GAAP in 2013.

Focus

- IFRS 13 contains some lengthy and complex definitions.
- Since 2015, there has been a new UK GAAP regime.

20.02 The International Valuation Standards Council

The International Valuation Standards Council (IVSC) is an independent non-profit-making organisation which states that it is committed to advancing quality in the valuation profession. Its stated primary objective is to build confidence and public trust in valuation by producing standards, and securing their universal adoption and implementation, for the valuation of assets across the world.

IVSC definitions and guidance are becoming increasingly common as the primary point of reference for valuations both in the UK and overseas. The valuations covered by the IVSC are not restricted to those required for financial reporting purposes but cover valuations whatever the reason that they are required.

At the time of writing, the current version of IVS (International Valuation Standards) is IVS 2017. However, the IVSC Standards Board is planning to issue an updated version in 2019. Electronic and hard copies of IVS may be obtained from www.ivsc.org.

International Valuation Standard (IVS) 104, 'Bases of Value', defines 'market value' as:

> 'the estimated amount for which an asset or liability should exchange on the valuation date between a willing buyer and a willing seller in an arm's length

transaction, after proper marketing and where the parties had each acted knowledgeably, prudently and without compulsion.'

Thus, to all intents and purposes, fair value under IFRS and UK GAAP's FRS 102 has a very similar meaning to 'market value' under IVS. It should also be noted that, in chapters of this book other than **Chapters 20**, **21** and **22**, the term 'fair value' has a different meaning. The term with a similar meaning in other sections of this book is either market value or open market value.

Focus

Fair value under IFRS and UK GAAP's FRS 102, ie for financial reporting purposes, has a similar meaning to market value under IVS and to open market value elsewhere in this book. It does not mean the same as fair value elsewhere in this book.

20.03 Overview of requirements of IFRS 13

The objectives of IFRS 13, 'Fair Value Measurement', are: to define fair value; to set out in a single IFRS a framework for measuring fair value; and to require disclosures about fair value measurements. It is part of the suite of standards developed at a similar time by the IASB that address points raised in a 2009 letter from the G20 group of global finance ministers to the IASB and FASB (Financial Accounting Standards Board: the body responsible for US GAAP) expressing concern about certain areas of financial reporting in the wake of the global financial crisis.

IFRS 13 does not set out when fair value measurements are required. A summary of some of the circumstances under which IFRS requires fair value measurements is set out at **20.04** below. Unless specifically noted as an exception, the IFRS 13 framework and its disclosure requirements are required to be followed in each of these circumstances.

IFRS 13 definitions

An overview of the definitions in IFRS 13 is set out at **20.01** above. The standard also addresses the sometimes complex notions of the principal market and the most advantageous market for an asset or liability. The principal market is defined as the market with the greatest volume and level of activity for the asset or liability. The most advantageous market is defined as the one that would maximise the amount received to sell an asset or minimise the amount paid to transfer a liability, after taking into account transaction costs and transport costs. Fair value is required to be measured by reference to the principal market to which the reporting entity has access, if there is a principal market, and by reference to the most advantageous market if there is no principal market.

For example, two different types of market that could typically exist are a retail and wholesale market. Some entities would have access only to one or other of these, whilst others would have access to both. Fair value measurement might be different in each market.

IFRS 13 also notes that fair value should be measured by reference to the highest and best use obtainable for a non-financial, eg tangible or intangible, asset. This may differ from the specific use an entity intends to put an asset to. For instance, land used to house a factory may have a different value from the same piece of land if it were vacant and available to be sold for redevelopment. Fair value would be measured by reference to the higher of the resulting two values.

Cost, market and income approaches

The single framework that IFRS 13 refers to includes reference to the three basic approaches to valuation. Valuation techniques virtually always fall within one of a cost approach, a market approach or an income approach.

The cost approach is defined as a valuation technique that reflects the amount that would be required currently to replace the service capacity of an asset (often referred to as current replacement cost).

Websites and software are sometimes valued using a cost approach. In the case of valuing shares, the cost approach is rarely appropriate, although it might be applied to value equity shortly after it was acquired, provided there had been no significant changes in the relevant micro- or macro-economic climate post acquisition.

The market approach is defined as a valuation technique that uses prices and other relevant information generated by market transactions involving identical or comparable (ie similar) assets, liabilities, or a group of assets and liabilities, such as a business.

Typical market approaches that could be used to value shares in a company would involve the use of market multiples such as enterprise value to EBIT(DA) (EBIT – earnings before interest and tax; EBITDA – earnings before interest, tax, depreciation and amortisation); see **11.02**. Market multiples could be derived either from the prices at which comparable quoted companies are trading on a stock market or from the prices paid for transactions in shares in comparable companies.

The income approach is defined as valuation techniques that convert future amounts (eg cash flows or income and expenses) to a single, current (ie discounted) amount. The fair value measurement is determined on the basis of the value indicated by current market expectations about those future amounts.

Discounted cash flow (DCF) is the most widely used method within the income approach to valuation.

The IFRS 13 fair value hierarchy

IFRS 13 sets out a fair value hierarchy that determines the reliability of the fair value measurement. The extent to which detailed disclosures about measurement of the valuation are required is linked directly to the deemed reliability of the valuation. Reliability is assessed by reference to the assumptions, known as inputs, underlying the valuation rather than to the approach (ie cost, market or income) adopted. Inputs are classified as either observable or unobservable. Observable inputs are defined as:

> 'inputs that are developed using market data, such as publicly available information about actual events or transactions, and that reflect the assumptions that market participants would use when pricing the asset or liability.'

Unobservable inputs are defined as:

> 'inputs for which market data are not available and that are developed using the best information available about the assumptions that market participants would use when pricing the asset or liability.'

Thus, observable inputs can be directly identified from data available to the public. Unobservable inputs, however, are based on management's best estimates and cannot be directly identified from the market. For instance, prices of equity quoted on the London Stock Exchange would be observable inputs. Similarly, yields to redemption on UK gilts would also be observable inputs: these are obtainable from a number of sources such as the *Financial Times* website or Bloomberg.

However, cash flow projections made by a company for a discounted cash flow exercise, such as projections of turnover, working capital needs or anticipated capital expenditure, are not available in the market. They would have to be estimated and would form unobservable inputs.

IFRS 13 requires that the valuer maximises the use of relevant observable inputs and minimises the use of unobservable inputs. IFRS 13 classifies inputs as representing Level 1, 2 or 3 in the hierarchy.

Level 1 inputs are the most reliable and are defined as

> 'quoted prices (unadjusted) in active markets for identical assets or liabilities that the entity can access at the measurement date.'

Level 2 inputs are defined as:

> 'inputs other than quoted prices included within Level 1 that are observable for the asset or liability, either directly or indirectly.'

Level 3 inputs are the least reliable and are defined as:

> 'unobservable inputs for the asset or liability.'

Thus, in performing a valuation for IFRS reporting purposes, the valuer needs to identify the inputs he has used and grade them as being at Level 1, 2 or 3 in the IFRS 13 hierarchy. The hierarchy level in its entirety is the level of the lowest level input that is significant to the fair value measurement. An input is considered to be significant to the fair value measurement if varying it within a reasonably possible range would change the resulting value significantly.

It can be seen that a valuation classified as Level 1 in its entirety has only one input and that input is the price of the asset in an active market.

A valuation classified as Level 2 in its entirety must comprise only Level 2 inputs and, possibly, insignificant Level 3 inputs.

Any valuation containing a significant Level 3 input will be classified as Level 3 in its entirety.

The resulting valuation level in its entirety directly affects the extent of disclosure required in the financial statements. For all valuations, the hierarchy level in its entirety is required to be disclosed.

- For Level 1 valuations, no further disclosures are required.
- For Level 2 valuations, a qualitative description is also required of the inputs.

- For Level 3 valuations, disclosures as for Level 2 are required and, additionally a quantitative description of significant unobservable inputs.
- For Level 3 valuations of a recurring nature (ie the valuations are required to be performed at every year-end rather than just on the occurrence of a specific event such as an acquisition), as well as all of the above, a qualitative sensitivity analysis is required.
- For Level 3 recurring valuations of financial instruments, as well as all of the above, a quantitative sensitivity analysis is required.

It is noteworthy that it is only at Level 3 that quantitative disclosures about inputs are required. In practice, these are the most sensitive for companies to make. However, the more that companies follow these disclosure requirements, the more likely it is that the reliability and consistency of valuations will improve as a result of improved transparency provided in the market.

Given that valuations of unquoted equity will almost certainly involve significant unobservable inputs and hence be at Level 3 in the IFRS 13 hierarchy, substantial disclosures are required of such valuations. In particular, quantitative sensitivity analysis is required to be disclosed for equity investments accounted for in accordance with IFRS 9, 'Financial Instruments'.

Focus

- Both IFRS and IVS explain that valuation methods for all assets follow one of three main approaches: cost, market or income.
- IFRS 13 sets out a reliability hierarchy for all valuations: Level 1 is the most reliable and Level 3 the least reliable.
- IFRS 13 requires that the hierarchy level is disclosed for assets measured at fair value; disclosures are more extensive for the less reliable valuations.

20.04 Overview of when IFRS requires fair value measurements

IFRS requires or permits certain assets and liabilities to be recognised at fair value in financial statements, whilst others must be recognised using cost-based or other measures. There are also requirements for certain items of income and expenditure to be measured at fair value. As noted above, IFRS 13 does not determine when fair value measurements are required (ie for which assets, liabilities, income and expenses, and in which circumstances) but sets out the requirements regarding the approach to be taken to measure fair value when other IFRSs require such measurement. Fair value measurements may be required for recording amounts in the balance sheet or profit or loss account, or purely for disclosure purposes in the notes to the financial statements.

A full analysis of when IFRS requires or permits that fair value measurement is used in financial statements is outside the scope of this book (reference should be made to the relevant IFRSs, obtainable from www.ifrs.org). However, some of the key standards that require fair value measurements are noted below with a brief description of some of the items that are to be measured at fair value.

The paragraphs that follow do not attempt to identify all the situations in which fair value measurement is required.

Focus

- IFRS 13 sets out the approach to be taken to fair value measurements and the disclosures required in respect of those measurements. Other IFRSs set out the requirements for when such fair value measurements are required.
- Occasionally, other IFRS set their own disclosure requirements that are different from the IFRS 13 requirements.

IFRS 2: 'Share-based Payment'

IFRS 2 requires that the profit or loss account charge for shares or share options awarded to employees as part of their remuneration package is recorded based on the 'modified grant date fair value' of the award. The application of IFRS 2 is described in more detail in **Chapter 22** of this book. It is noteworthy at this stage, however, that IFRS 2 is an exception to other extant IFRSs in that it uses the old definition of fair value before the introduction of IFRS 13; fair value measurements under IFRS 2 are specifically noted as being outside the scope of the IFRS 13 requirements.

IFRS 3: 'Business Combinations'

IFRS 3 requires (with a few exceptions) that all the assets, including intangible assets, and liabilities, including contingent liabilities, of an acquiree are measured at fair value when initially recognised in the consolidated financial statements of the acquirer. Also, the consideration for an acquisition must be measured at fair value: whilst this is a straightforward exercise when it comprises purely cash payable in full on completion, it becomes more complex in cases involving deferred or contingent consideration or consideration payable in the form of equity. Measurement of fair value in the context of IFRS 3 is described in more detail in **Chapter 21** of this book.

IFRS 5: 'Non-current Assets Held for Sale and Discontinued Operations'

IFRS 5 addresses, *inter alia*, the accounting for businesses and assets that are held subject to planned disposal within 12 months. These are required to be recognised at the lower of their carrying value and fair value less costs to sell.

IFRS 9: 'Financial Instruments'

IFRS 9 is a new standard, which replaced IAS 39, 'Financial Instruments' and took effect from January 2018. It represents the conclusion of several years' work by the IASB. Prior to 2018, UK IFRS reporters could choose whether to adopt IFRS 9 early or to continue applying IAS 39. Accounting for financial instruments under IAS 39 or IFRS 9 is complex and outside the scope of this book, but a few key points are set out below.

IFRS 9, as did its predecessor IAS 39, has different requirements for the accounting for investments in debt instruments (eg corporate or government bonds) from the accounting for investments in equity instruments (eg shares in other companies). Both set out conditions under which debt instruments may be accounted for at a cost-based measure known as 'amortised cost' and conditions under which debt instruments are either required or permitted to be recognised at fair value. IFRS 7, 'Financial Instruments: Disclosures' includes disclosure requirements such that the fair value of debt investments must be disclosed in the notes to the accounts, even where these have been recognised at amortised cost in the balance sheet. Thus, fair value must be determined for all debt investments regardless of the balance sheet measurement model applied.

IAS 39 required that investments in quoted equity were recognised at fair value, but permitted the recognition of unquoted equity investments at cost if it was not possible to measure their fair value reliably. IFRS 9, however, makes no such allowance for unquoted equity investments: all equity investments are required to be recognised at fair value regardless of whether they are quoted or unquoted. This reflects a trend in recently issued or updated IFRS to insist that fair value can always be measured reliably and to reduce the number of situations in which it may be deemed that fair value cannot be measured reliably. This is a result both of the introduction of IFRS 13 providing more guidance on the measurement of fair value and also an acknowledgment that, in recent years, techniques for the measurement of fair value have developed significantly. The International Valuation Standards Council (IVSC) has also been more active in issuing valuation guidance since 2009.

The IASB collaborates with the IVSC in the drafting of new and revised IFRS where fair value measurement is required. The IVSC also obtains input from the IASB when drafting valuation guidance in the context of IFRS reporting. Indeed, to strengthen this collaborative link, Sir David Tweedie, who was chairman of the IASB from 2001 to 2011, was appointed chairman of the IVSC in 2012.

IFRS 10: 'Consolidated Financial Statements'

IFRS 10 came into force in 2013. The standard primarily addresses the requirement to consolidate investments controlled by a parent company. IFRS 10 replaced the control requirements previously set out in IAS 27 and much of it relates to the identification of the controlling party in complex situations.

It includes requirements in respect of the treatment of investments held by investment entities. These are entities which, in summary, invest solely for capital appreciation or investment income or both, rather than to run their investments as businesses. Investment entities are not permitted to consolidate the investments that they control; instead they must recognise them in the balance at fair value with changes in fair value measurement recognised in the profit or loss account.

IFRS 12: 'Disclosures of Interests in Other Entities'

IFRS 12 sets out the disclosure requirements for investments in other entities that are addressed in IFRS 10, IFRS 11, 'Joint Arrangements', and IAS 28, 'Investments in Associates and Joint Ventures'. IFRS 12 includes a requirement that where a material joint venture or associate is accounted for using the equity method, its fair value is also disclosed if there is a quoted market price for the investment.

IAS 16: 'Property, Plant and Equipment'

This standard offers a choice of treatment for items of property, plant and equipment. Individual classes of property, plant and equipment may either be recognised under a cost model or, if fair value can be measured reliably, under a revaluation model.

If the revaluation model is used for a particular class of property, such as plant and equipment, fair value is measured at the revaluation date and accumulated depreciation and impairment losses are deducted from this amount. Revaluations must be performed sufficiently regularly that the carrying value at the period end does not differ materially from fair value.

Increases in fair value above original cost are recognised in 'Other comprehensive income', but decreases in fair value below original cost are recognised in the profit or loss account.

IAS 19: 'Employee Benefits'

This standard includes a section addressing the accounting for defined benefit pension schemes, which includes a requirement that pension fund assets are measured at fair value. The requirements of IFRS 13, 'Fair Value Measurement', apply to the measurement of the plan assets but the disclosures regarding the measurements are set out in IAS 19 rather than IFRS 13. The required disclosures include an analysis of the plan assets into classes reflecting the nature and risks of the assets involved, with each class subdivided into those that have a quoted market price in an active market and those that do not. An example of the potential disaggregation includes the following:

- cash and cash equivalents;
- equity instruments (subdivided by industry type, company, size and geography, etc);
- debt instruments (subdivided by type of issuer, credit quality, geography, etc);
- real estate (subdivided by geography, etc);
- derivatives (subdivided by type of underlying risk, eg interest rate contracts, foreign exchange rate contracts, equity contracts);
- investment funds (subdivided by type of fund);
- asset-backed securities; and
- structured debt.

Disclosures are also required of the fair values of:

- the entity's own transferable financial instruments (eg listed shares or listed corporate bonds); and
- plan assets comprising property occupied by, or other assets used by, the entity.

IAS 28: 'Investments in Associates and Joint Ventures'

Some key amendments to IAS 28 came into force in 2013. The amended standard addresses the accounting treatment of associates and joint ventures. IAS 28 provides an optional exemption from the equity accounting treatment otherwise required for associates and joint ventures, such that venture capital funds may choose to recognise these investments at fair value with changes in fair value measurement recognised in the profit or loss account.

IAS 36: 'Impairment of Assets'

IAS 36 sets out the impairment requirements for tangible assets, goodwill and intangible assets. It includes a test that relies on measuring the fair value of the assets being tested and, in some cases, the fair value of the cash-generating unit to which the asset belongs. The standard is discussed further in **Chapter 21** of this book.

IAS 38: 'Intangible Assets'

IAS 38 sets out the requirements for recognising intangible assets in the balance sheet. It includes an optional revaluation model, rarely used, for intangible assets that are traded in an active market. Where the revaluation model is applied, intangible assets are recognised at the revalued amount, being fair value at the revaluation date, less accumulated amortisation and impairment losses. Similarly to the revaluation model available under IAS 16 for items of property, plant and equipment, revaluations of intangible assets must be performed sufficiently regularly that the carrying value at the period end does not differ materially from fair value.

The guidance notes that the frequency of the revaluation depends on the volatility of the fair values of the intangible assets being revalued.

Revaluations above original cost are recognised in Other comprehensive income, whilst revaluations below original cost are recognised in the profit or loss account. The requirements in respect of intangible assets acquired as part of a business combination are addressed in **Chapter 21**.

IAS 40: 'Investment Properties'

IAS 40 sets out the required accounting treatment for investment properties, ie property held by the owner, or by the lessee under a finance lease, to earn rentals or for capital appreciation or both rather than for:

- use in the production or supply of goods or services or for administrative purposes; or
- sale in the ordinary course of business.

A company may choose either to apply the fair value model or a cost model to all its investment properties. If it applies the fair value model, investment properties are recognised at fair value at the balance sheet date and changes in fair value measurement are recognised in the profit or loss account.

IAS 40 provides some additional guidance to that in IFRS 13 regarding measurement of fair value. This includes that fair value measurement shall reflect, *inter alia*, rental income from current leases and other assumptions that market participants would use when pricing investment property under the prevailing market conditions. The standard also draws attention to the need to ensure that related assets or liabilities that are separately recognised in the financial statements are not double counted.

If a company chooses the cost model for investment property, it must follow the requirements of the cost model as set out in IAS 16, 'Property, Plant and Equipment'. A company applying the cost model is still required by IAS 40 to disclose in its notes the fair value of its investment property.

There is a rebuttable presumption that a company can always measure the fair value of its investment property reliably. In exceptional circumstances, where a company, which has elected to recognise its investment properties at fair value, acquires an investment property for which it cannot measure fair value reliably, it must account for such property using the IAS 16 cost model for the full period until it disposes of the property.

In addition to the IFRS 13 disclosures regarding fair value measurement, the following must be disclosed (including for those investment properties recognised under the cost model in the balance sheet):

- the extent, if any, to which fair value measurement is based on a valuation by an independent valuer who holds a recognised and relevant professional qualification and has recent experience in the location and category of the investment property being valued;
- any significant adjustments made to a valuation for the purpose of the financial statements; eg to avoid the double counting referred to above; and
- an explanation, when the presumption that the fair value of investment property can be measured reliably is rebutted, of why, together, if possible, with a range of estimates within which fair value is highly likely to lie.

As a generic point, fair value measurements exclude the transaction costs that would be involved in selling the underlying assets. Consequently, balance sheet amounts for investment property carried at fair value should be stated gross of any expected costs of disposing of these properties.

IAS 41: 'Agriculture'

This standard addresses the accounting for biological assets, such as living animals or plants; eg sheep, and agricultural produce, eg wool. These are required to be accounted for at fair value less costs to sell, unless they are agricultural produce for which there is no active market and fair value cannot be measured reliably. Changes in fair value measurement are required to be recognised in the profit or loss account.

IAS 41 excludes bearer plants from its scope – 'bearer plants' are defined as living plants that are used in the production or supply of agricultural produce, are expected to bear produce for more than one period, and have a remote likelihood of being sold as agricultural produce, except for incidental scrap sales.

Bearer plants are required to be accounted for similarly to property, plant and equipment under IAS 16, so they may be accounted for under a cost or revaluation model.

IAS 41 includes guidance to the effect that measuring the fair value of a biological asset or agricultural produce may be facilitated by grouping each category together according to significant attributes, such as age or quality; these are to be chosen to match pricing attributes used in the market.

The standard also notes that forward contracts for the sale of biological assets or agricultural produce may not necessarily be relevant to measuring fair value under market conditions at the valuation date. Cost is noted as sometimes approximating fair value especially when there has been little biological transformation since initial acquisition, or the impact of biological transformation is not expected to be significant.

It is noted that biological assets are often attached to land, eg trees in a plantation forest. Sometimes an active market will exist for the combined biological asset and land but not for the individual biological assets. In such cases, the fair value of the biological assets may be derived by deducting the fair value of the raw land from the fair value of the combined assets.

20.05 UK GAAP accounting and fair value measurement

A new regime for UK GAAP came into force in 2015, with revised standards issued in March 2018. Listed companies are required to follow IFRS, as are those listed on the Alternative Investment Market (AIM), in their consolidated financial statements.

Private companies, however, are free to follow UK GAAP. The key UK GAAP standards are now:

- FRS 101, Reduced Disclosure Framework;
- FRS 102, The Financial Reporting Standard applicable in the UK and Republic of Ireland;
- FRS 103, Insurance Contracts; and
- FRS 105, The Financial Reporting Standard applicable to the Micro-entities Regime.

The document, FRS 100, Application of Financial Reporting Requirements, explains which entities need to apply which of the above standards and what choices are available.

Private companies may elect to follow IFRS if they wish to. Alternatively, they may elect to follow FRS 101. This comprises the full recognition and measurement requirements of IFRS but with reduced note disclosure requirements. This standard is often followed by subsidiaries of listed companies. It allows subsidiaries to follow the same recognition and measurement requirements as their parent companies, ie to have the same accounting policies, but without the extensive note disclosures.

FRS 102 is the standard adopted by UK companies that are either too large or do not wish to adopt FRS 105 and that do not need and do not wish to adopt full IFRS, even with reduced disclosure. The requirements of FRS 102 are based on the IFRS for small and medium-sized entities (SMEs). Like the IFRS for SMEs, FRS 102 is one single standard covering the various different financial reporting topics, with individual topics set out in different sections.

Following a triennial review, an amended version of FRS 102 was issued in March 2018.

For those companies applying FRS 102, the requirements of FRS 103, 'Insurance Contracts', apply to any insurance contracts or financial instruments with discretionary participation features that they issue. The accounting requirements applicable to these complex and specialised contracts are outside the scope of this book.

FRS 105 applies to the financial statements of a 'micro-entity'. It follows the same general format as FRS 102, ie different sections for different topics. It includes the minimum accounting items that are presumed in law to be required to show a true and fair view of the micro-entity's financial position and profit or loss.

UK company law defines a micro-entity as satisfying two or more of the following three criteria:

- turnover no more than £632,000;
- balance sheet total (ie fixed plus current assets) no more than £316,000; and
- average number of employees no more than 10.

However, even if they satisfy the above requirements, certain types of entity are not permitted to be micro-entities. These include limited liability partnerships (LLPs), charities and public companies (PLCs).

The paragraphs that follow look briefly at the sections in FRS 102 and FRS 105 where fair value accounting is either required or is a permitted optional treatment. They are not intended to form comprehensive guidance to the requirements of fair value measurement in the context of UK GAAP: such guidance is outside the scope of this book. Reference should be made to UK GAAP, which can be obtained from the FRC at www.frc.org.uk.

As noted earlier, fair value is defined in FRS 102: Section 2, 'Concepts and Pervasive Principles', as:

> 'the amount for which an asset could be exchanged, a liability settled, or an equity instrument granted could be exchanged, between knowledgeable, willing parties in an arm's length transaction.'

The Appendix to Section 2 provides additional guidance on measuring fair value, including:

1 The best evidence of fair value is a quoted price for an identical (or similar) asset in an active market.
2 When quoted prices are unavailable, the price in a binding sales agreement or a recent transaction for an identical (or similar) asset in an arm's length transaction between knowledgeable, willing parties provides evidence of fair value. However, this price may not be a good estimate of fair value if there has been a significant change in economic circumstances or a significant period of time between the date of the binding sale agreement or the transaction, and the measurement date. If the entity can

demonstrate that the last transaction price is not a good estimate of fair value (eg because it reflects the amount that an entity would receive or pay in a forced transaction, involuntary liquidation or distress sale), that price is adjusted.

3 If the market for the asset is not active and any binding sale agreements or recent transactions for an identical (or similar) asset on their own are not a good estimate of fair value, an entity estimates fair value by using another valuation technique. The objective of using another valuation technique is to estimate what the transaction price would have been on the measurement date in an arm's length exchange motivated by normal business considerations.

Valuation techniques are noted as including the price in a binding sale agreement and recent arm's length market transactions for an identical asset between knowledgeable, willing parties. Reference is also made to the current fair value of another asset that is substantially the same as the asset being valued, discounted cash flow analysis and option pricing models. It is noted that, if there is a valuation technique commonly used in the market for the asset and that technique has been demonstrated to provide reliable estimates of prices obtainable in actual market transactions, such a technique should be used.

A valuation technique should maximise the use of market inputs, and rely as little as possible on entity-determined inputs. It is noted that a valuation technique would be expected to arrive at a reliable estimate of fair value if:

(a) it reasonably reflects how the market could be expected to price the asset; and
(b) the inputs to the valuation technique reasonably represent market expectations and measures of the risk return factors inherent in the asset.

Some guidance is provided on how to decide whether the fair value of an asset that does not have a quoted market price, is reliably measurable – this requires that:

(a) variability in the range of reasonable fair value estimates is not significant for that asset; or
(b) probabilities of the various estimates within the range can be reasonably assessed and used in estimating fair value.

It is noted that there are many situations in which the variability in the range of reasonable fair value estimates of assets that do not have a quoted market price is likely not to be significant, and also that it is normally possible to estimate the fair value of an asset that an entity has acquired from an outside party.

Focus

- The Appendix to FRS 102 Section 2 is the place where general guidance on fair value measurement is found in FRS 102.
- Disclosure requirements are set out in the individual sections dealing with the different types of asset and liability, but they are generally much less onerous than those set out in IFRS 13.

FRS 102

Section 9, 'Consolidated and Separate Financial Statements'

Section 9 makes provision for subsidiaries that are not consolidated because they are held exclusively with a view to resale and which have not previously been consolidated on application of FRS 102:

- If they are held as part of an 'investment portfolio', ie their value to the investor is through fair value as part of a basket of investments rather than so that the investor can run a business through them, they are carried in the balance sheet at fair value, with changes in fair value recognised in the profit or loss account.
- If they are not held as part of an investment portfolio, they must be measured according to an accounting policy established as described below for the separate (ie non-consolidated) financial statements of the parent entity.

In the separate financial statements of the parent, an accounting policy for the recognition of subsidiaries, associates and jointly controlled entities at one of the following is required:

- cost less impairment provisions;
- fair value with changes in fair value recognised in 'Other comprehensive income', provided such changes are above original cost, or in the profit or loss account for any changes below original cost; or
- fair value with changes in fair value recognised in the profit or loss account.

Section 11, 'Basic Financial Instruments', and Section 12, 'Other Financial Instruments Issues'

Sections 11 and 12 of FRS 102 address the accounting for financial instruments, with Section 11 addressing basic financial instruments and Section 12 addressing more complex financial instruments. FRS 102 permits entities to establish an accounting policy to adopt application of:

- Sections 11 and 12 in full;
- IAS 39 for recognition and measurement of financial instruments accompanied by Sections 11 and 12 of FRS 102 for disclosure purposes; or
- IFRS 9 and IAS 39, as amended following the issue of IFRS 9, for recognition and measurement of financial instruments accompanied by Sections 11 and 12 of FRS 102 for disclosure purposes.

As with IAS 39 and IFRS 9 referred to earlier in this chapter, accounting for financial instruments is complex and outside the scope of this book. The following paragraphs note some of the key points that would arise from application of FRS 102.

The instruments deemed to be basic and included within Section 11 include the following:

- cash;
- demand and fixed-term deposits when the entity is the depositor, eg bank accounts;
- accounts, notes and loans receivable and payable;
- bonds and similar debt instruments;
- investments in non-derivative financial instruments that are equity of the issuer (eg most ordinary shares and certain preference shares); and
- restricted commitments to receive or make a loan.

More complex financial instruments within the scope of Section 12 include the following:

- asset-backed securities, such as collateralised mortgage obligations, repurchase agreements and securitised packages of receivables;
- derivatives, eg options, rights, warrants, futures contracts, forward contracts and interest rate swaps;
- hedging instruments; and
- commitments to make or receive a loan that can be settled net in cash.

The FRS 102 Section 11 treatment is that most investments in basic debt instruments are recognised at cost or amortised cost, rather than fair value, although there is an option to recognise certain basic debt instruments at fair value, in which case this must be the accounting policy from initial recognition onwards.

Investments in basic equity rather than debt instruments are measured:

- at fair value, with changes in fair value recognised in the profit or loss account if they are publicly traded or fair value can otherwise be measured reliably; or
- at cost less impairment, unless they are investments in another group entity, in which case the accounting policy established for subsidiaries, associates or joint ventures in the separate accounts of their parent (see FRS 102 Section 9 above) is adopted – this may be fair value measurement.

Investments in complex, ie non-basic, financial instruments are recognised at fair value, with changes in fair value recognised in profit or loss, unless either:

- the investments are in equity instruments that are not publicly traded and whose fair value cannot otherwise be measured reliably – in which case they are measured at cost less impairment; or
- they are part of a recognised hedging transaction.

Where financial instruments are measured at fair value, the required disclosures include the basis for determining fair value; eg quoted market price in an active market or a valuation technique. Where a valuation technique has been used, the assumptions applied for determining fair value for each class of financial assets are to be disclosed; eg interest rates, discount rates, etc.

Section 14, 'Investments in Associates'

An investor that is a parent company, and holds an associate as part of an investment portfolio, is required to recognise the associate at fair value with changes in fair value recognised in the profit or loss account.

An investor that is a parent company and recognises an associate using the equity method must disclose the fair value of the investment if there are published price quotations.

An investor that is not a parent company may choose to apply an accounting policy to recognise investments in associates at fair value, with a further choice in accounting policy regarding whether changes in fair value are recognised in Other comprehensive income or in the profit or loss account.

For investments in associates accounted for at fair value, the disclosure requirements of FRS 102 Section 11 apply; ie the basis for determining fair value and assumptions applied must be disclosed.

Section 15, 'Investments in Joint Ventures'

A venturer that is a parent and holds investments in jointly controlled entities as part of an investment portfolio, is required to recognise such investments at fair value with changes in fair value recognised in the profit and loss account.

A venturer that is a parent and accounts for investments in jointly controlled entities using the equity method must disclose the fair value of such investments if there are published price quotations.

A venturer that is not a parent must adopt an accounting policy for all its interests in jointly controlled entities such that they are accounted for at one of cost; fair value with increases in fair value above original cost recognised in 'Other comprehensive income' and decreases in fair value below original cost recognised in the profit or loss account; or at fair value with changes in fair value recognised in the profit or loss account.

For jointly controlled entities accounted for at fair value, the disclosure requirements of FRS 102 Section 11 apply; ie the basis for determining fair value and assumptions applied must be disclosed.

Section 16, 'Investment Property'

Investment property is property held by the owner or by the lessee under a finance lease to earn rentals or for capital appreciation or both rather than for:

- use in the production or supply of goods or services or for administrative purposes; or
- sale in the ordinary course of business.

Investment property is to be measured at fair value at each balance sheet date, with changes in fair value recognised in the profit or loss account. There is, however, a choice of using the cost, rather than fair value, model for an entity that rents a property to another group company.

The following are required to be disclosed regarding fair value measurement:

- the methods and significant assumptions applied; and
- the extent, if any, to which the measurement is based on a valuation by an independent valuer holding a recognised and relevant professional qualification with recent experience in the location and class of the investment property valued.

Section 17, 'Property, Plant and Equipment'

Items of property, plant and equipment are measured under either the cost model or the revaluation model. The same model must be applied to items from the same class of property, plant and equipment. Under the revaluation model, subsequent accumulated depreciation and accumulated impairment losses are deducted from the fair value measurement. Revaluations are to be made with sufficient regularity that the carrying amount does not differ materially from that which would be determined using fair value at the end of the reporting period.

Revaluation changes above original cost are recognised in 'Other comprehensive income'. Revaluation changes below original cost are recognised in the profit or loss account.

The fair value of land and buildings is noted as usually being determined from market-based evidence from a valuation by a professionally qualified valuer. The fair value of items of plant and equipment is noted as usually being determined by appraisal.

It is noted that, if there is no market-based evidence of fair value as a result of the specialised nature of the property, plant or equipment, and the item is rarely sold except as part of a continuing business, fair value may need to be estimated using an income or depreciated replacement cost approach.

For items carried at revalued amounts, the disclosure requirements include:

- the effective date of the revaluation;
- whether an independent valuer was involved; and
- the methods and significant assumptions applied in estimating fair value.

Section 18, 'Intangible Assets other than Goodwill'

The basic approach for the recognition of intangible assets in the balance sheet is that they are carried at cost less accumulated amortisation and impairment charges. However, for intangible assets that come from an active market, there is the option of using the revaluation model, as there is under IAS 38. This revaluation model is similar to that for property, plant and equipment. However, it is very rare to find intangible assets that come from an active market and so the revaluation model is rarely, if ever, used for them.

The requirements for the accounting for intangible assets acquired as part of a business combination are set out in more detail in **Chapter 21** of this book.

Section 19, 'Business Combinations and Goodwill'

Similarly to IFRS 3, Section 19 of FRS 102 requires that (with a few exceptions) all the assets, including intangible assets, and liabilities, including contingent liabilities, of an acquiree are measured at fair value when initially recognised in the consolidated financial statements of the acquirer. This approach is described in more detail in **Chapter 21** of this book, which also identifies the key differences between IFRS and FRS 102 as regards accounting for business combinations.

Section 26, 'Share-based Payment'

Section 26 requires that the profit or loss account charge for shares or share options awarded to employees as part of their remuneration package is made based on the fair value of the award granted. The application of Section 26 is described in more detail in **Chapter 22** of this book, where the fair value measurement guidance of that Section is also set out. **Chapter 22** also looks at the differences between application of IFRS 2, Share-based Payment, and FRS 102, Section 26.

Section 27, 'Impairment of Assets'

Most of Section 27 is devoted to setting out the requirements for the impairment of tangible assets, intangible assets and goodwill. It includes a test that relies on measuring the fair value of the assets being tested and, in some cases, the fair value of the cash-generating unit to which the asset belongs. The required approach is set out in more detail in **Chapter 21** of this book, where the similarities and differences between IAS 36, 'Impairment of Assets', and FRS 102, Section 27 are also discussed.

Section 28, 'Employee Benefits'

Section 28 includes the requirements for accounting for defined benefit pension plans. These include a requirement that the plan assets are recognised at fair value. The guidance in the Appendix to Section 2 of FRS 102 is noted as being applicable to the measurement of the fair value of the plan assets.

Required disclosures include the percentage of the total fair value of plan assets in each of the following classes:

- equity instruments;
- debt instruments;
- property; and
- all other assets.

In addition, disclosure is required for amounts included in the fair value of plan assets for:

- each class of the entity's own financial instruments; and
- any property occupied by, or other assets used by, the entity.

Section 34, 'Specialised Activities'

Section 34 includes the requirements for the accounting for agricultural activity, including biological assets, such as living animals and plants, eg sheep, and agricultural produce such as wool. This section requires the establishment of an accounting policy for each class of such assets to recognise them either using a cost model or a fair value model.

If the fair value model is adopted, biological assets are required to be recognised at fair value less costs to sell. Changes in this measurement are recognised in the profit or loss account. Agricultural produce harvested from such biological assets is measured at the point of harvest at fair value less costs to sell, which is then used as the base for cost accounting for this produce as it becomes inventory.

The following guidance is provided regarding fair value measurement:

- If an active market exists for the biological asset or agricultural produce in its present location and condition, the quoted price in that market is the appropriate basis for determining fair value of the asset. If the entity has access to different active markets, it should use the price in the market it expects to use.
- If there is no active market for the asset, fair value should be measured using one or more of the following:
  - the most recent market transaction price, provided there has not been a significant change in economic circumstances between the date of that transaction and the balance sheet date;
  - market prices for similar assets with adjustments to reflect differences; and
  - sector benchmarks such as the value of an orchard per hectare, or the value of cattle per kilogram of meat.
- Reasons for differences in fair value reached using the three methods above are required to be considered to reach the most reliable estimate of fair value within a reasonably narrow range of reasonable estimates.
- If market prices are not available, it is noted that it may still be possible to measure fair value reliably by estimating the present value of expected net cash flows from the asset, discounted at a current market determined rate.

If fair value cannot be determined reliably, the cost model must be applied.

Required disclosures include the methods and significant assumptions applied in determining the fair value of:

- each class of biological asset; and
- at the point of harvest, each class of agricultural produce.

20.06 Fair value measurement and FRS 105

UK companies or groups, which are defined as micro-entities in the Companies Act 2006, have the option of preparing their accounts in accordance with FRS 105, The Financial Reporting Standard applicable to the Micro-Entities Regime. They can, if they wish, alternatively apply full IFRS, FRS 101 or FRS 102.

FRS 105 is based on FRS 102 but the accounting requirements are designed to satisfy only the legal requirements applicable to micro-entities and to reflect their smaller size and simpler nature.

The current version of FRS 105 was issued in March 2018 and is mandatorily effective from January 2019. FRS 105 is organised by section similarly to FRS 102.

'Fair value' is defined as:

> 'the amount at which an asset could be exchanged, a liability settled, or an equity instrument granted could be exchanged, between knowledgeable, willing parties in an arm's length transaction.'

Thus, the definition is the same as that used in FRS 102.

FRS 105 Section 2 notes that it requires fair value measurement only in limited circumstances and that, in the absence of any specific guidance provided in the relevant section of the FRS, the guidance in paragraph 2.31 is to be used in measuring fair value. This is as follows:

(a) The best evidence of fair value is the open market price for an identical or similar asset or liability in an active market.
(b) If an open market price is not available, the price of a recent transaction for an identical or similar asset or liability in an arm's length transaction between knowledgeable, willing parties provides evidence of fair value should be used. However, the price may not be a good estimate of fair value if there has been a significant change in economic circumstances or significant period of time between the date of the binding sale agreement or the transaction, and the measurement date.
(c) If neither (a) nor (b) are available, the fair value is to be estimated using another valuation technique. The objective of using a valuation technique is to estimate what the price of a recent transaction for an identical or similar asset or liability would have been on the measurement date in an arm's length exchange motivated by normal business considerations.

Thus, the guidance available is generic rather than assisting or describing different valuation methods and is very similar to that in the Appendix to FRS 102 Section 2.

Section 9 addresses financial instruments. The only reference to fair value is that impairment is required to be recognised in a derivative if its carrying value exceeds its fair value less costs to sell.

Section 17 addresses liabilities and equity instruments. This makes provision for the use of fair value measurement of the liability component if a micro-entity issues convertible debt.

Section 19 addresses government grants, and it notes that a micro-entity recognises government grants at the fair value of the asset receivable.

Section 22 addresses impairment of assets. It notes that the recoverable amount of an asset is the higher of its fair value less costs to sell and value in use. It notes that fair value less costs to sell is the amount obtainable from the sale of an asset in an arm's length transaction between knowledgeable, willing parties, less the costs of disposal:

- The best evidence of fair value less costs to sell of an asset is a price in a binding sale agreement in an arm's length transaction or an open market price in an active market. If there is no binding sale agreement or active market for an asset, fair value less costs to sell is based on the best information available to reflect the amount that a micro-entity could obtain, at the reporting date, from the disposal of the asset in an arm's length transaction between knowledgeable, willing parties, after deducting the costs of disposal. In determining this amount, a micro-entity considers the outcome of recent transactions for similar assets within the same industry.
- Consideration is to be given to any restrictions imposed on the asset.

> **Focus**
>
> The Small Companies (Micro-Entities' Accounts) Regulations 2013 state that micro-entities are not permitted to apply the Alternative Accounting Rules or the Fair Value Rules as set out in company law. Thus, micro-entities are only permitted to apply the Historical Cost Accounting Rules and there is minimal reference to fair value measurement in FRS 105.

In *HMRC v Smith & Nephew Overseas Limited, TP Limited, Smith & Nephew Finance Holdings Limited* [2018] UKUT 393 (TCC), a change in functional currency was considered:

> '2. Following a company reorganisation, Smith and Nephew Overseas Limited ("SN Overseas"), TP Limited ("TP") and Smith and Nephew Finance Holdings Limited ("SN Finance") (together "the S&N Companies") changed their functional currency from sterling to US dollars. They claimed in their tax returns for the accounting periods ending on 31 December 2008 that this gave rise to foreign exchange losses. In sterling terms the claimed losses amounted to £445,868,096, £138,188,096 and £90,652,234 respectively.
>
> 3. The companies claimed that the exchange losses arose as a result of revaluations included in the statement of total recognised gains and losses ("STRGL") of each of the companies in their respective accounts for the period ended 31 December 2008. The losses were said to arise as a result of the fall in the value of sterling against the US dollar.
>
> 4. HMRC did not accept that the losses arose for corporation tax purposes, and on 16 April 2014 issued closure notices under paragraph 34(2) of Schedule 18 to the Finance Act 1998 which disallowed the losses and made consequential amendments to the tax returns of each company.
>
> 5. The companies appealed to the FTT against the closure notices, and the appeals were heard together. The FTT (Judge Brooks and John Agboola) allowed the appeals, and concluded that:
>
> (1) The accounts of each company for the relevant year were drawn up in accordance with UK Generally Accepted Accounting Practice ("GAAP").
> (2) The claimed exchange differences gave rise to "exchange losses" within the meaning of the legislation.
> (3) Those exchange differences did "fairly represent" losses within the meaning of the legislation.
>
> 6. On 14 August 2017 HMRC applied for permission to appeal the Decision. The grounds of appeal were that the FTT had erred in law in reaching all three conclusions. In relation to the conclusion that the accounts were drawn up in accordance with GAAP, it was submitted that numerous findings of fact by the FTT gave rise to errors of law under the principles in *Edwards v Bairstow* [1956] AC 14.
>
> 7. The FTT (Judge Brooks) granted permission to appeal on all grounds.'

The Upper Tribunal agreed with the First Tier Tribunal that, using the foreign operations accounting method, there was a substantial foreign exchange loss.

HMRC claimed that the FTT erred in 'relying expressly' on HMRC's manuals and on the approval of the accounts by the auditors. That and other submissions by HMRC on this issue were dismissed.

The third issue in this case was HMRC's appeal against the FTT's decision that the exchange losses did 'fairly represent' losses of the companies, in accordance with UK GAAP, and the relevant losses were 'exchange losses'. HMRC claimed that those losses did not fairly represent losses of the company because the companies had no underlying foreign exchange exposure and suffered no real economic loss.

HMRC's case was disputed by the companies and upheld by the Upper Tribunal, distinguishing it from *HMRC v GDF Suez Teesside Limited* [2018] EWCA Civ 2075.

Chapter 21

Accounting for goodwill and intangible assets arising on an acquisition

Signposts

21.01 Introduction

The meaning of fair value in the context of financial reporting is explained in **20.01**, whilst **20.03** sets out some of the key IFRS and UK GAAP requirements for fair value measurement. This chapter looks at some of the specific requirements of IFRS and UK GAAP in the accounting for business combinations, which includes the recognition and measurement of goodwill and intangible assets. It is not intended to provide comprehensive coverage of either IFRS or UK GAAP requirements for the accounting for goodwill and intangible assets arising from an acquisition. Reference should be made to the underlying standards and guidance available respectively from the International Accounting Standards Board (IASB) website (www.ifrs.org), and the Financial Reporting Council (FRC) website (www.frc.org) for a full understanding of the financial reporting required.

21.02 Accounting for business combinations under IFRS

The following IFRSs are relevant to the accounting for business combinations under IFRS:

- IFRS 3, 'Business Combinations';
- IAS 36, 'Impairment of Assets'; and
- IAS 38, 'Intangible Assets'.

As explained in **20.02**, whenever fair value measurement is required by an IFRS, the requirements of IFRS 13, 'Fair Value Measurement', must be followed with regard to both the framework for measurement and the required disclosures, other than where specific exceptions are set out in the standard requiring the fair value measurement. Consequently, the guidance in IFRS 13 is relevant to the measurement of fair value in the context of business combinations.

IFRS 3 requires that all business combinations are accounted for using the acquisition method of accounting. Thus, one party must always be identified as the acquirer, and the other as acquiree. With a few exceptions, the fair values of the assets, including identifiable intangible assets, liabilities and contingent liabilities of the acquiree must be recognised in the consolidated financial statements of the acquirer at the acquisition date. IFRS 3 was originally issued in 2004. A comprehensive revision came into force in 2010 after the IASB had observed its application for several years. The project to revise IFRS 3 was a joint project with the FASB. The outcome was a largely converged standard: IFRS 3, 'Business Combinations', and ASC 805, 'Business Combinations', have the same requirements in most areas.

Measurement of consideration at fair value

IFRS 3 requires that the consideration for an acquisition is measured at fair value. This is straightforward if it comprises purely cash payable in full on completion. However, there are several potential complications to this, including any or all of:

- consideration may comprise equity (share-for-share transactions) instead of, or as well as, cash;
- deferred consideration may be involved; or
- contingent consideration may be involved.

Where some or all of the consideration comprises equity of the acquirer, the acquisition date fair value of that equity must be measured. This is a straightforward exercise if the underlying shares are traded in an active market, such as the London Stock Exchange: the fair value is simply the number of shares issued multiplied by the acquisition date share price.

For shares in a private company, fair value will have to be measured using a valuation technique, following a cost, market or income approach as set out in IFRS 13. This will also need to reflect the appropriate unit of account for the size of shareholding issued: in most cases this will be a non-controlling stake in the acquirer.

In some cases, share options will form part of the consideration. These will need to be valued using an option pricing model, such as the Black & Scholes model. This will be a particularly complex exercise where the underlying shares are not traded in an active market, ie are from a private company.

Another complication arises where employees of the acquiree had been granted share options in the acquiree before the transaction and these are to be exchanged for share options in the acquirer as part of the transaction agreement. Specific requirements, which are outside the scope of this book, apply in such cases.

Where cash consideration is deferred, the time value of money and credit risk involved in the delayed payment must be reflected by discounting the contractual proceeds at an appropriate rate.

Where some or all of the consideration is contingent upon future events, such as the achievement of a profit target, the fair value measurement at the acquisition date must reflect expectations of achieving the profit target as at the acquisition date.

Focus

- Measuring the fair value of the consideration for an acquisition can be complex if deferred or contingent consideration or equity derivatives, such as share options, are involved.
- It is also harder if a private company is using shares as consideration than if a listed company is doing so.

Non-controlling interest

If the acquirer owns less than 100% of the equity of the acquiree post-acquisition, the stake he does not own is known as a non-controlling interest. Before 2010, such a stake was referred to as a minority interest. However, transactions are frequently structured such that a stake of less than 50% (ie a minority) controls the acquiree, whilst the holder of the majority of the shares does not have control. These types of situations are generally achieved through the use of Shareholders' Agreements and/or specific terms in the Articles of Association that give one party the right, for example, to appoint and remove all the directors, regardless of the size of that party's shareholding. The terminology was changed from a minority interest to a non-controlling interest to reflect such situations.

IFRS 3 provides an optional treatment for how the non-controlling interest is recognised in the balance sheet; this can either be at:

- the non-controlling interest's proportionate share of net assets of the acquiree; or
- fair value.

One of the points of difference between IFRS and US GAAP with regard to accounting for business combinations is that US GAAP, ASC 805, 'Business Combinations', requires that the non-controlling interest is measured in the balance sheet at fair value and does not permit the optional treatment available under IFRS.

The IASB gave permission for the optional treatment which, under pressure from preparers of financial statements, does not involve fair value measurement. These preparers highlighted the difficulties of measuring the fair value of a non-controlling stake. Empirical evidence may be available of the fair value of a controlling stake from the transaction details, especially where the acquiree or acquirer is a listed entity. However, this would not translate directly into a fair value measurement for a non-controlling stake, as a result of the implicit control premium. In practice, most IFRS reporters have taken advantage of the simpler option to measure the non-controlling stake at proportionate share of net assets.

There is a complication to this option. Where part of the equity of the acquiree is not represented by a present interest in the net assets (such as would be the case where the non-controlling interest holds some unexercised share options), that part of the non-controlling interest must be measured at fair value and the option to measure at proportionate share of net assets is not available.

Focus

Whilst there is an option that any *shares* held by a non-controlling shareholder may be accounted for at their proportionate share of net assets, any *share options* held by a non-controlling shareholder must be measured at fair value.

Identifiable intangible assets

IFRS 3 defines an asset as identifiable if it is:

- separable, ie could be sold or licensed separately from the entity; or
- arises from contractual or other legal rights, regardless of whether those rights are transferable from the entity.

It is important to note that only one of the above conditions needs to be satisfied in order that an intangible asset is identifiable. Although, in practice, many intangible assets will be both separable and arise from legal rights, eg a trade mark, others such as an unpatented technical drawing, which would be separable but may not be legally secured, may fall into one or other category only.

IAS 38, 'Intangible Assets', requires that all identifiable intangible assets arising on an acquisition are recognised at fair value; there is no option of claiming that fair value cannot be measured reliably. IAS 38 makes specific provision for certain intangible assets to be valued together rather than separately: this assists with ensuring that the fair values of huge numbers of different intangible assets are not required to be measured separately:

- Paragraph 36 notes that some intangible assets are separable only together with a related contract, identifiable asset or liability. In such cases, the intangible asset is to be recognised separately from goodwill but together with the related item.
- Paragraph 37 allows companies to recognise a group of complementary intangible assets as a single asset, provided only that the underlying single

assets have similar useful lives. Typically, this could be applied to a brand name comprising a trade mark, the related trade name and, potentially, underlying technology.

The Illustrative Examples to IFRS 3 analyse the types of intangible asset that may arise on an acquisition as:

- marketing-related – eg trade marks, newspaper mastheads;
- customer-related – eg customer lists, customer contracts and related relationships;
- artistic-related – eg musical works, books, videos;
- contract-based – eg licences, lease agreements, franchise agreements;
- technology-based – eg patented and unpatented technology, databases.

Under IAS 38, intangible assets may have a finite or indefinite life. If they have a finite life, they must be amortised over that life and reviewed for impairment indicators each period. If they have an indefinite life, they are not amortised but, instead, are tested for impairment each year. In this regard, the treatment of indefinite-lived intangible assets is the same as that of purchased goodwill (see below).

The methods that can be used for valuing intangible assets are discussed later in this chapter. The disclosure requirements of IFRS 13 (see **20.03** and **20.04**) would need to be followed regarding the measurement of fair value of any intangible assets recognised following an acquisition. Thus, the level in the IFRS 13 fair value hierarchy into which each of the assumptions, or inputs, used in the valuation falls would need to be identified, together with the corresponding level of the fair value measurement in its entirety.

It is likely that most intangible asset valuations would fall into Level 3 of the IFRS 13 fair value hierarchy. Consequently, qualitative and quantitative disclosures of significant unobservable inputs would be required.

Focus

For intangible assets valued and recognised following a business combination, there must be disclosure of the significant unobservable inputs (assumptions) used in valuing them.

Measurement of goodwill arising on an acquisition

It is important to remember that goodwill is not measured at fair value. The IFRS definition of fair value (see **20.01**) refers to the price that would be received to sell an asset. However, by definition, goodwill cannot be sold separately from a business – if it could, it would be separable and, hence, identifiable and would then fall to be recognised as an identifiable intangible asset (see above). Consequently, goodwill is not measured at fair value. Instead it is measured according to the following formula set out in IFRS 3:

Amount of purchased goodwill =

(a) fair value of consideration for transaction; *plus*
(b) fair value of any pre-acquisition stake held in acquiree; *plus*

(c) amount of any non-controlling interest (as noted above, this may either be measured at fair value or at proportionate share of net assets); *less*
(d) net sum of fair values of identifiable assets (including intangible assets) and liabilities (including contingent liabilities).

For the simplest situations, where a transaction involves the acquisition of a 100% stake in the equity of the acquiree, ie the acquirer did not have any stake in the acquiree pre-acquisition and there is no non-controlling interest post-acquisition (ie (b) and (c) above are zero), it can be seen that goodwill is measured as the difference between the consideration paid and the net sum of the fair values of the identifiable assets acquired (ie (a) – (d)).

In effect, whatever the holdings pre and post-acquisition, an 'amount' is derived that represents 100% of the equity (by adding together (a), (b) and (c) above). It is not the fair value of 100% of the equity except where there was no pre-existing equity stake and no non-controlling interest. From this 'amount' representing 100% of the equity, the net sum of all the identifiable assets less liabilities is deducted.

If the result is positive, it is recognised as purchased goodwill in the balance sheet. It is not amortised but, instead, is reviewed for impairment each year (see **21.03** below).

If it is negative, it is described as a gain from a bargain purchase and recognised as a credit in the profit or loss account (and sometimes referred to as negative goodwill).

IFRS 3 does not permit the amortisation of goodwill; instead, goodwill is reviewed for impairment each period in accordance with IAS 36, Impairment of Assets.

In January 2010, the Financial Reporting Council (FRC: www.frc.org) issued a report entitled 'FRC Study: Accounting for Acquisitions'. This study reviewed the application of IFRS 3 to 20 acquisitions that had taken place in 2008/09. It found that, on average, intangible assets represented approximately 33% and goodwill represented 67% of the purchase price for the acquisitions, ie other recognised assets and liabilities approximately netted off to zero. The FRC commented on the significance of the accounting for goodwill and intangible assets as, on average on a combined basis, they represented the entirety of the purchase prices paid. The FRC also noted that it would have expected more intangible assets to have been identified separately from purchased goodwill.

Focus

- It is important to remember that goodwill is *not* measured at fair value: it is measured according to a formula set out in IFRS 3 and is, in effect, a residual amount.
- The FRC has made clear that it generally expects to see a larger amount recognised in the balance sheet for identifiable intangible assets than for purchased goodwill.

21.03 Impairment testing of goodwill and intangible assets under IFRS

IAS 36, 'Impairment of Assets' addresses the impairment testing of goodwill and intangible assets, as well as tangible fixed assets:

- For intangible assets having a finite life and for tangible fixed assets, the test comprises a review for indicators of impairment with the full impairment test being required only if an indicator of impairment is present.
- For intangible assets having an indefinite life and for goodwill, the full impairment test is required each year.

The purpose of the impairment test is to check that assets are not carried in the balance sheet at more than their 'recoverable amount'. The recoverable amount of an asset is defined in IAS 36 as:

> 'the higher of its fair value less costs of disposal and its value in use.'

Value in use is defined as:

> 'the present value of the future cash flows expected to be derived from an asset or cash-generating unit.'

Thus, recoverable amount is the higher of the amount obtainable through sale of the asset and the amount obtainable through use of the asset by the owning entity. The fact that the test is structured by reference to the higher of these two values means that there is flexibility in how it is applied. In some cases, it will be easier to test for impairment by reference to fair value less costs of disposal and, in other cases, it will be easier to test by reference to value in use. If an asset is found to have failed the impairment test by reference to one measure of recoverable amount, the alternative measure of recoverable amount can then be used. It is clear from their published accounts that listed companies use this flexibility extensively in the performance of the impairment test.

It must, however, always be remembered that the measurement of fair value requires market participant assumptions (see discussion of IFRS 13 at **20.3**). Contrastingly, value in use is, in principle anyway, an entity-specific valuation and, hence, does not rely on market participant assumptions. Value in use is discussed further in the later paragraphs in this chapter, which also highlight some of the areas where the measurement required by IAS 36 differs from a strict entity-specific value.

Measuring fair value less costs of disposal

If an intangible asset is to be tested for impairment by reference to its fair value less costs of disposal, the methods described later in this chapter for measuring the fair value of the intangible asset should be used. The expected costs of disposal of the asset should be deducted.

In some cases fair value less costs of disposal can be determined by reference to the asset alone, but in other cases this can be measured only by reference to a group of assets. In the latter cases, the test must be performed by reference to a 'cash-generating unit', defined in IAS 36 as:

> 'the smallest identifiable group of assets that generates cash inflows that are largely independent of the cash inflows from other assets or groups of assets.'

A cash-generating unit is, in effect, the smallest identifiable business unit containing the asset being tested for impairment. As, by definition, goodwill is not separable from a business and, hence, cannot be sold, any test of the fair value less costs of disposal of goodwill must be by reference to the cash-generating unit to which that goodwill belongs.

There are special requirements in IAS 36 for identifying the cash-generating unit to which goodwill belongs. These may involve some degree of apportionment of the total goodwill balance. Goodwill in the balance sheet of an entity may have arisen from several different business combinations, some of which may have been accounted for in accordance with IFRS 3 and some with previously applicable accounting standards. Thus, whilst purchased goodwill accounted for under IFRS 3 will not have been amortised and will have had identifiable intangible assets excluded from it, purchased goodwill arising before the application of IFRS 3 is likely to have been partly amortised and may include identifiable intangible assets. Also, goodwill arising from the same acquisition may represent quite different factors. This could happen if a global corporation were acquired with different activities in different parts of the world. For instance, a global distributor of motor vehicles might be involved in selling private cars in Australia and commercial vehicles in Eastern Europe. The component factors giving rise to the payment of an amount representing purchased goodwill would probably be quite different in the two different businesses in the different locations.

If a particular cash-generating unit to which goodwill has been allocated is to be tested for impairment by reference to fair value less costs of disposal, its fair value must be determined. The methods described earlier in this book for valuing businesses should be applied for determining the fair value, equivalent to open market value, of the cash-generating unit. The methods principally comprise either the market multiples method (a market approach to measuring fair value) or discounted cash flow (an income approach to measuring fair value). Disposal costs for the unit must then be deducted.

IAS 36 requires that fair value less costs of disposal of the cash-generating unit are compared with the total carrying value of the assets in the unit. Care should be taken at this stage that the comparison is made consistently. If debt is included in the total value of the unit, so that it has been valued on an 'enterprise value' basis, debt should not be deducted from the total carrying value of the assets in the unit. Conversely, if debt has been deducted from the total value of the unit so that this is valued on an 'equity' basis, debt must be deducted from the total carrying value of the assets in the unit.

If the fair value less costs of disposal of the unit is at least as high as the sum of the carrying values of the assets in the unit (measured on a consistent basis as described above), the impairment test is passed and there is no goodwill impairment loss to measure.

If the fair value less costs of disposal of the unit is less than the sum of the carrying values of the assets in the unit (measured on a consistent basis as described above), one or more of the assets in the unit are deemed to be impaired. The impairment loss is allocated in the first instance to goodwill. If any impairment remains to be allocated after goodwill has been impaired to a zero carrying value, the remaining impairment loss is apportioned to the other tangible and intangible assets in the unit except that any asset for which fair value less costs of disposal is known is not written down below such amount.

Measuring value in use

Impairment tests by reference to value in use are performed at the level of the cash-generating unit: the net present value of the cash flows expected to be generated by the unit are determined. Forecast cash flows are entity-specific rather than based on market participant assumptions. Thus, synergies not available to other market participants may be included in the forecasts used to measure value in use. This contrasts with forecasts of cash flows made if the discounted cash flow method is being used to measure the fair value of a unit. For fair value measurements, entity specific synergies cannot be included in the forecast; synergies can only be included if they would be available to other market participants. To maintain some rigour in the impairment test, IAS 36 places certain restrictions on how the cash flows are to be projected when measuring value in use.

First, the projections must be based on reasonable and supportable assumptions that represent management's best estimate of the range of economic conditions that will exist over the life of the unit. There is also a requirement that greater weight should be given to external evidence. Thus, it would be hard to justify, for example, turnover increasing at a rate of 5% per annum for the first three years of the forecast, if market research reports in the relevant industry indicated that zero growth was expected over that period.

Secondly, the projections must be based on the most recent financial budgets or forecasts approved by management, but must exclude any cash inflows or outflows expected to arise from future restructurings or from improving or enhancing an asset's performance. Thus, the cash flows are to be forecast based on the business as it currently stands rather than on how the business might appear following a possible restructuring.

Management budgets and forecasts on which the projections are based are to cover a maximum period of five years unless a longer period can be justified. IAS 36 guidance clarifies that a longer period may be justified if management can demonstrate, based on past experience, its ability to forecast cash flows accurately over a longer period. In practice, it would only seem appropriate to forecast cash flows for a longer period if the business has a natural economic cycle of more than five years. The length of the explicit forecast period is required to be disclosed in the financial statements.

Finally, the cash flow projections beyond the explicit forecast period are to be obtained by extrapolating the projections based on the budgets and forecasts using a steady or declining growth rate, unless an increasing rate can be justified. The growth rate is not to exceed the long-term average growth rate for the products, industries, or countries in which the entity operates unless a higher rate can be justified. In practice, this constraint tends to restrict the real long-term growth rate used in terminal value calculations to no more than 2.5% for developed economies.

Terminal value calculations are usually performed using the Gordon Growth model. If cash flow (C) were forecast for year 5 and projections into perpetuity made thereafter, the terminal value, TV, would be obtained as follows:

$$TV = C \times (1 + i) \times (1 + r) / [(1 + d) - \{(1 + i) \times (1 + r)\}]$$

where:

i represents forecast inflation for the perpetuity period;
r represents forecast real growth forecast for the perpetuity period;
d represents the discount rate applied to the forecast cash flows.

This calculated terminal value would represent the present value at the end of year 5 of the forecast cash flows. It would need to be discounted appropriately, ie multiplied by the factor $1/\{(1+d)^5\}$ to bring it to the net present value at the date of the impairment test.

As noted below, there are various simplifications that can easily be derived and that are frequently used in respect of the Gordon Growth model.

If g represents compound growth, then $(1 + g) = (1 + i) \times (1 + r)$ and the terminal value formula reduces to:

$$TV = C \times (1 + g)/(d - g)$$

It can also be simplified further still in cases where forecast growth is nil in the perpetuity period. In such cases:

$$TV = C/d$$

It is not unusual for the terminal value to represent as much as 75% or more of the net present value calculated, so the resulting net present value tends to be highly sensitive to the assumed terminal growth rate.

IAS 36 requires the cash flows to be forecast on a pre-tax basis and to be discounted at a pre-tax rate. The discount rate applied is required to be a market rate – this deviation from a strict entity-specific approach being to ensure that companies do not try to argue that their specific cost of capital is very low and consequently to overstate the net present value of their cash flows.

Impairment test disclosures

Extensive disclosures are required to support the results of the impairment tests of goodwill and intangible assets. Many of these disclosures are required even when the impairment test is passed and serve to demonstrate that the test has been performed reliably.

Changes were made to these disclosures to:

- reflect the introduction of IFRS 13 – although the IAS 36 impairment test disclosures are specifically included in IAS 36 and are outside the scope of IFRS 13, they were changed on the introduction of IFRS 13 to include factors such as the IFRS 13 fair value hierarchy; and
- align the disclosures required when measuring fair value less costs of disposal using the discounted cash flow method with those required when measuring value in use (which is always required to be measured using the discounted cash flow method).

Where an impairment loss has been recognised in an asset or a cash-generating unit, the disclosures include:

- the recoverable amount of the asset/cash-generating unit;
- whether the recoverable amount was measured by reference to fair value less costs of disposal or value in use;
- if the recoverable amount was measured by reference to fair value less costs of disposal, additional required disclosures include:
  - the level of the fair value hierarchy, as described in IFRS 13 (see **20.02**), within which the fair value measurement would have been categorised in its entirety;

  - for fair value measurements categorised at Level 2 or Level 3 in their entirety, a description of the valuation techniques used to measure fair value less costs of disposal, and reasons for any change in technique; and
  - for fair value measurements categorised at Level 2 or Level 3 in their entirety, each key assumption (ie those to which fair value measurement is most sensitive) made and the discount rate in the current and preceding period;
- if the recoverable amount was measured by reference to value in use, the discount rate in the current and preceding period must be disclosed.

For cash-generating units for which the carrying amounts of goodwill or indefinite-lived intangible assets are significant in comparison with the entity's total carrying amount of goodwill or indefinite-lived intangible assets, disclosures regarding the measurement of recoverable amount, regardless of whether an impairment is identified, include:

- If the unit's recoverable amount is based on fair value less costs of disposal:
  - the valuation technique used;
  - if fair value is not measured using a quoted price for an identical unit:
    - each key assumption made;
    - a description of management's approach to determining the value assigned to each key assumption – whether they reflect past experience or, if appropriate, are consistent with external sources of information and, if not, why;
    - the level of the fair value hierarchy, as described in IFRS 13 (see **20.02**), within which the fair value measurement would have been categorised in its entirety (ignoring the costs of disposal); and
    - any change in valuation technique applied and the reason for the change;
  - if fair value has been measured using discounted cash flow projections, disclosures must include:
    - the period over which management has projected cash flows;
    - the growth rate used to extrapolate cash flow projections; and
    - the discount rate applied.
- If the unit's recoverable amount is based on value in use:
  - each key assumption made in projecting cash flows;
  - a description of management's approach to determining the value assigned to each key assumption – whether they reflect past experience or, if appropriate, are consistent with external sources of information and, if not, why;
  - the period over which management has projected cash flows based on forecasts approved by management and, if a period of more than five years has been used an explanation of why a longer period was justified;
  - the growth rate used to extrapolate cash flow projections beyond the period covered by the most recent budgets/forecasts, and the justification for using any growth rates that exceed the long-term average growth rate for the products, industries or countries in which the entity operates; and
  - the discount rate applied to the cash flow projections.

- Sensitivity analysis is required if a reasonably possible change in a key assumption on which management has based its determination of the unit's recoverable amount would cause the impairment test to be failed with disclosures to include:
  - the amount by which the test would be failed;
  - the value assigned to the key assumption; and
  - the amount by which the value assigned to the key assumption would need to change in order for the unit's recoverable amount to be equal to its carrying value.

With regard to the required disclosures arising when assets or cash-generating units are measured at fair value less costs of disposal, because of their reliance on unobservable inputs:

- most intangible asset valuations would be at Level 3 in the fair value hierarchy, (see **21.07–21.10** for a discussion of valuation methods for intangible assets); and
- most cash-generating unit valuations would be at Level 3 in the fair value hierarchy – an obvious exception to this would be where a cash-generating unit comprised an investment in equity quoted in an active market.

Focus

- The impairment test can be performed by reference to fair value (a market participant measure) less costs of disposal or value in use (an entity specific measure) – or even both, if the asset fails the impairment test under the first measurement.
- When testing by reference to fair value less costs of disposal, measurement of fair value should be performed in accordance with IFRS 13 but disclosures made in accordance with IAS 36.
- When testing by reference to value in use, IFRS 13 is irrelevant: both measurement and disclosure should be in accordance with IAS 36 requirements, which includes specific rules on cash flow forecasting and discount rate determination.

21.04 Accounting for business combinations under UK GAAP

FRS 102: Sections 18 and 19

This section looks at the requirements of FRS 102: Section 18, 'Intangible Assets other than Goodwill', and Section 19, 'Business Combinations and Goodwill' regarding the fair value exercises required in the context of accounting for an acquisition. For the generic guidance in FRS 102 regarding fair value measurement, see **20.05**.

With limited exceptions, FRS 102 requires the purchase, or acquisition, method of accounting to be used for all business combinations. The approach to be adopted has many similarities with that required under IFRS 3, but is simpler in certain areas:

- The cost of a business combination includes the fair values of any cash and equity consideration and, in a difference from IFRS 3, it is permitted to add directly attributable costs to this amount, eg legal fees in connection with preparing the sale and purchase agreement, accountants' due diligence fees.
- Contingent consideration is treated differently from under IFRS 3 and only included in the cost of the combination if the adjustment is probable and can be measured reliably. If the adjustment becomes probable at a later date, it is treated as an adjustment to the cost of the combination at that later date.
- Similarly to IFRS 3, a fair value exercise is required of the acquiree's identifiable assets (including intangible assets) and liabilities (including contingent liabilities).

However, in the revised version of FRS 102 (issued in March 2018 and mandatory from January 2019), a relaxation regarding the number of intangible assets to recognise separately from goodwill was introduced. The required treatment is now that intangible assets are recognised separately from goodwill only if they satisfy three conditions:

i. it is probable that economic benefits will flow to the entity and the fair value of the asset can be measured reliably;
ii. the intangible asset arises from contractual or other legal rights; and
iii. the intangible asset is separable.

Thus, under the revised FRS 102, not all identifiable intangible assets are required to be recognised.

Following this relaxation, the Basis for Conclusions to FRS 102 suggests that the following types of intangible asset would be expected to satisfy all three conditions and, hence, still be recognised separately from goodwill:

- licences;
- copyrights;
- trademarks;
- internet domain names;
- patented technology; and
- legally protected trade secrets.

However, the following would not normally be expected to satisfy all three conditions:

- customer lists;
- customer relationships; and
- unprotected trade secrets, eg secret recipes or formulae.

It is interesting that the FRS 102 Basis for Conclusions is silent regarding whether customer contracts would need to be recognised separately, as would be required under IFRS 3. As many customer contracts would not be separable, since the counterparty would not accept this, it seems that they will often not be recognised under the revised FRS 102.

It should be noted that the accounting for intangible assets arising from business combinations that took place before the application of the revised 2018 version of FRS 102 is left unchanged. Thus, identifiable intangible assets that satisfy the first condition, but only either the second or third above, would remain separately recognised in the balance sheet. They are not subsumed within goodwill after adoption of the revised 2018 version of FRS 102.

FRS 102 also allows an entity to elect to recognise intangible assets separately from goodwill for which the first condition above, and either the second or third condition, is satisfied – ie to recognise all reliably measurable identifiable intangible assets separately from goodwill. If an entity chooses to do this, it must apply this policy consistently to all intangible assets from the same class and consistently across all business combinations:

- Contingent liabilities are required to be recognised at fair value, provided their fair value can be measured reliably.
- Goodwill is recognised as the difference between the cost of the acquisition (measured as described above) and the acquirer's interest in the net amount of the identifiable assets, liabilities and provisions for contingent liabilities of the acquiree. Thus the option, under IFRS 3, to measure the non-controlling interest at fair value is not available and the non-controlling interest is measured at their proportionate share of net assets.
- Negative goodwill is treated differently from under IFRS. It is required to be disclosed in the balance sheet immediately below goodwill. Subsequently, it is recognised in the profit or loss account as the underlying non-monetary assets are recovered, ie used or sold. Any negative goodwill exceeding the fair value of non-monetary assets acquired is recognised in the profit or loss account in the periods expected to benefit.

There is a significant difference between FRS 102 and IFRS 3 when it comes to determining the useful lives of goodwill and intangible assets. Under FRS 102, goodwill and intangible assets are always considered to have a finite useful life. If, exceptionally, it is not possible to make a reliable estimate of their useful life, it is not permitted to exceed ten years. By contrast, IFRS 3 allows intangible assets to have an indefinite useful life and prohibits the amortisation of goodwill.

Focus

- The 2018 revised version of FRS 102 has relaxed the requirement for the recognition of intangible assets separately from goodwill. However, certain intangible assets still need to be recognised at fair value separately from goodwill.
- FRS 102 defaults to a maximum of a ten-year life for both goodwill and separately recognised intangible assets if, exceptionally, a reliable estimate of their useful life cannot be made.

FRS 105

When a micro-entity effects a business combination by acquiring the trade and assets of another business, it does not recognise separately any intangible assets.

Goodwill is measured in the same way as under FRS 102 and is to be amortised systematically over its life. As for FRS 102, if, in exceptional cases, it is not possible to measure the useful life reliably, it is not permitted to exceed ten years.

21.05 Impairment testing of goodwill and intangible assets under UK GAAP

FRS 102: Section 27 addresses impairment of goodwill and intangible assets. At each year-end, a company must assess whether there are any indicators of impairment. A full impairment test is required only if there is an indicator of impairment.

Impairment is recognised if the recoverable amount of an asset is lower than its carrying amount. The recoverable amount of an asset or cash-generating unit is described as:

> 'the higher of its fair value less costs to sell and its value in use.'

Where it is not possible to estimate the recoverable amount of an individual asset, recoverable amount is required to be estimated by reference to the cash-generating unit containing the asset.

Fair value less costs to sell is described as:

> 'the amount obtainable from the sale of an asset or cash-generating unit in an arm's length transaction between knowledgeable, willing parties, less the costs of disposal.'

The best evidence of fair value less costs to sell of an asset is noted as being a price in a binding sale agreement in an arm's length transaction or a market price in an active market. If there is no binding sale agreement or active market for the asset, fair value less costs to sell is based on the best information available to reflect the amount that an entity could obtain, at the reporting date, from disposal of the asset in an arm's length transaction between knowledgeable, willing parties after deducting the costs of disposal. Entities are required to consider recent transactions for similar assets within the same industry.

Value in use is described as:

> 'the present value of the future cash flows expected to be derived from an asset or cash-generating unit.'

Value in use is required to reflect various factors including:

- expected possible variations in the amount and timing of future cash flows;
- the time value of money;
- the price for bearing uncertainty inherent in the asset; and
- other factors, such as illiquidity, that market participants would reflect in pricing the future cash flows expected to be derived from the asset.

It is required that estimates of future cash flow are based on use of the asset in its current condition. Thus, similarly to IAS 36, FRS 102 does not allow reflection of any future restructuring to which the entity is not yet committed, or improvements or enhancements to the asset's performance.

The discount rate is required to be a pre-tax rate reflecting current market assessments of the time value of money and the risks specific to the asset (or cash-generating unit) for which the future cash flow estimates have not been adjusted.

The FRS 102 disclosure requirements are far less onerous than the IAS 36 disclosure requirements. Whilst disclosure is required of the amount of impairment losses recognised, or reversed, by class of asset, including separately for goodwill and intangible assets, no disclosures are required in respect of how recoverable amount has been measured.

FRS 105 Section 22 addresses impairment testing and includes requirements that are very similar to FRS 102. However, there are no specific disclosure requirements.

Focus

- Similarly to IAS 36, the FRS 102 impairment test can be performed by reference to either fair value less costs to sell (a market participant measure) or value in use (an entity-specific measure).

21.06 Intangible asset valuation guidance issued by the International Valuation Standards Council

As described in **20.03**, IFRS 13 provides a framework for the measurement of fair value together with disclosure requirements that are particularly focused on the reliability of the underlying measurement. IFRS 13 does not, however, provide practical guidance on how to perform valuations.

Instead, the IASB provides input to the International Valuation Standards Council (IVSC) and is seen to support the IVSC's output with regard to valuation guidance generally. This support is also evident from the work of the FRC. In its January 2010 study, 'Accounting for Acquisitions', referred to at **21.02**, the FRC made reference to evolving guidance from the IVSC regarding intangible asset valuations.

The IVSC's current guidance on the valuation of intangible assets is set out in IVS 210, 'Intangible Assets'. This applies to the valuation of intangible assets for any purpose, not just financial reporting purposes, and can be obtained from the IVSC's website at www.ivsc.org.

The IVSC's previous guidance included in Technical Information Paper 3 ('TIP3') has been withdrawn.

Focus

- Neither IFRS nor UK GAAP contains any substantive guidance regarding how to measure the fair value of intangible assets. In 2011, the IASB commented publicly that it was happy to support the work of the IVSC with regard to guidance on fair value measurement.

21.07 Market, income and cost approaches to intangible asset valuation

In its standard, IVS 105, 'Valuation Approaches and Methods', the IVSC notes that the principal valuation approaches are:

(a) the market approach;
(b) the income approach; and
(c) the cost approach.

The rest of this chapter discusses methods of valuing intangible assets that can be used for financial reporting purposes in accordance with either IFRS or UK GAAP.

21.08 Market approach to intangible asset valuation

The market approach is based on valuing an intangible asset by reference to the prices at which transactions in similar assets have taken place in the market. Prices and implied valuation multiples are derived from these transactions to apply in the valuation of the intangible asset in question.

In practice, there are relatively few transactions in intangible assets for which information regarding price and financial and other parameters such as turnover, market share, sales volume, etc is available in the public domain. Also, given the unique properties of many intangible assets, it is likely that there will be substantial differences between the intangible assets involved in the transactions and the intangible asset being valued. Consequently, it is rare that a price in the market can be used as the only method to value an intangible asset. It is sometimes possible, however, to use the market transactions method to provide support to a value obtained by a different method. For instance, if a newspaper masthead were being valued and the price at which a less well-known masthead had been sold were known, the price of that less well-known masthead might be used as a floor for the value of the masthead in question.

Any transaction data used in the market transactions method of valuation in order to obtain a fair value suitable for financial reporting must either relate to arm's length transactions between knowledgeable, willing parties or, if it does not, be subject to appropriate adjustments.

21.09 Income approach to intangible asset valuation

The income approach is based on valuing an intangible asset by reference to the net present value of the income, cash flow or cost savings attributable to it over its economic life. The difficulty with the income approach is that the income stream used has to be refined sufficiently that it relates just to the intangible asset in question and excludes income derived from other tangible, intangible or financial assets.

There are three key income-based methods that are used in practice to value intangible assets. These are the relief-from-royalty method, the excess earnings method and the premium profits method.

Relief-from-royalty method

The relief-from-royalty method estimates the value of an intangible asset by reference to the value of hypothetical royalty payments that would be saved through owning the asset rather than licensing it from a third party. Conceptually, it is often viewed as a discounted cash flow method applied to the cash flows that the owner of the intangible asset could receive through licensing the asset to third parties.

The key steps involved are as follows:

1. forecast turnover that would, hypothetically, be achieved by a licensee using the intangible asset over its estimated useful life;
2. determine a suitable royalty rate to apply to these turnover projections;
3. apply the royalty rate to the forecast turnover;
4. estimate any additional expenses for which the owner of the intangible asset would be responsible – eg maintenance and development expenses for technology intellectual property, advertising for a brand;
5. deduct a tax charge that the hypothetical licensor would have to pay on royalty receipts;
6. determine the appropriate discount rate and capitalise the net royalty cash flows measured as above; and
7. add a tax amortisation benefit ('TAB') amount if appropriate – see below for explanation.

The hardest step is usually finding a suitable royalty rate. There are two possible ways of doing this – often, both are used and the results compared:

i. obtain royalty rates for similar intangible assets; and
ii. review the appropriate profit splits between licensor and licensee.

For the first method, some large organisations have proprietary databases developed from previous valuations they have performed. However, there are also several external, commercial databases that can be interrogated by anyone. They include:

- www.royaltysource.com (US database but includes UK companies involved in US licensing arrangements);
- www.royaltyrange.com (European and worldwide royalty rates from 2005);
- www.royaltystat.com (uses SEC and Canada's SEDAR archives – launched 2000);
- www.ktmine.com (based in Chicago); and
- www.valuationresources.com (lists further websites from which royalty rates can be obtained).

These databases typically allow the user, for a fee, to search royalty rates in licensing agreements relating to given industry types. Following such a search, it is often helpful to benchmark the different agreements identified, to compare them with the intangible asset being valued, across certain characteristics of the underlying intangible asset, eg sophistication of technology, geographical reach of intangible, exclusivity of licence, perception in the market (such as best in class, or a more middle-of-the-road level of recognition). By using a benchmarking exercise such as this, it is possible to whittle down the number and range of royalty rates identified to a smaller range that is most suitable for the intangible being valued.

In using the second method above to obtain a suitable royalty rate, various research reports are available.

In 1971, Goldscheider published research often known as the '25% rule', indicating that royalty rates tend to be around 25% of licensee operating profits.

In 1997, Degnan and Horton published a paper indicating that royalty rates tend to fall into the range of 10–15% of gross profits. As such:

- the licensor normally receives 10–15% of gross profits; and
- the licensee normally receives 85–90% of gross profits.

In 2012, the accountants KPMG published a report 'Profitability and royalty rates across industries: Some preliminary evidence 2012'. This document provides interesting results of research into royalty rates across different industries and identifies average royalty rates by industry, along with those industries for which relatively high or relatively low royalty rates would be expected. It also looks at the link between royalty rates, gross margins, EBIT and EBITDA (Earnings before interest, tax, interest, depreciation and amortisation) margins.

A wealth of other literature regarding how royalty rates follow different characteristics of an intangible asset can be obtained through an internet search.

IVS 210 provides some guidance on selecting a suitable discount rate to apply to the projections.

The tax amortisation benefit ('TAB') is an adjustment to the value of an intangible asset that is sometimes appropriate when using an income approach to valuation. Logically, if the value of an intangible asset is measured by reference to the net present value of the cash flows that the asset is expected to generate, if there are tax savings available through amortising the capitalised intangible asset, an additional component of value comprises the net present value of the expected tax relief on amortisation of the intangible asset.

As the tax relief, if available, will be so in respect of the value of the asset including the estimated capitalised tax relief, there is some circularity involved in measuring it. This can be overcome either by using an iterative method to estimate the size of the tax relief or using the 'goal-seek' function in Excel.

Of course, the decision must first be taken as to whether the TAB is appropriate for the intangible asset being valued. This will depend on whether tax relief would be available on the asset that is being measured. If an intangible asset is being acquired as part of a business combination in the UK, it is unlikely that tax relief on amortisation will be available on the capitalised intangible asset. This is because the intangible asset will be recognised only in the consolidated financial statements of the acquiring company, whilst the tax computations submitted to HMRC are based on the individual company financial statements, ie accounts that are not consolidated. However, as both IFRS and UK GAAP require that a market value (known as fair value for financial reporting purposes) is used in the recognition of intangible assets, in theory, at least for certain transactions, it is considered that an overseas purchaser may have been included in the pool of potential purchasers (known as market participants under IFRS) and that this would have pushed up the market value to one that includes a TAB adjustment. For this reason, some valuers (especially in respect of IFRS financial statements) include a TAB adjustment when measuring intangible assets using an income approach.

The relief-from-royalty method is often used to measure the fair values of intangible assets such as patented or unpatented technology, software, and brands.

Excess earnings method

Under the excess earnings method, the value of an intangible asset is estimated as the present value of the cash flows that it is expected to generate, after excluding the proportion of cash flows that are attributable to other assets involved in generating these expected cash flows. These other assets are known as 'contributory assets'.

The excess earnings method is more complex to perform than relief from royalty. Some detailed and meticulous analysis is required to apportion cash flows appropriately. In practice, it is a discounted cash flow exercise 'with bells and whistles'.

The key steps involved are as follows:

1. forecast the revenues and expenses expected to be generated by the line of business to which the intangible asset belongs, but exclude any cash outflows expected in respect of the development of new technology or other new intangible assets that are not required for the asset being valued – thus profit margins in forecasts used when applying the excess earnings method may be higher than those used for the business line more generally;
2. identify the contributory assets required to generate the forecast revenue and expenses – typically these will comprise working capital, fixed assets, the workforce and any intangible assets other than the one being valued;
3. determine the appropriate 'return' on each contributory asset (see later) and deduct the returns on the contributory assets from the forecast cash flows;
4. determine the appropriate discount rate and calculate the present value of the forecast cash flows after all deductions;
5. add a TAB (see under 'relief from royalty' above), if considered appropriate.

In the first step above, it is possible that some apportionment of overhead costs to the line of business in question will be required.

Contributory asset charges are considered as being either 'on' or 'of' the underlying contributory assets (or both). A charge 'on' the asset is made for all contributory assets. A charge 'of' the asset is made only for those contributory assets of a wasting nature, such as tangible fixed assets. Typically determining contributory asset charges is the hardest part of applying the excess earnings method to value an intangible asset.

Some examples of how contributory asset charges may be made are noted below. The following would be charged as a percentage return against the fair value of the underlying asset. In certain cases, this fair value may not be recognised in the balance sheet; for instance, a contributory asset charge is usually made on the workforce even though the workforce is not permitted to be recognised as an asset in the balance sheet. In such cases, the fair value of the underlying asset would need to be determined as well as the return on the asset:

1 A contributory asset charge on working capital may be made by reference to interest rates charged on working capital.
2 A contributory asset charge on tangible fixed assets, such as property, may be made by reference to the rate of interest at which finance would be provided on the asset.
3 A contributory asset charge of tangible fixed assets, such as property, may be made by reference to depreciation charged on the assets.
4 A contributory asset charge on the workforce component of goodwill may be made by reference to the weighted average cost of capital of the line of business to which the intangible asset being valued belongs.

As an alternative approach to determining a percentage return on and of the fair value of the underlying asset, a composite charge on and of a brand, or any other contributory asset for which a royalty rate could be estimated reliably, may be made by reference to the hypothetical royalty rate applied to turnover (or, occasionally, another financial parameter) that would be charged for use of the asset.

Estimating contributory asset charges requires careful thought and analysis. Tax must be treated consistently – thus, if contributory asset charges are estimated on a post-tax basis, they must be included in the discounted cash flow model after the tax charge. The Appraisal Foundation (TAF) in the USA published a document in 2010 entitled 'Best Practices for Valuations in Financial Reporting: Intangible Asset Working Group – Contributory Assets – The Identification of Contributory Assets and Calculation of Economic Rents'. The document can be obtained from the TAF website (www.appraisalfoundation.org) and provides helpful guidance and examples on the measurement of contributory asset charges. Although it was written to assist with valuing intangible assets using the excess earnings method for US GAAP purposes, much of it is appropriate to the valuation of intangible assets for IFRS or UK GAAP reporting purposes.

It is generally considered good practice to perform a weighted average return on assets (WARA) check to ensure that the contributory asset charges are consistent with the weighted average cost of capital for the relevant line of business. This check works by applying the contributory asset charge to the fair value of each component asset including the asset being valued and any identified components of goodwill – usually just the workforce – and reconciling the resultant weighted average charge to the weighted average cost of capital (WACC). The 'plug' in the WARA check is the return required on the non-identifiable component of goodwill – usually the goodwill amount excluding the workforce component. The return on this component is required to be above the WACC for the line of business.

As the excess earnings method measures the value of an intangible asset by reference to the residual cash flows generated after deducting contributions from other assets, it can only be used for one intangible asset arising from each line of business/income stream.

There has been some recent commentary that the excess earnings method should be applied to the primary intangible asset being valued – ie the one that generates most value in the business. This is because there is some concern that the relief from royalty approach does not capture all the income generated by an intangible asset and, hence, may under-value it.

The excess earnings method is used extensively in practice to measure the fair values of customer contracts, including related customer relationship intangible assets, for IFRS 3 purposes following an acquisition.

Premium profits method

The premium profits method is based on identifying the incremental profit that is generated by using the intangible asset, as compared with not using it, and capitalising that incremental profit.

The first step in applying the method involves comparing the income or cash flow that would be achieved using the intangible asset with that achievable without using the asset. This incremental profit or cash flow is forecast over the life of the asset and capitalised. As with other income methods of intangible asset valuation the appropriateness of adding a tax amortisation benefit adjustment must also be considered (see below).

The main difficulty in applying the method is in forecasting the corresponding income stream without use of the asset. Whilst it may be possible to forecast some parts of the income stream, it is usually difficult to find sufficient information in the public domain to forecast all parts of the income stream. For example, if a brand were being valued, the income expected to be generated both with and without using the brand name would need to be estimated. This could give rise to difficulties in estimating an income stream without any reliance on a brand name. Even if one could be found, whilst retail selling price and even volume information might be available in the public domain, it is unlikely that overhead expenditure in respect of a specific line of business, and hence margin information, would be available.

Consequently, this method is used much less frequently than either the relief-from-royalty method or the excess earnings method. It is, however, sometimes used to measure the fair value of non-compete agreements.

Focus

- Technology, software and brands are often valued using the relief from royalty method.
- Customer contracts and their related relationships are usually valued using the excess earnings method.
- The excess earnings method is more complex to apply than relief from royalty.
- There is a current view that the excess earnings method should be used for the primary intangible asset being valued following an acquisition under UK GAAP or IFRS.

21.10 Cost approach to intangible asset valuation

Under the cost approach, the value of an intangible asset is measured based on the replacement cost of a similar asset or an asset providing similar service potential or utility.

The cost approach is appropriate if it would be possible to recreate the asset with substantially the same utility sufficiently quickly that an entity would not be willing to pay a significant premium to use the asset immediately.

There are only a few types of intangible asset for which the cost of rebuilding can be estimated reliably and for which such cost is representative of the asset's fair value. For instance, a brand or newspaper masthead may have taken many years to establish and it may be impossible to measure the cost of development accurately. Moreover, it is likely to be impossible to rebuild the asset and the cost of development may have no bearing on the value of the related intangible asset.

Replacement cost is, however, sometimes used to value software, websites and film or other libraries. In the case of software, the cost of developing similar software with the same functionality may be determinable, although the time taken to redevelop the software might be a barrier to the cost approach being suitable.

Chapter 22

Accounting for equity awards to employees

Signposts

22.01 Introduction

IFRS 2, 'Share-based Payment', came into force in 2005. It requires that a charge is made in the profit or loss account when employees, including directors, are granted equity awards, such as shares or share options, as part of their remuneration package. A similar profit or loss account charge is also required under US GAAP, US Financial Accounting Standards Board (FASB ASC Topic 718), although there are differences in the application of the two standards.

FRS 20, 'Share-based Payment', was introduced into UK GAAP in 2006; this standard was identical to IFRS 2. However, from 2015, for those companies wishing to adopt FRS 102 rather than IFRS or FRS 101, the requirements of FRS 20 were replaced by FRS 102: Section 26.

Share-based payment awards to employees are often made in the form of share options rather than shares. A call option over shares is a right to buy the shares at one or more future dates at a given price known as the exercise price:

- If the exercise price of a call option is lower than the fair value of the underlying equity at any stage, the option is said to be 'in the money' as the option holder can exercise his option and sell the underlying share at a profit.
- If the exercise price of a call option is higher than the fair value of the underlying equity at any stage, the option is said to be 'out of the money', or 'under water', as the option holder would make a loss if he were to exercise his option and sell the underlying share.

Clearly, rational option holders will exercise their call options only when they are in the money.

Generally speaking, options are either put options, which allow the option holder to sell shares at a fixed or calculable price at a future date, or call options enabling the holder to buy shares at a fixed or calculable price at a future date. Employee share option awards comprise call, rather than put, options. A 'European' option may be exercised only at the expiry date. An 'American' option may be exercised at any time up to and including the expiry date. A 'Bermudan' option may be exercised during a specified window of exercise dates.

This chapter provides an overview of the requirements of IFRS 2, FRS 102: Section 26 and FRS 105: Section 21 in respect of equity awards to employees. It does not, however, cover all areas of either IFRS or UK GAAP requirements; readers should refer to the appropriate guidance from the IASB (www.ifrs.org) or the FRC (www.frc.org).

22.02 Accounting for employee equity awards under IFRS

Terminology

IFRS 2 addresses the accounting for both equity-settled share-based payments, such as shares and share options, and cash-settled share-based payments, such as share appreciation rights and phantom shares. For simplicity, however, this chapter considers only awards comprising shares or share options. The following paragraphs look at some of the terminology used in IFRS 2.

Fair value

IFRS 2 is outside the scope of IFRS 13, 'Fair Value Measurement', as regards both measurement and disclosure requirements. IFRS 2 defines the fair value of equity instruments differently from IFRS 13, as:

> 'the amount for which an asset could be exchanged, a liability settled, or an equity instrument granted, could be exchanged between knowledgeable, willing parties in an arm's length transaction.'

This definition is similar to the IFRS definition of fair value prior to the issue of IFRS 13. Throughout the rest of this chapter, fair value is assumed to be defined as above.

Grant date

The grant date of an award to an employee is the date on which the entity and the employee have a shared understanding of, and agree to, the terms and conditions of the share-based payment arrangement. At the grant date, the entity confers the equity instruments on the employee or third party, provided certain vesting conditions are met. If an agreement between the entity and the employee is subject to an approval process, such as shareholder approval at a general meeting, grant date is the date on which that approval is obtained.

Vesting conditions

Vesting conditions are the conditions that determine whether the entity has received the services that entitle the employee to the equity instruments awarded. Sometimes these relate just to a specified service period, such as the employee being required to work for the entity granting the award for, say, three years, (these are 'service conditions') and sometimes, as well as a service condition, they include performance targets such as a specified level of profit, earnings per share or share price which must be achieved (these are 'performance conditions').

Vesting period

The vesting period is the period during which all the specified vesting conditions are to be satisfied.

Market conditions

If the vesting conditions include a performance condition, that condition may relate to the price of the underlying equity awarded. For instance, a share price or total shareholder return (TSR) – generally defined as the sum of the increase in the share price and the dividends paid on the shares over a period of time – target relates to the price of the underlying equity, whilst a profit or earnings per share target does not relate to the price of the underlying equity. Performance conditions that relate to the price of the underlying equity are known as market conditions. Market conditions may include implicit service conditions.

Non-vesting conditions

Certain conditions attaching to awards made to employees are known as non-vesting conditions. These are conditions that affect the employee's right to receive an award, but not whether the employee has provided the services or satisfied a performance target that entitle him to the award. For instance, non-vesting conditions may relate to factors outside the employee's control, such as inflation targets or retail price index targets. Alternatively, they may relate to a requirement that the employee saves cash from his salary over the vesting period.

For example, a common type of UK employee reward scheme is the Save As You Earn (SAYE) scheme. Under this scheme, the employee is required to save a certain amount from his salary each month during the vesting period of the award. The amount saved is placed in an interest-bearing deposit account by the entity. At the end of the service period (typically three or five years) the employee is entitled to use his savings with interest and a tax bonus to exercise the number of options originally granted to him. If at any stage during the vesting period, the employee decides he wants to stop saving and draw out his accumulated balance to date including accrued interest, he can do so. If he does, this does not prevent him from providing the services to the entity over the vesting period that would entitle him to earn the award, but does mean he will not be entitled at the end of the vesting period to exercise the options originally granted to him. Thus, the savings condition is a 'non-vesting' condition.

Overall approach

IFRS 2 requires the determination of the fair value at grant date of an award, with this fair value being adjusted to reflect both market conditions and non-vesting conditions (as described above). This adjusted fair value at grant date is charged to the profit or loss account over the vesting period to the extent that vesting conditions other than market conditions are achieved.

The rest of this chapter looks at the valuation techniques for determining the fair value at grant date adjusted as described above. The requirement for the spreading of the profit or loss account charge over the vesting period to reflect the extent of achievement of non-market conditions is an accounting issue that is outside the scope of this share valuation book.

Measurement of fair value at grant date

IFRS 2 requires that the following approach is taken to the measurement of fair value:

- market prices must be used if they are available; or
- if market prices are not available, a valuation technique must be used; the valuation technique is to be consistent with generally accepted valuation methodologies for pricing financial instruments and is to incorporate all factors and assumptions that knowledgeable, willing market participants would consider in pricing them.

In both cases, the terms and conditions under which the shares or options were granted, including any market or non-vesting conditions, must be reflected in the fair value measurement.

Valuation of shares under IFRS 2

Typical factors that may need to be considered in measuring IFRS 2 fair value of the shares awarded include:

- whether the employee is entitled to dividends during the vesting period; and
- the impact on value of any transfer restrictions on the shares after vesting if these would affect the price that a knowledgeable, willing participant would pay for that share.

Valuation of share options under IFRS 2

IFRS 2 guidance regarding the valuation of share options includes the following:

- if traded options exist with similar terms and conditions to the employee options granted, the prices of the traded options must be used;
- if there are no traded options with similar terms and conditions to the options granted, an option-pricing model must be used; this is more likely to be the case as options granted to employees as part of their remuneration package are likely to contain transfer restrictions that would not apply to traded options.

IFRS 2 notes that all option-pricing models are required to reflect at a minimum the following six inputs:

1 the grant date fair value of the underlying shares;
2 the exercise price of the option;
3 the life of the option;
4 the expected risk-free rate of return over the life of the option;
5 the expected volatility of the underlying share price over the life of the option; and
6 any expected dividend payments prior to exercise of the option.

Other factors that may need to be reflected include:

- those periods when the employee is not permitted to exercise the option, eg the vesting period;
- the extent to which early exercise before the end of the option's life is permitted and expected; and
- any other factors that a knowledgeable, willing, market participant would consider in pricing the options.

Employee share options take many different forms. The SAYE options described under 'Non-vesting conditions' above often have lives of three years and six months and are structured such that they cannot be exercised for the first three years after grant date. After this time there is a six-month exercise window.

In contrast to typical SAYE options, other options, including those issued in accordance with Enterprise Management Incentive (EMI) schemes, typically have contractual lives of up to ten years. As with SAYE schemes, there is a vesting period, often three years, during which employees are not permitted to exercise the options. After the end of the vesting period, there is a window during which exercise can take place up to the end of the option's life.

If there are corresponding traded options in the market, the price of the traded options can be used to estimate the price of the employee options, provided that the traded options were granted with similar terms and conditions to the employee options. Typically, however, traded options:

- have significantly shorter lives than options granted as awards to employees;
- do not have vesting conditions attaching to them, whereas there are very likely to be vesting conditions comprising at least a service condition for options granted to employees; and
- are freely transferable, whereas employee awards are not transferable.

Hence, it is unlikely that the price of traded options will provide reliable evidence in respect of the price of employee options. In many cases, there will not be any traded options. Where traded options are not available or are not considered to provide a reliable indicator of value for the employee options, IFRS 2 requires that an option-pricing model is used.

Awards of shares without market conditions

In most cases, employee share awards will be subject to service conditions. Generally, the employee will not be entitled to receive dividends paid on the shares during the vesting period. Consequently, an adjustment is required to the grant date fair value in respect of dividends foregone during the vesting period. The impact of these can be determined through making a market-based estimate of the dividends payable over the period and the payment dates. The expected payments are brought to a present value at grant date by discounting them at the entity's cost of equity. The present value of expected dividends is deducted from the grant date fair value of the shares to give the grant date fair value of the award.

Awards of shares with market conditions

Typically, awards with market conditions are made to employees deemed to be of sufficient seniority that their actions may impact the share price. For instance, shares that will vest in three years' time subject to continued employment and a given increase in share price, might be awarded under a Directors' Performance Plan. The performance condition comprising the share price increase is a market condition. Sometimes market conditions are set in absolute terms or an absolute amount of increase, eg the share price must reach £5 or increase by £2 from its price at grant date. Sometimes market conditions are set relative to an index of share prices for a peer group of companies.

These conditions may be quite complex. For example, a market condition could be structured based on the TSR of the company over a three-year period compared to that of a peer group of 19 comparable companies, making a total of 20 companies under comparison. The position of the entity in the peer group might be measured by reference to the quartile into which it falls in a ranking of the peer group's TSR over a three-year period.

For instance, a particular director may be granted shares in a pattern similar to the attached:

- maximum award 1,000 shares and minimum award no shares;
- if the entity's TSR after three years is in the top quartile for the peer group, a sliding scale of 75% to 100% of the maximum award vests, with 75% being earned in position 5 and 100% being earned in position 1 in the peer group;
- if the entity's TSR after three years is in the second quartile for the peer group, a sliding scale of 25% to 50% of the maximum award vests, with 25% being earned in position 10 and 50% being earned in position 6; and
- if the entity's TSR after three years is in the third or fourth quartiles for the peer group, none of the award vests.

The issue for the valuer is to determine the grant date fair value of the award taking into account the likelihood of achieving these market conditions. In this case, determination of fair value is much more complicated than in situations where there are no market conditions. The technique generally used for incorporating market conditions into grant date fair value is Monte Carlo simulation.

Monte Carlo simulation

The details of how to apply Monte Carlo simulation are outside the scope of this book. However, in general terms, Monte Carlo simulation is a statistical technique used for solving complex problems, which do not have an easy formulaic solution. Monte Carlo simulation looks at a very large number of statistically possible outcomes and averages the results. So, in the example described above, possible outcomes for the number of shares awarded, and the price of such shares in three years' time, would depend on the returns on the shares in question and their relative positions compared with other companies in the peer group. This would need to reflect the expected share price movements of both the entity and the 19 peer group companies. The key statistical parameters involved would include the expected:

- risk-free rate of return over the three-year period;
- volatility of the entity's share price;
- volatilities of the prices of shares in the peer group;
- dividend yields for the entity and the peer group; and
- coefficients of correlation between expected movements in the entity's share price and those of the peer group.

The volatility of a share price is a measure of the extent to which it is expected to move up or down in consecutive periods. Statistically, share prices usually follow a lognormal distribution, ie their natural logarithms follow a statistical normal distribution. A statistical normal distribution is defined by its mean, or average, and its standard deviation. The mean return for a share is usually considered to be the risk-free interest rate. The volatility of a share price is the annualised standard deviation of movements in its natural logarithm. Techniques for estimating volatility are described at **22.03**.

Once values for the statistical parameters have been determined, possible outcomes for the value of the award on vesting date can be modelled. Very large numbers of statistically possible outcomes, known as trials, are run using random number generation. For each trial, the resulting value of the award after three years is calculated and brought to a present value at grant date by discounting at the risk-free rate of return. The average of the resulting present values is calculated. Typically, a Monte Carlo simulation will involve running 20,000 or more trials, so a computer programme will be required. It is possible to obtain Monte Carlo simulation programmes such as Risk Solver from www.solver.com, which run in Excel on a personal computer. Other useful websites include www.hearne.co.uk, www.palisade.com, and www.riskamp.com.

Focus

- Fair value is defined differently in IFRS 2 from in IFRS 13.
- Fair value measurement and disclosure requirements for employee equity awards are outside the scope of IFRS 13 and, hence, as an exception are set out in IFRS 2 rather than IFRS 13.
- Market conditions are reflected in the measurement of grant date fair value but non-market conditions are excluded.

22.03 Using option-pricing models

IFRS 2 refers to two option-pricing models that are used regularly: the Black-Scholes model and the binomial model. However, it makes clear that other option-pricing models may also be used provided they take account of, as a minimum, the six inputs listed at **22.02**. As Monte Carlo simulation can also be used to provide an option price, this is an alternative technique.

The six inputs required, at a minimum, in applying option-pricing models are each addressed below.

- the grant date fair value of the underlying shares should be measured using the guidance set out at **22.02**; and
- the exercise price of the option will be set out in the option agreement.

Life of option

An option will have a contractual life but may not be exercisable throughout the entirety of this life. Generally, options with longer lives have higher values than options with shorter lives, as there is more opportunity for the shares to increase in value and be exercised when they are substantially in the money. However, if a high dividend yield is expected on the equity, this can result in options becoming less valuable if they are held beyond a critical date as, after that date, the loss of value to the option holder (resulting from value being paid out in the form of dividends) restricts the size of potential share price increases. Thus, an option's life has a direct bearing on its value.

Share options normally have lives of no more than ten years but may not be exercisable for a certain period, depending on the terms of the scheme. SAYE options are often exercisable at any point within the six-month period commencing three years from grant date.

In the case of the SAYE options, there is a relatively short exercise window and, hence, the option's value if it had a three-year life is unlikely to be significantly different from its value if it had a three-and-a-half-year life.

However, with options which have a possible ten-year life, the value, if measured as having a life finishing at the start of the exercise window, eg assuming it has a three-year life, is likely to be substantially different from its value if measured as having a life finishing at the end of the possible seven-year exercise window, ie a ten-year life.

Thus, the option-pricing model that should be used for options with a potentially long exercise window needs to be able to deal with possible variations in exercise date which would not arise with an option with a relatively short exercise window, such as an SAYE option.

In practice, employee options are frequently exercised significantly earlier than the end of their contractual lives. This is for several reasons including:

- employees leaving the employment of the reporting entity may not be entitled to exercise their options when they are no longer employed by the entity;
- the options may not be transferable but the underlying shares may be transferable; and
- concerns that options which are in the money at a particular date may later become out of the money.

Generally, senior employees exercise their options later than junior employees. Consequently, it is sometimes appropriate to stratify populations of staff that have been granted options according to their seniority, with different option lives being assumed for different staff groups within the stratification.

Expected risk-free rate of return over the life of option

The expected risk-free rate of return over the life of the option can be measured by reference to yields to maturity on government bonds with the same life as that of the option, in those countries in which the entity conducts business. If the staff population has been stratified for purposes of estimating the life of an option, the risk-free rates of return should also be estimated by reference to the different expected option life for each group.

Expected volatility of underlying share price over life of option

As noted earlier in **22.02**, the volatility of a share price is a measure of the extent to which it is expected to move up or down in consecutive periods. Statistically, the volatility of a share price is the annualised standard deviation of movements in its natural logarithm.

The input required for an option-pricing model is the expected volatility over the life of the option. By using a process known as reverse engineering, the implied expected volatility over the life of a traded option can be deduced. Reverse engineering involves applying an option pricing model with assumptions for expected volatility that vary until the resulting option price is the same as that of the traded option. This will result in implied expected volatility over the life of the traded option, which may be significantly shorter than the life of the employee option being valued, as traded options tend to have relatively short lives, such as six months.

Expected volatility can also be estimated by reference to historical volatility with adjustments being made for expected differences between historical and prospective volatility. To determine historical volatility, the standard deviation of the movements in the natural logarithm of the share price must be measured. IFRS 2 suggests that a suitable time period over which to measure historical volatility should be the same as the estimated life of the option. Observations of share prices over the historical period will be taken at periodic intervals such as daily, weekly or monthly. The volatility calculated on a periodic basis can be brought to an annualised volatility through using the 'square root of time rule' described below.

To apply the square root of time rule to annualise calculated volatilities, the periodic volatility is multiplied by the square root of the number of observations that there would be in a year. Thus:

- daily volatility is multiplied by the square root of 252 to bring it to an annualised amount – this is because 252 is the generally accepted number of trading days in a year;
- weekly volatility is multiplied by the square root of 52 to bring it to an annualised amount; and
- monthly volatility is multiplied by the square root of 12 to bring it to an annualised amount.

For unlisted equity, historical share prices may be observable only at infrequent dates on which share transactions have taken place. Historical volatility may be calculated based on these infrequent observations; however, if there are relatively few observations, this figure may not be considered to be representative of expected future volatility. In such cases where insufficient company data is available, historical volatility can be determined for a peer group of quoted companies with a similar risk profile to that of the reporting entity.

Once historical volatility has been computed, it can be used to estimate future volatility over the life of the option. If there are anomalies in the historical period reviewed, such as abnormal variations arising from share price peaks during failed take-over bids, the historical data should be adjusted for these prior to being used to estimate future volatility. Adjustments may also be required to deal with abnormal share price fluctuations in the market.

Expected dividends over the life of the option

Dividends should be estimated by reference to market data regarding dividend expectations. For an unlisted company, management should be asked whether they expect to pay dividends over the option life.

The Black–Scholes option-pricing model

The choice of option-pricing model should be determined according to the terms of the options granted. The models used most frequently are the Black–Scholes model and the binomial model. Both use established share price theory and assume that share price movements are statistically distributed with a lognormal distribution.

The Black–Scholes model uses a formula to determine the value of an option. The exact formula is complicated but can be obtained from numerous text books and online references.

As a formula is used, one assumption only can be made for each of the six inputs required for the model. Consequently, this model is most suitable when no significant variations in any of the input assumptions are expected over the life of the option. Although the original Black–Scholes model was derived in 1973 and assumed that the entity issuing the options did not pay dividends, this model has now been adjusted so that it can also be used to determine option values for dividend-paying companies. There are websites available that license software, which run Black–Scholes model calculations for given input assumptions. Alternatively, by following the formula obtainable from a text book, an Excel spreadsheet can be set up to run the model.

In many cases, the Black–Scholes model will be suitable for application to options granted under terms similar to those of the SAYE scheme described earlier. As the exercise window at six months is relatively short, assumed exercise dates at different points within the exercise window are unlikely to result in significantly different option values. There would need to be an assumption that the dividend yield was not expected to vary significantly during the option life also as a constant dividend yield must be assumed when using the Black–Scholes model. For companies with an established history and relatively consistent dividend yield, this would appear to be reasonable.

The binomial option-pricing model

The binomial model does not use a formula to determine option values. Instead it breaks down the life of the option into a number of time periods and builds up a lattice or tree of possible share price movements for each period, under the assumption that in each period the share price can move either up or down. It is an iterative process working backwards through the binomial price tree from the option value of each final node through each earlier node to the first node in the price tree which is the value of the option. Building a binomial lattice model is relatively complex and requires a good understanding of statistics, probability and computer modelling – hence the details of these are outside the scope of this book. However, there are numerous textbooks and online resources which describe the theory in more detail and from which the computer software required to run a binomial model can be purchased, such as from www.fis-group.com.

Binomial lattice models are also known as binomial trees or a Cox, Ross and Rubinstein (CRR) binomial options pricing model, after the authors who first proposed the model in 1979.

Comparison of option-pricing models

As the binomial and Black–Scholes models are based on the same underlying share price theory, if they are run with identical assumptions (and in the limiting case where the binomial model were to use an infinite number of individual time periods), they would result in the same option value. In practice, if the binomial model is run with a large number of time periods and identical assumptions to a Black–Scholes model, the resulting option values are very close.

Whilst the binomial model is more complicated to build and run than the Black–Scholes model, it has the advantage of being more flexible and this flexibility is required in certain circumstances. For instance, certain options may have relatively long option exercise windows, say of seven years. The option value is likely to differ significantly according to whether a life at the start or the end of the exercise window is selected, ie either three or ten years, and this renders the Black–Scholes model unsuitable. Bespoke binomial models can be constructed that result in the option value being calculated such that exercise is possible only within a given exercise window.

Once a maximum expected life has been determined, which may be shorter than the full contractual life of the option for the reasons described at **22.03**, the binomial model requires no further refinement of the option life in order to determine the highest value of the option within the given exercise window. This is not achievable with the Black–Scholes model, which would require a best guess of one specific option exercise date to be included, rather than reflecting the potential exercise window.

Many entities will expect their dividend yield to change over the life of the option. This is particularly the case for start-up companies that may not expect to pay a dividend in the short term but would expect to pay a dividend after, say, three years. A variable pattern of dividends can be modelled relatively easily using a binomial model but cannot be modelled using a Black–Scholes model.

There are further variations that can be modelled with complex bespoke binomial models; for instance, for shares whose volatility is expected to vary over the option life. Again, this would not be possible using a Black–Scholes model.

There are a number of websites that provide Black–Scholes and/or binomial models, including www.fincad.com, www.hoadley.net and www.blobek.com.

As noted at **22.02**, Monte Carlo simulation can also be used to model the value of share options and, like the binomial model, can provide flexibility in model inputs over the life of the options.

As with any valuation calculation, the result is dependent on the validity of the chosen assumptions for the relevant variables and should be subject to an appropriate reasonableness check. Similarly, there should be a check when deciding whether or not to grant the award. Is it likely that there will be a sufficient share price increase in excess of the exercise price to incentivise the grantee, because, if not, the reward is a waste of time?

Awards of share options with market conditions

Certain market conditions, such as the award of shares subject to a specified share price being achieved, can be incorporated into bespoke binomial option pricing models but cannot be incorporated into Black–Scholes models. Such conditions can also be incorporated into Monte Carlo simulation models used for option pricing.

Simple example of Black–Scholes application

A company which is listed on the London Stock Exchange, Pangolin PLC, grants 100 options to employees at £2 per option at a time when the share price is £1.75. Suppose also that:

- the options have a life of 3.5 years with a three-year vesting period and are expected to be exercised at the end of 3.5 years, based on past history for similar employee awards;
- expected volatility over the 3.5 years based on analysing historical share price data is 30%;
- the risk-free rate of return over the period is 3%; and
- a constant 2% dividend yield is expected over the 3.5 years.

The Black–Scholes model could be used to determine the value of the option and this would result in a value of each of the 100 options of 29.76p and, hence, a fair value at grant date for the 100 options of £29.76. As noted earlier, there are specific accounting requirements regarding the extent to which this £29.76 is charged to the profit and loss account and over what periods; however, these are outside the scope of this book.

Focus

- The Black–Scholes model is the simplest model to apply but may not be appropriate for options with long exercise windows.
- The binomial model can be adapted to deal with changes in dividend assumptions over the life of the option.
- Monte Carlo simulation is usually used for complex awards with market conditions.

Disclosures required under IFRS 2

The required disclosures for share awards include:

- the number and weighted average fair value of equity instruments at the measurement date and information on how that fair value was measured including:
  - if fair value was not based on an observable market price, how it was determined;
  - whether and how expected dividends were incorporated into the fair value measurement; and
  - whether and how any other features of the equity instruments granted were incorporated into the fair value measurement.

The required disclosures for share option awards include:

- the number and weighted average exercise prices of share options analysed by those:
  - outstanding at the beginning and end of the period;
  - granted during the period;
  - forfeited during the period (ie for failing to satisfy non-market performance conditions);
  - exercised and expired during the period; and
  - exercisable at the end of the period.
- for share options granted during the period, the weighted average fair value at the measurement date and information on how fair value was measured including:
  - the option-pricing model used and inputs to the model including:
    - weighted average share price;
    - exercise price;
    - expected volatility, including an explanation of extent to which expected volatility is based on historical volatility;
    - option life;
    - expected dividends;
    - risk-free interest rate;
    - any other inputs including method used and assumptions made to incorporate effects of expected early exercise; and
    - whether and how any other features of the options granted, such as a market condition, were incorporated into the fair value measurement.

22.04 Accounting for employee equity awards under UK GAAP, FRS 102

Similarly to IFRS 2, FRS 102: Section 26 requires that the grant date fair value of equity instruments granted to employees as part of their remuneration package is charged to the profit or loss account. Also, similarly to IFRS 2, the grant date fair value must be adjusted to reflect market conditions and non-vesting conditions.

For awards of shares, the following three-tier measurement hierarchy is required to be applied:

(a) Use an observable market price for the shares if there is one.
(b) If there is no observable market price, base fair value on entity-specific observable market data such as:
   (i) a recent transaction in the entity's shares; or
   (ii) a recent independent fair valuation of the entity or its principal assets.
(c) If an observable market price is not available and obtaining a reliable measure of fair value under (ii) above is impracticable, measure the fair value of the shares indirectly by applying a valuation method that uses market data to the greatest extent practicable to estimate the price of the equity instruments on the grant date in an arm's length transaction between knowledgeable, willing parties. The entity's directors are to use their judgement to apply a generally accepted valuation methodology for valuing equity instruments that is appropriate to the circumstances of the entity.

For awards of share options, the following three-tier measurement hierarchy is to be applied:

(a) Use an observable market price for the share options if there is one.
(b) If there is no observable market price for the share options, base fair value on entity-specific observable market data such as a recent transaction in the share options.
(c) If an observable market price is not available and obtaining a reliable measure of fair value under (b) above is impracticable, measure the fair value of the share options indirectly using an alternative valuation method such as an option-pricing model. The inputs to the option-pricing model (see **22.02** for the six inputs involved) are to incorporate market data to the greatest extent possible. The grant date fair value of the underlying shares is to be measured according to the three-tier hierarchy described above. Expected volatility is to be determined on a basis consistent with the valuation method used to determine the fair value of the underlying shares.

Disclosures required for awards of shares or share options include information about how the fair value of the shares was determined including, if a valuation methodology was used, the method used and reason for choosing it.

Additional disclosures required for awards of share options include:

- the numbers and weighted average exercise prices of share options analysed (as under IFRS 2) by those:
  - outstanding at the beginning and end of the period;

- granted during the period;
- forfeited during the period (ie for failing to satisfy non-market performance conditions);
- exercised and expired during the period;
- outstanding at the period end; and
- exercisable at the period end.

Thus, FRS 102 does not require that the inputs to an option-pricing model are disclosed and is, therefore, much less onerous than IFRS 2 in this regard.

Focus

FRS 102 provides a different three-tier measurement hierarchy to apply to measure the fair values of shares or share options from IFRS 2.

22.05 Accounting for employee equity awards under UK GAAP, FRS 105

Unlike IFRS 2 and FRS 102, FRS 105: Section 21, Share-based Payment, does not require micro-entities to make a profit or loss account charge for the fair value of share and share option awards granted. Instead, accounting is required only for the ultimate number of shares or share options awarded at the award date. There is no fair value measurement requirement.

Chapter 23

Valuation in matrimonial proceedings

Signposts

23.01 Valuation principles

Although the basic principle to be adhered to when valuing unquoted shares for ancillary relief purposes in a matrimonial dispute is to arrive at open market value, the court, if values are contested to that level, has considerable discretion to impose a solution that it finds fair in the circumstances, under Part II of the Matrimonial Causes Act 1973 as amended up to 20 February 2019, in particular s 25.

Section 25 now reads as follows:

> **'Matters to which court is to have regard in deciding how to exercise its powers under ss 23, 24, 24A, 24B and 24E**
>
> (1) It shall be the duty of the court in deciding whether to exercise its powers under section 23, 24, 24A, 24B or 24E above and, if so, in what manner, to have regard to all the circumstances of the case, first consideration being given to the welfare while a minor of any child of the family who has not attained the age of eighteen.

(2) As regards the exercise of the powers of the court under section 23(1)(a), (b), or (c), 24, 24A, 24B or 24E above in relation to a party to the marriage, the court shall in particular have regard to the following matters –

(a) the income, earning capacity, property and other financial resources which each of the parties to the marriage has or is likely to have in the foreseeable future, including in the case of earning capacity any increase in that capacity which it would in the opinion of the court be reasonable to expect a party to the marriage to take steps to acquire;
(b) the financial needs, obligations and responsibilities which each of the parties to the marriage has or is likely to have in the foreseeable future;
(c) the standard of living enjoyed by the family before the breakdown of the marriage;
(d) the age of each party to the marriage and the duration of the marriage;
(e) any physical or mental disability of either of the parties to the marriage;
(f) the contributions which each of the parties has made or is likely in the foreseeable future to make to the welfare of the family, including any contribution by looking after the home or caring for the family;
(g) the conduct of each of the parties, if that conduct is such that it would in the opinion of the court be inequitable to disregard it;
(h) in the case of proceedings for divorce or nullity of marriage, the value to each of the parties to the marriage of any benefit … which, by reason of the dissolution or annulment of the marriage, that party will lose the chance of acquiring.

(3) As regards the exercise of the powers of the court under section 23(1)(d), (e) or (f), (2) or (4), 24 or 24A above in relation to a child of the family, the court shall in particular have regard to the following matters –

(a) the financial needs of the child;
(b) the income, earning capacity (if any), property and other financial resources of the child;
(c) any physical or mental disability of the child;
(d) the manner in which he was being and in which the parties to the marriage expected him to be educated or trained;
(e) the considerations mentioned in relation to the parties to the marriage in paragraphs (a), (b), (c) and (e) of subsection (2) above.

(4) As regards the exercise of the powers of the court under section 23(1)(d), (e) or (f), (2) or (4), 24 or 24A above against a party to a marriage in favour of a child of the family who is not the child of that party, the court shall also have regard –

(a) to whether that party assumed any responsibility for the child's maintenance, and, if so, to the extent to which, and the basis upon which, that party assumed such responsibility and to the length of time for which that party discharged such responsibility;
(b) to whether in assuming and discharging such responsibility that party did so knowing that the child was not his or her own;
(c) to the liability of any other person to maintain the child.'

That discretion allows the Court to deal with the following contentious areas, amongst others, in the manner it thinks fit the facts of the particular case:

(i) quasi partnerships;
(ii) minority holdings in family companies;
(iii) shares held in trust;

(iv) director's remuneration and/or dividends from the company form the family's main source of income; and
(v) illiquidity.

The cases summarised below address some of those issues but it has to be stressed that, in matrimonial proceedings, each case will turn on its own merits to an even greater degree than is usual for other purposes. Whether or not a divorce is to be a clean break will also influence the Court's attitude.

Focus

The Matrimonial Causes Act 1973 is the lynchpin of family litigation.

23.02 Fairness

In the House of Lords in the divorce cases *of Miller v Miller, McFarlane v McFarlane* [2006] UKHL 24, their Lordships laid down the matters to be taken into consideration in claims for ancillary relief following the breakdown of marriage.

Lord Nicholls of Birkenhead began his judgment with the following words:

> 'These two appeals concern that most intractable of problems: how to achieve fairness in the division of property following a divorce. In *White v White* [2001] 1 AC 596 your Lordships' house sought to assist judges who have the difficult task of exercising the wide discretionary powers conferred on the court by Part II of the Matrimonial Causes Act 1973. In particular the house emphasised that in seeking a fair outcome there is no place for discrimination between a husband and wife and their respective roles. Discrimination is the antithesis of fairness. In assessing the party's contributions to the family there should be no bias in favour of the money-earner and against the home-maker and the child-carer. This is a principal of universal application. It is applicable to all marriages.'

This concept of fairness has to be borne in mind by the valuer called upon to value shares or intangible assets for the purpose of matrimonial proceedings.

One of the factors that may have to be taken into account when considering the value of a minority interest in a family company or quasi-partnership is the extent to which it might be fair to apply a discount to a minority shareholding held by one of the parties to the marriage in circumstances where in practice the shares could not be sold to an outsider and decisions in running the company are taken by consensus following discussion rather than following a formal vote.

In the matrimonial dispute in *H v H* [2008] EWHC 935 (Fam), the professional business valuations for the parties were £1.7 million for the husband and £5 million for the wife, as a result of which the judge specified that the value of the business was £2.5 million. As the judge pointed out, quoting *McFarlane v McFarlane* [2006] UKHL 24 per Lord Nicholl, 'valuations are often a matter on which experts differ'.

In *Charman v Charman* [2007] EWCA Civ 503 the Court of Appeal regarded a Bermudan trust settled by Mr Charman, of which he and his family and others were beneficiaries, a resource for matrimonial purposes. Taking this into account, the total assets were approximately £131m and on the breakup of the marriage the wife was awarded 36.5% of the total, taking account of the exceptional contribution to the family wealth made by the husband; this was a 28-year marriage with two children. In *James Paul McCartney v Heather Ann Mills-McCartney* [2008] EWHC 401 (Fam) the award to the wife was £24.3m out of Sir Paul McCartney's estimated £400m of assets, which took into account the short-lived marriage and the huge premarital assets.

In *Prest v Petrodel Resources Ltd* [2013] UKSC 34, the Supreme Court, whilst accepting that the assets of various Isle of Man companies which had properties in the UK could be ordered to transfer the properties to the wife under the Matrimonial Causes Act 1973, ss 23–55, the court noted that 'the husband's conduct at the meetings has been characterised by persistent obstruction, obfuscation and deceit and a contumelious refusal to comply with the rules of Court and specific orders'. There is in this case an interesting discussion on whether the court had power to 'pierce the corporate veil'. Lord Neuberger did not dismiss the concept of piercing the corporate veil. The Supreme Court upheld that on the facts the companies held the properties in question in trust for the husband, and as he was beneficially entitled to them, they fell within the scope of the court's power to make transfer of property orders under the Matrimonial Causes Act 1973, s 24(1)(a).

Focus

The divorce courts seek to produce a result they consider to be as fair as possible.

23.03 Valuation in context of the overall settlement

In *D v D & Another* [2007] EWHC 278 (Fam), Mr Justice Charles in a lengthy judgment stated (at para 93):

> 'It was submitted to me, and I of course accept, that valuations carry an element of uncertainty and, for example, this is so in respect of the valuation of a matrimonial home. However I do not accept, as was again submitted on behalf of the wife, that this example of uncertainty is equivalent to and can be approached in the same way as the uncertainty that exists when the shares in a private company are valued. In my view that submission is one that ignores the reality of the nature of the relevant assets and in particular the likelihood that in respect of such a company, (a) there is no ready market and (b) highly competent valuers (using the same method of valuation) will reach widely different valuations. Such a variance between valuers is regularly encountered in this and other types of litigation and is a natural product of the effects of the elements of opinion applied by the valuers and thus of the exercise they carry out. The degree and nature of any such differences in valuation is not the same as those that can occur when there is an open market and comparables.
>
> To my mind this point and the point that private companies are often the goose that has laid the golden eggs in the form of income and benefits through a marriage have the consequences that when such companies are involved the "apples and pears" argument is likely to arise.

> Also the wish of a party and perhaps the requirements of fairness may mean that when private companies are involved one of the parties to a marriage should be permitted to continue running such a company. Thus the ability of the company to lawfully and sensibly (in both a business and general sense) pay sums of money to one or both of the parties will often arise. This will involve consideration of the relevant company and fiscal law and an assessment of the commercial situation and thus a commercial and practical approach by persons with the relevant expertise.'

He continued (at para 104):

> 'I therefore repeat my urging of those involved in ancillary relief cases involving private companies not to confine themselves to an approach based solely on valuation and liquidity (ie the ability to raise money to meet a lump sum payment) but to investigate and consider commercial alternatives and periodical payments. In my view it should be practical for this to be done without undue expense, in particular with cooperation and the formulation of the correct type of question. This is particularly so when it is remembered that rough and preliminary valuations on an earnings basis should be possible without incurring significant accountancy fees. The same point can be made in respect of the identification and preliminary views on commercial options if someone experienced in these matters and the fiscal consequences of various alternatives is consulted. In the case of an accountant it is important that he or she is instructed to consider and advise or report on the relevant issues. If the family law specialists instructed do not have the relevant expertise to identify such issues (or to ensure that they have been identified by the accountants) there are a number of lawyers who do and whose advice to my mind sadly is not sought regularly enough in ancillary relief proceedings.'

And (at para 119):

> 'I make the general point that these proceedings (and other ancillary relief proceedings) are not a situation when a willing buyer is by law to be assumed (as can be the case for tax valuations) or one where there is an identified buyer (eg as in a (CA 1985) s 459 petition). Rather, overall fairness is the goal and the valuation exercise is one that seeks to put a capital value on assets that are retained (or may be retained) to assess what orders to make under the MCA and in that respect the value in capital (and income terms) of assets if they are to be retained by one of the parties. Issues of and relating to extraction or conversion into cash of corporate assets and shares and of marketability are also relevant.'

Charles J explained (at para 152):

> 'If the commercial approach I advocate had taken place in this case something like the post hearing report should have been produced at an early stage of the litigation (although it would not have included the figures based on valuations). So at that stage it would have been known that:
>
> (i) the non-trading assets would have to be extracted.
> (ii) if they were, there was a good chance that the shares in the holding company (valued as the owner of the trading company) could be sold with an effective tax charge of 10%.
> (iii) to extract the non-trading assets in the affordable way suggested (dividend in specie) there would have to be sufficient distributable reserves / profits.
> (iv) the availability of such distributable reserves / profits was sufficiently affected by the provision made for the US customs claim and thus the detail of the merits of that claim.
> (v) Tax charges on the extraction needed to be addressed.

(vi) If the dividend in specie route was not to be available other strategies and methods of maximising value would have to be considered.

If this had been identified at an early stage the expert evidence could and no doubt would have been directed to it and the parties should have been in a position to present their case against the background of a proper description of the viable alternatives concerning the realisation of the value of the business assets.

They were not in a position to do this and consequently did not do so.'

And at para 176:

'I have concluded on the information and argument before me that neither of the results urged by the parties results in a clean break that can with sufficient confidence be said to be fair and I have not identified an alternative about which that can be said. In my view if I was to order a clean break now my order could justifiably be described as an under-informed guess. That is not an appropriate basis for making an order under the MCA to achieve a fair result.'

In *D v D*, Mr Justice Charles was returning to a theme he had addressed in *A v A* [2004] EWHC 2818 (Fam). He stated (at para 60):

'At the risk of being accused of seeking to revisit issues in *Parra* I make the general comment that it seems to me that in ancillary relief proceedings it is important for the parties and their advisers to look at issues concerning private companies through the eyes of both (a) persons with experience in, and of, matrimonial litigation and (b) persons with experience in, and of, business and business litigation. For example if this is done it may quickly become apparent (a) that there is a wide bracket of valuation and (b) that there may be a viable and pragmatic business solution which would avoid either or both of the uncertainties and difficulties of valuation and the raising of finance, albeit that it may not involve a clean break.

61 The business approach or a pragmatic approach by reference to the commercial reality would also highlight (a) the point that the recognition of the diverse benefits which flow from a controlling interest in a private company lead a number of litigants to fight hard to keep the company or a controlling interest therein and thus what they regard as the goose that lays or is capable of laying golden eggs of income, benefits and capital rather than accept a capital sum based on a valuation of their interest in the company. This is because they are of the view that those benefits outweigh the risks and uncertainties associated with the relevant business (b) the different advantages of greater certainty and immediate access to capital (together perhaps with the realisation that they can no longer work in the business or a different view of the prospects of the company) can be more attractive to some litigants if the price is acceptable to them (c) the need to consider carefully non-competition provisions on a sale of the company as a whole or in a buy-out of a shareholder (d) the difficulties in predicting the future of the company and thus the need for up-to-date, verified management information for the purposes of valuation and the consideration of liquidity and borrowing (e) the understandable reaction of a shareholder who is retaining shares, control of and a management role in the company to emphasise the risks and problems relating to the future rather than the reasoning behind his or her decision to seek a result in which he or she retains shares (f) the lack of an open market and the distinction between the value of shares (i) in the hands of a controlling shareholder or (ii) the value of a minority interest (unless a company is sold as a whole) and thus the potential for differences in value by reference to the positions of the transferor and potential transferees and (g) the problems relating to the raising of finance to buy out a shareholder.

> 62 Naturally many if not all of these problems are familiar to matrimonial lawyers but I suggest that a consideration of them from the business perspective rather than from what seems to be a common approach in ancillary relief proceedings of seeing how a clean break on the payment of a lump sum can be achieved by reference to snap-shot valuations may, in a number of cases, point the way to more flexibility of thought and a fair solution.
>
> 63 I accept that the problem with a business solution is that often it will not involve a clean break, and the considerable advantages which flow from that in the context of litigation relating to a divorce would therefore be lost if it was adopted. However it seems to me that the parties and their advisers should be clear why they are taking a course which involves the uncertainties and potential unfairness of a result dependent on valuation and the payment of a lump sum (which may have to be borrowed) or a sale.
>
> 64 In an assessment of a fair division of assets under the MCA problems obviously arise in respect of "snap-shot valuations". The greater the volatility in value or the potential for a wide range of valuation the greater the problem. In respect of private companies and shareholdings therein the difficulties and potential unfairness of a snap-shot valuation clearly arise and can do so in a stark form. Such valuations turn in part upon opinions as to prospects and what multiple and discount should be used in the valuation method adopted. They suffer from the background difficulty that there is generally no open market for the shares. This can regularly give rise to large differences between highly reputable valuers even when they are using the same methodology and these can be compounded by differing views on prospects and methodology. All this and other problems flow from the nature of the asset.'

Aspen v Hildesley [1982] STC 206 confirmed that disposals between spouses on divorce are usually subject to capital gains tax, following *Turven v Fallett* [1973] STC 148. The judge stated:

> 'Counsel for the Crown says, correctly, that if the disposal was made on 12 February 1976 the taxpayer and Mrs Hildesley were still then husband and wife, since a marriage subsists until dissolved by decree absolute. He therefore claims that they were connected persons on the material date. On the other hand, it is not possible for the taxpayer to take advantage of the general exemption applying to disposals between husband and wife under (FA 1971) para 20 of Sch 7, because that exemption applies only when they are living together. On one view that is a somewhat paradoxical state of affairs, but the material provisions are clear and there may well have been good reasons for them.
>
> The result to which they lead, submits counsel for the Crown, is that under the combined effect of s 22(4) and para 17(2) the taxpayer must be deemed to have disposed of his interest and Mrs Hildesley to have acquired it for a consideration equal to its market value. I accept counsel for the Crown's submission as to the combined effect of s 22(4) and para 17(2).'

In *O'Donnell v O'Donnell* [1975] 2 All ER 993 at 996, Ormrod LJ said:

> 'In approaching a case like the present the first stage should be to make as reliable an estimate as possible of the husband's current financial position and future prospects. In making this assessment the court is concerned with the reality of the husband's resources using that word in a broad sense to include not only what he is shown to have but also what could reasonably be made available to him if he so wished. Much would depend on the interpretation of accounts, balance sheets and so on which will require in many cases the expert guidance of

> accountants. It will rarely be possible arrive at arithmetically exact figures. The court must penetrate through the balance sheets and the profit and loss accounts to the underlying realities bearing in mind that prudent financial management and skilled presentation of accounts are unlikely to overstate the husband's real resources and on the other side that there may be a great difference between wealth on paper and true wealth. Valuations may overstate or understate the results of realisation of assets many of which may not be realisable within the immediate or foreseeable future.'

It may be necessary to consider very closely the real market in shares for the particular company involved in arriving at the appropriate value.

Focus

In order to divide the assets fairly, they need to be valued or divided in specie.

23.04 Shares held in trust

In the leading divorce case of *Charman v Charman* [2006] EWHC 1879 (Fam) the High Court judge considered this to be a huge money case and noted:

> ' ... by the wife's calculation the husband had generated wealth to the tune of £150m–£160m although by then it was by no means all in his name. So for example nearly £6m of that sum was in wife's name, £25m–£30m (or maybe more) was held in a trust for the parties' children. The remaining £125m or so was either in the husband's ownership (about £56m) or in a trust called the Dragon Holdings trust (£68m), the Dragon Trust.'

The husband 'asserts that the assets owned by the Dragon Trust should be left entirely out of account because they were deposited there by him as part of his long-term plan and intention to found a dynastic trust for the benefit of as yet unborn members of the family (the children having already been provided for by their own trusts)'. However the judge held:

> 'the failure to indicate any such dynastic plan on the face of any of the letters of wishes drafted at the time since Dragon's inception is quite frankly incredible if it underlay the trust's true purpose. At all times the trust has been in the hands of paid professional offshore trustees. Would they have allowed this fundamental matter to have remained undocumented. I think not.'

He continued (at para 79):

> 'The test is whether the assets in the trust should be regarded by the court as a "resource". That is a very broad definition. These assets are held in a discretionary trust in conventional form. I will not repeat the very helpful descriptive analysis of such a trust in the Jersey High Court adopted by Potter P in his judgement dismissing the husband's appeal against my order relating to letters of request (*Re Esteem Settlement* [2004] WTLR 1). It is a very useful description of general application in cases like this and as Lloyd LJ in the same occasion pointed out, the assets in the trust "could be available to him on demand without being his money" as Mr Singleton was constrained to agree.'

Focus

Whether or not trust assets need to be taken into account depends on the circumstances and, in the case of foreign trusts, there may be problems of enforceability.

23.05 Quoted shares and options

On the valuation issues the judge in *Charman* stated (at para 83):

> 'I turn to the valuation of Access share options and warrants within and without Dragon. Both sides have employed the services of household name accountancy firms to assist them, PricewaterhouseCoopers for the wife and KPMG for the husband. The extent of the overall difference between them is almost exactly £20m. It is nicely illustrated on a schedule which I shall annexe to this judgment entitled "comparison of experts' reports and conclusions as to valuation" which was prepared jointly by junior Counsel. It highlights the different discounts contended for by each side.
>
> 84 In support of the argument supported by each side I have careful written submissions. Mr Pointer in his opening notes summarises the main differences between the experts and the competing contentions from page 29. I annexe an edited version.
>
> 85 The approach to valuation issues in this division is and always has been to look at the reality of the situation in any given case. For decades the court has set its face against hypothetical valuations produced for different purposes (income tax, probate etc). Any other approach is quite simply unfair. Indeed the rigid adoption of CETVs in pension cases sometimes has that effect albeit that it is expedient for other reasons. Of course this often leads to spirited debate. So where for instance a case proceeds on the basis that a sale of less than true market value is inevitable to satisfy a likely court order then discounts at high levels are often appropriate. But where a sale can be avoided or delayed to enable full value to be extracted over a reasonable time that too must in fairness be properly reflected in valuation.
>
> 86 For that reason I reject the approach adopted by KPMG as being hypothetical and prefer PWC as being specific to the facts of this case. Exactly the same kind of considerations apply when looking at discounts for valuation of minority interests in private companies. Sometimes they apply, sometimes especially in a family situation they do not, see *G v G (Financial Provision: Equal Division)* [2002] EWHC 1339 (Fam).
>
> 87 I shall adopt the share price current at the time of the February hearing because it turns out the figure of $29.5 is a reasonable mid-price. As a preliminary matter it is also important to remember that Access is a company whose stock is quoted on the New York Stock Exchange. This is not a case about private company holdings where the "top line" is in issue before discounts are applied. So all the shares are (subject to a particular time restriction) freely tradable and in time therefore also the shares generated by the exercise of options. Great care therefore needs to be taken when discounting from readily available market value.
>
> 88 As to the discounts for delay or restriction on sale; I have no rational basis for the huge discounts (60% and 70%) contended for by KPMG. They accepted

> that they were in effect plucking figures out of the air. I do not understand their methodology at all. I reject it and prefer PWC's more measured approach.
>
> 89 As for the CEO selling discount, those arguments I consider nowadays normally be regarded as "old hat". There was a time when CEOs in the divorce courts were a rarity and the prospect of their having to find cash to meet settlements for wives was enough to send a shiver down the stock market's spine. Expert evidence was often led to predict the effect on the share price in the CEO's company of a sale following divorce. All recent evidence and experience shows that this is no longer the case. CEO's are now, sadly, frequenters of these courts and with the most minimal of careful public relations prior to a sale it is of no moment so far as the stock market is concerned. The recent Sorell case amongst others illustrates this. I would like to hope that these arguments are now an anachronistic and can be confined to forensic history. If that is removed for the discount debate there is really nothing between the experts so far as volume discounts are concerned.
>
> 90 The attempt by KPMG to apply a further discount for the departure of the "key man" cannot possibly now be sustained given the husband has announced his departure and the market responded by increasing the share's price. I again remind myself that this is a huge publicly quoted company where the departure of one man is self-evidently unlikely to rock the boat.
>
> 91 Overall I far prefer the evidence of Mr Clokey on all valuation issues at stake. His approach and discounts seemed carefully considered, rational and fair in contrast to KPMG where I had the distinct impression that straws were being clutched at every opportunity to depress the figures artificially. I shall adopt the PWC figures and have concluded them in the main schedule. Their overall value within and without Dragon is £73,117,406 broken down as appears on the schedule.
>
> 92 The husband seeks conclusion on the asset's schedule by way of a deduction of the potential (not actual) liability to tax which he asserts was saved by his emigration to Bermuda. He says the wife should not be allowed to benefit from that saving (both in relation to his assets or those in Dragon) because she did not make the move and accompany him. If there is anything in that argument the place for it is in relation to consideration of matters of conduct which I will revert to below. It is not a true monetary deduction at this state of the s 25 exercise. I shall remove it for now from the schedule.'

Schedule 2 reveals that this is a case where the value of options was based on the binominal valuation model (at para 62):

> 'Clokey runs the model having discounted the share price by 2% (being the figure he adopts for the CEO/volume or blockage discount) and reaches a single aggregate valuation for each of the options ie a value which includes the intrinsic value which is calculated using the same assumptions as set out under "Shares" above.
>
> …
>
> 64 Clokey explains the economic theory behind his approach justifying the assumption that H will retain the options to the expiry of their respective term. In simple terms the theory states that in the case of options where the holder does not receive dividends until the option is exercised (which these are) it is always advantageous to retain options for the maximum period unless the loss of dividends suffered on the unexercised options is so great as to outweigh the benefit of retaining the options. With an agreed dividend yield of 2% the benefit of retention clearly outweighs the dividend loss.'

With regard to warrants (at para 65):

> '... the valuation of the warrants involves similar consideration as to the valuation of options which will not be repeated here. The summary of the position is:
>
> Clokey incorporates in the binomial model (i) the 2% CEO / volume discount to obtain an aggregate value; and (ii) a 5% restriction on sale discount to represent the 12 months holding period during which the shares cannot be sold after the exercise of the warrants and thus produces an aggregate value (ie including the intrinsic and time/potential values of the warrants);
>
> This underlying share price may need to be modified in the light of H's retirement announcement on the CEO/volume discount.'

This judgment was approved by the Court of Appeal: [2007] EWCA Civ 503.

> **Focus**
>
> Where assets are not immediately realisable, their valuation can present problems.

23.06 Taxation: the powers of the court

In *G v G* [2002] EWHC 1339 (Fam), Coleridge J, on ordering the transfer of shares in an unlisted company from husband to wife on a divorce settlement, stated:

> 'this transfer is ordered on the footing that business hold-over relief will be available to the husband; that the wife will receive the shares at the husband's base value and that accordingly no liability to CGT will arise on the husband as a result of the transfer. I have seen an extract from an Inland Revenue manual which confirms that a court order transfer of business assets does in principle satisfy the conditions for a claim for holdover relief but which goes on to suggest that actual consideration given by the donee may reduce the gain potentially eligible to hold-over relief to nil. The view of the Inland Revenue appears to be that the actual consideration is the surrender by the donee of rights which he would otherwise be able to exercise to obtain alternative financial provision. I do not share their view about that and I have to say that this view seems to me to be based on a misconception. In an ancillary relief hearing neither party has any rights as such at all: all the powers are vested in the court which may or may not exercise them. The parties may make suggestions as to how these powers are to be exercised. That is all. So when I order a transfer of shares in favour of the wife on a clean break basis she is not "giving up" her claim for maintenance as a quid pro quo. I am simply exercising my statutory powers in the way I consider to be fair. This would be equally the case where the court was making a consent order, for, although the parties may have made their agreement, it is for the court independently to adjudge its fairness: see *Xydhias v Xydhias* [1999] 1 FLR 683 at 691 where Thorpe LJ stated "An even more singular feature of the transition from compromise to order in ancillary relief proceedings is that the court does not either automatically or invariably grant the application to give the bargain the force of an order. The court conducts an independent assessment to enable it to discharge its statutory function to make such orders as reflects the criteria listed in s 25 of the Matrimonial Causes Act 1973 as amended.

> Although I cannot of course ultimately bind the Inland Revenue I am satisfied that at least in this case the wife gives no consideration for the transfer of the shares I order in her favour and that accordingly hold-over relief should be available.'

Focus

Taxation on transfer of assets between former spouses has to be considered.

23.07 Valuation of start-up companies

In the matrimonial case of *P v P* [2005] 1 FLR 548 the assets to be valued for the purposes of the divorce consisted of shares in two private car dealership companies in which the husband held 50% and 51% respectively. The husband also held a 25% shareholding in RP Ltd, a computer software company designing websites. The two expert accountants valued the shares in RP Ltd at £10,000 and £68,000 respectively. The former finance director had recently sold his 16.67% shareholding for £5,000 although it was accepted that he was not in a good bargaining position. The higher value was arrived at on the basis of maintainable earnings of £65,000 (the profits for the first two years were £33,000 and £87,000 respectively) to which he applied a multiple of 6.5 to produce a whole company value of £422,500 and a 25% shareholding of £105,625, before a minority interest discount of 35% of £36,969 leaving a value of £68,656 rounded down to £68,000. The judge took account of the fact that the company was still in its start-up phase and its trading record and profitability had been somewhat erratic. He therefore considered the higher valuation of £68,000 to be too high whereas the other expert's valuation of £10,000 was obviously too low. He stated:

> 'In the light of this divergence and because I have no better evidence I propose to take the average of the valuations advanced, thus the husband's shareholding is valued at £39,000. That is some £35,000 after capital gains tax at 10%.'

Focus

A pragmatic solution may sometimes be the answer.

23.08 Use of the Private Company Price Index

So far as the car dealerships (Ps and H) in *P v P* are concerned, the two sides' expert witnesses agreed that the appropriate methodology was to value the companies:

> 'by reference to their utilisation of a multiple applied to the maintainable post-tax earnings of the companies being valued. This approach to then be considered against an asset based valuation with the higher of the two valuations being taken.'

The problem was that the range of P/E multiples advocated on each side varied from 2 to 17.7. In their final joint statement dated 25 June 2004 the accountants agreed that the post-tax earnings of (i) Ps was £447,000 subject to the sight of the documentation relating to the directors compensation package and (ii) H was £165,000. They could not agree the P/E multiple to be applied. The wife's accountant, Mr R, put forward a price earnings multiple of 9.9 for Ps and 8.4 for H: "In his analysis Mr R based his multiple on the Private Company Price Index (PCPI) as at Spring 2004 for the automobile and parts sector. This index is collated by Messrs BDO Stoy Hayward from information supplied to them from Thompson Financial. The index includes an industry specific break-down of the last three year average P/E multiples applying to all deals completed during the period to 31 December 2003. Complaint has been made that this index cannot be regarded as wholly appropriate because it is distorted by the sale of parts manufacturers. Whilst I accept that this may affect the multiples (and I have no evidence as to the extent of the variants to be applied) this defect does not make the index irrelevant.

The PCPI indicates a multiple of 9.9 for private company deals and 13.3 for quoted companies.

In addition to the index Mr R considered the quoted companies that had been advanced as illustrative by the husband's accountant in his first (and second) report. He came to the conclusion that the average P/E in relation to those companies was now some 10.5. He also used the SP deal as an indicator and calculated that p/e at 10.4.

Mr R considered a number of other factors to take account of the companies' own specific strengths and weaknesses and as a result reduced the P/E of H to 8.4. Mr R told the judge "that he had made enquiries and the "industry rule of thumb" (confirmed in an approved minute of his meeting with the managing director of a large motor dealership) was that sales often took place at asset value plus two to three times pre-tax profits".

Mr R 'reserved the right to revise the maintainable earnings figure once he had evidence of the hours worked by the husband and his cousin AP. Once this was available he considered that the maintainable earnings should be increased by £70,000 (ie £35,000 each) to reflect the fact that the husband was over-paid for the work that was undertaken and AP did not merit her entire salary'.

Mr T for the husband asserted "that Ps should be valued on an asset basis (plus a 25% uplift) because this valuation was higher (on his calculation) than the value on a price earnings basis. In my experience (and I have specialised in this field for some 28 years) I have never come across a P/E valuation which is less than the net asset base when the entity being valued is an active trading company such as a motor dealership. Thus although his analysis is careful I consider it to be fatally flawed". Mr T's multiples of earnings were six for Ps and four for H. The judge in considering these values stated: " I do not believe that the husband's remuneration is merited by the current work that he undertakes (although I have no doubt that his package is justified from an historical and ownership prospective). His salary and benefits total £128,000 but I consider that the market rate for a chairman and strategic adviser is more likely to be £55,000. However a managing director (such as Mr C) would merit a package of some £125,000. Thus the savings would be £73,000, (£128,000 – £55,000) whilst the extra cost would be £47,000 (£125,000 – £78,000). The overall sum to be added to maintainable earnings is therefore some £26,000

(£73,000 – £47,000)". The judge then applied a multiple of 8 to Ps and 7 to H arriving at a whole company value of £3.784m and £1.155m respectively and the husband's 50% interest in Ps was valued, without a discount for a less than 100% shareholding, at 50% ie £1.892m and in H 51% £589,000.

Baron J continued: "whilst I accept that the PCPI is the proper starting point for the assessment of the P/E ratio I consider that some deductions are necessary to reflect the special factors in this case. Thus the starting point of 9.9 requires a measure of adjustment to reflect the following concerns, in no order of importance". The judge made a final deduction of £430,000 from the value of the husband's shares as funds that could be extracted from the company net of tax without destroying its trading capability. He continued: "assuming that the funds extracted from the business reduce the value of the husband's current interest on a pound for pond basis and taking into account the division of assets the value of shares that fall for division is about £1,750,000 in the round. The shares in the companies will be divided between the parties in order to effect broad equality of assets taking account of the fact that the husband has a greater proportion of illiquid assets in the division."

Focus

The BDO PCPI can be downloaded free of charge by searching for BDO PCPI or www.bdo.co.uk/news/private-company-price-index-pcpi. From first quarter 2013 the PCPI incorporates the Enterprise Value to EBITDA (earnings before interest, tax depreciation and amortisation) instead of the Price to Earnings ratio used up to Q4 2012. This was to 'incorporate the level of debt in deals and to use a less subjective measure of profitability'. Note, however, further comments on PCPI at **15.8**.

23.09 Shareholders' agreements

The judge in *P v P* recognised that:

> 'The wife has been concerned that if she receives a shareholding in the company she may find her holding manipulated to her disadvantage. Having seen Mr C and the husband I accept this is a possibility. However her position can be protected by a carefully drafted shareholder agreement and a direction that upon sale she will be entitled to her relevant proportion of the overall value whether it is drawn out by way of extra-ordinary bonus or dividend. A time period may have to be included to avoid a transaction which takes place say within two years of a sale. I will hear submissions on this aspect of the case if terms cannot be agreed.'

Focus

The court recognised the potential weakness of a minority shareholder and suggested that this could be overcome by a shareholders' agreement.

23.10 Single joint expert

The judge in *P v P* also commented:

> 'I have found myself wondering whether the monies expended on this litigation would have been more effectively used to deal with the parties' real needs following upon divorce'

and went on to say:

> 'I have had the benefit of two expert accountants Mr R on behalf of the wife and Mr T on behalf of the husband. Each was loyal to their instructions and produced significantly different values for each business. I consider that it would have been of more assistance to me if there had been one jointly instructed expert. I so state because I consider that in a case such as this where the issues are relatively simple, the court should be slow to permit each party to have their own expert. In this case the experts have each produced a number of reports. In fact the expert bundle was so large that it had to be divided.
>
> As each accountant was coming to the valuation from a different perspective (one seeking the highest possible value / liquidity and the other the lowest) their evidence was inevitably coloured. It would have been so much better (and significantly cheaper) if one expert had been instructed to report on an unbiased basis for the court. By that I am not suggesting that either expert was biased, merely that they had a specific cause to advance.'

The revised Civil Procedure Rules (CPR) that came into effect on 26 April 1999 allowed the appointment of a single joint expert (SJE) in an attempt to reduce the cost of expert evidence. The SJE is subject to the same duties as any other expert witness. The overriding duty is to help the court in matters within his expertise, which overrides any obligation to the person from whom he has received instructions or by whom he has been paid. As the SJE's fees will be met equally by both parties, he should be under no pressure, explicit or implicit, to slant his valuation in favour of an instructing solicitor.

In matrimonial proceedings, an SJE is often appointed in cases where values are unlikely to scale the heights reached in *Charman* or *McFarlane*.

The values will nevertheless be significant to the parties and the SJE will often have to face and decide upon the contentious issues listed in **23.01**. His report must be written and should address all contentious issues and explain how he has dealt with them.

Common sense and fairness will probably play an even greater part than usual in the approach to be taken.

> **Focus**
>
> An SJE can reduce costs and save time in matrimonial, and other, cases. The difficulty then becomes agreeing the identity of the SJE.

23.11 Acting as an Expert Witness

[The following is based on an article which first appeared in Tax Adviser of February 2014.]

Acting as an Expert Witness

An Expert, under the Civil Procedure Rules, Part 35 (Experts and Assessors) and Practice Direction 35 (Experts and Assessors), is a person who has been instructed to give or prepare Expert evidence for the purpose of Court proceedings. An Expert may be a single joint Expert instructed to prepare a report for the court, which has to be restricted to that which is reasonably required to resolve the proceedings, on behalf of two or more of the parties, including the claimant, or each party may appoint their own Expert or Experts, as required or as the court may direct. It is their duty to help the court on matters within their Expertise, which overrides any obligation to the person from whom they have received their instructions or by whom they are paid.

The Experts are likely to be asked to clarify the taxation and valuation issues which are relevant and which are within their own area of expertise, or that of their colleagues whose opinions they rely upon, making clear the distinction.

The sort of cases likely to require expert evidence on taxation and allied issues include matrimonial disputes, partnership disputes, professional negligence claims, valuation of shares, goodwill, intellectual property, trust disputes, company reconstructions and acquisitions, disputes with HMRC, both civil and criminal, residence and domicile, etc.

The Expert is often asked to comment in addition on allied matters such as the ability of the company to supply liquidity for a divorce settlement and means of extraction, and also on the state of the market and whether assets are saleable. The Expert could be asked to give his opinion on a range of matters, and care must be taken only to give opinions in areas in which the Expert is competent. There is nothing 'wrong' with saying there is insufficient information, that the Expert has made particular assumptions in arriving at the conclusion, or particular matters are outside of the Expert's competence or experience.

Preparing an Expert Witness Report under CPR Part 35

When preparing an Expert Witness Report it is a good idea to keep in mind the Declaration and Statement of Truth that will have to be signed when it is completed.

DECLARATION AND STATEMENT OF TRUTH

I, [FULL NAME OF EXPERT] DECLARE THAT:

1 I understand that my duty is providing written reports and giving evidence to help the Court, and that this duty overrides any obligation to the party by whom I am engaged or the person who has paid or is liable to pay me. I confirm that I have complied and will continue to comply with my duty.

2 I confirm that I have not entered into any arrangement where the amount or payment of my fees is in any way dependent on the outcome of the case.
3 I know of no conflict of interest of any kind, other than any which I have disclosed in my report.
4 I do not consider that any interest of any kind which I have disclosed affects my suitability as an Expert witness on any issues on which I have given evidence.
5 I will advise the party by whom I am instructed if, between the date of my report and the trial, there is any change in circumstances which affect my answers to points 3 and 4 above.
6 I have shown the sources of all information I have used.
7 I have exercised reasonable care and skill in order to be accurate and complete in preparing this report.
8 I have endeavoured to include in my report those matters, of which I have knowledge or of which I have been made aware, that might adversely affect the validity of my opinion. I have clearly stated any qualifications to my opinion.
9 I have not, without forming an independent view, included or excluded anything which has been suggested to me by others, including my instructing lawyers.
10 I will notify those instructing me immediately and confirm in writing if, for any reason, my existing report requires any correction or qualification.
11 I understand that:
  11.1 my report will form the evidence to be given under oath or affirmation;
  11.2 questions may be put to me in writing for the purposes of clarifying my report and that my answers shall be treated as part of my report and covered by my statement of truth;
  11.3 the court may at any stage direct a discussion to take place between Experts for the purpose of identifying and discussing the Expert issues in the proceedings, where possible reaching an agreed opinion on those issues and identifying what action, if any, may be taken to resolve any of the outstanding issues between the parties;
  11.4 the court may direct that following a discussion between the Experts, a statement should be prepared showing those issues which are agreed, and those issues which are not agreed, together with a summary of the reasons for disagreeing;
  11.5 I may be required to attend court to be cross-examined on my report by a cross-examiner assisted by an Expert;
  11.6 I am likely to be the subject of public adverse criticism by the judge if the Court concludes that I have not taken reasonable care in trying to meet the standards set out above.
12 I have read Part 35 of the Civil Procedure Rules and the accompanying practice direction including the 'Guidance' for Instruction of Experts to give Evidence in Civil Claims and I have complied with their requirements.
13 I am aware of the practice direction on pre-action conduct. I have acted in accordance with the Code of Practice for Experts.

STATEMENT OF TRUTH

I confirm that I have made clear which facts and matters referred to in this report are within my own knowledge and which are not. Those that are within my own knowledge I confirm to be true. The opinions I have expressed represent my true and complete professional opinions on the matters to which they refer.

Professional bodies

There are two institutions, which provide guidance and training for their members, as follows:

The Expert Witness Institute (EWI)
Temple Chambers
Temple Avenue
London
EC4Y 0DA
T: 020 7936 2213
E: info@ewi.org.uk
E: events@ewi.org.uk
www.ewi.org.uk

The Academy of Experts (A of E)
3 Gray's Inn Square
London
WC1R 5AH
T: 020 7430 0333
E:admin@academy-experts.org
www.academyofexperts.org

There is also the Institute of Expert Witnesses which provides specialist advice and support in accident cases, contactable on 0117 986 2194 and enquiries@iew.org.uk. The Law Society of Scotland has issued a Code of Practice for Expert Witnesses, as there are some marked differences in practice between Scotland and England. This is available at www.lawscot.org.uk/members/business-support/expert-witness/expert-witness-code-of-practice.

Procedure

The EWI and A of E have produced a joint Code of Practice for Experts which was approved by the Master of the Rolls and Chairman of the Civil Justice Committee on 22 June 2005. This Code of Practice, the Civil Procedure Rules Part 35 and Practice Direction 35 and the Guidance for the Instruction of Experts to give Evidence in Civil Claims 2012 are all available online. On 26 June 2006 the Code of Practice for Experts was endorsed by the Master of the Rolls and the President of the Queen's Bench Division for use in criminal proceedings.

A typical Expert Report will set out the names of the Petitioner and the Respondent, cite the case number and refer to the Expert Report by the named Expert and the date.

Under CPR Part 35, Expert evidence is to be restricted to that which is reasonably required to resolve the proceedings. The Expert's duty is to help the Court on matters within their expertise, which overrides any obligation to the person from whom Experts have received instructions or by whom they are paid. The Court has to give permission for expert evidence to be adduced. The court may require the appointment of a single joint Expert or direct a discussion between each party's Expert and require them to propose a statement setting out those issues on which they agree, or the reasons for disagreeing. Experts may request the court for directions.

Practice Direction 35 supplements CPR Part 35 and requires Experts to assist the court by providing objective unbiased opinions on matters within their expertise and they should not assume the role of an advocate. They must consider all material facts and disclose where a question or issue falls outside their expertise. The Expert's report is addressed to the court not the instructing party.

It is essential, in practice, to circulate to the instructing solicitors a draft for confirmation of factual accuracy. This usually flushes out further questions or matters raised by a party that may then be addressed in the final Report.

Practice Direction 35 paragraph 3.2:

> 'An Expert's report must:
>
> 1 give details of the Expert's qualifications;
> 2 give details of any literature or other material which has been relied on in making the report;
> 3 contain a statement setting out the substance of all facts and instructions which are material to the opinions expressed in the report or upon which those opinions are based;
> 4 make clear which of the facts stated in the report are within the Expert's own knowledge;
> 5 say who carried out any examination, measurement, test or experiment which the Expert has used for the report, give the qualifications of that person, and say whether or not the test or experiment has been carried out under the Expert's supervision;
> 6 where there is a range of opinion on the matters dealt with in the report–
>   a) summarise the range of opinions; and
>   b) give reasons for the Expert's own opinion;
> 7 contain a summary of the conclusions reached;
> 8 if the Expert is not able to give an opinion without qualification, state the qualification; and
> 9 contain a statement that the Expert–
>   a) understands their duty to the Court, and has complied with that duty; and
>   b) is aware of the requirements of Part 35, this Practice Direction and the Guidance for Instruction of Experts to give Evidence in Civil Claims.'

The court may direct that access be given to available information. The court or the parties may require the Experts to discuss the case to identify areas of agreement or reasons for disagreement, and how these could be resolved and identify any further material issues not raised and the extent to which they are agreed. The Expert is in no way the advocate for the party instructing him and must be very careful not to try and "help" his instructing solicitors by taking a view which would not withstand cross-examination.

Cresswell J in *National Justice Cia Naviera SA v Prudential Assurance Co Ltd* (The Ikarian Reefer) [1993] 2 Lloyd's Rep 68 at 81–82 defined the duties of Expert Witnesses.

> 'The duties and responsibilities of Expert Witnesses in civil cases include the following:
>
> 1 Expert evidence presented to the court should be, and should be seen to be, the independent product of the Expert uninfluenced as to form or content by

the exigencies of litigation (*Whitehouse v Jordan* [1981] 1 WLR 246, 256 per Lord Wilberforce).

2 An Expert Witness should provide independent assistance to the court by way of objective unbiased opinion in relation to matters within his expertise (see *Polivitte Ltd v Commercial Union Assurance Co plc* [1981] 1 Lloyd's Rep 379, 386, per Garland J and *in Re J* [1990] FCR192 per Cazalet J). An Expert Witness … should never assume the role of an advocate.

3 An Expert Witness should state the facts or assumptions upon which his opinion is based. He should not omit to consider material facts which could detract from his concluded opinion (*in Re J*).

4 An Expert Witness should make it clear when a particular question or issue falls outside his expertise.

5 If an Expert's opinion is not properly researched because he considers that insufficient data is available, then this must be stated with an indication that the opinion is no more than a provisional one (*in Re J*). In cases where the Expert Witness who has prepared a report could not assert that the report contained the truth, the whole truth and nothing but the truth without some qualification, that qualification should be stated in the report (*Derby & Co Ltd v Weldon* The Times 9 November 1990, per Staughton LJ).

6 If, after exchange of reports, an Expert Witness changes his view on a material matter having read the other side's Expert's report or for any other reason, such change of view should be communicated (through legal representatives) to the other side without delay and, when appropriate, to the court.

7 Where expert evidence refers to photographs, plans, calculations, analyses, measurements, survey reports or other similar documents, these must be provided to the opposite party at the same time as the exchange of reports.'

Anglo Group Plc, Winther Brown and Co Ltd v Winther Brown and Co Ltd, BML (Office Computers) Ltd, Anglo Group Plc, BML (Office Computers) Ltd [2000] EWHC Technology 127 was heard by His Honour Judge Toulmin CMG QC who stated:

'108. In the case of *The Ikarian Reefer* [1993] 2 Lloyds Rep 68, at 81–82 Cresswell J analysed the role of the expert witness. The analysis, needs to be extended in accordance with the Woolf reforms of civil procedure. 109.

1. An expert witness should at all stages in the procedure, on the basis of the evidence as he understands it, provide independent assistance to the court and the parties by way of objective unbiased opinion in relation to matters within his expertise. This applies as much to the initial meetings of experts as to evidence at trial. An expert witness should never assume the role of an advocate.
2. The expert's evidence should normally be confined to technical matters on which the court will be assisted by receiving an explanation, or to evidence of common professional practice. The expert witness should not give evidence or opinions as to what the expert himself would have done in similar circumstances or otherwise seek to usurp the role of the judge.
3. He should co-operate with the expert of the other party or parties in attempting to narrow the technical issues in dispute at the earliest possible stage of the procedure and to eliminate or place in context any peripheral issues. He should co-operate with the other expert(s) in attending without prejudice meetings as necessary and in seeking to find areas of agreement and to define precisely arrears of disagreement to be set out in the joint statement of experts ordered by the court.

4. The expert evidence presented to the court should be, and be seen to be, the independent product of the expert uninfluenced as to form or content by the exigencies of the litigation.
5. An expert witness should state the facts or assumptions upon which his opinion is based. He should not omit to consider material facts which could detract from his concluded opinion.
6. An expert witness should make it clear when a particular question or issue falls outside his expertise.
7. Where an expert is of the opinion that his conclusions are based on inadequate factual information he should say so explicitly.
8. An expert should be ready to reconsider his opinion, and if appropriate, to change his mind when he has received new information or has considered the opinion of the other expert. He should do so at the earliest opportunity.

110. It is clear from the Judgment of Lord Woolf MR in *Stevens v Gullis* (Court of Appeal Transcript of 27 July 1999) that the new Civil Procedure Rules underline the existing duty which an expert owes to the Court as well as to the party which he represents.

111. The formulation set out above is also consistent with the judgment of Laddie J in *Cala Homes (South) Ltd v Alfred McAlpine Homes East Ltd* [1995] FSR 818 at 841 where Laddie J criticised a not dissimilar approach by an expert to that of FMC in this case. It is also consistent with the judgment of Pumfrey J in *Cantor Fitzgerald v Tradition UK Ltd* Judgment Transcript of 15 April 1999 paragraph 70 where he emphasised the particular importance of experts being scrupulously independent in highly technical cases like computer cases.

112. It needs to be recognised that a failure to take such an independent approach is not in the interest of the clients who retain the expert, since an expert taking a partisan approach, resulting in a failure to resolve before trial or at trial issues on which experts should agree, inflates the costs of resolving the dispute and may prevent the parties from resolving their disputes long before trial.'

He went on to find that neither of the experts named conducted themselves as independent expert witnesses in the manner acceptable to the court and he was unable to rely on their evidence in support of Winther Brown and Co Ltd as expert evidence.

Expert's Report

The Judicial Committee of the Academy of Experts produced a Model Form of Expert's Report because:

'1.1 Some senior judges have expressed concern at the length of many Experts' reports and at the tendency to mix matters of fact and opinion.

1.2 The Judicial Committee of the Academy has commented that the hallmarks of a good report include

1.2.1 a stand-alone, concise, user-friendly format, expressed in the first person singular by the person whose opinion has been given or who adopts as his own the opinion of others.
1.2.2 text which is arranged in short sentences and paragraphs.
1.2.3 judicious use of appendices.
1.2.4 matters of fact being kept separate from matters of opinion. Conclusions should be given in the final section of the report before appendices. They should be cross-referenced to the text which supports the Conclusions.

1.3 Each opinion expressed in the report must be the opinion of the writer whether it was formed by the writer or formed by others and adopted by the writer as his own.

1.4 The following must be identified separately and distinguished:

1.4.1 facts which the writer is asked to assume;
1.4.2 facts which the writer observed for himself eg the results of experiments, investigations, etc, carried out by the writer himself;
1.4.3 facts which others, acting on behalf of the writer, observed, identifying the persons concerned;
1.4.4 opinions of others upon which the writer relies in forming his own opinion;
1.4.5 opinions of others which the writer accepts but upon which the writer cannot comment authoritatively.

1.5 The Model Form of report has been developed with these comments in mind and with the aim of assisting both Experts and those instructing, to address the relevant issues in the most direct way.

1.6 The model is intended as a guideline only. There may be valid reasons for departing from it and/or introducing additional sections, depending on the nature of the instructions and the dispute.

1.7 Since the Model Form was first published, new Civil and Criminal Procedure Rules have been introduced in England and Wales and other jurisdictions. These have largely taken into account the Model Form which was commended in Lord Woolf's report "Access to Justice". Users of the Model Form must always take care to comply with the requirements of the jurisdiction in which the report will be used.'

The Academy of Experts has a Code of Practice with which an Expert should comply.

The Code

1 Experts shall not do anything in the course of practising as an Expert, in any manner which compromises or impairs or is likely to compromise or impair any of the following:

   a the Expert's independence, impartiality, objectivity and integrity,
   b the Expert's duty to the Court or Tribunal,
   c the good repute of the Expert or of Experts generally,
   d the Expert's proper standard of work,
   e the Expert's duty to maintain confidentiality.

2 An Expert who is retained or employed in any contentious proceeding shall not enter into any arrangement which could compromise his impartiality nor make his fee dependent on the outcome of the case nor should he accept any benefits other than his fee and expenses.

3 An Expert should not accept instructions in any matter where there is an actual or potential conflict of interests. Notwithstanding this rule, if full disclosure is made to the judge or to those appointing him, the Expert may in appropriate cases accept instructions when those concerned specifically acknowledge the disclosure. Should an actual or potential conflict occur

after instructions have been accepted, the Expert shall immediately notify all concerned and in appropriate cases resign his appointment.

4 An Expert shall for the protection of his client maintain with a reputable insurer proper insurance for an adequate indemnity.

5 Experts shall not publicise their practices in any manner which may reasonably be regarded as being in bad taste. Publicity must not be inaccurate or misleading in any way.

6 An Expert shall comply with all appropriate Codes of Practice and Guidelines.

The Expert Witness Institute has similar requirements.

Meeting of Experts

Where two or more Experts are involved, they would normally be expected to meet to discuss their draft reports to try and agree the matters covered by their expertise, and pinpoint the matters on which their views differ.

The Trial

When the dispute comes to trial, if it has not been settled, each Expert will be available for cross-examination and be given the chance to explain his or her opinion.

This should enable the court to endorse the matters on which they agree and make an informed view on where they differ to enable it to come to a view on the relevant matters and decide which of the differing views it prefers, or, quite likely, decide matters somewhere between the Experts' opinions.

Under cross-examination the Expert should listen carefully to the questions put to him, or her, and reply to the judge, not to counsel, which can be counter-intuitive. Some counsel like to take advantage of their greater experience in court protocol to try and wrong foot the Expert, who should remember that they are in court because they have a greater knowledge of the matters within their Expertise than either counsel or the judge. If this were not so their reports and Expert evidence would not have been necessary and the judge would not have given permission for Expert evidence to have been approved. An expert witness who fails to appreciate that his duty is to assist the court, which overrides any obligation to the person who instructs him, may have a costs order made against him, *Phillips v Symes* [2004] EWHC 2330 (Ch).

> **Focus**
>
> The primary duty of the expert is to assist the court.

23.12 Court's resolution of differences between experts

In *F v F* [2003] 1 FLR 847 the values of the shares in the family business formed the major portion of the spouses assets, so that a clean break was not feasible, appropriate or just. An order was made for a transfer of the matrimonial property, two endowment policies, a lump sum of less than £60,000 and a pension sharing order for 50% of the main pension fund, with periodical payments of £75,000 per annum, where the joint assets were worth about £3,480,000. The value of the shares in the principal company was put at £2.119m by the husband and £2.996m on behalf of the wife. In this case the points of substance between the expert valuers boiled down to a difference in the amount added back to reflect excessive remuneration, the second element of disagreement related to the choice of P/E ratio. The judgment continued:

> 'The second element of disagreement relates to the choice of the P/E ratio. The value of this disparity in terms of its effect upon the two valuations amounts to some £340,000. Mr Walton (for the wife) took as his base-point the Private Company Price Index in fact created and published by the firm of which Mr Nedas (for the husband) is a partner, BDO Stoy Hayward. He then applied a discount factor of 40% which he regarded as appropriate in the light of the general reduction in P/E ratios recently, the relatively small size of the company and the fact that it operates in a relatively narrow sector. He therefore discounted the ratio from 12.5 to 7.5, and applied the lower figure to what he regarded as future maintainable profits for the appropriate year. As that year he selected the current calendar year for which actual figures are available for the first 8 months, and a projection supplied for the last four.
>
> Mr Nedas arrived at a P/E ratio of 6.53 by a quite different route. His starting point was the FTSE Leisure Sector P/E ratio of 14.51 published at the beginning of the month. That relates to public quoted companies. To this he applied a discount of 55%. As to 45%, this was a deduction (in turn derived from two separate indexes) to allow for the fact that this is a private company, and as to 10% it was to reflect the small size of this company.
>
> I do have a question mark in my mind, developed since the conclusion of submissions and therefore not canvassed for comment at the time. Should not the 45% for the difference between public and private have been taken off first, and only then (from the resultant 55%) the 10% for size deducted, rather than both in the same calculation? That seems to me more logical. The effect would be to increase the P/E ratio Mr Nedas applied for the current year from 6.53 to 7.18 more than half way to Mr Walton's ratio of 7.5. I have not (I emphasise) heard argument on the point, and therefore I have disregarded it, nor have I allowed it to affect the conclusions at which I had already arrived (and which it would only serve marginally to fortify rather than to alter). If, however, it is sound, then it means that the valuation for the shares at which I have arrived is likely to be on the conservative side.
>
> That, however, was not the whole difference. For Mr Nedas took into account profits and/or projected profits not only for the calendar year 2002, but also for the calendar year 2003. To his own estimate of this year's profit (based on the same forecast but applying different add-backs) he applied the 6.53 P/E ratio. But in relation to the wholly prospective forecast profits he applied the lower P/E ratio of 5, on the basis that they have yet, in their entirety, to be earned and are therefore more speculative. He then took the average of the two figures.
>
> What I must confess still seems odd to me is that the result of applying a lower multiple for next year's forecast profits is to factor into the resulting average a valuation ingredient for next year which is some £340,000 less than his valuation would be if based only on the current year. Yet next year's forecast shows increased turnover and profits, and indeed (after add-backs) an increase in net

profitability for the company form £417,200 to £465,500. That is an 11.58% increase in adjusted profits, admittedly only forecast. The application of the lower P/E ratio of 5 as against 6.53 results, however, in a 23.43% decrease in the pro rata contribution made to the result by that year's projected enhanced out-turn, which reduced proportion Mr Nedas has incorporated into his ultimate valuation.

I find myself, therefore, more favourably inclined to the view of Mr Walton, who was not prepared in any event to base his valuation on next year's projection, but also disagreed with his colleague's methodology.

I have in fact conflated the second discrepancy (P/E methodology and selection) and the third (whether to rely on the 2003 projection). Together they account for roughly £500,000 of the difference between the two accountants.

I am simply not in a position to say, as between two experienced accountants, which of them is correct (or more correct) in asserting that their respective selected P/E ratio is "more scientific" than the other. I shall therefore adopt a P/E ratio of 7. But for the reasons which I hope I have clearly stated, I shall apply it to his year's adjusted net profit of £473,900 computed by Mr Walton, rather than the lower figure for which Mr Nedas contends. Net of disposal costs and CGT this produces a value for the parties' combined 94.7% shareholding in the principal company of £2,721,585. When the agreed net value of £72,000 for the associated company is added to this, the figure which I shall take as the net value of the company interests is £2.8m.'

In the event, in the two-month period between handing down of the judgment and the hearing to finalise the order, the husband offered and the wife accepted lump sum instalments totalling £1,062,500 in place of the £210,000 proffered during the hearing, so that in the event a clean break order was made.

In *S v S* [2006] EWHC 2339 (Fam) a company specialising in contracting work for local authorities had to be valued. Singer J stated (at para 32):

'In April 2004 the accountants were a mere £14m apart weighing in for W at £24.75m and for H at £10.61m. They briefly narrowed their differences when they reported jointly in July 2004 each moving about £1.m towards the other. Mr Nedas in his first report shortly before the abortive hearing before Baron J in June last year retreated to a value of £4.66m to which Mr Lobbenberg responded the following month with the revised valuation of £23.5m. But when they met to see what common ground there was they discovered that there was even less than had been apparent. Mr Nedas reducing his valuation to £4.35m while Mr Lobbenberg increased his to something over £30m (revised on the eve of the hearing down to £27.2m). By then however Mr Nedas valued H's shares in T Ltd at no pounds at all. For the purpose of the hearing however (and for reasons which do not matter for present purposes) the application preceded upon the basis that H's advisers took H's shares to be worth either £4.35m or £3.73m (to include the value of his own preference shares).

33 I said something about the difficulties which confront the parties and the judge in such a situation and my first instance decision in the case now revealed as *Miller: M v M (short marriage: clean break)* [2005] EWHC 528 from which I forebear to quote in this judgment. There the valuation differential was between £12m and £18m a mere 50% of the lower figure whereas here the difference is £23.47m, the difference between £3.73m and £27.2m is 630% of the lower figure.'

He continued (at para 44):

'It is of large significance that neither party's outcome suggestion depends on a finding as to the shares at current value. Both party's Counsel acknowledged this.

That did not however prevent vituperative contention between Mr Lobbenberg and Mr Nedas over many aspects of their respective approach to the exercise.

45 They did agree that the appraisal should be on the basis of T Ltd's net sustainable earnings. They disagreed as to the accounting periods to be taken (Mr Nedas relying more on forecast than did Mr Lobbenberg); the multiple to be applied to arrive at an enterprise value for the company (a capitalisation of its earnings); the net debt position of the company; what if any other companies might be illustrative comparables; and effect of differing assumptions as to the timing of repayments to the outside shareholders. All these taken together significantly contributed to the divergence in the value each attributed. But the major disagreement and one which gave rise to the most serious exchange of epithets related to the depreciation charges in T Ltd's accounts and forecast. Mr Nedas contended for an evaluation known as EBITA as the basis to establish maintainable earnings. The acronym signifies "Earnings Before Interest Tax and Amortisation" and involves writing back these three items. Mr Lobbenberg maintains strenuously that the appropriate methodology was to evaluate on the basis of EBITDA writing back in addition the depreciation charge in the accounts which he took to be £6m. If he is mistaken in that view on the multiple he adopted of 4.5 his valuation would reduce by £27m although on this changed basis he would have been entitled to reconsider the appropriate multiples.

46 Emphasising as I do that in the event any adjudication by me in this dispute does not affect the outcome of the case I confess that I am not persuaded by Mr Lobbenberg on the depreciation point. This company tends to spend each year on new and replacement plant and equipment an amount broadly equal to (and in 2001 to 2004 more than) the depreciation charged in the accounts in line with accounting and fiscal requirements. I am satisfied that the nature of its business requires this expenditure and that it is imperative, if the company is to continue to generate the "maintainable earnings" which are a basic constituent of each accountant's methodology. In the context of T Ltd, it seems to me, incurring the cost of necessary renewal and maintenance of plant and equipment is as much a pre-requisite of bringing in the turnover and the profit as paying the workforce. Mr Lobbenberg agreed that anyone interested in acquiring the company would take the depreciation into account recognising it as a recurring reality. He suggested that this would form part of the due diligence enquiry. Due diligence would show the expenditure as real and necessary and I do not understand why it should not be treated as a legitimate expense of the business and thus not to be added back in the search for a maintainable earnings figure.'

Focus

- The court proceedings often result in the parties coming to a compromise agreement, which the court will endorse if it considers it fair.
- Maintainable earnings need to take into account the company's requirements to replace its assets as they are used up.

23.13 Basis of valuation

In the divorce case of *C v C* on 9 January 2006 (Northern Ireland unreported judgments), Master Redpath stated:

'The exercise of valuing a minority shareholding in a private limited company can be a difficult and complex one. In virtually every case the articles of association will limit the right of the minority shareholder to dispose of his shares and in most cases they will limit that right to either selling the shares back to the company or to the other shareholders. There are a number of ways of valuing such shareholdings:

(1) dividend basis – this involves looking at the record of the company and paying dividends or profits to the shareholders and the likelihood of those profits being sustained so as such dividends and profits will be paid in the future. At that stage a multiplier is applied which is often in the region of 5 years.
(2) net assets basis – if a trading company is not performing particularly well this is the basis that is often used. This involves essentially looking at the assets of the company or companies in question and assessing what they will realise and then coming at a figure after deducting liabilities.
(3) earnings basis – this is often used in relation to more substantial concerns with a history of growth and potential growth. This will look at the earning power of the company rather than its assets.
(4) goodwill – this generally applies to smaller companies and an attempt will be made to value goodwill where it is essentially a price that a willing purchaser would pay to purchase the business on the base of its customer base and its profitability.'

Both accountants approached this case on the basis of valuing the company on a net assets basis. It is quite clear in this particular case that was the correct approach.

'The shares in XP Ltd are owned by XH Ltd. XH Ltd is owned 20% by the respondent, 10% by the petitioner, 20% by the respondent's brother with 10% to the respondent's brother's wife and the remaining 40% to the respondent's sisters.

… the accountant for the petitioner relied on a valuation of the land at £2.6m less £180,000 capital gains tax to which he added £1,479,133 to give a total valuation of £3,938,896. He did not discount this valuation as a result of the majority shareholdings. His report states at para 104:- "I note these shares are all held by a small number of members of the C family as shown in paragraph 12. The brothers are X and Z C and their wives own between 60% of the company and the remaining shares are held by their two sisters. In these circumstances that the company is owned entirely by one family with the majority concentrated in a smaller group I believe that the shareholdings will act in concert and it is appropriate that the value of the shares in J and C on a pro rata basis treating the company as a quasi-partnership …

It is clear that I will not be ordering a forced sale of the shares in either of these companies. Accordingly I am of the view that the property valuation exercise for the court to take is simply to value the holding on an open market basis.'

In *C v C*, Master Redpath also said that:

'… the simple fact of the matter is that the vast majority of these family owned companies operate as quasi-partnerships.

In fact this issue has been considered by the courts recently. In the case of *G v G (Financial Provision: Equal Division)* [2002] 2 FLR 1143 the case involved a valuation of the husband's shareholding in a private limited company not unlike this case. At page 1151 Coleridge J states: "I cannot seriously envisage a

> situation where the husband in this case will be forced to sell his interest in this company on the open market in circumstances which a discount would be forced upon him. It is just conceivable that he may sell to a friendly purchaser but in those circumstances I am sure he would get full value. Accordingly I think it is artificial to apply a discount to the husband's shares in this company or for that matter the wife's and I shall not do so."
>
> This point was also considered at length by Singer J in the recent case of *M v M (Short Marriage: Clean Break)* [2005] 2 FLR 533). I have no words to mirror the eloquence of Mr Justice Singer and accordingly I will quote at length what he has to say about cases of this type. The learned judge states at page 547 para 57 and thereafter: "this if I may say so seems even more an exercise in throwing dice or playing Russian roulette with one-armed bandits than does relying on a judge's instinct for what is fair when he weighs a gamut of circumstances and produces his or her result out of the hat of fair outcome. For in reality the uncertainty and the element of chance (or as the French would put it 'hazard') inherent in such a forensic valuation gamble are at least as daunting as the unpredictability of the product of the s 25 exercise".'

In *Hodge v Hodge* (Scottish Court Opinions, 28 November 2006) it was held, in a Scottish divorce case, that a 25% shareholding in a family company should, in the circumstances, be valued on the basis of a pro rata proportion of the company as a whole and then subject to a 30% discount for being a minority shareholding.

The Sheriff Principal commented:

> 'The value of the defender's 25% shareholding has to be determined in light of the nature of the shareholding. It is a minority shareholding. The defender has 25% of the voting rights in the company. When his shareholding is sold, albeit with the consent of the other shareholders, the purchaser will have the same voting rights as he has. Although the company is currently conducted on the basis of a quasi-partnership and no decision is taken without the full agreement of all four family members, there is no legal requirement for that situation to continue on sale. I do not accept the position put forward by Counsel for the Pursuer that the position of the purchaser would be exactly the same as that of the defender in respect that no decisions would be made without his consent. A purchaser would be a minority shareholder with a 25% voting right in the affairs of the company. I consider that the Sheriff was correct to take the view that a discount required to be considered in view of the minority nature of the defender's shareholding.'

It will be noted that the question of whether or not a discount is appropriate in valuing a minority interest of shares in a family company is far from clear. The case law is ambivalent with judges applying a discount in some cases but not others. The authors' opinion is that in the absence of a court order the reality is that shares in family companies run as a quasi partnership do not change hands to strangers on a discounted basis. Either the company is sold as a whole and the sale proceeds divided pro rata to the shareholding or an external shareholder is introduced into the company with the consent of all the shareholders to take an active role in running a company and effectively joining the quasi-partnership, or is brought in on the basis of particular skills and issued with new shares or options, or is acquiring an interest as a venture capitalist providing additional working capital and management advice in return for the issue of further shares with preferential rights and appropriate conversion rights.

Therefore if fairness is the goal to be sought in ancillary relief proceedings a discount for a minority interest may be inappropriate.

Focus

In a divorce, a discount for a minority shareholding may not be appropriate.

23.14 Expenditure on experts

Master Redpath in *C v C* (see **23.13**) continued to quote Mr Justice Singer's views on this topic:

> 'This is particularly so in a case such as this where the accountancy fees involved in producing 200 pages of forensic reports with such irreconcilable positions trenchantly maintained throughout are horrific. I do not have a separate figure for the forensic accountants' charges but my belief is they are likely to make up the lions share of the disbursements including VAT which total just over £200,000 at the commencement of the hearing before me.
>
> It does seem to me to be wholly wrong and artificial particularly in this case were I to be bound to apply the yardstick of equality as a measure of fairness to a matrimonial estate the scale of which depends so significantly on the hypothetical valuation arrived at by judicial evaluation of the experts and their methodology. That judicial evaluation must be formulated by reference to the highly sophisticated and abstracted and in many areas vehemently contradictory opinions of experts who end up £6m apart, 33⅓% of a maximum valuation of £18m what confidence can that give the judge or the parties in the validity of the exercise which can throw up such disparity but is yet to be the basis of fixing the matrimonial award fairly.
>
> The answer in my judgment and at least in this case is that I derive no assistance at all from the minutiae contained in these reports or from the oral evidence of the protagonists (for such they have become) in support of the soundness of their own position and the transparent baselessness of the others. Nor is the process of sifting wheat from chaff assisted by the sophistication which experienced Counsel bring to the fray each emphasising what may or may not be the weaknesses in the other experts presentation. If I may just put in a word for this charge: I have some pretence to a degree of numeracy and some acquaintance with the basic process of share valuation. But when confronted with expert witnesses of the degree of experience and sophistication in their rarefied specialities as Mr Nedas and Mr Clokey, each apparently as reasonable and persuasive in the witness box as the other, how am I to choose between them or independently to arrive at my own figure in contradiction to them both.
>
> I content myself in this case with the observation that they may both be right without either of them being wrong. The future value of these shares is unfathomable in this case in my view their present value is inestimable. But in any case, neither of these experts can conclude the possibility that events may dictate that all H gets from his shares is the £200,000 he paid for them. That outcome may not be probable but am I nevertheless bound to ignore it?
>
> Can I also ignore the even more potent consideration that at the present time the most obvious certainty is that H could not do anything to realise these shares

> at more than their par value. How then can it make sense to base so large an element of W's award on so uncertain a foundation. The reality is that the shares are in my view simply not susceptible to sensible valuation as at the date of hearing. It is pointless to try to ascribe a single value to them when the true range is form £1 to the limits of the sky. But I repeat neither party proposed treating W as a beneficiary of the proceeds of disposal of any specified number of shares, no doubt because she is not prepared to await the uncertain event at its unpredictable date and he may hope to achieve an award to her which is based on an underestimate of whatever may be their eventual proceeds.'

Master Redpath continued:

> 'There are great uncertainties in this case and whilst the accountants and the accountancy evidence was of some value to me it did not solve with any certainty any of the problems that I face in relation to making a decision in this case. Accordingly I intend to divide the assets initially on an equalisation of property basis only and to leave their respective parties with the respective shareholdings in both XP Ltd and XH Ltd.
>
> Another reason why I have adopted this approach is that I do not wish the respondent to become involved in a forced sale which could be regarded as reducing the value of his various shareholdings. I am aware that the result which I am arriving at in this case may not be to the liking of either party but that it's the hazard that is entered into when a decision is taken to run cases such as this. I also appreciate that it may not produce what might be regarded as a clean break between the parties but for reasons that I will return to later, a clean break may in fact be produced by this approach in due course.'

Focus

Sometimes, the value of the shares is so uncertain that the only course of action is to leave them where they are, but this in turn leads to problems of excluding the minority shareholder and the possibility of prejudicial conduct proceedings.

23.15 Date of valuation and other practical issues

In the divorce litigation of *N v N* [2001] 2 FLR 69, Coleridge J had to deal with a practical case which:

> 'has illustrated some of the very real practical difficulties which have to be confronted when the court strives to achieve the overall aim now set forth in the recent case of *White v White* [2000] 2 FLR 981 I would perhaps over paraphrase that aim as normally the achieving of a fair result by the adoption of a starting point / yardstick of broad equality of outcome for each party.'

The main problem was a company, X, in the services industry, which formed the most valuable asset in the case, which had been started before the parties were married but after their relationship had begun. In this case the husband had a 50.05% shareholding in the X companies and a 40% minority interest in the associated Z company which operated in a complementary area of the services industry. The valuers were broadly able to agree the maintainable income of the two companies but not the appropriate multiplier to be applied. The expert witness for the husband had produced three reports during which his multiplier had ranged from one to two and his precise methodology had also altered from time to time. The wife's expert valuer had increased his original multiplier from three to four after discussions with people he knew in the industry. The judge commented:

> 'It is evident from hearing both experts that this area of valuation task is somewhat subjective. Mr B candidly admitted that much of his opinion consisted of a sense of what he felt to be the correct multiplier. In the end I doubt whether Mr F's methodology is really any more sophisticated than that either.
>
> Adopting a multiplier of 4 the gross value of the company would be £6.3m or thereabouts. Adopting a multiplier of 3 the value of £4.4m and adopting a multiplier of 2, the value is £2.6m.'

The judge found that:

> 'a proper overall value for this company for the purposes of these proceedings is £4m gross. That presupposes a multiplier of 2.75 and I think that is perfectly realistic. So I shall take the husband's 50% shareholding as being worth about £2m. The capital gains tax calculation on various different valuations has been agreed. On this valuation of £2m it is about £250,000 so for the purposes of this part of the case, I propose to adopt the figure of £1.75m as the appropriate figure to be included in the schedule.'

It was argued on behalf of the husband that there had been a real increase in the value of X since the separation, whereas the wife argued that the traditional valuation date is that at the date when the hearing takes place. The judge commented:

> 'I am quite sure that even now in most cases that is the correct date when the valuation should be applied. But I think the court must have an eye to the valuation at the date of separation where there has been a very significant change accounted for by more than just inflation or deflation; natural inflationary pressures on particular assets, for instance the value of a house moving up or down in the housing market.
>
> In this case the increase in value is attributable to extra investment of time, effort and money by the husband since separation and I do take into account the exceptionally steep increase in the turnover figures since the date of separation. However having done so it must be put in the context of the wife's continuing contribution too which similarly, did not cease at the date of separation. She too has continued to play the valuable part that she had done throughout the marriage in looking after the home of the children.'

The judge also stated:

> 'Doing the very best I can to take into account all the complicated and inter-relating circumstances of this case and particularly bearing in mind the nature of the assets from which any sum which I order to be made has to be extracted, in my judgement fairness to each party is properly reflected in an overall sum payable to the wife of £1m. I have not forgotten the latent value of the accountancy practice or on the other hand the costs paid by the husband.'

The judge further commented:

> 'I am conscious also that it is not numerically precisely 50% of the value of the assets on the schedule (it is nearer 40%) but in my judgement the exercise

> upon which the court is engaged nowadays is not just one of adding all the assets together and dividing them simplistically by 2. The court has to look very carefully not only at the nature of the assets but also the steps necessary to achieve their liquidation. The target in all cases is fairness. In my judgment this is a fair figure.
>
> How and at what rate should that sum be paid? It is at this stage as I have said that the court needs to proceed with sensitivity and creativity so that the values upon which the court's assumptions have been made are in fact realised. That can only be done if opportunity is given for orderly and prudent disposal where appropriate. If that course is not adopted there is a danger that only forced sale values will be achieved which would greatly be to the detriment of the paying party and so unfair … the payment of the £1m, will be made in the following way and at the following rate. In the first place the former matrimonial home will be transferred to the wife. As that is currently mortgaged to the tune of £200,000, the only equity being transferred to her by that route is some £50,000. That transfer will take place as soon as reasonably practicable subject to the existing mortgages. No doubt the mortgagors (sic) will have to give their consent and the husband will have to provide the appropriate guarantee for the continuation of the payment of the mortgage until redemption by him.
>
> A further sum of £100,000 will be paid to the wife on or before 31 July 2001 to meet her shorter term needs. That will leave the sum of £850,000 to be paid by the husband. Of that sum £200,000 will be paid by the husband not later than 31 January 2002. That sum will be paid to redeem the mortgages on the former matrimonial home. In the meantime, as I have indicated, the husband must continue paying the instalments due on it.
>
> That will leave the sum of £650,000 which will be paid by the husband to the wife upon the sale of X and / or Z group or 30 April 2003 whichever shall first occur. There will be appropriate injunctions and charges over the husband's interests in the X / Z group to provide the wife with security for the outstanding sum.'

The judge also dealt with periodical payments and school fees.

Focus

Reaching a fair and practical solution, when assets are not readily realisable at full value, is not a simple matter.

Division B
Valuation examples

1. Mock valuation report in *Re Lynall, Lynall v IRC*
2. Mock valuation report in *Re Holt*
3. Sparkco Ltd – fair value
4. Diplodocus Ltd – valuation of deferred shares at 13 April 2004
5. Salamander Marketing Consultants Ltd – valuation of shares for tax purposes
6. Motorco – valuation of goodwill on incorporation
7. Logo Properties Limited – valuation of shares for inheritance tax purposes
8. Lavender Systems Limited – EMI valuation

Example 1

Mock valuation report in *Re Lynall, Lynall v IRC*

It would seem to make sense to try and reconcile the court decision with the kind of valuation report recommended in **Chapter 19**. It should be emphasised that this report has been compiled by the authors from published information and is not related to any actual reports prepared by the experts in that case. It should be remembered that the information to be made available was changed following the *Lynall* decision and the valuation is made on the assumption that information on a possible flotation was confidential. There was a placing of ordinary shares in July 1963 at an equivalent price of £7.16s. per share.

The executors of Mrs Nellie Lynall deceased.

Dear Sirs,
We have been asked to prepare a valuation of 67,980 ordinary shares of £1 each in Linread Ltd, 'the company', held by Mrs Nellie Lynall at the date of her death on 21 May 1962.

Purposes of valuation

The shares are to be valued for the purposes of estate duty.

Basis of valuation

The shares are to be valued in accordance with FA 1894, s 7(5) which provides:

> 'The principal value of any property shall be estimated to be the price which, in the opinion of the commissioners, such property would fetch if sold in the open market at the time of death of the deceased.'

Various principles emerge from case law which assist in the interpretation of these words:

(1) The test is what the purchaser would pay not what the vendor would receive after costs.
(2) The market must be an open market without specially excluding anyone or specially including anyone; *IRC v Crossman* [1937] AC 26 at 73.
(3) Where the articles of association, as here, restrict the right to transfer, nevertheless the market must be open in the sense that it is assumed that the hypothetical purchaser will be entered on the register of members, but

thereafter will hold the shares subject to the restrictions in the articles; *IRC v Crossman* [1937] AC 26.

(4) The sale to be assumed is a hypothetical sale between hypothetical parties. The fact that Mrs Lynall was a director has to be disregarded; *Re Aschrott* [1927] 1 Ch 313 at 322; *Winter (Sutherland's Trustees) v IRC* [1963] AC 235 at 256; *Duke of Buccleuch v IRC* [1967] 1 AC 506 at 524.

(5) Directors owe no duty to a shareholder-vendor to disclose either orally or by way of documents the secrets of the boardroom; *Percival v Wright* [1902] 2 Ch 421 at 425.

(6) The directors would be under a positive duty not to disclose confidential information. What the directors would be prepared to disclose is a question of fact.

(7) The hypothetical sale is deemed to take place at the time of death; *Duke of Buccleuch v IRC* [1967] 1 AC 506.

(8) Any subsequent placing of the ordinary shares unless it were known to be in contemplation at 21 May 1962 has no relevance since it would be a totally different sale in totally different conditions; *Earl of Ellesmere v IRC* [1918] 2 KB 735 at 739; *IRC v Marr's Trustees* (1906) 44 SLR 647; *Re Holt* (1953) 32 ATC 402.

(9) Subsequent accounts can only be used to see what sort of forecast would have been given if the purchaser had asked for one, not to find out what actually happened; *Salvesen's Trustees v IRC* (1930) 9 ATC 43. Nevertheless the court has in many cases considered the accounts for the period current at the valuation date.

(10) There are no implied warranties or conditions and no assumption is to be made that the employees will enter into service contracts.

Capital structure

Shares issued and fully paid:

241,700 ordinary shares of £1 each.

Shares held by Mrs Lynall:

67,980 ordinary shares of £1 each.

Percentage of ordinary shares held by Mrs Lynall:

28.126%

Restriction of rights

The articles of association of the company contain stringent restrictions on transfer, in particular article 8, which provides as follows:

> 'The Directors may in their absolute and uncontrolled discretion refuse to register any proposed transfer of shares and regulation 24 of Part I of Table "A" shall be modified accordingly and no preference or ordinary share in the company shall be transferable until it shall (by letter addressed and delivered to the secretary of the company) have been first offered to Ezra Herbert Lynall so long as he shall

> remain a director of the company and after he shall have ceased to be a director of the company to the members of the company at its fair value. The fair value of such share shall be fixed by the company in general meeting from time to time and where not so fixed shall be deemed to be the par value. The directors may from time to time direct in what manner any such option to purchase shares shall be dealt with by the secretary when communicated to him.'

At the time of Mrs Lynall's death a fair value had never been fixed.

Sources of information

The company's premises have been visited by us and we have discussed the company's prospects with the management. We have not been informed whether a public flotation is in prospect, nor have we received any information from the company's auditors, solicitors or insurance brokers. We have received copies of the company's audited accounts for the six years ended 31 July 1962, although the accounts for the year ended 31 July 1962 cover a period extending some two months beyond the date of Mrs Lynall's death and are only partly admissible.

Valuation approach

There are no previous arm's length transfers of shares to give any assistance in arriving at the market value. The shareholding represents an influential minority interest of 28% and the valuation is therefore based mainly on the prospective future dividends compared with the yield available on quoted companies. Although Linread Ltd is a private company it is one where a public flotation would be possible and therefore a comparison with quoted companies is not, in this case, unreasonable, and the discount for non-marketability is lower than would normally be the case.

However the company has, and may be expected to continue to have, a conservative dividend policy and it is therefore reasonable to take into account the earnings of the company, and to take some notice of the tangible asset backing represented by the net assets of the company.

General economic conditions

The general economic position at 21 May 1962 is that the UK is currently suffering from a deficit of visible trade largely offset by a surplus of invisibles. Unemployment is running at an acceptable level of between 1.6% and 2.0% of the working population. The general terms of trade have materially improved since 1954 by some 15%. However the growth in gross domestic product over the past decade is lower than nearly all other industrialised countries and the level of industrial investment is similarly lagging.

The general level of inflation is running at approximately 3% per annum.

The dividend yield on the Financial Times/Actuaries 500 Share Index at 29 June 1962 is 5.04%, on the All Share Index the yield is 4.57% and on 2½% consols the yield is 6.16%. The official rate of exchange is US$2.8 to £1.

Outlook for the industry

Linread Ltd is involved in the engineering industry and industrial production fell in the second half of 1961. The UK's share of manufactured goods in world markets is declining. The aircraft industry has suffered from the 1957 defence review although the civil market is reasonably buoyant. The motor industry is continuing to grow but the proportion of imports is also increasing.

Company history

The company was incorporated in England as a private company on 1 August 1925. The company, which was formed to start a new business in the manufacture of cold forged fasteners, has become one of the largest in this field in the UK as a supplier to the automobile, aircraft, domestic appliance, electrical, electronic and other industries. The company makes a wide range of screws, bolts and other fasteners, many of which are specially designed. An important part of the business consists of the production under licence of Phillips recessed head machine screws and self tapping screws. The company manufactures metal pressings and assemblies and its automobile courtesy light switches are fitted to most new British cars.

It has been the policy to spread sales, almost all of which are made direct to industrial consumers, over as many industries as possible. The company has specialist sales engineers and consultants giving advice to customers on fastening problems and has well equipped research and development facilities.

In recent years the company has been expanding its export business which, in the year to 31 July 1961, represented about 6% of the company's turnover. The principal export markets are in the Commonwealth, the USA, South Africa and Western Europe.

The company has three wholly owned subsidiaries of which one (incorporated in England) has never traded and the other two, which are not at present contributing a material proportion of combined profits, are the following:

(1) Linread Canada Limited ('Linread Canada'), which has an issued share capital of $Can 206,000 (£68,211), was incorporated on 15 November 1957, to carry on business as importers of the company's products. In 1958 it started local manufacture and about 95% of its sales now consist of its own products, the balance being imported from the company. The manufacturing business in Canada has expanded rapidly and, although initially operated at a loss, has been profitable since July, 1960.

(2) Linread Products Inc was incorporated in the state of New York on 12 May 1952, and imports certain of the company's products into the USA.

Premises and plant

The company has the following manufacturing premises, all within one mile of the centre of Birmingham:

(1) Sterling Works, Cox Street, Livery Street and St Paul's Square, Birmingham. These properties, which include the company's head office, have total site areas of 2⅓ acres, all of which are freehold except about

one-third of an acre held on leases expiring in 1991 and 2009 at rents totalling £100 per annum. There are about 3½ acres of working floor area, about one-half acre of which is occupied by tenants of the company under leases at a total rental of £2,750 per annum expiring in or before 1969.

(2) Premises near Sterling Works – These have a site area of over one-half acre and are occupied by the company on short leases expiring in or before 1965 at a total rent of £1,275 per annum. The expiry of these leases will have no material effect on the company's business.

(3) Factory premises, Hospital Street, Birmingham – These have a floor area of about one-quarter acre and were recently constructed by the company to house the aircraft products division. They are held on a lease expiring in 2036 at a rent of £500 per annum.

The company has two main distribution depots outside Birmingham:

(1) Colnbrook, Middlesex – These premises were built by the company in 1960 on a freehold site of about one-third of an acre. They are conveniently placed to serve many customers in the aircraft and other industries and have easy access to London airport.

(2) Stockport, Cheshire – A new depot is under construction on a freehold site of nearly 1½ acres, which will replace leasehold premises in Stockport held on a lease terminating in 1970 at a rent of £468 per annum.

The plant and machinery of the company is modern and well maintained, all plant maintenance being carried out by the company, which also makes its own specialised tools. The company's road vehicles link the factory with the depots and deliver to customers about 85% of all home sales.

Linread Canada owns a freehold site of 13/8 acres in Guelph, Ontario, on which its factory premises are built. The site is only partially developed and there is room for further expansion.

Management and staff

Mr E H Lynall (aged 69) has been with the company since its incorporation and was chairman and managing director from 1930 until recently. He remains an executive director and chairman of the board. Mr A H Lynall (aged 44), who was appointed a director on 30 June 1942, and Mr D G Lynall (aged 39) who was appointed a director on 24 March 1947, are joint managing directors of the company. Mr R A Ellis (aged 47) who joined the company in 1939, was appointed a director on 1 January 1958.

The company and Linread Canada have about 900 employees, including administrative staff. Relations between management and labour are excellent. The company has a contributory pension fund and life assurance scheme for all staff and workpeople; all men over 21 years of age and women over 30 years of age who have been with the company for more than a year must join. The company operates an apprentice scheme which includes a fully equipped training department under the control of a qualified training officer.

Working capital

The directors are satisfied that the company and its subsidiaries have sufficient working capital for their present requirements.

Financial information

The main figures from the company's audited accounts are summarised below. The directors consider that at 21 May 1962 their forecast of the profits for the year ending 31 July 1962 would be roughly in line with the preceding year and they expect the dividend to remain the same. On both counts we consider the board to be unduly pessimistic and we have estimated the post-tax profits for the year ended 31 July 1962 as being £170,000.

Capitalisation of dividends

The actual dividend paid for the year ended 31 July 1961 was 15%. Profits are increasing, there is the danger of a surtax direction if sufficient profits are not distributed and a dividend of 22½% might be anticipated.

The actual dividend yields of the motors and aircraft and engineering sectors of the Actuaries Investment Index at the time are 5.18% and 6.27% giving 5.725% as a reasonable dividend in this case.

Per share: £1 × 22.5 / 5.725 = £3.930

Capitalisation of earnings

	£	£
Projected post-tax earnings for year ended 31 July 1962	170,000 × 4	680,000
Year ended 31 July 1961	135,496 × 3	406,488
Year ended 31 July 1960	141,343 × 2	282,686
Year ended 31 July 1959	90,697 × 1	90,697
	10	1,459,871
Anticipated maintainable future post-tax earnings		145,987
say		145,000
P/E ratio of comparable quoted companies, say		10
Capitalised value		1,450,000
per share 1,450,000 / 241,700		5,999

Asset value

The net tangible assets at 31 July 1961 were £898,927 and by 21 May 1962 could be expected to have increased by approximately:

10/12 × £170,000 = £141,667 (anticipated net profit for year ended 31 July 1962)

To total	1,040,594, say £1,040,000
Per share 1,040,000/241,700	£4.303

Summary

	£	
Yield basis		
£3.930 × 0.6	2.358	
Earnings basis		
£5.999 × 0.3	1.799	
Assets basis		
£4.303 × 0.1	.430	
	4.587	
Discount for non-marketability (say) 24%	1.101	
	3.486	
say	3.50	per share

Conclusion

In our opinion the open market value for estate duty purposes of 67,980 £1 shares in Linread Ltd at 21 May 1962 amounts to £237,930.

Linread Ltd

Years ended 31 July

	1957	**1958**	**1959**	**1960**	**1961**	**1962**
	£	**£**	**£**	**£**	**£**	**£**
Turnover	979,000		1,267,000	1,604,000	1,607,000	1,801,000
Profits before depreciation and taxation	112,798		180,299	309,516	300,905	400,295
Depreciation			23,383	34,803	32,828	
Profit before taxation			156,916	274,713	268,077	
Taxation			66,219	133,370	132,581	
Profits available for dividend	35,456		90,697	141,343	135,496	180,067
Dividend paid	5%	5%	10%	15%	15%	15%
Dividend cover			6.1	6.4	6.1	8.1

Linread Ltd

Consolidated balance sheet at 31 July

	1957	1958	1959	1960	1961	1962
	£	£	£	£	£	£
Fixed assets						
Less depreciation						
Freehold land and buildings						303,642
Leasehold properties						4,581
Plant equipment and motor vehicles						176,504
	259,376				396,753	484,727
Current assets						
Stocks and work in progress					267,644	276,154
Debtors and prepayments					322,067	327,813
Tax reserve certificates	218,783				60,550	49,266
Cash at bank and in hand					202,650	239,870
					852,911	893,103
Less: Current liabilities						
Creditors					149,616	96,621
Mortgage	20,000	18,000	16,000	14,000	12,000	10,000
Current taxation					166,915	170,537
Proposed dividend			14,804	22,206	22,206	22,206
					350,737	299,364
Net current assets					502,174	593,739
					898,927	1,078,466
Reserve for future taxation					110,000	135,000
Net tangible assets					788,927	943,466
Ratios						
Current assets: current liabilities	1.7:1				2.4:1	3:1
Capital commitments					£105,000	£110,000

Example 2

Mock valuation report in *Re Holt*

An attempt has also been made to prepare a consistent valuation report from the details referred to in the *Holt* case. There was a placing of 650,000 5% first cumulative redeemable preference shares of £1 each at par on 21 September 1950.

The executors of Mr Robert L Holt (deceased),

Dear Sirs,

We have been asked to prepare a valuation of 43,698 ordinary shares of £1 each and 11,643 6½% preference shares of £1 each in John Holt & Co (Liverpool) Ltd held by the trustees of the Robert Longstaff Holt settlement, at the date of Mr Holt's death on 11 March 1948.

Purpose of valuation

The shares are to be valued for the purposes of estate duty.

Basis of valuation

The shares are to be valued in accordance with FA 1894, s 7(5) which provides:

> 'The principal value of any property shall be estimated to be the price which, in the opinion of the commissioners, such property would fetch if sold in the open market at the time of death of the deceased.'

Various principles emerge from case law which assist in the interpretation of these words:

(1) The test is what the purchaser would pay not what the vendor would receive after costs.

(2) The market must be an open market without specially excluding anyone or specially including anyone; *IRC v Crossman* [1937] AC 26 at 73.

(3) Where the articles of association, as here, restrict the right to transfer, nevertheless the market must be open in the sense that it is assumed that the hypothetical purchaser will be entered on the register of members, but thereafter will hold the shares subject to the restrictions in the articles; *IRC v Crossman* [1937] AC 26.

(4) The sale to be assumed is a hypothetical sale between hypothetical parties. Whether or not Mr R L Holt was a director is not material; *Re Aschrott* [1927] 1 Ch 313 at 322; *Winter (Sutherland's Trustees) v IRC* [1963] AC 235 at 256; *Duke of Buccleuch v IRC* [1967] 1 AC 506 at 524.

(5) Directors owe no duty to a shareholder-vendor to disclose either orally or by way of documents the secrets of the boardroom; *Percival v Wright* [1902] 2 Ch 421 at 425.
(6) The directors would be under a positive duty not to disclose confidential information. What the directors would be prepared to disclose is a question of fact.
(7) The hypothetical sale is deemed to take place at the time of death; *Duke of Buccleuch v IRC* [1967] 1 AC 506.
(8) Any subsequent placing of preference or ordinary shares has no relevance unless it were known to be in contemplation at 11 March 1948 since it would be a totally different sale in totally different conditions; *Earl of Ellesmere v IRC* [1918] 2 KB 735 at 739; *IRC v Marr's Trustees* (1906) 44 SLR 647.
(9) Subsequent accounts can only be used to see what sort of forecast would have been given if the purchaser had asked for one, not to find out what actually happened; *Salvesen's Trustees v IRC* (1930) 9 ATC 43. Nevertheless the court has in many cases considered the accounts for the period current at the valuation date.
(10) There are no implied warranties or conditions and no assumption is to be made that employees will enter into service contracts.

Capital structure

Shares issued and fully paid

697,680 ordinary shares of £1 each

139,140 6½% preference shares of £1 each

Shares held by Mr R L Holt

43,698 ordinary shares

11,643 6½% preference shares

Percentage of ordinary shares held by Mr R L Holt:

6.26%.

Shareholdings

All the shares are held by members of the Holt family and their family trusts.

Restriction of rights

The articles of association of the company contain restrictions on the transfer of shares on more or less familiar lines, the essential features being that unfettered transfer to non-members is prohibited as long as a member or person approved by the directors is willing to purchase the shares at the fair value to be certified (in the case of difference) by the company's auditor in accordance with article 26 of the articles of association. By article 31 the directors are given a general power to refuse to register a transfer.

Sources of information

The company's premises have been visited by us and we have discussed the company's prospects with the management. We have not been informed whether a public flotation is in prospect, nor have we received any information from the company's auditors, solicitors or insurance brokers. We have received copies of the company's accounts for the five years ended 30 September 1947.

Valuation approach

There are no previous arm's length transfers of shares to give any assistance in arriving at the market value. There were agreed values on death however of 17s. 6d. on 5 April 1943 and 20s. 0d. on 15 November 1945 and on 3 June 1946. The shareholding of ordinary shares represents a small and uninfluential minority interest and the valuation is therefore based mainly on the prospective future dividends compared with the yield available on quoted companies. Although John Holt & Co (Liverpool) Ltd is a private company, it is one where a public flotation would be possible and therefore comparison with quoted companies is not, in this case, unreasonable.

Since 1921 the practice of the company has been to limit distributions on the ordinary shares to 5%, less tax, and to build up its reserves by accumulating surplus profits in good years.

The earnings in the recent past, although greatly affected by the war years, would mean that the ability to pay an increased dividend is considerable and some allowance must be made for this growth potential. Similarly the very considerable asset cover cannot be ignored entirely.

General economic conditions

The world economy is gradually recovering from the devastating effects of the 1939–45 war. Inflation in the UK is running at some 8% per annum. The exchange rate is currently US$4.05 to £1 but the pound sterling is under considerable pressure. It appears that high commodity prices resulting from wartime shortages are unlikely to remain and sharp falls are expected in the near future.

Outlook for the business

The company is involved in the fluctuating business of trading in and with West Africa. The West African trade has had a bad reputation in the last 30 or 40 years and there were riots and a boycott of European traders in February 1948. Trade was also depressed by the devaluation of the French Colonial franc in January 1948. It appears that the seller's market is virtually disappearing and a recession in trade may be expected at any moment. As the company's reserves are largely in the form of current trading assets the company is extremely vulnerable to a material downturn in trade.

The West African territories are heavily dependent on agriculture and in some cases on some particular kind only, such as the culture of cocoa or groundnuts, so that they severely affected by the wide fluctuations in the prices of these products, and by growing conditions. The necessity of traders in West Africa to carry heavy stocks at times of high prices represents a tremendous danger where a break in prices appears imminent, as it did at 11 March 1948.

Another adverse factor is the growing tendency in West African countries to try to get trade away from European firms.

Company history

The company was incorporated in England on 29 March 1897, with the objects set out in its memorandum of association and in particular to acquire the business originally founded by John Holt in 1867. The company now carries on business as West African and General Merchants; this business comprises mainly the export and sale in the company's own establishments of merchandise of all kinds and the purchase and shipment as principals or agents of cocoa, palm oil products, groundnuts, hides and skins, and other West African produce.

History and business John Holt first sailed to West Africa in 1862, the year following the cession of the Lagos Colony to the British Crown; his original post was that of Assistant to the British Consul on the Spanish island of Fernando Po. In 1867, when he was 25 years of age, he commenced trading on his own account in Fernando Po and was joined the same year by his two younger brothers, Jonathan Holt and Thomas Holt; it was not, however, until 1884 that the first formal partnership was entered into by the brothers John and Jonathan.

Jonathan Holt obtained his Master's Certificate in October, 1868, and early in 1869 sailed the recently purchased 65 ton schooner *Maria* from Liverpool to Fernando Po. The advantage of operating their own water transport was early appreciated by the Holts; various vessels were chartered or purchased as the need grew with expanding trade, and in 1910 two steamers of 1,522 tons each were first built to the company's order. By 1929 the company's fleet of cargo liners had increased to five, and regular fortnightly sailings from Liverpool to West Africa were maintained. Only cargo owned by the company was carried, both outward and homewards, and the accommodation for 12 passengers in each vessel was used exclusively by the company's own staff. The country's shipping needs during the 1939–45 war caused this policy to be discontinued and, with the larger carrying capacity of the present fleet, it has not been renewed.

The early ownership of sea transport facilitated the opening of trading stations on the mainland, principally in the Gabon, Cameroons, Spanish Guinea and the palm oil ports of Nigeria. The severe discrimination against foreign companies by the French authorities towards the end of the nineteenth century, however, forced the company to concentrate on Nigeria and, following the withdrawal of the Charter of the Royal Niger Company in 1899, which resulted in the loss of the company's hitherto privileged position, expansion in Nigeria became more rapid. Trading stations as far inland as Lokoja (some 360 miles from the coast) were established in 1900 and by 1911 trading posts had been opened in the main market towns of Northern Nigeria. In the meantime a more liberal policy had been adopted by the French authorities and the company's main difficulties in trading in the French Colonies had been resolved by the end of 1912. The company now enjoys a considerable trade in all the French Colonies concerned.

The Spanish Civil War and the consequent financial and other controls made it necessary to cease trading in Spanish Territory, but the company still owns properties (which are let) in both Bata (Spanish Guinea) and Fernando Po. The opening of establishments in the Gold Coast in 1935 compensated for the closing of the trade outlet.

The company now owns stores and staff houses (mainly leasehold owing to local land tenure laws) in more than 50 trading branches throughout the Gold Coast, Togoland, Dahomey, Nigeria, British and French Cameroons and the Gabon, as well as freehold properties in the Lagos Colony, and in these French Colonies.

The wisdom of the policy, which was laid down by John Holt at the first annual general meeting of the company and which is still maintained, of 'making provision in the good years for the bad ones which must inevitably follow sooner or later' was proved in the slump period which followed the 1914–18 war, when the company was one of the very few concerns trading in West Africa which survived that economic blizzard, and also in the depression of the 1930s.

The company is having to restore practically the whole of its buildings in West Africa and before long will have to replace two of the five ships which were built in 1929.

The company and its subsidiaries directly employ over 4,400 men and women and have no difficulty in obtaining suitable staff.

Subsidiary companies The following are the principal subsidiary companies:

John Holt & Co Incorporated was formed in July 1947, in New York with the immediate object of taking over the agency work previously carried out on behalf of the company in the USA by various American firms. (The staff of the principal of these – W & A Leaman of New York – formed the nucleus of the staff of the new subsidiary company.) Since then, business outside the company's particular interests has been developed and it is hoped that the company's sterling exports to the dollar area, although at present relatively small in comparison with its West Africa trade, will show a steady increase.

John Holt (Overseas) et Cie was scheduled to commence business in Paris in September 1948, to take over the functions previously performed by the Paris branch of the company and to facilitate continental buying of goods required by the company's establishments in French Colonies and the sale of produce from those Colonies.

Trade investments The company has substantial ordinary shareholdings in the following companies established in Nigeria:

Costain (West Africa) Ltd – civil engineers and building contractors with a furniture factory at Lagos. Thomas Wyatt & Son (West Africa) Ltd – manufacturing stationers with a factory now established in Lagos.

Pension funds The company's managerial and clerical staff, both European and African, and certain steamer personnel are covered by contributory pension funds established from 1934 onwards. There are also widows' and orphans' benefits for the home and coast staff.

Continuity of management Over the 50 years of the company's existence, its affairs have been controlled by, in all, eighteen 18 directors (including the present nine) and of those only four have not been directly related to the founder. Of the present directorate, the chairman, the vice-chairman, and the two other executive directors are grandsons of the founder, three directors are nephews of his and two are not members of the family.

All the 6½% cumulative preference shares and all the ordinary shares are held by members of the family.

It will be seen that the business is a family one; it is the intention that the equity capital of the company shall remain in the hands of the family.

Financial information

The main figures from the company's audited accounts are summarised in annexures A and B. The directors consider that at 11 March 1948 the profit before tax for the year ended 30 September 1947 would be about £1,000,000 and the profits for the following year would not be expected to differ markedly.

Capitalisation of dividends

(1) Ordinary shares

The actual dividend paid for the year ended 30 September 1947 and for many years previously was 5% and it is unlikely that this will be increased in the near future.

The dividend yield for quoted shares in comparable companies is 4.89%.

Per share: £1 × 5 / 4.89 £1.022

(2) Preference shares

The actual dividend paid is 6½%. The average yield from the Actuaries Investment Index of 5% preference shares is just under 4%.

Per share £1 × 6½ / 4 £1.625

Capitalisation of earnings

	£	£
Projected pre-tax profits for		
Year ended 30 September 1947	1,000,000 × 4	4,000,000
Year ended 30 September 1946	681,745 × 3	2,045,235
Year ended 30 September 1945	630,022 × 2	1,260,044
Year ended 30 September 1944	629,951 × 1	629,951
	10	7,935,230
Anticipated maintainable future pre-tax profits		793,523
Less tax at likely future rates (to avoid distortion with wartime rates) – say 70%		555,466
		238,057
Less: applicable to preference dividend		
139,140 × 6½% = 9,044 less tax at 9s.0d.		4,972
		233,085
say		230,000
Price/earnings ratio, say,		7
Capitalised value		1,610,000
Per share 1.610,000/697,680		2.307

Asset value

The net tangible assets at 30 September 1947 were £2,946,000 and by 11 March 1948 could be expected to increase by approximately:

5/12 £230,000 = (anticipated net profit for year ended 30 September 1948)	£95,833
To total £3,041,833, say	£3,040,000
Per ordinary share: 3,040,000/697,680	£4.357

Summary

	£	
(1) Ordinary shares		
Yield basis £1.022 × 0.75	.766	
Earnings basis £2.307 × 0.15	.346	
Assets basis £4.357 × 0.05	.218	
Previous transfers £1.00 × 0.05	.050	
	1.380	
Less discount for non marketability, say, 31%	.427	
	.953	
say		.95 per share
(2) Preference shares	£	
Yield basis	1.625	
Less discount for non-marketability, say, 35%	.569	
	1.056	
say		1.05 per share

Conclusions

In our opinion the open market value for estate duty purposes of 43,698 £1 ordinary shares in John Holt & Co (Liverpool) Ltd at 11 March 1948 amounts to £41,513.10.

In our opinion the open market value for estate duty purposes of 11,643 6½% preference shares in John Holt & Co (Liverpool) Ltd at 11 March 1948 amounts to £12,036.15.

John Holt & Co (Liverpool) Ltd Years ended 30 September

	1943	1944	1945	1946	1947	1948
	£	£	£	£	£	£
Taxation						
Profits before taxation (as adjusted)	762,255	629,951	630,022	681,745	1,011,928	1,142,750
Dividend paid	5%	5%	5%	5%	5%	5%
Dividend cover					697,680	450,000
Ordinary shares in issue						
Asset backing per share of balance sheet values (see note 3)					£4.231	£6.883
Ratios				1.73:1	1.55:1	1.65:1
Current assets to liabilities						

John Holt & Co Ltd Consolidated balance sheet at 30 September

	1947	1948
	£	£
Fixed Assets		
Steamers, rivercraft and machinery (at cost)	1,272,941	1,277,396
Less: Provision for depreciation	489,622	500,242
	783,319	777,154
Land and buildings (at cost)	394,825	413,006
Less: Provision for depreciation	356,446	356,757
	44,379	56,249
Office furniture (at cost)	216	380
Less: Provision for depreciation	3	31
	213	349
At valuation	100	100
	313	449
	828,011	833,852
Trade Investment		
Shares (not officially quoted) at cost	17,920	65,103
Less: Provisions for depreciation	3,555	3,688
	14,365	61,415
Current Assets		
Stocks as valued by directors	3,385,870	3,890,003
Sundry debtors		
Less: Provision for doubtful debts	930,882	1,372,560
General investments (officially quoted)		
less provision for depreciation	527,087	106,907
Tax reserve certificates	250,450	225,250
Bank balances and cash in hand	1,204,983	1,276,416
	6,299,272	6,871,136
	7,141,648	7,716,404

Current Liabilities and Provisions		
Provisions for obligations to pensions funds	130,000	94,000
Provision for anticipated liabilities	4,857	41,932
Provision for deferred maintenance	31,593	–
Creditors, taxation, accrued charges and bills payable	2,903,068	3,119,080
Bank overdrafts	957,211	909,868
Dividends proposed (net)	24,160	7,425
	4,050,889	4,172,305
Net tangible assets	3,090,759	3,544,099
Cumulative preference shares	139,140	446,820
Applicable to ordinary shares	2,951,619	3,097,279

John Holt & Co (Liverpool) Ltd and subsidiary companies Profit and loss account for years ending 30 September

	1947		1948	
	£	£	£	£
Trading Profit for Year – on				
Steamers and Trading after deducting all expenses including the following (see Notes 6, 8 and 10):		1,171,247		1,033,450
Depreciation	71,354		70,784	
Insurance Reserve	6,842		7,875	
Doubtful Debts Provision	62,979		4,663	
Auditors' Fees	650		779	
Provision for Anticipated Liabilities	1,534		21,075	
	143,359		105,176	
Dividends and Interest Received				
Trade Investments	215		249	
Other Investments	1,650		4,579	
		1,865		4,828
Net Profit for Year Before Charging Taxation		1,173,112		1,038,278
UK and British Colonial Taxation				
(estimated to be payable on the net profits as shown above) (see Note 13):				
Excess Profits Tax	73,000		–	
Profits Tax (see Note 5)–		–		
UK Income Tax	250,839		364,184	
British Colonial Income Tax	278,000		188,000	
		601,839		552,184
Net Profit for Year		571,273		486,094
Balance Brought Forward From Previous Year		150,699		154,639

Total Available for Appropriation and Dividends		721,972		640,733
Appropriations				
To Contingency Reserve	418,173		268,597	
Provision for obligation to Pension Funds	125,000		–	
General Funds	–		163,000	
Investment Provision	–		5,839	
Provision for Anticipated Liabilities	–		16,000	
		543,173		453,436
		178,799		187,297
Dividends Paid and Proposed				
(Less: Income Tax at 9s in the £)				
Half year Pref Dividend to 31/3/48 (paid)	2,487		6,144	
Half year Pref Dividend to 30/9/48 (paid)	2,487		6,144	
Ordinary Dividend Interim at 2% (paid)	–		4,960	
Ordinary Dividend Final at 3% (proposed)	19,186		7,425	
		24,160		24,663
Balance Carried Forward to Balance Sheet		154,639		162,634

Note on the accounts of the holding company and its subsidiaries at 30 September 1948

(1) Liabilities under guarantees, etc

(a) There is a contingent liability in respect of uncalled capital on investments held by the holding company of £22,337.
(b) The holding company guarantees a revolving bank credit to a maximum amount of £20,000 for an associated company.
(c) The holding company has entered into guarantees in respect of pension schemes instituted by them.

(2) Contracts for capital expenditure

The approximate amounts for contracts for capital expenditure not provided for in the accounts are £33,000 for the holding company. There are no outstanding liabilities under this heading for subsidiary companies.

(3) Capital

During the year the basis of the authorised capital was altered by the holding company from:

150,000 6½% cumulative preference shares of £1 each 1,000,000 ordinary shares of £1 each to:

450,000 5% cumulative preference shares of £1 each
450,000 ordinary shares of £1 each
250,000 shares of £1 each

and under the capital reconstruction scheme carried out, in addition to the surrender by the shareholders of 139,140 6½% preference shares and 247,680 ordinary shares in exchange for 5% preference shares, on the basis of one for one 60,000 of the 5% preference shares were issued as a bonus to the existing shareholders, increasing the issued capital to £896,820. The legal and accountants' fees incurred on the above scheme, amounting to £523, have been charged against trading profits.

(4) Capital profit suspense

A number of investments were sold in 1948, which resulted in a profit to the holding company of £120,014, from which a capital cash bonus was paid of 1¼% to the ordinary shareholders, leaving a balance of £3,293 to be carried forward.

(5) Taxation

The reserve for future tax in the balance sheet of the holding company and the consolidated balance sheet at 30 September 1947 has been transferred to creditors for the income tax due on 1 January 1949. The estimated charge for profits tax on the profits as shown in the 1948 accounts amounting to £110,000 (1947 £94,000) is set off against Dominion tax relief, resulting in no charge to be made in the accounts. The UK tax liability has been finally settled with the Inland Revenue to the close of the accounting period ending 30 September 1944. The directors are of the opinion that the provisions held under the heading of creditors are adequate to cover any further liabilities which might arise.

(6) Reserves and provisions

(a) General Reserve Account for 1948:

	£	£
Balance forward from 1947		403,000
Bonus Issue of 60,000 Preference Shares	60,000	
10% Stamp Duty payable on Issue	6,000	
	66,000	
	337,000	
Appropriated from Profit and Loss Account		163,000
As per Balance Sheet		500,000

(b) A payment of £36,000 was made by the holding company in 1948 to the pension funds in part settlement of the liability to the schemes anticipated by the provisions made in 1947.

(c) During the year deferred maintenance to the extent of £94,113 has been carried out. This absorbed the provision of £31,593 at 30 September 1947, and the balance of £62,520 has been charged to the year's trading.

(7) Depreciation provisions

The Directors are of the opinion that there is no excess in these provisions which can be transferred to reserves.

(8) Current assets

In conformity with past policy, all maintenance stores and claims outstanding for losses etc which had not been met at the close of the period, have been charged against trading profits.

(9) Exchange and conversion rates

Currency values of current assets and liabilities in the balance sheet of the holding company, and in the consolidated balance sheet, have been taken at:

Colonial Francs	Fcs.	508.235 = £1
Metropolitan Francs	"	864.00 = £1
USA Dollars	$	4.03¼ = £1

The currencies, and day-to-day transactions, have been taken at the cost of remittances. The fixed assets have been taken at the rate ruling at the date of purchase.

(10) Exchange differences

On the devaluation of the Colonial and Metropolitan Franc in January 1948, due to the fortuitous position of Franc liabilities exceeding Franc current assets, a profit accrued to the holding company of £30,193. In 1947 certain Franc assets which had previously been devalued were paid by the French government at the rate ruling prior to the devaluation in 1945, resulting in a credit of £63,379. Both these items have been included in the trading profits of the years to which they appertain.

(11) Loan to officers

At 30 September 1948, there was £1,181 outstanding under this heading for advances made by the holding company.

(12) The comparative figures for 1947

In arriving at the corresponding figures for 1947 adjustments have been made where necessary to make them comparable with the 1948 figures.

(13) Consolidated accounts – foreign subsidiary companies

The profits from foreign subsidiary companies will be subject on remittance to UK taxes which will involve a further liability not provided for in these accounts.

	1946	1947	1948
Ordinary shares in issue		697,680	450,000
Asset backing per share at balance sheet values (see note 3)			
Ratios		£4.231	£6.883
Current assets to liabilities	1.73:1	1.55:1	1.65:1

Example 3

Sparkco Ltd – fair value

(1) Instructions

We have been asked to advise the trustees of two settlements made respectively on 22 and 28 May 1981 by Mrs Sparks and Mr W Sparks concerning the price of £100 per share at which it is proposed that Sparkco Ltd buys back the settlements' respective holdings of 7,382 and 2,200 £1 ordinary shares. The date of valuation has been taken as 16 June 1992.

(2) Basis of valuation

We have considered the appropriate value on the basis of the price that would be fair as between the parties to the particular transaction.

This valuation constitutes an estimation or opinion of value according to the information and documents made available to us and referred to or detailed herein. No investigation has been carried out into the activities or management of the company and no action has been taken to verify the information and statements that we have relied upon for the purposes of this valuation. This should not be taken to be the only valuation that could be determined and no responsibility can be assumed for loss occasioned through its use by the addressee or any other person.

(3) Company's activities

The company manufactures components for the motor vehicle, aircraft, gas ignition and ship building industries.

(4) Summary of financial results

The following figures are taken from the company's audited consolidated accounts.

		£000s		
Year ended 30 June	*1988*	*1989*	*1990*	*1991*
Turnover	16,249	20,342	22,370	24,671
Rent receivable	80	67	41	41
Interest payable	69	145	302	324
Directors remuneration	127	114	140	160
Profit before tax	508	1,051	524	344
Profit after tax	281	594	313	282
Extraordinary income (net)	556	–	–	–
Dividends payable	–	21	–	–

Management accounts kept by the company are treated as strictly confidential and have not been made available to us. We understand from Mr FS Sparks, the company's chairman, that the year to 30 June 1992 is expected to be 'no worse' than the year to 30 June 1991.

(5) Consolidated balance sheet at 30 June 1991

	£000
Tangible assets	4,591
Stocks	1,380
Debtors	6,433
Cash	2
Creditors due within one year	(7,176)
Creditors due after more than one year	(631)
Deferred taxation	(753)
	3,846
Called up share capital	21
Capital reserve	19
General reserve	8
Profit & loss account	3,798
Shareholders' funds	3,846
add 1992 estimated profit after tax	262
	4,108
Net assets per share	194.55

Tangible assets include freehold property at a book value of £1,863,974. The directors' report in the 1991 accounts states that the open market value is in excess of this figure.

(6) Capital structure

The company's issued share capital consists of 21,115 £1 ordinary shares.

The following purchases of its own shares have taken place:

January 1988:	2,020 shares for a total of £50,753
August 1988:	16,905 shares for a total of £1,005,000

(7) Valuation approach

There is no statutory or standard valuation method which governs the price at which a company can purchase its own shares. The company's articles of association provide that any member wishing to sell shares, other than to another member or a member of the shareholder's family, must first offer them to the other members at a fair value to be fixed by the company's auditors. There is no definition of fair value in the articles and no specific provision regarding the price at which shares should be bought back by the company.

In the circumstances, we have had regard to the price that in our view would be fair as between the parties to the transactions, that is to say the trustees as vendors and Mr FS Sparks as purchaser. Mr FS Sparks at present owns 54% of the issued share capital and as a result of the proposed buy-in will own 100% of the issued share capital.

With regard to the trustees of the settlement we have taken the following factors into account:

(a) In view of the close association between the two trusts, which have common trustees, we have considered the shareholding of each trust as a proportionate part of a combined shareholding of 9,582 shares, representing 45.3% of the issued share capital.
(b) The size of shareholding in point has the voting ability to block a special resolution but day-to-day control of the company rests in the hands of the 54.7% shareholder.
(c) The return by way of dividend over the past four years consists solely of a very small distribution in 1989.
(d) The value of the shares to the trust rests primarily in the hope of participating at some future date in a pro rata proportion of the sale proceeds of the company as a whole. We are not aware of any present intention of the controlling shareholder to consider a sale of the company.
(e) A sale of shares to the company at a fair price offers the trustees the opportunity to realise the value of the shareholding and convert it into an income producing asset.

As far as Mr FS Sparks is concerned, as a result of the proposed purchase of shares he will become the holder of 100% of the issued share capital. The company's net assets will nevertheless be reduced by the purchase price of the shares and future earnings will be affected by the interest payable on the sum required to carry out the buy-back.

In these circumstances we have considered the present open market values of 45.3% and 54.7% shareholdings and the open market value of a 100% shareholding after the buy-back of shares.

(8) Current value of a 45.3% shareholding

This shareholding has the ability to block a special resolution but does not entitle the holder to a directorship or to participation in the day-to-day running of the company, particularly as the remaining 54.7% of the shares are in the hands of one person. It would be usual to value an influential minority share-holding in these circumstances primarily by reference to dividend yield, but in the virtual absence of dividends such an approach is only possible by considering the level of dividends the company could pay if it were to adopt a dividend policy. The value arrived at on this basis would reflect a discount to allow for the lack of an actual dividend. Alternatively, the valuation can be approached by means of a multiple of maintainable earnings which would reflect the lack of dividends. This method is preferred in this case, in the virtual absence of a dividend record.

(a) Maintainable earnings

The motor industry, which is the biggest customer of Sparkco, has been affected particularly badly by the current recession and despite renewed optimism following the Budget and the general election, has yet to show any significant improvement. In these circumstances it is not appropriate to place much reliance on results achieved before the recession when considering the level of earnings that could be considered maintainable. We are of the opinion that a pre-tax profit of £350,000, £262,500 after corporation tax at the small companies rate of 25%, is a reasonable estimate in present conditions. £262,500 is equivalent to £12.43 per share.

(b) Price/earnings ratio

The average P/E ratio in the quoted motors sector at 16 June 1992 is 17.93. The P/E ratios of certain companies within that sector that manufacture motor vehicle components are as follows:

Company	*Share price*	*Historic P/E ratio*	*Prospective P/E ratio*
BBA Group	141	15.8	13.5
BSG	62½	21.8	15.2
Lucas	130	9.9	44.8
T & N	145	13.8	10.2

Historic P/E ratios are based on latest published results, whereas prospective P/E ratios are based on a consensus of brokers' forecasts for the current year. As the P/E ratio for Sparkco is to be applied to our estimate of future maintainable earnings, a comparison with prospective rather than historic P/E is appropriate.

The prospective P/E for Lucas appears to discount the collapse in earnings in the current year as a one-off event that will not be repeated.

If Sparkco were a quoted company, it is considered that a prospective P/E ratio in the range 10–12 would be appropriate. As it is an unquoted company with no significant dividend history, the following discounts are due:

Quoted P/E range	10	12
Lack of marketability discount (30%)	(3)	(3.6)
	7	8.4
Lack of dividends	(2.1)	(2.5)
	4.9	5.9

A P/E ratio in the range 5 to 6 is thus considered appropriate.

(c) Valuation

Applying a P/E in the range of 5 to 6 to maintainable earnings per share of £12.43 produces a value in the range £62.15 to £74.58 per share, say £68 per share.

(9) Current value of a 54.3% shareholding

This shareholding carries day-to-day control of the company but does not confer the power to wind the company up without the consent of the holders of a further 20.7% of the issued share capital.

It is again considered appropriate to value primarily by reference to earnings but with an added element to reflect the strength of the asset backing. Maintainable earnings are taken as at 8(a) above. As the owner of a holding of this size has the power to declare a dividend, if desired, a discount from the P/E ratio to allow for lack of dividends is not appropriate. We would also reduce the discount for lack of marketability to 15% to give a P/E ratio in the range 8.5 to 10.2. Applying that range to earnings of £12.43 per share produces a value on an earnings basis in the range £105.65 to £126, say £115 per share.

To introduce an element for the strength of the asset backing we would adopt the following weightings on a hybrid basis:

	£	*Weighting*	£
Value on an earnings basis	115	.8	92
Asset backing per share	194	.2	38
Value per share			130

Value of holding: £130 × 11,533 = £1,499,290

(10) Value of a 100% shareholding after a buy-back at £100 per share

(a) Maintainable earnings

Maintainable earnings will in the short term be reduced by the interest on £958,209, say £130,000 per annum, to £132,500 per annum.

(b) Price/earnings ratio

As the holding of 11,533 shares will give complete control of the company in all respects, a P/E ratio in the range 12 to 13 is considered appropriate, to give a value on an earnings basis in the range £1.59m to £1.72m, say £1.65m.

(c) Net assets

As a result of the buy-back, net assets will be reduced by £958,200 to £3,150,666.

(d) Hybrid value

As the holding has complete control of the company the following weightings are considered appropriate:

	Weighting	
Earnings basis: £1.65m	.5	£0.025m
Asset backing: £3.15m	.5	£1,575m
Value of holding		£2.4m

(11) Conclusion

In para (8) above we arrived at a value of £68 per share for a 45.3% shareholding in isolation. For Mr FS Sparks' current 54.7% shareholding, we estimate a current value of £130 per share. In the circumstances of the proposed sale it would be fair to put the sale price at a point midway between the values per share of each holding, which is £99 per share, an insignificant reduction from the proposed sale price of £100 per share.

As a result of a purchase of own shares at £100 per share our view is that the value of Mr FS Sparks' shareholding will increase by up to £900,000, which is considered reasonable in the circumstances.

Example 4

Diplodocus Ltd – valuation of deferred shares at 13 April 2014

Introduction

Diplodocus Ltd is a company incorporated in the UK which provides advisory services in the field of petroleum and natural gas.

The shareholding is:

A Brachiosaurus	20,000	Ordinary shares
	30,000	Deferred shares
P Teranadon	20,000	Ordinary shares
	30,000	Deferred shares
	100,000	

Deferred shares

The deferred shares have the following rights:

(3B) During the period of 15 years to 29 December 2013 the deferred ordinary shares:

(1) shall not entitle their holders as such to any votes at any general meetings of the company otherwise than upon Resolutions proposed for any of the following:
   (a) for winding up the company
   (b) for altering the rights attached to any shares in the company
   (c) for altering the objects of the company
   (d) for increasing the capital of the company
   (e) for reducing the capital of the company whether as a return of assets or otherwise
   (f) for consolidating or sub-dividing any shares in the capital of the company and the deferred ordinary shares shall not entitle their holders to receive notice or to attend and speak at any general meetings of the company except general meetings at which any such resolutions are to be proposed

(2) shall not entitle their holders as such to participate in the profits, property or assets of the company, whether in a winding up or on a return of capital or by way of dividend or otherwise.

(3C) Subject to the immediately preceding article, the ordinary shares and the deferred ordinary shares shall participate in all dividends and in the profits, property and assets of the company and shall in all respects rank *pari passu* and as one single class.

In view of the 15-year deferral of all valuable rights it is considered that each deferred ordinary share be valued on the basis of the value of an ordinary share discounted for 15 years at 15% per annum, ie 12.29% of the value of an ordinary share. 30,000 deferred ordinary shares would therefore be worth 3,687 ordinary shares.

Prior sales

There have been no prior sales of any shares in the company.

Assets

The net book value of assets at 31 December 2013, in accordance with the draft accounts, amounts to £165,895, which does not appear to require any material adjustment.

Earnings

The company has made the following pre-tax profits:

				£
2011	£201,674 ×	3	=	605,022
2012	£86,258 ×	2	=	172,516
2013	25,577 ×	1	=	25,777
		6		803,115
	Weighted average			133,852
	Less: corporation tax at 21%			(28,108)
	Post-tax earnings			105,744
	Apply price/earnings ratio of 5			528,720

Dividends

The company has paid no dividends. On available profits of £105,744 a reasonable dividend would be one-third, say £35,000 × 5⁄4 gross equivalent £43,750. If this is reduced by 50% as a notional dividend it becomes, say, £22,000. If the required gross yield is 10% and the equivalent share capital is £40,000 + £3,687 + £3,687 = £47,374 the capitalised value is

22,000 / 47,374 × 100 / 10 = 4.6438 per share

× 47,374 = £220,000

Weighting

30,000 deferred ordinary shares are equivalent to a minority interest.

Value *Valuation element*	*Amount*	*Weighting*	*Value*
	£		£
Assets	165,895	25%	41,474
Earnings	528,720	25%	132,180
Notional dividends	220,000	50%	110,000
			283,654
Less: discount for non-marketability	35%		99,279
			184,375
Equivalent share capital, shares			47,374
Value per share			3.89
Value of 30,000 deferred ordinary shares 3,687 × 3.89			14,342

Example 5

Salamander Marketing Consultants Ltd – valuation of shares for tax purposes

[This example pre-dates the introduction of 100% business property relief for most shareholdings for inheritance tax purposes, but is retained as an example of the valuation of the holdings of different sizes in the same company.]

2 July 1990
The Directors,
Salamander Marketing Consultants Ltd,
Phoenix House,
Griffin Street,
London EC1.

Dear Sirs,

We have been asked to value various shareholdings in Salamander Marketing Consultants Ltd, 'the company' on 2 July 1990.

Purpose of valuation

The shares are to be valued for the purposes of inheritance tax and capital gains tax.

Basis of valuation

The shares are to be valued for inheritance tax in accordance with IHTA 1984 s 160 which provides:

> 'Except; as otherwise provided by this Act, the value at any time of any property shall for the purposes of this Act be the price which the property might reasonably be expected to fetch if sold in the open market at that time; but that price shall not be assumed to be reduced on the grounds that the whole property is to be placed on the market at one and the same time.'

and IHTA 1984, s 168 which provides:

> '(1) In determining the price which unquoted shares or unquoted securities might reasonably be expected to fetch if sold in the open market it shall be assumed that in that market there is available to any prospective purchaser of the shares or securities all the information which a prudent prospective purchaser might reasonably require if he were proposing to purchase them from a willing vendor by private treaty and at arm's length.'

Under IHTA 1984, s 3(1) the chargeable transfer is the amount by which the estate is reduced by the transfer. Under IHTA 1984, s 3A the proposed transfers are potentially exempt transfers which will not become chargeable transfers unless the transferor dies within seven years of the date of transfer.

A reduction of 50% is available under IHTA 1984, s 105(1)(B) as the transfer is of unquoted shares which immediately before the transfer gave the transferor control of powers of voting on all questions affecting the company as a whole which if exercised would have yielded more than 25% of the votes capable of being exercised on them.

The shares to be valued for inheritance tax purposes are therefore:

Before transfer	
J Hobbs	27,000
B Sutcliffe	27,000
After transfer	
J Hobbs	10,000
B Sutcliffe	10,000

For capital gains tax purposes it is not necessary under FA 1985, s 71 [now TCGA 1992, s 19] to take into account any previous transfers.

The capital gains tax valuation provisions are contained in CGTA 1979, s 150(1) and (2) [now TCGA 1992, s 272] which provides:

> 'In this Act "market value" in relation to any assets means the price which those assets might reasonably be expected to fetch on a sale in the open market.
>
> In estimating the market value of any assets no reduction shall be made in the estimate on account of the estimate being made on the assumption that the whole of the assets is to be placed on the market at one and the same time.'

and CGTA 1979, s 152(3) [now TCGA 1992, s 273] which provides:

> 'For the purposes of a determination it shall be assumed that, in the open market which is postulated for the purposes of that determination, there is available to any prospective purchaser of the asset in question all the information which a prudent prospective purchaser of the asset might reasonably require if he were proposing to purchase it from a willing vendor by private treaty and at arm's length.'

Various principles emerge from case law which assist in the interpretation of these statutory provisions:

(1) The test is what the purchaser would pay not what the vendor would receive after costs.
(2) The market must be an open market without specially excluding anyone or specially including anyone: *IRC v Crossman* [1937] AC 26 at 73.
(3) Where the articles of association, as here, restrict the right to transfer, nevertheless the market must be open in the sense that it is assumed that the hypothetical purchaser will be entered on the register of members, but thereafter will hold the shares subject to the restrictions in the articles; *IRC v Crossman* [1937] AC 26.

(4) The sales to be assumed are hypothetical sales and the fact that the transferor is a director has to be disregarded, in *Re Aschrott* [1927] 1 Ch 313 at 322; *Winter (Sutherland's Trustees) v IRC* [1963] AC 235 at 256; *Duke of Buccleuch v IRC* [1967] 1 AC 506 at 524.

(5) Directors owe no duty to a shareholder-vendor to disclose either orally or by way of documents the secrets of the boardroom; *Percival v Wright* [1902] 2 Ch 421 at 425.

(6) The directors would be under a positive duty not to disclose confidential information. What the directors would be prepared to disclose in a sale by private treaty is a question of fact; *Re Lynall, Lynall v IRC* (1971) 47 TC 375.

(7) The hypothetical sale is deemed to take place at one time; *Duke of Buccleuch v IRC* [1967] 1 AC 506.

(8) Any subsequent placing of the ordinary shares except to the extent that it is known to be in contemplation at 2 July 1990 has no relevance since it would be a totally different sale in totally different conditions; *Earl of Ellesmere v IRC* [1918] 2 KB 735 at 739; *IRC v Marr's Trustees* (1906) 44 SLR 647.

(9) Subsequent accounts can only be used to see what sort of forecast would have been given if the purchaser had asked for one, not to find out what actually happened; *Salvesen's Trustees v IRC* (1930) 9 ATC 43.

Capital structure

Shares issued and fully paid:

75,000 ordinary shares of £1 each.
Shares held by each transferor:
27,000 ordinary shares of £1 each.
Percentage of ordinary shares to be valued:
10,000 = 13.33% for inheritance tax purposes
17,000 = 22.67% for capital gains tax purposes
27,000 = 36.00% for inheritance tax purposes

Shareholders	*No of shares*	*Percentages*
J Hobbs (age 48, joint managing director)	27,000	36
B Sutcliffe (age 46, joint managing director)	27,000	36
W Rhodes	21,000	28
	75,000	100

Transfer of shares

The instrument of transfer of any share shall be executed by or on behalf of the transferor and transferee, and the transferor shall be deemed to remain a holder of the share until the name of the transferee is entered in the register of members in respect thereof.

Subject to such of the restrictions of these regulations as may be applicable, any member may transfer all or any of his shares by instrument in writing in any usual or common form or any other form which the directors may approve.

The directors may also decline to register the transfer of a share (not being a fully paid share) to a person of whom they shall not approve, and they may also decline to register the transfer of a share on which the company has a lien.

The directors may also decline to recognise any instrument of transfer unless:

(a) a fee of 12½p or such lesser sum as the directors may from time to time require is paid to the company in respect thereof;
(b) the instrument of transfer is accompanied by the certificate of the shares to which it relates, and such other evidence as the directors may reasonably require to show the right of the transferor to make the transfer; and
(c) the instrument of transfer is in respect of only one class of shares.

If the directors refuse to register a transfer they shall within two months after the date on which the transfer was lodged with the company send to the transferee notice of the refusal.

The registration of transfers may be suspended at such times and for such periods as the directors may from time to time determine, provided always that such registration shall not be suspended for more than 30 days in any year.

The company shall be entitled to charge a fee not exceeding 12½p on the registration of every probate, letters of administration, certificate of death or marriage, power of attorney, noticc in lieu of distringas, or other instrument.

Transmission of shares

In case of the death of a member the survivor or survivors where the deceased was a joint holder, and the legal personal representatives of the deceased where he was a sole holder, shall be the only persons recognised by the company as having any title to his interest in the shares; but nothing herein contained shall release the estate of a deceased joint holder from any liability in respect of any share which had been jointly held by him with other persons.

Any person becoming entitled to a share in consequence of the death or bankruptcy of a member may, upon such evidence being produced as may from time to time properly be required by the directors and subject as hereinafter provided, elect either to be registered himself as holder of the share or to have some person nominated by him registered as the transferee thereof, but the directors shall, in either case, have the same right to decline or suspend registration as they would have had in the case of a transfer of the share by that member before his death or bankruptcy, as the case may be.

If the person so becoming entitled shall elect to be registered himself, he shall deliver or send to the company a notice in writing signed by him stating that he so elects. If he shall elect to have another person registered he shall testify his election by executing to that person a transfer of the share. All the limitations, restrictions and provisions of these regulations relating to the right to transfer and the registration of transfers of shares shall be applicable to any such notice or transfer as aforesaid as if the death or bankruptcy of the member had not occurred and the notice or transfer were a transfer signed by that member.

A person becoming entitled to a share by reason of the death or bankruptcy of the holder shall be entitled to the same dividends and other advantages to which he would be entitled if he were the registered holder of the share, except that he shall not, before being registered as a member in respect of the share, be entitled in respect of it to exercise any right conferred by membership in relation to meetings of the company.

Provided always that the directors may at any time give notice requiring any such person to elect either to be registered himself or to transfer the share, and if the notice is not complied with within 90 days the directors may thereafter withhold payment of all dividends, bonuses or other moneys payable in respect of the shares until the requirements of the notice have been complied with.

A member wishing to transfer shares to a person or corporation or other body who or which is not already a member of the company shall give written notice to the directors of the company of such intention accompanied by details of the shares which are proposed to be transferred. That written notice shall constitute the directors such member's agents for the sale of the shares in question or any of them to members of the company at a price to be agreed between such transferring member and the directors, or in the absence of agreement, at a price fixed as the fair value of such shares by the auditors of the company (acting as experts and not as arbitrators so that any provisions of law or of statute relating to arbitration shall not apply). If within 28 days from the date of the said written notice the directors are unable to find a member or members willing to purchase all such shares, the transferring member may (subject to the power of the directors in their absolute discretion and without assigning any reason therefore to decline to register any transfer of any share whether or not it is a fully paid share) dispose of so many of such shares as shall remain undisposed of in any manner he may think fit within six months from the date of the giving of the afore-mentioned written notice to the directors.

Any person becoming entitled to a share in consequence of the death or bankruptcy of a member may, upon such evidence being produced as may from time to time properly be required by the directors elect either to be registered himself as holder of the share or to have some person nominated by him registered as the transferee thereof.

The instruments of transfer of a fully paid share shall be signed by or on behalf of the transferor and in the case of shares which are not fully paid up, the instrument of transfer shall in addition be signed by or on behalf of the transferee. The transferor shall be deemed to remain a holder of the share until the name of the transferee is entered in the register of members in respect thereof.

Source of information

The company's premises have not been visited by us. We have discussed the company's future plans and prospects with the management. We have also discussed the company's plans with its auditors, Messrs Bradman Grace.

We have examined copies of the company's accounts for the four years ended 31 December 1989, and draft accounts for the six months to 30 June 1990.

Previous transfers

On 5 May 1986, 8,400 shares were sold by the executors of G Headley deceased, at a professional valuation, for £25,500 to W Rhodes. Subsequent bonus issues on 14 June and 30 December 1986 increased this holding to 21,000 shares, 28%. The capitalised value of the company on this basis would be:

£25,500 × 100 / 28 = £91,071

Valuation approach

The shareholdings to be valued represent various minority interests in the company and it appears reasonable to consider whether any quoted public companies are sufficiently comparable to give some guide to the value of the shares. A public flotation on the Unlisted Securities Market is contemplated for 1991. The company has no fixed assets valued materially in excess of book value.

General economic conditions

At 1 July 1990 the country's industry, in particular the construction and retail sectors, is suffering from high interest rates and falling consumer demand, as a result of the government's efforts to reduce inflation. After several years showing a constant fall in the level of unemployment, the seasonally adjusted figure for the number of people out of work is beginning to rise again.

The Financial Times Stock Exchange 100 Share Index at 2 July 1990 was 2372.0

UK clearing banks' base lending rate was:	15%
The yield on undated gilts was	10.65%
The rate of exchange against the dollar was:	£1 = $1.78

Financial advertising has increased in recent years to a considerable extent and there is no reason to suppose that this trend will not continue.

Company history

The company was incorporated on 14 October 1983 as Salamander Marketing Ltd, trading soon thereafter. The name was changed to Salamander Marketing Consultants Ltd on 11 November 1985. Audited accounts have been prepared for the years ended 31 December up to 1989 and draft accounts have been prepared for the six months ended 30 June 1990.

The company undertakes projects on a fee or retainer basis, the precise charging structure being negotiated with the individual client. All outside costs, such as print, are normally charged through to the client with the addition of a 10% fee to the consultancy.

Possible flotation

It is hoped that in early 1991 the company might be floated on the Unlisted Securities Market as part of the proposed Salamander Group plc.

The Salamander Group plc would be the holding company of four complementary and integrated companies which provide financial institutions – and other companies involved in the investment or lending of money – with a comprehensive range of services across the entire marketing spectrum. The four operating companies, each of which would be a wholly owned subsidiary of the Group, are:

Salamander Advertising Ltd
Salamander Graphics Ltd
Salamander Video Promotions Ltd
Salamander Financial Services Ltd

The Group would have a unique position in the financial world, due to the team of professionals that it would employ. These are people who have had many years' experience of working within the industry which they now advise, from an independent stance outside. They would be able to bring a new dimension to the marketing function: a detailed and informed understanding of a client's business. For this reason, the proposed Group companies attract clients not only from the City of London, where their offices are located, but also from countries such as the USA, Hong Kong, Bermuda, Gibraltar and the Netherlands.

These proposals are, however, some way from fruition and the flotation could fail to take place for numerous reasons.

In *Re Lynall, Lynall v IRC* (1971) 47 TC 375 it was held that the likelihood of a flotation would increase the market value of the shares by £1 from £3.50 to £4.50, ie by 28.571%.

The proposed flotation in this case appears more likely than that in *Lynall* and is thought to increase the value by approximately 30%.

Personnel

As co-founders and joint managing directors, Bert Sutcliffe and Jack Hobbs have always worked closely together to develop the long-term interests of the company and its associates. It is envisaged that this will continue to be the case, with both sharing the responsibility for the development of new business connections – in this country and overseas. They are also both constantly seeking to identify and recruit key personnel to strengthen the Salamander team.

Bert Sutcliffe (joint managing director)

Mr Sutcliffe has spent 25 years in the financial world – the first ten being with a leading life assurance company. He then spent two years as marketing director of a newly formed insurance company, before moving to a large insurance company – where, as marketing director he played a major role in developing new methods of marketing the company's traditional business.

At the corporate level his responsibilities include strategic long-term planning. He is 45.

Jack Hobbs (joint managing director)

Prior to co-founding Salamander in 1983, Mr Hobbs had worked closely with Mr Sutcliffe in executing the marketing and advertising functions for a large insurance company. In earlier years he had worked for a leading national marketing and publications agency, where he was responsible for a wide range of financial accounts.

His particular expertise is the creation and implementation of effective direct response financial advertising, especially for unit trust groups and other investment houses.

Other key personnel include:

Douglas Jardine

Before joining Salamander in September 1985, Mr Jardine worked for a sales promotion agency, as well as for the marketing and promotion departments of three different client companies.

He now heads one of the company's two account servicing divisions. He is principally responsible for ensuring the smooth day-to-day progress of projects being undertaken for a broad range of the company's clients, both in the UK and abroad.

His organisational ability has been a vital factor in the company's rapid expansion over the last 12 months. He is 34.

Bertha Morris

Ms Morris previously worked for a leading advertising agency – and joined Salamander in April 1988 to take responsibility for the second of the company's two account servicing divisions.

Her work now includes client handling and project co-ordination for several of the company's clients.

She has been instrumental in the creation of support systems to improve and extend the company's handling capability. She is 27.

The company employs, under the supervision of the joint managing director, four people, including:

Victor Trumper

Mr Trumper joined the company in April 1986 from a quality national newspaper, where he was assistant to the financial advertisement manager. His specialist skill in buying cost-effective advertising space in the City pages of the leading national newspapers has been instrumental in helping the Group's clients to achieve their direct response targets.

He is also responsible for a certain amount of client handling in his own right, as well as for introducing new financial advertising accounts to the Group. He is 26.

Gilbert Jessop

Mr Jessop is an experienced advertising media executive, who had previously worked for one of the largest advertising agencies in the country.

He joined the company in September 1987 to take responsibility for many aspects of the company's advertising business. He is 35.

Profit trends

The profits for the recent past have been:

Year ended			*Weighted average*
	£	£	£
31 December 1986		17,449 × 1	17,449
31 December 1987		31,506 × 2	63,012
31 December 1988		47,320 × 3	94,640
31 December 1989		75,221 × 4	150,442
Six months to 30 June 1990	95,206		
Annual equivalent 1990		190,412 × 5/15	952,060
			1,475,365
Weighted average			98,357

The profit trend is upwards and it is anticipated that the company should have a maintainable future pre-tax profit of:

	£180,000
Less corporation tax at 25%	£45,000
	£135,000

Dividends

The company has never paid a dividend.

Comparison with quoted companies

The company's main competitors are subsidiaries of quoted public companies which are not quoted in their own right.

Quoted advertising companies such as WPP are included in the miscellaneous section of the FT Actuaries Share Index which, on 2 July 1990 showed a gross dividend yield of 2.23% and a price/earnings ratio of 20.88. These figures are distorted, however, by three of the seventeen companies in the sector, which have exceptionally high price/earnings ratios and low dividend yields.

The FT Actuaries Industrial Group at this date showed a gross dividend yield of 4.48% and a price/earnings ratio of 11.50.

It is considered that a comparable quoted company at 2 July 1990 would have a dividend yield of 4.00% and a price/earnings ratio of 13.

On post-tax earnings of £135,000 the capitalised value would be £1,755,000.

Possible dividend

If the company had a post-tax profit of £135,000 and were to distribute one-third of its profits the net dividend would be £45,000, the gross equivalent of which would be £60,000.

On a yield of 4% the capitalised value would be:

60,000 100 / 4 = £1,500,000

As the company does not pay dividends this value should be discounted by, say, 50% to £750,000.

Asset value

The company's net assets at 30 June 1990 were:

	£
Fixed assets	126,201
Net current assets	84,347
	210,548

The fixed assets consist mainly of motor vehicles, furniture and equipment and capitalised expenses on leasehold property. The realisable value of these assets is unlikely to exceed book value.

Valuation

36% shareholding

	Amount	Weighting	Value
	£	%	£
Assets	210,548	20	42,109
Earnings	1,755,000	45	789,750
Dividends	750,000	35	262,500
		100	1,094,359
Less: Discount for non-marketability, say, 35%			383,025
			711,334
Plus: hope value for flotation, say, 30%			213,400
			924,734
Value of 27,000 shares out of 75,000			332,904
	Say		333,000

Valuation

22.67% shareholding

	Amount	Weighting	Value
	£	%	£
Assets	210,548	20	42,109
Earnings	1,755,000	30	526,500
Dividends	750,000	50	375,000
		100	943,609
Less: Discount for non-marketability, say, 35%			330,263
			613,346
Plus: hope value for flotation, say, 30%			184,003
			797,349
Value of 17,000 shares out of 75,000			180,732
	Say		180,000

Valuation

13.33% shareholding

	Amount	Weighting	Value
	£	%	£
Assets	210,548	20	42,109
Earnings	1,755,000	20	351,000
Dividends	750,000	60	450,000
		100	843,109
Less: Discount for non-marketability, say, 35%			295,088
			548,021
Plus: hope value for flotation, say, 30%			164,406
			712,427
Value of 10,000 shares out of 75,000			94,990
	Say		95,000

Example 6

Motorco – valuation of goodwill on incorporation

Instructions

We have been instructed to value the goodwill arising in Motorco ('Motorco' or 'the Partnership') as at 22 August 2012 for UK capital gains tax purposes. The valuation is required as the Partnership has incorporated and therefore there has been a disposal of goodwill.

Company background

Motorco was established in 2001 and is a vintage car dealership based in London. The Partnership is one of the largest and most established dealerships in the UK and specialises in older, classic cars.

As at 31 July 2012, the firm consisted of 21 staff (including three equity partners and one salaried partner).

Financial information

We have summarised below the reported profit and loss accounts for the Partnership for the financial years 2007 to 2011, together with the management accounts for the 12-month period to 31 July 2012.

Year ended 31 July	*2007*	*2008*	*2009*	*2010*	*2011*	*(Draft) 2012*
	£	£	£	£	£	£
Income	12,704,101	10,876,742	10,545,676	11,400,377	10,565,623	9,411,408
Expenses	(9,443,155)	(9,748,060)	(9,340,077)	(9,087,649)	(8,943,018)	(7,928,313)
Net income	3,260,946	1,128,682	1,205,599	2,312,728	1,622,605	1,483,095

Fee income has consistently exceeded £10 million per annum, in spite of the economic downturn, although we note that the draft financial statements for the year ended 31 July 2012 have dipped below this threshold, albeit the impact on net income is small. Profitability has varied and the firm has undertaken a cost-cutting exercise in order to reduce its overheads. We understand there is sufficient capacity to increase turnover without needing to recruit additional staff. The pre-incorporation budget for 2012/13 showed expected net profits of approximately £1.8m.

The Partnership's balance sheet as at 31 July 2012 is set out below:

Balance sheet as at 31 July 2012 (Draft)

	£	£
Fixed assets		6,257,253
Current assets:		
Sundry debtors, prepayments and work in progress	6,586,725	
Cash at bank and in hand	14,113	
	6,600,838	
Current liabilities:		
Sundry creditors	(3,652,078)	
Income tax provision	(158,670)	
	(3,810,748)	
Net current assets		2,790,090
Capital accounts		3,467,163

Valuation approach

As the business is profitable, we have valued the Partnership using a capitalisation of maintainable earnings. We have then deducted net assets from this value to arrive at a goodwill figure.

(a) Comparables

Motorco is a vintage car dealership operating in the UK. There are very few listed comparable companies, but we have identified five companies which are broadly comparable.

The latest price/earnings (PE) ratios for these companies are shown below:

Adjusted P/E

	Market cap as at valuation date	*Current*	*FY 2012*	*FY 2013*	*FY 2014*	*FY 2015*
Leopard plc	76.5	10.1x	9.5x	8.5x	N/A	N/A
Puma Group plc	34.5	9.0x	6.2x	6.0x	5.5x	5.2x
Tiger plc	14.8	9.4x	18.4x	12.6x	N/A	N/A
Mountain plc	185.3	9.8x	9.3x	8.0x	7.6x	N/A
Panther plc	13.6	38.5x	N/A	N/A	N/A	N/A
Low		9.0x	6.2x	6.0x	5.5x	5.2x
Mean		15.3x	10.9x	8.8x	6.6x	5.2x
Median		9.8x	9.4x	8.2x	6.6x	5.2x
High		38.5x	18.4x	12.6x	7.6x	5.2x

Based on the above and the nature of Motorco's business, we consider an unadjusted current P/E ratio of 11 to be most applicable. However, adjustments to this figure are required to reflect the relative size of the Firm, its non-quoted status and the fact that we are valuing the whole business. Following these adjustments, we have arrived at a revised P/E ratio of 11.5.

(b) Maintainable earnings

Though pre-tax profits have varied over time, the view was taken that in the current economic climate the maintainable level of annual profit is £1.7 million. An adjustment to this figure is required to reflect the salaries payable in respect of those individuals previously remunerated as equity partners. Motorco has advised that the average base pay is circa £85,000. Allowing for bonuses, we estimate that an average total salary package is in the region of £110,000 and that this would be an appropriate figure for the former equity partners. Given the current economic climate, a third-party acquirer would be unlikely to require the existing partner group in its entirety, as we understand that work generation and vehicle sourcing are undertaken by senior staff as well as partners. Therefore we have assumed additional costs for six employees. Therefore an adjustment to profit of £750,000 (including employer costs) has been made to reflect this additional salary cost, resulting in revised pre-tax profits of £950,000. Adjusting for tax at a rate of 25% gives a maintainable earnings figure of £712,500.

Applying a multiple of 11.5 results in a value for Motorco of £8.2 million. Net assets as at 31 July 2011 were approximately £3.5 million, resulting in a value for goodwill of £4.7 million.

(c) Revenue approach

An alternative valuation approach would be to consider the value of the partnership by reference to a multiple of revenue. A review of recent transactions in the public domain has not shown any businesses comparable to Motorco. However, our experience of private transactions in this sector would suggest that a revenue multiple of 0.7x to 1x revenue is not unreasonable. If we were to apply a multiple of 0.85 to estimated maintainable revenues of, say £10 million, this would give a value for Motorco of £8.5 million and a value for the goodwill of £5.0 million.

Accordingly, we would value the goodwill in Motorco at 22 August 2012 at £4.9 million.

Example 7

Logo Properties Limited – valuation of shares in a property company for IHT purposes

(1) Instructions

We have been instructed to value 200,000 'A' non-voting shares in Logo Properties Limited ('Logo' or 'the Company') as at 1 May 2014 (the 'Valuation Date'). The shares are currently held by a trust. We understand that the valuation is required for UK inheritance tax purposes as the shares may be transferred from the trust to the beneficiaries.

(2) Basis of valuation

This valuation constitutes an estimation or opinion of value according to the information and documents made available to us and referred to or detailed herein. No investigation has been carried out into the activities or management of the company and no action has been taken to verify the information and statements that we have relied upon for the purposes of this valuation. This should not be taken to be the only valuation that could be determined and no responsibility can be assumed for loss occasioned through its use by the addressee or any other person.

(3) Company's activities

Logo was incorporated on 18 June 1994 and is registered in London. Its principal activity is property investment and there have been no changes to its activities since the date of incorporation.

(4) Capital structure

The share capital of Logo is split into two classes of shares: ordinary shares and 'A' non-voting shares. At the valuation date, we understand that the number of shares in issue is as follows:

Share class	*Nominal value per share*	*Number of shares issued*
Ordinary shares	£1.00	100
'A' non-voting shares	£1.00	250,000

The trust holds 200,000 of the 250,000 'A' non-voting shares in issue.
We understand there have been no recent share transactions.

(5) Share rights

The rights attached to the 'A' non-voting shares, as set out in the written resolution dated 29 September 1997, are shown below:

- the holders do not have the right to receive notice of or to attend and vote at General Meetings of the Company;
- the holders have the right to participate in the distribution of profits by way of a dividend. Any dividend payment may be made independently to that paid to the holders of the ordinary shares. No dividend shall exceed the amount, if any, recommended at the absolute discretion of the Directors of the Company; and
- the holders have the right in winding up or on a return of capital repayment of the capital paid up or credited as paid up thereon after repayment in full of the capital paid up or credited as paid up on the ordinary shares but shall not confer on their holders any right to participate in the profits or assets of the Company.

(6) Summary of financial results

We have summarised below the financial information for Logo for the financial years ending 31 March 2011, 31 March 2012 and 31 March 2013:

	2011	*2012*	*2013*
	£	£	£
Turnover	220,980	226,012	246,751
Cost of sales	(87,857)	(81,452)	(58,645)
Gross profit	133,123	144,560	188,106
Administrative expenses	(14,058)	(59,177)	(62,947)
Operating profit	119,065	85,383	125,159
Interest receivable and similar income	–	61	66
Interest payable	(4,204)	–	–
Profit before tax	114,861	85,444	125,225
Tax	(33,680)	(18,031)	(25,350)
Profit after tax	**81,181**	**67,413**	**99.875**
Operating profit	119,065	85,383	125,159
Depreciation	1,883	1,694	1,525
EBITDA	**120,948**	**87,077**	**126,684**
Net assets	**2,440,671**	**2,508,084**	**7,686,638**

We note that the significant increase in asset value in the year ended 31 March 2013 arose due to a revaluation of the investment property portfolio of £5.1 million.

No draft financial information is currently available for the year ending 31 March 2014. However, we understand that turnover is expected to be slightly lower than that achieved in 2013, with profit after tax increasing slightly, to approximately £100,000.

(7) Dividends

We understand that no dividends have been paid since the year ending 31 March 2010, when £7,000 per Ordinary Share was paid. No dividends have ever been paid in respect of the 'A' non-voting shares.

(8) Valuation approach

We have determined the value of the 'A' non-voting shares with reference to the rights attached to those shares:

- The shareholders have the right to receive dividends. However, no dividends have been paid in either 2012 or 2013. Given the current low-level of profits being achieved by the Company it is not expected that any dividends will be paid in the near future, although we note that the Company does have distributable reserves.
- On an exit, the shareholders are not entitled to participate in the profits or assets of the Company. If such an event occurs, the shareholders will receive only the amount paid up on the shares held, once the ordinary shareholders have been repaid.

(9) Valuation conclusion

On this basis, our view is that the value of an 'A' non-voting share in Logo is not more than its nominal value, being £1.00 per share, or £200,000 for the trust's shareholding.

Example 8

Lavender Systems Limited – EMI valuation

We are writing to agree the current Unrestricted Market Value ('UMV') and the Actual Market Value ('AMV') of minority holdings of £1.00 B Ordinary shares in the Company to be awarded under the Company's Enterprise Management Incentive ('EMI') scheme.

Information provided

We enclose the following information in relation to the Company:

- Articles of Association for the Company (number 123456789) dated 1 October 2008 as amended by Written Resolution;
- Financial statements for the years ended 30 September 2010, 2011 and 2012;
- Draft financial statements for the year ended 30 September 2013;
- Management accounts including a budget for the year to 30 September 2014; and
- Form Val 231.

Company background

The Company operates in the information technology sector. Its activities include the resale of hardware and software from manufacturers such as Apple, IBM, Toshiba and Dell, and the provision of associated advisory services. The Company offers services to businesses at all stages of the IT lifecycle. In addition, the Company also supplies staff to businesses for short term contract work within the sector.

In the year to 30 September 2014, the company forecasts that approximately 85% of revenues will be attributable to the resale of products, with the balance generated from associated services.

Further information on the Company can be found on its website, www.Lavender-group.net.

Share capital

The Company's share capital is divided into two classes of shares; £1 A Ordinary and £1 B Ordinary. Both classes of shares carry an entitlement to vote. Holders of B Ordinary shares are not entitled to receive dividends or any proceeds apart from a return of capital on liquidation.

Minority shareholdings are subject to a 'drag along' clause which may require the holdings to be sold in the event of a sale of the Company.

The Company's current issued share capital is £7,910 comprised as follows:

- 6,550 £1 A Ordinary shares; and
- 1,360 £1 B Ordinary shares.

Options over 1,540 £1 B Ordinary shares remain unexercised at the current date.

Financial performance

We have summarised below the performance of the Company for the four years to 30 September 2013. The financial statements for the year to 30 September 2013 are currently in draft; however we understand that the Company does not anticipate any material changes to the draft figures.

£	*Restated*		*Restated*	
Year ended 30 September	*2010*	*2011*	*2012*	*2013*
Turnover	29,336,277	51,290,617	50,841,264	47,155,709
Cost of sales	(26,672,268)	(47,651,924)	(47,149,513)	(43,347,101)
Gross profit	**2,664,009**	**3,638,693**	**3,691,751**	**3,808,608**
Admin expenses	(3,233,184)	(2,529,260)	(2,601,226)	(3,774,379)
Operating profit	**(539,175)**	**1,109,433**	**1,090,525**	**34,229**
Interest receivable	348	209	381	432
Interest payable	(6,465)	(20,710)	(23,032)	(32,690)
Profit before taxation	**(545,292)**	**1,088,932**	**1,067,874**	**1,971**
Taxation	153,996	(309,425)	(277,179)	–
Profit for the year	(391,296)	779,507	790,695	1,971
EBITDA	**(378,060)**	**1,265,592**	**1,242,071**	**179,106**
Dividends paid	**108,075**	**–**	**196,500**	**818,750**

The balance sheet at 30 September 2013 shows net assets of £2,249,896 and net cash of £529,233.

An interim dividend of £818,750, equivalent to £125 per share, was paid to holders of 'A' Ordinary shares in the year to 30 September 2013. The purpose of this dividend was to clear the directors' loan accounts and is not expected to recur, particularly as profits have been in decline. We understand that there are no plans to pay any final dividend in respect of the year.

The forecast for the year to 30 September 2014 indicates a budgeted EBITDA of £985,000 and pre-tax profits of £582,000 on revenues of £94 million, resulting in a forecast EBITDA margin of 1% and pre-tax profit margin of 0.6%. The very thin trading margins of the Company mean that any small shortfall in forecast revenue would likely eliminate any positive EBITDA or profits for the period.

In arriving at an estimate of maintainable earnings, we have considered the volatility of earnings in recent years and the company's estimates for 2014. We understand that the Company generates a substantial portion of its revenues from a single customer and this relationship is based solely on goodwill without any contractual agreement. Consequentially, any hypothetical purchaser of the business would need to consider the significant risk surrounding this revenue stream and the associated impact on the Company's performance.

Having considered these factors, we consider a reasonable estimate for maintainable EBITDA to be £500,000.

Comparable companies

We have researched publicly listed companies which we consider comparable to Lavender Systems and analysed their current and forward EBITDA multiples below. In selecting comparable companies we have included both resellers of IT hardware and software as well as companies providing IT services and consulting.

	Financial year end	*Trailing 12 months*	*FY 2014*	*FY 2015*
Purple plc	31/12/2012	41.9x	N/A	N/A
Lilac plc	31/12/2012	6.0x	4.8x	4.6x
Mauve plc	31/12/2012	13.7x	N/A	N/A
Magenta plc	31/12/2012	15.7x	11.1x	9.5x
Low		6.0x	4.8x	4.6x
Mean		19.3x	7.9x	7.0x
Median		14.7x	7.9x	7.0x
High		41.9x	11.1x	9.5x

Forecast EV/EBITDA multiples are only available for FY 2014 for Lilac plc and Magenta plc. EBITDA margins for these two companies in FY 2014 are forecast to be 8.4% and 9.9% respectively, compared with 1% for Lavender Systems. As such, it is appropriate to select a lower multiple to reflect the narrow trading margins the Company operates on. We have therefore selected an unadjusted multiple of 4.0x. We have then adjusted this multiple to reflect the low margins of the business and its high dependence on one customer and to reflect that, in the first instance, we are valuing the whole Company. It is then appropriate to adjust the multiple to reflect the lack of liquidity in private company shares. Following these adjustments we arrive at a multiple of 3.75x.

Further information

We understand that there are no plans for an exit. An offer was made for the business when EBITDA was approximately £750,000 based on a multiple of 3.0x. However, this approach was not pursued.

Share valuation

Applying the selected multiple of 3.75x to estimated maintainable EBITDA of £500,000 results in an enterprise value for the Company of £1.875 million. To this we have added net cash (at September 2013) of £529,000 to arrive at an equity value of £2,400,000.

On a pro rata, fully diluted basis (assuming the exercise of 1,540 options) we arrive at a value per share of £254. We understand that the options to be acquired will represent around a 25% stake and therefore a discount is applicable to reflect the minority holdings being acquired. Accordingly, we arrive at a UMV of £114 and an AMV of £103 per share on the basis of a 55% and 65% discount which is deemed to be appropriate.

Division C

Appendices

A Financial Times/Stock Exchange Actuaries Share Indices
B Financial Times Actuaries Equity Indices (at 31 March 1982)
C Financial Times Actuaries Share Indices and their constituents (for 31 March 1982 valuations)
D Relevant estate duty and other obsolete legislation
E RICS Valuation – Global Standards: VPGA 3, VPGA 4, VPGA 6, VPGA 7 and VPGA 10 (1 July 2017)
F International Valuation Standards 2017, IPEV Guidelines (Appendix 1) and IVS 105
G Practice Note: Apportioning the Price Paid for a Business Transferred as a Going Concern
H Civil Procedure Rules, Part 35 (Experts and Assessors), Practice Direction 35 and Factsheet 53
I Parry's Valuation Tables – Present value of one pound
J Parry's Valuation Tables – Years' purchase or present value of one pound
K Summary of main relevant taxation Acts since 2014 that might affect a valuation
L Useful websites

Appendix A

Financial Times/Stock Exchange Actuaries Share Indices

Base Date 10 April 1962 = 100 (PER = Price Earnings Ratio, net basis)

Date	*Capital Goods*	*Consumer Goods Durable*	*Consumer Goods Non-durable*	*500 Share Index*	*Property*	*Goods*	*2½ % Consols*
29.6.62							
Index	86.39	84.77	90.64	89.91	93.69	89.23	
Earnings yield	11.39	8.12	7.87	9.41	3.08	–	
Dividend yield	5.74	4.56	4.32	5.04	2.85	4.57	6.16
28.9.62							
Index	89.49	86.68	89.76	91.93	93.65	90.11	
Earnings yield	10.86	7.26	7.85	9.03	3.04	–	
Dividend yield	5.48	4.46	4.35	4.95	2.97	4.55	5.55
31.12.62							
Index	95.50	91.11	92.64	97.24	86.09	94.54	
Earnings yield	9.62	5.97	7.52	8.28	3.41	–	
Dividend yield	5.09	4.12	4.26	4.68	3.31	4.35	5.59
28.3.63							
Index	100.66	98.65	97.27	102.32	82.79	98.15	
Earnings yield	8.58	5.87	7.25	7.82	3.55	–	
Dividend yield	4.82	3.92	4.09	4.52	3.45	4.27	5.79
28.6.63							
Index	100.71	96.86	98.22	103.28	80.30	98.09	
Earnings yield	8.26	5.65	7.28	8.00	3.99	–	
Dividend yield	4.82	4.01	4.14	4.51	3.80	4.32	5.39
30.9.63							
Index	106.92	103.15	105.23	110.66	82.73	103.84	
Earnings yield	7.76	5.28	6.83	7.45	3.91	–	
Dividend yield	4.56	3.81	3.94	4.28	3.73	4.14	5.43
27.12.63							
Index	115.75	111.24	110.06	116.99	81.91	108.54	
Earnings yield	7.18	6.22	6.59	7.18	4.09	–	
Dividend yield	4.37	3.66	3.86	4.18	3.89	4.08	5.81
31.3.64							
Index	115.26	110.28	104.00	113.47	72.04	104.61	
Earnings yield	7.30	6.67	7.17	7.57	4.54	–	
Dividend yield	4.46	3.82	4.14	4.37	4.44	4.29	5.88
29.6.64							
Index	116.64	111.99	105.22	114.45	76.63	105.65	
Earnings yield	7.73	7.30	7.63	8.08	4.48	–	
Dividend yield	4.71	4.10	4.28	4.61	4.38	4.49	6.07

Date	*Capital Goods*	*Consumer Goods Durable*	*Consumer Goods Non-durable*	*500 Share Index*	*Property*	*Goods*	*2½ % Consols*
29.9.64							
Index	121.66	114.46	105.59	117.41	79.24	108.59	
Earnings yield	7.54	7.51	7.91	8.12	4.53	–	
Dividend yield	4.63	4.09	4.34	4.63	4.34	4.50	6.05
30.12.64							
Index	106.79	102.30	96.01	105.40	58.63	97.07	
Earnings yield	8.95	9.34	8.80	9.26	6.31	–	
Dividend yield	5.56	4.76	4.90	5.32	5.89	5.18	6.31
31.3.65							
Index	114.60	104.92	93.71	106.18	60.67	98.22	
Earnings yield	8.92	9.76	9.13	9.57	6.04	–	
Dividend yield	5.43	4.83	5.22	5.53	5.75	5.36	6.39
30.6.65							
Index	108.84	93.79	88.91	100.39	60.88	93.42	
Earnings yield	10.06	11.56	10.02	10.75	6.21	–	
Dividend yield	5.80	5.53	5.57	5.91	5.74	5.69	6.66
29.9.65							
Index	113.28	100.86	95.72	106.63	65.60	99.55	
PER	12.47	11.53	13.41	12.46	21.27	–	
Dividend yield	5.59	5.17	5.24	5.60	5.36	5.40	6.21
30.12.65							
Index	113.84	104.71	100.44	110.74	67.14	103.74	
PER	12.33	11.87	13.99	12.86	21.54	–	
Dividend yield	5.58	5.01	5.05	5.43	5.27	5.22	6.48
30.3.66							
Index	114.70	100.30	100.05	112.53	64.24	104.90	
PER	12.48	11.82	13.90	13.23	20.63	–	
Dividend yield	5.63	5.29	5.15	5.41	5.36	5.24	6.68
29.6.66							
Index	123.06	110.45	106.94	119.59	71.47	111.20	
PER	13.84	13.57	14.83	14.60	22.36	–	
Dividend yield	5.18	4.78	4.84	5.08	4.79	4.94	6.89
29.9.66							
Index	99.27	88.61	89.10	99.59	62.64	93.32	
PER	11.49	10.85	12.45	12.30	20.32	–	
Dividend yield	6.49	5.91	5.80	6.06	5.43	5.86	7.01
29.12.66							
Index	103.07	89.86	88.27	99.63	60.82	94.03	
PER	12.33	12.92	12.41	12.60	19.73	–	
Dividend yield	6.08	5.83	5.79	6.02	5.40	5.78	6.66
31.3.67							
Index	108.82	94.49	92.64	105.14	59.85	98.01	
PER	14.06	13.18	13.07	13.46	19.36	–	
Dividend yield	5.71	5.37	5.50	5.61	5.47	5.46	6.41
30.6.67							
Index	118.13	101.80	103.72	114.20	70.52	106.42	
PER	15.65	14.37	14.83	14.60	23.19	–	
Dividend yield	5.26	4.80	4.87	5.13	4.67	5.00	6.80

Date	*Capital Goods*	*Consumer Goods Durable*	*Consumer Goods Non-durable*	*500 Share Index*	*Property*	*Goods*	*2½ % Consols*
29.9.67							
Index	127.13	119.88	111.11	123.10	74.13	114.67	
PER	16.27	18.25	15.91	15.74	23.51	–	
Dividend yield	4.71	4.07	4.57	4.74	4.48	4.63	6.85
28.12.67							
Index	129.43	134.30	112.52	129.10	74.93	121.13	
PER	17.29	20.60	16.61	16.95	23.98	–	
Dividend yield	4.55	3.54	4.58	4.61	4.45	4.38	7.06
29.3.68							
Index	145.98	153.02	125.86	147.79	86.78	139.43	
PER	19.57	23.79	18.03	19.25	27.54	–	
Dividend yield	4.08	3.11	4.14	3.99	3.90	3.85	7.16
28.6.68							
Index	157.40	173.51	142.32	166.10	98.65	154.49	
PER	20.67	26.09	20.39	21.13	30.42	–	
Dividend yield	3.77	2.73	3.67	3.55	3.38	2.48	7.75
30.9.68							
Index	172.42	184.16	144.97	174.21	106.94	160.72	
PER	22.80	25.82	20.15	21.65	32.46	–	
Dividend yield	3.47	2.52	3.67	3.43	3.09	3.39	7.46
30.12.68							
Index	169.71	186.91	150.47	186.02	136.66	173.21	
PER	21.27	24.39	20.56	22.44	37.00	–	
Dividend yield	3.54	2.61	3.58	3.25	2.50	3.19	7.99
31.3.69							
Index	155.91	178.04	144.56	176.21	124.09	164.01	
PER	19.10	21.89	18.93	19.07	32.93	–	
Dividend yield	3.85	2.82	3.81	3.50	2.79	3.44	8.69
30.6.69							
Index	129.77	147.04	122.32	153.39	115.23	142.00	
PER	16.30	17.69	15.89	16.62	31.24	–	
Dividend yield	4.67	3.44	4.55	4.08	3.03	4.02	9.12
30.9.69							
Index	128.61	149.81	122.91	148.76	125.35	139.50	
PER	16.00	17.37	15.65	15.82	31.75	–	
Dividend yield	4.70	3.38	4.54	4.20	2.80	4.09	9.00
31.12.69							
Index	132.60	172.53	133.82	157.35	137.14	147.34	
PER	16.40	19.75	17.04	16.67	32.68	–	
Dividend yield	4.44	2.90	4.12	3.93	2.71	3.85	8.76
31.3.70							
Index	134.24	163.56	130.45	152.66	148.93	144.02	
PER	16.27	16.94	16.58	15.81	34.95	–	
Dividend yield	3.34	3.55	4.42	4.18	2.55	4.07	8.50
30.6.70							
Index	114.59	128.61	117.41	132.87	128.65	125.65	
PER	13.94	12.61	14.94	13.67	29.53	–	
Dividend yield	5.07	4.65	4.91	4.84	3.02	4.72	9.47

Date	*Capital Goods*	*Consumer Goods Durable*	*Consumer Goods Non-durable*	*500 Share Index*	*Property*	*Goods*	*2½ % Consols*
30.9.70							
Index	127.02	142.15	123.77	144.98	151.10	138.70	
PER	15.40	13.58	15.62	14.80	32.90	–	
Dividend yield	4.56	4.21	4.70	4.46	2.62	4.31	9.25
31.12.70							
Index	117.04	131.15	123.12	141.72	157.97	136.26	
PER	13.77	13.27	14.96	14.21	32.77	–	
Dividend yield	4.90	4.46	4.78	4.58	2.59	4.39	9.79
				INDUSTRIAL GROUP			
31.3.71							
Index	115.09	132.22	131.16	133.25	156.30	142.68	
PER	12.63	14.92	14.71	14.45	29.24	–	
Dividend yield	4.99	3.82	4.50	4.43	2.75	4.20	8.92
30.6.71							
Index	136.80	154.44	153.93	155.47	195.48	167.95	
PER	14.72	17.93	17.25	16.79	33.87	–	
Dividend yield	4.33	3.28	3.94	3.88	2.32	3.64	9.25
30.9.71							
Index	156.07	179.59	165.63	170.21	223.66	181.25	
PER	16.52	20.88	18.32	18.15	36.55	–	
Dividend yield	3.83	2.89	3.69	3.57	2.21	3.40	8.69
31.12.71							
Index	178.72	205.51	182.40	187.05	253.53	193.39	
PER	18.42	25.20	19.71	19.71	43.43	–	
Dividend yield	3.43	2.71	3.39	3.31	2.04	3.25	8.46
30.3.72							
Index	193.86	219.12	209.58	207.48	289.13	217.69	
PER	19.77	21.95	21.59	21.01	48.63	–	
Dividend yield	3.24	2.83	3.00	3.07	1.85	2.96	8.72
30.6.72							
Index	177.62	201.73	200.99	197.26	266.18	206.42	
PER	16.69	19.80	18.88	18.62	40.09	–	
Dividend yield	3.66	3.19	3.27	3.36	2.04	3.22	9.33
29.9.72							
Index	165.74	189.59	197.25	191.16	266.43	199.00	
PER	14.83	16.33	17.68	17.17	36.62	–	
Dividend yield	4.01	3.41	3.39	3.51	2.16	3.40	9.46
29.12.72							
Index	184.82	207.34	211.99	206.59	308.35	218.18	
PER	15.96	17.07	18.53	18.03	39.05	–	
Dividend yield	3.64	3.18	3.25	3.31	1.88	3.15	9.84
30.3.73							
Index	166.15	178.93	178.97	180.04	256.83	189.56	
PER	16.34	15.38	17.70	17.57	41.19	–	
Dividend yield	4.10	3.55	3.97	3.87	2.24	3.69	10.24
29.6.73							
Index	172.25	181.23	180.66	182.37	295.31	191.95	
PER	15.60	14.37	15.85	16.07	44.40	–	
Dividend yield	4.03	3.39	3.96	3.86	2.05	3.67	10.43

Date	*Capital Goods*	*Consumer Goods Durable*	*Consumer Goods Non-durable*	*500 Share Index*	*Property*	*Goods*	*2½ % Consols*
28.9.73							
Index	162.26	170.59	171.76	173.44	291.19	181.43	
PER	13.00	12.28	13.87	14.03	38.02	–	
Dividend yield	4.33	3.62	4.25	4.12	2.12	3.93	11.40
31.12.73							
Index	120.88	128.03	145.64	139.87	210.63	149.76	
PER	9.50	8.79	11.46	11.02	26.87	–	
Dividend yield	5.83	4.86	5.12	5.15	2.99	4.77	12.25
29.3.74							
Index	99.26	85.73	107.00	108.71	144.46	118.31	
PER	7.49	6.24	8.12	7.87	18.47	–	
Dividend yield	7.09	7.40	6.98	6.72	4.42	6.17	14.77
28.6.74							
Index	90.01	78.79	98.78	99.90	120.93	105.35	
PER	6.14	5.70	6.97	6.74	16.32	–	
Dividend yield	8.11	8.58	7.89	7.66	5.59	7.31	15.58
30.9.74							
Index	66.70	52.42	72.53	72.78	119.71	76.92	
PER	4.20	3.74	4.99	4.75	17.46	–	
Dividend yield	11.03	12.80	10.79	10.62	5.22	10.15	15.01
31.12.74							
Index	55.43	42.19	65.42	63.75	98.65	66.89	
PER	3.48	3.25	4.59	4.18	14.29	–	
Dividend yield	13.50	14.14	11.81	12.12	6.69	11.71	17.20
27.3.75							
Index	103.47	77.80	114.29	112.12	179.78	118.32	
PER	6.49	6.02	7.92	6.89	26.13	–	
Dividend yield	7.40	7.74	6.85	6.95	3.31	6.70	14.13
30.6.75							
Index	108.94	78.78	120.90	118.20	158.69	128.21	
PER	6.96	6.61	8.50	7.38	30.19	–	
Dividend yield	7.38	7.80	6.86	6.99	3.74	6.51	14.89
30.9.75							
Index	122.47	98.55	137.83	134.40	165.20	144.66	
PER	7.96	8.40	9.96	8.83	45.70	–	
Dividend yield	6.66	6.25	6.15	6.29	3.50	5.91	14.46
31.12.75							
Index	142.01	120.46	149.57	149.96	174.49	158.08	
PER	9.23	9.77	11.07	10.03	65.95	–	
Dividend yield	5.93	5.20	5.81	5.77	2.78	5.47	14.67
31.3.76							
Index	154.75	136.13	151.81	159.06	162.50	164.61	
PER	10.07	10.41	10.72	10.53	58.72	–	
Dividend yield	5.54	4.56	5.85	5.53	3.03	5.35	13.96
30.6.76							
Index	141.28	122.95	144.47	149.08	154.94	155.41	
PER	9.12	8.79	10.32	10.11	51.73	–	
Dividend yield	6.39	5.48	6.33	6.21	3.39	5.91	13.87

Date	*Capital Goods*	*Consumer Goods Durable*	*Consumer Goods Non-durable*	*500 Share Index*	*Property*	*Goods*	*2½ % Consols*
30.9.76							
Index	120.71	99.72	123.62	127.43	128.28	135.00	
PER	6.85	6.54	8.43	7.88	38.16	–	
Dividend yield	7.70	7.00	7.79	7.57	4.27	7.12	14.90
31.12.76							
Index	131.99	115.65	135.57	140.13	138.65	151.96	
PER	6.92	6.94	8.83	8.10	30.26	–	
Dividend yield	7.29	6.19	7.25	7.03	4.03	6.42	14.17
31.3.77							
Index	165.43	149.76	159.77	168.13	179.42	176.51	
PER	8.03	8.29	9.81	9.11	39.56	–	
Dividend yield	6.07	5.25	6.31	6.06	3.15	5.69	12.10
30.6.77							
Index	184.54	172.37	170.25	182.95	189.05	190.69	
PER	8.24	8.86	8.86	8.80	36.65	–	
Dividend yield	5.77	4.97	6.19	5.86	3.12	5.53	12.97
30.9.77							
Index	217.08	202.90	207.70	216.95	227.09	224.45	
PER	9.10	9.51	10.40	9.74	70.83	–	
Dividend yield	5.20	4.26	5.17	5.16	2.59	4.89	10.40
30.12.77							
Index	208.95	193.59	203.79	208.74	244.71	214.53	
PER	8.35	8.42	9.63	8.88	66.67	–	
Dividend yield	5.60	4.71	5.44	5.52	2.79	5.28	10.46
31.3.78							
Index	201.44	185.41	194.65	199.83	231.44	205.27	
PER	7.90	7.88	8.51	8.06	66.21	–	
Dividend yield	5.81	5.15	5.96	5.88	2.93	5.64	11.42
30.6.78							
Index	210.34	192.51	198.13	206.20	226.25	210.67	
PER	7.69	7.96	8.32	8.04	47.77	–	
Dividend yield	5.76	5.01	5.92	5.82	3.29	5.65	12.41
29.9.78							
Index	241.92	213.49	214.23	227.35	257.26	228.35	
PER	8.60	8.68	8.68	8.67	50.66	–	
Dividend yield	5.16	4.96	5.73	5.52	2.95	5.43	12.33
29.12.78							
Index	230.71	207.15	206.66	216.21	267.42	220.22	
PER	7.90	7.84	8.06	7.99	43.80	–	
Dividend yield	5.63	5.21	6.17	6.02	3.07	5.79	12.33
30.3.79							
Index	270.05	242.93	252.05	257.20	344.07	266.28	
PER	8.99	8.92	9.32	9.06	49.22	–	
Dividend yield	5.01	4.45	5.18	5.20	2.38	4.94	10.74
29.6.79							
Index	242.67	229.08	234.21	235.32	342.22	247.88	
PER	7.48	8.58	7.82	7.79	49.15	–	
Dividend yield	5.55	4.87	5.78	5.73	2.57	5.32	11.42

Date	*Capital Goods*	*Consumer Goods Durable*	*Consumer Goods Non-durable*	*500 Share Index*	*Property*	*Goods*	*2½ % Consols*
28.9.79							
Index	241.30	240.55	240.22	240.50	367.05	254.73	
PER	7.12	8.09	7.55	7.59	44.11	–	
Dividend yield	5.99	4.86	5.95	5.92	2.58	5.96	10.68
31.12.79							
Index	213.41	190.39	203.74	207.70	316.73	229.79	
PER	6.27	6.53	6.30	6.53	34.41	–	
Dividend yield	7.22	6.38	7.37	7.22	3.39	6.87	11.82
31.3.80							
Index	229.96	204.95	209.49	217.46	356.91	240.38	
PER	6.58	7.39	6.36	6.55	39.32	–	
Dividend yield	6.83	6.17	7.37	7.18	3.13	6.91	12.56
30.6.80							
Index	252.88	219.18	227.98	238.49	404.68	269.54	
PER	6.91	8.14	6.64	6.86	42.01	–	
Dividend yield	6.38	5.86	7.03	6.79	2.86	6.40	11.96
30.9.80							
Index	279.56	235.69	237.96	251.30	454.08	290.26	
PER	7.70	8.76	6.98	7.39	44.57	–	
Dividend yield	5.92	5.33	6.80	6.53	2.63	6.12	11.68
31.12.80							
Index	287.41	232.76	238.14	253.44	445.03	291.99	
PER	8.00	8.99	7.31	7.63	42.09	–	
Dividend yield	5.75	5.21	6.72	6.45	2.76	6.10	12.11
		CONSUMER GROUP					
31.3.81							
Index	338.13	264.67		283.55	508.98	309.73	
PER	10.77	8.59		9.33	46.29	–	
Dividend yield	4.75	5.94		5.60	2.46	5.78	12.14
30.6.81							
Index	353.98	284.00		300.14	489.35	320.57	
PER	12.04	9.70		10.41	38.44	–	
Dividend yield	4.37	5.62		5.27	2.83	5.66	
30.9.81							
Index	310.43	247.47		262.38	396.23	278.69	
PER	10.77	8.77		9.63	27.86	–	
Dividend yield	5.10	6.54		6.06	3.59	6.58	
31.12.81							
Index	358.85	269.25		294.58	452.91	313.12	
PER	12.80	9.10		10.59	27.42	–	
Dividend yield	4.43	6.14		5.46	3.23	5.89	
31.3.82							
Index	370.64	303.72		320.67	460.26	326.59	
PER	12.61	10.06		10.73	28.40	–	
Dividend yield	4.29	5.50		5.13	3.24	5.80	
30.6.82							
Index	387.45	302.48		324.13	402.88	322.79	
PER	13.15	9.30		10.36	24.03	–	
Dividend yield	4.26	5.77		5.32	3.99	6.09	

Date	*Capital Goods*	*Consumer Goods Durable*	*Consumer Goods Non-durable*	*500 Share Index*	*Property*	*Goods*	*2½ % Consols*
30.9.82							
Index	433.10	373.03		377.95	399.56	361.81	
PER	13.93	11.07		11.65	22.86	–	
Dividend yield	3.89	4.69		4.60	4.13	5.50	
31.12.82							
Index	427.19	401.42		395.34	414.23	381.30	
PER	13.27	11.68		11.93	21.09	–	
Dividend yield	4.01	4.38		4.43	4.21	5.27	
31.3.83							
Index	444.41	413.58		414.27	462.75	411.94	
PER	14.26	11.98		12.89	23.64	–	
Dividend yield	3.84	4.32		4.24	3.78	4.94	
10.8.83							
Index	475.81	436.14		447.78	446.28	454.66	
PER	14.97	11.86		13.32	21.58	–	
Dividend yield	3.68	4.40		4.14	4.17	4.65	
30.9.83							
Index	448.12			434.83	464.89	445.53	
PER	14.01	11.67		12.81	21.75	–	
Dividend yield	3.95	4.47		4.31	4.05	4.80	
31.1.84							
Index	490.99	491.38		489.65	553.22	504.11	
PER	15.00	12.44		13.77	24.35	–	
Dividend yield	3.63	4.11		3.94	3.58	4.33	
30.4.84							
Index	529.37	543.25		531.83	584.61	534.84	
PER	14.51	12.83		13.41	25.93	–	
Dividend yield	3.51	3.94		3.84	3.42	4.36	
31.7.84							
Index	464.28	480.58		471.16	559.42	474.83	
PER	11.76	10.63		11.01	23.47	–	
Dividend yield	4.16	4.66		4.57	3.82	5.09	
31.10.84							
Index	529.98	562.82		547.11	625.53	543.48	
PER	12.93	11.90		12.25	26.05	–	
Dividend yield	3.80	4.09		4.03	3.48	4.63	
31.1.85							
Index	550.67	630.32		627.58	624.94	614.62	
PER	12.94	13.11		13.33	24.54	–	
Dividend yield	3.94	3.78		3.86	3.57	4.30	
31.4.85							
Index	550.16	641.88		635.79	633.34	622.11	
PER	12.27	12.50		12.85	23.70	–	
Dividend yield	4.05	3.87		3.96	3.64	4.52	
31.7.85							
Index	500.83	648.84		621.34	625.15	606.45	
PER	11.14	12.59		12.43	22.61	–	
Dividend yield	4.50	4.02		4.20	3.80	4.72	

Date	*Capital Goods*	*Consumer Goods Durable*	*Consumer Goods Non-durable*	*500 Share Index*	*Property*	*Goods*	*2½ % Consols*
31.10.85							
Index	558.05	745.58		693.21	694.27	670.64	
PER	12.10	14.49		13.77	24.73	–	
Dividend yield	4.07	3.60		3.83	3.49	4.35	
31.1.86							
Index	634.82	813.48		757.78	716.81	719.01	
PER	13.98	15.11		14.59	24.18	–	
Dividend yield	3.64	3.46		3.62	3.45	4.14	
30.4.86							
Index	753.28	934.29		868.61	767.44	816.40	
PER	16.26	17.08		16.53	25.36	–	
Dividend yield	3.21	3.00		3.20	3.26	3.73	
31.7.86							
Index	695.68	894.66		814.84	778.43	771.80	
PER	14.48	15.61		14.97	23.79	–	
Dividend yield	3.53	3.30		3.58	3.53	4.09	
31.10.86							
Index	661.38	934.54		833.01	787.55	807.27	
PER	13.86	15.64		15.03	22.85	–	
Dividend yield	3.86	3.32		3.63	3.58	4.05	
31.1.87							
Index	798.14	1088.88		983.50	839.09	941.18	
PER	15.98	19.04		17.05	22.87	–	
Dividend yield	3.30	2.90		3.18	3.50	3.58	
30.4.87							
Index	866.74	1191.32		1070.75	1026.69	1023.58	
PER	16.84	20.45		17.97	28.97	–	
Dividend yield	3.06	2.68		2.95	2.78	3.33	
31.7.87							
Index	1007.66	1363.47		1230.55	1303.32	1202.19	
PER	18.41	22.17		19.41	35.32	–	
Dividend yield	2.71	2.49		2.70	2.27	2.95	
31.10.87							
Index	688.43	995.56		872.72	894.13	856.05	
PER	12.27	15.34		13.33	23.82	–	
Dividend yield	4.12	3.54		3.91	3.32	4.28	
12.2.88							
Index	723.69	1008.84		907.66	1012.98	889.66	
PER	12.53	14.49		13.11	23.93	–	
Dividend yield	4.02	3.64		3.91	3.05	4.26	
4.5.88							
Index	763.77	1061.83		944.22	1165.76	925.47	
PER	12.34	14.59		13.03	26.88	–	
Dividend yield	3.95	3.50		3.83	2.66	4.20	
12.8.88							
Index	811.69	1098.99		981.13	1236.06	961.69	
PER	12.41	14.19		12.70	24.97	–	
Dividend yield	3.93	3.60		3.90	2.62	4.27	

Date	*Capital Goods*	*Consumer Goods Durable*	*Consumer Goods Non-durable*	*500 Share Index*	*Property*	*Goods*	*2½ % Consols*
4.11.88							
Index	823.10	1075.29		980.31	1245.37	958.61	
PER	11.75	13.42		12.22	23.20	–	
Dividend yield	4.10	3.74		4.02	2.66	4.42	
3.2.89							
Index	913.25	1185.27		1094.66	1324.89	1067.88	
PER	11.95	14.29		12.96	23.28	–	
Dividend yield	3.91	3.55		3.80	2.54	4.11	
3.5.89							
Index	951.98	1203.91		1123.93	1314.84	1088.10	
PER	11.62	14.07		12.77	21.57	–	
Dividend yield	4.06	3.63		3.89	2.75	4.23	
9.8.89							
Index	1009.91	1363.66		1250.53	1393.22	1200.27	
PER	11.66	15.71		13.59	20.90	–	
Dividend yield	3.98	3.13		3.58	2.82	3.94	
2.11.89							
Index	864.89	1233.83		1109.78	1137.56	1085.73	
PER	9.53	14.07		11.80	16.03	–	
Dividend yield	4.90	3.59		4.25	3.61	4.55	
5.2.90							
Index	895.87	1278.87		1169.12	1189.61	1172.59	
PER	9.60	14.12		11.77	16.41	–	
Dividend yield	4.76	3.72		4.28	3.62	4.40	
1.5.90							
Index	816.15	1158.49		1057.61	1062.15	1049.21	
PER	8.47	12.19		10.43	14.75–		
Dividend yield	5.55	4.23		4.91	4.23	5.15	
6.8.90							
Index	813.62	1229.68		1086.02	1037.90	1092.90	
PER	8.63	12.52		10.57	15.22	–	
Dividend yield	5.70	4.12		4.94	4.55	5.10	
6.11.90							
Index	689.68	1187.86		994.16	925.07	997.79	
PER	7.67	12.04		9.96	16.67	–	
Dividend yield	6.90	4.30		5.43	5.28	5.63	
5.2.91							
Index	732.94	1255.34		1064.15	962.85	1052.70	
PER	8.35	12.85		10.65	19.88	–	
Dividend yield	6.56	4.15		5.13	4.89	5.38	
7.5.91							
Index	849.92	1486.05		1251.39	988.13	1224.41	
PER	11.03	15.02		13.25	21.30	–	
Dividend yield	5.71	3.61		4.44	4.74	4.70	
1.8.91							
Index	828.79	1522.78		1269.55	923.96	1235.89	
PER	11.84	16.18		13.98	23.09	–	
Dividend yield	5.83	3.58		4.51	5.01	4.77	

Date	*Capital Goods*	*Consumer Goods Durable*	*Consumer Goods Non-durable*	*500 Share Index*	*Property*	*Goods*	*2½ % Consols*
4.11.91							
Index	811.09	1565.50		1272.62	894.81	1223.67	
PER	13.32	16.96		14.70	24.21	–	
Dividend yield	5.99	3.56		4.56	5.17	4.86	
3.2.92							
Index	785.38	1666.71		1300.94	785.64	1223.33	
PER	14.79	17.68		15.31	18.09	–	
Dividend yield	6.11	3.30		4.45	5.77	4.85	
5.5.92							
Index	888.58	1717.24		1384.29	724.25	1288.53	
PER	18.76	17.44		16.27	18.81	–	
Dividend yield	5.24	3.31		4.18	6.31	4.59	
3.8.92							
Index	742.32	1547.33		1236.36	547.00	1151.28	
PER	16.04	15.51		14.28	12.21	–	
Dividend yield	6.05	3.72		4.69	8.35	5.16	
3.11.92							
Index	767.73	1663.63		1333.74	593.77	1269.55	
PER	17.66	17.84		16.09	13.89	–	
Dividend yield	5.70	3.49		4.38	7.10	4.63	
2.2.93							
Index	925.55	1715.25		1444.81	701.76	1384.44	
PER	21.42	18.30		17.36	16.18	20.32	
Dividend yield	4.65	3.44		4.10	6.03	4.30	
5.5.93							
Index	981.92	1649.57		1430.42	777.39	1389.12	
PER	23.94	17.84		17.43	22.50	19.89	
Dividend yield	3.92	3.42		3.82	5.10	3.95	
3.8.93							
Index	1051.89	1641.96		1477.14	967.48	1457.25	
PER	32.83	17.84		19.24	32.07	21.92	
Dividend yield	3.79	3.51		3.79	4.21	3.81	
2.11.93							
Index	1073.72	1712.21		1560.42	1110.79	1562.16	
PER	33.39	18.45		20.35	36.30	23.18	
Dividend yield	3.81	3.44		3.65	3.65	3.62	

Date	*General Manufacturers*	*Consumer Goods*	*Non Financials*	*Property*	*All Share Index*
7.2.94					
Index	2190.67	2962.03	1826.41	1847.72	1719.48
PER	43.17	17.78	22.39	44.20	25.12
Dividend yield	3.36	3.77	3.37	3.34	3.29
3.5.94					
Index	2115.55	2765.83	1707.60	1636.96	1570.95
PER	29.17	15.75	20.49	33.07	20.04
Dividend yield	3.56	4.20	3.67	3.74	3.69

Date	*General Manufacturers*	*Consumer Goods*	*Non Financials*	*Property*	*All Share Index*
1.8.94					
Index	2020.45	2686.35	1677.79	1576.85	1551.22
PER	26.62	15.41	19.49	32.27	18.63
Dividend yield	3.76	4.33	3.82	3.82	3.83
7.11.94					
Index	1855.96	2723.26	1645.18	1448.07	1525.19
PER	23.40	15.63	18.62	28.04	17.80
Dividend yield	4.12	4.41	3.95	3.81	3.97
6.2.95					
Index	1803.54	2861.77	1636.57	1363.69	1508.21
PER	20.22	16.35	17.71	16.05	16.91
Dividend yield	4.33	4.27	4.04	4.41	4.07
1.5.95					
Index	1884.26	3042.87	1707.71	1341.72	1580.26
PER	18.16	17.12	17.13	23.44	16.23
Dividend yield	4.16	4.26	4.01	4.48	4.05
7.8.95					
Index	2001.87	3311.55	1841.12	1488.85	1715.47
PER	17.21	17.63	16.96	22.62	16.28
Dividend yield	4.06	3.97	3.83	4.14	3.84
6.11.95					
Index	1930.62	3464.27	1830.08	1366.40	1728.27
PER	15.89	17.70	16.57	20.71	16.05
Dividend yield	4.27	3.88	3.90	4.53	3.87
5.2.96					
Index	2035.48	3657.82	1940.84	1445.83	1838.74
PER	16.43	18.79	17.08	22.03	16.85
Dividend yield	4.06	3.75	3.76	4.31	3.71
7.5.96					
Index	2134.91	3463.69	2002.65	1566.46	1877.91
PER	16.70	16.72	17.22	23.51	16.27
Dividend yield	3.97	4.04	3.75	4.03	3.76
5.8.96					
Index	1986.52	3632.15	1975.06	1588.92	1872.28
PER	15.57	16.33	16.87	24.85	16.12
Dividend yield	4.36	3.87	3.88	4.03	3.90
4.11.96					
Index	2025.34	3654.68	2027.43	1645.45	1938.07
PER	17.29	16.38	17.89	25.22	17.10
Dividend yield	4.22	3.94	3.85	3.90	3.83
3.2.97					
Index	2027.78	3895.64	2134.92	1817.74	2079.60
PER	17.61	18.17	18.76	26.87	18.22
Dividend yield	3.80	3.72	3.61	3.51	3.54
6.5.97					
Index	1966.52	4366.97	2197.18	1934.97	2167.26
PER	16.13	19.77	18.59	29.01	18.18
Dividend yield	4.07	3.47	3.65	3.30	3.56

Date	*General Manufacturers*	*Consumer Goods*	*Non Financials*	*Property*	*All Share Index*
11.8.97					
Index	2070.74	4632.89	2351.42	2027.35	2357.52
PER	16.88	20.66	19.76	29.26	18.92
Dividend yield	3.86	3.31	3.47	3.23	3.33
3.11.97					
Index	2048.80	4539.25	2349.35	2185.90	2318.98
PER	16.76	20.52	19.68	30.86	18.86
Dividend yield	3.83	3.26	3.39	3.02	3.33
2.2.98					
Index	1909.80	5834.49	2559.16	2330.64	2589.06
PER	15.53	26.23	21.16	31.29	20.84
Dividend yield	4.02	2.62	3.14	2.77	3.00
5.5.98					
Index	2337.92	5828.68	2829.58	2377.21	2817.36
PER	18.00	27.23	23.16	31.31	22.22
Dividend yield	3.38	2.51	2.82	2.73	2.80
3.8.98					
Index	1949.52	5779.53	2770.45	1895.76	2721.09
PER	14.76	28.51	22.82	22.16	21.94
Dividend yield	3.71	2.53	2.85	3.41	2.91
2.11.98					
Index	1767.77	5781.76	2617.39	1746.33	2544.34
PER	13.56	27.53	21.22	20.53	20.12
Dividend yield	4.15	2.38	2.98	3.82	3.08

Date and category	**General Industrials**	**Consumer Goods**	**Non-Financials**	**Property**	**All Share**
03/02/1999					
Index	1882.02	5936.67	2791.76	1752.94	2730.31
PER	14.3	28.46	23.76	21.86	22.42
Div yield (gross)	3.87	2.25	2.78	3.56	2.85
19/05/1999		**Non cyclical consumer goods**		**Real estate**	
Index	140.34	5572.4	2933.34	1959.25	2887.91
PER	18.24	28.53	27.23	22.49	25.33
Div yield(actual)	2.55	2.24	2.28	2.89	2.35
03/08/1999					
Index	2224.58	5384.6	3016.76	2067.8	2946.58
PER	18.65	28.22	29.57	30.74	26.64
Yield	2.57	2.35	2.21	2.4	2.31
0/12/1999					
Index	2603.52	5166.56	2617.39	1848.88	3153.76
PER	19.01	27.78		21.99	27.83
Yield	2.66	2.39		3.36	2.18
2/02/2000					
Index	2384.41	4883.24	3190	1744.35	2984.25
PER	17.28	26.52		20.46	26.32
Yield	2.92	2.5		3.56	2.29

Date	*General Manufacturers*	*Consumer Goods*	*Non Financials*	*Property*	*All Share Index*
11/05/2000					
Index	2463.83	5996.36	3120	1881.05	2971.54
PER	16.95	18.96		20.33	25.31
Yield	2.91	1.69		2.78	2.21
01/08/2000					
Index	2608.26	5894.81	3193	2015.53	3102.86
PER					
Yield		2.37		2.76	2.34
01/11/2000					
Index	2190	5700.17	3078.01	2045.68	2977.26
PER					
Yield		2.59		2.93	2.4
01/02/2001					
Index	2093.14	5704.95	2792.71	2300.75	2992.06
PER					
Yield		2.59		2.51	
01/05/2001					
Index	2056.03	5316.82	2808.59	2279.16	2822.18
PER		12.62			
Yield				2.56	2.65
01/08/2001					
index	1970.39	5064.88	2424.14	2239.53	2628.57
PER					
Yield		12.62		2.69	2.99
01/11/2001					
Index	1605.41	4653.79	2397	2019.83	2406.13
PER		12.2			
yield				2.98	3.27
01/02/2002					
Index	1779.41	4467	2472.33	2091.92	2491.86
PER		12.92			
Yield				3.06	3.15
01/05/2002					
Index	1908.51	5319.92	2124.07	2382.12	2541.27
PER		12.19			
Yield				2.75	3.17
01/08/2002					
Index	1515.38	4455.54	1788.59	2076.64	1995.47
PER		11.62			
Yield				3.23	4.02
01/11/2002					
Index	1193.2	3839.82	1854.89	1948.82	1973.16
PER		11.16			
Yield				3.46	4.04
03/02/2003					
Index	1054.28	3459.78	1750.33	1829.28	1873.69
PER		11.16			
Yield					4.32

Date	*General Manufacturers*	*Consumer Goods*	*Non Financials*	*Property*	*All Share Index*
01/05/2003					
Index	1038.99	3791.61	1878.77		1823.96
PER		13.04			
Yield					4.45
01/08/2003					
Index	1283.63	4976.13	1973.46	2053.42	1991.57
PER		15.63			
Yield				5.51	4.02
03/11/2003					
Index	1440.34	6068.88	2142.38	2255.17	2113.66
PER					
Yield		17.33		5.118	3.8
2/02/2004					
Index	1385.89	5977.41	2161.16	2474.24	2224.74
PER		17.08			
Yield	3.91	3.05		5.05	3.69
04/05/2004					
Index	1539.79	5814.18	2139.91	2626.33	2235.85
PER		16.18			
Yield	3.32	1.82		4.58	3.62
02/08/2004					
Index	1519.34	5910.49	2241.64	2852.1	2198.68
PER		14.91			
Yield	3.35	3.06		2.9	3.82
01/11/2004					
Index	1642	5524.47	2316.62	2848.78	2324.52
PER		14.23			
Yield	3.2	3.34		3.34	3.57
01/02/2005					
Index	1784.8	6368.1	2383.84	3405.19	2426.86
PER					
Yield	2.92	2.9		2.8	3.53
03/05/2005					
Index	1708.83	5894.28	2546.83	3295.54	2479
PER					
Yield	3.13	4.51		2.86	3.72
01/08/2005					
Index	1983.25	6107.27	2593.75	3474.89	2644.75
Per	20.28	18.21	16.31	22.33	15.7
Yield	12.78	2.89	2.87	2.42	3.07
01/11/2005					
Index	2042.3	6388.81	2641.05	3508.83	2928.56
PER	23.89	18.72	15.23	19.85	15.24
Yield	2.77	2.77	2.85	2.38	3.09
01/02/2006					
Index	2475.22	7254.09	2869.47	4246.38	2928.56
PER	25.41	16.19	16.02	12.39	15.24
Yield	2.42	2.98	2.67	2.06	2.88

Date	*General Manufacturers*	*Consumer Goods*	*Non Financials*	*Property*	*All Share Index*
01/05/2006					
Index	2660.24	7520	3006.24	4594.77	3074.26
PER	21.35	13.66	14.72	9.05	14.37
Yield	2.39	2.97	2.71	2	2.92
01/08/2006					
Index	2480.12	7617.79	2948.06	4797.3	3004.28
PER	16.45	12.95	13.2	8.51	13.31
Yield	2.56	2.97	2.88	2.04	2.99
01/11/2006					
Index	2731.7	7889.54	3042.3	5273.33	3140.47
PER	20.7	13.09	13.92	8.48	13.83
Yield	2.23	2.98	2.79	1.72	2.97
01/02/2007					
Index	2912.86	8493.61	3108.84	5519.71	3211.84
PER	20.76	14.5	15.58	8.48	14.89
Yield	2.12	2.75	2.68	1.72	2.83
01/05/2007					
Index	3124.32	9086.76	3304.39	5409.47	3355.6
PER	22.89	16.54	15	5.06	13.86
Yield	2.03	2.53	2.59	1.75	2.78
01/08/2007					
Index	3047.97	8746.58	3294.99	4503.42	3289.12
PER	20.47	14.73	13.94	3.86	13.08
Yield	2	2.73	2.59	2.18	2.87
01/11/2007					
Index	3106.53	9244.1	3541.35	4130.31	3454.12
PER	19.62	15.93	14.35	3.38	13.1
Yield	2.02	2.67	2.48	2.51	2.79
01/02/2008					
Index	2567.99	8436.88	3140.59	3793.43	3000.1
PER	15.35	15.23	12.52	3.65	11.02
Yield	2.56	2.98	2.93	2.8	3.33
01/05/2008					
Index	2657.82	8673.02	3279.89	3464.82	3099.94
PER	15.1	15.73	12.52	18.57	11.95
Yield	2.95	3.16	3.08	3.51	3.6
01/08/2008					
Index	2382.32	7554.34	2958.1	2877.5	2749.21
PER	13.64	14.16	10.92	neg	11.05
Yield	3.37	3.83	3.57	4.5	4.26
01/09/2008					
Index	2596.91	8095.21	3071.41	3017.33	2855.12
PER	14.53	16.37	11.22	*	12.15
Yield	3.16	3.51	3.45	4.30	4.03
31/12/2008					
Index	1934.69	7565.98	2544.01	1853.87	2209.29
PER	11.10	17.11	9.05	*	9.09
Yield	4.13	3.76	4.21	6.81	4.49

Date	*General Manufacturers*	*Consumer Goods*	*Non Financials*	*Property*	*All Share Index*
31/03/2009					
Index	2699.60	9885.90	3353.80	1761.30	2910.20
PER	15.29	18.74	14.45	*	17.53
Yield	2.62	3.16	3.25	3.64	3.16
01/07/2009					
Index	1956.50	7396.90	2541.50	1562.30	2215.80
PER	14.92	18.52	9.76	*	10.95
Yield	3.75	3.82	4.33	6.70	4.47
01/10/2009					
Index	2327.00	8565.80	2890.20	2005.50	2593.80
PER	16.40	23.35	14.37	*	17.37
Yield	2.98	3.36	3.54	4.57	3.38
04/01/2010					
Index	2487.60	9348.20	3223.70	1808.70	2807.00
PER	16.79	22.15	16.10	*	19.36
Yield	2.76	3.13	3.24	3.49	3.15
01/04/2010					
Index	2739.40	9982.80	3394.40	1761.20	2943.90
PER	15.52	18.92	14.62	*	17.73
Yield	2.59	3.13	3.21	3.64	3.12
01/07/2010					
Index	2490.70	9037.50	2852.20	1506.70	2485.70
PER	13.90	14.91	10.82	*	12.80
Yield	2.84	3.50	3.46	3.62	3.42
01/10/2010					
Index	2841.20	9962.00	3315.20	1641.60	2889.70
PER	18.14	14.99	13.46	*	14.46
Yield	2.61	3.41	3.24	3.42	3.15
04/01/2011					
Index	3110.20	10696.10	3640.50	1678.50	3119.00
PER	19.83	15.41	12.01	*	13.14
Yield	2.39	3.20	2.85	3.38	2.84
01/04/2011					
Index	3157.10	10566.90	3636.80	1729.30	3116.80
PER	17.39	14.07	13.91	16.08	14.42
Yield	2.52	3.41	2.91	3.37	2.91
01/07/2011					
Index	3250.40	11239.50	3662.70	1871.80	3120.30
PER	17.63	14.67	11.24	18.45	12.09
Yield	2.46	3.26	2.97	3.06	2.96
03/10/2011					
Index	2679.95	10823.90	3175.97	1515.56	2628.41
PER	12.17	13.87	8.04	12.70	8.68
Yield	3.08	3.50	3.60	3.45	3.69
03/01/2012					
Index	3046.13	11915.37	3577.18	1574.69	2923.63
PER	14.01	14.97	10.38	11.07	10.85
Yield	2.93	3.23	3.34	3.06	3.44

Date	*General Manufacturers*	*Consumer Goods*	*Non Financials*	*Property*	*All Share Index*
02/04/2012					
Index	3424.49	12745.54	3669.36	1663.98	3053.42
PER	16.32	16.15	10.03	13.10	10.74
Yield	2.57	3.12	3.32	2.95	3.39
02/07/2012					
Index	3265.91	12791.17	3527.37	1640.80	2927.12
PER	15.22	16.05	10.20	17.78	10.93
Yield	2.81	3.15	3.58	3.15	3.65
01/10/2012					
Index	3486.31	13024.39	3625.20	1763.08	3038.34
PER	15.86	16.04	11.03	18.35	12.05
Yield	2.71	3.19	3.57	2.99	3.59
02/01/2013					
Index	3650.97	13541.56	3690.49	1903.43	3159.65
PER	16.26	16.41	11.53	20.75	12.59
Yield	2.64	3.09	3.56	2.77	3.50
02/04/2013					
Index	4171.29	15649.81	4004.05	2097.36	3420.02
PER	18.56	17.80	14.14	13.38	15.49
Yield	2.34	2.78	3.33	2.47	3.31
01/07/2013					
Index	4122.67	15073.68	3885.57	2318.04	3338.61
PER	19.21	17.01	12.67	16.85	13.70
Yield	2.40	2.90	3.52	2.15	3.48
01/10/2013					
Index	4423.84	14595.76	4007.71	2529.61	3445.08
PER	23.79	15.83	15.15	14.67	15.87
Yield	2.28	3.08	3.46	1.96	3.41
02/01/2014					
Index	4616.59	15110.94	4203.13	2663.45	3595.75
PER	24.55	16.44	14.05	13.90	14.83
Yield	2.18	3.03	3.33	1.71	3.29
01/04/2014					
Index	4617.77	15301.15	4216.27	2870.91	3584.47
PER	23.40	16.51	13.16	14.06	14.43
Yield	2.20	3.07	3.43	1.69	3.39
01/07/2014					
Index	4428.81	15961.96	4297.28	2646.09	3630.37
PER	21.85	17.51	13.78	13.08	14.85
Yield	2.36	2.95	3.25	1.65	3.24

[Figures for 2015 onwards are no longer produced in the same format.]

Appendix B

Financial Times Actuaries Equity Indices (at 31 March 1982)

These indices are the joint compilation of the Financial Times, the Institute of Actuaries and the Faculty of Actuaries.

EQUITY GROUPS & SUB-SECTIONS	Wed 31 March 1982					Tue Mar 20	Mon Mar 29	Fri Mar 26	Thur Mar 25	Year Ago (approx)
Figures in parenthesis show number of stocks per section	Index No.	Est Day's Change %	Gross Div Earnings Yield % (Max.)	Est Yield % (ACT at 30%)	P/E Ratio (Net)	Index No.	Index No.	Index No.	Index No.	Index No.
1 CAPITAL GOODS (206)	370.64	+1.1	9.82	4.29	12.61	316.73	383.98	366.12	361.45	342.27
2 Building Materials (23)	327.18	-0.7	13.54	5.25	8.88	329.60	329.40	330.66	532.75	307.60
3 Contracting, Construction (28)	607.03	+0.2	14.43	4.75	8.20	605.18	607.31	610.04	614.54	575.46
4 Electricals (31)	1288.40	+1.3	7.25	2.30	17.63	1271.38	1258.90	1265.09	1273.00	1083.97
5 Engineering Contractors (9)	496.11	+0.7	13.01	5.92	8.95	492.51	493.41	496.57	501.63	444.65
6 Mechanical Engineering (67)	196.40	+2.4	11.79	5.75	10.34	191.88	188.79	189.39	190.61	208.35
8 Metals and Metal Forming (11)	163.20	+2.0	9.76	7.26	13.20	159.95	154.21	161.04	162.57	156.13
9 Motors (21)	96.58	+0.6	2.60	6.88	–	95.90	95.70	94.24	96.11	94.30
10 Other Industrial Materials (18)	374.03	+0.8	9.75	5.66	12.41	371.23	369.21	373.54	376.15	355.29
21 CONSUMER GROUP (201)	303.72	+1.5	12.16	5.50	10.08	299.37	294.55	296.40	297.95	266.21
22 Brewers and Distillers (21)	304.27	+1.4	15.34	6.33	7.88	301.89	291.88	299.23	294.00	285.46
25 Food Manufacturing (22)	277.80	+1.3	15.32	6.53	7.85	274.18	271.51	271.72	273.60	261.35
26 Food Retailing (14)	607.35	+0.3	8.86	3.30	13.77	605.79	682.11	683.70	607.20	524.06
27 Health and Household Products (8)	395.52	+1.8	8.34	4.03	14.01	388.65	382.54	383.70	387.61	285.87
29 Leisure (24)	454.55	+2.6	9.90	4.99	12.49	462.87	438.52	407.85	444.61	407.27
32 Newspapers, Publishing (12)	526.71	+0.7	10.78	5.94	12.41	523.16	521.37	525.77	527.10	489.01
33 Packaging and Paper (14)	147.95	+1.5	13.29	7.16	9.00	145.79	146.01	147.37	148.32	138.48
34 Stores (45)	283.07	+1.3	10.05	4.74	13.33	279.36	277.12	275.59	276.63	266.70
35 Textiles (23)	176.18	+0.5	9.61	5.68	13.42	175.32	172.83	172.72	173.64	150.02
36 Tobaccos (3)	313.05	+2.3	19.57	8.33	5.82	306.93	304.65	303.16	304.32	219.38

EQUITY GROUPS & SUB-SECTIONS	Wed 31 March 1982					Tue Mar 20	Mon Mar 29	Fri Mar 26	Thur Mar 25	Year Ago (approx)
Figures in parenthesis show number of stocks per section	Index No.	Est Day's Change %	Gross Div Earnings Yield % (Max.)	Est Yield % (ACT at 30%)	P/E Ratio (Net)	Index No.	Index No.	Index No.	Index No.	Index No.
39 Other Consumer (15)	296.35	+0.5	1.52	5.33	–	294.90	291.83	294.06	293.39	273.87
41 OTHER GROUPS (78)	257.45	+1.0	13.09	6.04	9.21	254.88	253.32	253.91	254.31	221.68
42 Chemicals (16)	335.63	+1.6	13.29	6.88	8.99	139.42	328.00	324.33	334.47	259.25
44 Office Equipment (4)	126.85	-0.3	12.69	6.78	9.59	127.24	126.15	125.24	127.28	118.81
45 Shipping and Transport (13)	583.96	+1.0	18.79	6.33	6.31	578.02	575.08	578.08	500.08	611.83
46 Miscellaneous (45)	327.44	+0.7	11.31	5.00	10.82	325.27	322.93	324.16	325.45	289.91
49 INDUSTRIAL GROUP (487)	320.67	+1.2	11.43	5.13	10.73	316.71	314.08	314.79	316.75	285.88
51 Oils (13)	681.00	+0.7	18.34	8.50	6.36	676.22	862.22	692.64	682.47	782.54
59 500 SHARE INDEX	350.07	+1.2	12.50	5.65	9.70	346.04	342.49	345.58	346.57	325.54
61 FINANCIAL GROUP (117)	259.41	+0.6	–	6.20	–	257.78	256.31	257.98	258.99	256.44
62 Banks (6)	271.62	-1.1	38.82	7.87	2.82	274.76	272.62	274.23	275.89	234.21
63 Discount Houses (9)	232.06	–	–	9.34	–	232.05	234.96	234.90	234.33	304.68
65 Insurance (Life) (9)	288.94	+3.2	–	6.26	–	260.69	258.47	259.55	259.20	270.95
66 Insurance (Composite) (10)	164.31	+0.8	–	8.29	–	163.06	163.34	166.81	167.33	168.51
67 Insurance Brokers (7)	484.75	+1.7	10.88	5.14	12.55	476.51	478.35	488.65	469.14	353.66
68 Merchant Banks (12)	153.61	+2.9	–	5.46	–	149.28	148.04	145.63	145.83	158.67
69 Property (49)	480.26	+0.7	4.70	3.24	28.40	457.00	453.84	455.92	459.00	511.04
70 Other Financial (15)	179.90	-0.4	18.25	6.36	6.58	180.69	179.34	179.26	179.64	172.45
71 Investment Trusts (112)	298.53	+0.7	–	5.40	–	296.47	295.53	295.84	295.60	301.11
81 Mining Finance (4)	204.96	+0.3	16.53	6.93	7.35	204.30	203.33	204.68	287.85	290.32
99 Overseas Traders (17)	383.44	+0.4	13.65	8.30	8.94	381.88	390.61	381.64	343.51	440.04
99 ALL-SHARE INDEX (750)	326.59	+1.0	–	5.80	–	323.31	320.46	323.00	324.02	311.45

FIXED INTEREST						
	PRICE INDICES	**Wed Mar**	**Day's Change**	**Tue Mar**	**xd adj. today**	**xd adj. to date**
	British Government	**31**	**%**	**30**		**to date**
1	5 years	111.06	+0.32	110.71	–	2.89
2	5–15 years	110.94	+0.94	109.92	–	3.43
3	Over 15 years	115.34	+0.90	114.24	–	3.04
4	Irredeemables	122.45	+1.35	128.81	–	1.62
5	All stocks	112.35	+0.77	111.30	–	3.11
6	**Debentures & Loans**	87.83	+0.44	87.44	–	3.51
7	**Preference**	64.72	-0.00	64.72	–	2.52

AVERAGE GROSS REDEMPTION YIELDS			Wed Mar 31	Tue Mar 30	Year ago (approx.)
	British Government				
1	Low	5 years	11.69	11.91	11.40
2	Coupons	15 years	12.73	12.86	11.95
3		25 years	12.59	12.69	12.03
4	Medium	5 years	13.90	14.05	13.82
5	Coupons	15 years	13.73	13.88	13.43
6		25 years	13.27	13.41	13.11
7	High	5 years	13.87	14.02	13.02
8	Coupons	15 years	13.98	14.00	13.63
9		25 years	13.32	13.58	13.23
10	Irredeemables	‡	12.21	12.30	11.43
11	**Debts & Loans**	5 years	14.72	14.82	14.17
12		15 years	14.64	14.71	14.30
13		25 years	14.60	14.65	14.31
14	**Preference**	‡	15.39	15.19	14.37

‡ Flat yield, highs and lows received, bare dates, values and constituent changes are published in Saturday issues. A list of constituents is available from the Publishers: The Financial Times, Bracken House, Cannon Street, London WC4P 4BY.

Appendix C

Financial Times Actuaries Share Indices and their constituents (for 31 March 1982 valuations)

The following information is taken from the *Investors Chronicle* of 9 April 1982 and will be of particular interest when considering the value of shares at 31 March 1982 for capital gains tax re-basing and indexation purposes.

It should be noted that the P/E ratios shown here have been calculated on the fully taxed basis adopted by the *Investors Chronicle*. They reflect pre-tax profits less corporation tax at the then standard rate of 52%. The figure contained in brackets at the foot of the P/E ratios for each sector is the average using the *Investors Chronicle* method. The figure beneath the figure in brackets is the sector average P/E ratio published in the Financial Times Actuaries Share Indices.

High P	Low P	Stock	End Mar price P	Yield %	P/E ratio	Change on mth. %	Change on 3 mths. %	Change on year %	Rel change on yr. %	Mkt. cap. £m's
BUILDING MATERIALS										
66	32	Aaronson Bros. 10p	32	5.36	53.6	-3.0	-33.3	-44.8	-47.4	8.9
375	224	Aberthaw Cement	335	4.48	11.7	-8.2	-9.9	+48.2	+41.4	13.0
82	42	Alpine Holdings 5p	58	12.93	10.8	+3.5	+18.4	-29.3	-32.5	6.7
550	412	Blue Circle Inds. £1	450	5.00	7.8	-6.2	-11.1	+6.1	+1.2	478.8
418	228	B.P.B. Industries 50p	400	3.39	12.6	+6.4	+22.7	+42.9	+36.2	374.0
83	49	Carr, J. Doncaster	83	3.89	17.0	+10.7	+38.3	+33.9	+27.7	27.4
100	58	Ferguson Indl	98	8.02	10.9	+2.1	+25.6	+27.3	+21.4	20.6
23	16	Fobel Int'110p	19	2.93	63.1	-5.0	-15.6	-13.6	-17.6	3.3
116	87	Hepworth Ceramic	116	6.47	15.8	+7.4	+20.8	-7.6	-11.9	182.5
76	56	Ibstock Johnsen	73	8.81	30.0	+9.0	+12.3	-1.4	-5.9	20.8
80	68	Int. Timber	80	7.14	72.6	-3.6	-4.8	-12.1	-16.2	23.1
90	63	London Brick	83½	7.47	12.3	+7.1	+18.4	+3.1	-1.7	51.7
86	56	Macpherson, D.	83	7.23	12.0	+9.2	+23.9	+18.6	+13.1	15.0
174	126	Magnet & Sthms	166	4.30	18.2	+12.2	+23.9	+1.2	-3.5	176.0
172	123	Manders Hdgs	160	4.38	13.9	-1.8	+15.9	-1.2	-5.8	23.2
51	33	Marley	42½	7.56	13.0	-5.6	-6.6	-4.5	-8.9	86.7
88	50	Meyer, Montague L.	65	5.49	–	+4.8	-1.5	-24.4	-27.9	39.3
358	255	Pilkington Bros. £1	268	5.60	13.5	-2.5	+1.9	-13.5	-17.6	449.3
198	142	Redland	184	5.70	15.6	+6.4	+18.7	-3.7	-8.1	224.9
248	156	RMC Group	235	5.47	11.0	+2.2	+13.0	+15.2	+9.9	189.7
124	70	Ruberoid	124	4.55	12.0	+20.4	+37.8	+53.1	+46.0	14.6
98	68	Rugby Portland	85½	8.10	9.2	-6.0	+5.6	-1.2	-5.7	101.4
478	316	Tarmac	476	4.89	12.8	+9.7	+16.4	+44.2	+37.6	310.7
190	140	Travis & Arnold	176	3.20	12.8	+4.8	+7.3	+7.3	+2.3	30.0
79	46	UBM Group	54½	5.24	–	+0.9	+2.8	-27.8	-31.2	31.9
FTA				Index	5.25					
Sector	Index			327.18	8.86	(12.7)	+2.9	+8.4	+7.6	+2.09

High P	Low P	Stock	End Mar price P	Yield %	P/E ratio	Change on mth. %	Change on 3 mths. %	Change on year %	Rel change on yr. %	Mkt. cap. £m's
CONTRACTING & CONSTRUCTION										
222	155	Aberdeen Const.	220	4.23	13.0	+1.9	+19.6	+26.4	+20.6	24.3
231	162	Barratt Dev. 10p	231	6.28	12.7	+11.1	+29.5	+55.9	+48.7	208.4
101	60	Beltway	89	11.24	13.7	+6.0	+18.7	-3.3	-7.7	11.5
68	39	Bett Bros.20p	56	7.91	10.2	+21.7	+33.3	-3.4	-7.9	89.4
106	51	Bryant Holdings	106	4.51	11.8	+16.5	+35.9	+23.3	+17.5	42.4
1200	755	Burmett & Hallams	755	2.44	12.2	-9.9	-19.5	-39.3	-42.1	100.7
280	204	Costain Group	262	5.73	9.6	-2.2	+12.0	+11.0	+5.9	145.7
179	92	Crouch Group 20p	120	5.24	22.9	+9.1	+17.6	-30.9	-34.1	4.8
166	104	Fairclough Const.	158	4.97	10.7	+4.6	+20.6	+50.5	+43.5	69.4
137	71	Fairview Ests	107	6.15	12.5	+4.9	+9.2	-15.7	-19.7	35.9
106	62	French Kier Hdgs	107½	4.52	10.2	+3.9	+13.2	+70.6	+62.7	51.1
92	59	H.A.T. Group 10p	89½	4.39	18.3	+5.3	+26.1	+37.1	+30.7	55.0
48	25	Hewden-Stuart 10p	31	5.88	–	-11.4	+3.3	-31.1	-34.3	27.2
82	38	Laing, John 'A'	82	5.01	28.5	+6.5	+74.5	+67.3	+59.6	21.6
95	60	Leech (William) 20p	93	10.11	28.6	+1.1	+9.4	-10.6	-14.7	13.9
176	120	Lilley, F.J.C.	176	4.46	11.9	+6.0	+15.0	+23.9	+18.2	46.9
50	33	Ldn. & Nthm Grp	50	10.71	9.0	+17.6	+31.6	+14.9	+9.5	28.4
298	209	Lovell, Y.J.	298	3.84	14.1	+14.6	+28.5	+27.4	+21.5	25.6
140	92	Marchwiel	132	7.14	18.5	+4.8	+20.0	+10.0	+4.9	43.6
67	34	Monk, A.	62	6.34	5.2	-3.1	+6.9	+72.2	+64.2	6.7
194	133	Mowlem, John	184	6.87	10.4	-1.6	+3.4	+22.7	+17.0	36.4
579	133	Newarthill £1	572	1.75	13.0	+14.4	+30.6	+26.0	+20.2	57.2
94	61	Press, William 5p	73	5.64	15.4	+5.8	+14.1	+1.4	-3.3	43.7
182	118	S.G.B. Group	178	4.49	12.5	+6.0	+34.8	+11.3	+6.1	73.8
607	475	Taylor Woodrow	540	3.52	13.9	-0.9	+4.9	-5.1	-9.5	158.0
265	140	Vibroplant	172	12.06	21.2	-0.6	-7.0	-29.8	-33.1	10.3
207	108	Willson, Connolly	196	1.82	11.4	+8.9	+8.9	+79.8	+71.5	41.4
129	79	Wimpey (George)	105	3.47	10.7	+10.5	+9.4	-11.4	-15.5	268.8
FTA Sector Index	607.03	Index 4.75	8.20	(12.2) +5.6	+13.6	+6.3	+0.86			

ELECTRICALS										
343	218	BICC	325	4.56	17.6	+4.5	+15.7	+42.0	+35.4	613.3
230	148	Bowthorpe Hdgs 10p	230	2.12	17.2	+13.3	+29.2	+44.7	+37.9	92.0
27	15	Brown Boveri Kent	19	–	–	-15.6	-29.6	+5.6	+0.7	10.3
40	17	Chloride Group	28	–	–	-22.2	–	-6.7	-11.0	35.5
250	217	Comp. & Syst. Eng. 20p	240	1.88	20.5	+0.8	+4.3	–	–	16.4
83	54	Dale Elec. Intl. 10p	63	5.67	42.5	-11.3	+6.8	-12.5	-16.6	8.4
248	146	Diploma	246	2.32	28.1	+4.2	+20.0	+29.5	+23.5	64.0
32	22	Dowding & Milis 10p	31	7.60	12.4	–	+14.8	+34.8	+28.5	9.4
78	39	Dubllier	75	2.95	30.7	+15.4	+33.9	+36.4	+30.0	19.2
183	113	Electrocomponents 10p	160	1.74	22.6	+1.3	+1.3	+14.6	+9.3	160.0
399	230	Eurotherm Intl. 10p	389	1.84	28.3	+16.5	+45.1	+22.3	+16.7	44.0
168	95	Farnell Elect. 20p	168	1.17	31.2	+16.9	+23.8	+68.4	+60.6	104.2
692	455	Ferranti 50p	665	1.50	32.0	+3.1	+6.4	+12.7	+7.5	283.7
131	36	Forward Tech. Ind.	36	20.90	6.9	-20.0	-42.9	-72.5	-73.8	6.1
849	640	General Electric	826	1.90	18.7	+0.2	-0.1	+20.1	+14.5	4,532.3
51	21	ICL	48	–	–	+6.7	+41.2	+44.5	+37.8	128.2
280	140	Memec 10p	270	1.59	34.9	+14.9	+22.2	–	–	28.9
300	183	M.K. Electric	320	5.36	16.6	+17.2	+32.8	+42.2	+35.6	48.6
134	86	Muirheed	118	3.63	26.0	-7.8	+5.4	+7.3	+2.3	9.9
74	52	Pethow 10p	61	–	–	-3.2	-10.3	+13.0	+7.7	8.2
397	276	Plessey 50p	383	2.97	18.0	+4.9	+5.5	+14.7	+9.4	888.4
232	50	Quest Automation 10p	50	2.86	15.6	-44.4	-63.0	-67.1	-68.6	7.0
478	348	Racal Electronic	380	1.75	26.6	+7.0	-12.8	-0.8	-5.4	1,013.4
315	165	Scholes, George H.	298	8.88	10.1	+12.5	+26.8	+54.4	+47.2	12.8
104	36	Sound Diffusion 5p	104	0.83	–	+26.8	+82.5	+65.1	+57.4	48.0
544	377	Std. Tel. & Cables	512	3.77	21.1	+17.7	+17.7	-0.4	-5.0	512.0
282	179	Unitech	243	4.28	30.4	+7.0	+10.5	-3.6	-8.0	45.8
170	115	Victor Products	130	4.67	20.9	+4.8	+12.1	-8.5	-12.7	9.9
241	115	Vinten Group 20p	241	1.24	31.9	+12.1	+17.6	+89.8	+81.0	39.9
120	73	Ward & Goldstone	110	7.14	9.9	–	-3.5	+25.0	-19.2	16.5
265	164	Wholesale Ftngs 10p	220	2.75	20.1	+17.0	+8.9	-16.0	-19.9	30.8
FTA Sector Index	1,288.40	2.30	Index 17.63	+5.5	(20.3) +2.4	+19.7	+13.56			

High P	Low P	Stock	End Mar price P	Yield %	P/E ratio	Change on mth. %	Change on 3 mths. %	Change on year %	Rel change on yr. %	Mkt. cap. £m's
ENGINEERING CONTRACTORS										
77	52	Capper-Neill 10p	55½	10.81	7.4	-7.5	-2.6	-20.7	-24.4	16.0
75	58	Crown House	73½	10.20	23.8	+2.8	+7.3	+21.5	+15.9	16.5
194	134	Davy Corp.	143	7.36	11.1	-8.9	-18.5	-6.0	-10.3	135.0
243	127	Haden	223	4.13	10.6	+2.3	+10.9	+64.0	+56.4	34.8
224	153	Hall, Matthew	211	2.95	11.2	-4.1	+2.4	+15.9	+10.6	72.1
92	62	Nthn Eng. Inds	87	6.36	15.2	+0.6	+11.5	+10.3	+5.2	188.4
436	330	Simon Engg.	365	4.70	10.4	-4.2	-4.2	+8.0	+3.0	95.0
90	42	Whessoe	89	6.42	7.4	+17.1	+6.0	+107.0	+97.4	16.1
373	220	Wolseley-Hughes	373	5.43	11.9	+8.1	+22.3	+36.6	+30.3	59.4
FTA Sector Index	496.11	5.92	Index 8.85	-1.4	(12.3) +1.1	+15.0	+9.03			
MECHANICAL ENGINEERING										
50	26	Acrow 'A'	43	2.49	–	-4.4	+4.9	+4.9	–	26.5
200	122	Adwest Group	194	5.52	15.1	+1.0	+7.8	+12.8	+7.8	39.8
106	67	Anderson S'Clyde	106	5.53	10.9	+5.0	+19.1	+18.4	+12.9	50.3
298	213	A.P.V. Holdings 50p	263	5.21	10.1	-1.9	+12.9	+0.8	-3.9	80.1
35	13	Aurora Holdings	20	–	–	+17.6	+25.0	-39.4	-42.2	4.3
146	78	Babcock (Int')	106	9.43	17.6	+11.6	+17.6	-15.2	-19.1	118.0
105	70	Baker Parkins 50p	101	7.21	25.0	-1.0	+13.5	+16.1	+10.7	33.6
65	35	Benford Concrete 10p	64	5.86	17.1	+4.9	–	+82.9	+74.4	14.2
490	311	Bestobeli	358	5.19	14.6	+4.4	+3.5	-15.4	-19.3	57.7
32	18	Birmid Qualcast	31	6.91	16.4	+1.6	+19.2	+14.8	+9.5	20.4
46	16	Blackwood Hodge	15½	18.14	–	-16.0	-32.3	-61.8	-63.6	12.5
169	108	Brammer, H-20p	137	5.94	13.9	-2.8	+7.0	-8.1	-12.3	38.2
80	51	Bridon	74	4.63	40.6	+8.8	+5.7	+27.6	+21.7	40.2
252	170	Brit. Aerospace	194	5.74	11.4	+10.2	-6.7	-0.5	-5.1	388.0

129	81	Brit. Steam Spec. 20p	105	7.14	18.3	+8.2	+22.1	-4.5	-9.0	13.0
42	23	Brockhouse	36	3.97	–	-10.0	+9.1	+22.0	+16.4	6.2
101	53	Brown, John £1	57	10.65	8.2	-3.4	-3.6	-36.7	-39.6	74.6
124	80	Bruntona Mussel	117	11.55	12.8	–	+11.4	+25.8	+20.0	9.4
185	126	Bullough 20p	180	8.53	9.2	+2.9	+24.1	+9.8	+4.7	15.7
26	12	Central & Sherwood 5p	12½	12.00	–	–	-19.4	-50.0	-52.3	8.0
118	78	Chubb & Son 20p	118	6.57	29.1	+5.4	+13.5	+35.6	+29.3	71.7
49	25	Concentric 10p	44	10.75	16.7	-6.4	+12.8	+46.7	+39.9	8.3
130	83	Desoutter Bros.	100	8.14	10.5	-2.0	-2.0	-12.3	-16.3	9.4
119	72	Dobson Park Inds 10p	86½	8.60	15.5	+3.6	+2.4	-19.9	-23.6	71.6
203	112	Dowty Group 50p	129	3.78	18.0	+10.3	-6.5	-29.6	-32.9	260.9
151	94	EIS Group	120	4.94	12.6	+8.1	-0.8	+19.4	+13.8	17.8
213	86	Elliott, B.	88	8.12	11.2	-5.4	-8.3	-50.0	-52.3	15.1
75	48	Expanded metal	68	9.45	96.0	-2.9	+7.9	+38.0	+29.7	14.8
181	135	Fenner, J.H.	166	7.75	12.4	-0.6	+10.7	+0.6	-4.1	51.1
387	237	Flight Refuelling	250	2.14	25.1	+4.2	-8.1	-23.9	-27.5	36.8
24	12	Folloss Hefo 5p	13	13.74	–	-10.3	-3.7	-38.1	-41.0	1.7
87	63	G.E.I. Int. 20p	74	10.26	18.2	–	+10.4	–	-4.6	26.2
213	148	Hall Engineering 50p	164	6.63	7.8	+1.2	+5.1	-10.4	-14.5	22.6
112	71	Halma 10p	110	1.70	25.9	+1.9	+32.5	+41.0	+34.5	21.1
356	260	Hawker Siddeley	308	4.13	12.4	-6.1	-5.5	-3.1	-7.6	806.9
112	77	Hopkinsons Hdgs. 50p	112	7.21	8.5	+3.7	+8.7	+41.8	+35.2	12.5
34	13	Howard Machinery	21	–	–	-16.0	-16.0	-34.4	-37.4	6.0
165	127	Howden Group	157	3.76	12.1	-4.8	+3.3	+7.5	+2.5	47.7
64	40	Jones & Shipman	44	5.84	16.3	-8.3	+4.8	-29.0	-32.3	5.3
145	104	Laird Group	123	4.65	11.0	-0.8	-0.8	–	-4.7	96.6
270	213	Martonair Int. 20p	226	4.80	16.1	+2.7	+2.7	-8.5	-12.7	29.4
180	90	Mining Supplies 10p	135	2.12	–	+17.4	+21.6	-14.0	-18.0	32.3
55	42	Mitchell Cotts	44	14.46	9.5	-16.2	-9.3	-5.4	-9.8	36.8
183	122	Mollins	173	6.52	14.3	-4.9	+8.8	+39.5	+33.0	50.7
45	26	Neill, James Hdg.	33	–	–	-2.9	-10.8	-2.9	-7.4	5.9
210	142	Pegler-Hattersley	204	6.65	10.4	+6.3	+13.3	+20.0	+14.4	62.3
213	123	Ransomes, Sims	200	7.96	22.1	+17.0	+37.9	+26.6	+20.7	11.1

High P	Low P	Stock	End Mar price P	Yield %	P/E ratio	Change on mth. %	Change on 3 mths. %	Change on year %	Rel change on yr. %	Mkt. cap. £m's
65	39	Redman Heenan 10p	49	12.24	–	+2.1	+4.3	-15.5	-19.4	9.1
76	35	Renold £1	41	–	–	–	+5.1	-36.9	-39.3	16.5
94	47	RHP Group £1	66	8.66	16.5	+1.5	-2.9	-14.3	-18.3	23.3
535	375	Ricardo Con. Eng.	496	2.45	22.9	+13.2	+14.8	+2.3	-2.5	17.8
41	18	Richardsns, Wstgth 50p	25½	10.08	–	-7.3	+6.3	-15.0	-18.9	3.3
60	41	Rotork 10p	52	6.73	8.1	+18.2	+15.6	-8.8	-13.0	9.8
26	20	Senior Eng'g. 10p	25	8.57	10.3	+6.4	+16.3	+6.4	+1.5	21.2
81	55	600 Group	72	10.42	21.1	+7.5	+1.4	-7.7	-12.0	32.4
403	286	Smiths Inds. 50p	366	4.10	13.7	+9.3	+1.4	+6.1	+1.2	189.0
124	90	Spear & Jackson	113	8.31	25.9	+8.7	+20.2	+15.3	+10.0	6.0
177	126	Spirax-Sarco Eng.	144	4.56	15.0	+2.9	-4.0	-17.5	-21.3	53.8
240	92	Tube Investments £1	136	7.88	–	+13.3	+4.6	-35.8	-38.8	80.6
335	173	Utd. Scientific	328	1.31	36.0	+9.7	+14.5	+84.1	+75.6	176.6
208	141	Vickers £1	163	10.52	10.2	-1.8	+5.2	-4.7	-9.1	119.4
159	83	Vosper	140	1.02	–	-4.1	+2.2	+68.7	+60.9	8.0
86	63	Wagon Ind. Hdgs	71	10.06	13.8	-4.1	+12.7	-6.6	+60.9	14.2
64	18	Weir Group	63	4.20	3.5	+13.5	+15.8	168.1	155.7	15.7
59	43	Wellnan Eng.	44	10.88	26.9	-4.3	-10.2	-14.6	-18.5	5.8
155	81	Westland Aircraft	97	10.31	4.7	-6.7	-17.1	-33.1	-36.2	57.6
310	213	Yarrow 50p	305	3.82	29.5	+3.4	+7.0	+28.2	+22.2	12.2
FTA Sector Index	Index 196.40	5.75	(14.1) 10.34	+4.1	+1.3	-4.3	-9.22			
METALS & METAL FORMING										
615	227	Amal. Metal Corp.£1	556	2.05	33.4	–	–	+72.8	+64.7	35.1
36	22	Barton Group	30½	9.37	–	+3.4	-1.6	+13.0	+7.7	7.3
156	105	Brown & Tawse	144	6.35	16.3	-2.7	+11.6	+35.8	+29.6	15.0
63	38	Delta Group	46½	11.18	10.8	-6.1	+4.5	-13.9	-17.9	66.4

125	49	Ductile Steels	120	8.33	10.5	–	+23.7	+130.8	+120.1	15.6
119	74	Glynwed	111½	8.79	10.0	+11.2	+17.7	+31.3	+25.2	78.0
188	130	Guest, Keen £1	164	6.97	17.3	+3.8	–	+11.6	+6.4	271.6
75	48	IMI	55½	11.58	13.6	-7.5	+0.9	-8.3	-12.5	149.0
28	12	Johnson & F.B.	13	0.01	–	-13.3	-23.5	-40.9	-43.6	13.8
300	228	Johnson, Matthew £1	256	5.30	14.0	-3.8	-12.6	+1.2	-3.5	340.3
18	10	Lee, Arthur 12½p	16	3.93	–	-11.1	–	+48.8	+41.9	5.0
44	31	Lloyd, F.M.	39	1.83	–	-4.9	+5.4	+11.4	+6.3	9.4
127	85	Mckechnie Bros	100	10.39	9.9	-2.9	+5.3	-17.4	-21.2	49.7
FTA										
Sector	Index		(14.8)							
Index	163.20	7.26	13.20	+0.2	-2.4	+5.7	+0.20			
MOTORS										
66	34	AE	51	3.92	11.9	+5.2	+13.3	+14.6	+9.3	50.1
54	23	Armstrong Equip.	23½	7.88	–	-31.9	-23.0	-45.3	-47.9	12.1
75	42	Automotive Prods.	55	6.54	–	+3.8	+5.8	-3.5	-8.0	30.9
123	93	Avon Rubber £1	109	3.93	–	-1.8	+1.9	+5.8	+0.9	7.2
39	25	B.B.A. Group	34	7.31	11.6	-2.9	-5.6	+30.8	+24.7	19.6
88	56	Brit. Car Auction 10p	88	6.09	13.3	+10.0	+12.1	+17.3	+11.9	19.3
23	12	B.S.G.Int. 10p	14	1.02	–	-6.7	-15.5	-15.2	-19.1	9.2
30	10	Camford Eng'g	13½	–	–	-20.6	-18.2	-55.0	-57.1	2.4
97	73	Davis (G.) Hldgs	84	6.80	16.3	-6.7	-9.7	-4.5	-9.0	12.7
87	52	Dunlop 50p	77	6.22	–	+8.5	+16.7	+11.8	+6.4	111.9
113	36	Edbro Holdings	108	2.65	–	+11.3	+38.5	+200.0	+188.1	9.0
124	55	Henlys 20p	102	8.40	–	–11.3	-1.0	+8.5	+3.5	14.3
33	19	Heron Motor	32	1.79	–	–	+3.2	+14.3	+9.0	12.7
77	49	Holt Lloyd Int. 10p	50	9.06	8.9	-3.8	-12.3	-25.4	-28.8	18.1
88	56	Kenning Motor	58	8.62	9.9	-13.4	-20.5	-23.7	-27.2	18.3
112	44	Kwik-fit Hdgs.	53	3.68	15.5	+17.8	+8.2	-46.5	-49.0	26.4
123	85	Lex Service Group	110	9.09	9.5	–	+12.2	+2.8	-2.0	71.2
238	173	Lucas Industries £1	199	7.90	–	-5.7	-4.3	+0.5	-4.2	180.2
103	69	Perry, Harold	102	4.90	20.3	+7.4	+29.1	+34.2	+28.0	18.4

High P	Low P	Stock	End Mar price P	Yield %	P/E ratio	Change on mth. %	Change on 3 mths. %	Change on year %	Rel change on yr. %	Mkt. cap. £m's
58	33	Tecalemit	36	7.31	16.9	–	-8.9	-22.6	-26.2	12.3
46	26	Woodhead, Jonas	36	0.40	–	–	+2.9	-21.7	-25.4	5.3
FTA Sector Index	Index 96.58	6.88	(26.6) –	+1.6	+2.8	-0.4	-5.54			
OTHER INDUSTRIAL MATERIALS										
81	42	Bath & Portland	80	8.04	7.7	+2.6	+23.1	+63.3	+55.7	15.3
378	290	BTR	334	3.74	21.5	-8.7	-2.3	+3.9	+0.9	800.1
75	38	Canning, W.	62	9.17	18.0	-8.8	+10.7	-7.5	-11.8	8.1
84	52	Elect Holdings 10p	73	6.65	12.5	-3.9	+4.3	-2.7	-7.2	10.6
169	108	Eng. China Clays	154	6.68	10.5	-3.1	+0.7	+38.7	+32.3	249.6
258	178	Foseco Minsep	215	4.65	15.0	+3.4	+16.2	+2.5	-2.2	174.2
150	79	Huntleigh Group 10p	110	2.08	27.6	-3.5	+0.9	-17.9	-21.7	15.8
188	139	Lead Inds. Group 50p	180	7.67	221.	+2.3	+13.9	+25.0	+19.2	75.9
146	94	Morgan Crucible	125	8.57	17.3	-0.8	+2.5	-10.4	-14.6	65.4
23	9	Newman Inds.	9	–	–	-10.0	-30.8	-59.1	-61.0	3.6
111	82	Norcros	102½	7.69	10.7	-2.4	+17.8	+2.5	-2.3	99.2
242	173	Staveley Inds.£1	234	7.94	13.8	-2.5	+5.9	-8.6	-12.8	33.7
187	159	Steetley	175	8.57	12.9	+1.7	+9.4	-8.9	-13.1	112.1
184	132	Tilling, Thomas 20p	145	7.88	11.1	-6.5	-4.0	-10.5	-14.6	392.3
117	62	Turner & Newall £1	63	6.80	13.2	-36.4	-25.0	-25.9	-29.3	68.5
280	137	United Eng. Inds. 10p	253	21.7	39.1	–	-6.3	+80.7	+72.3	131.9
207	161	Watts, Blake &B.	170	2.83	16.1	–	-2.3	-7.1	-11.4	28.1
FTA Sector Index	324.03	Index 5.66	12.41	(15.3) -4.6	–	+6.0	+0.53			
BREWERS & DISTILLERS										
88	63	Allied-Lyons	88	8.12	12.0	+6.0	+23.9	+29.4	+23.4	557.6
252	184	Bass	232	5.83	11.2	+3.6	+12.1	+8.4	+3.4	742.6

188	110	Bell, Arthur & Sons 50p	188	3.70	10.6	+11.9	+22.1	+53.3	+46.2	131.1
165	136	Boddingtons	150	3.33	16.9	+1.4	-5.7	+7.9	+2.9	66.7
182	145	Brown, Matthew	158	5.74	12.3	-4.8	+1.3	+1.0	-3.7	32.4
393	194	Bulmer, H.P.	393	3.61	10.8	+19.8	+32.8	+99.5	+90.2	40.7
415	275	Burtonwood Brew	415	1.82	13.9	+3.7	+7.8	+50.9	+43.9	17.7
172	128	Clark, Mathew	158	6.78	11.0	-2.5	+11.3	+17.9	+12.4	6.8
159	99	Davenports Brew	159	3.85	16.4	+2.6	+34.7	+24.2	+18.5	12.9
235	161	Distillers 50p	181	8.48	8.8	+7.1	+9.7	-6.2	-10.6	657.3
222	152	Grand Metropolitan	218	4.87	13.4	+10.1	+16.0	+11.8	+6.6	1,137.1
165	104	Greenall Whitley	124	3.96	13.4	+14.8	-1.6	–	-4.6	128.7
296	238	Greene, King	296	3.19	18.4	–	+2.8	+21.3	+15.7	61.0
83	51	Guinness, Arthur	80	8.75	9.9	+6.7	+27.0	+3.9	-0.9	141.1
102	72	Highland Dist. 20p	78	4.76	19.2	–	-1.3	-19.6	-23.3	47.9
465	345	MacDonald Mart, 'A' 50p	345	4.76	17.8	-1.4	-6.8	-6.8	-11.1	7.9
79	59	Marston, Thompson	73	3.67	13.1	–	+5.8	+9.0	+3.9	37.3
69	46	Scot. & Newcastle	55	11.36	8.8	-1.8	+6.8	-15.4	-19.3	155.0
184	116	Vaux Breweries	136	7.88	10.5	+3.8	+7.9	-15.5	-19.4	44.0
128	87	Whitbread 'A'	107	6.10	13.3	+4.9	+15.1	+7.0	+2.0	388.4
252	192	Wolv'ton & Dudley	194	4.05	12.8	-7.6	-6.7	-8.5	-12.7	62.7
FTA Sector Index		Index 308.27	6.33	(11.7) 7.86	+8.1	+13.2	+6.6	+1.13		
FOOD MANUFACTURING										
159	118	Assd. Brit-Foods 5p	134	4.26	9.8	-9.5	-5.6	+4.7	-0.2	481.7
78	56	Assd. Fisheries	71	4.02	14.3	+2.9	–	+12.7	+7.5	12.5
300	223	Avana Group 5p	255	3.03	21.3	+3.7	-3.0	+4.9	+0.1	85.8
9	4	Barker & Dobson 20p	6½	–	23.0	-13.3	-13.3	+30.0	+24.0	8.0
73	50	Bassett. Geo.	69	5.18	9.6	+3.0	+7.8	+30.2	+24.2	8.3
370	210	Bibby, J. 50p	365	3.33	16.2	+9.0	+15.9	+22.5	+16.8	93.7

High P	Low P	Stock	End Mar price P	Yield %	P/E ratio	Change on mth. %	Change on 3 mths. %	Change on year %	Rel change on yr. %	Mkt. cap. £m's
450	290	Brit. Sugar Corp. 50p	450	7.94	11.0	+4.7	+20.6	+53.6	+46.5	270.0
58	43	Brooke Bond	54	10.33	9.3	-4.4	+10.2	+4.9	–	168.2
104	77	Cadbury Schwepps	104	6.32	12.1	+8.3	+20.9	+17.3	+11.9	461.9
344	286	Dalgety £1	323	9.73	13.3	-0.6	+12.2	+0.3	-4.3	249.6
114	55	Huntley & Palmer 20p	92	7.76	21.6	-12.4	-1.1	+35.3	+29.0	65.3
201	95	Matthews, Bernard	105	5.95	21.5	–	+10.5	-47.9	-50.3	16.8
270	180	Nichols (Vimto)	242	5.90	9.8	+30.8	+21.0	+18.0	+12.6	12.1
188	127	Northern Foods	168	4.25	16.0	+3.7	+7.7	-8.5	-12.7	341.5
218	140	Pauls & Whites	218	4.26	13.6	+7.9	+17.2	+52.4	+45.4	59.6
71	45	Ranks, Hovis	60	9.18	7.8	-4.8	–	+13.2	+8.0	165.2
193	146	Rowntree Mack. 50p	166	6.38	10.9	+1.2	–	-9.5	+13.7	225.2
220	154	Tate & Lyle £1	206	7.98	7.5	+1.0	+4.0	+19.1	+13.6	112.4
125	84	Unigate	90	10.32	7.9	-7.2	-10.0	-19.6	-23.4	196.6
670	498	Unilever	627	6.12	6.0	-5.7	+3.1	+21.7	+16.1	1,147.8
138	100	United Biscuits	123	6.10	13.0	-3.1	+6.0	+11.8	+6.6	380.3
FTA Sector Index	Index 277.60	6.53	(9.2) 7.85	-0.5	+5.3	+12.4	+6.58			
FOOD RETAILING										
132	81	Argyll Foods 5p	107	4.34	33.5	+7.0	+20.2	-18.3	-22.1	45.0
160	111	Assd. Dairies Grp	136	2.99	18.2	–	+1.5	-14.5	-18.4	45.0
131	81	Bejam Group 10p	118	3.33	23.0	-6.3	+6.3	+21.0	+15.4	114.0
205	130	Bishop's Group	140	3.06	–	–	-17.6	-6.7	-11.0	2.5
205	152	Clifford's Drs	195	3.66	15.0	-4.9	-2.5	+25.8	+20.0	3.4
86	55	Fitch Lovell 20p	74	10.04	13.0	-5.1	-2.6	+1.4	-3.3	49.0
172	114	Hillards 10p	172	2.39	20.9	+10.3	+18.2	+47.6	+40.8	42.0

280	173	Kwik Save Disct. 10p	254	3.37	19.3	-0.8	+17.1	+25.7	+19.9	172.8
58	43	Lennons Group 10p	54	7.01	15.9	+1.9	+5.9	+26.0	+20.1	21.0
198	133	Linfood Hdgs	195	8.79	21.0	+2.6	+10.8	+35.4	+29.1	86.8
210	144	Low, William 20p	198	5.41	14.6	-2.0	+23.8	+19.3	+13.7	13.7
176	113	Morrison, Wm. S/M 10p	168	1.11	23.3	+9.1	+6.3	+44.2	+37.5	77.5
154	98	Nurdin & Peacock 10p	154	2.26	17.9	+5.5	+14.1	+26.7	+20.9	89.6
585	387	Sainsbury, J.	565	2.09	26.9	-1.7	+11.9	+41.6	+35.0	954.1
71	48	Tesco Stores 5p	63	6.01	12.0	+10.5	+22.3	+5.9	+1.0	209.7
FTA Sector Index	Index 607.35	3.30	(20.2) 13.77	+2.0	+10.2	+17.9	+11.78			
HEALTH & HOUSEHOLD PRODS										
209	142	Amersham Int'l	209	2.39	27.9	+7.7	–	–	–	104.5
253	174	Beecham Group	237	4.38	18.9	+2.6	+7.7	+33.1	+27.0	1,546.7
526	300	Giaxo Hldgs. 50p	526	3.06	19.4	+8.7	+24.1	+70.8	+62.9	904.3
49	39	L.R.C. Int. 10p	48½	7.38	11.5	+5.4	+19.8	+6.6	+1.7	43.4
168	102	Macarthy's Pharm. 20p	164	6.10	9.4	+12.3	+54.7	-1.2	-5.8	21.6
306	208	Reckitt & Colman	292	4.79	12.3	+2.8	+16.8	+22.7	+17.0	360.5
85	33	Sangers	50	–	–	+11.1	+25.0	-28.6	-31.9	4.7
113	85	Smith & Nephew 10p	108	5.29	14.4	-2.7	+11.9	+12.0	+6.8	218.7
FTA Sector Index	Index 395.52	4.03	(17.3) 14.01	+7.5	+14.3	+40.9	+33.59			
LEISURE										
250	137	Amstrad Con. Elec.	235	2.59	19.2	+6.8	-2.1	+67.9	+60.1	21.9
132	76	Anglia T.V. 'A'	128	6.70	7.8	+4.9	+24.3	+40.7	+34.1	16.7
110	40	Assd. Communic. A	97	–	–	+11.5	+79.6	+98.0	+88.8	52.6
148	75	Assd. Leisure	107	7.01	15.2	+24.4	+30.5	-17.1	-20.9	28.0
65	44	Black & Decker 50p	53	2.70	–	+3.9	+1.9	+6.0	+1.1	9.9
88	40	BSR	74	1.93	46.0	-5.1	-8.3	+68.2	+60.4	85.2

High P	Low P	Stock	End Mar price P	Yield %	P/E ratio	Change on mth. %	Change on 3 mths. %	Change on year %	Rel change on yr. %	Mkt. cap. £m's
265	178	De Vere Hotels	183	4.68	67.2	+1.7	+1.1	-21.5	-25.1	21.2
121	80	Electronic Rent.	93	6.62	23.7	+1.1	+6.9	-18.4	-22.2	166.8
263	176	Granada Group 'A'	236	2.91	17.7	-0.8	+10.3	+5.4	+0.5	366.7
105	46	Hawley Group	81	4.88	17.3	+11.0	+32.8	-22.2	-25.8	31.0
403	178	Horizon Travel	403	2.13	12.6	+8.9	+39.9	+66.0	+58.3	85.1
138	74	H.T.V. Group N/V	129	11.63	5.0	+9.3	+20.6	+46.6	+39.8	13.0
175	120	Ladbroke Group 10p	169	6.26	14.8	+16.6	+31.0	+15.8	+10.4	242.4
153	88	LWT (Holdings) 'A'	153	9.40	11.9	+10.9	+28.6	+71.0	+63.9	24.9
217	97	Man. Agency & Music	115	10.87	10.9	+6.5	-6.5	-41.9	-44.6	8.6
230	112	Plessurama	225	3.02	10.5	+13.9	+50.0	+81.5	+73.0	29.3
176	93	Saga Holidays	152	3.63	19.6	-3.2	+6.3	+50.5	+43.5	27.4
206	160	Savoy Hotel 'A' 10p	196	0.84	–	–	+8.9	-2.0	-6.5	54.3
57	39	Stakis, Reo Org. 10p	56½	4.03	15.2	+5.6	+17.6	+14.6	+9.3	31.1
53	38	Telefusion 5p	51	4.68	16.7	+8.5	+15.9	+18.6	+13.1	14.8
501	324	Thorn EMI	433	4.83	16.2	-2.7	-5.5	+26.9	+22.9	754.6
90	36	Trident T.V.'A'	90	6.76	16.9	+7.1	+30.4	+93.5	+84.6	42.7
164	102	Trusthouse Forte	126	6.80	18.1	+9.6	+5.9	-11.9	-16.0	491.1
175	121	Wigfall, Henry	133	6.44	–	-1.5	-5.0	-17.9	-21.7	6.9
FTA Sector Index			Index 454.55	4.99	(18.5)	+4.6	+8.2	+14.1	+8.23	
NEWSPAPERS & PUBLISHING										
291	173	Assd. Newspapers	188	7.90	7.6	-2.6	+6.8	-34.3	-37.3	57.2
36	24	Ault & Wiborg Grp	32	5.58	20.6	-5.9	+10.3	-5.9	-10.2	6.3
105	72	B.P.M. Hidgs 'B'	72	11.46	11.1	-12.2	-19.1	-19.1	-22.9	8.9
37	14	Br. Printing & Comm	35½	–	–	+2.9	+36.5	+102.9	+93.5	42.3
73	32	Clay, Richard	73	1.96	–	+73.8	+73.8	+40.4	+33.9	6.5

261	160	Collins, Wm	245	4.37	14.5	+2.9	+14.0	+53.1	+46.0	10.1
118	75	East Mid. Press A	98	5.10	12.6	+7.7	+6.5	+2.1	-2.6	22.8
261	195	Link House Pubs. 20p	250	6.06	11.4	+0.8	–	+8.7	+3.7	30.0
162	110	Liverpool Post 50p	151	9.65	9.2	+4.1	+12.7	+37.3	+30.9	16.9
173	98	McCorquodale	168	6.80	9.1	+4.3	+23.5	+31.3	+25.2	27.4
480	318	Sharpe, W. N.	430	2.66	10.4	-9.5	–	+32.3	+26.2	23.9
226	155	Utd. Newspapers	171	10.03	15.0	+8.2	–	-12.8	-16.8	24.9
FTA										
Sector			Index		(10.7)					
Index			526.71	5.94	12.41	+3.6	+9.8	+8.7	+3.06	
PACKAGING & PAPER										
62	34	Assd. Paper Inds	62	5.53	18.9	+3.3	+44.2	+62.4	+73.9	8.9
206	108	Beatson, Clark	206	5.89	10.4	+7.3	+18.4	+87.3	+78.6	11.7
72	39	Bemrose Corp.	69	8.28	6.9	+30.2	+50.0	+68.3	+60.5	7.8
120	92	Blagden & Noakes	110	7.79	16.4	–	+14.6	+7.6	+2.8	11.7
286	191	Bowater Corp. £1	242	6.79	14.7	-2.0	+9.0	+1.7	-3.0	381.9
177	113	Bunzi	176	6.49	9.4	+4.1	+14.3	+23.9	+18.2	46.1
101	64	DRG	84	10.20	13.5	+12.0	+16.7	-11.6	-15.7	70.3
224	128	Metal Box £1	152	10.86	84.0	-10.6	-6.2	-20.0	-23.7	114.3
132	97	Metal Closures	128	6.36	9.9	+4.1	+16.4	+24.3	+18.5	27.0
200	95	Rediearn Glass	153	7.73	–	+10.9	+22.4	-10.0	-14.2	9.3
286	212	Reed Int. £1	284	6.54	7.6	+7.6	+17.4	+27.9	+22.0	334.1
79	42	Rockware Group	76	3.95	22.9	+24.7	+46.2	+10.1	+5.0	16.8
132	84	Waddington, J.	110	4.55	11.3	-6.8	+12.2	+7.8	+2.8	6.9
FTA										
Sector			Index		(11.3)					
Index			147.95	7.16	9.00	+3.0	+11.5	+7.5	+1.99	
STORES										
34	20	Aquascutum, 'A' 5p	33	8.87	13.4	+6.5	+26.9	-2.9	-7.4	5.5
76	48	Bambers Stores 10p	49	4.96	13.8	-12.5	-14.0	-30.0	-33.2	17.6

High P	Low P	Stock	End Mar price P	Yield %	P/E ratio	Change on mth. %	Change on 3 mths. %	Change on year %	Rel change on yr. %	Mkt. cap. £m's
176	115	Beattie, James 'A'	125	5.15	9.1	-6.0	+6.8	-17.8	-21.6	13.5
50	34	Bentalls 10p	40	4.82	25.1	-4.8	+5.3	+11.1	+6.0	16.6
256	189	Boots	230	4.66	15.0	+10.0	+16.8	-7.3	-11.6	832.7
184	110	Brit. Home Stores	159	4.04	17.0	+6.7	+30.3	+1.9	-2.8	326.1
186	105	Burton Group	186	5.38	15.3	+16.3	+39.8	+35.8	+29.5	149.0
49	34	Comb. Eng. Stores 12½p	36	12.50	17.6	–	–	-7.7	-12.0	17.6
163	99	Comet Group 5p	114	5.01	14.0	+8.6	+1.6	-23.0	-26.5	46.1
94	58	Courts (Fums.)	78	6.78	30.5	+8.3	+18.2	-7.1	-11.4	2.1
229	150	Currys Group	190	3.38	17.5	+2.2	+15.9	+5.6	+0.7	88.5
109	66	Debenhams	80	11.37	11.4	-1.2	+14.3	-13.0	-17.1	106.9
188	116	Dixons Photo 10p	178	2.86	12.7	-2.7	+6.0	+8.5	+3.5	89.5
140	60	Empire Stores	84	6.63	14.9	+7.7	+20.0	-38.2	-41.1	27.4
72	42	Fine Art Devs 5p	45	9.52	10.2	-4.3	-2.2	-33.0	-36.1	26.3
67	46	Foster Brothers	55	8.70	9.4	-8.3	+5.8	-37.5	-40.4	25.3
146	88	Freemans	140	4.23	15.6	+1.4	+20.7	+11.1	+6.0	97.2
89	46	Goldberg, A	57	13.16	15.0	+1.8	+18.7	-13.6	-17.6	9.7
110	72	Grattan	106	5.55	17.5	+6.0	+17.6	+43.2	+36.6	46.6
527	430	Gt. Univ. Stores	527	3.48	14.7	+9.8	+21.4	+9.3	+4.3	28.7
144	105	Habitat M'Care 10p	138	3.73	18.1	+13.1	+20.0	–	–	146.0
173	98	Harris Queensway	148	3.86	31.1	+15.6	+17.5	+8.8	+3.8	86.2
123	85	Hepworth, J	106	5.11	23.8	+20.5	+8.2	-13.8	-17.8	46.1
162	114	Home Charm	162	2.65	16.9	+14.1	+33.9	+33.9	+27.7	22.7
183	134	House of Fraser	164	5.75	16.6	-3.5	-1.2	+12.3	+7.1	247.0
155	106	Marks & Spencer	155	3.73	22.1	+9.9	+23.0	+24.0	+18.3	2,036.2
330	190	Martin Newsagent	325	4.62	11.7	+1.6	+25.0	+54.8	+47.6	21.4
247	160	Menzies, John	233	2.42	18.5	-0.9	+6.9	+44.7	+38.0	64.5
57	47	MFI Furniture 10p	66	5.67	16.7	+11.9	+10.0	+17.9	+12.4	112.4
190	125	NSS Newsagents 10p	176	3.04	13.8	-1.1	+16.6	+16.6	+11.2	30.0
271	156	Owen Owen	203	2.99	33.5	-4.7	-6.0	+28.5	+22.5	19.0

60	40	Ratners (Jewellers) 10p	43	7.64	18.9	-8.5	+4.9	-25.9	-29.3	12.8
75	36	Rayback	41	7.87	–	-4.7	+5.1	-36.9	-39.8	15.0
93	55	Reed, Austin Gp. A	76	6.32	16.4	+11.8	+22.6	-14.6	-18.6	11.4
162	100	Samuel, H. 'A'	109	8.19	14.4	-6.8	+9.0	-23.2	-26.8	48.8
70	43	Sears Holdings	64½	5.09	15.5	+0.8	+18.3	+5.7	+0.6	576.6
187	138	Smith, W. H. 'A'	176	3.81	25.8	+4.8	+15.0	+12.8	+7.6	125.4
81	45	Stanley, A. G. 5p	63	5.67	19.9	+5.0	+31.3	-20.3	-24.0	16.0
55	44	Stead & Simpson 'A'	55	9.09	18.3	+5.8	+7.8	+22.2	+16.6	15.0
180	110	Stylo	110	3.90	36.5	-12.0	-13.4	-23.1	-26.6	11.0
62	28	Time Products 10p	28	11.48	27.2	-9.7	-22.2	-53.3	-55.5	13.9
93	61	UDS Group	79	11.23	20.7	+3.9	+14.5	-1.2	-5.8	150.7
88	54	Walker, James	54	10.58	17.2	-11.5	-3.6	-38.6	-41.5	4.8
172	105	Waring & Gillow	105	7.48	4.2	-7.1	-6.3	-26.1	-29.5	16.4
69	43	Woolworth, F. W.	50½	12.05	10.4	-11.4	–	-14.4	-18.4	191.0
FTA Sector Index			Index 283.07	4.74	(16.8) 13.33	+8.5	+17.8	+6.3	+0.79	
TEXTILES										
222	134	Allied Textile	222	4.95	12.2	+6.2	+51.0	+57.4	+50.1	16.6
246	159	Baird, William £1	218	8.49	12.2	+6.3	+17.8	-6.0	-10.4	41.0
34	17	Carpets Int. 50p	19½	–	1.4	-15.2	-18.7	+14.7	+9.4	4.6
17	11	Carrington Viyella	13½	–	–	+8.0	–	–	-4.6	24.5
66	53	Coats Patons	63	9.07	4.9	+2.4	+5.0	-6.0	-10.3	174.3
68	30	Corah	46	9.01	17.6	+13.6	+41.5	+33.3	+27.2	13.5
89	49	Courtaukis	88	3.25	–	+8.6	+17.3	+41.9	+35.4	240.4
146	99	Dawson Int.	136	5.78	11.3	+0.7	+2.3	+14.6	+9.3	117.8
98	65	Dewhirst, I.J.	97	1.86	24.0	+5.4	+31.1	+77.1	+88.9	23.2
25	17	Ellis & Goldstein 15p	24	12.79	10.9	-4.0	+9.1	+37.1	+30.8	5.5
176	109	Fothergilt & Harvey	128	8.65	17.8	-5.9	+12.3	+15.5	+10.2	15.7
14	10	Illingworth M.A. 20p	14	–	–	+3.7	+3.7	+33.3	+27.2	4.2
210	107	Lee Cooper Group	125	3.25	6.3	–	-9.4	+24.2	-27.8	19.3
49	30	Lister & Co.	32	0.45	–	-11.1	+3.2	-20.0	-23.7	5.3

High P	Low P	Stock	End Mar price P	Yield %	P/E ratio	Change on mth. %	Change on 3 mths. %	Change on year %	Rel change on yr. %	Mkt. cap. £m's
174	119	Nottingham Mfg.	173	3.72	13.3	+8.1	+35.2	+31.1	+25.0	121.5
23	15	Readicut Int.	18	0.79	–	-14.3	+16.1	+16.1	+10.7	13.8
54	38	R.F.D. Group 10p	47	8.51	37.5	-6.9	+8.0	+6.6	+1.9	6.4
164	112	Scapa Group	147	6.56	8.2	-3.3	+5.0	+30.1	+24.1	47.0
16	9	Selincourt 5p	11½	13.87	23.4	+11.9	+20.5	-13.0	-17.0	6.1
130	80	Sirdar	129	4.15	11.1	+9.3	+8.4	+44.9	+38.2	30.9
39	25	Tootal	38	8.83	–	+13.4	+18.8	+35.7	+29.4	67.3
141	101	Vantona Group 20p	128	8.93	10.2	-0.8	+8.5	+18.5	+13.0	27.5
92	51	Wearwell 5p	61	6.15	9.8	+17.3	+8.9	-25.0	-28.5	19.8
FTA Sector Index			Index 176.18	5.68	(12.9) 13.42	+5.7	+12.6	+18.8	+12.65	
TOBACCO										
441	276	B.A.T. Inds.	418	7.18	6.5	-3.5	+17.4	+48.8	+41.6	1,519.4
93	53	Imperial Group	93	11.14	11.3	+6.3	+29.2	+29.2	+23.2	665.1
86	55	Rothmans int. 'B'	78½	6.92	5.0	+0.6	+4.7	+38.9	+32.5	108.5
FTA Sector Index			Index 313.05	8.33	(7.3) 5.82	+2.3	+20.0	+43.9	+35.82	
OTHER CONSUMER GOODS										
49	31	Chamberin Phipps 10p	49	9.04	11.4	+4.3	+16.7	+53.1	+46.0	11.8
59	30	Christie-Tyler 10p	30	14.29	–	-11.8	-21.1	-38.8	-41.6	2.9
107	84	Friedland Doggart.	97	7.51	8.4	+4.9	+10.9	+10.9	+5.7	5.9
45	22	Gomme Holdings	36	–	–	+63.6	+24.1	+2.9	-1.9	4.6
162	67	Hoover' A'	99	–	–	–	+25.3	-13.2	-17.2	12.1
28	12	Lesney Products 5p	13	–	–	-7.1	-27.6	-27.8	-31.1	3.8

29	12	Moben Group 10p	23	–	11.5	–	+35.3	-8.0	-12.3	3.8
50	27	M.Y. Dart	29½	13.93	50.0	-1.7	+5.3	-27.0	-30.4	5.2
169	122	Prestige Group	169	5.81	9.6	+13.4	+38.3	+19.0	+13.5	30.6
118	56	Silentnight Hdgs. 10p	116	5.54	11.3	+16.0	+31.8	+103.5	+94.1	26.1
120	77	Spear, J. W.	92	8.54	–	-1.1	+17.9	-21.4	-25.0	3.7
69	40	Valor	58	6.75	10.1	+3.6	-1.7	-1.7	-6.3	7.0
74	42	Ward White Group	64	9.37	10.3	+1.6	+39.1	+4.9	+0.1	19.7
92	66	Wedgwood	82½	7.23	7.1	+9.3	+5.1	1.9	-2.9	30.7
FTA Sector Index			Index 296.35	5.33	(12.6) –	+8.9	+19.6	+9.0	+3.35	
CHEMICALS										
197	115	Allied Colloids 10p	192	2.08	26.2	+8.5	+38.1	+41.2	+34.6	82.9
174	121	BOC Group	170	4.29	13.1	+4.3	+11.8	+28.8	+22.8	82.9
138	94	Brent Chemicals 10p	124	2.65	28.3	-5.3	-0.8	+16.5	+10.2	47.3
190	135	British Vita	148	5.21	10.5	-1.3	+4.2	-4.5	-8.9	39.7
133	95	Coalite Group	119	5.06	10.6	+1.7	-4.0	-6.3	-10.6	102.3
65	42	Coates Bros 'A'	63	6.80	8.8	-3.1	+26.0	+23.5	+17.6	14.7
85	38	Croda int. 10p	82	12.20	21.5	+6.5	+3.8	+105.0	+95.5	86.6
310	120	Fisons	310	4.61	27.5	+9.5	+96.2	+102.6	+93.2	115.6
246	158	Hickson & Welch 50p	235	4.56	13.7	+0.9	+15.8	+39.9	+33.4	45.4
350	236	Imp. Chem. Inds. £1	316	8.54	11.5	-4.2	+8.9	+30.3	+24.3	1,903.0
151	88	Laporte Inds. 50p	144	6.94	26.3	+0.7	+16.1	+56.5	+49.3	83.4
178	86	Leigh Interests 5p	94	8.56	19.5	-6.0	-14.5	-46.3	+48.8	9.5
175	127	Rentokil Group 10p	155	2.63	21.8	-2.5	+2.6	-1.3	-5.9	147.5
126	73	Stewart Plastics	125	2.36	15.3	+4.2	+15.8	+70.5	+62.6	21.3
125	100	Wolstenhoime Rink	125	7.14	9.9	+4.2	+8.7	+16.8	+11.4	6.1
47	26	Yorks, Chemical	44	1.62	–	+2.3	+4.8	+46.7	+39.9	5.9
FTA Sector Index			Index 335.63	6.88	(13.0) 8.99	+0.3	+11.1	+29.8	+22.13	

High P	Low P	Stock	End Mar price P	Yield %	P/E ratio	Change on mth. %	Change on 3 mths. %	Change on year %	Rel change on yr. %	Mkt. cap. £m's
OFFICE EQUIPMENT										
100	45	Gestetner 'A'	58	6.47	18.0	-10.8	+9.4	-31.8	-34.9	27.2
420	250	Office & Elec.	315	3.17	16.4	–	+5.0	-6.5	-10.9	19.3
218	130	Rank Org.	191	8.08	9.5	+2.7	+4.9	-3.5	-8.0	385.8
400	270	Tele. Rentals	338	3.49	21.1	+3.0	+5.3	+9.0	+4.0	131.2
FTA Sector Index			Index 126.85	6.73	(11.2) 9.59	+4.8	+5.3	+8.2	+2.66	
SHIPPING AND TRANSPORT										
400	263	Brit. & Commwlth.50p	396	4.87	9.4	-0.5	+22.6	+20.0	+14.4	128.3
108	63	European Ferries	84½	5.24	18.3	+3.0	+10.5	-16.6	-20.4	205.1
174	137	Fisher, James	166	2.26	20.1	+16.9	+19.4	-2.4	-6.9	37.6
42	27	Jacobs, John 1.20p	36	9.13	19.0	-4.0	+7.5	+2.9	-1.9	8.3
335	278	LEP Group 10p	325	7.25	12.6	+5.5	+16.1	+1.6	-3.1	22.8
63	31	Ldn. & Ossas. Freight	52	2.95	–	-8.0	-3.7	+20.9	+15.3	29.3
355	270	Lyle Shipping	272	4.99	5.8	-15.0	-4.6	-14.5	-18.4	26.9
151	92	Ocean Transport	124	10.37	10.3	+1.6	+13.8	-15.1	-19.0	139.7
164	95	Pen. & Orient Dfd. £1	142	8.05	13.4	+9.2	+10.9	-4.1	-8.5	201.6
192	87	Reardon Smith 50p	128	1.95	7.3	-6.6	+14.3	-30.8	-34.0	5.2
146	93	Runciman, W.	101	10.61	5.0	-1.0	+4.1	-26.3	-29.7	8.9
85	80	Transport Dev.	76	7.99	14.7	-3.2	+16.9	+4.1	-0.7	101.0
186	113	United Parcels 10p	177	2.99	16.8	-2.7	+12.0	+23.8	+18.0	45.3
FTA Sector Index			Index 583.96	6.33	(13.3) 6.31	+3.7	+12.4	-4.6	-9.57	

MISCELLANEOUS										
104	75	A.A.H.	83	8.41	10.4	-7.8	-10.8	-10.6	-14.9	23.9
285	178	AGB Research 10p	278	2.98	30.1	-0.7	+11.2	+23.6	+17.9	66.7
223	117	Automated Sec. 10p	223½	0.93	37.7	+34.2	+19.8	+28.8	+22.8	40.6
38	30	Barrow Hepbum	35	8.96	14.2	+2.9	+8.1	+12.9	+7.7	9.0
75	49	Booker McConnell 50p	75	6.67	12.1	+11.9	+23.0	+23.0	+17.3	93.8
60	38	Brengreen Holdgs 10p	47½	2.41	30.9	-1.0	+4.4	-2.8	-7.3	15.2
179	113	Brit. Elec. Tr. Dfd.	179	6.04	11.7	+20.9	+25.2	+27.0	+21.1	268.8
52	25	Brook St. Bureau 10p	26	5.49	–	–	-3.7	-36.6	-39.5	2.7
92	17	Brown & Jackson 20p	19	37.59	–	-24.0	-36.7	-72.1	-73.4	3.8
251	168	Cable & Wireless 50p	249	3.61	19.6	+7.3	+15.8	–	–	672.3
233	162	Cawoods Holdings	206	2.78	15.0	+5.1	+1.0	+14.3	+9.0	100.2
240	118	Christies Int. 10p	144	6.94	10.8	+12.5	+5.1	+39.5	-42.3	17.5
61	31	Cope Allman Int. 5p	41½	10.33	23.0	-5.7	+13.7	-6.7	-11.1	16.4
100	59	Crest Nicholson 10p	99	4.11	13.5	+4.2	+15.1	+12.5	+7.3	40.9
795	605	De La Rue	640	4.69	14.1	-9.2	-5.2	-8.6	-12.8	243.6
15	8	Duport	9½	–	–	-5.0	-13.6	+18.6	+13.3	4.0
288	161	Extel Group	285	4.01	15.4	+3.3	+21.3	+75.9	+67.8	35.5
70	44	Gramplan Hdgs.	59	10.90	14.3	-4.8	+25.5	+7.3	+2.3	8.0
164	113	Hanson Trust	159	4.49	10.4	+3.9	+10.4	+24.1	+18.4	359.7
57	32	Hargreaves Group 20p	55	8.31	30.6	+12.2	+22.2	+12.2	+7.0	19.3
49	31	Hestair	45	6.35	15.4	+15.4	+32.4	+32.4	+26.2	8.2
420	210	Hunting Ass. Inds.	242	2.95	14.7	-0.8	+7.6	-36.1	-39.1	292.8
281	184	Initial	265	5.12	14.2	-0.4	+9.5	+22.7	+17.0	140.8
256	185	Johnson Cleaners	189	5.82	12.5	-9.6	-12.9	-2.6	-7.1	20.5
74	56	L.C.P. Hdgs,	59	10.41	21.6	-6.3	+1.7	-9.2	-13.4	29.6
128	90	London & Mid Inds.	96	11.53	13.0	+1.1	+2.1	-19.3	-23.1	16.0
213	123	Low & Bonar Grp. 50p	123	8.13	9.0	-34.2	-16.3	-40.9	-43.6	17.2
138	107	More O'Ferrall 10p	133	3.52	14.2	-1.5	+2.3	+14.4	+9.1	21.8
258	185	Pearson S. & Son	252	5.67	7.8	+2.0	+19.4	+22.3	+16.7	178.2
29	11	Pentos 10p	13	–	–	-7.1	-13.3	-31.6	-34.8	5.8
545	425	Portals Holdings	508	3.59	15.4	+0.6	-1.4	+14.2	+8.9	91.7
286	225	Powell Duffryn 50p	231	6.81	10.5	-2.5	+0.9	-3.6	-8.2	72.2

High P	Low P	Stock	End Mar price P	Yield %	P/E ratio	Change on mth. %	Change on 3 mths. %	Change on year %	Rel change on yr. %	Mkt. cap. £m's
96	62	Pritchard Serv. 5p	90	3.97	23.5	+1.1	+4.7	+20.8	+15.2	72.9
128	84	Ropner Hdgs. 'A'	100	6.19	9.7	-3.8	-14.2	-5.3	-10.2	15.6
288	150	Royal Worcester	187	6.57	9.3	+10.0	-4.1	-30.7	-34.0	12.3
416	231	Saatchi & Saatchi 10p	416	2.06	22.6	+7.8	+15.2	+47.0	+40.2	33.5
226	151	Securicor Grp. 'A'	203	1.25	16.8	-6.0	+12.2	+22.3	+16.6	37.7
203	158	Slebe Gorman	168	6.17	13.4	–	-4.0	-8.2	-12.5	17.4
304	225	Sketchley	275	5.45	13.8	-1.1	-2.6	+8.3	+3.2	41.8
510	295	Sotheby Parke	340	5.25	9.4	+2.1	-13.5	-31.3	-34.5	38.7
121	80	Spring Grove	92	6.21	12.6	-1.1	+7.0	-11.5	-15.6	23.0
127	75	Trafaigar House 20p	126	7.03	12.4	+11.4	+23.3	+32.0	+25.9	302.2
74	29	Uko Internatinal	50	8.57	49.5	+6.4	+47.1	-15.3	-19.2	7.0
71	43	Whitecrolt	69	8.23	14.3	+13.1	+16.9	+13.1	+7.9	13.6
216	116	Wood Hall Trust	213	4.17	–	+4.9	+43.9	+42.0	+35.4	52.3
98	66	Yule Catto 10p	83	3.49	12.9	+2.5	–	+10.8	-14.9	15.6
FTA Sector Index			Index 327.44	5.00	(13.4) 10.82	+4.8	+11.0	+14.3	+8.42	
OILS										
304	208	Brit. Borneo Pet. 10p	220	8.02	14.0	–	-14.1	-27.4	-30.8	9.9
396	254	Brit. Petroleum	290	9.96	6.1	+2.8	-8.2	-19.7	-23.4	5,265.5
172	95	Burmah Oil £1	123	7.55	11.7	+6.0	-1.6	-20.6	-24.3	177.1
170	94	Carless Capel & L. 10p	165	2.38	55.4	+25.0	-2.9	+18.7	+13.2	81.4
94	56	Century Oils GRP 10p	93	4.30	15.4	+1.1	+6.1	+31.0	+24.9	21.4
92	60	Chartertise Petroleum	75	1.43	23.3	+5.6	-5.1	-1.3	-5.9	60.0
230	151	Imp. Cont. Gas £1	193	6.14	14.2	+2.7	-4.9	-11.5	-15.6	249.2
206	84	KCA International	90	6.73	5.8	-8.2	-33.3	-55.9	-57.9	32.4
624	262	Ldn. Scot. Mar. Oil	309	4.62	12.5	+3.3	-27.1	-46.4	-48.9	226.5

142	75	NCC Energy 10p	76	3.29	–	-20.0	-18.3	-46.5	-49.0	27.4
422	314	Shell Transport	382	7.67	6.1	+12.4	-4.5	+4.9	+0.1	4,220.5
296	168	Tricentrol	204	5.88	13.2	+9.7	-13.6	-26.8	-30.2	123.9
535	338	Ultrimar	388	4.79	4.3	+2.1	-22.1	-18.0	-21.8	417.3
FTA Sector Index			Index 681.62	8.50	(6.4) 6.36	-7.1	-5.4	+15.8	+9.83	
BANKS										
547	304	Bank of Scotland £1	432	6.45	6.9	-3.4	-16.4	+37.8	+31.2	140.1
511	378	Barclays Bank £1	448	8.42	5.0	-8.6	-1.1	+17.0	+11.5	1,266.6
500	323	Lloyds Bank £1	438	6.97	4.3	-8.0	+1.9	+32.7	+26.6	793.7
361	295	Midland Bank £1	326	10.52	4.9	-3.0	-6.9	+4.2	-0.7	538.6
480	338	Nat. West. Bank £1	418	8.61	3.6	-7.3	+2.5	+19.4	+13.9	991.2
200	107	Ryl Bank of Scot.	109	7.08	4.2	-7.8	-44.1	-20.4	-24.1	246.0
FTA Sector Index			Index 271.62	7.87	(4.4) 2.82	-7.1	-5.4	+15.8	+9.83	
DISCOUNT HOUSES										
255	194	Alexanders Disc. £1	217	12.18	–	-2.3	-12.1	-17.8	-21.6	10.7
328	280	Cater Allen Hdgs. £1	328	10.06	–	+6.5	+4.8	-18.4	-22.2	22.8
29	17	Clive Discount 20p	27	5.29	–	+8.0	+28.6	-42.6	-45.2	5.8
280	239	Gerrard & Nat.	267	7.49	–	–	-2.2	-14.1	-18.1	39.9
220	140	Gillett Bros £1	140	8.93	–	-6.7	-37.2	-51.4	-53.6	3.8
68	54	Jessel, Toynbee	60	11.90	–	+3.4	-6.2	-28.6	-31.9	7.9
104	77	King & Shaxson 20p	86	9.55	–	–	–	-14.0	-18.0	7.7
154	24	Smith, St. Aubyn	38	16.92	–	+8.6	-63.0	-72.2	-73.5	8.2
513	398	Union Discount £1	438	8.48	–	+3.5	+7.4	-13.8	-17.8	43.8
FTA Sector Index			Index 232.06	9.34	(–) –	+1.3	-5.9	-24.0	-27.92	

High P	Low P	Stock	End Mar price P	Yield %	P/E ratio	Change on mth. %	Change on 3 mths. %	Change on year %	Rel change on yr. %	Mkt. cap. £m's
INSURANCE (LIFE)										
302	238	Britannic Ass. 5p	276	8.33	–	+1.5	+6.2	+5.3	+0.5	53.0
452	354	Equity & Law Life 5p	410	5.23	–	-6.8	+7.9	+10.8	+5.7	82.2
432	297	Hambro Life Ass. 5p	305	4.73	–	-0.7	-3.8	-15.5	-19.4	305.8
266	200	Legal & General 5p	247	10.12	–	+12.8	+19.3	+0.4	-4.2	369.9
304	223	London & Manch. 5p	240	7.08	–	-15.5	-4.0	-5.5	-9.9	55.0
468	366	Pearl Assurance 5p	408	7.53	–	+3.0	+2.0	-11.7	-15.8	148.9
251	207	Prudential Corp. 5p	249	7.17	–	+5.1	+7.8	+2.5	-2.3	743.0
270	214	Refuge Ass. 5p	246	8.42	–	–	+7.9	+7.0	+2.0	51.4
344	274	Sun Life Ass. 5p	314	4.09	–	–	–	+11.7	+6.6	180.9
FTA Sector Index			Index 268.94	6.26	(–) –	+6.0	+6.7	+1.8	-3.46	
INSURANCE (COMPOSITE)										
185	124	Commercial Union	141	11.96	–	-5.4	+9.3	-16.6	-20.4	579.6
392	225	Eagle Star Hldgs	378	5.67	–	-0.3	+14.2	+55.6	+48.3	517.0
388	288	General Accident	320	7.25	–	-1.8	+1.3	-8.0	-12.3	525.4
378	269	Guardian Royal Ex.	302	8.28	–	-3.89	+0.7	-10.4	-14.6	474.7
230	173	London Utd. Invs. 20p	212	6.06	–	+5.0	–	+21.1	+15.5	18.7
93	57	Minister Assets	68	8.61	–	-5.6	-11.1	-17.6	-21.4	23.3
320	216	Phoenix Assurance	254	8.83	–	–	+11.4	-8.0	-12.2	154.3
418	326	Royal Insurance	360	10.02	–	-3.0	+7.1	-7.2	-11.5	678.3
£11	770	Sun Allnce. & Ldn £1	850	6.30	–	-6.0	+1.4	+4.4	-0.4	419.0
200	165	Trade Indemnity	170	5.81	–	–	+3.0	-10.5	-14.7	12.3
FTA Sector Index			Index 164.31	8.29	(–) –	+0.1	+6.0	+0.3	-4.87	

INSURANCE BROKERS										
336	233	Heath, C. E. 20p	336	4.68	13.2	+16.7	+20.0	+44.2	+37.5	104.0
116	92	Hogg Robinson	111	7.72	8.0	–	+1.8	-5.1	-9.5	37.8
175	102	Minet Holdings 20p	175	3.89	19.4	+10.1	+21.5	+69.9	+62.0	89.1
167	118	Sedgwick Group 10p	167	5.13	12.4	+9.2	+12.8	+41.5	+35.0	354.4
117	79	Stenhouse Hidgs	115	6.34	9.7	+8.5	+17.3	+45.6	+38.8	43.7
241	190	Stew. Wrightson 20p	206	8.32	13.4	-6.4	-7.6	-10.4	-14.6	37.8
460	306	Willis Faber	460	4.66	14.1	+12.7	+25.7	+48.4	+41.5	185.8
FTA Sector Index			Index 484.75	5.14	(12.4) 12.55	+12.4	+16.2	+37.3	+30.24	
MERCHANT BANKS										
22	12	Ansbacher, Henry 5p	16	3.13	23.1	-8.6	+16.4	-14.7	-18.6	15.8
242	178	Brown Shlpley £1	235	3.95	–	+0.9	+3.1	+22.1	+16.4	27.5
93	65	Charterhouse Grp	85	8.28	9.5	+6.2	+7.6	+1.2	-3.5	128.7
123	58	Gulnness Peat	78	2.29	–	+23.8	-16.1	-27.8	-31.1	52.2
193	120	Hambros	136	4.96	–	+2.3	-17.6	-9.9	-14.1	117.5
176	108	Hill Samuel Grp	157	6.64	–	+1.9	-2.5	+8.3	+3.3	107.6
265	215	Joseph, Leopold £1	230	6.49	–	–	-2.1	-4.2	-8.6	6.0
278	194	Kleinwort, Benson	242	5.90	–	+6.1	+5.2	-12.3	-16.4	130.7
295	186	Mercury Secs.	223	4.48	7.8	+4.7	+4.7	-4.3	-8.7	98.7
137	85	Rea Brothers	90	3.17	–	–	-12.6	-7.7	-12.0	14.7
500	357	Schroders £1	440	4.38	–	+4.0	+3.5	+20.5	+15.0	69.0
185	95	Wintrust 20p	179	2.66	19.0	-1.6	+44.4	+82.7	+74.2	15.1
FTA Sector Index			Index 153.61	5.46	(–) –	+5.4	-1.6	-2.8	-7.81	
PROPERTY										
101	50	Alid. London Prop.	88½	2.19	27.0	+6.0	-2.2	-10.2	-14.4	18.7
242	167	Allnatt Lon. Prop.	192	3.27	18.9	-1.0	-2.0	-19.3	-23.1	76.8
176	100	Apex Properties 10p	128	2.23	41.3	-1.5	–	-26.4	-29.6	13.8

High P	Low P	Stock	End Mar price P	Yield %	P/E ratio	Change on mth. %	Change on 3 mths. %	Change on year %	Rel change on yr. %	Mkt. cap. £m's
226	172	Bilton, Percy	213	4.63	21.9	+7.6	+18.3	-4.9	-9.3	79.7
252	160	Bradford Prop.	192	3.20	12.0	-4.0	+4.3	-21.3	-25.0	44.8
108	66	British Land	88½	0.81	13.0	-1.7	+10.6	-16.5	-220.4	92.0
133	101	Brixton Estate	111	3.81	36.6	+0.9	+2.8	-10.6	-14.7	86.2
130	89	Capital & Counties	130	3.96	18.5	+11.1	+18.2	+4.0	-0.8	99.8
208	155	Centrovincial 20p	184	2.59	44.7	-1.6	-5.2	-7.1	-11.4	28.9
395	280	Chesterfield	360	2.58	38.8	+2.9	+1.4	-7.7	-12.0	71.1
760	565	Churchbury Ests	655	2.73	72.1	+2.3	+1.6	+14.9	+9.6	49.3
63	42	Country & New Town 10p	49	2.48	–	+1.0	+1.0	-18.1	-21.9	22.2
210	100	Deajan Holdings	190	3.42	14.4	-6.0	+15.9	+1.1	-3.6	31.0
174	120	Estates Property 50p	148	6.76	19.5	+0.7	+1.4	-14.0	-17.9	28.0
80	58	Evans of Leeds	64	5.30	14.5	–	-8.6	-15.2	-19.2	21.0
160	94	Federated Land	145	3.63	52.6	+7.4	-7.6	+21.8	+16.2	15.8
218	147	Gt. Portland Est. 50p	186	3.84	31.4	+6.9	+5.7	-12.7	-16.7	224.5
207	133	Greycoat Estates	144	0.99	60.0	-2.0	-11.7	-30.1	-33.3	16.0
670	490	Hammerson Prop.A	655	2.07	50.6	–	+4.8	+1.6	-3.2	245.4
429	336	Haslemere Ests 10p	386	2.55	34.6	-3.0	+4.9	-7.8	-12.1	111.9
288	200	Imry Property	285	1.73	51.1	-1.9	–	-5.9	-10.3	36.5
75	49	Kent, M. P.	67	2.50	11.0	-1.5	-1.5	-8.2	-12.5	28.7
206	168	Laing Props.	196	3.28	26.1	+3.2	+3.2	+4.6	-0.2	109.1
69	44	Land Investors £1	54	2.65	45.3	-1.8	+1.9	-16.9	-20.8	52.6
347	257	Land Securities	293	3.71	29.1	-2.7	-1.7	-14.2	-18.2	1,014.8
490	310	Lon. & Prov. Shop 10p	480	0.71	97.1	–	+3.2	+6.0	+1.0	51.8
141	80	Ldn. Shop Prop.	120	5.06	22.0	–	-12.4	-12.1	-16.1	36.3
314	200	Lynton Hdgs 20p	234	2.17	55.9	+4.0	-1.3	-24.5	-28.0	23.0
150	107	McKay Secs. 20p	140	2.76	28.5	+2.2	-1.4	-3.4	-7.9	19.4
247	181	MEPC	226	4.11	25.2	+2.3	-5.5	-7.0	-11.4	461.0
127	77	Mucklow, A. & J. Grp	86	6.64	15.9	+7.5	+3.6	-32.3	-35.4	44.6
209	130	North Brft. Prop.	147	3.01	26.9	-0.7	-2.0	-27.9	-31.3	19.1

161	116	Peachey Property	150	5.00	17.2	-3.2	+4.2	-6.2	-10.6	43.7
172	113	Property Holding	154	3.25	30.1	-3.7	-1.3	-10.7	-14.8	58.7
186	125	Prop. & Revers	164	2.61	36.9	-1.2	-3.5	-8.9	-13.1	44.6
153	100	Prop. Security 50p	142	1.55	51.4	+3.6	+14.5	-4.4	-8.9	63.3
180	115	Regional Props A	152	2.11	28.2	-0.7	+2.7	-14.1	-18.1	24.6
330	205	Rosehaugh Co.10p	277	1.08	20.5	+8.6	+13.1	-13.4	-17.5	20.3
250	192	Rush & Tompkins	230	2.48	–	+4.1	+5.5	-7.3	-11.6	25.3
131	81	Samuel Props	107	5.74	19.8	+1.9	+9.2	-17.7	-21.5	30.9
114	79	Scot. Metrop. Prop	86	5.40	22.5	-4.4	-1.3	-23.8	-27.4	75.1
153	103	Slough Estates	141	3.37	31.3	+3.7	+11.9	-6.6	-11.0	200.2
380	300	Stock Conversion	335	1.71	31.9	+0.6	+1.5	-9.0	-13.2	175.4
50	33	Town Centre Sec.	42	2.83	36.2	+2.4	+5.0	-13.1	-17.1	30.6
33	18	Town & City Props 10p	30	0.05	–	-3.2	-5.5	-4.0	-8.4	104.3
184	118	Trafford Park	136	7.88	13.7	–	-5.6	-14.5	-18.4	14.5
535	400	Utd. Real Prop.	450	1.90	–	-3.8	-2.8	-13.5	-17.5	54.0
400	265	Warner Estate	308	3.71	37.4	+0.3	+1.0	-21.4	-25.1	30.9
500	350	Warnford Invs. 20p	400	3.93	24.5	+2.6	-1.2	-15.8	-19.7	38.4
FTA Sector Index			Index 460.26	3.24	(28.5) 28.40	+0.9	+1.6	-9.6	-14.24	
OTHER FINANCIAL										
196	148	Akroyd & Smithers	180	10.71	8.7	-4.3	+9.1	-5.8	-10.1	28.8
62	37	Britannia Arrow	43½	4.93	10.8	-7.4	-7.4	-9.4	-13.6	35.2
34	15	Cattles Holdings 10p	28½	6.08	17.6	-4.1	-4.1	-26.6	-30.0	6.8
214	130	English Assoc. Gp.	175	2.45	16.5	-7.9	+12.9	-17.2	-21.1	15.8
228	140	Exco Int. 10p	200	3.21	19.7	-11.5	+5.3	–	–	85.0
93	73	Gresham Inv. Trust	86½	5.45	12.7	+5.5	+6.8	+16.1	+10.7	13.9
243	153	Grindlays Holdings	173	3.41	10.9	-5.5	-16.8	-8.9	-13.2	58.8
410	182	Martin, R. P. 5p	330	3.96	9.8	-17.1	+4.8	+76.9	+68.7	30.8
525	287	Mercantile House	448	3.11	15.2	-4.7	+4.2	+55.9	+48.6	78.5
366	268	M. & G. Group (Hdg.) 9p	314	5.69	15.3	-0.9	-0.6	-9.8	-14.0	28.3
543	356	Mills & Allen Int. 50p	528	5.68	11.2	+3.9	+23.4	+47.5	+40.6	66.2

High P	Low P	Stock	End Mar price P	Yield %	P/E ratio	Change on mth. %	Change on 3 mths. %	Change on year %	Rel change on yr. %	Mkt. cap. £m's
147	93	Provident Fin.	134	8.00	10.9	+13.6	+12.6	-5.6	-10.0	52.3
714	557	Stand. Chartered £1	664	7.96	5.4	-2.2	-1.9	+1.5	-3.2	573.6
55	38	Wagon Finance	47	7.03	26.7	+9.3	+17.5	-14.5	-18.5	11.0
76	48	Westpool Inv. Trust	58	2.82	59.6	-3.4	+7.7	-23.3	-26.8	55.2
FTA Sector Index			Index 179.90	6.36	(15.7) 6.56	-2.6	+1.1	+4.3	-1.06	
INVESTMENT TRUSTS										
152	116	Aberdeen Trust	144	6.05	-17.7	-0.7	+13.4	+10.8	+11.7	48.0
56½	41	Ailsa Investment	44½	5.06	-18.4	-1.1	-14.4	+1.7	+2.5	22.3
114	88	Alliance Invest.	94	4.10	-18.9	+2.2	–	-5.1	-4.3	21.0
302	236	Alliance Trust	290	5.79	-25.8	-0.7	+7.4	+12.4	+13.3	145.2
75	55½	American Trust	64	5.02	-23.9	+1.6	+4.9	-7.2	-6.5	51.2
148	119	Anglo-Amer. Secs.	135	5.36	-26.5	-4.9	+3.1	+1.5	+2.3	77.3
75	58	Anglo-Scot. Trust	68½	5.01	-22.1	-0.7	+11.4	+2.2	+3.1	22.4
206	169	Ashdown Inv. Tst.	194	4.86	-27.1	-0.5	+9.0	+3.7	+4.6	21.1
74½	49½	Atlantic Assets	59	0.61	-18.9	-1.7	-4.8	-3.7	-2.9	68.8
101	78	Atlas Elec. & Gen.	93½	5.04	-27.3	-1.1	+8.1	+5.6	+6.5	101.0
89	63½	Bankers Inv. Tst.	89	5.55	-17.2	+6.0	+25.4	+20.3	+21.2	34.5
205	148	Berry Trust	156	1.56	-15.2	-7.1	-12.8	-7.7	-7.0	23.7
101	78	Bishopsgate Tst.	88	5.47	-27.6	-1.1	+4.8	-0.4	+0.4	20.8
93	73½	Border & Southern 10p	81	4.85	-26.7	-4.1	+1.3	-4.7	-3.9	79.5
55	41	Brit. Am. & General	53½	6.68	-22.8	+0.9	+11.5	+10.3	+11.2	26.8
115	87	British Assets	99	6.35	-16.9	+3.1	+3.1	+1.0	+1.8	94.4
203	167	Brit. Inv. Trust	190	6.65	-24.2	-2.1	+5.0	+5.6	+6.4	118.6
234	190	Broadstone 20p	200	5.32	-27.7	-4.8	+2.0	-2.0	-1.2	27.3
87	69	Brunner Inv. Tst.	78	5.49	-23.3	-1.3	+4.0	+3.3	+4.1	25.0

192	143	Capital & National	174	5.71	-26.1	-2.2	+15.2	+3.6	+4.4	26.1
102½	81½	Cardinal Inv. Dfd.	88	5.36	-25.5	-2.9	+2.3	-8.3	-7.6	20.2
106	78	Cedar Inv. Trust	106	6.20	-14.4	+10.4	+26.2	+14.0	+14.9	35.0
82	63½	Charter Trust	79½	6.20	-23.6	+1.9	+11.2	+10.4	+11.3	32.1
87	64	City Ldn. Brew. Dfd.	85	7.99	-21.8	+2.4	+16.4	+3.7	+4.5	40.6
145	110	Claverhouse 50p	130	7.20	-25.5	–	+6.6	+0.8	+1.6	13.0
112	84	C.L.R.P. Inv. Tst.	106	4.72	-21.1	+1.0	+16.5	+13.4	+14.3	14.8
296	240	Cont. & Industrial	268	6.18	-27.3	-0.7	+5.6	-4.3	-3.6	45.1
177	132	Cont. Union Trust	169	5.28	-23.0	-0.6	+17.4	+9.7	+10.6	27.0
126	101	Crossfriars Tst.	120	7.74	-22.7	+0.8	+16.5	+0.8	+1.6	12.0
190	144	Drayton Consol	164	6.88	-29.1	-6.8	+3.8	-6.8	-6.1	53.9
95½	61	Drayton Far Eastern	61	2.90	-14.4	-4.7	-23.7	-26.7	-26.1	10.2
176	135	Drayton Japan	149	7.05	-29.5	-9.7	+3.5	-7.5	-6.7	40.3
234	187	Drayton Premier	199	7.69	-31.0	-5.2	+3.1	-8.3	-7.8	58.5
100	83	Dundee & London	98	5.83	-19.9	+0.5	+10.1	+14.0	+14.9	16.5
128	87	Edin. Amer. Assets	95	1.20	-16.0	-5.0	–	-1.0	-0.3	35.0
77½	56	Edin. Inv. Trust	68	4.54	-13.2	–	-1.4	-2.9	-2.1	113.1
62½	47	Electra Inv. Tst.	59½	6.45	-16.8	+3.5	+13.3	+3.5	+4.3	87.3
132	106	Elec. & General	114	3.20	-27.5	-6.6	-1.7	-3.4	-2.6	20.6
102	80	English & New York	97	6.11	-25.8	-2.5	+12.8	+9.0	+9.9	38.8
83½	59	Eng. & Scot. Invrs.	62	4.15	-24.5	-4.6	-7.5	-10.8	-10.1	24.4
89½	73	Estate Duties	73	4.50	+130.3	-5.2	–	-10.7	-10.0	68.5
135	103	First Scot. Amer.	125	5.54	-23.9	-6.7	+5.0	+5.9	+6.8	39.2
77½	56	Foreign & Colonial	62½	4.65	-24.8	–	+0.8	-9.1	-8.4	164.0
126	100	General Consol	122	7.49	-23.8	+1.7	+16.2	+8.0	+8.8	22.7
358	270	General Funds	276	4.14	-23.5	-9.2	-4.8	-7.4	-6.6	17.2
193	157	Gen. Invrs. & Tstee	171	5.26	-25.4	-3.9	+1.8	-8.1	-7.3	26.3
86	67	Glasgow Stxhldrs	75	4.48	-23.0	-3.8	–	-3.8	-3.1	16.5
161	129	Globe Inv. Trust	141½	7.57	-23.9	+0.4	+£8	-4.4	-3.6	218.2
156	110	Great Northern	140	6.73	-22.2	-6.7	+12.0	+6.9	+7.7	67.9
404	275	G.T. Japan Inv.	287	2.24	-7.9	-6.5	-23.5	-5.9	-5.2	14.3
121	92	Guardian Inv. Tst.	109½	6.10	-28.4	-7.2	+8.4	+0.9	+1.7	55.4
105	79	Hambros. Inv. Tst.	89	4.82	-25.1	+1.1	-2.2	+0.6	+1.4	47.5

High P	Low P	Stock	End Mar price P	Yield %	P/E ratio	Change on mth. %	Change on 3 mths. %	Change on year %	Rel change on yr. %	Mkt. cap. £m's
137½	110	Hill, P. Inv. Trust	134	6.46	-25.2	+1.9	+8.9	+8.5	+9.4	130.2
84½	64½	Industrial & Gen.	77	5.57	-27.6	+1.3	+9.2	-3.1	-2.4	164.7
114	84	Internat. Inv. Tst.	98	6.27	-27.7	-10.9	+5.4	-1.0	-0.2	33.6
338	256	Inv. in Success	256	2.81	-19.5	-8.6	-9.2	-4.1	-3.4	15.7
132½	102	Investors Cap.	107	4.21	-25.9	-3.6	-3.6	-4.5	-3.7	66.2
174	133	Lake View Invest.	138	4.30	-22.4	-5.5	-2.8	-8.52	-7.9	62.0
167	133	Law Debenture	158	7.23	-18.3	-3.7	+11.3	+1.3	+2.1	17.9
171	133	Ldn. & Holyrood	158	5.20	-26.4	-4.8	+13.7	+5.3	+6.2	34.4
113	84	London & Lomond	102	5.60	-28.4	-2.9	+6.2	+2.0	+2.8	19.3
124	82	London & Montrose	120	4.54	-15.7	–	+29.0	+20.0	+21.0	28.8
177	124	London & Prov.	168	4.51	-15.6	–	+27.3	+17.5	+18.4	52.3
80½	64	London Trust	76½	6.54	-24.0	+2.7	+3.4	-10.0	-9.3	69.8
62½	48	Mercantile Inv.	59	6.30	-27.7	+0.9	+5.4	-1.7	-0.9	80.1
105½	84	Merchant Trust	98½	6.02	-26.1	-2.5	+9.4	+4.2	+5.1	50.2
77½	64	Monks Inv. Trust	70½	4.86	-25.3	-2.8	-2.1	-2.1	-1.3	54.7
79	59	Moorside Trust	67	7.46	-16.5	-5.6	+1.5	-9.5	-8.7	13.0
83	65	Murray Caledonian	78	7.33	-22.5	+4.0	+11.4	+4.7	+5.5	42.1
75½	57	Murray Clydesdale	64½	3.84	-29.8	-1.5	+2.4	-6.5	-5.8	56.5
150	118	Murray Glendevon	140	2.76	-22.2	-1.4	+6.1	+5.3	+6.1	14.0
99	68	Murray Northern	79	3.35	-24.7	-3.7	-3.7	-0.6	+0.2	21.8
91	68	Murray Western	83	4.30	-27.4	+0.6	+6.4	-0.6	+0.2	63.8
94	70	1928 Inv. Trust	89	7.06	-24.1	-2.2	+11.2	+5.3	+6.2	32.4
145	119	N. Atlantic Secs	135	2.91	-18.5	-1.5	-2.2	+7.1	+8.0	24.7
145	110	Nthn: Amer. Trust	135	5.29	-24.1	-5.6	+5.5	+7.1	+8.0	44.9
75	55	Outwich Inv. Tst.	63	5.01	-26.8	-3.1	–	-11.9	-11.2	31.8
175	136	Pentland Inv. Tst.	166	5.46	-20.9	-1.8	+9.9	+12.2	+13.1	29.0
174	130	Raeburn Inv. Tst.	164	6.01	-27.0	-2.4	+14.7	+7.2	+8.0	43.8
147	110	River & Mercantile	129	8.31	-22.9	+1.6	+5.7	+1.6	+2.4	31.0
134	100	River Plate Dfd.	113	6.95	-25.2	-0.9	-1.7	-8.1	-7.4	17.7

140	104	Romney Trust	116	5.42	-26.8	-4.1	-5.7	+0.9	+1.7	33.0
381	298	RIT 50p	372	5.38	-21.2	+5.4	+6.3	–	+0.8	90.9
170	141	St. Andrew Trust	160	5.80	-21.5	+3.2	+2.6	+8.1	+9.0	18.3
158	118	Scot. American 50p	137	4.55	-23.0	+1.5	+3.0	-7.4	-6.7	77.1
90	66	Scot. Eastern	83½	5.70	-24.5	+0.6	+6.4	+5.0	+5.9	88.7
158	117	Scottish Inv.	133	4.90	-24.8	-1.5	+4.7	-3.6	-2.9	113.5
184	137	Scot. Mortgage	153	4.92	-26.2	-3.8	-0.6	-3.2	-2.4	111.1
115	91	Scot. National	99	4.89	-28.7	-8.3	–	-10.0	-9.3	63.2
119	80	Scot. Northern	94	5.24	-25.7	+2.2	+2.2	-17.5	-16.9	49.6
90	72	Scottish Ontario	85	5.29	-19.8	-4.0	+8.3	+12.6	+13.5	23.5
67½	46	Scottish United	51½	4.44	-24.0	+1.0	-1.9	-13.4	-12.8	85.6
257	198	Second Alliance	243	5.38	-28.1	-2.0	+5.7	+11.5	+12.4	46.7
121	94	Secs. Trust Scot.	114	6.14	-23.9	–	+9.6	+8.6	+9.4	45.6
173	136	Sphere Inv. Trust	162	5.51	-27.4	-1.8	+12.5	+6.2	+7.1	48.1
248	183	Sterling Trust	222	6.11	-26.1	-4.3	+12.7	+5.2	+6.1	36.2
179	127	Stockholders I.T.	135	3.92	-23.3	–	-3.6	-12.3	-11.6	53.7
176	134	Technology Inv.	156	3.94	-22.9	-3.7	+2.0	+9.5	+10.3	30.8
67½	50½	Temple Bar	61	9.25	-20.2	+2.1	+7.5	-1.2	-0.4	34.8
127	92	Throgmorton Tst.	118	7.26	-22.5	+3.5	+8.8	+2.6	+3.4	49.8
91	68	Trans-Oceanic	77	4.64	-27.0	-7.2	–	-2.1	-1.3	27.7
112	82	Tribune Inv. Tst.	95	4.51	-29.0	-4.0	-9	-2.6	-1.8	24.3
78½	57½	Trustees Corporation	72	5.85	-26.0	–	+13.4	-3.4	-2.6	64.2
88	64	Trust Union	79	5.52	-26.8	-8.1	+9.7	+1.3	+2.1	34.1
178	139	United Br. Secs.	161	6.21	-26.9	-4.2	+4.5	-0.6	+0.2	71.3
120	88	U.S. Debenture	112	7.55	-25.5	-4.3	+8.7	+1.8	+2.6	77.0
322	228	U.S. & General	308	5.33	-14.6	-1.3	+25.7	+21.3	+22.2	25.0
114	68	Viking Resources	76	1.50	-12.9	–	-17.4	+21.6	-21.0	30.4
122	94	Whitbread Invest. Co.	106	6.00	-21.5	-3.6	+10.4	+6.0	+6.6	66.9
81	45	Winterbottom	54	1.72	-4.8	+5.9	-19.4	-22.4	-21.8	13.0
86	61	Witan Inv. Tst.	70	4.23	-25.6	-2.1	-0.7	-1.1	-0.3	119.4
135	104	Yeoman Inv. Tst.	129	7.59	-21.1	-1.5	+11.2	+0.8	+1.6	15.8
FTA Sector Index			Index 298.53	5.40	(n/a) n/a	-2.1	+4.4	+0.2	-5.00	

High P	Low P	Stock	End Mar price P	Yield %	P/E ratio	Change on mth. %	Change on 3 mths. %	Change on year %	Rel change on yr. %	Mkt. cap. £m's
MINING FINANCE										
231	203	Charter Cons. 2p	220	6.72	9.0	-1.3	-13.7	-0.5	-13.7	231.0
538	349	Consd. Goldfields	387	9.04	8.0	-4.9	-20.5	-18.2	-22.0	723.8
235	130	Hampt. Gold Min Areas	135	2.65	14.5	-9.4	-14.6	-40.0	-42.8	18.9
624	411	Rio Tinto-Zinc	417	5.48	9.5	-2.8	-6.3	-9.9	-14.1	1,022.4
FTA Sector Index			Index 204.98	6.93	(9.1) 7.35	-3.6	-13.2	-12.9	-17.36	
OVERSEAS TRADERS										
127	62	Barlow Holdings 10p	67	6.4	28.2	-1.5	-5.6	-38.5	-41.4	31.5
138	94	Berisford, S & W	135	7.94	10.2	+5.5	+8.9	+18.4	+12.9	226.1
28	10	Borthwick, Thomas 50p	14	0.10	–	-12.4	–	-48.1	-50.6	7.2
179	78	Boustead 10p	78	2.29	66.0	-10.3	-26.4	-55.7	-55.7	26.1
168	120	Esperanza 12½p	138	6.94	19.4	+2.2	-2.1	-8.6	-12.8	16.3
105	64	Finlay, James	93	6.40	14.7	-5.1	-6.1	+28.0	+22.0	53.7
237	137	Gill & Duffus	141	8.51	7.7	-0.7	-11.9	-23.8	-27.3	92.7
975	575	Harrisons & Cross £1	612½	6.53	20.3	-9.3	-21.0	-23.4	-27.0	382.0
475	248	Inchcape £1	310	8.36	10.6	+1.3	+15.7	-32.8	-35.9	262.6
420	360	Lawrie Plant Hid £1	392	7.29	9.1	-0.5	-0.8	+1.8	-2.9	10.0
97	68	Lonrho	73	17.61	6.7	-2.7	-5.2	-21.5	-25.1	191.1
118	73	Majedie Invs. 10p	78	5.17	19.1	-8.4	-15.6	-33.3	-36.4	11.8
380	230	McLeod Russel £1	340	3.47	–	-7.6	-9.3	+3.0	-1.7	13.7
54	34	Ocean Wilsons 20p	44	9.21	12.8	–	+10.0	-10.2	-14.4	11.6
167	112	Paterson Zoch 10p	133	4.65	4.8	-11.3	-4.3	-17.3	-21.1	32.5
237	140	Steel Bros	220	5.19	10.7	-2.2	-0.9	+40.1	+33.6	24.3
82	51	Tozer, Kemsley 20p	82	1.91	–	+10.8	+12.3	+57.7	+50.4	44.0
FTA Sector Index			Index 383.44	8.30	(11.0) 8.94	-0.2	-5.0	-14.0	-18.45	

1982 High p	Low p	Stock	End Mar price p	Change on month p	Yield %
GOLD MINES					
526	359	Blyvoor 25c	454	–14	..
£18½	£13¼	Buffels R1	£16¼	+£⅞	..
802	567	Doomfontein R1	659	–84	..
£12½	786	Driefontein R1	£10⅞	+£⅝	11.5
602	400	E. Rand Prp. R1	449	–19	..
120	77	Elsburg R1	95	–3	14.6
£17½	£10½	F.S. Geduld 50c	£12¾	–£1¾	25.7
668	503½	Harmony 50c	534xd	–71	21.0
£26¾	£17¾	Hartebeast R1	£21¾	–£1½	..
609	447	Kinross R1	471xd	–85	..
£16	£10¼	Kloof Gold R1	£12	–£1¼	..
126	78	Leslie 65c	87xd	–23	..
846	575	Libanon R1	701	–28	..
£18⅜	£13¼	President Brand 50c	£16	–£⅜	19.8
£16⅜	£10⅜	President Steyn 50c	£13⅜	–£⅜	20.1
£16⅜	£11	St Helens R1	£13⅜	–£⅜	22.8
£16¼	£10¾	Southvaal 50c	£12¾	–£⅝	15.0
789	579	Stilfontein 50c	674	–14	24.5
£35	£20¾	Vaal Reels 50c	£25	–£3⅞	..
550	359	Welkom 50c	421	–52	31.0
203	116	Western Areas R1	140	–14	15.2
£16⅞	£10¼	Western Deep R2	£13⅓	–£¼	16.0
£23⅛	£16½	Western Hidgs. 50c	£18¾	–£3½	29.8
£14¼	£10¾	Winkelhaak R1	£12xd	–£½	..
FTA Stock Index			Index 246.70	month ago 263.40	Change –16.70
COPPERS					
76	63	Bougainville I Kina	68	–5	5.7
325	195	Messina R0.50	205	–65	15.6
21	16	Zambia Copper $BD0.24	17	–3	..
RUBBERS					
92	89	Anglo-Indonesian	90	..	5.5
75	64	Bertam Con. 10p	65	..	1.9
50	44½	Cons Plants M50c	47	+1½	7.2
182	142	Harrisons Malay Est. 10p	145	–7	7.9
72	61	Highlands M50c	68	+4	5.3
280	240	Lon. Sumatra 10p	240	–30	4.8
TEAS					
245	235	Assam Dooars £1	245	+5	3.5
230	200	Assam Frontier £1	227	+19	6.3
90	90	Blantyre	90	..	7.9
425	398	Lunuva £1	400	–10	11.8

1982					
High p	**Low p**	**Stock**	**End Mar price p**	**Change on month p**	**Yield %**
290	285	Moran £1	290		2.5
65	58	Ruo Estates	60	+2	2.4
240	212	Williamson Tea £1	235	–2	7.6
TINS					
140	95	Geevor	95	–30	..
630	450	Gopeng Cons.	460	–65	5.3
98	80	Malaysia Mining $M0.10	64	–6	9.3
450	290	Pengkalen 10p	305	..	1.6
255	200	Tronoh SM1	200	–20	..

Fixed interest

1982						
High p	**Low p**	**Stock**	**End Mar price p**	**Change on month p**	**Yield %**	**Gross Red Yield %**
GOVERNMENT SECURITIES						
99¼	95¾	Treasury 12% 1983	99½	+½	12.11	12.96
89	80⅜	Treasury 8½% '84–86	89	+5½	9.55	11.85
63½	60¼	Transport 3% '78–88	63½	+1¾	4.78	11.52
91¾	77⅞	Treasury 11¾ % 1991	91⅛	+5	13.27	14.04
61¾	56¼	Funding 6% 1993	61¼	+2¾	9.84	12.48
114⅞	73	Treasury 15¼ % 1996	106¼xd	–¾	14.13	13.95
78½	66	Treasury 9½% 1999	77¾	+3⅞	12.60	13.16
99⅜	81¾	Treasury 12½% '03–05	98	+6¼	13.37	13.40
49⅜	44¼	Treasury 5½% '08–12	48½	+1⅞	11.42	11.81
20¼	17¾	Consols 2½%	20xd	+¼	12.48	..
30¼	26¾	War Loan 3½%	30	+1¼	12.13	..
F.T. Stock Index			Index 68.93	month ago 66.39	Change +2.54	

	Price p	**Flat Yield %**	**Gross Red. Yield %**
DEBENTURES			
Allied-Brew 7¼% 88–93	64xd	11.41	13.63
BOC Int. 11½% Tonnage 92	90¾	13.28	13.97
Bass 8¼% 87–92	69xd	12.06	14.12
Courtaulds 7¾% 89–94	63½2xd	12.31	14.31
Delta Group 10¾ % 95–99	77½2xd	13.81	14.20
Dunlop 6¾% 85–90	65½2xd	10.38	14.25
English Electric 7% 86–91	73¼	9.79	12.06
G.K.N. (U.K.) 10½% 90–95	78¾	13.94	14.74
M.E.P.C. 9¾ % 97–2002	72xd	13.67	14.04
Trusthouse Forte 10½% 91–96	76½2xd	13.70	14.37

	Price p	Flat Yield %	Gross Red. Yield %
UNSECURED LOAN STOCKS			
Dickinson Robinson 7¾% 86–91	66	12.19	15.00
Distillers 10½% 93–98	75xd	14.14	14.68
General Accident 7¾% 92–97	60½	13.35	14.64
I.C.I. 10¾ % 91–96	79¾	13.88	14.59
Imperial Group 10½% 90–95	74¾4xd	14.02	14.86
Land Securities 8½% 92–97	64xd	13.40	14.57
Midland Bank 10¾% 93–98	80	14.03	14.50
Nat. West. 9% 1993	71¼	13.16	14.75
Rank Org. 10¾% 97–	77¼	14.37	14.71
Unilever 7¾% 91–2006	58¼	13.89	14.31
PREFERENCE SHARES			
Bowaters 5½%	38½2xd	14.33	..
British-American Tobacco 5%	41½2xd	14.44	..
Brit. Petroleum 9%	66½	13.97	..
Hawker Siddeley 5½%	40½	14.01	..
I.C.I.5%	37½	13.75	..
Lewis (J.) Partnership 5%	36xd	13.70	..
Nat. West. 7%	51½	13.89	..
Rank Org. 6¼%	45½	14.36	..
Scottish & Newcastle 7¾%	55½2xd	13.94	..
Tilling (Thos.) 5¼%	54½	14.38	..

Warrants†

Company	Ord. Price	Warrant Price	Gearing
Britannia Arrow	43	12½	4.6
Burton Group	185	89	2.1
Consolidated Plantantions	47	117	1.6
International Inv. Trust	98	85	2.3
Ladbroke	169	119	1.4
Lex Services Group	110	29	3.8
New Throgmorton Capital	205	25	8.2
Redland	184	£75	3.1
Town & City Props	30	13	3.5

† Source: Earnshaw Haes.

Financial Times Share Information Service extract 15 October 2014

INDUSTRIAL ENGINEERING

	Price	+/-Chg	52 week High	52 week Low	Yld	P/E	Volume '000s
Bodycote†	574.00	16.50	832.00	548.00	2.35	14.08	1130.1
Castings	439.88	–0.13	525.00	411.00	2.84	11.12	0.7
Fenner	292.10	4.00	489.77	275.00	3.85	12.92	364.3
Goodwin	3406	1.00	4250	3200	1.04	12.88	2.2
Hill&Sm	525.00	–	574.00	450.00	3.05	18.14	35.4
IMI	1163	28.00	1801.14	1108	3.19	16.36	1185.8
MetroseInd†	246.80	3.60	382.20	234.50	3.34	20.19	3328.9
Renold	52.13	0.38	69.00	38.05	–	–10.64	22.8
Rotork	2489	44.00	2923	2331	1.93	22.03	202.1
Severfd	59.38	0.88	69.51	52.60	–	–66.56	31.2
SKF SKr	143.40	5.00	183.40	137.50	3.86	45.14	4307.6
Spirax-S†	2688	47.00	3214	2548	2.19	20.39	94.6
Tex	91.50	–	101.50	68.00	4.37	8.28	5.0
Trifast†	92.50	–3.75	134.00	67.35	1.30	16.05	483.2
Vitec†	564.50	–17.50	729.50	539.00	4.07	14.11	9.2
Weir†	2213	58.00	2848	2036	1.90	14.42	1328.5

INDUSTRIAL GENERAL

	Price	+/-Chg	52 week High	52 week Low	Yld	P/E	Volume '000s
BritPoly	605.00	3.00	742.61	565.00	2.40	13.35	14.6
JardnMt $*†	58.43	0.24	64.60	49.34	2.23	14.51	110.0
Jard Str $*†	34.39	–0.08	38.10	30.06	0.69	13.08	53.0
Macfrlne†	36.25	–0.50	49.50	33.00	4.41	12.16	96.5
REXAM	459.90	–2.00	603.00	453.70	4.26	11.45	3084.0
RPC	516.00	4.00	672.90	444.60	2.93	19.62	245.0
Smith DS†	241.30	1.20	359.10	236.31	3.61	15.88	3892.3
Smiths	1208	20.00	1535	1176	3.29	20.77	986.5
SmurfKap £†	15.70	-0.06	20.61	14.49	2.63	14.12	309.1
Vesuvius	413.70	10.30	523.50	399.00	3.63	10.29	143.3

INDUSTRIAL TRANSPORTATION

			52 week				Volume
	Price	**+/-Chg**	**High**	**Low**	**Yld**	**P/E**	**'000s**
Avation	142.00	1.50	165.00	97.00	1.52	10.09	57.0
BBA Aviat†	326.00	4.80	35.00	288.60	2.76	15.57	522.2
Braemar	460.00	33.50	585.00	398.00	5.65	15.03	52.7
Clarkson	2205	–14.00	2750	1839	2.54	22.13	0.4
Eurotunnl £	8.95	0.07	10.30	6.76	1.69	44.22	1165.0
Fisher J†	1197	–19.00	1565	1071.5	1.67	15.07	100.9
Flybe Grp	111.00	1.25	151.56	65.15	–	11.50	954.9
Goldenpt	307.50	2.50	500.00	300.00	–	-9.34	31.6
OceanWil	1102.5	25.00	1290	943.00	3.18	11.19	15.3
RoyalMail	399.90	6.20	618.00	388.00	–	3.13	4291.3
UK Mail	414.50	2.25	715.00	405.53	4.70	13.02	5.4

Appendix D

Relevant estate duty and other obsolete legislation

ESTATE DUTY

FA 1894, s 7(5)

The principal value of any property shall be estimated to be the price which, in the opinion of the commissioners, such property would fetch if sold in the open market at the time of the death of the deceased.

F(1909–10)A 1910, s 60(2)

In estimating the principal value of any property under subsection (5) of section seven of the principal Act, in the case of any person dying on or after the thirtieth day of April nineteen hundred and nine, the commissioners shall fix the price of the property according to the market price at the time of the death of the deceased, and shall not make any reduction in the estimate on account of the estimate being made on the assumption that the whole property is to be placed on the market at one and the same time:

Provided that where it is proved to the commissioners that the value of the property has been depreciated by reason of the death of the deceased, the commissioners in fixing the price shall take such depreciation into account.

FA 1940, s 55

Valuation for estate duty of shares and debentures of certain companies

(1) Where for the purposes of estate duty there pass, on the death of a person dying after the commencement of this Act, shares in or debentures of a company to which this section applies then if;
   (a) the deceased had the control of the company at any time during the (seven years) ending with his death;
   the principal value of the shares or debentures, in lieu of being estimated in accordance with the provisions of subsection (5) of section seven of the Finance Act 1894, shall be estimated by reference to the net value of the assets of the company in accordance with the provisions of the next succeeding subsection.

(2) For the purposes of such ascertainment as aforesaid;
   (a) the net value of the assets of the company shall be taken to be the principal value thereof estimated in accordance with the said subsection (5), less the like allowance for liabilities of the company as is provided by subsection (1) of section fifty of this Act in relation to the assets of a company passing on a death by virtue of section forty-six of this Act, but subject to the modification that allowance shall be made for such a liability as is mentioned in paragraph (b) of that subsection unless it also falls within paragraph (a) thereof;
   (b) the aggregate value of all the shares and debentures of the company issued and outstanding at the death of the deceased shall be taken to be the same as the net value of the assets of the company;
   (c) in a case in which there are both shares in and debentures of the company issued and outstanding at the death, or different classes of either, the net value of the assets of the company shall be apportioned between them with due regard to the rights attaching thereto respectively; and
   (d) the value of any share, or of any debenture, or of a share or debenture of any class, shall be a rateable proportion, ascertained by reference to a nominal amount, of the net value of the assets of the company as determined under paragraph (a) of this subsection, or, in the case mentioned in paragraph (c) of this subsection, of the part thereof apportioned under that paragraph to the shares of the company, or to its debentures, or to that class thereof, as the case may be.

(3) For the purposes of this section a person shall be deemed to have had control of a company at any time if he then had;
   (a) the control of powers of voting on all questions, or on any particular question, affecting the company as a whole which if exercised would have yielded a majority of the votes capable of being exercised thereon;

   or if he could have obtained such control … by an exercise at that time of a power exercisable by him or with his consent.

(4) This section shall not apply to the valuation of shares or debentures of a class as to which permission to deal has been granted by the committee of a recognised stock exchange in the United Kingdom and dealings in the ordinary course of business on that stock exchange have been recorded during the year ending with the death of the deceased, and, in making an apportionment under paragraph (c) of subsection (2) of this section in the case of a company having shares or debentures of such a class, the part of the value of the assets of the company to be apportioned to shares or debentures of that class shall be determined by reference to the prices recorded on such dealings.

(5) Control of a company which a person had in a fiduciary capacity shall be disregarded for the purposes of this section.

(6) In this section references to the assets of a company shall be construed as references to the assets that it had at the death of the deceased.

(7) Section thirty-seven of the Finance Act, 1930, shall not have effect in relation to a person dying after the commencement of this Act.

FA 1954, s 28

Reduced rate of duty on certain business assets

(1) Where a business or an interest passes on a death, any estate duty chargeable on the death in respect of industrial hereditaments used in and occupied for the purposes of the business or in respect of machinery or plant so used shall (except as hereinafter provided) be charged at fifty-five per cent of the estate rate.

(2) Where any shares in or debentures of a company in respect of which estate duty is chargeable on a death fall to be valued by reference to the value of the company's assets in accordance with section fifty-five of the Finance Act 1940, (or where paragraph (a) of subsection (3) of section sixty-six of the Finance Act 1960, operates to determine the principal value of any such shares or debentures);

  (a) the duty shall be charged in accordance with subsection (1) of this section on the relevant proportion of the net value of the shares or debentures; and

  (b) if the company is engaged in husbandry or forestry, the duty shall be charged at fifty-five per cent of the estate rate on such proportion of that net value as is attributable to the agricultural value (within the meaning of section 23 of the Finance Act 1925) of agricultural property occupied by the company for the purposes of that husbandry or forestry or, where the occupation is partly for those and partly for other purposes, the part of that agricultural value which ought justly to be apportioned to the occupation for those purposes.

(3) The reference in paragraph (a) of subsection (2) of this section to the relevant proportion of the net value of shares or debentures refers to such part of that value as is attributable to the value of any of the following namely;

  (a) industrial hereditaments used in and occupied for the purposes of the company's business and machinery and plant so used;

  (b) shares in or debentures of a subsidiary of the company in so far as their value is attributable;

    (i) to the value of industrial hereditaments used in and occupied for the purposes of the business of that or any other subsidiary of the company, or of machinery or plant so used; or

    (ii) to the value of any interest a subsidiary of the company has as lessor in property let to the company by the subsidiary and consisting either of industrial hereditaments used in and occupied for the purposes of the company's business or machinery or plant so used;

  (c) any interest the company has as lessor in any property let by the company to a subsidiary of it and consisting either of industrial hereditaments used in and occupied for the purposes of that subsidiary's business or of machinery or plant so used.

(4) Where subsection (2) of this section applies to shares in or debentures of a company passing on a death, any interest of the deceased as lessor in industrial hereditaments used in and occupied for the purposes of the

company's business or in machinery or plant so used shall, if chargeable with duty on his death, be charged in accordance with subsection (1) of this section; but save as aforesaid the said subsection (1) shall apply only to the interest of the person carrying on the business in question.

(5) In the case of company's business treated as passing on a death by virtue of section forty-six of the Finance Act 1940, duty shall be charged in accordance with subsection (1) of this section in respect of the company's assets in so far as they fall within paragraphs (b) and (c) of subsection (3) of this section (as well as assets falling within subsection (1)).

(6) The relief from estate duty conferred by this section in respect of, or by reference to the value of, machinery or plant used in any business shall, in the case of machinery or plant not used exclusively in that business, be such part only of the relief conferred apart from this subsection as appears to the Commissioners of Inland Revenue to be just and reasonable having regard to all the relevant circumstances of the case and, in particular, to the extent of any other use (whether for business purposes or not).

(7) Land or premises used in a business shall be treated for the purposes of this section as an industrial hereditament if it falls to be treated as an industrial hereditament (or industrial lands and heritages) for purposes of valuation for rating or, in the case of land or premises outside Great Britain, would fall to be so treated if situated in England. Provided that, in the case of land or premises occupied and used partly for industrial purposes and partly for other purposes, the value shall be apportioned between those purposes and the land or premises shall be treated according to that apportionment as partly being and partly not being an industrial hereditament.

(8) The value to be apportioned under the proviso to the last foregoing subsection is the next annual value for rating (or in the case of land or premises outside Great Britain, a corresponding value), and subsection (2) of section four of the Rating and Valuation (Apportionment) Act 1928, shall apply for the purposes of that proviso, but with the substitution for the reference to the net annual value not exceeding fifty pounds of a reference to the principal value not exceeding one thousand pounds and with the necessary adaptation in relation to land or premises outside Great Britain of other references to net annual value.

(9) In this section, 'business' does not include a business carried on in the exercise of a profession or vocation, or carried on otherwise than for gain.

(10) Nothing in this section shall apply

(a) to a business for the sale of which a binding contract has been entered into, other than a sale to a company formed for the purpose of carrying it on made in consideration wholly or mainly of shares in that company; or

(b) to the business of a company with respect to which a winding-up order has been made, or which has passed a resolution for voluntary winding-up (unless only with a view to a reconstruction or amalgamation), or which is otherwise in process of liquidation (unless only with that view);

nor to assets used in any such business, in or shares or debentures of any such company.

FA 1960, s 66

Valuation of assets of certain companies

(1) Subject to the provisions of this section, in the case of a person dying after the fourth day of April, nineteen hundred and sixty, the principal value of assets of a company which are used in, and in the case of land or buildings are occupied for the purposes of, a trade or business carried on by the company, shall be estimated for the purposes of section fifty-five of the Finance Act 1940 (valuation, by reference to assets, to shares and debentures of certain companies) on the footing that the sale by reference to which (in accordance with subsection (5) of section seven of the Finance Act 1894) the value of the assets is to be estimated is a sale of the business where the assets are subject to an enforceable restriction that they are to be used or occupied only for the purposes of that business.

(2) In the case of a company whose business consists wholly or mainly of one or more of the following, that is to say dealing in securities, stocks or shares, land or buildings or making or holding investments, subsection (1) of this section shall not apply to securities, stocks, shares, land or buildings belonging to the business at the time of the death.

(3) Subsection (1) of this section shall not have effect so as to reduce the principal value of shares or debentures below whichever is the lower of;
   (a) the amount at which it would have been estimated in accordance with subsection (5) of section seven of the Finance Act 1894.
   (b) the amount at which it would have been estimated (under section fifty-five of the Finance Act 1940) if this section had not been passed.

F(1909–10)A 1910, s 25 (re obsolete duties on land values)

(1) For the purposes of this part of this Act, the gross value of land means the amount which the fee simple of the land, if sold at the time in the open market by a willing seller in its then condition, free from incumbrances, and from any burden, charge, or restriction (other than rates of taxes) might be expected to realise.

(2) The full site value of land means the amount which remains after deducting from the gross value of the land the difference (if any) between that value and the value which the fee simple of the land, if sold at the time in the open market by a willing seller, might be expected to realise if the land were divested of any buildings and of any other structures (including fixed or attached machinery) on, in, or under the surface, which are appurtenant to or used in connection with any such buildings, and of all growing timber, fruit trees, fruit bushes, and other things growing thereon.

(3) The total value of land means the gross value after deducting the amount by which the gross value would be diminished if the land were sold subject to any fixed charges and to any public rights of way or any public rights of user, and to any right of common and to any easements affecting the land, and to any covenant or agreement restricting the use of the land entered into or made before the thirtieth day of April nineteen hundred and nine, and to any covenant or agreement restricting the use of the land entered

into or made on or after that date, if, in the opinion of the Commissioners, the restraint imposed by the covenant or agreement so entered into or made on or after that date was when imposed desirable in the interests of the public, or in view of the character and surroundings of the neighbourhood, and the opinion of the Commissioners shall in this case be subject to an appeal to the referee, whose decision shall be final.

(4) The assessable site value of land means the total value after deducting;

(a) The same amount as is to be deducted for the purposes of arriving at full site value from gross value; and

(b) Any part of the total value which is proved to the Commissioners to be directly attributable to works executed, or expenditure of a capital nature (including any expenses of advertisement) incurred bona fide by or on behalf of or solely in the interests of any person interested in the land for the purposes of improving the value of the land as building land, or for the purpose of any business, trade, or industry other than agriculture; and

(c) Any part of the total value which is proved to the commissioners to be directly attributable to the appropriation of any land or to the gift of any land by any person interested in the land for the purpose of streets, roads, paths, squares, gardens, or other open spaces for the use of the public; and

(d) Any part of the total value which is proved to the commissioners to be directly attributable to the expenditure of money on the redemption of any land tax, or any fixed charge, or on the enfranchisement of copyhold land or customary freeholds, or on effecting the release of any covenant or agreement restricting the use of land which may be taken into account in ascertaining the total value of the land; to goodwill or any other matter which is personal to the owner, occupier, or other person interested for the time being in the land; and

(e) Any sums which, in the opinion of the commissioners, it would be necessary to expend in order to divest the land of buildings, timber, trees, or other things of which it is to be taken to be divested for the purpose of arriving at the full site value from the gross value of the land and of which it would be necessary to divest the land for the purpose of realising the full site value.

Where any works executed or expenditure incurred for the purpose of improving the value of the land for agriculture have actually improved the value of the land as building land, or for the purpose of any business, trade, or industry other than agriculture, the works or expenditure shall, for the purpose of this provision, be treated as having been executed or incurred also for the latter purposes.

Any reference in this Act to site value (other than the reference to the site value of land on an occasion on which increment duty is to be collected) shall be deemed to be a reference to the assessable site value of the land as ascertained in accordance with this section.

(5) The provisions of this section are not applicable for the purpose of the valuation of minerals.

Appendix E

RICS Valuation – Global Standards: VPGA 3, VPGA 4, VPGA 6, VPGA 7 and VPGA 10 (1 July 2017)

VPGA 3 Valuation of businesses and business interests

This guidance is advisory and not mandatory in content. Where appropriate, however, it alerts *members* to relevant mandatory material contained elsewhere in these global standards, including the *International Valuation Standards*, using cross-references in bold type. These cross-references are for the assistance of *members* and do not alter the status of the material that follows below. *Members* are reminded that:

- this guidance cannot cover every circumstance, and they must always have regard to the facts and circumstances of individual assignments when forming valuation judgments
- they should remain alert to the fact that individual jurisdictions may have specific requirements that are not covered by this guidance.

1 Scope

1.1 The guidance below provides additional commentary on the *valuation* of businesses and business interest and the practical application of **IVS 200 Businesses and Business Interests**. Any cross-references to mandatory requirements are highlighted in **bold type**.

2 Introduction

2.1 For the purposes of this application, a 'partial interest' means ownership of a right or rights that represent less than all of the rights in a tangible or *intangible asset*, such as the right to use but not sell an asset or property. 'Fractional interest' means ownership of a percentage of the right or rights in a tangible or *intangible asset* (whether such rights are in the entirety of the asset, or a partial interest in the asset) such as the ownership of an asset which is vested in more than one party.

2.2 IVS 200 defines a business as 'a commercial, industrial, service or investment activity'. This VPGA is concerned with the *valuation* of entire businesses – whether companies, sole traders or partnerships (including limited liability partnerships) – together with interests therein, such as company stocks and shares or partnership interests.

2.3 This VPGA does not deal with the *valuation* of *intangible assets* (for which see VPGA 6), *plant and equipment* (for which see VPGA 5), land, or other tangible assets that may sometimes constitute part of a business. However, a business valuer may often be required to rely on the *valuation* of such assets provided by other specialist valuers, for example, of real estate, and of mineral rights.

2.4 *Valuation* of financial interests, loan capital, debentures, options, warrants, convertibles and fixed interest securities may form part of a business valuation assignment.

2.5 To satisfy **PS 2 section 2**, it is important that the valuer is regularly involved in business *valuation*, as practical knowledge of the factors affecting investment in any particular property, asset, business or share, is essential.

3 Scope of work and terms of engagement

3.1 The valuation knowledge of clients will vary widely. Some will have a thorough understanding of business *valuation*, while others will be unfamiliar with the terms and concepts used by business valuers.

3.2 It is important that both the scope of the work to be undertaken and the *terms of engagement* are understood and agreed between the valuer and the client prior to commencement of the assignment. The asset or liability, or the specific interest in the asset or liability that is to be valued, or the right (or rights to) that are to be appraised should be recorded. Such record should specify:

- the legal structure of the business entity
- whether the asset to be valued is the interest in its entirety or a fractional interest
- if the asset to be valued is confined to, or excludes, certain assets or liabilities, and
- the class (or classes) of shares concerned.

3.3 Any *assumptions* that are made must be clearly stated in compliance with **VPS 4 sections 8 and 9**. For example, the valuer should state whether he or she assumes that the owners of shares or partial interests are intending to sell or retain such interests, or whether certain assets or liabilities owned by the business are to be disregarded.

3.4 There may be situations where the interest in the asset to be valued is shared with others, i.e. common use or shared ownership, and in such cases, it should be clearly specified.

3.5 Valuers may wish to develop standard letters of engagement that can be used for any type of valuation instruction. Where a *valuation* has to comply with the RICS Red Book the valuer must produce *terms of engagement* that comply with the minimum terms set out in **PS 2 section 7** and **VPS 1**, adapted as necessary to refer to business *valuation*.

4 Businesses and business interests

4.1 A business *valuation* may either comprise the whole of the activity of an entity or a part of the activity. It is important to distinguish as necessary between the entirety value, the value of a partial interest (see paragraph 2.1 above), the values of specific assets or liabilities of the entity, and the intended use of the *valuation* (for example, for tax planning, or management's internal purposes), prior to commencing the *valuation*.

4.2 It is essential to be clear about the 'purpose' of the *valuation*, and its 'intended use'. Purpose may refer to the provision of an opinion in accordance with a specific *basis of value*, for example, *market value* or *fair value*. Intended use may refer to a type of transaction or activity, for example, financial reporting.

4.3 Where individual assets, divisions and liabilities are to be valued, and are capable of being independently transferred, they should, where possible, be valued at their respective *market values* rather than by apportionment of the entirety value of the business.

4.4 When valuing a business or interest in a business, the valuer should consider whether a higher value could be arrived at on a liquidation basis and, if so, consider the prospect of realising such value, having regard to the ownership interest.

4.5 Whatever the ownership interest – whether a proprietorship, a partnership, or in corporate form – the rights, privileges and conditions attaching to that interest have to be considered in the *valuation*. Ownership interests may be the entire business, or part or shares therein, and it may be important to distinguish between legal and beneficial ownership, rights and obligations inherent to the interest and those rights that may be contained in any agreement between current shareholders. Ownership rights will usually be set out in legally binding documents such as articles of association, articles of incorporation, business memoranda, bye-laws, partnership articles or other agreements, and shareholder agreements.

4.6 The documents referred to in paragraph 4.5 above may contain transfer restrictions and may state the *basis of value* that has to be used on a transfer of the business interest. It is important to distinguish between rights and obligations inherent in the interest to be valued. For example, the ownership documentation may require the *valuation* to be done on a pro-rata proportion of the entity value, regardless of size of interest. The valuer will then have to comply with such requirements and the rights attaching to any other class of interest. IVS 200 provides further commentary on ownership rights.

4.7 A non-controlling interest may have a lower value than a controlling one, although a majority interest does not necessarily control the entity. Voting control and other rights will be set out by the legal frameworks mentioned in paragraph 4.5 above and may give control or veto even to minority interests in certain circumstances. There are often different equity classes in a business, each with different rights.

4.8 The reason why the valuer has been instructed to perform a business *valuation* is important to understand, as the *valuation* may be required for a wide variety of purposes. Examples include financial reporting, taxation, public sector assignments, transactions and flotations, fairness opinions, banking arrangements, insolvency and administration, knowledge management, or portfolio review. The purpose will introduce various *bases of value*, some governed by statute and case law, and others by international and national standards of professional valuation practice.

4.9 *Bases of value* typically encountered for these *valuations* are *fair value*, fair market value, *market value*, open market value, *investment value*, owner value and net realisable value. It is important to check the precise terms of any *basis of value* that may be described, for example, in shareholders' agreements, legislation or regulations. Valuers should be mindful of the requirements of **PS 1 sections 3, 4 and 7**, relating to the use of a *basis of value* not recognised in the Red Book.

4.10 Depending on the rules and practice followed in respect of the *basis of value*, *valuations* of the same asset may be different. For example, because of the rules concerning tax *valuations*, a tax authority might view a *valuation* differently to a litigant, merger partner or *special purchaser*.

4.11 While the valuer should consider future returns likely to be received from the business, as well as the often theoretical aspects of *valuation* (particularly fiscal factors), ultimately the business that is to be valued is the one that actually exists, or the one that could exist on a commercial basis as at the *valuation date*. The valuer therefore needs to account for the future expectations of operation of the business. These expectations may be based partly on actual historic performance and partly on a notional unachieved one. They will be those of the market participants as identified by the valuer, following appropriate research as to the business and outlook for the industry, and discussions with the operators of the business as to their expectations.

4.12 As the underlying concept revolves around the profits that the purchaser might expect to accrue from ownership, these are generally measured after deducting the commercial costs of managing the business entity. Therefore, where a business entity does not bear actual management costs, the valuer will need to consider the deduction of notional management costs at a market rate in arriving at profitability for business valuation purposes.

4.13 In many cases the valuer may need to apply more than one valuation method, particularly where there is insufficient information or evidence to enable the valuer to rely on just one. In such cases, the valuer may use additional methods, to arrive at the final *valuation* indicating why preference is given to any one or more methodologies. The valuer should consider all valuation approaches, giving reasons why any particular approach has not been completed.

5 Information

5.1 Business *valuation* often depends on information received from the proprietors and their advisers or representatives. The valuer should specify what reliance has been placed on what information, as well as stating the rationale for accepting and using, without verification, information provided by the client or that person's representative. Some information may have to be verified in whole or in part, and this will need to be stated in the valuation report. Although the value may largely depend on future expectations, the history may assist in determining what these expectations might reasonably be.

5.2 The valuer needs to be aware of any relevant economic developments, industry trends and the context in which the *valuation* is being prepared, for example, political outlook, government policies, inflation and interest rates, and market activity. Such factors may affect businesses in different sectors in distinct ways.

5.3 The interest being valued will reflect the financial standing of the business at the *valuation date*. The nature of the assets and liabilities needs to be understood, and the valuer is expected to consider which ones are employed for income generation, and which ones are redundant to such activities at the *valuation date*. The valuer should also take account of off-balance sheet assets or liabilities where necessary.

6 Valuation investigation

6.1 As a minimum requirement, valuers should not contemplate carrying out a *valuation* in the absence of a detailed knowledge and understanding of the history of, and activities associated with, the business and or asset(s). They will also need a comprehensive understanding of, as appropriate, management structures and personnel, state of the subject industry, the general economic outlook and political factors. In addition, consideration must be given to such issues as the rights of minority shareholders. For these reasons, valuers should have appropriate competency in business *valuation*.

6.2 Typical information requirements to assist the valuer in understanding the subject company and/or asset(s) could include:

- most recent *financial statements*, and details of current and prior projections or forecasts
- description and history of the business or asset, including legal protections
- information about the business or asset and supporting intellectual property and intangibles (for example, marketing and technical know-how, research and development, documentation, design graphics and manuals, including any licences/approvals/consents/permits to trade, etc.)
- articles of association, company memorandum, shareholders' agreements, subscription agreements, other collateral agreements

- precise activities of the business, and its associated companies or subsidiaries
- class rights of all share and debenture classes (security over assets)
- previous valuation reports
- product(s) dealt in, supported or extended by the business and intangibles
- company's market(s) and competition, barriers to entry in such markets, business and marketing plans, due diligence
- strategic alliances and joint venture details
- whether contractual arrangements can be assigned or transferred in any *intangible asset* or royalty agreement
- major customers and suppliers
- objectives, developments or trends expected in the industry and how these are likely to affect the company or asset
- accounting policies
- strengths, weaknesses, opportunities and threats (SWOT) analysis
- key market factors (for example, monopoly or dominant market position, market share)
- major capital expenditure in prospect
- competitor positions
- seasonal or cyclical trends
- technological changes affecting the business or asset
- vulnerability of any source of raw materials or supplier arrangement
- whether there have been any recent acquisitions or mergers in the sector around the *valuation date*, and the criteria that were applied
- whether there have been any significant developments or changes to the business since the latest accounting date (for example, management information, budgets, forecasts)
- offers to acquire the business, or discussions with banks and other sponsors to go public
- management of research and development (for example, non-disclosure agreements, subcontractors, training and incentives)
- *valuations* of underlying assets.

6.3 Much of the information relied on will be derived from the client(s) and it may not be possible to verify it. In such cases, the valuation report should make this clear. It may, however, extend to information obtained from other specialist valuers or other comment or informed sources, as set out at paragraph 5.1 above, and it should be made clear if reliance has been placed on such information.

7 Valuation approaches and methodology

7.1 In broad terms, valuation theory recognises four distinct approaches in the *valuation* of shares and businesses. These are:

- the *market approach* (sometimes known as the direct market comparison approach)
- the *income approach*
- the *cost approach* and
- the asset-based approach.

7.2 While the *market* and *income approaches* can be used for the *valuation* of any business or business interest, the *cost approach* will not normally apply except where profits and cash flows cannot reliably be determined, for example, in start-up businesses and early stage companies.

7.3 An alternative that may be used for the *valuation* of businesses and interests in businesses is the asset-based approach, which is based on the underlying assets being revalued, if necessary. This would include, for example, property holding and investment companies, and investment businesses holding listed company shares.

7.4 Involvement of market participants, who are able to provide insights to transactions and market conditions that are critical to proper use of the data in analysis, is advisable wherever possible.

Market approach

7.5 The *market approach* measures the value of an asset by comparing recent sales or offerings of similar or substitute property and related market data to the business being valued.

7.6 The two primary *market approach* methods are the 'market multiple method' and the 'similar transactions method'. These are based on data derived from three principal sources:

- public stock markets
- the acquisition market where entire businesses are traded and
- prior transactions in the shares of the entity being valued, or offers for that subject business.

7.7 The market multiple method focuses on comparing the subject asset to guideline similar, publicly traded, companies and assets. In applying this method, valuation multiples are derived from historic and operating data of comparables. These are selected, where possible, from the same industry, or one affected by the same economic factors as that of the subject business, and are evaluated on both a qualitative and quantitative basis. The data is then adjusted having regard to the strengths and weaknesses of the subject asset relative to the selected companies, and applied to the appropriate operating data of the subject asset to arrive at an indication of value. Appropriate adjustments (as supported by market-derived information presented in the report) to reflect different properties or characteristics, are usually made to the derived data. Examples of such matters are differences in perceived risk and future expectations, and differences in ownership interest, including level of control, marketability and size of holding.

7.8 The similar transactions method uses valuation multiples based on historical transactions that have occurred in the subject company's shares and/or asset's direct or related industries. These derived multiples are then adjusted and applied to the appropriate operating data of the subject asset to arrive at an indication of value.

7.9 In certain industries, businesses are bought and sold on the basis of established market practices or rules of thumb, often (though not exclusively) derived from multiples or percentages of turnover, and not linked to profitability. Where such rules of thumb exist, and there is evidence that buyers and sellers in the actual market rely on them, the business valuer may need to consider them. However, it would be sensible to cross check the results arising from such market practices against one or more other methods. Care should be taken that the 'established market practice' has not been superseded by changes in circumstances over time.

Income approach

7.10 The *income approach* has a number of variants, but essentially this approach is based on the income that an asset is likely to generate over its remaining useful life or a specified period. This estimation is determined by reference to both historic performance and forecasts. Where these are not available, the single period capitalisation method may be appropriate instead.

7.11 The single period capitalisation method commonly estimates the value by capitalising that income. A thorough understanding of accounting and economic profits, their historical record based usually on historic financial statements, and forecasting is necessary in each case. Normalised profits after tax are determined and, if necessary, adjusted to reflect differences between actual historic profits and cash flows and those that could be expected to be received by a purchaser of the business at the *valuation date*.

7.12 Further adjustments may include restating non-arm's length transactions and costs incurred with related parties to commercial terms, and reflecting the effect of non-recurring events whether of income or cost. Examples of this include one-off redundancies, exceptional profits or losses. Comparison of depreciation and inventory accounting should be on a like-for-like basis.

7.13 Profits are then capitalised by the price to earnings (P/E) ratio. A similar exercise can be carried out by applying a suitable capitalisation multiple to normalised profits before tax. A suitable capitalisation multiple will often be applied to earnings before interest and tax (EBIT), or earnings before interest, tax, depreciation and amortisation (EBITDA). Care must be taken in these cases to distinguish between:

- enterprise value (which also considers the debt of the business and any liquid assets owned by the entity that might mitigate the acquirer's purchase price) and
- equity value (i.e. the value of the shares).

7.14 Business value is often derived by capitalising profits or cash flows before costs of servicing debt, using a capitalisation or discount rate that is the weighted average cost of capital (WACC) of a comparable mix of debt and equity. The equity value is the enterprise value less the *market value* of the net debt, but can be established by measuring the equity cash flow itself.

7.15 Present value techniques measure the value of an asset by the present value of its future economic cash flow, which is cash that is generated over a period of time by an asset, group of assets, or business enterprise. These can include earnings, cost savings, tax deductions, and proceeds from its disposition. When applied to business *valuation*, value indications are developed by discounting expected cash flows, estimated, where appropriate, to include growth and price inflation, to their net present value at a rate of return. The rate of return incorporates the risk-free rate for the use of funds, the expected rate of inflation and risks associated with the particular investment and the market. The discount rate selected is generally based on rates of return available from alternative investments of similar type and quality as at the *valuation date*. Expressions such as 'rate of return' may mean different things to different individuals so valuers should consider defining what is meant by such terms.

7.16 The values of redundant or surplus assets, namely those owned but not used in the business operations, need to be taken into account in enterprise or equity values.

7.17 The *income approach*, as applied using the dividend *basis of value*, is common in company *valuation*, principally in relation to minority shareholdings. For business *valuations*, value indicators are developed by determining a share's future dividends and prospect of dividends, and a rate of return, using dividend discount and initial yield models.

Cost approach

7.18 The *cost approach* indicates the value of an asset by the cost to create or replace the asset with another similar one, on the premise that a purchaser would not pay more for an asset than the cost to obtain one of equal usefulness. This method is frequently used in valuing investment companies or capital intensive firms. However, it would normally not be used except when the other two approaches have been considered but deemed not applicable, and the report would contain an explanation as to why this was so.

7.19 When applied to business *valuation*, obsolescence, maintenance and the time value of money are considerations. If the asset being valued is less attractive than a modern equivalent, by reason of age or obsolescence, the valuer may need to adjust the cost of the perceived modern equivalent, thus arriving at the depreciated replacement cost.

Asset-based approach

7.20 The asset-based approach measures the value of a business and asset by reference to the value of individual assets and liabilities. This approach is commonly adopted in the area of property investment and share investment portfolio situations (investment trusts). This approach is not normally the preferred one for trading businesses, except where they are failing to achieve an adequate return on the tangible assets used in the business, or where a trading business also has substantial investment activity or surplus cash. The net asset value per share can be discounted or enhanced by the addition of a premium.

7.21 The valuation *assumptions* and inputs may be based either on actual data or on assumed information. The *market approach* is likely to be based on actual inputs, such as prices achieved on sales of similar assets or businesses and actual income or profits generated. Assumed inputs might include cash flow forecasts or projections. For *valuations* adopting the cost approach, actual inputs might include the actual cost of an asset, whereas assumed inputs may have regard to an estimated cost of an asset and other factors, such as the perceived attitude to risk of other players in the market.

7.22 As a general rule, *valuation* by summation, sometimes known as *valuation* by assembly, should be avoided. Accordingly, when valuing the totality of various assets or component parts of an entity, the valuer must avoid arriving at the value of the whole merely by adding together the values indicated for the various separate assets or component parts.

8 Reports

8.1 Where the *valuation* has to comply with the RICS Red Book, the valuer must produce a report that complies with the minimum terms set out in **VPS 3**. Generally the report has a brief introductory section or executive summary that defines the assignment, summarises the conclusion and sets the stage for the details of the report. The structure should move from the general to the specific, providing a logical flow of data and analysis within which all the necessary considerations can be incorporated, leading to the valuation conclusions.

8.2 Most reports will have the following major sections, although not necessarily in this order:

- introduction
- purpose and *basis of value*
- *assumptions* and *special assumptions*
- subject of *valuation*
- description and history of the business

- accounting and accounting polices
- *financial statement* analysis
- business and marketing plan analysis, and prospects
- search results for comparables and comparative transactions
- industry in which the business operates, economic environment, yields and risk assessment
- environmental constraints
- valuation methods and conclusion
- caveats, disclaimers and limitations.

8.3 Some reports will have a separate section containing a general discussion of valuation methodology, which will often follow the introduction. If national, regional and economic data are important to the company and asset, each may have its own section.

8.4 Where appropriate, factual information, or sources thereof, should be identified either in the body of the report or in the appendices. Where the opinion of an expert is required for litigation purposes, the report must adhere to the requirements imposed by the local jurisdiction and must therefore contain all relevant disclosures including the statement of the expert's qualifications and the statement of truth.

9 Confidentiality

9.1 Information in respect of many business assets will be confidential. Valuers should use their best endeavours to preserve such confidentiality, particularly in relation to information obtained in respect of comparable assets. Where required by the client, business valuers will comply with any requests to enter into non-disclosure or similar agreements.

VPGA 4 Valuation of individual trade related properties

This guidance is advisory and not mandatory in content. Where appropriate, however, it alerts *members* to relevant mandatory material contained elsewhere in these global standards, including the *International Valuation Standards*, using cross-references in bold type. These cross-references are for the assistance of *members* and do not alter the status of the material that follows below. *Members* are reminded that:

- this guidance cannot cover every circumstance, and they must always have regard to the facts and circumstances of individual assignments when forming valuation judgments
- they should remain alert to the fact that individual jurisdictions may have specific requirements that are not covered by this guidance.

1 Background

1.1 Certain trade related properties are valued using the profits method (also known as the *income approach*) of *valuation*. The guidance below sets out the principles of this method of valuation but does not concern itself with the detailed approach to a *valuation*, which may vary according to the property to be valued.

1.2 This VPGA relates only to the *valuation* of an individual property that is valued on the basis of trading potential.

1.3 Some properties are normally bought and sold on the basis of their trading potential. Examples include hotels, pubs and bars, restaurants, nightclubs, fuel stations, care homes, casinos, cinemas and theatres, and various other forms of leisure property. The essential characteristic of this type of property is that it has been designed or adapted for a specific use, and the resulting lack of flexibility usually means that the value of the property interest is intrinsically linked to the returns that an owner can generate from that use. The value therefore reflects the trading potential of the property. It can be contrasted with generic property that can be occupied by a range of different business types, such as standard office, industrial or retail property.

1.4 The examples provided at 1.3 above are not intended to be exhaustive. Other types of properties (such as car parks, garden centres, caravan parks, crematoria, etc.) may also be best considered by reference to their trading potential and a profits-based approach. This will be a matter for valuer judgment having regard to the specific type, form and use of the property and market circumstances prevailing, and evolving, at the time.

1.5 Valuers who prepare *valuations* of *trade related property* usually specialise in this particular market. Knowledge of the operational aspects of the property *valuation*, and of the industry as a whole, is fundamental to the understanding of market transactions and the analysis required.

1.6 Comparable information may be derived from a wide variety of sources, not just transactional evidence. Also, information may be drawn from different operational entities with regard to the component parts of the profits *valuation*. The valuer should emphasise within the report that the *valuation* is assessed having regard to trading potential and should refer to the actual profits achieved. If the trading potential and/or the actual profits vary, there could be a change in the reported value (see **VPS 3 paragraphs 2.2(h)(4) and 2.2(o)**).

1.7 This VPGA assumes that the current trade related use of the property will continue. However, where it is clear that the property may have an alternative use that may have a higher value, an appropriate comment should be made in the report. Where such an alternative use value is provided, it should be accompanied by a statement that the *valuation* takes no account of the costs of business closure, disruption or any other costs associated with realising this value.

2 Terms used in this VPGA

2.1 The terms used in this VPGA may have different meanings when used by other professional disciplines.

Adjusted net profit

2.2 This is the valuer's assessment of the actual net profit of a currently trading operational entity. It is the net profit that is shown from the accounts once adjustments for abnormal and non-recurring expenditure, finance costs and depreciation relating to the property itself, as well as rent where appropriate, have been made. It relates to the existing operational entity and gives the valuer guidance when assessing the fair maintainable operating profit (FMOP).

Earnings before interest, taxes, depreciation and amortisation [EBITDA]

2.3 This term relates to the actual operating entity and may be different from the valuer's estimated FMOP.

Fair maintainable operating profit [FMOP]

2.4 This is the level of profit, stated prior to depreciation and finance costs relating to the asset itself (and rent if leasehold), that the reasonably efficient operator (REO) would expect to derive from the fair maintainable turnover (FMT) based on an assessment of the market's perception of the potential earnings of the property. It should reflect all costs and outgoings of the REO, as well as an appropriate annual allowance for periodic expenditure, such as decoration, refurbishment and renewal of the trade inventory.

Fair maintainable turnover [FMT]

2.5 This is the level of trade that an REO would expect to achieve on the *assumption* that the property is properly equipped, repaired, maintained and decorated.

Market rent

2.6 This is the estimated amount for which an interest in real property should be leased on the *valuation date* between a willing lessor and a willing lessee on appropriate lease terms in an arm's length transaction, after proper marketing and where the parties had each acted knowledgeably, prudently and without compulsion. Whenever *market rent* is provided the 'appropriate lease terms' that it reflects should also be stated.

Market value

2.7 This is the estimated amount for which an asset or liability should exchange on the *valuation date* between a willing buyer and a willing seller in an arm's length transaction after proper marketing and where the parties had each acted knowledgeably, prudently and without compulsion.

Operational entity

2.8 An operational entity usually includes:

- the legal interest in the land and buildings
- the trade inventory, usually comprising all trade fixtures, fittings, furnishings and equipment and
- the market's perception of the trading potential, together with an assumed ability to obtain/renew existing licences, consents, certificates and permits.

Consumables and stock in trade are normally excluded.

Personal goodwill [of the current operator]

2.9 This is the value of profit generated over and above market expectations that would be extinguished upon sale of the *trade related property*, together with financial factors related specifically to the current operator of the business, such as taxation, depreciation policy, borrowing costs and the capital invested in the business.

Reasonably efficient operator [REO]

2.10 This is a concept where the valuer assumes that the market participants are competent operators, acting in an efficient manner, of a business conducted on the premises. It involves estimating the trading potential rather than adopting the actual level of trade under the existing ownership, and it excludes personal goodwill.

Tenant's capital

2.11 This may include, for example, all consumables, purchase of the inventory, stock, and working capital.

Trade related property

2.12 This is any type of real property designed or adapted for a specific type of business where the property value reflects the trading potential for that business.

Trading potential

2.13 This is the future profit, in the context of a *valuation* of the property that an REO would expect to be able to realise from occupation of the property. This could be above or below the recent trading history of the property. It reflects a range of factors (such as the location, design and character, level of adaptation and trading history of the property within the market conditions prevailing) that are inherent to the property asset.

3 Profits method of valuation

3.1 The profits method of *valuation* involves the following steps:

Step 1: An assessment is made of the FMT that could be generated at the property by an REO.

Step 2: Where appropriate, an assessment is made of the potential gross profit, resulting from the FMT.

Step 3: An assessment is made of the FMOP. The costs and allowances to be shown in the assessment should reflect those to be expected of the REO – which will be the most likely purchaser or operator of the property if offered in the market.

Step 4:

(a) To assess the *market value* of the property the FMOP is capitalised at an appropriate rate of return reflecting the risk and rewards of the property and its trading potential. Evidence of relevant comparable market transactions should be analysed and applied.

(b) In assessing *market value* the valuer may decide that an incoming new operator would expect to improve the trading potential by undertaking alterations or improvements. This will be implicit within the valuer's estimate of FMT at step 1. In such instances, an appropriate allowance should be made from the figure resulting from step 4 to reflect the costs of completing the alterations or improvements and the delay in achieving FMT. Similarly, if the property is in need of repair and/or decoration to enable the REO to achieve the FMT, then an appropriate allowance should be made from the figure resulting from step 4(a) to reflect the cost of such repairs and decorations.

(c) To assess the *market rent* for a new letting, the rent payable on a rent review or the reasonableness of the actual rent passing (particularly when preparing an investment *valuation*), an allowance should be made from the FMOP to reflect a return on the tenant's capital invested in the operational entity – for example, the cost of trade inventory, stock and working capital. The resultant sum is referred to as the divisible balance. This is apportioned between the landlord and tenant having regard to the respective risks and rewards, with the landlord's proportion representing the annual rent.

3.2 Certain extended or more detailed approaches to a profits method of *valuation* may be appropriate, particularly for some larger or more complex *trade related properties*. Consideration of discounted cash flow assessments and different income streams may be adopted. Such knowledge will aid in the analysis and review of historic and current trading performance, as well as with forecasts that may show increases or decreases on actual trade. This can assist in forming an opinion of the FMT and FMOP considered achievable by a likely purchaser or REO.

3.3 It is important that the valuer is regularly involved in the relevant market for the class of property, as practical knowledge of the factors affecting the particular market is required.

3.4 When preparing a *trade related property valuation* it is essential that the valuer reviews the cumulative result of the different steps of the valuation process. The *valuation* should be considered having regard to the valuer's general experience and knowledge of the market.

4 Valuation special assumptions

4.1 A *trade related property* will usually be valued to *market value* or *market rent*, but valuers are commonly asked for a *valuation* subject to *special assumptions*.

Typical special assumptions are:

(a) on the basis that trade has ceased and no trading records are available to prospective purchasers or tenants

(b) on the same basis as (a) but also assuming the trade inventory has been removed

(c) as a fully equipped operational entity that has yet to trade (also known as 'day one' *valuation*) and

(d) subject to stated trade projections, assuming they are proven. This is appropriate when considering development of the property.

5 Valuation approach for a fully equipped operational entity

5.1 The *valuation* of a *trade related property* as a fully equipped operational entity necessarily assumes that the transaction will be either the letting or the sale of the property, together with the trade inventory, licences, etc., required to continue trading.

5.2 However, care must be taken because this *assumption* does not necessarily mean that the entire trade inventory is to be included in the *valuation* of the property. For example, some equipment may be owned by *third parties* and therefore would not form part of the interest being valued. Any *assumption* made about the trade inventory included in the *valuation* should be clearly set out in the report.

5.3 There may be tangible assets that are essential to the running of the operational entity but are either owned separately from the land and buildings, or are subject to separate finance leases or charges. In such cases, an *assumption* may need to be made that the owners or beneficiaries of any charge would consent to the transfer of the assets as part of a sale of the operational entity. If it is not certain that such an *assumption* can be made, the valuer must consider carefully the potential impact on the *valuation* that the lack of availability of those assets would have to anyone purchasing or leasing the operational entity and comment accordingly in the report.

5.4 When *trade related properties* are sold or let as fully equipped operational entities, the purchaser or operator normally needs to renew licences or other statutory consents and take over the benefit of existing certificates and permits. If the valuer is making any different *assumption*, it should be clearly stated as a *special assumption*.

5.5 Where it is not possible to inspect the licences, consents, certificates and permits relating to the property, or other information cannot be verified, the *assumptions* made should be identified in the report, together with a recommendation that their existence should be verified by the client's legal advisers.

6 Assessing the trading potential

6.1 There is a distinction between the *market value* of a *trade related property* and the *investment value* – or its *worth* – to the particular operator. The operator will derive *worth* from the current and potential net profits from the operational entity operating in the chosen format. While the present operator may be one potential bidder in the market, the valuer will need to understand the requirements and achievable profits of other potential bidders, along with the dynamics of the open market, to come to an opinion of value for that particular property.

6.2 A *trade related property* is considered to be an individual trading entity and is typically valued on the *assumption* that there will be a continuation of trading.

6.3 When assessing future trading potential, the valuer should exclude any turnover and costs that are attributable solely to the personal circumstances, or skill, expertise, reputation and/or brand name of the existing operator. However, the valuer should reflect additional trading potential that might be realised by an REO taking over the property at the *valuation date*.

6.4 The actual trading performance should be compared with similar types of *trade related property* and styles of operation. To do so the valuer needs a proper understanding of the profit potential of those property types and how they compare with one another. A *trade related property* valuer should test, by reference to market transactions and similar *trade related properties*, whether the present trade represents the FMT in current market conditions. When available, the actual trading accounts of the subject property and similar properties may need adjusting to reflect the circumstances of the REO.

6.5 For many trading entities, the vehicle for a transfer of the business will be the sale of a freehold or leasehold interest in the property. Such transactional evidence can be used as comparable evidence in the *valuation* of *trade related properties*, so long as the valuer is in a position to exclude the value of the component parts of the transaction that are not relevant. Examples include stock, consumables, cash, liabilities and *intangible assets* (such as brand names or contracts, to the extent they would not be available to the REO).

6.6 Changes in competition can have a dramatic effect on profitability, and hence value. The valuer should be aware of the impact of current and expected future levels of competition. If a significant change from existing levels is anticipated, the valuer should clearly identify this in the report and comment on the general impact it might have on profitability and value.

6.7 Outside influences, such as the construction of a new road or changes in relevant legislation, can also affect the trading potential and hence the value of the *trade related property*.

6.8 Where it is intended to reflect purchaser's costs in the *valuation* (usually in the case of investment *valuations*), the normal *market approach* is to be adopted and an appropriate comment should be made in the report.

6.9 Where the property is trading and the trade is expected to continue, the *valuation* should be reported as follows:

'Market value *[or market rent]* as a fully equipped operational entity having regard to trading potential subject to any agreed or special assumptions … *[which must be clearly set out]*.'

7 Valuation approach for a non-trading property

7.1 The valuation process for a non-trading property is the same as outlined in section 5 above, but where the property is empty either through cessation of trade, or because it is a new property with no established trading history, different *assumptions* are to be made. For example, an empty property may have been stripped of all or much of its trade inventory or a new property may not have the trade inventory installed, but either could still be valued having regard to its trading potential.

7.2 The cessation of an operational entity and the removal of some or all the trade inventory are likely to have an effect on the value of the property. It would therefore be appropriate to express the value on both the basis of one or more *special assumptions*, and a basis reflecting the status quo. This is often a requirement when advising a lender on the value of *trade related property* for loan security purposes. For example, the differences could reflect the cost and time involved in purchasing and installing the trade inventory, obtaining new licences, appointing staff and achieving FMT.

7.3 Where the property is empty, the *valuation* should be reported as follows:

'Market value *[or market rent]* of the empty property having regard to trading potential subject to the following special assumptions … *[which must be clearly set out].*'

8 Apportionment

8.1 The valuer may need, or may be requested, to provide an indicative apportionment of a *valuation* or a transaction price for:

- analysis as a comparable
- inclusion in *financial statements* to comply with the applicable accounting standards
- secured lending or
- tax purposes.

8.2 Any such apportionment of *market value* would usually relate to:

- the land and buildings reflecting the trading potential and
- the trade inventory.

8.3 When considering the apportionment of a transaction price, particularly where the sale is through share transfer in a limited company, the valuer should proceed with caution as the transaction may, in addition to that listed in paragraph 8.2, reflect the following:

- the *trading stock*, consumables and cash
- *intangible assets* and

- liabilities, such as salaries, taxes, debts, etc.

8.4 Apportionments for tax purposes have to be in accordance with specific legislation and are outside the scope of this VPGA.

9 Valuation for investment purposes

9.1 The basic approach to an investment *valuation* of *trade related property* is the same as for any other category of property. Where the investment is a portfolio or group of properties VPGA 9 will be relevant.

9.2 When valuing a *trade related property* investment, the valuer will need to carry out the assessment of the FMT and FMOP as set out in paragraph 3.1. It is also necessary to assess the *market rent* of the property so as to determine the security of the income stream and growth potential. The rent payable and the rent review will be determined by the terms of the subsisting or proposed lease.

9.3 The capitalisation rate adopted for investment *valuations* differs from that for vacant possession *valuations*. The investment rate of return will generally be determined by market transactions of similar *trade related property* investments. Clearly, due to the differing characteristics of *trade related property* and the wide variety of lease terms, careful analysis of comparable transactions is essential.

9.4 The valuer will include the landlord's fixtures and fittings with the land and buildings, but probably not the trade inventory, which is usually owned by the occupational tenant. However, the valuer should highlight the importance of the trade inventory to the trading potential and value of the property.

VPGA 6 Valuation of intangible assets

This guidance is advisory and not mandatory in content. Where appropriate, however, it alerts *members* to relevant mandatory material contained elsewhere in these global standards, including the *International Valuation Standards*, using cross-references in bold type. These cross-references are for the assistance of *members* and do not alter the status of the material that follows below. *Members* are reminded that:

- this guidance cannot cover every circumstance, and they must always have regard to the facts and circumstances of individual assignments when forming valuation judgments
- they should remain alert to the fact that individual jurisdictions may have specific requirements that are not covered by this guidance.

1 Scope

1.1 The guidance below provides additional commentary on the *valuation* of *intangible assets* and the practical application of **IVS 210 Intangible Assets**. Any mandatory requirements are highlighted in **bold type**.

It covers the *valuation* of *intangible assets* in respect of acquisitions, mergers and sale of businesses or parts of businesses and purchases and sales of *intangible assets*.

2 Introduction

2.1 An *intangible asset* is defined as a non-monetary asset that manifests itself by its economic properties. It does not have physical substance but grants rights and/or economic benefits to its owner. It is therefore an asset that is capable of being separated or divided from a business entity and sold, transferred, licensed, rented or exchanged individually or with a related asset, liability or contract. Non-identifiable *intangible assets* arising from contractual or legal rights that may or may not be separable from the entity, or other rights and obligations, are generally termed *'goodwill'*.

2.2 Identified *intangible assets* include:

- marketing related assets: typically associated with, and primarily used in, the marketing or promotion of a company's products or services (trademarks, brands, trade names, trade dress, internet domain names, newspaper mastheads, non-compete agreements)

- customer or supplier related assets: arise from relationships with, or knowledge of, customers and suppliers, and are used in the development, procurement, management and maintenance of a company's customers (customer lists, order or production backlog, customer contracts and related relationships, non-contractual customer relationships)
- artistic related assets: arise from artistic products or services that are protected by a contractual or legal right (copyright and design), and give rise to benefits including royalties from artistic works (plays, operas, ballet, books, magazines, newspapers, musical works, pictures, photographs, videos, films, television programmes)
- technology related assets: these represent the value of technological innovation or advancements, and can arise from non-contractual rights to use technology, or be protected through legal or contractual rights (patented technology, computer software, unpatented technology, databases, trade secrets, in-process research and development, manufacturing processes and know-how).

2.3 *Intangible assets* may be either contractual or non-contractual. Contract-based assets represent the value of rights that arise from contractual arrangements (licensing, royalty, and standstill agreements; contracts for advertising, construction, management, service or supply lease agreements; construction permits; franchise agreements; operating and broadcasting rights; contractual use rights other than those expressly classified or properly regarded as tangible assets; servicing contracts; and employment contracts).

2.4 A major *intangible asset* is *goodwill*, which is defined as any future economic benefit arising from a business, an interest in a business or the use of a group of assets that is not separable. The benefits that may form part of *goodwill* include synergies that follow a business combination and are company specific. Examples of this include:

- economies of scale not otherwise reflected in the values of other assets
- growth opportunities, such as expansion into other markets and
- organisational capital, for instance the benefits obtained from an assembled network.

Goodwill is sometimes defined as the amount remaining after the value of all separable and identifiable assets have been deducted from the overall value of the business. This definition is commonly used for accounting purposes.

2.5 *Intangible assets* are differentiated from one another by characteristics such as ownership, function, market position and image. For example, ladies' fashion shoe brands may be characterised by use of particular colours and styles, as well as price. In addition, while *intangible assets* within the same class will inevitably have similar characteristics, there will also be aspects that differentiate them from other similar ones.

2.6 It is important that the valuer is regularly involved in *intangible asset valuation*, as practical knowledge of the factors affecting investing in any particular asset is essential (see **PS 2 section 2**).

3 Terms of engagement

3.1 The valuation knowledge of clients will vary widely. Some will have a thorough understanding of intangible property rights and *intangible asset valuation*, while others will be unfamiliar with the terms and concepts used by valuers of *intangible assets*.

3.2 It is imperative that the *terms of engagement* are understood and agreed between the valuer and the client prior to commencement of the assignment. Any supplementary or contributory assets should be identified and agreement reached on whether they are to be included or not. Contributory assets are those used in conjunction with the subject asset to generate cash flows. Where contributory assets are not to be valued, it is important to clarify whether the intention is therefore for the principal asset to be valued on a stand-alone basis.

3.3 There may be situations where the interest in the asset to be valued is shared with others, and in such cases, it should be clearly specified.

3.4 Valuers may wish to develop standard letters of engagement that can be used for any type of valuation instruction. Where a *valuation* has to comply with the RICS Red Book, the valuer must produce *terms of engagement* that comply with the minimum terms set out in **PS 2 section 7** and **VPS 1**.

4 Valuation concepts

4.1 The reason why the valuer has been instructed to perform a *valuation* is important to understand, as the *intangible asset valuation* may be required for a wide variety of purposes. Examples include financial reporting, tax, public sector assignments, transactions and flotations, fairness opinions, banking arrangements, insolvency and administration, knowledge management, or portfolio review. The answer will introduce various concepts of value, some governed by statute and case law, and others by international and national standards of professional valuation practice.

4.2 Valuation bases typically encountered for these types of *valuations* (not all of which are recognised by the IVS or the Red Book) are *fair value*, fair market value, *market value*, and open market value. Valuers should be mindful of the requirements of **PS 1 section 1**, where a written *valuation* is provided.

4.3 Depending on the rules and practice followed in respect of the concept, the valuation conclusion in respect of the same asset may be different. For example, because of the rules concerning tax *valuations*, a tax authority could view *valuation* differently to how a litigant, merger partner or *special purchaser* would.

4.4 Except in the case where there are strong indications to the contrary, the presumption is that of a 'going concern' and that the asset will continue to have a useful life for the foreseeable future. In some cases, this period will be based on what is specified either by law, or under the terms of any relevant agreements or protocols that govern the asset. However, for financial reporting purposes the value of an *intangible asset* that is to be disposed of, or abandoned, might have to be considered.

4.5 In many cases it may be necessary to apply more than one valuation method, particularly where there is insufficient information or evidence to enable the valuer to rely on just one. In such cases, the valuer may use additional methods to arrive at the final *valuation*, indicating why preference is given to any one or more methodologies. The valuer should consider all valuation approaches, giving reasons why any particular approach has not been completed.

5 Valuation due diligence

5.1 In line with **PS 2 section 2**, valuers should have appropriate competency in *intangible asset valuation*. As a minimum requirement, a valuer should not contemplate carrying out a *valuation* in the absence of a detailed knowledge and understanding of such issues as:

- the rights of the owners of the asset(s)
- the history of, and activities associated, with the asset(s)
- as appropriate, the state of the subject industry, the general economic outlook and political factors.

5.2 Typical information requirements to assist the valuer in understanding the subject asset(s) could include:

- most recent income statements associated with the subject asset, and details of current and prior projections or forecasts
- description and history of the subject asset, including legal protections and rights associated with it (the extent to which such legal rights have been assessed should be disclosed)
- information about the asset and supporting documentation (for example, registrations, territorial applications, marketing, technical research and development, documentation, design graphics and manuals)
- other collateral agreements
- details of the precise activities exploiting the *intangible asset*
- previous valuation reports
- product(s) dealt in, supported or extended by the business and intangibles
- whether anyone else is permitted to use the *intangible asset*(s), and whether there are plans to do so
- the company's market(s) and competition, barriers to entry in such markets, business and marketing plans, due diligence

- licensing, strategic alliances and joint venture detail
- whether contractual arrangements can be assigned or transferred in any *intangible asset* or royalty agreement
- major customers and suppliers
- objectives, developments or trends expected in the industry and how these are likely to affect the company or asset
- accounting policies
- strengths, weaknesses, opportunities and threats (SWOT) analysis
- key market factors (for example, monopoly or dominant market position, market share)
- major capital expenditure in prospect
- competitor positions
- seasonable or cyclical trends
- technological changes affecting the asset
- vulnerability of any source of raw materials or supplier arrangement
- whether there have been any recent acquisitions or mergers in this sector around the *valuation date*, and the criteria that were applied
- management of research and development (non-disclosure agreements, subcontractors, training and incentives)
- whether there is an intellectual property asset schedule setting out the extent of intellectual property right (IPR) ownership, and the interests of *third parties* (if any)
- examination of comparable licensing of similar assets.

5.3 The valuer should, as far as it is possible, verify facts and information used in arriving at the *valuation* and benchmark, where possible, inputs to the *valuation*.

5.4 Much of the information relied on by the valuer will be provided by the client(s), and it may not be possible to verify it. In such cases, the valuation report should make this clear.

6 Valuation approaches

6.1 In broad terms, valuation theory recognises three distinct approaches in *valuation*, including for intangibles. These are the *market approach* (sometimes known as the direct market comparison approach), the *income approach*, and the *cost approach*.

6.2 Each approach requires the valuer to adopt an estimate of the asset's remaining useful life. This could be a finite period set by the length of a contract or normal life expectancy in the sector, or it could be indefinite. A number of factors will have to be considered in determining life expectancy, including legal, technical, economic and functional aspects. The presumed life expectancy of an asset that has been licensed for a particular period may be shorter if a superior competitor product is likely to reach the market before the licence expiration. In such case, the valuer would need to take a view on this.

Market approach

6.3 The *market approach* measures the value of an asset by comparing recent sales or offerings of similar or substitute property and related market data. However, it is rarely possible to find such evidence relating to identical assets.

6.4 The two primary *market approach* methods are the 'market multiple method' and the 'similar transactions method'.

6.5 The market multiple method focuses on comparing the subject asset with guideline data such as industry royalty rates. In applying this method, matters such as royalty rates are evaluated and adjusted based on the strengths and weaknesses of the subject asset relative to similar assets. They are then applied to the appropriate operating data of the subject asset to arrive at an indication of value. Appropriate adjustments to reflect different properties or characteristics are usually made to the derived data.

6.6 The similar transactions method uses valuation data based on historical transactions that have occurred in the subject asset's direct or related industries. The derived data are then adjusted and applied to the appropriate operating data of the subject asset to arrive at an indication of value.

6.7 In certain industries, assets are bought and sold on the basis of established market practices or rules of thumb, often (though not exclusively) derived from data or percentages of turnover, and not directly linked to profit generation. Care should be taken that the 'established market practice' has not been superseded by changes in circumstances over time. Where such rules of thumb exist, they may need to be considered by the valuer.

Income approach

6.8 The *income approach* has a number of variants. When applied (using, for example, the discounted cash flow (DCF) method), it measures the value of an asset by the present value of its future economic benefits. These benefits can include earnings, cost savings, tax deductions, and proceeds from its disposal.

6.9 When applied to an *intangible asset valuation*, value indications are developed by discounting expected cash flows to their present value at a rate of return that incorporates the risk-free rate for the use of funds, the expected rate of inflation, and risks associated with the particular investment. The discount rate selected is generally based on rates of return available from alternative investments of similar type and quality as at the *valuation date*.

6.10 The *income approach* also embraces methods such as the relief-from-royalty method, defined in IVS 210 Intangible Assets as one that estimates 'the value of an *intangible asset* … determined by reference to the value of the hypothetical royalty payments that would be saved through owning the asset, as compared with licensing the *intangible asset* from a third party'.

6.11 There is also the 'multi period excess earnings' method. This is a method of estimating the economic benefits of an *intangible asset* over multiple time periods by identifying the cash flows associated with the use of the asset and deducting a periodic charge reflecting a fair return for the use of contributory assets.

6.12 The *income approach*, as applied using the capitalised earnings *basis of value*, is common in *intangible asset valuation*. A thorough understanding of accounting and economic profits, their historical record and forecasting is necessary in each case.

6.13 Appraisal of *intangible assets* and IPR includes techniques to identify the earnings specifically associated with the subject asset, such as gross profit differential, excess profits and relief from royalty. A thorough understanding of the historic and forecast earnings is necessary.

Cost approach

6.14 The *cost approach* indicates the value of an asset by the cost to create or replace it with another similar asset. When applied to *intangible asset valuation*, obsolescence, maintenance and the time value of money are considerations. When the *basis of value* in the *valuation* is *market value*, the indications of obsolescence must be supported by market data.

7 Present value techniques

7.1 Present value techniques (PVT) measure the value of an asset by the present value of its future economic cash flow, which is cash that is generated over a period of time by an asset, group of assets, or business enterprise.

7.2 Issues to consider in relation to this technique include:

- the number of years over which the cash flow is applied
- the capitalisation rate or discount rate applied at the end of the term
- the discount rate(s) adopted
- whether inflation is built into the cash flow
- what other variables need to be considered in respect of the cash flow in the future
- the trading profile of the asset
- initial and running yields, internal rate of return (IRR) and the terminal value.

7.3 Where a PVT approach is applied, it is important that market transactions (i.e. comparables) reflecting the same approach to *valuation* are taken into consideration. The details of market transactions may be more difficult to obtain where a PVT approach is adopted. However, such transactions will assist in assessing the discount rate to be adopted, the IRR sought and the general approach taken by the market.

7.4 If the *valuation* is for a specific *intangible asset*, before undertaking the detailed cash flow modelling, the valuer is required to quantify the remaining useful life and deterioration rate associated specifically with the use of the asset. Typically this remaining useful life analysis will quantify the shortest of the following:

- physical life (for example, of an underlying tangible asset)
- functional life (for example, of an underlying tangible asset)
- technological life
- economic life
- legal life.

7.5 PVT *valuation* will thus involve these key components: a financial forecast identifying specific intellectual capital and associated earnings, and the discount rate (cost of capital). Unsystematic and systematic risk will be considered, and the discount rate determination in its basic application will require identification and application of the cost of capital to known and projected cash flows.

7.6 Discounting appropriately at the weighted average cost of capital (WACC) will be adopted. The two basic elements of the cost of capital are the cost of debt and the cost of equity. To aid the calculation of an appropriate rate of return and discount rates, the valuer uses a number of different methodologies, including capital asset pricing model (CAPM), arbitrage pricing theory and hybrids, depending on the particular circumstances.

7.7 Valuers may be required to consider *intangible assets* in a licensing context, for example, the licensing in or out of technology or patents. Much of what has been covered in this VPGA is relevant in the calculation of an appropriate rate of return in royalty rate calculations. In practice the rate is estimated by reference to some or all of the following:

- existing licences for the intangibles (the comparables approach)
- industry norms for licences for similar assets (the *market approach*)
- allocation of economic benefits derived from the use of, for example, the patented invention (sometimes referred to as the available profits or analytical approach)
- licensing practice (rule of thumb approaches).

7.8 Licensing appraisal examines specifics such as:

- how other relevant licences were negotiated
- *intangible asset* and support
- length of the licence agreement
- exclusivity

- special terms for special deals
- geography
- sector in which the *intangible asset* is licensed
- any special relationships.

Even if previous licensing practice is comparable, it can only provide a benchmark. Intangibles, by their nature, are unique and may involve carrying out numerous required adjustments to make a fair comparison.

7.9 PVT models the approaches such as the relief-from-royalty method (see paragraph 6.10 above, under *Income approach*).

8 Reports

8.1 Where the *valuation* has to comply with the Red Book, the valuer must produce a report that complies with the minimum terms set out in **VPS 3**. Generally the report has a brief introductory section or executive summary that defines the assignment, summarises the conclusion and sets the stage for the details of the report. The structure should move from the general to the specific, providing a logical flow of data and analysis within which all the necessary considerations can be incorporated, leading to the valuation conclusions.

8.2 Most situations will easily form into major sections as follows, although not necessarily in this order:

- introduction
- purpose and *basis of value*
- *assumptions* and *special assumptions*
- subject of *valuation*
- description and history of the asset(s), and the business entity in which it has (they have) been used
- accounting and accounting polices
- *financial statement* analysis, if appropriate
- business and marketing plan analysis, and prospects
- search results for comparative transactions
- industry in which the asset is used
- economic context and environment, yields and risk assessment
- valuation methods and conclusion
- caveats, disclaimer, and limitations.

8.3 Some reports will have a separate section containing a general discussion of valuation methodology, which will often follow the introduction. If national, regional and economic data are important to the company and asset, each may have its own section.

8.4 Where appropriate, factual information, or sources thereof, should be identified either in the body of the report or in the appendices. Where the report is that of an expert required for litigation purposes, it must adhere to the requirements imposed by the local jurisdiction and must therefore contain all relevant disclosures including the statement of the expert's qualifications and the 'statement of truth'.

9 Confidentiality

9.1 Information in respect of many *intangible assets* will be confidential. Valuers should use their best endeavours to preserve such confidentiality, including information obtained in respect of comparable assets. Where required by the client, valuers of *intangible assets* will comply with any requests to enter into non-disclosure or similar agreements.

VPGA 7 Valuation of personal property, including arts and antiques

This guidance is advisory and not mandatory in content. Where appropriate, however, it alerts *members* to relevant mandatory material contained elsewhere in these global standards, including the *International Valuation Standards*, using cross-references in bold type. These cross-references are for the assistance of *members* and do not alter the status of the material that follows below. *Members* are reminded that:

- this guidance cannot cover every circumstance, and they must always have regard to the facts and circumstances of individual assignments when forming valuation judgments
- they should remain alert to the fact that individual jurisdictions may have specific requirements that are not covered by this guidance.

1 Introduction and scope

1.1 This guidance provides additional commentary on the application of the International Valuation Standards and **VPS 1–5** to '*personal property*', being those assets (or liabilities) specified in 1.2 below.

1.2 For the purpose of this VPGA, '*personal property*' means assets (or liabilities) not permanently attached to land or buildings:

- **including**, but not limited to, fine and decorative arts, antiques, paintings, gems and jewellery, collectables, fixtures and furnishings, and other general contents
- **excluding** trade fixtures and fittings, *plant and equipment*, businesses or business interests, or *intangible assets*.

Valuations of *personal property* may arise in many different contexts and for a variety of purposes which may include, but are not restricted to, the following:

- insurance coverage
- damage or loss
- taxation (charitable contribution, gift tax, estate tax, casualty loss)
- financial reporting

- business transactions
- litigation, including claims of fraud
- estate planning, equitable distribution, and probate
- pre-nuptial agreements
- dissolution of marriage
- dissolution of business
- advice on the acquisition or disposition of property
- loan collateral
- bankruptcy
- inventory *valuation*.

1.3 This list is not definitive, as national or regional variations may exist. Statutory requirements within a given jurisdiction will take precedence. This may especially be the case where *valuations* are prepared for the assessment of tax liabilities, including probate.

1.4 It is essential to be clear about the purpose of the *valuation*, which will often dictate the particular *basis of value* to be used. See **VPS 1**.

2 Terms of engagement

2.1 To properly define the valuation assignment and, as well, the valuer's responsibilities, the valuer should identify the client and any others who might rely on the *valuation* (i.e. the intended users) to ensure that the *valuation* is both meaningful to them and not misleading.

2.2 The *terms of engagement*, including the minimum terms set out in **VPS 1**, will generally be agreed between the valuer and the client prior to the commencement of the valuation engagement. When it is necessary to commence work prior to the *terms of engagement* being fully documented, all matters concerning those terms must be brought to the client's attention and documented before the report is issued (see **VPS 1**).

2.3 When agreeing the *terms of engagement*, the valuer should advise the client of the possible effect on value of any other relevant matters (for example, the provenance of the object, or the impact of a group of objects being valued as a collection, rather than individually). Not to do so could be misleading, in breach of **VPS 3**.

3 Identifying the market

3.1 *Valuations* are based on an understanding of the market in which the *valuation* takes place. Valuers should assess the nature and state of the market that provides the context for their investigations and value conclusions.

Considerations that the valuer should take into account include the level of activity, confidence and trends.

3.2 *Personal property* valuers should recognise that there are different markets within which a particular asset may be traded and that each may generate its own sales data. In particular, an asset may have a different value at the wholesale level of trade, the retail level of trade, or when trading at auction. The valuer should identify and analyse the relevant market consistent with the asset being valued and the purpose of the *valuation* undertaken. It should be recognised that *valuations* undertaken for the purpose of advising on a sale between businesses that trade in a particular form of asset may differ from that between a business and an individual.

3.3 In identifying the market, *personal property* valuers should be aware that the method of sale could affect the resultant sale price. For example, online auctions and other forms of e-commerce have loosened many transactional constraints, expanding the pool of potential purchasers for some types of items. However, valuers should be aware that the quality of information and matters such as commissions and costs of sale associated with some online platforms, where these are not associated with offline sales, can render the sales data unreliable as a source of comparable evidence.

3.4 In *personal property*, groups of assets are often held as collections which, if divided, may be worth significantly more or less per item than when held collectively. The valuer will need to assess whether holding assets collectively has any impact on their *valuation*, and advise accordingly.

4 Inspection, research and analysis

4.1 Valuers of *personal property* should collect, verify and analyse pertinent sales data; they should analyse pertinent economic and market conditions; furthermore they should consider any additional related information necessary to generate realistic value conclusions. **VPS 2** sets out the requirements for conducting investigations.

4.2 *Personal property* valuers should always be aware that the degree of reliability of previous sales data may be limited and should always assess the reliability of data used to support the analysis. They should document the sources of information used in the analysis. As noted in paragraph 3.3 above, valuers should take particular care when using information obtained from online platforms and internet sources.

4.3 Any limitations or conditions that impede the *inspection*, research, and/or analysis should be taken into account by the valuer. If there are such limitations the valuer may need to make *assumptions/special assumptions*. **VPS 4** sets out the requirements relating to *assumptions* and *special assumptions*. Any *assumptions* must be discussed and agreed with the client prior to the conclusion of the *valuation* and clearly documented in both the *terms of engagement* and the report.

4.4 The valuer should consider economic and market data, such as supply and demand in the marketplace and market movements. When there is a degree of uncertainty with respect to the information used, or the state of the market, the valuer should refer to **VPS 3**.

4.5 When the valuer consults other specialists or professionals, the valuer should, to the extent necessary for the purpose of the *valuation*, ensure that the specialist or professional is appropriately qualified, and that the services are carried out competently.

5 Valuation

Valuation approaches and applications

5.1 The three approaches to arriving at *market value* (as defined at IVS 104 paragraph 30.1) for *personal property* are:

- the sales comparison approach
- the *cost approach* and
- the *income approach*.

5.1.1 The sales comparison approach

This provides an indication of value by comparing the subject asset to similar assets for which sales data are available. This approach is the most commonly used in the *valuation* of *personal property*. When applying this approach, the valuer should be careful in the analysis of the appropriate comparable sales data.

5.1.2 The cost approach

This provides an indication of value based on the estimated current costs to reproduce or create a property of equal quality, utility, and marketability. This approach includes replacement with a replica and replacement with a facsimile. A replica is a copy of the original item, as near as possible to the original in terms of nature, quality and age of materials, but created by means of modern construction or fabrication methods. A facsimile is an exact copy of the original item, created with materials of a closely similar nature, quality and age, using construction or fabrication methods of the original period. Both of these approaches (i.e. replica or facsimile) are usually only adopted for insurance purposes. When applying the *cost approach*, the valuer should analyse pertinent and appropriate cost data to estimate the cost of replacement.

5.1.3 The income approach

This provides an indication of value by calculating the anticipated monetary benefits (such as a stream of income) for the subject asset. When applying this approach, the valuer should analyse pertinent and appropriate data to reliably estimate the income in the relevant marketplace of the property. Valuers should base projections of anticipated monetary benefits on an analysis of past and current data, trends and competitive factors.

5.1.4 In all approaches, the valuer should use prudent and well-informed judgment to synthesise the analysis into a logical value conclusion.

5.1.5 All valuation conclusions should be reasonably based and clearly supported by appropriate evidence. If more than one valuation approach has been used in the analysis, the valuer should include both and then reconcile the results.

5.1.6 RICS does not prescribe the method(s) that a valuer should use. However, the valuer should be prepared to justify the rationale for the approach and method adopted.

Other valuation considerations

5.2 In addition to the requirements of **VPS 3**, the valuer's research and analysis should consider:

- the extent of the information that should be communicated to the client and other intended users. The valuer should take account of the fact that the valuation knowledge of clients will vary and should communicate information that can be understood by all intended users of the report
- the interest to be valued (there may be situations in which the interest in *personal property* to be valued is shared with others, and in such cases, it should be clearly specified)
- the characteristics required to establish the identity of the property (including, but not limited to, artist or maker, material or medium, size, title, origin, style, age, provenance or history, condition, exhibition history, and citations in the literature)
- the *basis of value* to be adopted (for example, *market value*, replacement value, etc.) and the source of the definition for that value
- any special assignment conditions or regulatory requirements
- restrictions, encumbrances, leases, covenants, contracts, or any other such considerations that may affect the *valuation* or ownership of the *personal property* to be valued
- the degree to which third-party information can be verified and relied on
- the relationship of the object to any real property or *intangible assets* that may affect the *valuation* of the property
- the importance of individual assets in an instruction that includes multiple objects with a wide range of values
- analysis of prior sales of the property being valued, if relevant
- the degree to which the current market conditions and the economy affect the level of certainty of the valuation conclusion.

6 Reports

6.1 It is the responsibility of the valuer to ensure that the valuation report is clear and accurate, and that no element of it is ambiguous or misleading. It should be prepared with independence, integrity and objectivity (see **PS 2**).

6.2 The valuer should comply with the minimum requirements listed in **VPS 3**, and incorporate all the valuation considerations listed in paragraph 5.2 above (Other valuation considerations). Additionally, when the valuer has consulted a specialist or professional individual or firm in the process of preparing the *valuation*, the sources and credentials should in each instance be identified and the nature of the input acknowledged (see paragraph 4.5 above).

6.3 The level of detail provided in the valuation report should adequately address the needs of the client and the intended user(s), the nature of the property, and the intended use of the *valuation*. The terminology used in the report should be understood by all intended users.

6.4 The valuer should state any limitations or conditions regarding *inspection*, research or analysis and explain any effect on the valuer's conclusions.

6.5 The purpose of the *valuation* (for example, equitable distribution), the *basis of value* (for example, *market value*), and the market in which the (notional or actual) transaction is presumed to take place (for example, auction) should be set out clearly within the report.

6.6 The valuer should report, if necessary, that the conclusion complies with any special requirements of the client, regulatory rules or pertinent laws.

6.7 The valuer should summarise the research conducted and the data used in the analysis. The valuer should state the valuation approach(es) used (i.e. comparison, cost or income) as well as the rationale for choosing it (them). The valuer should also state why other approaches were considered but rejected. If multiple approaches were used in the analysis, these should be detailed in the report and a reconciliation of the results should be included.

6.8 When arriving at a *valuation* based on any *special assumptions* (such as when an aggregated value is being determined), these should be specifically stated together with the effect on value, if any, of the *special assumptions*.

6.9 The valuer should comment on any issues affecting the certainty of the *valuation*. The extent of the commentary will vary, depending on the purpose of the *valuation* and the knowledge of the user.

6.10 Photographs should be appropriate and used as required by the assignment. If any alterations were made to the photographs, these should be noted.

VPGA 10 Matters that may give rise to material valuation uncertainty

This guidance is advisory and not mandatory in content. Where appropriate, however, it alerts *members* to relevant mandatory material contained elsewhere in these global standards, including the *International Valuation Standards*, using cross-references in bold type. These cross-references are for the assistance of *members* and do not alter the status of the material that follows below. *Members* are reminded that:

- this guidance cannot cover every circumstance, and they must always have regard to the facts and circumstances of individual assignments when forming valuation judgments
- they should remain alert to the fact that individual jurisdictions may have specific requirements that are not covered by this guidance.

1 Scope

1.1 This guidance provides additional commentary on matters that may give rise to material valuation uncertainty in accordance with **VPS 3 paragraph 2.1(o)**.

2 Examples

2.1 It is not possible to provide an exhaustive list of circumstances in which material uncertainty may arise – however, the examples in 2.2, 2.3 and 2.4 represent the three most common circumstances.

2.2 The asset or liability itself may have very particular characteristics that make it difficult for the valuer to form an opinion of the likely value, regardless of the approach or method used. For example, it may be a very unusual, or even unique, type. Similarly, the quantification of how purchasers would reflect a potential significant change, such as a potential planning permission, may be highly dependent on the *special assumptions* made.

2.3 Where the information available to the valuer is limited or restricted, either by the client or the circumstances of the *valuation*, and the matter cannot be sufficiently addressed by adopting one or more reasonable *assumptions*, less certainty can be attached to the *valuation* than would otherwise be the case.

2.4 Markets can be disrupted by relatively unique factors. Such disruption can arise due to unforeseen financial, macro-economic, legal, political or even natural events. If the *valuation date* coincides with, or is in the immediate aftermath of, such an event there may be a reduced level of certainty that can be attached to a *valuation*, due to inconsistent, or an absence of, empirical data, or to the valuer being faced with an unprecedented set of circumstances on which to base a judgment. In such situations demands placed on valuers can be unusually testing. Although valuers should still be able to make a judgment, it is important that the context of that judgment is clearly expressed.

3 Reporting

3.1 The overriding requirement is that a valuation report must not be misleading or create a false impression. The valuer should expressly draw attention to, and comment on, any issues resulting in material uncertainty in the *valuation* as at the specified *valuation date*. Such comment should not be about the general risk of future market movements or the inherent risk involved in forecasting future cash flows – both of which can and should be considered and reflected as part of the valuation process (for example, the *valuation* of an investment property that is subject to a very uncertain future cash flow could nevertheless be underpinned by a depth of consistent comparable transaction information) – but should be related to the risk surrounding the *valuation* of that asset.

3.2 Where material uncertainty exists, it will normally be expressed in qualitative terms, indicating the valuer's confidence in the valuation opinion offered by use of a suitable form of words. Indeed this may be the only realistic way in which to do so, given that the very conditions that create valuation uncertainty will frequently mean there is an absence of empirical data to inform or support a quantitative estimate.

3.3 In most cases it is either inappropriate or impractical to reflect material uncertainty in the valuation figure quantitatively, and indeed any attempt to do so might well seem contradictory. If a mathematical measure of uncertainty is included in any report, it is **essential** that the method or model used is adequately explained, with any limitations appropriately highlighted. In some limited circumstances a sensitivity analysis may be judged appropriate in order to illustrate the effect that clearly stated changes to specified variables could have on the reported *valuation*, which should be accompanied by suitable explanatory comment. It will be appreciated that the inherent risk with quantification of any sort is that it might convey an impression of precision that could be misleading.

3.4 In other cases, where the valuer can reasonably foresee that different values may arise under different but well-defined circumstances, an alternative approach would be for the valuer to enter into a dialogue with the client to consider alternative *valuations* using *special assumptions* that reflect those different circumstances. However, *special assumptions* may only be used if they can be regarded as realistic, relevant and valid in connection with the circumstances of the *valuation*. Where different values arise under different circumstances, they can be reported separately on the stated *special assumptions*.

3.5 It would not normally be acceptable for a valuation report to have a standard caveat to deal with material valuation uncertainty. The degree to which an opinion is uncertain will normally be unique to the specific *valuation*, and the use of standard clauses can devalue or bring into question the authority of the advice given. The task is to produce authoritative and considered professional advice within the report. Issues that affect the degree of certainty should be reported in this context.

3.6 Unless specifically requested, the expression of values within a stated range is not good practice and would not normally be regarded as an acceptable form of disclosure. In most cases the valuer has to provide a single figure in order to comply with the client's requirements and *terms of engagement*. Similarly, the use of qualifying words such as 'in the region of' would not normally be appropriate or adequate to convey material uncertainty without further explicit comment, and is again actively discouraged. Where different values may arise under different circumstances it is preferable to provide them on stated *special assumptions* (see paragraph 3.4 above).

3.7 Attention is drawn to the fact that financial reporting standards may, and often do, have specific disclosure requirements in relation to valuation uncertainty, though that particular term may not be expressly used. Compliance with those requirements is **mandatory** in cases to which they apply.

Appendix F

International Valuation Standards 2017, IPEV Guidelines (Appendix 1) and IVS 105

INTERNATIONAL VALUATION STANDARDS 2017 (FROM 1 JULY 2017)

Meaning of terms:
 Approaches:

1. The market approach is to compute the comparable price or royalty rate which could be obtained by a similar business in the market.
2. The income approach determines the estimated future income likely to be generated by the intellectual property assets over its expected life.
3. The cost approach is used to determine the reproduction or replacement cost of the intellectual property at the date of the valuation.

INTERNATIONAL PRIVATE EQUITY AND VENTURE CAPITAL VALUATION (IPEV) GUIDELINES, APPENDIX 1 (DECEMBER 2018)

1. The Concept of Fair Value

1.1 Fair Value is the price that would be received to sell an asset in an Orderly Transaction between Market Participants at the Measurement Date.

1.2 A Fair Value measurement assumes that a hypothetical transaction to sell an asset takes place in the Principal Market or in its absence, the Most Advantageous Market for the asset.

1.3 For actively traded (quoted) Investments, available market prices will be the exclusive basis for the measurement of Fair Value for identical instruments.

1.4 For Unquoted Investments, the measurement of Fair Value requires the Valuer to assume the Investment is realised or sold at the Measurement Date whether or not the instrument or the Investee Company is prepared for sale or whether its shareholders intend to sell in the near future.

1.5 Some Funds invest in multiple securities or tranches of the same Investee Company. If a Market Participant would be expected to transact all positions in the same underlying Investee Company simultaneously, for example separate Investments made in series A, series B, and series C, then Fair Value would be estimated for the aggregate Investment in the Investee Company. If a Market Participant would be expected to transact separately, for example purchasing series A independent from series B and series C, or if Debt Investments are purchased independent of equity, then Fair Value would be more appropriately determined for each individual financial instrument.

1.6 Fair Value should be estimated using consistent Valuation Techniques from Measurement Date to Measurement Date unless there is a change in market conditions or Investment-specific factors, which would modify how a Market Participant would determine value. The use of consistent Valuation Techniques for Investments with similar characteristics, industries, and/or geographies would also be expected.

1.7 Unit of Account

1.7 To estimate Fair Value the Unit of Account must be determined. The Unit of Account represents the specific Investment that is being measured at Fair Value.

2. Principles of Valuation

2.1 The Fair Value of each Investment should be assessed at each Measurement Date.

2.2 In estimating Fair Value for an Investment, the Valuer should apply a technique or techniques that is/are appropriate in light of the nature, facts, and circumstances of the Investment and should use reasonable current market data and inputs combined with Market Participant assumptions.

2.3 Fair Value is estimated using the perspective of Market Participants and market conditions at the Measurement Date irrespective of which Valuation Techniques are used.

2.4 Allocating Enterprise Value

2.4 Generally, for Private Capital Investments, Market Participants determine the price they will pay for individual equity instruments using Enterprise Value estimated from a hypothetical sale of the equity which may be determined by considering the sale of the Investee Company, as follows:

i. Determine the Enterprise Value of the Investee Company using the Valuation Techniques;
ii. Adjust the Enterprise Value for factors that a Market Participant would take into account such as surplus assets or excess liabilities and other contingencies and relevant factors, to derive an Adjusted Enterprise Value for the Investee Company;
iii. Deduct from this amount the value, from a Market Participant's perspective, of any financial instruments ranking ahead of the highest-ranking instrument of the Fund in a sale of the Investee Company.
iv. Take into account the effect of any instrument that may dilute the Fund's Investment to derive the Attributable Enterprise Value;
v. Apportion the Attributable Enterprise Value between the Investee Company's relevant financial instruments according to their ranking;
vi. Allocate the amounts derived according to the Fund's holding in each financial instrument, representing their Fair Value.

2.5 Exercising Prudent Judgement

2.5 Because of the uncertainties inherent in estimating Fair Value for Private Capital Investments, care should be applied in exercising judgement and making the necessary estimates. However, the Valuer should be wary of applying excessive caution.

2.6 Calibration

2.6 When the price of the initial Investment in an Investee Company or instrument is deemed Fair Value (which is generally the case if the entry transaction is considered an Orderly Transaction, then the Valuation Techniques that are expected to be used to estimate Fair Value in the future should be evaluated using market inputs as of the date the Investment was made. This process is known as Calibration. Calibration validates that the Valuation Techniques using contemporaneous market inputs will generate Fair Value at inception and therefore that the Valuation Techniques using updated market inputs as of each subsequent Measurement Date will generate Fair Value at each such date.

2.7 Backtesting

2.7 Valuers should seek to understand the substantive differences that legitimately occur between the exit price and the previous Fair Value assessment. This concept is known as Backtesting.

Backtesting seeks to articulate:

i. What information was known or knowable as of the Measurement Date;
ii. Assess how such information was considered in coming to the most recent Fair Value estimates; and
iii. Determine whether known or knowable information was properly considered in determining Fair Value given the actual exit price results.

3. Valuation Methods

3.1 General

3.1 (i) In determining the Fair Value of an Investment, the Valuer should use judgement. This includes consideration of those specific terms of the Investment that may impact its Fair Value. In this regard, the Valuer should consider the economic substance of the Investment, which may take precedence over the strict legal form.

3.1 (ii) Where the reporting currency of the Fund is different from the currency in which the Investment is denominated, translation into the reporting currency for reporting purposes should be done using the bid spot exchange rate prevailing at the Measurement Date.

3.2 Apply Judgement in Selecting Valuation Techniques

3.2 The Valuer should exercise their judgement to select the Valuation Technique or techniques most appropriate for a particular Investment.

3.3 Selecting the Appropriate Valuation Technique

3.3 The Valuer should use one or more of the following Valuation Techniques as of each Measurement Date, taking into account Market Participant assumptions as to how Value would be determined:

A. Market Approach
   a. Multiples (3.4)
   b. Industry Valuation Benchmarks (3.5)
   c. Available Market Prices (3.6)
B. Income Approach
   a. Discounted Cash Flows (3.7, 3.8)
C. Replacement Cost Approach
   a. Net Assets (3.9)

The Price of a Recent Investment, if resulting from an orderly transaction, generally represents Fair Value as of the transaction date. At subsequent Measurement Dates, the Price of a Recent Investment may be an appropriate starting point for estimating Fair Value. However, adequate consideration must be given to the current facts and circumstances, including, but not limited to, changes in the market or changes in the performance of the Investee Company.

Inputs to Valuation Techniques should be calibrated to the Price of a Recent Investment, to the extent appropriate (3.10).

3.4 Multiples

3.4 Depending on the stage of development of an Enterprise, its industry, and its geographic location, Market Participants may apply a multiple of earnings or revenue. In using the multiples Valuation Technique to estimate the Fair Value of an Enterprise, the Valuer should:

i. Apply a multiple that is appropriate and reasonable (given the size, risk profile and earnings growth prospects of the underlying company) to the applicable indicator of value (earnings or revenue) of the Investee Company;
ii. Adjust the Enterprise Value for surplus or non-operating assets or excess liabilities and other contingencies and relevant factors to derive an Adjusted Enterprise Value for the Investee Company;
iii. Deduct from this amount any financial instruments ranking ahead of the highest-ranking instrument of the Fund in a liquidation scenario (e.g. the amount that would be paid) and taking into account the effect of any instrument that may dilute the Fund's Investment to derive the Attributable Enterprise Value;
iv. Apportion the Attributable Enterprise Value appropriately between the relevant financial instruments using the perspective of potential Market Participants. Judgement is required in assessing a Market Participant perspective.

3.5 Industry Valuation Benchmarks

3.5 The use of industry benchmarks is only likely to be reliable and therefore appropriate as the main basis of estimating Fair Value in limited situations and is more likely to be useful as a sanity check of values produced using other techniques.

3.6 (i) Quoted Investments

3.6 (i) Instruments quoted on an Active Market should be valued at the price within the bid / ask spread that is most representative of Fair Value on the Measurement Date. The Valuer should consistently use the most representative point estimate in the bid /ask spread.

3.6 (ii/iii) Blockage Factors and Discounts

3.6 (ii) Blockage Factors that reflect size as a characteristic of the reporting entity's holding (specifically, a factor that adjusts the quoted price of an asset because the market's normal daily trading volume is not sufficient to absorb the quantity held by the entity) should not be applied.

3.6 (iii) Discounts may be applied to prices quoted in an Active Market if there is some contractual, governmental, or other legally enforceable restriction attributable to the security, not the holder, resulting in diminished Liquidity of the instrument that would impact the price a Market Participant would pay at the Measurement Date.

3.6 (iv) Observable Prices

3.6 (iv) In the absence of an Active Market for financial instruments, but where observable prices are available, the Valuer should consider observable prices in conjunction with estimating Fair Value utilising one or more of the other Valuation Techniques.

3.7 Discounted Cash Flows or Earnings (of Investee Company)

3.7 In using the Discounted Cash Flows or Earnings (of Investee Company) Valuation Technique to estimate the Fair Value of an Investment, the Valuer should:

i. Derive the Enterprise Value of the company, using reasonable assumptions and estimations of expected future cash flows (or expected future earnings) and the terminal value, and discounting to the present by applying the appropriate risk-adjusted rate that captures the risk inherent in the projections;
ii. Adjust the Enterprise Value for surplus or non-operating assets or excess liabilities and other contingencies and relevant factors to derive an Adjusted Enterprise Value for the Investee Company;
iii. Deduct from this amount any financial instruments ranking ahead of the highest-ranking instrument of the Fund in a liquidation scenario (e.g. the amount that would be paid) and taking into account the effect of any instrument that may dilute the Fund's Investment to derive the Attributable Enterprise Value; and
iv. Apportion the Attributable Enterprise Value appropriately between the relevant financial instruments using the perspective of Market Participants. Judgement is required in assessing a Market Participant perspective.

3.8 Discounted Cash Flows (from an Investment)

3.8 In using the Discounted Cash Flows (from an Investment) Valuation Technique to estimate the Fair Value of an Investment, the Valuer should derive the present value of the cash flows from the Investment using reasonable assumptions and estimations of expected future cash flows, the terminal value or maturity amount, date, and the appropriate risk-adjusted rate that captures the risk inherent to the Investment. This Valuation Technique would generally be applied to Debt Investments or Investments with characteristics similar to debt.

3.9 Net Assets

3.9 In using the Net Assets Valuation Technique to estimate the Fair Value of an Investment, the Valuer should:

i. Derive an Enterprise Value for the company using the perspective of a Market Participant to value its assets and liabilities (adjusting, if appropriate, for non-operating assets, excess liabilities, and contingent assets and liabilities);
ii. Deduct from this amount any financial instruments ranking ahead of the highest-ranking instrument of the Fund in a liquidation scenario (e.g. the amount that would be paid) and taking into account the effect of any instrument that may dilute the Fund's Investment to derive the Attributable Enterprise Value; and

iii. Apportion the Attributable Enterprise Value appropriately between the relevant financial instruments using the perspective of potential Market Participants. Judgement is required in assessing a Market Participant perspective.

3.10 Calibrating to the Price of a Recent Investment

3.10 The Fair Value indicated by a recent transaction in the Investee Companies equity is used to calibrate inputs used with various valuation methodologies. The Valuer should assess at each Measurement Date whether changes or events subsequent to the relevant transaction would imply a change in the Investment's Fair Value. The Price of a Recent Investment should not be considered a standalone Valuation Technique.

4. Valuing Fund Interests

4.1 General

4.1 In measuring the Fair Value of an interest in a Fund the Valuer may base their estimate on their attributable proportion of the reported Fund Net Asset Value (NAV) if NAV is derived from the Fair Value of underlying Investments and is as of the same Measurement Date as that used by the Valuer of the Fund interest, except as follows:

i. if the Fund interest is actively traded, Fair Value would be the actively traded price; and
ii. if management of the interest in the Fund has made the decision to sell the Fund interest or portion thereof and the interest will be sold for an amount other than NAV, Fair Value would be the expected sales price.

4.2 Adjustments to Net Asset Value

4.2 If the Valuer has determined that the reported NAV is an appropriate starting point for determining Fair Value, it may be necessary to make adjustments based on the best available information at the Measurement Date. Although the Valuer may look to the Fund Manager for the mechanics of their Fair Value estimation procedures, the Valuer needs to have appropriate processes and related controls in place to enable the Valuer to assess and understand the valuations received from the Fund Manager. If NAV is not derived from the Fair Value of underlying Investments and / or is not as of the same Measurement Date as that used by the Valuer of the Fund interest, then the Valuer will need to assess whether such differences are significant, resulting in the need to adjust reported NAV.

4.3 Secondary Transactions

4.3 When a Valuer of an interest knows the relevant terms of a Secondary Transaction in that particular Fund and the transaction is orderly, the Valuer must consider the transaction price as one component of the information used to measure the Fair Value of a Fund Interest.

4.4 Other Valuation Approaches for Fund Interests

4.4 When NAV is not or cannot be used as a starting point to estimate the Fair Value of a Fund Interest and market information is not available an income-based Valuation Technique would be used to estimate Fair Value of a Fund Interest.

IVS 105 Valuation Approaches and Methods

Contents **Paragraphs**

10. Introduction

10.1. Consideration *must* be given to the relevant and appropriate valuation approaches. The three approaches described and defined below are the main approaches used in valuation. They are all based on the economic principles of price equilibrium, anticipation of benefits or substitution. The principal valuation approaches are:

(a) market approach,

(b) income approach, and

(c) cost approach.

10.2. Each of these valuation approaches includes different, detailed methods of application.

10.3. The goal in selecting valuation approaches and methods for an *asset* is to find the most appropriate method under the particular circumstances. No one method is suitable in every possible situation. The selection process *should* consider, at a minimum:

(a) the appropriate basis(es) of value and premise(s) of value, determined by the terms and *purpose of the valuation* assignment,

(b) the respective strengths and weaknesses of the possible valuation approaches and methods,

(c) the appropriateness of each method in view of the nature of the *asset*, and the approaches or methods used by *participants* in the relevant market, and

(d) the availability of reliable information needed to apply the method(s).

10.4. *Valuers* are not required to use more than one method for the valuation of an *asset*, particularly when the *valuer* has a high degree of confidence in the accuracy and reliability of a single method, given the facts and circumstances of the valuation engagement. However, *valuers should* consider the use of multiple approaches and methods and more than one valuation approach or method *should* be considered and *may* be used to arrive at an indication of value, particularly when there are insufficient factual or observable inputs for a single method to produce a reliable conclusion. Where more than one approach and method is used, or even multiple methods within a single approach, the conclusion of value based on those multiple approaches and/or methods *should* be reasonable and the process of analysing and reconciling the differing values into a single conclusion, without averaging, *should* be described by the *valuer* in the report.

10.5. While this standard includes discussion of certain methods within the Cost, Market and Income approaches, it does not provide a comprehensive list of all possible methods that *may* be appropriate. Some of the many methods not addressed in this standard include option pricing methods (OPMs), simulation/Monte Carlo methods and probability-*weighted* expected-return methods (PWERM). It is the *valuer's* responsibility to choose the appropriate method(s) for each valuation engagement. Compliance with IVS *may* require the *valuer* to use a method not defined or mentioned in the IVS.

10.6. When different approaches and/or methods result in widely divergent indications of value, a *valuer should* perform procedures to understand why the value indications differ, as it is generally not appropriate to simply *weight* two or more divergent indications of value. In such cases, *valuers should* reconsider the guidance in para 10.3 to determine whether one of the approaches/methods provides a better or more reliable indication of value.

10.7. *Valuers should* maximise the use of relevant observable market information in all three approaches. Regardless of the source of the inputs and assumptions used in a valuation, a *valuer must* perform appropriate analysis to evaluate those inputs and assumptions and their appropriateness for the *valuation purpose*.

10.8. Although no one approach or method is applicable in all circumstances, price information from an active market is generally considered to be the strongest evidence of value. Some bases of value *may* prohibit a *valuer* from making subjective adjustments to price information from an active market. Price information from an inactive market *may* still be good evidence of value, but subjective adjustments *may* be needed.

20. Market Approach

20.1. The market approach provides an indication of value by comparing the *asset* with identical or comparable (that is similar) *assets* for which price information is available.

20.2. The market approach *should* be applied and afforded *significant weight* under the following circumstances:

(a) the subject *asset* has recently been sold in a transaction appropriate for consideration under the basis of value,

(b) the subject *asset* or substantially similar *assets* are actively publicly traded, and/or

(c) there are frequent and/or recent observable transactions in substantially similar *assets*.

20.3. Although the above circumstances would indicate that the market approach *should* be applied and afforded *significant weight*, when the above criteria are not met, the following are additional circumstances where the market approach *may* be applied and afforded *significant weight*. When using the market approach under the following circumstances, a *valuer should* consider whether any other approaches can be applied and *weighted* to corroborate the value indication from the market approach:

(a) Transactions involving the subject *asset* or substantially similar *assets* are not recent enough considering the levels of volatility and activity in the market.

(b) The *asset* or substantially similar *assets* are publicly traded, but not actively.

(c) Information on market transactions is available, but the comparable *assets* have *significant* differences to the subject *asset*, potentially requiring subjective adjustments.

(d) Information on recent transactions is not reliable (ie, hearsay, missing information, synergistic purchaser, not arm's-length, distressed sale, etc).

(e) The critical element affecting the value of the *asset* is the price it would achieve in the market rather than the cost of reproduction or its income-producing ability.

20.4. The heterogeneous nature of many *assets* means that it is often not possible to find market evidence of transactions involving identical or similar *assets*. Even in circumstances where the market approach is not used, the use of market-based inputs *should* be maximised in the application of other approaches (eg, market-based valuation metrics such as effective yields and rates of return).

20.5. When comparable market information does not relate to the exact or substantially the same *asset*, the *valuer must* perform a comparative analysis of qualitative and quantitative similarities and differences between the comparable *assets* and the subject *asset*. It will often be necessary to make adjustments based on this comparative analysis. Those adjustments *must* be reasonable and *valuers must* document the reasons for the adjustments and how they were quantified.

20.6. The market approach often uses market multiples derived from a set of comparables, each with different multiples. The selection of the appropriate multiple within the range requires judgement, considering qualitative and quantitative factors.

30. Market Approach Methods

Comparable Transactions Method

30.1. The comparable transactions method, also known as the guideline transactions method, utilises information on transactions involving *assets* that are the same or similar to the subject *asset* to arrive at an indication of value.

30.2. When the comparable transactions considered involve the subject *asset*, this method is sometimes referred to as the prior transactions method.

30.3. If few recent transactions have occurred, the *valuer may* consider the prices of identical or similar *assets* that are listed or offered for sale, provided the relevance of this information is clearly established, critically analysed and documented. This is sometimes referred to as the comparable listings method and *should* not be used as the sole indication of value but can be appropriate for consideration together with other methods. When considering listings or offers to buy or sell, the *weight* afforded to the listings/offer price *should* consider the level of commitment inherent in the price and how long the listing/offer has been on the market. For example, an offer that represents a binding commitment to purchase or sell an *asset* at a given price *may* be given more *weight* than a quoted price without such a binding commitment.

30.4. The comparable transaction method can use a variety of different comparable evidence, also known as units of comparison, which form the basis of the comparison. For example, a few of the many common units of comparison used for real property interests include price per square foot (or per square metre), rent per square foot (or per square metre) and capitalisation rates. A few of the many common units of comparison used in business valuation include EBITDA (Earnings Before Interest, Tax, Depreciation and Amortisation) multiples, earnings multiples, revenue multiples and book value multiples. A few of the many common units of comparison used in financial instrument valuation include metrics such as yields and interest rate spreads. The units of comparison used by *participants* can differ between *asset* classes and across industries and geographies.

30.5. A subset of the comparable transactions method is matrix pricing, which is principally used to value some types of financial instruments, such as debt securities, without relying exclusively on quoted prices for the specific securities, but rather relying on the securities' relationship to other benchmark quoted securities and their attributes (ie, yield).

30.6. The key steps in the comparable transactions method are:

(a) identify the units of comparison that are used by *participants* in the relevant market,

(b) identify the relevant comparable transactions and calculate the key valuation metrics for those transactions,

(c) perform a consistent comparative analysis of qualitative and quantitative similarities and differences between the comparable *assets* and the subject *asset*,

(d) make necessary adjustments, if any, to the valuation metrics to reflect differences between the subject *asset* and the comparable *assets* (see para 30.12(d)),

(e) apply the adjusted valuation metrics to the subject *asset*, and

(f) if multiple valuation metrics were used, reconcile the indications of value.

30.7. A *valuer should* choose comparable transactions within the following context:

(a) evidence of several transactions is generally preferable to a single transaction or event,

(b) evidence from transactions of very similar *assets* (ideally identical) provides a better indication of value than *assets* where the transaction prices require *significant* adjustments,

(c) transactions that happen closer to the valuation date are more representative of the market at that date than older/dated transactions, particularly in volatile markets,

(d) for most bases of value, the transactions *should* be "arm's length" between unrelated parties,

(e) sufficient information on the transaction *should* be available to allow the *valuer* to develop a reasonable understanding of the comparable *asset* and assess the valuation metrics/comparable evidence,

(f) information on the comparable transactions *should* be from a reliable and trusted source, and

(g) actual transactions provide better valuation evidence than intended transactions.

30.8. A *valuer should* analyse and make adjustments for any material differences between the comparable transactions and the subject *asset*. Examples of common differences that could warrant adjustments *may* include, but are not limited to:

(a) material characteristics (age, size, specifications, etc),

(b) relevant restrictions on either the subject *asset* or the comparable *assets*,

(c) geographical location (location of the *asset* and/or location of where the *asset* is likely to be transacted/used) and the related economic and regulatory environments,

(d) profitability or profit-making capability of the *assets*,

(e) historical and expected growth,

(f) yields/coupon rates,

(g) types of collateral,

(h) unusual terms in the comparable transactions,

(i) differences related to marketability and control characteristics of the comparable and the subject *asset*, and

(j) ownership characteristics (eg, legal form of ownership, amount percentage held).

Guideline publicly-traded comparable method

30.9. The guideline publicly-traded method utilises information on publicly-traded comparables that are the same or similar to the subject *asset* to arrive at an indication of value.

30.10. This method is similar to the comparable transactions method. However, there are several differences due to the comparables being publicly traded, as follows:

(a) the valuation metrics/comparable evidence are available as of the valuation date,

(b) detailed information on the comparables are readily available in public filings, and

(c) the information contained in public filings is prepared under well understood accounting standards.

30.11. The method *should* be used only when the subject *asset* is sufficiently similar to the publicly-traded comparables to allow for meaningful comparison.

30.12. The key steps in the guideline publicly-traded comparable method are to:

(a) identify the valuation metrics/comparable evidence that are used by *participants* in the relevant market,

(b) identify the relevant guideline publicly-traded comparables and calculate the key valuation metrics for those transactions,

(c) perform a consistent comparative analysis of qualitative and quantitative similarities and differences between the publicly-traded comparables and the subject *asset*,

(d) make necessary adjustments, if any, to the valuation metrics to reflect differences between the subject *asset* and the publicly-traded comparables,

(e) apply the adjusted valuation metrics to the subject *asset*, and

(f) if multiple valuation metrics were used, *weight* the indications of value.

30.13. A *valuer should* choose publicly-traded comparables within the following context:

(a) consideration of multiple publicly-traded comparables is preferred to the use of a single comparable,

(b) evidence from similar publicly-traded comparables (for example, with similar market segment, geographic area, size in revenue and/or *assets*, growth rates, profit margins, leverage, liquidity and diversification) provides a better indication of value than comparables that require *significant* adjustments, and

(c) securities that are actively traded provide more meaningful evidence than thinly-traded securities.

30.14. A *valuer should* analyse and make adjustments for any material differences between the guideline publicly-traded comparables and the subject *asset*. Examples of common differences that could warrant adjustments *may* include, but are not limited to:

(a) material characteristics (age, size, specifications, etc),

(b) relevant discounts and premiums (see para 30.17),

(c) relevant restrictions on either the subject *asset* or the comparable *assets*,

(d) geographical location of the underlying company and the related economic and regulatory environments,

(e) profitability or profit-making capability of the *assets*,

(f) historical and expected growth,

(g) differences related to marketability and control characteristics of the comparable and the subject *asset*, and

(h) type of ownership.

Other Market Approach Considerations

30.15. The following paragraphs address a non-exhaustive list of certain special considerations that *may* form part of a market approach valuation.

30.16. Anecdotal or "rule-of-thumb" valuation benchmarks are sometimes considered to be a market approach. However, value indications derived from the use of such rules *should* not be given substantial *weight* unless it can be shown that buyers and sellers place *significant* reliance on them.

30.17. In the market approach, the fundamental basis for making adjustments is to adjust for differences between the subject *asset* and the guideline transactions or publicly-traded securities. Some of the most common adjustments made in the market approach are known as discounts and premiums.

(a) Discounts for Lack of Marketability (DLOM) *should* be applied when the comparables are deemed to have superior marketability to the subject *asset*. A DLOM reflects the concept that when comparing otherwise identical *assets*, a readily marketable *asset* would have a higher value than an *asset* with a long marketing period or restrictions on the ability to sell the *asset*. For example, publicly-traded securities can be bought and sold nearly instantaneously while shares in a private company *may* require a *significant* amount of time to identify potential buyers and complete a transaction. Many bases of value allow the consideration of restrictions on marketability that are inherent in the subject *asset* but prohibit consideration of marketability restrictions that are specific to a particular owner. DLOMs *may* be quantified using any reasonable method, but are typically calculated using option pricing models, studies that compare the value of publicly-traded shares and restricted shares in the same company, or studies that compare the value of shares in a company before and after an initial public offering.

(b) Control Premiums (sometimes referred to as *Market Participant Acquisition Premiums* or *MPAPs*) and Discounts for Lack of Control (DLOC) are applied to reflect differences between the comparables and the subject *asset* with regard to the ability to make decisions and the changes that can be made as a result of exercising control. All else being equal, *participants* would generally prefer to have control over a subject *asset* than not. However, *participants*' willingness to pay a Control Premium or DLOC will generally be a factor of whether the ability to exercise control enhances the economic benefits available to the owner of the subject *asset*. Control Premiums and DLOCs *may* be quantified using any reasonable method, but are typically calculated based on either an analysis of the specific cash flow enhancements or reductions in risk associated with control or by comparing observed prices paid for controlling interests in publicly-traded securities to the publicly-traded price before such a transaction is announced. Examples of circumstances where Control Premiums and DLOC *should* be considered include where:

1. shares of public companies generally do not have the ability to make decisions related to the operations of the company (they lack control). As such, when applying the guideline public comparable method to value a subject *asset* that reflects a controlling interest, a control premium *may* be appropriate, or

2. the guideline transactions in the guideline transaction method often reflect transactions of controlling interests. When using that method to value a subject *asset* that reflects a minority interest, a DLOC *may* be appropriate.

(c) Blockage discounts are sometimes applied when the subject *asset* represents a large block of shares in a publicly-traded security such that an owner would not be able to quickly sell the block in the public market without negatively influencing the publicly-traded price. Blockage discounts *may* be quantified using any reasonable method but typically a model is used that considers the length of time over which a *participant* could sell the subject shares without negatively impacting the publicly-traded price (ie, selling a relatively small portion of the security's typical daily trading volume each day). Under certain bases of value, particularly fair value for financial reporting *purposes*, blockage discounts are prohibited.

40. Income Approach

40.1. The income approach provides an indication of value by converting future cash flow to a single current value. Under the income approach, the value of an *asset* is determined by reference to the value of income, cash flow or cost savings generated by the *asset*.

40.2. The income approach *should* be applied and afforded *significant weight* under the following circumstances:

(a) the income-producing ability of the *asset* is the critical element affecting value from a *participant* perspective, and/or

(b) reasonable projections of the amount and timing of future income are available for the subject *asset*, but there are few, if any, relevant market comparables.

40.3. Although the above circumstances would indicate that the income approach *should* be applied and afforded *significant weight*, the following are additional circumstances where the income approach *may* be applied and afforded *significant weight*. When using the income approach under the following circumstances, a *valuer should* consider whether any other approaches can be applied and *weighted* to corroborate the value indication from the income approach:

(a) the income-producing ability of the subject *asset* is only one of several factors affecting value from a *participant* perspective,

(b) there is *significant* uncertainty regarding the amount and timing of future income-related to the subject *asset*,

(c) there is a lack of access to information related to the subject *asset* (for example, a minority owner *may* have access to historical financial statements but not forecasts/budgets), and/or

(d) the subject *asset* has not yet begun generating income, but is projected to do so.

40.4. A fundamental basis for the income approach is that investors expect to receive a return on their investments and that such a return *should* reflect the perceived level of risk in the investment.

40.5. Generally, investors can only expect to be compensated for systematic risk (also known as "market risk" or "undiversifiable risk").

50. Income Approach Methods

50.1. Although there are many ways to implement the income approach, methods under the income approach are effectively based on discounting future amounts of cash flow to present value. They are variations of the Discounted Cash Flow (DCF) method and the concepts below apply in part or in full to all income approach methods.

Discounted Cash Flow (DCF) Method

50.2. Under the DCF method the forecasted cash flow is discounted back to the valuation date, resulting in a present value of the *asset*.

50.3. In some circumstances for long-lived or indefinite-lived *assets*, DCF *may* include a terminal value which represents the value of the *asset* at the end of the explicit projection period. In other circumstances, the value of an *asset may* be calculated solely using a terminal value with no explicit projection period. This is sometimes referred to as an income capitalisation method.

50.4. The key steps in the DCF method are:

(a) choose the most appropriate type of cash flow for the nature of the subject *asset* and the assignment (ie, pre-tax or post-tax, total cash flows or cash flows to equity, real or nominal, etc),

(b) determine the most appropriate explicit period, if any, over which the cash flow will be forecast,

(c) prepare cash flow forecasts for that period,

(d) determine whether a terminal value is appropriate for the subject *asset* at the end of the explicit forecast period (if any) and then determine the appropriate terminal value for the nature of the *asset*,

(e) determine the appropriate discount rate, and

(f) apply the discount rate to the forecasted future cash flow, including the terminal value, if any.

Type of Cash Flow

50.5. When selecting the appropriate type of cash flow for the nature of *asset* or assignment, *valuers must* consider the factors below. In addition, the discount rate and other inputs *must* be consistent with the type of cash flow chosen.

(a) Cash flow to whole *asset* or partial interest: Typically cash flow to the whole *asset* is used. However, occasionally other levels of income *may* be used as well, such as cash flow to equity (after payment of interest and principle on debt) or dividends (only the cash flow distributed to equity owners). Cash flow to the whole *asset* is most commonly used because an *asset should* theoretically have a single value that is independent of how it is financed or whether income is paid as dividends or reinvested.

(b) The cash flow can be pre-tax or post-tax: If a post-tax basis is used, the tax rate applied *should* be consistent with the basis of value and in many instances would be a *participant* tax rate rather than an owner-specific one.

(c) Nominal versus real: Real cash flow does not consider inflation whereas nominal cash flows include expectations regarding inflation. If expected cash flow incorporates an expected inflation rate, the discount rate has to include the same inflation rate.

(d) Currency: The choice of currency used *may* have an impact on assumptions related to inflation and risk. This is particularly true in emerging markets or in currencies with high inflation rates.

50.6. The type of cash flow chosen *should* be in accordance with *participant's* viewpoints. For example, cash flows and discount rates for real property are customarily developed on a pre-tax basis while cash flows and discount rates for businesses are normally developed on a post-tax basis. Adjusting between pre-tax and post-tax rates can be complex and prone to error and *should* be approached with caution.

50.7. When a valuation is being developed in a currency ("the valuation currency") that differs from the currency used in the cash flow projections ("the functional currency"), a *valuer should* use one of the following two currency translation methods:

(a) Discount the cash flows in the functional currency using a discount rate appropriate for that functional currency. Convert the present value of the cash flows to the valuation currency at the spot rate on the valuation date.

(b) Use a currency exchange forward curve to translate the functional currency projections into valuation currency projections and discount the projections using a discount rate appropriate for the valuation currency. When a reliable currency exchange forward curve is not available (for example, due to lack of liquidity in the relevant currency exchange markets), it *may* not be possible to use this method and only the method described in para 50.7(a) can be applied.

Explicit Forecast Period

50.8. The selection criteria will depend upon the *purpose of the valuation*, the nature of the *asset*, the information available and the required bases of value. For an *asset* with a short life, it is more likely to be both possible and relevant to project cash flow over its entire life.

50.9. *Valuers should* consider the following factors when selecting the explicit forecast period:

(a) the life of the *asset*,

(b) a reasonable period for which reliable data is available on which to base the projections,

(c) the minimum explicit forecast period which *should* be sufficient for an *asset* to achieve a stabilised level of growth and profits, after which a terminal value can be used,

(d) in the valuation of cyclical *assets*, the explicit forecast period *should* generally include an entire cycle, when possible, and

(e) for finite-lived *assets* such as most financial instruments, the cash flows will typically be forecast over the full life of the *asset*.

50.10. In some instances, particularly when the *asset* is operating at a stabilised level of growth and profits at the valuation date, it *may* not be necessary to consider an explicit forecast period and a terminal value *may* form the only basis for value (sometimes referred to as an income capitalisation method).

50.11. The intended holding period for one investor *should* not be the only consideration in selecting an explicit forecast period and *should* not impact the value of an *asset*. However, the period over which an *asset* is intended to be held *may* be considered in determining the explicit forecast period if the objective of the valuation is to determine its investment value.

Cash Flow Forecasts

50.12. Cash flow for the explicit forecast period is constructed using prospective financial information (PFI) (projected income/inflows and expenditure/outflows).

50.13. As required by para 50.12, regardless of the source of the PFI (eg, management forecast), a *valuer must* perform analysis to evaluate the PFI, the assumptions underlying the PFI and their appropriateness for the *valuation purpose*. The suitability of the PFI and the underlying assumptions will depend upon the *purpose of the valuation* and the required bases of value. For example, cash flow used to determine market value *should* reflect

PFI that would be anticipated by *participants*; in contrast, investment value can be measured using cash flow that is based on the reasonable forecasts from the perspective of a particular investor.

50.14. The cash flow is divided into suitable periodic intervals (eg, weekly, monthly, quarterly or annually) with the choice of interval depending upon the nature of the *asset*, the pattern of the cash flow, the data available, and the length of the forecast period.

50.15. The projected cash flow *should* capture the amount and timing of all future cash inflows and outflows associated with the subject *asset* from the perspective appropriate to the basis of value.

50.16. Typically, the projected cash flow will reflect one of the following:

(a) contractual or promised cash flow,

(b) the single most likely set of cash flow,

(c) the probability-*weighted* expected cash flow, or

(d) multiple scenarios of possible future cash flow.

50.17. Different types of cash flow often reflect different levels of risk and *may* require different discount rates. For example, probability-*weighted* expected cash flows incorporate expectations regarding all possible outcomes and are not dependent on any particular conditions or events (note that when a probability-*weighted* expected cash flow is used, it is not always necessary for *valuers* to take into account distributions of all possible cash flows using complex models and techniques. Rather, *valuers may* develop a limited number of discrete scenarios and probabilities that capture the array of possible cash flows). A single most likely set of cash flows *may* be conditional on certain future events and therefore could reflect different risks and warrant a different discount rate.

50.18. While *valuers* often receive PFI that reflects accounting income and expenses, it is generally preferable to use cash flow that would be anticipated by *participants* as the basis for valuations. For example, accounting non-cash expenses, such as depreciation and amortisation, *should* be added back, and expected cash outflows relating to capital expenditures or to changes in working capital *should* be deducted in calculating cash flow.

50.19. *Valuers must* ensure that seasonality and cyclicality in the subject has been appropriately considered in the cash flow forecasts.

Terminal Value

50.20. Where the *asset* is expected to continue beyond the explicit forecast period, *valuers must* estimate the value of the *asset* at the end of that period. The terminal value is then discounted back to the valuation date, normally using the same discount rate as applied to the forecast cash flow.

50.21. The terminal value *should* consider:

(a) whether the *asset* is deteriorating/finite-lived in nature or indefinite-lived, as this will influence the method used to calculate a terminal value,

(b) whether there is future growth potential for the *asset* beyond the explicit forecast period,

(c) whether there is a pre-determined fixed capital amount expected to be received at the end of the explicit forecast period,

(d) the expected risk level of the *asset* at the time the terminal value is calculated,

(e) for cyclical *assets*, the terminal value *should* consider the cyclical nature of the *asset* and *should* not be performed in a way that assumes "peak" or "trough" levels of cash flows in perpetuity, and

(f) the tax attributes inherent in the *asset* at the end of the explicit forecast period (if any) and whether those tax attributes would be expected to continue into perpetuity.

50.22. *Valuers may* apply any reasonable method for calculating a terminal value. While there are many different approaches to calculating a terminal value, the three most commonly used methods for calculating a terminal value are:

(a) Gordon growth model/constant growth model (appropriate only for indefinite-lived *assets*),

(b) market approach/exit value (appropriate for both deteriorating/finite-lived *assets* and indefinite-lived *assets*), and

(c) salvage value/disposal cost (appropriate only for deteriorating/ finite-lived *assets*).

Gordon Growth Model/Constant Growth Model

50.23. The constant growth model assumes that the *asset* grows (or declines) at a constant rate into perpetuity.

Market Approach/Exit Value

50.24. The market approach/exit value method can be performed in a number of ways, but the ultimate goal is to calculate the value of the *asset* at the end of the explicit cash flow forecast.

50.25. Common ways to calculate the terminal value under this method include application of a market-evidence based capitalisation factor or a market multiple.

50.26. When a market approach/exit value is used, *valuers should* comply with the requirements in the market approach and market approach methods section of this standard (sections 20 and 30). However, *valuers should* also consider the expected market conditions at the end of the explicit forecast period and make adjustments accordingly.

Salvage Value/Disposal Cost

50.27. The terminal value of some *assets may* have little or no relationship to the preceding cash flow. Examples of such *assets* include wasting *assets* such as a mine or an oil well.

50.28. In such cases, the terminal value is typically calculated as the salvage value of the *asset*, less costs to dispose of the *asset*. In circumstances where the costs exceed the salvage value, the terminal value is negative and referred to as a disposal cost or an *asset* retirement obligation.

Discount Rate

50.29. The rate at which the forecast cash flow is discounted *should* reflect not only the time value of money, but also the risks associated with the type of cash flow and the future operations of the *asset*.

50.30. *Valuers may* use any reasonable method for developing a discount rate. While there are many methods for developing or determining the reasonableness of a discount rate, a non-exhaustive list of common methods includes:

(a) the capital *asset* pricing model (CAPM),

(b) the *weighted* average cost of capital (WACC),

(c) the observed or inferred rates/yields,

(d) the internal rate of return (IRR),

(e) the *weighted* average return on *assets* (WARA), and

(f) the build-up method (generally used only in the absence of market inputs).

50.31. In developing a discount rate, a *valuer should* consider:

(a) the risk associated with the projections made in the cash flow used,

(b) the type of *asset* being valued. For example, discount rates used in valuing debt would be different to those used when valuing real property or a business,

(c) the rates implicit in transactions in the market,

(d) the geographic location of the *asset* and/or the location of the markets in which it would trade,

(e) the life/term of the *asset* and the consistency of inputs. For example, the risk-free rate considered would differ for an *asset* with a three-year life versus a 30-year life,

(f) the type of cash flow being used (see para 50.5), and

(g) the bases of value being applied. For most bases of value, the discount rate *should* be developed from the perspective of a *participant*.

60. Cost Approach

60.1. The cost approach provides an indication of value using the economic principle that a buyer will pay no more for an *asset* than the cost to obtain an *asset* of equal utility, whether by purchase or by construction, unless undue time, inconvenience, risk or other factors are involved. The approach provides an indication of value by calculating the current replacement or reproduction cost of an *asset* and making deductions for physical deterioration and all other relevant forms of obsolescence.

60.2. The cost approach *should* be applied and afforded *significant weight* under the following circumstances:

(a) *participants* would be able to recreate an *asset* with substantially the same utility as the subject asset, without regulatory or legal restrictions, and the *asset* could be recreated quickly enough that a *participant* would not be willing to pay a *significant* premium for the ability to use the subject *asset* immediately,

(b) the *asset* is not directly income-generating and the unique nature of the *asset* makes using an income approach or market approach unfeasible, and/or

(c) the basis of value being used is fundamentally based on replacement cost, such as replacement value.

60.3. Although the circumstances in para 60.2 would indicate that the cost approach *should* be applied and afforded *significant weight*, the following are additional circumstances where the cost approach *may* be applied and afforded *significant weight*. When using the cost approach under the following circumstances, a *valuer should* consider whether any other approaches can be applied and *weighted* to corroborate the value indication from the cost approach:

(a) *participants* might consider recreating an *asset* of similar utility, but there are potential legal or regulatory hurdles or *significant* time involved in recreating the *asset*,

(b) when the cost approach is being used as a reasonableness check to other approaches (for example, using the cost approach to confirm whether a business valued as a going-concern might be more valuable on a liquidation basis), and/or

(c) the *asset* was recently created, such that there is a high degree of reliability in the assumptions used in the cost approach.

60.4. The value of a partially completed *asset* will generally reflect the costs incurred to date in the creation of the *asset* (and whether those costs contributed to value) and the expectations of *participants* regarding the value of the property when complete, but consider the costs and time required to complete the *asset* and appropriate adjustments for profit and risk.

70. Cost Approach Methods

70.1. Broadly, there are three cost approach methods:

(a) replacement cost method: a method that indicates value by calculating the cost of a similar *asset* offering equivalent utility,

(b) reproduction cost method: a method under the cost that indicates value by calculating the cost to recreating a replica of an *asset*, and

(c) summation method: a method that calculates the value of an *asset* by the addition of the separate values of its component parts.

Replacement Cost Method

70.2. Generally, replacement cost is the cost that is relevant to determining the price that a *participant* would pay as it is based on replicating the utility of the *asset*, not the exact physical properties of the *asset*.

70.3. Usually replacement cost is adjusted for physical deterioration and all relevant forms of obsolescence. After such adjustments, this can be referred to as depreciated replacement cost.

70.4. The key steps in the replacement cost method are:

(a) calculate all of the costs that would be incurred by a typical *participant* seeking to create or obtain an *asset* providing equivalent utility,

(b) determine whether there is any deprecation related to physical, functional and external obsolescence associated with the subject *asset*, and

(c) deduct total deprecation from the total costs to arrive at a value for the subject *asset*.

70.5. The replacement cost is generally that of a modern equivalent *asset*, which is one that provides similar function and equivalent utility to the *asset* being valued, but which is of a current design and constructed or made using current cost-effective materials and techniques.

Reproduction Cost Method

70.6. Reproduction cost is appropriate in circumstances such as the following:

(a) the cost of a modern equivalent *asset* is greater than the cost of recreating a replica of the subject *asset*, or

(b) the utility offered by the subject *asset* could only be provided by a replica rather than a modern equivalent.

70.7. The key steps in the reproduction cost method are:

(a) calculate all of the costs that would be incurred by a typical *participant* seeking to create an exact replica of the subject *asset*,

(b) determine whether there is any deprecation related to physical, functional and external obsolescence associated with the subject *asset*, and

(c) deduct total deprecation from the total costs to arrive at a value for the subject *asset*.

Summation Method

70.8. The summation method, also referred to as the underlying *asset* method, is typically used for investment companies or other types of *assets* or entities for which value is primarily a factor of the values of their holdings.

70.9. The key steps in the summation method are:

(a) value each of the component *assets* that are part of the subject *asset* using the appropriate valuation approaches and methods, and

(b) add the value of the component *assets* together to reach the value of the subject *asset*.

Cost Considerations

70.10. The cost approach *should* capture all of the costs that would be incurred by a typical *participant*.

70.11. The cost elements *may* differ depending on the type of the *asset* and *should* include the direct and indirect costs that would be required to replace/ recreate the *asset* as of the valuation date. Some common items to consider include:

(a) direct costs:

1. materials, and

2. labour.

(b) indirect costs:

1. transport costs,

2. installation costs,

3. professional fees (design, permit, architectural, legal, etc),

4. other fees (commissions, etc),

5. overheads,

6. taxes,

7. finance costs (eg, interest on debt financing), and

8. profit margin/entrepreneurial profit to the creator of the *asset* (eg, return to investors).

70.12. An *asset* acquired from a third party would presumably reflect their costs associated with creating the *asset* as well as some form of profit margin to provide a return on their investment. As such, under bases of value that assume a hypothetical transaction, it *may* be appropriate to include an assumed profit margin on certain costs which can be expressed as a target profit, either a lump sum or a percentage return on cost or value. However, financing costs, if included, *may* already reflect *participants*' required return on capital deployed, so *valuers should* be cautious when including both financing costs and profit margins.

70.13. When costs are derived from actual, quoted or estimated prices by third party suppliers or contractors, these costs will already include a third parties' desired level of profit.

70.14. The actual costs incurred in creating the subject *asset* (or a comparable reference *asset*) *may* be available and provide a relevant indicator of the cost of the *asset*. However, adjustments *may* need to be made to reflect the following:

(a) cost fluctuations between the date on which this cost was incurred and the valuation date, and

(b) any atypical or exceptional costs, or savings, that are reflected in the cost data but that would not arise in creating an equivalent.

80. Depreciation/Obsolescence

80.1. In the context of the cost approach, "depreciation" refers to adjustments made to the estimated cost of creating an *asset* of equal utility to reflect the impact on value of any obsolescence affecting the subject *asset*. This meaning is different from the use of the word in financial reporting or tax law where it generally refers to a method for systematically expensing capital expenditure over time.

80.2. Depreciation adjustments are normally considered for the following types of obsolescence, which *may* be further divided into subcategories when making adjustments:

(a) Physical obsolescence: Any loss of utility due to the physical deterioration of the *asset* or its components resulting from its age and usage.

(b) Functional obsolescence: Any loss of utility resulting from inefficiencies in the subject *asset* compared to its replacement such as its design, specification or technology being outdated.

(c) External or economic obsolescence: Any loss of utility caused by economic or locational factors external to the *asset*. This type of obsolescence can be temporary or permanent.

80.3. Depreciation/obsolescence *should* consider the physical and economic lives of the *asset*:

(a) The physical life is how long the *asset* could be used before it would be worn out or beyond economic repair, assuming routine maintenance but disregarding any potential for refurbishment or reconstruction.

(b) The economic life is how long it is anticipated that the *asset* could generate financial returns or provide a non-financial benefit in its current use. It will be influenced by the degree of functional or economic obsolescence to which the *asset* is exposed.

80.4. Except for some types of economic or external obsolescence, most types of obsolescence are measured by making comparisons between the subject *asset* and the hypothetical *asset* on which the estimated replacement or reproduction cost is based. However, when market evidence of the effect of obsolescence on value is available, that evidence *should* be considered.

80.5. Physical obsolescence can be measured in two different ways:

(a) curable physical obsolescence, ie, the cost to fix/cure the obsolescence, or

(b) incurable physical obsolescence which considers the *asset*'s age, expected total and remaining life where the adjustment for physical obsolescence is equivalent to the proportion of the expected total life consumed. Total expected life *may* be expressed in any reasonable way, including expected life in years, mileage, units produced, etc.

80.6. There are two forms of functional obsolescence:

(a) excess capital cost, which can be caused by changes in design, materials of construction, technology or manufacturing techniques resulting in the availability of modern equivalent *assets* with lower capital costs than the subject *asset*, and

(b) excess operating cost, which can be caused by improvements in design or excess capacity resulting in the availability of modern equivalent *assets* with lower operating costs than the subject *asset*.

80.7. Economic obsolescence *may* arise when external factors affect an individual *asset* or all the *assets* employed in a business and *should* be deducted after physical deterioration and functional obsolescence. For real estate, examples of economic obsolescence include:

(a) adverse changes to demand for the products or services produced by the *asset*,

(b) oversupply in the market for the *asset*,

(c) a disruption or loss of a supply of labour or raw material, or

(d) the *asset* being used by a business that cannot afford to pay a market rent for the *assets* and still generate a market rate of return.

80.8. Cash or cash equivalents do not suffer obsolescence and are not adjusted. Marketable *assets* are not adjusted below their market value determined using the market approach.

Appendix G

Practice Note: Apportioning the Price Paid for a Business Transferred as a Going Concern

Practice Note
Apportioning the Price Paid for a Business Transferred as a Going Concern

Index

1. Background

1.1 An apportionment of the price paid for a business as a going concern between the underlying assets may be required for tax purposes in a number of instances, for example:

a. For the purpose of calculating the capital gain arising on the disposal of the separate assets in accordance with the Taxation of Chargeable Gains Act (TCGA) 1992.

b. On an acquisition for the purpose of calculating the Stamp Duty Land Tax (SDLT) due on the interest in the land and buildings only.

c. On an acquisition for the purpose of calculating the allowances available under the Capital Allowances Act 2001, such as Machinery and Plant Allowances.

d. On acquisition of goodwill for the purpose of Part 8, Corporation Tax Act 2009 (formerly Schedule 29 of the Finance Act 2002).

1.2 The price paid for a business sold as a going concern may include any or all of the following assets:

a. The land and buildings including landlord's fixtures ('the property').

b. The trade fixtures, fittings, furniture, furnishings and equipment ('the chattels').

c. Any transferable licences.

d. Goodwill

e. Other separately identifiable intangible assets (e.g. registered trade marks).

The purchaser may also separately acquire consumables and stock but these are usually valued separately and will not normally be included in the sale price to be apportioned.

1.3 Some of the principles set out in this Practice Note are applicable to apportionments for all types of businesses but the note deals mainly with the particular issues that have arisen where the property is a 'trade related property' valued using a profits approach, e.g. public houses, hotels, petrol filling stations, cinemas, restaurants, care homes etc (see paragraph 4 below). In these cases there can be particular difficulties in identifying the sum attributable to 'goodwill' and this is fundamental to the apportionment.

2. The Statutory Provisions

2.1 For the purposes of calculating a capital gain s.52 of the TCGA 1992 provides that any apportionment shall be on a 'just and reasonable' basis.

2.2 For the purposes of calculating any SDLT due paragraph 4, Schedule 4, FA 2003 similarly provides that any apportionment shall be on a 'just and reasonable' basis (subject to other provisions of the Capital Allowances Act).

2.3 For the purposes of calculating any Capital Allowances claimed s.562 CAA 2001 similarly provides that any apportionment should be on a just and reasonable basis unless other specific provisions disapply the application of s.562 in whole or in part.

2.4 For the purpose of calculating the cost of purchased goodwill Part 8 of the Corporation Tax Act 2009 (CTA 2009) provides that 'goodwill' has the meaning it has for accounting purposes[1]. Accounting guidance (FRS[2] 10) provides that 'purchased goodwill' should be taken to be the "difference between the cost of an acquired entity and the aggregate of the fair values of that entity's identifiable assets and liabilities" (see paragraph 12 below).

2.5 Unlike the Capital Gains, SDLT and Capital Allowances provisions which provide for an apportionment approach, the starting point for Part 8 of CTA 2009 is to consider whether the accounts are prepared in accordance with generally accepted accounting practice (GAAP)[3]. Where accounts are not GAAP compliant the "purchased goodwill" is to be calculated as if the company has prepared GAAP compliant accounts.

An apportionment adjustment under s.856(4) CTA 2009 can only be made in the circumstances where assets have been acquired together with other assets as part of one bargain and the values allocated to those particular assets have not already been allocated a value in accordance with GAAP i.e. fair value.

In practice, apportionment is only required in limited circumstances. For example if a company has not applied acquisition accounting, or not applied acquisition accounting correctly, and that failure is material (i.e. accounts are not GAAP compliant) the adjustment is to be made under section 717(1) CTA 2009. However, if that failure is not material (so the accounts remain GAAP compliant) then the adjustment will be made under section 856(4) CTA 2009.

2.6 The various statutory provisions do not define the method of arriving at a 'just and reasonable' apportionment but any apportionment should generally seek to apportion the price paid between the underlying assets included in the sale on the basis of their relative values and the contribution they make to the price that is being apportioned.

3. Legal Definitions of Goodwill

3.1 Halsbury's Laws of England, 4th edition, Vol. 35 at page 1206 states that:

"The goodwill of a business is the whole advantage of the reputation and connection with customers together with the circumstances whether of habit or

---

[1] Section 715(3) CTA 2009.

[2] Financial Reporting Standard.

[3] This note does not take account of the recently issued UK accounting standard, FRS 102, approved by the Financial Reporting Council in March 2013. This is only mandatory for accounting periods beginning on or after 1 January 2015, although it may be adopted early if desired. It is not expected there should be significant differences in practice to the principles applicable under existing UK GAAP.

otherwise, which tend to make that connection permanent . It represents in connection with any business or business product the value of the attraction to the customers which the name and reputation possesses ."

3.2 The definition contained in the Shorter Oxford Dictionary is:

"Goodwill is the privilege granted by the seller of a business to a purchaser of trading as his recognised successor; the possession of a ready-formed connection with customers considered as a separate element in the saleable value of a business."

3.3 The leading legal authority on the meaning of goodwill is found in *IRC v Muller & Co Margarine Limited* [1901] AC 217. In answer to the question "what is goodwill?" Lord Macnaghten said:

"It is a thing very easy to describe, very difficult to define. It is the benefit and advantage of the good name, reputation and connection of a business. It is the attractive force which brings in custom. It is the one thing which distinguishes an old-established business from a new business at its first stage."

Lord Macnaghten went on to say that:

"Goodwill is composed of a variety of elements. It differs in its composition in different trades and in different businesses in the same trade. One element may preponderate here; and another there."

3.4 In the decision of the Special Commissioners in *Balloon Promotions Ltd v Wilson*, SpC 524 [2006] STC (SCD) 167, goodwill for CG purposes was construed in accordance with legal rather than accountancy principles.

3.5 Traditionally goodwill has been subdivided into different types such as 'inherent goodwill', 'adherent goodwill' and 'free goodwill'. These subdivisions are no longer considered helpful as they tend to cause confusion. 'Inherent' and 'adherent' goodwill are not really goodwill at all as they form part of the value of the property asset and are properly reflected within such.

4. Trade Related Properties

4.1 'Trade related property' (TRP) is defined in the Royal Institution of Chartered Surveyors (RICS) Guidance Note 2 (GN2) as "any type of real property designed for a specific type of business where the property value reflects the trading potential for that business"[6]. Examples include hotels, public houses, restaurants, nightclubs, casinos, cinemas, theatres, care homes and petrol filling stations.

4.2 The essential characteristic of this type of property is that it has been designed or adapted for a specific use where the property value is usually

---

[4] See *Trego v Hunt* [1896] AC 7 at 16, 17, 23, 27, HL and *H P Bulmer Ltd and Showerings Ltd v J Bollinger SA* [1977] 2 CMLR 625, CA.

[5] *R J Reuter Co Ltd v Ferd Mulhens* [1954] Ch 50 at 89, [1953] 2 All ER 1160 at 1179, CA per Evershed MR.

[6] © Royal Institution of Chartered Surveyors (RICS)

intrinsically linked to the returns an owner or occupier can generate from such use.

4.3 TRPs are often individual and exhibit unique features in terms of their location, character, size, consents and levels of adaptation or construction specific to their particular use. It is these features that lead to the need for specific valuation treatment within the valuation profession, often utilising a profits based methodology to determine market value. (This involves estimating the 'trading potential' of the property.)

4.4 'Trading potential' is defined in the RICS GN2 as "the future profit, in the context of a valuation of the property, that a reasonably efficient operator would expect to be able to realise from occupation of the property. This could be above or below the recent trading history of the property. It reflects a range of factors such as the location, design and character, level of adaptation and trading history of the property within the market conditions prevailing that are inherent to the property asset"[7].

4.5 'Reasonably efficient operator' (REO) is defined as "a concept where the valuer assumes that the market participants are competent operators, acting in an efficient manner, of a business conducted on the premises. It involves estimating the trading potential rather than adopting the actual level of trade under the existing ownership, and it excludes personal goodwill"[8]. Assessing the trading potential of the property will therefore entail a review of the existing operator's trading accounts and comparing the actual trading performance with that of similar trade related property types and styles of operation. The trading performance expected by a reasonably efficient operator may be the same as, greater than or less than the actual trading performance.

5. Goodwill in Trade Related Properties

5.1 It has in the past been argued that because the business in TRPs is usually largely or wholly incapable of being sold separately from the property there is little or no goodwill (see the Lands Tribunal decision in Coles Executors v IRC (1973) concerning the valuation of a public house for Estate Duty). On the sale of a business operated from such properties, unless there were other separately identifiable intangible assets included in the sale, the whole of the purchase price would normally be apportioned to the property and chattels, it being argued that there was no goodwill.

5.2 The above view was often put forward by purchasers seeking to claim Capital Allowances on fixtures which formed part of the property. However, since the introduction of SDLT and the provisions now contained in Part 8 CTA 2009, HMRC has seen increasingly large sums apportioned to goodwill (away from the underlying property) in order to maximise the claim under Part 8 CTA 2009 and minimise the amount of SDLT payable.

5.3 HMRC accept that if a business is sold as a going concern the sale may include some element of goodwill. The question to be answered is not whether

[7] © Royal Institution of Chartered Surveyors (RICS)

[8] © Royal Institution of Chartered Surveyors (RICS)

goodwill exists, but what is the value of that goodwill? That question has to be decided on the facts of each individual case and will vary depending on the type of property and use. In some cases the value of the goodwill may be nominal but in some it may be substantial.

6. Valuing Goodwill

6.1 There is a broad measure of agreement across the valuation, accountancy and legal professions that the value of goodwill is represented by the difference between the value of a business as a going concern and the value of the separately identifiable assets included in the sale. HMRC consider that the value of any goodwill in trade related properties should be arrived at by deducting the value of the separately identifiable assets included in the sale from the value of the business as a going concern.

6.2 The value of a business as a going concern will usually be represented by the actual sale price achieved in the open market. However, if it is necessary to value a business as a going concern, because the sale price was not at arm's length, then this is the responsibility of HMRC (SAV).

6.3 The value of the tangible assets is the responsibility of the VOA. If it is necessary to value any other intangible assets (e.g. registered trademarks) included in the sale then this is the responsibility of HMRC Shares and Assets Valuation.

6.4 When the deductive method of arriving at the value of goodwill is adopted difficulties may arise over the appropriate assumptions to be adopted when arriving at a valuation of the other business assets. This is addressed in the paragraphs below.

7. Valuing the Tangible Assets - Assumptions

7.1 Difficulties relating to the assumptions to be adopted when valuing the tangible assets often arise in cases involving TRPs. Some of the reasons for this are:

a. The established approach to valuation of this type of property typically relies on 'the profits method' (see paragraph 8 below). In applying this valuation method there can sometimes be confusion in distinguishing the income and trading potential that runs with the operational property from any additional income arising from the actual operator's business.

b. The value of such properties is often significantly reduced if the property ceases to be occupied for any length of time because customers go elsewhere and the purchaser has to rebuild the level of trade. The enhanced value that arises as a result of the property having been occupied by the vendor and any predecessors for the particular use (ie. the property's trading history) is part of what was previously described as 'adherent' goodwill but is properly part of the property value and is reflected in the property's 'trading potential',

c. The property value is often significantly reduced if the property is stripped of chattels because the purchaser has to re-fit the premises before being ready to trade.

d. It can sometimes be difficult to obtain new licences where these have been lost.

7.2 The valuation of the tangible assets must reflect the facts at the valuation date and not, for example, treat the property as stripped of chattels and empty of occupiers when it was not. There should be no assumption of an empty and bare property unless that is representative of the facts. If, contrary to the evident facts, it were to be assumed for the purposes of valuation that the property has lost any licences, been stripped of chattels and left vacant for a period of time then the value will be significantly reduced and the value of goodwill in the final apportionment, arrived at by deduction, would be unreasonably inflated.

An assumption of vacant possession does not imply that the property is empty, but that physical and legal possession will pass on completion. Any parts of the property occupied by third parties is a matter of fact for consideration within the valuation. For example, in relation to care homes the presence of residents occupying under short terms licences at the valuation date will be a consequence of the property's established use and a fact to be reflected in the property valuation. The valuer, or a purchaser, would nevertheless still have to make a judgement as to how many residents may choose to remain on a change of ownership. This may affect the timing and level of anticipated income to be reflected in the valuation.

7.3 When arriving at the value of goodwill using the approach outlined in paragraph 6 above, if all the tangible assets are included in the sale, it will usually be appropriate to value all the tangible assets together for sale as an 'operational entity' so that a purchaser can, if they wish, trade from the day of purchase . It is critical that this possibility is reflected to ensure a fair apportionment of the sale price (and any premium arising from a sale of combined assets) between the tangible and intangible elements so as to avoid any over or understatement.

7.4 The valuation of the property should have regard to any established use or trading history up to the valuation date as this may influence both the timing and level of future income a purchaser would expect. A property that has been operational up to the date of valuation is likely to have a higher value than one that has been empty for six months because the purchaser will anticipate greater certainty and immediacy of a trading income stream due to continued customer patronage. Established use provides the likelihood of sustaining a level of use and income generation for the REO and reduces the risk of delay - a running start rather than a cold start.

7.5 Where the business is sold as a going concern, the benefit of contracts entered into by the vendor with customers, staff and suppliers will normally pass to the purchaser and be reflected in the price paid for the business. However, these contracts do not form part of the tangible assets so, if they add any value, the added value should not be reflected in the valuation of the tangible assets. For example, in relation to a care home, prior to the sale the residents would have contracts with the owner to reside at the property and those contracts cannot be assumed to pass to a purchaser of the property.

However, many of the existing residents may wish to continue to reside in the property following any change of ownership and those residents would be free to enter into new contracts with the purchaser. Equally the purchaser of the property may be prepared to pay an additional sum to the vendor (over and above the property value) to acquire these contracts if it is perceived they provide greater certainty and immediacy of full trading incomes (that is goodwill or business value).

7.6 When arriving at the value of goodwill using the approach outlined in paragraph 6 above it is considered appropriate to assume that the benefit of any contracts with customers, staff and suppliers would either have to be acquired separately from the vendor or the purchaser would have to make their own arrangements. It would be open to a purchaser to make their own arrangements with any existing customers, staff and suppliers who would be likely to be happy entering into new contracts following a change of ownership. For example, in relation to a public house, the existing operator may be achieving a higher than expected profit margin because of a favourable supply contract with a brewery. It cannot be assumed that the contract with the brewery would pass to a purchaser of the property but the purchaser may be able to enter into a similar contract with the existing supplier or another brewery in which event this will be reflected within the market bid for the property interest. This will be a matter of judgement on the facts and the market prevailing.

7.7 Applying the assumptions in paragraph 7.4 will have different effects depending on the facts in each particular case. For example:

a. A small public house to be run by the purchaser with help from part-time bar staff. The purchaser has acquired the business as a going concern but there are no contracts with customers and the purchaser wishes to enter their own contracts with suppliers and employ their own staff. In such a case there may be no identifiable difference between the price paid for the business as a going concern and the price that a purchaser would pay to acquire all the tangible assets. In such a case the value of the goodwill may be nominal.

b. A specialist care home that is fully occupied by residents and is to be run by the purchaser with the help of full-time qualified staff. There may be a difference between the price paid for such a business as a going concern and the price a purchaser would pay to acquire all the tangible assets, depending on the degree of difficulty the purchaser might anticipate in securing full occupancy and staffing (see paragraph 8.3 below). In such a case the value of the goodwill may be more substantial.

7.8 When purchasing such a business as a going concern the purchaser will often have obtained a valuation of the tangible assets as an 'operational entity' in accordance with the RICS GN2 (see paragraph 10 below). In addition, an alternative valuation of the property based on special assumptions (e.g. vacant following a failure of the business, no accounts providing evidence of trade, stripped of chattels and licences lost) may also be obtained for bank lending purposes. For the purposes of calculating the value of goodwill it would not be appropriate to deduct a valuation based on such special assumptions that do not reflect the actual circumstances prevailing at the valuation date. It is important to recognise that the valuation of the property as an 'operational entity' is a value of the property with chattels and readily available licences and is not a valuation of the actual business as a going concern (see paragraph 10 below). Whilst GN2 states that it does not apply to apportionments for tax purposes, HMRC/VOA consider that for the purpose of arriving at the value of goodwill (see paragraph 11.2, Step 2, below), it should normally be acceptable to deduct a GN2 valuation of the 'operational entity' as reflecting the established valuation approach to properties of this nature. RICS UKGN 3 provides guidance on valuations and apportionments for tax purposes and HMRC/VOA consider that, if all the tangible assets are prudently lotted together as an operational entity, a valuation in accordance with UKGN 3 would not give a lower figure.

8. Valuing the Tangible Assets – the Profits Approach

8.1 When valuing the tangible assets of an operational TRP, the aim should normally be to arrive at a capital value that fairly represents the price that an owner-occupier purchaser would be prepared to pay to acquire all the tangible assets together, having regard to the circumstances existing at the valuation date. Having decided on the appropriate assumptions (see paragraphs 7.3 - 7.6 above) it is then necessary to consider the most appropriate method of valuation. The appropriate method of valuation is a matter for the valuer having regard to the facts, but most TRPs are valued using the profits method of valuation. This valuation method requires consideration of both the level and timing of estimated trading income and is described in detail in the RICS GN2 but essentially it involves the following:

- The valuer makes an assessment of the fair maintainable turnover (FMT) that could be generated by a reasonably efficient operator (REO) of the 'operational entity' that is fully equipped and ready to trade.
- From this an assessment is made of the fair maintainable operating profit (FMOP) reflecting the costs to be expected by a REO.
- The market value of the property as an operational entity is then assessed by capitalising the FMOP at an appropriate rate of return reflecting the risks and rewards of the property and its trading potential.

8.2 A valuation of the tangible assets using the profits method has the following advantages:

a. it is widely used in the market to arrive at both going concern values and valuations of the tangible assets as an operational entity under the RICS GN2.

b. it represents the value to an owner-occupier purchaser.

c. the purchase price paid for the going concern and any GN2 valuation of the tangible assets as an operational entity can be analysed to provide evidence of the FMT/FMOP and a multiplier for the actual subject property at the valuation date.

d. it produces a value for all the tangible assets to be valued together as a single operational entity.

8.3 When assessing the FMT/FMOP it must be remembered that in cases where the existing contracts with customers, staff and suppliers are of some additional value it is necessary to have regard to this in the valuation. A valuer looking to determine the value of the operational property alone may have to make difficult judgements on whether staff and customers would choose to stay with the property or would realistically take their custom elsewhere if the property were to change hands. Whether this affects the value of the property or not will depend on the facts of the case and the market conditions prevailing at the valuation date. In cases where it is considered that there may be some delay before the REO could achieve the expected FMT/FMOP, this may either be reflected in the rate of return at which the FMT/FMOP is capitalised or a more specific discount may be made to reflect the reduced FMT/FMOP during the period whilst the trade is built up to the expected level.

9. Valuing the Tangible Assets – the Investment Method

9.1 A valuation based on the investment method (capitalising an estimated rental value) may be useful in some cases but as a primary method of valuation in apportionment cases the difficulties and flaws of this method are as follows:

a. arriving at the capital value involves making difficult judgements not only about the FMT/FMOP but also the percentage of profits to adopt as the rental value and the appropriate investment yield, both of which can only be derived from comparison with lettings and sales of other properties at different dates, which significantly increase the scope for disputes over the analysis and comparability of the evidence.

b. the available comparable rental evidence will relate to new lettings of properties that have either not previously been let, have been vacant or have had rent reviews/renewals that disregard the occupation of the property by the tenant and predecessors in title in accordance with s.34 Landlord and Tenant Act 1954.

c. the approach requires the valuer to assume a hypothetical lease is in place which introduces the possibility of a range of hypothetical assumptions as to the nature of the lease and associated terms, each of which could result in a different valuation conclusion.

d. the comparable rental evidence will relate to lettings where the tenant has had to provide the chattels and the return on this capital and risk is reflected in the rents paid.

e. the valuation using this approach represents the value of the property to an investor not an owner-occupier: the RICS GN2, paragraph 8.3, notes that the capitalisation rate adopted for investment valuations differs from that for vacant possession values.

f. the valuation produces a valuation of the property only to which it is then necessary to add a valuation of the chattels. It will not include the premium value to an occupier of acquiring the tangible assets together as a package with the enhanced trading potential due to the established trading history and the ability to continue trading from day one. Isolating the bare property asset may unfairly apportion any premium or share of marriage value away and overstate the intangible elements.

9.2 However, in cases where there are particular difficulties in arriving at a valuation using the profits method the investment method may provide a guide as to the minimum value of the property to an incoming purchaser.

Example

A simple example of the problems with the rental approach may be illustrated by considering a small public house like the one described in paragraph 7.7(a) above:

Say the property was trading at no more than FMT/FMOP level, it had been sold as a going concern for £1m and an analysis of this sale price was say FMOP £125k pa x 8YP (Years Purchase).

For illustration purposes, the rental value on a new letting without chattels may be say £62,500 and an investment yield may be say 8%. This would give a capital value of £781,250 leaving a balance of £218,750. If the in situ value of the chattels was say £50,000 this would leave a sum of £168,750 being attributed to the goodwill when in reality most valuers would agree that the purchaser had acquired nothing of any value beyond the value of the tangible assets. The excess is artificially created because the valuation of the property reflects its notional investment value whereas, just as with some other classes of property, the owner-occupier market is influenced by different factors and the price an owner-occupier may pay is not always the same as an investor.

10. RICS Red Book GN2 - Valuations of the 'Operational Entity'

10.1 As indicated above, when purchasing a business operated from a TRP as a going concern the purchaser will often have obtained a valuation of the tangible assets as an 'operational entity' in accordance with the RICS Red Book GN2 - Valuation of Individual Trade Related Properties. The new GN2 (issued in May 2011) has helpfully clarified some of the areas of uncertainty that existed in the old GN1 that it replaced.

10.2 The guidance makes it clear that a valuation in accordance with GN2 should relate only to the valuation of an individual property valued on the basis of trading potential. The valuation is of the property as a 'place to do business', not a valuation of the actual business itself. Valuations of businesses are covered in separate guidance. GN2 makes it clear that the trading potential of the property should be properly reflected within the property value and that the current operator's goodwill (personal goodwill) is not to be reflected.

10.3 GN2 also makes it clear that the 'operational entity' "usually includes:

- the legal interest in the land and buildings;
- the trade inventory, usually comprising all trade fixtures, fittings, furnishings and equipment; and

- the market's perception of the trading potential, together with an assumed ability to obtain/renew existing licences, consents, certificates and permits."[9]

10.4 Whilst GN2 states that it does not apply to apportionments for tax purposes, HMRC/VOA consider that for the purpose of arriving at the value of goodwill (see paragraph 11.2, Step 2, below), it should normally be acceptable to deduct a GN2 valuation of the 'operational entity' as reflecting the established valuation approach to properties of this nature.

10.5 GN2 provides guidance on the valuation of individual TRPs. When establishing the value of a portfolio of properties (whether they be TRPs or not), it is important to consider whether the sum of individual values would be enhanced by a portfolio premium (see RICS GN3).

11. Apportionment Approach – CGT and SDLT cases

11.1 In CGT and SDLT cases the apportionment of the sale price paid for a business as a going concern should be approached by first identifying the value of any goodwill (and other separately identifiable intangibles assets) along the lines described in paragraphs 6 – 10 above. After deducting this from the total sale price, the in-situ value of the chattels may then be deducted to leave the value of the property.

11.2 In practice, to arrive at the sum attributable to the property, the approach outlined in paragraph 11.1 above will involve the following steps:

Step 1 - Estimate the market value of all the tangible assets together as an operational entity having regard to the guidance above. (See paragraph 11.3 below.)

Step 2 - Identify the sum attributable to goodwill and any other intangible assets included in the sale by deducting the value of the property, licences and chattels (Step 1 value) from the sale price (or market value) of the business as a going concern. (See paragraph 11.4 below.)

Step 3 - Identify the sum attributable to the chattels by estimating their 'in-situ' value (i.e. the value to an incoming purchaser. (See paragraph 11.5 below).

Step 4 - Identify the sum attributable to the property by deducting the value of the chattels (Step 3 value) from the Step 1 value. (See paragraph 11.6 below).

Step 5 - Stand back and consider whether the answer produced is reasonable in the particular circumstances of the case. (See paragraph 11.7 below).

11.3 **Step 1**

[9] © Royal Institution of Chartered Surveyors (RICS)

The market value of the tangible assets should be assessed as at the date of disposal/sale on the basis defined in UKGN3 (Valuations for CGT, IHT and SDLT) reflecting the assumptions in paragraphs 7.2 and 7.4 above. HMRC/VOA consider that, for the purpose of arriving at the value of goodwill, it should normally be acceptable to deduct a GN2 valuation of the 'operational entity'.

In particular the valuation should reflect the following:

a. the market's perception of the trading potential of the property excluding the actual operator's goodwill (and any 'super profits' beyond the expected FMT).

b. the benefit of any transferable licences, consents and certificates. (If any of the licences etc have been lost or are in jeopardy at the valuation date that fact should be reflected in the valuation)[10].

c. all the facts pertaining at the valuation date such as the availability of possession, the fact that the property is fully equipped and ready to trade, the fact that the property was in use up to point of transfer etc.

d. the assumption that any accounts available to the purchaser are available at the valuation date to inform judgments as to reasonable future trading potential.

e. that the purchaser may either bring in their own staff or seek to re-employ some of the existing staff.

f. that the purchaser will take into account the likelihood of any future bookings sticking with the property if they choose to run the business in the same manner as the vendor.

g. that the purchaser will take into account the likelihood of any existing care home residents opting to stay with the property if they choose to run the business in the same manner as the vendor.

11.4 **Step 2**

The sum attributable to goodwill and any other intangible assets included in the sale should be arrived at by deducting the value of the tangible assets (from Step 1 above) from the sale price (or market value) of the business.

11.5 **Step 3**

The sum attributable to any chattels included in the sale should be arrived at by estimating the value of the chattels to an incoming purchaser. The value of the chattels to an incoming purchaser will normally be based on their depreciated replacement cost but in some cases they may be of no value, for example, if the purchaser intends to refit the premises.

[10] Some licences may be a separate asset for CGT purposes

11.6 **Step 4**

The sum attributable to the property should be arrived at by deducting the value of the chattels (the Step 3 value) from the value of the tangible assets (the Step 1 value).

11.7 **Step 5**

Caseworkers should always stand back and consider whether the answer produced by the above approach is reasonable in the particular circumstances of the case. For instance, if a business is sold in an arms length transaction at a price that is significantly in excess of the market value of the business as a going concern it may be appropriate to firstly value the business and then apportion the excess sale price on a pro-rata basis.

<u>Example:</u>

Sale price	=	£600,000
Market value of business	=	£500,000
Property	=	£450,000
Chattels	=	£ 20,000
Goodwill	=	<u>£ 30,000</u> (i.e. £500,000 – (£450,000 + £20,000))
Total	=	<u>£ 500,000</u>

Pro-rata apportionment:

Property	=	450/500 x £600,000	=	£540,000
Chattels	=	20/500 x £600,000	=	£ 24,000
Goodwill	=	30/500 x £600,000	=	<u>£ 36,000</u>
Total			=	<u>£600,000</u>

11.8 A criticism of the above approach may be that it adopts a deduction approach and such an approach was criticised by the High Court in the case of Bostock v Totham (HMIT). However, the above approach does not just consider the value of one element - the taxpayer's approach which was criticised in the Bostock case – but rather it considers the value of all elements on a basis that reflects the contribution of the various elements to the price being apportioned. If one were to value all of the elements in strict isolation then the apportionment may become artificially distorted to the extent that the answer may not be just and reasonable. For instance, the property value in isolation may be less than when it is lotted with the other tangible assets, the value of the chattels if not sold in-situ with the property may be little more than scrap value and any goodwill may be of nominal value if the business is not sold with the property as a going concern.

11.9 Taxpayers may also challenge the above approach based on the Special Commissioner's decision in the case of Balloon Promotions Limited v Wilson (Insp of Taxes) in which it was suggested that goodwill should be looked at as a whole and that the value of adherent goodwill was not automatically subsumed in the property value. The decision of the Special Commissioner in the Balloon case concerned appeals against a refusal to grant rollover relief under S152 of the Taxation of Chargeable Gains Act 1992 in respect of chargeable gains following the sale of the Company's franchised Pizza

Express restaurants to the franchisor. Whilst the decision includes discussion of existing legal authorities dealing with goodwill the conclusions reflect the particular circumstances of the case. It is worth noting that in this case the values of the property interests submitted by the taxpayers were not challenged and there was no evidence to demonstrate whether or not those values included adherent goodwill. As previously mentioned, the subdivisions of goodwill that were previously used are no longer considered helpful as they tend to cause confusion. The view now is that what used to be referred to as 'inherent' and 'adherent' goodwill are, in reality, attributes which add value to the property in which a business is carried on and that they do not represent goodwill at all.

12. Residual Approach – Part 8 CTA 2009 cases

12.1 As noted above (paragraph 2.4), for the purpose of calculating the cost of purchased goodwill Part 8 CTA 2009 provides that 'goodwill' has the meaning it has for accounting purposes. UK GAAP (FRS10 *Goodwill and intangible assets*) provides that 'purchased goodwill' should be taken to be the "difference between the cost of an acquired entity and the aggregate of the fair values of that entity's identifiable assets and liabilities. Positive goodwill arises when the acquisition cost of the entity exceeds the aggregate fair values of the identifiable assets and liabilities. Negative goodwill arises when the aggregate fair values of the identifiable assets and liabilities of the entity exceed the acquisition cost". Thus, purchased goodwill recognised for accounting purposes is a 'residual'[11]. For the avoidance of doubt, purchased goodwill only arises for accounting purposes where there has been a business acquisition (combination).

12.2 UK GAAP (FRS 7 *Fair values in acquisition accounting*) requires fair values to be used in measuring the identifiable assets and liabilities of an acquired business at the date of acquisition and that the identifiable net assets which should be recognised (as forming part of the business combination) to be measured at fair values that reflect conditions at the date of acquisition.

FRS 7, para. 9 requires that the fair value of a tangible fixed asset should be based on:

a. market value, if assets similar in type and condition are bought and sold on an open market [as here]; or

b. depreciated replacement cost [generally not applicable here].

12.3 In determining what is meant by 'market value' within FRS 7, FRS 15 (*Tangible fixed assets*) is instructive, paragraphs 53 and 56 in particular (notwithstanding they are in the section of the standard dealing with revalued properties). FRS 15 is authoritative literature which explains what is meant by 'market value' in the context of valuing property. Paragraph 85 also provides support that for TRPs trading potential is reflected within the value of, and is inseparable from, the property.

[11] IFRS 3, (Appendix A) defines goodwill as; "[a]n asset representing the future economic benefits arising from other assets acquired in a business combination that are not individually identified and separately recognised".

- FRS 15, para. 53 (inter alia) states:

  "The following valuation bases should be used for revalued properties that are not impaired:
  (a) non-specialised properties should be valued on the basis of existing use value (EUV) …".

- FRS 15, para. 56 states:

  "Certain types of non-specialised properties are bought and sold, and therefore valued, as businesses. The EUV of a property valued as an operational entity is determined by having regard to trading potential, but excludes personal goodwill that has been created in the business by the present owner or management and is not expected to remain with the business in the event of the property being sold".

- FRS 15, para. 85 states:

  "It would not be appropriate, however, to treat the trading potential associated with a property that is valued as an operational entity, such as a public house or hotel, as a separate component where the value and life of any such trading potential is inherently inseparable from that of the property".

Therefore, for non-specialised properties (which include TRPs), HMRC considers the use of an EUV basis of valuation is required by UK GAAP in the context of the fair value exercise in a business acquisition.

Furthermore, there is support for using EUV to determine the fair value of non-specialised properties in PwC's Manual of accounting (UK GAAP). This, inter alia, states that "in acquisition accounting, properties that would normally be valued under the alternative accounting rules [i.e. within the revaluation option within FRS 15[12]] on an existing use value basis in the acquired company's financial statements (that is those occupied for the purpose of the business) would also usually be valued on this basis in the fair value exercise"[13].

Although PwC add that "there may be some confusion as to what market value means… The most commonly used bases are market value and existing use value"[14], they go on to comment that "existing use value is the basis normally used for valuing properties that are occupied in the company's business …"[15].

12.4 For companies preparing accounts under IFRS[16], the relevant accounting standards are IFRS 3 (*Business Combinations*), IFRS 13 (*Fair Value Measurement*) and IAS 16 (*Property, Plant and Equipment*). In general, though in particular circumstances there may be exceptions (e.g. market value and fair value may not be the same), it is not considered likely in relation to TRPs there will be substantial differences between accounts drawn up under

[12] HMRC comment within parentheses.
[13] 2012 edition, see paragraph 25.267.
[14] 2012 edition, see paragraph 25.262.
[15] 2012 edition, see paragraph 25.265.
[16] International Financial Reporting Standards.

UK GAAP and IFRS (unless, in IFRS, market or other factors suggest that a different use by market participants would maximise the value of the asset).

12.5 'Negative goodwill' (i.e. a gain resulting from a bargain purchase) can arise, under both UK GAAP and IFRS. Within UK GAAP, negative goodwill is carried on the balance sheet and recognised in the profit and loss account in the periods in which non-monetary assets are recovered (by depreciation or disposal) or in which the benefits are expected to be realised. Within IFRS, however, the gain resulting from a bargain purchase is recognised in profit or loss on the acquisition date.

12.6 In HMRC's view, for TRPs, the EUV of the tangible assets required for the purpose of calculating the cost of purchased goodwill under Part 8 CTA 2009 will normally be represented by the market value of the assets as an operational entity, in accordance with the guidance contained in the RICS GN2.

13. Leasehold Interests

13.1 In some cases it will be necessary to apportion the price paid for a leasehold interest but the same principles apply. The valuations and apportionment should be approached using the same assumptions and approach described above.

13.2 It should be borne in mind that for TRPs it is not uncommon for leasehold interests to be sold for substantial premiums even when the rent has recently been reviewed. The premium in such cases may be attributable to any or all of the following:

a. The reviewed rent may not reflect the full rental value because it may disregard the enhanced trading potential attributable to the occupation of the property by the tenant and predecessors (in accordance with s.34 LTA 1954).

b. The reviewed rent may not reflect the value of improvements carried out by the tenant or predecessors when fitting out the property (in some cases the rent may only represent a shell rent).

c. The value of the chattels and fittings belonging to the tenant.

d. The premium value to an occupier of offering the tangible assets together as a package with the enhanced trading potential due to the established trading history and the ability to continue trading from day one.

e. There may be some element of goodwill, particularly if the business is trading at above FMT level and contracts of some value are included in the sale.

f. There may be other separately identifiable intangible assets included in the sale (eg. registered trade marks).

g. Market perception and prevailing conditions whereby it is expected there will be some 'key money' or premium to acquire the interest in order to move in to this market sector or specific trading location.

13.3 The value of any goodwill and other intangible assets included in the sale should be determined by adopting the same valuation assumptions and approach outlined in paragraphs 7 and 8 above.

14. Examples

14.1 Examples illustrating the application of the approaches outlined in paragraphs 11 and 12 above are set out in Appendix 1.

APPENDIX 1

Examples

All the figures used in the examples below are for illustrative purposes only.

Example 1

The Facts

A owns and runs a public house. The business has been struggling for some years because the owner is nearing retirement and has lost interest in the business. The level of trade has fallen over the last 2 years and profit margins are low because wage costs are higher than would be expected due to overstaffing.

The Figures

The salient figures are as follows:-

- FMT – the actual trade based on an average of the last two years accounts is only £445k pa but the estimated FMT (assuming a reasonably efficient operator[17]) is £500k pa.
- FMOP – the actual operating profit is only £70k pa but the estimated FMOP[18], reflecting lower wage costs, is £125k pa.
- The business has been sold as a going concern for £875k. This price reflects the potential to increase the trade up to the FMOP level but also the possible delay before this level of trade could be achieved.
- The chattels are included in the accounts at a net book value of £25k but their market value to an incoming purchaser would be £35k.
- The market value of the property as an operational entity is £875k. This is based on a FMOP of £125k pa x 7 Years Purchase (YP).
- The market value of the property based on 'special assumptions' is £450k (this assumes that the property has been empty and closed for 6 months, no trading accounts are available, the chattels have all been removed, the licences have been lost and a sale is required within 180 days).
- The purchaser claims that the sum that should be attributed to goodwill is the purchase price less the separate values of the property (assuming it to be empty etc) and the chattels, ie. £875k – (£450k + £25k) = £400k.

Apportionment for SDLT Purposes

[17] 'Reasonably efficient operator' is defined as "a concept where the valuer assumes that the market participants are competent (but not exceptional) operators, acting in an efficient manner, of a business conducted on the premises. It involves estimating the trading potential rather than adopting the actual level of trade under the existing ownership". (© Royal Institution of Chartered Surveyors).

[18] 'Fair Maintainable Operating Profit (FMOP)' is defined as "the level of profit, stated prior to depreciation and finance costs relating to the asset itself (and rent if leasehold), that the reasonably efficient operator (REO) would expect to derive from the fair maintainable turnover (FMT) based on an assessment of the market's perception of the potential earnings of the property. It should reflect all costs and outgoings of the REO, as well as an appropriate annual allowance for periodic expenditure, such as decoration, refurbishment and renewal of the trade inventory" (© Royal Institution of Chartered Surveyors).

The HMRC/VOA approach to the apportionment required for SDLT purposes would be as follows:

- The value of the goodwill, reflecting its value when sold with the property, is the sale price paid for the business as a going concern less the value of all the tangible assets as an operational entity. In this case that would be £875k - £875k = nil. However, as the business has been sold as a going concern something needs to be apportioned to goodwill so a nominal sum of £1 is adopted, leaving a net sale price of £874,999.
- The sum attributed to the property is in this case the net sale price (£874,999) less the value of the chattels, reflecting their value when sold with the property (£35k), which is £839,999.

Calculation of Goodwill Figure for Relief Under Part 8 CTA 2009

The HMRC/VOA approach to the calculation of the sum paid for goodwill for the purposes of relief under Part 8 CTA 2009 would be as follows:

- Price paid for the going concern less the value of the tangible assets as an operational entity, ie. £875k - £875k = nil.

Example 2

The Facts

B owns and runs a public house. The business has been exceptionally well run for a number of years. The level of trade and profits are much higher than would be expected for a similar pub in this location.

The Figures

The salient figures are as follows:-

- FMT – the actual trade based on an average of the last two years accounts is £600k pa but the estimated FMT (assuming a reasonably efficient operator) is only £500k pa.
- FMOP – the actual operating profit is £180k pa but the estimated FMOP, reflecting typical profit margins, is only £125k pa.
- The business has been sold as a going concern for £1.1m. This price reflects the purchaser's belief that they can continue to operate the business in the same manner as the vendor and sustain at least a proportion of the exceptional actual level of profits.
- The chattels are included in the accounts at a net book value of £25k but their market value to an incoming purchaser would be £40k.
- The market value of the property as an operational entity (excluding exceptional profits) is £950k. This is based on a FMOP of £125k pa x 7.6 Years Purchase (YP) based on evidence of other sales and reflecting a sustainable volume of trade for the property.
- The market value of the property based on 'special assumptions' is £550k (this assumes that the property has been empty for 6 months, no trading accounts are available, the chattels have all been removed, the licences have been lost and a sale is required within 180 days).

- The purchaser claims that the sum that should be attributed to goodwill is the purchase price less the separate values of the property (assuming it to be empty etc) and the chattels, ie. £1.1m – (£550k + £25k) = £525k.

Apportionment for SDLT Purposes

The HMRC/VOA approach to the apportionment required for SDLT purposes would be as follows:

- The value of the goodwill, reflecting its value when sold with the property, is the sale price paid for the business as a going concern less the value of all the tangible assets as an operational entity. In this case that would be £1.1m - £950k = £150k.
- The sum attributed to the property is in this case the value of the tangible assets as an operational entity (£950k) less the value of the chattels, reflecting their value when sold with the property (£35k), which is £915k.

Calculation of Goodwill Figure for Relief Under Part 8 CTA 2009

The HMRC/VOA approach to the calculation of the sum paid for goodwill for the purposes of relief under Part 8 CTA 2009 would be as follows:

- Price paid for the going concern less the value of the tangible assets as an operational entity, ie. £1.1m - £950k = £150k.

Example 3

The Facts

A owns and runs a modern residential care home. The business has been run in a reasonably efficient but not exceptional manner for a number of years. The occupancy rate, fees and level of profits are what would be expected for a similar residential care home in this location.

The Figures

The salient figures are as follows:-

- FMT – the actual trade based on an average of the last two years accounts is £935k pa and this accords with the valuers estimate of FMT (assuming a reasonably efficient operator)
- FMOP – the actual operating profit is £330k pa and the estimated FMOP is also £330k pa.
- The business has been sold as a going concern for £2.3m. This price reflects the purchaser's belief that they can continue to operate the business in the same manner as the vendor and maintain the actual level of trade. This is based on the actual operating profit of £330k pa x 7 Years Purchase (YP).
- The chattels are included in the accounts at a net book value of £75k and their market value to an incoming purchaser would be £75k.
- The market value of the property as an operational entity is £2.2m. This is based on a FMOP of £330k pa x 6.7 Years Purchase (YP). The YP reflects the risk that on a change of ownership some residents and staff may choose to move elsewhere and there may therefore be some delay before the full FMOP is achieved.

- The market value of the property based on 'special assumptions' is £1.4m (this assumes that the property has been closed for 3 months, no trading accounts are available, the chattels have all been removed, the licences have been lost and a sale is required within 180 days).
- The purchaser claims that the sum that should be attributed to goodwill is the purchase price less the separate values of the property (assuming it to be empty etc) and the chattels, ie. £2.3m – (£1.4m + £75k) = £825k.

Apportionment for SDLT Purposes

The HMRC/VOA approach to the apportionment required for SDLT purposes would be as follows:

- The value of the goodwill, reflecting its value when sold with the property, is the sale price paid for the business as a going concern less the value of all the tangible assets as an operational entity. In this case that would be £2.3m - £2.2m = £100k.
- The sum attributed to the property is in this case the value of the tangible assets as an operational entity (£2.2m) less the value of the chattels, reflecting their value when sold with the property (£75k), which is £2.125m.

Calculation of Goodwill Figure for Relief Under Part 8 CTA 2009

The HMRC/VOA approach to the calculation of the sum paid for goodwill for the purposes of relief under Part 8 CTA 2009 would be as follows:

- Price paid for the going concern less the value of the tangible assets as an operational entity, ie. £2.3m - £2.2m = £100k.

Example 4

The Facts

B owns and runs a modern residential care home. The business has been very well run for a number of years with the owner working all hours. Whilst the occupancy rates, fees and level of profits are all higher than would be expected for a similar residential care home in this location, wage costs are lower than considered appropriate.

The Figures

The salient figures are as follows:-

- FMT – the actual trade based on an average of the last two years accounts is £950k pa but the estimated FMT is only £900k pa.
- FMOP – the actual operating profit is £400k pa but the estimated FMOP is only £330k pa.
- The business has been sold as a going concern for £2.525 m. This price reflects the purchaser's belief that they can continue to operate the business in the same exceptional manner as the vendor and maintain the actual level of occupancy, fees and profits. This is based on the actual operating profit of £400k pa x 6.3 Years Purchase (YP).
- The chattels are included in the accounts at a net book value of £50k and their market value to an incoming purchaser would be £50k.

- The market value of the property as an operational entity is £2.3m. This is based on a FMOP of £330k pa x 6.95 Years Purchase (YP). The YP reflects the risk that on a change of ownership some residents and staff may choose to move elsewhere and there may therefore be some delay before the full FMOP is achieved.
- The market value of the property based on 'special assumptions' is £1.575m (this assumes that the property has been closed for 3 months, no trading accounts are available, the chattels have all been removed, the licences have been lost and a sale is required within 180 days).
- The purchaser claims that the sum that should be attributed to goodwill is the purchase price less the separate values of the property (assuming it to be empty etc) and the chattels, ie. £2.525m – (£1.575m + 50k) = £1m.

<u>Apportionment for SDLT Purposes</u>

The HMRC/VOA approach to the apportionment required for SDLT purposes would be as follows:

- The value of the goodwill, reflecting its value when sold with the property, is the sale price paid for the business as a going concern less the value of all the tangible assets as an operational entity. In this case that would be £2.525m - £2.3m = £225k.
- The sum attributed to the property is in this case the value of the tangible assets as an operational entity (£2.3m) less the value of the chattels, reflecting their value when sold with the property (£50k), which is £2.25m.

<u>Calculation of Goodwill Figure for Relief Under Part 8 CTA 2009</u>

The HMRC/VOA approach to the calculation of the sum paid for goodwill for the purposes of relief under Part 8 CTA 2009 would be as follows:

- Price paid for the going concern less the value of the tangible assets as an operational entity, ie. £2.525m - £2.3m = £225k.

Appendix H

Civil Procedure Rules, Part 35 (Experts and Assessors), Practice Direction 35 and Factsheet 53

Duty to restrict expert evidence

35.1 Expert evidence shall be restricted to that which is reasonably required to resolve the proceedings.

Interpretation and definitions

35.2

(1) A reference to an 'expert' in this Part is a reference to a person who has been instructed to give or prepare expert evidence for the purpose of proceedings.

(2) 'Single joint expert' means an expert instructed to prepare a report for the court on behalf of two or more of the parties (including the claimant) to the proceedings.

Experts – overriding duty to the court

35.3

(1) It is the duty of experts to help the court on matters within their expertise.

(2) This duty overrides any obligation to the person from whom experts have received instructions or by whom they are paid.

Court's power to restrict expert evidence

35.4

(1) No party may call an expert or put in evidence an expert's report without the court's permission.

(2) When parties apply for permission they must provide an estimate of the costs of the proposed expert evidence and identify –
  (a) the field in which expert evidence is required and the issues which the expert evidence will address; and
  (b) where practicable, the name of the proposed expert.

(3) If permission is granted it shall be in relation only to the expert named or the field identified under paragraph (2). The order granting permission may specify the issues which the expert evidence should address.

(3A) Where a claim has been allocated to the small claims track or the fast track, if permission is given for expert evidence, it will normally be given for evidence from only one expert on a particular issue.

(3B) In a soft tissue injury claim, permission –
  (a) may normally only be given for one expert medical report;
  (b) may not be given initially unless the medical report is a fixed cost medical report. Where the claimant seeks permission to obtain a further medical report, if the report is from a medical expert in any of the following disciplines –
    (i) Consultant Orthopaedic Surgeon;
    (ii) Consultant in Accident and Emergency Medicine;
    (iii) General Practitioner registered with the General Medical Council; or
    (iv) Physiotherapist registered with the Health and Care Professions Council, the report must be a fixed cost medical report.

(3C) In this rule, 'fixed cost medical report' and 'soft tissue injury claim' have the same meaning as in paragraph 1.1(10A) and (16A), respectively, of the RTA Protocol.

(Paragraph 7 of Practice Direction 35 sets out some of the circumstances the court will consider when deciding whether expert evidence should be given by a single joint expert.)

(4) The court may limit the amount of a party's expert's fees and expenses that may be recovered from any other party.

General requirement for expert evidence to be given in a written report

35.5

(1) Expert evidence is to be given in a written report unless the court directs otherwise.

(2) If a claim is on the small claims track or the fast track, the court will not direct an expert to attend a hearing unless it is necessary to do so in the interests of justice.

Written questions to experts

35.6

(1) A party may put written questions about an expert's report (which must be proportionate) to –

(a) an expert instructed by another party; or
(b) a single joint expert appointed under rule 35.7.

(2) Written questions under paragraph (1) –
(a) may be put once only;
(b) must be put within 28 days of service of the expert's report; and
(c) must be for the purpose only of clarification of the report,
unless in any case –
(i) the court gives permission; or
(ii) the other party agrees.

(3) An expert's answers to questions put in accordance with paragraph (1) shall be treated as part of the expert's report.

(4) Where –
(a) a party has put a written question to an expert instructed by another party; and
(b) the expert does not answer that question,
the court may make one or both of the following orders in relation to the party who instructed the expert –
(i) that the party may not rely on the evidence of that expert; or
(ii) that the party may not recover the fees and expenses of that expert from any other party.

Court's power to direct that evidence is to be given by a single joint expert

35.7

(1) Where two or more parties wish to submit expert evidence on a particular issue, the court may direct that the evidence on that issue is to be given by a single joint expert.

(2) Where the parties who wish to submit the evidence ('the relevant parties') cannot agree who should be the single joint expert, the court may –
(a) select the expert from a list prepared or identified by the relevant parties; or
(b) direct that the expert be selected in such other manner as the court may direct.

Instructions to a single joint expert

35.8

(1) Where the court gives a direction under rule 35.7 for a single joint expert to be used, any relevant party may give instructions to the expert.

(2) When a party gives instructions to the expert that party must, at the same time, send a copy to the other relevant parties.

(3) The court may give directions about –
(a) the payment of the expert's fees and expenses; and
(b) any inspection, examination or experiments which the expert wishes to carry out.

(4) The court may, before an expert is instructed –
  (a) limit the amount that can be paid by way of fees and expenses to the expert; and
  (b) direct that some or all of the relevant parties pay that amount into court.
(5) Unless the court otherwise directs, the relevant parties are jointly and severally liable for the payment of the expert's fees and expenses.

Power of court to direct a party to provide information

35.9 Where a party has access to information which is not reasonably available to another party, the court may direct the party who has access to the information to –
(a) prepare and file a document recording the information; and
(b) serve a copy of that document on the other party.

Contents of report

35.10
(1) An expert's report must comply with the requirements set out in Practice Direction 35.
(2) At the end of an expert's report there must be a statement that the expert understands and has complied with their duty to the court.
(3) The expert's report must state the substance of all material instructions, whether written or oral, on the basis of which the report was written.
(4) The instructions referred to in paragraph (3) shall not be privileged against disclosure but the court will not, in relation to those instructions –
  (a) order disclosure of any specific document; or
  (b) permit any questioning in court, other than by the party who instructed the expert,

  unless it is satisfied that there are reasonable grounds to consider the statement of instructions given under paragraph (3) to be inaccurate or incomplete.

Use by one party of expert's report disclosed by another

35.11 Where a party has disclosed an expert's report, any party may use that expert's report as evidence at the trial.

Discussions between experts

35.12
(1) The court may, at any stage, direct a discussion between experts for the purpose of requiring the experts to –
  (a) identify and discuss the expert issues in the proceedings; and
  (b) where possible, reach an agreed opinion on those issues.

(2) The court may specify the issues which the experts must discuss.
(3) The court may direct that following a discussion between the experts they must prepare a statement for the court setting out those issues on which –
  (a) they agree; and
  (b) they disagree, with a summary of their reasons for disagreeing.
(4) The content of the discussion between the experts shall not be referred to at the trial unless the parties agree.
(5) Where experts reach agreement on an issue during their discussions, the agreement shall not bind the parties unless the parties expressly agree to be bound by the agreement.

Consequence of failure to disclose expert's report

35.13 A party who fails to disclose an expert's report may not use the report at the trial or call the expert to give evidence orally unless the court gives permission.

Expert's right to ask court for directions

35.14
(1) Experts may file written requests for directions for the purpose of assisting them in carrying out their functions.
(2) Experts must, unless the court orders otherwise, provide copies of the proposed requests for directions under paragraph (1) –
  (a) to the party instructing them, at least 7 days before they file the requests; and
  (b) to all other parties, at least 4 days before they file them.
(3) The court, when it gives directions, may also direct that a party be served with a copy of the directions.

Assessors

35.15
(1) This rule applies where the court appoints one or more persons under section 70 of the Senior Courts Act 19811 or section 63 of the County Courts Act 19842 as an assessor.
(2) An assessor will assist the court in dealing with a matter in which the assessor has skill and experience.
(3) An assessor will take such part in the proceedings as the court may direct and in particular the court may direct an assessor to –
  (a) prepare a report for the court on any matter at issue in the proceedings; and
  (b) attend the whole or any part of the trial to advise the court on any such matter.
(4) If an assessor prepares a report for the court before the trial has begun –
  (a) the court will send a copy to each of the parties; and
  (b) the parties may use it at trial.

(5) The remuneration to be paid to an assessor is to be determined by the court and will form part of the costs of the proceedings.
(6) The court may order any party to deposit in the court office a specified sum in respect of an assessor's fees and, where it does so, the assessor will not be asked to act until the sum has been deposited.
(7) Paragraphs (5) and (6) do not apply where the remuneration of the assessor is to be paid out of money provided by Parliament.

Footnotes
1 1981 c 54.
2 1984 c.28.

PRACTICE DIRECTION 35 EXPERTS AND ASSESSORS

This Practice Direction supplements CPR Part 35

Introduction

1 Part 35 is intended to limit the use of oral expert evidence to that which is reasonably required. In addition, where possible, matters requiring expert evidence should be dealt with by only one expert. Experts and those instructing them are expected to have regard to the guidance contained in the Guidance for the Instruction of Experts in Civil Claims 2018 at www.judiciary.gov.uk. (Further guidance on experts is contained in Annex C to the Practice Direction (Pre-Action Conduct)).

Expert Evidence – General Requirements

2.1 Expert evidence should be the independent product of the expert uninfluenced by the pressures of litigation.
2.2 Experts should assist the court by providing objective, unbiased opinions on matters within their expertise, and should not assume the role of an advocate.
2.3 Experts should consider all material facts, including those which might detract from their opinions.
2.4 Experts should make it clear –
   (a) when a question or issue falls outside their expertise; and
   (b) when they are not able to reach a definite opinion, for example because they have insufficient information.
2.5 If, after producing a report, an expert's view changes on any material matter, such change of view should be communicated to all the parties without delay, and when appropriate to the court.
2.6
   (1) In a soft tissue injury claim, where permission is given for a fixed cost medical report, the first report must be obtained from an accredited medical expert selected via the MedCo Portal (website at: www.medco.org.uk).

(2) The cost of obtaining a further report from an expert not listed in rule 35.4(3C)(a) to (d) is not subject to rules 45.19(2A)(b) or 45.29I(2A)(b), but the use of that expert and the cost must be justified.

(3) 'Accredited medical expert', 'fixed cost medical report', 'MedCo', and 'soft tissue injury claim' have the same meaning as in paragraph 1.1(A1), (10A), (12A) and (16A), respectively, of the RTA Protocol.

Form and Content of an Expert's Report

3.1 An expert's report should be addressed to the court and not to the party from whom the expert has received instructions.

3.2 An expert's report must:

(1) give details of the expert's qualifications;

(2) give details of any literature or other material which has been relied on in making the report;

(3) contain a statement setting out the substance of all facts and instructions which are material to the opinions expressed in the report or upon which those opinions are based;

(4) make clear which of the facts stated in the report are within the expert's own knowledge;

(5) say who carried out any examination, measurement, test or experiment which the expert has used for the report, give the qualifications of that person, and say whether or not the test or experiment has been carried out under the expert's supervision;

(6) where there is a range of opinion on the matters dealt with in the report –

(a) summarise the range of opinions; and

(b) give reasons for the expert's own opinion;

(7) contain a summary of the conclusions reached;

(8) if the expert is not able to give an opinion without qualification, state the qualification; and

(9) contain a statement that the expert –

(a) understands their duty to the court, and has complied with that duty; and

(b) is aware of the requirements of Part 35, this practice direction and the Guidance for the Instruction of Experts in Civil Claims 2018.

3.3 An expert's report must be verified by a statement of truth in the following form –

'I confirm that I have made clear which facts and matters referred to in this report are within my own knowledge and which are not. Those that are within my own knowledge I confirm to be true. The opinions I have expressed represent my true and complete professional opinions on the matters to which they refer.'

(Part 22 deals with statements of truth. Rule 32.14 sets out the consequences of verifying a document containing a false statement without an honest belief in its truth.)

Information

4 Under rule 35.9 the court may direct a party with access to information, which is not reasonably available to another party to serve on that other party a document, which records the information. The document served must include sufficient details of all the facts, tests, experiments and assumptions which underlie any part of the information to enable the party on whom it is served to make, or to obtain, a proper interpretation of the information and an assessment of its significance.

Instructions

5 Cross-examination of experts on the contents of their instructions will not be allowed unless the court permits it (or unless the party who gave the instructions consents). Before it gives permission the court must be satisfied that there are reasonable grounds to consider that the statement in the report of the substance of the instructions is inaccurate or incomplete. If the court is so satisfied, it will allow the cross-examination where it appears to be in the interests of justice.

Questions to Experts

6.1 Where a party sends a written question or questions under rule 35.6 direct to an expert, a copy of the questions must, at the same time, be sent to the other party or parties.

6.2 The party or parties instructing the expert must pay any fees charged by that expert for answering questions put under rule 35.6. This does not affect any decision of the court as to the party who is ultimately to bear the expert's fees.

Single joint expert

7 When considering whether to give permission for the parties to rely on expert evidence and whether that evidence should be from a single joint expert the court will take into account all the circumstances in particular, whether:

(a) it is proportionate to have separate experts for each party on a particular issue with reference to –
   (i) the amount in dispute;
   (ii) the importance to the parties; and
   (iii) the complexity of the issue;

(b) the instruction of a single joint expert is likely to assist the parties and the court to resolve the issue more speedily and in a more cost-effective way than separately instructed experts;

(c) expert evidence is to be given on the issue of liability, causation or quantum;

(d) the expert evidence falls within a substantially established area of knowledge which is unlikely to be in dispute or there is likely to be a range of expert opinion;
(e) a party has already instructed an expert on the issue in question and whether or not that was done in compliance with any practice direction or relevant pre-action protocol;
(f) questions put in accordance with rule 35.6 are likely to remove the need for the other party to instruct an expert if one party has already instructed an expert;
(g) questions put to a single joint expert may not conclusively deal with all issues that may require testing prior to trial;
(h) a conference may be required with the legal representatives, experts and other witnesses which may make instruction of a single joint expert impractical; and
(i) a claim to privilege (GL) makes the instruction of any expert as a single joint expert inappropriate.

Orders

8 Where an order requires an act to be done by an expert, or otherwise affects an expert, the party instructing that expert must serve a copy of the order on the expert. The claimant must serve the order on a single joint expert.

Discussions between experts

9.1 Unless directed by the court discussions between experts are not mandatory. Parties must consider, with their experts, at an early stage, whether there is likely to be any useful purpose in holding an experts' discussion and if so when.

9.2 The purpose of discussions between experts is not for experts to settle cases but to agree and narrow issues and in particular to identify:
(i) the extent of the agreement between them;
(ii) the points of and short reasons for any disagreement;
(iii) action, if any, which may be taken to resolve any outstanding points of disagreement; and
(iv) any further material issues not raised and the extent to which these issues are agreed.

9.3 Where the experts are to meet, the parties must discuss and if possible agree whether an agenda is necessary, and if so attempt to agree one that helps the experts to focus on the issues which need to be discussed. The agenda must not be in the form of leading questions or hostile in tone.

9.4 Unless ordered by the court, or agreed by all parties, and the experts, neither the parties nor their legal representatives may attend experts' discussions.

9.5 If the legal representatives do attend –
(i) they should not normally intervene in the discussion, except to answer questions put to them by the experts or to advise on the law; and

(ii) the experts may if they so wish hold part of their discussions in the absence of the legal representatives.

9.6 A statement must be prepared by the experts dealing with paragraphs 9.2(i)–(iv) above. Individual copies of the statements must be signed by the experts at the conclusion of the discussion, or as soon thereafter as practicable, and in any event within 7 days. Copies of the statements must be provided to the parties no later than 14 days after signing.

9.7 Experts must give their own opinions to assist the court and do not require the authority of the parties to sign a joint statement.

9.8 If an expert significantly alters an opinion, the joint statement must include a note or addendum by that expert explaining the change of opinion.

Assessors

10.1 An assessor may be appointed to assist the court under rule 35.15. Not less than 21 days before making any such appointment, the court will notify each party in writing of the name of the proposed assessor, of the matter in respect of which the assistance of the assessor will be sought and of the qualifications of the assessor to give that assistance.

10.2 Where any person has been proposed for appointment as an assessor, any party may object to that person either personally or in respect of that person's qualification.

10.3 Any such objection must be made in writing and filed with the court within 7 days of receipt of the notification referred to in paragraph 10.1 and will be taken into account by the court in deciding whether or not to make the appointment.

10.4 Copies of any report prepared by the assessor will be sent to each of the parties but the assessor will not give oral evidence or be open to cross-examination or questioning.

Concurrent expert evidence

11.1 At any stage in the proceedings the court may direct that some or all of the evidence of experts from like disciplines shall be given concurrently. The procedure set out in paragraph 11.4 shall apply in respect of any part of the evidence which is to be given concurrently.

11.2 To the extent that the expert evidence is not to be given concurrently, the court may direct the evidence to be given in any appropriate manner. This may include a direction for the experts from like disciplines to give their evidence and be cross-examined on an issue-by-issue basis, so that each party calls its expert or experts to give evidence in relation to a particular issue, followed by the other parties calling their expert or experts to give evidence in relation to that issue (and so on for each of the expert issues which are to be addressed in this manner).

11.3 The court may set an agenda for the taking of expert evidence concurrently or on an issue-by-issue basis, or may direct that the parties agree such an agenda subject to the approval of the court. In either case, the agenda should be based upon the areas of disagreement identified in the experts' joint statements made pursuant to rule 35.12.

11.4 Where expert evidence is to be given concurrently, then (after the relevant experts have each taken the oath or affirmed) in relation to each issue on the agenda, and subject to the judge's discretion to modify the procedure–

(1) the judge will initiate the discussion by asking the experts, in turn, for their views in relation to the issues on the agenda. Once an expert has expressed a view the judge may ask questions about it. At one or more appropriate stages when questioning a particular expert, the judge may invite the other expert to comment or to ask that expert's own questions of the first expert;

(2) after the process set out in (1) has been completed for any issue (or all issues), the judge will invite the parties' representatives to ask questions of the experts. Such questioning should be directed towards:

(a) testing the correctness of an expert's view;

(b) seeking clarification of an expert's view; or

(c) eliciting evidence on any issue (or on any aspect of an issue) which has been omitted from consideration during the process set out in (1); and

(3) after the process set out in (2) has been completed in relation to any issue (or all issues), the judge may summarise the experts' different positions on the issue and ask them to confirm or correct that summary.

Factsheet 53: Guidance for the instruction of experts in civil claims

Last reviewed: April 2018

This guidance began life in 2005 (amended 2009) as the *Protocol for the Instruction of Experts to give Evidence in Civil Claims*. It was created when the Civil Justice Council took the initiative to establish a single, authoritative set of guidance for expert witnesses working under the Civil Procedure Rules (CPR) in England and Wales. It has now evolved into *Guidance for the instruction of experts in civil claims*, and this revision came into force on 1 December 2014 (see https://www.judiciary.gov.uk/related-offices-and-bodies/advisory-bodies/cjc/cjc-publications/guidance-for-the-instruction-of-experts-in-civil-claims).

Guidance

Introduction

1. The purpose of this guidance is to assist litigants, those instructing experts and experts to understand best practice in complying with Part 35 of the Civil Procedure Rules (CPR) and court orders. Experts and those who instruct them should ensure they are familiar with CPR 35 and the Practice Direction (PD35). This guidance replaces the Protocol for the instruction of experts in civil claims (2005, amended 2009).

2. Those instructing experts, and the experts, must also have regard to the objectives underpinning the Pre-Action Protocols to:
(a) encourage the exchange of early and full information about the expert issues involved in the prospective claim;
(b) enable the parties to avoid or reduce the scope of the litigation by agreeing the whole or part of an expert issue before proceedings are started; and
(c) support the efficient management of proceedings where litigation cannot be avoided.

3. Additionally, experts and those instructing them should be aware that some cases will be governed by the specific pre-action protocols and some may be 'specialist proceedings' (CPR 49) where specific rules may apply.

Selecting and Instructing Experts

The need for experts

4. Those intending to instruct experts to give or prepare evidence for the purpose of civil proceedings should consider whether expert evidence is necessary, taking account of the principles set out in CPR Parts 1 and 35, and in particular whether 'it is required to resolve the proceedings' (CPR 35.1).

5. Although the court's permission is not generally required to instruct an expert, the court's permission is required before an expert's report can be relied upon or an expert can be called to give oral evidence (CPR 35.4).

6. Advice from an expert before proceedings are started which the parties do not intend to rely upon in litigation is likely to be confidential; this guidance does not apply then. The same applies where, after the commencement of proceedings, experts are instructed only to advise (e.g. to comment upon a single joint expert's report) and not to prepare evidence for the proceedings. The expert's role then is that of an expert advisor.

7. However this guidance does apply if experts who were formerly instructed only to advise, are later instructed as an expert witness to prepare or give evidence in the proceedings.

8. In the remainder of this guidance, a reference to an expert means an expert witness to whom Part 35 applies.

Duties and obligations of experts

9. Experts always owe a duty to exercise reasonable skill and care to those instructing them, and to comply with any relevant professional code. However when they are instructed to give or prepare evidence for civil proceedings they have an overriding duty to help the court on matters within their expertise (CPR 35.3). This duty overrides any obligation to the person instructing or paying them. Experts must not serve the exclusive interest of those who retain them.

10. Experts should be aware of the overriding objective that courts deal with cases justly and that they are under an obligation to assist the court in this respect. This includes dealing with cases proportionately (keeping the work and costs in proportion to the value and importance of the case to the parties), expeditiously and fairly (CPR 1.1).

11. Experts must provide opinions that are independent, regardless of the pressures of litigation. A useful test of 'independence' is that the expert would express the same opinion if given the same instructions by another party. Experts should not take it upon themselves to promote the point of view of the party instructing them or engage in the role of advocates or mediators.

12. Experts should confine their opinions to matters which are material to the disputes and provide opinions only in relation to matters which lie within their expertise. Experts should indicate without delay where particular questions or issues fall outside their expertise.

13. Experts should take into account all material facts before them. Their reports should set out those facts and any literature or material on which they have relied in forming their opinions. They should indicate if an opinion is provisional, or qualified, or where they consider that further information is required or if, for any other reason, they are not satisfied that an opinion can be expressed finally and without qualification.

14. Experts should inform those instructing them without delay of any change in their opinions on any material matter and the reasons for this (see also paragraphs 64–66).

15. Experts should be aware that any failure to comply with the rules or court orders, or any excessive delay for which they are responsible, may result in the parties who instructed them being penalised in costs, or debarred from relying upon the expert evidence (see also paragraphs 89–92).

The appointment of experts

16. Before experts are instructed or the court's permission to appoint named experts is sought, it should be established whether the experts:

(a) have the appropriate expertise and experience for the particular instruction;
(b) are familiar with the general duties of an expert;
(c) can produce a report, deal with questions and have discussions with other experts within a reasonable time, and at a cost proportionate to the matters in issue;
(d) are available to attend the trial, if attendance is required; and
(e) have no potential conflict of interest.

17. Terms of appointment should be agreed at the outset and should normally include:
(a) the capacity in which the expert is to be appointed (e.g. party appointed expert or single joint expert);
(b) the services required of the expert (e.g. provision of an expert's report, answering questions in writing, attendance at meetings and attendance at court);
(c) time for delivery of the report;
(d) the basis of the expert's charges (e.g. daily or hourly rates and an estimate of the time likely to be required, or a fixed fee for the services). Parties must provide an estimate to the court of the costs of the proposed expert evidence and for each stage of the proceedings (R 35.4(2));
(e) travelling expenses and disbursements;
(f) cancellation charges;
(g) any fees for attending court;
(h) time for making the payment;
(i) whether fees are to be paid by a third party;
(j) if a party is publicly funded, whether the expert's charges will be subject to assessment; and
(k) guidance that the expert's fees and expenses may be limited by the court (note expert's recoverable fees in the small claims track cannot exceed £750: see PD27 paragraph 7).

18. When necessary, arrangements should be made for dealing with questions to experts and discussions between experts, including any directions given by the court.

19. Experts should be kept informed about deadlines for all matters concerning them. Those instructing experts should send them promptly copies of all court orders and directions that may affect the preparation of their reports or any other matters concerning their obligations.

Instructions

20. Those instructing experts should ensure that they give clear instructions (and attach relevant documents), including the following:
(a) basic information, such as names, addresses, telephone numbers, dates of incidents and any relevant claim reference numbers;
(b) the nature of the expertise required;
(c) the purpose of the advice or report, a description of the matter(s) to be investigated, the issues to be addressed and the identity of all parties;
(d) the statement(s) of case (if any), those documents which form part of disclosure and witness statements and expert reports that are relevant to the advice or report, making clear which have been served and which are drafts and when the latter are likely to be served;
(e) where proceedings have not been started, whether they are contemplated and, if so, whether the expert is being asked only for advice;
(f) an outline programme, consistent with good case management and the expert's availability, for the completion and delivery of each stage of the expert's work; and
(g) where proceedings have been started, the dates of any hearings (including any case/costs management conferences and/or pre-trial reviews), the dates fixed by the court or agreed between the parties for the exchange of experts' reports and any other relevant deadlines to be adhered to, the name of the court, the claim number, the track to which the claim has been allocated and whether there is a specific budget for the experts' fees.

21. Those instructing experts should seek to agree, where practicable, the instructions for the experts, and that they receive the same factual material.

Acceptance of instructions

22. Experts should confirm without delay whether they accept their instructions.

23. They should also inform those instructing them (whether on initial instruction or at any later stage) without delay if:
(a) instructions are not acceptable because, for example, they require work that falls outside their expertise, impose unrealistic deadlines, or are insufficiently clear. Experts who do not receive clear instructions should request clarification and may indicate that they are not prepared to act unless and until such clear instructions are received;
(b) they consider that instructions are insufficient to complete the work;
(c) they become aware that they may not be able to fulfil any of the terms of appointment;
(d) the instructions and/or work have, for any reason, placed them in conflict with their duties as an expert. Where an expert advisor is approached to act as an expert witness they will need to consider carefully whether they can accept a role as expert witness; or
(e) they are not satisfied that they can comply with any orders that have been made.

24. Experts must neither express an opinion outside the scope of their field of expertise, nor accept any instructions to do so.

25. Where an expert identifies that the basis of his instruction differs from that of another expert, he should inform those instructing him.

26. Experts should agree the terms on which they are to be paid with those instructing them. Experts should be aware that they will be required to provide estimates for the court and that the court may limit the amount to be paid as part of any order for budgeted costs (CPR 35.4(2) and (4) and 35.15).

Experts' Withdrawal

27. Where experts' instructions are incompatible with their duties, through incompleteness, a conflict between their duty to the court and their instructions, or for any other reason, the experts may consider withdrawing from the case. However, experts should not do so without first discussing the position with those who instruct them and considering whether it would be more appropriate to make a written request for directions from the court. If experts do withdraw, they must give formal written notice to those instructing them.

Experts' right to ask court for directions

28. Experts may request directions from the court to assist them in carrying out their functions (CPR 35.14), for example, if experts consider that they have not been provided

with information they require. Experts should normally discuss this with those who instruct them before making a request. Unless the court otherwise orders, any proposed request for directions should be sent to the party instructing the expert at least seven days before filing any request with the court, and to all other parties at least four days before filing it.

29. Requests to the court for directions should be made by letter clearly marked 'expert's request for directions' containing:
(a) the title of the claim;
(b) the claim number;
(c) the name of the expert;
(d) why directions are sought; and
(e) copies of any relevant documentation.

Experts' access to information held by the parties

30. Experts should try to ensure that they have access to all relevant information held by the parties, and that the same information has been disclosed to each expert in the same discipline. Experts should seek to confirm this soon after accepting instructions, notifying instructing solicitors of any omissions.

31. If a solicitor sends an expert additional documents before the report is finalised the solicitor must tell the expert whether any witness statements or expert reports are updated versions of those previously sent and whether they have been filed and served.

32. Experts should be specifically aware of CPR 35.9. This provides that, where one party has access to information that is not readily available to the other party, the court may direct the party who has access to the information to prepare, file and copy to the other party a document recording the information. If experts require such information which has not been disclosed, they should discuss the position with those instructing them without delay, so that a request for the information can be made, and, if not forthcoming, an application can be made to the court.

33. Any request for further information from the other party made by an expert should be in a letter to the expert's instructing party and should state why the information is necessary and the significance in relation to the expert issues in the case.

Single joint experts

34. CPR 35.7–8 and PD35 paragraph 7 deal with the instruction and use of joint experts by the parties and the powers of the court to order their use. The CPR encourage the use of joint experts. Wherever possible a joint report should be obtained. Single joint experts are the norm in cases allocated to the small claims track and the fast track.

35. In the early stages of a dispute, when investigations, tests, site inspections, photographs, plans or other similar preliminary expert tasks are necessary, consideration should be given to the instruction of a single joint expert, especially where such matters are not expected to be contentious. The objective should be to agree or to narrow issues.

36. Experts who have previously advised a party (whether in the same case or otherwise) should only be proposed as single joint experts if the other parties are given all relevant information about the previous involvement.

37. The appointment of a single joint expert does not prevent parties from instructing their own experts to advise (but the cost of such expert advisors will not be recoverable from another party).

Joint instructions

38. The parties should try to agree joint instructions to single joint experts, but in default of agreement, each party may give instructions. In particular, all parties should try to agree what documents should be included with instructions and what assumptions single joint experts should make.

39. Where the parties fail to agree joint instructions, they should try to agree where the areas of disagreement lie and their instructions should make this clear. If separate instructions are given, they should be copied to the other instructing parties.

40. Where experts are instructed by two or more parties, the terms of appointment should, unless the court has directed otherwise, or the parties have agreed otherwise, include:
(a) a statement that all the instructing parties are jointly and severally liable to pay the experts' fees and, accordingly, that experts' invoices should be sent simultaneously to all instructing parties or their solicitors (as appropriate); and
(b) a copy of any order limiting experts' fees and expenses (CPR 35.8(4)(a)).

41. Where instructions have not been received by the expert from one or more of the instructing parties, the expert should give notice (normally at least 7 days) of a deadline for their receipt. Unless the instructions are received within the deadline the expert may begin work. If instructions are received after the deadline but before the completion of the report the expert should consider whether it is practicable to comply without adversely affecting the timetable for delivery of the report and without greatly increasing the costs and exceeding any court approved budget. An expert who decides to issue a report without taking into account instructions received after the deadline must inform the parties, who may apply to the court for directions. In either event the report must show clearly that the expert did not receive instructions within the deadline, or, as the case may be, at all.

Conduct of the single joint expert

42. Single joint experts should keep all instructing parties informed of any material steps that they may be taking by, for example, copying all correspondence to those instructing them.

43. Single joint experts are Part 35 experts and so have an overriding duty to the court. They are the parties' appointed experts and therefore owe an equal duty to all parties. They should maintain independence, impartiality and transparency at all times.

44. Single joint experts should not attend a meeting or conference that is not a joint one, unless all the parties have agreed in writing or the court has directed that such a meeting may be held. There also needs to be agreement about who is to pay the experts' fees for the meeting.

45. Single joint experts may request directions from the court (see paragraphs 28–29).

46. Single joint experts should serve their reports simultaneously on all instructing parties. They should provide a single report even though they may have received

instructions that contain conflicts. If conflicting instructions lead to different opinions (for example, because the instructions require the expert to make different assumptions of fact), reports may need to contain more than one set of opinions on any issue. It is for the court to determine the facts.

Cross-examination of the single joint expert

47. Single joint experts do not normally give oral evidence at trial but if they do, all parties may ask questions. In general, written questions (CPR 35.6) should be put to single joint experts before requests are made for them to attend court for the purpose of cross-examination.

Experts' reports

48. The content of experts' reports should be governed by their instructions and general obligations, any court directions, CPR 35 and PD35, and the experts' overriding duty to the court.

49. In preparing reports, experts should maintain professional objectivity and impartiality at all times.

50. PD35, paragraph 3.1 provides that experts' reports should be addressed to the court and gives detailed directions about their form and content. All experts and those who instruct them should ensure that they are familiar with these requirements.

51. Model forms of experts' reports are available from bodies such as the Academy of Experts and the Expert Witness Institute and a template for medical reports has been created by the Ministry of Justice.

52. Experts' reports must contain statements that they:
(a) understand their duty to the court and have complied and will continue to comply with it; and
(b) are aware of and have complied with the requirements of CPR 35 and PD35 and this guidance.

53. Experts' reports must also be verified by a statement of truth. The form of the statement of truth is:

'I confirm that I have made clear which facts and matters referred to in this report are within my own knowledge and which are not. Those that are within my own knowledge I confirm to be true. The opinions I have expressed represent my true and complete professional opinions on the matters to which they refer.'

54. The details of experts' qualifications in reports should be commensurate with the nature and complexity of the case. It may be sufficient to state any academic and professional qualifications. However, where highly specialised expertise is called for, experts should include the detail of particular training and/or experience that qualifies them to provide that specialised evidence.

55. The mandatory statement of the substance of all material instructions should not be incomplete or otherwise tend to mislead. The imperative is transparency. The term 'instructions' includes all material that solicitors send to experts. These should be listed, with dates, in the report or an appendix. The omission from the statement of 'off-the-record' oral instructions is not permitted. Courts may allow cross-examination about the instructions if there are reasonable grounds to consider that the statement may be inaccurate or incomplete.

56. Where tests of a scientific or technical nature have been carried out, experts should state:
(a) the methodology used; and
(b) by whom the tests were undertaken and under whose supervision, summarising their respective qualifications and experience.

57. When addressing questions of fact and opinion, experts should keep the two separate. Experts must state those facts (whether assumed or otherwise) upon which their opinions are based; experts should have primary regard to their instructions (paragraphs 20–25 above). Experts must distinguish clearly between those facts that they know to be true and those facts which they assume.

58. Where there are material facts in dispute experts should express separate opinions on each hypothesis put forward. They should not express a view in favour of one or other disputed version of the facts unless, as a result of particular expertise and experience, they consider one set of facts as being improbable or less probable, in which case they may express that view and should give reasons for holding it.

59. If the mandatory summary of the range of opinion is based on published sources, experts should explain those sources and, where appropriate, state the qualifications of the originator(s) of the opinions from which they differ, particularly if such opinions represent a well-established school of thought.

60. Where there is no available source for the range of opinion, experts may need to express opinions on what they believe to be the range that other experts would arrive at if asked. In those circumstances, experts should make it clear that the range that they summarise is based on their own judgement and explain the basis of that judgement.

Prior to service of reports

61. Before filing and serving an expert's report solicitors must check that any witness statements and other experts' reports relied upon by the expert are the final served versions.

Conclusions of reports

62. A summary of conclusions is mandatory. Generally the summary should be at the end of the report after the reasoning. There may be cases, however, where the court would find it helpful to have a short summary at the beginning, with the full conclusions at the end. For example, in cases involving highly complex matters which fall outside the general knowledge of the court the judge may be assisted in the comprehension of the facts and analysis if the report explains at the outset the basis of the reasoning.

Sequential exchange of experts' reports

63. Where there is to be sequential exchange of reports then the defendant's expert's report usually will be produced in response to the claimant's. The defendant's report should then:
(a) confirm whether the background set out in the claimant's expert report is agreed, or identify those parts that in the defendant's expert's view require revision, setting out the necessary revisions. The defendant's expert need not repeat information that is adequately dealt with in the claimant's expert report;
(b) focus only on those material areas of difference with the claimant's expert's opinion. The defendant's report should identify those assumptions of the claimant's expert that they

consider reasonable (and agree with) and those that they do not; and
(c) in particular where the experts are addressing the financial value of heads of claim (for example, the costs of a care regime or loss of profits), the defendant's report should contain a reconciliation between the claimant's expert's loss assessment and the defendant's, identifying for each assumption any different conclusion to the claimant's expert.

Amendment of reports

64. It may become necessary for experts to amend their reports:
(a) as a result of an exchange of questions and answers;
(b) following agreements reached at meetings between experts; or
(c) where further evidence or documentation is disclosed.

65. Experts should not be asked to amend, expand or alter any parts of reports in a manner which distorts their true opinion, but may be invited to do so to ensure accuracy, clarity, internal consistency, completeness and relevance to the issues. Although experts should generally follow the recommendations of solicitors with regard to the form of reports, they should form their own independent views on the opinions and contents of their reports and not include any suggestions that do not accord with their views.

66. Where experts change their opinion following a meeting of experts, a signed and dated note to that effect is generally sufficient. Where experts significantly alter their opinion, as a result of new evidence or for any other reason, they must inform those who instruct them and amend their reports explaining the reasons. Those instructing experts should inform other parties as soon as possible of any change of opinion.

Written questions to experts

67. Experts have a duty to provide answers to questions properly put. Where they fail to do so, the court may impose sanctions against the party instructing the expert, and, if there is continued non-compliance, debar a party from relying on the report. Experts should copy their answers to those instructing them.

68. Experts' answers to questions become part of their reports. They are covered by the statement of truth, and form part of the expert evidence.

69. Where experts believe that questions put are not properly directed to the clarification of the report, or have been asked out of time, they should discuss the questions with those instructing them and, if appropriate, those asking the questions. Attempts should be made to resolve such problems without the need for an application to the court for directions, but in the absence of agreement or application for directions by the party or parties, experts may themselves file a written request to court for directions (see paragraphs 28–29).

Discussions between experts

70. The court has the power to direct discussions between experts for the purposes set out in the Rules (CPR 35.12). Parties may also agree that discussions take place between their experts at any stage. Discussions are not mandatory unless ordered by the court.

71. The purpose of discussions between experts should be, wherever possible, to:
(a) identify and discuss the expert issues in the proceedings;
(b) reach agreed opinions on those issues, and, if that is not possible, narrow the issues;
(c) identify those issues on which they agree and disagree and summarise their reasons for disagreement on any issue; and
(d) identify what action, if any, may be taken to resolve any of the outstanding issues between the parties.

They are not to seek to settle the proceedings.

72. Where single joint experts have been instructed but parties have, with the permission of the court, instructed their own additional Part 35 experts, there may, if the court so orders or the parties agree, be discussions between the single joint experts and the additional Part 35 experts. Such discussions should be confined to those matters within the remit of the additional Part 35 experts or as ordered by the court.

73. Where there is sequential exchange of expert reports, with the defendant's expert's report prepared in accordance with the guidance at paragraph 63 above, the joint statement should focus upon the areas of disagreement, save for the need for the claimant's expert to consider and respond to material, information and commentary included within the defendant's expert's report.

74. Arrangements for discussions between experts should be proportionate to the value of cases. In small claims and fast-track cases there should not normally be face to face meetings between experts: telephone discussion or an exchange of letters should usually suffice. In multi-track cases discussion may be face to face but the practicalities or the proportionality principle may require discussions to be by telephone or video-conference.

75. In multi-track cases the parties, their lawyers and experts should cooperate to produce an agenda for any discussion between experts, although primary responsibility for preparation of the agenda should normally lie with the parties' solicitors.

76. The agenda should indicate what has been agreed and summarise concisely matters that are in dispute. It is often helpful to include questions to be answered by the experts. If agreement cannot be reached promptly or a party is unrepresented, the court may give directions for the drawing up of the agenda. The agenda should be circulated to experts and those instructing them to allow sufficient time for the experts to prepare for the discussion.

77. Those instructing experts must not instruct experts to avoid reaching agreement (or to defer doing so) on any matter within the experts' competence. Experts are not permitted to accept such instructions.

78. The content of discussions between experts should not be referred to at trial unless the parties agree (CPR 35.12(4)). It is good practice for any such agreement to be in writing.

79. At the conclusion of any discussion between experts, a joint statement should be prepared setting out:
(a) issues that have been agreed and the basis of that agreement;
(b) issues that have not been agreed and the basis of the disagreement;
(c) any further issues that have arisen that were not included in the original agenda for discussion; and

(d) a record of further action, if any, to be taken or recommended, including if appropriate a further discussion between experts.

80. The joint statement should include a brief re-statement that the experts recognise their duties (or a cross-reference to the relevant statements in their respective reports). The joint statement should also include an express statement that the experts have not been instructed to avoid reaching agreement (or otherwise defer from doing so) on any matter within the experts' competence.

81. The joint statement should be agreed and signed by all the parties to the discussion as soon as practicable.

82. Agreements between experts during discussions do not bind the parties unless the parties expressly agree to be bound (CPR 35.12(5)). However, parties should give careful consideration before refusing to be bound by such an agreement and be able to explain their refusal should it become relevant to the issue of costs.

83. Since April 2013 the court has had the power to order at any stage that experts of like disciplines give their evidence at trial concurrently, not sequentially with their party's evidence as has been the norm hitherto: PD35 paragraphs 11.1–11.4 (this is often known as 'hot–tubbing'). The experts will then be questioned together, firstly by the judge based upon disagreements in the joint statement, and then by the parties' advocates. Concurrent evidence can save time and costs, and assist the judge in assessing the difference of views between experts. Experts need to be told in advance of the trial if the court has made an order for concurrent evidence.

Attendance of experts at court

84. Those instructing experts should ascertain the availability of experts before trial dates are fixed; keep experts updated with timetables (including the dates and times experts are to attend), the location of the court and court orders; consider, where appropriate, whether experts might give evidence via video-link; and inform experts immediately if trial dates are vacated or adjourned.

85. Experts have an obligation to attend court and should ensure that those instructing them are aware of their dates to avoid and that they take all reasonable steps to be available.

86. Experts should normally attend court without the need for a witness summons, but on occasion they may be served to require their attendance (CPR 34). The use of witness summonses does not affect the contractual or other obligations of the parties to pay experts' fees.

87. When a case has been concluded either by a settlement or trial the solicitor should inform the experts they have instructed.

Experts and conditional and contingency fees

88. Payment of experts' fees contingent upon the nature of the expert evidence or upon the outcome of the case is strongly discouraged. In *ex parte Factortame (No 8)* [2003] *QB* 381 at [73], the court said 'we consider that it will be a rare case indeed that the court will be prepared to consent to an expert being instructed under a contingency fee agreement'.

Sanctions

89. Solicitors and experts should be aware that sanctions might apply because of a failure to comply with CPR 35, the PD or court orders.

90. Whether or not court proceedings have been commenced a professional instructing an expert, or an expert, may be subject to sanction for misconduct by their professional body/ regulator.

91. If proceedings have been started the court has the power under CPR 44 to impose sanctions:
(a) cost penalties against those instructing the expert (including a wasted costs order) or the expert (such as disallowance or reduction of the expert fee) (CPR 35.4(4) and CPR 44).
(b) that an expert's report/evidence be inadmissible.

92. Experts should also be aware of other possible sanctions:
(a) In more extreme cases, if the court has been misled it may invoke general powers for contempt in the face of the court. The court would then have the power to fine or imprison the wrongdoer.
(b) If an expert commits perjury, criminal sanctions may follow.
(c) If an expert has been negligent there may be a claim on their professional indemnity insurance.

Commentary

What follows is a refresher on the CJC guidance. References in the form §1 represent the paragraph number.

Purpose

The purpose of the guidance is to allow litigants, experts and those who instruct them to '*... understand best practice in complying with Part 35 and court orders*' (§1).

Pre-action protocol

Experts and those instructing them (so not the lawyer's client) must have regard to the objectives underlying the pre-action protocols. These are:

- to ensure **early and full disclosure of the expert issues**
- to **agree as many of the expert issues before proceedings** begin, and
- to **support efficient management** of the proceedings (§2).

Specialist proceedings

Experts, and those who instruct them, must be aware of other court guidance and of specialist proceedings in some cases (§3).

Judicial notice and limitation

The 2007 guidance warned that the courts could take account of any failure to comply with the protocol, and stated that if complying with the protocol would time bar a case, then the protocol could be bypassed but the court had to be told of such abrogation. The CJC must have felt that both are self-evident truths because both were removed from the 2014 update.

Need for experts

Of course, proportionality is now paramount in the civil justice system's pursuit of justice. So §4 requires those intending to instruct experts specifically to consider whether, bearing in mind Civil Procedure Rules (CPR) Parts 1 and 35, such evidence '*... is required to resolve the proceedings...*'. We are reminded that the court's permission is required to use expert evidence in court proceedings, but that in general the parties are free to instruct an expert for their own private purposes without any particular permission (§5).

Expert advisors

There is helpful emphasis given to the important difference between expert witnesses instructed under CPR 35 and expert advisors – upon whose opinions the parties do not intend to rely (§6). There is also implicit acceptance that an expert advisor can later take on the role of expert witness proper (§7). The remainder of the guidance does not apply to expert advisors (§8).

Duties and obligations of experts

Experts have a duty to exercise reasonable care, must comply with any professional codes and have an overriding duty to the court (§9).

The overriding objective: Experts are reminded of their obligation to help the court achieve the overriding objective set out in CPR 1.1. Helpfully, a meaning of '*proportionate*' is spelt out – '*... keeping the work and costs in proportion to the value and importance of the case to the parties...*' (§10). Previous guidance asked experts not to stray into mediation or otherwise trespass on the court's function, and clearly that must still apply.

Other duties: An expert has a duty to independence (§11), to stay within their area of expertise (§12), to take into account all material facts (§13) and to promptly flag up any change of opinion (§14).

Sanction: Any failure to comply with court rules or court judgments may have consequences (§15). The guidance speaks of sanctions on the parties, and these are dealt with in §89–92.

Appointment of experts

Before instructing an expert, a lawyer must establish that the expert:

- has the **appropriate expertise**
- **understands the duties** of an expert witness
- has the **capacity to perform the work to the required timescale** and **at a cost proportionate to the matters** in issue
- can **attend trial** if needed, and
- has **no potential conflict of interest** (§16).

Terms of appointment: Terms must be agreed at the outset of the instruction. They must include setting out the nature of the instruction (i.e. party expert, SJE or advisor), the services required, the timescale, the basis for the expert fees and payment terms. Both cancellation fees and the acceptance, or otherwise, of any fee reduction based on court assessment should also be defined. Furthermore, the expert should be reminded that the court has powers to limit the expert fee (§17). Parties are also reminded that CPR 35.4(2) requires them to provide estimates of the cost of the proposed expert evidence in every case. Arrangements must also be made for dealing with questions to experts and expert discussions (§18), and those instructing experts are under a duty to keep experts informed about deadlines and court orders that touch on the work of the expert (§19).

Instructions

Clear instructions must be given (§20). When disclosing documents, the solicitor must make '*... clear which have been served and which are drafts and when the latter are likely to be served...*'. This should help experts to avoid pulling quotes from a draft witness statement which change in the final version – something that has made more than one expert look foolish in the witness box!

But there is a long-standing problem with lawyers sending experts 'background material' that should not be cited in the expert report. The practice is unhelpful and risks putting experts in breach of their duty under CPR 35.10(3) to state the '*... substance of all material instructions*'. Whether a document attracts legal privilege is a legal issue outside the competence of expert witnesses. If an expert is shown evidence that is relevant to the opinion given in the expert report, the source of that evidence must be noted in the report. Alternatively, if a lawyer sends an expert material that should not be cited, in our view the expert should return it unread. But what an expert should never do is ignore known evidence relevant to the opinion.

Agreed instructions: Those who instruct experts must try to agree the instructions and use the same factual material as the baseline (§21). It's a helpful reminder to non-lawyers that a reason experts may come to radically different opinions could be because they are given different evidence to consider at the outset! Experts must highlight where such evidential discrepancies occur (§25).

Acceptance of instructions: Experts should be prompt in confirming, or otherwise, their willingness to accept the instruction to act (§22). If circumstances change to cast doubt over an expert's ability to complete the instructions, he must advise his instructing solicitor promptly (§23). Experts should say if their instructions are insufficiently clear, impose an unrealistic timeframe, or fall outside the expert's area of expertise.

The potential difficulties that can arise when an expert advisor – a partisan advisor to a party – moves to the role of expert witness – instructed under CPR 35 with an overriding duty to independence and the court – are noted explicitly. Experts must also stay within their area of expertise (§24).

Agreed payment terms: In an attempt to reduce the perennial problem of experts and lawyers bickering over fees, the guidance states that experts should agree payment terms with those who instruct them (§26). But experts are reminded that they are always required to provide cost estimates, and the court has the power to limit the amount paid as part of an order for budgeted costs. It seems to us that the latter power applies only in multi-track cases and relates to costs between the parties – it does not override the fees due under the contract agreed between the expert and the solicitor.

Withdrawal from an instruction

§27 offers guidance for experts on withdrawing from instructions. Possible reasons may include a personal or professional conflict of interest, incomplete instructions, etc. Experts must first discuss their concerns with their instructing solicitor(s).

Asking the court for directions

An expert can take advantage of the power contained in CPR 35.14 to ask the court for directions. An example is included of when such a request might be needed (§28). There is also advice to include the phrase '*expert's request for directions*' on any request (§29). It remains to be seen whether that will remove the confusion such requests are reported to have created hitherto in court offices.

Access to all information

What should an expert do if it is felt that required information is being withheld? There is a duty on the expert to identify both missing information and those cases where experts are working on a dissimilar evidence base. If such problems are identified, the expert is required simply to tell the instructing solicitor (§30).

There is also a duty upon the solicitor to specifically alert experts if any documents being sent are updated versions of material sent previously, and to note whether they have been filed with the court and/or served on the other party (§31).

The expert's attention is drawn to the power under CPR 35.9 for the court to require that information be disclosed by another party. First, the expert must inform the instructing solicitor of what is needed and its significance to the expert issue. It is then for the lawyer to decide on proportionality (§32). Any request for further information should be put to the expert's own instructing solicitor in writing, and should set out why it is needed and its importance to the expert issues (§33).

Single joint experts

There is a standing assumption that single joint experts (SJEs) should be used in small claims and fast-track cases (§34), with the aim being to agree or narrow issues that are not contentious (§35). The redeployment of a party-appointed expert as an SJE requires full disclosure of the expert's prior involvement in the case (§36). Party-appointed experts can be assigned to 'shadow' an SJE, but costs associated with such an expert cannot be recovered from another party (§37).

Parties are strongly advised to agree joint instructions for an SJE (§38). If that isn't possible, then separate instructions can be given, but the parties should then try to agree on their disagreements and set them out in the instructions (§39). What happens when the parties disagree on their disagreements is covered in a moment!

An SJE has a right to joint and several liability for payment from all parties (§40), and any order limiting an expert's fee must be copied to the expert.

So what's an expert to do when the parties are unable to agree on anything? If left waiting for instructions, the expert can set a deadline (normally 7 days hence), after which work will commence. If that approach means a report is written that fails to take into account instructions received after the deadline, then that is acceptable but the expert must clearly disclose that limitation (§41).

SJEs must keep all parties informed at all times (§42); they must have an equal duty to all the parties which is subservient to the overriding duty to the court (§43); and meetings with just one party (e.g. conference with counsel) must be agreed by all parties, as well as who is to pay the expert for attending such a meeting (§44).

An SJE, like a party expert, may seek directions from the court (§45), while the SJE report should be served on all parties simultaneously (§46).

It should be noted that even if there are multiple sets of instructions, only one report should be prepared, even if it contains multiple opinions necessitated by conflicting assumptions of fact.

SJEs are open to cross-examination by all the parties on the rare occasion that an SJE steps into the witness box (§47).

Expert reports

The content of the expert report is governed by the instructions, the general obligations, CPR 35 and its practice direction, and the expert's overriding duty to the court. But the need to follow any court directions is spelt out in §48. Objectivity and impartiality must be maintained (§49), and the report should be addressed to the court and comply with the CPR 35 guidance on form and content (§50). Reference to various model forms of report are extended to include the template for medical reports created by the Ministry of Justice (§51).

The mandatory statements must be included in every report. An expert must state that he understands his duties and complies, and continues to comply, with these duties. In addition, an expert must confirm his awareness of CPR 35, its practice direction and the CJC guidance (§52). Naturally, the statement of truth as set out in CPR 35 PD 3.3 must also appear in the report (§53). It reads:

> *'I confirm that I have made clear which facts and matters referred to in this report are within my own knowledge and which are not. Those that are within my own knowledge I confirm to be true. The opinions I have expressed represent my true and complete professional opinions on the matters to which they refer.'*

§54 offers guidance on defining qualifications: the level of detail should reflect the complexity of the case.

Material instructions: Guidance about the mandatory statement on the substance of all material instructions stresses transparency. If an expert is shown something that is relevant to his opinion, it must feature in the summary of instructions given (§55).

Tests: Where tests are carried out, details of the methodology, and information about any technician who conducted such tests, must be provided (§56).

Facts: Facts must be separated from opinion, and opinion must be linked to the underlying facts. Experts must distinguish those facts they know to be true from those they are asked to assume (§57). When it comes to the facts, the guidance adds stress to the point that experts must be guided primarily by their instructions – which is a warning to experts to restrict themselves to their letter of instruction.

Experts are required to offer multiple opinions when the material facts are in dispute. In such cases, experts should only express a view that favours one version of the facts over others if they do so based on their expertise. Exactly why they hold such a view must be explained fully in their report (§58). Experts must cite the published sources that support their mandatory statement of the range of opinion (§59). When no source for the range exists, experts must say what they believe the range would be (§60).

Service of the report: Before filing and serving an expert report, solicitors must check that any witness statements and other expert reports relied upon by the expert are the final served versions (§61).

Conclusions of the report: A summary of the conclusions is mandatory and is usually put at the end of the report. However, if the complexity of the case so demands, an 'executive summary' at the front of the report is permitted (§62).

Sequential exchange of expert reports: The defendant's expert report will usually be produced in response to the claimant's (§63). The defendant's report must work towards narrowing the issues in dispute and minimising unnecessary repetition of agreed background and other materials.

Amendment of reports

The basis upon which a report may require amendment (i.e. following questions, an expert meeting or the disclosure of new evidence) is considered in §64, as is the prohibition on asking experts to alter their opinions. Naturally, requests to change reports to ensure accuracy, clarity, internal consistency, completeness and relevance to the issues are permitted (§65).

If an expert's opinion changes following a meeting of experts, then a short, signed and dated note will generally suffice. If the change of opinion is based on new evidence, however, the expert must amend the report, explaining the reasons. Furthermore, those instructing the expert must inform the other parties (§66).

Written questions to experts

Experts have a duty to answer questions that have been 'properly put' under the CPR, with the party instructing them risking sanctions if the expert refuses (§67). The answers given form part of the report (§68). Guidance about what happens when an expert has doubts about whether questions have been properly put stresses the point that asking the court to help resolve the issue should be an approach of last resort; experts should first discuss the matter with those who instruct them, and then with those asking the questions (§69).

Discussions between experts

The court has the power to direct discussions between experts for the purposes set out in CPR 35.12. In addition, the parties have the ability to agree that discussions can take place between their experts at any stage. Note that discussions are not mandatory unless ordered by the court (§70).

The purpose of such discussions is to:

(i) **identify and discuss the expert issues** in the proceedings

(ii) **reach agreed opinions** on those issues and, if that is not possible, **narrow the issues**

(iii) **identify those issues on which they agree and disagree,** and summarise their reasons for disagreement on any issue, and

(iv) **identify what action, if any, may be taken to resolve any of the outstanding issues** between the parties.

The purpose of such discussions is 'not to seek to settle the proceedings' (§71).

When an SJE meets with a party-appointed expert (one who has been authorised by the court), the remit of any meeting will normally be limited by the remit of the party-appointed expert (§72).

§73 sets out that where there is sequential exchange of expert reports, with the defendant's expert report prepared in accordance with the guidance at §61, the joint statement should focus on the areas of disagreement. The only exception accommodates the need for the claimant's expert to consider and respond to material, information and commentary included within the defendant's expert report.

There is a need to balance the cost of holding discussions against the value of the case (§74), so telephone discussions will be the norm in anything other than higher value multi-track cases. The parties, their lawyers and experts should co-operate to produce an agenda, but this is restricted to multi-track cases (§75). There's no guidance on what happens in the vast majority of lower value cases.

The agenda should indicate what has been agreed and summarise concisely the matters in dispute, and it is often helpful to include questions to be answered by the experts. If agreement cannot be reached promptly or a party is unrepresented, the court may give directions for the drawing up of the agenda.

The agenda should be circulated to experts and those instructing them to allow sufficient time for the experts to prepare for the discussion (§76). There is a prohibition on telling experts not to reach agreement in meetings (§77), and a bar on the content of discussions between experts being referred to at trial unless the parties agree (§78).

The joint statement should set out (§78):

(i) **issues that have been agreed** and the basis of that agreement

(ii) **issues that have not been agreed** and the basis of the disagreement

(iii) **any further issues** that have arisen that were not included in the original agenda for discussion, and

(iv) **a record of further action,** if any, to be taken or recommended, including, if appropriate, a further discussion between experts.

The joint statement should include a brief re-statement that the experts recognise their duties, as well as an express statement that the experts have not been instructed to avoid reaching agreement on any matter within their competence (§80).

It should be agreed and signed by all the parties to the discussion as soon as practicable. Sadly, there is still no explicit guidance on what an expert should do when faced with another expert who refuses to follow the guidance!

Agreements reached by experts following discussions do not bind the parties, although this is accompanied by the warning that in refusing to be bound the party runs the risk of subsequent cost sanctions (§82).

In the hot tub

§83 offers guidance on the use of concurrent evidence: so-called 'hot tubbing'. It explains how the process works, and outlines its benefits, before noting that experts need to be told in advance of the trial if the court has made an order for concurrent evidence.

Attendance at court

Solicitors should:

- ascertain the **availability** of experts before trial dates are fixed
- keep experts **updated with timetables** (including the dates and times experts are to attend court), the **location of the court** and the **content of court orders**, and
- **inform experts immediately if trial dates are vacated or adjourned** (§84).

Experts are reminded that they have an obligation to attend court, and should take proper steps to ensure their availability (§85). The witness summons can be used to help achieve this (NB It does not affect the contractual obligations of the party to pay its expert.) (86).

When a case has concluded, by either a settlement or trial, the solicitor should inform the instructed expert(s) (§87). We won't be holding our breath!

Conditional and contingency fees

The 2014 guidance inexplicably, and unhelpfully, weakened the previous total ban on payments to experts that depend on the outcome of the case. In the 2007 guidance such terms could be neither offered nor accepted; to do so would '*... contravene experts' overriding duty to the court and compromise their duty of Independence*'. But in the 2014 guidance we have only strong discouragement (§88). The guidance remains firmly against such fees, but we wonder why it was felt necessary to weaken the previous absolute ban.

Sanctions

Sanctions can apply to solicitors or experts (§89). In the case of the expert, there could be recourse to a professional body (§90). Once proceedings have started, the sanctions can include the court reducing (even to zero) the fee the expert will receive, or the expert report can be ruled inadmissible (§91).

Experts are also alerted to the more serious sanctions they could face: contempt of court proceedings, perjury proceedings or a claim against their professional indemnity insurance.

J S Publications can be contacted at:
PO Box 505, Newmarket, Suffolk CB8 7TF
Tel: 01638 561590 • Fax: 01638 560924 • e-mail: ukrew@jspubs.com

Appendix I

Parry's Valuation Tables – Present value of one pound

Receivable at the expiration of a given Number of Years at Rates of Interest ranging from 2% to 28% (ie, the amount which must be invested now in order to accumulate to £1 at Compound Interest)

$$V_{\overline{n}|i}\ (1 + i)^{-n}$$

(From Parry's Valuation Tables)

Note: No allowance has been made for the effect of income tax on interest accumulations.

No Income Tax

PRESENT VALUE OF £1

Rate Per Cent

Yrs.	**2**	**2.25**	**2.5**	**2.75**	**3**	**Yrs.**
1	.9803922	.9779951	.9756098	.9732360	.9708738	**1**
2	.9611688	.9564744	.9518144	.9471883	.9425959	**2**
3	.9423223	.9354273	.9285994	.9218378	.9151417	**3**
4	.9238454	.9148433	.9059506	.8971657	.8884870	**4**
5	.9057308	.8947123	.8838543	.8731540	.8626088	**5**
6	.8879714	.8750243	.8622969	.8497849	.8374843	**6**
7	.8705602	.8557695	.8412652	.8270413	.8130915	**7**
8	.8534904	.8369383	.8207466	.8049064	.7894092	**8**
9	.8367553	.8185216	.8007284	.7833638	.7664167	**9**
10	.8203483	.8005101	.7811984	.7623979	.7440939	**10**
11	.8042630	.7828950	.7621448	.7419931	.7224213	**11**
12	.7884932	.7656675	.7435559	.7221344	.7013799	**12**
13	.7730325	.7488190	.7254204	.7028072	.6809513	**13**
14	.7578750	.7323414	.7077272	.6839973	.6611178	**14**
15	.7430147	.7162263	.6904656	.6656908	.6418619	**15**
16	.7284458	.7004658	.6736249	.6478742	.6231669	**16**
17	.7141626	.6850521	.6571951	.6305345	.6050164	**17**
18	.7001594	.6699776	.6411659	.6136589	.5873946	**18**
19	.6864308	.6552348	.6255277	.5972350	.5702860	**19**
20	.6729713	.6408165	.6102709	.5812506	.5536758	**20**
21	.6597758	.6267154	.5953863	.5656940	.5375493	**21**
22	.6468390	.6129246	.5808647	.5505538	.5218925	**22**
23	.6341559	.5994372	.5666972	.5358187	.5066917	**23**
24	.6217215	.5862467	.5528754	.5214781	.4919337	**24**
25	.6095309	.5733464	.5393906	.5075213	.4776056	**25**
26	.5975793	.5607300	.5262347	.4939380	.4636947	**26**

No Income Tax

PRESENT VALUE OF £1

Rate Per Cent

Yrs.	2	2.25	2.5	2.75	3	Yrs.
27	.5858620	.5483912	.5133997	.4807182	.4501891	**27**
28	.5743746	.5363239	.5008778	.4678523	.4370768	**28**
29	.5631123	.5245221	.4886613	.4553307	.4243464	**29**
30	.5520709	.5129801	.4767427	.4431442	.4119868	**30**
31	.5412460	.5016920	.4651148	.4312839	.3999871	**31**
32	.5306333	.4906523	.4537706	.4197410	.3883370	**32**
33	.5202287	.4798556	.4427030	.4085071	.3770262	**33**
34	.5100282	.4692964	.4319053	.3975738	.3660449	**34**
35	.5000276	.4589696	.4213711	.3869331	.3553834	**35**
36	.4902232	.4488700	.4110937	.3765773	.3450324	**36**
37	.4806109	.4389927	.4010670	.3664986	.3349829	**37**
38	.4711872	.4293327	.3912849	.3566896	.3252262	**38**
39	.4619482	.4198853	.3817414	.3471432	.3157535	**39**
40	.4528904	.4106458	.3724306	.3378522	.3065568	**40**
41	.4440102	.4016095	.3633469	.3288099	.2976280	**41**
42	.4353041	.3927722	.3544848	.3200097	.2889592	**42**
43	.4267688	.3841293	.3458389	.3114449	.2805429	**43**
44	.4184007	.3756765	.3374038	.3031094	.2723718	**44**
45	.4101968	.3674098	.3291744	.2949970	.2644386	**45**
46	.4021537	.3593250	.3211458	.2871017	.2567365	**46**
47	.3942684	.3514181	.3133129	.2794177	.2492588	**47**
48	.3865376	.3436852	.3056712	.2719394	.2419988	**48**
49	.3789584	.3361224	.2982158	.2646612	.2349503	**49**
50	.3715279	.3287261	.2909422	.2575778	.2281071	**50**
51	.3642430	.3214925	.2838461	.2506840	.2214632	**51**
52	.3571010	.3144181	.2769230	.2439747	.2150128	**52**
53	.3500990	.3074994	.2701688	.2374450	.2087503	**53**
54	.3432343	.3007329	.2635793	.2310900	.2026702	**54**
55	.3365042	.2941153	.2571505	.2249051	.1967672	**55**
56	.3299061	.2876433	.2508786	.2188858	.1910361	**56**
57	.3234374	.2813137	.2447596	.2130275	.1854719	**57**
58	.3170955	.2751235	.2387898	.2073260	.1800698	**58**
59	.3108779	.2690694	.2329657	.2017772	.1748251	**59**
60	.3047823	.2631486	.2272836	.1963768	.1697331	**60**
61	.2988061	.2573580	.2217401	.1911210	.1647894	**61**
62	.2929472	.2516949	.2163318	.1860058	.1599897	**62**
63	.2872031	.2461564	.2110554	.1810276	.1553298	**63**
64	.2815717	.2407397	.2059077	.1761825	.1508057	**64**
65	.2760507	.2354423	.2008856	.1714672	.1464133	**65**
66	.2706379	.2302614	.1959859	.1668780	.1421488	**66**
67	.2653313	.2251945	.1912058	.1624117	.1380085	**67**
68	.2601287	.2202391	.1865422	.1580649	.1339889	**68**
69	.2550282	.2153928	.1819924	.1538345	.1300863	**69**
70	.2500276	.2106531	.1775536	.1497173	.1262974	**70**
71	.2451251	.2060177	.1732230	.1457102	.1226188	**71**
72	.2403187	.2014843	.1689980	.1418104	.1190474	**72**
73	.2356066	.1970507	.1648761	.1380150	.1155800	**73**
74	.2309869	.1927146	.1608548	.1343212	.1122136	**74**
75	.2264577	.1884739	.1569315	.1307262	.1089452	**75**

No Income Tax

PRESENT VALUE OF £1

Rate Per Cent

Yrs.	**2**	**2.25**	**2.5**	**2.75**	**3**	**Yrs.**
76	.2220174	.1843266	.1531039	.1272275	.1057721	**76**
77	.2176641	.1802705	.1493697	.1238224	.1026913	**77**
78	.2133962	.1763036	.1457265	.1205084	.0997003	**78**
79	.2092119	.1724241	.1421722	.1172831	.0967964	**79**
80	.2051097	.1686299	.1387046	.1141441	.0939771	**80**
81	.2010880	.1649192	.1353215	.1110892	.0912399	**81**
82	.1971451	.1612902	.1320210	.1081160	.0885824	**82**
83	.1932795	.1577410	.1288010	.1052224	.0860024	**83**
84	.1894897	.1542700	.1256595	.1024062	.0834974	**84**
85	.1857742	.1508753	.1225946	.0996654	.0810655	**85**
86	.1821316	.1475553	.1196045	.0969980	.0787043	**86**
87	.1785604	.1443083	.1166873	.0944019	.0764120	**87**
88	.1750592	.1411329	.1138413	.0918753	.0741864	**88**
89	.1716266	.1380272	.1110647	.0894164	.0720256	**89**
90	.1682614	.1349900	.1083558	.0870232	.0699278	**90**
91	.1649622	.1320195	.1057130	.0846942	.0678911	**91**
92	.1617276	.1291145	.1031346	.0824274	.0659136	**92**
93	.1585565	.1262733	.1006191	.0802213	.0639938	**93**
94	.1554475	.1234947	.0981650	.0780743	.0621299	**94**
95	.1523995	.1207772	.0957707	.0759847	.0603203	**95**
96	.1494113	.1181195	.0934349	.0739510	.0585634	**96**
97	.1464817	.1155203	.0911560	.0719718	.0568577	**97**
98	.1436095	.1129783	.0889326	.0700456	.0552016	**98**
99	.1407936	.1104922	.0867636	.0681709	.0535938	**99**
100	.1380330	.1080608	.0846474	.0663463	.0520328	**100**

No Income Tax

PRESENT VALUE OF £1

Rate Per Cent

Yrs.	**3.25**	**3.5**	**3.75**	**4**	**4.25**	**Yrs.**
1	.9685230	.9661836	.9638554	.9615385	.9592326	**1**
2	.9380368	.9335107	.9290173	.9245562	.9201272	**2**
3	.9085102	.9019427	.8954383	.8889964	.8826160	**3**
4	.8799130	.8714422	.8630731	.8548042	.8466341	**4**
5	.8522160	.8419732	.8318777	.8219271	.8121190	**5**
6	.8253908	.8135006	.8018098	.7903145	.7790111	**6**
7	.7994100	.7859910	.7728287	.7599178	.7472528	**7**
8	.7742470	.7594116	.7448952	.7306902	.7167893	**8**
9	.7498760	.7337310	.7179712	.7025867	.6875676	**9**
10	.7262722	.7089188	.6920205	.6755642	.6595373	**10**
11	.7034113	.6849457	.6670077	.6495809	.6326497	**11**
12	.6812700	.6617833	.6428990	.6245970	.6068582	**12**
13	.6598257	.6394042	.6196617	.6005741	.5821182	**13**
14	.6390564	.6177818	.5972643	.5774751	.5583868	**14**
15	.6189408	.5968906	.5756764	.5552645	.5356228	**15**
16	.5994584	.5767059	.5548688	.5339082	.5137868	**16**
17	.5805892	.5572038	.5348133	.5133732	.4928411	**17**
18	.5623140	.5383611	.5154827	.4936281	.4727493	**18**
19	.5446141	.5201557	.4968508	.4746424	.4534765	**19**

No Income Tax

PRESENT VALUE OF £1

Rate Per Cent

Yrs.	3.25	3.5	3.75	4	4.25	Yrs.
20	.5274713	.5025659	.4788923	.4563869	.4349895	**20**
21	.5108680	.4855709	.4615830	.4388336	.4172561	**21**
22	.4947874	.4691506	.4448993	.4219554	.4002456	**22**
23	.4792130	.4532856	.4288186	.4057263	.3839287	**23**
24	.4641288	.4379571	.4133191	.3901215	.3682769	**24**
25	.4495195	.4231470	.3983799	.3751168	.3532632	**25**
26	.4353699	.4088377	.3839806	.3606892	.3388616	**26**
27	.4216658	.3950122	.3701018	.3468166	.3250471	**27**
28	.4083930	.3816543	.3567246	.3334775	.3117958	**28**
29	.3955380	.3687482	.3438309	.3206514	.2990847	**29**
30	.3830877	.3562784	.3314033	.3083187	.2868918	**30**
31	.3710292	.3442303	.3194249	.2964603	.2751959	**31**
32	.3593503	.3325897	.3078794	.2850579	.2639769	**32**
33	.3480391	.3213427	.2967512	.2740942	.2532153	**33**
34	.3370839	.3104761	.2860253	.2635521	.2428923	**34**
35	.3264735	.2999769	.2756870	.2534155	.2329903	**35**
36	.3161971	.2898327	.2657224	.2436687	.2234919	**36**
37	.3062441	.2800316	.2561180	.2342968	.2143807	**37**
38	.2966045	.2705619	.2468607	.2252854	.2056409	**38**
39	.2872683	.2614125	.2379380	.2166206	.1972575	**39**
40	.2782259	.2525725	.2293379	.2082890	.1892158	**40**
41	.2694682	.2440314	.2210486	.2002779	.1815020	**41**
42	.2609862	.2357791	.2130588	.1925749	.1741026	**42**
43	.2527711	.2278059	.2053579	.1851682	.1670049	**43**
44	.2448146	.2201023	.1979353	.1780463	.1601966	**44**
45	.2371086	.2126592	.1907811	.1711984	.1536658	**45**
46	.2296451	.2054679	.1838854	.1646139	.1474012	**46**
47	.2224166	.1985197	.1772389	.1582826	.1413921	**47**
48	.2154156	.1918065	.1708327	.1521948	.1356279	**48**
49	.2086349	.1853202	.1646580	.1463411	.1300987	**49**
50	.2020677	.1790534	.1587065	.1407126	.1247949	**50**
51	.1957073	.1729984	.1529701	.1353006	.1197073	**51**
52	.1895470	.1671482	.1474411	.1300967	.1148272	**52**
53	.1835806	.1614959	.1421119	.1250930	.1101460	**53**
54	.1778020	.1560347	.1369753	.1202817	.1056556	**54**
55	.1722054	.1507581	.1320244	.1156555	.1013483	**55**
56	.1667849	.1456600	.1272524	.1112072	.0972166	**56**
57	.1615350	.1407343	.1226529	.1069300	.0932533	**57**
58	.1564503	.1359752	.1182197	.1028173	.0894516	**58**
59	.1515257	.1313770	.1139467	.0988628	.0858049	**59**
60	.1467562	.1269343	.1098282	.0950604	.0823069	**60**
61	.1421367	.1226418	.1058585	.0914042	.0789515	**61**
62	.1376627	.1184945	.1020323	.0878887	.0757328	**62**
63	.1333295	.1144875	.0983443	.0845084	.0726454	**63**
64	.1291327	.1106159	.0947897	.0812580	.0696838	**64**
65	.1250680	.1068753	.0913636	.0781327	.0668430	**65**
66	.1211312	.1032611	.0880613	.0751276	.0641180	**66**
67	.1173184	.0997692	.0848784	.0722381	.0615041	**67**
68	.1136255	.0963954	.0818105	.0694597	.0589967	**68**

No Income Tax

PRESENT VALUE OF £1
Rate Per Cent

Yrs.	3.25	3.5	3.75	4	4.25	Yrs.
69	.1100489	.0931356	.0788535	.0667882	.0565916	**69**
70	.1065849	.0899861	.0760033	.0642194	.0542845	**70**
71	.1032299	.0869431	.0732562	.0617494	.0520714	**71**
72	.0999806	.0840030	.0706084	.0593744	.0499486	**72**
73	.0968335	.0811623	.0680563	.0570908	.0479123	**73**
74	.0937855	.0784177	.0655964	.0548950	.0459591	**74**
75	.0908334	.0757659	.0632255	.0527837	.0440854	**75**
76	.0879742	.0732038	.0609402	.0507535	.0422882	**76**
77	.0852051	.0707283	.0587376	.0488015	.0405642	**77**
78	.0825231	.0683365	.0566145	.0469245	.0389105	**78**
79	.0799255	.0660256	.0545682	.0451197	.0373242	**79**
80	.0774097	.0637929	.0525959	.0433843	.0358026	**80**
81	.0749730	.0616356	.0506948	.0417157	.0343430	**81**
82	.0726131	.0595513	.0488625	.0401112	.0329430	**82**
83	.0703275	.0575375	.0470964	.0385685	.0316000	**83**
84	.0681138	.0555918	.0453941	.0370851	.0303117	**84**
85	.0659698	.0537119	.0437533	.0356588	.0290760	**85**
86	.0638932	.0518955	.0421719	.0342873	.0278906	**86**
87	.0618821	.0501406	.0406476	.0329685	.0267536	**87**
88	.0599342	.0484450	.0391784	.0317005	.0256629	**88**
89	.0580476	.0468068	.0377623	.0304813	.0246167	**89**
90	.0562205	.0452240	.0363974	.0293089	.0236132	**90**
91	.0544508	.0436946	.0350818	.0281816	.0226505	**91**
92	.0527369	.0422170	.0338138	.0270977	.0217271	**92**
93	.0510769	.0407894	.0325916	.0260555	.0208414	**93**
94	.0494691	.0394101	.0314136	.0250534	.0199917	**94**
95	.0479120	.0380774	.0302782	.0240898	.0191767	**95**
96	.0464039	.0367897	.0291838	.0231632	.0183949	**96**
97	.0449432	.0355456	.0281290	.0222724	.0176450	**97**
98	.0435285	.0343436	.0271123	.0214157	.0169257	**98**
99	.0421584	.0331822	.0261323	.0205920	.0162357	**99**
100	.0408314	.0320601	.0251878	.0198000	.0155738	**100**

No Income Tax

PRESENT VALUE OF £1
Rate Per Cent

Yrs.	4.5	4.75	5	5.25	5.5	Yrs.
1	.9569378	.9546539	.9523810	.9501188	.9478673	**1**
2	.9157300	.9113641	.9070295	.9027257	.8984524	**2**
3	.8762966	.8700374	.8638376	.8576966	.8516137	**3**
4	.8385613	.8305846	.8227055	.8149136	.8072167	**4**
5	.8024510	.7929209	.7835262	.7742647	.7651344	**5**
6	.7678957	.7569650	.7462154	.7356435	.7252458	**6**
7	.7348285	.7226396	.7106813	.6989486	.6874368	**7**
8	.7031851	.6898708	.6768394	.6640842	.6515989	**8**
9	.6729044	.6585879	.6446089	.6309589	.6176293	**9**
10	.6439277	.6287235	.6139133	.5994859	.5854306	**10**
11	.6161987	.6002134	.5846793	.5695828	.5549105	**11**
12	.5896639	.5729960	.5568374	.5411713	.5259815	**12**

No Income Tax

PRESENT VALUE OF £1
Rate Per Cent

Yrs.	**4.5**	**4.75**	**5**	**5.25**	**5.5**	**Yrs.**
13	.5642716	.5470129	.5303214	.5141770	.4985607	**13**
14	.5399729	.5222080	.5050680	.4885292	.4725694	**14**
15	.5167204	.4985280	.4810171	.4641608	.4479330	**15**
16	.4944693	.4759217	.4581115	.4410079	.4245811	**16**
17	.4731764	.4543405	.4362967	.4190098	.4024465	**17**
18	.4528004	.4337380	.4155207	.3981091	.3814659	**18**
19	.4333018	.4140696	.3957340	.3782509	.3615791	**19**
20	.4146429	.3952932	.3768895	.3593833	.3427290	**20**
21	.3967874	.3773682	.3589424	.3414568	.3248616	**21**
22	.3797009	.3602561	.3418499	.3244245	.3079257	**22**
23	.3633501	.3439199	.3255713	.3082418	.2918727	**23**
24	.3477035	.3283245	.3100679	.2928664	.2766566	**24**
25	.3327306	.3134362	.2953028	.2782578	.2622337	**25**
26	.3184025	.2992231	.2812407	.2643780	.2485628	**26**
27	.3046914	.2856545	.2678483	.2511905	.2356045	**27**
28	.2915707	.2727012	.2550936	.2386608	.2233218	**28**
29	.2790150	.2603353	.2429463	.2267561	.2116794	**29**
30	.2670000	.2485301	.2313774	.2154452	.2006440	**30**
31	.2555024	.2372603	.2203595	.2046985	.1901839	**31**
32	.2444999	.2265015	.2098662	.1944879	.1802691	**32**
33	.2339712	.2162305	.1998725	.1847866	.1708712	**33**
34	.2238959	.2064253	.1903548	.1755692	.1619632	**34**
35	.2142544	.1970647	.1812903	.1668116	.1535196	**35**
36	.2050282	.1881286	.1726574	.1584909	.1455162	**36**
37	.1961992	.1795977	.1644356	.1505851	.1379301	**37**
38	.1877504	.1714537	.1566054	.1430738	.1307394	**38**
39	.1796655	.1636789	.1491480	.1359371	.1239236	**39**
40	.1719287	.1562567	.1420457	.1291564	.1174631	**40**
41	.1645251	.1491711	.1352816	.1227139	.1113395	**41**
42	.1574403	.1424068	.1288396	.1165928	.1055350	**42**
43	.1506605	.1359492	.1227044	.1107770	.1000332	**43**
44	.1441728	.1297844	.1168613	.1052513	.0948182	**44**
45	.1379644	.1238992	.1112965	.1000012	.0898751	**45**
46	.1320233	.1182809	.1059967	.0950130	.0851897	**46**
47	.1263381	.1129173	.1009492	.0902737	.0807485	**47**
48	.1208977	.1077970	.0961421	.0857707	.0765389	**48**
49	.1156916	.1029088	.0915639	.0814924	.0725487	**49**
50	.1107096	.0982423	.0872037	.0774274	.0687665	**50**
51	.1059422	.0937874	.0830512	.0735652	.0651815	**51**
52	.1013801	.0895345	.0790964	.0698957	.0617834	**52**
53	.0970145	.0854745	.0753299	.0664092	.0585625	**53**
54	.0928368	.0815985	.0717427	.0630967	.0555095	**54**
55	.0888391	.0778984	.0683264	.0599493	.0526156	**55**
56	.0850135	.0743660	.0650728	.0569590	.0498726	**56**
57	.0813526	.0709938	.0619741	.0541178	.0472726	**57**
58	.0778494	.0677745	.0590229	.0514183	.0448082	**58**
59	.0744970	.0647012	.0562123	.0488535	.0424722	**59**
60	.0712890	.0617672	.0535355	.0464166	.0402580	**60**
61	.0682191	.0589663	.0509862	.0441013	.0381593	**61**

No Income Tax

PRESENT VALUE OF £1
Rate Per Cent

Yrs.	4.5	4.75	5	5.25	5.5	Yrs.
62	.0652815	.0562924	.0485583	.0419015	.0361699	62
63	.0624703	.0537398	.0462460	.0398114	.0342843	63
64	.0597802	.0513029	.0440438	.0378256	.0324969	64
65	.0572059	.0489765	.0419465	.0359388	.0308028	65
66	.0547425	.0467556	.0399490	.0341461	.0291970	66
67	.0523852	.0446354	.0380467	.0324428	.0276748	67
68	.0501294	.0426114	.0362349	.0308246	.0262321	68
69	.0479707	.0406791	.0345095	.0292870	.0248645	69
70	.0459050	.0388345	.0328662	.0278261	.0235683	70
71	.0439282	.0370735	.0313011	.0264381	.0223396	71
72	.0420366	.0353924	.0298106	.0251194	.0211750	72
73	.0402264	.0337875	.0283910	.0238664	.0200711	73
74	.0384941	.0322553	.0270391	.0226759	.0190247	74
75	.0368365	.0307927	.0257515	.0215448	.0180329	75
76	.0352502	.0293964	.0245252	.0204701	.0170928	76
77	.0337323	.0280634	.0233574	.0194490	.0162017	77
78	.0322797	.0267908	.0222451	.0184789	.0153571	78
79	.0308897	.0255759	.0211858	.0175571	.0145565	79
80	.0295595	.0244162	.0201770	.0166814	.0133976	80
81	.0282866	.0233090	.0192162	.0158493	.0130783	81
82	.0270685	.0222520	.0183011	.0150587	.0123965	82
83	.0259029	.0212430	.0174296	.0143076	.0117502	83
84	.0247874	.0202797	.0165996	.0135939	.0111376	84
85	.0237200	.0193601	.0158092	.0129158	.0105570	85
86	.0226986	.0184822	.0150564	.0122715	.0100066	86
87	.0217211	.0176441	.0143394	.0116594	.0094850	87
88	.0207858	.0168440	.0136566	.0110778	.0089905	88
89	.0198907	.0160802	.0130063	.0105253	.0085218	89
90	.0190342	.0153510	.0123869	.0100002	.0080775	90
91	.0182145	.0146549	.0117971	.0095014	.0076564	91
92	.0174302	.0139904	.0112353	.0090275	.0072573	92
93	.0166796	.0133560	.0107003	.0085772	.0068789	93
94	.0159613	.0127503	.0101907	.0081493	.0065203	94
95	.0152740	.0121721	.0097055	.0077428	.0061804	95
96	.0146163	.0116202	.0092433	.0073566	.0058582	96
97	.0139868	.0110933	.0088031	.0069897	.0055528	97
98	.0133845	.0105902	.0083840	.0066410	.0052633	98
99	.0128082	.0101100	.0079847	.0063097	.0049889	99
100	.0122566	.0096515	.0076045	.0059950	.0047288	100

No Income Tax

PRESENT VALUE OF £1
Rate Per Cent

Yrs.	5.75	6	6.25	6.5	6.75	Yrs.
1	.9456265	.9433962	.9411765	.9389671	.9367681	1
2	.8942094	.8899964	.8858131	.8816593	.8775346	2
3	.8455881	.8396193	.8337065	.8278491	.8220464	3
4	.7996105	.7920937	.7846649	.7773231	.7700669	4
5	.7561329	.7472582	.7385082	.7298808	.7213742	5

No Income Tax

PRESENT VALUE OF £1
Rate Per Cent

Yrs.	**5.75**	**6**	**6.25**	**6.5**	**6.75**	**Yrs.**
6	.7150193	.7049605	.6950665	.6853341	.6757603	**6**
7	.6761411	.6650571	.6541803	.6435062	.6330308	**7**
8	.6393770	.6274124	.6156991	.6042312	.5930031	**8**
9	.6046118	.5918985	.5794815	.5673532	.5555064	**9**
10	.5717369	.5583948	.5453943	.5327260	.5203807	**10**
11	.5406496	.5267875	.5133123	.5002122	.4874760	**11**
12	.5112526	.4969694	.4831175	.4696829	.4566520	**12**
13	.4834539	.4688390	.4546988	.4410168	.4277771	**13**
14	.4571669	.4423010	.4279518	.4141002	.4007279	**14**
15	.4323091	.4172651	.4027782	.3888265	.3753892	**15**
16	.4088029	.3936463	.3790853	.3650953	.3516526	**16**
17	.3865749	.3713644	.3567862	.3428125	.3294170	**17**
18	.3655554	.3503438	.3357988	.3218897	.3085873	**18**
19	.3456789	.3305130	.3160459	.3022438	.2890748	**19**
20	.3268831	.3118047	.2974550	.2837970	.2707961	**20**
21	.3091093	.2941554	.2799576	.2664761	.2536731	**21**
22	.2923020	.2775051	.2634895	.2502123	.2376329	**22**
23	.2764085	.2617973	.2479901	.2349411	.2226069	**23**
24	.2613792	.2469785	.2334025	.2206020	.2085311	**24**
25	.2471671	.2329986	.2196729	.2071380	.1953453	**25**
26	.2337277	.2198100	.2067510	.1944958	.1829932	**26**
27	.2210191	.2073680	.1945892	.1826252	.1714222	**27**
28	.2090015	.1956301	.1831427	.1714790	.1605829	**28**
29	.1976374	.1845567	.1723696	.1610132	.1504289	**29**
30	.1868911	.1741101	.1622303	.1511861	.1409170	**30**
31	.1767292	.1642548	.1526873	.1419587	.1320066	**31**
32	.1671198	.1549574	.1437057	.1332946	.1236596	**32**
33	.1580329	.1461862	.1352524	.1251592	.1158403	**33**
34	.1494401	.1379115	.1272964	.1175204	.1085155	**34**
35	.1413145	.1301052	.1198084	.1103478	.1016539	**35**
36	.1336308	.1227408	.1127608	.1036130	.0952261	**36**
37	.1263648	.1157932	.1061278	.0972892	.0892048	**37**
38	.1194939	.1092389	.0998850	.0913513	.0835642	**38**
39	.1129966	.1030555	.0940094	.0857759	.0782803	**39**
40	.1068526	.0972222	.0884795	.0805408	.0733305	**40**
41	.1010426	.0917190	.0832748	.0756251	.0686937	**41**
42	.0955486	.0865274	.0783763	.0710095	.0643500	**42**
43	.0903533	.0816296	.0737659	.0666756	.0602811	**43**
44	.0854404	.0770091	.0694267	.0626062	.0564694	**44**
45	.0807947	.0726501	.0653428	.0587852	.0528987	**45**
46	.0764016	.0685378	.0614991	.0551973	.0495538	**46**
47	.0722474	.0646583	.0578815	.0518285	.0464205	**47**
48	.0683191	.0609984	.0544767	.0486652	.0434852	**48**
49	.0646043	.0575457	.0512722	.0456951	.0407356	**49**
50	.0610916	.0542884	.0482562	.0429062	.0381598	**50**
51	.0577698	.0512154	.0454176	.0402875	.0357469	**51**
52	.0546286	.0483164	.0427460	.0378286	.0334865	**52**
53	.0516583	.0455816	.0402315	.0355198	.0313691	**53**
54	.0488495	.0430015	.0378649	.0333519	.0293856	**54**

No Income Tax

PRESENT VALUE OF £1
Rate Per Cent

Yrs.	5.75	6	6.25	6.5	6.75	Yrs.
55	.0461933	.0405674	.0356376	.0313164	.0275275	**55**
56	.0436816	.0382712	.0335413	.0294051	.0257869	**56**
57	.0413065	.0361049	.0315682	.0276104	.0241563	**57**
58	.0390605	.0340612	.0297113	.0259252	.0226289	**58**
59	.0369367	.0321332	.0279636	.0243429	.0211980	**59**
60	.0349283	.0303143	.0263187	.0228572	.0198576	**60**
61	.0330291	.0285984	.0247705	.0214622	.0186020	**61**
62	.0312332	.0269797	.0233134	.0201523	.0174257	**62**
63	.0295350	.0254525	.0219420	.0189223	.0163239	**63**
64	.0279290	.0240118	.0206513	.0177675	.0152917	**64**
65	.0264104	.0226526	.0194365	.0166831	.0143248	**65**
66	.0249744	.0213704	.0182932	.0156648	.0134190	**66**
67	.0236165	.0201608	.0172171	.0147088	.0125705	**67**
68	.0223324	.0190196	.0162044	.0138110	.0117756	**68**
69	.0211181	.0179430	.0152512	.0129681	.0110310	**69**
70	.0199698	.0169274	.0143540	.0121766	.0103335	**70**
71	.0188840	.0159692	.0135097	.0114335	.0096801	**71**
72	.0178572	.0150653	.0127150	.0107356	.0090680	**72**
73	.0168862	.0142125	.0119671	.0100804	.0084946	**73**
74	.0159681	.0134081	.0112631	.0094652	.0079575	**74**
75	.0150998	.0126491	.0106006	.0088875	.0074543	**75**
76	.0142788	.0119331	.0099770	.0083451	.0069830	**76**
77	.0135024	.0112577	.0093901	.0078357	.0065414	**77**
78	.0127682	.0106204	.0088378	.0073575	.0061278	**78**
79	.0120740	.0100193	.0083179	.0069085	.0057403	**79**
80	.0114175	.0094522	.0078286	.0064868	.0053774	**80**
81	.0107967	.0089171	.0073681	.0060909	.0050373	**81**
82	.0102096	.0084124	.0069347	.0057192	.0047188	**82**
83	.0096545	.0079362	.0065268	.0053701	.0044204	**83**
84	.0091295	.0074870	.0061428	.0050423	.0041409	**84**
85	.0086331	.0070632	.0057815	.0047346	.0038791	**85**
86	.0081637	.0066634	.0054414	.0044456	.0036338	**86**
87	.0077198	.0062862	.0051213	.0041743	.0034040	**87**
88	.0073001	.0059304	.0048201	.0039195	.0031888	**88**
89	.0069031	.0055947	.0045365	.0036803	.0029872	**89**
90	.0065278	.0052780	.0042697	.0034557	.0027983	**90**
91	.0061729	.0049793	.0040185	.0032448	.0026213	**91**
92	.0058372	.0046974	.0037821	.0030467	.0024556	**92**
93	.0055198	.0044315	.0035597	.0028608	.0023003	**93**
94	.0052197	.0041807	.0033503	.0026862	.0021549	**94**
95	.0049359	.0039441	.0031532	.0025222	.0020186	**95**
96	.0046675	.0037208	.0029677	.0023683	.0018910	**96**
97	.0044137	.0035102	.0027931	.0022238	.0017714	**97**
98	.0041737	.0033115	.0026288	.0020880	.0016594	**98**
99	.0039468	.0031241	.0024742	.0019606	.0015545	**99**
100	.0037322	.0029472	.0023287	.0018409	.0014562	**100**

No Income Tax

PRESENT VALUE OF £1

Rate Per Cent

Yrs.	7	7.25	7.5	7.75	8	Yrs.
1	.9345794	.9324009	.9302326	.9280742	.9259259	1
2	.8734387	.8693715	.8653326	.8613218	.8573388	2
3	.8162979	.8106028	.8049606	.7993706	.7938322	3
4	.7628952	.7558068	.7488005	.7418753	.7350299	4
5	.7129862	.7047150	.6965586	.6885153	.6805832	5
6	.6663422	.6570769	.6479615	.6389933	.6301696	6
7	.6227497	.6126591	.6027549	.5930333	.5834904	7
8	.5820091	.5712439	.5607022	.5503789	.5402689	8
9	.5439337	.5326284	.5215835	.5107925	.5002490	9
10	.5083493	.4966232	.4851939	.4740533	.4631935	10
11	.4750928	.4630519	.4513432	.4399567	.4288829	11
12	.4440120	.4317500	.4198541	.4083125	.3971138	12
13	.4149644	.4025641	.3905620	.3789443	.3676979	13
14	.3878172	.3753512	.3633135	.3516884	.3404610	14
15	.3624460	.3499778	.3379660	.3263930	.3152417	15
16	.3387346	.3263196	.3143870	.3029169	.2918905	16
17	.3165744	.3042607	.2924530	.2811294	.2702690	17
18	.2958639	.2836930	.2720493	.2609090	.2502490	18
19	.2765083	.2645156	.2530691	.2421429	.2317121	19
20	.2584190	.2466346	.2354131	.2247266	.2145482	20
21	.2415131	.2299623	.2189890	.2085629	.1986557	21
22	.2257132	.2144171	.2037107	.1935619	.1839405	22
23	.2109469	.1999227	.1894983	.1796398	.1703153	23
24	.1971466	.1864081	.1762775	.1667191	.1576993	24
25	.1842492	.1738071	.1639791	.1547277	.1460179	25
26	.1721955	.1620579	.1525387	.1435988	.1352018	26
27	.1609304	.1511029	.1418964	.1332703	.1251868	27
28	.1504022	.1408885	.1319967	.1236848	.1159137	28
29	.1405628	.1313646	.1227876	.1147886	.1073275	29
30	.1313671	.1224845	.1142210	.1065324	.0993773	30
31	.1227730	.1142046	.1062521	.0988700	.0920160	31
32	.1147411	.1064845	.0988392	.0917587	.0852000	32
33	.1072347	.0992862	.0919434	.0851589	.0788889	33
34	.1002193	.0925746	.0855288	.0790337	.0730453	34
35	.0936629	.0863166	.0795616	.0733492	.0676345	35
36	.0875355	.0804817	.0740108	.0680735	.0626246	36
37	.0818088	.0750412	.0688473	.0631772	.0579857	37
38	.0764569	.0699685	.0640440	.0586332	.0536905	38
39	.0714550	.0652387	.0595758	.0544159	.0497134	39
40	.0667804	.0608286	.0554194	.0505020	.0460309	40
41	.0624116	.0567167	.0515529	.0468696	.0426212	41
42	.0583286	.0528827	.0479562	.0434985	.0394641	42
43	.0545127	.0493078	.0446104	.0403698	.0365408	43
44	.0509464	.0459747	.0414980	.0374662	.0338341	44
45	.0476135	.0428668	.0386028	.0347714	.0313279	45
46	.0444986	.0399691	.0359096	.0322705	.0290073	46
47	.0415875	.0372672	.0334043	.0299494	.0268586	47
48	.0388668	.0347480	.0310738	.0277953	.0248691	48
49	.0363241	.0323990	.0289058	.0257961	.0230269	49
50	.0339478	.0302089	.0268891	.0239407	.0213212	50

No Income Tax

PRESENT VALUE OF £1
Rate Per Cent

Yrs.	**7**	**7.25**	**7.5**	**7.75**	**8**	**Yrs.**
51	.0317269	.0281668	.0250131	.0222187	.0197419	**51**
52	.0296513	.0262628	.0232680	.0206206	.0182795	**52**
53	.0277115	.0244874	.0216447	.0191375	.0169255	**53**
54	.0258986	.0228321	.0201346	.0177610	.0156717	**54**
55	.0242043	.0212887	.0187299	.0164835	.0145109	**55**
56	.0226208	.0198496	.0174231	.0152979	.0134360	**56**
57	.0211410	.0185078	.0162076	.0141976	.0124407	**57**
58	.0197579	.0172567	.0150768	.0131764	.0115192	**58**
59	.0184653	.0160901	.0140249	.0122287	.0106659	**59**
60	.0172573	.0150024	.0130464	.0113491	.0098759	**60**
61	.0161283	.0139883	.0121362	.0105329	.0091443	**61**
62	.0150732	.0130427	.0112895	.0097753	.0084670	**62**
63	.0140871	.0121610	.0105019	.0090722	.0078398	**63**
64	.0131655	.0113389	.0097692	.0084197	.0072590	**64**
65	.0123042	.0105724	.0090876	.0078141	.0067213	**65**
66	.0114993	.0098578	.0084536	.0072520	.0062235	**66**
67	.0107470	.0091914	.0078638	.0067304	.0057625	**67**
68	.0100439	.0085701	.0073152	.0062463	.0053356	**68**
69	.0093868	.0079907	.0068048	.0057971	.0049404	**69**
70	.0087727	.0074506	.0063301	.0053801	.0045744	**70**
71	.0081988	.0069469	.0058884	.0049931	.0042356	**71**
72	.0076625	.0064773	.0054776	.0046340	.0039218	**72**
73	.0071612	.0060394	.0050954	.0043007	.0036313	**73**
74	.0066927	.0056312	.0047399	.0039914	.0033623	**74**
75	.0062548	.0052505	.0044093	.0037043	.0031133	**75**
76	.0058457	.0048956	.0041016	.0034378	.0028827	**76**
77	.0054632	.0045647	.0038155	.0031906	.0026691	**77**
78	.0051058	.0042561	.0035493	.0029611	.0024714	**78**
79	.0047718	.0039684	.0033017	.0027481	.0022884	**79**
80	.0044596	.0037001	.0030713	.0025505	.0021188	**80**
81	.0041679	.0034500	.0028570	.0023670	.0019619	**81**
82	.0038952	.0032168	.0026577	.0021968	.0018166	**82**
83	.0036404	.0029993	.0024723	.0020388	.0016820	**83**
84	.0034022	.0027966	.0022998	.0018921	.0015574	**84**
85	.0031796	.0026075	.0021393	.0017560	.0014421	**85**
86	.0029716	.0024313	.0019901	.0016297	.0013352	**86**
87	.0027772	.0022669	.0018512	.0015125	.0012363	**87**
88	.0025955	.0021137	.0017221	.0014037	.0011447	**88**
89	.0024257	.0019708	.0016019	.0013028	.0010600	**89**
90	.0022670	.0018376	.0014902	.0012091	.0009814	**90**
91	.0021187	.0017133	.0013862	.0011221	.0009087	**91**
92	.0019801	.0015975	.0012895	.0010414	.0008414	**92**
93	.0018506	.0014895	.0011995	.0009665	.0007791	**93**
94	.0017295	.0013888	.0011158	.0008970	.0007214	**94**
95	.0016164	.0012950	.0010380	.0008325	.0006679	**95**
96	.0015106	.0012074	.0009656	.0007726	.0006185	**96**
97	.0014118	.0011258	.0008982	.0007170	.0005727	**97**
98	.0013194	.0010497	.0008355	.0006654	.0005302	**98**
99	.0012331	.0009787	.0007773	.0006176	.0004910	**99**
100	.0011525	.0009126	.0007230	.0005732	.0004546	**100**

No Income Tax

PRESENT VALUE OF £1
Rate Per Cent

Yrs.	8.25	8.5	8.75	9	9.25	Yrs.
1	.9237875	.9216590	.9195402	.9174312	.9153318	**1**
2	.8533834	.8494553	.8455542	.8416800	.8378323	**2**
3	.7883449	.7829081	.7775211	.7721835	.7668946	**3**
4	.7282632	.7215743	.7149620	.7084252	.7019630	**4**
5	.6727605	.6650454	.6574363	.6499314	.6425291	**5**
6	.6214877	.6129451	.6045391	.5962673	.5881273	**6**
7	.5741226	.5649264	.5558980	.5470342	.5383316	**7**
8	.5303673	.5206694	.5111706	.5018663	.4927520	**8**
9	.4899467	.4798797	.4700419	.4604278	.4510316	**9**
10	.4526067	.4422854	.4322225	.4224108	.4128436	**10**
11	.4181124	.4076363	.3974460	.3875329	.3778889	**11**
12	.3862470	.3757017	.3654675	.3555347	.3458937	**12**
13	.3568102	.3462688	.3360621	.3261786	.3166075	**13**
14	.3296168	.3191418	.3090226	.2992465	.2898009	**14**
15	.3044959	.2941399	.2841587	.2745380	.2652640	**15**
16	.2812895	.2710967	.2612954	.2518698	.2428046	**16**
17	.2598517	.2498587	.2402716	.2310732	.2222468	**17**
18	.2400478	.2302845	.2209394	.2119937	.2034295	**18**
19	.2217532	.2122438	.2031627	.1944897	.1862055	**19**
20	.2048528	.1956164	.1868163	.1784309	.1704398	**20**
21	.1892405	.1802916	.1717851	.1636981	.1560090	**21**
22	.1748180	.1661674	.1579633	.1501817	.1428000	**22**
23	.1614947	.1531497	.1452536	.1377814	.1307094	**23**
24	.1491868	.1411518	.1335665	.1264049	.1196425	**24**
25	.1378169	.1300938	.1228198	.1159678	.1095125	**25**
26	.1273135	.1199021	.1129377	.1063925	.1002403	**26**
27	.1176106	.1105089	.1038508	.0976078	.0917531	**27**
28	.1086472	.1018515	.0954950	.0895484	.0839846	**28**
29	.1003670	.0938723	.0878115	.0821545	.0768738	**29**
30	.0927177	.0865183	.0807462	.0753711	.0703650	**30**
31	.0856515	.0797403	.0742494	.0691478	.0644073	**31**
32	.0791238	.0734934	.0682753	.0634384	.0589541	**32**
33	.0730936	.0677359	.0627819	.0582003	.0539625	**33**
34	.0675229	.0624294	.0577305	.0533948	.0493936	**34**
35	.0623768	.0575386	.0530855	.0489861	.0452116	**35**
36	.0576229	.0530310	.0488142	.0449413	.0413836	**36**
37	.0532314	.0488765	.0448866	.0412306	.0378797	**37**
38	.0491745	.0450474	.0412751	.0378262	.0346725	**38**
39	.0454268	.0415184	.0379541	.0347030	.0317368	**39**
40	.0419647	.0382658	.0349003	.0318376	.0290497	**40**
41	.0387664	.0352680	.0320922	.0292088	.0265901	**41**
42	.0358120	.0325051	.0295101	.0267971	.0243388	**42**
43	.0330826	.0299586	.0271357	.0245845	.0222781	**43**
44	.0305613	.0276116	.0249524	.0225545	.0203918	**44**
45	.0282322	.0254485	.0229447	.0206922	.0186653	**45**
46	.0260805	.0234548	.0210986	.0189837	.0170849	**46**
47	.0240929	.0216173	.0194010	.0174162	.0156384	**47**
48	.0222567	.0199238	.0178400	.0159782	.0143143	**48**
49	.0205605	.0183630	.0164046	.0146589	.0131023	**49**
50	.0189935	.0169244	.0150847	.0134485	.0119930	**50**

No Income Tax

PRESENT VALUE OF £1
Rate Per Cent

Yrs.	**8.25**	**8.5**	**8.75**	**9**	**9.25**	**Yrs.**
51	.0175459	.0155985	.0138710	.0123381	.0109776	**51**
52	.0162087	.0143765	.0127549	.0113194	.0100481	**52**
53	.0149734	.0132502	.0117287	.0103847	.0091974	**53**
54	.0138323	.0122122	.0107850	.0095273	.0084186	**54**
55	.0127781	.0112555	.0099172	.0087406	.0077058	**55**
56	.0118042	.0103737	.0091193	.0080189	.0070534	**56**
57	.0109046	.0095610	.0083856	.0073568	.0064562	**57**
58	.0100735	.0088120	.0077109	.0067494	.0059096	**58**
59	.0093058	.0081217	.0070904	.0061921	.0054092	**59**
60	.0085966	.0074854	.0065199	.0056808	.0049512	**60**
61	.0079414	.0068990	.0059954	.0052118	.0045320	**61**
62	.0073362	.0063585	.0055130	.0047814	.0041483	**62**
63	.0067771	.0058604	.0050694	.0043866	.0037971	**63**
64	.0062606	.0054013	.0046615	.0040244	.0034756	**64**
65	.0057834	.0049781	.0042864	.0036921	.0031813	**65**
66	.0053427	.0045881	.0039416	.0033873	.0029120	**66**
67	.0049355	.0042287	.0036244	.0031076	.0026654	**67**
68	.0045593	.0038974	.0033328	.0028510	.0024397	**68**
69	.0042119	.0035921	.0030646	.0026156	.0022332	**69**
70	.0038909	.0033107	.0028181	.0023996	.0020441	**70**
71	.0035943	.0030513	.0025913	.0022015	.0018710	**71**
72	.0033204	.0028123	.0023828	.0020197	.0017126	**72**
73	.0030673	.0025920	.0021911	.0018530	.0015676	**73**
74	.0028336	.0023889	.0020148	.0017000	.0014349	**74**
75	.0026176	.0022018	.0018527	.0015596	.0013134	**75**
76	.0024181	.0020293	.0017036	.0014308	.0012022	**76**
77	.0022338	.0018703	.0015666	.0013127	.0011004	**77**
78	.0020636	.0017238	.0014405	.0012043	.0010072	**78**
79	.0019063	.0015887	.0013246	.0011049	.0009219	**79**
80	.0017610	.0014643	.0012180	.0010136	.0008439	**80**
81	.0016268	.0013496	.0011200	.0009299	.0007724	**81**
82	.0015028	.0012438	.0010299	.0008532	.0007070	**82**
83	.0013883	.0011464	.0009470	.0007827	.0006472	**83**
84	.0012825	.0010566	.0008708	.0007181	.0005924	**84**
85	.0011848	.0009738	.0008008	.0006588	.0005422	**85**
86	.0010945	.0008975	.0007363	.0006044	.0004963	**86**
87	.0010110	.0008272	.0006771	.0005545	.0004543	**87**
88	.0009340	.0007624	.0006226	.0005087	.0004158	**88**
89	.0008628	.0007027	.0005725	.0004667	.0003806	**89**
90	.0007971	.0006476	.0005265	.0004282	.0003484	**90**
91	.0007363	.0005969	.0004841	.0003928	.0003189	**91**
92	.0006802	.0005501	.0004452	.0003604	.0002919	**92**
93	.0006284	.0005070	.0004093	.0003306	.0002672	**93**
94	.0005805	.0004673	.0003764	.0003033	.0002466	**94**
95	.0005362	.0004307	.0003461	.0002783	.0002239	**95**
96	.0004954	.0003970	.0003183	.0002553	.0002049	**96**
97	.0004576	.0003659	.0002927	.0002342	.0001876	**97**
98	.0004227	.0003372	.0002691	.0002149	.0001717	**98**
99	.0003905	.0003108	.0002475	.0001971	.0001571	**99**
100	.0003608	.0002864	.0002275	.0001809	.0001438	**100**

No Income Tax

PRESENT VALUE OF £1
Rate Per Cent

Yrs.	9.5	10	10.5	11	12	Yrs.
1	.9132420	.9090909	.9049774	.9009009	.8928571	1
2	.8340110	.8264463	.8189841	.8116224	.7971939	2
3	.7616539	.7513148	.7411620	.7311914	.7117802	3
4	.6955743	.6830135	.6707349	.6587310	.6355181	4
5	.6352277	.6209213	.6069999	.5934513	.5674269	5
6	.5801166	.5644739	.5493212	.5346408	.5066311	6
7	.5297868	.5131581	.4971232	.4816584	.4523492	7
8	.4838236	.4665074	.4498853	.4339265	.4038832	8
9	.4418480	.4240976	.4071360	.3909248	.3606100	9
10	.4035142	.3855433	.3684489	.3521845	.3219732	10
11	.3685061	.3504939	.3334379	.3172833	.2874761	11
12	.3365353	.3186308	.3017537	.2858408	.2566751	12
13	.3073381	.2896644	.2730803	.2575143	.2291742	13
14	.2806741	.2633313	.2471315	.2319948	.2046198	14
15	.2563234	.2393920	.2236484	.2090043	.1826963	15
16	.2340853	.2176291	.2023968	.1882922	.1631217	16
17	.2137765	.1978447	.1831645	.1696326	.1456443	17
18	.1952297	.1798588	.1657597	.1528222	.1300396	18
19	.1782920	.1635080	.1500088	.1376776	.1161068	19
20	.1628237	.1486436	.1357546	.1240339	.1036668	20
21	.1486974	.1351306	.1228548	.1117423	.0925596	21
22	.1357968	.1228460	.1111808	.1006687	.0826425	22
23	.1240153	.1116782	.1006161	.0906925	.0737880	23
24	.1132560	.1015256	.0910553	.0817050	.0658821	24
25	.1034301	.0922960	.0824030	.0736081	.0588233	25
26	.0944567	.0839055	.0745729	.0663136	.0525208	26
27	.0862619	.0762777	.0674867	.0597420	.0468936	27
28	.0787779	.0693433	.0610740	.0538216	.0418693	28
29	.0719433	.0630394	.0552706	.0484879	.0373833	29
30	.0657017	.0573086	.0500186	.0436828	.0333779	30
31	.0600015	.0520987	.0452657	.0393539	.0298017	31
32	.0547959	.0473624	.0409644	.0354540	.0266087	32
33	.0500419	.0430568	.0370719	.0319405	.0237577	33
34	.0457004	.0391425	.0335492	.0287752	.0212123	34
35	.0417355	.0355841	.0303613	.0259236	.0189395	35
36	.0381146	.0323492	.0274763	.0233546	.0169103	36
37	.0348079	.0294083	.0248654	.0210402	.0150985	37
38	.0317880	.0267349	.0225026	.0189551	.0134808	38
39	.0290302	.0243044	.0203644	.0170767	.0120364	39
40	.0265116	.0220949	.0184293	.0153844	.0107468	40
41	.0242115	.0200863	.0166781	.0138598	.0095954	41
42	.0221109	.0182603	.0150933	.0124863	.0085673	42
43	.0201926	.0166002	.0136591	.0112489	.0076494	43
44	.0184408	.0150911	.0123612	.0101342	.0068298	44
45	.0168409	.0137192	.0111866	.0091299	.0060980	45
46	.0153798	.0124720	.0101236	.0082251	.0054447	46
47	.0140455	.0113382	.0091616	.0074100	.0048613	47
48	.0128269	.0103074	.0082911	.0066757	.0043405	48
49	.0117141	.0093704	.0075032	.0060141	.0038754	49
50	.0106978	.0085186	.0067903	.0054182	.0034602	50

No Income Tax

PRESENT VALUE OF £1
Rate Per Cent

Yrs.	9.5	10	10.5	11	12	Yrs.
51	.0097697	.0077441	.0061450	.0048812	.0030894	**51**
52	.0089221	.0070401	.0055611	.0043975	.0027584	**52**
53	.0081480	.0064001	.0050327	.0039617	.0024629	**53**
54	.0074411	.0058183	.0045545	.0035691	.0021990	**54**
55	.0067955	.0052894	.0041217	.0032154	.0019634	**55**
56	.0062060	.0048085	.0037300	.0028968	.0017530	**56**
57	.0056675	.0043714	.0033756	.0026097	.0015652	**57**
58	.0051758	.0039740	.0030548	.0023511	.0013975	**58**
59	.0047268	.0036127	.0027646	.0021181	.0012478	**59**
60	.0043167	.0032843	.0025019	.0019082	.0011141	**60**
61	.0039422	.0029857	.0022641	.0017191	.0009947	**61**
62	.0036002	.0027143	.0020490	.0015487	.0008881	**62**
63	.0032878	.0024675	.0018543	.0013953	.0007930	**63**
64	.0030026	.0022432	.0016781	.0012570	.0007080	**64**
65	.0027421	.0020393	.0015186	.0011324	.0006322	**65**
66	.0025042	.0018539	.0013743	.0010202	.0005644	**66**
67	.0022869	.0016853	.0012437	.0009191	.0005040	**67**
68	.0020885	.0015321	.0011256	.0008280	.0004500	**68**
69	.0019073	.0013929	.0010186	.0007460	.0004018	**69**
70	.0017419	.0012662	.0009218	.0006720	.0003587	**70**
71	.0015907	.0011511	.0008342	.0006054	.0003203	**71**
72	.0014527	.0010465	.0007549	.0005454	.0002860	**72**
73	.0013267	.0009513	.0006832	.0004914	.0002553	**73**
74	.0012116	.0008649	.0006183	.0004427	.0002280	**74**
75	.0011065	.0007862	.0005595	.0003988	.0002035	**75**
76	.0010105	.0007148	.0005064	.0003593	.0001817	**76**
77	.0009228	.0006498	.0004583	.0003237	.0001623	**77**
78	.0008427	.0005907	.0004147	.0002916	.0001449	**78**
79	.0007696	.0005370	.0003753	.0002627	.0001294	**79**
80	.0007029	.0004882	.0003396	.0002367	.0001155	**80**
81	.0006419	.0004438	.0003074	.0002132	.0001031	**81**
82	.0005862	.0004035	.0002782	.0001921	.0000921	**82**
83	.0005353	.0003668	.0002517	.0001731	.0000822	**83**
84	.0004889	.0003334	.0002278	.0001559	.0000734	**84**
85	.0004465	.0003031	.0002062	.0001405	.0000655	**85**
86	.0004077	.0002756	.0001866	.0001265	.0000585	**86**
87	.0003724	.0002505	.0001688	.0001140	.0000522	**87**
88	.0003401	.0002277	.0001528	.0001027	.0000466	**88**
89	.0003106	.0002070	.0001383	.0000925	.0000416	**89**
90	.0002836	.0001882	.0001251	.0000834	.0000372	**90**
91	.0002590	.0001711	.0001132	.0000751	.0000332	**91**
92	.0002365	.0001556	.0001025	.0000677	.0000296	**92**
93	.0002160	.0001414	.0000927	.0000609	.0000265	**93**
94	.0001973	.0001286	.0000839	.0000549	.0000236	**94**
95	.0001802	.0001169	.0000760	.0000495	.0000211	**95**
96	.0001645	.0001062	.0000687	.0000446	.0000188	**96**
97	.0001503	.0000966	.0000622	.0000401	.0000168	**97**
98	.0001372	.0000878	.0000563	.0000362	.0000150	**98**
99	.0001253	.0000798	.0000509	.0000326	.0000134	**99**
100	.0001144	.0000726	.0000461	.0000294	.0000120	**100**

No Income Tax

PRESENT VALUE OF £1

Rate Per Cent

Yrs.	13	14	15	16	17	Yrs.
1	.8849558	.8771930	.8695652	.8620690	.8547009	**1**
2	.7831467	.7694675	.7561437	.7431629	.7305136	**2**
3	.6930502	.6749715	.6575162	.6406577	.6243706	**3**
4	.6133187	.5920803	.5717532	.5522911	.5336500	**4**
5	.5427599	.5193687	.4971767	.4761130	.4561112	**5**
6	.4803185	.4555865	.4323276	.4104423	.3898386	**6**
7	.4250606	.3996373	.3759370	.3538295	.3331954	**7**
8	.3761599	.3505591	.3269018	.3050255	.2847824	**8**
9	.3328848	.3075079	.2842624	.2629530	.2434037	**9**
10	.2945883	.2697438	.2471847	.2266836	.2080374	**10**
11	.2606977	.2366174	.2149432	.1954169	.1778097	**11**
12	.2307059	.2075591	.1869072	.1684628	.1519741	**12**
13	.2041645	.1820694	.1625280	.1452266	.1298924	**13**
14	.1806766	.1597100	.1413287	.1251953	.1110192	**14**
15	.1598908	.1400965	.1228945	.1079270	.0948882	**15**
16	.1414962	.1228917	.1068648	.0930405	.0811010	**16**
17	.1252179	.1077997	.0929259	.0802074	.0693171	**17**
18	.1108123	.0945611	.0808051	.0691443	.0592454	**18**
19	.0980640	.0829484	.0702653	.0596071	.0506371	**19**
20	.0867823	.0727617	.0611003	.0513855	.0432796	**20**
21	.0767985	.0638261	.0531307	.0442978	.0369911	**21**
22	.0679633	.0559878	.0462006	.0381878	.0316163	**22**
23	.0601445	.0491121	.0401744	.0329205	.0270225	**23**
24	.0532252	.0430808	.0349343	.0283797	.0230961	**24**
25	.0471020	.0377902	.0303776	.0244653	.0197403	**25**
26	.0416831	.0331493	.0264153	.0210908	.0168720	**26**
27	.0368877	.0290783	.0229699	.0181817	.0144205	**27**
28	.0326440	.0255073	.0199738	.0156739	.0123253	**28**
29	.0288885	.0223748	.0173685	.0135120	.0105344	**29**
30	.0255651	.0196270	.0151031	.0116482	.0090038	**30**
31	.0226239	.0172167	.0131331	.0100416	.0076955	**31**
32	.0200212	.0151024	.0114201	.0086565	.0065774	**32**
33	.0177179	.0132477	.0099305	.0074625	.0056217	**33**
34	.0156795	.0116208	.0086352	.0064332	.0048049	**34**
35	.0138757	.0101937	.0075089	.0055459	.0041067	**35**
36	.0122794	.0089418	.0065295	.0047809	.0035100	**36**
37	.0108667	.0078437	.0056778	.0041215	.0030000	**37**
38	.0096165	.0068804	.0049372	.0035530	.0025641	**38**
39	.0085102	.0060355	.0042932	.0030629	.0021916	**39**
40	.0075312	.0052943	.0037332	.0026405	.0018731	**40**
41	.0066647	.0046441	.0032463	.0022763	.0016010	**41**
42	.0058980	.0040738	.0028229	.0019623	.0013683	**42**
43	.0052195	.0035735	.0024547	.0016916	.0011695	**43**
44	.0046190	.0031346	.0021345	.0014583	.0009996	**44**
45	.0040876	.0027497	.0018561	.0012572	.0008544	**45**
46	.0036174	.0024120	.0016140	.0010838	.0007302	**46**
47	.0032012	.0021158	.0014035	.0009343	.0006241	**47**
48	.0028329	.0018560	.0012204	.0008054	.0005334	**48**
49	.0025070	.0016280	.0010612	.0006943	.0004559	**49**
50	.0022186	.0014281	.0009228	.0005986	.0003897	**50**

No Income Tax

PRESENT VALUE OF £1
Rate Per Cent

Yrs.	13	14	15	16	17	Yrs.
51	.0019634	.0012527	.0008024	.0005160	.0003331	**51**
52	.0017375	.0010989	.0006978	.0004448	.0002847	**52**
53	.0015376	.0009639	.0006068	.0003835	.0002433	**53**
54	.0013607	.0008455	.0005276	.0003306	.0002080	**54**
55	.0012042	.0007417	.0004588	.0002850	.0001777	**55**
56	.0010656	.0006506	.0003990	.0002457	.0001519	**56**
57	.0009430	.0005707	.0003469	.0002118	.0001298	**57**
58	.0008345	.0005006	.0003017	.0001826	.0001110	**58**
59	.0007385	.0004392	.0002623	.0001574	.0000948	**59**
60	.0006536	.0003852	.0002281	.0001357	.0000811	**60**
61	.0005784	.0003379	.0001983	.0001170	.0000693	**61**
62	.0005118	.0002964	.0001725	.0001008	.0000592	**62**
63	.0004530	.0002600	.0001500	.0000869	.0000506	**63**
64	.0004008	.0002281	.0001304	.0000749	.0000433	**64**
65	.0003547	.0002001	.0001134	.0000646	.0000370	**65**
66	.0003139	.0001755	.0000986	.0000557	.0000316	**66**
67	.0002778	.0001539	.0000858	.0000480	.0000270	**67**
68	.0002458	.0001350	.0000746	.0000414	.0000231	**68**
69	.0002176	.0001185	.0000648	.0000357	.0000197	**69**
70	.0001925	.0001039	.0000564	.0000308	.0000169	**70**
71	.0001704	.0000911	.0000490	.0000265	.0000144	**71**
72	.0001508	.0000800	.0000426	.0000229	.0000123	**72**
73	.0001334	.0000701	.0000371	.0000197	.0000105	**73**
74	.0001181	.0000615	.0000322	.0000170	.0000090	**74**
75	.0001045	.0000540	.0000280	.0000146	.0000077	**75**
76	.0000925	.0000473	.0000244	.0000126	.0000066	**76**
77	.0000818	.0000415	.0000212	.0000109	.0000056	**77**
78	.0000724	.0000364	.0000184	.0000094	.0000048	**78**
79	.0000641	.0000320	.0000160	.0000081	.0000041	**79**
80	.0000567	.0000280	.0000139	.0000070	.0000035	**80**
81	.0000502	.0000246	.0000121	.0000060	.0000030	**81**
82	.0000444	.0000216	.0000105	.0000052	.0000026	**82**
83	.0000393	.0000189	.0000092	.0000045	.0000022	**83**
84	.0000348	.0000166	.0000080	.0000039	.0000019	**84**
85	.0000308	.0000146	.0000069	.0000033	.0000016	**85**
86	.0000272	.0000128	.0000060	.0000029	.0000014	**86**
87	.0000241	.0000112	.0000052	.0000025	.0000012	**87**
88	.0000213	.0000098	.0000046	.0000021	.0000010	**88**
89	.0000189	.0000086	.0000040	.0000018	.0000009	**89**
90	.0000167	.0000076	.0000034	.0000016	.0000007	**90**
91	.0000148	.0000066	.0000030	.0000014	.0000006	**91**
92	.0000131	.0000058	.0000026	.0000012	.0000005	**92**
93	.0000116	.0000051	.0000023	.0000010	.0000005	**93**
94	.0000102	.0000045	.0000020	.0000009	.0000004	**94**
95	.0000091	.0000039	.0000017	.0000008	.0000003	**95**
96	.0000080	.0000034	.0000015	.0000006	.0000003	**96**
97	.0000071	.0000030	.0000013	.0000006	.0000002	**97**
98	.0000063	.0000027	.0000011	.0000005	.0000002	**98**
99	.0000056	.0000023	.0000010	.0000004	.0000002	**99**
100	.0000049	.0000020	.0000009	.0000004	.0000002	**100**

No Income Tax

PRESENT VALUE OF £1
Rate Per Cent

Yrs.	**18**	**19**	**20**	**21**	**22**	**Yrs.**
1	.8474576	.8403361	.8333333	.8264463	.8196721	**1**
2	.7181844	.7061648	.6944444	.6830135	.6718624	**2**
3	.6086309	.5934158	.5787037	.5644739	.5507069	**3**
4	.5157889	.4986688	.4822531	.4665074	.4513991	**4**
5	.4371092	.4190494	.4018776	.3855433	.3699993	**5**
6	.3704315	.3521423	.3348980	.3186308	.3032781	**6**
7	.3139250	.2959179	.2790816	.2633313	.2485886	**7**
8	.2660382	.2486705	.2325680	.2176291	.2037611	**8**
9	.2254561	.2089668	.1938067	.1798588	.1670173	**9**
10	.1910645	.1756024	.1615056	.1486436	.1368994	**10**
11	.1619190	.1475650	.1345880	.1228460	.1122127	**11**
12	.1372195	.1240042	.1121567	.1015256	.0919776	**12**
13	.1162877	.1042052	.0934639	.0839055	.0753915	**13**
14	.0985489	.0875674	.0778866	.0693433	.0617963	**14**
15	.0835160	.0735861	.0649055	.0573086	.0506527	**15**
16	.0707763	.0618370	.0540879	.0473624	.0415186	**16**
17	.0599799	.0519639	.0450732	.0391425	.0340316	**17**
18	.0508304	.0436671	.0375610	.0323492	.0278948	**18**
19	.0430766	.0366951	.0313009	.0267349	.0228646	**19**
20	.0365056	.0308362	.0260841	.0220949	.0187415	**20**
21	.0309370	.0259128	.0217367	.0182603	.0153619	**21**
22	.0262178	.0217754	.0181139	.0150911	.0125917	**22**
23	.0222185	.0182987	.0150949	.0124720	.0103211	**23**
24	.0188292	.0153770	.0125791	.0103074	.0084599	**24**
25	.0159569	.0129219	.0104826	.0085186	.0069343	**25**
26	.0135228	.0108587	.0087355	.0070401	.0056839	**26**
27	.0114660	.0091250	.0072796	.0058183	.0046589	**27**
28	.0097119	.0076681	.0060663	.0048085	.0038188	**28**
29	.0082304	.0064437	.0050553	.0039740	.0031301	**29**
30	.0069749	.0054149	.0042127	.0032843	.0025657	**30**
31	.0059110	.0045503	.0035106	.0027143	.0021030	**31**
32	.0050093	.0038238	.0029255	.0022432	.0017238	**32**
33	.0042452	.0032133	.0024379	.0018539	.0014129	**33**
34	.0035976	.0027002	.0020316	.0015321	.0011582	**34**
35	.0030488	.0022691	.0016930	.0012662	.0009493	**35**
36	.0025837	.0019068	.0014108	.0010465	.0007781	**36**
37	.0021896	.0016024	.0011757	.0008649	.0006378	**37**
38	.0018556	.0013465	.0009797	.0007148	.0005228	**38**
39	.0015725	.0011315	.0008165	.0005907	.0004285	**39**
40	.0013327	.0009509	.0006804	.0004882	.0003512	**40**
45	.0005825	.0003985	.0002734	.0001882	.0001300	**45**
50	.0002546	.0001670	.0001099	.0000726	.0000481	**50**
55	.0001113	.0000700	.0000442	.0000280	.0000178	**55**
60	.0000486	.0000293	.0000177	.0000108	.0000066	**60**
65	.0000213	.0000123	.0000071	.0000042	.0000024	**65**
70	.0000093	.0000051	.0000029	.0000016	.0000009	**70**
75	.0000041	.0000022	.0000012	.0000006	.0000003	**75**
80	.0000018	.0000009	.0000005	.0000002	.0000001	**80**
90	.0000003	.0000002	.0000001	.0000000	.0000000	**90**
100	.0000001	.0000000	.0000000	.0000000	.0000000	**100**

No Income Tax

PRESENT VALUE OF £1

Rate Per Cent

Yrs.	23	24	25	26	28	Yrs.
1	.8130081	.8064516	.8000000	.7936508	.7812500	**1**
2	.6609822	.6503642	.6400000	.6298816	.6103516	**2**
3	.5373839	.5244873	.5120000	.4999060	.4768372	**3**
4	.4368975	.4229736	.4096000	.3967508	.3725290	**4**
5	.3552012	.3411077	.3276800	.3148816	.2910383	**5**
6	.2887815	.2750869	.2621440	.2499060	.2273737	**6**
7	.2347817	.2218443	.2097152	.1983381	.1776357	**7**
8	.1908794	.1789067	.1677722	.1574112	.1387779	**8**
9	.1551865	.1442796	.1342177	.1249295	.1084202	**9**
10	.1261679	.1163545	.1073742	.0991504	.0847033	**10**
11	.1025755	.0938343	.0858993	.0786908	.0661744	**11**
12	.0833947	.0756728	.0687195	.0624530	.0516988	**12**
13	.0678006	.0610264	.0549756	.0495659	.0403897	**13**
14	.0551224	.0492149	.0439805	.0393380	.0315544	**14**
15	.0448150	.0396894	.0351844	.0312206	.0246519	**15**
16	.0364350	.0320076	.0281475	.0247783	.0192593	**16**
17	.0296219	.0258126	.0225180	.0196653	.0150463	**17**
18	.0240829	.0208166	.0180144	.0156074	.0117549	**18**
19	.0195796	.0167876	.0144115	.0123868	.0091835	**19**
20	.0159183	.0135384	.0115292	.0098308	.0071746	**20**
21	.0129417	.0109180	.0092234	.0078022	.0056052	**21**
22	.0105217	.0088049	.0073787	.0061922	.0043791	**22**
23	.0085543	.0071007	.0059030	.0049145	.0034211	**23**
24	.0069547	.0057264	.0047224	.0039004	.0026728	**24**
25	.0056542	.0046180	.0037779	.0030955	.0020881	**25**
26	.0045969	.0037242	.0030223	.0024568	.0016313	**26**
27	.0037373	.0030034	.0024179	.0019498	.0012745	**27**
28	.0030385	.0024221	.0019343	.0015475	.0009957	**28**
29	.0024703	.0019533	.0015474	.0012282	.0007779	**29**
30	.0020084	.0015752	.0012379	.0009747	.0006077	**30**
31	.0016328	.0012704	.0009904	.0007736	.0004748	**31**
32	.0013275	.0010245	.0007923	.0006140	.0003709	**32**
33	.0010793	.0008262	.0006338	.0004873	.0002898	**33**
34	.0008775	.0006663	.0005071	.0003867	.0002264	**34**
35	.0007134	.0005373	.0004056	.0003069	.0001769	**35**
36	.0005800	.0004333	.0003245	.0002436	.0001382	**36**
37	.0004715	.0003495	.0002596	.0001933	.0001080	**37**
38	.0003834	.0002818	.0002077	.0001534	.0000843	**38**
39	.0003117	.0002273	.0001662	.0001218	.0000659	**39**
40	.0002534	.0001833	.0001329	.0000966	.0000515	**40**
45	.0000900	.0000625	.0000436	.0000304	.0000150	**45**
50	.0000320	.0000213	.0000143	.0000096	.0000044	**50**
55	.0000114	.0000073	.0000047	.0000030	.0000013	**55**
60	.0000040	.0000025	.0000015	.0000010	.0000004	**60**
65	.0000014	.0000008	.0000005	.0000003	.0000001	**65**
70	.0000005	.0000003	.0000002	.0000001	.0000000	**70**
75	.0000002	.0000001	.0000001	.0000000	.0000000	**75**
80	.0000001	.0000000	.0000000	.0000000	.0000000	**80**
90	.0000000	.0000000	.0000000	.0000000	.0000000	**90**
100	.0000000	.0000000	.0000000	.0000000	.0000000	**100**

Rule for extending the Table of

PRESENT VALUE OF ONE POUND

Rule—

P.V. of £1 receivable in N years × P.V. of £1 receivable in M years = P.V. of £1 receivable in N + M years.

Example—

What is the present value of £1 receivable in 120 years at 4 per cent?

Answer—

P.V. of £1 receivable in 20 years at 4% = .4563869
P.V. of £1 receivable in 100 years at 4% = .0198000
P.V. of £1 receivable in 120 years at 4%

= (.4563869 × .0198000)} = .009036 *Ans.*

Appendix J

Parry's Valuation Tables – Years' purchase or present value of one pound

Receivable at the end of each year after allowing for a sinking fund to accumulate at the same rate of interest as that which is required on the invested capital and ignoring the effect of income tax on that part of the income used to provide the annual sinking fund instalment.

At Rates of Interest from 2% to 28%

$$A_{\overline{n}|i} \quad \frac{I - (I + i)^{-n}}{i}$$

(From Parry's Valuation Tables)

No Income Tax **Single Rate**

YEARS' PURCHASE

Rate Per Cent

Yrs.	**2**	**2.25**	**2.5**	**2.75**	**3**	**3.25**	**3.5**	**3.75**	Yrs.
1	0.9804	0.9780	0.9756	0.9732	0.9709	0.9685	0.9662	0.9639	**1**
2	1.9416	1.9345	1.9274	1.9204	1.9135	1.9066	1.8997	1.8929	**2**
3	2.8839	2.8699	2.8560	2.8423	2.8286	2.8151	2.8016	2.7883	**3**
4	3.8077	3.7847	3.7620	3.7394	3.7171	3.6950	3.6731	3.6514	**4**
5	4.7135	4.6795	4.6458	4.6126	4.5797	4.5472	4.5151	4.4833	**5**
6	5.6014	5.5545	5.5081	5.4624	5.4172	5.3726	5.3286	5.2851	**6**
7	6.4720	6.4102	6.3494	6.2894	6.2303	6.1720	6.1145	6.0579	**7**
8	7.3255	7.2472	7.1701	7.0943	7.0197	6.9462	6.8740	6.8028	**8**
9	8.1622	8.0657	7.9709	7.8777	7.7861	7.6961	7.6077	7.5208	**9**
10	8.9826	8.8662	8.7521	8.6401	8.5302	8.4224	8.3166	8.2128	**10**
11	9.7868	9.6491	9.5142	9.3821	9.2526	9.1258	9.0016	8.8798	**11**
12	10.5753	10.4148	10.2578	10.1042	9.9540	9.8071	9.6633	9.5227	**12**
13	11.3484	11.1636	10.9832	10.8070	10.6350	10.4669	10.3027	10.1424	**13**
14	12.1062	11.8959	11.6909	11.4910	11.2961	11.1060	10.9205	10.7396	**14**
15	12.8493	12.6122	12.3814	12.1567	11.9379	11.7249	11.5174	11.3153	**15**
16	13.5777	13.3126	13.0550	12.8046	12.5611	12.3244	12.0941	11.8702	**16**
17	14.2919	13.9977	13.7122	13.4351	13.1661	12.9049	12.6513	12.4050	**17**
18	14.9920	14.6677	14.3534	14.0488	13.7535	13.4673	13.1897	12.9205	**18**
19	15.6785	15.3229	14.9789	14.6460	14.3238	14.0119	13.7098	13.4173	**19**
20	16.3514	15.9637	15.5892	15.2273	14.8775	14.5393	14.2124	13.8962	**20**
21	17.0112	16.5904	16.1845	15.7929	15.4150	15.0502	14.6980	14.3578	**21**
22	17.6580	17.2034	16.7654	16.3435	15.9369	15.5450	15.1671	14.8027	**22**
23	18.2922	17.8028	17.3321	16.8793	16.4436	16.0242	15.6204	15.2315	**23**
24	18.9139	18.3890	17.8850	17.4008	16.9355	16.4883	16.0584	15.6448	**24**
25	19.5235	18.9624	18.4244	17.9083	17.4131	16.9379	16.4815	16.0432	**25**
26	20.1210	19.5231	18.9506	18.4023	17.8768	17.3732	16.8904	16.4272	**26**

No Income Tax **Single Rate**

YEARS' PURCHASE

Rate Per Cent

Yrs.	**2**	**2.25**	**2.5**	**2.75**	**3**	**3.25**	**3.5**	**3.75**	**Yrs.**
27	20.7069	20.0715	19.4640	18.8830	18.3270	17.7949	17.2854	16.7973	**27**
28	21.2813	20.6078	19.9649	19.3508	18.7641	18.2033	17.6670	17.1540	**28**
29	21.8444	21.1323	20.4535	19.8062	19.1885	18.5988	18.0358	17.4978	**29**
30	22.3965	21.6453	20.9303	20.2493	19.6004	18.9819	18.3920	17.8292	**30**
31	22.9377	22.1470	21.3954	20.6806	20.0004	19.3529	18.7363	18.1487	**31**
32	23.4683	22.6377	21.8492	21.1003	20.3888	19.7123	19.0689	18.4565	**32**
33	23.9886	23.1175	22.2919	21.5088	20.7658	20.0603	19.3902	18.7533	**33**
34	24.4986	23.5868	22.7238	21.9064	21.1318	20.3974	19.7007	19.0393	**34**
35	24.9986	24.0458	23.1452	22.2933	21.4872	20.7239	20.0007	19.3150	**35**
36	25.4888	24.4947	23.5563	22.6699	21.8323	21.0401	20.2905	19.5807	**36**
37	25.9695	24.9337	23.9573	23.0364	22.1672	21.3463	20.5705	19.8369	**37**
38	26.4406	25.3630	24.3486	23.3931	22.4925	21.6429	20.8411	20.0837	**38**
39	26.9026	25.7829	24.7303	23.7402	22.8082	21.9302	21.1025	20.3217	**39**
40	27.3555	26.1935	25.1028	24.0781	23.1148	22.2084	21.3551	20.5510	**40**
41	27.7995	26.5951	25.4661	24.4069	23.4124	22.4779	21.5991	20.7720	**41**
42	28.2348	26.9879	25.8206	24.7269	23.7014	22.7389	21.8349	20.9851	**42**
43	28.6616	27.3720	26.1664	25.0384	23.9819	22.9917	22.0627	21.1905	**43**
44	29.0800	27.7477	26.5038	25.3415	24.2543	23.2365	22.2828	21.3884	**44**
45	29.4902	28.1151	26.8330	25.6365	24.5187	23.4736	22.4955	21.5792	**45**
46	29.8923	28.4744	27.1542	25.9236	24.7754	23.7032	22.7009	21.7631	**46**
47	30.2866	28.8259	27.4675	26.2030	25.0247	23.9256	22.8994	21.9403	**47**
48	30.6731	29.1695	27.7732	26.4749	25.2667	24.1411	23.0912	22.1111	**48**
49	31.0521	29.5057	28.0714	26.7396	25.5017	24.3497	23.2766	22.2758	**49**
50	31.4236	29.8344	28.3623	26.9972	25.7298	24.5518	23.4556	22.4345	**50**
51	31.7878	30.1559	28.6462	27.2479	25.9512	24.7475	23.6286	22.5875	**51**
52	32.1449	30.4703	28.9231	27.4918	26.1662	24.9370	23.7958	22.7349	**52**
53	32.4950	30.7778	29.1932	27.7293	26.3750	25.1206	23.9573	22.8770	**53**
54	32.8383	31.0785	29.4568	27.9604	26.5777	25.2984	24.1133	23.0140	**54**
55	33.1748	31.3727	29.7140	28.1853	26.7744	25.4706	24.2641	23.1460	**55**
56	33.5047	31.6603	29.9649	28.4042	26.9655	25.6374	24.4097	23.2733	**56**
57	33.8281	31.9416	30.2096	28.6172	27.1509	25.7989	24.5504	23.3959	**57**
58	34.1452	32.2167	30.4484	28.8245	27.3310	25.9554	24.6864	23.5141	**58**
59	34.4561	32.4858	30.6814	29.0263	27.5058	26.1069	24.8178	23.6281	**59**
60	34.7609	32.7490	30.9087	29.2227	27.6756	26.2537	24.9447	23.7379	**60**
61	35.0597	33.0063	31.1304	29.4138	27.8404	26.3958	25.0674	23.8438	**61**
62	35.3526	33.2580	31.3467	29.5998	28.0003	26.5335	25.1859	23.9458	**62**
63	35.6398	33.5042	31.5578	29.7808	28.1557	26.6668	25.3004	24.0442	**63**
64	35.9214	33.7449	31.7637	29.9570	28.3065	26.7959	25.4110	24.1389	**64**
65	36.1975	33.9803	31.9646	30.1285	28.4529	26.9210	25.5178	24.2303	**65**
66	36.4681	34.2106	32.1606	30.2953	28.5950	27.0421	25.6211	24.3184	**66**
67	36.7334	34.4358	32.3518	30.4578	28.7330	27.1594	25.7209	24.4032	**67**
68	36.9936	34.6560	32.5383	30.6158	28.8670	27.2731	25.8173	24.4851	**68**
69	37.2486	34.8714	32.7203	30.7697	28.9971	27.3831	25.9104	24.5639	**69**
70	37.4986	35.0821	32.8979	30.9194	29.1234	27.4897	26.0004	24.6399	**70**
71	37.7437	35.2881	33.0711	31.0651	29.2460	27.5929	26.0873	24.7132	**71**
72	37.9841	35.4896	33.2401	31.2069	29.3651	27.6929	26.1713	24.7838	**72**
73	38.2197	35.6866	33.4050	31.3449	29.4807	27.7897	26.2525	24.8518	**73**
74	38.4507	35.8794	33.5658	31.4792	29.5929	27.8835	26.3309	24.9174	**74**
75	38.6771	36.0678	33.7227	31.6100	29.7018	27.9744	26.4067	24.9807	**75**
76	38.8991	36.2522	33.8758	31.7372	29.8076	28.0623	26.4799	25.0416	**76**
77	39.1168	36.4324	34.0252	31.8610	29.9103	28.1475	26.5506	25.1003	**77**
78	39.3302	36.6087	34.1709	31.9815	30.0100	28.2301	26.6190	25.1569	**78**
79	39.5394	36.7812	34.3131	32.0988	30.1068	28.3100	26.6850	25.2115	**79**

No Income Tax **Single Rate**

YEARS' PURCHASE

Rate Per Cent

Yrs.	2	2.25	2.5	2.75	3	3.25	3.5	3.75	Yrs.
80	39.7445	36.9498	34.4518	32.2129	30.2008	28.3874	26.7488	25.2641	**80**
81	39.9456	37.1147	34.5871	32.3240	30.2920	28.4624	26.8104	25.3148	**81**
82	40.1427	37.2760	34.7192	32.4321	30.3806	28.5350	26.8700	25.3637	**82**
83	40.3360	37.4337	34.8480	32.5374	30.4666	28.6053	26.9275	25.4108	**83**
84	40.5255	37.5880	34.9736	32.6398	30.5501	28.6734	26.9831	25.4562	**84**
85	40.7113	37.7389	35.0962	32.7394	30.6312	28.7394	27.0368	25.4999	**85**
86	40.8934	37.8864	35.2158	32.8364	30.7099	28.8033	27.0887	25.5421	**86**
87	41.0720	38.0307	35.3325	32.9308	30.7863	28.8652	27.1388	25.5827	**87**
88	41.2470	38.1719	35.4463	33.0227	30.8605	28.9251	27.1873	25.6219	**88**
89	41.4187	38.3099	35.5574	33.1121	30.9325	28.9831	27.2341	25.6597	**89**
90	41.5869	38.4449	35.6658	33.1992	31.0024	29.0394	27.2793	25.6961	**90**
91	41.7519	38.5769	35.7715	33.2838	31.0703	29.0938	27.3230	25.7312	**91**
92	41.9136	38.7060	35.8746	33.3663	31.1362	29.1466	27.3652	25.7650	**92**
93	42.0722	38.8323	35.9752	33.4465	31.2002	29.1976	27.4060	25.7976	**93**
94	42.2276	38.9558	36.0734	33.5246	31.2623	29.2471	27.4454	25.8290	**94**
95	42.3800	39.0766	36.1692	33.6006	31.3227	29.2950	27.4835	25.8592	**95**
96	42.5294	39.1947	36.2626	33.6745	31.3812	29.3414	27.5203	25.8884	**96**
97	42.6759	39.3102	36.3538	33.7465	31.4381	29.3864	27.5558	25.9166	**97**
98	42.8195	39.4232	36.4427	33.8165	31.4933	29.4299	27.5902	25.9437	**98**
99	42.9603	39.5337	36.5295	33.8847	31.5469	29.4720	27.6234	25.9698	**99**
100	43.0984	39.6417	36.6141	33.9510	31.5989	29.5129	27.6554	25.9950	**100**
PERP	50.0000	44.4444	40.0000	36.3636	33.3333	30.7692	28.5714	26.6667	**PERP**

No Income Tax **Single Rate**

YEARS' PURCHASE

Rate Per Cent

Yrs.	4	4.25	4.5	4.75	5	5.25	5.5	5.75	Yrs.
1	0.9615	0.9592	0.9569	0.9547	0.9524	0.9501	0.9479	0.9456	**1**
2	1.8861	1.8794	1.8727	1.8660	1.8594	1.8528	1.8463	1.8398	**2**
3	2.7751	2.7620	2.7490	2.7361	2.7232	2.7105	2.6979	2.6854	**3**
4	3.6299	3.6086	3.5875	3.5666	3.5460	3.5255	3.5052	3.4850	**4**
5	4.4518	4.4207	4.3900	4.3596	4.3295	4.2997	4.2703	4.2412	**5**
6	5.2421	5.1997	5.1579	5.1165	5.0757	5.0354	4.9955	4.9562	**6**
7	6.0021	5.9470	5.8927	5.8392	5.7864	5.7343	5.6830	5.6323	**7**
8	6.7327	6.6638	6.5959	6.5290	6.4632	6.3984	6.3346	6.2717	**8**
9	7.4353	7.3513	7.2688	7.1876	7.1078	7.0294	6.9522	6.8763	**9**
10	8.1109	8.0109	7.9127	7.8163	7.7217	7.6288	7.5376	7.4481	**10**
11	8.7605	8.6435	8.5289	8.4166	8.3064	8.1984	8.0925	7.9887	**11**
12	9.3851	9.2504	9.1186	8.9896	8.8633	8.7396	8.6185	8.5000	**12**
13	9.9856	9.8325	9.6829	9.5366	9.3936	9.2538	9.1171	8.9834	**13**
14	10.5631	10.3909	10.2228	10.0588	9.8986	9.7423	9.5896	9.4406	**14**
15	11.1184	10.9265	10.7395	10.5573	10.3797	10.2065	10.0376	9.8729	**15**
16	11.6253	11.4403	11.2340	11.0332	10.8378	10.6475	10.4622	10.2817	**16**
17	12.1657	11.9332	11.7072	11.4876	11.2741	11.0665	10.8646	10.6683	**17**
18	12.6593	12.4059	12.1600	11.9213	11.6896	11.4646	11.2461	11.0338	**18**
19	13.1339	12.8594	12.5933	12.3354	12.0853	11.8428	11.6077	11.3795	**19**
20	13.5903	13.2944	13.0079	12.7307	12.4622	12.2022	11.9504	11.7064	**20**
21	14.0292	13.7116	13.4047	13.1080	12.8212	12.5437	12.2752	12.0155	**21**
22	14.4511	14.1119	13.7844	13.4683	13.1630	12.8681	12.5832	12.3078	**22**
23	14.8568	14.4958	14.1478	13.8122	13.4886	13.1763	12.8750	12.5842	**23**
24	15.2470	14.8641	14.4955	14.1405	13.7986	13.4692	13.1517	12.8456	**24**
25	15.6221	15.2173	14.8282	14.4540	14.0939	13.7475	13.4139	13.0927	**25**
26	15.9828	15.5562	15.1466	14.7532	14.3752	14.0118	13.6625	13.3265	**26**

No Income Tax **Single Rate**

YEARS' PURCHASE
Rate Per Cent

Yrs.	4	4.25	4.5	4.75	5	5.25	5.5	5.75	Yrs.
27	16.3296	15.8812	15.4513	15.0389	14.6430	14.2630	13.8981	13.5475	**27**
28	16.6631	16.1930	15.7429	15.3116	14.8981	14.5017	14.1214	13.7565	**28**
29	16.9837	16.4921	16.0219	15.5719	15.1411	14.7285	14.3331	13.9541	**29**
30	17.2920	16.7790	16.2889	15.8204	15.3725	14.9439	14.5337	14.1410	**30**
31	17.5885	17.0542	16.5444	16.0577	15.5928	15.1486	14.7239	14.3178	**31**
32	17.8736	17.3182	16.7889	16.2842	15.8027	15.3431	14.9042	14.4849	**32**
33	18.1476	17.5714	17.0229	16.5004	16.0025	15.5279	15.0751	14.6429	**33**
34	18.4112	17.8143	17.2468	16.7068	16.1929	15.7034	15.2370	14.7923	**34**
35	18.6646	18.0473	17.4610	16.9039	16.3742	15.8703	15.3906	14.9337	**35**
36	18.9083	18.2708	17.6660	17.0920	16.5469	16.0287	15.5361	15.0673	**36**
37	19.1426	18.4852	17.8622	17.2716	16.7113	16.1793	15.6740	15.1937	**37**
38	19.3679	18.6908	18.0500	17.4431	16.8679	16.3224	15.8047	15.3131	**38**
39	19.5845	18.8881	18.2297	17.6068	17.0170	16.4583	15.9287	15.4261	**39**
40	19.7928	19.0773	18.4016	17.7630	17.1591	16.5875	16.0461	15.5330	**40**
41	19.9931	19.2588	18.5661	17.9122	17.2944	16.7102	16.1575	15.6340	**41**
42	20.1856	19.4329	18.7235	18.0546	17.4232	16.8268	16.2630	15.7296	**42**
43	20.3708	19.5999	18.8742	18.1905	17.5459	16.9376	16.3630	15.8199	**43**
44	20.5488	19.7601	19.0184	18.3203	17.6628	17.0428	16.4579	15.9054	**44**
45	20.7200	19.9137	19.1563	18.4442	17.7741	17.1428	16.5477	15.9862	**45**
46	20.8847	20.0611	19.2884	18.5625	17.8801	17.2378	16.6329	16.0626	**46**
47	21.0429	20.2025	19.4147	18.6754	17.9810	17.3281	16.7137	16.1348	**47**
48	21.1951	20.3382	19.5356	18.7832	18.0772	17.4139	16.7902	16.2031	**48**
49	21.3415	20.4683	19.6513	18.8861	18.1687	17.4954	16.8628	16.2678	**49**
50	21.4822	20.5931	19.7620	18.9844	18.2559	17.5728	16.9315	16.3288	**50**
51	21.6175	20.7128	19.8679	19.0782	18.3390	17.6464	16.9967	16.3866	**51**
52	21.7476	20.8276	19.9693	19.1677	18.4181	17.7163	17.0585	16.4412	**52**
53	21.8727	20.9377	20.0663	19.2532	18.4934	17.7827	17.1170	16.4929	**53**
54	21.9930	21.0434	20.1592	19.3348	18.5651	17.8458	17.1726	16.5417	**54**
55	22.1086	21.1447	20.2480	19.4127	18.6335	17.9057	17.2252	16.5879	**55**
56	22.2198	21.2420	20.3330	19.4870	18.6985	17.9627	17.2750	16.6316	**56**
57	22.3267	21.3352	20.4144	19.5580	18.7605	18.0168	17.3223	16.6729	**57**
58	22.4296	21.4247	20.4922	19.6258	18.8195	18.0682	17.3671	16.7120	**58**
59	22.5284	21.5105	20.5667	19.6905	18.8758	18.1171	17.4096	16.7489	**59**
60	22.6235	21.5928	20.6380	19.7523	18.9293	18.1635	17.4499	16.7839	**60**
61	22.7149	21.6717	20.7062	19.8112	18.9803	18.2076	17.4880	16.8169	**61**
62	22.8028	21.7475	20.7715	19.8675	19.0288	18.2495	17.5242	16.8481	**62**
63	22.8873	21.8201	20.8340	19.9213	19.0751	18.2893	17.5585	16.8777	**63**
64	22.9685	21.8898	20.8938	19.9726	19.1191	18.3271	17.5910	16.9056	**64**
65	23.0467	21.9566	20.9510	20.0215	19.1611	18.3631	17.6218	16.9320	**65**
66	23.1218	22.0208	21.0057	20.0683	19.2010	18.3972	17.6510	16.9570	**66**
67	23.1940	22.0823	21.0581	20.1129	19.2391	18.4297	17.6786	16.9806	**67**
68	23.2635	22.1413	21.1082	20.1555	19.2753	18.4605	17.7049	17.0029	**68**
69	23.3303	22.1978	21.1562	20.1962	19.3098	18.4898	17.7297	17.0240	**69**
70	23.3945	22.2521	21.2021	20.2351	19.3427	18.5176	17.7533	17.0440	**70**
71	23.4563	22.3042	21.2460	20.2721	19.3740	18.5440	17.7756	17.0629	**71**
72	23.5156	22.3542	21.2881	20.3075	19.4038	18.5692	17.7968	17.0807	**72**
73	23.5727	22.4021	21.3283	20.3413	19.4322	18.5930	17.8169	17.0976	**73**
74	23.6276	22.4480	21.3668	20.3736	19.4592	18.6157	17.8359	17.1136	**74**
75	23.6804	22.4921	21.4036	20.4044	19.4850	18.6372	17.8539	17.1287	**75**
76	23.7312	22.5344	21.4389	20.4338	19.5095	18.6577	17.8710	17.1430	**76**
77	23.7800	22.5750	21.4726	20.4618	19.5329	18.6772	17.8872	17.1565	**77**
78	23.8269	22.6139	21.5049	20.4886	19.5551	18.6956	17.9026	17.1692	**78**
79	23.8720	22.6512	21.5358	20.5142	19.5763	18.7132	17.9172	17.1813	**79**

No Income Tax **Single Rate**

YEARS' PURCHASE

Rate Per Cent

Yrs.	4	4.25	4.5	4.75	5	5.25	5.5	5.75	Yrs.
80	23.9154	22.6870	21.5653	20.5386	19.5965	18.7299	17.9310	17.1927	**80**
81	23.9571	22.7213	21.5936	20.5619	19.6157	18.7457	17.9440	17.2035	**81**
82	23.9972	22.7543	21.6207	20.5842	19.6340	18.7608	17.9564	17.2137	**82**
83	24.0358	22.7859	21.6466	20.6054	19.6514	18.7751	17.9682	17.2234	**83**
84	24.0729	22.8162	21.6714	20.6257	19.6680	18.7887	17.9793	17.2325	**84**
85	24.1085	22.8453	21.6951	20.6451	19.6838	18.8016	17.9899	17.2412	**85**
86	24.1428	22.8732	21.7178	20.6635	19.6989	18.8139	17.9999	17.2493	**86**
87	24.1758	22.8999	21.7395	20.6812	19.7132	18.8255	18.0094	17.2570	**87**
88	24.2075	22.9256	21.7603	20.6980	19.7269	18.8366	18.0184	17.2643	**88**
89	24.2380	22.9502	21.7802	20.7141	19.7399	18.8471	18.0269	17.2712	**89**
90	24.2673	22.9738	21.7992	20.7295	19.7523	18.8571	18.0350	17.2778	**90**
91	24.2955	22.9965	21.8175	20.7441	19.7641	18.8666	18.0426	17.2840	**91**
92	24.3226	23.0182	21.8349	20.7581	19.7753	18.8757	18.0499	17.2898	**92**
93	24.3486	23.0390	21.8516	20.7715	19.7860	18.8842	18.0567	17.2953	**93**
94	24.3737	23.0590	21.8675	20.7842	19.7962	18.8924	18.0633	17.3005	**94**
95	24.3978	23.0782	21.8828	20.7964	19.8059	18.9001	18.0694	17.3055	**95**
96	24.4209	23.0966	21.8974	20.8080	19.8151	18.9075	18.0753	17.3101	**96**
97	24.4432	23.1142	21.9114	20.8191	19.8239	18.9145	18.0809	17.3145	**97**
98	24.4646	23.1312	21.9248	20.8927	19.8323	18.9211	18.0861	17.3187	**98**
99	24.4852	23.1474	21.9376	20.8398	19.8403	18.9274	18.0911	17.3227	**99**
100	24.5050	23.1630	21.9499	20.8494	19.8479	18.9334	18.0958	17.3264	**100**
PERP	25.0000	23.5294	22.2222	21.0526	20.0000	19.0476	18.1818	17.3913	**PERP**

No Income Tax **Single Rate**

YEARS' PURCHASE

Rate Per Cent

Yrs.	6	6.25	6.5	6.75	7	7.25	7.5	7.75	Yrs.
1	0.9434	0.9412	0.9390	0.9368	0.9346	0.9324	0.9302	0.9281	**1**
2	1.8334	1.8270	1.8206	1.8143	1.8080	1.8018	1.7956	1.7894	**2**
3	2.6730	2.6607	2.6485	2.6363	2.6243	2.6124	2.6005	2.5888	**3**
4	3.4651	3.4454	3.4258	3.4064	3.3872	3.3682	3.3493	3.3306	**4**
5	4.2124	4.1839	4.1557	4.1278	4.1002	4.0729	4.0459	4.0192	**5**
6	4.9173	4.8789	4.8410	4.8036	4.7665	4.7300	4.6938	4.6582	**6**
7	5.5824	5.5331	5.4845	5.4366	5.3893	5.3426	5.2966	5.2512	**7**
8	6.2098	6.1488	6.0888	6.0296	5.9713	5.9139	5.8573	5.8016	**8**
9	6.8017	6.7283	6.6561	6.5851	6.5152	6.4465	6.3789	6.3124	**9**
10	7.3601	7.2737	7.1888	7.1055	7.0236	6.9431	6.8641	6.7864	**10**
11	7.8869	7.7870	7.6890	7.5929	7.4987	7.4062	7.3154	7.2264	**11**
12	8.3838	8.2701	8.1587	8.0496	7.9427	7.8379	7.7353	7.6347	**12**
13	8.8527	8.7248	8.5997	8.4774	8.3577	8.2405	8.1258	8.0136	**13**
14	9.2950	9.1528	9.0138	8.8781	8.7455	8.6158	8.4892	8.3653	**14**
15	9.7122	9.5555	9.4027	9.2535	9.1079	8.9658	8.8271	8.6917	**15**
16	10.1059	9.9346	9.7678	9.6051	9.4466	9.2921	9.1415	8.9946	**16**
17	10.4773	10.2914	10.1106	9.9346	9.7632	9.5964	9.4340	9.2757	**17**
18	10.8276	10.6272	10.4325	10.2432	10.0591	9.8801	9.7060	9.5367	**18**
19	11.1581	10.9433	10.7347	10.5322	10.3356	10.1446	9.9591	9.7788	**19**
20	11.4699	11.2407	11.0185	10.8030	10.5940	10.3912	10.1945	10.0035	**20**
21	11.7641	11.5207	11.2850	11.0567	10.8355	10.6212	10.4135	10.2121	**21**
22	12.0416	11.7842	11.5352	11.2943	11.0612	10.8356	10.6172	10.4057	**22**
23	12.3034	12.0322	11.7701	11.5169	11.2722	11.0355	10.8067	10.5853	**23**
24	12.5504	12.2656	11.9907	11.7255	11.4693	11.2220	10.9830	10.7520	**24**
25	12.7834	12.4852	12.1979	11.9208	11.6536	11.3958	11.1469	10.9067	**25**
26	13.0032	12.6920	12.3924	12.1038	11.8258	11.5578	11.2995	11.0503	**26**

No Income Tax **Single Rate**

YEARS' PURCHASE
Rate Per Cent

Yrs.	6	6.25	6.5	6.75	7	7.25	7.5	7.75	Yrs.
27	13.2105	12.8866	12.5750	12.2752	11.9867	11.7089	11.4414	11.1836	**27**
28	13.4062	13.0697	12.7465	12.4358	12.1371	11.8498	11.5734	11.3073	**28**
29	13.5907	13.2421	12.9075	12.5862	12.2777	11.9812	11.6962	11.4221	**29**
30	13.7648	13.4043	13.0587	12.7272	12.4090	12.1037	11.8104	11.5286	**30**
31	13.9291	13.5570	13.2006	12.8592	12.5318	12.2179	11.9166	11.6275	**31**
32	14.0840	13.7007	13.3339	12.9828	12.6466	12.3244	12.0155	11.7192	**32**
33	14.2302	13.8360	13.4591	13.0987	12.7538	12.4236	12.1074	11.8044	**33**
34	14.3681	13.9633	13.5766	13.2072	12.8540	12.5162	12.1929	11.8834	**34**
35	14.4982	14.0831	13.6870	13.3088	12.9477	12.6025	12.2725	11.9568	**35**
36	14.6210	14.1958	13.7906	13.4041	13.0352	12.6830	12.3465	12.0249	**36**
37	14.7368	14.3020	13.8879	13.4933	13.1170	12.7581	12.4154	12.0880	**37**
38	14.8460	14.4018	13.9792	13.5768	13.1935	12.8280	12.4794	12.1467	**38**
39	14.9491	14.4958	14.0650	13.6551	13.2649	12.8933	12.5390	12.2011	**39**
40	15.0463	14.5843	14.1455	13.7284	13.3317	12.9541	12.5944	12.2516	**40**
41	15.1380	14.6676	14.2212	13.7971	13,3941	13.0108	12.6460	12.2985	**41**
42	15.2245	14.7460	14.2922	13.8615	13.4524	13.0637	12.6939	12.3420	**42**
43	15.3062	14.8197	14.3588	13.9218	13.5070	13.1130	12.7385	12.3823	**43**
44	15.3832	14.8892	14.4214	13.9782	13.5579	13.1590	12.7800	12.4198	**44**
45	15.4558	14.9545	14.4802	14.0311	13.6055	13.2018	12.8186	12.4546	**45**
46	15.5244	15.0160	14.5354	14.0807	13.6500	13.2418	12.8545	12.4868	**46**
47	15.5890	15.0739	14.5873	14.1271	13.6916	13.2791	12.8879	12.5168	**47**
48	15.6500	15.1284	14.6359	14.1706	13.7305	13.3138	12.9190	12.5446	**48**
49	15.7076	15.1796	14.6816	14.2113	13.7668	13.3462	12.9479	12.5704	**49**
50	15.7619	15.2279	14.7245	14.2495	13.8007	13.3764	12.9748	12.5943	**50**
51	15.8131	15.2733	14.7648	14.2852	13.8325	13.4046	12.9998	12.6165	**51**
52	15.8614	15.3161	14.8026	14.3187	13.8621	13.4309	13.0231	12.6372	**52**
53	15.9070	15.3563	14.8382	14.3501	13.8898	13.4553	13.0447	12.6563	**53**
54	15.9500	15.3942	14.8715	14.3795	13.9157	13.4782	13.0649	12.6741	**54**
55	15.9905	15.4298	14.9028	14.4070	13.9399	13.4995	13.0836	12.6905	**55**
56	16.0288	15.4633	14.9322	14.4328	13.9626	13.5193	13.1010	12.7058	**56**
57	16.0649	15.4949	14.9598	14.4569	13.9837	13.5378	13.1172	12.7200	**57**
58	16.0990	15.5246	14.9858	14.4796	14.0035	13.5551	13.1323	12.7332	**58**
59	16.1311	15.5526	15.0101	14.5008	14.0219	13.5712	13.1463	12.7454	**59**
60	16.1614	15.5789	15.0330	14.5206	14.0392	13.5862	13.1594	12.7568	**60**
61	16.1900	15.6037	15.0544	14.5392	14.0553	13.6002	13.1715	12.7673	**61**
62	16.2170	15.6270	15.0746	14.5567	14.0704	13.6132	13.1828	12.7771	**62**
63	16.2425	15.6489	15.0935	14.5730	14.0845	13.6254	13.1933	12.7862	**63**
64	16.2665	15.6696	15.1113	14.5883	14.0976	13.6367	13.2031	12.7946	**64**
65	16.2891	15.6890	15.1280	14.6026	14.1099	13.6473	13.2122	12.8024	**65**
66	16.3105	15.7073	15.1436	14.6160	14.1214	13.6571	13.2206	12.8097	**66**
67	16.3307	15.7245	15.1583	14.6286	14.1322	13.6663	13.2285	12.8164	**67**
68	16.3497	15.7407	15.1721	14.6404	14.1422	13.6749	13.2358	12.8226	**68**
69	16.3676	15.7560	15.1851	14.6514	14.1516	13.6829	13.2426	12.8284	**69**
70	16.3845	15.7703	15.1973	14.6617	14.1604	13.6903	13.2489	12.8338	**70**
71	16.4005	15.7838	15.2087	14.6714	14.1686	13.6973	13.2548	12.8388	**71**
72	16.4156	15.7966	15.2195	14.6805	14.1763	13.7038	13.2603	12.8434	**72**
73	16.4298	15.8085	15.2295	14.6890	14.1834	13.7098	13.2654	12.8477	**73**
74	16.4432	15.8198	15.2390	14.6969	14.1901	13.7154	13.2701	12.8517	**74**
75	16.4558	15.8304	15.2479	14.7044	14.1964	13.7207	13.2745	12.8554	**75**
76	16.4678	15.8404	15.2562	14.7114	14.2022	13.7256	13.2786	12.8589	**76**
77	16.4790	15.8498	15.2641	14.7179	14.2077	13.7301	13.2825	12.8621	**77**
78	16.4897	15.8586	15.2714	14.7240	14.2128	13.7344	13.2860	12.8650	**78**
79	16.4997	15.8669	15.2783	14.7298	14.2175	13.7384	13.2893	12.8678	**79**

No Income Tax **Single Rate**

YEARS' PURCHASE
Rate Per Cent

Yrs.	**6**	**6.25**	**6.5**	**6.75**	**7**	**7.25**	**7.5**	**7.75**	**Yrs.**
80	16.5091	15.8747	15.2848	14.7352	14.2220	13.7421	13.2924	12.8703	**80**
81	16.5180	15.8821	15.2909	14.7402	14.2262	13.7455	13.2952	12.8727	**81**
82	16.5265	15.8890	15.2966	14.7449	14.2301	13.7487	13.2979	12.8749	**82**
83	16.5344	15.8956	15.3020	14.7493	14.2337	13.7517	13.3004	12.8769	**83**
84	16.5419	15.9107	15.3070	14.7535	14.2371	13.7545	13.3027	12.8788	**84**
85	16.5489	15.9075	15.3118	14.7573	14.2403	13.7571	13.3048	12.8806	**85**
86	16.5556	15.9129	15.3162	14.7610	14.2433	13.7596	13.3068	12.8822	**86**
87	16.5619	15.9181	15.3204	14.7644	14.2460	13.7618	13.3087	12.8837	**87**
88	16.5678	15.9229	15.3243	14.7676	14.2486	13.7639	13.3104	12.8851	**88**
89	16.5734	15.9274	15.3280	14.7706	14.2511	13.7659	13.3120	12.8864	**89**
90	16.5787	15.9317	15.3315	14.7734	14.2533	13.7678	13.3135	12.8876	**90**
91	16.5837	15.9357	15.3347	14.7760	14.2554	13.7695	13.3149	12.8887	**91**
92	16.5884	15.9395	15.3377	14.7784	14.2574	13.7711	13.3161	12.8898	**92**
93	16.5928	15.9430	15.3406	14.7807	14.2593	13.7726	13.3173	12.8908	**93**
94	16.5970	15.9464	15.3433	14.7829	14.2610	13.7739	13.3185	12.8917	**94**
95	16.6009	15.9495	15.3458	14.7849	14.2626	13.7752	13.3195	12.8925	**95**
96	16.6047	15.9525	15.3482	14.7868	14.2641	13.7764	13.3205	12.8933	**96**
97	16.6082	15.9553	15.3504	14.7886	14.2655	13.7776	13.3214	12.8940	**97**
98	16.6115	15.9579	15.3525	14.7902	14.2669	13.7786	13.3222	12.8946	**98**
99	16.6146	15.9604	15.3545	14.7918	14.2681	13.7796	13.3230	12.8953	**99**
100	16.6175	15.9627	15.3563	14.7932	14.2693	13.7805	13.3237	12.8958	**100**
PERP	16.6667	16.0000	15.3846	14.8148	14.2857	13.7931	13.3333	12.9032	**PERP**

No Income Tax **Single Rate**

YEARS' PURCHASE
Rate Per Cent

Yrs.	**8**	**8.25**	**8.5**	**8.75**	**9**	**9.5**	**10**	**11**	**Yrs.**
1	0.9259	0.9238	0.9217	0.9195	0.9174	0.9132	0.9091	0.9009	**1**
2	1.7833	1.7772	1.7711	1.7651	1.7591	1.7473	1.7355	1.7125	**2**
3	2.5771	2.5655	2.5540	2.5426	2.5313	2.5089	2.4869	2.4437	**3**
4	3.3121	3.2938	3.2756	3.2576	3.2397	3.2045	3.1699	3.1024	**4**
5	3.9927	3.9665	3.9406	3.9150	3.8897	3.8397	3.7908	3.6959	**5**
6	4.6229	4.5880	4.5536	4.5196	4.4859	4.4198	4.3553	4.2305	**6**
7	5.2064	5.1621	5.1185	5.0755	5.0330	4.9496	4.8684	4.7122	**7**
8	5.7466	5.6925	5.6392	5.5866	5.5348	5.4334	5.3349	5.1461	**8**
9	6.2469	6.1825	6.1191	6.0567	5.9952	5.8753	5.7590	5.5370	**9**
10	6.7101	6.6351	6.5613	6.4889	6.4177	6.2788	6.1446	5.8892	**10**
11	7.1390	7.0532	6.9690	6.8863	6.8052	6.6473	6.4951	6.2065	**11**
12	7.5361	7.4394	7.3447	7.2518	7.1607	6.9838	6.8137	6.4924	**12**
13	7.9038	7.7962	7.6910	7.5879	7.4869	7.2912	7.1034	6.7499	**13**
14	8.2442	8.1259	8.0101	7.8969	7.7862	7.5719	7.3667	6.9819	**14**
15	8.5595	8.4304	8.3042	8.1810	8.0607	7.8282	7.6061	7.1909	**15**
16	8.8514	8.7116	8.5753	8.4423	8.3126	8.0623	7.8237	7.3792	**16**
17	9.1216	8.9715	8.8252	8.6826	8.5436	8.2760	8.0216	7.5488	**17**
18	9.3719	9.2115	9.0555	8.9035	8.7556	8.4713	8.2014	7.7016	**18**
19	9.6036	9.4333	9.2677	9.1067	8.9501	8.6496	8.3649	7.8393	**19**
20	9.8181	9.6381	9.4633	9.2935	9.1285	8.8124	8.5136	7.9633	**20**
21	10.0168	9.8274	9.6436	9.4653	9.2922	8.9611	8.6487	8.0751	**21**
22	10.2007	10.0022	9.8098	9.6233	9.4424	9.0969	8.7715	8.1757	**22**
23	10.3711	10.1637	9.9629	9.7685	9.5802	9.2209	8.8832	8.2664	**23**
24	10.5288	10.3129	10.1041	9.9021	9.7066	9.3341	8.9847	8.3481	**24**
25	10.6748	10.4507	10.2342	10.0249	9.8226	9.4376	9.0770	8.4217	**25**
26	10.8100	10.5780	10.3541	10.1379	9.9290	9.5320	9.1609	8.4881	**26**

No Income Tax **Single Rate**

YEARS' PURCHASE
Rate Per Cent

Yrs.	**8**	**8.25**	**8.5**	**8.75**	**9**	**9.5**	**10**	**11**	**Yrs.**
27	10.9352	10.6956	10.4646	10.2417	10.0266	9.6183	9.2372	8.5478	**27**
28	11.0511	10.8043	10.5665	10.3372	10.1161	9.6971	9.3066	8.6016	**28**
29	11.1584	10.9046	10.6603	10.4250	10.1983	9.7690	9.3696	8.6501	**29**
30	11.2578	10.9974	10.7468	10.5058	10.2737	9.8347	9.4269	8.6938	**30**
31	11.3498	11.0830	10.8266	10.5800	10.3428	9.8947	9.4790	8.7331	**31**
32	11.4350	11.1621	10.9001	10.6483	10.4062	9.9495	9.5264	8.7686	**32**
33	11.5139	11.2352	10.9678	10.7111	10.4644	9.9996	9.5694	8.8005	**33**
34	11.5869	11.3028	11.0302	10.7688	10.5178	10.0453	9.6086	8.8293	**34**
35	11.6546	11.3651	11.0878	10.8219	10.5668	10.0870	9.6442	8.8552	**35**
36	11.7172	11.4228	11.1408	10.8707	10.6118	10.1251	9.6765	8.8786	**36**
37	11.7752	11.4760	11.1897	10.9156	10.6530	10.1599	9.7059	8.8996	**37**
38	11.8289	11.5252	11.2347	10.9569	10.6908	10.1917	9.7327	8.9186	**38**
39	11.8786	11.5706	11.2763	10.9948	10.7255	10.2207	9.7570	8.9357	**39**
40	11.9246	11.6125	11.3145	11.0297	10.7574	10.2472	9.7791	8.9511	**40**
41	11.9672	11.6513	11.3498	11.0618	10.7866	10.2715	9.7991	8.9649	**41**
42	12.0067	11.6871	11.3823	11.0913	10.8134	10.2936	9.8174	8.9774	**42**
43	12.0432	11.7202	11.4123	11.1184	10.8380	10.3138	9.8340	8.9886	**43**
44	12.0771	11.7508	11.4399	11.1434	10.8605	10.3322	9.8491	8.9988	**44**
45	12.1084	11.7790	11.4653	11.1663	10.8812	10.3490	9.8628	9.0079	**45**
46	12.1374	11.8051	11.4888	11.1874	10.9002	10.3644	9.8753	9.0161	**46**
47	12.1643	11.8292	11.5104	11.2068	10.9176	10.3785	9.8866	9.0235	**47**
48	12.1891	11.8514	11.5303	11.2247	10.9336	10.3913	9.8969	9.0302	**48**
49	12.2122	11.8720	11.5487	11.2411	10.9482	10.4030	9.9063	9.0362	**49**
50	12.2335	11.8910	11.5656	11.2562	10.9617	10.4137	9.9148	9.0417	**50**
51	12.2532	11.9085	11.5812	11.2700	10.9740	10.4235	9.9226	9.0465	**51**
52	12.2715	11.9247	11.5956	11.2828	10.9853	10.4324	9.9296	9.0509	**52**
53	12.2884	11.9397	11.6088	11.2945	10.9957	10.4405	9.9360	9.0549	**53**
54	12.3041	11.9535	11.6210	11.3053	11.0053	10.4880	9.9418	9.0585	**54**
55	12.3186	11.9663	11.6323	11.3152	11.0140	10.4548	9.9471	9.0617	**55**
56	12.3321	11.9781	11.6427	11.3244	11.0220	10.4610	9.9519	9.0646	**56**
57	12.3445	11.9890	11.6522	11.3327	11.0294	10.4667	9.9563	9.0672	**57**
58	12.3560	11.9991	11.6610	11.3404	11.0361	10.4718	9.9603	9.0695	**58**
59	12.3667	12.0084	11.6692	11.3475	11.0423	10.4766	9.9639	9.0717	**59**
60	12.3766	12.0170	11.6766	11.3541	11.0480	10.4809	9.9672	9.0736	**60**
61	12.3857	12.0250	11.6835	11.3601	11.0532	10.4848	9.9701	9.0753	**61**
62	12.3942	12.0323	11.6899	11.3656	11.0580	10.4884	9.9729	9.0798	**62**
63	12.4020	12.0391	11.6958	11.3706	11.0624	10.4917	9.9753	9.0782	**63**
64	12.4093	12.0453	11.7012	11.3753	11.0664	10.4947	9.9776	9.0795	**64**
65	12.4160	12.0511	11.7061	11.3796	11.0701	10.4975	9.9796	9.0806	**65**
66	12.4222	12.0565	11.7107	11.3835	11.0735	10.5000	9.9815	9.0816	**66**
67	12.4280	12.0614	11.7150	11.3871	11.0766	10.5022	9.9831	9.0826	**67**
68	12.4333	12.0659	11.7189	11.3905	11.0794	10.5043	9.9847	9.0834	**68**
69	12.4382	12.0702	11.7224	11.3935	11.0820	10.5062	9.9861	9.0841	**69**
70	12.4428	12.0741	11.7258	11.3964	11.0844	10.5080	9.9873	9.0848	**70**
71	12.4471	12.0776	11.7288	11.3990	11.0867	10.5096	9.9885	9.0854	**71**
72	12.4510	12.0810	11.7316	11.4013	11.0887	10.5110	9.9895	9.0860	**72**
73	12.4546	12.0840	11.7342	11.4035	11.0905	10.5124	9.9905	9.0864	**73**
74	12.4580	12.0869	11.7366	11.4055	11.0922	10.5136	9.9914	9.0869	**74**
75	12.4611	12.0895	11.7388	11.4074	11.0938	10.5147	9.9921	9.0873	**75**
76	12.4640	12.0919	11.7408	11.4091	11.0952	10.5157	9.9929	9.0876	**76**
77	12.4666	12.0941	11.7427	11.4107	11.0965	10.5166	9.9935	9.0880	**77**
78	12.4691	12.0962	11.7444	11.4121	11.0977	10.5174	9.9941	9.0883	**78**
79	12.4714	12.0981	11.7460	11.4134	11.0988	10.5182	9.9946	9.0885	**79**

No Income Tax **Single Rate**

YEARS' PURCHASE

Rate Per Cent

Yrs.	8	8.25	8.5	8.75	9	9.5	10	11	Yrs.
80	12.4735	12.0999	11.7475	11.4147	11.0998	10.5189	9.9951	9.0888	**80**
81	12.4755	12.1015	11.7488	11.4158	11.1008	10.5196	9.9956	9.0890	**81**
82	12.4773	12.1030	11.7501	11.4168	11.1016	10.5201	9.9960	9.0892	**82**
83	12.4790	12.1044	11.7512	11.4177	11.1024	10.5207	9.9963	9.0893	**83**
84	12.4805	12.1057	11.7523	11.4186	11.1031	10.5212	9.9967	9.0895	**84**
85	12.4820	12.1069	11.7532	11.4194	11.1038	10.5216	9.9970	9.0896	**85**
86	12.4833	12.1079	11.7541	11.4202	11.1044	10.5220	9.9972	9.0898	**86**
87	12.4845	12.1090	11.7550	11.4208	11.1050	10.5224	9.9975	9.0899	**87**
88	12.4857	12.1099	11.7557	11.4215	11.1055	10.5227	9.9977	9.0900	**88**
89	12.4868	12.1108	11.7564	11.4220	11.1059	10.5230	9.9979	9.0901	**89**
90	12.4877	12.1116	11.7571	11.4226	11.1064	10.5233	9.9981	9.0902	**90**
91	12.4886	12.1123	11.7577	11.4230	11.1067	10.5236	9.9983	9.0902	**91**
92	12.4895	12.1130	11.7582	11.4235	11.1071	10.5238	9.9984	9.0903	**92**
93	12.4903	12.1136	11.7587	11.4239	11.1074	10.5240	9.9986	9.0904	**93**
94	12.4910	12.1142	11.7592	11.4243	11.1077	10.5242	9.9987	9.0904	**94**
95	12.4917	12.1147	11.7596	11.4246	11.1080	10.5244	9.9988	9.0905	**95**
96	12.4923	12.1152	11.7600	11.4249	11.1083	10.5246	9.9989	9.0905	**96**
97	12.4928	12.1157	11.7604	11.4252	11.1085	10.5247	9.9990	9.0905	**97**
98	12.4934	12.1161	11.7607	11.4255	11.1087	10.5249	9.9991	9.0906	**98**
99	12.4939	12.1165	11.7610	11.4257	11.1089	10.5250	9.9992	9.0906	**99**
100	12.4943	12.1168	11.7613	11.4260	11.1091	10.5251	9.9993	9.0906	**100**
PERP	12.5000	12.1212	11.7647	11.4286	11.1111	10.5263	10.0000	9.0909	**PERP**

No Income Tax **Single Rate**

YEARS' PURCHASE

Rate Per Cent

Yrs.	12	13	14	15	16	17	18	19	Yrs.
1	0.8929	0.8850	0.8772	0.8696	0.8621	0.8547	0.8475	0.8403	**1**
2	1.6901	1.6681	1.6467	1.6257	1.6052	1.5852	1.5656	1.5465	**2**
3	2.4018	2.3612	2.3216	2.2832	2.2459	2.2096	2.1743	2.1399	**3**
4	3.0373	2.9745	2.9137	2.8550	2.7982	2.7432	2.6901	2.6386	**4**
5	3.6048	3.5172	3.4331	3.3522	3.2743	3.1993	3.1272	3.0576	**5**
6	4.1114	3.9975	3.8887	3.7845	3.6847	3.5892	3.4976	3.4098	**6**
7	4.5638	4.4226	4.2883	4.1604	4.0386	3.9224	3.8115	3.7057	**7**
8	4.9676	4.7988	4.6389	4.4873	4.3436	4.2072	4.0776	3.9544	**8**
9	5.3282	5.1317	4.9464	4.7716	4.6065	4.4506	4.3030	4.1633	**9**
10	5.6502	5.4262	5.2161	5.0188	4.8332	4.6586	4.4941	4.3389	**10**
11	5.9377	5.6869	5.4257	5.2337	5.0286	4.8364	4.6560	4.4865	**11**
12	6.1944	5.9176	5.6603	5.4206	5.1971	4.9884	4.7932	4.6105	**12**
13	6.4235	6.1218	5.8424	5.5831	5.3423	5.1183	4.9095	4.7147	**13**
14	6.6282	6.3025	6.0021	5.7245	5.4675	5.2293	5.0081	4.8023	**14**
15	6.8109	6.4624	6.1422	5.8474	5.5755	5.3242	5.0916	4.8759	**15**
16	6.9740	6.6039	6.2651	5.9542	5.6685	5.4053	5.1624	4.9377	**16**
17	7.1196	6.7291	6.3729	6.0472	5.7487	5.4746	5.2223	4.9897	**17**
18	7.2497	6.8399	6.4674	6.1280	5.8178	5.5339	5.2732	5.0333	**18**
19	7.3658	6.9380	6.5504	6.1982	5.8775	5.5845	5.3162	5.0700	**19**
20	7.4694	7.0248	6.6231	6.2593	5.9288	5.6278	5.3527	5.1009	**20**
21	7.5620	7.1016	6.6870	6.3125	5.9731	5.6648	5.3837	5.1268	**21**
22	7.6446	7.1695	6.7429	6.3587	6.0113	5.6964	5.4099	5.1486	**22**
23	7.7184	7.2297	6.7921	6.3988	6.0442	5.7234	5.4321	5.1668	**23**
24	7.7843	7.2829	6.8351	6.4338	6.0726	5.7465	5.4509	5.1822	**24**
25	7.8431	7.3300	6.8729	6.4641	6.0971	5.7662	5.4669	5.1951	**25**
26	7.8957	7.3717	6.9061	6.4906	6.1182	5.7831	5.4804	5.2060	**26**

No Income Tax **Single Rate**

YEARS' PURCHASE
Rate Per Cent

Yrs.	12	13	14	15	16	17	18	19	Yrs.
27	7.9426	7.4086	6.9352	6.5135	6.1364	5.7975	5.4919	5.2151	**27**
28	7.9844	7.4412	6.9607	6.5335	6.1520	5.8099	5.5016	5.2228	**28**
29	8.0218	7.4701	6.9830	6.5509	6.1656	5.8204	5.5098	5.2292	**29**
30	8.0552	7.4957	7.0027	6.5660	6.1772	5.8294	5.5168	5.2347	**30**
31	8.0850	7.5183	7.0199	6.5791	6.1872	5.8371	5.5227	5.2392	**31**
32	8.1116	7.5383	7.0350	6.5905	6.1959	5.8437	5.5277	5.2430	**32**
33	8.1354	7.5560	7.0482	6.6005	6.2034	5.8493	5.5320	5.2462	**33**
34	8.1566	7.5717	7.0599	6.6091	6.2098	5.8541	5.5356	5.2489	**34**
35	8.1755	7.5856	7.0700	6.6166	6.2153	5.8582	5.5386	5.2512	**35**
36	8.1924	7.5979	7.0790	6.6231	6.2201	5.8617	5.5412	5.2531	**36**
37	8.2075	7.6087	7.0868	6.6288	6.2242	5.8647	5.5434	5.2547	**37**
38	8.2210	7.6183	7.0937	6.6338	6.2278	5.8673	5.5452	5.2561	**38**
39	8.2330	7.6268	7.0997	6.6380	6.2309	5.8695	5.5468	5.2572	**39**
40	8.2438	7.6344	7.1050	6.6418	6.2335	5.8713	5.5482	5.2582	**40**
41	8.2534	7.6410	7.1097	6.6450	6.2358	5.8729	5.5493	5.2590	**41**
42	8.2619	7.6469	7.1138	6.6478	6.2377	5.8743	5.5502	5.2596	**42**
43	8.2696	7.6522	7.1173	6.6503	6.2394	5.8755	5.5510	5.2602	**43**
44	8.2764	7.6568	7.1205	6.6524	6.2409	5.8765	5.5517	5.2607	**44**
45	8.2825	7.6609	7.1232	6.6543	6.2421	5.8773	5.5523	5.2611	**45**
46	8.2880	7.6645	7.1256	6.6559	6.2432	5.8781	5.5528	5.2614	**46**
47	8.2928	7.6677	7.1277	6.6573	6.2442	5.8787	5.5532	5.2617	**47**
48	8.2972	7.6705	7.1296	6.6585	6.2450	5.8792	5.5536	5.2619	**48**
49	8.3010	7.6730	7.1312	6.6596	6.2457	5.8797	5.5539	5.2621	**49**
50	8.3045	7.6752	7.1327	6.6605	6.2463	5.8801	5.5541	5.2623	**50**
51	8.3076	7.6772	7.1339	6.6613	6.2468	5.8804	5.5544	5.2624	**51**
52	8.3103	7.6789	7.1350	6.6620	6.2472	5.8807	5.5545	5.2625	**52**
53	8.3128	7.6805	7.1360	6.6626	6.2476	5.8809	5.5547	5.2626	**53**
54	8.3150	7.6818	7.1368	6.6631	6.2479	5.8811	5.5548	5.2627	**54**
55	8.3170	7.6830	7.1376	6.6636	6.2482	5.8813	5.5549	5.2628	**55**
56	8.3187	7.6841	7.1382	6.6640	6.2485	5.8815	5.5550	5.2628	**56**
57	8.3203	7.6851	7.1388	6.6644	6.2487	5.8816	5.5551	5.2629	**57**
58	8.3217	7.6859	7.1393	6.6647	6.2489	5.8817	5.5552	5.2629	**58**
59	8.3229	7.6866	7.1397	6.6649	6.2490	5.8818	5.5552	5.2630	**59**
60	8.3240	7.6873	7.1401	6.6651	6.2492	5.8819	5.5553	5.2630	**60**
61	8.3250	7.6879	7.1404	6.6653	6.2493	5.8819	5.5553	5.2630	**61**
62	8.3259	7.6884	7.1407	6.6655	6.2494	5.8820	5.5554	5.2630	**62**
63	8.3267	7.6888	7.1410	6.6657	6.2495	5.8821	5.5554	5.2631	**63**
64	8.3274	7.6892	7.1412	6.6658	6.2495	5.8821	5.5554	5.2631	**64**
65	8.3281	7.6896	7.1414	6.6659	6.2496	5.8821	5.5554	5.2631	**65**
66	8.3286	7.6899	7.1416	6.6660	6.2497	5.8822	5.5555	5.2631	**66**
67	8.3291	7.6902	7.1418	6.6661	6.2497	5.8822	5.5555	5.2631	**67**
68	8.3296	7.6904	7.1419	6.6662	6.2497	5.8822	5.5555	5.2631	**68**
69	8.3300	7.6906	7.1420	6.6662	6.2498	5.8822	5.5555	5.2631	**69**
70	8.3303	7.6908	7.1421	6.6663	6.2498	5.8823	5.5555	5.2631	**70**
71	8.3307	7.6910	7.1422	6.6663	6.2498	5.8823	5.5555	5.2631	**71**
72	8.3310	7.6911	7.1423	6.6664	6.2499	5.8823	5.5555	5.2631	**72**
73	8.3312	7.6913	7.1424	6.6664	6.2499	5.8823	5.5555	5.2631	**73**
74	8.3314	7.6914	7.1424	6.6665	6.2499	5.8823	5.5555	5.2631	**74**
75	8.3316	7.6915	7.1425	6.6665	6.2499	5.8823	5.5555	5.2631	**75**
76	8.3318	7.6916	7.1425	6.6665	6.2499	5.8823	5.5555	5.2631	**76**
77	8.3320	7.6917	7.1426	6.6665	6.2499	5.8823	5.5555	5.2631	**77**
78	8.3321	7.6918	7.1426	6.6665	6.2499	5.8823	5.5555	5.2632	**78**
79	8.3323	7.6918	7.1426	6.6666	6.2499	5.8823	5.5555	5.2632	**79**

No Income Tax **Single Rate**

YEARS' PURCHASE
Rate Per Cent

Yrs.	12	13	14	15	16	17	18	19	Yrs.
80	8.3324	7.6919	7.1427	6.6666	6.2500	5.8823	5.5555	5.2632	**80**
81	8.3325	7.6919	7.1427	6.6666	6.2500	5.8823	5.5555	5.2632	**81**
82	8.3326	7.6920	7.1427	6.6666	6.2500	5.8823	5.5555	5.2632	**82**
83	8.3326	7.6920	7.1427	6.6666	6.2500	5.8823	5.5555	5.2632	**83**
84	8.3327	7.6920	7.1427	6.6666	6.2500	5.8823	5.5556	5.2632	**84**
85	8.3328	7.6921	7.1428	6.6666	6.2500	5.8823	5.5556	5.2632	**85**
86	8.3328	7.6921	7.1428	6.6666	6.2500	5.8823	5.5556	5.2632	**86**
87	8.3329	7.6921	7.1428	6.6666	6.2500	5.8823	5.5556	5.2632	**87**
88	8.3329	7.6921	7.1428	6.6666	6.2500	5.8823	5.5556	5.2632	**88**
89	8.3330	7.6922	7.1428	6.6666	6.2500	5.8823	5.5556	5.2632	**89**
90	8.3330	7.6922	7.1428	6.6666	6.2500	5.8823	5.5556	5.2632	**90**
91	8.3331	7.6922	7.1428	6.6666	6.2500	5.8823	5.5556	5.2632	**91**
92	8.3331	7.6922	7.1428	6.6666	6.2500	5.8823	5.5556	5.2632	**92**
93	8.3331	7.6922	7.1428	6.6667	6.2500	5.8824	5.5556	5.2632	**93**
94	8.3331	7.6922	7.1428	6.6667	6.2500	5.8824	5.5556	5.2632	**94**
95	8.3332	7.6922	7.1428	6.6667	6.2500	5.8824	5.5556	5.2632	**95**
96	8.3332	7.6922	7.1428	6.6667	6.2500	5.8824	5.5556	5.2632	**96**
97	8.3332	7.6923	7.1428	6.6667	6.2500	5.8824	5.5556	5.2632	**97**
98	8.3332	7.6923	7.1428	6.6667	6.2500	5.8824	5.5556	5.2632	**98**
99	8.3332	7.6923	7.1428	6.6667	6.2500	5.8824	5.5556	5.2632	**99**
100	8.3332	7.6923	7.1428	6.6667	6.2500	5.8824	5.5556	5.2632	**100**
PERP	8.3333	7.6923	7.1429	6.6667	6.2500	5.8824	5.5556	5.2632	**PERP**

No Income Tax **Single Rate**

YEARS' PURCHASE
Rate Per Cent

Yrs.	20	21	22	23	24	25	26	28	Yrs.
1	0.8333	0.8264	0.8197	0.8130	0.8065	0.8000	0.7937	0.7812	**1**
2	1.5278	1.5095	1.4915	1.4740	1.4568	1.4400	1.4235	1.3916	**2**
3	2.1065	2.0739	2.0422	2.0114	1.9813	1.9520	1.9234	1.8684	**3**
4	2.5887	2.5404	2.4936	2.4483	2.4043	2.3616	2.3202	2.2410	**4**
5	2.9906	2.9260	2.8636	2.8035	2.7454	2.6893	2.6351	2.5320	**5**
6	3.3255	3.2446	3.1669	3.0923	3.0205	2.9514	2.8850	2.7594	**6**
7	3.6046	3.5079	3.4155	3.3270	3.2423	3.1611	3.0833	2.9370	**7**
8	3.8372	3.7256	3.6193	3.5179	3.4212	3.3289	3.2407	3.0758	**8**
9	4.0310	3.9054	3.7863	3.6731	3.5655	3.4631	3.3657	3.1842	**9**
10	4.1925	4.0541	3.9232	3.7993	3.6819	3.5705	3.4648	3.2689	**10**
11	4.3271	4.1769	4.0354	3.9018	3.7757	3.6564	3.5435	3.3351	**11**
12	4.4392	4.2784	4.1274	3.9852	3.8514	3.7251	3.6059	3.3868	**12**
13	4.5327	4.3624	4.2028	4.0530	3.9124	3.7801	3.6555	3.4272	**13**
14	4.6106	4.4317	4.2646	4.1082	3.9616	3.8241	3.6949	3.4587	**14**
15	4.6755	4.4890	4.3152	4.1530	4.0013	3.8593	3.7261	3.4834	**15**
16	4.7296	4.5364	4.3567	4.1894	4.0333	3.8874	3.7509	3.5026	**16**
17	4.7746	4.5755	4.3908	4.2190	4.0591	3.9099	3.7705	3.5177	**17**
18	4.8122	4.6079	4.4187	4.2431	4.0799	3.9279	3.7861	3.5294	**18**
19	4.8435	4.6346	4.4415	4.2627	4.0967	3.9424	3.7985	3.5386	**19**
20	4.8696	4.6567	4.4603	4.2786	4.1103	3.9539	3.8083	3.5458	**20**
21	4.8913	4.6750	4.4756	4.2916	4.1212	3.9631	3.8161	3.5514	**21**
22	4.9094	4.6900	4.4882	4.3021	4.1300	3.9705	3.8223	3.5558	**22**
23	4.9245	4.7025	4.4985	4.3106	4.1371	3.9764	3.8273	3.5592	**23**
24	4.9371	4.7128	4.5070	4.3176	4.1428	3.9811	3.8312	3.5619	**24**
25	4.9476	4.7213	4.5139	4.3232	4.1474	3.9849	3.8342	3.5640	**25**
26	4.9563	4.7284	4.5196	4.3278	4.1511	3.9879	3.8367	3.5656	**26**

No Income Tax **Single Rate**

YEARS' PURCHASE
Rate Per Cent

Yrs.	**20**	**21**	**22**	**23**	**24**	**25**	**26**	**28**	**Yrs.**
27	4.9636	4.7342	4.5243	4.3316	4.1542	3.9903	3.8387	3.5669	**27**
28	4.9697	4.7390	4.5281	4.3346	4.1566	3.9923	3.8402	3.5679	**28**
29	4.9747	4.7430	4.5312	4.3371	4.1585	3.9938	3.8414	3.5687	**29**
30	4.9789	4.7463	4.5338	4.3391	4.1601	3.9950	3.8424	3.5693	**30**
31	4.9824	4.7490	4.5359	4.3407	4.1614	3.9960	3.8432	3.5697	**31**
32	4.9854	4.7512	4.5376	4.3421	4.1624	3.9968	3.8438	3.5701	**32**
33	4.9878	4.7531	4.5390	4.3431	4.1632	3.9975	3.8443	3.5704	**33**
34	4.9898	4.7546	4.5402	4.3440	4.1639	3.9980	3.8447	3.5706	**34**
35	4.9915	4.7559	4.5411	4.3447	4.1644	3.9984	3.8450	3.5708	**35**
36	4.9929	4.7569	4.5419	4.3453	4.1649	3.9987	3.8452	3.5709	**36**
37	4.9941	4.7578	4.5426	4.3458	4.1652	3.9990	3.8454	3.5710	**37**
38	4.9951	4.7585	4.5431	4.3462	4.1655	3.9992	3.8456	3.5711	**38**
39	4.9959	4.7591	4.5435	4.3465	4.1657	3.9993	3.8457	3.5712	**39**
40	4.9966	4.7596	4.5439	4.3467	4.1659	3.9995	3.8458	3.5712	**40**
41	4.9972	4.7600	4.5441	4.3469	4.1661	3.9996	3.8459	3.5713	**41**
42	4.9976	4.7603	4.5444	4.3471	4.1662	3.9997	3.8459	3.5713	**42**
43	4.9980	4.7606	4.5446	4.3472	4.1663	3.9997	3.8460	3.5713	**43**
44	4.9984	4.7608	4.5447	4.3473	4.1663	3.9998	3.8460	3.5714	**44**
45	4.9986	4.7610	4.5449	4.3474	4.1664	3.9998	3.8460	3.5714	**45**
46	4.9989	4.7612	4.5450	4.3475	4.1665	3.9999	3.8461	3.5714	**46**
47	4.9991	4.7613	4.5451	4.3476	4.1665	3.9999	3.8461	3.5714	**47**
48	4.9992	4.7614	4.5451	4.3476	4.1665	3.9999	3.8461	3.5714	**48**
49	4.9993	4.7615	4.5452	4.3477	4.1666	3.9999	3.8461	3.5714	**49**
50	4.9995	4.7616	4.5452	4.3477	4.1666	3.9999	3.8461	3.5714	**50**
51	4.9995	4.7616	4.5453	4.3477	4.1666	4.0000	3.8461	3.5714	**51**
52	4.9996	4.7617	4.5453	4.3477	4.1666	4.0000	3.8461	3.5714	**52**
53	4.9997	4.7617	4.5453	4.3478	4.1666	4.0000	3.8461	3.5714	**53**
54	4.9997	4.7617	4.5454	4.3478	4.1666	4.0000	3.8461	3.5714	**54**
55	4.9998	4.7618	4.5454	4.3478	4.1666	4.0000	3.8461	3.5714	**55**
56	4.9998	4.7618	4.5454	4.3478	4.1666	4.0000	3.8461	3.5714	**56**
57	4.9998	4.7618	4.5454	4.3478	4.1666	4.0000	3.8461	3.5714	**57**
58	4.9999	4.7618	4.5454	4.3478	4.1667	4.0000	3.8461	3.5714	**58**
59	4.9999	4.7618	4.5454	4.3478	4.1667	4.0000	3.8461	3.5714	**59**
60	4.9999	4.7619	4.5454	4.3478	4.1667	4.0000	3.8462	3.5714	**60**
61	4.9999	4.7619	4.5454	4.3478	4.1667	4.0000	3.8462	3.5714	**61**
62	4.9999	4.7619	4.5454	4.3478	4.1667	4.0000	3.8462	3.5714	**62**
63	4.9999	4.7619	4.5454	4.3478	4.1667	4.0000	3.8462	3.5714	**63**
64	5.0000	4.7619	4.5454	4.3478	4.1667	4.0000	3.8462	3.5714	**64**
65	5.0000	4.7619	4.5454	4.3478	4.1667	4.0000	3.8462	3.5714	**65**
66	5.0000	4.7619	4.5454	4.3478	4.1667	4.0000	3.8462	3.5714	**66**
67	5.0000	4.7619	4.5454	4.3478	4.1667	4.0000	3.8462	3.5714	**67**
68	5.0000	4.7619	4.5454	4.3478	4.1667	4.0000	3.8462	3.5714	**68**
69	5.0000	4.7619	4.5454	4.3478	4.1667	4.0000	3.8462	3.5714	**69**
70	5.0000	4.7619	4.5455	4.3478	4.1667	4.0000	3.8462	3.5714	**70**
71	5.0000	4.7619	4.5455	4.3478	4.1667	4.0000	3.8462	3.5714	**71**
72	5.0000	4.7619	4.5455	4.3478	4.1667	4.0000	3.8462	3.5714	**72**
73	5.0000	4.7619	4.5455	4.3478	4.1667	4.0000	3.8462	3.5714	**73**
74	5.0000	4.7619	4.5455	4.3478	4.1667	4.0000	3.8462	3.5714	**74**
75	5.0000	4.7619	4.5455	4.3478	4.1667	4.0000	3.8462	3.5714	**75**
76	5.0000	4.7619	4.5455	4.3478	4.1667	4.0000	3.8462	3.5714	**76**
77	5.0000	4.7619	4.5455	4.3478	4.1667	4.0000	3.8462	3.5714	**77**
78	5.0000	4.7619	4.5455	4.3478	4.1667	4.0000	3.8462	3.5714	**78**
79	5.0000	4.7619	4.5455	4.3478	4.1667	4.0000	3.8462	3.5714	**79**

No Income Tax **Single Rate**

YEARS' PURCHASE
Rate Per Cent

Yrs.	20	21	22	23	24	25	26	28	Yrs.
80	5.0000	4.7619	4.5455	4.3478	4.1667	4.0000	3.8462	3.5714	**80**
81	5.0000	4.7619	4.5455	4.3478	4.1667	4.0000	3.8462	3.5714	**81**
82	5.0000	4.7619	4.5455	4.3478	4.1667	4.0000	3.8462	3.5714	**82**
83	5.0000	4.7619	4.5455	4.3478	4.1667	4.0000	3.8462	3.5714	**83**
84	5.0000	4.7619	4.5455	4.3478	4.1667	4.0000	3.8462	3.5714	**84**
85	5.0000	4.7619	4.5455	4.3478	4.1667	4.0000	3.8462	3.5714	**85**
86	5.0000	4.7619	4.5455	4.3478	4.1667	4.0000	3.8462	3.5714	**86**
87	5.0000	4.7619	4.5455	4.3478	4.1667	4.0000	3.8462	3.5714	**87**
88	5.0000	4.7619	4.5455	4.3478	4.1667	4.0000	3.8462	3.5714	**88**
89	5.0000	4.7619	4.5455	4.3478	4.1667	4.0000	3.8462	3.5714	**89**
90	5.0000	4.7619	4.5455	4.3478	4.1667	4.0000	3.8462	3.5714	**90**
91	5.0000	4.7619	4.5455	4.3478	4.1667	4.0000	3.8462	3.5714	**91**
92	5.0000	4.7619	4.5455	4.3478	4.1667	4.0000	3.8462	3.5714	**92**
93	5.0000	4.7619	4.5455	4.3478	4.1667	4.0000	3.8462	3.5714	**93**
94	5.0000	4.7619	4.5455	4.3478	4.1667	4.0000	3.8462	3.5714	**94**
95	5.0000	4.7619	4.5455	4.3478	4.1667	4.0000	3.8462	3.5714	**95**
96	5.0000	4.7619	4.5455	4.3478	4.1667	4.0000	3.8462	3.5714	**96**
97	5.0000	4.7619	4.5455	4.3478	4.1667	4.0000	3.8462	3.5714	**97**
98	5.0000	4.7619	4.5455	4.3478	4.1667	4.0000	3.8462	3.5714	**98**
99	5.0000	4.7619	4.5455	4.3478	4.1667	4.0000	3.8462	3.5714	**99**
100	5.0000	4.7619	4.5455	4.3478	4.1667	4.0000	3.8462	3.5714	**100**
PERP	5.0000	4.7619	4.5455	4.3478	4.1667	4.0000	3.8462	3.5714	**PERP**

Appendix K

Summary of main relevant taxation Acts since 2014 that might affect a valuation

Revenue Scotland and Tax Powers Act 2014

This Act defines Revenue Scotland (RS) and its various powers and responsibilities and those of the Scottish Tax Tribunals and Judicial Review, the powers and enforcement of RS and its Practice and Procedure, including Tribunal rules, practice directions, administration and interpretation. The Scottish General anti-avoidance rule is covered as are tax returns, enquiries and assessments, etc, as well as the investigatory powers of RS, penalties and appeals.

Taxation of Pensions Act 2014

This Act deals with lump sums, pension flexibility, annuities, uncrystallised funds, pensions, death of a pension scheme member, lump sum benefits etc.

Wales Act 2014

This Act deals with delegated matters of finance etc.

Corporation Tax (Northern Ireland) Act 2015

This Act modifies the research and development (R&D) expenditure rules, as well as film tax relief and television and theatrical production reliefs, and profits arising from the exploitation of patents etc.

Finance Act 2015

This Act makes the usual changes to the tax law, including s 26 which amends CTA 2009, s 746 and inserts s 849B to restrict tax relief for goodwill etc acquired from related parties.

R&D expenditure credits are increased from 10% to 11%, and the additional deductions for R&D incurred by SMEs are increased. Film tax relief is amended as is television tax relief. Entrepreneurs' relief is amended. Non-UK companies avoiding a UK taxable presence may be caught by ss 86 and 87 and diverted profits by ss 88–92. The non-resident capital gains tax rules in Schedule 7 are amended.

Penalties in connection with offshore matters and offshore transfers are dealt with in Schedules 20 and 21.

Finance (No 2) Act 2015

R&D expenditure credits are denied to ineligible companies such as higher education establishments, charities or other companies defined by Treasury regulations.

The intangible fixed asset reliefs in CTA 2009, Part 8, ss 711 to 906 do not apply to goodwill, customer records etc, unregistered trademarks and licences.

From 8 July 2015, controlled foreign companies (CFCs) are not able to set UK losses against a CFC charge. Restitution interest is dealt with at length and is taxable under CTA 2010, ss 357YA–357YW.

The valuation of trading stock on cessation and transfers of intangible assets not at arm's length are valued at the higher of normal transfer pricing rules on the market value. New rules are introduced for carried interest under TCGA 1992, ss 103KA–103KF and various terms are defined. Client notification agreements to improve compliance are introduced.

Schedules specify the rate of tax charged on transfers of value. Amendments are made to the Enterprise Investment Scheme (EIS), Value Capital trusts, loan relationships and derivative contracts. Schedule 8 enables HMRC to collect tax and tax credit debts from taxpayers' bank accounts.

Finance Act 2016

Sections 14 inserts ITEPA 2003, ss 339A and 688B and PAYE Regulations 2003 (SI 2003/2682), Chapter 3B, to recover PAYE debts from employment intermediaries, inserting regulations 97ZG–97ZM; and ITEPA 2003, s 688B applies to travel expenses of workers providing services through intermediaries to recover unpaid tax. The recovery of such tax and consequential National Insurance contributions could result in substantial charges which would affect the value of the company and its shareholders.

Section 37 inserts ITA 2007, Part 13, Chapter 5F, taxing income-based carried interest, derivatives and hedging.

Sections 52 and 53 amend CTA 2009 to prevent arrangements designed to bring pre-1 April 2002 intellectual property within the tax-relieved amortisation rules.

The anti-avoidance rules affecting profits from the exploitation of patents etc are extended by s 64, amending CTA 2010, s 357A and inserting ss 357BF–357BQ, and are extended to transferred trades by CTA 2010, s 357GCA.

CTA 2010, Part 8ZB is inserted to bring certain profits and gains from the disposal of UK land within the tax net which may impact on the value of the shares in the chargeable company.

The general anti-abuse rule (GAAR) in FA 2015, Schedule 20 is strengthened, and promoters of tax avoidance schemes are increased in FA 2016, ss 157 (inserting FA 2013, Schedules 43A and 43B to 160. Administration, enforcement and supplementary powers are in ss 167–178 and, in ss 184–189 and Schedule 25, the Office of Tax Simplification's duties are amended.

Scotland Act 2016

This Act allows the Scottish Parliament to set tax rates etc, with constitutional arrangements made under the Scottish Fiscal Commission Act 2016.

Tax Collection and Management (Wales) Act 2016

This Act introduces the Welsh Revenue Authority.

Criminal Finances Act 2017

Where an employee, agent or service provider of a body corporate, such as a limited company or partnership, engages in tax or NIC evasion on its behalf, the relevant body can be held liable under sections 44–58. Failure to prevent facilitation of tax evasion offences is an offence, unless measurable prevention procedures are in force. Guidance is available in the main text of the book at **4.07**.

Finance Act 2017

Employee shareholder shares issued to employees are to be treated as earnings from employment on the market value of the shares acquired from 1 or 2 December 2016 under sections 12–15 and Schedule 2.

Promoters of tax avoidance schemes, threshold provisions are amended by section 24, and overseas pensions by section 9 and Schedule 3.

Finance (No 2) Act 2017

The provisions in this Act which are particularly relevant for this book are contained in sections 65 (Penalties for enablers of defeated tax avoidance) and 67 (Requirement to correct certain offshore tax non-compliance); Schedules 2 (Trades and property businesses: calculation of profits) and 3 (Trading and property allowances); and Schedule 4 (Relief for carried-forward losses), including Part 10 (Northern Ireland trading losses etc) and Part 11 (Minor and consequential amendments). Schedule 5 introduces a corporate interest restriction.

The following Schedules are also relevant:

- Schedule 6 (Relief for production of museum and art gallery exhibitions);
- Schedule 8 (Deemed domicile: income tax and capital gains tax);
- Schedule 9 (Settlements and transfer of assets abroad: value of benefits);
- Schedule 10 (Inheritance tax on overseas property representing UK residential property);

- Schedule 11 (Employment income provided through third parties: loans etc outstanding on 5 April 2019);
- Schedule 12 (Trading income provided through third parties: loans etc outstanding on 5 April 2019);
- Schedule 13 (Third country goods fulfilment businesses: penalty);
- Schedule 14 (Digital reporting and record-keeping for income tax etc: further amendments);
- Schedule 15 (Partial closure notices);
- Schedule 16 (Penalties for enablers of defeated tax avoidance);
- Schedule 17 (Disclosure of avoidance schemes: VAT and other indirect taxes); and
- Schedule 18 (Requirement to correct certain offshore tax non-compliance).

If a scheme or arrangement seems too good to be true, it probably is.

Finance Act 2018

Sections 11 to 17 and Schedule 2 relate to disguised remuneration, aimed at employment income and trading income provided through third parties. Enterprise investment schemes and venture capital trusts require a risk-to-capital condition to apply in order to obtain the claimed tax relief under Schedules 4 and 5.

Section 26 freezes the indexation allowance for gains subject to corporation tax etc.

Section 30 reduces the double taxation relief for foreign tax on the profits of overseas permanent establishments, introducing TIOPA 2010, ss 71A and 71B; and s 81 is replaced to counter the effect of avoidance arrangements.

Section 23 and Schedule 7 are aimed at hybrid and other mismatches. Section 35 and Schedule 10 are aimed at tax avoidance through settlements under TCGA 1992 and ITTOIA 2005, which are amended accordingly.

The main anti-avoidance provisions in this Act are sections 30 (Reduction of relief in cases where losses relieved sideways etc), 31 (Countering effect of avoidance arrangements), 32 (Double taxation arrangements specified by Order in Council) and 35 (Settlements: anti-avoidance etc). Schedules 1 and 2 are aimed at employment income provided through third parties and trading income provided through third parties where there are loans etc outstanding on 5 April 2019, such as Schedules 3 (Pension schemes), 4 (EIS and VCT reliefs: knowledge-intensive companies) and 5 (Venture capital trusts: further amendments). Schedule 6 relates to partnerships, where there are bare trusts, and notional trades or businesses where there is an indirect partner, and the information to be included in returns including returns of overseas partners in investment partnerships etc. Returns are conclusive as to shares of profits and losses.

Schedule 8 amends the corporate interest restriction. Schedule 10 introduces further anti-avoidance rules for capital gains tax and income tax.

Finance Act 2019

Section 13 and Schedule 1 tax the gains from the disposal of UK land by non-UK resident companies which will, from 6 April 2019, be subject to corporation tax, and the charge to tax on ATED-related gains (Annual Tax on Enveloped Dwellings) is abolished from that date. TCGA 1992, Schedules 1A to 1C are inserted, as are TCGA 1992, Schedules 4AA and 5AAA, with consequential amendments.

Section 14 and Schedule 2 introduce further reporting and payment on account obligations on the disposal of UK land etc from 6 April 2020.

Section 15 and Schedule 3 are introduced with effect from 6 April 2019, to charge non-UK persons on receipts in respect of intangible property by reference to the extent to which such receipts are referable to the sale of goods or services in the UK. A new Chapter 2A is inserted into ITTOIA 2005 as ss 608A–608Z.

Section 16 and Schedule 4 counter avoidance involving profit fragmentation arrangements of UK business profits with the intention of benefiting from low or non-existent tax charges in a foreign jurisdiction, which is likely to be a tax haven.

Section 17 and Schedule 5 apply to non-UK resident companies carrying on UK property businesses etc, with effect from 6 April 2020. The UK taxable income includes the profits on loan relationships and on derivative contracts regarded as other UK property income, as defined. There are extensive supplementary and consequential amendments. Losses which have arisen during the income tax regime, which previously applied, may be carried forward into the corporation tax regime.

Section 18 and Schedule 6 amend the diverted profits tax legislation in FA 2015, Part 3, ss 82–85, and new TIOPA 2010, s 111A is introduced and TIOPA 2010, ss 73 and 101 are amended, and new ss 101A and 101B are introduced to close tax planning opportunities.

Section 19 introduces amendments to the hybrid and other mismatches regime in TIOPA 2010, Part 6A, in particular ss 259HA, 259HC, and 259N.

Section 20 amends the Controlled Foreign Companies (CFC) regime in TIOPA 2010, Part 9A in respect of the finance company exemption and the definition of control.

Section 21 amends the definition of a Permanent Establishment (PE) under CTA 2010, s 1143 where non-resident companies artificially fragment their operations to take advantage of the exemption.

Section 22 and Schedule 7 relate to capital gains tax exit charges to introduce a capital gains tax (CGT) charge on trusts ceasing to be UK resident or where non-UK residents trade through a UK branch or agency in order to defer CGT if a trust ceases to be UK resident or where assets cease to be used in a UK trade carried on through a UK branch. Newly inserted TMA 1970, s 59BB introduces new TMA 1970, Sch 3ZAA which enables a CGT exit charge to spread the consequential tax charge for European Economic Area (EEA) resident individuals who have been carrying on a trade in the UK through a branch or agency and an exit charge arises on a deemed disposal if the trade ceases and the assets become situated outside the UK, in order to comply with Article 49 of the Treaty on the Functioning of the European Union. The exit charge may be spread over six equal instalments, plus interest.

Section 23 and Schedule 8 give rise to corporation tax exit charges to comply with the EU Anti-Tax Avoidance Directive from 1 January 2020. TMA 1970, Sch 3ZB is introduced and replaces TCGA 1992, s 187 to postpone the exit charge under TCGA 1992, s 185.

Section 24 defines 'UK related' company for the purposes of group relief.

Section 26 amends the degrouping charge on intangible fixed assets under CTA 2009, Part 8, s 782A, with consequential amendments to s 785.

Section 27 and Schedule 10 amend the corporation tax relief for carried-forward losses under CTA 2010, Part 7ZA, to restrict relief for certain carried-forward losses and allow these to be used more flexibly.

Section 28 and Schedule 11 restrict certain corporate interest relief under TIOPA 2010, Sch 7A, to align the taxation of profits with the location of economic activity consistent with a more territorial approach to corporate taxation.

Section 29 and Schedule 12 prevent a tax mismatch where two linked loan relationships would otherwise be taxed on a different basis due to one of them having hybrid features.

Section 30 amends the Capital Allowances Act 2001 to provide allowances for qualifying expenditure incurred on or after 29 October 2018 on the construction of a building or structure for a qualifying use.

Section 31 reduces the rate of special writing down allowance for new and relieved expenditure on plant and machinery from 8% to 6% from 1 or 6 April 2019.

Section 32 and Schedule 13 increase the maximum amount of the annual investment allowance to £1 million from 1 January 2019 to 31 December 2020.

Section 33 ends the first year allowance from April 2020 on all products on the Energy or Water Technology Lists, under CAA 2001, ss 45A to 45C, 45H to 45I and 262A, and Sch A1.

Section 36 and Schedule 14 implement changes resulting from the adoption of IFRS 16 or FRS 101.

Section 39 and Schedule 16 amend entrepreneurs' relief to extend the qualifying period and amend the definition of a personal company, and to allow the relief up to the date at which a shareholding is diluted below 5%.

Section 80 increases the assessment time limits for offshore income and gains to 12 years for income tax and capital gains tax, where a tax loss arises in respect of offshore tax.

Section 81 follows section 80 and applies to inheritance tax.

Section 82 amends the Construction Industry Scheme to require security for corporation tax and construction scheme deductions.

Section 83 introduces statutory powers to implement the EU Directive on tax dispute resolution mechanisms.

Section 84 provides for regulations to require disclosure of information to HMRC about certain cross-border tax arrangements, to give effect to international rules.

Appendix L

Useful websites

Website	*Address*	*Free/paid*	*Information provided*
Companies House	www.gov.uk/government/organisations/companies-house	Free	Company filings
Financial Times	https://markets.ft.com/data/archive	Subscription	Data Archive contains FTASI indices
International Valuation Standards Council (IVSG)	www.ivsc.org	Paid	Access to IVSC publications and Standards
IRS	www.irs.gov/irm/part4/irm_04-048-004.html	Free	Business valuation guidelines
OECD	www.oecd.org/ctp/transfer-pricing	Free	Transfer pricing guidance
FASB	www.fasb.org/home	Paid	US Accounting Standards
IFRS	www.ifrs.org/Pages/default.aspx	Free	International Accounting Standards
HMRC	www.hmrc.gov.uk/manuals/svmanualnew/Index.htm	Free	Shares and Assets Valuation Manual
	www.hmrc.gov.uk/shareschemes/val231.pdf	Free	EMI form VAL231
	www.hmrc.gov.uk/forms/val232form.htm	Free	ESS form VAL232
BDO Private Company Price Index	www.bdo.co.uk/news/private-company-price-index-pcpi	Free	Quarterly analysis of transaction data
Financial Conduct Authority	www.fca.org.uk	Free	Information provided by the FCA including details of regulated entities and the Stock Exchange Listing Rules
Prudential Regulation Authority	www.bankofengland.co.uk/pra/Pages/default.aspx	Free	Information provided by the PRA

Website	*Address*	*Free/paid*	*Information provided*
London Stock Exchange	www.londonstockexchange.com/home/homepage.htm	Free	Share price information including share prices for probate purposes
Bloomberg	www.bloomberg.com	Free/ subscription	Different levels of access to financial data
CapitalIQ	www.capitaliq.com/home.aspx	Subscription	Extensive source of financial information
	www.capitaliq.com	Paid	Corporate financial information for listed companies, interest rates and volatility data
Morningstar	www.morningstar.co.uk/uk	Paid	Company and financial information
Thomson Reuters	thomsonreuters.com/	Paid	Financial information including analyst reports
Factiva companies and executives	www.dowjones.com/factiva	Paid	Company- and industry-specific research and analyst reports
D&B	www.dnb.co.uk/	Paid	Past accounts for all companies incorporated in the UK
Merger Market	www.mergermarket.com	Paid	M&A intelligence tool
Mintel	http://reports.mintel.com	Paid	Sector data
OANDA	www.oanda.com	Free	Currency conversion
IBIS World	http://clients1.ibisworld.co.uk/user/setupusercontact.aspx?return=%2f	Paid	Company filings, reformatted company financials, shareholder information, subsidiaries, registered address and analyst reports

Index

All references are to paragraph number, Example number in Division B, and Appendix in Division C.

Milton Keynes UK
Ingram Content Group UK Ltd.
UKHW020609090823
426575UK00001B/1